LEAGUE
Publications Ltd

RUGBY LEAGUE 2004-05
Scandals and sell-outs

League Publications Ltd

First published in Great Britain in 2004 by
League Publications Ltd
Wellington House
Briggate
Brighouse
West Yorkshire HD6 1DN

A CIP catalogue record for this book is available from the British Library
ISBN 1-901347-13-3

Designed and Typeset by League Publications Limited
Printed by ColourBooks Ltd, Dublin, Eire

Contributing Editor	Tim Butcher
Statistics, production and design	Daniel Spencer
Contributors	Gareth Walker
	Malcolm Andrews
	Mike Latham
	John Drake
	Raymond Fletcher
	Tony Hannan
	Steve Kilgallon
	Mike Sterriker
	Alex Shirvani
	Martyn Sadler
Pictures	Andy Howard
	Varley Picture Agency
	Action Photographics, Australia
	Vicky Matthers
	Graham Lynch
	Dave Williams
	Sig Kasatkin
	Max Flego
	Gordon Clayton

CONTENTS

Foreword	6
Acknowledgments	8
Introduction	9

1. Personalities of 2004 — 13
Andy Farrell — 14
Darren Lockyer — 15
Danny McGuire — 16
Shaun McRae — 17
Tommy Martyn — 18

2. The 2004 Season — 19
December 2003 — 20
January — 24
February — 28
March — 34
April — 41
Challenge Cup Final — 49
May — 53
June — 59
July — 65
August — 71
September — 78

3. Super League Play-offs 2004 — 83
Play-offs week by week — 84
Super League Grand Final — 91
Super League award winners — 96

4. National League 2004 — 113
by Gareth Walker
National League One Season — 114
National League Two Season — 123
National League Cup Final — 130
National League Play-offs — 131
National League Grand Finals — 133
National League award winners — 136

5. International 2004 — 137
Gillette Tri-Nations 2004 — 138
Other Internationals — 158
Season Down Under — 165
by Malcolm Andrews

6. Statistical review 2004 — 193
Super League Players 1996-2004 — 194
Super League IX club by club — 203
Super League IX round by round — 228
Super League IX
Opta Index Analysis — 244
National League One 2004
club by club — 254
National League Two 2004
club by club — 264
National League One 2004
round by round — 274
National League Two 2004
round by round — 284
National League Cup 2004
round by round — 294
Challenge Cup 2004
round by round — 302
2004 Amateur/Academy round-up — 308
Super League 2005 Fixtures — 310
National League 2005 Fixtures — 312
Grand Final History — 314
2004 Statistical round-up — 318

FOREWORD

2004 may go down as a breakthrough year for Rugby League. The game has always been able to demonstrate a strong national presence at its domestic showpiece occasions, but in 2004 it re-established itself back on the international scene. The quality of play, intensity and sheer drama of all of the Gillette Tri-Nations games demonstrated that the game is alive and well.

Gillette has been taking an increasingly higher profile within the game over the past few years, and we have chosen to associate ourselves with Rugby League for several reasons.

It forms a major part of our overall sports marketing programme. We have market-leading innovative global brands and therefore choose to be associated with sports that have both a national and international presence. We would like to think that our support has helped raise the profile of both Rugby League and its players.

When we choose a sport to partner we do so on two levels. Firstly via the event, and secondly via a nominated "ambassador" for the relevant sport. Within Rugby League that role is fulfilled by Paul Sculthorpe. I would like to publicly thank Paul on behalf of Gillette, for his tremendous energy and levels of professionalism. He is a world-class athlete and as a "face " of Gillette he is rightly gaining the national profile that he and the game deserve.

The Gillette Tri-Nations co-incided with a major global product launch for Gillette, our new system razor M3 Power. Sport is a vibrant and increasingly important medium to reach target consumers, and Rugby League has proved that it can deliver on this essential requirement.

I would like to thank all the coaches, players and officials of all three competing nations. They were a pleasure to work with and their support in making the tournament as much a success off the field as on, should not be underestimated. I would also like to thank Chris Green and Graham Clay for their tireless work, skill and tenacity in ensuring the "Activation" of the tournament achieved our goals. A special mention also to all at League Publications for their support over the past few years.

Finally, a thank you to you the Rugby League supporters (and Gillette consumers!) for your support and feedback during the Tri-Nations.

Enjoy the read and continue to support the game of Rugby League.

Tony Colquitt, Sales Director, Gillette UK

One try.
One conversion.

New!

Gillette's Best Shave

Gillette
M3POWER
& MACH3
INNOVATION

Paul Sculthorpe – St. Helens and Great Britain & Ireland

Gillette®

The Best a Man Can Get

ACKNOWLEDGEMENTS

Rugby League 2004-2005 is the ninth in League Publications Ltd's annual series of Rugby League Yearbooks, the second year with the backing of Gillette.

Without the hard work and dedication of all the contributors to Rugby Leaguer & Rugby League Express and Rugby League World magazine, who provide such a tremendous service to the game of Rugby League, there could be no yearbook of this stature.

We are also fortunate to be able to include some wonderful action photography provided by, in particular, Rugby Leaguer & League Express's former staff photographer Andy Howard, Varley Picture Agency, Col Whelan of Action Photographics in Sydney, and Dave Williams of Rugby League Photos.

Co-editor Daniel Spencer has once again handled the statistical sections and the design. And Colourbooks of Dublin deserve some mention for the speed with which they produce the hard copies of the book.

Special mentions for Gareth Walker, Malcolm Andrews, Raymond Fletcher, Alex Shirvani, Steve Kilgallon and Mike Latham, who have contributed so much to the writing of this book; to Opta Index, who provided the Opta Index Analysis in our mind-boggling statistical section; and to John Drake, webmaster of the excellent totalrl.com website, for his help with proofing.

Tim Butcher
Editor, Rugby League 2004-2005

INTRODUCTION

This yearbook went to press two days after the Gillette Tri-Nations final at Elland Road.

After three performances of great promise and improvement, including a rare win over Australia, Great Britain were blown away yet again by the Kangaroos in a decider.

It was hard at half-time of that game to contemplate the completion of a book looking back at the last 12 months of Rugby League. Nothing else seemed to matter that much.

But in the following days it became obvious that the Tri-Nations was just the last chapter in what had been another wonderful story, full of so many sub-plots, twists and turns.

For a start, the Tri-Nations itself had been a big success, drawing big crowds to six ultra-competitive games (and a big crowd to a not so competitive game), with plenty of positive media coverage.

And before that there was drama aplenty - the most gripping the so-called 'betting scandal' that rocked the world of Rugby League – with the inevitable over-reaction eventually subsiding.

When St Helens' pair Sean Long and Martin Gleeson were caught betting against their own team, on a day when they knew it had no chance of success, there were many wishing to cast the game as corrupt to the core. The Rugby Football League's lengthy enquiry into the matter decided that this was not the case, but nevertheless hit the pair with lengthy bans that effectively ended St Helens' chances of winning back the Super League title they last lifted in 2002.

Before that they had secured their fourth Challenge Cup of the summer era when they bettered their greatest rivals Wigan, on a wonderful afternoon in Cardiff, in front of a sell-out crowd.

(Wigan themselves experienced their own trauma at the time of that game when it was revealed coach Mike Gregory was suffering from a serious debilitating injury that would mean he couldn't continue in his job).

2004 was the year when the term 'sell-out crowd' almost became a cliché in Rugby League, with the Tetley's Super League Grand Final and three Tri-Nations matches all needing the adjective. Plus a few club Super League games too.

Three of them were at Headingley where Leeds Rhinos attracted the best support in the game on their march to the League Leaders and eventually the Super League Championship Trophy.

And at the centre of their road to success was Danny McGuire – who fought out a season-long battle with the Bulls' Lesley Vainikolo to be the top-try-scorer of 2004, eventually ending with 39 tries each. McGuire was the stand-off British supporters had been praying for and they couldn't wait to see him take on the Aussies and the Kiwis at the end of the year. Come the Final, he wasn't given his head, coming off the bench after 24 minutes with the cause already lost.

Vainikolo was himself a huge star on the domestic scene, netting a monster five-try haul against Wigan at Odsal on the very first night of Super League IX.

That came a week after the Bulls had become world champions with a 22-4 win over NRL champions Penrith Panthers on a memorable night in Huddersfield

The Bulls had a rough ride in terms of injuries, losing centre Toa Kohe-Love and winger Tevita Vaikona for almost all the season, but to their credit they came strong at the end to almost pip Leeds in another compelling Grand Final.

For Wigan, it was goodbye to a number of familiar faces. Former Kiwi international prop Quentin Pongia called it a day when he was virtually forced out of the game after being diagnosed with the infectious Hepatitis B virus - which for a few weeks in May became the most talked about medical condition in Rugby League history. And at the end of the season, fellow prop Craig Smith had also retired and Terry O'Connor had been allowed to leave the JJB Stadium.

Hull's injury woes were even worse than last year although they finished in third spot after missing the play-offs in 2003. Shaun McRae had to throw some inexperienced players into the fray and they rewarded them with another fine season before he headed home to take the reins at South Sydney.

Wakefield Trinity had their best ever season in Super League, not only making the play-offs for the first time, but eliminating Hull, away from home, before almost doing the same to Wigan. In David Solomona they had netted the overseas signing of the season and their coach Shane McNally was rewarded with the Coach of the Year award.

Warrington Wolves made a complete success of their move to their new Halliwell Jones Stadium, at least after a first-night hiccup when ticketing problems meant hundreds were locked out of their win against Wakefield. Later in the season the Wolves tailed off, but they were gearing up for Super League X well before the end of the season, with their big transfer-fee signing of Martin Gleeson one of the stories of the year.

But the Wolves couldn't replicate their play-off achievements of 2003, and neither could London Broncos, who were in relegation danger until late in the season, although they had some real highlights as they saved their skins, including wins over St Helens and Wigan. They also took a point off Leeds Rhinos, and not many teams could say that in Super League IX. But at the end of the campaign the Broncos saw the departure of the bedrock of their side, and the impact of their new signings is going to be one of the most interesting aspects of Super League X.

Huddersfield Giants made real progress under new coach Jon Sharp - despite a disappointing second half of the season - taking some sizeable scalps along the way. And although the loss of Brandon Costin is a blow, they too have made some positive acquisitions.

Salford's objective of avoiding immediate relegation on their return to Super League was achieved, and with a move to new stadium still on the near horizon, a bright future beckons for the City Reds.

Super League survival wasn't Widnes' major objective when the season kicked off, but it had become so half way through the season, and coach Neil Kelly was the second head coach to lose his job.

The first had been Graham Steadman, whose close-season recruitment, which had promised so much, turned to dust as injuries to key players eventually led to the Tigers' relegation after a dramatic last Saturday night in Round 28. Most people among the 11,000-plus crowd at the Jungle that night, when neighbours Wakefield finally condemned the Tigers to National League One next season, will share the view that Super League will be a poorer competition without Castleford.

Supporters of Leigh Centurions might not agree, as their side finally won promotion with a nail-biting win over Whitehaven in the NL1 Grand Final. And Barrow came up from NL2 after tying up that particular title.

Anyway. Why am I rattling on? It's all in the following 300 or so pages. I'll leave you to it.

Tim Butcher
Editor, Rugby League 2004-2005

The Gillette Rugby League yearbook 2004-2005 has an in-depth statistical section, featuring every team in the Rugby Football League, chapters on all the major competitions both here and abroad and a record of every game in Super League and the National Leagues One and Two.

It also contains details of the international season, with full coverage of the Gillette Tri-Nations and other international fixtures during the season.

And this year we have included an historical record of all the Grand Finals played since they were introduced in 1998

Once again we have selected five individuals who we judge to have made the biggest impact on Rugby League in 2004.

This book contains a whole host of information that no serious Rugby League fan can afford to be without, and you can enjoy over 200 full colour and black and white photographs along the way.

League Publications produces the weekly newspaper 'Rugby Leaguer & Rugby League Express', as well as the monthly glossy magazine 'Rugby League World' and the website 'totalrugbyleague.com'.

We hope you enjoy looking back over 2004 with us, and looking forward - you can find your club's fixtures for next season at the back of the yearbook.

1
PERSONALITIES OF 2004

Andy Farrell

On an individual performance level, 2004 could hardly have gone much better for captain-fantastic Andy Farrell.

The Wigan skipper had felt the brunt of what all well-placed observers felt was undeserved criticism for several years. But he answered all of those critics - in spades - with a sensational year for club and country.

Farrell missed the start of the season with the knee injury he had played with throughout the 2003 Ashes series, but made an immediate impact on his return.

With the Warriors going through a massive injury crisis, the 29-year-old was soon forced to make the unfamiliar switch to prop, and it was a move that he thrived on.

Farrell gained countless man of the match awards with courageous performances up front. And few will forget Wigan's home game with Leeds in June, when Farrell - with his broken nose dramatically strapped to his face - returned to the field to inspire his team to victory.

He later claimed to be "embarrassed" at the media attention that incident received - a mark of the humility of the man.

But he earned more column inches later in the year as he made a virtual clean sweep of the end-of-season individual awards.

First came the Man of Steel - for the second time in his career - and then the Players' Player award.

And after some typically inspirational performances in his role as Great Britain captain, he was crowned the International Forward of the Year, and ultimately, given the Golden Boot as the world's leading player.

Farrell was handed his award by the only other British player to win the Golden Boot - his former Wigan idol Ellery Hanley.

It was fitting that one Rugby League great was there to present the coveted award to another.

The only disappointment for Farrell was to be that both Wigan and Great Britain fell just short of ultimate glory.

Darren Lockyer

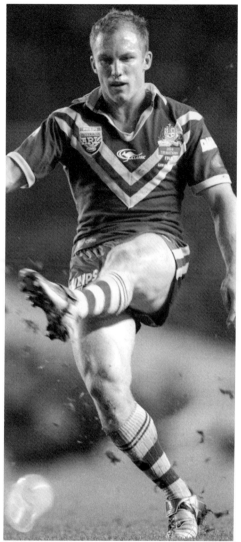

Even Australian coach Wayne Bennett had run out of superlatives to describe Darren Lockyer, his on-field talisman, in the aftermath of the Gillette Tri-Nations Final.

Bennett has seen Lockyer produce the goods for almost a decade for club, state and country, and develop into one of the modern greats of our game.

In the Final at Elland Road, Lockyer was at his breath-taking best.

Returning from a rib injury that had kept him out for almost a month, Lockyer inspired the Kangaroos to their first-half onslaught in Leeds.

Now a fully fledged stand-off after initially making his mark in the senior game at fullback, Lockyer scored one try and directly created four others as the Aussies swept into an unassailable 38-0 interval lead.

His try - when he took Nathan Hindmarsh's offload on halfway and then arced brilliantly between Paul Wellens and Brian Carney to score - was vintage Lockyer.

In the end, Bennett decided to plump for "outstanding" when asked about the qualities of his captain in the Final press conference.

And who could argue with that?

For years he had been seen as a world-class player - one with the ability to break any defence with his smooth, gliding running style and supreme awareness.

But in the Ashes series of 2003 and the Tri-Nations of 2004, Lockyer has added unrivalled leadership to his bow - confirming he was the man primarily responsible for keeping Australia on top of the world.

There were still those who would have had you believe that the 2004 Kangaroos were not a patch on some of their predecessors.

But those who have been fortunate enough to watch Darren Lockyer in the flesh over the last two years will understand he compares with any of the greats of the past.

A living Rugby League legend, Lockyer, in 2004 was at the peak of his powers.

15

Danny McGuire

This was always going to be something of a make or break season for Danny McGuire - 39 tries in all competition for Grand Final winners Leeds suggests it definitely fell into the "made it" bracket.

The Rhinos' multi-talented youngster had shown numerous flashes of unlimited potential before 2004, but with Tony Smith taking over the coaching reins at Headingley, he was immediately installed as the Rhinos' starting stand-off.

McGuire thrived on the responsibility, and developed into the type of player everyone in the British game had been crying out for for years - a young English stand-off with the ability to strike fear into the hearts of any defence in the world.

McGuire, who started at the East Leeds amateur club before progressing through the Rhinos' Academy - set Super League IX alight with his breath-taking attacking skills.

His electric pace, stunning side-step and Shaun Edwards-esque support play had crowds across the country rising to their feet.

McGuire passed Paul Newlove's record for tries in a Super League regular season against Wakefield in Round 21, though he was eventually overtaken - just - by Bradford's Lesley Vainikolo.

It couldn't take the shine off a remarkable year.

After being reduced to a bit-part in Great Britain's opening Gillette Tri-Nations to defeat to Australia, McGuire was handed a starting place against New Zealand the following week.

He repaid coach Brian Noble's initial faith - producing a typically dazzling stepping run to lay on a crucial try for Stuart Reardon.

But he was then a surprise omission from the starting line-up for the final. By the time he entered the action, the game was all but over, with the Kangaroos leading 26-0.

It was hard to remember at times that McGuire was still only 22 years old. He looked destined to spend many, many more years sporting the red-white and blue.

From the moment he arrived at St Helens as the new head coach, Shaun McRae was busy winning friends and admirers in British Rugby League.

Shaun McRae

There have been few figures in the game - particularly from Australia - that have become as popular as the man affectionately referred to as "Bomber".

A Super League and Challenge Cup winner with Saints, he then moved onto Gateshead, where his partnership with chief executive Shane Richardson began to blossom.

Though McRae performed a minor miracle in guiding Thunder to sixth place, the club was forced to close, and the duo teamed up again at Hull, where they sparked a revival at the famous old club.

Hull were firmly established among Super League's leading lights by the time McRae, midway through the 2004 season, confirmed he was to return Down Under as coach of troubled South Sydney, where Richardson had just taken over as CEO.

It was a significant blow to the Black and Whites, who at the time were flying high in Super League and looking like genuine Grand Final contenders.

Unfortunately for McRae, a spate of injuries - the kind that have blighted Hull since their switch to the KC Stadium - severely dented their aspirations.

With key duo Richard Horne and Paul King sidelined, they crashed to a home defeat to Wakefield Trinity Wildcats in the play-offs, robbing McRae of his perfect send-off.

But that defeat will do nothing to affect Bomber's popularity in this country - both among supporters and the media, who appreciated his honest, always-available approach.

McRae's departure to the NRL was a definite loss to Super League - but domestic fans were counting on him talking up the quality of the British game and its players once he'd settled in again in Sydney.

17

Tommy Martyn

Tommy Martyn could hardly have written a more perfect script for his last scene as a professional player.

Stand-off Martyn - who won every major honour in the domestic game in a trophy-laden spell with St Helens - had signed for his hometown club Leigh at the end of 2003, with the aim of guiding the Centurions into Super League.

Though they failed - losing to Salford in the Grand Final that year - Martyn was again the on-field figurehead of their 2004 bid, as well as being coach Darren Abram's assistant.

Everything appeared to be going to plan until the closing weeks of the league campaign, when Martyn suffered a serious arm injury in a heavy defeat at Halifax - two incidents that threatened to derail Leigh's promotion challenge.

Martyn's hopes of being fit for the Grand Final appeared initially slim, and his fitness was the subject of intense speculation leading up to the all-important clash with Whitehaven.

He wasn't on the first team sheet handed to the press at the Halton Stadium - but just half an hour before kick-off, a new list arrived with Martyn's name at number seven (he still refused to wear the number six jersey following a spate of injuries to players at St Helens in that shirt).

Later he revealed that he had been inspired to play in the week leading up to the Grand Final when the Centurions had been overlooked for the National League Club of the Year title, which went to 'Haven.

Martyn played like a man possessed in the Final, scoring one try and then producing two moments of absolute magic in extra-time as the Centurions eventually won through.

After the game he confirmed his retirement - and what a fitting ending it was. He was to remain as Abram's number two as Leigh began their attempt to survive in the top flight.

2
THE 2004 SEASON

DECEMBER 2003
Missed opportunity

Once again British Rugby League entered December still chasing the Ashes, in the knowledge this time that all three of the Tests against Australia could, and should have been won.

For his part in the remarkable late victories, Kangaroo skipper Darren Lockyer was awarded the Golden Boot by Rugby League World magazine as the best player in the world.

The 2003 Ashes Series proved to be David Waite's swansong as Great Britain coach, with the name of the successor he had recommended to the RFL a closely-guarded secret.

Whilst on-field success at senior level remained elusive, for the second year in succession a junior England team got the better of Australian tourists, as the England Under-17 Academy team completed a two-nil whitewash of the touring Australian Institute of Sport (AIS) Rugby League side.

The under-17s - made up of 22 players contracted to Tetley's Rugby Super League clubs - beat the touring AIS team 28-22 in the first game at South Leeds Stadium and followed that up with a 34-14 win at Featherstone.

"We would like to offer our congratulations to all members of the England Academy under-17s squad. They have produced tremendous results against top level international opposition," said RFL Executive Chairman Richard Lewis. "The victories are a clear indication of the quality and effectiveness of the Academy structures in this country, which is highly pleasing both for the RFL and the clubs who are partners in the programmes."

Bradford Bulls breathed a sigh of relief when their Great Britain winger Leon Pryce escaped jail after pleading guilty to attacking Salford conditioner Eddie McGuinness in a Bradford pub in 2002.

Pryce was ordered instead to complete 120 hours of community service after the attack on McGuinness, formerly on Bradford's staff, which left his victim needing 48 stitches in facial injuries.

Further negative news surfaced with the Kangaroos' tour management reporting that almost 4,000 Australian dollars had been stolen from four of their players' hotel rooms during their tour to Great Britain. They were unable to identify the thief, despite reported suspicions among some players that the culprit could be one of the touring party. "All that I can confirm is that we have had reports that money has gone missing," Australian Rugby League chief executive Geoff Carr told a Sydney newspaper.

Salary cap restrictions forced angry Wigan chairman Maurice Lindsay to release two of the Warriors' star players. "We have released Paul Johnson and Shaun Briscoe, who both had a year to go on their contracts," Lindsay told Rugby Leaguer & League Express. "We have had to make some adjustments to contracts for several of our players, in the light of what they have achieved this season, but that has meant that we have been unable to reward all our players, despite the fact that we would have liked to have done so. Recently we uplifted Brian Carney's contract when we gave him a new three-year deal, we signed Danny Orr, and we gave Quentin Pongia another year. We have tied up Kevin Brown for three years, and some of our other younger stars have had their contracts uplifted. But those deals all increase our outlay next season."

Lindsay suggested that the salary cap regulations should be amended to reward clubs who develop young talent, and to punish those who don't. "I would like to see an allowance for clubs who produce players who go on to play for Great Britain, and I think clubs should be penalised who don't invest in youth," said Lindsay.

One club who appeared to have no money troubles was London Broncos who based their pre-season training camp in Dubai. The Broncos added more players to the camp with Leigh scrum-half Lee Sanderson and Sheffield prop Mitchell Stringer linking up with Tony Rea's squad.

Also London-bound was Wests Tigers' threequarter Mark O'Halloran, set to join former teammates Steve Trindall and Troy Wozniak at Griffin Park. However Wozniak decided to head elsewhere, with Widnes Vikings - preparing to represent Britain in the 2004 World Sevens - reported to be interested in his services.

While in Dubai the Broncos took part in the Invitation Sevens with chief executive Nick Cartwright calling for more Rugby League teams to enter the event: "We would certainly like to get a few other teams over here next year, whether it's getting into the main event, or getting a Rugby League tournament started. There is no reason why we shouldn't get both Australian and English teams."

Christmas shopping proved difficult for some in 2003 - angry English Rugby League fans finding copies of the new Super League computer game - made down under - almost impossible to buy. Eager fans found the Playstation 2 version of the game hard to find in shops, even if they pre-ordered weeks before, while distributor Alternative Software admitted the PC and X-Box versions would also be in short supply.

The festive season of course meant that clubs could display their new signings - with former Great Britain scrum-half Bobbie Goulding once again on the move, returning to Rugby League as player-coach of Rochdale Hornets. The National League One club were without a coach following the departure of Martin Hall - after a consortium he was fronting failed in a bid to take over at Spotland.

Also back on the Rugby League scene was Leeds' Great Britain threequarter Chev Walker, who was released from prison before Christmas. Walker and Ryan Bailey both played in the full-blooded 20-12 Boxing Day victory over Castleford, which also saw the first appearance in the blue and amber of Leeds' only recruit of the off-season, PNG star Marcus Bai.

But it was fullback Richard Mathers who earned the fullest admiration of new Rhinos coach Tony Smith. Teenager Mathers lost his mother on Christmas Eve after a battle against cancer, but insisted on figuring in the Rhinos' win.

"Richard Mathers had the option to pull out at any stage but he wasn't having it," Smith said. "And even at the end when he copped a knock there was no way he was leaving the field and he deserves a special mention for that effort."

At Wilderspool on Boxing Day, a try eight minutes from time by centre Richard Varkulis earned Warrington a share of the spoils - 26-26 - in an entertaining friendly with local rivals Widnes. Warrington's tries came through Nick Owen, Jon Clarke, Phil Berry, Dean Gaskell and Varkulis, with Adam Flanagan, David Mills, Paul Devlin, Chris Giles and trialist winger Nick Royle scoring for Widnes.

Batley Bulldogs hammered local rivals Dewsbury Rams 46-12 at Mount Pleasant; Wakefield Trinity Wildcats defeated Featherstone Rovers 34-14 at the Lionheart Stadium; while Whitehaven beat Oldham 18-4 to claim the first 'Seat Challenge' Trophy.

At the Lionheart Stadium Featherstone had forward Jim Carlton dismissed in the 50th minute after an altercation with Michael Korkidas, while Sid Domic and Semi Tadulala marked their Wildcats debuts with tries.

Just as Christmas comes around every year December also saw another spat between the Rugby Football League and the British Amateur Rugby League Association.

This time the row centred on who should take over as BARLA chief executive from Ian Cooper, who resigned from the job earlier in the year. The RFL had initially suggested that, as a stopgap measure, the RFL Director of Coach Education, Ray Unsworth, based at the BARLA HQ, should take over.

According to Rugby Football League Executive Chairman Richard Lewis: "The BARLA board objected to the process, I spoke to them and they then approved it, but the BARLA General Assembly then overturned it. It wasn't a political issue, but it was made into one."

BARLA also had other difficulties. Prior to their unification with the RFL they were audited by Sport England, who qualified the amateur body as being "not fit for purpose", implying that no more funds would come to BARLA from public sources.

POWERGEN CHALLENGE CUP PRELIMINARY ROUND

Saturday 15th November 2003
Castleford Lock Lane 56 York Acorn 0; East Leeds 18 Huddersfield Sharks 12; Oulton Raiders 28 Wigan St Judes 18; Ovenden 10 West Hull 28; Queensbury 16 Castleford Panthers 18; Siddal 56 Millom 10; Stanley Rangers 18 Sharlston Rovers 37; Waterhead 10 West Bowling 24; Wath Brow Hornets 60 Skirlaugh 14; Widnes St Maries (walkover) v Dublin Blues; Wigan St Patricks 20 Thornhill Trojans 12

POWERGEN CHALLENGE CUP FIRST ROUND

Saturday 29th November 2003
Army 12 East Hull 22; Birkenshaw 22 St Albans 10; Bradford Dudley Hill 38 Embassy 8; Castleford Lock Lane 48 Batley Victoria 8; Castleford Panthers 18 Shaw Cross Sharks 10; Cottingham (walkover) v Charleston Knights; East Leeds 20 Queens 6; Elland 26 Kells 12; Hensingham 10 Wath Brow Hornets 18; Hunslet Warriors 9 Orrell St James 8; Leigh East 28 Milford Marlins 10; Leigh Miners Rangers 52 Blackbrook 24; Normanton Knights 14 Royal Navy 20; Oldham St Annes 19 Hull Dockers 12; Oulton Raiders 40 Loughborough University 22;; RAF 16 Huddersfield Underbank 12; Saddleworth Rangers 0 Rochdale Mayfield 51; Sheffield Hillsborough Hawks 2 Crosfields 31; Siddal 14 Halton Simms Cross 2; Walney Central 8 Thatto Heath Crusaders 12; West Hull 30 Askam 8; Widnes Albion Bulls 2 Eastmoor Dragons 21; Widnes St Maries 6 Sharlston Rovers 20; Wigan St Patricks 12 Ideal Isberg 17

Sunday 30th November 2003
Aberavon Irish 6 Ince Rosebridge 28; Featherstone Lions 60 Coventry Bears 21; Heworth 34 Edinburgh Eagles 8; South London Storm 4 West Bowling 36

Saturday 6th December 2003
Warrington Woolston 18 Eccles & Salford Juniors 22

Dinamo Mascow carved their own little niche of Rugby League history when they became the first ever Russian side to win a Challenge Cup tie.

A late try from centre Sergei Dobrynine secured a thrilling 22-18 win for Dinamo in Bradford against West Bowling with New Zealander Lee Finnerty providing a crucial guiding influence and also kicking three goals.

Second-rower Kirill Koulemine scored two tries and winger Vladimir Trofimov one as the Russians made the third round draw.

Russian Champions Lokomotiv Moscow, and a quartet of French clubs - UTC, Villeneuve, Pia and Limoux - joined Dinamo in the third round draw of the Powergen sponsored competition, whilst the Royal Navy and the Royal Air Force demonstrated the growing strength of forces Rugby League with wins against established BARLA clubs in round one.

POWERGEN CHALLENGE CUP SECOND ROUND

Saturday 13th December 2003
Birkenshaw 6 Bradford Dudley Hill 46; Castleford Lock Lane 13 Ideal Isberg 6; Cottingham Tigers 12 Crosfields 20; East Hull 46 Royal Navy 18; East Leeds 12 Featherstone Lions 18; Eccles & Salford Juniors 6 Castleford Panthers 11; Elland 28 Eastmoor Dragons 4; Ince Rosebridge 28 Hunslet Warriors 14; Leigh Miners Rangers 34 Siddal 6; Rochdale Mayfield 20 Leigh East 10; Sharlston Rovers 14 Oldham St Annes 9; West Hull 76 Heworth 4

Sunday 14th December 2003
Royal Air Force 0 Thatto Heath Crusaders 32; West Bowling 18 Dinamo Moscow 22

Saturday 20th December 2003
Wath Brow Hornets 10 Oulton Raiders 18

JANUARY
New year, no change

The lack of headlines for Rugby League made the headlines as we entered the new year.

In the first issue of Rugby Leaguer & League Express of 2004, Rugby Football League Executive Chairman Richard Lewis slammed the absence of any Rugby League personalities from the New Year's Honours List.

"Half a dozen nominations have been in the system for a while now," Lewis said, "but we just seem to be ignored. I don't think this is deliberate prejudice, but I think there is a lack of awareness as to how big the sport of Rugby League is."

The results of a poll conducted by MORI on behalf of leading rugby union sponsor Zurich supported Lewis's claim. It showed that League had enjoyed a 50 per cent gain in popularity during 2003. The results of a previous poll in January of that year had shown that just 10 per cent of the population was interested in Rugby League, but that proportion had risen to 15 per cent by December.

One man who was enjoying game-wide popularity was Wigan and Great Britain winger Brian Carney, who scooped the Rugby League & League Express Readers' Player of the Year Award. Carney edged 2003 Man of Steel Jamie Peacock for the accolade, largely due to his sensational displays for Great Britain in the autumn Ashes Series.

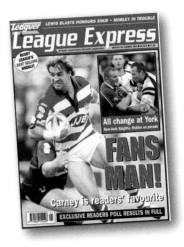

Fellow Test player Adrian Morley's career looked a bit shaky for a while when it was revealed that he had picked up a drink-driving conviction during the Ashes series, though his manager denied the Sydney Roosters star had been involved in a scuffle with police. Morley completed 40 hours of community service and was also banned from driving for six months.

But the RFL backed away from reports they were preparing to impose a six-month worldwide suspension on Morley for bringing the game into disrepute. (The Tests against Australia were sponsored by the anti-drink-driving campaign Think – Don't Drive!, and Great Britain players had agreed, as part of their contract to represent their country, not to drive while under the influence of alcohol). Morley's apology was accepted.

The RFL lost its third marketing director inside three years when Chris Green resigned from the job, citing "personal reasons" for his decision to quit. There would be no rush to appoint a replacement.

The Rugby League International Federation met and agreed to play the next World Cup in Australia in 2008, to commemorate the 100th anniversary of the New South Wales Rugby League. Wigan Chairman Maurice Lindsay was tipped to play a leading role in organising the competition, though no firm details of how the tournament would be structured were announced. Richard Lewis, who succeeded Lindsay as vice-chairman of the RLIF, said he was 'mystified' to read reports that Great Britain as a single entity would represent the home nations. "If that happens, what would be the point of having the European Nations Cup," Lewis told 'Rugby Leaguer & League Express'.

The RLIF also rubber stamped the continuation of the Mediterranean Cup, the Victory Cup, to be held again in Russia, and a Pacific Nations Cup. Also on the agenda was the format of the autumn's Tri-Nations between Great Britain, Australia and New Zealand.

On the domestic front, clubs were gearing up for Super League IX.

Huddersfield chief executive Ralph Rimmer - buoyed by encouraging early season ticket sales - was confident that the Giants had a chance of breaking a 6,000 average attendance if the Giants could enjoy some success on the field.

But Huddersfield's plans to renovate their ancestral home, Fartown, were stymied by planning wrangles and the club was ordered by the RFL to play its Academy games elsewhere in the future. New coach Jon Sharp also suffered a blow as young halfback Paul White broke a leg in the Giants' 36-0 friendly win over Castleford.

Widnes Vikings signed three new players, while confirming veteran fullback Stuart Spruce - suffering from a long-term hand and wrist injury - had retired from playing (coach Neil Kelly had signed St Helens youngster Steve Rowlands who could cover the role).

Australian Troy Wozniak joined the Vikings after turning his back on a three-year deal at London, and was joined at the Halton Stadium by 19-year-old Nicky Royle - a winger who impressed as a trialist in friendlies against Warrington and the 'Widnes Barbarians' - and Leigh Centurions' highly-rated young forward Adam Bibey.

The Vikings were also to trial former Barrow Raiders Australian Andrew Henderson, a Scottish International, during their trip to Australia for the World Sevens.

However things didn't go entirely to plan down under. Stand-off Jules O'Neill was accused of trying to set fire to a boy wearing a rubber and foam dolphin suit during a pleasure boat trip in Port Macquarie, north of where the Vikings were holding their pre-season training camp on the NSW north coast.

O'Neill claimed the owners of the boat were just trying to generate publicity for their tourist attraction by making public a letter of complaint they had fired off to the Widnes club. Nothing further came of the matter.

In the Sevens - acclaimed again as a great success - the Vikings lost all three games, losing 21-18 to NSW Country, 34-13 to Cronulla Sharks and 35-11 to eventual runners-up Parramatta Eels. West Tigers beat the Eels in the final 18-7. France won the 'International Cup', beating Fiji 26-18 in the final.

The following Friday the Vikings were no match for the Tigers at 13-a-side when they went down 40-6 in a friendly, with winger Paul Devlin suffering a knee injury that was to keep him out for most of the rest of the season.

Back home, St Helens announced the signings of two Samoan rugby union stars - Dom Feaunati and Maurie Fa'asavalu. Neither player would count as quota players - both qualifying under the Kolpak ruling - which allowed players (and indeed other individuals seeking work) from countries with reciprocal employment agreements with the European Union the right to earn their living in this country. Coach Ian Millward suggested it was time the RFL considered giving Super League clubs cap dispensation to sign established union stars, a system which operated in the Australian NRL. Both Samoans made highly-promising debuts in a 38-20 friendly win at Barrow.

Wakefield Trinity Wildcats also netted a Samoan in 22-year-old former Sydney Roosters hooker or halfback Albert Talipeau, who played for Samoa in the World Cup in 2000. Talipeau had been sidelined with a broken leg in 2003.

Saints announced that Paul Sculthorpe would be the club's new captain, succeeding long-serving Chris Joynt, who had held the position since 1997. The appointment put to bed a report in the 'News of the World' newspaper that Bradford Bulls had made a £400,000 bid for the St Helens loose forward. The 'News of the World' said the Bulls' offer had been flatly rejected by Saints, and quoted Sculthorpe as saying "I'm flattered, but I like it here". But Bradford football manager Stuart Duffy told 'Rugby Leaguer & League Express': "It's absolute rubbish: there is no truth whatsoever in this story. If we were to make a move for Paul how could we fit him under the salary cap?"

London Broncos were rocked by the news that Australian back-rower Bill Peden, 34, who had agreed a new one-year contract with the Broncos and had been on their training camp in Dubai, was to take up a three-year coaching contract with his hometown club Newcastle Knights. Former South Sydney back-rower Andrew Hart, who had been searching for a club since being cut by the Rabbitohs at the end of the previous season, agreed a one-year contract with London.

New Zealand Warriors' Australian centre John Carlaw pulled out after agreeing to join Salford City Reds, who spent a warm-weather training camp in Florida. Family reasons were cited and Carlaw subsequently turned out for St George Illawarra in the NRL. The Reds were also linked with former centre Nathan McAvoy - who had left Bradford for rugby union - but claimed they would struggle to get him under the salary cap.

New Castleford Tigers signing Paul Newlove was booked in to see a specialist after picking up a foot injury. The former Great Britain centre's hopes of making his Tigers' debut in a friendly at Odsal, his former home ground, were dashed at the eleventh hour, when he limped out of the final training session the day before. Vice-captain Sean Rudder and former Halifax centre Ryan Clayton also missed the game through injury, as the Tigers conceded ten tries in a 56-18 demolition at the hands of Bradford. Winger Paul Mellor was stretchered off after only 12 minutes of the game, which was played as former Bulls prop Brian McDermott's Testimonial.

Another fine prop, though not yet retired, Mark Hilton enjoyed a testimonial game as the Wolves beat Super League hopefuls Leigh Centurions 34-16. The Wolves were given a civic reception ahead of the opening of the Halliwell Jones Stadium, and also unveiled new signings Chris Leikvoll, Danny Lima and John Wilshere.

Hull FC chief executive David Plummer backed Hull Kingston Rovers' bid to secure a Super League place, after the two clubs registered a bumper crowd of 15,064 for a friendly match - billed as the Clive Sullivan Memorial Trophy - at the KC Stadium. Hull won a tightly contested game 18-6. Hull coach Shaun McRae was in talks to extend his contract at Hull which was due to run out at the end of Super League IX.

Wigan added youngster Bob Beswick to their first team squad, after making no off-season signings, instead putting faith in the Academy production line that had helped take them in the Grand Final the previous year. But there was still some doubt about the future of Adrian Lam, who had undergone surgery to a cruciate ligament injury down under.

Leeds Rhinos parted company with Darren Robinson, the only full-time sports psychologist employed by a Super League club and played neighbours Hunslet Hawks in the revived Lazenby Cup at the South Leeds Stadium, and York City Knights. The Rhinos allowed the National League clubs to keep the proceeds from the games. Matt Diskin was the gamestar in a 24-6 home win over Wakefield at the end of the month.

Another famous name from Leeds was about to make a re-entry into the game as National League Three was expanded to 14 clubs in its second season, with one of the new clubs being Bramley, who went out of the League in 1999. The RFL also announced the inclusion of Carlisle, Birmingham and Essex in the 2004 competition.

The RFL also revealed that 19 new teams were to join a 68-team TotalRL.com Conference, sponsored for the third successive year by League Publications, the publishers of 'Rugby Leaguer & League Express' and 'Rugby League World' magazine. Rugby League Ireland was also on track to launch its new Conference that summer, despite rugby union opposition.

The month ended with RFL boss Richard Lewis confident that he would soon be able to announce the signing of a new deal with BSkyB.

FEBRUARY
Champions of the World

Bradford Bulls reclaimed the World Club Champions tag, two years after they first won the title, on a great night for British Rugby League in Huddersfield. And the 22-4 victory over NRL Champions Penrith Panthers was even more convincing than their 41-26 success over Newcastle Knights on the same venue in 2002. It was certainly light years away from Sydney Roosters' 38-0 mauling of St Helens 12 months before.

Penrith didn't trot out the excuses of previous vanquished Australian sides. They'd arrived over a week before the game to acclimatise and get over jet lag, and their coach John Lang and chief executive Shane Richardson conceded they had been beaten by the better team on the night.

The Bulls were too strong, too clever, and too quick for their opponents, with utility Karl Pratt - deputising for Paul Deacon, ruled out with an eye injury - producing a perfect kicking game in only his second match at scrum-half in two years. Superbly-placed high kicks led to two of Bradford's tries, and then a booming 40-20 gained the position from which Pratt sent Rob Parker charging in for the late try that crowned a magnificent victory.

The win, and the nature of it, increased calls for Bulls coach Brian Noble to be given the Great Britain coaching job - with David Waite having stepped down after the previous autumn's Ashes series.

Another pre-match injury setback for Bradford was the loss of captain Robbie Paul, whose arm injury carried over from the previous season was causing some consternation among the Bulls medical team. Leon Pryce filled the stand-off role and he caused a threat every time he was in possession, striding in for a brilliant solo try from 40 metres out in the 24th minute.

The retirement of James Lowes had left Noble with another huge gap to fill, and he put his faith in young Aaron Smith at hooker, who stood out in only his fourth senior game.

Michael Withers, who grew up in Penrith, took the man of the match award, back to his exciting best after injury had restricted him to only six matches in 2003.

Bradford's Paul Anderson swamped by the Penrith defence

Penrith were unlucky not be awarded a try in the 15th minute when a brilliant raid down the left ended with Paul Whatuira adjudged by the video referee to have made a double movement after being tackled by Tevita Vaikona. The Panthers looked even more dejected a few minutes later when the video referee ruled in Lesley Vainikolo's favour when the winger snatched the ball from Rhys Wesser's grasp as they both jumped to field Pratt's kick.

Pryce scored his 24th minute try, and after Withers had kicked a penalty goal Bradford took a 16-0 interval lead with Logan Swann's converted try on his club debut. After another Withers penalty goal in the 44th minute, Penrith scored a scrambled try from Luke Priddis off Preston Campbell's high kick to the corner, and the Panthers went all out for another try. But the Bulls held out magnificently before breaking away and sealing victory with Parker's 78th minute touchdown.

WORLD CLUB CHALLENGE

Friday 13th February 2004

BRADFORD BULLS 22 PENRITH PANTHERS 4

BULLS: 6 Michael Withers; 2 Tevita Vaikona; 16 Paul Johnson (D); 4 Shontayne Hape; 5 Lesley Vainikolo; 3 Leon Pryce; 15 Karl Pratt; 10 Paul Anderson; 24 Aaron Smith; 29 Stuart Fielden; 11 Lee Radford; 12 Jamie Peacock (C); 13 Logan Swann (D). Subs (all used): 8 Joe Vagana; 27 Rob Parker; 19 Jamie Langley; 17 Stuart Reardon.
Tries: Vainikolo (19), L Pryce (24), Swann (35), Parker (78); **Goals:** Withers 3/5.
PANTHERS: 1 Rhys Wesser; 2 Brett Howland; 3 Luke Lewis; 4 Paul Whatuira; 5 Luke Rooney; 6 Preston Campbell; 7 Craig Gower (C); 8 Joel Clinton; 9 Luke Priddis; 10 Martin Lang; 11 Joe Galuvao; 12 Tony Puletua; 13 Trent Waterhouse. Subs (all used): 14 Ben Ross; 15 Shane Rodney; 16 Colin Ward; 17 Luke Swain.
Try: Priddis (48); **Goals:** Campbell 0/1.
Rugby Leaguer & League Express Men of the Match: *Bulls:* Michael Withers; *Panthers:* Tony Puletua.
Penalty count: 8-4; **Half-time:** 16-0;
Referee: Steve Ganson (England);
Attendance: 18,962 *(at McAlpine Stadium, Huddersfield).*

February

Bradford chairman Chris Caisley was quick to use the Bulls' magnificent World Club Challenge victory in a simmering argument over the level at which the Salary Cap should be set.

A reduction in the cap from its level of £1.8 million per year was on the cards at a two-day meeting to thrash out a strategic direction for Super League, with a small majority of clubs thought to be in favour of a figure of £1.5 million per year.

Caisley asserted that a reduction in the salary cap would ensure that no British club would again win the World Club Challenge. "If we expect clubs like Bradford to come here and play against allegedly the best club side in the world, then we can't carry on dumbing down to the lowest common denominator," said the Bulls boss.

"This is the hardest physical contact sport in the world, and you can't pay players peanuts. They have to be paid a wage that is commensurate with what other people are paid in other sports. How could I go into the dressing room after they've worked so hard to win this match, and tell the players that they will all have to take a 20 per cent cut in their salaries? How many of the chief executives in Super League clubs have taken a pay cut in the last five years? And yet we are asking players to take pay cuts."

Caisley said he would refuse to attend the Super League meeting, claiming that a "cabal" of clubs was pushing to lower the cap "irrespective of what's best for the competition or the good of the game."

The Bulls denied stories they were ready to sign former Leeds Rhinos skipper Iestyn Harris, with speculation rife that the Rhinos would be ready to transfer Harris to the Bulls for a fee.

Caisley did confirm that the Bulls would be prepared to allow coach Brian Noble to take charge of Great Britain in the autumn for the Tri-Nations series - if the terms and conditions were right.

RFL Executive Chairman Richard Lewis admitted that Noble was in the frame. Lewis also conceded that the first game of the series would take place in New Zealand, rather than England, as was originally planned.

He also revealed the Rugby League International Federation had approved a junior Tri-Nations tournament in New Zealand later in the year. "We had given a commitment to send an English team to New Zealand at the end of this year as part of our agreement to receive the New Zealand 'A' team in the UK at the end of last year, but this scheme has been expanded to take in Australia," explained Lewis. "Now we're currently working through the age level at which we will aim the tournament, as well as the fixture dates and venues. We're excited by the progress being made by the Federation, and the importance the game globally is now placing on the development of the international game." The RLIF also agreed to discontinue BARLA's associate membership of the Federation after the amateur body's unification with the RFL in 2003.

Meanwhile, Wales, Ireland and Scotland Rugby League officials made pleas for their inclusion in the 2008 World Cup after suggestions that ARL boss and RLIF chairman Colin Love favoured a ten-team competition. Ireland's biggest name player, Brian Carney, backed the prospect of a standalone Irish side in 2008. "Having an Ireland team involved as a separate entity has to be the best way forward," said Carney. "Having an Irish team involved in any World Cup creates a great atmosphere – and that'll be no different in Rugby League. When we call upon our second-generation players we have a great deal of strength – as we showed in 2000 – and hopefully by the time of 2008 we should have even more home-grown players pushing through the new competition back in Ireland."

In the last of the pre-season friendlies, the Bulls beat Wakefield 26-12; Leeds beat Huddersfield 28-0 in Francis Cummins' Testimonial; Richard Whiting starred for Hull in a 26-14 win over Leeds in Lee Jackson's Testimonial; and Saints beat Salford 20-10, with Paul Sculthorpe the star on the back of an appearance on BBC TV's 'Question of Sport' programme.

● *Before the big kick-off, both the RFL and NRL took measures designed to prevent players taking too much time converting tries or penalties. Stuart Cummings, RFL Technical Executive, informed English clubs that, once the whistle had been blown following the awarding of a try or penalty, referees would call time off after one minute had elapsed - stopping the match clock. Down under, clubs were to be fined $2,000 if kickers took longer that 90 seconds.*

Cummings also told English clubs that play would stop immediately when the hooter sounded at half-time or full-time. "If the hooter is sounded while the ball is still in play, the referee will presume the time-keeper was attempting to sound the hooter at the previous tackle, and will blow the whistle immediately to end the game," said Cummings.

Super League IX kicked off on Friday 20 February 2004 as Lesley Vainikolo scored five outstanding tries when the Bulls defeated Wigan 34-6 at Odsal. Wigan were without Andy Farrell, Adrian Lam, Mick Cassidy and David Hodgson (who had suffered an Achilles tendon injury in Terry O'Connor's Testimonial match against London Broncos at Orrell). Danny Orr scored Wigan's only try on his debut for the club but Wigan were second best. "Part of our job was to show that we could control Vainikolo, and obviously we came up short there," reflected Wigan coach Mike Gregory.

The big event of the opening weekend was the opening of Warrington's Halliwell Jones Stadium, and the Wolves celebrated with a 34-20 win over Wakefield Trinity Wildcats.

February

The event was hit by a spate of forged tickets which ruined the night for over a hundred Wolves supporters, some of whom had bought season tickets but couldn't gain admission to the ground. The match was a 14,206 sellout, but many supporters watched it on big screens at local pubs after the police closed the gates once the capacity had been reached. An estimated 500 fans with genuine tickets were unable to get in, although some scaled the walls of the new stadium to see the game, with fans spilling over onto the pitch behind the advertising hoardings at one end of the stadium.

The first try at the new stadium was scored by Nathan Wood, whose halfback partner Lee Briers was making his comeback for the Wolves after eight months out with a broken wrist.

Hull's 2003 injury nightmare looked set to continue into 2004, after centre Michael Eagar broke his arm on debut in the 30-16 Friday night defeat at St Helens. Jason Smith was already facing a three-month lay-off after a shoulder operation.

Francis Cummins' run of 179 consecutive first-team appearances ended when coach Tony Smith left him out of the Leeds side that beat London 58-14. Cummins was replaced by hat-trick winger Marcus Bai, Keith Senior and Chev Walker also claiming two tries each.

Castleford Tigers coach Graham Steadman was gutted after his side gave away a late matchwinning try to Huddersfield Giants at the McAlpine Stadium. The Giants defeated the Tigers 26-22, although Steadman was adamant the winning try came after a knock-on.

The Tigers were waiting for an appeal hearing date from the RFL to plead the innocence of their teenage back-row signing, Rob Lunt, who was suspended for two years after testing positive for a banned steroid.

And at the Willows Salford City Reds coach Karl Harrison called for Andy Coley to receive international honours after his dynamic prop helped the Reds make a sparkling return to Super League with a 24-12 win over Widnes. Salford turned round an 8-2 half-time deficit with three tries in the second period.

"Too many performances like that and we are going to make someone look very smart," Vikings coach Neil Kelly said, responding to pre-season predictions in Rugby League World magazine that Widnes would be relegated come the end of the season.

SUPER LEAGUE TABLE - *Sunday 22nd February*

	P	W	D	L	F	A	D	PTS
Leeds Rhinos	1	1	0	0	58	14	44	2
Bradford Bulls	1	1	0	0	34	6	28	2
Warrington Wolves	1	1	0	0	34	20	14	2
St Helens	1	1	0	0	30	16	14	2
Salford City Reds	1	1	0	0	24	12	12	2
Huddersfield Giants	1	1	0	0	26	22	4	2
Castleford Tigers	1	0	0	1	22	26	-4	0
Widnes Vikings	1	0	0	1	12	24	-12	0
Wakefield T Wildcats	1	0	0	1	20	34	-14	0
Hull FC	1	0	0	1	16	30	-14	0
Wigan Warriors	1	0	0	1	6	34	-28	0
London Broncos	1	0	0	1	14	58	-44	0

● *THE opening weekend of the Tetley's Super League smashed all previous crowd records for the competition, with 69,499 supporters turning out to watch the weekend's six matches.*

The previous record of 61,982 supporters for a six-match round was set in the second round of Super League VIII. And, for the first time in its history, Super League registered four individual crowds of more than 10,000 in a single round.

The Cup had already produced its fair share of shocks by the fourth round stage when the Super League clubs made their entry - a week after Super League IX had started.

In the third round three amateur teams had bettered professional opposition

At Featherstone's Lionheart Stadium, Dewsbury Rams crashed out to Sharlston Rovers, inspired by 1998 Wembley winner Martyn Wood, by 30-28. Conference Division Two leaders East Hull proved two strong for Swinton Lions at their new Park Lane home, winning 26-14. And Keighley Cougars lost at home 14-16 to Bradford Dudley Hill.

French clubs UTC, Limoux and Pia all progressed. But the two Russian sides, Dinamo Moscow and Locomotiv Moscow, went down to heavy defeats at Rochdale and Chorley.

All three amateur teams fell in round four, East Hull putting up the best fight in a postponed midweek game, before falling 14-4 to NL1 Whitehaven at Craven Park in Hull. Sharlston didn't disgrace themselves, losing 24-4 at Oldham, again in midweek, but Dudley Hill were defeated heavily at Batley by 76-14.

St Helens upset World Champions Bradford Bulls 30-10 at Odsal in the Sunday TV game, with Lee Gilmour scoring his first try for his new club against the club he left the season before.

But the real upset came at the Stade de l'Aguille in southern France, where Limoux shocked Halifax 19-18. UTC followed up their win at Hull KR in the third round by testing Castleford, who needed two tries from substitute Jamie Thackray to overcome Steve Deakin's side at the Jungle, although the third French side, Pia, were well beaten at Huddersfield.

London Broncos recovered from their Super League opening day thrashing at Leeds to beat Salford 24-8 at Griffin Park, while Hull had Paul McNicholas sent off for a high tackle, and were down to eleven men at one stage as they needed a late Richard Whiting field goal to see off NL1 Leigh 21-14. Wigan beat Widnes 38-12 at the JJB but lost winger Brian Carney in the first half with a broken leg.

Earlier that week, in a joint announcement with the BBC, the RFL confirmed the Challenge Cup Final would be moved from 2005 from May to late August, with the BBC paying around £2 million per year for the Challenge Cup and highlights of Super League and international Rugby League until the end of 2007. Tied into the deal was increased promotion of the Challenge Cup by the BBC, beginning in 2005.

The main TV contract was a new agreement with BSkyB Television - a five-year deal, the value not revealed, but widely accepted to be worth £53 million. The new agreement covered the period between 2004 and 2009 and included the Super League, Test and International Rugby League, and the new Tri-Nations tournament to be staged in the autumn.

But the RFL confirmed that the deal did not include the proposed World Cup, scheduled for 2008.

MARCH
TV times

The game was on the up. March commenced with the news that the opening match of the Super League season between Bradford Bulls and Wigan had attracted a record opening night audience for a Super League game, with almost a 10 per cent increase compared to the previous season's opener between St Helens and Bradford Bulls.

An audience of 230,000 viewers, according to the British Audience Research Bureau, watched the game, compared to 210,000 who watched the season's opener a year before.

It followed a figure of 240,000 that watched the World Club Challenge clash between the Bulls and Penrith Panthers a week earlier.

BSkyB, in the first year of its new five-year contract, were also considering making the Varsity Match a regular TV event after they screened this year's clash - won 29-16 by Oxford University - live for the first time in its 24-year history.

After the one-weekend break for the Challenge Cup, Round Two of Super League IX produced three more 10,000-plus gates.

One of them was at Castleford, who registered a record Super League home crowd of 11,731 as the Rhinos came to town. Leeds went home with a 34-8 victory under their belt thanks in the main to a brilliant three-try show from stand-off Danny McGuire, who went near to scoring five tries and had a big say in two others.

Tigers winger Waine Pryce suffered a hernia in the defeat and was forecast to be out for several weeks, whilst centre Paul Newlove spent the previous weekend in Devon having specialist treatment to the nerve endings in an injured foot.

Another club suffering early injuries was Hull, who registered their first league points with a less than straightforward 24-18 home win over Warrington Wolves. Young winger Richie Barnett Jnr, signed from Gateshead in the close-season, and on debut, scored two tries. But Hull forward sub Richard Fletcher suffered a broken leg, ending his comeback from seven months on the sidelines with a knee problem, after only 11 minutes on the field.

Hull had been hit in midweek when the RFL fined them £10,000 - £7,500 suspended until December 31st - for a post-game incident the previous September, when a Leeds supporters bus was stoned as it was leaving the KC Stadium.

St Helens were emerging as the early-season form team and they were 18-0 up at half-time of the Saturday TV game in London. Paul Sculthorpe was the classiest of a string of class players in the black shirt of Saints as they eventually collected the points with a 26-12 win.

The Widnes players were booed off the pitch at Halton Stadium as Huddersfield Giants hammered the Vikings 38-6.

Neil Kelly, Coach of the Year in 2002, was facing the hardest test of his coaching career, with games against Saints and Leeds next up. "We are in a dark cloud," Kelly admitted. "And a lot of it is our own creation. All the players are feeling sorry for themselves but the solution is in the changing room. There are players in there more than capable of getting a result against Huddersfield. They (the Giants) can be proud of their win but they shouldn't be doing that to us."

Kelly's job was not in danger, according to Vikings Chairman Tony Chambers, keen to dispel speculation his coach would be leaving the Halton Stadium that week.

"Neil has done a good job for us for the last two years, and we are not going to overlook all that good work on the basis of a single result," said Chambers.

Widnes were without Adam Hughes and Ryan McDonald, who'd been fortunate to escape relatively unharmed from a serious car accident the previous week, although former Melbourne centre Aaron Moule, who had come out of retirement, made a promising debut.

But the Giants' win was all the more creditable as they were without the injured Brandon Costin and Darren Turner. Turner pulled out just before kick-off when his injured back stiffened up again on the bus journey over, allowing Phil Joseph to make an accomplished Super League debut. Halfback Paul March was in inspirational form, collecting a 22-point haul.

Salford caused Wigan Warriors a real scare at the JJB before going down 20-10. Two tries from loose forward and man of the match Sean O'Loughlin saved Wigan - who had Senior Academy captain Chris Melling making his debut off the bench.

Bradford's injury problems meant they gave a debut at hooker to 20-year-old Richard Colley, as they bounced back from their Cup exit with a 40-6 win at Wakefield, Tevita Vaikona and Lesley Vainikolo scoring two tries each. The game turned out to be Toa Kohe-Love's last in Bradford colours, as he suffered knee ligament damage early in the second half.

Castleford Tigers' board were to 'review the position' of their coach Graham Steadman after the Tigers suffered a disappointing 26-0 Cup exit at the hands of Hull at the KC Stadium.

Tigers' chief executive Richard Wright admitted that he and his fellow directors were "very disappointed" with the performance, with Tigers' supporters growing increasingly restless on the club's official messageboard and local radio stations after the club's disappointing start to the season.

March

Cas had no answer to the black and whites' invention and pace, which resulted in four excellently-worked tries, including a hat-trick from man of the match Colin Best. And the Tigers suffered another injury blow at Hull, when scrum-half Ryan Sheridan left the field with a shoulder injury at half-time after scoring an apparent try that was disallowed by a touch-judge.

Richard Agar's York City Knights produced the story of the fifth round as they battled against adversity to win 29-26 at Featherstone.

The NL2 Knights were down to 15 fit players after a series of injuries and suspensions, and with some players being cup-tied. As a result, the retired Richie Hayes dug his boots out after calling it quits with a persistent shoulder injury the month before, and Danny Seal - who hadn't trained with the Knights for several weeks - had special permission to have time off work in London and travelled up to the game. Even then, the Knights were up against it when Australian centre Aaron Wood was sent off in the tenth minute. But their twelve men battled against the odds, and winger Alex Godfrey's 79th minute try sealed a gripping contest.

York's reward was a trip to Huddersfield in the quarter-finals after the Giants beat Doncaster 36-12 in a scrappy game at the McAlpine Stadium.

The last French club bowed out of the competition when Wigan defeated Limoux in southern France, 80-20, with the help of a hat-trick of tries from scrum-half Luke Robinson, and 24 points from Chris Melling, who scored a try and ten goals on his full debut for the club.

Warrington were many people's tip for the final after they accounted for Oldham at Boundary Park, scoring nine tries in a 44-10 win. The faced a trip to Whitehaven in the next round after the Cumbrians won at Batley 29-6.

Two-try Jamie Rooney carved London Broncos apart with 17 points as the Wildcats booked their place in the quarter-finals with a 29-10 win at Griffin Park.

And on the Saturday St Helens won an enthralling Knowsley Road battle with Leeds 24-14, with Willie Talau racing over for the game-clinching try nine minutes from time.

Paul Wellens, whose 2003 season had been blighted by a knee injury, finished with two crucial tries in an impressive all-round game.

St Helens did well to come back after Leeds had taken a 14-8 lead in the 36th minute after Danny McGuire had opened their scoring with a classical stand-off's try, though after that he was well marshalled by opposite number Jason Hooper.

Leeds were still well in the game until the 70th minute when a handling mistake cost them dearly.

McGuire had just saved a certain try when he brought down Feaunati with a flying dive, causing the winger to lose the ball as Keith Senior added his weight to the tackle. The video referee ruled no try and Leeds should have been relieved. But following the 20-metre tap they lost possession at a sloppy play-the-ball. Andrew Dunemann's pass went to ground after Mick Higham cleverly caught his arm, and Jon Wilkin snapped up the ball to send Talau racing clear for the match-breaking score.

Bradford Bulls captain Robbie Paul was back in action in the 20-6 victory against previously unbeaten Huddersfield Giants at the McAlpine Stadium. Paul - who broke his arm in 2003 against St Helens, and returned as a substitute in the Grand Final against Wigan, only to discover that the injury hadn't healed properly and needed further treatment - made his return unscathed from the bench at hooker.

The Bulls, who went second on points difference after slugging it out in icy wind, rain and hail, had ordered their 17-year-old centre Matt Cook to pull out of the England under-19 rugby union squad to help their injury crisis. They were without five injured players (Shontayne Hape, Michael Withers, Logan Swann, Toa Kohe-Love and Karl Pratt) at the McAlpine

The club also confirmed that it had received a letter from the Rugby Football League asking whether their coach Brian Noble would be available to coach Great Britain in the autumn Tri-Nations series against Australia and New Zealand.

The Giants' defeat left St Helens as the only undefeated side in all competitions after their 38-20 win at home over Widnes.

Deputising as captain for the injured Paul Sculthorpe, Sean Long shouldered the extra responsibility without a problem, clocking up 20 points from two tries and six goals, having a hand in two more of his side's six-try tally.

Widnes were much better than the side that subsided to the dismal home defeat by Huddersfield two weeks before, and well deserved a 14-6 lead after half an hour's play. The Vikings even fought back to 20-20 early in the second half, despite having their captain Robert Relf in the sin bin, before Long's genius took the game away from them.

First Long, deemed to have been obstructed by Relf in one of a number of decisions by referee Ashley Klein that perplexed Vikings coach Neil Kelly, supplied a superb short pass that led to Jason Hooper cutting through for the gamebreaking try. Long then got on the end of a move fashioned by props Ricky Bibey, making a long-awaited debut after injury, and Nick Fozzard and streaked away for his second try.

A Brent Grose interception try, as Castleford were in the lead and pressing for points, decided a game at the Halliwell Jones Stadium that went in the favour of the Wolves by 32-18. Two early Michael Smith bursts created tries for Jon Hepworth and Ryan Hudson, as Cas led 12-0 after eight minutes. But two John Wilshere tries pegged the score at 12-10 at the break and Grose's interception try on the hour was followed by further tries from props Mark Hilton and Paul Wood.

Wakefield, on a gusty night at the Willows, claimed their first victory - by 27-20 - in Super League IX, despite a rousing revival from the City Reds in the Saturday night game.

The victory was won in the first half as the Yorkshire club built a 22-4 lead with tries from Sid Domic, Darrell Griffin and Ben Jeffries. Salford - who looked shot to pieces - recovered their composure, but it came too late to save the Reds.

Hull produced a nine-try rout of London Broncos at the KC Stadium, with

London reject Peter Lupton the main thorn in the visitors' side. Colin Best and Richie Barnett Jnr each scored twice.

And on the Friday night at Headingley the Rhinos maintained their unbeaten Super League charge with a polished performance to down Wigan 36-24, with Jamie Jones-Buchanan and Danny McGuire each scoring two tries.

The Warriors - still without captain Andy Farrell - suffered another injury blow as Chris Melling was forced off in the opening minute with medial ligament damage. He didn't appear in first grade again in 2004. They also lost prop Danny Sculthorpe, who was suspended for two games after being referred for use of the forearm in the defeat at Headingley.

St Helens emerged as clear favourites to win the Powergen Rugby League Challenge Cup after the weekend's quarter-final ties on the last weekend of March.

A magnificent Saturday-afternoon 31-26 victory over Hull FC in front of the BBC TV cameras impressed the bookies, who slapped short odds on the Saints.

With the scores deadlocked at 26-26 for much of the second half of a see-sawing encounter, Paul Sculthorpe stamped his authority in the final nine minutes, coolly slotting a field goal and using his familiar strength to force home from dummy-half at the death

An intriguing sub-plot was the shoot-out between the halfbacks Sean Long and Richard Horne. Both produced wonderful performances and gave healthy indication of a battle to come for the Great Britain spot.

Hull led 14-2 after Shaun Briscoe and Horne tries, and then by 26-16 when Briscoe got his second try two minutes after half-time.

But by the 51st minute Saints had wiped out the difference.

Running the ball audaciously, Long hurled a looping long pass left at full tilt to find Willie Talau. The New Zealand centre thundered out of his own half with the chasers trailing, with Long running parallel to his break to take the return pass and run home. Then Keiron Cunningham demolished the defence from close range. Long's conversion bounced away from the posts, leaving the scores square for the final half hour.

Twice Hull fired off field-goal attempts, but it was Sculthorpe who hit the target before crashing over for his try two minutes from time.

The prospects of an auld firm derby were still alive as Wigan had beaten Wakefield 20-4 on a murky, drizzly night at the JJB on the Friday night.

Great Britain skipper Andy Farrell came through his comeback match with no reported problems, playing his first game at second row at club level since moving to loose forward as a teenager.

The return of Farrell and Mick Cassidy after injury for their first games of the season certainly stiffened the Wigan side, even though both players looked

Andy Farrell offloads under pressure from Wakefield's Jason Demetriou during Wigan's quarter final win

rusty at times. And Cassidy was placed on report after Gareth Ellis, the Wildcats captain and easily their best player on the night, was left in a crumpled heap in back-play. He received a one-match suspension.

For long spells in the first half the Wildcats looked the better side. But they failed to break through a dogged home defence when they held the ascendancy, and they had only two Jamie Rooney penalties to show for their efforts. Kevin Brown's opportunist try just before the hour and two tries in three minutes by Martin Aspinwall enabled the Warriors to ward off the Wildcats' determined challenge.

Huddersfield booked their first Challenge Cup semi-final for 33 years - taking a 38-6 interval lead - but NL2 York City Knights retained their pride with a big second-half effort before going out 50-12.

Giants stand-off Brandon Costin took the Powergen man of the match award after playing a major role in Huddersfield taking full command in the first quarter, scoring a try and having a hand in three of their first four touchdowns.

And it was a red letter day in west Cumbria as over 5,000 filled the Recreation Ground and Whitehaven got a taste of what Super League could bring to the town.

There was no fairytale in front of the BBC cameras, as Warrington brought Whitehaven's unbeaten record for the season to an end. Former coach Paul Cullen knew plenty about Whitehaven's star players and he masterminded a 42-10 victory, although the Cumbrians put up a stern fight.

Huddersfield's Julian Bailey on the charge against York as the Giants reach the Challenge Cup semi-finals

As March came to a close, London Broncos moved to squash speculation that coach Tony Rea's job was on the line after a poor start to the season, even though the Broncos moved off the foot of the Tetley's Super League table following their win over Salford City Reds at Griffin Park. (The game was brought forward from round 17, as Griffin Park was to be unavailable in July because of pitch re-seeding). The Broncos won a crucial victory to drag themselves off the foot of the table, winning a 12-try thriller 35-30, Jim Dymock sealing the win with a last-minute field goal.

Former Australia coach Chris Anderson, currently out of work and taking legal action against his former club Cronulla Sharks, was linked to the club and was at the Salford game. But Broncos' chief executive Nic Cartwright denied he was taking Rea's job. "Tony Rea has got the safest job in the whole of Super League, because without Tony there is no London Broncos," said Cartwright, who claimed that the Broncos were "100 per cent" behind Rea, and sacking their coach of five years was "not even on the radar". There was some change though, with the Broncos releasing the much-travelled Radney Bowker, and replacing him with the loan acquisition of Leeds youngster Scott Murrell.

Bradford Bulls denied media reports in Australia that South Sydney's Test back-rower Bryan Fletcher was set to join the Bulls for the 2005 season to replace Logan Swann, whose contract ran to the end of Super League IX.

And on the international front, Scotland coach Billy McGinty urged the RFL to announce details of the European Nations Cup quickly - allowing developing nations such as the Scots a chance to structure their long-term future.

SUPER LEAGUE TABLE - *Sunday 28th March*

	P	W	D	L	F	A	D	PTS
Leeds Rhinos	3	3	0	0	128	46	82	6
Bradford Bulls	3	3	0	0	94	18	76	6
St Helens	3	3	0	0	94	48	46	6
Hull FC	3	2	0	1	86	52	34	4
Warrington Wolves	3	2	0	1	84	62	22	4
Huddersfield Giants	3	2	0	1	70	48	22	4
Salford City Reds	4	1	0	3	84	94	-10	2
Wigan Warriors	3	1	0	2	50	80	-30	2
Wakefield T Wildcats	3	1	0	2	53	94	-41	2
London Broncos	4	1	0	3	65	160	-95	2
Castleford Tigers	3	0	0	3	48	92	-44	0
Widnes Vikings	3	0	0	3	38	100	-62	0

APRIL
A safe bet?

There may have been question marks about the experience of former St Helens assistant Jon Sharp when he was named as Tony Smith's successor at Huddersfield, but not after the Giants registered their third win out of four games - a 26-10 victory over Wigan at the McAlpine Stadium. Fullback Paul Reilly was in spectacular form, capping a gamestar performance with a try a minute from time.

Utility forward Bob Beswick made a bench debut for Wigan, after Gregory lost forward Harrison Hansen for six weeks with a broken scaphoid, and teenage forward Dave Allen was sidelined with an ankle injury.

That weekend Warriors Chairman Maurice Lindsay categorically denied reports in the Sydney media that former Australian Test coach Chris Anderson was being lined up to take over at the JJB Stadium.

At the bottom of the table the Vikings claimed they had missed out on a Kiwi halfback they were trailing as a replacement for the departed Dean Lawford, released to join Batley in March.

Widnes denied they were interested in New Zealand Warriors' giant prop Mark Tookey, who hadn't figured in the Warriors' senior side in 2004.

On the field there was little joy either for Widnes and they were not in the same ballpark as visitors Leeds Rhinos, still unbeaten in the league. Leeds won 46-0 - the first time they had nilled a side in the summer era - in a clinical nine-try demolition, with Matt Diskin involved in virtually every Leeds attack.

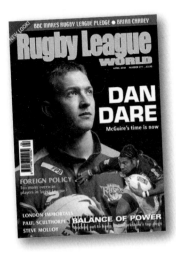

Besides the Vikings, only Castleford Tigers were searching for their first win, although there was much promise in the 22-14 home defeat by St Helens, themselves maintaining a one hundred per cent record. Castleford had fought back from 12-0 down to be only four points behind, and were looking set to snatch the lead when Jason Hooper finished them off with two quickfire strikes midway through the second half.

It could have been a try under the Saints' post as Cas halfback Jon Hepworth popped out a pass, only for it to go straight to Hooper and none in the Cas team could catch him as he set off on an 85-metre gallop to the line. Five minutes later

Hooper struck again, breaking down the left before sending Paul Wellens away to the posts.

A typical bulldozing try from winger Lesley Vainikolo seven minutes from time broke Salford's heroic resistance and maintained Bradford's winning start to Super League IX. The City Reds led from the opening minute of the game until deep into the second half with their halfback combination of Gavin Clinch and Cliff Beverley - who scored a hat-trick - in great form. Salford coach Karl Harrison confirmed he had made an offer of a one-year deal to the Manly centre Kevin McGuinness.

Wakefield captain Gareth Ellis was playing his way back into the Great Britain squad - according to Wildcats coach Shane McNally - as he starred in Trinity's 21-27 defeat at home to Hull on the Saturday night.

Prop Garreth Carvell - moved up to the starting line-up from the bench just minutes before kick-off, when Ewan Dowes was forced to pull out with a leg injury - swung a see-saw game decisively in Hull's favour to earn the Black and Whites' first away win since May 2003. He scored the decisive try eight minutes from the end, latching onto Paul Cooke's off-balance kick to touch down.

Warrington stayed in the top-six with a telling 36-24 win at London, sub Jerome Guisset's two tries in ten minutes making a match-winning impact. But the Wolves lost winger John Wilshere, who went off with a damaged cheek in the opening minutes of the game.

That week Warrington chief executive Andy Gatcliffe said he was "investigating" the identity of an April Fool prankster who convinced some national media outlets that the Wolves had signed Iestyn Harris.

An official-sounding press release from a spoof email address purporting to be that of Wolves press officer Gina Coldrick - accompanied by a picture which proved to be Harris' head glued on to the body of prop Mark Hilton - was responsible. The Internet prankster later sent an emailed apology to Coldrick, who had to spend many hours denying the reports.

A good-natured war of words broke out between Wigan chairman Maurice Lindsay and Leeds Rhinos chief executive Gary Hetherington after the first part of the Easter Holiday programme over whether the Leeds-Bradford or Saints-Wigan derby was now the bigger game.

The Rhinos thanked their fans for creating the first ever sold out game for the club, with a capacity crowd of 21,225 attending Headingley on the Thursday night to watch the Rhinos defeat the Bulls 26-18. "It was a special night in the history of the Rhinos," said Hetherington.

"Has Gary never heard of Good Friday?" asked Lindsay. "I can't remember our Good Friday game ever being less than an epic contest. It always will be the biggest derby in Rugby League."

Rugby Leaguer & League Express match reporter Mike Latham would have sided with Lindsay after Saints and Wigan fought out a monster 21-21 draw at Knowsley Road - only the tenth draw in 215 league games between the rivals. 'For raw passion, unending excitement and the full roller-coaster of emotions, this game was in the top echelon - it had just about everything, with wonderfully-fashioned tries, tremendous bone-jarring defence, great ball skills and the mother of all brawls, all played before a captivated near-16,000 crowd with the kick-off delayed for ten minutes.'

Sean Long's improvised field goal two minutes from time salvaged a point for Saints and preserved their unbeaten start to the season, as they trailed by a point after Andrew Farrell's 30-metre field goal eight minutes from time. Then Long instigated one last raid and Lee Gilmour looked set for his hat-trick try down the right, only to be denied by Brett Dallas's sharp tackle.

And the game will be long remembered for a mass 59th-minute brawl that Karl Kirkpatrick put on report, as well sin-binning the initial transgressors, Wigan hooker Terry Newton and Saints' Jon Wilkin. The following Wednesday Dom Feaunati was suspended for three games for punching, Andy Farrell was fined £500 for his part in the brawl, while Saints captain Paul Sculthorpe was found not guilty.

At Headingley Danny McGuire scored a thrilling brace of tries after coming off the bench as Leeds beat a side that had beaten them on all five occasions in 2003. Seemingly knocked out on the half-hour, and receiving lengthy treatment, his next touch five minutes later saw McGuire temptingly tease the visiting defence, before searing around Paul Johnson for a glorious solo score which made it 10-6 at the break.

His second solo glide, on the blind side 40 metres out from the base of a scrum in the 64th minute, gave his side breathing space in a breathless clash.

In the Good Friday Mersey derby the Vikings got off the mark as they stunned the Wolves 24-16 at the HJ Stadium. It was Widnes's first win since September 2003.

Aaron Moule sparkled on his first derby outing, making several breaks and looking a continuous threat with his footwork and agility in the centres, and Stephen Myler belied his first team inexperience with a confident display at halfback. But it was Jules O'Neill who played the leading role - "a masterclass in how to kick the ball where you intend to kick it, gain field position and screw a side into the floor on the back of it" was Paul Cullen's summation.

Hull beat Castleford 26-4 at the KC Stadium on the Thursday night in a virtual re-run of the Challenge Cup-tie the two sides contested less than a month earlier. From the sixth minute, when Hull centre Kirk Yeaman raced over off man of the match Paul Cooke's pass for the home side's first of four first-half tries, the Tigers faced an uphill struggle.

Huddersfield Giants' reawakening continued, but a 24-16 win over Salford was harder than expected. In fact, Salford were poised to take over after recovering from being 12-2 down early on to be only two points behind when Julian Bailey shattered their revival with a superb long-distance try in the 55th minute.

April

Tony Rea's policy of bringing in young English players, talented but unproven, looked to be backfiring after the Broncos fell to their fifth loss out of six games - a 39-16 home defeat by Wakefield Trinity Wildcats. Two-try David Wrench narrowly shaded the gamestar rating from David Solomona.

At the start of the month the RFL announced a new sponsor, LHF Healthplan, for National Leagues One, Two and Three for the 2004 season.

St Helens' Jason Hooper was the first winner of the 'Rugby Leaguer & League Express' Readers' Poll as the Super League Player of the Month for the first four rounds. Hooper outpolled Leeds Rhinos' stars Danny McGuire and Matt Diskin, Huddersfield Giants' halfback Paul March, and Bradford Bulls' winger Lesley Vainikolo.

As Rugby League fans enjoyed a Sunday off in preparation for Easter Monday, there was no indication of the storm that was about to hit the game.

For the first time in its history, Rugby Leaguer & League Express produced an Easter Special edition. It turned out to be a wise move, if only to accommodate the sacks full of letters expressing outrage at the events at Odsal on Easter Monday afternoon.

The match-up between the Bulls and St Helens was eagerly anticipated, but the game turned out to be wholly one-sided as Saints coach Ian Millward made 11 changes from the team that drew 21-21 with Wigan on Good Friday, fielding five Academy debutants in a side that went down 56-8 to the Bulls. And they were down to 12 men after Jon Wilkin, one of the few who played four days earlier, was sent off after only ten minutes for a late challenge on Paul Deacon - which later earned him a four-match suspension.

Millward was slammed in several sections of the media, and by supporters of both clubs. "We prepared to fight George Foreman and got George Formby," was Bradford coach Brian Noble's reaction to the mis-match. But Millward was backed by the St Helens board and the RFL also confirmed that they would not take any further action against the club, as they did in 2002, when they fined Saints £25,000 for fielding a weakened team - again at Bradford - ahead of a Challenge Cup semi-final. The fine was later rescinded.

"Following the Tetley's Rugby Super League Round 6 fixture between Bradford Bulls and St Helens, the Rugby Football League (RFL) has received and examined the official team sheets from the game," a statement read. "The RFL can confirm that the St Helens club had submitted relevant documentation relating to participating players prior to that fixture and all players who took part in the game had been approved to play at Super League level. This was in accordance with bye-laws relating to the Tetley's Rugby Super League competition."

Saints cancelled their weekly press conference on the Tuesday, but chief executive Sean McGuire issued a public backing of his coach.

"The club's executive management team fully supports the selections made by the medical and coaching team," McGuire said. "Good Friday saw a fantastic effort from the 17 involved and, coupled with the intense Cup run, we have had a very testing start to the season. It was great to see Martin Gleeson, Tim Jonkers and James Graham back in action following serious injury.

"The team has received fantastic support so far this season, and everyone connected with the Saints appreciates that backing – our average home attendance so far this season is over 12,000, and that is a testament to our supporters."

The episode re-opened the debate around a two-game programme over Easter with most clubs' coaches almost unanimous in their opposition to the congested weekend. But the RFL insisted it would continue with the policy of having two games over the Easter period because the clubs wanted it, and a two-match programme was now written into the television contract with BSkyB.

The furore at Bradford overshadowed the rest of the Easter Monday programme, but there were other significant results. Saints' first defeat of the season allowed Leeds to stretch two points clear at the top of the table after a 44-0 hammering of Salford at the Willows; Widnes stunned Hull at the Halton Stadium 32-18 to move four points off the bottom; and the Giants strode clear in third place after a 24-17 win at Wakefield. And a try from Danny Tickle four minutes from time gave Wigan - with Adrian Lam making his comeback off the bench - a dramatic 26-24 win over the Wolves at the JJB.

And on Easter Tuesday boos echoed around The Jungle as London won a televised basement battle 42-34 to pile more agony on beleaguered Cas boss Graham Steadman. The Broncos went four points clear of the Tigers, who remained the only point-less team in the competition, a Dennis Moran try 12 minutes from time finally killing off the Tigers.

The defeat was to have repercussions for Steadman, but the fall-out from the Bulls-Saints game was to have far greater repercussions. Saints coach Millward told Rugby Leaguer & Leaguer Express that he didn't want to dwell on the match. "I just want to move on now - the club and RFL have made statements and it's a closed case now," he said.

Not quite.

On Friday 16 April, the Daily Mail newspaper ran a two-page exclusive that claimed two St Helens players, Sean Long and Martin Gleeson - who played in the game and scored the opening try - had placed thousand pound bets on Bradford Bulls to win the game between the Bulls and Saints on Easter Monday - breaking Rugby Football League bye-laws.

Huddersfield chief executive Ralph Rimmer suggested optimistically the pair should both be suspended by the RFL from the following Sunday's Powergen Challenge Cup semi-final between the Giants and Saints at Warrington's Halliwell Jones Stadium. The RFL did confirm that Long and Gleeson had been sent letters by Norman Sarsfield, the Disciplinary Commissioner, informing them that they were under investigation. Both players were to be invited to meetings with the investigators "in the near future."

Sarsfield appealed for anybody who might think they had relevant information about the case to contact him via RFL HQ "on a strictly confidential basis".

The events left the Saints fans in a disappointing 7,649 Knowsley Road crowd in muted mood and the awful weather - with continuous rain making for monsoon-like pitch conditions - hardly helped lift the gloom, as Paul Sculthorpe scored a hat-trick in a routine 40-4 win over Salford. 'And Salford (playing their fourth game in 14 days), facing up to another familiar battle against relegation, just looked plain knackered - their resources, physical and mental drained to the dregs by a punishing fixture list', wrote Mike Latham in Rugby Leaguer & League Express. Long and Gleeson were among the Saints' injured list but Ian Millward confirmed that both would be considered for selection for the Cup semi-final if fit.

Huddersfield were brought down to earth at Leeds - coach Jon Sharp had hit out earlier in the week at the hectic nature of the Easter schedule, branding it "disgraceful", with the trip to Headingley the Giants' fourth Super League match in 13 days. Rob Burrow's introduction from the bench and a Chev Walker hat-trick were the significant factors in a 38-6 home victory.

London Broncos rose to the heady heights of eighth position after a 34-18 win over Widnes at Griffin Park. Dennis Moran scored one try and set up another five for the Broncos.

And in the Saturday game, Castleford fans staged a "mini sit-in protest" after their 10-42 home defeat to neighbours Wakefield. Coach Graham Steadman calmed the situation when he addressed the supporters after the game.

Cas stand-off Sean Rudder suffered concussion and the Wildcats lost influential halfback Jamie Rooney with a broken fibula after only 23 minutes. But Wakefield battled back from being 10-6 down on 30 minutes to shoot the Tigers to pieces with a rapid burst of six second-half tries.

The following Tuesday Steadman was sacked after seven straight Super League defeats and 15 years as player and coach at the Jungle.

Round Eight of Super League IX belonged to Hull and in particular their young fullback Shaun Briscoe. Shaun McRae had snapped up Briscoe at the end of the 2003 season when he was released by Wigan, and it paid great dividends in Hull's stunning 26-18 win at Bradford, as Briscoe scored four tries. It was Hull's first win at Bradford for over a decade.

Bradford were without wingers Lesley Vainikolo (on Anzac Day Test duty for New Zealand along with skipper Robbie Paul) and Tevita Vaikona (whose knee injury sustained in the rout over St Helens looked likely to keep him out for the season).

Widnes coach Neil Kelly was widely linked with the vacancy at Castleford Tigers but he made the job - regardless of who eventually took it - significantly harder, by inflicting the Tigers' eighth successive Super League defeat, by 29-18 at Halton Stadium.

Tigers' caretaker coach Gary Mercer threw his hat into the ring to take the job on a permanent basis - and insisted the Tigers would not be relegated while he was at the club. Despite the defeat, the side was cheered at the end of the game by the club's travelling support.

Wakefield had their biggest home crowd (7,680) since entering Super League in 1999 for the visit of Leeds Rhinos, who made it eight wins from eight games with a 36-12 success. Keith Senior celebrated his 28th birthday a day early by taking over the captaincy for the first time from the injured Kevin Sinfield and scored two well-taken tries in addition to assisting with Danny McGuire's second try.

Warrington held onto sixth position in the table with a 37-18 win at the Willows on the Saturday. Paul Cullen's patched-up men were well worth their victory - but the result would have been different if a crucial call by referee Russell Smith had gone the way of the home side. With the scoreline at 18-18, Salford were in the ascendancy, but after acting skipper Sean Rutgerson was adjudged to have knocked the ball on in his own half, Paul Wood took full advantage and the Wolves never looked back.

TV replays showed that second-row Rutgerson re-gathered the ball before it touched Danny Lima, and a knock-on should not have been awarded. Lee Briers added a field goal before Mark Gleeson and Richard Varkulis crossed late on. And Wigan moved up a place into seventh after a 64-8 hammering of London Broncos at the JJB Stadium. Wigan started with the much-anticipated halfback partnership of Danny Orr and Adrian Lam - finally given a contract to the end of the season - for the first time. Adding to a growing feelgood factor at the JJB was an encouraging wing debut from 18-year-old Londoner Desi Williams.

Warrington were back in action the following Tuesday in a round seven catch up game against Bradford.

"It's a long season and moments like this can be defining," said Brian Noble as his Bradford team staged a second-half revival to take a point from a 22-all draw, which seemed unlikely for much of a rainy evening in Warrington. A jet-lagged Lesley Vainikolo, who flew halfway across the world after the ANZAC Test to collect a nasty facial injury in the first half but returned to the field with a closed swollen eye, levelled the scores with a try three minutes from time. Bulls skipper Robbie Paul was missing after damaging an ankle during New Zealand's defeat by Australia in the Test.

The Bulls pack been battered by the rampant Wolves forwards, Mark Hilton and Danny Lima to the fore. Lima, already a crowd favourite, enhanced his reputation, bouncing off tackles in a series of thumping charges upfield, although some suspect tackles booked him a date at an RFL Disciplinary hearing a week later, He was banned for three games.

Lee Briers - playing with broken fingers - had a fine match, hurdling the barriers to applaud his own first-half try from the stands.

SUPER LEAGUE TABLE - *Tuesday 27th April*

	P	W	D	L	F	A	D	PTS
Leeds Rhinos	8	8	0	0	318	82	236	16
Bradford Bulls	8	5	1	2	231	118	113	11
St Helens	7	5	1	1	185	141	44	11
Hull FC	7	5	0	2	183	127	56	10
Huddersfield Giants	7	5	0	2	150	129	21	10
Warrington Wolves	8	4	1	3	219	176	43	9
Wigan Warriors	7	3	1	3	171	159	12	7
Wakefield T Wildcats	8	3	0	5	184	207	-23	6
Widnes Vikings	8	3	0	5	141	232	-91	6
London Broncos	9	3	0	6	189	351	-162	6
Salford City Reds	9	1	0	8	140	264	-124	2
Castleford Tigers	8	0	0	8	128	253	-125	0

The Rugby Football League was accused of a lack of ambition after selecting two venues with a combined capacity of only just over 26,000 for the Powergen Challenge Cup semi-finals

The RFL confirmed all four clubs had agreed to the venues - Warrington's new Halliwell Jones stadium and Widnes's Halton Stadium - after extensive talks. RFL Executive Chairman Richard Lewis came out fighting in defence of the decisions. "It is easy to underestimate the importance of full stadia when you are on television, and I feel strongly that we should be playing in front of full stadia," Lewis told 'Rugby Leaguer & League Express'.

And this year the RFL reverted to playing the ties on separate weekends - on Sundays 18 and 25 April - as Wigan and St Helens booked their places at Cardiff.

In the first semi at Widnes that drew a crowd of 11,175, winger Brett Dallas scored a thrilling hat-trick of tries to sink the challenge of Warrington Wolves, by 30-18. Dallas had rejected the opportunity of a two-and-a-half year contract from Cronulla at the end of 2003 in favour of trying to earn another contract with Wigan, despite a run of injuries - cheekbone, knee cruciate ligaments and then recurring hamstring problems - that had marred his time at the JJB.

Mike Gregory, the Wigan coach, reflected: "To be honest I think Warrington with the ball were the better team. But defensively we were magnificent."

A week later, on a warm and sunny spring afternoon at Warrington, the returning Sean Long was in magnificent form with a virtuoso 58-minute performance, as Saints rampaged through to Cardiff, beating the Giants 46-6.

Long had a hand in four of his side's five first-half tries, and then broke the second-half deadlock with a typically impudent effort of his own, as Saints opened up a 32-6 lead on their way to their fifth Challenge Cup Final of the summer era, and their sixth Final overall against old enemies Wigan.

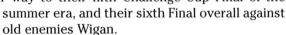

Both Long and Martin Gleeson would be available for the Final, with the report on their alleged betting scandal by the RFL not expected to be finalised before 15 May.

The Giants, appearing in their first semi-final since 1971, and looking for their first Challenge Cup win over Saints for 36 years, were never really in the hunt.

Meanwhile, the Super League clubs postponed a decision on whether to allow French club Union Treiziste Catalane into Super League in 2006.

CHALLENGE CUP FINAL
Another Long story

St Helens registered their ninth Challenge Cup victory, beating their great rivals 32-16 on a blistering day in Cardiff.

Saints had beaten Super League big guns at every stage of the competition, and they were worthy winners of the Powergen Challenge Cup in 2004. And nobody enjoyed the sweet moment more than Sean Long - Lance Todd Trophy winner for the second time in four years - whose kicking game wore down a mighty Wigan effort.

Long was even better than in the 13-6 win over Bradford in 2001. But there were plenty of other contenders. Paul Wellens was solid at the back, and a constant thorn with the ball in hand; Paul Sculthorpe hit the line with ferocity; and Willie Talau still looked every inch an international centre. Plus there was the industry of props Keith Mason, Nick Fozzard and Mark Edmondson, who - eventually - got the better of their 30-something front-row opponents.

Wigan were equal to Saints for the first half at least, but found themselves ten points adrift at half-time after 40 marvellous minutes that left the capacity crowd breathless. When Saints stretched into a 26-10 lead on 50 minutes, the game was up, and the more they tried the more the Warriors gave up possession.

Captain Andrew Farrell couldn't have given any more to the cause; Brett Dallas, scoring two tries, was fast and elusive; and Terry Newton was always dangerous from dummy-half.

But there was to be no repeat of Edinburgh 2002, when Wigan defied the odds after Saints went into the final as overwhelming favourites.

Saints were in the lead after only three minutes. In Wigan's second set of the game they were looking at completing successfully again with a kick from their own 40-metre line.

As Newton fed Danny Orr for the downtown, and he passed on to Kris Radlinski for the kick, Jason Hooper was around his legs like a flash, the ball went to ground, and Talau scooped it up and tore towards the Wigan line. The Kiwi had the coolness to feed Lee Gilmour in support on his left, and the back-rower - a substitute for the Bulls in the 2003 Final win on the same ground – had the pace to race over on the left. Long converted magnificently.

Farrell was convinced he had created the equaliser when he made a tilt for the line after eight minutes, only for the ball to shoot forward out of his arms, before Newton hurdled a pile of bodies to ground the ball just short of the dead ball line. Farrell and his teammates claimed that Paul Sculthorpe had dislodged the ball from his hands as he went for the line – in a two-man tackle – and there had been no knock-on. Video referee David Asquith thought otherwise, and called a Saints 20-metre tap.

But Wigan scented a breakthrough, and Orr trapped Ade Gardner in-goal before the Warriors got points on the board in spectacular fashion. Farrell dropped Gareth Hock inside 50 metres from the Saints line. Super League's Young Player of 2003 produced a trademark hop and skip, enough to draw in two defenders in Mason and Fozzard, and slipped a perfectly-timed pass to the trailing Radlinski. Hooper managed to tackle the Wigan fullback, but Radlinski popped a ball around him to the speeding Adrian Lam.

Lam was away, but Wellens stood in his way and the supporting Terry Newton was crowded out by Saints defenders. Instinctively Lam chipped ahead, was blocked by Wellens, but Newton won the race to the kick, collected at speed, juggled the ball and dived under the posts. Farrell converted. Three minutes later Wigan looked to have taken the lead when Keiron Cunningham, on one of his destructive forays 40 metres from his own line, tried an overhead offload and the ball ended loose on the ground. Kevin Brown reacted first, scooped up the ball and showed Long a clean pair of heels on his way to the posts. But the video referee was called to adjudicate, and in the midfield scramble Craig Smith was seen to have knocked the ball forward.

POWERGEN CHALLENGE CUP FINAL

Saturday 15th May 2004

ST HELENS 32 WIGAN WARRIORS 16

SAINTS: 1 Paul Wellens; 2 Ade Gardner; 3 Martin Gleeson; 4 Willie Talau; 5 Darren Albert; 6 Jason Hooper; 7 Sean Long; 8 Nick Fozzard; 9 Keiron Cunningham; 16 Keith Mason; 11 Chris Joynt; 12 Lee Gilmour; 13 Paul Sculthorpe (C). Subs: 18 Mark Edmondson for Mason (16); 22 Dom Feaunati for Gardner (24); Mason for Edmondson (36); Gardner for Feaunati (HT); Edmondson for Joynt (48); 21 Jon Wilkin for Mason (60); Feaunati for Gardner (66); Mason for Edmondson (70); 20 Ricky Bibey for Fozzard (70); Gardner for Feaunati (72); Joynt for Wilkin (75).
Tries: Gilmour (3), Talau (23, 68), Wellens (39), Sculthorpe (50); **Goals:** Long 6/7.
On report: Feaunati (31) - high tackle on Brown.
WARRIORS: 1 Kris Radlinski; 4 David Hodgson; 15 Sean O'Loughlin; 21 Kevin Brown; 2 Brett Dallas; 6 Danny Orr; 7 Adrian Lam; 10 Craig Smith; 9 Terry Newton; 18 Quentin Pongia; 12 Danny Tickle; 20 Gareth Hock; 13 Andy Farrell (C). Subs: 8 Terry O'Connor for Smith (19); 16 Danny Sculthorpe for Pongia (20); 11 Mick Cassidy for Tickle (28); Smith for Sculthorpe (48); 19 Stephen Wild for Hock (52); Pongia for O'Connor (55); Tickle for Cassidy (61); Sculthorpe for Smith (66); Hock for Pongia (70).
Tries: Newton (13), Dallas (33, 65); **Goals:** Farrell 2/3.
Rugby Leaguer & League Express Men of the Match: *Saints:* Sean Long; *Warriors:* Andy Farrell.
Penalty count: 2-4; **Half-time:** 20-10;
Referee: Karl Kirkpatrick (Warrington);
Attendance: 73,734 *(at Millennium Stadium, Cardiff).*

The disallowing of Brown's try was a turning point. Within two minutes Saints were back on the Wigan '20', and Quentin Pongia handed them two points with a high tackle on Wellens, 30 metres in front of the posts. Long made it 8-6, and after Brett Dallas - who that week received offers from Brisbane and Cronulla to return to the NRL in 2005 - made a searing break down the left, but to most observers' astonishment was brought back for a forward pass, Long grubbered into the in-goal towards the left centre. Talau steamed onto the ball, as David Hodgson stumbled, to claim the try. Long converted for a 14-6 lead.

On the half-hour mark Saints looked to have extended the lead when, after a brilliant Gilmour offload in midfield, the ball was worked left by Long, Hooper

Martin Gleeson, Keith Mason and Paul Sculthorpe combine to halt Danny Sculthorpe

and Talau, and Darren Albert eluded two tackles down the wing. The touch judge was unsighted, but the video proved that the winger had stepped on the touchline.

A Dom Feaunati high tackle on Brown – the giant Samoan started on the bench and was interchanged several times during the game on the right wing with Ade Gardner – was put on report, and Wigan were able to make their way downfield.

A magical Danny Sculthorpe offload caused chaos in the Saints defence, but when the sub's next pass went to ground five metres from the Saints line, the danger seemed over. But as Gleeson ran the ball out, Farrell dislodged the ball from his grasp and Newton pounced. Farrell went into dummy-half, slung a superb long ball out to Lam in the left centre, and the halfback timed a wonderful pass to put Dallas into the left corner. Farrell hit the post with the conversion attempt, but at 14-10 it was anyone's game.

51

Challenge Cup Final

Saints engineered a crucial score just before the break. They gained a repeat set when a Long chip took a lucky ricochet 30 metres out, and made it count. They worked the ball left through Hooper and Talau, and then back to the right again with crisp short passing from Gilmour, Sculthorpe and finally Mason, before Wellens forced his way through Radlinski and Hock's tackle just to the left of the posts. The hooter sounded as Long stroked over his fourth goal.

On 46 minutes Albert looked a certain scorer as he was released by Mason and Talau 40 metres out, and Radlinski, initially covering for the inside pass, had to perform a miracle to catch and tackle the Aussie flyer into touch.

Wigan were under pressure and their prayers for relief seemed to have been answered on 50 minutes, when a Cunningham pass went to ground and Brown collected to tear away from his own line. The pass that Brown attempted out of the tackle to Dallas is likely to be the subject of a recurring nightmare for the young centre.

The ball went to ground, Paul Sculthorpe collected and, although he was tackled by Lam, from the play-the ball he made himself available from Long's dummy-half pass and crashed through the tackle of Newton. Long converted, and four minutes later added a 20-metre penalty after Craig Smith went high on Edmondson.

Brown's confidence looked shot to pieces – after his rush of blood he spilled a high pass straight from a scrum in a big Martin Gleeson tackle. But he showed his composure on 65 minutes when Craig Smith's pass sent him racing down field from his own quarter and his measured inside ball sent Dallas to the posts. Farrell converted and 28-16, with 15 minutes left on the clock, gave Wigan a glimmer of hope. It was snuffed out three minutes later.

Just as the press were submitting their votes for the Lance Todd Trophy winner, Long chipped from halfway, collected on the run and Gilmour linked to send in Talau. Long missed the conversion, but it couldn't detract from his match-winning contribution.

St Helens - 2004 Challenge Cup Winners

MAY
Tigers find their feet

As Britain looked forward to the Mayday holiday weekend, Leeds were beginning to look unbeatable.

They weren't. The Rhinos went to Knowsley Road as unbeaten leaders of Super League, having conceded just 14 tries in eight games. They left it still top, but humbled, having conceded nine tries in a 56-10 defeat. Saints' front three of Nick Fozzard, Keith Mason and Keiron Cunningham played a massive role, punching holes in the Leeds defence all night. They owned the opening quarter during which Saints established a commanding 16-point lead. Jason Hooper's containment of Danny McGuire and his two-try, two-goal contribution earned him the gamestar rating.

Just as in March's Powergen Challenge Cup tie between these two sides, too many of Leeds talented squad failed to hit their best form but Leeds coach Tony Smith, who was missing hooker Matt Diskin for the first time, promised: "We'll come back stronger, we always do. It's a long, long season. We've learnt some very good lessons tonight."

Meanwhile Saints were reported to be favourites to capture the signature of Ali Lauitiiti, who had been released by the New Zealand Warriors.

There was an even more one-sided contest the following Sunday at the KC Stadium as Hull humiliated Salford 82-6. After the victory at Odsal, Hull director of rugby Shaun McRae had asked his men not to drop their guard and his team responded in style, running in 15 tries. After his Odsal four-try heroics, Shaun Briscoe scored three tries in four minutes either side of half-time.

Huddersfield continued to demonstrate their credentials as they came away from Warrington with a 26-20 victory. Their 21-year-old giant Eorl Crabtree had a stormer and Sean Penkywicz's speed from dummy-half and kicking game were decisive in the Giants' victory.

"We're doing it tough," admitted Paul Cullen, as the Wolves played their third game in nine days, with Leeds to come five days later. "But we've allowed ourselves to become victims of the circumstances we've found ourselves in."

Gary Mercer, in his second match in charge, saw his injury-hit Tigers give easily their best performance of the year, scoring 28 points against Cup-final bound Wigan Warriors, only to go down to their ninth successive league defeat of the season by 42-28. Castleford led 24-20 going into the last quarter - Paul Mellor collecting a hat-trick of tries from high kicks - before falling to a late Wigan surge. Gamestar Terry Newton grabbed two tries and just missed a hat-trick in a totally-involved display.

Wakefield gained a first win of the season on home soil at a sun-drenched

Belle Vue - by 40-10 - and their first victory over Widnes in seven Super League meetings. Five tries in 23 second-half minutes sealed the points that took Trinity to the verge of top six as Shane McNally gave debuts off the bench to second-rower Mark Applegarth - who scored the Wildcats' last try - and former Halifax halfback Liam Finn.

And on Mayday Monday Bradford got back to winning ways with a far from straightforward 24-12 win at cold, windy and wet London. The Broncos, missing nine regulars, were forced to beg, steel and borrow replacements for this game after their hammering at Wigan Warriors, with Dwayne Barker and Jason Netherton brought in on loan from Leeds Rhinos, while former Bulls junior, Welshman Steve Thomas - who played two games for Warrington in 2001 - arrived via union side Penzance & Newlyn. And they pushed the Bulls - who also had Andy Smith on debut on the wing - all the way until Stuart Reardon's try seven minutes from time finally killed off any hopes the Broncos had of a late comeback.

That weekend, Wigan players were stunned by the news that coach Mike Gregory was suffering from a debilitating illness, and would fly to the USA after the Powergen Challenge Cup Final to have treatment.

Bradford coach Brian Noble was finally unveiled as the coach of Great Britain on a three-year part-time contract. And the following Sunday a four-try supershow from Stuart Reardon - playing on the wing - helped move the rampaging Bulls into second place in the table and left the injury-ravaged Castleford Tigers - who lost Jamie Thackray with a broken arm - still looking for their first win of the season, 44-18 the scoreline.

Leeds Rhinos had won the battle to sign giant Kiwi forward Ali Lauitiiti. St Helens had earlier emerged as favourites as they too had a spare quota spot, but their efforts were derailed because they could not match Leeds' offer and stay under the salary cap.

That weekend the Rhinos bounced back from their Knowsley Road mauling with a 23-10 win over injury-hit Warrington at Headingley, Kevin Sinfield's 71st minute field goal decisive. Wolves coach Paul Cullen was a proud man in defeat. "I'm delighted with the response on the back of a month that has punished us to the point of abuse," he said, as the Wolves dropped out of the top-six for the first time.

Wigan jumped over them into the play-off spots after their 26-8 home win over Widnes - their fifth successive win - though it was a scrappy encounter, evenly littered with 22 penalties. There was a try-scoring return to action for David Hodgson, playing his first game since tearing his Achilles in the pre-season friendly with London. And Mike Gregory handed a debut off the bench to 19-year-old winger Liam Colbon. Vikings' Adam Bibey, the 18-year-old younger brother of Saints prop Ricky, will long remember his Super League debut, being despatched for holding-down within a minute of taking the field. Neil Kelly also gave a debut to 20-year-old Phil Wood, impressive in deputising for injured hooker Shane Millard.

A late disallowed David March try prevented Wigan's Cup Final opponents Saints from dropping just their third point of the Super League season, as they hung on for a 26-20 home win over Wakefield.

Embarrassment turned to elation for Salford City Reds coach Karl Harrison as his side bounced back from a ten-game losing streak in style to beat London Broncos 30-12. After the previous week's 82-6 hammering at Hull, the vultures were gathering around the Willows, but a four-try blast inside 15 first-half minutes ensured Harrison would sleep a little easier. Kevin McGuinness made a positive impression on debut.

And Hull followed up the 15-try rout of Salford by nilling Huddersfield at McAlpine Stadium 20-0. But the Giants ran them much closer than the scoreline suggested, having three try-claims overruled, while Hull opened with a very dubious touchdown. All this after Huddersfield had lost their key player, Brandon Costin, in the opening minutes with a hamstring injury. But it was a tremendous defensive effort from Hull, that produced their first Super League clean sheet since 1998.

Wigan winger Brett Dallas was named as the 'Rugby Leaguer & League Express' readers' Player of the Month for April, narrowly edging out a strong challenge from Keiron Cunningham, Richard Swain, Jules O'Neill and Lee Briers.

After the wonderful Challenge Cup Final weekend put League in the spotlight, there was more national exposure to come the weekend after. A report in the 'News of the World' newspaper claimed that Wigan had tried to cover up the fact that Wigan prop forward Quentin Pongia was diagnosed with the Hepatitis B virus before the start of the season.

Wigan chairman Maurice Lindsay strongly refuted the claim, adamant that he'd informed the Rugby Football League within 24 hours of Pongia's condition being diagnosed.

Pongia received the result of a blood test showing that he had the virus in January, and had since undergone treatment for the condition, which can be passed on by blood-to-blood contact. But Pongia, who is thought to have had the condition since he was born, had continued to play, after the club received advice that the risk of transmission in a Rugby League game was minimal.

An RFL spokesman was reluctant to be drawn on why the RFL had apparently not taken action on being informed of Pongia's condition.

Later that week the RFL issued all clubs with a six-page document, with a recommendation that all players be inoculated against the disease.

Pongia never appeared in Wigan colours again - the former New Zealand Test captain had played in all 14 of Wigan's games, but was absent as Wigan edged the Wildcats by 20-14 at Belle Vue.

Almost unnoticed in the furore, veteran Gary Connolly played in the right centre position he once made his own, following his surprise return to the JJB Stadium from Leeds. But Kevin Brown suffered a cracked fibia in the closing stages of the game. Denis Betts was in sole charge of Wigan for the first time due to Mike Gregory's absence in Texas to begin treatment of his medical condition.

St Helens coach Ian Millward called for Martin Gleeson's inclusion in the Great Britain side for the autumn's Tri-Nations after the centre produced a superb performance in Saints' 50-20 win at Warrington on the Saturday night. Seven days after lifting the Powergen Challenge Cup in Cardiff, Millward's side produced another clinical display to run in nine tries against the Wolves.

Huddersfield got back in the winning groove with a 30-6 win over London at Griffin Park; and Widnes Vikings gave Bradford a run for their money at the Halton Stadium before going down 30-20.

The Saturday TV game from the KC Stadium was one of the best matches of the season as the Rhinos ended Hull's unbeaten home record with a 23-12 win. Few could remember a time they'd seen a Super League match with a 0-0 scoreline at half-time. And certainly nobody could recall a more gripping and exciting scoreless 40 minutes. A standing ovation from both sets of supporters in a crowd of 16,528 showed how much the efforts of both teams had been appreciated. Rob Burrow's second try of the night five minutes from time finally settled the issue.

Castleford plunged deeper into relegation trouble despite the arrival of the legendary Ellery Hanley as 'coaching consultant', when they sank to a 36-32 defeat at the hands of Salford at the Jungle. Gary Mercer, in charge as head coach for the first time since being promoted from caretaker following Graham Steadman's departure, said: "There are 17 games to go and I'm not giving up."

Salford exposed all the Tigers' old failings as they moved six points clear of rock-bottom Castleford, who had now lost all 11 league games. And twice the Reds hit back after Castleford looked set take command. Andy Johnson's 77th minute converted try finally clinched victory for Salford. Even the early loss of Chris Charles with a head wound and inspirational captain Malcolm Alker with a rib injury could not hold Salford back. Joel Caine moved up from fullback to hooker and finished with a try and six goals in a splendid all-round display. Wayne Godwin continued his rapid progress as Castleford's hooker with a similar performance, also scoring a try and six goals. But Luke Robinson made a quiet start to his loan spell from Wigan Warriors. Nathan McAvoy also had a quite game on the Salford wing after returning for a second debut following his time at Bradford Bulls and Saracens RU.

Castleford's next match was to be at London Broncos the following Friday and Mercer said: "We've got to win it. If we don't, we might as well go get an ice cream van and sell ice creams."

There were celebrations in France when the news came through that UTC had finally won admission to Super League in 2006 - by a majority of seven votes to five at a Super League meeting on Wednesday 26 May (the meeting also decided that the Salary Cap would remain unchanged despite pressure from some clubs to see it lowered).

The French club would have two years' protection from relegation, although a decision on how many teams would play in Super League from 2006 was deferred.

As if to emphasise the urgency of providing a career path for French players, reports emerged that Warrington Wolves' French international forward Jérôme Guisset was to move to rugby union at the end of the season.

One of Rugby League's greats said his goodbyes to the game as Castleford Tigers' Paul Newlove announced his retirement from Rugby League at the age of 32 after a first-grade career spanning 16 seasons. Newlove's injury had been one of several that had dogged Castleford Tigers' Super League IX season. But after the Friday night of round 12 things didn't look quite so gloomy down Wheldon Road way as the Tigers registered their first win of the season at London, beating the Broncos 12-10.

The Tigers had Luke Robinson in great form, even though he was harshly sin-binned for a professional foul. Liam Botham, on loan at Griffin Park from Leeds Rhinos - with Jason Netherton and Dwayne Barker returned to Headingley - kicked a penalty goal on his debut from in front of the posts to level the scores.

But Wayne Godwin landed a straight 42-metre penalty five minutes from time to edge the Tigers home.

Nathan Wood scored the first hat-trick of his professional career with a thrilling display of running football from halfback in a shock 34-18 home win over Wigan. His celebration to his second try – leaping the fence and heading down the tunnel into the concourses behind the stadium, before re-entering through another - earned him a quiet ticking off from referee Steve Ganson.

A few years before, Wood had been understudy to Adrian Lam at Sydney Roosters, but Lam was very quiet before being substituted on 25 minutes. "I wouldn't call it tactical," said Wigan caretaker coach Denis Betts. "We had to get someone on that was going to run, kick and pass." In the week Lam had pleaded with Wigan not to sign New Zealand Test scrum-half Stacey Jones, telling the club that his understudy Luke Robinson, currently on loan to Castleford, would be ready to be their front-line halfback next year. Wigan Chairman Maurice Lindsay denied that his club was in the market for Jones. Reports claimed Hull would also be in position to offer Jones a sizeable deal for next season, with both Jason Smith and Richie Barnett due to retire.

St George star Mark Gasnier was also linked with Wigan. Gasnier had been dropped from the NSW Origin side after making a lewd phone call to a woman he did not know.

Wigan coach Mike Gregory returned from the United States. Wigan launched a fund-raising campaign to help fund the cost of Gregory's trip, as his medical insurance would not meet the bill. Warrington, the club for which Gregory played his entire professional career, said they would help with the fundraising initiative.

St Helens did their best to erase memories of the controversial Easter Monday mismatch with a 35-30 win over the Bulls at Knowsley Road, a 34-18 lead that Saints established midway through the second half proving just too much for the Bulls to overhaul. The star of the St Helens display was Jason Hooper, probably the most consistent performer in Super League IX. Hooper grabbed a superb hat-trick, including two long-distance efforts right out of the top drawer. Hooper scored twice in the first five minutes, and again to make it 34-18 - just keeping Saints' noses in front of a never-say-die Bradford outfit.

Leeds moved three points clear at the top with a 34-6 home win over Salford, a crowd of over 14,000 at Headingley to witness the debut of Ali Lauitiiti. A wonderful sleight of hand that slipped an offload to Andrew Dunemann on the runaround gave a glimpse of the second-rower's ability. Salford also had a debutant - Lancashire Academy centre Tim Hartley.

Huddersfield Giants forward Eorl Crabtree signed a three-year contract

Shaun Briscoe touches down during Hull's 70-4 rout of Widnes on Bank Holiday Monday

extension to remain with his hometown club until the end of the 2007 season but the Giants were no match for the rampant Wildcats, who ran in seven tries on the way to a 38-6 victory at the McAlpine Stadium. Centre Jason Demetriou scored twice for the Wildcats to seal the game in the second half.

And on a sun-soaked Bank Holiday Monday, Hull humiliated Widnes Vikings with a 70-4 win at the KC Stadium.

After putting up some stern resistance in the first quarter, the Vikings wilted away and suffered the biggest loss in the club's hundred year-plus history. Hull, watched by another TV audience, played some of the most exciting football seen for a long time.

Richard Horne produced a masterly display at scrum-half to suggest he must be given an opportunity in the middle of Great Britain's attack in the autumn's Tri-Nations. Skipper Jason Smith returned from injury after over a year on the sidelines and showed he'd lost none of his guile and inventiveness. Michael Eagar also made a return after breaking his arm in the opening round of Super League at St Helens. Leeds prop Nick Scruton - on a month's loan - made a debut off the bench. Scruton was signed after the news that Scott Logan had been released from his contract to undergo treatment in Australia for persistent ankle problems that had prevented him playing in 2004.

SUPER LEAGUE TABLE - *Monday 31st May*

	P	W	D	L	F	A	D	PTS
Leeds Rhinos	12	11	0	1	408	166	242	22
St Helens	11	9	1	1	352	221	131	19
Bradford Bulls	12	8	1	3	359	203	156	17
Hull FC	11	8	0	3	367	160	207	16
Huddersfield Giants	11	7	0	4	212	213	-1	14
Wigan Warriors	11	6	1	4	277	243	34	13
Warrington Wolves	12	5	1	6	303	293	10	11
Wakefield T Wildcats	12	5	0	7	296	269	27	10
Salford City Reds	13	3	0	10	218	424	-206	6
Widnes Vikings	12	3	0	9	183	398	-215	6
London Broncos	13	3	0	10	229	447	-218	6
Castleford Tigers	12	1	0	11	218	385	-167	2

JUNE
Hull on the rise

As news filtered from south Wales that former Rhinos star Iestyn Harris had told the Welsh Rugby Union he was to return to Rugby League, his former club was stretching away at the top of Super League after a 26-12 win at Bradford - the club that was hotly tipped to have signed the erstwhile Leeds skipper, although they denied they had offered him a contract.

Harris, who signed with the WRU and the Cardiff Blues rugby union club in August 2001 when he left the Rhinos, had instructed solicitors to start negotiations to release him from his contract. David Moffett, the WRU group chief executive - and former NRL boss - was critical of the contract signed for the WRU by his predecessor, which had seen it pay a fee to Leeds - thought to be £850,000 - when he signed the deal, although the WRU would receive nothing when Harris returned to play Rugby League. "It is the most bizarre contract I have ever seen in my life," Moffett said.

In round 13 the Bulls narrowly failed to break the Super League attendance record for a regular-season match – a crowd of 23,375 crammed into Odsal - and on the field they failed by a bigger margin to dent the progress of the Rhinos.

They lost Leon Pryce after 12 minutes with a rib cartilage injury, and there were question marks against the Rhinos' first two tries - Kevin Sinfield looked offside when he collected Andrew Dunemann's kick to create the first try for Keith Senior, and Willie Poching could have knocked on before touching down for the second. And, for the third, the Rhinos knew it was their day when Keith Senior kicked the ball back and it fell neatly into the hands of Ali Lauitiiti for the killer try just before half-time.

Danny McGuire didn't figure on the scoresheet but that week the star stand-off signed a new contract to keep him at Headingley until the end of 2007.

On the Friday night at the JJB Stadium, Wigan did Leeds a favour by beating second-placed St Helens 30-14, sub Danny Sculthorpe determining the outcome of the game with virtually his first two touches of the ball. The two superb offloads led to tries by Adrian Lam and Martin Aspinwall in the 21st and 22nd minutes and suddenly Wigan were 14-2 in the lead. Saints, lacking Keiron Cunningham and Micky Higham, weren't going to get back into the game.

Wigan coach Mike Gregory was back from his treatment in America, but wasn't well enough to attend the Cup Final rematch.

Chairman Maurice Lindsay praised caretaker coach Denis Betts and scrum-half Adrian Lam, after Lam's gamestar performance, six days after being ignominiously substituted against Warrington. Meanwhile Wigan continued to be linked with New Zealand Warriors halfback Stacey Jones.

Widnes Chairman Tony Chambers gave his backing to coach Neil Kelly, despite admitting his reaction was one of "shock and horror" at the Vikings' 70-4 defeat at Hull eight days before. Chambers, speaking before the Shane Millard-inspired 31-10 round 13 defeat of Warrington at the Halton Stadium, dismissed suggestions that the Vikings were relegation candidates.

Chambers said the record defeat had not affected the club's drawn-out negotiations with Kelly over an extension to his contract, due to expire at the end of the season.

Papua New Guinea World Cup star Stanley Gene recovered from a groin operation in record time to make the difference in a close, error-strewn game at the Willows. A game that could have gone either way, was decided when Paul March slotted over a field goal in the final minute to seal a 25-18 win. Aussie James Evans made his Giants debut.

David Solomona capped a superb individual show by crossing four times at Belle Vue as Wakefield produced a barnstorming finish to gain successive wins for the first time in Super League IX. Trinity blitzed the Broncos with 34-unanswered points in the closing 24 minutes to end 48-18 winners and leave the Broncos looking nervously over their shoulder at Castleford, four points behind them at the foot of the table.

Luckily for them, the Tigers couldn't back up their win in the capital the week before, coaching consultant Ellery Hanley apologising to Tigers fans and criticising his players after they suffered a 52-18 defeat at home to Hull. Castleford handed a debut to New Zealand Test halfback Motu Tony.

But it was another impressive display of all-out attacking play by Hull, highlighted by a hat-trick from reinstated winger Gareth Raynor - left out of the Widnes game for disciplinary reasons after unintentionally missing a training session. Following Hull's 70-4 thrashing of Widnes Vikings it took their points tally to 122 in two matches, and lifted them to third place in the Tetley's Super League.

RFL Match Officials Director Stuart Cummings confirmed he had given instructions to referees to clamp down on "grapple tackles", in which players wrestle their opponents to the ground by gripping them in a headlock. The decision followed similar moves in Australia.

And after round 14 Cummings was at the centre of a storm as he came to the defence of referee Ian Smith, after Smith gave five separate penalties for players not attempting to play the ball with their foot on the Friday night at Headingley, as Leeds beat Widnes 48-24. And on the Sunday Salford coach Karl Harrison claimed official Ronnie Laughton had cost his side a famous victory against Bradford Bulls when he disallowed a 70th minute try by Andy Coley for the same offence. Almost immediately, Lesley Vainikolo set off on a storming run down the left to touch down in the corner and the Bulls emerged from the Willows with a 35-28 victory.

On the Friday night, Danny McGuire entered another line in the Headingley history books, equalling the Super League record, and creating a summer-era club record by romping in for five tries.

Vikings coach Neil Kelly announced that he had relinquished his international role as the coach of Wales - a job he had held since the 2000 World Cup - with immediate effect.

Warrington chief executive Andy Gatcliffe promised that two big appointments would translate into on-field success for the club.

Events promoter Simon Moran took a 73 per cent majority shareholding in the club, and the Halliwell Jones stadium, while the Wolves also signed up head coach Paul Cullen to a new three-year deal.

In the Saturday night game the Wolves recorded a comfortable 42-14 home victory over London. Broncos coach Tony Rea insisted his side had no fears of relegation from Super League after his team slid to a seventh consecutive defeat. Broncos youngsters Paul Sykes, Rob Purdham (three years) and hooker Neil Budworth (two-years) signed new long-term deals with the club.

Paul Wellens produced a convincing case for international selection with an outstanding individual display as Saints rediscovered their attacking fluency after their derby defeat at Wigan with a 52-8 win over Castleford. The Tigers that weekend maintained they had not signed their former halfback Brad Davis, though they admitted an interest in bringing the veteran halfback back to the Jungle. Thirty-six-year-old Davis had already signed a contract with NL1 club Halifax after a season as player-coach at French side Villeneuve.

Wigan leapfrogged the Giants into fifth place and avenged their 10-26 defeat at the McAlpine in early April with a 40-18 win over the Giants at the JJB Stadium.

Brett Dallas and Kris Radlinski each scored two tries and also made important defensive contributions at the end of a week in which Quentin Pongia announced his retirement, having not played since the Hepatitis B controversy broke earlier in the year.

Canberra halfback Brad Drew was that week announced as the Giants' first new signing for 2005 after penning a two-year contract.

Richard Horne was voted the 'Rugby Leaguer & League Express' readers Player of the Month for May, narrowly defeating Sean Long, and he celebrated with a 28-24 home win over Wakefield. Young centre Kirk Yeaman's capped another fine game with two tries.

On Thursday evening, 17th June, a RFL disciplinary panel suspended St Helens players Sean Long and Martin Gleeson for three and four months respectively for their part in placing bets on the game played on Easter Monday between Bradford Bulls and St Helens at Odsal. The two players were fined £7,500 each, and were ordered to pay costs of £2,205 each. Both players would not be paid by St Helens for the duration of their suspension, a decision which was thought likely to cost Long an additional £50,000, and Gleeson around £40,000.

June

RFL Executive Chairman Richard Lewis was confident that no permanent damage had been done to Rugby League's reputation. Lewis, who played no part in the disciplinary process, didn't believe that the actions of the two players represented a wider problem.

"When you look at the way the case has been dealt with, when you look at the outcome of the investigation, and the fact that it has been taken seriously by the game, it has been a setback for the image of the sport, but not a lasting one," said Lewis. "The two players have now acknowledged what they did, and admitted that it was inappropriate. There were a number of rumours circulating in the aftermath of the specific allegations. This investigation has shown that these were not true or unproven. Indeed, the investigation only uncovered evidence of betting of this nature by these two players. The RFL has no evidence that betting which contravenes the rules of the sport is a widespread problem."

And Lewis confirmed that both Long and Gleeson, when they had served their suspensions, could then be considered for selection for Great Britain in the autumn's Gillette Tri-Nations series.

Saints came through their first test after the bans with a 40-12 win over the Vikings at Halton Stadium in the Friday night TV game. Ian Millward switched Darren Albert to fullback, with Paul Wellens covering for Long at scrum-half, while Lee Gilmour reverted to his old centre position in place of Gleeson, with Dom Feaunati returning from injury on the bench. Widnes coach Neil Kelly had the consolation of a top show from Aaron Moule, who scored his first try since joining the club.

There was another big story that weekend as Wigan inflicted a second defeat of the season on Leeds. Warriors skipper Andy Farrell left a lasting image on a huge TV audience when he suffered a broken nose in a clash with teammate Danny Sculthorpe after 30 minutes, as the pair tackled Leeds captain Kevin Sinfield. In the second half he came back onto the pitch wearing a mask to protect his nose - kicking the two penalties that finally separated the two sides - before being treated in hospital for the break. For sheer bravery and wonderful skills the game had the lot, with the Rhinos playing their full part in a captivating spectacle that had the 14,000-plus crowd on the edge of their seats to the end.

Wigan boss Maurice Lindsay was reportedly stepping up efforts to land the signature of St George-Illawarra's former Test centre Mark Gasnier, and was also tipped to sign Canberra's veteran Kiwi forward Ruben Wiki.

In other games Bradford fought their way past an injury-decimated but spirited Huddersfield - who gave debuts off the bench to Bolu Fagborun and Jason Southwell - at Odsal by 40-12; Ben Westwood scored a well-taken hat-trick in torrential rain at the Jungle, Ellery Hanley again critical of his players after a 32-10 defeat; and Wakefield were lucky to emerge with a 21-20 win over Salford at Belle Vue, a Ben Jeffries field goal ultimately the difference.

The win completed a positive week for Wakefield as young back-rower Mark Applegarth signed a new three-and-a-half year contract after the club came out of its three-year CVA.

Hull coach Shaun McRae was expected to open talks with the Airlie Birds about the futures of himself and his coaching staff, being widely tipped to replace Paul Langmack, recently sacked as the coach of NRL club South Sydney.

That weekend Hull inflicted London's record equalling eighth successive defeat in an "On the Road" game at Leicester Tigers' Welford Road ground. Richard Whiting scored two tries in a 42-26 win in front of 3,589 supporters.

Meanwhile Hull's recruitment plans for 2005 were thrown into confusion, after reports that the club was about to sign Stacey Jones from the New Zealand Warriors. But although Warriors chief executive Mick Watson had previously said the club would not stand in Jones' way if he wanted to leave, the club were now likely to try to hold Jones to the final two years of his contract. There had been friction between Jones and previous coach Daniel Anderson, but new mentor Tony Kemp was a Jones fan.

Paul Sculthorpe became the public face of Rugby League for Gillette after signing a marketing agreement with the company. Sculthorpe became only the second British sports star, after footballer David Beckham, to represent Gillette.

In Saturday night's home game against Warrington, Sculthorpe's break for Darren Albert to supply a slick finish from 20 metres hauled Saints back to parity at 8-8 nine minutes into the second half, Sculthorpe adding a fine touchline conversion as Saints went on to a 28-8 win.

The Tigers' relegation SOS for Brad Davis was completed with Castleford and Halifax - who had signed him from French club Villeneuve but for whom he had not played, agreeing an undisclosed fee. Davis made his second debut for the club in a 30-14 defeat at Salford.

The Reds, who insisted they were keen to hang onto forward Andy Coley, strongly linked with a close-season move to Wigan, were now six points clear of the Tigers.

Fortunately for Castleford, the other sides immediately above them were also on losing streaks.

London fell 35-22 at Huddersfield - a club record ninth successive defeat - the Giants forced to dig deep and come from behind three times to get back on the winning track and consolidate their top six spot. Former Giants and Broncos halfback Chris Thorman denied reports that he could be about to return to England from Parramatta before the end of the season to join a Super League club.

And Widnes threatened one of the greatest comebacks in Super League history at Odsal, but ultimately fell just short after Bradford's devastating opening half saw them hold on for a 38-30 success. New Widnes signing from South Sydney Willie Peters missed out after arriving in England too late to be considered by Kelly, who gave a debut to former St Helens and England Academy prop Bruce Johnson.

Widnes were able to secure Peters' signature when a place on the overseas

Leeds' Ali Lauitiiti crashes past Gareth Raynor to score against Hull

quota became available due to the shock retirement of prop Robert Relf. The tough Australian called it a day after news that he required operations on both of his ankles.

Relf bowed out after making his 74th appearance in a Widnes shirt against St Helens. He missed just one game after joining the Vikings from North Queensland Cowboys in 2002.

Maurice Lindsay was in Sydney closing in on the signature of Mark Gasnier as the Warriors had to withstand a determined revival from the Wildcats, before winning 28-22 at the JJB Stadium. In the absence of broken-nose victim Andy Farrell, stand-in skipper Kris Radlinski was in his usual dominant form, his brace taking his tally to twelve tries in his last eleven games, as Wigan completed their run of four successive home games. Wigan's win came at a price, with prop Terry O'Connor suffering a broken hand, likely to keep him out for a month.

Ali Lauitiiti scored two tries as Leeds bounced back from defeat at Wigan with a 28-24 home win over Hull. That weekend Rhinos prop Danny Ward expressed surprise at rumours surfacing in Australia linking him with a possible move to Wests Tigers.

And in the round seven game on the last Tuesday in June postponed because of Wigan's cup commitments the Warriors came away from Hull with a 20-20 draw, after leading 18-4 at half-time. The black and whites - inspired by prop Paul King - produced an unbelievable transformation to score three, unanswered second-half tries and lead 20-18 as the match went into the last five minutes. But the game still had a final twist when Wigan skipper Andy Farrell landed his third penalty of the match to leave the scores tied at the final hooter.

SUPER LEAGUE TABLE - *Tuesday 29th June*

	P	W	D	L	F	A	D	PTS
Leeds Rhinos	16	14	0	2	532	252	280	28
St Helens	15	12	1	2	486	279	207	25
Hull FC	16	11	1	4	533	276	257	23
Bradford Bulls	16	11	1	4	484	299	185	23
Wigan Warriors	16	10	2	4	421	339	82	22
Huddersfield Giants	15	9	0	6	302	333	-31	18
Warrington Wolves	16	7	1	8	395	374	21	15
Wakefield T Wildcats	16	7	0	9	411	363	48	14
Salford City Reds	17	4	0	13	314	519	-205	8
Widnes Vikings	16	4	0	12	280	534	-254	8
London Broncos	17	3	0	14	307	614	-307	6
Castleford Tigers	16	1	0	15	268	551	-283	2

JULY
Coming home

It was one of the worst kept secrets of the year, and on Thursday 1 July, Bradford Bulls duly unveiled Iestyn Harris at a press conference at Odsal.

Leeds chief executive Gary Hetherington threatened to launch a lawsuit against Harris immediately, and urged the Rugby Football League to investigate the circumstances in which the Rhinos' bitter rivals came to sign the former Rhinos star on a four-and-a-half year contract after his three years spent playing rugby union.

The Rhinos claimed that the Bulls "coerced" Harris into signing a contract, and that it had "caused anger and disappointment at Leeds Rhinos. It was at Iestyn's insistence that we released him two-years early from his original contract with us in 2001, and part of the agreement with himself, Cardiff and the WRU was his return to the Rhinos on specified terms from the 2004 Super League season. A copy of this contract has been made available to the RFL today."

The RFL would only confirm that the Bulls had a standard Rugby League contract with Harris - and he was therefore now a Bulls player.

"We are grateful to the Rugby Football League for arriving at a speedy acceptance of Iestyn's registration," said Bulls Chairman Chris Caisley. "As far as we are concerned that aspect of the matter is closed, although we are looking into the very serious associated matter of the defamatory comments made of our club yesterday by the Chief Executive of the Leeds Rugby League Club."

Iestyn Harris arrives at Odsal Stadium

July

The following Sunday Harris watched on as Lesley Vainikolo led Bulls' try rush with four and Paul Deacon collected 24 points with a try and ten goals from 11 kicks, in the Bulls' 60-12 thrashing of the Tigers at the Jungle. Paul Johnson suffered a broken arm.

Castleford's problems also mounted with Sean Ryan stretchered off after sustaining a leg injury and Jon Hepworth being an early casualty with a shoulder injury. The Tigers signed out of favour New Zealand Warriors prop forward Mark Tookey after terminating the contract of former Newcastle Knights stand-off Sean Rudder after 14 appearances.

Leeds stayed five points clear of the pack, with Danny McGuire coming off he bench to score two second-half tries in a 38-22 win at Warrington.

Hull coach Shaun McRae, who had returned from Australia, where he had been visiting his father in hospital, confirmed to 'Rugby Leaguer & League Express' he would be leaving the club at the end of the 2004 season to take up a two-year contract with Australian club South Sydney. Contrary to reports in Australia, he would not be taking Richard Horne with him.

McRae's assistant John Kear was expected to step up to the head coach's position with the Airlie Birds.

On the Sunday, Hull moved into second place of Super League with another magnificent victory - a 40-12 home win over Huddersfield Giants, though centre Michael Eagar broke the same arm which saw him side-lined for a dozen games earlier in the campaign. Gareth Raynor produced his best display since his return from rugby union, capped by a brilliant individual try.

That week the Giants had announced that Rocky Turner had played his last game for the club. The Challenge Cup winner with Sheffield in 1998 needed a knee reconstruction that ruled him out for the remainder of the season, and they would not be offering the 29 year old a new deal.

Another coach on the way out - this time with immediate effect, was Neil Kelly the morning after the Vikings' disappointing 56-8 defeat by Wigan at the Halton Stadium on the Saturday. Vikings Chairman Tony Chambers said his board had made the decision with some regret. "What is sad is that Neil (Super League coach of the year in 2002) has done a fantastic job at Widnes, and we wouldn't be in Super League if it weren't for him," he said. "We are grateful for everything he's done." Willie Peters made his Widnes debut that night and the Vikings handed a three-year contract to Academy prop Stephen Nash. Kelly's assistant Stuart Spruce was appointed caretaker coach

Terry Newton could take part of the blame for Kelly's dismissal as he scored four tries, while halfbacks Adrian Lam and, in particular Danny Orr, were outstanding. The Warriors had gone into the game with just one recognised prop - Craig Smith - after Quentin Pongia's retirement and injuries to Danny Sculthorpe and Terry O'Connor. Andy Farrell, two weeks after breaking his nose against Leeds, had to leave the field just before half-time after a tackle by Widnes captain Andy Hay did further damage. Hay received a one-match ban for the reckless challenge the following Tuesday.

Wakefield's Belle Vue home of 125 years was re-titled the 'Atlantic Solutions Stadium' and the Wildcats duly humbled St Helens 41-22 on the Friday night, with Ben Jeffries getting two tries in a gamestar performance.

Saints, who were strongly tipped to sign Melbourne Storm's New Zealand Test forward Steve Kearney for 2005, allowed Tim Jonkers - struggling to hold down a regular first team place after undergoing a knee reconstruction - to join Salford City Reds on a month's loan. The Reds had a free weekend, having played their away game at London earlier in the season.

The Broncos moved to sign their former forward Russell Bawden, who had been playing for French club UTC in that weekend's French Championship Final, for a third time. The club also suggested they were likely to appeal against relegation if they finished at the foot of the Super League table. "We bring a huge amount to Super League and our plans are just taking seed," said chief executive Nic Cartwright.

On the Wednesday night leading up to round 17, St Helens star Darren Albert clinched the inaugural Powergen Fastest Man in Rugby League title in Wigan.

Albert won the Final in a time of 11.37 seconds, in a competition run in full kit, boots, and carrying a ball, just edging out Whitehaven youngster Craig Calvert in the Final, with Leeds' David Doherty coming in third. Wigan's Brett Dallas and Mark Calderwood of Leeds were late withdrawals, and hundreds were locked out of the Robin Park Arena, the organisers underestimating the appeal of the event.

Iestyn Harris made his re-entry into Rugby League from the bench after 52 minutes of the Bulls' home 36-26 win over Wakefield Trinity Wildcats on the Sunday night. By that time the Bulls had been reduced to 12 men, following the dismissal of Karl Pratt for his part in a first-half brawl that also saw the sin-binning of Bradford's Leon Pryce and Wakefield's Semi Tadulala.

Tadulala and Pryce received one-match bans, although Pryce's suspension was lifted on appeal, reduced to a straight fine. Bulls' Karl Pratt also got three games and Wakefield's Olivier Elima two for their part in the melee.

Meanwhile former Bulls and now Canberra coach Matt Elliott dismissed suggestions that Bradford's Test prop Stuart Fielden, who played his 200th game for the Bulls against Wakefield, was poised to join the Raiders.

Willie Poching was the Rugby Leaguer & League Express Player of the Week for his three-try performance - the first hat-trick of his career - in the Rhinos' Friday night 46-14 defeat of Castleford Tigers at Headingley. Tigers' Brad Davis was by now assisting coach Gary Mercer after the departure of consultant coach Ellery Hanley in the week. New recruit Mark Tookey watched the Tigers' defeat from the Headingley stand.

Wigan Warriors missed out on Kiwi Test captain Ruben Wiki, who decided to join the other Warriors, in Auckland, instead snaring his Canberra teammate, prop Luke Davico. And Salford City Reds prop Andy Coley escaped their clutches as he signed a three-year deal to stay with the Reds, although Sean O'Loughlin signed a new two-year contract. Andy Farrell was missing from the Wigan teamsheet that Sunday at the Willows after receiving a nose injury in training, but Wigan hardly missed him at all as halfback Danny Orr put on a master-class in a 32-16 victory, and Brian Carney made his first start of Super League IX. Salford gave a debut to on-loan Saints second row Tim Jonkers.

London spent three days training with the Army at Dover, in preparation for their trip to Knowsley Road, but went down 30-10 in a forgettable game. Saints had already bounced back from their Wakefield defeat in a round eight catch-up game at Huddersfield the Wednesday before with skipper Paul Sculthorpe producing another masterclass, underpinning his side's 50-8 runaway win with a 22-point haul from a try and nine goals from as many attempts. The two wins put Saints in second spot in the table.

The Giants remained four points clear in sixth after their 26-20 win over the improving Vikings, Stuart Jones netting two tries. And Hull's Richard Whiting was the star of a 28-18 win at fading Warrington.

The 12 Super League clubs met in Wakefield on Wednesday 13 July and made a near-unanimous decision to drop two teams from the top flight in 2005 to accommodate the arrival of Perpignan, and to keep promotion and relegation for clubs in National League One.

Despite Widnes' push for an expansion to 14 clubs, and fears from National League teams that promotion might be suspended for a season, the meeting was strongly in favour of relegating two teams.

And BARLA's six-match tour of Australia to take on the indigenous Aboriginals in a goodwill exchange ended in disgrace, with players fighting and one of them in court. Four players were despatched home early for disciplinary reasons at the start of the last week of the tour and the final game against the Police/Correctional Services team was cancelled at the last minute. The RFL launched an investigation.

Widnes Vikings coach Stuart Spruce, who was appointed as caretaker after the sacking of head coach Neil Kelly two weeks before, launched a scathing attack on some of his players after Widnes's 15-14 home defeat to relegation rivals Salford at the Halton Stadium. "I'd love to stay here coaching, but definitely not with this bunch of blokes," said Spruce. "There's seven in contract, but most of the ones who aren't in contract won't be getting a new deal - if I'm coach, anyway, they won't be."

A Gavin Clinch field goal six minutes from time took the Reds to the brink of survival. And the result left Widnes third from bottom of Super League on eight points, just one point ahead of London Broncos, and four ahead of bottom club Castleford with nine rounds to go.

Spirits were lifted at the Jungle though as the Tigers recorded a 24-20 victory over Huddersfield Giants - only the Tigers' second win of the season, with prop Mark Tookey making his debut off the bench and loanee Luke Robinson the gamestar. The Tigers were keeping their fingers crossed that they would be able to keep their on-loan halfback until the end of the season. But Wigan's loss of their first choice scrum-half Adrian Lam meant Robinson was likely to be called back to the JJB Stadium.

Lam and Craig Smith - Wigan's one remaining fit prop - both suffered knee injuries in the 32-16 win over Bradford Bulls at the JJB Stadium on the Friday night. Andy Farrell again led from the front with another towering display, this time at prop, as the Warriors extended their unbeaten run to eight games. Good news for the club was that prop Danny Sculthorpe - out through injury - had signed a new contract to keep him at the JJB Stadium for three more years.

Liam Botham, on loan at London Broncos and about to sign a new League-only one-year contract at Headingley, kicked a late conversion at Griffin Park to take a surprise point off the Rhinos. Botham had an outstanding game, scoring twelve points from a try and four goals, as the Broncos held the league leaders to a 36-36 draw. As well as the shock at Brentford, the Rhinos were facing a wave of protest about the decision to switch the date of their derby against Bradford Bulls at Headingley, from Friday 20 August to Sunday 22 August, with a kick-off at 7.35pm. They had been forced to make the switch by Sky Sports.

Paul Sculthorpe was expected to be sidelined for a minimum of six weeks, after the Saints skipper's hamstring lasted just 25 minutes of the 34-6 defeat at the KC Stadium on the Saturday night. Hull - strongly linked with Bradford Bulls' New Zealand centre Shontayne Hape - leapfrogged Saints back into second place in the table and came within three minutes of becoming the first side to ever nil St Helens in Super League, Lee Gilmour saving the visitors' record.

Before the kick-off, both sets of fans applauded the retired Steve Prescott on to the pitch, in true appreciation of his magnificent service to both clubs.

That week hooker Richard Swain signed an extension to his contract to keep him at the KC Stadium for the 2006 Super League season.

Wakefield Trinity Wildcats back-rower David Solomona was voted the readers 'Rugby Leaguer & League Express' Player of the Month for June, and his side closed in on the Giants in sixth spot with a 32-26 home win over Warrington, a Justin Ryder try two minutes from time giving Wakefield the win. The Wildcats gave a debut to Australian forward Duncan MacGillivray from French club Carcassonne, to replace Dallas Hood who had gone back to Australia after an injury-hit season. Salford had been favourites to sign MacGillivray and that week they confirmed they would not be signing UTC's highly-rated French forward Djamel Fakir either, because of injury.

The Wolves did make a key signing, in Kiwi Henry Fa'afili on a three-year deal. The Samoan was thought likely to arrive at the Halliwell Jones stadium before the end of the current season. Meanwhile Warrington's French international Jerome Guisset admitted he wanted to remain in Rugby League, despite fielding offers from a number of French union clubs.

There was no doubting the big story of the last week in July as the news broke that Warrington had signed St Helens' international centre Martin Gleeson, suspended until the end of the domestic season for his part in the 'betting scandal' of 2004.

Funded by the publicity-shy concert promoter Simon Moran, the Wolves made an unsolicited bid for Gleeson, who signed on a four-year deal, believed to be worth up to £200,000 to St Helens. Gleeson would be training with Warrington in the hope of making the Great Britain squad for the Tri-Nations. St Helens coach Ian Millward admitted he had not been consulted by the club board about the move.

The Wolves meanwhile revived their hopes of a play-off spot with a 34-18 win at sixth-placed Huddersfield - who that week had announced that Brisbane Broncos and Australian Test star Michael De Vere would be joining them for

2005. Wolves' dogged defence, clinical finishing and a moment of pure magic from Lee Briers brought to an end a run of four successive defeats.

St Helens, though, looked as though they had hit the wall and the traumatic events of the season had finally taken their toll. They were hammered 70-0 at Headingley on the Friday, Marcus Bai and Danny McGuire each scoring hat-tricks, and Kevin Sinfield kicking 11 goals. As a result Saints plummeted to fifth.

Hull stayed second, with Kirk Yeaman scoring a first-half hat-trick in a 44-20 win at Salford; and Bradford moved up to fourth with a relatively comfortable 44-16 victory against London at Odsal, Lesley Vainikolo getting two tries.

And Widnes had a priceless 25-24 win at home to Wakefield, taking them six points clear of Castleford and three points clear of the Broncos. It was the Vikings' first win in seven games, Willie Peters' field goal five minutes from time securing the points.

Castleford got the expected hammering at Wigan, Brett Dallas scoring four tries in a 48-18 Warriors win. Halfback Luke Robinson, returned to the Warriors after his loan spell with the Tigers, re-stated his desire to win a new contract with the club. Another player who was out of contract at the end of the year committed his future to the Warriors when Danny Tickle signed a new deal until the end of 2006.

As the month came to a close it emerged that the Rugby Football League had moved the deadline for clubs being able to carry out negotiations with players from other clubs coming out of contract. The deadline had been June 30, for some years, but in June the Super League clubs had moved the deadline to August 31 with immediate effect.

According to Wigan, Ireland and Great Britain prop Terry O'Connor, many Super League players were up in arms at the decision. "Nobody came to the players to ask whether they agree with this," O'Connor said. "Players who finish out of the top six this season will play their final games in the middle of September, and that means that, with the current deadline, players coming out of contract will have two weeks to work out their futures before the season ends. Who is it (the decision) supposed to benefit?

"The lads give their best, they play as professionals, they give their all playing through injury, and they should be treated with respect by the people who run the game."

SUPER LEAGUE TABLE - *Sunday 25th July*

	P	W	D	L	F	A	D	PTS
Leeds Rhinos	20	17	1	2	722	324	398	35
Hull FC	20	15	1	4	689	332	357	31
Wigan Warriors	20	14	2	4	589	397	192	30
Bradford Bulls	20	14	1	5	640	385	255	29
St Helens	20	14	1	5	594	442	152	29
Huddersfield Giants	20	10	0	10	386	501	-115	20
Wakefield T Wildcats	20	9	0	11	534	472	62	18
Warrington Wolves	20	8	1	11	495	500	-5	17
Salford City Reds	20	5	0	15	365	609	-244	10
Widnes Vikings	20	5	0	15	347	655	-308	10
London Broncos	20	3	1	16	369	724	-355	7
Castleford Tigers	20	2	0	18	336	725	-389	4

AUGUST
In the heat of the fight

Good news stories were dominating the headlines at the height of the summer, with Rugby League World magazine revealing after an audit conducted by the RFL's Development Department that grass roots participation in Rugby League had virtually doubled in two years. The RFL also reported its finances were in the black for the first time in ten years, following two years of profits and increasing financial support from Sport England.

And August was the month that England's under-18's Academy side inflicted a 33-24 defeat on the Combined Australian High Schools in Sydney. It was the Aussie Schoolboys' first-ever defeat on home soil and followed up the Academy's 1-1 series draw with the Junior Kiwis earlier in the month, and their 2-0 series victory against the Australians in England in 2002. A try four minutes from time by Leeds Rhinos winger David Doherty gave England a thrilling victory in the one-off Test after the Aussies had led at the interval.

It was certainly good news time for Leeds Rhinos and for Danny McGuire in particular, who on the first day of August broke Paul Newlove's Super League try record, set in Super League I in 1996, crossing the line in the 31st minute of the game against Wakefield for his 29th try of Super League IX. The Rhinos were given a tough contest by a fired-up Wildcats on the hottest day of the season before winning 46-28 in front of a bumper 15,629 crowd.

The shock of the day was Wigan's 22-20 defeat by London Broncos - who had a new assistant coach in Rowan Smith - the son of Parramatta coach Brian and nephew of Leeds boss Tony. Smith had been on the coaching staff at New Zealand Warriors. A late converted try by Dennis Moran sealed the Broncos' first win in 12 games.

An injury-hit Wigan, with teenagers Paul Prescott and Bryn Hargreaves playing the whole game at prop forward, picked up another raft of injuries. Brian Carney and Gary Connolly suffered hamstring problems, while Kevin Brown only lasted 15 minutes before suffering a recurrence of a painful broken bone in his leg. Danny Orr was already out for six weeks with a hamstring, and Mick Cassidy was ruled out on the Saturday morning of the game with a knee injury.

London's victory soured celebrations over the weekend at Castleford, who were now still three points behind the Broncos at the bottom of the Super League table with seven games remaining, with the Broncos just one point behind both Widnes and Salford. Brad Davis was in vintage form in an emphatic 42-8 defeat of Widnes Vikings. The stand-off scored their first try, and had a big say in the next five, as he took total command with his superb distribution and excellent kicking game. Francis Maloney, returned after a nine-match lay-off.

Hull had a thrilling 25-14 win at the KC Stadium against Bradford Bulls, and now looked certain to finish in second place. Hull - expected to announce the appointment of Richard Agar as their new assistant coach later that week - trailed 6-8 at the break but two tries in ten minutes in the third quarter saw them storm into a 10-point lead. And, despite a revival by the visitors which saw them reduce Hull's lead to 18-14, Ewan Dowes' 68th minute try ended the Bulls' hopes.

The Wolves unveiled record signing Martin Gleeson to a delighted home faithful, and dispatched Salford by 46-20 to move within a point of Huddersfield, who had been thrashed 50-10 by St Helens on the Friday night. Saints were barely recognisable from the 70-0 Headingley debacle.

Off the field Tetley's were rumoured to be ending their title sponsorship of Super League and settle for a subsidiary backing of the competition from 2005, leaving the RFL's new commercial director Paul Kimberley to seek a new headline backer.

And the British Amateur Rugby League Association accepted the conclusions of the 'Genesis Report' for a re-structuring of 'Community Rugby League'. The report proposed a new 'Community Board' be set up to administer all aspects of the game outside the full and part-time professional set-ups.

The RFL confirmed that the age for out-of-contract players to move clubs without compensation had been reduced to 22 - affecting a host of Super League players due to come out of contract at the end of the season.

National League 3 clubs Coventry Bears, Bramley Buffaloes and Hemel Stags were immediate candidates to fill a 34th professional place to be made available by the RFL, who were preparing to admit an extra club as early as 2006 to balance up the three divisions when Perpignan joined Super League.

On another hot weekend, Leeds were five points clear again at the end of the straight home and away series as they beat Huddersfield 42-10 at the newly re-named 'Galpharm Stadium', and Hull were held at the JJB Stadium.

Hull and Wigan fought out a 13-13 draw as Andrew Farrell and Richard Horne exchanged field goals in the last five minutes to leave the spoils shared for the second time in six weeks. The 20-20 draw at the KC Stadium had been a classic, but this was even better. Hull proved their top-two credentials with a great comeback after they were threatened with being over-run by Wigan's brilliant attacking play in the first half-hour.

The charging Rhinos had given prop forward Danny Ward permission to speak to other clubs, with Bradford rumoured to be interested, while agreeing new contracts with Richard Mathers (two years) and Willie Poching (one year), and confirming that Matt Adamson would leave the club to join Canberra Raiders at the end of the season.

Leeds chief executive Gary Hetherington was confident that an agreement to sell the Headingley cricket ground to Yorkshire cricket club for £15 million would mean the adjacent rugby ground would at last see a modernisation plan.

Bradford Bulls re-signed their New Zealand stars Shontayne Hape and Joe Vagana for Super League X, despite speculation that both players would be leaving Odsal, with Hape in particular having been linked strongly with Hull. But their Kiwi teammate Logan Swann, who joined the Bulls on a one-year deal at the start of the season, and prop forward Paul Anderson, would both be allowed to leave Odsal after the play-offs.

Warrington Wolves' new signing Henry Fa'afili was catapulted straight into Super League action against the Bulls at Odsal, just three days after arriving from New Zealand Warriors. The Bulls moved up to third place in Super League, leapfrogging Wigan and St Helens, with a 36-22 win thanks to a clinical second-half performance that saw them pull away.

The Wolves dropped to eighth after Wakefield beat Castleford 39-18, 'Rugby Leaguer & League Express' Player of the Month for July Ben Jeffries inspiring the Wildcats. The Tigers' new recruit, former Sydney Roosters back row forward Steven Crouch, made a try-scoring debut.

Jason Hooper was taken to hospital with neck and jaw problems after suffering injury in Saints' shock 20-30 defeat to Salford City Reds at the Willows, in a game that saw the return of Saints hooker Micky Higham after a 19-week absence. It was Salford's first Super League victory over St Helens for seven years.

Former Wakefield winger Paul Sampson made his debut for London in a vital 38-24 win at Widnes that leapfrogged the Broncos over the Vikings into tenth place. A woeful first quarter, which saw Widnes leak four tries without reply, cost the Vikings any chance of winning the crucial bottom of the table clash at the Halton Stadium. A section of the home crowd staged a vocal protest after a shambolic opening which saw the Broncos race 22 points clear at a point a minute. Welsh Rugby Union defensive coach Clive Griffiths was the latest coach to be linked with the Widnes Vikings' vacant coaching position.

A second victory in less than a month over the troubled Giants - this time on their own patch, by 29-12 - put bottom club Castleford Tigers within two points of Widnes Vikings.

The basement dwellers' third win in six games came courtesy of their most dominant spell of the whole troubled season - in an opening 25 minutes, aided by an 8-1 penalty count and their own almost faultless handling. By the time Huddersfield managed to get any decent share of possession they were already trailing 14-0, and staring a fifth straight defeat in the face. "I'm very proud of the way the players responded to what we talked about during the week, and I believe that we are going to win more games than we lose at the back end of the

Andy Lynch makes a break during Castleford's win at Huddersfield

season," said Tigers coach Gary Mercer, who, if he did manage to save the Tigers' Super League life would be without centre Paul Mellor, set to take up a one-year contract with his former club Cronulla in 2005.

Salford, who agreed an extended deal for three years with Australian centre Kevin McGuinness, and also signed Parramatta's former St George and Melbourne centre Junior Langi for 2005, inflicted a hammer blow on Widnes with their second one-point victory over the Vikings - this time by 14-13 at the Willows. A dramatic late try from Andy Johnson virtually guaranteed Salford City Reds' Super League status.

The Vikings were hoping that former Wigan coach Frank Endacott could save them from relegation, after contracting him to examine the club's playing strength, while caretaker coach Stuart Spruce was to continue in the role until the end of the season.

London, who were ready to concede defeat in their attempts to keep inspirational skipper Jim Dymock, looked as safe as houses after a 28-22 win at Knowsley Road on the Friday night. Prop Steele Retchless - also uncontracted for 2005 - made his 200th appearance for the Broncos, as Dennis Moran sank the Saints - who had Paul Sculthorpe back - with a clinical hat-trick.

St Helens meanwhile had made an offer to former Kangaroo centre Jamie Lyon as a replacement for Martin Gleeson.

Bradford looked like the side that began the season in awesome style when they avenged their 32-16 defeat at Wigan with a 38-12 win over the Warriors at Odsal. Despite being without front-row juggernauts Paul Anderson and Joe

Vagana, their pack dominated throughout and Karl Pratt made a significant impact when he went on as a 24th minute substitute.

In the week the Bulls firmly dismissed a Leeds offer for Jamie Peacock, contracted at Odsal until the end of 2005, and agreed a new three-year contract with scrum-half Paul Deacon, keeping him at Odsal until the end of the 2007 season.

The Rhinos maintained a five-point cushion at the top of the table with a 44-12 win at Warrington as Danny Ward and Jamie Jones-Buchanan both agreed new one-year contracts.

Hull stayed second after a 38-24 win over Wakefield - their third win over the Wildcats in 2004 - and confirmed they had signed St George-Illawarra winger Nathan Blacklock on a two-year contract. He was to join Kiwi second-rower Stephen Kearney at the KC Stadium next season. Shaun Briscoe and Paul King celebrated signing two-year extensions to their contracts with magnificent contributions as Hull FC finally overcame a spirited Wildcats side, that gave a second debut to Leeds prop Chris Feather, on loan until the end of the season.

Trinity also confirmed they had made a formal new contract offer to club captain Gareth Ellis, insisting they would do "everything they can" to keep the Great Britain International at the club.

Castleford Tigers led the fight against relegation, as three of the bottom four teams recorded vital wins in what looked like being a scramble to the last round of Super League.

The Tigers continued their recent resurgence with a fourth win in six games by surprisingly defeating Hull 21-14 at the Jungle. Ryan Hudson produced a non-stop display in attack and defence, with Brad Davis kicking a crucial field goal, before being sin-binned - to a standing ovation from Cas fans.

The theme tune to "The Great Escape" was becoming the anthem at the Jungle but unfortunately for Castleford, Widnes's victory over Huddersfield left the Tigers still at the foot of Super League - with the Vikings and Tigers due to clash at the Halton Stadium on September 12 in what was building to be the season's decisive relegation battle. The Vikings bettered Huddersfield 24-18 at the Halton Stadium, with Matt Whitaker, on loan from the Giants, scoring two tries.

Wigan inflicted a 27-18 defeat on Saints at the JJB Stadium - St Helens' sixth defeat in nine games. Their 18-year-old substitute James Roby scored two tries in three minutes to leave Saints three points behind just before the hour, and a comeback seemed possible. But the old combination of Kris Radlinski and Andy Farrell ensured it was not, with a decisive 61st minute Wigan try. Hooker Terry Newton was later suspended for two matches for a high tackle on Jon Wilkin.

RFL Match Officials Director Stuart Cummings gave his backing to the 'mousetrap' tactic employed by Saints at the play-the-ball. Saints effectively used two acting halfbacks, with the foremost player not picking up the ball, and leaving it for the second player. "It used to be illegal, when the attacking team used to have to retreat five metres, but it no longer has to," explained Cummings. "That rule was abolished five years ago by the Rugby League International Federation. Ian Millward used it in the Huddersfield game three weeks ago, and he telephoned me beforehand to ask me whether I thought it was OK."

That week came the announcement that Wigan youngsters David Hodgson and Luke Robinson were to join Salford for 2005 and that Wigan's veteran Kiwi prop forward Craig Smith would retire at the end of the season, while Mark Smith signed a 12-month contract.

After their 40-12 humiliation of Bradford Bulls at Headingley on the Sunday night - Danny McGuire scoring his first try of two after 49 seconds - Leeds Rhinos said they were still waiting to hear formally from the Bulls in response to their offer for Jamie Peacock. It came in a week in which the continuing row between Leeds and Bradford over Iestyn Harris took more twists and turns, with the Rhinos now confirming that they were pursuing legal action against Harris after Leeds CEO Gary Hetherington was forced to make an apology to the Bulls over earlier comments in which he had claimed that the Bulls had "coerced" Harris into signing for them. Meanwhile the Rhinos announced new one-year contracts for forwards Barrie McDermott and Liam Botham.

The Broncos celebrated their tenth birthday with a fourth successive victory - a 34-26 home win over the Wolves - to all but secure their Super League future, Lee Greenwood's second try in the last minute securing the win. The Broncos had Kiwis Mal Kaufusi and Zebastian Luisi on debut, while London owner David Hughes admitted that the club was in talks with New Zealand Warriors Eric Watson about a possible takeover.

The Wakefield-Salford clash was nicely poised until just before half-time. With the scores level, Joel Caine allowed a ball which seemed to be going dead to bounce, then watched horrified as it changed direction and spun back into the arms of a grateful Semi Tadulala, who touched down. Wakefield seized on their good fortune to come out and score six more tries, four in the third quarter, to claim a 46-18 victory, and a decisive edge in the race for the remaining play-off place.

On the night of Friday 27 August the Rhinos ensured that they would win the 'League Leaders Shield' with an overwhelming 64-12 victory over Castleford Tigers at Headingley. Danny McGuire missed the chance to equal the Super League record of scoring a try in nine consecutive games, when he sat out the game through a dead-leg injury. He had crossed the try line in eight successive matches, racking up 13 tries. Four other players had scored tries in nine successive Super League matches - Paul Newlove (1996), Paul Sterling (1997), Anthony Sullivan (1999) and Brandon Costin (2003).

It was the Tigers' heaviest ever defeat. The club's previous worst result was a 62-12 defeat by St Helens in 1986, and to make matters worse, the Vikings opened up a four-point advantage over them the day after with a shock 20-16 win over Wigan. The decision to bring Frank Endacott to the Halton Stadium already looked like a masterstroke, with two wins in eight days since his arrival. Widnes led 20-4 after 65 minutes before resisting a stirring Wigan comeback.

Wakefield were sitting pretty in sixth after their 24-16 win in London, with David Solomona, who scored four tries against the Broncos at Belle Vue in June, adding another two to his tally.

Joe Mbu, Steele Retchless and Dennis Moran combine to upend Ian Sibbit as London defeat Warrington

The Giants were now four points off the Wildcats after a 48-12 defeat at Knowsley Road on the Friday night.

Saints supporters saw a little piece of history, when they witnessed the youngest try-scorer in Super League history - 16-year-old scrum-half Scott Moore, who had made his debut the week before at Wigan - touching down on 19 minutes. And, for good measure, they saw a debut try by their latest overseas signing, Gray Viane. Saints were without Samoan winger Dom Feaunati, who, it emerged, had been bailed to appear in the town's magistrates court the following month to answer charges of 'assault and malicious wounding of a child'.

Back-to-back defeats - the second a round 25, 32-6 hammering by the Wolves - put Salford back into real relegation danger. The Wolves dominated the match from start to finish to keep up their chase for sixth spot, Ian Sibbit - playing in the second row - the gamestar.

And on the Bank Holiday Monday the Bulls strengthened their hold on a top-three finish when they beat Hull at the KC Stadium. The third 2004 meeting of the two sides will be remembered for Lesley Vainikolo's power-packed hat-trick, and the 76th minute set-to between Stuart Fielden and an already battered Jason Smith.

SUPER LEAGUE TABLE - *Monday 30th August*

	P	W	D	L	F	A	D	PTS
Leeds Rhinos	25	22	1	2	958	398	560	45
Hull FC	25	17	2	6	791	430	361	36
Bradford Bulls	25	17	1	7	766	496	270	35
St Helens	25	16	1	8	752	549	203	33
Wigan Warriors	25	15	3	7	677	508	169	33
Wakefield T Wildcats	25	12	0	13	695	608	87	24
Warrington Wolves	25	10	1	14	633	640	-7	21
Huddersfield Giants	25	10	0	15	448	694	-246	20
London Broncos	25	7	1	17	507	840	-333	15
Salford City Reds	25	7	0	18	453	766	-313	14
Widnes Vikings	25	7	0	18	436	783	-347	14
Castleford Tigers	25	5	0	20	458	862	-404	10

SEPTEMBER
Last day drama

"Edge of the abyss" was the dramatic headline on the front page of Rugby Leaguer & League Express on the first Monday of September. Castleford's hopes of avoiding relegation from Super League were fading fast after a 24-22 home defeat to Salford City Reds on a balmy late summer Sunday evening. Brad Davis was the key man in the Tigers' two first-half tries, while Paul Mellor scored a hat-trick in a losing cause. But Chris Charles's four conversions proved the difference with Wayne Godwin's last attempt from the touchline drifting just the wrong side of the near post.

Karl Fitzpatrick was Salford's hero with two tries and a brilliant defensive effort, the ageless Gavin Clinch, playing the final game of his career, defied concussion to produce another top display and Andy Coley and Malcolm Alker led the forward effort.

The Reds had finally shaken off the threat of relegation, having confirmed they were to make an offer to Australian Test halfback and hooker Craig Gower to join the Reds for the 2006 season, when the club expected to move into a new stadium in the Barton area of the city.

But the Tigers, looking down the barrel of relegation, now had to win their last two games - with a trip to Widnes next up - and hope Widnes lost at Hull in round 28, while also making up a deficit of 25 points difference.

The Vikings couldn't follow up their heroics against Wigan as they fell to a 40-6 defeat at Wakefield - who were now almost certain of a sixth-placed finish. A stirring second-half display, scoring 28 unanswered points, took the Wildcats to their seventh successive home win (their last defeat was by Wigan on May 7). Halfback Paul Handforth backed up a midweek game in the under-21s with two tries and three goals.

Warrington's play-off hopes were ended when they saw Paul Sculthorpe steal a 26-24 win at the Halliwell Jones Stadium. With St Helens facing a sixth defeat in seven games, Sculthorpe coolly and expertly hit Jason Hooper with a pass which sent the Australian in for a game-levelling score with a little over a minute to play, before nervelessly hitting home the conversion which turned one competition point into two.

The win kept Saints in fourth, with Wigan drawing 12-12 with Leeds in a cracking game at the JJB Stadium, Danny McGuire scoring twice to make it 35 in Super League IX. Andrew Farrell's fourth goal rescued a point for Wigan with 12 minutes remaining.

Wigan's run of just one win (and two draws) from their last six games had dampened hopes of a top-two finish. And Brian Carney's continued hamstring problems were another worry for Wigan. After his superb try he had to leave the field in the 22nd minute after feeling his hamstring tighten and only returned just after the hour.

Bradford leapfrogged Hull with an ominous 60-18 win over London at Odsal, in-form Shontayne Hape scoring a hat-trick. On the Saturday afternoon Hull had suffered their second defeat in six days, sinking to a late 22-20 defeat at Huddersfield. "They (his players) have got to face the firing squad," said Hull FC coach Shaun McRae, accusing his side of stupidity and lack of courage after watching them give up a 20-10 lead with less than five minutes left. And that with Hull having a 12-11 player advantage following a triple sin-binning, Jim Gannon and Richard Horne off after a 72nd minute bust-up and Paul March accompanying them for giving an unwanted opinion to referee Ian Smith.

Brandon Costin inspired the Giants to one of Super League's greatest escapes to end a seven-match losing run. The club's Australian talisman had that week announced he was to leave at the end of the season with a year still remaining on his contract. "Brandon Costin has been probably the best player this club's had for 40 years," said Huddersfield coach Jon Sharp after the Giants' remarkable late comeback.

Widnes and Castleford's relegation scrap would go down to the last round of the season after the Tigers' nail-biting 7-6 win at the Halton Stadium on the Saturday night,

The Vikings were left two points ahead of Castleford at the foot of the table, but they had to travel to Hull, while the Tigers were due to entertain Wakefield at the Jungle. The Vikings had a 23-points better points difference.

Castleford showed enormous courage and patience in a dour arm-wrestle of a game as Francis Maloney kept his cool to pot a 30-metre field goal ten minutes from time. But the travelling Tigers fans had their hearts in their mouths 69 seconds from the end as Jules O'Neill's swirling cross-field kick from 40 metres out for once eluded Waine Pryce. Adam Hughes rushed up and looked set to score by the flag, but the ball agonisingly slipped out of his clutches.

Salford City Reds pushed lacklustre Hull all the way with 12 men after Andy Coley was sent off for punching Airlie Birds' loose forward Richard Whiting in the 25th minute, although he escaped a ban. Hull's 12-8 win at the Willows ended a three-match losing run. A 57th minute try from Kirk Yeaman settled the issue.

The Broncos home support bade farewell to a departing quartet of long-serving veterans: Steele Retchless and Rusty Bawden (who didn't play), Mat Toshack and Jim Dymock (who did), after a 26-22 defeat by Wigan at Griffin Park. Andy Farrell stole the show with another awesome all-round display.

The win saw Wigan jump over St Helens into fourth spot in the table after the Rhinos produced a stunning second-half revival at Knowsley Road on the Friday evening.

Danny McGuire's try-scoring exploits had spearheaded their table-topping campaign but Leeds' 19-1 scoring advantage after the break was achieved with McGuire sitting on the sidelines, nursing a dead-leg. McGuire was forced off at the interval with Saints, leading 18-6, seemingly on the way to their third win of the season over the Rhinos at Knowsley Road. Matt Diskin's late try sealed

Rhinos' second-half revival and a 25-19 win.

Wakefield sealed a play-off spot with a fiery 21-20 home win over the Giants on the Friday night, Ben Jeffries' 74th minute field goal separating the teams.

Bradford retained second place with a nervous 28-27 win at Warrington. Paul Deacon kicked two field goals in the closing minutes to Lee Briers' one, the last one sailing over almost as the hooter called time on an intriguing contest. French international Jerome Guisset made his last home appearance for the Wolves after announcing he was heading to French rugby union at the end of the season, slamming the 20/20 rule that constrained Super League clubs. After Warrington decided not to renew his contract, Guisset claimed that rugby union was the only option available to him.

"I'm a League man through and through, and I think the '20/20' rule is absolute rubbish," said Guisset.

Castleford Tigers' relegation - their first since they joined the Rugby League in 1926 - was confirmed on Saturday 18 September, after their 28-32 home defeat to Wakefield, with Widnes Vikings surviving the drop, despite their 20-18 defeat at Hull.

The Hull-Widnes game had been selected as the SkyTV game that night, with the RFL deciding that Castleford would have to play their game at the same time.

It was an evening at full of emotion and high drama at the Jungle. The Tigers, in front of a near-capacity crowd of 11,055, fought to the dying seconds, even though the news coming in from Hull made it clear that Widnes would not lose by a big enough margin to keep them up even if they did win.

Wakefield offered their neighbours no helping hand, despite being already assured of a top-six play-off place. After going 18-10 down inside 23 minutes they swept to victory with four tries - with Castleford halfback Brad Davis withdrawn at half-time with a hamstring injury. There were plenty of Castleford players who gave it their best shot, but none could match the outstanding performance of Wakefield's David Solomona - who confirmed himself as the best overseas recruit of the season by turning the game with two quick tries before creating another.

Tigers chief executive Richard Wright conceded there would be a number of departures from the Jungle - with the likes of Ryan Hudson, Andy Lynch and Wayne Godwin already having been linked with a host of their rivals. Coach Gary Mercer, who had guided the club to five wins from ten games, said he wanted to stay with the club.

The Vikings lost 20-18 to Hull in an emotionally-charged game at the KC Stadium, but knew they were safe four minutes from time when Castleford's defeat by Wakefield was confirmed.

Hull were already assured of third place after Bradford's win on the Friday - a result that one club official reckoned cost at least 3,000 fans on the gate. But their five-try win (they failed to kick a single goal) confirmed a huge improvement on 2003, despite another crippling injury list - Shaun McRae reckoning 11 players who would have been first choice at the start of the year were out injured.

The Bulls had given Saints a 64-24 hiding at Odsal. For Saints, Sean Long

Michael Smith is distraught as Castleford suffer relegation from Super League

made a successful return to action - his first match back after a three-month ban imposed for backing Bradford to beat a virtual Saints reserve side on Easter Monday - and he was jeered throughout by unforgiving Bulls fans. There had been much debate about whether Long should have been able to play - his ban due to expire on the 17 September - the date of the game - although no time had been specified. The RFL eventually confirmed the suspension ended at midnight, 16 September. Long showed flashes of his brilliant best, including a superb run that set up St Helens' second try, before being substituted in the 72nd minute.

Lesley Vainikolo broke the Super League try record - his fifth hat-trick of the season swept the powerful winger to the top of the Tetley's Super League try chart with 36 for the season. He began the game needing three to overtake Danny McGuire's 35, and it soon became clear his colleagues were determined to help him get them, knowing the injured Leeds Rhinos player could not add to his total.

Vainikolo's first try was gift-wrapped by Shontayne Hape, who ignored the chance to touch down nearer the posts to complete his own hat-trick and passed to Vainikolo in the in-goal area, but he needed no help with the second two.

Brandon Costin, Julian Bailey and Darren Fleary bade their farewells to the Huddersfield public after a 28-22 home win over Salford City Reds. And it was one of the Giants' most promising youngsters - Paul White, who began the season with a broken leg - who came up with two winning plays in the final minutes of a supposedly 'nothing game' that had almost everything. White claimed the winning try in a keenly-contested match and then scuppered Salford's hopes of snatching what might have been a deserved draw with a wonderful try-saving tackle, which also deprived Stuart Littler of a hat-trick, in the dying seconds.

September

The genius of Adrian Lam took Wigan to a hard-earned 21-16 home win over the Wolves that guaranteed fourth spot, and a home play-off tie with Saints. With captain Andrew Farrell, suffering from flu, sitting out the second half, Lam was the man who ensured Wigan's unbeaten home record was left intact. With the Wolves deservedly leading 16-12 after a quick-fire brace of tries by Brent Grose and Daryl Cardiss, the little genius from PNG took the game into his own hands. Lam's sharp pass allowed Sean O'Loughlin to send Danny Tickle slicing through on the right for a try that tied things up again with twelve minutes left, Tickle's conversion drifting agonisingly wide. Then, after Mark Smith's break from deep, and Terry O'Connor's charge had set up the position, Lam safely negotiated a field goal with seven minutes left on the clock.

Lam then collected Luke Robinson's pass to spirit Kevin Brown over on the left. But Tickle's third miss at goal left the door slightly ajar, and the Wolves, backed by a 5,000-strong army of fans who lent a carnival atmosphere to proceedings, almost snatched a chance of victory right at the end, Lee Briers' cross-field kick to the left agonisingly eluding Dean Gaskell's clutches.

A 17,000-plus crowd gathered at Headingley on the same Friday night as the Rhinos were presented with the 'League Leaders Shield', the current team receiving a guard of honour from almost 50 former Leeds players. Then Leeds ended the campaign as they had

Leeds Rhinos - 2004 League Leaders

started it, comfortably defeating the much-improved Broncos - who gave a debut off the bench to teenaged Londoner Ade Adebisi - by 42-14 to maintain their one hundred per cent home record, and finish nine points clear of second-placed Bradford.

Leeds' attendance figure guaranteed a new aggregate total of over 16,000 per match to make the Rhinos the best supported club of a summer era season. And Super League crowds as a whole had risen for the third season in a row, with the average attendance at a regular season Super League match 8,573, a rise of more than five per cent on the previous season.

The six 'loop' fixtures added on at the end of the season, which replicated matches played earlier in the season, didn't lose their attraction. The total attendance for the last six weeks of the season was 312,899, with the same fixtures earlier in the year having attracted an almost identical 313,065 spectators.

FINAL SUPER LEAGUE TABLE - *Sunday 19th September*

	P	W	D	L	F	A	D	PTS
Leeds Rhinos	28	24	2	2	1037	443	594	50
Bradford Bulls	28	20	1	7	918	565	353	41
Hull FC	28	19	2	7	843	478	365	40
Wigan Warriors	28	17	4	7	736	558	178	38
St Helens	28	17	1	10	821	662	159	35
Wakefield T Wildcats	28	15	0	13	788	662	126	30
Huddersfield Giants	28	12	0	16	518	757	-239	24
Warrington Wolves	28	10	1	17	700	715	-15	21
Salford City Reds	28	8	0	20	507	828	-321	16
London Broncos	28	7	1	20	561	968	-407	15
Widnes Vikings	28	7	0	21	466	850	-384	14
Castleford Tigers	28	6	0	22	515	924	-409	12

3
SUPER LEAGUE PLAY-OFFS 2004

Super League Play-offs

Wakefield blasted into the Elimination semi-final on the first Friday of the play-offs with a tremendous second-half performance as injury-hit Hull fell at the first hurdle by 18-28. Halfback Ben Jeffries - in doubt until the day of the game with an ankle injury picked up at Castleford the week before - was once again in magnificent form, his kicking tormenting the Hull defence, one uncannily-accurate kick to the left setting up Semi Tadulala for the try that put daylight between the two sides.

Tadulala was also a standout and though there were heroes all over the park in red, white and blue, none stood taller than prop Michael Korkidas. It was his monster run as he returned Hull's second-half restart, in which he ran round and through five defenders before finally being halted on halfway, that lifted the Wildcats, after they trailed 14-6 at the break.

The Wildcats could have gone ahead in the very first minute of the game when Rob Spicer regathered a loose ball to storm over after a Jeffries kick. But after going to the screen, referee Karl Kirkpatrick penalised Colum Halpenny for tackling Gareth Raynor whilst he was off the ground.

Jeffries was sin-binned for interference at the play-the-ball after his tackle had halted Shaun Briscoe just short of the Wakefield line, and skipper Gareth Ellis joined him in the bin after 12 minutes. In between, David March scooted blind from dummy-half, stepped through attempted tackles by Kirk Yeaman and Briscoe and resisted Gareth Raynor's last-ditch tackle to open the visitors' account. The clever hooker also added the conversion and the 12-man Wildcats led 6-0 after seven minutes.

Hull exploited the numerical advantage, Richard Swain racing through a depleted line and Peter Lupton adding the conversion to level the scores. Five minutes later skipper Paul Cooke, also back from injury, made a 40-metre break down the left flank. Young Wakefield fullback Mark Field scythed him down with a super cover tackle. But the excellent Richard Whiting used the position on the next play to step through and send Shayne McMenemy over with a great inside pass as he fell to the floor. Lupton added his second conversion and also landed a penalty nine minutes from the break to leave Hull 14-6 ahead at the interval.

The match was transformed in the third quarter when Wakefield ran in three tries without reply. Within five minutes of Korkidas's miracle run, winger Colum Halpenny touched down after Kirk Yeaman had failed to deal with another teasing crossfield kick by Jeffries. Seven minutes later, Chris Feather managed to get the ball down in the right corner, despite the attentions of four Hull defenders – and substitute Paul Handforth's conversion put the Wildcats ahead for the first time. Then, roared on by a near two-thousand-strong Wakefield following packed into the North Stand, Tadulala out-jumped Colin Best and collected Jeffries' kick cleanly to score in the opposite corner. This time Handforth couldn't add the goal points but he increased his side's lead in the

65th minute when Whiting was penalised for not standing square, which left Hull needing two scores.

They got one 12 minutes from time when Ewan Dowes crashed over, and although Lupton couldn't convert, Hull only trailed 18-22. And in a frenetic final ten minutes they nearly snatched victory three times. But it was to be the Wildcats' night – and centre Jason Demetriou sealed a famous win, racing 30 metres up the middle and stepping Briscoe off Handforth's inside pass for their fifth try.

The elimination meant a sad end to Shaun McRae's five years in charge of Hull. "It's disappointing for us but at the same time we've had a very good season and I think you'd all agree the future is pretty rosy," McRae concluded after he waved goodbye to the black and white faithful.

On the Saturday night St Helens' miserable run against Wigan at the JJB was extended to nine losing games and their season ended, as it did last year, in defeat against their old enemy, this time by 18-12.

Wigan's defence was magnificent throughout and, sparked by the youthful exuberance of Sean O'Loughlin and Luke Robinson in attack, they conjured up three tries in an inspired ten-minute spell either side of half-time.

Saints were left to rue a couple of borderline video refereeing decisions that went against them, notably the decision to disallow Ian Hardman's 11th-minute "try", as they slipped out of the play-offs at their earliest stage in the seven-year history of the competition.

Wigan, losing 6-0 after 25 minutes when they were 7-2 behind on the penalty count, somehow recovered to lead 12-6 at the interval and scored again within 87 seconds of the re-start.

Salford-bound Robinson went it alone from the tap penalty, cutting between Jason Hooper and Chris Joynt for the first Wigan score. Andrew Farrell converted and was on target again five minutes later after Robinson had instigated a flowing move that was continued when Adrian Lam sent Gareth Hock through a hole for Kevin Brown to finish clinically.

Within two minutes of the resumption Farrell's bullet pass on halfway found his brother-in-law, the outstanding O'Loughlin, with a one-on-one against Paul Sculthorpe. O'Loughlin backed himself, taking on the Saints captain on the outside and then supplying the perfect inside pass for Farrell to cross, despite Lee Gilmour's despairing cover tackle.

At 18-6 ahead, Wigan then failed to land the killer blow, missing three field-goal attempts through Farrell and Lam (twice). Saints almost made them pay, despite losing Ade Gardner to a head knock (though he later returned) from a Terry Newton tackle. In the 50th minute a towering Sculthorpe kick was lost by Brown under his own posts and Sean Long swooped, only to lose the ball.

Just six minutes remained when Saints finally made their pressure tell, Sculthorpe running across the face of the Wigan defensive line to create the opportunity for Paul Wellens to send the returned Gardner over, Long hitting the difficult conversion to set up a nerve-wracking finale.

Saints were roused for one last effort when Dallas put down a Lam pass on his own 40-metre line with three minutes left. But their last chance effectively disappeared when Long's bouncing kick was grabbed by O'Loughlin five metres from his own line.

The visitors were left to reflect on failing to take their chances in a dominant opening when Long's three penalties - all from close range - were their only reward for sustained spells of pressure. Saints were also denied a classic breakaway score by the video referee after 11 minutes when Willie Talau was judged to be accidentally offside after Orr's kick rebounded off the covering Mick Higham. Higham had sparked a thrilling 90-metre counter-attack, racing away to combine with the supporting Jason Hooper to send Hardman streaking away for what looked like the opener - until they were cruelly recalled.

Higham was also denied on 28 minutes by one of the tackles of the season by Kris Radlinski, despite suffering from concussion that forced his withdrawal at the break.

St Helens coach Ian Millward had promised that Saints were set to peak at the right time, and the way they dominated large portions of both halves at the JJB Stadium backed up that view.

"Still, it's been a great season," he said. "We gave five kids under 18 a run and the Challenge Cup was great. We were great up to round 19."

The Wildcats - tipped at the start of the year in some quarters to be embroiled once again in the relegation battle - went very close to making the penultimate game of the season.

They squandered a 14-0 lead, saw a contentious video referee decision to disallow a try go against them at a crucial stage in the second half, had David Solomona unluckily sin-binned, and ended the game pounding the Wigan line as their hosts were hanging on the ropes at 18-14.

The sides had already met four times in 2004, Wigan winning all four, though the margins in the last three games had been just six, six and four points.

Denis Betts lost Sean O'Loughlin, who was taken to hospital after a nasty bang on the ribs in the 12th minute, while Brian Carney suffered another setback on his comeback trail. Carney managed just 12 minutes either side of the interval before suffering a recurrence of his hamstring problems.

The tension even seemed to affect Wigan captain Andrew Farrell, who missed three shots at goal and put his side under severe pressure with a knock-on with less than three minutes left. Wigan survived that, but then faced a nerve-shredding final minute after Kevin Brown also knocked-on on his own line from acting halfback.

In a thrilling start, Brett Dallas had a try disallowed for a double movement after the ball came loose from Gareth Ellis's tackle on Gareth Hock close to the line, video referee Geoff Berry making the first of several decisions on a busy night for him.

Terry Newton and Stephen Wild halt Colum Halpenny during the Elimination Semi-Final

But suddenly it was all Wildcats after they hit the front, when Halpenny's rushed kick on the last tackle created something out of nothing. Semi Tadulala made a nuisance of himself, Sid Domic grabbed the loose ball, and Halpenny took his pass off his toes and stretched over by the post for the opening try, confirmed after a lengthy deliberation. Two minutes later the Wildcats moved further ahead after Hock lost the ball in a double tackle by Jason Demetriou and Spicer. Duncan MacGillivray collected David March's pass from first receiver, went through Terry Newton's half-hearted tackle and crossed out wide. But this time March was unable to convert.

Then, with the away end still filling up after horrendous turnstile problems, the Wildcats fans were in dreamland as Solomona extended their lead to 14-0, loping over after Tadulala challenged Martin Aspinwall to a Jeffries kick, the video referee satisfied that the ball rebounded backwards off his arm. Again, though, March was off-target, and Paul Handforth later sent a penalty kick wide of the posts to leave his team ruing missed opportunities of putting the game away.

Kris Radlinski led Wigan's comeback with a typically inspiring display, miraculously getting the ball down one-handed by the flag on the right in a massed tackle. Terry Newton's bullet pass from dummy-half then allowed Brown to squeeze over on the left to leave Wigan just four points behind.

There it stayed for 26 minutes until Farrell potted a penalty, but missed two more, and with Danny Tickle - playing, despite the death of his father earlier in the week - having a score ruled out, the frustrations grew for the Wigan faithful.

With ten minutes remaining, though, Danny Orr's run off a Danny Sculthorpe offload was halted just short of the line, and Lam cleverly drove over on the angle from dummy-half for what proved to be the match-winner, Farrell converting.

Super League Play-offs

Bradford Bulls, for the fifth time in six years took the direct route to Old Trafford, this time by shattering Leeds' previously unbeaten home record.

The 26-12 win was built on an exceptional scrambling defence – particularly in the second quarter as Bradford spectacularly defended a dream start which had seen Shontayne Hape cross for a brace of tries. Leading the charge was 2003 Man of Steel Jamie Peacock, back to his best, with a series of awe-inspiring charges and tackles, ably backed up by Lesley Vainikolo.

Bradford crowned new heroes in the form of Rob Parker – who produced an unbelievable try and match-saving ankle tap to deny Chris McKenna – and Lee Radford, in arguably his best performance until a calf injury struck.

Behind them, Bulls' halfbacks dominated, Paul Deacon with his roving darts and astute kicks - which eventually broke the deadlock. And his partner, Iestyn Harris, was even more influential. "Everybody complemented each other, but Iestyn's contribution was huge, I honestly didn't think he would be quite as impressive as he is now, he's fitted in really quickly," coach Brian Noble said.

The hottest ticket in town to see two sides at full strength ensured a tremendous atmosphere and another sell-out crowd - but Bradford muted the Leeds hordes with a sensational start.

Deacon's hurried grubber at the end of the Bulls' first set was fumbled by Andrew Dunemann, Harris, as he did so often, mopping up. And after Hape and Paul had taken possession to the home line, Harris, Deacon, Radford and Logan Swann combined on the power play for Hape to scamper across on the overlap.

Matt Adamson went close on the crash ball, but Richard Mathers lost possession when being spun round in the tackle. And Bradford expertly exploited the left-hand side after David Furner had spilt the ball in his own quarter, Paul's weaving cross-field run sowing the seeds for Deacon's long pass to put Hape in at a canter. When Danny McGuire latched onto the tireless Matt Diskin's grubber, Sinfield made it 6-8 at the interval with the extras.

In the space of four second-half minutes, the contest was summed up and decided. Willie Poching stormed to the Bradford line, only for Harris to collect the ball following a massive tackle from Leon Pryce. Bradford's subsequent set, led by Deacon's vision and Vainikolo's power, took them into dangerous territory, David Furner knocking on Harris's pin-point cross-field kick on the last tackle as Chev Walker seemingly strode away into the clear. From the scrum, Deacon and Harris found the ground to enable Robbie Paul – whose second stint was central to victory – to twist his way over from acting halfback.

With the dam breached, Bulls struck on the last tackle of the following set, this time Deacon's towering bomb, again to the left, evading Vainikolo's chase, the ball taking a jag backwards on the bounce for Radford to pluck it out of the grasp of Danny McGuire to establish a 20-6 lead. And they could have increased their lead when Withers, Paul and Deacon found Pryce in space but his pass went into touch.

And after Bradford had been penalised for interference, Ali Lauitiiti and Mathers were heavily involved in the interplay, allowing McKenna to send Sinfield careering towards the posts, his flick on the inside seeing Poching crash over.

But the Bulls finished as they had begun. Keith Senior lost possession in his own quarter attempting to play catch up. From the scrum Paul, on the runaround with Harris, found Hape, who sent the deserving Vainikolo over out wide, Deacon adding the conversion for good measure.

The defeat left Leeds desperate to avoid becoming the first league leaders not to make the Grand Final.

The Rhinos ignored a week of taunts at being "chokers" and dispatched Wigan, 40-12, with an exuberant display. They maintained the pressure all night through ferocious defence, with Danny Ward and David Furner prominent; a vastly improved kicking game which ensured repeat sets; and a clinical finish which included one of the tries of the season, almost inevitably to Danny McGuire.

Chris McKenna was outstanding in the pack; Mark Calderwood excellent on the wing; Chev Walker a dominating presence in the middle; and Marcus Bai became one of the few players to qualify for a Grand Final in both hemispheres with another stunning hat-trick – bringing his tally to 26 touchdowns in 29 games.

Defeat for the cherry and whites meant emotional farewells to a number of the game's finest, not least Adrian Lam, who tirelessly tried to fashion a rescue act. He was ably supported by fellow retiree Craig Smith, together with skipper Andy Farrell - four days later named Man of Steel - who constantly searched for work and nearly started a comeback with a touchdown at the end of the first half.

In 2003, the Grand Final proved to be the game too far for the Warriors and although they produced a mighty effort at the start of the second period to haul the margin back to ten points, the defensive exertions during the Rhinos' blistering start took their toll in the last quarter.

Tries to Bai, Walker, McGuire and Richard Mathers, and three Sinfield conversions had Leeds 22-0 up after 33 minutes. McGuire's was a beauty.

It began with an enormous hit from Ward on a kick return by Radlinski which eventually forced Danny Orr into a hurried, early punt to clear the congested lines. Mathers brought the ball back into play, his superbly-judged flick out of Stephen Wild's tackle releasing Bai to half way. McGuire appeared effortlessly on the inside with precision timing to split the cover and gloriously complete a fatal length-of-the-field riposte.

With their first real attack of a shattering half, and on the back of a huge hit by Gareth Hock which caused Barrie McDermott to spill the ball, Farrell gave Wigan a lifeline from Orr's perfectly-placed grubber behind the sticks.

In an all-or-nothing start to the second half the Warriors went for broke, aided by the Rhinos' propensity to attack at every opportunity. Lam was instrumental in straightening and directing the attack, Wild, Sean O'Loughlin and Terry O'Connor turned up the pressure. And after Farrell had sent Terry Newton close, Luke Robinson twisted his way over.

The Warriors sensed a chance of redemption, Keith Senior just denying Danny Tickle before Newton and Robinson gave O'Loughlin a run to the corner; McGuire, Senior and Bai producing a stunning try-saver in the corner.

Lam ghosted through two would-be defenders to send Tickle into the clear, Bai denying him with a bone-jarring challenge before Newton sent Smith rumbling for glory, Walker and Calderwood forcing him to just lose control of the ball as he rolled over for the try.

That was the nearest Wigan came as Leeds improvised an excellent last-tackle play, Calderwood showing great presence and awareness to keep a move on the right going with a shimmy and cut inside, Ali Lauitiiti plucking McGuire's cross kick to send Bai over with an audacious flick pass.

Radlinski just won the race to McKenna's kick for Calderwood, but the die had been cast, Diskin, McGuire and Mathers giving Lauitiiti space to send Bai stepping across to make it 34-12.

Five minutes from time, O'Loughlin fumbled Diskin's grubber to the posts, under pressure from Calderwood after a period of sustained Leeds attack, and Ryan Bailey was on hand to pick up and plunge over and double his career try-tally.

Kevin Brown grounded by David Furner and Keith Senior during the Final Eliminator

SUPER LEAGUE
GRAND FINAL
Year of the Rhino

Danny McGuire scored the try in the 75th minute of the Super League decider that settled a gripping first all-Yorkshire Grand Final.

When McGuire slid over in trademark style right in front of the Leeds end, a game which the Rhinos had dominated tactically without ever looking totally secure was in the bag.

And McGuire's try drew him level with the Bulls' man-mountain Lesley Vainikolo at the top of the try-scoring lists - 39 each for the season in all competitions - to ensure him a lasting spot in the season's records.

It was Leeds' first Championship since Alan Hardisty's side carried off the old trophy after their win over St Helens in 1972, achieved not too far away from Old Trafford, at Station Road.

"Both teams were determined not to let the other side get across the line, and that is finals football," said Leeds coach Tony Smith, who had delivered all that had been asked of him when he replaced Daryl Powell as coach at Headingley at the end of last year, and later extended his Headingley contract by a year to the end of 2006.

"I'm proud. Very, very proud. It's great to be involved with this team. They are a special bunch of guys and it's a pleasure to work with them. I'm really proud to be the Rhinos coach."

Until McGuire's clincher, with the Rhinos leading only 10-8, the game could have gone either way.

Leeds' player of the year Matt Diskin collected the Harry Sunderland Trophy; McGuire himself could have sneaked the award, if only for his enthusiasm in defence, although he also played a part in Leeds' relentless kicking game. Marcus Bai was explosive; Richard Mathers was as calm and collected as an international fullback ten years his senior; and Mark Calderwood resoundingly answered pre-match questions about his ability to contain Vainikolo.

The Volcano was an obvious target for the

Leeds defence. He spent the whole of the first half returning Rhinos kicks, being trapped in-goal, and finding himself swamped when he tried to burst out of dummy-half.

Vainikolo emerged from all the pressure with great credit, and there was a mighty effort throughout a Bulls side that at times lacked composure. There was the usual wholehearted show from Jamie Peacock, the halves Iestyn Harris and Paul Deacon also worked hard, and Shontayne Hape ran strongly. Bradford lost Michael Withers at half-time with a quad injury and Joe Vagana also picked up a shoulder injury just after the ten-minute mark, even though he returned to almost carry six men over the Leeds line midway through the second half.

The Bulls were already missing Leon Pryce with a dislocated shoulder, and Paul Johnson slotted into the right centre, with Paul Anderson coming onto the bench – although he only lasted ten minutes in the first half before appearing to limp off.

For the first time all season, Tony Smith selected the same side for two matches running, showing faith in the side that had beaten Wigan the week before to earn the right to have a second crack at the Bulls. Chev Walker stayed in the centre with Chris McKenna in the second row, meaning no places for Matt Adamson, Wayne McDonald or Andrew Dunemann.

Deacon's perfect kick-off signalled that the Bulls were primed to collect their third title in four years, the high kick allowing the Bulls defence to pen Leeds inside their own 20-metre area for the first four tackles.

Kevin Sinfield's clearing kick to half way looked less than promising, but Vainikolo spilled the ball in Dave Furner, Diskin and McGuire's tackle, and in the next set of six Vagana was penalised for stripping the ball from Diskin right under the Bulls posts. Sinfield stepped up to kick the first of his four goals from four attempts and give Leeds a 2-0 lead.

A great McGuire kick to the posts had Vainikolo tracking back again, although the pressure was relieved when Bai was pulled up by referee Steve Ganson for lying on the Tongan.

The Bulls-machine clicked into gear, and at the other end Iestyn Harris put up a magnificent bomb. Mathers collected superbly right under his crossbar, but he was hammered into the in-goal and then dead by Deacon. From the drop-out Bradford were in the lead.

Robbie Paul took the ball from dummy-half on a teasing lateral run to the left. He offloaded to Lee Radford who hit the line and managed to find Paul on the runaround. In the blink of an eye, Paul audaciously looped the ball around his back to Shontayne Hape, who fed Vainikolo. From a yard out, Vainikolo stepped inside the cover and dived over in front of the despairing Leeds support.

It took the Rhinos seven minutes to edge back in front. Sinfield's kick to the corner saw Vainikolo trapped in-goal by the effervescent Calderwood; Mathers stepped inside Harris, and was just brought down. McGuire couldn't hold onto the pass from the play-the-ball, and Logan Swann lifted the siege when he dropped on the loose ball. On the next Leeds set Sinfield put in the first poor kick of the night, when he sliced a bomb and Walker was caught in possession, throwing a frantic pass into touch. But from the scrum a jarring tackle from

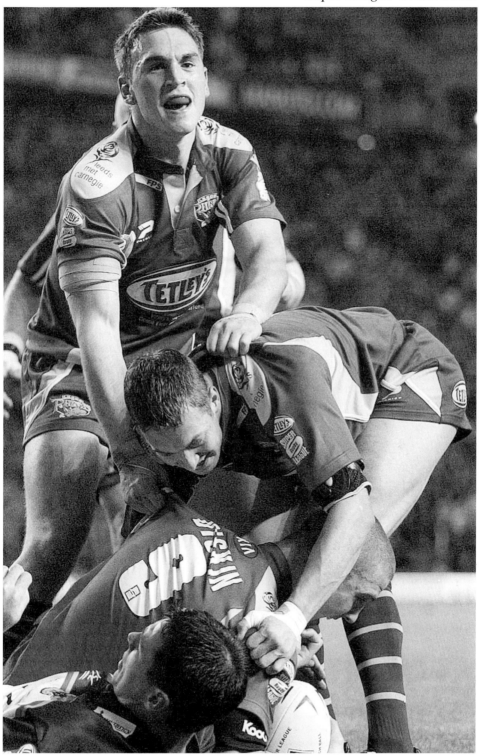

Kevin Sinfield and Danny McGuire congratulate Matt Diskin on scoring

Super League Grand Final

Furner – a Grand Final winner on both sides of the world – caused Radford to spill the ball as he hit the ground on his own 40-metre line.

Three tackles later, Diskin ambled left from dummy-half, Stuart Fielden hung back while Peacock moved up, and the hooker ghosted through the gap and over the line just to the left of the posts. Sinfield converted.

The Bulls needed to get more possession near the Leeds line, but instead their last-tackle options let them down for the rest of the first half. Swann was tackled on the last just inside the Leeds half; sub Karl Pratt's pass from dummy-half 15 metres out, and again on the sixth, was forward; Deacon's stab to the posts was collected by Mathers in front of his own line – after a wonderful Peacock charge down the middle; and Parker was penalised for delaying Rob Burrow too long at the play-the-ball. A Pratt kick to the in-goal that went straight into dead summed up Bradford's fortunes in attack.

TETLEY'S SUPER LEAGUE GRAND FINAL

Saturday 16th October 2004

BRADFORD BULLS 8 LEEDS RHINOS 16

BULLS: 6 Michael Withers; 17 Stuart Reardon; 16 Paul Johnson; 4 Shontayne Hape; 5 Lesley Vainikolo; 18 Iestyn Harris; 7 Paul Deacon; 8 Joe Vagana; 1 Robbie Paul (C); 29 Stuart Fielden; 12 Jamie Peacock; 13 Logan Swann; 11 Lee Radford. Subs: 10 Paul Anderson for Vagana (14); 15 Karl Pratt for Paul (23); 27 Rob Parker for Anderson (24); 19 Jamie Langley for Peacock (32); Paul for Withers (ht); Peacock for Radford (48); Radford for Swann (54); Vagana for Parker (56); Parker for Fielden (63); Fielden for Vagana (67); Swann for Langley (68).
Tries: Vainikolo (7), Hape (43); **Goals:** Deacon 0/2.
RHINOS: 21 Richard Mathers; 18 Mark Calderwood; 5 Chev Walker; 4 Keith Senior; 22 Marcus Bai; 13 Kevin Sinfield (C); 6 Danny McGuire; 19 Danny Ward; 9 Matt Diskin; 8 Ryan Bailey; 3 Chris McKenna; 29 Ali Lauitiiti; 11 David Furner. Subs: 16 Willie Poching for Furner (19); 10 Barrie McDermott for Ward (22); Ward for Bailey (29); 7 Rob Burrow for Lauitiiti (30); Bailey for McDermott (41); 20 Jamie Jones-Buchanan for McKenna (48); Lauitiiti for Ward (50); Furner for Sinfield (60); McKenna for Poching (63); Sinfield for Diskin (67); Poching for McKenna (72); Ward for Bailey (73).
Tries: Diskin (15), McGuire (75); **Goals:** Sinfield 4/4.
Rugby Leaguer & League Express Men of the Match:
Bulls: Lesley Vainikolo; *Rhinos:* Richard Mathers.
Penalty count: 5-5; **Half-time:** 4-10;
Referee: Steve Ganson (St Helens);
Attendance: 65,547 *(at Old Trafford, Manchester).*

On 27 minutes, one last-tackle play looked to have worked out, when Deacon's bomb to the left went loose as Walker and Calderwood both tried to collect. Vainikolo picked up and fed inside to Radford. Radford fell to Barrie McDermott's tackle and landed on his back, popped a pass up to Vainikolo, whose long pass put in Hape into the left corner.

But video referee David Campbell ruled, correctly, that Radford's ball-carrying arm had touched the deck and the tackle had been completed. The penalty went to Leeds, and the siege was lifted again.

The only other score of the half went to Leeds, when Harris was penalised for stealing the ball from Willie Poching, just as Stuart Fielden came in to assist – one of several 50/50 decisions. Sinfield converted the penalty from 30 metres out to give the Rhinos a 10-4 half-time lead.

Both coaches described the game as an arm-wrestle, and in the second half it was certainly that – with two points separating the sides for 30 minutes after the Bulls had got to within two points, four minutes from the restart.

Leeds conceded two penalties – the first when Calderwood held down Vainikolo, as he returned Ryan Bailey's bomb, and the second when they were adjudged offside at the ten-metre tap.

And for the only time in the game, Leeds ran out of numbers, and as the ball was moved left, Swann put Hape through the centre for the try. Crucially Deacon missed the conversion attempt.

Parker spilled the ball two tackles after the re-start to kill off any Bulls momentum, allowing Leeds to regather their composure. Stuart Reardon – at fullback after Withers' withdrawal – was taken over the dead-ball line by Danny Ward from Diskin's kick in-goal. Then Bai was stopped just short from a powerplay by Pratt and Harris.

Leeds had a good chance to stretch their lead when Swann was left wobbly after a Bailey charge, but they failed to exploit the gap in the line as Calderwood's hurried inside pass ten metres out dribbled forwards.

A lovely scissors pass from Johnson gave Pratt – now on the right wing – some daylight and after the ball was moved left Swann's kick through was just fumbled by Vainikolo.

But Leeds dominated territory and twice more forced drop-outs as Poching trapped Pratt in-goal in the right corner, and then Harris just scooped the ball dead as Calderwood tore onto McGuire's kick to the posts. A couple of 50/50 calls saw a penalty to either side for dissent, and both sides liberally surrendered possession.

Ali Lauitiiti and Keith Senior got Bai away down the left, but Peacock got across to scythe him down.

The Bulls were running out of time, and needed something special to steal the game. They looked to have it when Deacon skipped through the line and tore down field. Leeds scrambled magnificently and forced the halfback left, where he found Vainikolo charging down the wing. With 40 metres to go and little cover in sight the Volcano was a definite chance, at least until Walker took him down with a textbook front-on tackle.

It was Bradford's last hurrah as Bai took Harris's bomb on the next play and raced 40 metres into the Bulls' half. The pressure was back on Bradford and it showed, when Paul, in his own '20', inexplicably dropped the ball as he tried to pass.

On the second tackle from the scrum, McGuire was over, feeding Senior for a crash at the line and then taking his return pass to dance over. Sinfield's kick completed the scoring.

"People have asked us 'could we do it this year?" asked Tony Smith at the post-match press conference. His answer was succinct: "Yes.

Danny McGuire dives past Stuart Reardon and Paul Johnson to score the winning try

TETLEY'S MAN OF STEEL AWARD WINNERS

MAN OF STEEL -
Andy Farrell (Wigan Warriors)
PLAYERS' PLAYER OF THE YEAR -
Andy Farrell (Wigan Warriors)
COACH OF THE YEAR -
Shane McNally
(Wakefield Trinity Wildcats)
YOUNG PLAYER OF THE YEAR -
Shaun Briscoe (Hull FC)
REFEREE OF THE YEAR -
Steve Ganson
SPECIAL AWARDS
FOR SERVICE TO SUPER LEAGUE -
Shaun McRae, Mike Forshaw
& Paul Newlove
TOP TRY SCORER -
Lesley Vainikolo (Bradford Bulls)
METRE MAKER -
Michael Korkidas (Wakefield Trinity
Wildcats) for making 4,084 metres
HIT MAN -
Richard Swain (Hull FC)
for making 933 Super League tackles

**TETLEY'S SUPER LEAGUE
DREAM TEAM 2004**
1 Shaun Briscoe (Hull FC)
2 Lesley Vainikolo (Bradford Bulls)
3 Keith Senior (Leeds Rhinos)
4 Sid Domic
(Wakefield Trinity Wildcats)
5 Marcus Bai (Leeds Rhinos)
6 Danny McGuire (Leeds Rhinos)
7 Richard Horne (Hull FC)
8 Andy Farrell (Wigan Warriors)
9 Matt Diskin (Leeds Rhinos)
10 Paul King (Hull FC)
11 Ali Lauitiiti (Leeds Rhinos)
12 David Solomona
(Wakefield Trinity Wildcats)
13 Paul Sculthorpe (St Helens)

The 2004 Super League Dream Team

2004 SUPER LEAGUE SEASON

ROUND BY ROUND

Gillette®

ABOVE: Nathan Wood shows his joy at scoring the first try at Warrington's new Halliwell Jones Stadium with teammates Brent Grose and Jon Clarke as the Wolves defeat Wakefield

ABOVE: Marcus Bai charges towards the try line on his way to a debut hat-trick for Leeds against London

RIGHT: Lesley Vainikolo crashes over for one of his five tries, despite the attentions of Martin Aspinwall, as Bradford take apart Wigan in the opening game of Super League IX

ROUND 2

BELOW: Danny McGuire goes over for a try as Leeds race past Castleford at a packed Jungle

ABOVE: Richie Barnett held up by Mark Hilton and Mike Forshaw during Hull's win over Warrington

ROUND 3

ABOVE: Wakefield's David March dumped by Salford's Andy Coley as the Wildcats edge a close encounter at a wind-swept Willows

RIGHT: Danny Orr gets to grips with Marcus St Hilaire as Wigan are stunned by Huddersfield

ROUND 4

CHALLENGE CUP

ROUND 4

ABOVE: Sean Long congratulated on scoring by Jason Hooper as St Helens eliminate Bradford

QUARTER FINALS

ABOVE: Keith Mason closes down Richard Horne as St Helens edge a thriller with Hull

BELOW: Howard Hill makes a break as Whitehaven put up a brave fight in defeat against Warrington

ROUND 5

ABOVE: Coach Richard Agar and Danny Brough are jubilant as York earn a last-gasp win at Featherstone

SEMI FINALS

ABOVE: Danny Orr and Quentin Pongia combine to dump Danny Lima as Wigan defeat Warrington

ABOVE: Lee Gilmour shakes off Paul March to score as St Helens deny Huddersfield

ROUND 5

ABOVE: Chris Feather wrapped up by Jamie Langley as Leeds come out on top against Bradford

ABOVE: Kris Radlinski feels the force of Mark Edmondson and Nick Fozzard during a physical Good Friday stalemate between St Helens and Wigan

RIGHT: Wakefield's Michael Korkidas collared by Castleford's Andy Lynch as the Wildcats tame the Tigers

ROUND 7

ROUND 6

RIGHT: Lesley Vainikolo sends Ian Hardman and James Roby flying on the way to a try during a highly controversial encounter between Bradford and St Helens on Easter Monday

ROUND 10

ROUND 8

LEFT: Four-try hero Shaun Briscoe looks for a way through during Hull's win at Bradford

ABOVE: Andy Coley brought down as Salford defeat London

BELOW: Keiron Cunningham and Jason Hooper corner Rob Burrow during St Helens' big win over Leeds

ROUND 9

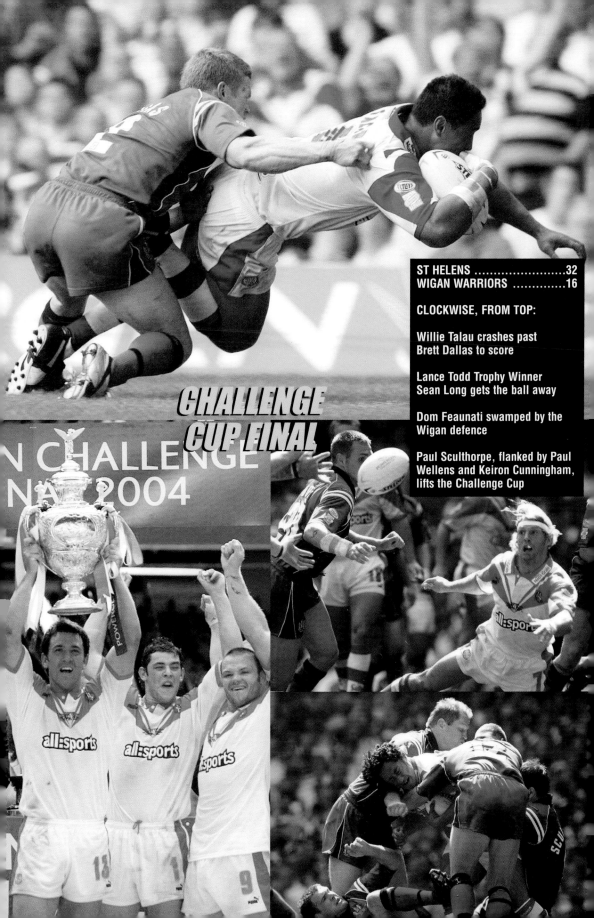

CHALLENGE CUP FINAL

ST HELENS 32
WIGAN WARRIORS 16

CLOCKWISE, FROM TOP:

Willie Talau crashes past
Brett Dallas to score

Lance Todd Trophy Winner
Sean Long gets the ball away

Dom Feaunati swamped by the
Wigan defence

Paul Sculthorpe, flanked by Paul
Wellens and Keiron Cunningham,
lifts the Challenge Cup

ROUND 11

RIGHT: Matt Adamson on the charge as Leeds edge past Hull at the KC Stadium

BELOW: Craig Greenhill, Waine Pryce and Michael Smith lead the Castleford celebrations after the Tigers' first Super League IX win, at London

BOTTOM: Nathan Wood weaves past Danny Tickle as Warrington down Wigan

RIGHT: Ali Lauitiiti celebrates his first Leeds try as the Rhinos roll past Bradford at Odsal

ROUND 12

RIGHT: Widnes' Julian O'Neill surrounded by the Warrington defence as the Vikings enjoy a derby win

ROUND 13

ABOVE: Colin Best takes on Wakefield's Jason Demetriou as Hull edge a close one

ROUND 14

LEFT: Dennis Moran feels the force of Gareth Raynor as London take on Hull 'On The Road' in Leicester

ROUND 15

ABOVE: Wigan skipper Andy Farrell displays the scars of battle as the Warriors shade Leeds in a JJB Stadium thriller

RIGHT: Andy Coley tackled by returning Tiger Brad Davis as Salford win a crucial relegation battle with Castleford

ROUND 16

ROUND 18

ROUND 17

ABOVE: Sid Domic caught high by Paul Sculthorpe during Wakefield's big home win over St Helens

ABOVE: League returnee Iestyn Harris takes on Ben Jeffries as Bradford edge out Wakefield

ROUND 19

ABOVE: London's Mark O'Halloran upended by Leeds' Andrew Dunemann as the Broncos roar back to share the spoils with the Rhinos

ROUND 20

ABOVE: Leeds' Danny McGuire dives over to score despite the challenge of Darren Albert as the Rhinos race to a 70-0 win over St Helens

BELOW: Salford's Sean Rutgerson tackled by St Helens duo Ade Gardner and John Stankevitch as the Reds stun the Saints

ROUND 21

ABOVE: Lee Greenwood looks for a way past Brian Carney and Martin Aspinwall during London's win over Wigan

ROUND 22

ROUND 23

ABOVE: Robbie Paul goes past Craig Smith as Bradford down Wigan

ABOVE: Ryan Hudson congratulates Darren Rogers on scoring as Castleford defeat Hull

ROUND 24

ROUND 25

RIGHT: Warrington's Jerome C... collars John Stankevitch as St Helens inflict a loss on the W...

LEFT: Shontayne Hape moves in on Richard Swain as Bradford blitz Hull

ROUND 28

BELOW: Coaching consultant Frank Endacott leads the Widnes celebrations as the Vikings stay in Super League despite losing at Hull

ABOVE: Tom Saxton, Jon Hepworth and Paul Mellor reflect on Castleford's loss to Wakefield - and relegation from Super League

ROUND 26

RIGHT: Francis Maloney kicks the winning field goal for Castleford as the Tigers beat Widnes 7-6

ROUND 27

ABOVE: Terry Newton makes a break through the St Helens defence as Wigan knock out their old rivals

ABOVE: Gareth Ellis and Colum Halpenny celebrate as Wakefield eliminate Hull

ELIMINATION PLAY-OFFS

LEFT: Kevin Brown shows his delight at scoring as Wigan are made to battle their way through against Wakefield

ELIMINATION SEMI-FINAL

ABOVE: Leeds' Chev Walker on the burst as the League Leaders down Wigan to book their place at Old Trafford

LEFT: Lee Radford, Leon Pryce and Iestyn Harris halt Danny McGuire as Bradford reach their fourth consecutive Grand Final with a win at Leeds

QUALIFYING SEMI-FINAL

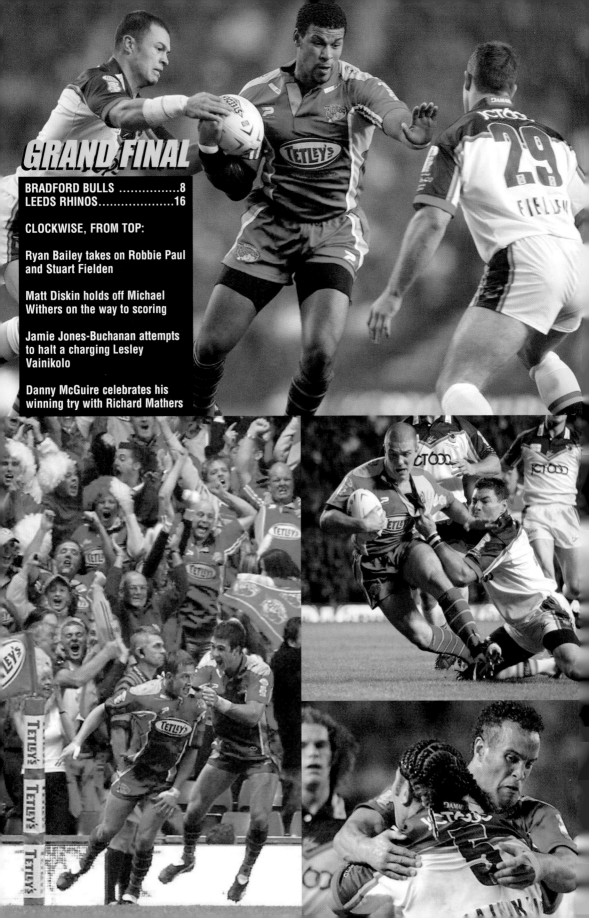

GRAND FINAL

BRADFORD BULLS 8
LEEDS RHINOS....................16

CLOCKWISE, FROM TOP:

Ryan Bailey takes on Robbie Paul and Stuart Fielden

Matt Diskin holds off Michael Withers on the way to scoring

Jamie Jones-Buchanan attempts to halt a charging Lesley Vainikolo

Danny McGuire celebrates his winning try with Richard Mathers

4
NATIONAL LEAGUE 2004

NATIONAL LEAGUE ONE SEASON
Super Leigh!

After five years on the brink, **LEIGH CENTURIONS** finally realised their Super League dream at the end of a memorable and eventful campaign.

On a dramatic night in Widnes, the Centurions beat their closest rivals Whitehaven in a thrilling NL1 Grand Final that went to extra-time, before Leigh emerged victorious 32-16.

Darren Abram's side also lifted the League Leaders shield after pipping Haven on points difference, and the Arriva Trains Cup, comprehensively defeating Hull KR at Spotland in July.

It meant the end of years of heartbreak for the club's faithful supporters - though it certainly wasn't all plain sailing.

Heavy defeats at home to Rochdale and away at Halifax threatened to upset Leigh's momentum - with Abram even considering resignation after the 58-30 setback at the Shay. But they recovered their composure well to ensure they rejoined the top flight for the first time since 1994.

Abram had a host of consistent performers in his ranks. His assistant coach and on-field leader Tommy Martyn was inspirational at times - especially in the matches when it mattered most. He was nominated for the competition's Player of the Year title and made the NL1 All Stars team,

Neil Turley

Tommy
Martyn

as did Paul Rowley, who had another top season at hooker.

At least three others could count themselves desperately unlucky not to join them - fullback Neil Turley, and seconds-rowers Oliver Wilkes and David Larder.

Turley provided another record-breaking season, notching a mammoth 468 points and winning the man of the match award in the Grand Final. The second-rowers proved to be an outstanding combination - Wilkes a rugged competitor, and Larder an intelligent wide runner, while prop Simon Knox also deserves a mention.

115

Craig
Walsh.

Though the campaign ended in Grand Final despair, **WHITEHAVEN** made huge strides under Steve McCormack in 2004.

McCormack was crowned NL1 Coach of the Year after leading the Cumbrians into second place - and the first ever major final in the club's history.

They also had the division's outstanding performer in Australian Sam Obst, a shrewd mid-season capture who finished as the NL1 Player of the Year, and Players' Player. His organisational skills and ability to break the defensive line were key factors in Haven's success.

Obst was supported throughout by prolific loose forward Craig Walsh, whose transformation from occasional threequarter to NL1's best number 13 mirrored the club's overall progression. Both were members of the All Stars team, along with free-scoring centre Mick Nanyn and tough, experienced second rower Howard Hill. McCormack also had models of consistency in reliable fullback Gary Broadbent, and non-stop Kiwi front-rowers Aaron Lester at hooker, and David Fatialofa at prop.

The club also continued to develop off the field - with their crowds continuing to rise and their community work being rewarded with the National League Club of the Year title. And the fact they were given the green light for Super League before their Grand Final defeat boded well for 2005.

Paul Mansson

Jamie Bovill

It was a strange season for **HULL KINGSTON ROVERS**, full of peaks and troughs.

The year started on a major high, with the appointment of "dream team" coaching duo of Malcolm Reilly and Martin Hall raising hopes that the Robins could reach the top flight for the first time in a decade.

But the partnership never really clicked, despite the club reaching the Arriva Trains Final. And come the closing weeks of the league season, Hall was in sole charge, with Reilly eventually leaving.

Hall inspired a late revival as Rovers pushed up the table to third, and then dumped Doncaster out of the play-offs. But their season ended in disappointment and anti-climax the following week, with a home defeat to Featherstone.

The best performers over the course of the year were generally their props - with All Stars member Makali Aizue, Frank Watene, Jamie Bovill and Paul Fletcher all having big years.

Paul Parker was the Rugby League World Player of the Month for September after a string of consistent displays at centre, winger Alasdair McClarron finished the season strongly, and halfbacks Paul Mansson and in particular the impressive Phil Hasty both had their moments.

They would have another new coach for 2005 - after Hall decided not to take up a new contract offer - with former player Harvey Howard taking the reins in October.

Jon Goddard

A lack of consistency again haunted **OLDHAM**, whose season ended with the departure of player-coach Steve Molloy.

The former Great Britain prop guided the Roughyeds to fourth place in NL1 despite battling against injury problems for much of the year. But an opening weekend play-off exit at home to Featherstone was hugely disappointing - especially after a close-season recruitment drive that had promised much.

Of the players that Molloy brought in, scrum-half Ian Watson showed his undoubted class at this level, and prop Paul Southern impressed despite playing most of the year in need of a groin operation. Loose forward Lee Marsh was also a success after making a loan switch from Salford permanent - as was winger Nick Johnson, who finished as the club's top try scorer.

But the real stars of the season were fullback Jon Goddard - who deservedly made the NL1 All Stars team - and Australian forward Dane Morgan, who rarely allowed his performance levels to drop.

Molloy's exit prompted a month-long search for a coach that ended with the appointment of Kiwi Gary Mercer, sacked by relegated Castleford, who will be keen to realise the Roughyeds' unquestionable potential.

Matt Wray

FEATHERSTONE ROVERS were one of the big improvers in 2004, with Gary Price earning a nomination for Coach of the Year after his efforts in turning the club's fortunes around.

They started shakily - losing an amazing four times to NL2 side York in the Arriva Trains Cup and Challenge Cup. Then their opening league match saw them thrashed at Oldham. But Price's influence became apparent soon after, and after steadily climbing the league ladder, they finished just one game short of making the Grand Final.

Rovers supporters will long remember away play-off wins at Oldham and Hull KR, with lively French scrum-half Maxime Greseque a key figure in both, following his mid-season switch from Pia. Winger Matt Wray made the All Stars team, and props Ian Tonks and in particular Salford-bound Stuart Dickens were inspirational up front.

Hooker Paul Darley guided his side around the field well, while Adam Hayes and Andy McNally proved quality additions to the squad. And with the close season already providing much more stability than last year's, Rovers' progression under Price looks set to continue.

119

Marlon Billy

DONCASTER DRAGONS' season promised much at the halfway mark of the league campaign, as they stood joint top of NL1 with just two defeats from nine games.

But their form turned upside down in the second half of the year - they won just two more matches before crashing out of the play-offs with a heavy defeat at Hull KR.

St John Ellis - the longest serving coach in the professional game - had prolific try scorers in wingers Marlon Billy and Dean Colton, who was nominated for the Young Player of the Year award.

But it was their defence that often let the Dragons down during the closing weeks of the campaign, leading to some one-sided set-backs.

Little blame could be laid at the feet of ever-consistent second-rowers Peter Green and Martin Ostler, who rarely let the Dragons down. Andy Fisher proved to be a shrewd signing after leaving the coaching position at Dewsbury, becoming one of the most effective forwards in the competition, despite his advancing years.

And hooker Craig Cook was a real find for Ellis, developing into one of the best dummy-halves in the league.

BATLEY BULLDOGS were another side who started the season strongly, before a major mid-season slump saw them dragged into the relegation battle.

They avoided the bottom two courtesy of excellent away wins at Featherstone and Rochdale, as the Bulldogs started to realise the potential they had shown at the start of the year under rookie coach Gary Thornton. He took over from previous boss Paul Storey, and the Bulldogs kicked off the year in fine style in the Arriva Trains Cup, losing just one of their eight group games.

Andy Spink

The were knocked out in the quarter-finals by Whitehaven - who were also their conquerors in the Challenge Cup - before winning five of their first six league matches to sit level top of NL1. Eight defeats from nine sent them sliding down the table, before their mini-recovery eased any relegation fears.

Scrum-half Barry Eaton was again the Bulldogs' talisman, while second-rower Andy Spink was named in the All Stars side after scoring 14 tries in 29 games. Danny Maun had another top season in the centres and Bryn Powell impressed on the wing after joining on loan from Salford.

And prop David Rourke was one of the success stories of the competition, making a terrific transition from the back row with a string of hard-working displays.

The 2004 season may go down as one of the most important in **ROCHDALE HORNETS'** long history.

At the end of the 2003, Hornets' existence was in genuine danger due to financial problems, and with coach Martin Hall and his entire squad of players having left, the future was bleak.

The club took something of a gamble in appointing the much-travelled Bobbie Goulding as player-coach on a voluntary basis. But he paid them back in spades.

After a difficult start - Hornets were the only NL1 team not to make the second phase of the ATC and were smashed 80-0 at Warrington in the Cup - Goulding's team of amateurs, Academy players, student internationals and a sprinkling of experience started to gel.

They hauled themselves off the bottom of NL1 with a run of five straight wins in August, and could still make the play-offs with two games remaining.

They fell just short - but Goulding's infectious enthusiasm had re-ignited the whole club, and the Coach of the Year nominee set his sights on the play-offs in 2005.

Tommy Hodgkinson

Veteran Tommy Hodgkinson epitomised Hornets' season by coming from the amateur game to deservedly take his place in the All Stars team, while other top performers included NL1 Young Player of the Year Michael Platt, Dave Cunliffe, captain Andy Gorski, Lee Birdseye and Darren Robinson.

National League One Season

HALIFAX started the season as one of the favourites for promotion - and finished it needing a dramatic last ten minutes against York to preserve their NL1 status.

Fax were forced to play in the controversial NL1 Qualifying play-offs after slumping to ninth, and only three tries in six incredible minutes in the Final against the Knights prevented them from suffering a second successive relegation.

That was some kind of reward for the hard work of their player-coach Anthony Farrell, who took over when Australian Tony Anderson was dismissed in May. Anderson made a raft of close season signings in an attempt to lift the club back up to Super League at the first attempt, but their early-season form was poor, and Farrell took over facing a scrap for survival.

The vastly experienced prop was Fax's most consistent figure throughout the year, and their performances improved notably under him. He was helped by the signing of Australian halfback Ben Black, who scored ten tries in ten games after his mid-season arrival, and also brought the best out of fellow countryman Pat Weisner.

Winger Rikki Sheriffe was selected in the All Stars team, while James Haley was unlucky not to be nominated for the Young Player of the Year. Centres Alan Hadcroft and James Bunyan were among Fax's best, while Jamie Bloem's experience came to the fore late in the campaign.

KEIGHLEY COUGARS struggled almost from the off after promotion from National League Two - though to the credit of their coach Gary Moorby, they never allowed their heads or spirit to drop.

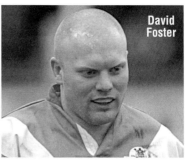

David Foster

The Cougars finished with just two league points in NL1 - from an early-season home win against Featherstone that raised hopes of an unlikely survival push.

But they were rarely hammered, and in Matt Foster they had the competition's top try-scorer (in league matches only), earning the Cougar favourite a place in the All Stars team.

Prop Phil Stephenson swept the board at the club's awards night after another season of doing the hard yards up front, where he was well supported by Richard Mervill, Danny Ekis and Jason Clegg. Hooker Simeon Hoyle again gave his all throughout the campaign, despite interest from other clubs, while centre David Foster had few peers defensively.

The club backed Moorby to bring success on their return to NL2 in 2005 - and they would be boosted by a host of promising youngsters coming through the ranks, like Jordan Ross, Chris Roe and Matt Steel.

NATIONAL LEAGUE TWO SEASON
Barrow raid title

FEW pundits predicted that **BARROW RAIDERS** would finish top of LHF Healthplan National League Two - but under experienced coach Peter Roe, they defied the critics with a superb campaign.

The Raiders earned automatic promotion to NL1 by losing just three of their 18 league games - twice to York and at home to Swinton.

But the Raiders kept their noses ahead of closest rivals the Knights by displaying greater week-to-week consistency, including a handful of crucial wins against the likes of Sheffield and Workington.

Roe's achievement in leading another lower league side to promotion (he did the same with Halifax in 1991, Keighley in 1993 and Swinton in 1996) - despite having one of the smallest squads in the competition - deservedly saw him pick up the NL2 Coach of the Year accolade.

His on-field general Darren Holt was crowned Player of the Year, just edging out his teammate James King, the influential Australian second-rower and captain.

Veteran Phil Atkinson and young gun Chris Archer also played their parts, as did late-season signings Matt McConnell and Matt Gardner, as the Raiders' squad was tested to its limits. Centre Paul Jones and fullback Craig Bower helped provide the tries, and Mike Whitehead and hooker Dave Clark the graft up front, during a campaign that helped re-awaken the famous Cumbrian club.

Barrow start the promotion party

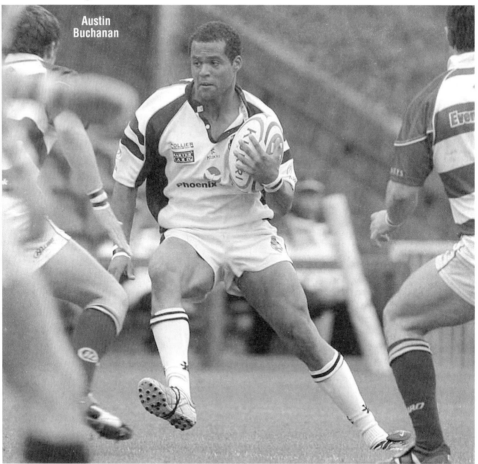

Austin
Buchanan

YORK CITY KNIGHTS' season lacked nothing in terms of excitement and incident - but ultimately ended in disappointment for one of the game's most forward-thinking clubs.

A superb Arriva Trains Cup campaign saw the Knights progress through a tough group, past NL1 side Halifax in the quarter-finals, before losing out at Hull KR. In amongst that, they also reached the quarter-finals of the Challenge Cup for the first time in 20 years, putting up a commendable performance before being well beaten by Super League side Huddersfield.

But promotion was always the aim of the Knights and their highly-regarded young coach Richard Agar. They missed out on the automatic place, league defeats against Hunslet (twice), Chorley and Workington costing them dear.

The Knights then reached the final of the NL1 Qualifying play-offs by thumping Workington, only to go down to Halifax in heart-breaking circumstances in the final ten minutes of the match.

They had some of the best performers in NL2 in halfbacks Scott Rhodes and Danny Brough, hooker Lee Jackson, centre Chris Langley, back-rower Simon Friend and Young Player of the Year Austin Buchanan.

Agar, Brough and Buchanan have all departed for Hull - but a link-up with Leeds Rhinos should ensure that York continue to progress in 2005.

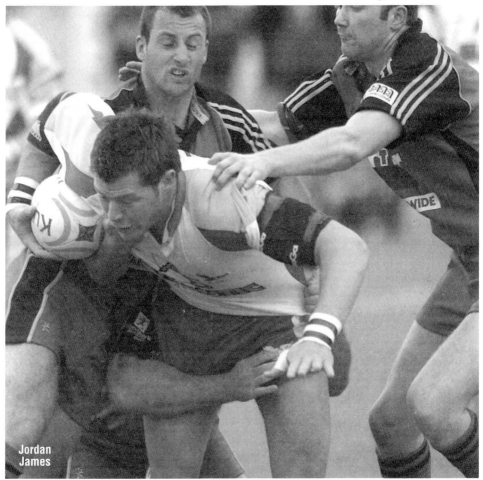

Jordan James

SHEFFIELD EAGLES had higher expectations than third place and an opening weekend play-off exit, but there was still much to be positive about at the Don Valley Stadium.

After losing out in the closing stages of the 2003 NL2 Grand Final, the Eagles had their sights firmly set on promotion. But three consecutive home defeats in June and July - to Barrow, Swinton and Chorley - set them back significantly, and despite a late-season recovery they failed to emulate 2003's first placed finish.

Still, coach Mark Aston continued to show he has a real eye for talented young players - with second-rower Jordan James the latest one to attract attention from higher divisions after being handed his chance with the Eagles.

There were also high hopes for Irish winger Carl De Chenu, and the trio of Dickinson brothers (Sean, Alex and Ryan) that Aston signed from Bradford Dudley Hill mid-season.

Second-rower Andy Raleigh and prop Jon Bruce were again towers of strength in the Sheffield pack, while fullback Andy Poynter retained his position as the club's top try scorer.

The loss of key playmaker Gavin Brown to injury late in the campaign hit Sheffield hard - but they were again expected to challenge in 2005.

Wayne
English

SWINTON LIONS made genuine strides under rookie coach Paul Kidd - the youngest boss in the professional game.

The Lions progressed from seventh in 2003 to fourth, though their play-off campaign ended after just one week in a high-scoring game with Workington.

The Lions had two members of the NL2 All Stars team in top try-scorer Chris Maye - a former St Helens Academy centre - and loyal fullback Wayne English, who again proved to be one of the most reliable performers in the competition.

Halfback Michael Coates also had an accomplished year while on loan from Leigh, as did hard-working loose forward Ian Hodson.

The season also marked the Lions moving to yet another new home. The club moved its base from Moor Lane, the home of Salford City FC, to Sedgley Park RU's Park Lane, a compact, tidy ground that was generally well received.

With several high-profile recruits already secured for the new campaign, including popular returning duo Marlon Billy and Ian Watson, the Lions will be confident of developing further next year.

The 2004 season could yet go down as the year that re-ignited a famous old flame in **WORKINGTON TOWN**.

The Cumbrians came from having no coach and few players to within one game of the NL1 Qualifying Play-offs Final, increasing their crowds dramatically on the way.

Their progression can be put down to the decision to appoint New Zealand A coach Gerard Stokes to the Derwent Park hot seat. Stokes brought with him three outstanding countrymen - fullback Lusi Sione, hooker Jonny Limmer and forward John Tuimaualuga.

Free-scoring Sione and All Stars member Limmer had particularly big impacts, along with experienced halfback Tane Manihera, once he returned to the club following a spell playing rugby union.

Town weren't short of local heroes either - prop Matt Tunstall, winger Neil Frazer and loose forward Brett Smith among them. And perhaps most promisingly of all, young talents such as Dean Burgess, Richard George and Martyn Wilson all impressed.

The campaign finished on something of a downer with a 70-10 play-off defeat at York - but with the vast majority of their squad having been retained, they should have started 2005 as one of the favourites for promotion.

Tane Manihera

It was something of an up-and-down season for **HUNSLET HAWKS**, who promised much at times, but ultimately failed to scale the heights they were capable of.

A significant reason for that was the injury situation that coach Roy Sampson had to deal with - arguably the worst at any National League club. As a result, Sampson was without several of his key players for the crucial season run-in.

They did lift themselves in the play-offs, when experienced scrum-half Latham Tawhai inspired a stunning away win at Sheffield, before losing out after a brave performance at Workington.

Winger George Rayner was their best player over the course of the season, finishing as top try-scorer and being selected in the All Stars line-up.

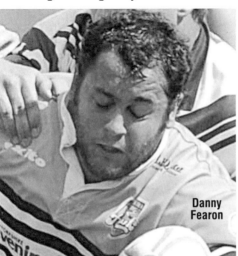

Danny Fearon

Strong running second-rower Jonlee Lockwood and evergreen veterans Mick Coyle and the retiring Steve Pryce were all constants in the Hawks pack. Winger or fullback Chris Hall looked a shrewd capture from the rugby union ranks, while Danny Fearon had his moments from loose forward.

But ultimately, missing class acts such as Craig Ibbetson - whose entire season was written off with a shoulder injury - and hooker Jamaine Wray in crucial matches cost the Hawks dear.

It proved to be the end of an era for **CHORLEY LYNX**, as their major backer withdrew his support for the club at the end of a typically-eventful campaign.

Chris Ramsdale

The club will be reborn yet again as Blackpool in 2005 - but the fact that professional Rugby League will no longer be played at Victory Park will bring sadness to many.

At least Mark Lee's side managed to finish on a major high - completing an amazing late comeback against high-flying York when stand-off Brian Capewell landed a long-distance field goal to complete an emotional 21-20 win. Lee impressed throughout the campaign, after having to completely rebuild a side that had finished second in 2003. But the Lynx just missed out on the play-offs, with inconsistency their biggest downfall.

Prop Ian Parry made the NL2 All Stars team, just edging out his equally impressive front row partner John Hill. Fullback Lee Patterson finished as Lynx's top try scorer, closely followed by centre Jamie Stenhouse.

Capewell also proved to be a cornerstone of the side, as did league ever presents Martin Gambles and Chris Ramsdale.

LONDON SKOLARS were among 2004's big achievers, hauling themselves off the foot of NL2 and recording five wins in the process.

They ensured New River Stadium was a difficult place for any side to visit - as Sheffield and Swinton, among others, discovered. And they also improved their form away from home, notching a win at Gateshead early in the league campaign.

The Skolars had NL2's top try-scorer in loose forward Mark Cantoni, who enjoyed an outstanding first season in the professional game. He was unlucky to miss out on selection for the NL2 All Stars - but the Skolars did have a

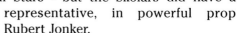

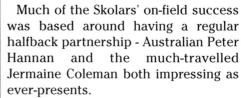

Peter Hannan

representative, in powerful prop Rubert Jonker.

Much of the Skolars' on-field success was based around having a regular halfback partnership - Australian Peter Hannan and the much-travelled Jermaine Coleman both impressing as ever-presents.

Fullback Joel Osborn and player coach Alex Smits - who took joint charge of the team with Marcus Tobin - were other constants in a hugely promising year for the Skolars.

For **DEWSBURY RAMS**, it was generally a year to forget.

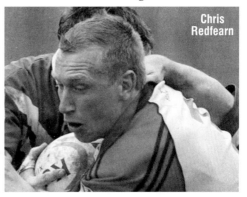

Chris Redfearn

They started the campaign with player coach Andy Fisher at the helm, but he made his exit after a string of disappointing results, and was replaced by Andy Kelly. The former Wakefield, Gateshead and Featherstone boss had a difficult task on his hands from the off - dealing with a small, largely inexperienced squad. And he was hardly helped by a spate of long-term injuries to key players such as Kurt Rudder, Mick Senior, Graham Law and Mick Hill.

There were bright spots of course - several promising young players were given their first chances at senior level, with forward Mark Stubley the pick. Captain Kevin Crouthers gave his all every time he took the field, even in the most trying circumstances, while Adam Thaler did remarkably well to register 13 league tries in a losing side. With Wayne McHugh, Chris Redfearn and the ever-reliable Paul Hicks also providing moments of relief, it wasn't a totally disastrous year for the Rams faithful.

And Kelly looked set to spearhead a more positive future - with the club having apparently overcome the financial difficulties of recent years, making a string of high-profile captures for 2005, including Ryan Sheridan, Francis Maloney, Warren Jowitt and Richard Chapman.

GATESHEAD THUNDER endured another difficult campaign in the North East, though they finished they year with bright prospects.

Under coach Seamus McCallion, they won just one game all year - a 22-4 defeat of Dewsbury Rams at the Thunderdome in August. They also picked up a series of heavy defeats along the way, as McCallion worked valiantly with limited resources.

But their talented young local players did bring some relief - particularly non-stop loose forward Stephen Bradley, whose efforts were recognised by opposition coaches when he was voted onto the NL2 All Stars team.

The Thorman brothers, stand-off Paul and halfback-turned-hooker Neil, again stood up to the challenge on a weekly basis, while winger Robin Peers ran in his fair share of tries.

Neil & Paul Thorman

Losing twice to fellow development club London Skolars will have disappointed Thunder - but they have since appointed former Sheffield conditioner Dean Thomas as their new coach. And with a host of signings on board for next season, hopes were high that the admirable club could finally start to haul itself up the league ladder.

ARRIVA TRAINS CUP FINAL
Steaming ahead

Leigh Centurions laid down a mid-season marker with an accomplished all-round display in the Final of the Arriva Trains Cup.

Inspired by brilliant halfback Tommy Martyn, the Centurions brushed aside a gallant Hull KR in front of over 4,000 supporters at Spotland. Two tries inside the first ten minutes set the tone for Darren Abram's side, as Danny Halliwell and Simon Knox both scored. Halliwell completed a double inside the opening quarter, and with Ben Cooper crossing and Neil Turley booting nine points and Martyn one, the Centurions led 26-8 at the break.

Robins fullback Craig Poucher had contributed his side's sole try in the opening half, though they briefly dragged themselves back into the game when Australian hooker Scott Thorburn crossed to close the gap to 12 points. But this was always going to be the Centurions' day.

Turley glided under the posts to re-establish Leigh's control, and further tries from Martyn and Knox sealed their impressive win.

"Win or lose we didn't want this game to distract us from where we want to go and that is Super League," Abram said after the game. "It was just one step but hopefully the lads will remember the feeling of winning a final."

They did. Sixteen of the side that took the field against Hull KR lined up for the Centurions again three months later in the NL1 Grand Final.

ARRIVA TRAINS CUP FINAL

Sunday 18th July 2004

HULL KINGSTON ROVERS 14 LEIGH CENTURIONS 42

ROVERS: 1 Craig Poucher; 2 Nick Pinkney; 3 Paul Parker; 4 Marvin Golden; 5 Lynton Stott; 6 Paul Mansson; 7 Phil Hasty; 8 Makali Aizue; 9 Scott Thorburn; 10 Jon Aston; 11 Dale Holdstock; 12 Andy Smith; 13 Tommy Gallagher. Subs (all used): 14 Matt Calland; 15 Anthony Seibold; 16 Frank Watene; 17 Paul Fletcher.
Tries: Poucher (28), Thorburn (45); **Goals:** Stott 3/3.
CENTURIONS: 1 Neil Turley; 2 Dan Potter; 3 Danny Halliwell; 4 Ben Cooper; 5 Rob Smyth; 6 John Duffy; 7 Tommy Martyn; 8 Simon Knox; 9 Paul Rowley; 10 Matt Sturm; 11 David Larder; 12 Oliver Wilkes; 13 Ian Knott. Subs (all used): 14 Dave McConnell; 15 Willie Swann; 16 Richard Marshall; 17 Heath Cruckshank.
Tries: Halliwell (2, 19), Knox (10, 75), Cooper (37), Turley (51), Martyn (71); **Goals:** Turley 6/9;
Field goals: Martyn, Turley.
Rugby Leaguer & League Express Men of the Match:
Rovers: Phil Hasty; *Centurions:* Tommy Martyn.
Penalty count: 4-5; **Half-time:** 8-26; **Referee:** Colin Morris (Huddersfield); **Attendance:** 4,383 *(at Spotland, Rochdale).*

Neil Turley takes on Paul Parker

NATIONAL LEAGUE PLAY-OFFS
The road to glory

NATIONAL LEAGUE ONE

Oldham and Doncaster were the first two casualties of the NL1 play-offs, going down to defeats against Featherstone and Hull KR respectively.

Oldham's was the more surprising - having finished fourth, they were at home to Fev and started the game as marginal favourites. But at the end of a see-saw encounter in which the lead exchanged hands four times, Andy McNally's late try proved decisive in Rovers' Maxime Greseque-inspired 33-28 win at Boundary Park.

The result was much more clear cut at Craven Park, where Hull KR had the game won by half-time, leading a disappointing Dragons outfit 30-10.

Lee Doran looks for support during Oldham's play-off clash with Featherstone

None of the previous trouble between the clubs surfaced during the game - but the Robins did provide a dazzling attacking display, Alasdair McClarron and Nick Pinkney scoring two tries each as Paul Mansson starred in the 63-22 win.

The Robins' play-off run would last for just one more week however - as Featherstone recorded their second successive away win in another thriller. Martin Hall's side actually scored three tries to two - but the goal kicking of Stuart Dickens and man of the match Greseque - who kicked the decisive field goal - proved to be the difference.

On the same day, Leigh Centurions took the direct route to the Grand Final with a 30-16 win over closest rivals Whitehaven. The game was much closer than the score suggests - there were just six points in it with five minutes left, before late scores from Dave Alstead and Dave Larder sealed matters.

That set up a Final Eliminator between Whitehaven and Featherstone at the Recreation Ground. It was the Cumbrians who prevailed, loose forward Craig Walsh scoring twice in their 30-2 win.

NATIONAL LEAGUE ONE QUALIFYING SERIES

Sheffield Eagles, one of the pre-season favourites for the NL2 title, crashed out of the play-offs on the opening weekend at home to Hunslet.

The Hawks, who finished sixth in the league, produced one of their best performances of the campaign, as Latham Tawhai led them to a 39-16 win at the Don Valley Stadium.

Also making an early exit was Swinton Lions - though not before a thrilling clash with Workington Town. The two teams shared 14 tries in an end-to-end encounter at Park Lane. In the end, eight goals from as many attempts by Tane Manihera proved crucial, as did two Jonny Limmer tries in Town's 44-38 win.

That gave Town a home clash with Hunslet. Manihera again put in a dazzling performance, though the game was in the balance on the hour mark, with Town leading just 15-13. Late tries from Scott Chilton and Limmer sent the Hawks out of the competition though, and Town onto a Final Eliminator clash at York.

Meanwhile, Halifax - the team who finished ninth in NL1 - went straight into the Final with a polished 37-20 win over York at the Shay. Captain Pat Weisner led his side from the front, scoring one of Fax's seven tries and creating two others.

That left the Knights with a home game against Workington to make the Final - and they did it in style, thrashing the Cumbrians 70-10 in a surprisingly one-sided affair. Substitute Mark Cain scored five tries in the rout, which ended a season of genuine progression on a disappointing note for Town.

York's Craig Farrell moves in on Workington's John Tuimaualuga during the City Knights' 70-10 win

NATIONAL LEAGUE GRAND FINALS
Tommy's magic

Tommy Martyn produced a fairytale end to his playing career as Leigh Centurions finally realised their Super League dream, in the most dramatic of circumstances against gallant Whitehaven.

The Cumbrian side were just four minutes from promotion themselves, leading 16-15 with the clock ticking down. But man of the match Neil Turley then stepped forward to slot a superb field goal to take the game into extra-time.

And the Centurions pulled away from their opponents, with converted tries to Ben Cooper and Turley, plus one-pointers from Paul Rowley and the inspirational Martyn, taking them to the promised land of the top flight.

"It caps a top year for us," coach Darren Abram gasped after the game.
"We've got three trophies in the cabinet, but more importantly we've got Leigh into Super League. This season we've built up the mental toughness to grind out wins, rather than just think Leigh Centurions can score tries from anywhere. Discipline was a factor as well. We said that at the first meeting this season, and our discipline held out again, which is crucial in a major final."

It was the perfect script for veteran halfback Martyn, who had been missing for the Centurions since defeat at Halifax in August, with damaged tendons in his arm threatening to cut short his glittering career. But Martyn defied doctors orders to play - even though he wasn't named on the initial teamsheet - and produced a handful of moments of brilliance that were crucial to the Centurions' win.

"It's very hard to take," Whitehaven coach Steve McCormack conceded. "But I'm proud of the players, not only for they way they performed today, but how they have done all season. I honestly thought going into extra time that we could still get the game. But they stepped it up, we didn't, and fair play to them."

LHF HEALTHPLAN NATIONAL LEAGUE ONE GRAND FINAL

Sunday 10th October 2004

LEIGH CENTURIONS 32 WHITEHAVEN 16
(After extra time)

CENTURIONS: 1 Neil Turley; 2 Rob Smyth; 3 Danny Halliwell; 4 Ben Cooper; 5 David Alstead; 6 John Duffy; 7 Tommy Martyn; 8 Simon Knox; 9 Paul Rowley; 10 Matt Sturm; 11 David Larder; 12 Oliver Wilkes; 13 Ian Knott. Subs (all used): 14 Dave McConnell; 15 Heath Cruckshank; 16 Richard Marshall; 17 Willie Swann.
Tries: Cooper (27, 83), Martyn (61), Turley (87);
Goals: Turley 6/8; **Field goals:** Turley 2, Rowley, Martyn.
WHITEHAVEN: 1 Gary Broadbent; 2 Craig Calvert; 3 David Seeds; 4 Mick Nanyn; 5 Wesley Wilson; 6 Leroy Joe; 7 Sam Obst; 8 Marc Jackson; 9 Aaron Lester; 10 David Fatialofa; 11 Paul Davidson; 12 Howard Hill; 13 Craig Walsh. Subs (all used): 14 Spencer Miller; 15 Carl Sice; 16 Chris McKinney; 17 Ryan Tandy.
Tries: Wilson (2, 71), Calvert (45); **Goals:** Nanyn 2/6.
Rugby Leaguer & League Express Men of the Match:
Centurions: Neil Turley; *Whitehaven:* Aaron Lester.
Penalty count: 5-9; **Half-time:** 7-6;
Referee: Ronnie Laughton (Barnsley);
Attendance: 11,005 *(at Halton Stadium, Widnes).*

No escaping the Whitehaven defence for Leigh's John Duffy

Leigh could hardly have made a worse start. In their first set of six, Rob Smyth was bundled into touch on halfway, and on the last tackle of the ensuing set, Whitehaven took the lead when Mick Nanyn sent Wesley Wilson over.

The Centurions drew level through Ben Cooper's well-taken first try, created when John Duffy's intelligent reverse kick was collected by Turley. The Leigh fullback's first field goal made it 7-6 to his side at the break, but Haven were soon back in front after the try of the match. Aaron Lester put David Seeds through a gap inside his own half, and his kick was weighted perfectly for speedster Craig Calvert to touch down.

Leigh responded when Martyn took on a retreating Haven defence to stretch out and score, before Haven regained the lead again - Leroy Joe and Nanyn combining for Wilson's second. Leigh's dreams looked to be over when Turley unusually missed a penalty that would have put his side back in front, but he regained his composure to send the game beyond 80 minutes.

And after Joe booted the ball out on the full at the end of the first set, the Centurions grasped their opportunity with both hands to provide Martyn with a fitting end to his glittering playing career.

NATIONAL LEAGUE ONE QUALIFYING SERIES - FINAL

Halifax clung onto their NL1 status, and avoided a second consecutive relegation, with a stunning late comeback in a controversial clash against York.

Fax looked out on their feet, and out of NL1, as they trailed 30-16 to an impressive City Knights side, with just over ten minutes remaining of a fascinating clash.

It was then that centre Alan Hadcroft forced his way over the line for a decision that was referred to video referee Steve Cross by Robert Connolly - in his last game before retirement. Cross ruled that Hadcroft had managed to ground the ball, to many people's surprise - including the Fax threequarter, who was preparing to play the ball believing he had been held up.

But a try was awarded, Jamie Bloem converted, and three minutes later, James Bunyan was sent crashing over to close the gap to two points.

As the Knights visibly wilted, a revitalised Fax poured forward, and the outstanding Scott Grix threw an outrageous dummy to slice over underneath the posts and seal a thrilling comeback. "I looked up at the scoreboard with ten minutes to go, and a lot can happen in ten minutes," Fax player-coach Anthony Farrell explained. "It's all down to character and a lot of positive thinking.

"It's a game of swings and roundabouts. We've been asking them to show character all year, and when we really needed it they came out with it."

His opposite number Richard Agar felt that the Hadcroft video ref decision provided a crucial turning point - but wasn't looking for excuses. "It was a big call," Agar reflected. "It must have been an extra long blade of grass. We thought there was daylight, and from the Halifax players' reaction they did as well - I don't think Alan Hadcroft thought for one minute he had the ball down. But we were still eight points up at that time and had the chance to close the game off."

After recovering from a slow start, the Knights had looked certain to clinch promotion, having just missed out on the NL2 title to Barrow. Early tries from Alan Hadcroft, James Bunyan and Rikki Sheriffe helped Fax into a 16-6 lead, with York's response coming from the hard-working Jim Elston. But by half-time, York were level, winger Austin Buchanan making amends for an earlier error by scoring twice out wide.

The Knights then grasped the initiative after the break, Mark Cain plunging over from close range, and Buchanan swooping on a mistake from Sheriffe to send Chris Langley over.

But the Knights' joy would soon turn to despair as the dramatic closing stages unfolded.

NATIONAL LEAGUE ONE QUALIFYING SERIES - FINAL

Sunday 10th October 2004

HALIFAX 34 YORK CITY KNIGHTS 30

HALIFAX: 1 Scott Grix; 5 James Haley; 3 James Bunyan; 4 Alan Hadcroft; 2 Rikki Sheriffe; 6 Simon Grix; 7 Ben Black; 8 Jon Simpson; 9 Mark Moxon; 10 Chris Birchall; 11 Jamie Bloem; 12 Ged Corcoran; 13 Pat Weisner. Subs (all used): 14 Ben Feehan; 15 Anthony Farrell; 16 David Bates; 17 Gareth Greenwood.
Tries: Hadcroft (2, 71), Bunyan (9, 74), Sheriffe (22), Scott Grix (76); **Goals:** Bloem 5/7.
CITY KNIGHTS: 1 Scott Walker; 2 Austin Buchanan; 3 Chris Langley; 4 Chris Spurr; 5 Craig Farrell; 6 Scott Rhodes; 7 Danny Brough; 8 Richard Wilson; 9 Lee Jackson; 10 Yusuf Sozi; 11 John Smith; 12 Simon Friend; 13 Jimmy Elston. Subs (all used): 14 Mark Cain; 15 Albert Talipeau; 16 Adam Sullivan; 17 Craig Forsyth.
Tries: Elston (16), Buchanan (30, 37), Cain (61), Langley (64); **Goals:** Brough 5/7.
Rugby Leaguer & League Express Men of the Match: *Halifax:* Jamie Bloem; *City Knights:* Danny Brough.
Penalty count: 6-5; **Half-time:** 16-16; **Referee:** Robert Connolly (Wigan). *(at Halton Stadium, Widnes).*

LHF HEALTHPLAN NATIONAL LEAGUE AWARDS

NATIONAL LEAGUE ONE

PLAYER OF THE YEAR
Sam Obst (Whitehaven)
Nominees:
Makali Aizue (Hull Kingston Rovers)
Tommy Martyn (Leigh Centurions)

YOUNG PLAYER OF THE YEAR
Michael Platt (Rochdale Hornets)
Nominees:
Jamie Bovill (Hull Kingston Rovers)
Dean Colton (Doncaster Dragons)

COACH OF THE YEAR
Steve McCormack (Whitehaven)
Nominees:
Darren Abram (Leigh Centurions)
Bobbie Goulding (Rochdale Hornets)
Gary Price (Featherstone Rovers)

GMB RLPA PLAYERS' PLAYER OF THE YEAR
Sam Obst (Whitehaven)

RUGBY LEAGUE WORLD ALL STARS TEAM
1 Jon Goddard (Oldham)
2 Rikki Sheriffe (Halifax)
3 Mick Nanyn (Whitehaven)
4 Matt Foster (Keighley Cougars)
5 Matthew Wray (Featherstone Rovers)
6 Tommy Martyn (Leigh Centurions)
7 Sam Obst (Whitehaven)
8 Makali Aizue (Hull Kingston Rovers)
9 Paul Rowley (Leigh Centurions)
10 Tommy Hodgkinson (Rochdale Hornets)
11 Howard Hill (Whitehaven)
12 Andy Spink (Batley Bulldogs)
13 Craig Walsh (Whitehaven)

NATIONAL LEAGUE TWO

PLAYER OF THE YEAR
Darren Holt (Barrow Raiders)
Nominees:
Andy Raleigh (Sheffield Eagles)
Scott Rhodes (York City Knights)

Sam Obst and Steve McCormack with their awards

YOUNG PLAYER OF THE YEAR
Austin Buchanan (York City Knights)
Nominees: Chris Maye (Swinton Lions)
Barry Pugh (Barrow Raiders)

COACH OF THE YEAR
Peter Roe (Barrow Raiders)
Nominees:
Richard Agar (York City Knights)
Paul Kidd (Swinton Lions)

RUGBY LEAGUE WORLD ALL STARS TEAM
1 Wayne English (Swinton Lions)
2 Austin Buchanan (York City Knights)
3 Chris Langley (York City Knights)
4 Chris Maye (Swinton Lions)
5 George Rayner (Hunslet Hawks)
6 Scott Rhodes (York City Knights)
7 Darren Holt (Barrow Raiders)
8 Rubert Jonker (London Skolars)
9 Jonny Limmer (Workington Town)
10 Ian Parry (Chorley Lynx)
11 Andy Raleigh (Sheffield Eagles)
12 James King (Barrow Raiders)
13 Steven Bradley (Gateshead Thunder)

NATIONAL LEAGUE CLUB OF THE YEAR
Whitehaven

NATIONAL LEAGUE BEST COMMUNITY PROGRAMME: York City Knights

NATIONAL LEAGUE REFEREE OF THE YEAR: Ronnie Laughton
Nominees: Robert Connolly, Ben Thaler

MATCH OFFICIAL ACHIEVER OF THE YEAR
The Neil Whittaker Trophy - Paul Stockman

5
INTERNATIONAL YEAR

GILLETTE TRI-NATIONS
Razor-sharp Roos

There were surprise omissions and inclusions when Brian Noble read out his first squad as Great Britain coach - but the new Lions boss had no doubts about the quality of the players selected, and the quality of the opposition, as New Zealand and Australia had kicked off the competition the Saturday before in Auckland.

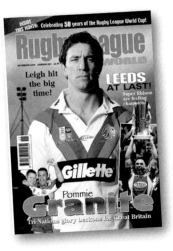

There was no Kevin Sinfield or Paul Deacon - 17 caps between them - and Noble included nine uncapped players.

Among the nine new caps were St Helens hooker Mick Higham and Wigan centre or second-rower Steve Wild. And Leeds hooker Matt Diskin was also included, after the open secret of him missing out in Noble's initial 40-man squad.

Richard Horne, Paul King, Lee Gilmour, Nick Fozzard, Leon Pryce and Keiron Cunningham were all ruled out through injury and at the time a 25th man was to be added to the squad from Karl Harrison's England side, although that never happened.

Noble also made the decision to retain Andy Farrell as captain - one that the recently crowned Man of Steel admitted he thanked him for.

GAME ONE

The Tri-Nations Tournament got off to a gripping start with a 16-all draw between Australia and New Zealand in Auckland. It was a real nail-biting finish to an enthralling encounter that proved to all the doom-and-gloom merchants that the international game was very much alive and kicking.

Even torrential rain that whipped around the North Harbour Stadium failed to dampen the enthusiasm of the 19,000 hardy souls on hand to witness the opening hostilities of the Gillette series. The Aussies left for the Northern Hemisphere pleased to put behind them what had become a nightmare venue. They had been to North Harbour on five occasions and had won only one encounter.

Before kick-off they had been white hot favourites to overwhelm a Kiwi side that, while boasting an impressive pack, seemed outclassed, on paper at least, in the backline. There was Warriors scrum-half Thomas Leuluai who had been plucked from where he was languishing in the Bartercard Cup local competition and stand-off Vinnie Anderson who had never played at No. 6 since his schoolboy days.

Yet the Kiwis lifted – inspired by pre-match speeches by Matt Utai, Tony Puletua and Joe Galuvao, who were all about to go under the surgeon's knife and would miss the remainder of the tournament.

The Kiwis' defence was awesome as they ignored the top-notch credentials of their opponents.

The New Zealanders scored first after managing a second set of six tackles in the opening minutes. Leuluai manoeuvred a runaround before fullback Brent Webb sent a cut-out pass to Vinnie Anderson, who scored out wide. Webb's conversion had the Kiwis in front 6-0.

However, the Aussies were not to be denied. Debutant winger Luke Rooney stepped out of a would-be tackle by Vinnie Anderson and out-sped boom youngster Sonny Bill Williams in a 55-metre dash for the tryline. Almost from the restart the visitors were in again. Clever passing from the halves Craig Gower and Darren Lockyer created an overlap and fullback Anthony Minichiello wrong-footed Francis Meli to score.

There was more to come. Lockyer and Gower combined again and some quick hands from centre Willie Tonga gave Rooney a clear run to the line for his second try. The Aussies were now leading 18-6 and there were worries among media that the expected slaughter was about to take place.

Perish the thought!

The Kiwis had no intention of throwing in the towel. Just before half-time Nathan Cayless was grassed short of the line. But from the play-the-ball, dummy-half debutant Louis Anderson, the younger of the two brothers, dived over next to the posts. The conversion had the Kiwis trailing by just four points as they

TRI-NATIONS SQUADS

GREAT BRITAIN
Ryan Bailey (Leeds Rhinos), Brian Carney (Wigan Warriors), Matt Diskin (Leeds Rhinos), Gareth Ellis (Wakefield Trinity Wildcats), Andy Farrell (Wigan Warriors) (C), Stuart Fielden (Bradford Bulls), Martin Gleeson (Warrington Wolves), Iestyn Harris (Bradford Bulls), Mick Higham (St Helens), Paul Johnson (Bradford Bulls), Sean Long (St Helens), Danny McGuire (Leeds Rhinos), Adrian Morley (Sydney Roosters), Terry Newton (Wigan Warriors), Sean O'Loughlin (Wigan Warriors), Jamie Peacock (Bradford Bulls), Kris Radlinski (Wigan Warriors), Stuart Reardon (Bradford Bulls), Paul Sculthorpe (St Helens), Keith Senior (Leeds Rhinos), Chev Walker (Leeds Rhinos), Danny Ward (Leeds Rhinos), Paul Wellens (St Helens), Stephen Wild (Wigan Warriors).

Karl Pratt (Bradford Bulls) was drafted into the squad after GB's first game but then withdrew

AUSTRALIA
Anthony Minichiello (Sydney Roosters), Matt Bowen (North Queensland Cowboys), Luke Rooney (Penrith Panthers), Matt Sing (North Queensland Cowboys), Shaun Berrigan (Brisbane Broncos), Matt Cooper (St George-Illawarra Dragons), Willie Tonga (Bulldogs), Brent Tate (Brisbane Broncos), Darren Lockyer (Brisbane Broncos) (C), Scott Hill (Melbourne Storm), Craig Gower (Penrith Panthers), Brett Kimmorley (Cronulla Sharks), Petero Civoniceva (Brisbane Broncos), Mark O'Meley (Bulldogs), Jason Ryles (St George-Illawarra Dragons), Shane Webcke (Brisbane Broncos), Danny Buderus (Newcastle Knights), Craig Fitzgibbon (Sydney Roosters), Nathan Hindmarsh (Parramatta Eels), Willie Mason (Bulldogs), Andrew Ryan (Bulldogs), Ben Kennedy (Newcastle Knights), Tonie Carroll (Brisbane Broncos), Craig Wing (Sydney Roosters), Shaun Timmins (St George-Illawarra Dragons).

Michael Crocker (Sydney Roosters) was chosen but withdrew threw injury and was replaced by Timmins

NEW ZEALAND
Original squad chosen for Auckland game: Brent Webb (New Zealand Warriors); Francis Meli (New Zealand Warriors), Nigel Vagana (Cronulla Sharks), Paul Whatuira (Penrith Panthers), Matt Utai (Bulldogs); Vinnie Anderson (New Zealand Warriors), Thomas Leuluai (New Zealand Warriors); Jason Cayless (Sydney Roosters), Louis Anderson (New Zealand Warriors), Ruben Wiki (Canberra Raiders) (C), Tony Puletua (Penrith Panthers), Joe Galuvao (Penrith Panthers), Sonny Bill Williams (Bulldogs). Interchange: Motu Tony (Castleford Tigers), Roy Asotasi (Bulldogs), Nathan Cayless (Parramatta Eels), David Kidwell (Melbourne Storm).

Utai, Puletua, Galuvao and Tony did not travel to England

Added to the team for English leg:
Lesley Vainikolo (Bradford Bulls), Shontayne Hape (Bradford Bulls), Robbie Paul (Bradford Bulls), Henry Fa'afili (Warrington Wolves), Ali Lauitiiti (Leeds Rhinos), Clinton Toopi (New Zealand Warriors), Jamaal Lolesi (Bulldogs), Dene Halatau (Wests Tigers), Paul Rauhihi (North Queensland Cowboys), Alex Chan (Melbourne Storm), Wairangi Koopu (New Zealand Warriors).

trooped off the pitch at the break.

With the rain still tumbling down, the second half was a tight affair, with some wonderful defence by each side.

Eight minutes after the resumption of play, Williams, who had recovered from a heavy knock early in the proceedings, was tackled short of the line. From the

Ben Kennedy tackled by Thomas Leuluai

play-the-ball David Kidwell appeared to be over the line for a try. But the video replays showed he had been held-up by Gower and Nathan Hindmarsh.

The fans were beginning to chant: 'Kiwis, Kiwis, Kiwis.'

The shouts provided inspiration for the toilers on the pitch. In the 55th minute, it was Leuluai's turn to be tackled centimetres from the tryline. This time, however, Meli managed to burrow his way under three defenders to score. This try was to be the only score in the second half, with a spate of field goal attempts missing as the clock wound down.

The Australian halves, Gower and Lockyer, combined wonderfully throughout the match and their kicking game was spot-on. Among the forwards Hindmarsh and Shane Webcke were the pick of the crop. Minichiello was dangerous every time he got the ball, making around 230 metres with his kick-returns during the game.

For the Kiwis none was better than Williams, in a preview of some wonderful displays during the tournament. His defence was brutal, his off-loads miraculous and when he burst through the rucks at full speed the fans rose as one to pay homage to this superstar of the future.

"It just shows that we aren't a second-string side and there's a lot of pride and commitment in that black-and-white jersey," Williams explained about the shock result.

Jason Cayless and Louis Anderson tackled their hearts out and Puletua and Utai played as if there was no tomorrow. Webb was safe for his adopted country – and helped out regularly at dummy-half.

It was a classic contest, as Australia's coach Wayne Bennett readily recognised: "If that's the standard we're going to set...well, I can tell you...Test football is only going to get better."

He was not wrong!

Saturday 16th October 2004

NEW ZEALAND 16 AUSTRALIA 16

NEW ZEALAND: 1 Brent Webb (New Zealand Warriors); 2 Francis Meli (New Zealand Warriors); 3 Nigel Vagana (Cronulla Sharks); 4 Paul Whatuira (Penrith Panthers); 5 Matt Utai (Bulldogs); 6 Vinnie Anderson (New Zealand Warriors); 7 Thomas Leuluai (New Zealand Warriors); 8 Jason Cayless (Sydney Roosters); 9 Louis Anderson (New Zealand Warriors); 10 Ruben Wiki (Canberra Raiders) (C); 11 Tony Puletua (Penrith Panthers); 12 Joe Galuvao (Penrith Panthers); 13 Sonny Bill Williams (Bulldogs). Subs (all used): 14 Motu Tony (Castleford Tigers); 15 Roy Asotasi (Bulldogs); 16 Nathan Cayless (Parramatta Eels); 17 David Kidwell (Melbourne Storm).
Tries: V Anderson (5), L Anderson (36), Meli (55); **Goals:** Webb 2/3.
AUSTRALIA: 1 Anthony Minichiello (Sydney Roosters); 2 Luke Rooney (Penrith Panthers); 3 Shaun Berrigan (Brisbane Broncos); 4 Willie Tonga (Bulldogs); 5 Matt Sing (North Queensland Cowboys); 6 Darren Lockyer (Brisbane Broncos) (C); 7 Craig Gower (Penrith Panthers); 8 Shane Webcke (Brisbane Broncos); 9 Danny Buderus (Newcastle Knights); 10 Jason Ryles (St George-Illawarra Dragons); 11 Willie Mason (Bulldogs); 12 Nathan Hindmarsh (Parramatta Eels); 13 Tonie Carroll (Brisbane Broncos). Subs (all used): 14 Craig Wing (Sydney Roosters); 15 Petero Civoniceva (Brisbane Broncos); 16 Ben Kennedy (Newcastle Knights); 17 Andrew Ryan (Bulldogs).
Tries: Rooney (13, 21), Minichiello (18); **Goals:** Lockyer 2/3.
Rugby Leaguer & League Express Men of the Match:
New Zealand: Sonny Bill Williams; *Australia:* Shane Webcke.
Half-time: 12-16; **Referee:** Russell Smith (England); **Attendance:** 19,118 *(at North Harbour Stadium, Auckland).*

GAME TWO

Australia provided Great Britain with a timely reminder of their ability to clinically kill off sides, as the Kangaroos came from behind to notch their opening Gillette Tri-Nations win on a damp autumn night at Loftus Road.

Australia's fleet-footed stand-off Darren Lockyer turned the game with a brilliant individual try just after half-time, after New Zealand had threatened a shock win on a memorable night in London. Lockyer produced the game's crucial play after his side had stared at the prospect of defeat - and the potentially fatal return of just one point from their opening two games, as the Kiwis led 12-8 at half-time.

Lockyer then laid on a score for centre Willie Tonga, before retiring to the sidelines with an aggravated rib injury that put him in doubt for at least the next game.

Coach Wayne Bennett acknowledged Lockyer's contribution to their crucial win. "That's what you make him captain for," Bennett reflected.

Lockyer's combinations with halfback partner Craig Gower were central to most things the Aussies did well, while forwards Shaun Webcke and Nathan Hindmarsh stood up to another almighty challenge from the physical Kiwi forwards. There was also much to be positive about for New Zealand, particularly in a first half in which they scored three tries to one.

Sonny Bill Williams, the most talked about teenager in the game, gave British fans a taste of his unlimited potential with some special touches, while fullback Brent Webb and stand-off Vinnie Anderson both had their moments. But as their coach Daniel Anderson acknowledged, their inability to control the ball after the break - allied to an inferior kicking game - cost them dear.

Thousands of Aussie and Kiwi backpackers and bar workers descended on Loftus Road, to help create a capacity crowd and a unique atmosphere.

They witnessed an enthralling, at times brutal first half that saw New Zealand go in 12-8 ahead.

The Kiwis struck first, with less than three minutes on the clock.

Loose forward Williams had already bust the line down the right when he provided a superb flick pass, allowing Nigel Vagana to send Webb over. Webb's conversion hit the right upright and bounced out.

Australia hit back within four minutes. Their score came down New Zealand's right side - an area they had raided with much success in the 16-all draw in North Harbour seven days earlier.

There was great fluidity in their handling as Gower and Lockyer linked with Anthony Minichiello, before Tonga brought Luke Rooney on the inside to score. Craig Fitzgibbon added the difficult conversion, and a 30-metre penalty soon after, when Ruben Wiki was penalised for interference on Gower.

Then followed a passage of play where the two opposing sets of forwards ripped into each other with a series of massive tackles. Logan Swann set the tone with a shoulder charge on Nathan Hindmarsh after he had released a pass, leaving the Parramatta star dazed for some time.

He recovered well enough to put in a huge hit of his own that dislodged the ball from Williams' grasp, before Willie Mason threw himself at David Kidwell.

New Zealand scrum-half Thomas Leuluai also got in on the act - his perfectly-executed tackle forcing a mistake from Tonie Carroll and leading to the Kiwi's second score. Leuluai was also involved in the move that led to the try, helping move the ball left to Webb, before Vinnie Anderson's perfect floated pass put Lesley Vainikolo over in the left corner.

Fitzgibbon missed a second penalty attempt, and the Kiwis soon scored again. Swann was the architect, charging through a hole in the left centre on the last tackle, and then providing a brilliant inside ball for the supporting Vinnie Anderson to dive over.

Webb missed his third conversion attempt to leave the score at 12-8 - a lead New Zealand only preserved after a huge backs-to-the-wall defensive effort right on the hooter, after Francis Meli had dropped the kick-off under his own posts. That mistake was a prelude to events that would swing the game in Australia's favour.

Webb came up with an uncharacteristic error just moments into the second half, failing to hold onto Williams' ambitious offload. With a minute, Lockyer was regaining the lead for the Aussies, gliding onto Gower's inside ball and arcing around Robbie Paul to score. Paul almost made amends when he attacked the Australian line, only to be forced into touch by Tonga's last-gasp cover tackle.

The Kangaroos then began to turn the screw. Aided by two penalties taking them downfield, Gower and Lockyer again combined smoothly, the stand-off then bringing Tonga crashing onto a short ball and taking three New Zealand defenders over the line with him.

Lockyer converted, with Fitzgibbon now off the field with a shoulder problem. He did so again on the hour mark, when Gower's smart grubber into the in-goal was touched down by Berrigan.

The Australians were now firmly on control, leading 26-12 - so much so that Lockyer was able to retire with a rib injury.

It mattered little, as his side wrapped matters up in the closing stages, another Gower kick taking a lucky deflection, with prop Petero Civoniceva this time the grateful recipient.

Saturday 23rd October 2004

AUSTRALIA 32 NEW ZEALAND 12

AUSTRALIA: 1 Anthony. Minichiello (Sydney Roosters); 5 Matt Sing (North Queensland Cowboys); 3 Shaun Berrigan (Brisbane Broncos); 4 Willie Tonga (Bulldogs); 2 Luke Rooney (Penrith Panthers); 6 Darren Lockyer (Brisbane Broncos) (C); 7 Craig Gower (Penrith Panthers); 8 Shane Webcke (Brisbane Broncos); 9 Danny Buderus (Newcastle Knights); 10 Jason Ryles (St George-Illawarra Dragons); 11 Craig Fitzgibbon (Sydney Roosters); 12 Nathan Hindmarsh (Parramatta Eels); 13 Tonie Carroll (Brisbane Broncos). Subs (all used): 14 Craig Wing (Sydney Roosters); 15 Petero Civoniceva (Brisbane Broncos); 16 Willie Mason (Bulldogs); 17 Shaun Timmins (St George-Illawarra Dragons). **Tries:** Rooney (7), Lockyer (42), Tonga (55), Berrigan (59), Civoniceva (73); **Goals:** Fitzgibbon 3/4, Lockyer 2/2, Berrigan 1/1.
NEW ZEALAND: 1 Brent Webb (New Zealand Warriors); 2 Francis Meli (New Zealand Warriors); 3 Nigel Vagana (Cronulla Sharks); 4 Paul Whatuira (Penrith Panthers); 5 Lesley Vainikolo (Bradford Bulls); 6 Vinnie Anderson (New Zealand Warriors); 7 Thomas Leuluai (New Zealand Warriors); 8 Jason Cayless (Sydney Roosters); 9 Louis Anderson (New Zealand Warriors); 10 Nathan Cayless (Parramatta Eels); 11 Logan Swann (Bradford Bulls); 12 Ruben Wiki (Canberra Raiders) (C); 13 Sonny Bill Williams (Bulldogs). Subs (all used): 14 Robbie Paul (Bradford Bulls); 15 Roy Asotasi (Bulldogs); 16 Paul Rauhihi (North Queensland Cowboys); 17 David Kidwell (Melbourne Storm). **Tries:** Webb (3), Vainikolo (30), V Anderson (36); **Goals:** Webb 0/3.
Rugby Leaguer & League Express Men of the Match: *Australia:* Darren Lockyer; *New Zealand:* Vinnie Anderson. **Penalty count:** 7-4; **Half-time:** 8-12; **Referee:** Russell Smith (England); **Attendance:** 16,750 *(at Loftus Road, London).*

GAME THREE

Luke Rooney's second try, 35 seconds from the end of a great Test at City of Manchester Stadium, spelt heartbreak once again for British fans.

The script was familiar and virtually identical from the Tests in 2003 as Britain suffered a 3-0 series defeat when they could so easily have won all three games.

As both sides had battered each other to near submission and a field goal looked the likeliest way to decide a compelling contest, Britain worked the position for one more pot at goal. But captain Andrew Farrell's angled attempt was charged down by the alert Nathan Hindmarsh, who then managed to re-gather the ball and set up the Kangaroos for one last attack.

Hindmarsh's remarkable energy in the last embers of a draining encounter was rewarded. Brett Kimmorley eschewed a chance at a field goal from 30 metres out and instead ran the ball. Anthony Minichiello joined the line for one last time and his elusive angled run set up Willie Tonga to send Rooney over in the left corner.

Rooney, who had now scored five tries in his first three Tests, did remarkably well to ground the ball left-handed in Paul Wellens' challenge by the flag.

Both coaches agreed a draw would have been the fair result.

Stuart Fielden was the official choice as man of the match for a typically involved 61-minute stint in the front row. And Bulls clubmate Jamie Peacock, who had spent the previous Friday in bed with 'flu - which hung around the GB training camp for the first two weeks of their tournament - was another who confirmed his stature as one of the world's best second-rowers.

Saturday 30th October 2004

GREAT BRITAIN 8 AUSTRALIA 12

GREAT BRITAIN: 1 Paul Wellens (St Helens); 2 Brian Carney (Wigan Warriors); 3 Martin Gleeson (Warrington Wolves); 4 Keith Senior (Leeds Rhinos); 5 Stuart Reardon (Bradford Bulls); 6 Paul Sculthorpe (St Helens); 7 Sean Long (St Helens); 8 Stuart Fielden (Bradford Bulls); 9 Terry Newton (Wigan Warriors); 10 Adrian Morley (Sydney Roosters); 11 Jamie Peacock (Bradford Bulls); 12 Andy Farrell (Wigan Warriors) (C); 13 Gareth Ellis (Wakefield Trinity Wildcats). Subs (all used): 14 Chev Walker (Leeds Rhinos); 15 Stephen Wild (Wigan Warriors); 16 Ryan Bailey (Leeds Rhinos); 17 Danny McGuire (Leeds Rhinos).
Tries: Gleeson (13), Carney (33); **Goals:** Farrell 0/2.
AUSTRALIA: 1 Anthony Minichiello (Sydney Roosters); 5 Matt Sing (North Queensland Cowboys); 3 Shaun Berrigan (Brisbane Broncos); 4 Willie Tonga (Bulldogs); 2 Luke Rooney (Penrith Panthers); 6 Craig Gower (Penrith Panthers); 7 Brett Kimmorley (Cronulla Sharks); 8 Shane Webcke (Brisbane Broncos); 9 Danny Buderus (Newcastle Knights) (C); 10 Jason Ryles (St George-Illawarra Dragons); 11 Andrew Ryan (Bulldogs); 12 Nathan Hindmarsh (Parramatta Eels); 13 Tonie Carroll (Brisbane Broncos). Subs (all used): 14 Craig Wing (Sydney Roosters); 15 Petero Civoniceva (Brisbane Broncos); 16 Willie Mason (Bulldogs); 17 Shaun Timmins (St George-Illawarra Dragons).
Tries: Mason (40), Rooney (51, 80); **Goals:** Kimmorley 0/3.
Rugby Leaguer & League Express Men of the Match:
Great Britain: Stuart Fielden; *Australia:* Anthony Minichiello.
Penalty count: 4-3; **Half-time:** 8-4;
Referee: Glen Black (New Zealand);
Attendance: 38,572 *(at City Of Manchester Stadium).*

Lions coach Brian Noble had to delete Sean O'Loughlin from his plans when he reported sick four hours before kick-off, and Kris Radlinski was ruled out - for the rest of the Tri-Nations - by a back injury. Paul Wellens was named at fullback and went on to have a fine game with the Saints pair of Paul Sculthorpe and Sean Long at halfback. Bulls utility back Stuart Reardon came in for his Test debut on the left wing with another four new boys on the bench - Chev Walker, Stephen Wild, Ryan Bailey and McGuire.

The Kangaroos made two changes to their side from the game at Loftus Road with skipper Darren Lockyer and goal-kicking second row Craig Fitzgibbon ruled out by injury.

Kimmorley was recalled on the back of a superb midweek performance at Workington against the ANZACs. And Bulldogs second row Andrew Ryan was handed his second cap. Shaun Timmins recovered from the virus that ruled him out of the ANZACs game, with Danny Buderus assuming the captaincy.

Australia's domination of the early stages suggested the Lions were in for a long, hard evening but to their enormous credit they kept their line intact. Twice the home side had to concede goal-line drop-outs, first when Wellens dived to his left to knock the ball dead as Craig Gower's spearing kick to the corner sought out Matt Sing. Then Carney had to kick the ball behind his own dead-ball line after Gower's kick took a ricochet off Ryan.

Farrell, captaining GB for the 26th consecutive time, made a typically-inspiring contribution with a flying tackle out of the defensive line on Kimmorley. Then the alert Reardon was again safe and secure in defence after Gower's kick for Sing. Kimmorley's raking kick then just bounced dead with Wellens under pressure from Rooney.

GB broke the siege, with Sculthorpe spearing a kick to the right corner flag in their first real attack on 11 minutes, the ball just eluding Carney's despairing clutches after he had hared down the touchline. But Australia cleared the danger from the ensuing scrum and Gower's long kick again pinned the home side back.

But from nowhere the Lions came up with a marvellous opening try.

Sculthorpe's superb inside pass 20 metres from his own line took out Ryan and Gower and set Peacock on a rampaging 40-metre run. Terry Newton was in support and provided the link for Martin Gleeson, playing his first game for over four months, to take the scoring pass 20 metres out and beat off the attentions of three covering defenders. Farrell, though, was off-target with the angled conversion.

Britain survived more pressure after Newton conceded the first penalty, for lifting Shane Webcke in the tackle; then Kimmorley offended with a high tackle on Fielden and from the ensuing pressure Gower was just able to keep in-field from a testing Long kick.

GB moved further ahead with another try out of nothing, Carney shocking the Kangaroos with a thrilling direct run from dummy-half from just inside his own half. The Irishman backed himself, his speed off the mark taking him past the diving Willie Tonga and round the covering Minichiello to the corner for a score out of the top drawer.

Farrell was again off-target with the difficult conversion. Gareth Ellis was then hauled down in front of the posts from good approach play by Newton as the Kangaroos looked rocky.

But with just 53 seconds of the half remaining Australia grabbed a lifeline, Willie Mason charging down the blind-side from first receiver in a rampaging run that saw him fight off attempted tackles by Sculthorpe and Gleeson and bounce off Wellens by the line to reduce the arrears to 8-4 at the interval.

Carney went off five minutes after the re-start, disappearing straight down the tunnel for treatment on his hamstring, and Australia looked as though they had got the equalising score when Sing seized on a loose ball on halfway after Ellis put down a Newton pass, only for referee Glen Black to have blown his whistle too early. Feed at the ensuing scrum was scarce consolation for the Kangaroos.

But three minutes later they did equalise. Bailey was harshly adjudged to have held down Shane Webcke and from the penalty Australia worked the position for Gower to shrug off three tackles and combine with Tonga and Minichiello to get Rooney over in the corner, though the fullback's last pass looked decidedly forward. Kimmorley was again off-target and the game was then deadlocked for 28 minutes until Rooney's dramatic second try.

Sculthorpe's field-goal attempt hit the underside of the bar, via an Australian hand, with 15 minutes remaining and Newton, following up, was just unable to get to the ball before it ran dead.

Kimmorley sent a similar effort, from only 15 metres, bouncing straight back off the bar with eight minutes left before Long pulled a 30-metre effort well wide of the near post. Kimmorley

Shane Webcke upended by Adrian Morley

then sent a 30-metre effort high and wide with four minutes remaining.

As Britain poured forward again, Long and Ellis worked an opening for Keith Senior down the left but his kick through was safely gathered by Minichiello five metres from his own line. Then came Farrell's field-goal effort and, as the seconds ticked down, another heart-wrenching tale unfolded for British eyes.

Australia had now won their last seven Tests against the old enemy and dispersed around Europe for a few days off, safe in the knowledge their final place was assured.

And as far as the man in the stand was concerned, inexperienced referee, New Zealander, Glen Black, the centre of a wrangle in the weeks leading up to the game between the RFL and ARL, had justified the principle of neutral referees for international games.

GAME FOUR

"A mighty pack and halfbacks eager to work off them. This is beginning to look like a very good Great Britain side," wrote Rugby Leaguer & League Express reporter Raymond Fletcher as Great Britain beat the Kiwis in Huddersfield to take them one win away from the Gillette Tri-Nations final.

All that seemed a long way off when they trailed 12-2 at half-time in the 100th meeting between the two countries. Two superb tries by the Kiwis and a magnificent first-half performance by wonder boy Sonny Bill Williams had Britain rocking. But with a few reassuring words from coach Brian Noble during the interval they returned fired up and a quick three tries in eight minutes swept them into a 16-12 lead and on to victory.

It was essentially a tremendous team effort by Britain. But it was two dazzling pieces of play from their halfbacks that lit up their second-half performance.

Above all it was Danny McGuire's electrifying burst to set up the try that put them in front. McGuire had been fizzing away for most of the match until he suddenly popped in the 51st minute. He began with his familiar jink in midfield as if he was stepping over hot coals. It took him away from a clutch of grasping hands and he was into the open. Head back, he curved away to the left and when fullback Brent Webb threatened to cut him off McGuire sent a long, looping pass out to the wing. The ball started to fall short of its target until Stuart Reardon scooped it up near his toes, while virtually on his knees, regained his balance and went over in the corner. Even faster quick thinking saw McGuire leap high to flick on the ball in the move that had led to Reardon's first try a few minutes earlier.

It would be easy to say now that if Noble had given him more time against Australia a week earlier, McGuire might have swung the close game Britain's way. Then again, perhaps his 20-minute international breaking-in spell primed him for this game and many more Tests.

Completing an exciting new halfback pairing was Long. Like McGuire, the St Helens scrum-half was a constant threat without quite making a decisive move until his explosive burst of action that led to Britain's equalising try in the 48th minute. Long seemed about to be grounded a couple of times as he was buffeted by

defenders near the Kiwis' line, but somehow he retained his feet and pushed out a lobbed pass that McGuire flipped on to Keith Senior, who put Reardon over in the corner. Reardon did well to take it and then step inside a defender to get the ball over the line.

The entire British pack, superbly led once again by flu victim Andrew Farrell, was magnificent with Terry Newton scoring Great Britain's all-important first try just three minutes after the interval. From a play-the-ball close to the opposition line, he straightened up, looked around and flashed a dummy before ducking under a defender to grab the touchdown. Paul Sculthorpe's goal made it 8-12 and the buzz around the ground suggested the crowd wanted more. They got it.

The official man of the match award went to Paul Wellens, the fullback following up his outstanding game against Australia with another faultless showing.

But the most memorable performance was given by Sonny Bill Williams – if only for 40 minutes. His first-half contribution confirmed all that has been written about the 19-year-old loose forward being the most exciting prospect in world rugby. He had a major role in both of the New Zealand tries, including touching down for the second, as he combined all of his abilities in an awe-inspiring four-minute burst.

He set up the first try in the 23rd minute with a gem of a pass out of a tackle near half way that sparked off a blistering piece of New Zealand rugby at its exhilarating best. Ali Lauitiiti took the pass in his long stride before handing on to Clinton Toopi. The centre ran strongly down the left to link with his winger, Shontayne Hape, and Lauitiiti was there again to finish off the move near the posts.

Four minutes later Williams added the finishing touch in great style. When the Kiwis, unloading at every opportunity, decided to run the ball after the fifth tackle, Louis Anderson did well to keep it alive with a speculative toss back that Williams latched on to. The loose forward then combined his power with the agility of a halfback to twist and turn his way through two defenders for another touchdown near the posts.

With Webb adding the simple goals to both tries, New Zealand took a well-deserved 12-2 interval lead and should have been sitting pretty. Instead, things turned ugly as for the second successive time in this series they self-destructed. They had led 12-8 against Australia at Loftus Road following an impressive first-half performance before falling away badly in the next 40 minutes.

Saturday 6th November 2004

GREAT BRITAIN 22 NEW ZEALAND 12

GREAT BRITAIN: 1 Paul Wellens (St Helens); 2 Brian Carney (Wigan Warriors); 3 Martin Gleeson (Warrington Wolves); 4 Keith Senior (Leeds Rhinos); 5 Stuart Reardon (Bradford Bulls); 6 Danny McGuire (Leeds Rhinos); 7 Sean Long (St Helens); 8 Stuart Fielden (Bradford Bulls); 9 Terry Newton (Wigan Warriors); 10 Adrian Morley (Sydney Roosters); 11 Jamie Peacock (Bradford Bulls); 12 Andy Farrell (Wigan Warriors) (C); 13 Paul Sculthorpe (St Helens). Subs (all used): 14 Gareth Ellis (Wakefield Trinity Wildcats); 15 Ryan Bailey (Leeds Rhinos); 16 Paul Johnson (Bradford Bulls); 17 Iestyn Harris (Bradford Bulls).
Tries: Newton (43), Reardon (48, 51);
Goals: Farrell 2/2, Sculthorpe 1/3, Harris 2/2.
NEW ZEALAND: 1 Brent Webb (New Zealand Warriors); 2 Francis Meli (New Zealand Warriors); 3 Nigel Vagana (Cronulla Sharks); 4 Clinton Toopi (New Zealand Warriors); 5 Shontayne Hape (Bradford Bulls); 6 Vinnie Anderson (New Zealand Warriors); 7 Thomas Leuluai (New Zealand Warriors); 8 Jason Cayless (Sydney Roosters); 9 Louis Anderson (New Zealand Warriors); 10 Ruben Wiki (Canberra Raiders) (C); 11 Logan Swann (Bradford Bulls); 12 David Kidwell (Melbourne Storm); 13 Sonny Bill Williams (Bulldogs). Subs (all used): 14 Robbie Paul (Bradford Bulls); 15 Nathan Cayless (Parramatta Eels); 16 Paul Rauhihi (North Queensland Cowboys); 17 Ali Lauitiiti (Leeds Rhinos).
Tries: Lauitiiti (23), Williams (27); **Goals:** Webb 2/2.
Rugby Leaguer & League Express Men of the Match:
Great Britain: Stuart Reardon; *New Zealand:* Sonny Bill Williams.
Penalty count: 14-8; **Half-time:** 2-12;
Referee: Tim Mander (Australia);
Attendance: 20,372 *(at Galpharm Stadium, Huddersfield).*

Lack of composure and the concession of a series of penalties for niggling offences cost them dearly.

With Britain leading only 16-12, the last ten minutes should have been nail-biting, with New Zealand setting themselves for a rousing finish. Instead, they switched off, with Britain penalties coming like the drip of a tap - all of them simple efforts. Farrell popped one over in the 71st minute and Iestyn Harris another five minutes later before adding his second to put the Kiwis to sleep seconds before the final hooter.

Great Britain captain Farrell again set a magnificent example. He looked as if he should have been wrapped up in bed, but still gave a whole-hearted first 27 minutes before retiring to recuperate for another stint in the second half.

147

GAME FIVE

Great Britain ran up their highest home score in the long history of clashes with Australia to stride gloriously into the Gillette Tri-Nations final.

Going right back to the first meeting in 1908 through the eras of the legendary Harold Wagstaff, Jim Sullivan, Ernest Ward, Eric Ashton and other much-acclaimed Lions teams, Britain had never scored more than 23 points on home soil against the old enemy.

Great Britain's 24 points beat their previous highest home score against Australia set twice in 1948 when they won the first Test 23-21 at Headingley and the third Test 23-9 at Odsal Stadium.

This win was an amazing way to avoid going down to a record-equalling seventh successive home defeat against Australia, with coach Wayne Bennett describing his side's performance the best so far.

Although it is Britain's highest score that goes into the record books, most people will remember the game for their tremendous defence. Captain Andy Farrell said it was one of the best defensive efforts he had been involved in at international level.

It was certainly something exceptional, especially in the second half when Australia put the home line under intensive prolonged pressure.

Yet the half had begun ominously for Great Britain. They came out with an 18-6 lead, but when Mark O'Meley strode through a big gap for a debut try between the posts within four minutes of the restart, the majority of the capacity 25,004 crowd heaved a collective despondent sigh of "Here we go again".

All too often they had seen Britain squander similar leads over the years once Australia increased the tempo. It happened last year when they lost after leading 20-8 in the second Test and only two weeks before an 8-0 lead went down the pan. This time there was to be no collapse. Britain defended their 18-12 lead as if their life depended on it as time and again Australia were held inches short by desperate last-ditch tackling.

There were times when Britain seemed to be feeling the effects of the energy-sapping virus that has swept through the camp. Drained bodies looked as if they could hardly raise a gallop. Then Paul Sculthorpe would charge into battle or bring off a shattering tackle and his colleagues would respond with renewed vigour.

Sculthorpe's main contribution on attack was the little kick he slotted through that led to Terry Newton winning the scramble to score Britain's first try in the 22nd minute, not long after Australia had taken a 6-0 lead. An even better kick almost led to Danny McGuire scoring a sensational second-half try when the stand-off collected Sculthorpe's delicately-judged lobbed kick on the bounce but failed to finish off the move after an electrifying run.

Another player to set a magnificent example up front was Farrell, who somehow rose above even the high standard he has set himself since first taking charge of Great Britain eight years before. He was always there right in the middle of the battle, leading his men by example and when needed adding the odd subtle touch.

The pass he sent out for Stuart Reardon to squeeze in at the corner for Britain's second try was sheer class. It was a rare time when Britain decided not to kick after the fifth tackle and Farrell seized the opportunity to throw a long pass close to the visitors' line that cut out Keith Senior and gave Reardon his chance.

Once again the winger took it in great style, just as he had done twice against New Zealand a week earlier. Although Reardon was only a few metres from the line he still had to step inside Matt Sing and force back Anthony Minichiello to get the ball down to the satisfaction of the video referee.

Farrell then stepped up to complement his part in the try by landing a towering kick from almost off the touchline. He went on to finish with four out of four to take his Great Britain career total to 54 and lift him into fourth place in the all-time list behind Neil Fox, 93, Lewis Jones, 66 and Jim Sullivan, 64.

Newton's biggest contribution on attack was his central role in Britain's wonderful third try - one to rank among the very best in international rugby. Britain were leading 12-6 after 36 minutes, but were just coming out of some sustained Australia pressure when Sean Long launched the attack from deep inside his own half. Martin Gleeson took his pass in full stride to race down the right before passing inside to McGuire. With the defence suddenly closing in, the stand-off transferred to Newton and he carried on the move until timing his pass perfectly to send Stuart Fielden pounding for the line. Although Minichiello's despairing dive brought down Fielden, the prop's momentum carried him over for a try worth wearing out the video tape.

As important as Newton's part was in the try, equally as vital was his tackle that stopped Craig Wing heading for what looked like a certain try between the posts a few minutes earlier. Wing was an immediate threat when he went on as a substitute and zipped through into what should have been empty space, but Newton suddenly appeared in the fullback position to bring off a terrific try-saving tackle.

Saturday 13th November 2004

GREAT BRITAIN 24 AUSTRALIA 12

GREAT BRITAIN: 1 Paul Wellens (St Helens); 2 Brian Carney (Wigan Warriors); 3 Martin Gleeson (Warrington Wolves); 4 Keith Senior (Leeds Rhinos); 5 Stuart Reardon (Bradford Bulls); 6 Danny McGuire (Leeds Rhinos); 7 Sean Long (St Helens); 8 Stuart Fielden (Bradford Bulls); 9 Terry Newton (Wigan Warriors); 10 Adrian Morley (Sydney Roosters); 11 Jamie Peacock (Bradford Bulls); 12 Andy Farrell (Wigan Warriors) (C); 13 Paul Sculthorpe (St Helens). Subs (all used): 14 Paul Johnson (Bradford Bulls); 15 Ryan Bailey (Leeds Rhinos); 16 Sean O'Loughlin (Wigan Warriors); 17 Gareth Ellis (Wakefield Trinity Wildcats).
Tries: Newton (22), Reardon (25), Fielden (36), Senior (76);
Goals: Farrell 4/4.
On report: Brawl (78).
AUSTRALIA: 1 Anthony Minichiello (Sydney Roosters); 5 Matt Sing (North Queensland Cowboys); 3 Shaun Berrigan (Brisbane Broncos); 4 Willie Tonga (Bulldogs); 2 Luke Rooney (Penrith Panthers); 6 Scott Hill (Melbourne Storm); 7 Brett Kimmorley (Cronulla Sharks); 8 Shane Webcke (Brisbane Broncos); 9 Danny Buderus (Newcastle Knights) (C); 10 Petero Civoniceva (Brisbane Broncos); 11 Craig Fitzgibbon (Sydney Roosters); 12 Nathan Hindmarsh (Parramatta Eels); 13 Tonie Carroll (Brisbane Broncos). Subs (all used): 14 Craig Wing (Sydney Roosters); 15 Andrew Ryan (Bulldogs); 16 Willie Mason (Bulldogs); 17 Mark O'Meley (Bulldogs).
Tries: Rooney (13), O'Meley (44);
Goals: Fitzgibbon 1/1, Kimmorley 1/1.
On report: Brawl (78).
Rugby Leaguer & League Express Men of the Match:
Great Britain: Paul Sculthorpe; *Australia:* Brett Kimmorley.
Penalty count: 7-2; **Half-time:** 18-6; **Referee:** Glen Black (New Zealand); **Attendance:** 25,004 *(at JJB Stadium, Wigan)*.

Stuart Fielden dives past Anthony Minichiello to score

At 18-12 there was always the fear for Britain that Brett Kimmorley would pull of the match-winning magic that foiled them late on in last year's Ashes series. He did not manage that this time but was a key figure in both of their tries.

It was his high kick to the corner that led to Luke Rooney opening the scoring in the 13th minute after getting the nod from the video referee. The winger took it superbly before producing a typically powerful finishing touch from ten metres out that brought him his sixth try of the series in four matches. Craig Fitzgibbon added the goal and Australia looked set to take control until Britain fired in with the tries from Newton, Reardon and Fielden, all goaled by the reliable Farrell.

The nearest Australia came to cracking the impregnable British defence in the last half hour was when Nathan Hindmarsh tried to touch down Kimmorley's kick in the 70th minute and was ruled offside. And it was Sculthorpe who came up with the ball on that occasion.

Then after being robbed by Australia in the last few minutes of their previous four meetings, Keith Senior completed the dramatic turnaround of fortunes by gratefully receiving Kangaroos stand-off Scott Hill's pass to race 60 metres for a try between the posts.

There was only four minutes left and Farrell sealed the memorable victory with his fourth goal.

A couple of minutes from the end there was a brief brawl following Fitzgibbon's heavy handling of Sculthorpe that was put on report, and Mark O'Meley was later in the week was later found guilty of punching, but escaped a ban.

GAME SIX

An exhilarating performance by Brian Carney highlighted Great Britain's victory at Hull that put them in good heart for the Gillette Tri-Nations final against Australia.

While coach Brian Noble rested a few players in preparation for the final showdown, the Wigan Warriors winger insisted he did not want to sit out the game against New Zealand and responded with all the enthusiasm of a youngster out to impress on his debut. First-class finishing earned him two tries and he brought the often subdued crowd to life every time he had the ball.

Britain had trailed yet again at the interval, 12-4, with only Carney having given the Kiwis much trouble.

All New Zealand had to do in the second half was keep it simple and not kick to Carney. They did neither. Within three minutes of the restart a clearance kick went straight to Carney. It was as good as a pass. The Irishman set off, the crowd rose in anticipation and the opposition paid the price for their naivety. A weaving 40-metre run had the visitors' defence in a tangle and though it did not end in a try one was soon forthcoming.

From the position gained, Britain moved the ball swiftly back to the right where Martin Gleeson cleverly sent Carney darting in unopposed at the corner. Andrew Farrell landed a terrific goal from near the touchline and followed up by converting his own try a few minutes later. Then Carney struck again with a copy of his first touchdown after another perfect pass from centre partner Gleeson.

The irrepressible winger still had not finished. A few minutes later he was revealing his try-making ability as he was the central figure in a dazzling 60-metre raid. Gleeson unleashed him from 60 metres out this time and away he went down the right, stepping away from Hape's attempted tackle but hardly breaking his stride. As the cover cut across Carney looked for support inside and found it in Paul Johnson, who curved away towards the posts.

Carney looked set for a well-deserved hat-trick five minutes from time when he hared for the corner again only to be taken into touch with a flying tackle by Shontayne Hape.

Brian Noble said after the game that he had already decided on his halfback partnership for the final, expected to revert to the Danny McGuire-Sean Long partnership. Long was rested and with McGuire moving to scrum-half, Iestyn Harris was given his chance to stake a halfback claim at stand-off.

McGuire had his quietest game of the series but his well-judged long cut out pass gave club colleague Keith Senior a clear run in for Britain's first try and he set off on a searching cross-field run that launched Britain's superb last try by Johnson.

Matt Diskin's quiet desperation to push for a Final place turned to disaster when the youngster's Great Britain debut was cut short in the 17th minute as he was carried off with a knee injury.

Mick Higham was then given his chance as a replacement and did enough on his Test debut to suggest he could come off the bench to face Australia.

Danny Ward also went on for his Great Britain debut, 22 years after his father David made his last Test appearance, and the prop did solidly enough to suggest he justified the call up.

But without Paul Sculthorpe and Jamie Peacock, both rested, Britain's pack did not produce the fire of previous games. There was no lack of commitment, however, and certainly not from Andy Farrell, again leading by example and highlighting his performance with a try, only his fourth in 33 Test and World Cup appearances. It was a good one, too, taking the ball ten metres from the Kiwi line and giving a slight dummy before charging over fullback Brent Webb to touch down.

Farrell also landed three goals to lift him into fourth place in Britain's all-time point scoring list with 134. Ahead of him were three legends: Neil Fox (228), Garry Schofield (149) and Lewis Jones (147).

The "dead rubber" followed a similar pattern to the previous clash of the two countries. Two weeks earlier at Huddersfield New Zealand had led 12-2 at half-time and within 11 minutes of the restart were behind and heading for defeat.

The Kiwis squandered an eight-point half-time lead after only ten minutes going through the same wasteful motions. They had also led 12-8 at the interval in their second game against Australia.

New Zealand had looked impressive enough in the first half with their eager unloading game, but there remained a sloppiness and lack of concentration in defence.

They were best served by Paul Rauhihi, who stepped up as captain and replacement for the injured Ruben Wiki. Rauhihi put in some mighty charges and added good handling ability to set up the opening try after 18 minutes. He took a lot of holding when he crashed into the home front line and managed to push out a pass that was deflected off a British defender for Ali Lauitiiti to send Vinnie Anderson dodging over near the posts.

Webb tagged on the goal and Britain were on the back foot until they decided to run the ball after the fifth tackle from 40 metres out and were rewarded with Senior's 27th minute try.

Saturday 20th November 2004

GREAT BRITAIN 26 NEW ZEALAND 24

GREAT BRITAIN: 1 Paul Wellens (St Helens); 2 Brian Carney (Wigan Warriors); 3 Martin Gleeson (Warrington Wolves); 4 Keith Senior (Leeds Rhinos); 5 Stuart Reardon (Bradford Bulls); 6 Iestyn Harris (Bradford Bulls); 7 Danny McGuire (Leeds Rhinos); 8 Stuart Fielden (Bradford Bulls); 9 Matt Diskin (Leeds Rhinos); 10 Adrian Morley (Sydney Roosters); 11 Gareth Ellis (Wakefield Trinity Wildcats); 12 Andy Farrell (Wigan Warriors) (C); 13 Sean O'Loughlin (Wigan Warriors). Subs (all used): 14 Mick Higham (St Helens); 15 Chev Walker (Leeds Rhinos); 16 Paul Johnson (Bradford Bulls); 17 Danny Ward (Leeds Rhinos).
Tries: Senior (27), Carney (43, 56), Farrell (50), Johnson (59); **Goals:** Farrell 3/5.
NEW ZEALAND: 1 Brent Webb (New Zealand Warriors); 2 Francis Meli (New Zealand Warriors); 3 Nigel Vagana (Cronulla Sharks); 4 Clinton Toopi (New Zealand Warriors); 5 Shontayne Hape (Bradford Bulls); 6 Vinnie Anderson (New Zealand Warriors); 7 Thomas Leuluai (New Zealand Warriors); 8 Jason Cayless (Sydney Roosters); 14 Louis Anderson (New Zealand Warriors); 10 Paul Rauhihi (North Queensland Cowboys) (C); 11 Logan Swann (Bradford Bulls); 12 Ali Lauitiiti (Leeds Rhinos); 17 Wairangi Koopu (New Zealand Warriors). Subs (all used): 9 Dene Halatau (Wests Tigers); 16 Roy Asotasi (Bulldogs); 16 Nathan Cayless (Parramatta Eels); 19 Alex Chan (Melbourne Storm).
Tries: V Anderson (18), Vagana (39), Chan (67), Hape (77); **Goals:** Webb 4/5.
Rugby Leaguer & League Express Men of the Match:
Great Britain: Brian Carney; *New Zealand:* Paul Rauhihi.
Penalty count: 6-4; **Half-time:** 4-12;
Referee: Tim Mander (Australia); **Attendance:** 23,377
(at Kingston Communications Stadium, Hull).

New Zealand still looked the more dangerous with their adventurous approach and gained their 12-4 lead just before the interval. Webb fluffed an easy penalty shot at goal. But it turned into six points as within five tackles of the Great Britain drop out Webb was adding the goal to a try between the posts. It was a typical piece of Kiwi play, with the ball being kept alive at every opportunity, Lauitiiti's off-loading ability again being a central part of the move that finished with Clinton Toopi putting co-centre Nigel Vagana over with a miraculous pass.

But the old script was still being adhered to with only a slight change in timing.

It was the first time Britain had won three successive matches since 1994 and a small consolation for New Zealand was that it was the most points they have scored in defeat against Britain.

No way through for Andy Farrell

GILLETTE TRI-NATIONS - FINAL TABLE

	P	W	D	L	F	A	D	Pts
Great Britain	4	3	0	1	80	60	20	6
Australia	4	2	1	1	72	60	12	5
New Zealand	4	0	1	3	64	96	-32	1

TOUR MATCHES

Wednesday 27th October 2004

CUMBRIA 12 ANZACS 64

CUMBRIA: 1 Gary Broadbent (Whitehaven) (C); 5 Ade Gardner (St Helens); 4 Matt Gardner (Leeds Rhinos); 3 David Seeds (Whitehaven); 2 Craig Calvert (Whitehaven); 6 Jon Roper (Oldham); 7 Craig Walsh (Whitehaven); 8 Dean Burgess (Workington Town); 9 Carl Sice (Whitehaven); 10 Marc Jackson (Whitehaven); 11 Howard Hill (Whitehaven); 12 Oliver Wilkes (Leigh Centurions); 13 Craig McDowell (Keighley Cougars). Subs (all used): 14 Wesley Wilson (Whitehaven); 15 Chris McKinney (Whitehaven); 16 Jamie Beaumont (Workington Town); 17 Shaun Lunt (Castleford Tigers); 18 Paul Davidson (Whitehaven).
Tries: Calvert (32, 51), Wilkes (57); **Goals:** Roper 0/3.
ANZACS: 1 Matt Bowen (A) (North Queensland Cowboys); 14 Jamaal Lolesi (NZ) (Bulldogs); 4 Shontayne Hape (NZ) (Bradford Bulls); 13 Brent Tate (A) (Brisbane Broncos); 18 Matt Cooper (A) (St George-Illawarra Dragons); 6 Scott Hill (A) (Melbourne Storm); 7 Brett Kimmorley (A) (Cronulla Sharks) (C); 8 Mark O'Meley (A) (Bulldogs); 9 Dean Halatau (NZ) (Wests Tigers); 11 Paul Rauhihi (NZ) (North Queensland Cowboys); 17 Clinton Toopi (NZ) (New Zealand Warriors); 12 Wairangi Koopu (NZ) (New Zealand Warriors). Subs (all used): 15 Ben Roarty (A) (Huddersfield Giants); 16 Henry Fa'afili (NZ) (Warrington Wolves); 3 Luisi Sione (NZ) (Workington Town); 2 Chris Nero (A) (Huddersfield Giants).
Tries: Bowen (9), O'Meley (13, 44, 80), Cooper (19), Hape (22, 70), Halatau (36), Hill (47), Tate (65), Fa'afili (68);
Goals: Kimmorley 9/10, Bowen 1/1.
Rugby Leaguer & League Express Men of the Match:
Cumbria: Carl Sice; *ANZACS:* Brett Kimmorley.
Penalty count: 4-8; **Half-time:** 4-28; **Referee:** Glen Black (New Zealand); **Attendance:** 4,203 *(at Derwent Park, Workington).*

Thursday 11th November 2004

FRANCE 20 NEW ZEALAND 24

FRANCE: 1 Renaud Guigue; 2 Freddie Zitter; 3 Damien Couturier; 4 Jerome Hermet; 5 Claude Sirvent; 6 Maxime Greseque; 7 Julien Rinaldi; 8 Adel Fellous; 9 David Berthezene; 10 David Ferriol; 11 Djamel Fakir; 12 Olivier Elima; 13 Gregory Mounis. Subs (all used): 14 Cedric Gay; 15 Sebastien Raguin; 16 Olivier Pramil; 17 Laurent Carrasco.
Tries: Greseque (6), Sirvent (39), Zitter (56); **Goals:** Greseque 4/4.
NEW ZEALAND: 1 Jamaal Lolesi (Bulldogs); 2 Nigel Vagana (Cronulla Sharks); 3 Paul Whatuira (Penrith Panthers); 4 Clinton Toopi (New Zealand Warriors); 5 Shontayne Hape (Bradford Bulls); 6 Henry Fa'afili (Warrington Wolves); 7 Robbie Paul (Bradford Bulls); 8 Paul Rauhihi (North Queensland Cowboys); 9 Dean Halatau (Wests Tigers); 10 Alex Chan (Melbourne Storm); 11 Ali Lauitiiti (Leeds Rhinos); 12 Roy Asotasi (Bulldogs); 13 Wairangi Koopu (New Zealand Warriors). Subs (all used): 14 Ruben Wiki (Canberra Raiders) (C); 15 Louis Anderson (New Zealand Warriors); 16 Nathan Cayless (Parramatta Eels); 17 Jason Cayless (Sydney Roosters).
Tries: Toopi (20, 46), Hape (25), Wiki (71), Lauitiiti (76);
Goals: Paul 2/5.
Rugby Leaguer & League Express Men of the Match:
France: Maxime Greseque; *New Zealand:* Clinton Toopi.
Penalty count: 7-7; **Half-time:** 12-8; **Referee:** Russell Smith (England); **Attendance:** 8,000 *(at Stade Albert Domec, Carcassonne).*

Sunday 21st November 2004

FRANCE 30 AUSTRALIA 52

FRANCE: 1 Renaud Guigue; 2 Freddie Zitter; 3 Damien Couturier; 4 Jerome Hermet; 5 Michael Van Snick; 6 Maxime Greseque; 7 Julien Rinaldi; 8 Adel Fellous; 9 David Berthezene; 10 David Ferriol; 11 Djamel Fakir; 12 Olivier Elima; 13 Gregory Mounis. Subs (all used): 14 Olivier Pramil; 15 Remi Casty; 16 Laurent Carrasco; 17 Said Tamghart; 18 Claude Sirvent.
Tries: Fellous (5), Fakir (17), Greseque (20), Zitter (48, 62), Couturier (66); **Goals:** Greseque 3/7.
AUSTRALIA: 1 Matt Bowen (North Queensland Cowboys); 2 Brent Tate (Brisbane Broncos); 3 Shaun Berrigan (Brisbane Broncos); 4 Tonie Carroll (Brisbane Broncos); 5 Matt Cooper (St George-Illawarra Dragons); 6 Darren Lockyer (Brisbane Broncos) (C); 7 Brett Kimmorley (Cronulla Sharks); 16 Jason Ryles (St George-Illawarra Dragons); 9 Craig Wing (Sydney Roosters); 10 Mark O'Meley (Bulldogs); 11 Craig Fitzgibbon (Sydney Roosters); 12 Shaun Timmins (St George-Illawarra Dragons); 13 Ben Kennedy (Newcastle Knights). Subs (all used): 8 Willie Mason (Bulldogs); 14 Scott Hill (Melbourne Storm); 15 Petero Civoniceva (Brisbane Broncos); 17 Willie Tonga (Bulldogs).
Tries: Ryles (8), Cooper (26), Fitzgibbon (28, 77), Tate (35), Lockyer (38), Carroll (50), Civoniceva (74), Kennedy (80);
Goals: Lockyer 4/5, Fitzgibbon 4/4.
Rugby Leaguer & League Express Men of the Match:
France: Djamel Fakir; *Australia:* Darren Lockyer.
Penalty count: 7-2; **Half-time:** 16-28; **Referee:** Karl Kirkpatrick (England); **Attendance:** 8,000 *(at Stade Ernest-Wallon, Toulouse).*

GILLETTE TRI-NATIONS FINAL

The Kangaroos swiftly dampened British plans of a night of hope and glory in Leeds with an outstanding team display fit to rank among the best in any of their predecessors in the green and gold.

Led magnificently by Darren Lockyer, fit again after damaged ribs curtailed his involvement in the Tri-Series, they put on a mesmerising first-half display that at one time threatened to re-write the history books.

Lockyer had once again proved himself the outstanding Rugby League player of his generation. With one marvellous try and a hand or foot in five others Lockyer led his team magnificently from the front, masterminding their incredible surge to a mind-numbing 44-0 lead after 43 minutes.

Britain at least salvaged some pride to quell the scoring and reply with the only score from the remaining 37 minutes of an embarrassingly one-sided contest.

Even the 1982 Kangaroos that re-wrote the way the game was played and approached in this country could do no better than the 40-4 victory they inflicted in the first Test at Boothferry Park. The feelings of British supporters afterwards mirrored those that gathered that day in Hull 22 years ago - the prevailing emotion one of numbness and shock at the way the British challenge was so astonishingly swept aside by a team playing Rugby League from another planet.

Britain went into the final with justifiable hopes of victory on the back of four impressive displays in the series and by virtue of finishing top of the group table. But the Australians were simply awesome; they stepped up several levels in a first-half display that ranked with the finest exhibitions of the greatest game.

And the home side, with its abominable kicking game and one-dimensional attack simply failed to respond. The skill level of the Kangaroos was simply sensational, their execution clinical, their desire plainly there for all to see, their team-work exemplary.

As Lockyer kicked-off to Paul Wellens British hopes ran high, even though Brian Noble's selection of the halfback pairing of Sean Long and Iestyn Harris brought groans from those urging him to put Leeds crowd favourite Danny McGuire on from the start.

Without the injured Jason Ryles and Craig Gower, Australia's iconic prop Shane Webcke played through the pain barrier with a floating bone in his knee and Andrew Ryan was given a starting place - one he justified with a superb display.

There were more groans from home fans as Paul Sculthorpe sent the first British kick straight down the throat of Kangaroos fullback Anthony Minichiello. And then Adrian Morley, coming into the tackle as second man, appeared to accidentally catch Luke Rooney with his

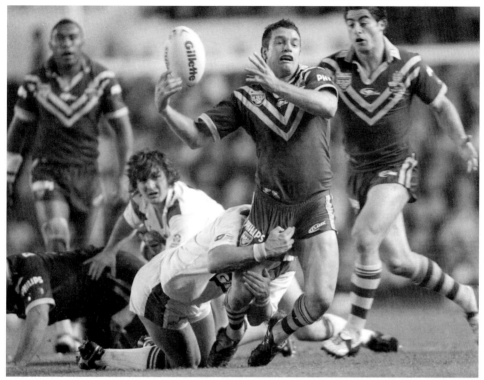

Danny Buderus cuts through the Great Britain defence

knees. The winger soldiered on before quitting the action midway through the first half, looking decidedly groggy as he was examined by the medical staff on the touch-line.

Then the onslaught began - Britain penalised twice in succession, first for Terry Newton flopping on Brett Kimmorley in the tackle, then for dissent by Andy Farrell. Lockyer stroked home the fourth-minute penalty from 12 yards.

Britain's response might have changed the course of the game - maybe. Long's cross-field kick was the best they had managed in the series but the bouncing ball agonisingly missed the on-rushing Wellens' clutches - he would have been a certain scorer had he gathered - and Rooney was able to sweep up.

Within a twinkling of an eye the Australians were back on the offensive, Matt Sing sent away by Shaun Berrigan down the right only for Stuart Fielden to effect a terrific cover tackle in front of the dug-outs - a great effort, especially by a prop forward, stirring stuff.

But a minute later Sing had bagged the first try. Harris's offload on halfway was rushed and put to ground by Morley and the Kangaroos fed off the scraps. Lockyer's crisp pass gave Minichiello that crucial extra second of time and his perfectly judged kick from just outside the '20' split two home defenders for Sing to ground.

Stuart Reardon's tackle on Berrigan saved a certain try and ended a compelling sustained passing move as the Australians demonstrated their offloading game to perfection. No matter, for in the next assault Lockyer's inside pass sent Minichiello cutting over.

Then Lockyer pulled another rabbit out of the hat, floating an inch-perfect cross-field kick to the left from 15 metres out, with Willie Tonga timing his leap above the isolated Brian Carney to perfection to grab his side's third try.

Farrell then went close to a riposte, hauled back from the line by a clutch of defenders after Petero Civoniceva had lost possession in a juddering Newton tackle from the deep kick-off.

Any doubts the game had gone were soon dispelled as, with Lockyer and Kimmorley in command, the Australians piled on the agony.

Kimmorley's pass found his captain, he found Berrigan on the inside and Minichiello, again timing his run perfectly, went over in Wellens' tackle.

Saturday 27th November 2004

FINAL

GREAT BRITAIN 4 AUSTRALIA 44

GREAT BRITAIN: 1 Paul Wellens (St Helens); 2 Brian Carney (Wigan Warriors); 3 Martin Gleeson (Warrington Wolves); 4 Keith Senior (Leeds Rhinos); 5 Stuart Reardon (Bradford Bulls); 6 Iestyn Harris (Bradford Bulls); 7 Sean Long (St Helens); 8 Stuart Fielden (Bradford Bulls); 9 Terry Newton (Wigan Warriors); 10 Adrian Morley (Sydney Roosters); 11 Jamie Peacock (Bradford Bulls); 12 Andy Farrell (Wigan Warriors) (C); 13 Paul Sculthorpe (St Helens). Subs: 14 Danny McGuire (Leeds Rhinos) for Long (24); 15 Paul Johnson (Bradford Bulls) for Peacock (21); 16 Ryan Bailey (Leeds Rhinos) for Morley (20); 17 Sean O'Loughlin (Wigan Warriors) for Newton (36); Morley for Fielden (29); Newton for Sculthorpe (41); Peacock for Johnson (53); Fielden for Bailey (55); Long for Harris (58); Johnson for Newton (68); Bailey for Morley (75).
Try: Reardon (45); **Goals:** Farrell 0/1.
AUSTRALIA: 1 Anthony Minichiello (Sydney Roosters); 5 Matt Sing (North Queensland Cowboys); 3 Shaun Berrigan (Brisbane Broncos); 4 Willie Tonga (Bulldogs); 2 Luke Rooney (Penrith Panthers); 6 Darren Lockyer (Brisbane Broncos); 7 Brett Kimmorley (Cronulla Sharks); 8 Shane Webcke (Brisbane Broncos); 9 Danny Buderus (Newcastle Knights); 10 Petero Civoniceva (Brisbane Broncos); 11 Andrew Ryan (Bulldogs); 12 Nathan Hindmarsh (Parramatta Eels); 13 Tonie Carroll (Brisbane Broncos). Subs: 14 Craig Wing (Sydney Roosters) for Rooney (19); 15 Mark O'Meley (Bulldogs) for Civoniceva (23); 16 Craig Fitzgibbon (Sydney Roosters) for Buderus (33); 17 Willie Mason (Bulldogs) for Webcke (20); Webcke for Hindmarsh (34); Civoniceva for Webcke (51); Hindmarsh for O'Meley (57); Buderus for Wing (58); O'Meley for Mason (65); Mason for Civoniceva (68); Civoniceva for O'Meley (71); O'Meley for Ryan (77).
Tries: Sing (8), Minichiello (13, 24), Tonga (17, 35), Lockyer (27), Mason (43); **Goals:** Lockyer 6/6, Fitzgibbon 2/2.
Rugby Leaguer & League Express Men of the Match:
Great Britain: Martin Gleeson; *Australia:* Darren Lockyer.
Penalty count: 5-7; **Half-time:** 0-38; **Referee:** Russell Smith (England); **Attendance:** 39,120 *(at Elland Road, Leeds).*

McGuire came on for Long at this point; the Australians had re-jigged with Tonga switching to the left wing and Tonie Carroll to centre while Mark O'Meley and Willie Mason made huge impacts off the bench.

With Britain in disarray, Nathan Hindmarsh's offload just inside his own half found Lockyer in support; and the Kangaroos captain glided over the turf with most of the British defence trailing behind on an arcing run and still having the strength to go over in a double-tackle by Carney and Wellens.

All the time Lockyer was tagging on the goals; six from six and 16 points in the bag. He looked certain to surpass Michael O'Connor's individual record of 22 points against Great Britain. But the Kangaroos seemed unconcerned by individual glory and Lockyer passed on the marksman's role to Craig Fitzgibbon when he emerged from the bench.

Briefly, Britain threatened again as Farrell's kick pinned back Minichiello behind his own line and Sing did well to gather Sculthorpe's high kick before Ryan, gathering an outrageously long bullet pass from Lockyer, supplied a superb cut-out pass of his own for Tonga to score in the corner.

38-0 at half-time became 44-0 three minutes after the break as Kimmorley's kick fell perfectly for the on-rushing Mason behind the line.

By now the crowd was long stunned into periods of silence, resorting to Mexican waves to rouse their spirits.

Two minutes later they at least had a home score to cheer, Reardon capitalising on Sing's hesitancy in his own in-goal area after McGuire, from first

Paul Sculthorpe and Brian Carney show the pain of defeat

receiver, dabbed a kick to the corner.

The final half-hour was played out in an unreal, almost eerie atmosphere; the Kangaroos doing little more than go through the motions, seemingly content with their lot.

It was Britain, without the injured Sculthorpe for the second half after his back injury fired up again, that went closest to a further score.

Paul Johnson's burst and Wellens' pass looked to have created a try for Carney but the final pass was forward.

Just after the hour Newton drove over from dummy-half after McGuire and Martin Gleeson had gone close, but was deemed not to have managed to ground the ball in a massed tackle.

Gleeson's footwork caused the Kangaroos defence plenty of concerns - he looked dangerous every time he got the ball and his right-wing partnership with Carney was one of the highlights of the series. Farrell, Fielden, Morley and Jamie Peacock never stopped toiling in the pack.

But Britain's capitulation caused thousands of supporters in the sell-out crowd to begin to leave the stadium after Willie Mason's try - Australia's seventh - in the third minute of the second half.

Rugby Football League Executive Chairman Richard Lewis dismissed any suggestion that he would be calling for Brian Noble's resignation after Great Britain's humiliating performance, or that the result affected the future of the Tri-Nations tournament.

OTHER INTERNATIONALS
Aussies fire warning

ANZAC TEST

One of the bravest coaching decisions in the past quarter of a century must be that of Wayne Bennett at the start of the 2004 season to switch Darren Lockyer from fullback to stand-off.

The previous year a team of respected international Rugby League journalists and media commentators had awarded Lockyer the Golden Boot as the finest player in the world. They rated him up there with great Australian fullbacks in history such as Clive Churchill, Graeme Langlands and Graeme Eadie.

Bennett decided his Brisbane Broncos club needed Lockyer at stand-off. And Locky was such a success that when selectors sat down to choose Australia's Test side, which Bennett also coached, they had no hesitation in picking him to wear No 6 on his green and gold strip, too.

Lockyer did not disappoint, showing just why he was handed the Golden Boot.

What a remarkable young man he is! The success of Australia in the 2003 Ashes series in Great Britain rested firmly on his shoulders.

The same was the case in Newcastle in the first international encounter for 2004 as Australia piled on 26 points in the final 29 minutes to crush a gallant bunch of Kiwis, whose side had been hit by injury and suspension.

Lockyer snapped a field goal as the siren sounded for half-time to give the Australians an 11-10 lead and you could almost imagine the relief in Bennett's mind.

The Kiwis had tried to worry the Australian captain with every means at their disposal. Yet the more they tried, the more he seemed to relish his new role. And, with more than a little help from scrum-half Craig Gower and dummy-half Danny Buderus, Lockyer toyed with his tormentors. "Awesome," Gower said of his new halfback mate. "I hope we have a lot more games together."

The Kiwis went into the match with a makeshift line-up after veteran half Stacey Jones ruled himself out of the picture because of poor form, fullback David Vaealiki was injured and captain Ruben Wiki suspended. Then they lost stand-in captain Nathan Cayless early in the proceedings and the side's third skipper in a week, Bradford's Robbie Paul, was a passenger for most of the match. Cayless suffered concussion after just four minutes from a head clash with his brother Jason. Paul was knocked out by Buderus with a crunching tackle in the 15th minute. And, as Paul hit the turf, he injured an ankle. Both he and Cayless eventually returned – but they were only making up the numbers.

Kiwi coach Daniel Anderson reckoned it was a real double blow. "It hurts your focus and direction," he said. "Leaders drive players. But everyone saw a gutsy Kiwi side."

158

Certainly the spare-parts New Zealanders were gutsy. They had held the Australians for so long. And had they held onto their passes they may have established a good early lead.

They were the first to score when late inclusion David Kidwell celebrated his 27th birthday and his return to the Test arena after a five-year absence with a classic try off a clever pass from scrum-half Thomas Leuluai.

The Australians hit back with a try to Anthony Minichiello. It was lucky that Minichiello managed to get over the line as he had ignored an unmarked Lockyer inside him. A Minichiello mistake led to the Kiwis' second try. The Aussie fullback fumbled the ball from a kick into touch before Bradford winger Lesley Vainikolo wrestled his way past Timana Tahu and Minichiello to score. Tahu made amends with a try a few minutes later.

It was nip and tuck for the rest of the half before Lockyer snapped his field goal right on half-time. "In the first half we didn't give ourselves the opportunity because we turned it over too much," Lockyer explained. "In the second half we were a little bit more patient. We put the kicks in-goal for repeat sets. The defence got tired and the rest looked after itself."

It took just 11 minutes for the dam to burst. When Brent Tate pushed off Clinton Toopi to score it was the beginning of the end. Lockyer grabbed a try after a great break by Parramatta's Nathan Hindmarsh. Gower ducked under an attempted tackle by Sione Faumuina and out of a groping attempt to stop him by Joe Galuvao to touch down. Hindmarsh pulled off a sensational tackle on Francis Meli to dislodge the ball. Moments later Michael De Vere had scored. And substitute Michael Crocker brought the curtain down on the Kiwis with a try right on full-time off an inside pass from Lockyer.

ANZAC TEST - *Friday, April 23, 2004, at EnergyAustralia Stadium, Newcastle*

AUSTRALIA 37 ....**NEW ZEALAND 10**
Australia: Tries – Anthony Minichiello (11), Timana Tahu (25), Brent Tate (51), Darren Lockyer (55), Craig Gower (63), Michael De Vere (69), Michael Crocker (80); Goals – Michael De Vere 4; Field goal - Darren Lockyer
New Zealand: Tries – David Kidwell (6), Lesley Vainikolo (17); Goal – Sione Faumuina
Australia: Anthony Minichiello (Sydney Roosters); Timana Tahu (Newcastle Knights), Matthew Gidley (Newcastle Knights), Brent Tate (Brisbane Broncos), Michael De Vere (Brisbane Broncos); Darren Lockyer (Brisbane Broncos) (c), Craig Gower (Penrith Panthers); Shane Webcke (Brisbane Broncos), Danny Buderus (Newcastle Knights), Joel Clinton (Penrith Panthers), Nathan Hindmarsh (Parramatta Eels), Steve Price (Bulldogs), Shaun Timmins (St George Illawarra Dragons). Subs: Shaun Berrigan (Brisbane Broncos), Michael Crocker (Sydney Roosters), Trent Waterhouse (Penrith Panthers), Luke Bailey (St George Illawarra Dragons).
New Zealand: Nigel Vagana (Cronulla Sharks); Lesley Vainikolo (Bradford Bulls), Paul Whatuira (Penrith Panthers), Clinton Toopi (New Zealand Warriors), Francis Meli (New Zealand Warriors); Sione Faumuina (New Zealand Warriors), Thomas Leuluai (New Zealand Warriors), Jason Cayless (Sydney Roosters), Robbie Paul (Bradford Bulls), Nathan Cayless (Parramatta Eels) (c), Tony Puletua (Penrith Panthers), Joe Galuvao (Penrith Panthers), David Kidwell (Melbourne Storm). Subs: Jerry Seuseu (New Zealand Warriors), Sonny Bill Williams (Bulldogs), Tevita Latu (New Zealand Warriors), Stephen Kearney (Melbourne Storm).
Half-time: 11-10; **Referee:** Sean Hampstead (Australia)
Video referee: Tim Mander (Australia); **Attendance:** 21,537
Rugby Leaguer & League Express Men of the Match: Darren Lockyer (Australia) & Joe Galuvao (New Zealand)

Nigel Vagana, chosen out of position at fullback, had a nightmare of a night for the Kiwis. He fumbled the kick-off and from then on things went from bad to worse. "It's the worst game I've had in a long time," said Vagana. "I couldn't catch anything and I couldn't tackle. It was one of those games where the harder I tried the worse it got. The fullback position didn't worry me before the game. I'd been training there all week and training well. I went in really confidently. But nothing worked."

The Kiwi coach wasn't too downhearted. "This was very encouraging for October and the Tri-Series," Anderson said. "I'm rapped for when we next get a crack at them [the Australians]."

But Australian mentor Bennett was even more upbeat – especially about the Tri-Nations Tournament: "I'm looking forward to the tour actually. We've got them [the players] together for a month. And I think we can play some real football."

They proved to be ominous words.

EUROPEAN NATIONS CHAMPIONSHIP

England retained their Euro Nations crown with an accomplished win over gritty Ireland in the Final at the Halliwell Jones Stadium.

Karl Harrison's side had stampeded over the top of Russia and France in their qualifying group, but found the Irish a somewhat different proposition.

The young English side were never in real danger of losing, however - particularly after a first half that saw them establish a 24-0 lead. Man of the Match and winner of the Jean Galia Medal Paul Reilly grabbed a quickfire double, with Leeds duo Rob Burrow and Mark Calderwood also crossing. Ireland fought back after the break, inspired by Rhinos prop Barrie McDermott, who dragged them back into the contest with a powerful try.

Rob Parker's effort effectively sealed matters for England, but Ireland battled on, Halifax's David Bates crashing over.

Harrison's side put a seal on their win with Nick Scruton's last minute effort.

"The competition has been a really good exercise," Harrison said. "We've been to some strange places, some good places and it's been like a club atmosphere. The guys have been very close and there hasn't been one clique in the camp. The competition has been good for maturing young players - they need this kind of experience to progress to a higher level.

"Ireland tried really hard - they slowed the ruck and encroached at the ten-metres but they were allowed to, so good luck to them. They never gave in and showed plenty of spirit."

His Ireland counterpart Daryl Powell added: "The team as a whole in the second half got plenty of credibility for Irish Rugby League. For Rugby League to grow and develop, the international game has to be at the forefront. When we start out and play in one-sided games against England there is a tendency to say it's not working, but persistence will pay dividends."

England had earned their place in the Final after thrashing Russia and France in two one-sided games.

The first was a trip to Moscow, where, with hooker Wayne Godwin in fine form, Harrison's side ran in 17 tries in a 98-4 win. Godwin booted 15 goals and crossed for a try for a personal haul of 34 points, while Andy Coley and Gareth Raynor both ran in hat-tricks.

London's Lee Greenwood opened the scoring in the very first minute, though it was a full 17 minutes before they scored again, through the impressive Luke Robinson. Further tries from Ben Westwood, Godwin, Kirk Yeaman, Coley (2) and Robinson's second gave England an imposing 46-0 half-time lead.

The procession continued after the break, with Westwood, Raynor (3), Eorl Crabtree, Stuart Jones and Richard Whiting running in more tries. Russia - who had a non-stop performer in hooker Roman Ovtchinnikov - grabbed a late consolation try through centre Nikolai Zagoskin.

A week later, it was Rob Burrow and Calderwood recording the hat-tricks in a 42-4 win over France in Avignon.

The pair grabbed a brace each in the first half, as England established an unassailable 28-4 lead. Second-rower Coley scored the other, against France's sole effort from centre Claude Sirvent.

Coach Harrison was less than pleased with the performance of the French, who he described as "niggly", but his side still ran in three more tries after the break, to Calderwood, Burrow and Raynor.

The opening weekend had seen France beat Russia 58-10 in Moscow. Fourcade Abasse, Sebastien Raguin and Arnaud Dulac all scored two tries each, while Jean-Christophe Borlin was also a try scorer in a man of the match performance. Other try scorers in the one-sided win were Djamel Fakir, Renaud Guigue, David Berthezene and Julien Rinaldi, while Laurent Frayssinous kicked seven goals. Russia battled bravely, and ran in tries through Aidar Akmetshin and classy stand-off Oleg Ghukov.

In the other group, the three Homes Nations sides, Wales, Scotland and Ireland, fought out three well-matched contests.

The opening game saw Ireland get off to a winning start with a 25-12 win over Wales in Aberavon. Halifax's Australian-born halfback Pat Weisner enjoyed a sparkling International debut, as the Irish built a commanding half-time lead of 18-0 through tries to Phil Cantillon, Anthony Stewart, Stuart Littler and Carl De Chenu.

Littler's second, on 54 minutes, looked to have sealed matters, with Daryl Powell's side now leading 22-0. But two converted tries in three minutes to Jordan James and Mark Lennon closed the gap to ten points. It was left to Weisner, with three late field goals, to seal the match in Ireland's favour.

Wales went down again seven days later, as Scotland got their campaign off to a winning start with a 30-22 victory on Glasgow. It was another International debutant that proved the Dragons' nemesis - this time York halfback Danny Brough.

Brough booted five goals from as many attempts and was accomplished with ball in hand, as Steve McCormack's side capitalised on an 18-6 half-time lead to book a showdown with Ireland.

An early try from Glasgow Bulls winger Andy McPhail had them ahead, and Spencer Miller and Dave McConnell crossed just before half-time, after Ian Watson had scored for Stuart Wilkinson's Wales. Tries from Steve Thomas, Aled James and Bryn Powell brought the Welsh level, before Jason Roach's 72nd minute effort clinched Scotland's win.

That set up a winner-takes-all clash for the Scots with Ireland in Navan - and they looked set for the Final, as Miller's first-half try and three Brough goals gave them a 10-3 half-time lead.

But the Irish then ran in 30 unanswered points in the second half, with Salford halfback Karl Fitzpatrick the star of the show. Fitzpatrick scored twice, while hooker and captain Phil Cantillon raced in for four tries in 28 minutes. Halifax forward Ged Corcoran completed the rout, to book Ireland a place in the Final against England.

EUROPEAN NATIONS CHAMPIONSHIP - FINAL STANDINGS

Group One

	P	W	D	L	F	A	D	Pts
Ireland	2	2	0	0	68	22	46	4
Scotland	2	1	0	1	40	65	-25	2
Wales	2	0	0	2	34	55	-21	0

Group Two

	P	W	D	L	F	A	D	Pts
England	2	2	0	0	140	8	132	4
France	2	1	0	1	62	52	10	2
Russia	2	0	0	2	14	156	-142	0

Other Internationals

EUROPEAN NATIONS CHAMPIONSHIP

Saturday 16th October 2004

GROUP TWO

RUSSIA 10 FRANCE 58

RUSSIA: 1 Oleg Sokolov; 2 Oleg Logunov; 3 Alexander Lysenkov; 4 Robert Illiassov; 5 Nikolai Zagoskin; 6 Oleg Ghukov; 7 Artem Grigorian; 8 George Vinogradov; 9 Roman Ovtchinnikov; 10 Jan Gvozdev; 11 Aidar Akhmetshin; 12 Evgeny Boghukov; 13 Maxim Romanov. Subs (all used): 14 Andrey Kukarin; 15 Alexander Chulkov; 16 Sergei Sidorov; 17 Sergei Dobrynin.
Tries: Ghukov, Akhmetshin;
Goals: Grigorian 1/2.
FRANCE: 1 Renaud Guigue; 2 Fourcade Abasse; 3 Claude Sirvent; 4 Teddy Saddaoui; 5 Jerome Hermet; 6 Laurent Frayssinous; 7 Julien Rinaldi; 8 Jean-Christophe Borlin; 9 David Berthezene; 10 Adel Fellous; 11 Djamel Fakir; 12 Olivier Elima; 13 Arnaud Dulac. Subs (all used): 14 Bouatou Coulibaly; 15 Maxime Greseque; 16 Sebastien Raguin; 17 Laurent Carrasco.
Tries: Abasse 2, Raguin 2, Dulac 2, Fakir, Guigue, Berthezene, Borlin, Rinaldi;
Goals: Frayssinous 7/11.
Rugby Leaguer & League Express
Men of the Match: *Russia:* Oleg Ghukov;
France: Jean-Christophe Borlin.
Penalty count: 7-7; **Half-time:** 6-20;
Referee: Ashley Klein (England);
Attendance: 2,000
(at Olympic Stadium, Moscow).

Sunday 17th October 2004

GROUP ONE

WALES 12 IRELAND 25

WALES: 1 Damian Gibson (Castleford Tigers) (C); 2 Hefin O'Hare (Huddersfield Giants); 3 Kris Tassell (unattached); 4 Adam Hughes (Widnes Vikings); 5 Bryn Powell (Salford City Reds); 6 Mark Lennon (Manly Sea Eagles); 7 Ian Watson (Oldham); 8 Damien Hudd (Torfaen Tigers); 9 Dave Clark (Barrow Raiders); 10 Gareth Dean (Workington Town); 11 Jordan James (Sheffield Eagles); 12 Steve Thomas (London Broncos); 13 Barry Pugh (Barrow Raiders). Subs (all used): 14 Kevin Ellis (Bridgend Blue Bulls); 15 Neil Davies (Aberavon Fighting Irish); 16 Nathan Strong (Bridgend Blue Bulls); 17 Aled James (Sheffield Eagles).
Tries: J James (59), Lennon (62);
Goals: Lennon 2/2.
IRELAND: 1 Anthony Stewart (Salford City Reds); 2 Carl De Chenu (Sheffield Eagles); 3 Stuart Littler (Salford City Reds); 4 Chris Maye (Swinton Lions); 5 Ian Dowling (Kilkenny Wildcats); 6 Karl Fitzpatrick (Salford City Reds); 7 Pat Weisner (Halifax); 8 Paul Southern (Oldham); 9 Phil Cantillon (Halifax); 10 David Bates (Halifax); 11 Matt McConnell (Barrow Raiders); 12 Mick Cassidy (Wigan Warriors) (C); 13 Tommy Gallagher (Leeds Rhinos). Subs (all used): 14 Paul Darley (Featherstone Rovers); 15 Declan Foy (Kerry Kings); 16 Phil Purdie (Clontarf Bulls); 17 Simon Manuel (Kilkenny Wildcats).
Tries: Cantillon (21), Stewart (29), De Chenu (33), Littler (37, 54); **Goals:** Weisner 1/5;
Field goals: Weisner 3.
Rugby Leaguer & League Express
Men of the Match: *Wales:* Mark Lennon;
Ireland: Pat Weisner.
Penalty count: 7-9; **Half-time:** 0-18;
Referee: Ian Smith (Australia); **Attendance:** 1,296 *(at Talbot Athletic Ground, Aberavon).*

Sunday 24th October 2004

GROUP ONE

SCOTLAND 30 WALES 22

SCOTLAND: 1 Nathan Graham (Batley Bulldogs) (C); 2 Jason Roach (Swinton Lions); 3 Iain Marsh (Oldham); 4 Jamie Bloem (Halifax); 5 Andy McPhail (Glasgow Bulls); 6 Dave McConnell (Leigh Centurions); 7 Danny Brough (York City Knights); 8 Jack Howieson (Sheffield Eagles); 9 Andrew Henderson (Wests Tigers); 10 Matthew Tunstall (Workington Town); 11 Alex Szostak (Bradford Bulls); 12 Neil Lowe

(Featherstone Rovers); 13 Spencer Miller (Whitehaven). Subs: 14 Peter Shaw (Scotland Students); 15 Andy Brown (Fife Lions); 16 Chris Birchall (Halifax); 17 Ross Marshall (Scotland Students) (not used).
Tries: McPhail (14), Miller (35), McConnell (39), Roach (72); **Goals:** Bloem 2/3, Brough 5/5.
WALES: 1 Damian Gibson (Castleford Tigers) (C); 2 Hefin O'Hare (Huddersfield Giants); 3 Kris Tassell (unattached); 4 Adam Hughes (Widnes Vikings); 5 Bryn Powell (Salford City Reds); 6 Mark Lennon (Manly Sea Eagles); 7 Ian Watson (Oldham); 8 Gareth Price (Rochdale Hornets); 9 Dave Clark (Barrow Raiders); 10 Gareth Dean (Workington Town); 11 Jordan James (Sheffield Eagles); 12 Steve Thomas (London Broncos); 13 Barry Pugh (Barrow Raiders). Subs (all used): 14 Nathan Strong (Bridgend Blue Bulls); 15 Aled James (Sheffield Eagles); 16 Lewis Taylor (Leeds Rhinos); 17 Tom Brown (Coventry RU).
Tries: Watson (21), Thomas (46), A James (55), Powell (67); **Goals:** Lennon 3/4.
Rugby Leaguer & League Express
Men of the Match: *Scotland:* Danny Brough; *Wales:* Damian Gibson.
Penalty count: 10-7; **Half-time:** 18-6;
Referee: Thierry Alibert (France);
Attendance: 1,047 *(at Old Anniesland, Glasgow).*

GROUP TWO

RUSSIA 4 ENGLAND 98

RUSSIA: 1 Oleg Sokolov; 2 Oleg Logunov; 3 Alexander Lysenkov; 4 Robert Illiassov; 5 Nikolai Zagoskin; 6 Oleg Ghukov; 7 Artem Grigorian; 8 George Vinogradov; 9 Roman Ovtchinnikov; 10 Jan Gvozdev; 11 Aidar Akhmetshin; 12 Evgeny Boghukov; 13 Maxim Romanov. Subs (all used): 14 Andrey Kukarin; 15 Alexander Chulkov; 16 Sergei Sidorov; 17 Sergei Dobrynin.
Try: Zagoskin. **Goals:** Grigorian 0/1.
ENGLAND: 1 Shaun Briscoe (Hull FC); 2 Lee Greenwood (London Broncos); 3 Ben Westwood (Warrington Wolves); 4 Kirk Yeaman (Hull FC); 5 Gareth Raynor (Hull FC); 6 Richard Whiting (Hull FC); 7 Luke Robinson (Wigan Warriors); 8 Andy Lynch (Castleford Tigers); 9 Wayne Godwin (Castleford Tigers); 10 Ewan Dowes (Hull FC); 11 Rob Parker (Bradford Bulls) (C); 12 Andy Coley (Salford City Reds); 13 Jamie Langley (Bradford Bulls). Subs (all used): 14 Rob Burrow (Leeds Rhinos); 15 Eorl Crabtree (Huddersfield Giants); 16 Stuart Jones (Huddersfield Giants); 17 Nick Scruton (Leeds Rhinos).
Tries: Greenwood 2, Robinson 2, Westwood 2, Godwin, Yeaman, Coley 3, Raynor 3, Crabtree, Jones, Whiting; **Goals:** Godwin 15/17.
Rugby Leaguer & League Express
Men of the Match: *Russia:* Roman Ovtchinnikov; *England:* Wayne Godwin.
Penalty count: 5-9; **Half-time:** 0-46;
Referee: Jean-Pierre Boulagnon (France);
Attendance: 1,000
(at Olympic Stadium, Moscow).

Friday 29th October 2004

GROUP ONE

IRELAND 43 SCOTLAND 10

IRELAND: 1 Stuart Littler (Salford City Reds); 2 Carl De Chenu (Sheffield Eagles); 3 Chris Maye (Swinton Lions); 4 Lee Doran (Oldham); 5 Ian Dowling (Kilkenny Wildcats); 6 Karl Fitzpatrick (Salford City Reds); 7 Pat Weisner (Halifax); 8 Paul Southern (Oldham); 9 Phil Cantillon (Halifax) (C); 10 Barrie McDermott (Leeds Rhinos); 11 Matt McConnell (Barrow Raiders); 12 Ged Corcoran (Halifax); 13 David Bates (Halifax). Subs (all used): 14 Declan Foy (Kerry Kings); 15 Paul Darley (Featherstone Rovers); 16 Martin McLoughlin (Oldham); 17 Tommy Gallagher (Leeds Rhinos).
Tries: Fitzpatrick (45, 64), Cantillon (52, 70, 78, 80), Corcoran (75); **Goals:** Weisner 5/5, Fitzpatrick 2/2; **Field goal:** Weisner.
SCOTLAND: 1 Nathan Graham (Batley Bulldogs) (C); 2 Jason Roach (Swinton Lions); 3 Iain Marsh (Oldham); 4 Jamie Bloem (Halifax); 5 Andy McPhail (Glasgow Bulls); 6 Dave McConnell (Leigh Centurions); 7 Danny Brough (York City Knights); 8 Chris Birchall (Halifax); 9 Andrew Henderson (Wests Tigers); 10 Matthew Tunstall (Workington Town); 11 Duncan MacGillivray (Wakefield Trinity Wildcats); 12 Neil Lowe (Featherstone Rovers); 13 Spencer Miller

(Whitehaven). Subs: 14 Andy Brown (Fife Lions); 15 Jack Howieson (Sheffield Eagles); 16 Ian Sinfield (Swinton Lions); 17 Alex Szostak (Bradford Bulls).
Try: Miller (30); **Goals:** Brough 3/3.
Sin bin: Lowe (42) - late challenge on Fitzpatrick.
Rugby Leaguer & League Express
Men of the Match: *Ireland:* Karl Fitzpatrick; *Scotland:* Andrew Henderson.
Penalty count: 7-7; **Half-time:** 3-10;
Referee: Ashley Klein (England);
Attendance: 600 *(at Navan RUFC).*

Saturday 30th October 2004

GROUP TWO

FRANCE 4 ENGLAND 42

FRANCE: 1 Renaud Guigue; 2 Jerome Hermet; 3 Claude Sirvent; 4 Arnaud Dulac; 5 Fourcade Abasse; 6 Laurent Frayssinous; 7 Julien Rinaldi; 8 Adel Fellous; 9 David Berthezene; 10 Jean-Christophe Borlin; 11 Djamel Fakir; 12 Sebastien Raguin; 13 Olivier Elima. Subs (all used): 14 David Ferriol; 15 Bouatou Coulibaly; 16 Maxime Greseque; 17 Olivier Pramil.
Try: Sirvent (12); **Goals:** Frayssinous 0/1.
ENGLAND: 1 Shaun Briscoe (Hull FC); 2 Mark Calderwood (Leeds Rhinos); 3 Kirk Yeaman (Hull FC); 4 Ben Westwood (Warrington Wolves); 5 Gareth Raynor (Hull FC); 6 Jon Wilkin (St Helens); 7 Luke Robinson (Wigan Warriors); 8 Ewan Dowes (Hull FC); 9 Wayne Godwin (Castleford Tigers); 10 Andy Lynch (Castleford Tigers); 11 Rob Parker (Bradford Bulls) (C); 12 Andy Coley (Salford City Reds); 13 Jamie Langley (Bradford Bulls). Subs (all used): 14 Rob Burrow (Leeds Rhinos); 15 Eorl Crabtree (Huddersfield Giants); 16 Paul Reilly (Huddersfield Giants); 17 Nick Scruton (Leeds Rhinos).
Tries: Coley (8), Burrow (28, 40, 55), Calderwood (30, 36, 51), Raynor (77);
Goals: Godwin 5/8.
Rugby Leaguer & League Express
Men of the Match: *France:* Olivier Elima; *England:* Ben Westwood.
Penalty count: 7-6; **Half-time:** 4-28;
Referee: Tim Mander (Australia);
Attendance: 4,000
(at Parc des Sports, Avignon).

Sunday 7th November 2004

FINAL

ENGLAND 36 IRELAND 12

ENGLAND: 1 Paul Reilly (Huddersfield Giants); 2 Mark Calderwood (Leeds Rhinos); 3 Ben Westwood (Warrington Wolves); 4 Kirk Yeaman (Hull FC); 5 Lee Greenwood (London Broncos); 6 Jon Wilkin (St Helens); 7 Luke Robinson (Wigan Warriors); 8 Ewan Dowes (Hull FC); 9 Wayne Godwin (Castleford Tigers); 10 Andy Lynch (Castleford Tigers); 11 Rob Parker (Bradford Bulls) (C); 12 Andy Coley (Salford City Reds); 13 Jamie Langley (Bradford Bulls). Subs (all used): 9 Richard Whiting (Hull FC); 15 Eorl Crabtree (Huddersfield Giants); 16 Shaun Briscoe (Hull FC); 17 Nick Scruton (Leeds Rhinos).
Tries: Reilly (9, 18), Burrow (20), Calderwood (24), Parker (65), Scruton (79);
Goals: Burrow 6/6.
IRELAND: 1 Stuart Littler (Salford City Reds); 2 Carl De Chenu (Sheffield Eagles); 3 Martin McLoughlin (Oldham); 4 Lee Doran (Oldham); 5 Ian Dowling (Kilkenny Wildcats); 6 Karl Fitzpatrick (Salford City Reds); 7 Pat Weisner (Halifax); 8 David Bates (Halifax); 9 Phil Cantillon (Halifax) (C); 10 Barrie McDermott (Leeds Rhinos); 11 Matt McConnell (Barrow Raiders); 12 Ged Corcoran (Halifax); 13 Tommy Gallagher (Leeds Rhinos). Subs (all used): 14 John Gallagher (Leeds Rhinos); 15 Paul Darley (Featherstone Rovers); 16 Declan Foy (Kerry Kings); 17 Paul Southern (Oldham).
Tries: McDermott (47), Bates (68);
Goals: Weisner 2/2.
Rugby Leaguer & League Express
Men of the Match: *England:* Paul Reilly; *Ireland:* Barrie McDermott.
Penalty count: 5-4; **Half-time:** 24-0; **Referee:** Richard Frileux (France); **Attendance:** 3,582 *(at Halliwell Jones Stadium, Warrington).*

England's Jon Wilkin held up against Ireland during the Euro Nations Final

● The England Academy under-18s ended the Australian Schoolboys' 100 per cent record on their own soil in August with a 33-24 victory at St Mary's in west Sydney.

Tries from Leeds' John Gallagher and Joel Tomkins gave the tourists an early 12-0 advantage.

Australia snatched back the momentum and hit back with three tries - Blake Green, Greg Inglis, Steven Michaels crossing before half-time - to take an 18-12 lead into the break.

England started the second half as it did the first with Bradford's Matt Cook and Wigan's Harrison Hansen crossing and Leeds fullback Lee Smith kicking two more goals and a decisive field goal to give the visitors a 25-18 lead.

Australia edged back within a point when Bulldogs signing Nathan Armit crossed in the 57th minute. But Cook claimed his second try and the Rhinos' David Doherty - who earlier that year finished third in the Rugby League sprint challenge - sealed the win four minutes from full-time.

Earlier in the month, the Academy and the Junior Kiwis drew one-all in their series. England won the opening match 22-20 and the Junior Kiwis bounced back to win 22-12, both games at North Harbour Stadium.

Other Internationals

● Host country Lebanon sealed a hat-trick of Mediterranean Cups with a commanding 42-14 victory over a France Espoirs team in Tripoli, after beating Morocco (48-14) and Serbia-Montenegro (64-4) on the way. France had bettered Morocco 46-6 (it was 72-0 in the corresponding fixture the previous year) and Serbia-Montenegro 18-4, although that match was abandoned after 26 minutes for bad light after a mix-up meant the lights at Tripoli's Olympic Stadium weren't available.

In this year's decider Lebanese winger Ahmed Al Masri streaked in to score in the first minute of the game, went on to score a hat-trick, and carried off the man of the tournament award. Samer El Masri lived up to the family name as he notched seven goals out of seven attempts. Christophe Calegary scored two of the French tries, but they were out of the contest at the break when they trailed 30-8.

In the third place play-off Serbia-Montenegro and Morocco fought out a fiery 20-20 draw.

● Greece made a historic tour of New Caledonia in March, emerging victorious 58-8 from an entertaining game against the hosts played just north of Noumea.

They went onto to play a full international against Italy in Sydney in October, losing 58-14.

ITALY 58 GREECE 14

Italy 58 (Paul Franze 3, Jason Commisso 3, Daniel Sorbello, Steve Carlon, Andrew Dallalana, Aaron Lewis, Andrew Kaleopa tries; Dallalana 6, Franze goals) d. Italy 14 (Nick Kouparitsas, George Kouparitsas, Andrew Georgiadis tries; Georgiadis goal) at Marconi Stadium. Referee: Ben Everill. Crowd: 1500. Penalties: Greece 13-5. Official Man of the Match: Jason Commisso (Italy). Dismissal: Michael Russo (Italy) 18th minute. Sin bin: Nick Kouparitsas (Greece).

● The touring British Police lost a two-match series against the New Zealand Police 40-26 and 36-28.

● Cook Islands were crowned Pacific Cup champions in October after beating New Zealand Maori 46-4 in the grand final held at North Harbour Stadium, Auckland.

The previous month the Cooks won a two-match series in Fiji, with 36-24 and 22-14 Test wins capping a successful tour.

● Fiji A beat Malta 40-24 in Sydney.

● The Glen Mills Bulls won the 2004 United States Rugby League (AMNRL) premiership after they beat defending premiers Connecticut Wildcats 32-24 in the grand final.

AMNRL GRAND FINAL 2004

Glen Mills Bulls 32 (Kevin Deal, Mike Edwards, Chris Craig, David Niu, Marcus Vassilakopoulos tries; David Niu 6 goals) d. Connecticut Wildcats 24 (Danny Bull, Mike Mulvihill, Gareth Griggs, Nate Smith, Ben Mathers tries; Mulvihill 2 goals) at Jack Pearson Stadium, Glen Mills. Crowd: 3000.

Former Leeds, Hunslet and Sheffield player Marcus Vassilakopoulos secured victory when he scored with just two minutes left on the clock.

● Russia went one better than last year and won the second Victory Cup, despite a brave effort from the BARLA Great Britain Lions, who went down 26-4 in the final in Moscow in front of a 17,000 crowd.

In April Russia had completed a successful four-match tour of New Zealand with a 2-2 win record.

They recorded their first every victory on New Zealand soil when they defeated West Coast by 40-32.

SEASON DOWN UNDER
Year of the Dogs

When sporting historians look back on the 2004 NRL season they will remember it as the year in which the Bulldogs dominated the headlines from start to finish – first for all the wrong reasons and finally because they were the best side in the competition.

Two years earlier the club, which the fans still call Canterbury, had been stripped of 37 competition points for cheating on the salary cap, a demotion from top of the table to the wooden spoon.

But that shame was nothing to what engulfed the Bulldogs during the 2004 pre-season period.

While on a visit to Coffs Harbour, a resort town on the NSW north coast, the Bulldogs were the centre of a major sex scandal – that was splashed across the front pages of the nation's newspapers. Police revealed that a woman had accused up to six players of raping her at the resort hotel at which they were staying. Eventually, after all the players and officials were questioned by police and DNA taken, no charges were laid. The police said there was not sufficient evidence to lead to any convictions.

Sadly for the Bulldogs, in the aftermath, the mud stuck. The club was fined by the NRL, not for the sexual accusations but for the way the players conducted themselves in public during the scandal. The Bulldogs chief executive Steve Mortimer was forced to resign and another of the club's favourite sons, Garry Hughes, was sacked from his job as football manager. Several players were fined by the Bulldogs management.

There was also plenty of controversy surrounding Test forward Willie Mason, who just couldn't keep from generating bad press coverage. So much so that he was repeatedly jeered by the fans in later Origin matches.

But talk about a turn-around! Mason finished the season as one of the pin-up boys. He received a very public kiss from Joyce Churchill, the widow of 'The Little Master' when she presented him with the Clive Churchill Medal as Man of the Match after the grand final. And NSW Origin coach Phil Gould even talked about him being a future captain of the Blues.

It was the fourth occasion in five years that the Sydney Roosters were in the season finale, after taking out the Minor Premiership. And for the third time, they came away vanquished.

The fairytale finish to the 16-year career of Brad Fittler, captaining his beloved Roosters for the 200th time, did not eventuate as they were beaten 16-13 by the Bulldogs in a challenging, if mistake-ridden, Grand Final. Winning coach Steve Folkes summed up the encounter succinctly. "Both sides made a lot of mistakes," said Folkes. "It wasn't the greatest of Grand Finals. But it certainly was tough."

The Roosters led 13-6 at half-time, but the Bulldogs were able to hold them scoreless in the second stanza while adding two tries themselves. "We stayed in there as they kept coming," is the way the Bulldogs' scrum-half Brent Sherwin described the victory.

As rain tumbled down, the Bulldogs had been on the back foot right from the kick-off. The Roosters were first on the scoreboard when Fittler fooled the defence with a reverse 'banana' kick behind the Bulldogs' tryline. Winger Chris Walker steamed through at full pace to touch down. And Craig Fitzgibbon's conversion had the Minor Premiers ahead 6-0. It was the enigmatic Walker's one positive effort on a night in which he kept fumbling the ball and missing tackles.

Kiwi Test star Matt Utai took full advantage of Walker's miscues. Utai made a spectacular 60-metre burst along the sideline from near his own line and a few minutes later scored the Bulldogs' first try. Sherwin, realising that Walker had strayed infield, fired the ball at the Bulldogs' new captain Andrew Ryan who threw a long pass to an unmarked Utai, who was over before Walker had realised his mistake. Hazem El Masri made a rare miss with the conversion – but then kicked a penalty to lock up the scores.

Moments later, much to the amazement of the majority of the capacity crowd of 82,127, Roosters scrum-half Brett Finch snapped a field goal. And when the Roosters scored a length-of-the-field try straight from the restart, they were sitting pretty. Walker had run the ball back to the 30-metre line. From the ensuing ruck exciting young substitute Anthony Tupou split the defences, shrugging off attempted tackles from Tony Grimaldi and Corey Hughes. Anthony Minichiello was in support and scored between the posts.

Only minutes later, Minichiello touched down again – but the video referee denied him a try, ruling that there had been obstruction by teammate Chris Flannery. Flannery had been lucky to have even made it onto the pitch for the grand final. He had ruptured a testicle the previous weekend, underwent surgery on the Monday and only played with a protective support, designed by one of Australia's leading cricketers.

It was a different scenario after the break. It took only two minutes for the Bulldogs to score, again finding out the defensive weaknesses of Walker, as Utai powered across the whitewash for his second try.

The Bulldogs now trailed by just a point. And they went to the lead for the first time, after 52 minutes, when El Masri showed great strength to score. He had been tackled over the line by Minichiello and Ryan Cross, who tried to hold him up. But El Masri wrenched his arms clear of the tackle and banged the ball down over the top of the pair. El Masri failed to convert his own try.

It was to be the last points scored in the Grand Final.

The scenes of jubilation among the Bulldogs at full-time had to be seen to be believed. Young substitute Johnathan Thurston gave his Premiership-winner's ring to Steve Price, the club captain forced to miss the Grand Final through injury. But it was later returned as the Bulldogs' management decided to have replicas made for those who were involved in the season, but did not play in the Grand Final.

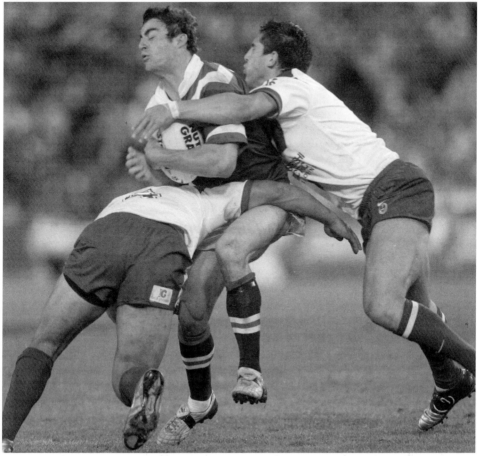

Anthony Minichiello tackled by Braith Anasta during the NRL Grand Final

Sonny Bill Williams, one of the youngest players ever to appear in a Grand Final, was left shaking his head: "This is unbelievable...I'm honoured...I'm proud. These are such a great bunch of blokes...such a great coach. It's awesome."

Mason admitted: "It's unreal. It's been an incredible year for me, both on and off the field. I could retire tomorrow and be a happy man."

It was Price's last appearance for the Bulldogs. He would be leading the Warriors in 2005. Price kept the Bulldogs on an even keel in 2004, both on and off the pitch.

The club's Player of the Year award went to second-rower Andrew Ryan, who was also rewarded with a spot in Australia's Tri-Nations squad, together with Mason, centre Willie Tonga and prop Mark 'Shrek' O'Meley. Williams, Utai, centre Jamaal Lolesi (who missed out on the Grand Final after a spell on the sideline with injury) and utility forward Roy Asotasi made the Kiwi squad.

The Roosters were disappointed again. Scrum-half Brett Finch was named their Player of the Year. And fullback Anthony Minichiello, utility Craig Wing and forwards Craig Fitzgibbon and Michael Croker wore the green and gold, while Jason Cayless turned out for New Zealand and Adrian Morley for Great Britain in the international arena.

Here's how the other clubs fared:

PENRITH PANTHERS (3rd): Few modern clubs have been able to win back-to-back Premierships, but the Panthers went close, eliminated by a red-hot Bulldogs outfit in their preliminary final. But this time the Panthers had to put up with a run of serious injuries and suspensions that cost them dearly. Captain Courageous Craig Gower was their Player of the Year and led the club's international charge, too. Others to play for Australia were winger Luke Rooney, loose forward Trent Waterhouse and prop Joel Clinton, while the second-row partnership of Tony Puletua and Joe Galuvao and centre Paul Whatuira turned out for the Kiwis. Mention should also be made of the exciting Amos Roberts, who joined the club unheralded from the Dragons and played on the wing, fullback and scrum-half (when Gower was injured). He netted 23 tries in as many appearances.

Craig Gower

NORTH QUEENSLAND COWBOYS (4th): They provided the real success story of 2004 as they made the play-offs for the first time in their ten-year history. The Cowboys were in sixth place on the final Premiership Ladder. They then scored a shock 30-22 victory over the Bulldogs in the opening round of the finals' series. This forced a hurried relocation of their next match to Townsville where a capacity crowd of just under 25,000 packed the ground (and a 100 per cent television audience in Townsville tuned in to the box) to see them beat Brisbane 10-0. And had a couple of contentious refereeing decisions gone their way, the Cowboys could well have been into the Grand Final. But the Roosters got the nod 19-16. Player of the Year was back-rower Luke O'Donnell. Rookie was 'Man Mountain' Shane Tronc. And there were three who made the Tri-Nations squads – Matt Sing and Matt Bowen (Australia) and Paul Rauhihi (New Zealand).

Matt Bowen

MELBOURNE STORM (5th): The year saw the departure of the man who set up the club, John Ribot, and a concerted Sydney push for the Storm to be relocated to a 'League' stronghold such as the Gold Coast. If nothing else, the Sydney carping galvanised the Storm players. They scored a shock 31-14 victory over Brisbane in the opening weekend of the play-offs but then came up against a fired-up Bulldogs outfit and were bundled out of the finals 43-18. Fullback Billy Slater became a folk hero around the country with some electrifying displays, including one of the best tries ever seen in an Origin game. The Storm's Player of the Year was scrum-half Matt Orford and their Rookie of the Year, centre Matt King.

Billy Slater

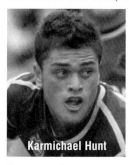
Karmichael Hunt

BRISBANE BRONCOS (6th): At the start of the season coach Wayne Bennett made one of the boldest moves in the history of the club. He switched the world's best player, Rugby League World Golden Boot winner Darren Lockyer, from fullback to stand-off. Critics reckoned he was mad. But the move was a real success, with Lockyer starring in his new role – but missing vital stages of the season through a chronic rib injury. His place as fullback was taken by 17-year-old Karmichael Hunt, who was also a great success and named Dally M Rookie of the Year. The Broncos however stumbled in the finals, losing first to Melbourne and then to North Queensland. Petero Civoniceva was the Broncos' Player of the Year. He, Lockyer, Shane Webcke, Tonie Carroll, Brent Tate and Shaun Berrigan all made Australia's Tri-Nations squad, while Michael De Vere also wore the green and gold in the Anzac Test against the Kiwis.

ST GEORGE-ILLAWARRA DRAGONS (7th): The Dragons were one of the real disappointments of 2004 – promising so much and delivering so little. In their defence they were hit badly by injuries. But this was a side that included internationals Trent Barrett, Shaun Timmins, Mark Gasnier, Nathan Blacklock, Jason Ryles and Luke Bailey (with Matt Cooper to be chosen in the Tri-Nations squad at the end of the season) and a host of Origin players and was at one stage touted as Grand Final material. The Dragons went into the play-offs in fifth spot but were knocked out on the first weekend by Penrith. They never recovered from an

Matt Cooper

early blitz that had the Panthers ahead 24-0 after 17 minutes, to just fail by 31-30. Scrum-half Matthew Head was Dragons Player of the Year.

169

CANBERRA RAIDERS (8th): The Raiders sneaked into the play-offs after thrashing South Sydney 62-22 in the final round. Once there, they were no match for the Roosters, who sent them on their way with a 38-12 drubbing. But they had never looked likely to challenge to top sides at any stage of the season. Fullback Clinton Schifcofske was Canberra's Player of the Year, even though he was overlooked for Queensland Origin selection. The critics were already dubbing the Raiders 'Dad's Army' with the signing for 2005 of veterans Jason Smith and Matt Adamson from Britain's Super League and the extension of Jason Croker's contract for another two years, even though he will turn 32 in March.

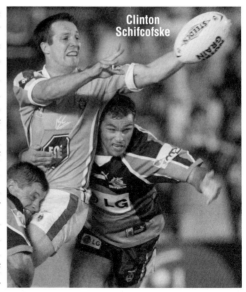

Clinton Schifcofske

WESTS TIGERS (9th): A finals appearance remains just as elusive as ever for the merged club. The Tigers threw away their chance of a landmark appearance in the play-offs by losing their last three games of the season after posting an impressive 56-6 victory over the Rabbitohs. Brett Hodgson was Player of the Year and young utility star Dean Halatau made it into the Kiwis' squad for the end-of-season Tri-Nations Tournament.

NEWCASTLE KNIGHTS (10th): The Knights suffered dearly for the loss of captain Andrew Johns with a season-ending knee injury in Round Three. And internationals Timana Tahu, Steve Simpson, Ben Kennedy and Robbie O'Davis all spent significant periods on the sideline injured too. In the end, Newcastle missed the finals for the first time since 1996. It was through no fault of their replacement skipper Danny Buderus, who won the Dally M Award as NRL Player of the Year, captained NSW to victory in the Origin series and took over as Australia's captain when Darren Lockyer was injured during the Tri-Nations Tournament.

CRONULLA SHARKS (11th): Former Castleford and Wigan coach Stuart Raper had a tough baptism into the NRL coaching scene. Despite having a side that included internationals Brett Kimmorley, Nigel Vagana, Jason Stevens, Phil Bailey, Andrew Lomu and David Peachey, the Sharks never really looked like challenging the leading lights of the Premiership. Stevens was named the club's Player of the Year. But there was some light at the end of the tunnel, with the Sharks only just missing out on success in the Jersey Flegg (under-20's) Premiership Grand Final.

PARRAMATTA EELS (12th): Yet another disappointing season for Brian Smith's Eels. Their season started with a 48-14 thrashing by the Bulldogs and they never got back on track. Test centre Jamie Lyon walked out on his rich contract after just one appearance. Captain Nathan Cayless broke an arm after just a handful of matches. The one bright spot was the wonderful form of second-rower Nathan Hindmarsh, the NRL Second-rower of the Year who topped both the tackle count (an average of 41 per game) and runs (average 17) as well as trailing only fullback Wade McKinnon in the metres gained (average 125).

MANLY SEA EAGLES (13th): As club stalwart Ken Arthurson severed his final ties with his beloved Sea Eagles, the players were left licking their wounds after yet another disastrous season, including the worst defeat in the club's history, 72-12 to Penrith. But Manly did unearth a future superstar in fullback Brett Stewart, who scored 14 tries in his 17 appearances and made the Junior Kangaroos side.

NEW ZEALAND WARRIORS (14th): Twelve months before, the Warriors were only eliminated in the penultimate weekend of the Premiership, going down narrowly to Penrith, who went on to win the Grand Final a week later. No wonder Kiwi journalist Peter Jessup wrote during the 2004 season: "If sport comes down to the top two inches of the head, the Warriors' top two inches this season are bone." The Warriors sacked coach Daniel Anderson mid-year, had a clean-out of personnel at the end of the season and bought veteran props Steve Price (Bulldogs) and Ruben Wiki (Raiders) as well as livewire half Nathan Fein (Cowboys) in an effort to instil a new spirit for 2005.

● *FORMER Test captains Brad Fittler and Gorden Tallis led an impressive list of players who called it a day in the NRL at the end of 2004 after making more than 100 senior appearances. Most retired but a handful continued their careers in Super League.*

Nathan Blacklock ● : 140 games, five for Eastern Suburbs Roosters (1995), 23 for St George Dragons (1997-98), 112 for St George Illawarra Dragons (1999-2004).

Michael Buettner: 263 games, 129 for Parramatta Eels (1992-95 & 2001-02), 95 for North Sydney Bears (1996-99), 23 for Northern Eagles (2000) and 16 for Wests Tigers (2003-04)

Kevin Campion: 240 games, 44 for Gold Coast Seagulls (1993-95), 20 for St George Dragons (1996), 14 for Adelaide Rams (1997), 80 for Brisbane Broncos (1998-2000), 44 for New Zealand Warriors (2001-02), 38 for North Queensland Cowboys (2003-04)

Luke Davico: 176 games for Canberra Raiders (1994-2004)

Jason Death: 201 games, 59 for Canberra Raiders (1991-95), 45 for North Queensland Cowboys (1996-98), 53 for Auckland Warriors (1999-2001), 44 for South Sydney Rabbitohs (2002-04)

Michael De Vere ● : 162 games for Brisbane Broncos (1997-2004)

Brad Fittler ● : 336 games, 119 for Penrith Panthers (1989-95), 217 for Sydney Roosters (1996-2004)

Ryan Girdler ● : 227 games, 23 for Illawarra Steelers (1991-92), 204 for Penrith Panthers (1993-2004)

Rodney Howe ● : 156 games, 10 for Newcastle Knights (1992-93), 40 for Western Reds (1995-97), 105 for Melbourne Storm (1998-2004)

Stephen Kearney ● : 264 games, 46 for Western Suburbs Magpies (1992-94), 80 for Auckland Warriors (1995-98), 138 for Melbourne Storm (1999-2004)

Martin Lang: 176 games, 109 for Cronulla Sharks (1996-2001), 67 for Penrith Panthers (2003-04)

Robbie O'Davis ● : 223 games for Newcastle Knights (1992-2004)

Russell Richardson ● : 121 games, 92 for Cronulla Sharks (1996-2001), 22 for South Sydney Rabbitohs (2002-03), seven for Newcastle Knights (2004)

Scott Sattler: 203 games, six for Gold Coast Seagulls (1992-93), one for Eastern Suburbs Roosters (1994), eight for South Queensland Crushers (1995-96), 166 for Penrith Panthers (1997-2003), 22 for Wests Tigers (204)

Darren Senter: 226 games, 30 for Canterbury Bulldogs (1992-94), 100 for Balmain (1995-99), 96 for Wests Tigers (2000-04)

Jerry Seuseu ● : 131 for Auckland/New Zealand Warriors (1997-2004)

Gorden Tallis ● : 214 games, 54 for St George Dragons (1992-95), 160 for Brisbane Broncos (1997-2004)

● *Internationals*

SOUTH SYDNEY RABBITOHS (15th): Once again the Rabbitohs were the whipping boys of the competition. They won only five matches and collected the wooden spoon on points-difference from the Warriors after conceding more than 800 (an average of 34 per game). Ashley Harrison, the club's Player of the Year, was a notable exception to a long list of Souths' under-performing footballers. Coach Paul Langmack was shown the door mid-season and the Rabbitohs turned to Shaun McRae for 2005 in the hope that he could reproduce the success he had with St Helens and Hull in Super League.

NRL SCOREBOARD

FINAL PREMIERSHIP TABLE

	P	W	L	D	B	F	A	Pts
Sydney Roosters	24	19	5	0	2	710	368	42
Bulldogs	24	19	5	0	2	760	491	42
Brisbane Broncos	24	16	7	1	2	602	533	37
Penrith Panthers	24	15	9	0	2	672	567	34
St George-Illawarra Dragons	24	14	10	0	2	624	415	32
Melbourne Storm	24	13	11	0	2	684	517	30
North Queensland Cowboys	24	13	11	1	2	526	514	29
Canberra Raiders	24	11	13	0	2	554	613	26
Wests Tigers	24	10	14	0	2	509	534	24
Newcastle Knights	24	10	14	0	2	516	617	24
Cronulla Sharks	24	10	14	0	2	528	645	24
Parramatta Eels	24	9	15	0	2	517	626	22
Manly Sea Eagles	24	9	15	0	2	615	754	22
New Zealand Warriors	24	6	18	0	2	427	693	16
South Sydney Rabbitohs	24	5	17	2	2	455	812	16

QUALIFYING FINALS

PENRITH PANTHERS 31 ....**ST GEORGE-ILLAWARRA DRAGONS 30**
Panthers: T – Trent Waterhouse (2, 6), Preston Campbell (12, 44), Luke Priddis (56); G – Ryan Girdler 5; FG – Craig Gower
Dragons: T – Nathan Blacklock (33), Ben Hornby (37), Shaun Timmins (52), Lance Thompson (66), Dean Young (77); G – Mathew Head 5
Half-time: 10-12; Referee: Sean Hampstead
Video referees: Graeme Wests & Phil Cooley
Attendance: 21,963 at Penrith Football Stadium (September 10)

BRISBANE BRONCOS 14 ....**MELBOURNE STORM 31**
Broncos: T – Tonie Carroll (17), Brent Tate (66); G – Darren Lockyer 3
Storm: T – Scott Hill (41), Steven Bell (45), Matt King (49), Billy Slater (59), Matt Orford (69), Matt Geyer (79); G – Matt Orford 3; FG – Matt Orford
Half-time: 8-0; Referee: Steve Clark
Video referees: Chris Ward & Steve Chiddy
Attendance: 31,100 at Suncorp Stadium (September 11)

BULLDOGS 22 ....**NORTH QUEENSLAND COWBOYS 30**
Bulldogs: T – Sonny Bill Williams (32), Matt Utai (62), Ben Harris (65), Willie Tonga (75); G – Hazem El Masri 3
Cowboys: T – Luke O'Donnell (12), Matt Sing (19, 27, 78), Matt Bowen (55); G – Josh Hannay 5
Half-time: 6-18; Referee: Tim Mander
Video referees: Phil Cooley & Mick Stone
Attendance: 21,963 at Telstra Stadium (September 11)

SYDNEY ROOSTERS 38 ....**CANBERRA RAIDERS 12**
Roosters: T – Craig Fitzgibbon (21), Chris Walker (35), Justin Hodges (37), Brad Fittler (43), Anthony Minichiello (48, 52), Chris Flannery (74); G – Craig Fitzgibbon 5
Raiders: T – Nathan Smith (70), Marshall Chalk (80); G – Clinton Schifcofske 2
Half-time: 14-0; Referee: Paul Simpkins
Video referee: Mick Stone & Chris Ward
Attendance: 18,335 at Aussie Stadium (September 12)

(Canberra Raiders & St George Illawarra Dragons eliminated)

SEMI-FINALS

BRISBANE BRONCOS 0 ....**NORTH QUEENSLAND COWBOYS 10**
Cowboys: T – David Myles (25); G – Josh Hannay 3
Half-time: 0-8; Referee: Tim Mander
Video referees: Graeme West & Mick Stone
Attendance: 24,989 at Dairy Farmers Stadium (September 18)

BULLDOGS 43.....................................**MELBOURNE STORM 18**
Bulldogs: T – Adam Perry (3), Andrew Ryan (8), Hazem El Masri (11), Willie Tonga (35), Johnathan Thurston (47, 79), Luke Patten (52); G – Hazem El Masri 7; FG – Brent Sherwin
Storm: T – Steven Bell (16, 56), Billy Slater (58); G – Matt Orford 3
Half-time: 22-6; Referee: Paul Simpkins
Video referees: Chris Ward & Phil Cooley
Attendance: 23,750 at Aussie Stadium (September 19)

(Brisbane Broncos & Melbourne Storm eliminated)

PRELIMINARY FINALS

PENRITH PANTHERS 14 ....**BULLDOGS 30**
Panthers: T – Rhys Wesser (35), Preston Campbell (70); G – Ryan Girdler 3
Bulldogs: T – Hazem El Masri (24, 65, 71), Braith Anasta (43), Reni Maitua (53); G – Hazem El Masri 5
Half-time: 8-4; Referee: Tim Mander
Video referees: Graeme West & Mick Stone
Attendance: 37,868 at Aussie Stadium (September 25)

SYDNEY ROOSTERS 19 ....**NORTH QUEENSLAND COWBOYS 16**
Roosters: T – Ryan Cross (10), Brad Fittler (54); G – Craig Fitzgibbon 5
Cowboys: T – Paul Bowman (18), Leigh McWilliams (45, 60): G – Josh Hannay 2
Half-time: 10-6; Referee: Paul Simpkins
Video referee: Chris Ward & Phil Cooley
Attendance: 43,048 at Telstra Stadium (September 26)

(Penrith Panthers & North Queensland Cowboys eliminated)

GRAND FINAL

SYDNEY ROOSTERS **13**
BULLDOGS **16**
Roosters: T – Chris Walker (14), Anthony Minichiello (35); G – Craig Fitzgibbon 2; FG – Brett Finch
Bulldogs: T – Matt Utai (23, 42), Hazem El Masri (52); G – Hazem El Masri 2
Roosters: Anthony Minichiello; Shannon Hegarty, Ryan Cross, Justin Hodges, Chris Walker; Brad Fittler (c), Brett Finch; Jason Cayless, Craig Wing, Peter Cusack, Adrian Morley, Michael Crocker, Craig Fitzgibbon. Subs: Chad Robinson, Chris Flannery, Ned Catic, Anthony Tupou.
Bulldogs: Luke Patten; Hazem El Masri, Ben Harris, Willie Tonga, Matt Utai; Braith Anasta, Brent Sherwin; Mark O'Meley, Adam Perry, Willie Mason, Andrew Ryan (c), Reni Maitua, Tony Grimaldi. Subs: Corey Hughes, Roy Asotasi, Sonny Bill Williams, Johnathan Thurston.
Half-time: 13-6; **Referee:** Tim Mander
Video referees: Graeme West & Chris Ward
Clive Churchill Medal: Willie Mason (Bulldogs)
Attendance: 82,127 *at Telstra Stadium (October 3)*
Rugby Leaguer & League Express Men of the Match
Roosters: Craig Fitzgibbon, *Bulldogs:* Willie Mason

TOP POINTSCORERS

	T	G	FG	Pts
Hazem El Masri (Bulldogs) ●	16	139	-	342
Josh Hannay (North Queensland Cowboys)	8	96	-	224
Brett Hodgson (Wests Tigers)	11	74	-	192
Andrew Walker (Manly Sea Eagles)	5	80	-	180
Michael De Vere (Brisbane Broncos)	8	65	-	162
Amos Roberts (Penrith Panthers)	23	32	-	156
Craig Fitzgibbon (Sydney Roosters)	2	72	-	152
Kurt Gidley (Newcastle Knights)	12	50	2	150

● Premiership record for a season

TOP TRYSCORERS

Amos Roberts (Penrith Panthers)	23
Steven Bell (Melbourne Storm)	18
Ryan Cross (Sydney Roosters)	18
Scott Donald (Manly Sea Eagles)	18
Anthony Minichiello (Sydney Roosters)	18
Willie Tonga (Bulldogs)	18
Matt Cooper (St George-Illawarra Dragons)	17

MINOR GRADES GRAND FINALS

PREMIER LEAGUE

ST GEORGE-ILLAWARRA DRAGONS 8 ....**SYDNEY ROOSTERS 30**
Dragons: T – Andrew Frew, Wes Naiqama; G – Luke Dorn 5
Roosters: T – Gavin Lester 3, Tyrone Smith, Tevita Metuisla; G – Luke Dorn 5
Half-time: 8-16; Referee: Gavin Badger

JERSEY FLEGG TROPHY *(Under-20s)*

SYDNEY ROOSTERS 14...............................**CRONULLA SHARKS 13**
(After 'golden point' extra time)
Roosters: T – Jermaine Ale, Peter Taylor; G – Jamie Soward 2; FG – Jamie Soward 2
Sharks: T – Bryson Goodwin 2; G – Travis Burns 2; FG – Scott Porter
Half-time: 0-8; Referee: Ben Cummins

DALLY M AWARDS

Dally M Medal (NRL Player of the Year):
Danny Buderus (Newcastle Knights)

Fullback: Anthony Minichiello (Sydney Roosters)
Winger: Amos Roberts (Penrith Panthers)
Centre: Willie Tonga (Bulldogs)
Stand-off: Darren Lockyer (Brisbane Broncos)
Scrum-half: Brett Finch (Sydney Roosters)
Prop: Paul Rauhihi (North Queensland Cowboys)
Hooker: Danny Buderus (Newcastle Knights)
Second-rower: Nathan Hindmarsh (Parramatta Eels)
Loose-forward: Shaun Timmins (St George-Illawarra Dragons)
Coach: Steve Folkes (Bulldogs)
Captain: Steve Price (Bulldogs)
Rookie: Karmichael Hunt (Brisbane Broncos)
Representative Player: Craig Fitzgibbon (Sydney Roosters)

Provan-Summons Medal (Fans' Choice):
Darren Lockyer (Brisbane Broncos)

STATE OF ORIGIN SERIES

When Brad Fittler bowed out of representative Rugby League at the end of 2001 it wasn't quite the fairytale ending the pundits had been predicting. Freddy did lead Australia to victory in the Ashes series against Great Britain. But he had also been the captain of the NSW Blues who had failed to wrest the State of Origin crown from the Queenslanders.

Fittler's good mate and mentor, NSW coach Phil Gould, had always reckoned he deserved better. So when there was the chance to invite Fittler back into the Origin arena three years later, Gould grabbed it with both hands.

After the Blues won the opening encounter, two of NSW's top stand-offs, the Dragons pair of Shaun Timmins and Trent Barrett, were unavailable for Origin II. Gould ignored the credentials of the Melbourne's Storm's Scott Hill and, usurping the job of the selectors, telephoned Fittler and asked him to return. And even when Barrett was available for the final (and deciding) match, Gould kept Fittler in the side and played the St George Illawarra star out of position at scrum-half.

It gave Fittler the farewell he wanted as NSW took out the series two matches to one. And Gould bowed out as the most successful coach in Origin history – but with a few choice words aimed at those in the media who had dared to question him over his decisions while holding the reins of NSW.

Shaun Timmins, playing at stand-off for NSW, snapped a field goal two minutes into extra time to break an 8-all deadlock and win the first State of Origin clash for the Blues. It was the first time the so-called 'golden point' had been used to separate sides in an Origin encounter. And, predictably, it left the Queenslanders gutted.

"It's an unsatisfactory way to end a great spectacle," said Maroons captain Shane Webcke. "We slogged it out for 80 minutes and we arrived at 8-all. Then it comes down to more or less a field-goal shoot-out to see who can get there first. I fail to see how that's a real great point for Rugby League."

But, if nothing else, the golden point provided a fairytale finish for Timmins, who several times in the past few years had thought his career was over because of a degenerative knee condition.Timmins battled on with his suspect knees – and reaped the reward. He potted the winner from 40 metres out having returned to the fray, after a short break, when the match went into extra time (and each side is allowed another two substitutes).

Queensland scored two tries to one, but goalkicker Cameron Smith missed with two difficult conversion attempts from wide out. On the other hand, Craig Fitzgibbon, NSW's kicker and arguably the best player on the pitch, booted two goals from three attempts.

NSW hammered the Queenslanders early in the encounter, with Blues captain Danny Buderus held up over the line by former Leeds Rhino Tonie Carroll in the second minute. Fourteen minutes into the game, Blues winger Michael De Vere grounded the ball after a kick along the ground by fullback Ben Hornby. But the video referees ruled Timmins had knocked on while trying to grab the ball before De Vere.

It seemed a miracle that the Maroons were able to weather the storm. But when they got their own chances they took full advantage. In the 20th minute Melbourne Storm winger Billy Slater couldn't get to a kick from Brent Tate before it reached the dead ball line. Then two minutes later Carroll was grassed a metre or so from the NSW tryline. Almost immediately, scrum-half Scott Prince caught the defence napping with a fine dummy as he dived over from the play-the-ball.

NSW hit the front soon after the break when Timmins, although tackled on the tryline by Carroll and Prince, showed tremendous strength to reach over backwards to make a miraculous touchdown. A penalty goal to Fitzgibbon in the 50th minute stretched the lead to 8-4.

However, the Queenslanders struck back with Prince making a sensational break before lobbing a long, overhead pass to an unmarked Tate, to score and lock up the match 8-all with ten minutes remaining.

It was a nail-biting countdown to the siren with several field-goal attempts going astray. It would have been fitting for the game to have ended in a draw. But the rules introduced last year forced it into extra time.

'Bustling' Billy Slater was the toast of Queensland after his two-try effort to help the Maroons win the second State of Origin and send the series back to Sydney for the decider.

Not even the sour grapes of the New South Welshmen who claimed he was offside when scoring his second try – which swung the momentum of the game – could detract from his effort. Indeed, most critics described that try as one of the greatest in the quarter of a century of Origin encounters.

It came 22 minutes into the second half. From near halfway, Queensland captain Darren Lockyer put in a kick along the ground. The bounce was perfect for Slater, who sliced through on his way to the tryline. When confronted by NSW fullback Anthony Minichiello, Slater thought of attempting a side-step but instead put in a reverse chip over the custodian's head. All that was left was to use his blinding speed to be first to the ball and dive over to score.

It put the Queenslanders ahead for the first time in the encounter. "It was just a spur of the moment thing," Slater explained. "I've got Lockyer inside me. He puts the ball where you want it. And you do your best to finish it off."

Quite simply really!

Referees' boss Robert Finch later gave it his stamp of approval saying that because Slater had one foot behind Lockyer under the rules he was on-side.

With 56 per cent of possession, the New South Welshmen had the best of play for most of the first half and were unlucky not to have been ahead by a much greater margin than their 12-6. Winger Timana Tahu had scored after three and a half minutes off a long cut-out pass from half Brett Finch, drafted into the side only three days earlier after a hamstring injury to Brett Kimmorley. The scores were tied up after Maroons fullback Rhys Wesser juggled the ball before turning it back inside to a speeding Slater. Then less than a minute before the break, Tahu was over again in the corner off a clever pass from his Newcastle team-mate Matthew Gidley.

The Maroons were never going to throw in the towel and when newcomer Willie Tonga grabbed a long pass from Lockyer to score four minutes into the second half they trailed by just two.

Then came Slater's gamebreaker.

NSW fought back. Fittler was held up over the line before Tahu had the ball jolted out of his hands as he was about the touch down. Within seconds the Maroons had the ball up at the other end of the pitch. Lockyer put up a bomb, Tahu fumbled and Dane Carlaw was quick to grab the loose ball and race over to score.

The Maroons now led 20-12 and had some breathing space – but not enough to prevent a nail-biting finish. Seven minutes from the end a break begun by Willie Mason finished with NSW winger Luke Rooney scoring wide out.

But it was too little, too late to overtake the Queenslanders.

The Gus Gould era came to an end in Sydney. The most successful coach in State of Origin history bowed out a winner in the decider at the old Olympic headquarters.

But Gould was hardly gracious in victory. At a moment when he should have been grinning from ear to ear – as was his partner in success, Brad Fittler – Gould took time out at the post-match press conference to vent his spleen on a group of journalists he described as "insecure or immature" and "intimidated by the own lack of knowledge or what they don't understand."

Gould snarled: "I don't deserve the s— youse have f—ing dished up to me."

And there were later a couple more four-letter words, too. The outburst took the gloss of what was a fine win by the Blues. The decider in front of a capacity crowd of 82,487 did not have the intensity of the Origin I at the same arena or the razzle-dazzle excitement of the second encounter at Lang Park. It was just a clinical carve-up of a Queensland side that was outclassed on the night.

2004 STATE OF ORIGIN SERIES

ORIGIN I - *Wednesday, May 26, at Telstra Stadium, Sydney*

NEW SOUTH WALES 9 ....**QUEENSLAND 8**
(Two minutes into 'golden point' extra time)
NSW: Try – Shaun Timmins (46); Goals – Craig Fitzgibbon 2; Field goal – Shaun Timmins
Queensland: Tries – Scott Prince (22), Brent Tate (61)
NSW: 1 Ben Hornby (Dragons); 2 Luke Rooney (Panthers), 3 Michael De Vere (Broncos), 4 Matthew Gidley (Knights), 5 Luke Lewis (Panthers); 6 Shaun Timmins (Dragons), 7 Craig Gower (Panthers); 8 Ryan O'Hara (Raiders), 9 Danny Buderus (Knights) (c), 10 Mark O'Meley (Bulldogs), 11 Nathan Hindmarsh (Eels), 12 Andrew Ryan (Bulldogs), 13 Craig Fitzgibbon (Roosters). Subs: 14 Willie Mason (Bulldogs), 15 Brent Kite (Dragons), 16 Trent Waterhouse (Panthers), 17 Craig Wing (Roosters).
Queensland: 1 Rhys Wesser (Panthers); 2 Justin Hodges (Roosters), 3 Paul Bowman (Cowboys), 4 Brent Tate (Broncos), 5 Billy Slater (Storm); 6 Chris Flannery (Roosters), 7 Scott Prince (Tigers); 8 Shane Webcke (Broncos) (c), 9 Cameron Smith (Storm), 10 Steve Price (Bulldogs), 11 Michael Crocker (Roosters), 12 Dane Carlaw (Broncos), 13 Tonie Carroll (Broncos). Subs: 14 Ben Ross (Panthers), 15 Petero Civoniceva (Broncos), 16 Travis Norton (Cowboys), 17 Matt Bowen (Cowboys).
Half-time: 0-4; **Referee:** Sean Hampstead
Video referees: Graeme West & Steve Clark; **Attendance:** 68,344
Rugby Leaguer & League Express Men of the Match:
Craig Fitzgibbon (NSW) & Steve Price (Qld)

ORIGIN II - *Wednesday, June 16, at Suncorp Stadium, Brisbane*

QUEENSLAND 22 ....**NEW SOUTH WALES 18**
Queensland: Tries – Billy Slater (33, 62), Willie Tonga (44), Dane Carlaw (67); Goals - Cameron Smith 2, Scott Prince
NSW: Tries – Timana Tahu (4, 39), Luke Rooney (73); Goals – Craig Fitzgibbon 3
Queensland: 1 Rhys Wesser (Panthers); 2 Matt Sing (Cowboys), 3 Paul Bowman (Cowboys), 4 Willie Tonga (Bulldogs), 5 Billy Slater (Storm); 6 Darren Lockyer (Broncos) (c), 7 Scott Prince (Tigers); 8 Shane Webcke (Broncos), 9 Cameron Smith (Storm), 10 Steve Price (Bulldogs), 11 Petero Civoniceva (Broncos), 12 Dane Carlaw (Broncos), 13 Tonie Carroll (Broncos). Subs: 14 Ben Ross (Panthers), 15 Corey Parker (Broncos), 16 Chris Flannery (Roosters), 17 Matt Bowen (Cowboys).
NSW: 1 Anthony Minichiello (Roosters); 2 Timana Tahu (Knights), 3 Matthew Gidley (Knights), 4 Luke Lewis (Panthers), 5 Luke Rooney (Panthers); 6 Brad Fittler (Roosters), 7 Brett Finch (Roosters); 8 Jason Stevens (Sharks), 9 Danny Buderus (Knights) (c), 10 Mark O'Meley (Bulldogs), 11 Nathan Hindmarsh (Eels), 12 Andrew Ryan (Bulldogs), 13 Craig Fitzgibbon (Roosters). Subs: 14 Willie Mason (Bulldogs), 15 Brent Kite (Dragons), 16 Trent Waterhouse (Panthers), 17 Craig Wing (Roosters).
Half-time: 6-12; **Referee:** Sean Hampstead; **Video referees:** Graeme West & Tim Mander; **Attendance:** 52,478 *(Ground record)*
Rugby Leaguer & League Express Men of the Match:
Billy Slater (Qld) & Nathan Hindmarsh (NSW)

ORIGIN III - *Wednesday, July 7, at Telstra Stadium, Sydney*

NEW SOUTH WALES 36 ....**QUEENSLAND 14**
NSW: Tries - Mark Gasnier (11, 35), Trent Barrett (33), Luke Rooney (55), Anthony Minichiello (61), Brad Fittler (73); Goals – Craig Fitzgibbon 6
Queensland: Tries – Billy Slater (22), Matt Bowen (77); Goals – Cameron Smith 3
NSW: 1 Anthony Minichiello (Roosters); 2 Luke Rooney (Panthers), 3 Matt Cooper (Dragons), 4 Mark Gasnier (Dragons), 5 Luke Lewis (Panthers); 6 Brad Fittler (Roosters), 7 Trent Barrett (Dragons); 8 Jason Ryles (Dragons), 9 Danny Buderus (Knights) (c), 10 Mark O'Meley (Bulldogs), 11 Nathan Hindmarsh (Eels), 12 Andrew Ryan (Bulldogs), 13 Shaun Timmins (Dragons). Subs: 14 Willie Mason (Bulldogs), 15 Brent Kite (Dragons), 16 Ben Kennedy (Knights), 17 Craig Wing (Roosters).
Queensland: 1 Rhys Wesser (Panthers); 2 Matt Sing (Cowboys), 3 Brent Tate (Broncos), 4 Willie Tonga (Bulldogs), 5 Billy Slater (Storm); 6 Darren Lockyer (Broncos) (c), 7 Scott Prince (Tigers); 8 Shane Webcke (Broncos), 9 Cameron Smith (Storm), 10 Steve Price (Bulldogs), 11 Michael Crocker (Roosters), 15 Petero Civoniceva (Broncos), 12 Dane Carlaw (Broncos). Subs: 13 Chris Flannery (Roosters), 14 Ben Ross (Panthers), 16 Corey Parker (Broncos), 17 Matt Bowen (Cowboys).
Half-time: 18-8; **Referee:** Paul Simpkins
Video referees: Graeme West & Sean Hampstead; **Attendance:** 82,487
Rugby Leaguer & League Express Men of the Match:
Trent Barrett (NSW) & Darren Lockyer (Qld)

Rhys Wesser outjumped for a high ball in Origin III

The match was won in the forwards, with sensational efforts from back-rowers Fitzgibbon, Hindmarsh and young prop Mark O'Meley, and around the base of the scrum where the three veterans, Fittler, Barrett playing an unaccustomed role as scrum-half, and loose forward Timmins drew on every ounce of their vast experience.

And with plenty of ball Mark Gasnier, the centre who had been the focus of Wigan's attention in the preceding weeks, had a wonderful Origin debut, scoring two tries and saving a couple, too.

Gould decided to target Slater, the hero of Origin II. In the second minute, Slater was hit by a spear tackle. And in the ninth minute he knocked on after some incredible pressure. From the next set of six, Gasnier was over for the first of his brace of tries.

Midway through the first half, the Queenslanders came back. Matt Sing deserved a penalty try after being blatantly stopped from grounding a rolling ball over the tryline. But it mattered not as a couple of tackles later Slater was over the whitewash for a try and the Maroons were back in the lead 8-6.

That was as good as it got for Queensland. Two tries in the space of as many minutes sealed Queensland's fate. Barrett touched down after a wonderful run from 15 metres out. And Fittler orchestrated Gasnier's second try.

It was 18-8 at the interval – and NSW never looked back. Sing smashed his jaw in an accidental clash of heads with Fittler moments after play resumed in the second half. Fittler was then held up over the tryline before the procession began. Winger Rooney showed his considerable strength in a bullocking run to the line. Minichiello, making up for some indifferent form early in the match, grabbed another try and the Blues were cruising at 28-8.

All that was left was for the try for which the NSW fans had been waiting. With seven minutes left Fittler sliced through the tired Queensland defence, raised his left arm and pointed to the sky as he grounded the ball between the posts.

A fitting farewell for Freddy! Queensland managed a late consolation try to substitute winger Matt Bowen. But it was the Blues' night.

Fittler, lured out of representative retirement for Origin II was elated to finish his Origin career a winner. "Call it a fairytale, call it what you like," he said. "But it was a great way to finish for me."

It was a bit different from his words after the second encounter: "I've never believed in fairytales. It's no longer in my vocabulary." Well, not for three weeks, anyway!

Gillette
RUGBY LEAGUE
TRI-NATIONS
2004

FINAL

GREAT BRITAIN 4
AUSTRALIA 44

Australian skipper Darren Lockyer lifts the Tri-Nations trophy after the Kangaroos' comprehensive defeat of Great Britain

Gillette®

Gillette RUGBY LEAGUE TRI-NATIONS 2004

GAME SIX

GREAT BRITAIN 26
NEW ZEALAND 24

CLOCKWISE, FROM TOP:
Gareth Ellis takes on Wairangi
Koopu; Thomas Leuluai can't stop
Brian Carney from scoring; Paul
Rauhihi and Nathan Cayless get
to grips with Sean O'Loughlin

GAME FIVE

GREAT BRITAIN 24
AUSTRALIA 12

CLOCKWISE, FROM TOP: Keith
Senior races away from Shaun
Berrigan to score the winning try;
and is mobbed by Sean Long,
Paul Wellens and Paul
Sculthorpe; Andy Farrell fends off
the challenge of Brett Kimmorley

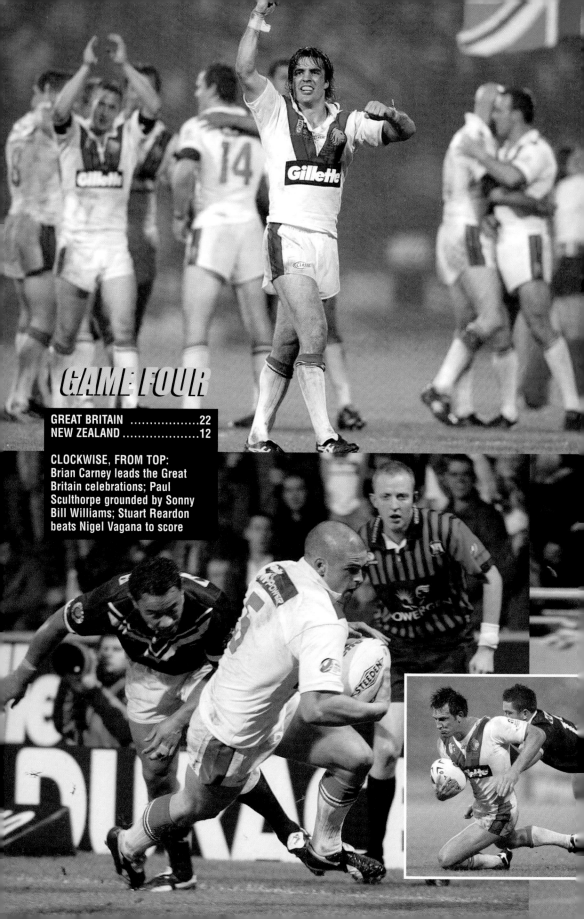

GAME FOUR

GREAT BRITAIN 22
NEW ZEALAND 12

CLOCKWISE, FROM TOP:
Brian Carney leads the Great
Britain celebrations; Paul
Sculthorpe grounded by Sonny
Bill Williams; Stuart Reardon
beats Nigel Vagana to score

Gillette
RUGBY LEAGUE
TRI-NATIONS
2004

GAME THREE

GREAT BRITAIN 8
AUSTRALIA 12

ABOVE: Brian Carney goes past Anthony Minichiello to score

BELOW: Luke Rooney dives in at the corner, past Paul Wellens, to score his last-gasp winning try

Gillette RUGBY LEAGUE TRI-NATIONS 2004

GAME TWO

AUSTRALIA 32
NEW ZEALAND 12

RIGHT: Darren Lockyer looks for support under pressure from Logan Swann

ABOVE: Scott Hill held up by Gary Broadbent during the ANZACs' win over Cumbria

GAME ONE

NEW ZEALAND 16
AUSTRALIA 16

LEFT: Danny Buderus upends Sonny Bill Williams

INSET: Ben Kennedy, Andrew Ryan, Nathan Hindmarsh and Shane Webcke lead the Australian side from the field

EUROPEAN NATIONS CUP

RIGHT:
Ireland's David Bates collared by Wales' Jordan James

ENGLAND	36
IRELAND	12

ABOVE: England's Mark Calderwood tackled by Ireland's Pat Weisner

BELOW: England celebrate their European Nations Cup Final win

EUROPEAN NATIONS CUP FINAL

-WINNERS 2004-

LEFT: Shannon Hegarty dumped by the North Queensland Cowboys defence as the Sydney Roosters reach the Grand Final

BELOW: Josh Hannay celebrates North Queensland's play-off victory over Brisbane with the Cowboys fans

ABOVE: Sonny Bill Williams smashes into Joel Clinton as the Bulldogs book their spot in the NRL decider by defeating Penrith

NRL SEASON

RIGHT: Gorden Tallis leaves the Suncorp Stadium field for the last time after Brisbane's play-off game with Melbourne

STATE OF ORIGIN

ANZAC TEST

ABOVE: Craig Gower shrugs off Penrith teammate Joe Galuvao to score

ABOVE: Trent Barrett and Brad Fittler celebrate New South Wales' State Of Origin Series win

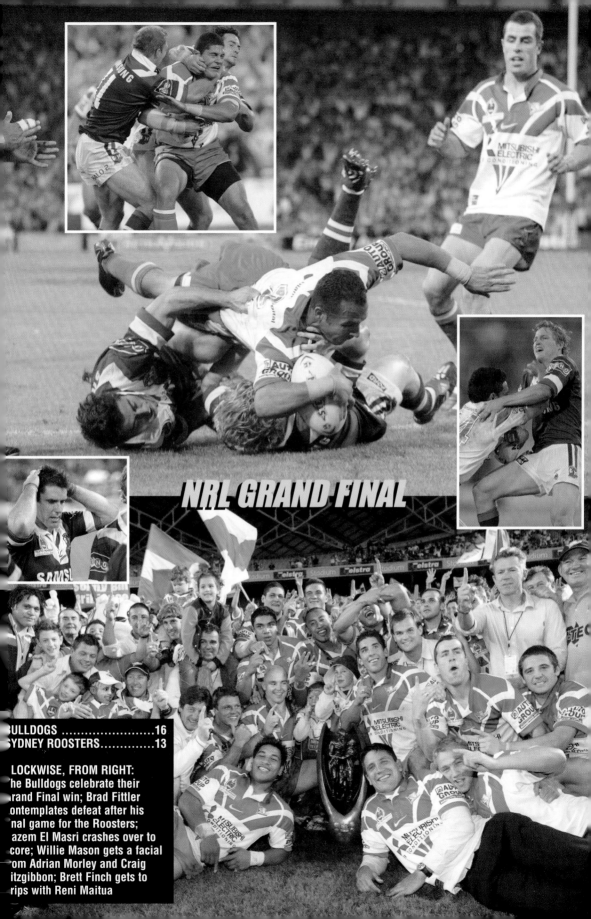

NRL GRAND FINAL

BULLDOGS **16**
SYDNEY ROOSTERS..............**13**

CLOCKWISE, FROM RIGHT:
The Bulldogs celebrate their
Grand Final win; Brad Fittler
contemplates defeat after his
final game for the Roosters;
Hazem El Masri crashes over to
score; Willie Mason gets a facial
from Adrian Morley and Craig
Fitzgibbon; Brett Finch gets to
grips with Reni Maitua

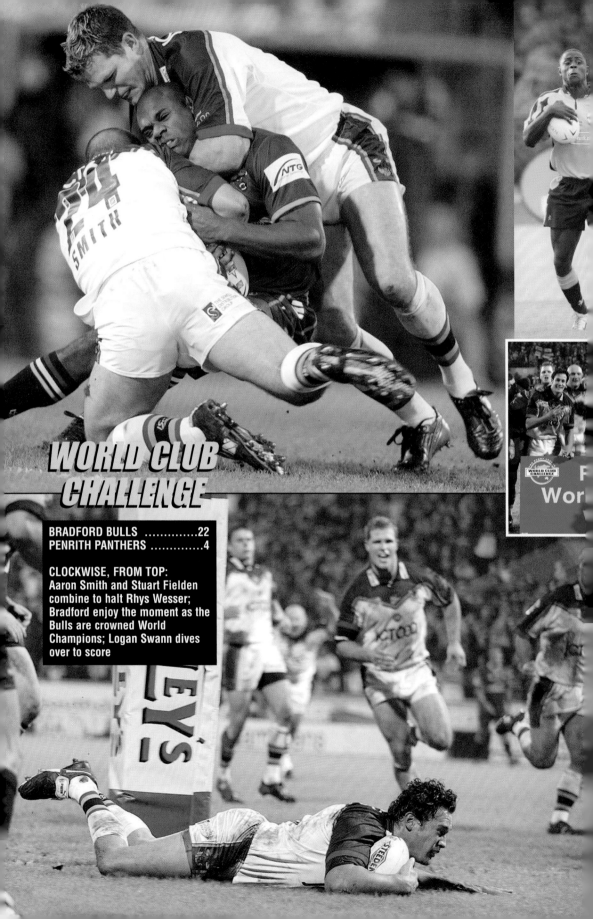

WORLD CLUB CHALLENGE

BRADFORD BULLS 22
PENRITH PANTHERS 4

CLOCKWISE, FROM TOP:
Aaron Smith and Stuart Fielden combine to halt Rhys Wesser; Bradford enjoy the moment as the Bulls are crowned World Champions; Logan Swann dives over to score

ABOVE: Powergen Fastest Man winner Darren Albert leads the way from Ade Adebisi, Dean Colton and Mark Stevens

League Challenge s 2004

Melbourne's Matt King shows off his 'unusual' hair style

RIGHT: Widnes' Jules O'Neill grounded against the New South Wales Country side

WORLD SEVENS

ABOVE: Lebanon picked up the Mediterranean Cup

LEFT: Wests Tigers - World Sevens Winners

RIGHT: West Indies - York 9's Winners

LEFT: Italy celebrate victory over Greece

Andy Spink earned selection in the Rugby League World All-Stars team after a big season with Batley

NATIONAL LEAGUE ONE SEASON

ABOVE: Paul Fletcher swamped by the Doncaster defence as Hull KR eliminate the Dragons

BELOW: Featherstone's Jim Carlton outnumbered by the Oldham defence during the play-offs

Bobbie Goulding guided Rochdale Hornets through an eventful season

Jason Clegg had a stand-out season for Keighley despite the Cougars' relegation

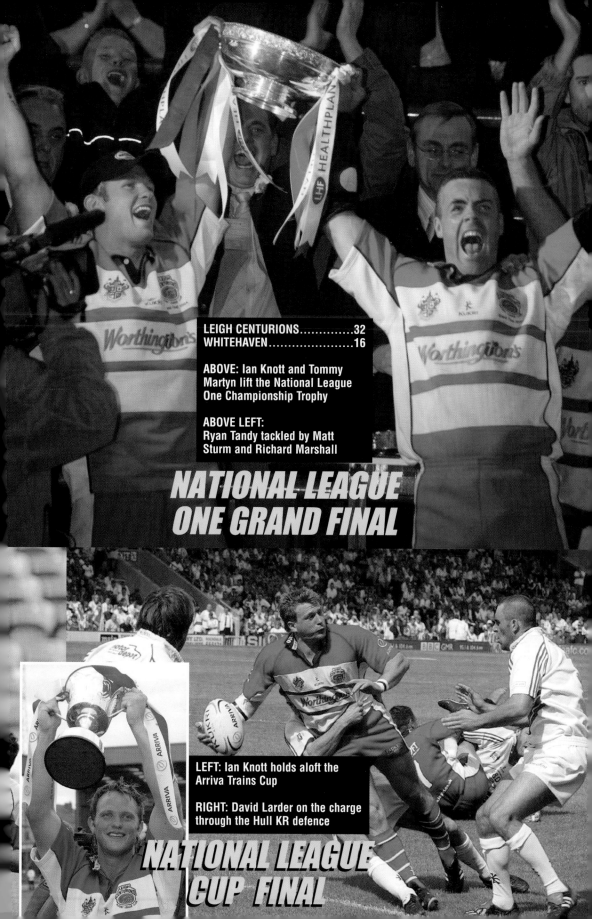

LEIGH CENTURIONS..............32
WHITEHAVEN.....................16

ABOVE: Ian Knott and Tommy Martyn lift the National League One Championship Trophy

ABOVE LEFT:
Ryan Tandy tackled by Matt Sturm and Richard Marshall

NATIONAL LEAGUE ONE GRAND FINAL

LEFT: Ian Knott holds aloft the Arriva Trains Cup

RIGHT: David Larder on the charge through the Hull KR defence

NATIONAL LEAGUE CUP FINAL

Barrow's Darren Holt lifts the National League Two Championship Trophy

Workington's Scott Chilton held up against Hunslet in the play-offs

Alex Smits led London Skolars to a much-improved season

NATIONAL LEAGUE TWO SEASON

ABOVE: Chorley celebrate their thrilling last-day win over York, the Lynx's last game at Victory Park

ABOVE: Swinton's Chris Irwin dumped by York's Chris Langley

ABOVE: Things get physical between Sheffield and Dewsbury

NATIONAL LEAGUE ONE QUALIFYING FINAL

HALIFAX 34
YORK CITY KNIGHTS 30

CLOCKWISE, FROM TOP:
Richard Wilson offloads under pressure from the Halifax defence; Paul Dixon congratulates Anthony Farrell; Halifax celebrate their National League One survival; Simon Friend is distraught as the City Knights are denied promotion

RIGHT: Coventry's four-try hero Kurt Johnson on the charge

BELOW LEFT: Coventry celebrate National League Three Grand Final glory

National League Three Grand Final Winners 2004

NATIONAL LEAGUE THREE GRAND FINAL

BARLA NATIONAL CONFERENCE
ABOVE: Siddal - Arriva Trains
Conference Champions
RIGHT: No way through the West Hull
defence for Siddal's Johnny Lawless

BARLA NATIONAL CUP
LEFT: Paul Davidson looks for a way
through the Oldham St Annes defence
BELOW: Wath Brow and fans celebrate
winning the BARLA National Cup

TOTALRL.COM CONFERENCE
ABOVE: Paea Liku powers forward
against West London Sharks
ABOVE LEFT:
Widnes Saints celebrate their
Harry Jepson Trophy win
LEFT: Cardiff Demons - RLC
Shield Winners

6
STATISTICAL REVIEW

SUPER LEAGUE PLAYERS
1996-2004

PLAYER	CLUB	YEAR	APP	TRIES	GOALS	FG	PTS
Carl Ablett	Leeds	2004	(1)	0	0	0	0
Darren Abram	Oldham	1996-97	25(2)	11	0	0	44
Darren Adams	Paris	1996	9(1)	1	0	0	4
Guy Adams	Huddersfield	1998	1(2)	0	0	0	0
Matt Adamson	Leeds	2002-04	54(8)	9	0	0	36
Phil Adamson	St Helens	1999	(1)	0	0	0	0
Ade Adebisi	London	2004	(1)	0	0	0	0
Jamie Ainscough	Wigan	2002-03	30(2)	18	0	0	72
Glen Air	London	1998-2001	57(13)	27	0	1	109
Darren Albert	St Helens	2002-04	81	52	0	0	208
Paul Alcock	Widnes	2003	1(3)	0	0	0	0
Neil Alexander	Salford	1998	(1)	0	0	0	0
Malcolm Alker	Salford	1997-2002, 2004	145(1)	33	0	1	133
Chris Allen	Castleford	1996	(1)	0	0	0	0
David Allen	Wigan	2003	(1)	0	0	0	0
Gavin Allen	London	1996	10	0	0	0	0
John Allen	Workington	1996	20(1)	6	0	0	24
Ray Allen	London	1996	5(3)	3	0	0	12
Richard Allwood	Gateshead	1999	(4)	0	0	0	0
Sean Allwood	Gateshead	1999	3(17)	1	0	0	4
David Alstead	Warrington	2000-02	23(10)	3	0	0	12
Asa Amone	Halifax	1996-97	32(7)	10	0	0	40
Grant Anderson	Castleford	1996-97	15(6)	3	0	0	12
Paul Anderson	Bradford	1997-2004	74(104)	30	0	0	120
	Halifax	1996	5(1)	1	0	0	4
Paul Anderson	Sheffield	1999	3(7)	1	0	0	4
	St Helens	1996-98	2(28)	4	1	0	18
Phil Anderton	St Helens	2004	1	0	0	0	0
Eric Anselme	Halifax	1997	(2)	0	0	0	0
Mark Applegarth	Wakefield	2004	12(1)	1	0	0	4
Graham Appo	Warrington	2002-04	51(5)	30	72	0	264
	Huddersfield	2001	7	4	0	0	16
Colin Armstrong	Workington	1996	11(2)	1	0	0	4
Richard Armswood							
	Workington	1996	5(1)	1	0	0	4
Danny Arnold	Salford	2001-02	26(13)	13	0	0	52
	Huddersfield	1998-2000	55(7)	26	0	0	104
	Castleford	2000	(4)	0	0	0	0
	St Helens	1996-97	40(1)	33	0	0	132
Martin Aspinwall	Wigan	2001-04	59(12)	22	0	0	88
Mark Aston	Sheffield	1996-99	67(6)	6	243	6	516
Paul Atcheson	Widnes	2002-04	16(35)	4	0	0	16
	St Helens	1998-2000	58(4)	18	0	0	72
	Oldham	1996-97	40	21	0	0	84
David Atkins	Huddersfield	2001	26(1)	4	0	0	16
Brad Attwood	Halifax	2003	(3)	0	0	0	0
Warren Ayres	Salford	1999	2(9)	1	2	0	8
Jerome Azema	Paris	1997	(1)	0	0	0	0
Marcus Bai	Leeds	2004	29	26	0	0	104
David Baildon	Hull	1998-99	26(2)	4	0	0	16
Andy Bailey	Hull	2004	2(7)	1	0	0	4
Julian Bailey	Huddersfield	2003-04	47	13	0	0	52
Ryan Bailey	Leeds	2002-04	36(19)	1	0	0	4
Simon Baldwin	Salford	2004	8(13)	1	0	0	4
	Sheffield	1999	7(15)	2	0	0	8
	Halifax	1996-98	41(15)	16	0	1	65
Rob Ball	Wigan	1998-2000	3(4)	0	0	0	0
Michael Banks	Bradford	1998	(1)	0	0	0	0
Frederic Banquet	Paris	1996	16(2)	7	4	0	36
Lee Bardauskas	Castleford	1996-97	(2)	0	0	0	0
Craig Barker	Workington	1996	(2)	0	0	0	0
Dwayne Barker	London	2004	3	1	0	0	4
	Hull	2003	(1)	0	0	0	0
Mark Barlow	Wakefield	2002	(1)	0	0	0	0
Danny Barnes	Halifax	1999	2	0	0	0	0
Richie Barnett	Hull	2003-04	31(1)	17	0	0	68
	London	2001-02 *	31(4)	13	0	0	52
Richie Barnett Jnr	Hull	2004	15(5)	14	0	0	56
David Barnhill	Leeds	2000	20(8)	5	0	0	20
Paul Barrow	Warrington	1996-97	1(10)	1	0	0	4
Scott Barrow	St Helens	1997-2000	9(13)	1	0	0	4
Steve Barrow	London	2000	2	0	0	0	0
	Hull	1998-99	4(17)	1	0	0	4
	Wigan	1996	(8)	3	0	0	12
Ben Barton	Huddersfield	1998	1(6)	1	0	0	4
Danny Barton	Salford	2001	1	0	0	0	0
Wayne Bartrim	Castleford	2002-03	41(2)	9	157	0	350
Greg Barwick	London	1996-97	30(4)	21	110	2	306
David Bastian	Halifax	1996	(2)	0	0	0	0
David Bates	Castleford	2001-02	(4)	0	0	0	0
	Warrington	2001	1(2)	0	0	0	0
Nathan Batty	Wakefield	2001	1(1)	0	0	0	0
Russell Bawden	London	1996-97, 2002-04	50(49)	15	0	0	60
Neil Baxter	Salford	2001	1	0	0	0	0
Neil Baynes	Salford	1999-2002, 2004	84(19)	10	0	0	40
	Wigan	1996-98	(10)	1	0	0	4
Robbie Beazley	London	1997-99	48(15)	13	0	0	52
Robbie Beckett	Halifax	2002	27	15	0	0	60
Dean Bell	Leeds	1996	1	1	0	0	4
Ian Bell	Hull	2003	(1)	0	0	0	0
Mark Bell	Wigan	1998	22	12	0	0	48
Paul Bell	Leeds	2000	1	0	0	0	0
Troy Bellamy	Paris	1997	5(10)	0	0	0	0
Adrian Belle	Huddersfield	1998	10(2)	0	0	0	0
	Oldham	1996	19	8	0	0	32
Jamie Benn	Castleford	1998, 2000	3(8)	1	15	0	34
Andy Bennett	Warrington	1996	6(5)	1	0	0	4
Mike Bennett	St Helens	2000-04	32(40)	5	0	0	20
John Bentley	Huddersfield	1999	13(4)	3	0	0	12
	Halifax	1996, 1998	22(3)	24	0	0	96
Phil Bergman	Paris	1997	20(1)	14	0	0	56
Joe Berry	Huddersfield	1998-99	25(14)	3	0	0	12
Colin Best	Hull	2003-04	57	34	0	0	136
Roger Best	London	1997-98	15(5)	1	0	0	4
Bob Beswick	Wigan	2004	(6)	0	0	0	0
Mike Bethwaite	Workington	1996	17(3)	1	0	0	4
Denis Betts	Wigan	1998-2001	82(24)	33	0	0	132
Cliff Beverley	Salford	2004	21(1)	10	0	0	40
Adam Bibey	Widnes	2004	(1)	0	0	0	0
Ricky Bibey	St Helens	2004	4(14)	0	0	0	0
	Wigan	2001-03	5(29)	0	0	0	0
Chris Birchall	Halifax	2002-03	24(22)	4	0	0	16
	Bradford	2000	(1)	0	0	0	0
Deon Bird	Widnes	2003-04	39(6)	9	0	0	36
	Wakefield	2002	10(1)	1	0	0	4
	Hull	2000-02	37(22)	20	0	0	80
	Gateshead	1999	19(3)	13	0	0	52
	Paris	1996-97	30	12	2	0	52
Richie Blackmore	Leeds	1997-2000	63	25	0	0	100
Matthew Blake	Wakefield	2003-04	1(5)	0	0	0	0
Steve Blakeley	Salford	1997-2002	103(5)	26	241	2	588
	Warrington	2000	4(3)	1	9	0	22
Richard Blakeway	Castleford	2002-04	1(14)	0	0	0	0
Ian Blease	Salford	1997	(1)	0	0	0	0
Jamie Bloem	Huddersfield	2003	18(4)	3	11	0	34
	Halifax	1998-2002	82(25)	25	100	2	302
Vea Bloomfield	Paris	1996	4(14)	3	0	0	12
Pascal Bomati	Paris	1996	17(1)	10	0	0	40
Simon Booth	Hull	1998-99	15(9)	2	0	0	8
	St Helens	1996-97	10(4)	1	0	0	4
Steve Booth	Huddersfield	1998-99	16(4)	2	3	0	14
Alan Boothroyd	Halifax	1997	2(3)	0	0	0	0
John Boslem	Paris	1996	(5)	0	0	0	0
Liam Bostock	St Helens	2004	1	0	0	0	0
Liam Botham	London	2004	6(2)	3	6	0	24
	Leeds	2003-04	1(1)	0	0	0	0
Frano Botica	Castleford	1996	21	5	84	2	190
Hadj Boudebza	Paris	1996	(2)	0	0	0	0
David Boughton	Huddersfield	1999	26(1)	4	0	0	16
David Bouveng	Halifax	1997-99	66(2)	19	0	0	76
Tony Bowes	Huddersfield	1998	3(2)	0	0	0	0
Radney Bowker	London	2004	3	1	0	0	4
	St Helens	2001	(1)	0	0	0	0
David Boyle	Bradford	1999-2000	36(13)	15	0	1	61
Andy Bracek	St Helens	2004	(1)	0	0	0	0
David Bradbury	Hudds-Sheff	2000	21(2)	1	0	0	4
	Salford	1997-99	23(10)	6	0	0	24
	Oldham	1996-97	19(6)	9	0	0	36
John Braddish	St Helens	2001-02	1(1)	0	3	0	6
Graeme Bradley	Bradford	1996-98	62(1)	29	0	0	116
Darren Bradstreet	London	1999-2000	1(3)	0	0	0	0
Dominic Brambani	Castleford	2004	2(2)	0	0	0	0
Liam Bretherton	Wigan	1999	(5)	2	0	0	8
	Warrington	1997	(2)	0	0	0	0
Johnny Brewer	Halifax	1996	4(2)	2	0	0	8

194

PLAYER	CLUB	YEAR	APP	TRIES	GOALS	FG	PTS
Chris Bridge	Bradford	2003-04	2(14)	4	6	0	28
Lee Briers	Warrington	1997-2004	167(11)	54	494	39	1243
	St Helens	1997	3	0	11	0	22
Carl Briggs	Salford	1999	8(5)	3	0	1	13
	Halifax	1996	5(3)	1	0	0	4
Mike Briggs	Widnes	2002	1(2)	1	0	0	4
Shaun Briscoe	Hull	2004	29	22	0	0	88
	Wigan	2002-03	23(5)	11	0	0	44
Darren Britt	St Helens	2002-03	41	3	0	0	12
Gary Broadbent	Salford	1997-2002	117(2)	22	0	0	88
Paul Broadbent	Wakefield	2002	16(5)	0	0	0	0
	Hull	2000-01	40(9)	3	0	0	12
	Halifax	1999	26(1)	2	0	0	8
	Sheffield	1996-98	63(1)	6	0	0	24
Andrew Brocklehurst							
	Salford	2004	1(4)	0	0	0	0
	London	2004	12(6)	2	0	0	8
	Halifax	2001-03	37(8)	2	0	0	8
Justin Brooker	Wakefield	2001	25	9	0	0	36
	Bradford	2000	17(4)	11	0	0	44
Darren Brown	Salford	1999-2001	47(9)	11	6	0	56
Gavin Brown	Leeds	1996-97	5(2)	1	2	0	8
Kevin Brown	Wigan	2003-04	18(11)	14	0	0	56
Lee Brown	Hull	1999	(1)	0	0	0	0
Michael Brown	London	1996	(2)	0	0	0	0
Todd Brown	Paris	1996	8(1)	2	0	0	8
Adrian Brunker	Wakefield	1999	17	6	0	0	24
Justin Bryant	Paris	1996	4(1)	0	0	0	0
	London	1996	7(8)	1	0	0	4
Austin Buchanan	London	2003	3(1)	2	0	0	8
Neil Budworth	London	2002-04	56(10)	4	1	0	18
James Bunyan	Huddersfield	1998-99	8(7)	2	0	0	8
Andy Burgess	Salford	1997	3(12)	0	0	0	0
Darren Burns	Warrington	2002-04	66(6)	19	0	0	76
Gary Burns	Oldham	1996	6	1	0	0	4
Paul Burns	Workington	1996	5(2)	1	0	0	4
Rob Burrow	Leeds	2001-04	40(62)	38	35	1	223
Dean Busby	Warrington	1999-2002	34(34)	7	0	0	28
	Hull	1998	8(6)	0	0	0	0
	St Helens	1996-98	1(7)	0	0	0	0
Ikram Butt	London	1996	5(1)	0	0	0	0
Shane Byrne	Huddersfield	1998-99	1(5)	0	0	0	0
Didier Cabestany	Paris	1996-97	20(6)	2	0	0	8
Joel Caine	Salford	2004	24	8	13	0	58
	London	2003	6	4	1	0	18
Mark Calderwood	Leeds	2001-04	88(9)	61	0	0	244
Mike Callan	Warrington	2002	(4)	0	0	0	0
Matt Calland	Huddersfield	2003	2	0	0	0	0
	Hull	1999	1	0	0	0	0
	Bradford	1996-98	44(5)	24	0	0	96
Dean Callaway	London	1999-2000	26(24)	12	0	0	48
Laurent Cambres	Paris	1996	(1)	0	0	0	0
Chris Campbell	Warrington	2000	7(1)	2	0	0	8
Logan Campbell	Hull	1998-99, 2001	70(13)	14	0	0	56
	Castleford	2000	14(2)	3	0	0	12
	Workington	1996	7(1)	1	0	0	4
Blake Cannova	Widnes	2002	(1)	0	0	0	0
Phil Cantillon	Widnes	2002-03	27(21)	18	0	0	72
	Leeds	1997	(1)	0	0	0	0
Daryl Cardiss	Warrington	2003-04	23(2)	3	4	0	20
	Halifax	1999-2003	91(8)	39	4	0	164
	Wigan	1996-98	12(6)	4	0	0	16
Dale Cardoza	Warrington	2002	5	1	0	0	4
	Halifax	2001	3	1	0	0	4
	Huddersfield	2000-01	20(9)	11	0	0	44
	Sheffield	1998-99	11(7)	3	0	0	12
Paul Carige	Salford	1999	24(1)	7	0	0	28
Jim Carlton	Huddersfield	1999	3(11)	2	0	0	8
Brian Carney	Wigan	2001-04	76(10)	37	0	0	148
	Hull	2000	13(3)	7	0	0	28
	Gateshead	1999	3(2)	2	0	0	8
Martin Carney	Warrington	1997	(1)	0	0	0	0
Paul Carr	Sheffield	1996-98	45(5)	15	0	0	60
Bernard Carroll	London	1996	2(1)	1	0	0	4
Mark Carroll	London	1998	15(3)	1	0	0	4
Tonie Carroll	Leeds	2001-02	42(2)	30	0	0	120
Darren Carter	Workington	1996	10(3)	0	1	0	2
Steve Carter	Widnes	2002	14(7)	4	0	0	16
John Cartwright	Salford	1997	9	0	0	0	0
Garreth Carvell	Hull	2001-04	19(56)	12	0	0	48
	Leeds	1997-2000	(4)	0	0	0	0
	Gateshead	1999	4(4)	1	0	0	4
Garen Casey	Salford	1999	13(5)	3	23	0	58
Mick Cassidy	Wigan	1996-2004	184(36)	30	0	0	120
Chris Causey	Warrington	1997-99	(18)	1	0	0	4
Arnaud Cervello	Paris	1996	4	4	0	0	16
Gary Chambers	Warrington	1996-2000	65(28)	2	0	0	8
Pierre Chamorin	Paris	1996-97	27(3)	8	3	0	38
Chris Chapman	Leeds	1999	(1)	0	0	0	0
Damien Chapman	London	1998	6(2)	3	4	1	21
David Chapman	Castleford	1996-98	24(6)	8	0	0	32
Jaymes Chapman	Halifax	2002-03	5(8)	1	0	0	4
Richard Chapman	Sheffield	1996	1	2	0	0	8
Chris Charles	Salford	2004	24(3)	3	68	0	148
	Castleford	2001	1(4)	1	0	0	4
Andy Cheetham	Huddersfield	1998-99	30	11	0	0	44
Kris Chesney	London	1998	1(2)	0	0	0	0
Chris Chester	Hull	2002-04	45(12)	8	0	0	32
	Wigan	1999-2001	21(22)	8	5	0	20
	Halifax	1996-99	47(14)	16	15	1	95
Lee Chilton	Workington	1996	10(3)	6	0	0	24
Gary Christie	Bradford	1996-97	4(7)	1	0	0	4
Dean Clark	Leeds	1996	11(2)	3	0	0	12
Des Clark	St Helens	1999	4	0	0	0	0
	Halifax	1998-99	35(13)	6	0	0	24
Greg Clarke	Halifax	1997	1(1)	0	0	0	0
John Clarke	Oldham	1996-97	27(4)	5	0	0	20
Jon Clarke	Warrington	2001-04	97(2)	17	1	0	70
	London	2000-01	19(11)	2	0	0	8
	Wigan	1997-99	13(10)	3	0	0	12
Ryan Clayton	Castleford	2004	11(6)	3	0	0	12
	Halifax	2000, 2002-03	28(12)	6	0	0	24
Gavin Clinch	Salford	2004	21(1)	1	0	1	5
	Halifax	1998-99, 2001-02	88(2)	26	45	5	199
	Hudds-Sheff	2000	18(2)	5	0	1	21
	Wigan	1999	10(2)	4	12	0	40
John Clough	Salford	2004	(1)	0	0	0	0
Bradley Clyde	Leeds	2001	7(5)	1	0	0	4
Evan Cochrane	London	1996	5(1)	1	0	0	4
Liam Colbon	Wigan	2004	1(3)	0	0	0	0
Anthony Colella	Huddersfield	2003	5(1)	2	0	0	8
Andy Coley	Salford	2001-02, 2004	44(25)	13	0	0	52
Richard Colley	Bradford	2004	1	0	0	0	0
Steve Collins	Hull	2000	28	17	0	0	68
	Gateshead	1999	20(4)	13	0	0	52
Wayne Collins	Leeds	1997	21	3	0	0	12
Gary Connolly	Wigan	1996-2002, 2004	168(10)	70	5	0	290
	Leeds	2003-04	27	6	0	0	24
Mick Cook	Sheffield	1996	9(10)	2	0	0	8
Paul Cook	Huddersfield	1998-99	11(6)	2	13	0	34
	Bradford	1996-97	14(8)	7	38	1	105
Peter Cook	St Helens	2004	(1)	0	0	0	0
Paul Cooke	Hull	1999-2004	116(27)	23	171	1	435
Ben Cooper	Huddersfield	2000-01, 2003-04	28(12)	3	0	0	12
Ged Corcoran	Halifax	2003	1(11)	0	0	0	0
Wayne Corcoran	Halifax	2003	4(2)	0	0	0	0
Mark Corvo	Salford	2002	7(5)	0	0	0	0
Brandon Costin	Huddersfield	2001, 2003-04	69	42	93	3	357
	Bradford	2002	20(1)	8	0	0	32
Wes Cotton	London	1997-98	12	3	0	0	12
Phil Coussons	Salford	1997	7(2)	3	0	0	12
Alex Couttet	Paris	1997	1	0	0	0	0
Nick Couttet	Paris	1997	1	0	0	0	0
Jamie Coventry	Castleford	1996	1	0	0	0	0
Jimmy Cowan	Oldham	1996-97	2(8)	0	0	0	0
Will Cowell	Warrington	1998-2000	6(8)	1	0	0	4
Neil Cowie	Wigan	1996-2001	116(27)	10	0	1	41
Mark Cox	London	2003	(3)	0	0	0	0
Eorl Crabtree	Huddersfield	2001, 2003-04	11(28)	2	0	0	8
Andy Craig	Halifax	1999	13(7)	1	3	0	10
	Wigan	1996	5(5)	2	0	0	8
Scott Cram	London	1999-2002	65(7)	4	0	0	16
Steve Craven	Hull	1998-2003	53(42)	4	0	0	16
Nicky Crellin	Workington	1996	(2)	0	0	0	0
Jason Critchley	Wakefield	2000	7(1)	4	0	0	16
	Castleford	1997-98	27(3)	11	0	0	44
Martin Crompton	Salford	1998-2000	30(6)	11	6	2	58
	Oldham	1996-97	36(1)	16	0	3	67
Paul Crook	Oldham	1996	4(9)	0	3	0	6
Lee Crooks	Castleford	1996-97	27(2)	2	14	0	36
Alan Cross	St Helens	1997	(2)	0	0	0	0
Steve Crouch	Castleford	2004	4(1)	2	0	0	8
Kevin Crouthers	Warrington	2001-03	12(1)	4	0	0	16
	London	2000	6(4)	1	0	0	4
	Wakefield	1999	4(1)	1	0	0	4
	Bradford	1997-98	3(9)	2	0	0	8
Matt Crowther	Hull	2001-03	48	20	166	0	412
	Hudds-Sheff	2000	10(4)	5	22	0	64
	Sheffield	1996-99	43(4)	22	10	0	108
Heath Cruckshank	Halifax	2003	19(1)	0	0	0	0
	St Helens	2001	1(12)	0	0	0	0
Paul Cullen	Warrington	1996	19	3	0	0	12
Francis Cummins	Leeds	1996-2004	217(10)	120	26	2	534
Keiron Cunningham							
	St Helens	1996-2004	214(5)	98	0	0	392
Andy Currier	Warrington	1996-97	(2)	1	0	0	4
Joe Dakuitoga	Sheffield	1996	6(3)	0	0	0	0
Brett Dallas	Wigan	2000-04	110	68	0	0	272
Paul Darbyshire	Warrington	1997	(6)	0	0	0	0
Maea David	Hull	1998	1	0	0	0	0
Paul Davidson	Halifax	2001-03	22(30)	10	0	0	40
	London	2000	6(10)	4	0	0	16
	St Helens	1998-99	27(16)	7	0	0	28
	Oldham	1996-97	17(18)	14	0	1	57
Gareth Davies	Warrington	1996-97	1(6)	0	0	0	0
Wes Davies	Wigan	1998-2001	22(22)	11	0	0	44
Brad Davis	Castleford	1997-2000, 2004	96	29	41	10	208
	Wakefield	2001-03	51(12)	15	22	5	109
	Hull	2000	17(1)	7	0	0	28
	Gateshead	1999	30	25	0	0	100
Paul Deacon	Bradford	1998-2004	136(43)	42	492	14	1166
	Oldham	1997	(2)	0	0	0	0
Craig Dean	Halifax	1996-97	25(11)	12	1	1	51
Gareth Dean	London	2002	(4)	0	0	0	0
Yacine Dekkiche	Hudds-Sheff	2000	11(3)	3	0	0	12
Jason Demetriou	Wakefield	2004	29(1)	13	2	0	56
	Widnes	2002-03	47(1)	15	1	0	62
Martin Dermott	Warrington	1997	1	0	0	0	0

Super League Players 1996-2004

PLAYER	CLUB	YEAR	APP	TRIES	GOALS	FG	PTS
David Despin	Paris	1996	(1)	0	0	0	0
Fabien Devecchi	Paris	1996-97	17(10)	2	0	0	8
Paul Devlin	Widnes	2002-04	32	16	0	0	64
Matt Diskin	Leeds	2001-04	88(10)	20	0	0	80
Kirk Dixon	Hull	2004	(1)	0	0	0	0
Paul Dixon	Sheffield	1996-97	5(9)	1	0	0	4
Gareth Dobson	Castleford	1998-2000	(10)	0	0	0	0
Michael Docherty	Hull	2000-01	(6)	0	0	0	0
Sid Domic	Wakefield	2004	30	22	0	0	88
	Warrington	2002-03	41(4)	17	0	0	68
Glen Donkin	Hull	2002-03	(10)	1	0	0	4
Stuart Donlan	Huddersfield	2004	24(2)	2	0	0	8
	Halifax	2001-03	65(2)	22	0	0	88
Jason Donohue	Bradford	1996	(4)	0	0	0	0
Jeremy Donougher	Bradford	1996-99	40(21)	13	0	0	52
Justin Dooley	London	2000-01	37(18)	2	0	0	8
Dane Dorahy	Halifax	2003	20	7	45	0	118
	Wakefield	2000-01	16(2)	4	19	1	55
Ewan Dowes	Hull	2003-04	30(16)	6	0	0	24
	Leeds	2001-03	1(9)	0	0	0	0
Adam Doyle	Warrington	1998	9(3)	4	0	0	16
Rod Doyle	Sheffield	1997-99	52(10)	10	0	0	40
Damien Driscoll	Salford	2001	23(1)	1	0	0	4
John Duffy	Salford	2000	3(11)	0	1	1	3
	Warrington	1997-99	12(12)	2	0	0	8
Andrew Duncan	London	1997	2(4)	2	0	0	8
	Warrington	1997	(1)	0	0	0	0
Andrew Dunemann	Leeds	2003-04	49(2)	8	0	2	34
	Halifax	1999-2002	68	19	0	1	77
Matt Dunford	London	1997-98	18(20)	3	0	1	13
Jamie Durbin	Warrington	2003	(1)	0	0	0	0
James Durkin	Paris	1997	(5)	0	0	0	0
Bernard Dwyer	Bradford	1996-2000	65(10)	14	0	0	56
Jim Dymock	London	2001-04	94(1)	15	0	1	61
Leo Dynevor	London	1996	8(11)	5	7	0	34
Jason Eade	Paris	1997	9	4	0	0	16
Michael Eagar	Hull	2004	6	2	0	0	8
	Castleford	1999-2003	130(2)	60	0	0	240
	Warrington	1998	21	6	0	0	24
Barry Eaton	Widnes	2002	25	2	49	4	110
	Castleford	2000	1(4)	0	3	0	6
Greg Ebrill	Salford	2002	15(6)	1	0	0	4
Cliff Eccles	Salford	1997-98	30(5)	1	0	0	4
Chris Eckersley	Warrington	1996	1	0	0	0	0
Steve Edmed	Sheffield	1997	15(1)	0	0	0	0
Mark Edmondson	St Helens	1999-2004	26(59)	6	0	0	24
Diccon Edwards	Castleford	1996-97	10(5)	1	0	0	4
Peter Edwards	Salford	1997-98	35(2)	4	0	0	16
Shaun Edwards	London	1997-2000	32(8)	16	1	0	66
	Bradford	1998	8(2)	4	0	0	16
	Wigan	1996	17(3)	12	1	0	50
Danny Ekis	Halifax	2001	(1)	0	0	0	0
Abi Ekoku	Bradford	1997-98	21(4)	6	0	0	24
	Halifax	1996	15(1)	5	0	0	20
Olivier Elima	Wakefield	2003-04	4(22)	3	0	0	12
	Castleford	2002	(1)	1	0	0	4
Abderazak Elkhalouki	Paris	1997	(1)	0	0	0	0
Gareth Ellis	Wakefield	1999-2004	86(17)	21	0	2	88
Danny Ellison	Castleford	1998-99	7(16)	6	0	0	24
	Wigan	1996-97	15(1)	13	0	0	52
Patrick Entat	Paris	1996	22	2	0	0	8
Jason Erba	Sheffield	1997	1(4)	0	0	0	0
James Evans	Huddersfield	2004	17	10	0	0	40
Paul Evans	Paris	1997	18	8	0	0	32
Wayne Evans	London	2002	11(6)	2	0	0	8
Richie Eyres	Warrington	1997	2(5)	0	0	0	0
	Sheffield	1997	2(3)	0	0	0	0
Henry Fa'afili	Warrington	2004	7	4	0	0	16
Sala Fa'alogo	Widnes	2004	(3)	1	0	0	4
Maurie Fa'asavalu	St Helens	2004	3(13)	2	0	0	8
Bolouagi Fagborun	Huddersfield	2004	2(1)	0	0	0	0
Esene Faimalo	Salford	1997-99	23(25)	2	0	0	8
	Leeds	1996	3(3)	0	0	0	0
Joe Faimalo	Salford	1998-2000	23(47)	7	0	0	28
	Oldham	1996-97	37(5)	7	0	0	28
Karl Fairbank	Bradford	1996	17(2)	4	0	0	16
David Fairleigh	St Helens	2001	26(1)	8	0	0	32
Jim Fallon	Leeds	1996	10	5	0	0	20
Danny Farrar	Warrington	1998-2000	76	13	0	0	52
Andy Farrell	Wigan	1996-2004	230	77	1026	16	2376
Anthony Farrell	Widnes	2002-03	24(22)	4	1	0	18
	Leeds	1997-2001	99(23)	18	0	0	72
	Sheffield	1996	14(5)	5	0	0	20
Craig Farrell	Hull	2000-01	1(3)	0	0	0	0
Abraham Fatnowna	London	1997-98	7(2)	2	0	0	8
	Workington	1996	5	2	0	0	8
Vince Fawcett	Wakefield	1999	13(1)	2	0	0	8
	Warrington	1998	4(7)	1	0	0	4
	Oldham	1997	5	3	0	0	12
Danny Fearon	Huddersfield	2001	(1)	0	0	0	0
	Halifax	1999-2000	5(6)	0	0	0	0
Chris Feather	Wakefield	2001-02, 2004	20(21)	8	0	0	32
	Leeds	2003-04	10(29)	5	0	0	20
Dom Feaunati	St Helens	2004	10(7)	7	0	0	28
Luke Felsch	Hull	2000-01	46(6)	7	0	0	28
	Gateshead	1999	28(1)	2	0	0	8
Leon Felton	Warrington	2002	4(2)	0	0	0	0
	St Helens	2001	1(1)	0	0	0	0
Jamie Field	Wakefield	1999-2004	108(44)	14	0	0	56
	Huddersfield	1998	15(5)	0	0	0	0
	Leeds	1996-97	3(11)	0	0	0	0
Mark Field	Wakefield	2003-04	10(4)	2	0	0	8
Jamie Fielden	London	2003	(1)	0	0	0	0
	Huddersfield	1998-2000	4(8)	0	0	0	0
Stuart Fielden	Bradford	1998-2004	93(78)	29	0	0	116
Lafaele Filipo	Workington	1996	15(4)	3	0	0	12
Salesi Finau	Warrington	1996-97	16(15)	8	0	0	32
Liam Finn	Wakefield	2004	1(1)	0	1	0	2
	Halifax	2002-03	16(5)	2	30	1	69
Lee Finnerty	Halifax	2003	18(2)	5	2	0	24
Phil Finney	Warrington	1998	1	0	0	0	0
Simon Finnigan	Widnes	2003-04	29(15)	9	0	0	36
Matt Firth	Halifax	2000-01	12(2)	0	0	0	0
Andy Fisher	Wakefield	1999-2000	31(8)	4	0	0	16
Karl Fitzpatrick	Salford	2004	16(9)	4	2	0	20
Darren Fleary	Huddersfield	2003-04	43(8)	4	0	0	16
	Leeds	1997-2002	98(9)	3	0	0	12
Greg Fleming	London	1999-2001	64(1)	40	2	0	164
Richard Fletcher	Hull	1999-2004	11(56)	5	0	0	20
Greg Florimo	Halifax	2000	26	6	4	0	32
	Wigan	1999	18(2)	7	1	0	30
Jason Flowers	Salford	2004	6(1)	0	0	0	0
	Halifax	2002	24(4)	4	0	0	16
	Castleford	1996-2001	119(19)	33	0	1	133
Stuart Flowers	Castleford	1996	(3)	0	0	0	0
Adrian Flynn	Castleford	1996-97	19(2)	10	0	0	40
Wayne Flynn	Sheffield	1997	3(5)	0	0	0	0
Adam Fogerty	Warrington	1998	4	0	0	0	0
	St Helens	1996	13	1	0	0	4
Carl Forber	St Helens	2004	1(1)	0	6	0	12
Paul Forber	Salford	1997-98	19(12)	4	0	0	16
Mike Ford	Castleford	1997-98	25(12)	5	0	3	23
	Warrington	1996	3	0	0	0	0
Jim Forshaw	Salford	1999	(1)	0	0	0	0
Mike Forshaw	Warrington	2004	20(1)	5	0	0	20
	Bradford	1997-2003	162(7)	32	0	0	128
	Leeds	1996	11(3)	5	0	0	20
Mark Forster	Warrington	1996-2000	102(1)	40	0	0	160
David Foster	Halifax	2000-01	4(9)	0	0	0	0
Nick Fozzard	St Helens	2004	24(1)	2	0	0	8
	Warrington	2002-03	43(11)	2	0	0	8
	Huddersfield	1998-2000	24(8)	2	0	0	8
	Leeds	1996-97	6(16)	3	0	0	12
David Fraisse	Workington	1996	8	0	0	0	0
Daniel Frame	Widnes	2002-04	75(4)	19	0	0	76
Andrew Frew	Halifax	2003	17	5	0	0	20
	Wakefield	2002	21	8	0	0	32
	Huddersfield	2001	26	15	0	0	60
Dale Fritz	Castleford	1999-2003	120(4)	9	0	0	36
David Furner	Leeds	2003-04	45	8	23	0	78
	Wigan	2001-02	51(2)	21	13	0	110
David Furness	Castleford	1996	(1)	0	0	0	0
Tommy Gallagher	Widnes	2004	(6)	0	0	0	0
	London	2003	1(9)	1	0	0	4
Mark Gamson	Sheffield	1996	3	0	0	0	0
Jim Gannon	Huddersfield	2003-04	44(8)	7	0	0	28
	Halifax	1999-2002	83(4)	14	0	0	56
Steve Garces	Salford	2001	(1)	0	0	0	0
Jean-Marc Garcia	Sheffield	1996-97	35(3)	22	0	0	88
Ade Gardner	St Helens	2002-04	48(11)	23	0	0	92
Matt Gardner	Castleford	2004	1	1	0	0	4
Steve Gartland	Oldham	1996	1(1)	0	1	0	2
Daniel Gartner	Bradford	2001-03	74(1)	26	0	0	104
Dean Gaskell	Warrington	2002-04	44	9	0	0	36
Richard Gay	Castleford	1996-2002	94(16)	39	0	0	156
Andrew Gee	Warrington	2000-01	33(1)	4	0	0	16
Stanley Gene	Huddersfield	2001, 2003-04	52(4)	21	0	0	84
	Hull	2000-01	5(23)	6	0	0	24
Steve Georgallis	Warrington	2001	5(1)	2	0	0	8
Shaun Geritas	Warrington	1997	(5)	1	0	0	4
Anthony Gibbons	Leeds	1996	9(4)	2	0	1	9
David Gibbons	Leeds	1996	3(4)	2	0	0	8
Scott Gibbs	St Helens	1996	9	3	0	0	12
Damian Gibson	Castleford	2003-04	40(3)	5	0	0	20
	Salford	2002	28	3	0	0	12
	Halifax	1998-2001	104(1)	39	0	0	156
	Leeds	1997	18	3	0	0	12
Ian Gildart	Oldham	1996-97	31(7)	0	0	0	0
Chris Giles	Widnes	2003-04	35	12	0	0	48
	St Helens	2002	(1)	0	0	0	0
Peter Gill	London	1996-99	75(6)	20	0	0	80
Carl Gillespie	Halifax	1996-99	47(36)	13	0	0	52
Michael Gillett	London	2001-02	23(21)	12	2	0	52
Simon Gillies	Warrington	1999	28	6	0	0	24
Lee Gilmour	St Helens	2004	25	9	0	0	36
	Bradford	2001-03	44(31)	20	0	0	80
	Wigan	1997-2000	44(39)	22	0	0	88
Marc Glanville	Leeds	1998-99	43(3)	5	0	0	20
Eddie Glaze	Castleford	1996	1	0	0	0	0
Paul Gleadhill	Leeds	1996	4	0	0	0	0
Mark Gleeson	Warrington	2000-04	7(43)	8	0	0	32
Martin Gleeson	St Helens	2002-04	56(1)	25	0	0	100
	Huddersfield	1999-2001	47(9)	18	0	0	72
Jonathan Goddard	Castleford	2000-01	(2)	0	0	0	0
Richard Goddard	Castleford	1996-97	11(3)	2	10	0	28
Brad Godden	Leeds	1998-99	47	15	0	0	60
Wayne Godwin	Castleford	2001-04	30(33)	18	56	0	184
Marvin Golden	Widnes	2003	4	1	0	0	4
	London	2001	17(2)	1	0	0	4
	Halifax	2000	20(2)	5	0	0	20
	Leeds	1996-99	43(11)	19	0	0	76
Brett Goldspink	Halifax	2000-02	64(5)	2	0	0	8
	Wigan	1999	6(16)	1	0	0	4
	St Helens	1998	19(4)	2	0	0	8
	Oldham	1997	13(2)	0	0	0	0

PLAYER	CLUB	YEAR	APP	TRIES	GOALS	FG	PTS
Luke Goodwin	London	1998	9(2)	3	1	1	15
	Oldham	1997	16(4)	10	17	2	76
Andy Gorski	Salford	2001-02	(2)	0	0	0	0
Bobbie Goulding	Salford	2001-02	31(1)	2	56	4	124
	Wakefield	2000	12	3	25	3	65
	Huddersfield	1998-99	27(1)	3	65	4	146
	St Helens	1996-98	42(2)	9	210	4	460
James Graham	St Helens	2003-04	1(7)	0	0	0	0
Nathan Graham	Bradford	1996-98	17(28)	4	0	1	17
Nick Graham	Wigan	2003	13(1)	2	0	0	8
Jon Grayshon	Huddersfield	2003-04	3(22)	1	0	0	4
Brett Green	Gateshead	1999	10(2)	0	0	0	0
Toby Green	Huddersfield	2001	3(1)	1	0	0	4
Craig Greenhill	Castleford	2004	21(4)	1	0	0	4
	Hull	2002-03	56	3	2	0	16
Brandon Greenwood							
	Halifax	1996	1	0	0	0	0
Gareth Greenwood	Huddersfield	2003	(1)	0	0	0	0
	Halifax	2002	1	0	0	0	0
Lee Greenwood	London	2004	25(1)	17	0	0	68
	Halifax	2000-03	38(2)	17	0	0	68
	Sheffield	1999	1(1)	0	0	0	0
Darrell Griffin	Wakefield	2003-04	27(14)	3	1	0	14
Jonathan Griffiths	Paris	1996	(4)	1	0	0	4
Andrew Grima	Workington	1996	2(9)	2	0	0	8
Tony Grimaldi	Hull	2000-01	56(1)	14	0	0	56
	Gateshead	1999	27(2)	10	0	0	40
Danny Grimley	Sheffield	1996	4(1)	1	0	0	4
Simon Grix	Halifax	2003	2(4)	0	0	0	0
Brett Grogan	Gateshead	1999	14(7)	3	0	0	12
Brent Grose	Warrington	2003-04	54	29	0	0	116
Jerome Guisset	Warrington	2000-04	59(65)	21	0	0	84
Reece Guy	Oldham	1996	3(4)	0	0	0	0
Gareth Haggerty	Salford	2004	1(24)	3	0	0	12
	Widnes	2002	1(2)	1	0	0	4
Andy Haigh	St Helens	1996-98	20(16)	11	0	0	44
Carl Hall	Leeds	1996	7(2)	3	0	0	12
Martin Hall	Halifax	1998	2(10)	0	0	0	0
	Hull	1999	7	0	0	0	0
	Castleford	1998	4	0	0	0	0
	Wigan	1996-97	31(5)	7	6	0	40
Steve Hall	Widnes	2004	1	0	0	0	0
	London	2002-03	35(3)	10	0	0	40
	St Helens	1999-2001	36(22)	19	0	0	76
Graeme Hallas	Huddersfield	2001	1	0	0	0	0
	Hull	1998-99	30(10)	6	39	1	103
	Halifax	1996	11(4)	5	0	0	20
Danny Halliwell	Halifax	2000-03	17(8)	4	0	0	16
	Warrington	2002	9(1)	8	0	0	32
	Wakefield	2002	3	0	0	0	0
Colum Halpenny	Wakefield	2003-04	52(1)	16	0	0	64
	Halifax	2002	22	12	0	0	48
Jon Hamer	Bradford	1996	(1)	0	0	0	0
Andrew Hamilton	London	1997, 2003	1(20)	3	0	0	12
John Hamilton	St Helens	1998	3	0	0	0	0
Karle Hammond	Halifax	2002	10(2)	2	14	0	36
	Salford	2001	2(3)	1	0	0	4
	London	1999-2000	47	23	2	3	99
	St Helens	1996-98	58(8)	28	4	0	116
Anthony Hancock	Paris	1997	8(6)	1	0	0	4
Michael Hancock	Salford	2001-02	12(24)	7	0	0	28
Gareth Handford	Castleford	2001	7(2)	0	0	0	0
	Bradford	2000	1(1)	0	0	0	0
Paul Handforth	Wakefield	2000-04	17(44)	10	13	0	66
Paddy Handley	Leeds	1996	1(1)	2	0	0	8
Dean Hanger	Warrington	1999	7(11)	3	0	0	12
	Huddersfield	1998	20(1)	5	0	0	20
Harrison Hansen	Wigan	2004	(6)	1	0	0	4
Lee Hansen	Wigan	1997	10(5)	0	0	0	0
Shontayne Hape	Bradford	2003-04	55	35	0	0	140
Lionel Harbin	Wakefield	2001	(1)	0	0	0	0
Ian Hardman	St Helens	2003-04	10(8)	5	0	0	20
Jeff Hardy	Hudds-Sheff	2000	20(5)	6	0	1	25
	Sheffield	1999	22(4)	7	0	0	28
Spencer Hargrave	Castleford	1996-99	(6)	0	0	0	0
Bryn Hargreaves	Wigan	2004	1(1)	0	0	0	0
Lee Harland	Castleford	1996-2004	148(35)	20	0	0	80
Neil Harmon	Halifax	2003	13(3)	0	0	0	0
	Salford	2001	6(5)	0	0	0	0
	Bradford	1998-2000	15(13)	2	0	0	8
	Huddersfield	1998	12	1	0	0	4
	Leeds	1996	10	1	0	0	4
Iestyn Harris	Bradford	2004	12(1)	6	3	0	30
	Leeds	1997-2001	111(7)	57	490	6	1214
	Warrington	1996	16	4	63	2	144
Karl Harrison	Hull	1999	26	2	0	0	8
	Halifax	1996-98	60(2)	2	0	0	8
Andrew Hart	London	2004	12(1)	2	0	0	8
Tim Hartley	Salford	2004	(3)	0	0	0	0
Carlos Hassan	Bradford	1996	6(4)	2	0	0	8
Phil Hassan	Wakefield	2002	9(1)	0	0	0	0
	Halifax	2000-01	25(4)	3	0	0	12
	Salford	1998	15	2	0	0	8
	Leeds	1996-97	38(4)	12	0	0	48
Tom Haughey	London	2003-04	10(8)	1	0	0	4
	Wakefield	2001-02	5(12)	0	0	0	0
Simon Haughton	Wigan	1996-2002	63(46)	32	0	0	128
Andy Hay	Widnes	2003-04	50(2)	7	0	0	28
	Leeds	1997-2002	112(27)	43	0	0	172
	Sheffield	1996-97	17(3)	5	0	0	20
Adam Hayes	Hudds-Sheff	2000	2(1)	0	0	0	0
Joey Hayes	Salford	1999	9	2	0	0	8
	St Helens	1996-98	11(6)	7	0	0	28
Mitch Healey	Castleford	2001-03	68(1)	10	16	0	72
Ricky Helliwell	Salford	1997-99	(2)	0	0	0	0
Bryan Henare	St Helens	2000-01	4(12)	1	0	0	4
Richard Henare	Warrington	1996-97	28(2)	24	0	0	96
Brad Hepi	Castleford	1999, 2001	9(21)	3	0	0	12
	Salford	2000	3(5)	0	0	0	0
	Hull	1998	15(1)	3	0	0	12
Jon Hepworth	Castleford	2003-04	19(23)	7	8	0	44
	Leeds	2003	(1)	0	0	0	0
	London	2002	(2)	0	0	0	0
Ian Herron	Hull	2000	9	1	17	0	38
	Gateshead	1999	25	4	105	0	226
Jason Hetherington							
	London	2001-02	37	9	0	0	36
Gareth Hewitt	Salford	1999	2(1)	0	0	0	0
Andrew Hick	Hull	2000	9(9)	1	0	0	4
	Gateshead	1999	12(5)	2	0	0	8
Paul Hicks	Wakefield	1999	(1)	0	0	0	0
Darren Higgins	London	1998	5(6)	2	0	0	8
Iain Higgins	London	1997-98	1(7)	2	0	0	8
Liam Higgins	Hull	2003-04	(16)	0	0	0	0
Mick Higham	St Helens	2001-04	35(48)	25	0	0	100
Chris Highton	Warrington	1997	1(1)	0	0	0	0
David Highton	London	2004	5(18)	1	0	0	4
	Salford	2002	4(5)	2	0	0	8
	Warrington	1998-2001	18(14)	2	0	0	8
Paul Highton	Salford	1998-2002, 2004	85(56)	10	0	0	40
	Halifax	1996-97	12(18)	2	0	0	8
Andy Hill	Huddersfield	1999	(4)	0	0	0	0
	Castleford	1999	4(4)	0	0	0	0
Danny Hill	Hull	2004	(3)	0	0	0	0
Howard Hill	Oldham	1996-97	22(12)	4	0	0	16
John Hill	St Helens	2003	(1)	0	0	0	0
	Halifax	2003	1(2)	0	0	0	0
	Warrington	2001-02	(4)	0	0	0	0
Mark Hilton	Warrington	1996-2000, 2002-04	116(31)	6	0	0	24
Andy Hobson	Widnes	2004	5(13)	0	0	0	0
	Halifax	1998-2003	51(85)	8	0	0	32
Gareth Hock	Wigan	2003-04	31(28)	10	0	0	40
Andy Hodgson	Wakefield	1999	14(2)	2	1	0	10
	Bradford	1997-98	8(2)	4	0	0	16
David Hodgson	Wigan	2000-04	90(19)	43	0	0	172
	Halifax	1999	10(3)	5	0	0	20
Darren Hogg	London	1996	(1)	0	0	0	0
Michael Hogue	Paris	1997	5(7)	0	0	0	0
Chris Holden	Warrington	1996-97	2(1)	0	0	0	0
Stephen Holgate	Halifax	2000	1(10)	0	0	0	0
	Hull	1999	1	0	0	0	0
	Wigan	1997-98	11(26)	2	0	0	8
	Workington	1996	19	3	0	0	12
Martyn Holland	Wakefield	2000-03	52(3)	6	0	0	24
Tim Holmes	Widnes	2004	7	0	0	0	0
Graham Holroyd	Huddersfield	2003	3(5)	0	0	0	0
	Salford	2000-02	40(11)	8	75	5	187
	Halifax	1999	24(2)	3	74	5	165
	Leeds	1996-98	40(26)	22	101	8	298
Dallas Hood	Wakefield	2003-04	18(9)	1	0	0	4
Jason Hooper	St Helens	2003-04	46(4)	24	14	0	124
Sean Hoppe	St Helens	1999-2002	69(16)	32	0	0	128
Graeme Horne	Hull	2003-04	8(24)	6	0	0	24
Richard Horne	Hull	1999-2004	138(9)	53	12	2	238
John Hough	Warrington	1996-97	9	2	0	0	8
Sylvain Houles	Wakefield	2003	4	1	0	0	4
	London	2001-02	17(10)	11	0	0	44
	Hudds-Sheff	2000	5(2)	1	0	0	4
Harvey Howard	Wigan	2001-02	25(27)	1	0	0	4
	Bradford	1998	4(2)	1	0	0	4
	Leeds	1996	8	0	0	0	0
Kim Howard	London	1997	4(5)	0	0	0	0
Stuart Howarth	Workington	1996	(2)	0	0	0	0
Phil Howlett	Bradford	1999	5(1)	2	0	0	8
Craig Huby	Castleford	2003-04	(12)	0	3	0	6
Ryan Hudson	Castleford	2002-04	73(6)	21	0	0	84
	Wakefield	2000-01	42(9)	11	0	1	45
	Huddersfield	1998-99	12(7)	0	0	0	0
Adam Hughes	Widnes	2002-04	79(1)	39	51	0	258
	Halifax	2001	8(8)	8	0	0	32
	Wakefield	1999-2000	43(3)	21	34	0	152
	Leeds	1996-97	4(5)	4	0	0	16
Ian Hughes	Sheffield	1996	9(8)	4	0	0	16
Steffan Hughes	London	1999-2001	1(13)	1	0	0	4
David Hulme	Salford	1997-99	53(1)	5	0	0	20
	Leeds	1996	8(1)	2	0	0	8
Paul Hulme	Warrington	1996-97	23(1)	2	0	0	8
Gary Hulse	Warrington	2001-04	20(28)	8	0	1	33
Alan Hunte	Salford	2002	19(2)	9	0	0	36
	Warrington	1999-2001	83	49	0	0	196
	Hull	1998	21	7	0	0	28
	St Helens	1996-98	30(2)	28	0	0	112
Nick Hyde	Paris	1997	5(5)	1	0	0	4
Andy Ireland	Hull	1998-99	22(15)	0	0	0	0
	Bradford	1996	1	0	0	0	0
Kevin Iro	St Helens	1999-2001	76	39	0	0	156
	Leeds	1996	16	9	0	0	36
Andrew Isherwood	Wigan	1998-99	(5)	0	0	0	0
Olu Iwenofu	London	2000-01	2(1)	0	0	0	0
Chico Jackson	Hull	1999	(4)	0	0	0	0
Lee Jackson	Hull	2001-02	37(9)	12	1	0	50
	Leeds	1999-2000	28(24)	7	0	0	28
Michael Jackson	Sheffield	1998-99	17(17)	2	0	0	8
	Halifax	1996-97	27(6)	11	0	0	44

Super League Players 1996-2004

PLAYER	CLUB	YEAR	APP	TRIES	GOALS	FG	PTS
Paul Jackson	Castleford	2003-04	7(21)	0	0	0	0
	Wakefield	1999-2002	57(41)	2	0	0	8
	Huddersfield	1998	(11)	0	0	0	0
Rob Jackson	London	2002-04	26(14)	9	0	0	36
Wayne Jackson	Halifax	1996-97	17(5)	2	0	0	8
Aled James	Widnes	2003	3	0	0	0	0
Andy James	Halifax	1996	(4)	0	0	0	0
Pascal Jampy	Paris	1996-97	3(2)	0	0	0	0
Ben Jeffries	Wakefield	2003-04	49(6)	27	1	4	114
Mick Jenkins	Hull	2000	24	2	0	0	8
	Gateshead	1999	16	3	0	0	12
Ed Jennings	London	1998-99	1(2)	0	0	0	0
Matthew Johns	Wigan	2001	24	3	0	1	13
Andy Johnson	Salford	2004	7(20)	7	0	0	28
	Castleford	2002-03	32(16)	11	0	0	44
	London	2000-01	24(21)	12	0	0	48
	Huddersfield	1999	5	1	0	0	4
	Wigan	1996-99	24(20)	19	0	0	76
Bruce Johnson	Widnes	2004	(3)	0	0	0	0
Jason Johnson	St Helens	1997-99	2	0	0	0	0
Mark Johnson	Salford	1999-2000	22(9)	16	0	0	64
	Hull	1998	10(1)	4	0	0	16
	Workington	1996	12	4	0	0	16
Nick Johnson	London	2003	(1)	0	0	0	0
Paul Johnson	Bradford	2004	18(5)	8	0	0	32
	Wigan	1996-2003	74(46)	54	0	0	216
Danny Jones	Halifax	2003	1	0	0	0	0
David Jones	Oldham	1997	14(1)	5	0	0	20
Mark Jones	Warrington	1996	8(11)	2	0	0	8
Phil Jones	Wigan	1999-2001	14(7)	6	25	0	74
Stuart Jones	Huddersfield	2004	25(3)	5	0	0	20
	St Helens	2003	(18)	2	0	0	8
	Wigan	2002	5(3)	1	0	0	4
Jamie Jones-Buchanan	Leeds	1999-2004	9(43)	9	0	0	36
Tim Jonkers	Salford	2004	(5)	0	0	0	0
	St Helens	1999-2004	41(64)	12	0	0	48
Darren Jordan	Wakefield	2003	(1)	0	0	0	0
Phil Joseph	Huddersfield	2004	7(6)	0	0	0	0
Warren Jowitt	Hull	2003	(2)	0	0	0	0
	Salford	2001-02	17(4)	2	0	0	8
	Wakefield	2000	19(3)	8	0	0	32
	Bradford	1996-99	13(25)	5	0	0	20
Chris Joynt	St Helens	1996-2004	201(14)	68	0	0	272
Gregory Kacala	Paris	1996	7	1	0	0	4
Andy Kain	Castleford	2004	2(2)	1	0	0	4
Mal Kaufusi	London	2004	1(3)	0	0	0	0
Damon Keating	Wakefield	2002	7(17)	1	0	0	4
Shaun Keating	London	1996	1(3)	0	0	0	0
Mark Keenan	Workington	1996	3(4)	1	0	0	4
Tony Kemp	Wakefield	1999-2000	15(5)	2	0	1	9
	Leeds	1996-98	23(2)	5	0	2	22
Damien Kennedy	London	2003	5(11)	1	0	0	4
Ian Kenny	St Helens	2004	(1)	0	0	0	0
Shane Kenward	Wakefield	1999	28	6	0	0	24
	Salford	1998	1	0	0	0	0
Jason Keough	Paris	1997	2	1	0	0	4
Martin Ketteridge	Halifax	1996	7(5)	0	0	0	0
Ronnie Kettlewell	Warrington	1996	(1)	0	0	0	0
David Kidwell	Warrington	2001-02	14(12)	9	0	0	36
Andrew King	London	2003	23(1)	15	0	0	60
Dave King	Huddersfield	1998-99	11(17)	2	0	0	8
Kevin King	Castleford	2004	(1)	0	0	0	0
Paul King	Hull	1999-2004	96(44)	16	0	1	65
Andy Kirk	Salford	2004	20	5	0	0	20
	Leeds	2001-02	4(4)	0	0	0	0
John Kirkpatrick	London	2004	14(1)	3	0	0	12
	St Helens	2001-03	10(11)	10	0	0	40
	Halifax	2003	4	1	0	0	4
Wayne Kitchin	Workington	1996	11(6)	3	17	1	47
Ian Knott	Wakefield	2002-03	34(5)	7	79	0	186
	Warrington	1996-2001	68(41)	24	18	0	132
Matt Knowles	Wigan	1996	(3)	0	0	0	0
Phil Knowles	Salford	1997	1	0	0	0	0
Simon Knox	Halifax	1999	(6)	0	0	0	0
	Salford	1998	1(1)	0	0	0	0
	Bradford	1996-98	9(19)	7	0	0	28
Toa Kohe-Love	Bradford	2004	1(1)	0	0	0	0
	Hull	2002-03	42	19	0	0	76
	Warrington	1996-2001	114(2)	69	0	0	276
Paul Koloi	Wigan	1997	1(2)	1	0	0	4
Michael Korkidas	Wakefield	2003-04	51(3)	9	0	0	36
David Krause	London	1996-97	22(1)	7	0	0	28
Ben Kusto	Huddersfield	2001	21(4)	9	0	1	37
Adrian Lam	Wigan	2001-04	105(2)	40	1	9	171
Mark Lane	Paris	1996	(2)	0	0	0	0
Allan Langer	Warrington	2000-01	47	13	4	0	60
Kevin Langer	London	1996	12(4)	2	0	0	8
Chris Langley	Huddersfield	2000-01	18(1)	3	0	0	12
Jamie Langley	Bradford	2002-04	10(35)	10	0	0	40
Andy Last	Hull	1999-2004	15(10)	4	0	0	16
Dale Laughton	Warrington	2002	15(1)	0	0	0	0
	Huddersfield	2000-01	36(2)	4	0	0	16
	Sheffield	1996-99	48(22)	5	0	0	20
Ali Lauitiiti	Leeds	2004	14(5)	9	0	0	36
Jason Laurence	Salford	1997	1	0	0	0	0
Graham Law	Wakefield	1999-2002	34(30)	6	40	0	104
Neil Law	Wakefield	1999-2000	83	39	0	0	156
	Sheffield	1998	1(1)	1	0	0	4
Dean Lawford	Widnes	2003-04	17(1)	5	2	4	28
	Halifax	2001	1(1)	0	0	0	0
	Leeds	1997-2000	15(8)	2	3	0	14
	Huddersfield	1999	6(1)	0	6	1	13
	Sheffield	1996	9(5)	2	1	1	11
Johnny Lawless	Halifax	2001-03	73(1)	10	0	0	40
	Hudds-Sheff	2000	19(6)	3	0	0	12
	Sheffield	1996-99	76(4)	11	0	0	44
Leroy Leapai	London	1996	2	0	0	0	0
Jim Leatham	Hull	1998-99	20(18)	4	0	0	16
	Leeds	1997	(1)	0	0	0	0
Andy Leathem	Warrington	1999	2(8)	0	0	0	0
	St Helens	1996-98	20(1)	1	0	0	4
Danny Lee	Gateshead	1999	16(2)	0	0	0	0
Jason Lee	Halifax	2001	10(1)	2	0	0	8
Mark Lee	Salford	1997-2000	25(11)	1	0	4	8
Robert Lee	Hull	1999	4(3)	0	0	0	0
Matthew Leigh	Salford	2000	(6)	0	0	0	0
Chris Leikvoll	Warrington	2004	13(7)	1	0	0	4
Jim Lenihan	Huddersfield	1999	19(1)	10	0	0	40
Mark Lennon	Castleford	2001-03	30(21)	10	21	0	82
Gary Lester	Hull	1998-99	46	17	0	0	68
Stuart Lester	Wigan	1997	1(3)	0	0	0	0
Afi Leuila	Oldham	1996-97	17(3)	2	0	0	8
Simon Lewis	Castleford	2001	4	3	0	0	12
Jon Liddell	Leeds	2001	1	0	0	0	0
Jason Lidden	Castleford	1997	15(1)	7	0	0	28
Danny Lima	Warrington	2004	13(12)	4	0	0	16
Stuart Littler	Salford	1998-2002, 2004	99(12)	31	0	0	124
Peter Livett	Workington	1996	3(1)	0	0	0	0
Scott Logan	Hull	2001-03	27(20)	5	0	0	20
David Lomax	Huddersfield	2000-01	45(9)	4	0	0	16
	Paris	1997	19(2)	1	0	0	4
Dave Long	London	1999	(1)	0	0	0	0
Karl Long	London	2003	(1)	0	0	0	0
	Widnes	2002	4	1	0	0	4
Sean Long	St Helens	1997-2004	146(6)	86	593	8	1538
	Wigan	1996-97	1(5)	0	0	0	0
Davide Longo	Bradford	1996	1(3)	0	0	0	0
Gary Lord	Oldham	1996-97	28(12)	3	0	0	12
Paul Loughlin	Huddersfield	1998-99	34(2)	4	4	0	24
	Bradford	1996-97	36(4)	15	8	0	76
Karl Lovell	Hudds-Sheff	2000	14	5	0	0	20
	Sheffield	1999	22(4)	8	0	0	32
James Lowes	Bradford	1996-2003	205	84	2	2	342
Laurent Lucchese	Paris	1996	13(5)	2	0	0	8
Zebastian Luisi	London	2004	1	1	0	0	4
Peter Lupton	Hull	2003-04	14(19)	8	3	0	38
	London	2000-02	10(15)	2	2	0	12
Andy Lynch	Castleford	1999-2004	78(48)	15	0	0	60
Duncan MacGillivray	Wakefield	2004	5(7)	1	0	0	4
Brad Mackay	Bradford	2000	24(2)	8	0	0	32
Graham Mackay	Hull	2002	27	18	24	0	120
	Bradford	2001	16(3)	12	1	0	50
	Leeds	2000	12(8)	10	2	0	44
Steve Maden	Warrington	2002	3	0	0	0	0
Mateaki Mafi	Warrington	1996-97	7(8)	7	0	0	28
Brendan Magnus	London	2000	3	1	0	0	4
Mark Maguire	London	1996-97	11(4)	7	13	0	54
Adam Maher	Hull	2000-03	88(4)	24	0	0	96
	Gateshead	1999	21(5)	3	0	0	12
Lee Maher	Leeds	1996	4(1)	0	0	0	0
Shaun Mahony	Paris	1997	5	0	0	0	0
David Maiden	Hull	2000-01	32(10)	11	0	0	44
	Gateshead	1999	5(16)	8	0	0	32
Craig Makin	Salford	1999-2001	24(20)	2	0	0	8
Brady Malam	Wigan	2000	5(20)	1	0	0	4
Francis Maloney	Castleford	1998-99, 2003-04	71(7)	24	33	3	165
	Salford	2001-02	45(1)	26	5	0	114
	Wakefield	2000	11	1	1	0	6
	Oldham	1996-97	39(2)	12	91	2	232
George Mann	Warrington	1997	14(5)	1	0	0	4
	Leeds	1996	11(4)	2	0	0	8
David March	Wakefield	1999-2004	119(13)	28	77	0	266
Paul March	Huddersfield	2003-04	44(4)	10	36	1	113
	Wakefield	1999-2001	32(23)	14	18	0	92
Nick Mardon	London	1997-98	14	2	0	0	8
Oliver Marns	Halifax	1996-2002	54(19)	23	0	0	92
Paul Marquet	Warrington	2002	23(2)	0	0	0	0
Iain Marsh	Salford	1998-2001	1(4)	0	0	0	0
Lee Marsh	Salford	2001-02	3(4)	0	0	0	0
Richard Marshall	London	2002-03	33(11)	1	0	0	4
	Huddersfield	2000-01	35(14)	1	0	0	4
	Halifax	1996-99	38(34)	2	0	0	8
Jason Martin	Paris	1997	15(2)	3	0	0	12
Scott Martin	Salford	1997-99	32(18)	8	0	0	32
Tony Martin	London	1996-97, 2001-03	97(1)	36	170	1	485
Mick Martindale	Halifax	1996	(4)	0	0	0	0
Tommy Martyn	St Helens	1996-2003	125(20)	87	63	12	486
Dean Marwood	Workington	1996	9(6)	0	22	0	44
Martin Masella	Warrington	2001	10(14)	5	0	0	20
	Wakefield	2000	14(8)	4	0	0	16
	Leeds	1997-1999	59(5)	1	0	0	4
Colin Maskill	Castleford	1996	8	1	1	0	6
Keith Mason	St Helens	2003-04	30(12)	4	0	0	16
	Wakefield	2000-01	5(17)	0	0	0	0
Vila Matautia	St Helens	1996-2001	31(68)	9	0	0	36
Barrie-Jon Mather	Castleford	1998, 2000-02	50(12)	21	0	0	84
Richard Mathers	Leeds	2002-04	42(2)	8	0	0	32
	Warrington	2002	4(3)	0	0	0	0
Jamie Mathiou	Leeds	1997-2001	31(82)	3	0	0	12
Terry Matterson	London	1996-98	46	15	90	6	246
Casey Mayberry	Halifax	2000	1(1)	0	0	0	0

PLAYER	CLUB	YEAR	APP	TRIES	GOALS	FG	PTS
Chris Maye	Halifax	2003	3(4)	0	0	0	0
Joe Mbu	London	2003-04	15(12)	3	0	0	12
Danny McAllister	Gateshead	1999	3(3)	1	0	0	4
	Sheffield	1996-97	33(7)	10	0	0	40
John McAtee	St Helens	1996	2(1)	0	0	0	0
Nathan McAvoy	Salford	1997-98, 2004	43	16	0	0	64
	Bradford	1998-2002	67(22)	45	0	0	180
Dave McConnell	London	2003	(4)	0	0	0	0
	St Helens	2001-02	3(2)	4	0	0	16
Robbie McCormack	Wigan	1998	24	2	0	0	8
Steve McCurrie	Widnes	2002-04	55(22)	10	0	0	40
	Warrington	1998-2001	69(26)	31	0	0	124
Barrie McDermott	Leeds	1996-2004	158(46)	22	0	0	88
Brian McDermott	Bradford	1996-2002	138(32)	33	0	0	132
Wayne McDonald	Leeds	2002-04	33(42)	14	0	0	56
	St Helens	2001	7(11)	4	0	0	16
	Hull	2000	5(8)	4	0	0	16
	Wakefield	1999	9(17)	8	0	0	32
Ryan McDonald	Widnes	2002-03	6(4)	0	0	0	0
Craig McDowell	Huddersfield	2003	(1)	0	0	0	0
	Warrington	2002	(1)	0	0	0	0
	Bradford	2000	(1)	0	0	0	0
Wes McGibbon	Halifax	1999	1	0	0	0	0
Billy McGinty	Workington	1996	1	0	0	0	0
Kevin McGuinness	Salford	2004	17	2	0	0	8
Danny McGuire	Leeds	2001-04	46(22)	58	0	1	233
Gary McGuirk	Workington	1996	(4)	0	0	0	0
Richard McKell	Castleford	1997-98	22(7)	2	0	0	8
Chris McKenna	Leeds	2003-04	42(3)	12	0	0	48
Phil McKenzie	Workington	1996	4	0	0	0	0
Chris McKinney	Oldham	1996-97	4(9)	2	0	0	8
Shayne McMenemy	Hull	2003-04	31(2)	5	0	0	20
	Halifax	2001-03	63	11	0	0	44
Andy McNally	London	2004	5(3)	0	0	0	0
	Castleford	2001, 2003	2(5)	1	0	0	4
Steve McNamara	Huddersfield	2001, 2003	41(9)	3	134	1	281
	Wakefield	2000	15(2)	2	32	0	72
	Bradford	1996-99	90(3)	14	348	7	759
Paul McNicholas	Hull	2004	23(3)	3	0	0	12
Neil McPherson	Salford	1997	(1)	0	0	0	0
Duncan McRae	London	1996	11(2)	3	0	1	13
Derek McVey	St Helens	1996-97	28(4)	6	1	0	26
Dallas Mead	Warrington	1997	2	0	0	0	0
Robert Mears	Leeds	2001	23	6	0	0	24
Paul Medley	Bradford	1996-98	6(35)	9	0	0	36
Chris Melling	Wigan	2004	1(1)	0	1	0	2
Paul Mellor	Castleford	2003-04	36(3)	18	0	0	72
Craig Menkins	Paris	1997	4(5)	0	0	0	0
Gary Mercer	Castleford	2002	(1)	0	0	0	0
	Leeds	1996-97, 2001	40(2)	9	0	0	36
	Warrington	2001	18	2	0	0	8
	Halifax	1998-2001	73(2)	16	0	0	64
Tony Mestrov	London	1996-97, 2001	59(8)	4	0	0	16
	Wigan	1998-2000	39(39)	3	0	0	12
Keiran Meyer	London	1996	4	1	0	0	4
Gary Middlehurst	Widnes	2004	(2)	0	0	0	0
Simon Middleton	Castleford	1996-97	19(3)	8	0	0	32
Shane Millard	Widnes	2003-04	53	15	0	0	60
	London	1998-2000	72(14)	11	1	0	46
David Mills	Widnes	2002-04	16(58)	8	0	0	32
Lee Milner	Halifax	1999	(1)	0	0	0	0
John Minto	London	1996	13	4	0	0	16
Martin Moana	Salford	2004	6(3)	1	0	0	4
	Halifax	1996-2001, 2003	126(22)	62	0	1	249
	Wakefield	2002	19(2)	10	0	0	40
	Huddersfield	2001	3(3)	2	0	0	8
Steve Molloy	Huddersfield	2000-01	26(20)	3	0	0	12
	Sheffield	1998-99	32(17)	3	0	0	12
Chris Molyneux	Huddersfield	2000-01	1(18)	0	0	0	0
	Sheffield	1999	1(2)	0	0	0	0
Adrian Moore	Huddersfield	1998-99	1(4)	0	0	0	0
Danny Moore	London	2000	7	0	0	0	0
	Wigan	1998-99	49(3)	18	0	0	72
Jason Moore	Workington	1996	(5)	0	0	0	0
Richard Moore	Bradford	2002-04	1(26)	0	0	0	0
	London	2002, 2004	5(9)	2	0	0	8
Scott Moore	St Helens	2004	2	1	0	0	4
Dennis Moran	London	2001-04	107(2)	74	2	5	305
Willie Morganson	Sheffield	1997-98	18(12)	5	3	0	26
Paul Moriarty	Halifax	1996	3(2)	0	0	0	0
Adrian Morley	Leeds	1996-2000	95(14)	25	0	0	100
Chris Morley	Salford	1999	3(5)	0	0	0	0
	Warrington	1998	2(8)	0	0	0	0
	St Helens	1996-97	21(16)	4	0	0	16
Iain Morrison	Huddersfield	2003-04	11(18)	0	0	0	0
	London	2001	(1)	0	0	0	0
Gareth Morton	Leeds	2001-02	1(1)	0	0	0	0
Aaron Moule	Widnes	2004	16	2	0	0	8
Wilfried Moulinec	Paris	1996	1	0	0	0	0
Mark Moxon	Huddersfield	1998-2001	20(5)	1	0	1	5
Brett Mullins	Leeds	2001	5(3)	1	0	0	4
Damian Munro	Widnes	2002	8(2)	1	0	0	4
	Halifax	1996-97	9(6)	8	0	0	32
Matt Munro	Oldham	1996-97	26(5)	8	0	0	32
Craig Murdock	Salford	2000	(2)	0	0	0	0
	Hull	1998-99	21(6)	8	0	2	34
	Wigan	1996-98	18(17)	14	0	0	56
Justin Murphy	Widnes	2004	5	1	0	0	4
Doc Murray	Warrington	1997	(2)	0	0	0	0
	Wigan	1997	6(2)	0	0	0	0
Scott Murrell	London	2004	3(3)	2	0	0	8
David Mycoe	Sheffield	1996-97	12(13)	1	0	0	4
Rob Myler	Oldham	1996-97	19(2)	6	0	0	24
Stephen Myler	Widnes	2003-04	20(10)	5	23	0	66
Vinny Myler	Salford	2004	(4)	0	0	0	0
	Bradford	2003	(1)	0	0	0	0
Matt Nable	London	1997	2(2)	1	0	0	4
Brad Nairn	Workington	1996	14	4	0	0	16
Frank Napoli	London	2000	14(6)	2	0	0	8
Carlo Napolitano	Salford	2000	(3)	1	0	0	4
Jim Naylor	Halifax	2000	7(6)	2	0	0	8
Scott Naylor	Salford	1997-98, 2004	30(1)	9	0	0	36
	Bradford	1999-2003	127(1)	51	0	0	204
Mike Neal	Salford	1998	(1)	0	0	0	0
	Oldham	1996-97	6(4)	3	0	0	12
Jonathan Neill	Huddersfield	1998-99	20(11)	0	0	0	0
	St Helens	1996	1	0	0	0	0
Chris Nero	Huddersfield	2004	22(3)	5	0	0	20
Jason Netherton	London	2003-04	6	0	0	0	0
	Halifax	2002	2(3)	0	0	0	0
	Leeds	2001	(3)	0	0	0	0
Paul Newlove	Castleford	2004	5	1	0	0	4
	St Helens	1996-2003	162	106	0	0	424
Richard Newlove	Wakefield	2003	17(5)	8	0	0	32
Terry Newton	Wigan	2000-04	134(6)	53	0	0	212
	Leeds	1996-1999	55(14)	4	0	0	16
Gene Ngamu	Huddersfield	1999-2000	29(2)	9	67	0	170
Sonny Nickle	St Helens	1999-2002	86(18)	14	0	0	56
	Bradford	1996-98	25(16)	9	0	0	36
Jason Nicol	Salford	1996-2002	52(7)	11	0	0	44
Tawera Nikau	Warrington	2000-01	51	7	0	0	28
Rob Nolan	Hull	1998-99	20(11)	6	0	0	24
Paul Noone	Warrington	2000-04	46(41)	10	17	0	74
Chris Norman	Halifax	2003	13(3)	2	0	0	8
Paul Norman	Oldham	1996	(1)	0	0	0	0
Andy Northey	St Helens	1996-97	8(17)	2	0	0	8
Danny Nutley	Warrington	1998-2001	94(1)	3	0	0	12
Tony Nuttall	Oldham	1996-97	1(7)	0	0	0	0
Clinton O'Brien	Wakefield	2003	(2)	0	0	0	0
Matt O'Connor	Paris	1997	11(4)	1	26	2	58
Terry O'Connor	Wigan	1996-2004	177(45)	9	0	0	36
Jarrod O'Doherty	Huddersfield	2003	26	3	0	0	12
David O'Donnell	Paris	1997	21	3	0	0	12
Martin Offiah	Salford	2000-01	41	20	0	2	82
	London	1996-99	29(3)	21	0	0	84
	Wigan	1996	8	7	0	0	28
Mark O'Halloran	London	2004	22	8	0	0	32
Hefin O'Hare	Huddersfield	2001, 2003-04	52(8)	21	0	0	84
Hitro Okesene	Hull	1998	21(1)	0	0	0	0
Anderson Okiwe	Sheffield	1997	1	0	0	0	0
Jamie Olejnik	Paris	1997	11	8	0	0	32
Kevin O'Loughlin	Halifax	1997-98	2(4)	0	0	0	0
	St Helens	1997	(3)	0	0	0	0
Sean O'Loughlin	Wigan	2002-04	63(18)	16	0	0	64
Jules O'Neill	Widnes	2003-04	45(1)	13	143	6	344
	Wigan	2002-03	29(1)	12	72	0	192
Julian O'Neill	Widnes	2002-04	47(26)	2	0	0	8
	Wakefield	2001	24(1)	2	0	0	8
	St Helens	1997-2000	28(8)	5	0	0	20
Steve O'Neill	Gateshead	1999	1(1)	0	0	0	0
Tom O'Reilly	Warrington	2001-02	8(6)	1	0	0	4
Chris Orr	Huddersfield	1998	19(3)	2	0	0	8
Danny Orr	Wigan	2004	24	7	7	0	42
	Castleford	1997-2003	150(18)	65	279	3	821
Jason Palmada	Workington	1996	12	2	0	0	8
Junior Paramore	Castleford	1996	5(5)	3	0	0	12
Paul Parker	Hull	1999-2002	23(18)	9	0	0	36
Rob Parker	Bradford	2000, 2002-04	12(60)	11	0	0	44
	London	2001	9	1	0	0	4
Wayne Parker	Halifax	1996-97	12(1)	0	0	0	0
Ian Parry	Warrington	2001	(1)	0	0	0	0
Jules Parry	Paris	1996	10(2)	0	0	0	0
Regis Pastre-Courtine	Paris	1996	4(3)	4	0	0	16
Andrew Patmore	Oldham	1996	8(5)	3	0	0	12
Henry Paul	Bradford	1999-2001	81(5)	29	350	6	822
	Wigan	1996-98	60	37	23	0	194
Junior Paul	London	1996	3	1	0	0	4
Robbie Paul	Bradford	1996-2004	181(19)	112	2	0	452
Danny Peacock	Bradford	1997-99	32(2)	15	0	0	60
Jamie Peacock	Bradford	1999-2004	131(25)	29	0	0	116
Martin Pearson	Wakefield	2001	21(1)	3	60	3	135
	Halifax	1997-98, 2000	55(6)	24	181	0	458
	Sheffield	1999	17(6)	9	36	2	110
Jacques Pech	Paris	1996	16	0	0	0	0
Mike Pechey	Warrington	1998	6(3)	2	0	0	8
Bill Peden	London	2003	21(3)	7	0	0	28
Sean Penkywicz	Huddersfield	2004	19(9)	6	0	0	24
	Halifax	2000-03	29(27)	8	0	0	32
Julian Penni	Salford	1998-99	4	0	0	0	0
Lee Penny	Warrington	1996-2003	140(5)	54	0	0	216
Paul Penrice	Workington	1996	11(2)	2	0	0	8
Chris Percival	Widnes	2002-03	26	6	0	0	24
Apollo Perelini	St Helens	1996-2000	103(16)	27	0	0	108
Mark Perrett	Halifax	1996-97	15(4)	4	0	0	16
Adam Peters	Paris	1997	16(3)	0	0	0	0

PLAYER	CLUB	YEAR	APP	TRIES	GOALS	FG	PTS
Dominic Peters	London	1998-2003	58(11)	12	0	0	48
Mike Peters	Warrington	2000	2(12)	1	0	0	4
	Halifax	2000	1	0	0	0	0
Willie Peters	Widnes	2004	9	3	0	2	14
	Wigan	2000	29	15	5	6	76
	Gateshead	1999	27	11	1	6	52
Adrian Petrie	Workington	1996	(1)	0	0	0	0
Rowland Phillips	Workington	1996	22	1	0	0	4
Nathan Picchi	Leeds	1996	(1)	0	0	0	0
Ian Pickavance	Hull	1999	4(2)	2	0	0	8
	Huddersfield	1999	3(14)	0	0	0	0
	St Helens	1996-98	12(44)	6	0	0	24
James Pickering	Castleford	1999	1(19)	0	0	0	0
Nick Pinkney	Salford	2000-02	64	29	0	0	116
	Halifax	1999	26(2)	13	0	0	52
	Sheffield	1997-98	33	10	0	0	40
Michal Piscuonov	Paris	1996	1(1)	1	0	0	4
Darryl Pitt	London	1996	2(16)	4	0	1	17
Andy Platt	Salford	1997-98	20(3)	1	0	0	4
Michael Platt	Salford	2001-02	3	1	0	0	4
Willie Poching	Leeds	2002-04	32(51)	28	0	0	112
	Wakefield	1999-2001	65(4)	20	0	0	80
Quentin Pongia	Wigan	2003-04	15(10)	0	0	0	0
Dan Potter	Widnes	2002-03	34(2)	6	0	0	24
	London	2001	1(3)	1	0	0	4
Craig Poucher	Hull	1999-2002	31(5)	5	0	0	20
Bryn Powell	Salford	2004	1(1)	0	0	0	0
Daio Powell	Sheffield	1999	13(1)	2	0	0	8
	Halifax	1997-98	30(3)	17	0	0	68
Daryl Powell	Leeds	1998-2000	49(30)	12	0	2	50
Karl Pratt	Bradford	2003-04	23(13)	12	0	0	48
	Leeds	1999-2002	62(12)	33	0	0	132
Paul Prescott	Wigan	2004	1(2)	0	0	0	0
Steve Prescott	Hull	1998-99, 2001-03	99	46	191	3	569
	Wakefield	2000	22(1)	3	13	0	38
	St Helens	1996-97	32	15	17	0	94
Lee Prest	Workington	1996	(1)	0	0	0	0
Gareth Price	Salford	2002	(2)	0	0	0	0
	London	2002	2(2)	3	0	0	12
	St Helens	1999	(11)	2	0	0	8
Gary Price	Wakefield	1999-2001	55(13)	11	0	0	44
Richard Price	Sheffield	1996	1(2)	0	0	0	0
Tony Priddle	Paris	1997	11(7)	3	0	0	12
Karl Pryce	Bradford	2003-04	2(2)	0	0	0	0
Leon Pryce	Bradford	1998-2004	136(23)	73	0	0	292
Waine Pryce	Castleford	2000-04	81(12)	39	0	0	156
Andrew Purcell	Castleford	2000	15(5)	3	0	0	12
	Hull	1999	27	4	0	0	16
Rob Purdham	London	2002-04	38(10)	6	1	1	27
Scott Quinnell	Wigan	1996	6(3)	1	0	0	4
Lee Radford	Bradford	1999-2004	49(65)	14	12	0	80
	Hull	1998	(7)	2	0	0	8
Kris Radlinski	Wigan	1996-2004	217	125	1	0	502
Adrian Rainey	Castleford	2002	4(7)	1	0	0	4
Jean-Luc Ramondou	Paris	1996	1(1)	1	0	0	4
Craig Randall	Halifax	1999	8(11)	4	0	0	16
	Salford	1997-98	12(18)	4	0	0	16
Scott Ranson	Oldham	1996-97	19(2)	7	0	0	28
Aaron Raper	Castleford	1999-2001	48(4)	4	2	1	21
Ben Rauter	Wakefield	2001	15(6)	4	0	0	16
Gareth Raynor	Hull	2001-04	80	47	0	0	188
	Leeds	2000	(3)	0	0	0	0
Tony Rea	London	1996	22	4	0	0	16
Stuart Reardon	Bradford	2003-04	39(11)	20	0	0	80
	Salford	2002	7(1)	3	0	0	12
Mark Reber	Wigan	1999-2000	9(9)	5	0	0	20
Alan Reddicliffe	Warrington	2001	1	0	0	0	0
Tahi Reihana	Bradford	1997-98	17(21)	0	0	0	0
Paul Reilly	Huddersfield	1999-2001, 2003-04	89(6)	17	0	0	68
Robert Relf	Widnes	2002-04	68(2)	5	0	0	20
Steve Renouf	Wigan	2000-01	55	40	0	0	160
Steele Retchless	London	1998-2004	177(6)	13	0	0	52
Scott Rhodes	Hull	2000	2	0	0	0	0
Phillipe Ricard	Paris	1996-97	2	0	0	0	0
Andy Rice	Huddersfield	2000-01	2(13)	1	0	0	4
Basil Richards	Huddersfield	1998-99	28(17)	1	0	0	4
Craig Richards	Oldham	1996	1	0	0	0	0
Andy Richardson	Hudds-Sheff	2000	(2)	0	0	0	0
Sean Richardson	Widnes	2002	2(18)	1	0	0	4
	Wakefield	1999	5(1)	1	0	0	4
	Castleford	1996-97	3(8)	1	0	0	4
Shane Rigon	Bradford	2001	14(11)	12	0	0	48
Craig Rika	Halifax	1996	2	0	0	0	0
Peter Riley	Workington	1996	7(5)	0	0	0	0
Julien Rinaldi	Wakefield	2002	(3)	1	0	0	4
Dean Ripley	Castleford	2004	3(4)	1	0	0	4
Leroy Rivett	Warrington	2002	9	1	0	0	4
	Hudds-Sheff	2000	5(1)	1	0	0	4
	Leeds	1996-2000	39(15)	21	0	0	84
Jason Roach	Warrington	1998-99	29(7)	15	0	0	60
	Castleford	1997	7	4	0	0	16
Ben Roarty	Huddersfield	2003-04	38	4	0	0	16
Mark Roberts	Wigan	2003	(3)	0	0	0	0
Robert Roberts	Huddersfield	2001	(1)	0	0	0	0
	Halifax	2000	(3)	0	0	0	0
	Hull	1999	24(2)	4	13	4	46
Jason Robinson	Wigan	1996-2000	126(1)	87	0	1	349
Jeremy Robinson	Paris	1997	10(3)	1	21	0	46
John Robinson	Widnes	2003-04	7	1	0	0	4
Luke Robinson	Wigan	2002-04	17(25)	9	6	1	49
	Castleford	2004	9	4	3	0	22
Will Robinson	Hull	2000	22	4	0	0	16
	Gateshead	1999	28	9	0	0	36
James Roby	St Helens	2004	8(8)	5	0	0	20
Mike Roby	St Helens	2004	(1)	0	0	0	0
Carl Roden	Warrington	1997	1	0	0	0	0
Matt Rodwell	Warrington	2002	10	3	0	0	12
Darren Rogers	Castleford	1999-2004	162(1)	81	0	0	324
	Salford	1997-98	42	16	0	0	64
Jamie Rooney	Wakefield	2003-04	27(2)	14	96	8	256
	Castleford	2001	2(1)	0	6	0	12
Jonathan Roper	Castleford	2001	13	7	12	0	52
	Salford	2000	1(4)	1	3	0	10
	London	2000	4	0	0	0	0
	Warrington	1996-2000	75(8)	33	71	0	274
Scott Roskell	London	1996-97	30(2)	16	0	0	64
Steve Rosolen	London	1996-98	25(9)	10	0	0	40
Adam Ross	London	1996	(1)	0	0	0	0
Paul Round	Castleford	1996	(3)	0	0	0	0
Steve Rowlands	Widnes	2004	9(3)	1	0	0	4
	St Helens	2003	(1)	0	0	0	0
Paul Rowley	Huddersfield	2001	24	3	0	0	12
	Halifax	1996-2000	107(3)	27	1	3	113
Nigel Roy	London	2001-04	100	39	0	0	156
Nicky Royle	Widnes	2004	13	7	0	0	28
Chris Rudd	Warrington	1996-98	31(17)	10	16	0	72
Sean Rudder	Castleford	2004	9(3)	2	0	0	8
James Rushforth	Halifax	1997	(4)	0	0	0	0
Danny Russell	Huddersfield	1998-2000	50(13)	8	0	0	32
Ian Russell	Oldham	1997	1(3)	1	0	0	4
	Paris	1996	3	0	0	0	0
Richard Russell	Castleford	1996-98	37(4)	2	0	0	8
Robert Russell	Salford	1998-99	2(1)	0	1	0	2
Sean Rutgerson	Salford	2004	23(2)	1	0	0	4
Chris Ryan	London	1998-99	44(3)	17	10	0	88
Sean Ryan	Castleford	2004	11(5)	2	0	0	8
	Hull	2002-03	53	8	0	0	32
Justin Ryder	Wakefield	2004	19(3)	11	0	0	44
Matt Salter	London	1997-99	14(34)	0	0	0	0
Ben Sammut	Hull	2000	20	4	67	0	150
	Gateshead	1999	26(2)	6	17	0	58
Dean Sampson	Castleford	1996-2003	124(28)	24	0	0	96
Paul Sampson	London	2004	1(2)	1	0	0	4
	Wakefield	2000	17	8	0	0	32
Lee Sanderson	London	2004	1(5)	1	7	0	18
Jason Sands	Paris	1996-97	28	0	0	0	0
Lokeni Savelio	Halifax	2000	2(11)	0	0	0	0
	Salford	1997-98	18(20)	0	0	0	0
Tom Saxton	Castleford	2002-04	37(12)	11	0	0	44
Jonathan Scales	Halifax	2000	1	0	0	0	0
	Bradford	1996-98	46(4)	24	0	0	96
Andrew Schick	Castleford	1996-98	45(13)	10	0	0	40
Garry Schofield	Huddersfield	1998	(2)	0	0	0	0
Gary Schubert	Workington	1996	(1)	0	0	0	0
Matt Schultz	Hull	1998-99	23(9)	2	0	0	8
	Leeds	1996	2(4)	0	0	0	0
John Schuster	Halifax	1996-97	31	9	127	3	293
Nick Scruton	Hull	2004	2(16)	3	0	0	12
	Leeds	2002, 2004	(2)	0	0	0	0
Danny Sculthorpe	Wigan	2002-04	9(32)	5	0	0	20
Paul Sculthorpe	St Helens	1998-2004	173(1)	83	274	6	886
	Warrington	1996-97	40	6	0	0	24
Mick Seaby	London	1997	3(2)	1	0	0	4
Danny Seal	Halifax	1996-99	8(17)	3	0	0	12
Matt Seers	Wakefield	2003	11(1)	2	0	0	8
Anthony Seibold	London	1999-2000	33(19)	5	0	0	20
Keith Senior	Leeds	1999-2004	142(1)	75	0	0	300
	Sheffield	1996-99	90(2)	40	0	0	160
Fili Seru	Hull	1998-99	37(1)	13	0	0	52
Anthony Seuseu	Halifax	2003	1(11)	1	0	0	4
Darren Shaw	Salford	2002	5(9)	1	0	0	4
	London	1996, 2002	22(8)	3	0	0	12
	Castleford	2000-01	50(6)	1	0	0	4
	Sheffield	1998-99	51(1)	3	0	1	13
Mick Shaw	Halifax	1999	5	1	0	0	4
	Leeds	1996	12(2)	7	0	0	28
Phil Shead	Paris	1996	3(2)	0	0	0	0
Richard Sheil	St Helens	1997	(1)	0	0	0	0
Kelly Shelford	Warrington	1996-97	25(3)	4	0	2	18
Michael Shenton	Castleford	2004	1(2)	0	0	0	0
Ryan Sheridan	Castleford	2004	2	0	0	0	0
	Widnes	2003	14(3)	2	0	0	8
	Leeds	1997-2002	123(7)	46	0	1	185
	Sheffield	1996	9(3)	5	0	1	21
Rikki Sheriffe	Halifax	2003	6(1)	3	0	0	12
Ian Sherratt	Oldham	1996	5(3)	1	0	0	4
Peter Shiels	St Helens	2001-02	44(3)	11	0	0	44
Gary Shillabeer	Huddersfield	1999	(2)	0	0	0	0
Mark Shipway	Salford	2004	18(6)	1	0	0	4
Ian Sibbit	Warrington	1999-2001, 2003-04	63(18)	24	0	0	96
Mark Sibson	Huddersfield	1999	2	2	0	0	8
Jon Simms	St Helens	2002	(1)	0	0	0	0
Craig Simon	Hull	2000	23(2)	8	0	0	32
	Gateshead	1999	25(4)	6	0	0	24
Darren Simpson	Huddersfield	1998-99	17(1)	5	0	0	20
Robbie Simpson	London	1999	6(7)	0	0	0	0
Kevin Sinfield	Leeds	1997-2004	137(25)	26	325	6	760
Wayne Sing	Paris	1997	18(1)	2	0	0	8
Fata Sini	Salford	1997	22	7	0	0	28
Ben Skerrett	Castleford	2003	(1)	0	0	0	0
Kelvin Skerrett	Halifax	1997-99	31(6)	2	0	0	8
	Wigan	1996	1(8)	0	0	0	0
Troy Slattery	Wakefield	2002-03	33(5)	4	0	0	16
	Huddersfield	1999	3	1	0	0	4

PLAYER	CLUB	YEAR	APP	TRIES	GOALS	FG	PTS
Mick Slicker	Huddersfield	2001,					
		2003-04	16(41)	2	0	0	8
	Sheffield	1999	(3)	1	0	0	4
	Halifax	1997	2(5)	0	0	0	0
Ian Smales	Castleford	1996-97	10(8)	5	0	0	20
Aaron Smith	Bradford	2003-04	12(1)	3	0	0	12
Andy Smith	Bradford	2004	6(2)	2	0	0	8
Byron Smith	Castleford	2004	(9)	0	0	0	0
	Halifax	2003	6(1)	0	0	0	0
Chris Smith	Hull	2001-02	12	3	0	0	12
	St Helens	1998-2000	62(9)	26	0	0	104
	Castleford	1996-97	36(1)	12	0	0	48
Craig Smith	Wigan	2002-04	77(3)	10	0	0	40
Damien Smith	St Helens	1998	21(1)	8	0	0	32
Danny Smith	Paris	1996	10(2)	1	15	0	34
	London	1996	2(1)	1	0	0	4
Darren Smith	St Helens	2003	25(1)	14	0	0	56
Gary Smith	Castleford	2001	(1)	0	0	0	0
Hudson Smith	Bradford	2000	8(22)	2	0	0	8
	Salford	1999	23(2)	5	0	0	20
James Smith	Salford	2000	23(3)	6	0	0	24
Jamie Smith	Hull	1998-99	24(6)	6	12	0	48
	Workington	1996	5(3)	0	1	0	2
Jason Smith	Hull	2001-04	61(3)	17	0	1	69
Kris Smith	London	2001	(1)	0	0	0	0
	Halifax	2001	(1)	0	0	0	0
Leigh Smith	Workington	1996	9	4	0	0	16
Mark Smith	Wigan	1999-2004	35(77)	8	0	0	32
Michael Smith	Castleford	1998,					
		2001-04	86(33)	32	0	0	128
	Hull	1999	12(6)	3	0	0	12
Paul Smith	Huddersfield	2004	14(6)	3	0	0	12
Paul Smith	Warrington	2001	(1)	0	0	0	0
	Castleford	1997-2000	6(37)	3	0	0	12
Paul Smith	London	1997	7(1)	2	0	0	8
Peter Smith	Oldham	1996	2	0	0	0	0
Richard Smith	Wakefield	2001	8(1)	1	0	0	4
	Salford	1997	(1)	1	0	0	4
Tony Smith	Hull	2001-03	43(5)	26	0	0	104
	Wigan	1997-2000	66(5)	46	0	0	184
	Castleford	1996-97	18(2)	10	0	0	40
Tony Smith	Workington	1996	9	1	0	0	4
Rob Smyth	Warrington	2000-03	65	35	20	0	180
	London	1998-2000	32(2)	9	15	0	66
	Wigan	1996	11(5)	16	0	0	64
Steve Snitch	Wakefield	2002-04	4(40)	2	0	0	8
Bright Sodje	Wakefield	2000	15	4	0	0	16
	Sheffield	1996-99	54	34	0	0	136
David Solomona	Wakefield	2004	29	14	0	0	56
Alfred Songoro	Wakefield	1999	8(5)	4	0	0	16
Romain Sort	Paris	1997	(1)	0	0	0	0
Paul Southern	Salford	1997-2002	79(33)	6	13	0	50
	St Helens	2002	1(1)	0	0	0	0
Roy Southernwood							
	Wakefield	1999	1	0	0	0	0
	Halifax	1996	2	0	0	0	0
Jason Southwell	Huddersfield	2004	(1)	0	0	0	0
Waisale Sovatabua	Wakefield	2001-03	44(3)	19	0	0	76
	Hudds-Sheff	2000	23(1)	8	0	0	32
	Sheffield	1996-99	56(17)	19	0	1	77
Yusef Sozi	London	2000-01	(5)	0	0	0	0
Andy Speak	Castleford	2001	4(4)	0	0	0	0
	Wakefield	2000	6(5)	2	0	0	8
	Leeds	1999	4	1	0	0	4
Tim Spears	Castleford	2003	(3)	0	0	0	0
Ady Spencer	London	1996-99	8(36)	5	0	0	20
Rob Spicer	Wakefield	2002-04	18(14)	2	0	0	8
Stuart Spruce	Widnes	2002-03	45(4)	19	0	0	76
	Bradford	1996-2001	107(2)	57	0	0	228
Lee St Hilaire	Castleford	1997	4(2)	0	0	0	0
Marcus St Hilaire	Huddersfield	2003-04	50(1)	19	0	0	76
	Leeds	1996-2002	59(33)	31	0	0	124
Dylan Stainton	Workington	1996	2(3)	0	0	0	0
Mark Stamper	Workington	1996	(1)	0	0	0	0
John Stankevitch	St Helens	2000-04	74(40)	25	0	0	100
Gareth Stanley	Bradford	2000	1	1	0	0	4
Graham Steadman	Castleford	1996-97	11(17)	5	0	0	20
Jamie Stenhouse	Warrington	2000-01	9(3)	3	0	0	12
Gareth Stephens	Sheffield	1997-99	23(6)	2	0	0	8
David Stephenson	Hull	1998	11(7)	3	0	0	12
	Oldham	1997	10(8)	2	0	0	8
Francis Stephenson							
	London	2002-04	35(28)	5	0	0	20
	Wigan	2001	2(9)	0	0	0	0
	Wakefield	1999-2000	50(1)	6	0	0	24
Paul Sterling	Leeds	1997-2000	79(12)	50	0	0	200
Paul Stevens	Oldham	1996	2(1)	0	0	0	0
	London	1996	(1)	0	0	0	0
Warren Stevens	Warrington	1996-99,					
		2002-04	17(59)	1	0	0	4
	Salford	2001	(8)	0	0	0	0
Anthony Stewart	Salford	2004	26	6	0	0	24
	St Helens	1997-2003	93(23)	44	0	0	176
Troy Stone	Widnes	2002	18(6)	1	0	0	4
	Huddersfield	2001	12(1)	1	0	0	4
Lynton Stott	Wakefield	1999	21	4	6	1	29
	Sheffield	1996-98	40(4)	15	0	0	60
Mitchell Stringer	London	2004	10(17)	0	0	0	0
Graham Strutton	London	1996	9(1)	2	0	0	8
Matt Sturm	Warrington	2002-04	1(18)	0	0	0	0
	Huddersfield	1998-99	46	8	0	0	32
Anthony Sullivan	St Helens	1996-2001	137(2)	105	0	0	420
Phil Sumner	Warrington	1996	(5)	0	0	0	0
Simon Svabic	Salford	1998-2000	13(5)	3	19	0	50
Richard Swain	Hull	2004	29	2	0	0	8
Anthony Swann	Warrington	2001	3	1	0	0	4
Logan Swann	Bradford	2004	25	6	0	0	24
Willie Swann	Warrington	1996-97	25(2)	6	0	0	24
Nathan Sykes	Castleford	1996-2004	158(52)	3	0	0	12
Paul Sykes	London	2001-04	66(1)	14	101	1	259
	Bradford	1999-2002	5(4)	2	3	0	14
Wayne Sykes	London	1999	(2)	0	0	0	0
Semi Tadulala	Wakefield	2004	26	9	0	0	36
Whetu Taewa	Sheffield	1997-98	33(7)	8	0	0	32
Alan Tait	Leeds	1996	3(3)	1	0	0	4
Willie Talau	St Helens	2003-04	33(1)	12	0	0	48
Ian Talbot	Wakefield	1999	9(5)	2	31	0	70
	Wigan	1997	3	1	0	0	4
Albert Talipeau	Wakefield	2004	2(3)	0	0	0	0
Gael Tallec	Halifax	2000	5(19)	3	0	0	12
	Castleford	1998-99	19(21)	3	0	0	12
	Wigan	1996-97	8(12)	3	0	0	12
Joe Tamani	Bradford	1996	11(3)	4	0	0	16
Andrew Tangata-Toa							
	Huddersfield	1999	15	2	0	0	8
Kris Tassell	Wakefield	2002	24	10	0	0	40
	Salford	2000-01	35(10)	12	0	0	48
Shem Tatupu	Wigan	1996	(3)	0	0	0	0
Tony Tatupu	Wakefield	2000-01	20	2	0	0	8
	Warrington	1997	21(1)	6	0	0	24
Joe Taylor	Paris	1997	9(5)	2	0	0	8
Lawrence Taylor	Sheffield	1996	(1)	0	0	0	0
Frederic Teixido	Sheffield	1999	(4)	0	0	0	0
	Paris	1996-97	2(3)	1	0	0	4
Jason Temu	Hull	1998	13(2)	1	0	0	4
	Oldham	1996-97	25(3)	1	0	0	4
Paul Terry	London	1997	(1)	0	0	0	0
Jamie Thackray	Castleford	2003-04	7(11)	3	0	0	12
	Halifax	2000-02	10(38)	3	0	0	12
Adam Thaler	Castleford	2002	(1)	0	0	0	0
Giles Thomas	London	1997-99	1(2)	0	0	0	0
Steve Thomas	London	2004	4(2)	0	0	0	0
	Warrington	2001	2	0	0	0	0
Alex Thompson	Sheffield	1997	4(11)	0	0	0	0
Bobby Thompson	Salford	1999	28	5	2	0	24
Chris Thorman	London	2003	26(1)	7	81	1	191
	Huddersfield	2000-01	38(13)	10	2	0	44
	Sheffield	1999	5(13)	2	8	1	25
Tony Thorniley	Warrington	1997	(5)	0	0	0	0
Danny Tickle	Wigan	2002-04	56(20)	20	68	1	217
	Halifax	2000-02	25(17)	10	91	2	224
Kris Tickle	Warrington	2001	(1)	0	0	0	0
John Timu	London	1998-2000	57(3)	11	0	0	44
Kerrod Toby	London	1997	2(2)	0	0	0	0
Tulsen Tollett	London	1996-2001	105(5)	38	49	1	251
Glen Tomlinson	Wakefield	1999-2000	41(5)	8	0	0	32
	Hull	1998	5	1	0	0	4
	Bradford	1996-97	27(13)	12	0	0	48
Ian Tonks	Castleford	1996-2001	32(50)	11	13	0	70
Motu Tony	Castleford	2004	8(1)	1	0	0	4
Mark Tookey	Castleford	2004	2(8)	1	0	0	4
Paul Topping	Oldham	1996-97	23(10)	1	19	0	42
Patrick Torreilles	Paris	1996	9(1)	1	25	0	54
Mat Toshack	London	1998-2004	120(21)	24	0	0	96
Darren Treacy	Salford	2002	24(1)	6	1	0	26
Dean Treister	Hull	2003	16(1)	3	0	0	12
Steve Trindall	London	2003-04	20(15)	2	0	0	8
George Truelove	Wakefield	2002	2	1	0	0	4
	London	2000	2	1	0	0	4
Va'aiga Tuigamala	Wigan	1996	21	10	3	0	46
Fereti Tuilagi	St Helens	1999-2000	43(15)	21	0	0	84
	Halifax	1996-98	55(3)	27	0	0	108
Sateki Tuipulotu	Leeds	1996	6(3)	1	2	0	8
Darren Turner	Huddersfield	2000-01,					
		2003-04	42(13)	13	0	0	52
	Sheffield	1996-99	41(29)	15	0	0	60
Ian Turner	Paris	1996	1(1)	1	0	0	4
Gregory Tutard	Paris	1996	1(1)	0	0	0	0
Brendon Tuuta	Warrington	1998	18(2)	4	0	0	16
	Castleford	1996-97	41(1)	3	0	0	12
Mike Umaga	Halifax	1996-97	38(1)	16	5	0	74
Kava Utoikamanu	Paris	1996	6(3)	0	0	0	0
Joe Vagana	Bradford	2001-04	106(8)	9	0	0	36
Nigel Vagana	Warrington	1997	20	17	0	0	68
Tevita Vaikona	Bradford	1998-2004	145(2)	89	0	0	356
Lesley Vainikolo	Bradford	2002-04	69(4)	70	0	0	280
Eric Van Brussell	Paris	1996	2	0	0	0	0
Richard Varkulis	Warrington	2004	4(1)	3	0	0	12
Marcus Vassilakopoulos							
	Sheffield	1997-99	15(11)	3	10	2	34
	Leeds	1996-97	1(3)	0	0	0	0
Phil Veivers	Huddersfield	1998	7(6)	1	0	0	4
	St Helens	1996	1(1)	0	0	0	0
Eric Vergniol	Paris	1996	14(1)	6	0	0	24
Gray Viane	St Helens	2004	4	1	0	0	4
Adrian Vowles	Castleford	1997-2001,					
		2003	125(1)	29	1	1	119
	Wakefield	2002-03	24(3)	6	1	0	26
	Leeds	2002	14(3)	2	0	0	8
Michael Wainwright							
	Wakefield	2004	13(7)	6	0	0	24
Mike Wainwright	Warrington	1996-99,					
		2003-04	101(13)	16	0	0	64
	Salford	2000-02	72(3)	9	0	0	36
Ben Walker	Leeds	2002	23(1)	8	100	0	232
Chev Walker	Leeds	1999-2004	92(16)	53	0	0	212

Super League Players 1996-2004

PLAYER	CLUB	YEAR	APP	TRIES	GOALS	FG	PTS
Matt Walker	Huddersfield	2001	3(6)	0	0	0	0
Anthony Wall	Paris	1997	9	3	3	0	18
Mark Wallace	Workington	1996	14(1)	3	0	0	12
Kerrod Walters	Gateshead	1999	10(12)	2	1	0	10
Kevin Walters	Warrington	2001	1	0	0	0	0
Barry Ward	St Helens	2002-03	20(30)	4	0	0	16
Danny Ward	Leeds	1999-2004	46(46)	6	0	1	25
Phil Waring	Salford	1997-99	6(8)	2	0	0	8
Brett Warton	London	1999-2001	49(7)	14	133	0	322
Kyle Warren	Castleford	2002	13(14)	3	0	0	12
Frank Watene	Wakefield	1999-2001	24(37)	6	0	0	24
Dave Watson	Sheffield	1998-99	41(4)	4	0	0	16
Ian Watson	Salford	1997, 2002	24(17)	8	3	5	43
	Workington	1996	4(1)	1	15	0	34
Kris Watson	Warrington	1996	11(2)	2	0	0	8
Michael Watts	Warrington	2002	3	0	0	0	0
Jason Webber	Salford	2000	25(1)	10	0	0	40
Paul Wellens	St Helens	1998-2004	150(23)	58	17	1	267
Jon Wells	London	2004	19(1)	7	0	0	28
	Wakefield	2003	22(1)	1	0	0	4
	Castleford	1996-2002	114(14)	49	0	0	196
Dwayne West	St Helens	2000-02	8(16)	6	0	0	24
	Wigan	1999	1(1)	0	0	0	0
Craig Weston	Widnes	2002, 2004	23(9)	2	1	2	12
	Huddersfield	1998-99	46(1)	15	15	0	90
Ben Westwood	Warrington	2002-04	51(1)	22	0	0	88
	Wakefield	1999-2002	31(7)	8	1	0	34
Andrew Whalley	Workington	1996	(2)	0	0	0	0
Matt Whitaker	Widnes	2004	2(6)	4	0	0	16
	Huddersfield	2003-04	3(14)	0	0	0	0
David White	Wakefield	2000	(1)	0	0	0	0
Josh White	Salford	1998	18(3)	5	5	1	31
	London	1997	14(2)	8	0	1	33
Paul White	Huddersfield	2003-04	6(15)	8	16	0	64
Richard Whiting	Hull	2004	17(10)	12	3	1	55
Danny Whittle	Warrington	1998	(2)	0	0	0	0
David Whittle	St Helens	2002	1(2)	0	0	0	0
	Warrington	2001	1(2)	0	0	0	0
Jon Whittle	Wigan	2003	1	0	0	0	0
Stephen Wild	Wigan	2001-04	41(18)	18	0	0	72
Oliver Wilkes	Huddersfield	2000-01	1(6)	0	0	0	0
	Sheffield	1998	(1)	0	0	0	0
Jon Wilkin	St Helens	2003-04	21(11)	9	0	0	36
Alex Wilkinson	Hull	2003-04	11(4)	1	0	0	4
	Huddersfield	2003	8	4	0	0	16
	London	2002	5(1)	0	0	0	0
	Bradford	2000-01	3(3)	1	0	0	4
Bart Williams	London	1998	5(3)	1	0	0	4
Desi Williams	Wigan	2004	2	0	0	0	0
Jonny Williams	London	2004	(4)	0	0	0	0
John Wilshere	Warrington	2004	5	2	0	0	8
Craig Wilson	Hull	2000	2(16)	1	0	1	5
	Gateshead	1999	17(11)	5	0	1	21
George Wilson	Paris	1996	7(2)	3	0	0	12
Richard Wilson	Hull	1998-99	(13)	0	0	0	0
Scott Wilson	Warrington	1998-99	23(2)	6	0	0	24
Johan Windley	Hull	1999	2(2)	1	0	0	4
Paul Wingfield	Warrington	1997	5(3)	6	1	0	26
Michael Withers	Bradford	1999-2004	111(4)	75	15	4	334
Jeff Wittenberg	Huddersfield	1998	18(1)	1	0	0	4
	Bradford	1997	8(9)	4	0	0	16
Martin Wood	Sheffield	1997-98	24(11)	4	18	2	54
Nathan Wood	Warrington	2002-04	67	24	0	3	99
	Wakefield	2002	11	2	0	0	8
Paul Wood	Warrington	2000-04	44(54)	19	0	0	76
Phil Wood	Widnes	2004	2(1)	0	0	0	0
David Woods	Halifax	2002	18(2)	8	0	0	32
Rob Worrincy	Castleford	2004	1	0	0	0	0
Troy Wozniak	Widnes	2004	13(7)	1	0	0	4
Matthew Wray	Wakefield	2002-03	13(3)	2	0	0	8
David Wrench	Wakefield	2002-04	21(32)	5	0	0	20
	Leeds	1999-2001	7(17)	0	0	0	0
Craig Wright	Castleford	2000	1(9)	0	0	0	0
Nigel Wright	Huddersfield	1999	4(6)	1	0	0	4
	Wigan	1996-97	5(5)	2	0	1	9
Ricky Wright	Sheffield	1997-99	2(13)	0	0	0	0
Vincent Wulf	Paris	1996	13(4)	4	0	0	16
Andrew Wynyard	London	1999-2000	34(6)	4	0	0	16
Bagdad Yaha	Paris	1996	4(4)	2	4	0	16
Malakai Yasa	Sheffield	1996	1(3)	0	0	0	0
Kirk Yeaman	Hull	2001-04	47(16)	25	0	0	100
Grant Young	London	1998-99	22(2)	2	0	0	8
Ronel Zenon	Paris	1996	(4)	0	0	0	0
Nick Zisti	Bradford	1999	6(1)	0	0	0	0

SUPER LEAGUE IX
Club by Club

KEY DATES - BRADFORD BULLS

16 April 2004 - Tevita Vaikona to miss the remainder of 2004 after suffering serious knee ligament damage in the Bulls controversial round six 54-8 win over St Helens.

3 May 2004 - Brian Noble emerges as favourite for the Great Britain head coaching job.

7 May 2004 - Iestyn Harris rumoured to be on his way to Odsal after announcing he will be returning to Rugby League.

21 May 2004 - Minister for Sport Richard Caborn MP visits Odsal Stadium to help launch the 'Bradford Bulls Foundation', a new charitable body that will focus on developing work in the community.

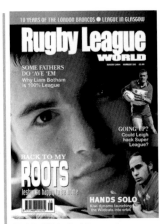

3 December 2003 - Bulls sign Great Britain utility player Paul Johnson from Wigan on a three-year contract.

15 January 2004 - planning application lodged to turn Odsal Stadium and adjacent land into a sporting village.

13 February 2004 - Bulls crowned World Club champions after a 22-4 win over Penrith Panthers at Huddersfield.

7 March 2004 - Michael Withers damages a shoulder as Bradford beat Wakefield Wildcats 40-6 at Belle Vue.

11 March 2004 - Bradford centre Toa Kohe-Love plays his last Bulls game, suffering knee ligament damage against Wakefield.

18 March 2004 - Robbie Paul makes Bulls return at Huddersfield in round three after missing the start of the season with a broken arm suffered the previous June.

4 April 2004 - Robbie Paul and Lesley Vainikolo are called up for New Zealand in the ANZAC tests versus Australia.

1 July 2004 - Iestyn Harris to join the Bulls on a four-and-a-half year contract after a three-year spell in Welsh rugby union.

12 July 2004 - Paul Deacon signs a new three-year contract, securing his future at the club until the end of the 2007 season.

13 July 2004 - Karl Pratt and Leon Pryce are suspended for their parts in a brawl in the 36-26 home win over Wakefield Trinity Wildcats.

19 August 2004 - centre Shontayne Hape signs a new contract until 2006.

15 September 2004 - Bulls sign Australian 24-year-old international Brad Meyers from Brisbane Broncos on a three-year contract.

22 September 2004 - Kiwi prop Joe Vagana signs a new two-year contract and will remain at Odsal until the end of the 2006 Super League season.

2 October 2004 - Bulls stampede past local rivals Leeds Rhinos and into the Grand Final with an accomplished 26-12 win at Headingley.

16 October 2004 - Bulls fall to the Rhinos 16-8 in the Tetley's Super League Grand Final.

21 October 2004 - Bulls sign Ryan Hudson on a two-year contract and Andy Lynch on a three-year deal from Castleford Tigers, who sign Bulls hooker Aaron Smith.

Stuart Fielden

BRADFORD BULLS

DATE	FIXTURE	RESULT	SCORERS	LGE	ATT
13/2/04	Penrith (WCC) ●	W22-4	t:Vainikolo,L Pryce,Swann,Parker g:Withers(3)	N/A	18,962
20/2/04	Wigan (h)	W34-6	t:Withers,Vainikolo(5),Aaron Smith g:Withers(3)	2nd	17,267
29/2/04	St Helens (h) (CCR4)	L10-30	t:Deacon,Radford g:Deacon	N/A	12,215
7/3/04	Wakefield (a)	W6-40	t:Vaikona(2),Vainikolo(2),Bridge(2),Johnson,Reardon g:Deacon(4)	2nd	6,472
21/3/04	Huddersfield (a)	W6-20	t:Johnson(2),Deacon g:Deacon(4)	2nd	8,039
2/4/04	Salford (h)	W25-18	t:Deacon,L Pryce,Johnson,Vainikolo g:Deacon(4) fg:Withers	2nd	11,976
8/4/04	Leeds (a)	L26-18	t:Vainikolo,Hape,Vaikona g:Deacon(3)	3rd	21,225
12/4/04	St Helens (h)	W54-8	t:Radford,Vaikona(2),Vainikolo(2),Langley,Hape(3),Withers(2) g:Withers(3),Deacon,Paul	2nd	15,623
23/4/04	Hull (h)	L18-26	t:Hape,Deacon g:Deacon(5)	3rd	12,684
27/4/04	Warrington (a)	D22-22	t:Aaron Smith,Withers(2),Vainikolo g:Deacon(3)	2nd	8,111
3/5/04	London (a)	W12-24	t:Deacon,Langley,L Pryce,Reardon(2) g:Deacon(2)	2nd	3,987
9/5/04	Castleford (h)	W44-18	t:Reardon(4),Langley(2),Vainikolo(2) g:Deacon(6)	2nd	12,877
23/5/04	Widnes (a)	W20-30	t:L Pryce(2),Johnson,Hape,Aaron Smith g:Deacon(5)	2nd	6,615
29/5/04	St Helens (a)	L35-30	t:Anderson,Parker,Pratt(3) g:Deacon(5)	3rd	10,933
5/6/04	Leeds (h)	L12-26	t:Vainikolo,Reardon g:Deacon(2)	4th	23,375
13/6/04	Salford (a)	W28-35	t:Hape,Johnson(2),Vainikolo(2),Bridge g:Withers,Bridge(4) fg:Withers	4th	5,006
20/6/04	Huddersfield (h)	W40-12	t:Hape(2),Swann,Fielden,Reardon g:Deacon(10)	4th	11,069
27/6/04	Widnes (h)	W38-30	t:Johnson,Pratt(2),Andy Smith,L Pryce,Paul(2) g:Deacon(3),Bridge(2)	3rd	11,137
4/7/04	Castleford (a)	W12-60	t:L Pryce,Vainikolo(4),Hape(2),Deacon,Peacock,Parker g:Deacon(10)	3rd	6,606
11/7/04	Wakefield (h)	W36-26	t:Peacock,Reardon,Deacon,Vainikolo(2),Parker g:Deacon(6)	4th	12,670
16/7/04	Wigan (a)	L32-16	t:Peacock,Swann,Hape g:Deacon(2)	5th	15,102
25/7/04	London (h)	W44-16	t:Andy Smith,Vainikolo(2),Paul,Swann,Langley,Reardon,Fielden g:Deacon(4),Harris(2)	4th	10,283
1/8/04	Hull (a)	L25-14	t:Hape,Paul g:Deacon(3)	5th	14,124
8/8/04	Warrington (h)	W36-22	t:Hape,Reardon,Vainikolo(3),Bridge g:Deacon(6)	3rd	12,981
13/8/04	Wigan (h)	W38-12	t:L Pryce,Paul,Langley,Vainikolo,Harris(2),Hape g:Deacon(4),Harris	3rd	12,610
22/8/04	Leeds (a)	L40-12	t:Swann,Harris g:Deacon(2)	3rd	21,225
30/8/04	Hull (h)	W12-26	t:Vainikolo(3),Langley,Harris g:Deacon(3)	3rd	13,593
5/9/04	London (h)	W60-18	t:Hape(3),Fielden,Swann(2),Withers,Parker(2),Vagana g:Deacon(10)	2nd	11,319
12/9/04	Warrington (a)	W27-28	t:Langley,Vainikolo,Hape,Harris(2) g:Deacon(3) fg:Deacon(2)	2nd	10,008
17/9/04	St Helens (h)	W64-24	t:Hape(2),Reardon(3),Vainikolo(3),Peacock,Withers,Deacon g:Deacon(10)	2nd	13,127
2/10/04	Leeds (a) (QSF)	W12-26	t:Hape(2),Paul,Radford,Vainikolo g:Deacon(3)	N/A	21,225
16/10/04	Leeds (GF) ●●	L8-16	t:Vainikolo,Hape	N/A	65,547

● Played at McAlpine Stadium, Huddersfield
●● Played at Old Trafford, Manchester

		APP		TRIES		GOALS		FG		PTS	
	D.O.B.	ALL	SL	ALL	SL	ALL	SL	ALL	SL	ALL	SL
Paul Anderson	25/10/71	10(14)	8(14)	1	1	0	0	0	0	4	4
Chris Bridge	5/7/84	2(12)	2(11)	4	4	6	6	0	0	28	28
Richard Colley	9/1/84	1	1	0	0	0	0	0	0	0	0
Paul Deacon	13/2/79	29	28	8	7	124	123	2	2	282	276
Stuart Fielden	14/9/79	30(2)	28(2)	3	3	0	0	0	0	12	12
Shontayne Hape	30/1/82	27	26	24	24	0	0	0	0	96	96
Iestyn Harris	25/6/76	12(1)	12(1)	6	6	3	3	0	0	30	30
Paul Johnson	25/11/78	20(5)	18(5)	8	8	0	0	0	0	32	32
Toa Kohe-Love	2/12/74	2(1)	1(1)	0	0	0	0	0	0	0	0
Jamie Langley	21/12/83	10(20)	9(19)	8	8	0	0	0	0	32	32
Richard Moore	2/2/81	(10)	(10)	0	0	0	0	0	0	0	0
Rob Parker	5/9/81	9(23)	9(21)	6	5	0	0	0	0	24	20
Robbie Paul	3/2/76	22(4)	22(4)	6	6	1	1	0	0	26	26
Jamie Peacock	14/12/77	32	30	4	4	0	0	0	0	16	16
Karl Pratt	18/7/80	8(8)	7(8)	5	5	0	0	0	0	20	20
Karl Pryce	27/7/86	2(1)	2(1)	0	0	0	0	0	0	0	0
Leon Pryce	9/10/81	29(1)	27(1)	8	7	0	0	0	0	32	28
Lee Radford	26/3/79	24(6)	22(6)	3	2	0	0	0	0	12	8
Stuart Reardon	13/10/81	25(7)	25(5)	15	15	0	0	0	0	60	60
Aaron Smith	10/9/82	11(1)	9(1)	3	3	0	0	0	0	12	12
Andy Smith	6/7/84	6(2)	6(2)	2	2	0	0	0	0	8	8
Logan Swann	10/2/75	26	25	7	6	0	0	0	0	28	24
Joe Vagana	21/1/75	20(9)	20(7)	1	1	0	0	0	0	4	4
Tevita Vaikona	18/8/74	8	6	5	5	0	0	0	0	20	20
Lesley Vainikolo	4/5/79	28	26	39	38	0	0	0	0	156	152
Michael Withers	16/5/76	23	21	7	7	10	7	2	2	50	44

LEAGUE RECORD
P28-W20-D1-L7
(2nd, SL/Grand Final Runners Up)
F918, A565, Diff+353
41 points.

CHALLENGE CUP
Round Four

ATTENDANCES
Best - v Leeds (SL - 23,375)
Worst - v London (SL - 10,283)
Total (SL only) - 188,998
Average (SL only) - 13,500
(Down by 1,759 on 2003)

TOP TACKLES
Jamie Peacock 614

TOP CARRIES
Jamie Peacock 395

TOP METRES
Lesley Vainikolo 3593

TOP BREAKS
Lesley Vainikolo 40

TOP OFFLOADS
Stuart Fielden 46

TOP BUSTS
Lesley Vainikolo 132

KEY DATES - CASTLEFORD TIGERS

21 April 2004 - Tigers part company with coach Graham Steadman "by mutual consent". Widnes coach Neil Kelly is linked with the vacant position.

12 May 2004 - Tigers hand two-year contracts to their trialists from London, wing/fullback Rob Worrincy and prop Alex Rowe.

20 May 2004 - Caretaker coach Gary Mercer is handed head coach's job, with Ellery Hanley coming in as coaching consultant.

25 May 2004 - Tigers and former Great Britain centre Paul Newlove announces his retirement due to a persistent foot tendon injury after just five Super League games.

6 November 2003 - Tigers complete the signing of England A centre/second-rower Ryan Clayton from Halifax on a two-year contract.

11 December 2003 - Castleford recruit Byron Smith for the 2004 from Halifax.

7 January 2004 - Tigers sign under-18s, centre Kevin King, prop Craig Cawthray and scrum-half Dominic Brambani on professional contracts.

22 January 2004 - Graham Steadman hands debuts to new signings Paul Newlove, Craig Greenhill and Sean Ryan in friendly against Bradford.

29 January 2004 - Andy Lynch and Ryan Clayton are ruled out of Super League opener at Huddersfield Giants, as the Tigers lose 26-22.

7 March 2004 - New Super League record home attendance of 11,731 for the Leeds Rhinos clash in Round Two.

22 March 2004 - scrum-half Ryan Sheridan is ruled out for at least three months with a shoulder injury.

23 March 2004 - Academy player Rob Lunt's appeal against a two-year suspension for a breach of the RFL's Doping Control regulations in February, is dismissed.

14 June 2004 - Brad Davis re-signs for Castleford after a cash settlement between the Tigers and Halifax.

15 June 2004 - Luke Robinson has his loan-spell at Castleford Tigers extended for another month.

2 July 2004 - Sean Rudder to leave the club after only 14 appearances.

6 July 2004 - Ellery Hanley parts company with the Tigers.

8 July 2004 - Tigers confirm the signing of New Zealand Warriors prop Mark Tookey until the end of the season.

22 July 2004 - Tigers sign the Leeds Rhinos under-21's centre Matt Gardner on a month's loan.

27 July 2004 - Second-rower Sean Ryan to leave after a hamstring injury ends his 2004 season.

19 August 2004 - Tigers keep hopes of Super League survival alive as Francis Maloney pots a field goal for a 7-6 win at Widnes.

19 September 2004 - The Tigers are relegated from Super League, after going down 28-32 at home to Wakefield Trinity Wildcats.

26 September 2004 - The Tigers announce that they are planning to run a full-time team in LHF Healthplan National League One - as they look to bounce back into Super League at the first attempt.

22 October 2004 - Sign hooker Aaron Smith from Bradford after Wayne Godwin signs for Wigan. Andy Lynch and Ryan Hudson leave to join Bradford Bulls.

Ryan Hudson

CASTLEFORD TIGERS

DATE	FIXTURE	RESULT	SCORERS	LGE	ATT
22/2/04	Huddersfield (a)	L26-22	t:Rogers,Pryce,Clayton,Saxton g:Godwin(3)	7th	5,326
28/2/04	Union Treiziste Catalane (h) (CCR4)	W32-20	t:Godwin,Gibson,Rudder,Thackray(2),Pryce g:Godwin(3),Hepworth	N/A	3,435
7/3/04	Leeds (h)	L8-34	t:Clayton g:Godwin(2)	9th	11,731
14/3/04	Hull (a) (CCR5)	L26-0	No Scorers	N/A	11,443
21/3/04	Warrington (a)	L32-18	t:Hepworth(2),Hudson g:Godwin(3)	10th	8,902
2/4/04	St Helens (h)	L14-22	t:Hudson,Godwin g:Godwin(3)	11th	6,876
8/4/04	Hull (a)	L26-4	t:M Smith	12th	10,971
13/4/04	London (h)	L34-42	t:Hudson,Rogers,Saxton,Rudder,Ryan,Newlove,Saxton g:Maloney(3)	12th	4,710
17/4/04	Wakefield (h)	L10-42	t:Ryan,Ripley g:Maloney	12th	5,427
25/4/04	Widnes (a)	L29-18	t:Rogers,Saxton,Thackray g:Maloney(3)	12th	5,274
1/5/04	Wigan (h)	L28-42	t:Mellor(3),Saxton,Thackray g:Godwin(3),Maloney	12th	6,222
9/5/04	Bradford (a)	L44-18	t:Rogers,Godwin,Mellor g:Godwin(3)	12th	12,877
23/5/04	Salford (h)	L32-36	t:Godwin,M Smith,Harland,Kain,Hudson g:Godwin(6)	12th	6,961
28/5/04	London (a)	W10-12	t:Robinson,Mellor g:Godwin(2)	12th	2,562
6/6/04	Hull (h)	L18-52	t:Clayton,Rudder,Mellor g:Hepworth(2),Godwin	12th	8,084
11/6/04	St Helens (a)	L52-8	t:Hudson g:Godwin(2)	12th	8,397
20/6/04	Warrington (h)	L10-32	t:Robinson(2) g:Godwin	12th	6,111
27/6/04	Salford (a)	L30-14	t:Mellor,Lynch g:Godwin(3)	12th	3,313
4/7/04	Bradford (h)	L12-60	t:Godwin,Rogers g:Godwin(2)	12th	6,606
9/7/04	Leeds (a)	L46-14	t:Lynch,Greenhill,Tony g:Godwin	12th	13,922
18/7/04	Huddersfield (h)	W24-20	t:Mellor,Robinson,Hudson,Rogers g:Robinson(3),Godwin	12th	5,321
23/7/04	Wigan (h)	L48-18	t:Pryce,Lynch,Gardner,Rogers g:Hepworth	12th	10,032
31/7/04	Widnes (h)	W42-8	t:Davis,Mellor(2),M Smith,Hudson,Maloney,Godwin,Rogers g:Godwin(5)	12th	5,517
8/8/04	Wakefield (a)	L39-18	t:Hepworth,Crouch,Davis g:Hepworth(2),Godwin	12th	6,673
15/8/04	Huddersfield (a)	W12-29	t:Pryce(2),Hudson,Tookey g:Godwin(6) fg:Maloney	12th	3,231
22/8/04	Hull (h)	W21-14	t:Rogers,Gibson g:Godwin(5),Hepworth fg:Davis	12th	8,054
27/8/04	Leeds (a)	L64-12	t:Crouch,Davis g:Hepworth(2)	12th	14,605
5/9/04	Salford (h)	L22-24	t:Mellor(3),Maloney g:Godwin(2),Maloney	12th	5,809
11/9/04	Widnes (a)	W6-7	t:Hepworth g:Godwin fg:Maloney	12th	7,005
18/9/04	Wakefield (h)	L28-32	t:Gibson,Saxton,Mellor(2),M Smith,Godwin g:Maloney(2)	12th	11,055

	D.O.B.	APP ALL	APP SL	TRIES ALL	TRIES SL	GOALS ALL	GOALS SL	FG ALL	FG SL	PTS ALL	PTS SL
Richard Blakeway	22/7/83	(1)	(1)	0	0	0	0	0	0	0	0
Dominic Brambani	10/5/85	2(2)	2(2)	0	0	0	0	0	0	0	0
Ryan Clayton	22/11/82	13(6)	11(6)	3	3	0	0	0	0	12	12
Steve Crouch	24/12/77	4(1)	4(1)	2	2	0	0	0	0	8	8
Brad Davis	13/3/68	13	13	3	3	0	0	1	1	13	13
Matt Gardner	24/8/84	1	1	1	1	0	0	0	0	4	4
Damian Gibson	14/5/75	22(1)	20(1)	3	2	0	0	0	0	12	8
Wayne Godwin	13/3/82	23(3)	22(2)	7	6	59	56	0	0	146	136
Craig Greenhill	14/2/72	23(4)	21(4)	1	1	0	0	0	0	4	4
Lee Harland	4/9/74	20(3)	18(3)	1	1	0	0	0	0	4	4
Jon Hepworth	25/12/82	15(15)	15(13)	4	4	9	8	0	0	34	32
Craig Huby	21/5/86	(3)	(3)	0	0	0	0	0	0	0	0
Ryan Hudson	20/11/79	29	27	8	8	0	0	0	0	32	32
Paul Jackson	29/9/78	7(15)	6(14)	0	0	0	0	0	0	0	0
Andy Kain	1/9/85	2(2)	2(2)	1	1	0	0	0	0	4	4
Kevin King	18/1/85	(1)	(1)	0	0	0	0	0	0	0	0
Andy Lynch	20/10/79	23(4)	23(3)	3	3	0	0	0	0	12	12
Francis Maloney	26/5/73	18	17	2	2	11	11	2	2	32	32
Paul Mellor	21/8/74	19	19	15	15	0	0	0	0	60	60
Paul Newlove	10/8/71	5	5	1	1	0	0	0	0	4	4
Waine Pryce	3/10/81	16	15	5	4	0	0	0	0	20	16
Dean Ripley	13/9/83	3(4)	3(4)	1	1	0	0	0	0	4	4
Luke Robinson	25/7/84	9	9	4	4	3	3	0	0	22	22
Darren Rogers	6/5/74	28(1)	26(1)	9	9	0	0	0	0	36	36
Sean Rudder	13/2/79	11(3)	9(3)	3	2	0	0	0	0	12	8
Sean Ryan	23/8/73	13(5)	11(5)	2	2	0	0	0	0	8	8
Tom Saxton	3/10/83	23(2)	21(2)	6	6	0	0	0	0	24	24
Michael Shenton	22/7/86	1(2)	1(2)	0	0	0	0	0	0	0	0
Ryan Sheridan	24/5/75	4	2	0	0	0	0	0	0	0	0
Byron Smith	5/3/84	(9)	(9)	0	0	0	0	0	0	0	0
Michael Smith	10/5/76	20(3)	19(2)	4	4	0	0	0	0	16	16
Nathan Sykes	8/9/74	6(15)	5(15)	0	0	0	0	0	0	0	0
Jamie Thackray	30/9/79	6(6)	6(4)	4	2	0	0	0	0	16	8
Motu Tony	29/5/81	8(1)	8(1)	1	1	0	0	0	0	4	4
Mark Tookey	9/3/77	2(8)	2(8)	1	1	0	0	0	0	4	4
Rob Worrincy	9/7/85	1	1	0	0	0	0	0	0	0	0

LEAGUE RECORD
P28-W6-D0-L22
(12th, SL)
F515, A924, Diff-409
12 points.

CHALLENGE CUP
Round Five

ATTENDANCES
Best - v Leeds (SL - 11,731)
Worst - v Union Treiziste Catalane
(CC - 3,435)
Total (SL only) - 98,484
Average (SL only) - 7,035
(Down by 164 on 2003)

TOP TACKLES
Ryan Hudson 780

TOP CARRIES
Andy Lynch 408

TOP METRES
Andy Lynch 3296

TOP BREAKS
Darren Rogers 19

TOP OFFLOADS
Andy Lynch 61

TOP BUSTS
Michael Smith 74

KEY DATES - HUDDERSFIELD GIANTS

6 May 2004 - Paul Reilly lands a new two-year deal to extend his contract until the end of 2006.

26 May 2004 - Giants sign James Evans from Canberra Raiders on an 18-month deal.

2 June 2004 - Marcus St Hilaire extends his contract by one year.

8 June 2004 - Canberra Raiders halfback or hooker Brad Drew signs for 2005 on a two-year contract.

26 June 2004 - Jim Gannon pens a two-year contract extension to keep him at the Giants until the end of the 2006 season.

30 June 2004 - Darren Turner is ruled out for the rest of the season with a recurring knee injury, and will not be offered a new contract by Huddersfield.

20 July 2004 - Giants sign Australian Test centre Michael De Vere for 2005 on a two-year contract.

28 July 2004 - Giants sign Chris Thorman from Parramatta for the 2005 season on a two-year contract.

12 August 2004 - Paul White signs a contract extension to keep him at the newly re-named Galpharm Stadium until the end of next season.

6 November 2003 - prop forward Stuart Jones, 21, signs a one-year loan deal from Saints to join the Giants.

30 January 2004 - scrum-half Paul White to miss the first two months of the new season after suffering a broken and dislocated leg in pre-season friendly.

12 February 2004 - assistant coach Billy McGinty resigns.

29 April 2004 - Giants prop Mick Slicker signs a two-year contract extension to tie him to the Giants until the end of 2006.

4 May 2004 - Paul March signs a new-two-year contract.

1 September 2004 - Brandon Costin announces he is leaving Huddersfield Giants at the end of this season despite having a year left on his contract.

8 September 2004 - Scottish International back row Iain Morrison signs a one-year extension.

4 October 2004 - Hefin O'Hare signs a new one-year deal with the Giants.

12 October 2004 - Stuart Jones agrees a permanent two-year deal.

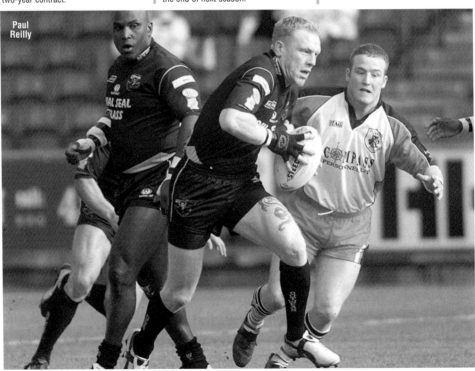

Paul Reilly

HUDDERSFIELD GIANTS

DATE	FIXTURE	RESULT	SCORERS	LGE	ATT
22/2/04	Castleford (h)	W26-22	t:St Hilaire(2),March,Jones,Costin g:Costin(3)	6th	5,326
29/2/04	Pia (h) (CCR4)	W50-16	t:St Hilaire(2),March,Gene,Cooper,Jones,Reilly,Donlan,Roarty(2) g:Costin(3),March(2)	N/A	1,392
5/3/04	Widnes (a)	W6-38	t:March(2),Gene(2),Bailey,Nero g:March(7)	3rd	5,412
14/3/04	Doncaster (h) (CCR5)	W36-12	t:O'Hare,Slicker,Donlan,Penkywicz,Jones,Smith,March g:March(4)	N/A	3,134
21/3/04	Bradford (h)	L6-20	t:Turner g:March	6th	8,039
28/3/04	York (h) (CCQF)	W50-12	t:Roarty(3),Costin(2),Penkywicz,Cooper,O'Hare,St Hilaire,Bailey g:March(5)	N/A	4,286
4/4/04	Wigan (h)	W26-10	t:Costin,Jones,Turner,Reilly g:March(5)	5th	5,175
9/4/04	Salford (h)	W24-16	t:O'Hare,St Hilaire,Bailey,Nero g:March(4)	5th	4,062
12/4/04	Wakefield (a)	W17-24	t:Roarty,O'Hare,Penkywicz,Turner g:March(4)	3rd	4,702
16/4/04	Leeds (a)	L38-6	t:St Hilaire g:Costin	4th	11,701
25/4/04	St Helens (CCSF) ●	L6-46	t:March g:March	N/A	13,134
2/5/04	Warrington (a)	W20-26	t:Bailey,Roarty,Crabtree,Nero g:March(5)	4th	8,792
7/5/04	Hull (h)	L0-20	No Scorers	5th	4,064
23/5/04	London (a)	W6-30	t:Penkywicz,Jones,O'Hare,Donlan,St Hilaire,Reilly g:March(3)	5th	2,627
30/5/04	Wakefield (h)	L6-38	t:Penkywicz g:March	5th	4,419
6/6/04	Salford (a)	W18-25	t:Smith,O'Hare,Gene,Penkywicz g:March(4) fg:March	5th	3,271
13/6/04	Wigan (a)	L40-18	t:Slicker,Evans,Nero g:White(3)	6th	9,162
20/6/04	Bradford (h)	L40-12	t:Evans,White g:White(2)	6th	11,069
27/6/04	London (h)	W35-22	t:Evans(2),Nero,St Hilaire(2),Gene g:Costin(4),White fg:Costin	6th	3,009
4/7/04	Hull (a)	L40-12	t:White,Gannon g:White(2)	6th	9,706
7/7/04	St Helens (h)	L8-50	t:Gannon g:White(2)	6th	3,506
11/7/04	Widnes (h)	W26-20	t:Jones(2),Evans,Costin g:Costin(5)	6th	3,566
18/7/04	Castleford (a)	L24-20	t:Evans,Penkywicz,O'Hare g:Costin(4)	6th	5,321
24/7/04	Warrington (h)	L18-34	t:Donlan,Bailey,Smith g:Costin(2),March	6th	4,038
30/7/04	St Helens (a)	L50-10	t:Smith,St Hilaire g:Costin	6th	7,218
8/8/04	Leeds (h)	L10-42	t:Costin,Evans g:White	7th	6,011
15/8/04	Castleford (h)	L12-29	t:White,Evans g:Costin(2)	7th	3,231
22/8/04	Widnes (a)	L24-18	t:Costin(2),Gannon g:Costin(2),March	7th	4,881
27/8/04	St Helens (a)	L48-12	t:Costin,St Hilaire g:Costin(2)	8th	6,095
4/9/04	Hull (h)	W22-20	t:St Hilaire,Costin,Evans g:Costin(5)	7th	3,541
10/9/04	Wakefield (a)	L21-20	t:Penkywicz,Gannon,White g:Costin(4)	7th	4,311
19/9/04	Salford (h)	W28-22	t:Grayshon,Evans,St Hilaire,White g:Costin(6)	7th	3,083

● Played at Halliwell Jones Stadium, Warrington

		APP		TRIES		GOALS		FG		PTS	
	D.O.B.	ALL	SL	ALL	SL	ALL	SL	ALL	SL	ALL	SL
Julian Bailey	17/11/78	23	19	5	4	0	0	0	0	20	16
Ben Cooper	8/10/79	2(5)	1(3)	2	0	0	0	0	0	8	0
Brandon Costin	23/6/72	25	22	10	8	44	41	1	1	129	115
Eorl Crabtree	2/10/82	7(17)	7(13)	1	1	0	0	0	0	4	4
Stuart Donlan	29/8/78	26(5)	24(4)	4	2	0	0	0	0	16	8
James Evans	5/11/78	17	17	10	10	0	0	0	0	40	40
Bolouagi Fagborun	28/3/86	2(1)	2(1)	0	0	0	0	0	0	0	0
Darren Fleary	2/12/72	22(6)	19(6)	0	0	0	0	0	0	0	0
Jim Gannon	16/6/77	20(7)	19(6)	4	4	0	0	0	0	16	16
Stanley Gene	11/5/74	23(2)	19(2)	5	4	0	0	0	0	20	16
Jon Grayshon	10/5/83	1(12)	1(12)	1	1	0	0	0	0	4	4
Stuart Jones	7/12/81	29(3)	25(3)	7	5	0	0	0	0	28	20
Phil Joseph	10/1/85	8(6)	7(6)	0	0	0	0	0	0	0	0
Paul March	25/7/79	26	22	6	3	48	36	1	1	121	85
Iain Morrison	6/5/83	3(7)	3(7)	0	0	0	0	0	0	0	0
Chris Nero	14/2/81	26(3)	22(3)	5	5	0	0	0	0	20	20
Hefin O'Hare	2/6/79	23(7)	19(7)	7	5	0	0	0	0	28	20
Sean Penkywicz	18/5/82	20(12)	19(9)	8	6	0	0	0	0	32	24
Paul Reilly	10/5/76	24(1)	21(1)	3	2	0	0	0	0	12	8
Ben Roarty	5/2/75	25(1)	22	7	2	0	0	0	0	28	8
Mick Slicker	16/8/78	11(7)	7(7)	2	1	0	0	0	0	8	4
Paul Smith	17/5/77	14(9)	14(6)	4	3	0	0	0	0	16	12
Jason Southwell	14/7/85	(1)	(1)	0	0	0	0	0	0	0	0
Marcus St Hilaire	26/1/77	27(1)	23(1)	14	11	0	0	0	0	56	44
Darren Turner	13/10/73	7(1)	5	3	3	0	0	0	0	12	12
Matt Whitaker	6/3/82	1(2)	1(2)	0	0	0	0	0	0	0	0
Paul White	7/12/82	4(10)	4(10)	5	5	11	11	0	0	42	42

LEAGUE RECORD
P28-W12-D0-L16
(7th, SL)
F518, A757, Diff-239
24 points.

CHALLENGE CUP
Semi Finalists

ATTENDANCES
Best - v Bradford (SL - 8,039)
Worst - v Pia (CC - 1,392)
Total (SL only) - 61,070
Average (SL only) - 4,362
(Down by 360 on 2003)

TOP TACKLES
Stuart Jones 660

TOP CARRIES
Paul Reilly 374

TOP METRES
Paul Reilly 2807

TOP BREAKS
Brandon Costin 15

TOP OFFLOADS
Ben Roarty 33

TOP BUSTS
Paul Reilly 58

KEY DATES - HULL F.C.

22 June 2004 - captain Jason Smith signs a one-year deal with the Canberra Raiders after four seasons at Hull.

14 July 2004 - sign Kiwi back row forward Stephen Kearney for 2005 on a one-year deal, with an option for a further year.

16 July 2004 - Richard Swain signs an extension to his current two-year contract that will keep him at Hull until the end of the 2006 Super League season.

4 November 2003 - loanee Alex Wilkinson signs from Bradford on a two-year deal.

5 December 2003 - Hull sign Shaun Briscoe on a three-year contract after he was released by Wigan.

4 March 2004 - Hull are fined £10,000 following a breach of RFL bye-laws concerning crowd misbehaviour the previous season.

8 March 2004 - Second-row forward Richard Fletcher out for up to four months with a broken leg.

25 April 2004 - sign Leeds youngster Nick Scruton on a month's loan.

18 May 2004 - fullback Steve Prescott is released from the remainder of his contract by mutual consent.

21 June 2004 - coach Shaun McRae is to leave at the end of the season to take up a two-year contract with South Sydney Rabbitohs.

23 July 2004 - Hull confirm the appointment of John Kear as head coach for the next two seasons, with an option for a third year.

12 August 2004 - Hull announce the signing of St George Illawarra star winger Nathan Blacklock on a two-year contract.

3 September 2004 - Alex Wilkinson and Ryan Benjafield to leave the club at the end of the current season.

7 September 2004 - Danny Hill signs for two further years and Liam Higgins for one.

9 September 2004 - centre Kirk Yeaman extends his contract to 2007.

13 September 2004 - York coach Richard Agar to become John Kear's assistant for the 2005 and 2006 Super League seasons.

20 September 2004 - sign Castleford utility player Motu Tony on a two-year contract.

22 September 2004 - Great Britain international Richard Horne signs a two-year extension to his contract, tying him to Hull until at least 2008.

23 September 2004 - complete the signing of Castleford Tigers' Jamie Thackray on a one-year contract.

20 October 2004 - sign highly-rated Castleford threequarter Tom Saxton on a two-year contract.

Colin Best

HULL F C

HULL F.C.

DATE	FIXTURE	RESULT	SCORERS	LGE	ATT
20/2/04	St Helens (a)	L30-16	t:Raynor,Best(2) g:Cooke(2)	10th	12,532
29/2/04	Leigh (a) (CCR4)	W14-21	t:Yeaman,Carvell,Best,Briscoe g:Cooke(2) fg:Lupton	N/A	3,324
7/3/04	Warrington (h)	W24-18	t:Barnett,Barnett Jnr(2),Briscoe,Yeaman g:Cooke(2)	7th	12,124
14/3/04	Castleford (h) (CCR5)	W26-0	t:Best(3),Whiting g:Cooke(5)	N/A	11,443
21/3/04	London (h)	W46-4	t:Barnett,Best(2),Lupton,Cooke,Barnett Jnr(2),Carvell,Whiting g:Cooke(5)	4th	9,040
28/3/04	St Helens (a) (CCQF)	L31-26	t:Briscoe(2),R Horne,Barnett g:Cooke(5)	N/A	11,184
3/4/04	Wakefield (a)	W21-27	t:Barnett(2),Barnett Jnr,Carvell g:Cooke(5) fg:R Horne	4th	4,337
8/4/04	Castleford (h)	W26-4	t:Yeaman,Lupton,Best,Barnett g:Cooke(5)	4th	10,971
12/4/04	Widnes (a)	L32-18	t:Briscoe,McMenemy,Cooke g:Cooke(3)	5th	6,059
23/4/04	Bradford (a)	W18-26	t:Briscoe(4) g:Cooke(5)	4th	12,684
2/5/04	Salford (h)	W82-6	t:Whiting(2),Raynor(2),Carvell(2),Briscoe(3),Swain,R Horne, Yeaman,Lupton,Barnett Jnr,King g:Cooke(11)	3rd	9,869
7/5/04	Huddersfield (a)	W0-20	t:McNicholas,Whiting,G Horne g:Cooke(4)	4th	4,064
21/5/04	Leeds (h)	L12-23	t:R Horne,Cooke g:Cooke(2)	4th	16,528
31/5/04	Widnes (h)	W70-4	t:Barnett Jnr(2),Chester(2),Smith,McMenemy,Briscoe(2),Lupton, R Horne,Best,Yeaman g:Cooke(11)	4th	9,946
6/6/04	Castleford (a)	W18-52	t:R Horne,Smith,King,Best,Raynor(3),Yeaman(2),Whiting g:Cooke(5),King	3rd	8,084
13/6/04	Wakefield (h)	W28-24	t:Yeaman(2),Raynor(2),King,Best g:Cooke(2)	3rd	9,928
20/6/04	London (a) ●	W26-42	t:Briscoe,Whiting(2),McNicholas,Best,R Horne,Raynor,Lupton g:Cooke(4),Whiting	3rd	3,589
25/6/04	Leeds (a)	L28-24	t:R Horne,Scruton,Briscoe,Best g:Cooke(4)	4th	15,153
29/6/04	Wigan (h)	D20-20	t:McNicholas,Eagar,Best g:Cooke(4)	3rd	11,042
4/7/04	Huddersfield (h)	W40-12	t:Raynor,Eagar,Lupton,Dowes,R Horne,Whiting,Briscoe g:Cooke(6)	2nd	9,706
11/7/04	Warrington (a)	W18-38	t:Barnett Jnr,Raynor,Whiting,Scruton,Briscoe,Smith g:Cooke(7)	3rd	8,166
17/7/04	St Helens (h)	W34-6	t:R Horne,Briscoe,Yeaman(2),Best,Raynor g:Cooke(5)	2nd	12,949
25/7/04	Salford (a)	W20-44	t:Yeaman(3),Briscoe(2),Barnett Jnr(2),Best,R Horne g:Cooke(4)	2nd	3,515
1/8/04	Bradford (h)	W25-14	t:Barnett Jnr,Briscoe,G Horne,Dowes g:Cooke(4) fg:Whiting	2nd	14,124
6/8/04	Wigan (a)	D13-13	t:Briscoe,R Horne g:Whiting,Cooke fg:R Horne	2nd	12,074
15/8/04	Wakefield (h)	W38-24	t:R Horne,Yeaman,Briscoe(2),Scruton,Cooke,Bailey g:Cooke(5)	2nd	11,048
22/8/04	Castleford (a)	L21-14	t:Cooke,Yeaman,Barnett Jnr g:Cooke	2nd	8,054
30/8/04	Bradford (a)	L12-26	t:Best,Smith g:Cooke(2)	2nd	13,593
4/9/04	Huddersfield (a)	L22-20	t:Carvell,King,Whiting g:Cooke(4)	3rd	3,541
12/9/04	Salford (a)	W8-12	t:Raynor,Yeaman g:Cooke(2)	3rd	3,307
18/9/04	Widnes (h)	W20-18	t:Whiting(2),Barnett Jnr,Lupton,Best	3rd	9,544
24/9/04	Wakefield (h) (EPO)	L18-28	t:Swain,McMenemy,Dowes g:Lupton(3)	N/A	10,550

● Played at Welford Road, Leicester

		APP		TRIES		GOALS		FG		PTS	
	D.O.B.	ALL	SL	ALL	SL	ALL	SL	ALL	SL	ALL	SL
Andy Bailey	15/10/82	2(8)	2(7)	1	1	0	0	0	0	4	4
Richie Barnett	21/4/72	12(1)	9(1)	6	5	0	0	0	0	24	20
Richie Barnett Jnr	26/4/81	17(5)	15(5)	14	14	0	0	0	0	56	56
Colin Best	22/11/78	32	29	19	15	0	0	0	0	76	60
Shaun Briscoe	23/2/83	32	29	25	22	0	0	0	0	100	88
Garreth Carvell	21/4/80	6(10)	6(8)	6	5	0	0	0	0	24	20
Chris Chester	8/10/78	9(7)	8(5)	2	2	0	0	0	0	8	8
Paul Cooke	17/4/81	31	28	5	5	127	115	0	0	274	250
Kirk Dixon	19/7/84	(1)	(1)	0	0	0	0	0	0	0	0
Ewan Dowes	4/3/81	30(1)	27(1)	3	3	0	0	0	0	12	12
Michael Eagar	15/8/73	6	6	2	2	0	0	0	0	8	8
Richard Fletcher	17/5/81	1(8)	1(8)	0	0	0	0	0	0	0	0
Liam Higgins	19/7/83	(17)	(15)	0	0	0	0	0	0	0	0
Danny Hill	31/10/84	(3)	(3)	0	0	0	0	0	0	0	0
Graeme Horne	22/3/85	2(11)	2(11)	2	2	0	0	0	0	8	8
Richard Horne	16/7/82	30	27	12	11	0	0	2	2	50	46
Paul King	28/6/79	25(3)	22(3)	4	4	0	0	0	0	16	16
Andy Last	25/3/81	(1)	(1)	0	0	0	0	0	0	0	0
Peter Lupton	7/3/82	12(13)	10(12)	7	7	3	3	1	0	35	34
Shayne McMenemy	19/7/76	31	28	3	3	0	0	0	0	12	12
Paul McNicholas	26/5/75	26(3)	23(3)	3	3	0	0	0	0	12	12
Gareth Raynor	24/2/78	18	17	13	13	0	0	0	0	52	52
Nick Scruton	24/12/84	2(16)	2(16)	3	3	0	0	0	0	12	12
Jason Smith	14/3/72	13(1)	13(1)	4	4	0	0	0	0	16	16
Richard Swain	2/7/75	32	29	2	2	0	0	0	0	8	8
Richard Whiting	20/12/84	17(13)	17(10)	13	12	3	3	1	1	59	55
Alex Wilkinson	9/10/82	1(3)	(3)	0	0	0	0	0	0	0	0
Kirk Yeaman	15/9/83	29(2)	27(1)	17	16	0	0	0	0	68	64

LEAGUE RECORD
P28-W19-D2-L7
(3rd, SL/Elimination Play-Off)
F843, A478, Diff+365
40 points.

CHALLENGE CUP
Quarter Finalists

ATTENDANCES
Best - v Leeds (SL - 16,528)
Worst - v London (SL - 9,040)
Total (SL, inc play-offs) - 170,962
Average (SL, inc play-offs) - 11,397
(Down by 201 on 2003)

TOP TACKLES
Richard Swain 933

TOP CARRIES
Ewan Dowes 439

TOP METRES
Colin Best 3310

TOP BREAKS
Kirk Yeaman 29

TOP OFFLOADS
Colin Best 53

TOP BUSTS
Colin Best 84

KEY DATES - LEEDS RHINOS

5 July 2004 - Leeds launch a lawsuit against Iestyn Harris.

1 August 2004 - Danny McGuire breaks Super League record of tries scored in a season, with his 29th of the season in the 46-28 home win over Wakefield.

2 August 2004 - Liam Botham returns after his loan spell at London Broncos.

3 August 2004 - Matt Adamson announces he will leave the Rhinos at the end of the season after three years at Headingley to join Canberra Raiders.

11 November 2003 - Kevin Sinfield signs a new five-year contract with the Rhinos.

4 December 2003 - Great Britain centre Keith Senior agrees a new four-year contract.

15 December 2003 - Leeds welcome Chev Walker back to training after his release from a young offenders institute.

8 April 2004 - Rhinos' clash against Bradford Bulls is sold out. Leeds win 26-12.

10 May 2004 - Rhinos sign giant Kiwi forward Ali Lauitiiti.

7 June 2004 - Rhinos issue a statement following the speculation surrounding former captain Iestyn Harris's return to Rugby League.

8 June 2004 - Leeds Rhinos are forced to make three of their upcoming Super League games, against Hull, St Helens and Bradford, all ticket.

2 July 2004 - chief executive Gary Hetherington hits out over Bradford's announcement that they have signed Iestyn Harris, claiming he is still in contract with Leeds.

5 August 2004 - Richard Mathers, 20, lands a new two-year contract which will keep him at Headingley until at least the end of the 2006 Super League season.

6 August 2004 - Samoan international Willie Poching, 30, agrees a one-year extension to his contract.

11 August 2004 - second row Jamie Jones-Buchanan agrees a one-year extension to his contract, keeping him at Headingley until at least the end of the 2005 Super League season.

13 August 2004 - Danny Ward signs new one-year contract which will keep the prop at Headingley until at least the end of the 2005 Super League season.

13 August 2004 - Barrie McDermott agrees a new one-year contract and is awarded a testimonial.

20 August 2004 - The Rhinos issue a statement making an apology to Bradford - while confirming that they are to press ahead with legal action against the Bulls and Iestyn Harris.

18 August 2004 - Liam Botham, 26, agrees a new one-year Rugby League only deal.

16 September 2004 - David Furner announces he will return to Australia to join Canberra at the end of the season.

17 September 2004 - Rhinos finish nine points clear at the top of the table.

16 October 2004 - A late try from Danny McGuire seals a compelling Grand Final win for Leeds Rhinos to end their 32-year title drought.

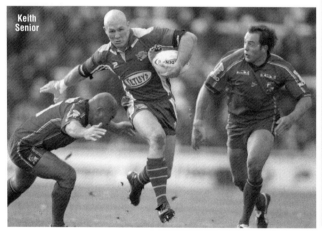

Keith Senior

LEEDS RHINOS

DATE	FIXTURE	RESULT	SCORERS	LGE	ATT
22/2/04	London (h)	W58-14	t:Burrow(2),Senior(2),Bai(3),Walker(2),Calderwood g:Sinfield(9)	1st	15,119
29/2/04	Workington (a) (CCR4)	W18-68	t:McDermott,Calderwood(2),Poching,Cummins(2),McKenna,Burrow, Jones-Buchanan,Walker,Feather,Diskin g:Sinfield(9),Burrow	N/A	4,829
7/3/04	Castleford (a)	W8-34	t:McGuire(3),Bai,Connolly,Senior g:Sinfield(5)	1st	11,731
13/3/04	St Helens (a) (CCR5)	L24-14	t:McGuire,Bailey g:Sinfield(3)	N/A	13,699
19/3/04	Wigan (h)	W36-24	t:Jones-Buchanan(2),McGuire(2),Walker,Diskin g:Sinfield(6)	1st	18,124
4/4/04	Widnes (a)	W0-46	t:Diskin,Bai(2),McGuire,Cummins,Sinfield,Feather,Burrow,McDermott g:Sinfield(3),Burrow(2)	1st	7,325
8/4/04	Bradford (h)	W26-18	t:Dunemann,McGuire(2),Bai,Feather g:Sinfield(3)	1st	21,225
12/4/04	Salford (a)	W0-44	t:Walker(2),McKenna,Bai(2),Poching,Dunemann,Calderwood,McGuire g:Sinfield(4)	1st	5,462
16/4/04	Huddersfield (h)	W38-6	t:Mathers,Walker(3),Furner(2),McGuire g:Sinfield(5)	1st	11,701
23/4/04	Wakefield (a)	W12-36	t:Senior(2),McGuire(2),Cummins,Furner(2) g:Furner(4)	1st	7,680
30/4/04	St Helens (a)	L56-10	t:Burrow,Feather g:Sinfield	1st	11,059
7/5/04	Warrington (h)	W23-10	t:Bai(2),Calderwood,McGuire g:Sinfield(2),Furner fg:Sinfield	1st	16,065
21/5/04	Hull (a)	W12-23	t:Mathers,Burrow(2),McGuire g:Sinfield(3) fg:Sinfield	1st	16,528
28/5/04	Salford (h)	W34-6	t:Sinfield,Diskin,Calderwood,Senior,Cummins,McGuire g:Sinfield(5)	1st	14,239
5/6/04	Bradford (a)	W12-26	t:Senior,Poching,Lauitiiti,Dunemann g:Sinfield(5)	1st	23,375
11/6/04	Widnes (h)	W48-24	t:Calderwood(2),McGuire(5),Lauitiiti,Burrow g:Furner(5),Burrow	1st	13,419
19/6/04	Wigan (a)	L26-22	t:Bai,Lauitiiti,Jones-Buchanan g:Sinfield(5)	1st	14,140
25/6/04	Hull (h)	W28-24	t:Lauitiiti(2),Senior,Walker,Jones-Buchanan g:Sinfield,Burrow(3)	1st	15,153
4/7/04	Warrington (a)	W22-38	t:Bai,Walker,Diskin,Cummins,McGuire(2),McKenna g:Sinfield(4),Burrow	1st	10,404
9/7/04	Castleford (h)	W46-14	t:Bai,McGuire(2),Diskin,Poching(3),Calderwood g:Sinfield(7)	1st	13,922
18/7/04	London (a)	D36-36	t:McGuire,Bai(2),McDonald,Sinfield,McKenna g:Sinfield(6)	1st	5,058
23/7/04	St Helens (h)	W70-0	t:Bai(3),McGuire(3),McDonald(2),Diskin,Mathers,Lauitiiti,Senior g:Sinfield(11)	1st	16,635
1/8/04	Wakefield (h)	W46-28	t:Ward,Poching(2),McGuire,Burrow(2),Senior,McKenna g:Sinfield(6),Burrow	1st	15,629
8/8/04	Huddersfield (a)	W10-42	t:McDonald,Bai,McKenna(2),Burrow,McGuire,Poching g:Sinfield(5),Burrow(2)	1st	6,011
15/8/04	Warrington (a)	W12-44	t:Diskin,Walker,McDermott,Bai,McGuire,Mathers,Sinfield g:Sinfield(8)	1st	9,360
22/8/04	Bradford (h)	W40-12	t:McGuire(2),McKenna(2),Lauitiiti,Bai,Jones-Buchanan g:Sinfield(6)	1st	21,225
27/8/04	Castleford (h)	W64-12	t:Burrow(2),Senior,Walker(4),Bai,Poching(2),Dunemann,McDonald g:Sinfield(8)	1st	14,605
3/9/04	Wigan (a)	D12-12	t:McGuire(2) g:Sinfield(2)	1st	14,288
10/9/04	St Helens (a)	W19-25	t:Walker,Mathers,Senior,Diskin g:Sinfield(4) fg:Sinfield	1st	11,265
17/9/04	London (h)	W42-14	t:Senior,Calderwood(2),Walker,Lauitiiti(2),Diskin(2) g:Sinfield(5)	1st	17,329
2/10/04	Bradford (h) (QSF)	L12-26	t:McGuire,Poching g:Sinfield(2)	N/A	21,225
8/10/04	Wigan (h) (FE)	W40-12	t:Bai(3),Walker,McGuire,Mathers,Bailey g:Sinfield(5),Furner	N/A	20,119
16/10/04	Bradford (GF) ●	W8-16	t:Diskin,McGuire g:Sinfield(4)	N/A	65,547

● Played at Old Trafford, Manchester

		APP		TRIES		GOALS		FG		PTS	
	D.O.B.	ALL	SL	ALL	SL	ALL	SL	ALL	SL	ALL	SL
Carl Ablett	19/12/85	(1)	(1)	0	0	0	0	0	0	0	0
Matt Adamson	14/8/72	12(6)	11(6)	0	0	0	0	0	0	0	0
Marcus Bai	11/10/72	30	29	26	26	0	0	0	0	104	104
Ryan Bailey	11/11/83	21(7)	21(6)	2	1	0	0	0	0	8	4
Liam Botham	26/8/77	(1)	(1)	0	0	0	0	0	0	0	0
Rob Burrow	26/9/82	13(19)	11(19)	13	12	11	10	0	0	74	68
Mark Calderwood	25/10/81	17	15	11	9	0	0	0	0	44	36
Gary Connolly	22/6/71	3	2	1	1	0	0	0	0	4	4
Francis Cummins	12/10/76	20(2)	19(2)	6	4	0	0	0	0	24	16
Matt Diskin	27/1/82	31	29	12	11	0	0	0	0	48	44
Andrew Dunemann	10/6/76	22(4)	22(2)	4	4	0	0	0	0	16	16
Chris Feather	7/12/81	10(4)	10(3)	4	3	0	0	0	0	16	12
David Furner	6/2/70	20	18	4	4	11	11	0	0	38	38
Jamie Jones-Buchanan	1/8/81	4(12)	4(11)	6	5	0	0	0	0	24	20
Ali Lauitiiti	13/7/79	14(5)	14(5)	9	9	0	0	0	0	36	36
Richard Mathers	24/10/83	29	28	6	6	0	0	0	0	24	24
Barrie McDermott	22/7/72	12(18)	10(18)	3	2	0	0	0	0	12	8
Wayne McDonald	3/9/75	14(12)	12(12)	5	5	0	0	0	0	20	20
Danny McGuire	6/12/82	28(2)	26(2)	39	38	0	0	0	0	156	152
Chris McKenna	29/10/74	23(2)	22(2)	9	8	0	0	0	0	36	32
Willie Poching	30/8/73	7(22)	6(21)	12	11	0	0	0	0	48	44
Nick Scruton	24/12/84	(1)	(1)	0	0	0	0	0	0	0	0
Keith Senior	24/4/76	30	29	13	13	0	0	0	0	52	52
Kevin Sinfield	12/9/80	31	29	4	4	152	140	3	3	323	299
Chev Walker	9/10/82	26	24	19	18	0	0	0	0	76	72
Danny Ward	15/6/80	14(12)	14(10)	1	1	0	0	0	0	4	4

LEAGUE RECORD
P28-W24-D2-L2
(1st, SL, Grand Final Winners, Champions)
F1037, A443, Diff+594
50 points.

CHALLENGE CUP
Round Five

ATTENDANCES
Best - v Bradford
(SLR5, SLR24, QSF - 21,225)
Worst - v Huddersfield (SL - 11,701)
Total (SL, inc play-offs) - 265,734
Average (SL, inc play-offs) - 16,608
(Up by 3,465 on 2003)

TOP TACKLES
Matt Diskin 685

TOP CARRIES
Richard Mathers 438

TOP METRES
Marcus Bai 3746

TOP BREAKS
Marcus Bai 44

TOP OFFLOADS
Wayne McDonald 58

TOP BUSTS
Richard Mathers 78

3 November 2003 - Broncos sign young halfbacks Radney Bowker and Lee Sanderson on one-year deals.

10 November 2003 - Broncos sign Halifax star and Britain Academy player Andrew Brocklehurst on a two-year deal.

18 November 2003 - London Broncos trial Australian back row forward Troy Wozniak from Wests Tigers and give two-month trial to 21-year-old Castleford utility back Andrew McNally.

24 November 2003 - Broncos play in the Dubai Sevens while on camp in the Gulf and sign Salford hooker Dave Highton.

1 December 2003 - Sheffield prop Mitchell Stringer and Wests Tigers back Mark O'Halloran join London.

7 January 2004 - Troy Wozniak leaves and signs for Widnes Vikings.

8 January 2004 - Broncos are rocked by the retirement of Australian forward Bill Peden, who decides to take up a coaching role with former club Newcastle Knights.

26 January 2004 - Former Rabbitohs back-rower Andrew Hart signs a one-year deal.

12 February 2004 - Broncos beat 'London Barbarians', consisting of players from Skolars, St Albans, Hemel Stags and South London Storm, by 98-0.

8 March 2004 - London tie up new sponsorship deal with Bartercard UK after the deal with Virgin comes to an end.

23 March 2004 - Broncos part company with former Salford stand-off Radney Bowker five weeks into the new season.

KEY DATES - LONDON BRONCOS

3 April 2004 - Academy centre Matt King suffers serious neck injury during the under-18s clash with Halifax at the Shay.

7 April 2004 - Neil Budworth extends his contract by two seasons.

24 April 2004 - coach Tony Rea looks set bring London Skolar Rubert Jonker into his team to face Bradford Bulls at Griffin Park.

25 May 2004 - Leeds player Liam Botham joins the club on a one-month loan.

2 June 2004 - London take Bradford Bulls prop forward Richard Moore on loan for the rest of the season.

9 June 2004 - Paul Sykes and Rob Purdham sign new three-year deals.

8 July 2004 - Russell Bawden arrives for his third spell in the capital, signing from UTC.

9 August 2004 - Former Wakefield winger Paul Sampson signs a deal with the Broncos, keeping him at the club until the end of the 2004 season.

14 August 2004 - Jim Dymock announces he will leave the Broncos at the end of the season.

17 August 2004 - London take 19-year-old New Zealand utility Zebastian "Lucky" Luisi and Mal Kaufusi on trial for the remainder of the season.

16 August 2004 - Broncos linked with a possible buy-out from Eric Watson, owner of New Zealand Warriors.

23 August 2004 - Broncos lose Joe Mbu for the remainder of the season after he breaks his arm and suffers a dislocated wrist against Warrington.

1 September 2004 - Steele Retchless announces he will leave at the end of Super League IX after seven years at the club.

3 September 2004 - club captain Mat Toshack returns from injury after a long absence due to an injured calf muscle.

10 September 2004 - Toshack announces he is to leave the club at the end of the season.

8 November 2004 - Broncos sell halfback Dennis Moran to Wigan and sign Mark McLinden from Canberra Raiders.

15 November 2004 - sign second-rower Solomon Haumono.

Jim Dymock

LONDON BRONCOS

DATE	FIXTURE	RESULT	SCORERS	LGE	ATT
22/2/04	Leeds (a)	L58-14	t:Moran,Brocklehurst,Bowker g:Sykes	12th	15,119
29/2/04	Salford (h) (CCR4)	W24-8	t:Mbu,Roy,Moran,Hart g:Sykes(4)	N/A	2,454
6/3/04	St Helens (h)	L12-26	t:Sykes,Roy g:Sykes(2)	12th	4,757
14/3/04	Wakefield (h) (CCR5)	L10-29	t:Wells,Sykes g:Sykes	N/A	2,654
21/3/04	Hull (a)	L46-4	t:Greenwood	12th	9,040
28/3/04	Salford (h)	W35-30	t:Dymock,Moran,Greenwood,Budworth,O'Halloran,Murrell g:Sykes(5) fg:Dymock	10th	2,198
4/4/04	Warrington (h)	L24-36	t:Moran(2),Hart,Sykes g:Sykes(4)	10th	3,162
8/4/04	Wakefield (h)	L16-39	t:Wells,Greenwood,Highton g:Sykes(2)	11th	2,486
13/4/04	Castleford (a)	W34-42	t:Greenwood(2),Mbu,Wells,Moran(2),Murrell,Roy g:Sykes(5)	10th	4,710
18/4/04	Widnes (h)	W34-18	t:Roy,Mbu,Haughey,Moran,Retchless,Greenwood g:Sykes(5)	8th	2,923
25/4/04	Wigan (a)	L64-8	t:Wells,Roy	10th	9,132
3/5/04	Bradford (h)	L12-24	t:Moran,Barker g:Sanderson(2)	10th	3,987
8/5/04	Salford (a)	L30-12	t:Greenwood(2) g:Sanderson(2)	10th	2,529
23/5/04	Huddersfield (h)	L6-30	t:O'Halloran g:Moran	11th	2,627
28/5/04	Castleford (h)	L10-12	t:Greenwood,Brocklehurst g:Botham	11th	2,562
6/6/04	Wakefield (a)	L48-18	t:Sanderson,Budworth,Botham g:Sanderson(3)	11th	3,104
12/6/04	Warrington (a)	L42-12	t:Moran,O'Halloran g:Sykes(2)	11th	7,123
20/6/04	Hull (h) ●	L26-42	t:Botham,Jackson(2),O'Halloran,Mbu g:Sykes(3)	11th	3,589
27/6/04	Huddersfield (a)	L35-22	t:Kirkpatrick,Moran,Sykes g:Sykes(5)	11th	3,009
10/7/04	St Helens (a)	L30-10	t:Jackson,Wells g:Sykes	11th	6,828
18/7/04	Leeds (h)	D36-36	t:Roy,Greenwood(2),Kirkpatrick,O'Halloran,Moran,Botham g:Botham(4)	11th	5,058
25/7/04	Bradford (a)	L44-16	t:Hart,Jackson,Moran g:Sykes,Botham	11th	10,283
1/8/04	Wigan (h)	W22-20	t:O'Halloran,Trindall,Wells,Moran g:Sykes(3)	11th	4,352
8/8/04	Widnes (a)	W24-38	t:Wells(2),Dymock,Purdham,O'Halloran(2),Kirkpatrick g:Sykes(5)	10th	4,829
13/8/04	St Helens (a)	W22-28	t:Moran(3),Sykes g:Sykes(6)	10th	6,637
22/8/04	Warrington (h)	W34-26	t:Sykes,Roy,Purdham,Retchless,Greenwood(2) g:Sykes(5)	9th	3,526
29/8/04	Wakefield (h)	L16-24	t:Purdham,Greenwood,Roy g:Sykes(2)	9th	3,035
5/9/04	Bradford (a)	L60-18	t:Moran,Greenwood(2) g:Sykes(3)	10th	11,319
12/9/04	Wigan (h)	L22-26	t:Roy,Luisi,Greenwood,Trindall g:Sykes(3)	10th	4,151
17/9/04	Leeds (a)	L42-14	t:Purdham,Sampson,Moran g:Budworth	10th	17,329

● Played at Welford Road, Leicester

		APP		TRIES		GOALS		FG		PTS	
	D.O.B.	ALL	SL	ALL	SL	ALL	SL	ALL	SL	ALL	SL
Ade Adebisi	7/1/86	(1)	(1)	0	0	0	0	0	0	0	0
Dwayne Barker	21/9/83	3	3	1	1	0	0	0	0	4	4
Russell Bawden	24/7/73	(2)	(2)	0	0	0	0	0	0	0	0
Liam Botham	26/8/77	6(2)	6(2)	3	3	6	6	0	0	24	24
Radney Bowker	5/2/79	5	3	1	1	0	0	0	0	4	4
Andrew Brocklehurst	6/3/83	12(8)	12(6)	2	2	0	0	0	0	8	8
Neil Budworth	10/3/82	26(3)	24(3)	2	2	1	1	0	0	10	10
Jim Dymock	4/4/72	19	17	2	2	0	0	1	1	9	9
Lee Greenwood	28/9/80	25(1)	25(1)	17	17	0	0	0	0	68	68
Andrew Hart	9/3/76	14(1)	12(1)	3	2	0	0	0	0	12	8
Tom Haughey	30/1/82	8(7)	8(6)	1	1	0	0	0	0	4	4
David Highton	31/1/80	5(18)	5(18)	1	1	0	0	0	0	4	4
Rob Jackson	4/9/81	11(4)	10(4)	4	4	0	0	0	0	16	16
Mal Kaufusi	31/5/73	1(3)	1(3)	0	0	0	0	0	0	0	0
John Kirkpatrick	3/1/79	14(1)	14(1)	3	3	0	0	0	0	12	12
Zebastian Luisi	22/12/84	4	4	1	1	0	0	0	0	4	4
Joe Mbu	6/11/83	13(8)	11(8)	4	3	0	0	0	0	16	12
Andy McNally	9/1/82	6(3)	5(3)	0	0	0	0	0	0	0	0
Richard Moore	2/2/81	5(2)	5(2)	0	0	0	0	0	0	0	0
Dennis Moran	22/1/77	30	28	19	18	1	1	0	0	78	74
Scott Murrell	5/9/85	3(3)	3(3)	2	2	0	0	0	0	8	8
Jason Netherton	5/10/82	3	3	0	0	0	0	0	0	0	0
Mark O'Halloran	6/3/81	24	22	8	8	0	0	0	0	32	32
Rob Purdham	14/4/80	9(1)	9(1)	4	4	0	0	0	0	16	16
Steele Retchless	16/6/71	27	25	2	2	0	0	0	0	8	8
Nigel Roy	15/3/74	21	19	9	8	0	0	0	0	36	32
Paul Sampson	12/7/77	1(2)	1(2)	1	1	0	0	0	0	4	4
Lee Sanderson	16/12/81	1(6)	1(5)	1	1	7	7	0	0	18	18
Francis Stephenson	20/1/76	7(9)	7(7)	0	0	0	0	0	0	0	0
Mitchell Stringer	1/11/83	10(19)	10(17)	0	0	0	0	0	0	0	0
Paul Sykes	11/8/81	27	25	6	5	68	63	0	0	160	146
Steve Thomas	26/9/79	4(2)	4(2)	0	0	0	0	0	0	0	0
Mat Toshack	18/2/73	3(1)	3(1)	0	0	0	0	0	0	0	0
Steve Trindall	23/4/73	22(8)	20(8)	2	2	0	0	0	0	8	8
Jon Wells	23/9/78	21(1)	19(1)	8	7	0	0	0	0	32	28
Jonny Williams	23/8/85	(4)	(4)	0	0	0	0	0	0	0	0

LEAGUE RECORD
P28-W7-D1-L20
(10th, SL)
F561, A968, Diff-407
15 points.

CHALLENGE CUP
Round Five

ATTENDANCES
Best - v Leeds (SL - 5,058)
Worst - v Salford (SL - 2,198)
Total (SL only) - 48,413
Average (SL only) - 3,458
(Down by 88 on 2003)

TOP TACKLES
Steele Retchless 694

TOP CARRIES
Steele Retchless 424

TOP METRES
Steele Retchless 2653

TOP BREAKS
Dennis Moran 32

TOP OFFLOADS
Mitchell Stringer 39

TOP BUSTS
Dennis Moran 51

3 November 2003 - Bryn Powell signs for Reds from Hunslet Hawks on a one-year deal.

10 November 2003 - Reds sign old boy Scott Naylor on a one-year deal.

15 December - CEO Dave Tarry reveals plans for Salford's new stadium at Barton

19 December 2003 - St Helens winger Anthony Stewart joins Salford on a 12-month loan.

5 January 2004 - Reds travel to Jacksonville, Florida for ten day training camp.

22 March 2004 - Salford are fined £250 and deducted four league points after breaching Academy regulations by fielding two players aged over 21 instead of one.

4 April 2004 - sign Manly centre Kevin McGuinness on a one-year deal.

26 April 2004 - coach Karl Harrison complains to the RFL about refereeing calls against the Reds.

5 May 2004 - City Reds re-sign former centre Nathan McAvoy after a spell in rugby union.

10 May 2004 - Karl Harrison denies interest in Leigh hooker Paul Rowley.

21 May 2004 - Reds linked with move for Carcassonne's Aussie forward Duncan MacGillivray.

6 June 2004 - Karl Harrison slams referee Richard Silverwood after 25-18 defeat by the Giants at the Willows.

KEY DATES - SALFORD CITY REDS

9 June 2004 - prop Neil Baynes found guilty of illegally using his knees after being placed on report during the Reds' 25-18 Super League defeat by Huddersfield, but avoids a ban.

11 June 2004 - Reds sign Sheffield winger Danny Mills on a month's loan.

21 June 2004 - Reds chase UTC forward Djamel Fakir and release loose forward Martin Moana.

28 June 2004 - Salford City Reds insist they are keen to hang on to key forward Andy Coley, despite reports linking him with a close-season move to Wigan.

5 July 2004 - St Helens forward Tim Jonkers joins Reds on a month's loan.

8 July 2004 - Andy Coley signs a new three-year deal, keeping him at Salford City Reds until 2007.

26 July 2004 - admit interest in London halfback Dennis Moran and Adrian Morley for 2006.

2 August 2004 - Reds sign former Halifax forward Andrew Brocklehurst from London.

18 August 2004 - Reds sign Wigan Warriors' David Hodgson on a two year-deal beginning at the start of the 2005 season.

22 August 2004 - Wigan stars Luke Robinson and David Hodgson come to the Willows on two-year deals.

27 August 2004 - confirm winger Joel Caine will not take up second year of his contract.

5 September 2004 - 24-22 win at Castleford ensures Super League survival.

6 September 2004 - football director Steve Simms targets Aussie Test halfback Craig Gower and Canberra fullback Clinton Schifcofske.

14 September 2004 - sign Ian Sibbit from Warrington Wolves on a two-year deal from 2005.

23 September 2004 - winger Anthony Stewart signs permanent deal with the Reds.

8 October 2004 - Reds sign Stuart Dickens from Featherstone Rovers.

18 October 2004 - James Lowes linked with move to the Willows as assistant coach.

Kevin McGuinness

SALFORD CITY REDS

DATE	FIXTURE	RESULT	SCORERS	LGE	ATT
22/2/04	Widnes (h)	W24-12	t:Littler,Clinch,Coley g:Caine(5),Charles	5th	5,049
29/2/04	London (a) (CCR4)	L24-8	t:Alker,Stewart	N/A	2,454
7/3/04	Wigan (a)	L20-10	t:Stewart,Littler g:Charles	6th	11,172
20/3/04	Wakefield (a)	L20-27	t:Kirk(2),Fitzpatrick,Johnson g:Charles(2)	7th	2,825
28/3/04	London (a)	L35-30	t:Baldwin,Stewart,Beverley(2),Haggerty,Moana g:Fitzpatrick(2),Caine	7th	2,198
2/4/04	Bradford (a)	L25-18	t:Beverley(3) g:Charles(3)	7th	11,976
9/4/04	Huddersfield (a)	L24-16	t:Stewart,Beverley g:Charles(4)	9th	4,062
12/4/04	Leeds (h)	L0-44	No Scorers	11th	5,462
16/4/04	St Helens (a)	L40-4	t:Littler	11th	7,649
24/4/04	Warrington (h)	L18-37	t:Johnson,Beverley,Fitzpatrick g:Charles(3)	11th	3,624
2/5/04	Hull (a)	L82-6	t:Littler g:Charles	11th	9,869
8/5/04	London (h)	W30-12	t:Littler,Caine,Beverley,Stewart,Charles g:Charles(5)	11th	2,529
23/5/04	Castleford (a)	W32-36	t:Baynes,Caine,Highton,Haggerty,Stewart,Johnson g:Caine(6)	10th	6,961
28/5/04	Leeds (a)	L34-6	t:Baynes g:Charles	10th	14,239
6/6/04	Huddersfield (h)	L18-25	t:Haggerty,McGuinness,Johnson g:Charles(3)	10th	3,271
13/6/04	Bradford (h)	L28-35	t:Alker,Beverley,Caine,Coley g:Charles(6)	10th	5,006
20/6/04	Wakefield (a)	L21-20	t:Littler,Beverley,Coley g:Charles(4)	10th	3,426
27/6/04	Castleford (h)	W30-14	t:Coley,Alker(2),Charles,Shipway g:Charles(5)	9th	3,313
11/7/04	Wigan (h)	L16-32	t:Kirk,Johnson,Stewart g:Charles(2)	9th	6,037
18/7/04	Widnes (a)	W14-15	t:Caine,Kirk g:Charles(3) fg:Clinch	9th	5,573
25/7/04	Hull (h)	L20-44	t:Charles,Coley,Baynes g:Charles(3),Caine	9th	3,515
1/8/04	Warrington (a)	L46-20	t:McGuinness,McAvoy,Johnson,Littler g:Charles(2)	9th	8,641
8/8/04	St Helens (h)	W30-20	t:Alker(2),Caine,Littler,Baynes g:Charles(5)	9th	4,897
14/8/04	Widnes (h)	W14-13	t:Kirk,Caine,Johnson g:Charles	9th	3,067
22/8/04	Wakefield (a)	L46-18	t:Coley(2),Caine g:Charles(3)	10th	3,641
29/8/04	Warrington (h)	L6-32	t:Littler g:Charles	10th	4,019
5/9/04	Castleford (a)	W22-24	t:Alker,Fitzpatrick(2),Coley g:Charles(4)	9th	5,809
12/9/04	Hull (h)	L8-12	t:Alker g:Charles(2)	9th	3,307
19/9/04	Huddersfield (a)	L28-22	t:Littler(2),Rutgerson,Caine g:Charles(3)	9th	3,083

		APP		TRIES		GOALS		FG		PTS	
	D.O.B.	ALL	SL	ALL	SL	ALL	SL	ALL	SL	ALL	SL
Malcolm Alker	4/11/78	27	26	8	7	0	0	0	0	32	28
Simon Baldwin	31/3/75	8(13)	8(13)	1	1	0	0	0	0	4	4
Neil Baynes	14/9/77	16(1)	16(1)	4	4	0	0	0	0	16	16
Cliff Beverley	25/3/77	22(1)	21(1)	10	10	0	0	0	0	40	40
Andrew Brocklehurst	6/3/83	1(4)	1(4)	0	0	0	0	0	0	0	0
Joel Caine	18/9/78	24	24	8	8	13	13	0	0	58	58
Chris Charles	7/3/76	25(3)	24(3)	3	3	68	68	0	0	148	148
Gavin Clinch	13/9/74	22(1)	21(1)	1	1	0	0	1	1	5	5
John Clough	13/9/84	(1)	(1)	0	0	0	0	0	0	0	0
Andy Coley	7/7/78	27(1)	26(1)	8	8	0	0	0	0	32	32
Karl Fitzpatrick	13/9/80	16(10)	16(9)	4	4	2	2	0	0	20	20
Jason Flowers	30/1/75	7(1)	6(1)	0	0	0	0	0	0	0	0
Gareth Haggerty	8/9/81	2(24)	1(24)	3	3	0	0	0	0	12	12
Tim Hartley	2/1/86	(3)	(3)	0	0	0	0	0	0	0	0
Paul Highton	10/11/76	16(10)	16(9)	1	1	0	0	0	0	4	4
Andy Johnson	14/6/74	7(21)	7(20)	7	7	0	0	0	0	28	28
Tim Jonkers	3/7/81	(5)	(5)	0	0	0	0	0	0	0	0
Andy Kirk	2/8/82	21	20	5	5	0	0	0	0	20	20
Stuart Littler	19/2/79	27	26	11	11	0	0	0	0	44	44
Nathan McAvoy	31/12/76	7	7	1	1	0	0	0	0	4	4
Kevin McGuinness	10/11/76	17	17	2	2	0	0	0	0	8	8
Martin Moana	13/8/73	6(4)	6(3)	1	1	0	0	0	0	4	4
Vinny Myler	20/3/83	(4)	(4)	0	0	0	0	0	0	0	0
Scott Naylor	2/2/72	8	7	0	0	0	0	0	0	0	0
Bryn Powell	5/9/79	1(1)	1(1)	0	0	0	0	0	0	0	0
Sean Rutgerson	19/2/76	24(2)	23(2)	1	1	0	0	0	0	4	4
Mark Shipway	3/5/76	19(6)	18(6)	1	1	0	0	0	0	4	4
Anthony Stewart	5/3/79	27	26	7	6	0	0	0	0	28	24

LEAGUE RECORD
P28-W8-D0-L20
(9th, SL)
F507 A828, Diff-321
16 points.

CHALLENGE CUP
Round Four

ATTENDANCES
Best - v Wigan (SL - 6,037)
Worst - v London (SL - 2,529)
Total (SL only) - 55,921
Average (SL only) - 3,994
(Up by 1,672 on 2003, NL1)

TOP TACKLES
Malcolm Alker 849

TOP CARRIES
Joel Caine/Andy Coley 368

TOP METRES
Andy Coley 2869

TOP BREAKS
Karl Fitzpatrick/Stuart Littler 18

TOP OFFLOADS
Stuart Littler 43

TOP BUSTS
Andy Coley 66

KEY DATES - ST HELENS

14 April 2004 - Jon Wilkin suspended for four matches by the RFL Disciplinary Committee after being sent off in the ninth minute of Saints' 54-8 defeat at Bradford.

16 April 2004 - Sean Long and Martin Gleeson under investigation by RFL Disciplinary Commissioner after Daily Mail reveals the two placed bets on Saints losing the Bradford game.

26 May 2004 - form prop Keith Mason will miss two games after being referred and found guilty of a deliberate high tackle in the 50-20 at Warrington.

17 June 2004 - Saints and RFL find Sean Long and Martin Gleeson guilty of misconduct.

6 January 2004 - Samoan rugby union internationals Maurie Fa'asavalu and Dom Feaunati sign two-year contracts with St Helens.

20 January 2004 - Paul Sculthorpe is unveiled as the new Saints captain, taking over from Chris Joynt, who stepped down after seven years in the role.

17 February 2004 - St Helens ordered to pay £20,000 for Wigan's Ricky Bibey by Rugby Football League Tribunal hearing.

2 March 2004 - John Stankevitch's season in doubt because of a serious shoulder injury picked up in previous years play-off defeat by Wigan.

2 March 2004 - Mike Bennett sustains knee injury in Saints' 30-10 Powergen Challenge Cup win at Bradford.

18 March 2004 - former Wigan prop Ricky Bibey makes his Super League debut in the 38-20 win over Widnes.

12 April 2004 - Saints chairman Eamonn McManus admits the club has 'no concrete proposal or definite plans' for a new stadium.

13 April 2004 - Dominic Feaunati to miss the Challenge Cup semi-final after being found guilty of punching in Saints' 22-all draw with Wigan.

18 June 2004 - RFL suspend Sean Long for three months and Martin Gleeson for four, but St Helens record a vital 40-12 win at Widnes Vikings.

30 June 2004 - Darren Albert clinches the inaugural Powergen Fastest Man in Rugby League title in a time of 11.37 seconds over 100 metres.

7 July 2004 - Saints' problems continue to mount, with Chris Joynt and Keiron Cunningham added to growing injury list.

23 July 2004 - Martin Gleeson signs a four-year deal with Warrington Wolves, with a £200,000 transfer fee heading to Knowsley Road.

16 August 2004 - Saints buy out former Kangaroo centre Jamie Lyon's Parramatta contract for £60,000. He signs a two-year deal from 2005.

26 August 2004 - Saints sign Gray Viane, a 22 year-old centre or second-rower from Wests Tigers, on a two-year contract.

17 September 2004 - Sean Long returns from suspension at Odsal as Saints slump to a 64-24 round 28 defeat.

1 October 2004 - Saints sign Bulls and Great Britain prop Paul Anderson on a one-year contract.

5 October 2004 - Saints sign James Roby, Ian Hardman and Ade Gardner on new contracts and Paul Wellens puts pen to paper on a four-year deal.

14 October 2004 - second-rower Michael Smith signs on a two-year contract from relegated Castleford Tigers.

Keiron Cunningham

ST HELENS

DATE	FIXTURE	RESULT	SCORERS	LGE	ATT
20/2/04	Hull (h)	W30-16	t:Talau,Hooper,Fozzard(2),Cunningham,Feaunati g:Long(3)	4th	12,532
29/2/04	Bradford (a) (CCR4)	W10-30	t:Edmondson,Long,Gilmour,Gleeson,Sculthorpe g:Long(4),Sculthorpe	N/A	12,215
6/3/04	London (a)	W12-26	t:Feaunati,Cunningham,Wilkin,Gardner(2) g:Long(3)	4th	4,757
13/3/04	Leeds (h) (CCR5)	W24-14	t:Wellens(2),Feaunati,Talau g:Long(4)	N/A	13,699
19/3/04	Widnes (h)	W38-20	t:Gardner,Long(2),Albert,Hooper,Gilmour g:Long(6),Hooper	3rd	10,549
28/3/04	Hull (h) (CCQF)	W31-26	t:Hooper(2),Long,Cunningham,Sculthorpe g:Long(5) fg:Sculthorpe	N/A	11,184
2/4/04	Castleford (a)	W14-22	t:Cunningham,Wellens(2),Hooper g:Long(3)	3rd	6,876
9/4/04	Wigan (h)	D21-21	t:Gilmour(2),Wilkin,Talau g:Long(2) fg:Long	2nd	15,964
12/4/04	Bradford (a)	L54-8	t:Gleeson,Feaunati	4th	15,623
16/4/04	Salford (h)	W40-4	t:Albert(2),Sculthorpe(3),Higham,Fa'asavalu g:Forber(6)	2nd	7,649
25/4/04	Huddersfield (CCSF) ●	W6-46	t:Cunningham,Hooper,Gilmour,Talau,Gardner(2),Long g:Long(3),Sculthorpe(4)	N/A	13,134
30/4/04	Leeds (h)	W56-10	t:Gardner,Gilmour,Hooper(2),Sculthorpe,Albert,Talau,Hardman,Edmondson g:Long(8),Hooper(2)	2nd	11,059
7/5/04	Wakefield (h)	W26-20	t:Feaunati,Albert,Cunningham,Talau,Hardman g:Long(3)	3rd	9,191
15/5/04	Wigan (CCF) ●●	W32-16	t:Gilmour,Talau(2),Wellens,Sculthorpe g:Long(6)	N/A	73,734
22/5/04	Warrington (a)	W20-50	t:Cunningham,Wilkin,Albert(3),Long,Hooper,Gleeson,Gilmour g:Long(7)	3rd	11,328
29/5/04	Bradford (h)	W35-30	t:Hooper(3),Long,Gilmour g:Long(7) fg:Sculthorpe	2nd	10,933
4/6/04	Wigan (a)	L30-14	t:Gleeson,Sculthorpe g:Long(3)	2nd	17,194
11/6/04	Castleford (h)	W52-8	t:Hooper,Albert(2),Wellens(2),Long,Joynt(2),Sculthorpe g:Long(6),Sculthorpe(2)	2nd	8,397
18/6/04	Widnes (a)	W12-40	t:Gilmour,Albert,Cunningham,Hardman,Mason,Sculthorpe,Wilkin g:Sculthorpe(6)	2nd	7,482
26/6/04	Warrington (h)	W28-8	t:Albert,Hardman,Talau,Fa'asavalu,Hooper g:Sculthorpe(4)	2nd	8,783
2/7/04	Wakefield (a)	L41-22	t:Sculthorpe,Gardner,J Roby,Talau g:Sculthorpe(3)	4th	4,151
7/7/04	Huddersfield (a)	W8-50	t:Stankevitch,Albert,Wellens,Gilmour,Sculthorpe,Wilkin,Gardner,Feaunati g:Sculthorpe(9)	2nd	3,506
10/7/04	London (h)	W30-10	t:Stankevitch,J Roby,Feaunati,Wellens,Mason g:Sculthorpe(5)	2nd	6,828
17/7/04	Hull (a)	L34-6	t:Gilmour g:Hooper	3rd	12,949
23/7/04	Leeds (a)	L70-0	No Scorers	5th	16,635
30/7/04	Huddersfield (h)	W50-10	t:Albert,Stankevitch(2),Cunningham,Mason,Talau(2),Hooper,Gardner g:Hooper(7)	3rd	7,218
8/8/04	Salford (a)	L30-20	t:Gardner(2),Albert,Higham g:Wellens(2)	5th	4,897
13/8/04	London (h)	L22-28	t:Hooper,Wellens,Albert,Talau g:Hooper(3)	4th	6,637
20/8/04	Wigan (a)	L27-18	t:Hooper,J Roby(2) g:Sculthorpe(3)	5th	16,424
27/8/04	Huddersfield (h)	W48-12	t:Stankevitch,Talau(2),Moore,Hooper,Hardman,Cunningham(2),Viane,J Roby g:Sculthorpe(4)	4th	6,095
5/9/04	Warrington (a)	W24-26	t:Sculthorpe,Wellens,Higham,Hooper g:Sculthorpe(5)	4th	11,930
10/9/04	Leeds (h)	L19-25	t:Wilkin,Edmondson,Wellens g:Sculthorpe(3) fg:Sculthorpe	5th	11,265
17/9/04	Bradford (a)	L64-24	t:Stankevitch,Bennett,Feaunati,Gardner g:Long(4)	5th	13,127
25/9/04	Wigan (a) (EPO)	L18-12	t:Gardner g:Long(4)	N/A	20,052

● Played at Halliwell Jones Stadium, Warrington
●● Played at Millennium Stadium, Cardiff

		APP		TRIES		GOALS		FG		PTS	
	D.O.B.	ALL	SL	ALL	SL	ALL	SL	ALL	SL	ALL	SL
Darren Albert	28/2/76	31	26	16	16	0	0	0	0	64	64
Phil Anderton	19/1/84	1	1	0	0	0	0	0	0	0	0
Mike Bennett	9/5/80	4(9)	3(9)	1	1	0	0	0	0	4	4
Ricky Bibey	22/9/81	4(17)	4(14)	0	0	0	0	0	0	0	0
Liam Bostock	1/2/84	1	1	0	0	0	0	0	0	0	0
Andy Bracek	21/3/84	(1)	(1)	0	0	0	0	0	0	0	0
Peter Cook	31/10/84	(1)	(1)	0	0	0	0	0	0	0	0
Keiron Cunningham	28/10/76	28	23	11	9	0	0	0	0	44	36
Mark Edmondson	3/11/79	13(16)	11(13)	3	2	0	0	0	0	12	8
Maurie Fa'asavalu	12/1/80	3(13)	3(13)	2	2	0	0	0	0	8	8
Dom Feaunati	14/6/78	13(8)	10(7)	8	7	0	0	0	0	32	28
Carl Forber	17/3/85	1(1)	1(1)	0	0	6	6	0	0	12	12
Nick Fozzard	22/7/77	29(1)	24(1)	2	2	0	0	0	0	8	8
Ade Gardner	24/6/83	27(3)	25(1)	13	11	0	0	0	0	52	44
Lee Gilmour	12/3/78	30	25	12	9	0	0	0	0	48	36
Martin Gleeson	28/5/80	11	8	4	3	0	0	0	0	16	12
James Graham	10/9/85	1(6)	1(6)	0	0	0	0	0	0	0	0
Ian Hardman	8/12/84	10(8)	10(7)	5	5	0	0	0	0	20	20
Mick Higham	18/9/80	7(9)	6(7)	3	3	0	0	0	0	12	12
Jason Hooper	14/10/77	31	26	20	16	14	14	0	0	108	92
Tim Jonkers	3/7/81	1	1	0	0	0	0	0	0	0	0
Chris Joynt	7/12/71	23(3)	19(2)	2	2	0	0	0	0	8	8
Ian Kenny	11/10/84	(1)	(1)	0	0	0	0	0	0	0	0
Sean Long	24/9/76	18	13	8	5	81	59	1	1	195	139
Keith Mason	20/1/82	23(8)	19(7)	3	3	0	0	0	0	12	12
Scott Moore	23/1/88	2	2	1	1	0	0	0	0	4	4
James Roby	22/11/85	8(8)	8(8)	5	5	0	0	0	0	20	20
Mike Roby	2/4/86	(1)	(1)	0	0	0	0	0	0	0	0
Paul Sculthorpe	22/9/77	27	22	13	10	49	44	3	2	153	130
John Stankevitch	6/11/79	10(5)	10(5)	6	6	0	0	0	0	24	24
Willie Talau	25/1/76	32	27	15	11	0	0	0	0	60	44
Gray Viane	19/2/82	4	4	1	1	0	0	0	0	4	4
Paul Wellens	27/2/80	33	28	12	9	2	2	0	0	52	40
Jon Wilkin	11/1/83	16(10)	16(7)	6	6	0	0	0	0	24	24

LEAGUE RECORD
P28-W17-D1-L10
(5th, SL/Elimination Play-Off)
F821, A662, Diff+159
35 points.

CHALLENGE CUP
Winners

ATTENDANCES
Best - v Wigan (SL - 15,964)
Worst - v Huddersfield (SL - 6,095)
Total (SL only) - 133,100
Average (SL only) - 9,507
(Down by 136 on 2003)

TOP TACKLES
Keiron Cunningham 606

TOP CARRIES
Paul Wellens 511

TOP METRES
Paul Wellens 3556

TOP BREAKS
Paul Sculthorpe 25

TOP OFFLOADS
Keiron Cunningham 29

TOP BUSTS
Paul Wellens 52

20 November 2003 - Jamie Rooney signs a new contract to keep him at the club until November 2006.

3 December 2003 - sign Liam Finn from Halifax and promote Mark Applegarth from the Academy, both on one-year deals.

11 December 2003 - confirm the signings of new wingers Justin Ryder and Semi Tadulala for the 2004 season.

8 January 2004 - Trinity complete their ninth and final signing of the close-season with the capture of Samoan international Albert Talipeau.

19 April 2004 - both Jamie Rooney and David Wrench suffer broken legs in 42-10 victory at Castleford.

24 April 2004 - Michael Korkidas signs a new contract to the end of 2006.

30 May 2004 - David Solomona receives a one-match ban for fighting in the Wildcats 36-12 defeat at London.

8 July 2004 - French forward Olivier Elima signs a new contract which will keep him at Belle Vue until the end of 2007.

8 July 2004 - sign Australian forward Duncan MacGillivray from Carcassonne on a one-year contract, with prop Dallas Hood leaving Belle Vue.

13 July 2004 - Semi Tadulala, one game, and Olivier Elima, two, are suspended for their parts in a brawl in the defeat at Bradford.

KEY DATES - WAKEFIELD TRINITY WILDCATS

6 August 2004 - Leeds Rhinos prop forward Chris Feather joins Wildcats on loan until the end of the season.

12 August 2004 - talks open with skipper Gareth Ellis over a new contract.

24 September 2004 - win 28-18 in play-off eliminator at Hull.

1 October 2004 - edged in elimination semi-final, 18-14, at Wigan.

13 October 2004 - Shane McNally named Super League coach of the year.

Sid Domic

Michael Korkidas

WAKEFIELD T WILDCATS

DATE	FIXTURE	RESULT	SCORERS	LGE	ATT
21/2/04	Warrington (a)	L34-20	t:Jeffries,Ryder,Rooney,Halpenny g:Rooney(2)	9th	14,206
27/2/04	Chorley (a) (CCR4)	W6-88	t:Jeffries(5),Tadulala(2),Korkidas,Ellis(2),Domic,Rooney(3),March, Hood g:Rooney(12)	N/A	696
7/3/04	Bradford (h)	L6-40	t:Tadulala g:Rooney	11th	6,472
14/3/04	London (a) (CCR5)	W10-29	t:Ryder,Rooney(2),Domic(2) g:Rooney(4) fg:Rooney	N/A	2,654
20/3/04	Salford (a)	W20-27	t:Domic(2),Griffin,Jeffries,Halpenny g:Rooney(3) fg:Rooney	9th	2,825
26/3/04	Wigan (a) (CCQF)	L20-4	g:Rooney(2)	N/A	9,728
3/4/04	Hull (h)	L21-27	t:Ryder(2),Griffin g:Rooney(4) fg:Rooney	9th	4,337
8/4/04	London (a)	W16-39	t:Wrench(2),Jeffries,Domic,Wainwright(2) g:Rooney(7) fg:Jeffries	7th	2,486
12/4/04	Huddersfield (h)	L17-24	t:Rooney,Halpenny g:Rooney(4) fg:Rooney	8th	4,702
17/4/04	Castleford (a)	W10-42	t:Ellis(2),Jeffries(2),Tadulala(2),Demetriou,Korkidas g:Rooney,March(4)	7th	5,427
23/4/04	Leeds (h)	L12-36	t:Domic,Solomona g:March(2)	8th	7,680
2/5/04	Widnes (h)	W40-10	t:Elima,Halpenny,J Field,Domic,March,Jeffries,Applegarth g:March(6)	8th	4,136
7/5/04	St Helens (a)	L26-20	t:Ellis,Ryder,Korkidas g:March(3),Griffin	8th	9,191
23/5/04	Wigan (h)	L14-20	t:Ryder,Domic g:March(3)	8th	5,118
30/5/04	Huddersfield (a)	W6-38	t:J Field(2),Jeffries,Demetriou(2),Korkidas,Ryder g:March(5)	8th	4,419
6/6/04	London (h)	W48-18	t:Solomona(4),Elima,March,Domic,Jeffries g:March(8)	7th	3,104
13/6/04	Hull (a)	L28-24	t:Jeffries,Korkidas,Wainwright,Ryder g:March(4)	8th	9,928
20/6/04	Salford (h)	W21-20	t:Ryder,Domic(2),Ellis g:March(2) fg:Jeffries	8th	3,426
25/6/04	Wigan (a)	L28-22	t:Domic,J Field,March,Solomona g:March(3)	8th	9,274
2/7/04	St Helens (h)	W41-22	t:Domic,Jeffries(2),Wainwright,Snitch,Tadulala g:March(7),Handforth fg:Jeffries	7th	4,151
11/7/04	Bradford (a)	L36-26	t:Elima,J Field,Solomona,Ellis,Spicer g:March(2),Handforth	7th	12,670
18/7/04	Warrington (h)	W32-26	t:Jeffries,Wainwright,Domic,Solomona,Ryder g:March(6)	7th	4,309
25/7/04	Widnes (a)	L25-24	t:Ryder,Rooney,Jeffries,Domic g:March(3),Rooney	7th	5,104
1/8/04	Leeds (a)	L46-28	t:Rooney,Wainwright,Solomona,Demetriou(2),Jeffries g:March,Rooney	8th	15,629
8/8/04	Castleford (h)	W39-18	t:Demetriou(2),Jeffries(2),Domic,Ellis g:Rooney(7) fg:Rooney	6th	6,673
15/8/04	Hull (h)	L38-24	t:Jeffries,Domic(2),Demetriou g:Rooney,March(3)	6th	11,048
22/8/04	Salford (h)	W46-18	t:Domic(2),Tadulala(2),Demetriou(2),M Field,Ryder,Feather g:March(4),Demetriou	6th	3,641
29/8/04	London (a)	W16-24	t:Domic,Solomona(2),Jeffries,Demetriou g:March,Finn	6th	3,035
5/9/04	Widnes (h)	W40-6	t:Domic(2),Ellis,Handforth(2),Demetriou,Jeffries g:March(2),Handforth(3),Demetriou	6th	5,198
10/9/04	Huddersfield (h)	W21-20	t:Domic,Halpenny,Tadulala g:March(3),Handforth fg:Jeffries	6th	4,311
18/9/04	Castleford (a)	W28-32	t:Tadulala,Halpenny(2),Solomona(2),Handforth g:March(3),Handforth	6th	11,055
24/9/04	Hull (a) (EPO)	W18-28	t:March,Halpenny,Feather,Tadulala,Demetriou g:March,Handforth(3)	N/A	10,550
1/10/04	Wigan (a) (ESF)	L18-14	t:Halpenny,MacGillivray,Solomona g:March	N/A	16,179

		APP		TRIES		GOALS		FG		PTS	
	D.O.B.	ALL	SL	ALL	SL	ALL	SL	ALL	SL	ALL	SL
Mark Applegarth	10/12/84	12(1)	12(1)	1	1	0	0	0	0	4	4
Matthew Blake	17/3/83	1(2)	1(2)	0	0	0	0	0	0	0	0
Jason Demetriou	13/1/76	31(2)	29(1)	13	13	2	2	0	0	56	56
Sid Domic	8/2/75	33	30	25	22	0	0	0	0	100	88
Olivier Elima	19/5/83	6(17)	3(17)	3	3	0	0	0	0	12	12
Gareth Ellis	3/5/81	30	27	9	7	0	0	0	0	36	28
Chris Feather	7/12/81	7(1)	7(1)	2	2	0	0	0	0	8	8
Jamie Field	12/12/76	19(8)	19(6)	5	5	0	0	0	0	20	20
Mark Field	21/3/84	10(1)	10(1)	1	1	0	0	0	0	4	4
Liam Finn	2/11/83	1(1)	1(1)	0	0	1	1	0	0	2	2
Darrell Griffin	19/6/81	16(11)	14(10)	2	2	1	1	0	0	10	10
Colum Halpenny	25/4/79	27(1)	24(1)	9	9	0	0	0	0	36	36
Paul Handforth	6/10/81	(15)	(14)	3	3	10	10	0	0	32	32
Dallas Hood	11/12/77	2(9)	1(7)	1	0	0	0	0	0	4	0
Ben Jeffries	4/9/80	33	30	24	19	0	0	4	4	100	80
Michael Korkidas	12/1/81	30(1)	29	5	4	0	0	0	0	20	16
Duncan MacGillivray	25/10/76	5(7)	5(7)	1	1	0	0	0	0	4	4
David March	25/7/79	33	30	5	4	77	77	0	0	174	170
Jamie Rooney	17/3/80	14	11	9	4	50	32	5	4	141	84
Justin Ryder	14/7/80	22(3)	19(3)	12	11	0	0	0	0	48	44
Steve Snitch	22/2/83	(20)	(19)	1	1	0	0	0	0	4	4
David Solomona	26/1/78	32	29	14	14	0	0	0	0	56	56
Rob Spicer	22/9/84	12(8)	12(8)	1	1	0	0	0	0	4	4
Semi Tadulala	3/3/78	29	26	11	9	0	0	0	0	44	36
Albert Talipeau	5/8/81	3(5)	2(3)	0	0	0	0	0	0	0	0
Michael Wainwright	4/11/80	13(7)	13(7)	6	6	0	0	0	0	24	24
David Wrench	3/1/79	8(7)	6(6)	2	2	0	0	0	0	8	8

LEAGUE RECORD
P28-W15-D0-L13
(6th, SL/Elimination Semi Finalists)
F788, A662, Diff+126
30 points.

CHALLENGE CUP
Quarter Finalists

ATTENDANCES
Best - v Leeds (SL - 7,680)
Worst - v London (SL - 3,104)
Total (SL only) - 67,258
Average (SL only) - 4,804
(Up by 787 on 2003)

TOP TACKLES
David March 811

TOP CARRIES
Michael Korkidas 463

TOP METRES
Michael Korkidas 4084

TOP BREAKS
Ben Jeffries 29

TOP OFFLOADS
David Solomona 81

TOP BUSTS
Sid Domic 69

KEY DATES - WARRINGTON WOLVES

8 April 2004 - Ben Westwood, Paul Wood, Jon Clarke, Mark Hilton and Mike Wainwright all pen new contracts.

29 April 2004 - Danny Lima is referred to the RFL Disciplinary Committee for an alleged head high tackle during a Super League fixture against Bradford Bulls.

27 November 2003 - sign John Wilshere from St George and Danny Lima from Manly on two-year contracts.

10 January 2004 - extend contracts of Paul Wood to November 2006 and loose forward Mike Wainwright until November 2005.

13th January 2004 - Wolves announce record season-ticket sales as they prepare for their first game at the new Halliwell Jones Stadium.

21 February 2004 - celebrate the opening of the Halliwell Jones Stadium with a 34-20 win in front of a capacity crowd, with hundreds locked out.

6 April 2004 - John Wilshere is ruled out for six to eight weeks after fracturing his cheekbone in the opening minutes of Warrington's 36-24 round four win at London Broncos.

16 May 2004 - Danny Lima misses Warrington's visit to Super League leaders Leeds after being banned for four matches for head high tackles during the 22-22 home draw with Bradford Bulls.

10 June 2004 - Paul Cullen agrees a three-year extension, to the end of the 2007 season, to his current deal.

24 June 2004 - fullback Daryl Cardiss signs a two-year extension to his contract, keeping him at the Wolves until 2006.

15 July 2004 - Wolves sign Kiwi international winger Henry Fa'afili from New Zealand Warriors on a three-year deal.

23 July 2004 - Wolves confirm the £200,000 capture of St Helens and Great Britain centre Martin Gleeson on a four-year contract.

9 August 2004 - Wolves label reports that they are poised to sign Sydney Roosters forward Adrian Morley as "complete and utter rubbish".

9 September 2004 - bring centre Toa Kohe-Love back to the club on a one-year deal, and former Bulls teammate Logan Swann on a two-year contract.

23 September 2004 - Wolves confirm the signing of Halifax Academy star Simon Grix on a two-year contract.

8 October 2004 - £125,000 offer to sign Wakefield Trinity Wildcats captain Gareth Ellis is turned down.

Paul Wood

WARRINGTON WOLVES

DATE	FIXTURE	RESULT	SCORERS	LGE	ATT
21/2/04	Wakefield (h)	W34-20	t:N Wood,Gaskell,Briers,P Wood(2) g:Briers(7)	3rd	14,206
2/3/04	Rochdale (a) (CCR4) ●	W0-80	t:Appo(2),P Wood(2),Wilshere(2),Guisset,Westwood(2),Grose, Gaskell,Sibbit,Noone,Hulse,N Wood,Cardiss g:Appo(3),Wilshere(5)	N/A	6,761
7/3/04	Hull (a)	L24-18	t:Grose(2),Lima g:Briers(3)	5th	12,124
14/3/04	Oldham (a) (CCR5)	W10-44	t:Burns,Sibbit,Guisset,Hulse(2),Grose,Varkulis,Westwood,Gaskell g:Wilshere,Noone(3)	N/A	2,859
21/3/04	Castleford (h)	W32-18	t:Wilshere(2),Noone,Grose,P Wood,Hilton g:Briers(4)	5th	8,902
28/3/04	Whitehaven (a) (CCQF)	W10-42	t:Wilshere,Westwood,N Wood(2),Sibbit,Grose,P Wood,Stevens g:Briers(5)	N/A	5,328
4/4/04	London (a)	W24-36	t:Wainwright,Clarke,Forshaw,Guisset(2),Noone g:Noone(5) fg:N Wood,Hulse	6th	3,162
9/4/04	Widnes (h)	L16-24	t:Guisset(2),Lima g:Noone(2)	6th	11,413
12/4/04	Wigan (a)	L26-24	t:Hulse,Gaskell,Varkulis,Clarke g:Noone(4)	6th	13,822
18/4/04	Wigan (CCSF) ●●	L18-30	t:Westwood,Burns,Forshaw g:Briers(3)	N/A	11,175
24/4/04	Salford (a)	W18-37	t:Burns,N Wood,Briers,P Wood,Gleeson,Varkulis g:Briers(5),Noone fg:Briers	6th	3,624
27/4/04	Bradford (h)	D22-22	t:Briers,Varkulis,Grose(2),Gaskell g:Briers	6th	8,111
2/5/04	Huddersfield (h)	L20-26	t:Clarke,Guisset,Gaskell g:Briers(4)	6th	8,792
7/5/04	Leeds (a)	L23-10	t:Briers g:Briers(3)	7th	16,065
22/5/04	St Helens (h)	L20-50	t:Westwood,Wainwright,Grose,Clarke g:Briers(2)	7th	11,328
28/5/04	Wigan (h)	W34-18	t:Forshaw,N Wood(3),Wainwright,Briers g:Briers(5)	7th	10,062
6/6/04	Widnes (a)	L31-10	t:Forshaw g:Briers(3)	8th	8,315
12/6/04	London (h)	W42-12	t:Appo,N Wood,Noone(2),Westwood(2),Grose g:Briers(7)	7th	7,123
20/6/04	Castleford (a)	W10-32	t:Westwood,Gaskell,Grose,N Wood g:Noone(3),Appo	7th	6,111
26/6/04	St Helens (a)	L28-8	t:N Wood g:Noone,Cardiss	7th	8,783
4/7/04	Leeds (h)	L22-38	t:Grose,N Wood,Burns,Noone g:Briers(3)	8th	10,404
11/7/04	Hull (h)	L18-38	t:Leikvoll,Grose,Wainwright g:Briers(3)	8th	8,166
18/7/04	Wakefield (a)	L32-26	t:P Wood,Forshaw,Lima,Burns(2) g:Briers(3)	8th	4,309
24/7/04	Huddersfield (a)	W18-34	t:Gaskell,Briers(2),P Wood,Gleeson,Lima g:Briers(5)	8th	4,038
1/8/04	Salford (h)	W46-20	t:Hulse(2),Forshaw,Burns(2),Westwood,Appo,Guisset g:Briers(7)	7th	8,641
8/8/04	Bradford (a)	L36-22	t:N Wood(2),Grose,Gleeson g:Briers(3)	8th	12,981
15/8/04	Leeds (h)	L12-44	t:Fa'afili,Stevens g:Briers(2)	8th	9,360
22/8/04	London (a)	L34-26	t:Clarke,Fa'afili(2),Westwood,Sibbit g:Appo(3)	8th	3,526
29/8/04	Salford (a)	W6-32	t:Fa'afili,Grose,Hilton,Hulse,P Wood,Sibbit g:Appo(4)	7th	4,019
5/9/04	St Helens (h)	L24-26	t:Gaskell,N Wood,Wainwright(2),Appo g:Appo(2)	8th	11,930
12/9/04	Bradford (h)	L27-28	t:Sibbit,Appo,P Wood,Grose,Gaskell g:Briers(3) fg:Briers	8th	10,008
17/9/04	Wigan (a)	L21-16	t:Guisset,Grose,Cardiss g:Briers(2)	8th	15,132

● Played at Halliwell Jones Stadium
●● Played at Halton Stadium, Widnes

		APP		TRIES		GOALS		FG		PTS	
	D.O.B.	ALL	SL	ALL	SL	ALL	SL	ALL	SL	ALL	SL
Graham Appo	11/7/74	18(1)	17(1)	6	4	13	10	0	0	50	36
Lee Briers	14/6/78	23	21	7	7	83	75	2	2	196	180
Darren Burns	17/5/74	18(4)	16(4)	8	6	0	0	0	0	32	24
Daryl Cardiss	13/7/77	19(2)	16(2)	2	1	1	1	0	0	10	6
Jon Clarke	4/4/79	30	27	5	5	0	0	0	0	20	20
Jamie Durbin	7/9/84	(1)	0	0	0	0	0	0	0	0	0
Henry Fa'afili	30/5/80	7	7	4	4	0	0	0	0	16	16
Mike Forshaw	5/10/70	22(1)	20(1)	6	5	0	0	0	0	24	20
Dean Gaskell	12/4/83	26	23	10	8	0	0	0	0	40	32
Mark Gleeson	16/6/82	3(24)	2(22)	3	3	0	0	0	0	12	12
Brent Grose	11/9/79	28	25	17	14	0	0	0	0	68	56
Jerome Guisset	29/8/78	5(21)	4(18)	9	7	0	0	0	0	36	28
Mark Hilton	31/3/75	24(4)	21(4)	2	2	0	0	0	0	8	8
Gary Hulse	20/1/81	11(10)	10(9)	7	4	0	0	1	1	29	17
Chris Leikvoll	4/12/75	14(7)	13(7)	1	1	0	0	0	0	4	4
Danny Lima	27/7/75	16(13)	13(12)	4	4	0	0	0	0	16	16
Paul Noone	22/4/81	19(2)	16(1)	6	5	19	16	0	0	62	52
Ian Sibbit	15/10/80	15(10)	12(9)	6	3	0	0	0	0	24	12
Warren Stevens	4/10/78	(19)	(15)	2	1	0	0	0	0	8	4
Matt Sturm	13/12/72	(1)	(1)	0	0	0	0	0	0	0	0
Richard Varkulis	21/5/82	4(2)	4(1)	4	3	0	0	0	0	16	12
Mike Wainwright	25/2/75	30	26	6	6	0	0	0	0	24	24
Ben Westwood	25/7/81	26	22	13	8	0	0	0	0	52	32
John Wilshere	5/5/78	8	5	5	2	6	0	0	0	32	8
Nathan Wood	24/1/72	29	25	15	12	0	0	1	1	61	49
Paul Wood	10/10/81	21(5)	19(5)	11	8	0	0	0	0	44	32

LEAGUE RECORD
P28-W10-D1-L17
(8th, SL)
F700, A715, Diff-15
21 points.

CHALLENGE CUP
Semi Finalists

ATTENDANCES
Best - v Wakefield (SL - 14,206)
Worst - v London (SL - 7,123)
Total (SL only) - 138,446
Average (SL only) - 9,889
(Up by 2,858 on 2003)

TOP TACKLES
Mike Wainwright 587

TOP CARRIES
Paul Wood 354

TOP METRES
Danny Lima 3081

TOP BREAKS
Brent Grose 24

TOP OFFLOADS
Mike Forshaw 66

TOP BUSTS
Dean Gaskell 69

30 October 2003 - Vikings secure the services of prop forward Andy Hobson from relegated Halifax, on a one-year deal.

1 November 2003 - Aussie halfback Jason Ferris pulls out of a move to Widnes.

7 January 2004 - snap up Australian second-row forward Troy Wozniak, a fortnight after he quit London Broncos, on a three-year deal.

17 February 2004 - winger Paul Devlin faces up to six months on the sidelines due to knee surgery after picking up an injury in a pre-season friendly with Wests Tigers.

9 March 2004 - Vikings booed off the pitch after shock 38-6 home defeat by Huddersfield.

11 March 2004 - Widnes board gives full backing to coach Neil Kelly despite the club's dismal start to the Tetley's Super League season, with the promise of a new two-year contract.

11 March 2004 - halfback Dean Lawford released.

26 April 2004 - Neil Kelly confirms that contract talks with current club Widnes have stepped up, after a week of speculation linking him with the vacant Castleford Tigers post.

27 April 2004 - Vikings sign Aussie utility back Craig Weston, for a third time, until the end of the season.

14 June 2004 - Neil Kelly relinquishes his role as coach of Wales with immediate effect.

KEY DATES - WIDNES VIKINGS

25 June 2004 - prop Robert Relf announces his retirement after being told he needs operations on both ankles.

3 July 2004 - South Sydney scrum-half Willie Peters make Vikings debut in 56-8 defeat by his former club Wigan Warriors at Halton Stadium.

4 July 2004 - Neil Kelly sacked by the Vikings after four wins from 17 Super League matches.

6 July 2004 - Stuart Spruce appointed caretaker coach.

6 July 2004 - captain Andy Hay banned for one game for a reckless high tackle on Wigan skipper Andy Farrell.

12 July 2004 - centre Aaron Moule likely to miss the rest of the season with a knee injury.

27 July 2004 - new signing, Fijian winger Wise Kativerata, will not join the Vikings.

4 August 2004 - sign ex-St Helens winger Steve Hall until the end of the Super League season.

12 August 2004 - Vikings accept offer of help from former Wigan boss Frank Endacott to look at the club's playing strengths, while confirming caretaker coach Stuart Spruce will continue in his role until the end of the season.

20 August 2004 - sign Justin Murphy after the 26-year-old threequarter was released by New Zealand Warriors.

28 August 2004 - record crucial 20-16 win over Wigan Warriors to ease relegation fears.

30 August 2004 - Frank Endacott drops hint that he could be Widnes coach next season - if the Vikings stay up.

31 August 2004 - confirm signing of Samoan Sala Fa'alogo from Counties Manukau.

1 September 2004 - announce the signing of Wigan duo Terry O'Connor and Mick Cassidy for 2005 on one-year deals.

18 September 2004 - secure Super League status, despite going down 20-18 at Hull in round 28 at the KC Stadium.

22 September 2004 - beat off a challenge from Manly Sea Eagles to keep Aussie centre Aaron Moule on a two-year deal.

22 September 2004 - part company with stand-off Jules O'Neill, off to join a French rugby union club, but keep Sala Fa'alogo on a one year deal.

4 October 2004 - sign Warrington utility Gary Hulse on a one-year deal.

8 October 2004 - 20-year-old fullback Steve Rowlands signs a two-year contract.

18 October 2004 - Frank Endacott takes charge on a two-year deal, and signs veteran centre Gary Connolly, on a one-year contract, from Wigan.

23 November 2004 - Announce the capture of Mark Smith from Wigan Warriors.

Daniel Frame

WIDNES VIKINGS

DATE	FIXTURE	RESULT	SCORERS	LGE	ATT
22/2/04	Salford (a)	L24-12	t:Mills,Giles g:Jules O'Neill(2)	8th	5,049
29/2/04	Wigan (a) (CCR4)	L38-12	t:Jules O'Neill,Bird g:Jules O'Neill(2)	N/A	6,737
5/3/04	Huddersfield (h)	L6-38	t:Jules O'Neill g:Jules O'Neill	10th	5,412
19/3/04	St Helens (a)	L38-20	t:Hughes,Mills,Frame g:Jules O'Neill(4)	11th	10,549
4/4/04	Leeds (a)	L0-46	No Scorers	12th	7,325
9/4/04	Warrington (a)	W16-24	t:Giles,Finnigan,Royle,Millard g:Jules O'Neill(4)	10th	11,413
12/4/04	Hull (h)	W32-18	t:Hughes,Giles,Royle,McCurrie,Jules O'Neill g:Jules O'Neill(5) fg:Jules O'Neill(2)	9th	6,059
18/4/04	London (a)	L34-18	t:Millard,Hughes(2),Royle g:Jules O'Neill	10th	2,923
25/4/04	Castleford (h)	W29-18	t:Royle,Myler,McCurrie,Jules O'Neill g:Jules O'Neill(6) fg:Jules O'Neill	9th	5,274
2/5/04	Wakefield (a)	L40-10	t:Jules O'Neill(2) g:Jules O'Neill	9th	4,136
7/5/04	Wigan (a)	L26-8	t:Bird,Royle	9th	10,145
23/5/04	Bradford (h)	L20-30	t:Finnigan,Bird,Wozniak g:Jules O'Neill(4)	9th	6,615
31/5/04	Hull (a)	L70-4	t:Finnigan	10th	9,946
6/6/04	Warrington (h)	W31-10	t:Hughes(2),Royle,Millard,Hay g:Jules O'Neill(4),Myler fg:Jules O'Neill	9th	8,315
11/6/04	Leeds (a)	L48-24	t:Finnigan,Royle,Giles(2) g:Myler(4)	9th	13,419
18/6/04	St Helens (h)	L12-40	t:Rowlands,Moule g:Jules O'Neill(2)	9th	7,482
27/6/04	Bradford (a)	L38-30	t:Finnigan,Moule,Hay,Frame,Jules O'Neill g:Jules O'Neill(5)	10th	11,137
3/7/04	Wigan (a)	L8-56	t:Millard,Jules O'Neill	10th	6,012
11/7/04	Huddersfield (a)	L26-20	t:Peters,Hughes,Giles g:Jules O'Neill(4)	10th	3,566
18/7/04	Salford (h)	L14-15	t:Myler,Frame g:Jules O'Neill(2),Myler	10th	5,573
25/7/04	Wakefield (h)	W25-24	t:Frame(2),Peters,Finnigan g:Myler(4) fg:Peters	10th	5,104
31/7/04	Castleford (a)	L42-8	t:Millard g:Myler(2)	10th	5,517
8/8/04	London (h)	L24-38	t:Devlin(2),Hughes,Mills g:Myler(4)	11th	4,829
14/8/04	Salford (a)	L14-13	t:Robinson,Jules O'Neill g:Jules O'Neill(2) fg:Peters	11th	3,067
22/8/04	Huddersfield (h)	W24-18	t:Murphy,Whitaker(2),Peters g:Jules O'Neill(4)	11th	4,881
28/8/04	Wigan (h)	W20-16	t:McCurrie,Whitaker,Finnigan g:Jules O'Neill(3),Myler	11th	6,456
5/9/04	Wakefield (a)	L40-6	t:Finnigan g:Jules O'Neill	11th	5,198
11/9/04	Castleford (h)	L6-7	t:Myler g:Jules O'Neill	11th	7,005
18/9/04	Hull (a)	L20-18	t:Frame,Whitaker,Fa'alogo g:Jules O'Neill(3)	11th	9,544

		APP		TRIES		GOALS		FG		PTS	
	D.O.B.	ALL	SL	ALL	SL	ALL	SL	ALL	SL	ALL	SL
Paul Atcheson	17/5/73	6(6)	5(6)	0	0	0	0	0	0	0	0
Adam Bibey	30/4/86	(1)	(1)	0	0	0	0	0	0	0	0
Deon Bird	27/1/76	22(6)	21(6)	3	2	0	0	0	0	12	8
Paul Devlin	19/2/81	8	8	2	2	0	0	0	0	8	8
Sala Fa'alogo	20/9/77	(3)	(3)	1	1	0	0	0	0	4	4
Simon Finnigan	8/12/81	22(4)	21(4)	8	8	0	0	0	0	32	32
Daniel Frame	7/6/75	20(4)	20(4)	6	6	0	0	0	0	24	24
Tommy Gallagher	10/9/83	(6)	(6)	0	0	0	0	0	0	0	0
Chris Giles	26/12/81	22	21	6	6	0	0	0	0	24	24
Steve Hall	10/7/79	1	1	0	0	0	0	0	0	0	0
Andy Hay	5/11/73	26(1)	25(1)	2	2	0	0	0	0	8	8
Andy Hobson	26/12/78	5(14)	5(13)	0	0	0	0	0	0	0	0
Tim Holmes	29/9/82	7	7	0	0	0	0	0	0	0	0
Adam Hughes	1/10/77	25(1)	25	8	8	0	0	0	0	32	32
Bruce Johnson	26/1/84	(3)	(3)	0	0	0	0	0	0	0	0
Dean Lawford	9/5/77	3	2	0	0	0	0	0	0	0	0
Steve McCurrie	1/6/73	12(16)	11(16)	3	3	0	0	0	0	12	12
Ryan McDonald	24/2/78	(1)	0	0	0	0	0	0	0	0	0
Gary Middlehurst	24/10/83	(2)	(2)	0	0	0	0	0	0	0	0
Shane Millard	30/7/75	26	25	5	5	0	0	0	0	20	20
David Mills	1/6/81	13(15)	13(14)	3	3	0	0	0	0	12	12
Aaron Moule	20/6/77	16	16	2	2	0	0	0	0	8	8
Justin Murphy	14/2/78	5	5	1	1	0	0	0	0	4	4
Stephen Myler	21/7/84	18(7)	18(7)	3	3	17	17	0	0	46	46
Jules O'Neill	14/10/72	26	25	9	8	61	59	4	4	162	154
Julian O'Neill	24/7/73	19(4)	18(4)	0	0	0	0	0	0	0	0
Willie Peters	1/3/79	9	9	3	3	0	0	2	2	14	14
Robert Relf	29/1/71	15	14	0	0	0	0	0	0	0	0
John Robinson	18/12/83	7	6	1	1	0	0	0	0	4	4
Steve Rowlands	9/9/83	10(3)	9(3)	1	1	0	0	0	0	4	4
Nicky Royle	25/9/83	13	13	7	7	0	0	0	0	28	28
Craig Weston	20/12/73	4(4)	4(4)	0	0	0	0	0	0	0	0
Matt Whitaker	6/3/82	2(6)	2(6)	4	4	0	0	0	0	16	16
Phil Wood	25/10/83	2(1)	2(1)	0	0	0	0	0	0	0	0
Troy Wozniak	6/1/78	13(7)	13(7)	1	1	0	0	0	0	4	4

LEAGUE RECORD
P28-W7-D0-L21
(11th, SL)
F466, A850, Diff-384
14 points.

CHALLENGE CUP
Round Four

ATTENDANCES
Best - v Warrington (SL - 8,315)
Worst - v London (SL - 4,829)
Total (SL only) - 86,342
Average (SL only) - 6,167
(Down by 344 on 2003)

TOP TACKLES
Shane Millard 881

TOP CARRIES
Shane Millard 408

TOP METRES
Shane Millard 2726

TOP BREAKS
Adam Hughes/Jules O'Neill 14

TOP OFFLOADS
Julian O'Neill 41

TOP BUSTS
Jules O'Neill 44

KEY DATES - WIGAN WARRIORS

26 May 2004 - Mark Smith avoids suspension after being placed on report and found guilty of a dangerous tackle in the 20-14 win at Wakefield.

1 June 2004 - chairman Maurice Lindsay rejects calls to recall Luke Robinson from Castleford, after Adrian Lam's withdrawal from the action at Warrington in Wigan's 34-18 round 16 defeat.

7 June 2004 - Wigan favourites to re-sign Brett Dallas for next season, despite reports that the winger would head back to Australia at the end of the season.

8 June 2004 - Quentin Pongia, who has not played since the Hepatitis B revelations, announces his retirement from the game.

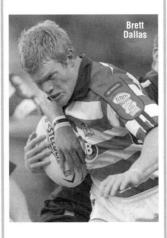

Brett Dallas

21 June 2004 - Maurice Lindsay expected to step up efforts to land the signature of St George-Illawarra's former Test centre Mark Gasnier.

22 June 2004 - Gareth Hock extends his contract until the end of the 2005 season.

30 June 2004 - Danny Sculthorpe could be out of action for up to three months with a shoulder injury after the Warrior's draw 20-20 at Hull.

10 July 2004 - Canberra Raiders release hard-working prop Luke Davico to take up a contract with Wigan for the 2005 season.

13 July 2004 - Danny Sculthorpe signs a new three-year contract, keeping him at the JJB Stadium until at least the end of 2007.

22 July 2004 - Danny Tickle signs a new two-year contract which will keep him at Wigan until the end of 2006.

27 July 2004 - Warriors confirm the signing of Parramatta Eels centre David Vaealiki on a three-year contract.

10 August 2004 - Kiwi prop forward Craig Smith announces he will retire from the game at the end of the 2004 season.

12 August 2004 - Brett Dallas, Mark Smith and Stephen Wild all extend their contracts. Young props Bryn Hargreaves and Paul Prescott also sign for a further two years.

28 August 2004 - youngsters Liam Colbon and Chris Melling both sign new two-year contracts.

13 October 2004 - Andy Farrell is Man of Steel for the second time, also voted player of the year by his fellow professionals.

13 October 2004 - sign hooker Wayne Godwin from Castleford Tigers on a two-year contract.

8 November 2004 - sign halfback Denis Moran from London Broncos on two-year contract. Adrian Lam to become assistant coach.

22 November 2004 - Andy Farrell wins the Golden Boot award.

5 February 2004 - Wigan Chairman Maurice Lindsay confirms interest in New Zealand Warriors' Test prop forward Jerry Seuseu for the 2005 season.

1 March 2004 - Brian Carney breaks ankle during 38-12 Powergen Challenge Cup win over Widnes.

23 March 2004 - prop forward Danny Sculthorpe ruled out of Cup quarter-final against Wakefield with two-match ban after being found guilty of use of the forearm in the 36-24 defeat at Leeds.

31 March 2004 - Mick Cassidy to miss Super League game at Huddersfield after being handed a one-match ban for striking in Wigan's 20-4 win over Wakefield.

26 April 2004 - Wigan reveal coach Mike Gregory has developed a chronic bacterial infection which will require hospital for treatment in America.

26 April 2004 - Brian Carney suffers setback in his efforts to recover from a broken ankle after an X-ray reveals his bone has not reformed.

22 May 2004 - News of the World reveals Wigan's New Zealand star Quentin Pongia has been playing with the contagious disease Hepatitis B.

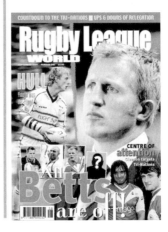

WIGAN WARRIORS

DATE	FIXTURE	RESULT	SCORERS	LGE	ATT
20/2/04	Bradford (a)	L34-6	t:Orr g:Orr	11th	17,267
29/2/04	Widnes (h) (CCR4)	W38-12	t:Aspinwall,M Smith(2),O'Loughlin,Newton,Brown,Orr g:Tickle(4),Robinson	N/A	6,737
7/3/04	Salford (h)	W20-10	t:Aspinwall,O'Loughlin(2),Newton g:Orr,Melling	8th	11,172
14/3/04	Limoux (a) (CCR5)	W20-80	t:Melling,Newton,Aspinwall,O'Loughlin,Hock(2),Orr,Radlinski,Brown, Robinson(3),M Smith,Dallas g:Orr(2),Melling(10)	N/A	2,500
19/3/04	Leeds (h)	L36-24	t:Brown,Wild(2),Aspinwall g:Tickle(4)	8th	18,124
26/3/04	Wakefield (h) (CCQF)	W20-4	t:Radlinski,Brown,Aspinwall(2) g:Farrell(2)	N/A	9,728
4/4/04	Huddersfield (a)	L26-10	t:Tickle,Dallas g:Orr	8th	5,175
9/4/04	St Helens (a)	D21-21	t:Brown,Orr,Newton g:Farrell(4) fg:Farrell	8th	15,964
12/4/04	Warrington (h)	W26-24	t:Aspinwall,Dallas(2),Tickle g:Farrell(5)	7th	13,822
18/4/04	Warrington (CCSF) ●	W18-30	t:Dallas(3),Radlinski,Wild g:Farrell(5)	N/A	11,175
25/4/04	London (h)	W64-8	t:Dallas,Orr,Radlinski(2),Brown,O'Loughlin,Farrell,Newton(3),C Smith g:Farrell(10)	7th	9,132
1/5/04	Castleford (a)	W28-42	t:Dallas(2),Brown,Newton(2),Lam,C Smith,Radlinski g:Farrell(5)	7th	6,222
7/5/04	Widnes (h)	W26-8	t:Wild,Tickle,Orr,Hodgson,Hock g:Farrell(3)	6th	10,145
15/5/04	St Helens (CCF) ●●	L32-16	t:Newton,Dallas(2) g:Farrell(2)	N/A	73,734
23/5/04	Wakefield (a)	W14-20	t:O'Loughlin,Brown,Radlinski g:Farrell(4)	6th	5,118
28/5/04	Warrington (a)	L34-18	t:C Smith,Aspinwall,M Smith g:Farrell(3)	6th	10,062
4/6/04	St Helens (h)	W30-14	t:Lam,Aspinwall,Radlinski(2) g:Farrell(5),Tickle(2)	6th	17,194
13/6/04	Huddersfield (h)	W40-18	t:Farrell,Radlinski(2),Dallas(2),Sculthorpe,Orr g:Farrell(6)	5th	9,162
19/6/04	Leeds (h)	W26-22	t:Radlinski,Newton,Hock,O'Loughlin g:Farrell(4),Tickle	5th	14,140
25/6/04	Wakefield (h)	W28-22	t:Radlinski(2),Orr,Dallas,Hodgson g:Tickle(4)	5th	9,274
29/6/04	Hull (a)	D20-20	t:Wild,Farrell,Orr g:Farrell(4)	5th	11,042
3/7/04	Widnes (a)	W8-56	t:Lam,Newton(4),Wild(2),O'Loughlin,M Smith g:Farrell(5),Tickle,Orr(4)	5th	6,012
11/7/04	Salford (a)	W16-32	t:Dallas(2),Tickle,Aspinwall,Hansen,O'Loughlin g:Tickle(4)	5th	6,037
16/7/04	Bradford (h)	W32-16	t:Farrell,Dallas,Cassidy,Radlinski,C Smith g:Farrell(6)	4th	15,102
23/7/04	Castleford (h)	W48-18	t:Dallas(4),Robinson,Aspinwall,Newton(2) g:Farrell(7),Tickle	3rd	10,032
1/8/04	London (a)	L22-20	t:Robinson,Radlinski,Aspinwall g:Farrell(4)	4th	4,352
6/8/04	Hull (h)	D13-13	t:Wild,Tickle g:Farrell(2) fg:Farrell	4th	12,074
13/8/04	Bradford (a)	L38-12	t:Aspinwall,Carney g:Farrell(2)	5th	12,610
20/8/04	St Helens (h)	W27-18	t:Dallas,Lam,O'Loughlin,Radlinski g:Farrell(5) fg:Farrell	4th	16,424
28/8/04	Widnes (a)	L20-16	t:Connolly,Wild,Lam g:Farrell(2)	5th	6,456
3/9/04	Leeds (h)	D12-12	t:Carney g:Farrell(4)	5th	14,288
12/9/04	London (a)	W22-26	t:Dallas,C Smith,Wild,Farrell g:Farrell(5)	4th	4,151
17/9/04	Warrington (h)	W21-16	t:Farrell,Aspinwall,Tickle,Brown g:Farrell,Tickle fg:Lam	4th	15,132
25/9/04	St Helens (h) (EPO)	W18-12	t:Robinson,Brown,Farrell g:Farrell(3)	N/A	20,052
1/10/04	Wakefield (h) (ESF)	W18-14	t:Radlinski,Brown,Lam g:Farrell(3)	N/A	16,179
8/10/04	Leeds (a) (FE)	L40-12	t:Farrell,Robinson g:Farrell(2)	N/A	20,119

● Played at Halton Stadium, Widnes
●● Played at Millennium Stadium, Cardiff

		APP		TRIES		GOALS		FG		PTS	
	D.O.B.	ALL	SL	ALL	SL	ALL	SL	ALL	SL	ALL	SL
David Allen	15/9/85	(1)	0	0	0	0	0	0	0	0	0
Martin Aspinwall	21/10/81	30	26	14	10	0	0	0	0	56	40
Bob Beswick	8/12/84	(6)	(6)	0	0	0	0	0	0	0	0
Kevin Brown	2/10/84	19(3)	14(3)	11	8	0	0	0	0	44	32
Brian Carney	23/7/76	9(1)	8(1)	2	2	0	0	0	0	8	8
Mick Cassidy	8/7/73	11(13)	9(12)	1	1	0	0	0	0	4	4
Liam Colbon	30/9/84	1(3)	1(3)	0	0	0	0	0	0	0	0
Gary Connolly	22/6/71	12(6)	12(6)	1	1	0	0	0	0	4	4
Brett Dallas	18/10/74	36	31	24	18	0	0	0	0	96	72
Andy Farrell	30/5/75	29	26	8	8	113	104	3	3	261	243
Harrison Hansen	26/10/85	(6)	(6)	1	1	0	0	0	0	4	4
Bryn Hargreaves	14/11/85	1(1)	1(1)	0	0	0	0	0	0	0	0
Gareth Hock	5/9/83	28(7)	24(6)	4	2	0	0	0	0	16	8
David Hodgson	8/8/81	10(5)	9(5)	2	2	0	0	0	0	8	8
Adrian Lam	25/8/70	23(2)	22(1)	6	6	0	0	1	1	25	25
Chris Melling	21/9/84	2(1)	1(1)	1	0	11	1	0	0	26	2
Terry Newton	7/11/78	29	24	17	14	0	0	0	0	68	56
Terry O'Connor	13/10/71	14(13)	13(9)	0	0	0	0	0	0	0	0
Sean O'Loughlin	24/11/82	36	31	10	8	0	0	0	0	40	32
Danny Orr	17/5/78	29	24	9	7	9	7	0	0	54	42
Quentin Pongia	9/7/70	9(5)	5(4)	0	0	0	0	0	0	0	0
Paul Prescott	1/1/86	1(2)	1(2)	0	0	0	0	0	0	0	0
Kris Radlinski	9/4/76	33	28	18	15	0	0	0	0	72	60
Luke Robinson	25/7/84	10(8)	7(8)	7	4	1	0	0	0	30	16
Danny Sculthorpe	8/9/79	2(18)	1(15)	1	1	0	0	0	0	4	4
Craig Smith	31/10/71	30(3)	26(2)	5	5	0	0	0	0	20	20
Mark Smith	18/8/81	7(23)	7(19)	5	2	0	0	0	0	20	8
Danny Tickle	10/3/83	28(7)	26(5)	6	6	22	18	0	0	68	60
Stephen Wild	26/4/81	27(6)	24(5)	10	9	0	0	0	0	40	36
Desi Williams	24/9/85	2	2	0	0	0	0	0	0	0	0

LEAGUE RECORD
P28-W17-D4-L7
(4th, SL/Final Eliminator)
F736, A558, Diff+178
38 points.

CHALLENGE CUP
Runners Up

ATTENDANCES
Best - v St Helens (EPO - 20,052)
Worst - v Widnes (CC - 6,737)
Total (SL, inc play-offs) - 213,324
Average (SL, inc play-offs) - 13,333
(Up by 2,116 on 2003)

TOP TACKLES
Sean O'Loughlin 792

TOP CARRIES
Andy Farrell 468

TOP METRES
Brett Dallas 3617

TOP BREAKS
Brett Dallas 28

TOP OFFLOADS
Andy Farrell 55

TOP BUSTS
Brett Dallas 77

SUPER LEAGUE IX
Round by Round

ROUND 1

Friday 20th February 2004

BRADFORD BULLS 34 WIGAN WARRIORS 6

BULLS: 6 Michael Withers; 2 Tevita Vaikona; 16 Paul Johnson; 4 Shontayne Hape; 5 Lesley Vainikolo; 3 Leon Pryce; 15 Karl Pratt; 10 Paul Anderson; 24 Aaron Smith; 29 Stuart Fielden; 11 Lee Radford; 12 Jamie Peacock (C); 19 Jamie Langley. Subs (all used): 8 Joe Vagana; 27 Rob Parker; 14 Toa Kohe-Love (D); 17 Stuart Reardon.
Tries: Withers (27), Vainikolo (38, 50, 60, 76, 79), Aaron Smith (54); **Goals:** Withers 3/6, Pratt 0/2.
WARRIORS: 1 Kris Radlinski (C); 2 Brett Dallas; 3 Martin Aspinwall; 19 Stephen Wild; 5 Brian Carney; 6 Danny Orr (D); 14 Luke Robinson; 18 Quentin Pongia; 9 Terry Newton; 10 Craig Smith; 20 Gareth Hock; 12 Danny Tickle; 15 Sean O'Loughlin. Subs (all used): 8 Terry O'Connor; 21 Kevin Brown; 16 Danny Sculthorpe; 17 Mark Smith.
Try: Orr (65); **Goals:** Orr 1/1.
Sin bin: Robinson (19) – persistent offside.
Rugby Leaguer & League Express Men of the Match: *Bulls:* Lesley Vainikolo; *Warriors:* Terry Newton.
Penalty count: 12-6; **Half-time:** 12-0; **Referee:** Russell Smith (Castleford); **Attendance:** 17,267.

ST HELENS 30 HULL FC 16

SAINTS: 1 Paul Wellens; 5 Darren Albert; 3 Martin Gleeson; 4 Willie Talau; 22 Dom Feaunati (D); 6 Jason Hooper; 7 Sean Long; 8 Nick Fozzard (D); 9 Keiron Cunningham; 18 Mark Edmondson; 11 Chris Joynt; 12 Lee Gilmour (D); 13 Paul Sculthorpe (C). Subs: 14 Mick Higham; 16 Keith Mason; 15 Mike Bennett; 25 Ian Hardman (not used).
Tries: Talau (5), Hooper (15), Fozzard (18, 26), Cunningham (49), Feaunati (73); **Goals:** Long 3/7.
HULL: 32 Shaun Briscoe (D); 2 Colin Best; 3 Richie Barnett (C); 4 Michael Eagar (D); 5 Gareth Raynor; 16 Paul Cooke; 6 Richard Horne; 10 Paul King; 9 Richard Swain (D); 18 Ewan Dowes; 14 Kirk Yeaman; 15 Shayne McMenemy; 17 Chris Chester. Subs (all used): 20 Garreth Carvell; 23 Paul McNicholas (D); 25 Peter Lupton; 19 Alex Wilkinson.
Tries: Raynor (41), Best (45, 52); **Goals:** Cooke 2/4.
Sin bin: Raynor (18) - holding down.
Rugby Leaguer & League Express Men of the Match: *Saints:* Sean Long; *Hull:* Colin Best.
Penalty count: 10-8; **Half-time:** 20-2; **Referee:** Richard Silverwood (Dewsbury); **Attendance:** 12,532.

Saturday 21st February 2004

**WARRINGTON WOLVES 34
WAKEFIELD TRINITY WILDCATS 20**

WOLVES: 5 Graham Appo; 2 John Wilshere (D); 3 Brent Grose; 4 Ben Westwood; 20 Dean Gaskell; 6 Lee Briers (C); 7 Nathan Wood; 8 Chris Leikvoll (D); 9 Jon Clarke; 10 Mark Hilton; 11 Darren Burns; 23 Mike Wainwright; 13 Mike Forshaw (D). Subs (all used): 14 Mark Gleeson; 16 Paul Wood; 22 Danny Lima (D); 18 Paul Noone.
Tries: N Wood (5), Gaskell (22), Briers (45), P Wood (49, 57); **Goals:** Briers 7/7.
WILDCATS: 1 Jason Demetriou (D); 2 Justin Ryder (D); 3 Gareth Ellis (C); 4 Sid Domic (D); 5 Semi Tadulala (D); 6 Jamie Rooney; 7 Ben Jeffries; 8 Darrell Griffin; 9 David March; 10 Michael Korkidas; 11 David Solomona (D); 12 Dallas Hood; 13 Jamie Field. Subs (all used): 14 Colum Halpenny; 15 David Wrench; 16 Steve Snitch; 25 Albert Talipeau (D).
Tries: Jeffries (26), Ryder (60), Rooney (65), Halpenny (69); **Goals:** Rooney 2/3, Ellis 0/1, Halpenny 0/1.
Sin bin: Wrench (51) - holding down.
Rugby Leaguer & League Express Men of the Match: *Wolves:* Lee Briers; *Wildcats:* Sid Domic.
Penalty count: 13-10; **Half-time:** 14-8;
Referee: Ian Smith (Oldham); **Attendance:** 14,206.

Sunday 22nd February 2004

HUDDERSFIELD GIANTS 26 CASTLEFORD TIGERS 22

GIANTS: 1 Paul Reilly; 2 Hefin O'Hare; 3 Stuart Donlan (D); 4 Julian Bailey; 34 Marcus St Hilaire; 6 Stanley Gene; 9 Paul March; 25 Darren Fleary (C); 15 Darren Turner; 12 Ben Roarty; 11 Chris Nero (D); 14 Stuart Jones (D); 13 Brandon Costin. Subs: 7 Sean Penkywicz (D); 8 Mick Slicker; 18 Eorl Crabtree; 5 Ben Cooper (not used).
Tries: St Hilaire (24, 71), March (37), Jones (53), Costin (77); **Goals:** Costin 3/6.
On report: Turner (63) - alleged biting.
TIGERS: 20 Tom Saxton; 2 Waine Pryce; 1 Damian Gibson; 14 Ryan Clayton (D); 5 Darren Rogers; 6 Sean Rudder (D); 7 Ryan Sheridan; 8 Craig Greenhill (D); 9 Wayne Godwin; 15 Nathan Sykes; 18 Jamie Thackray; 11 Lee Harland; 13 Ryan Hudson (C). Subs (all used): 17 Paul Jackson; 23 Michael Smith; 16 Jon Hepworth; 12 Sean Ryan (D).
Tries: Rogers (3), Pryce (16), Clayton (42), Saxton (57); **Goals:** Godwin 3/4, Hepworth 0/2.
Sin bin: Rogers (51) - persistent infringements; Greenhill (79) - dissent.
Rugby Leaguer & League Express Men of the Match: *Giants:* Paul March; *Tigers:* Ryan Sheridan.
Penalty count: 14-9; **Half-time:** 10-12; **Referee:** Ronnie Laughton (Barnsley); **Attendance:** 5,326.

LEEDS RHINOS 58 LONDON BRONCOS 14

RHINOS: 1 Gary Connolly; 22 Marcus Bai (D); 5 Chev Walker; 4 Keith Senior; 18 Mark Calderwood; 6 Danny McGuire; 7 Rob Burrow; 8 Ryan Bailey; 9 Matt Diskin; 10 Barrie McDermott; 11 David Furner; 12 Matt Adamson; 13 Kevin Sinfield (C). Subs (all used): 19 Danny Ward; 16 Willie Poching; 17 Wayne McDonald; 14 Andrew Dunemann.
Tries: Burrow (10, 13), Senior (26, 43), Bai (31, 53, 73), Walker (41, 68), Calderwood (50); **Goals:** Sinfield 9/10.
BRONCOS: 1 Paul Sykes; 2 Jon Wells (D); 21 Rob Jackson; 4 Mark O'Halloran (D); 3 Nigel Roy; 20 Radney Bowker (D); 7 Dennis Moran; 10 Steve Trindall; 9 Neil Budworth; 12 Steele Retchless; 16 Joe Mbu; 18 Andrew Hart (D); 13 Jim Dymock (C). Subs (all used): 8 Francis Stephenson; 14 Andrew Brocklehurst (D); 15 Mitchell Stringer (D); 17 Tom Haughey.
Tries: Moran (21), Brocklehurst (36), Bowker (47); **Goals:** Sykes 1/3, Moran 0/1.
Sin bin: Sykes (35) – interference.
Rugby Leaguer & League Express Men of the Match: *Rhinos:* Matt Diskin; *Broncos:* Radney Bowker.
Penalty count: 12-7; **Half-time:** 24-10;
Referee: Robert Connolly (Wigan); **Attendance:** 15,119.

SALFORD CITY REDS 24 WIDNES VIKINGS 12

CITY REDS: 1 Jason Flowers; 2 Joel Caine (D); 3 Stuart Littler; 5 Anthony Stewart (D); 4 Andy Kirk; 6 Cliff Beverley; 7 Gavin Clinch; 8 Andy Coley; 9 Malcolm Alker (C); 17 Gareth Haggerty; 10 Sean Rutgerson (D); 18 Mark Shipway (D); 16 Martin Moana. Subs (all used): 15 Karl Fitzpatrick; 12 Andy Johnson (D); 13 Chris Charles; 14 Paul Highton.
Tries: Littler (43), Clinch (52), Coley (80);
Goals: Caine 5/5, Charles 1/1.
VIKINGS: 1 Paul Atcheson; 22 John Robinson; 14 Deon Bird; 4 Adam Hughes; 5 Chris Giles; 6 Jules O'Neill; 7 Dean Lawford; 8 Robert Relf; 9 Shane Millard; 10 Julian O'Neill; 11 Steve McCurrie; 12 Andy Hay (C); 18 Simon Finnigan. Subs (all used): 23 Steve Rowlands (D); 15 Troy Wozniak (D); 16 Andy Hobson (D); 17 David Mills.
Tries: Mills (34), Giles (73); **Goals:** Jules O'Neill 2/3.
Rugby Leaguer & League Express Men of the Match: *City Reds:* Andy Coley; *Vikings:* David Mills.
Penalty count: 4-8; **Half-time:** 2-8;
Referee: Steve Ganson (St Helens); **Attendance:** 5,049.

ROUND 2

Friday 5th March 2004

WIDNES VIKINGS 6 HUDDERSFIELD GIANTS 38

VIKINGS: 1 Paul Atcheson; 22 John Robinson; 14 Deon Bird; 3 Aaron Moule (D); 5 Chris Giles; 6 Jules O'Neill; 7 Dean Lawford; 8 Robert Relf; 9 Shane Millard; 10 Julian O'Neill; 11 Steve McCurrie; 12 Andy Hay (C); 13 Daniel Frame. Subs (all used): 17 David Mills; 16 Andy Hobson; 18 Simon Finnigan; 15 Troy Wozniak.
Try: Jules O'Neill (28); **Goals:** Jules O'Neill 1/2.
Sin bin: Millard (17) - swinging arm.
GIANTS: 1 Paul Reilly; 2 Hefin O'Hare; 4 Julian Bailey; 3 Stuart Donlan; 34 Marcus St Hilaire; 6 Stanley Gene; 9 Paul March; 8 Mick Slicker; 22 Phil Joseph; 25 Darren Fleary (C); 12 Ben Roarty; 14 Stuart Jones; 11 Chris Nero. Subs (all used): 5 Ben Cooper; 7 Sean Penkywicz; 17 Paul Smith (D); 18 Eorl Crabtree.
Tries: March (13, 60), Gene (21, 40), Bailey (41), Nero (69); **Goals:** March 7/8.
Sin bin: Fleary (6) - late tackle;
Reilly (26) - holding down.
On report: Fleary (6) - late tackle;
Slicker (33) - high tackle.
Rugby Leaguer & League Express Men of the Match: *Vikings:* None; *Giants:* Paul March.
Penalty count: 9-7; **Half-time:** 6-20;
Referee: Steve Ganson (St Helens); **Attendance:** 5,412.

Saturday 6th March 2004

LONDON BRONCOS 12 ST HELENS 26

BRONCOS: 1 Paul Sykes; 2 Jon Wells; 3 Nigel Roy; 4 Mark O'Halloran; 21 Rob Jackson; 20 Radney Bowker; 7 Dennis Moran; 12 Steele Retchless; 9 Neil Budworth; 10 Steve Trindall; 18 Andrew Hart; 16 Joe Mbu; 13 Jim Dymock (C). Subs (all used): 14 Andrew Brocklehurst; 15 Mitchell Stringer; 8 Francis Stephenson; 22 Lee Sanderson (D).
Tries: Sykes (43), Roy (57); **Goals:** Sykes 2/3.
SAINTS: 1 Paul Wellens; 22 Dom Feaunati; 5 Darren Albert; 4 Willie Talau; 2 Ade Gardner; 6 Jason Hooper; 7 Sean Long; 8 Nick Fozzard; 9 Keiron Cunningham; 16 Keith Mason; 11 Chris Joynt; 12 Lee Gilmour; 13 Paul Sculthorpe (C). Subs (all used): 14 Mick Higham; 18 Mark Edmondson; 21 Jon Wilkin; 24 James Graham.
Tries: Feaunati (9), Cunningham (22), Wilkin (35), Gardner (63, 70); **Goals:** Long 3/5.
Rugby Leaguer & League Express Men of the Match: *Broncos:* Andrew Hart; *Saints:* Paul Sculthorpe.
Penalty count: 7-7; **Half-time:** 0-18; **Referee:** Richard Silverwood (Dewsbury); **Attendance:** 4,757.

Sunday 7th March 2004

WIGAN WARRIORS 20 SALFORD CITY REDS 10

WARRIORS: 1 Kris Radlinski (C); 3 Martin Aspinwall; 19 Stephen Wild; 21 Kevin Brown; 2 Brett Dallas; 6 Danny Orr; 14 Luke Robinson; 8 Terry O'Connor; 9 Terry Newton; 10 Craig Smith; 20 Gareth Hock; 12 Danny Tickle; 15 Sean O'Loughlin. Subs (all used): 16 Danny Sculthorpe; 17 Mark Smith; 18 Quentin Pongia; 26 Chris Melling (D).
Tries: Aspinwall (16), O'Loughlin (38, 77), Newton (67);
Goals: Orr 1/2, Melling 1/2.
CITY REDS: 15 Karl Fitzpatrick; 4 Andy Kirk; 20 Scott Naylor; 3 Stuart Littler; 5 Anthony Stewart; 6 Cliff Beverley; 7 Gavin Clinch; 8 Andy Coley; 9 Malcolm Alker (C); 14 Paul Highton; 18 Mark Shipway; 10 Sean Rutgerson; 16 Martin Moana. Subs (all used): 11 Simon Baldwin; 17 Gareth Haggerty; 12 Andy Johnson; 13 Chris Charles.
Tries: Stewart (3), Littler (53);
Goals: Charles 1/1, Fitzpatrick 0/1.
Rugby Leaguer & League Express Men of the Match: *Warriors:* Sean O'Loughlin; *City Reds:* Karl Fitzpatrick.
Penalty count: 5-10; **Half-time:** 10-4;
Referee: Ian Smith (Oldham); **Attendance:** 11,172.

HULL FC 24 WARRINGTON WOLVES 18

HULL: 32 Shaun Briscoe; 2 Colin Best; 3 Richie Barnett (C); 14 Kirk Yeaman; 26 Richie Barnett Jnr (D); 16 Paul Cooke; 6 Richard Horne; 20 Garreth Carvell; 9 Richard Swain; 18 Ewan Dowes; 15 Shayne McMenemy; 23 Paul McNicholas; 25 Peter Lupton. Subs (all used): 17 Chris Chester; 11 Richard Fletcher; 30 Richard Whiting; 27 Liam Higgins.
Tries: Barnett (7), Barnett Jnr (11, 65), Briscoe (14), Yeaman (57); **Goals:** Cooke 2/5.
WOLVES: 5 Graham Appo; 2 John Wilshere; 3 Brent Grose; 4 Ben Westwood; 20 Dean Gaskell; 6 Lee Briers (C); 7 Nathan Wood; 8 Chris Leikvoll; 9 Jon Clarke; 10 Mark Hilton; 11 Darren Burns; 23 Mike Wainwright; 13 Mike Forshaw. Subs (all used): 14 Mark Gleeson; 22 Danny Lima; 1 Daryl Cardiss; 16 Paul Wood.
Tries: Grose (61, 73), Lima (69); **Goals:** Briers 3/3.
Rugby Leaguer & League Express Men of the Match: *Hull:* Richie Barnett Jnr; *Wolves:* Brent Grose.
Penalty count: 7-8; **Half-time:** 16-0; **Referee:** Russell Smith (Castleford); **Attendance:** 12,124.

CASTLEFORD TIGERS 8 LEEDS RHINOS 34

TIGERS: 1 Damian Gibson; 5 Darren Rogers; 14 Ryan Clayton; 19 Francis Maloney; 2 Waine Pryce; 6 Sean Rudder; 7 Ryan Sheridan; 8 Craig Greenhill; 9 Wayne Godwin; 15 Nathan Sykes; 23 Michael Smith; 12 Sean Ryan; 13 Ryan Hudson (C). Subs (all used): 16 Jon Hepworth; 17 Paul Jackson; 11 Lee Harland; 18 Jamie Thackray.
Try: Clayton (17); **Goals:** Godwin 2/3.
Sin bin: Godwin (35) - striking.
RHINOS: 1 Gary Connolly; 22 Marcus Bai; 5 Chev Walker; 4 Keith Senior; 18 Mark Calderwood; 6 Danny McGuire; 7 Rob Burrow; 8 Ryan Bailey; 9 Matt Diskin; 10 Barrie McDermott; 11 David Furner; 16 Willie Poching; 13 Kevin Sinfield (C). Subs (all used): 19 Danny Ward; 20 Jamie Jones-Buchanan; 17 Wayne McDonald; 14 Andrew Dunemann.
Tries: McGuire (4, 23, 68), Bai (61), Connolly (64), Senior (72); **Goals:** Sinfield 5/6.
Rugby Leaguer & League Express Men of the Match: *Tigers:* Ryan Hudson; *Rhinos:* Danny McGuire.
Penalty count: 7-8; **Half-time:** 8-12; **Referee:** Karl Kirkpatrick (Warrington); **Attendance:** 11,731.

**WAKEFIELD TRINITY WILDCATS 6
BRADFORD BULLS 40**

WILDCATS: 14 Colum Halpenny; 2 Justin Ryder; 3 Gareth Ellis (C); 4 Sid Domic; 5 Semi Tadulala; 7 Ben Jeffries; 6 Jamie Rooney; 10 Michael Korkidas; 9 David March; 18 Olivier Elima; 11 David Solomona; 13 Jamie Field; 25 Albert Talipeau. Subs (all used): 15 David Wrench; 12 Dallas Hood; 8 Darrell Griffin; 1 Jason Demetriou.
Try: Tadulala (23); **Goals:** Rooney 1/3.
BULLS: 6 Michael Withers; 2 Tevita Vaikona; 14 Toa Kohe-Love; 16 Paul Johnson; 5 Lesley Vainikolo; 3 Leon Pryce; 7 Paul Deacon; 8 Joe Vagana; 31 Richard Colley (D); 29 Stuart Fielden; 27 Rob Parker; 12 Jamie Peacock (C); 11 Lee Radford. Subs (all used): 26 Chris Bridge; 17 Stuart Reardon; 19 Jamie Langley; 10 Paul Anderson.
Tries: Vaikona (6, 63), Vainikolo (27, 49), Bridge (52, 72), Johnson (60), Reardon (77);
Goals: Deacon 4/7, Withers 0/1.
Rugby Leaguer & League Express Men of the Match: *Wildcats:* Michael Korkidas; *Bulls:* Leon Pryce.
Penalty count: 10-4; **Half-time:** 6-10; **Referee:** Ronnie Laughton (Barnsley); **Attendance:** 6,472.

ROUND 3

Friday 19th March 2004

LEEDS RHINOS 36 WIGAN WARRIORS 24

RHINOS: 21 Richard Mathers; 22 Marcus Bai; 5 Chev Walker; 4 Keith Senior; 2 Francis Cummins; 6 Danny McGuire; 14 Andrew Dunemann; 8 Ryan Bailey; 9 Matt Diskin; 19 Danny Ward; 11 David Furner; 20 Jamie Jones-Buchanan; 13 Kevin Sinfield (C). Subs (all used): 17 Wayne McDonald; 15 Chris Feather; 7 Rob Burrow; 16 Willie Poching.
Tries: Jones-Buchanan (7, 29), McGuire (12, 37), Walker (48), Diskin (67); **Goals:** Sinfield 6/8.
WARRIORS: 1 Kris Radlinski (C); 26 Chris Melling; 3 Martin Aspinwall; 21 Kevin Brown; 2 Brett Dallas; 6 Danny Orr; 14 Luke Robinson; 10 Craig Smith; 9 Terry Newton; 18 Quentin Pongia; 20 Gareth Hock; 12 Danny Tickle; 15 Sean O'Loughlin. Subs (all used): 19 Stephen Wild; 8 Terry O'Connor; 16 Danny Sculthorpe; 17 Mark Smith.
Tries: Brown (33), Wild (53, 56), Aspinwall (76);
Goals: Tickle 4/6, Robinson 0/1.
Rugby Leaguer & League Express Men of the Match: *Rhinos:* Matt Diskin; *Warriors:* Sean O'Loughlin.

Penalty count: 9-10; **Half time:** 24-12; **Referee:** Richard Silverwood (Dewsbury); **Attendance:** 18,124.

ST HELENS 38 WIDNES VIKINGS 20

SAINTS: 1 Paul Wellens; 2 Ade Gardner; 5 Darren Albert; 25 Ian Hardman; 22 Dom Feaunati; 6 Jason Hooper; 7 Sean Long (C); 8 Nick Fozzard; 9 Keiron Cunningham; 16 Keith Mason; 11 Chris Joynt; 12 Lee Gilmour; 21 Jon Wilkin. Subs (all used): 14 Mick Higham; 18 Mark Edmondson; 20 Ricky Bibey (D); 26 James Roby (D).
Tries: Gardner (21), Long (39, 63), Albert (40), Hooper (57), Gilmour (74); **Goals:** Long 6/6, Hooper 1/1.
VIKINGS: 23 Steve Rowlands; 22 John Robinson; 4 Adam Hughes; 3 Aaron Moule; 5 Chris Giles; 6 Jules O'Neill; 20 Stephen Myler; 8 Robert Relf (C); 9 Shane Millard; 17 David Mills; 18 Simon Finnigan; 13 Daniel Frame; 14 Deon Bird. Subs: 1 Paul Atcheson (not used); 10 Julian O'Neill; 11 Steve McCurrie; 16 Andy Hobson.
Tries: Hughes (8), Mills (12), Frame (50);
Goals: Jules O'Neill 4/4.
Sin bin: Relf (47) - obstruction.
Rugby Leaguer & League Express Men of the Match:
Saints: Sean Long; *Vikings:* Robert Relf.
Penalty count: 14-7; **Half-time:** 18-14;
Referee: Ashley Klein (London); **Attendance:** 10,549.

Saturday 20th March 2004

SALFORD CITY REDS 20
WAKEFIELD TRINITY WILDCATS 27

CITY REDS: 6 Cliff Beverley; 4 Andy Kirk; 20 Scott Naylor; 3 Stuart Littler; 5 Anthony Stewart; 7 Gavin Clinch; 15 Karl Fitzpatrick; 8 Andy Coley; 9 Malcolm Alker (C); 14 Paul Highton; 18 Mark Shipway; 10 Sean Rutgerson; 16 Martin Moana. Subs (all used): 13 Chris Charles; 17 Gareth Haggerty; 12 Andy Johnson; 11 Simon Baldwin.
Tries: Kirk (32, 44), Fitzpatrick (53), Johnson (73);
Goals: Fitzpatrick 0/1, Charles 2/3.
WILDCATS: 14 Colum Halpenny; 2 Justin Ryder; 1 Jason Demetriou; 4 Sid Domic; 5 Semi Tadulala; 6 Jamie Rooney; 7 Ben Jeffries; 8 Darrell Griffin; 9 David March; 18 Olivier Elima; 11 David Solomona; 15 David Wrench; 3 Gareth Ellis (C). Subs (all used): 12 Dallas Hood; 13 Jamie Field; 16 Steve Snitch; 25 Albert Talipeau.
Tries: Domic (4, 50), Griffin (21), Jeffries (26), Halpenny (40); **Goals:** Rooney 3/5; **Field goal:** Rooney.
Rugby Leaguer & League Express Men of the Match:
City Reds: Karl Fitzpatrick; *Wildcats:* Colum Halpenny.
Penalty count: 9-4; **Half-time:** 4-22;
Referee: Robert Connolly (Wigan); **Attendance:** 2,825.

Sunday 21st March 2004

HUDDERSFIELD GIANTS 6 BRADFORD BULLS 20

GIANTS: 1 Paul Reilly; 2 Hefin O'Hare; 11 Chris Nero; 4 Julian Bailey; 34 Marcus St Hilaire; 6 Stanley Gene; 9 Paul March; 8 Mick Slicker; 15 Darren Turner; 25 Darren Fleary (C); 14 Stuart Jones; 12 Ben Roarty; 13 Brandon Costin. Subs (all used): 3 Stuart Donlan; 7 Sean Penkywicz; 17 Paul Smith; 18 Eorl Crabtree.
Try: Turner (62); **Goals:** March 1/3.
Sin bin: Penkywicz (43) - interference;
O'Hare (67) - not standing square at play-the-ball.
BULLS: 17 Stuart Reardon; 2 Tevita Vaikona; 26 Chris Bridge; 16 Paul Johnson; 5 Lesley Vainikolo; 3 Leon Pryce; 7 Paul Deacon; 8 Joe Vagana; 24 Aaron Smith; 29 Stuart Fielden; 12 Jamie Peacock; 27 Rob Parker; 11 Lee Radford. Subs (all used): 1 Robbie Paul (C); 22 Karl Pryce; 19 Jamie Langley; 10 Paul Anderson.
Tries: Johnson (45, 74), Deacon (71); **Goals:** Deacon 4/5.
Sin bin: Vaikona (34) - obstruction;
Fielden (35) - not standing square at play-the-ball.
Rugby Leaguer & League Express Men of the Match:
Giants: Ben Roarty; *Bulls:* Leon Pryce.
Penalty count: 11-13; **Half-time:** 2-4;
Referee: Russell Smith (Castleford); **Attendance:** 8,039.

WARRINGTON WOLVES 32 CASTLEFORD TIGERS 18

WOLVES: 1 Daryl Cardiss; 2 John Wilshere; 3 Brent Grose; 18 Paul Noone; 12 Ian Sibbit; 6 Lee Briers (C); 7 Nathan Wood; 10 Mark Hilton; 9 Jon Clarke; 16 Paul Wood; 13 Mike Forshaw; 23 Mike Wainwright; 11 Darren Burns. Subs (all used): 14 Mark Gleeson; 17 Warren Stevens; 15 Jerome Guisset; 22 Danny Lima.
Tries: Wilshere (18, 22), Noone (50), Grose (60), P Wood (72), Hilton (77); **Goals:** Briers 4/6.
TIGERS: 20 Tom Saxton; 5 Darren Rogers; 19 Francis Maloney; 14 Ryan Clayton; 1 Damian Gibson; 6 Sean Rudder; 16 Jon Hepworth; 8 Craig Greenhill; 9 Wayne Godwin; 17 Paul Jackson; 23 Michael Smith; 18 Jamie Thackray; 13 Ryan Hudson (C). Subs (all used): 28 Dean Ripley (D); 10 Andy Lynch; 12 Sean Ryan; 25 Craig Huby.
Tries: Hepworth (3, 54), Hudson (8); **Goals:** Godwin 3/3.
Rugby Leaguer & League Express Men of the Match:
Wolves: Lee Briers; *Tigers:* Michael Smith.
Penalty count: 7-9; **Half-time:** 10-12;
Referee: Ian Smith (Oldham); **Attendance:** 8,902.

HULL FC 46 LONDON BRONCOS 4

HULL: 32 Shaun Briscoe; 2 Colin Best; 3 Richie Barnett (C); 14 Kirk Yeaman; 26 Richie Barnett Jnr; 16 Paul Cooke; 6 Richard Horne; 10 Paul King; 9 Richard Swain; 18 Ewan Dowes; 15 Shayne McMenemy; 23 Paul McNicholas; 25 Peter Lupton. Subs (all used): 17 Chris Chester; 20 Garreth Carvell; 30 Richard Whiting; 27 Liam Higgins.
Tries: Barnett (4), Best (20, 45), Lupton (51), Cooke (57), Barnett Jnr (65, 67), Carvell (78), Whiting (80);
Goals: Cooke 5/10.
BRONCOS: 1 Paul Sykes; 23 Lee Greenwood (D); 4 Mark O'Halloran; 3 Nigel Roy; 24 Andy McNally; 20 Radney Bowker; 7 Dennis Moran; 10 Steve Trindall; 9 Neil Budworth; 12 Steele Retchless; 18 Andrew Hart; 16 Joe Mbu; 13 Jim Dymock (C). Subs (all used): 14 Andrew Brocklehurst; 15 Mitchell Stringer; 8 Francis Stephenson; 17 Tom Haughey.
Try: Greenwood (10); **Goals:** Sykes 0/1.
Rugby Leaguer & League Express Men of the Match:
Hull: Peter Lupton; *Broncos:* Paul Sykes.
Penalty count: 10-9; **Half-time:** 12-4; **Referee:** Ronnie Laughton (Barnsley); **Attendance:** 9,040.

ROUND 4

Friday 2nd April 2004

BRADFORD BULLS 25 SALFORD CITY REDS 18

BULLS: 6 Michael Withers; 2 Tevita Vaikona; 26 Chris Bridge; 16 Paul Johnson; 5 Lesley Vainikolo; 3 Leon Pryce; 7 Paul Deacon; 8 Joe Vagana; 24 Aaron Smith; 29 Stuart Fielden; 27 Rob Parker; 12 Jamie Peacock; 11 Lee Radford. Subs (all used): 17 Stuart Reardon; 1 Robbie Paul (C); 19 Jamie Langley; 10 Paul Anderson.
Tries: Deacon (21), L Pryce (36), Johnson (49), Vainikolo (73); **Goals:** Deacon 4/5; **Field goal:** Withers.
CITY REDS: 15 Karl Fitzpatrick; 4 Andy Kirk; 20 Scott Naylor; 3 Stuart Littler; 5 Anthony Stewart; 6 Cliff Beverley; 7 Gavin Clinch; 19 Neil Baynes; 9 Malcolm Alker (C); 10 Sean Rutgerson; 11 Simon Baldwin; 18 Mark Shipway; 13 Chris Charles. Subs (all used): 16 Martin Moana; 12 Andy Johnson; 14 Paul Highton; 17 Gareth Haggerty.
Tries: Beverley (1, 33, 43); **Goals:** Charles 3/3.
Rugby Leaguer & League Express Men of the Match:
Bulls: Robbie Paul; *City Reds:* Cliff Beverley.
Penalty count: 9-7; **Half-time:** 10-12; **Referee:** Russell Smith (Castleford); **Attendance:** 11,976.

CASTLEFORD TIGERS 14 ST HELENS 22

TIGERS: 1 Damian Gibson; 20 Tom Saxton; 19 Francis Maloney; 14 Ryan Clayton; 5 Darren Rogers; 6 Sean Rudder; 16 Jon Hepworth; 8 Craig Greenhill; 9 Wayne Godwin; 17 Paul Jackson; 23 Michael Smith; 18 Jamie Thackray; 13 Ryan Hudson (C). Subs (all used): 28 Dean Ripley; 10 Andy Lynch; 12 Sean Ryan; 25 Craig Huby.
Tries: Hudson (44), Godwin (72); **Goals:** Godwin 3/3.
SAINTS: 1 Paul Wellens; 2 Ade Gardner; 5 Darren Albert; 4 Willie Talau; 22 Dom Feaunati; 6 Jason Hooper; 7 Sean Long; 8 Nick Fozzard; 9 Keiron Cunningham; 20 Ricky Bibey; 12 Lee Gilmour; 11 Chris Joynt; 13 Paul Sculthorpe (C). Subs (all used): 18 Mark Edmondson; 14 Mick Higham; 23 Maurie Fa'asavalu (D); 21 Jon Wilkin.
Tries: Cunningham (24), Wellens (32, 65), Hooper (60);
Goals: Long 3/4.
Rugby Leaguer & League Express Men of the Match:
Tigers: Wayne Godwin; *Saints:* Jason Hooper.
Penalty count: 12-15; **Half-time:** 0-12;
Referee: Ian Smith (Oldham); **Attendance:** 6,876.

Saturday 3rd April 2004

WAKEFIELD TRINITY WILDCATS 21 HULL FC 27

WILDCATS: 14 Colum Halpenny; 2 Justin Ryder; 1 Jason Demetriou; 4 Sid Domic; 5 Semi Tadulala; 7 Ben Jeffries; 6 Jamie Rooney; 8 Darrell Griffin; 9 David March; 10 Michael Korkidas; 11 David Solomona; 15 David Wrench; 3 Gareth Ellis (C). Subs (all used): 12 Dallas Hood; 13 Jamie Field; 17 Paul Handforth; 18 Olivier Elima.
Tries: Ryder (6, 13), Griffin (42); **Goals:** Rooney 4/5;
Field goal: Rooney.
HULL: 32 Shaun Briscoe; 26 Richie Barnett Jnr; 14 Kirk Yeaman; 3 Richie Barnett (C); 2 Colin Best; 16 Paul Cooke; 6 Richard Horne; 20 Garreth Carvell; 9 Richard Swain; 10 Paul King; 15 Shayne McMenemy; 23 Paul McNicholas; 25 Peter Lupton. Subs (all used): 17 Chris Chester; 27 Liam Higgins; 30 Richard Whiting; 31 Danny Hill (D).
Tries: Barnett (10, 22), Barnett Jnr (25), Carvell (72);
Goals: Cooke 5/6; **Field goal:** R Horne.
Rugby Leaguer & League Express Men of the Match:
Wildcats: Gareth Ellis; *Hull:* Paul King.
Penalty count: 10-10; **Half-time:** 10-16; **Referee:** Ronnie Laughton (Barnsley); **Attendance:** 4,337.

Sunday 4th April 2004

HUDDERSFIELD GIANTS 26 WIGAN WARRIORS 10

GIANTS: 1 Paul Reilly; 2 Hefin O'Hare; 11 Chris Nero; 4 Julian Bailey; 34 Marcus St Hilaire; 13 Brandon Costin; 9 Paul March; 25 Darren Fleary (C); 15 Darren Turner; 8 Mick Slicker; 14 Stuart Jones; 12 Ben Roarty; 6 Stanley Gene. Subs (all used): 3 Stuart Donlan; 7 Sean Penkywicz; 10 Jim Gannon; 18 Eorl Crabtree.
Tries: Costin (24), Jones (32), Turner (55), Reilly (79);
Goals: March 5/5.
WARRIORS: 1 Kris Radlinski; 3 Martin Aspinwall; 19 Stephen Wild; 21 Kevin Brown; 2 Brett Dallas; 6 Danny Orr; 14 Luke Robinson; 8 Terry O'Connor; 9 Terry Newton; 10 Craig Smith; 12 Danny Tickle; 13 Andy Farrell (C); 15 Sean O'Loughlin. Subs (all used): 17 Mark Smith; 18 Quentin Pongia; 20 Gareth Hock; 24 Bob Beswick (D).
Tries: Tickle (19), Dallas (67); **Goals:** Orr 1/1, Farrell 0/1.
Rugby Leaguer & League Express Men of the Match:
Giants: Paul Reilly; *Warriors:* Andy Farrell.
Penalty count: 5-6; **Half-time:** 14-4;
Referee: Steve Ganson (St Helens); **Attendance:** 5,175.

LONDON BRONCOS 24 WARRINGTON WOLVES 36

BRONCOS: 1 Paul Sykes; 3 Nigel Roy; 4 Mark O'Halloran; 24 Andy McNally; 23 Lee Greenwood; 13 Jim Dymock (C); 7 Dennis Moran; 12 Steele Retchless; 9 Neil Budworth; 15 Mitchell Stringer; 14 Andrew Brocklehurst; 10 Steve Trindall; 18 Andrew Hart. Subs (all used): 16 Joe Mbu; 17 Tom Haughey; 19 David Highton; 25 Scott Murrell.
Tries: Moran (8, 59), Hart (24), Sykes (53).
Goals: Sykes 4/4.
WOLVES: 1 Daryl Cardiss; 2 John Wilshere; 3 Brent Grose; 12 Ian Sibbit; 4 Ben Westwood; 14 Mark Gleeson; 7 Nathan Wood (C); 10 Mark Hilton; 9 Jon Clarke; 16 Paul Wood; 13 Mike Forshaw; 23 Mike Wainwright; 19 Paul Noone. Subs (all used): 5 Graham Appo; 15 Jerome Guisset; 19 Gary Hulse; 22 Danny Lima.
Tries: Wainwright (4), Clarke (26), Forshaw (29), Guisset (45, 55), Noone (77);
Goals: Noone 5/6; **Field goals:** N Wood, Hulse.
Rugby Leaguer & League Express Men of the Match:
Broncos: Andrew Brocklehurst; *Wolves:* Mark Hilton.
Penalty count: 11-13; **Half-time:** 12-18; **Referee:** Richard Silverwood (Dewsbury); **Attendance:** 3,162.

WIDNES VIKINGS 0 LEEDS RHINOS 46

VIKINGS: 23 Steve Rowlands; 22 John Robinson; 4 Adam Hughes; 3 Aaron Moule; 5 Chris Giles; 6 Jules O'Neill; 20 Stephen Myler; 8 Robert Relf (C); 9 Shane Millard; 17 David Mills; 18 Simon Finnigan; 13 Daniel Frame; 14 Deon Bird. Subs (all used): 12 Andy Hay; 16 Andy Hobson; 11 Steve McCurrie; 15 Troy Wozniak.
Sin bin: Moule (25) - holding down.
RHINOS: 21 Richard Mathers; 2 Francis Cummins; 5 Chev Walker; 4 Keith Senior; 22 Marcus Bai; 6 Danny McGuire; 14 Andrew Dunemann; 8 Ryan Bailey; 9 Matt Diskin; 15 Chris Feather; 11 David Furner; 20 Jamie Jones-Buchanan; 13 Kevin Sinfield (C). Subs (all used): 7 Rob Burrow; 10 Barrie McDermott; 19 Danny Ward; 16 Willie Poching.
Tries: Diskin (4), Bai (17, 79), McGuire (25), Cummins (38), Sinfield (42), Feather (50), Burrow (52), McDermott (75); **Goals:** Sinfield 3/6, Burrow 2/3.
Rugby Leaguer & League Express Men of the Match:
Vikings: Daniel Frame; *Rhinos:* Matt Diskin.
Penalty count: 5-4; **Half-time:** 0-18; **Referee:** Karl Kirkpatrick (Warrington); **Attendance:** 7,325.

ROUND 5

Thursday 8th April 2004

HULL FC 26 CASTLEFORD TIGERS 4

HULL: 32 Shaun Briscoe; 2 Colin Best; 3 Richie Barnett (C); 14 Kirk Yeaman; 26 Richie Barnett Jnr; 16 Paul Cooke; 6 Richard Horne; 10 Paul King; 9 Richard Swain; 20 Garreth Carvell; 15 Shayne McMenemy; 23 Paul McNicholas; 25 Peter Lupton. Subs (all used): 17 Chris Chester; 18 Ewan Dowes; 30 Richard Whiting; 27 Liam Higgins.
Tries: Yeaman (6), Lupton (8), Best (31), Barnett (36);
Goals: Cooke 5/6.
TIGERS: 1 Damian Gibson; 20 Tom Saxton; 19 Francis Maloney; 4 Paul Newlove; 5 Darren Rogers; 6 Sean Rudder; 16 Jon Hepworth; 8 Craig Greenhill; 9 Wayne Godwin; 10 Andy Lynch; 12 Sean Ryan; 23 Michael Smith; 13 Ryan Hudson (C). Subs (all used): 18 Jamie Thackray; 17 Paul Jackson; 14 Ryan Clayton; 11 Lee Harland.
Try: M Smith (60); **Goals:** Maloney 0/1.
Rugby Leaguer & League Express Men of the Match:
Hull: Paul Cooke; *Tigers:* Michael Smith.
Penalty count: 14-5; **Half-time:** 22-0;
Referee: Ashley Klein (London); **Attendance:** 10,971.

LEEDS RHINOS 26 BRADFORD BULLS 18

RHINOS: 21 Richard Mathers; 22 Marcus Bai; 5 Chev Walker; 4 Keith Senior; 2 Francis Cummins; 6 Danny McGuire; 14 Andrew Dunemann; 8 Ryan Bailey; 9 Matt Diskin; 15 Chris Feather; 11 David Furner; 3 Chris McKenna; 13 Kevin Sinfield (C). Subs (all used): 19 Danny Ward; 16 Willie Poching; 10 Barrie McDermott; 7 Rob Burrow.
Tries: Dunemann (11), McGuire (35, 64), Bai (42), Feather (66); **Goals:** Sinfield 3/5.
BULLS: 6 Michael Withers; 2 Tevita Vaikona; 16 Paul Johnson; 4 Shontayne Hape; 5 Lesley Vainikolo; 1 Robbie Paul (C); 7 Paul Deacon; 8 Joe Vagana; 24 Aaron Smith; 29 Stuart Fielden; 12 Jamie Peacock; 27 Rob Parker; 19 Jamie Langley. Subs (all used): 10 Paul Anderson; 3 Leon Pryce; 30 Richard Moore; 17 Stuart Reardon.
Tries: Vainikolo (15), Hape (54), Vaikona (71);
Goals: Deacon 3/3.
Rugby Leaguer & League Express Men of the Match:
Rhinos: Chris Feather; *Bulls:* Robbie Paul.
Penalty count: 5-2; **Half-time:** 10-6;
Referee: Steve Ganson (St Helens); **Attendance:** 21,225.

LONDON BRONCOS 16
WAKEFIELD TRINITY WILDCATS 39

BRONCOS: 1 Paul Sykes; 23 Lee Greenwood; 24 Andy McNally; 3 Nigel Roy; 2 Jon Wells; 13 Jim Dymock (C); 7 Dennis Moran; 15 Mitchell Stringer; 9 Neil Budworth; 10 Steve Trindall; 14 Andrew Brocklehurst; 16 Joe Mbu; 12 Steele Retchless. Subs (all used): 18 Andrew Hart; 19 David Highton; 25 Scott Murrell; 17 Tom Haughey.
Tries: Wells (35), Greenwood (42), Highton (52);
Goals: Sykes 2/3.
WILDCATS: 14 Colum Halpenny; 24 Michael Wainwright (D); 1 Jason Demetriou; 4 Sid Domic; 5 Semi Tadulala; 6

Jamie Rooney; 7 Ben Jeffries; 8 Darrell Griffin; 9 David March; 10 Michael Korkidas; 11 David Solomona; 15 David Wrench; 3 Gareth Ellis (C). Subs (all used): 12 Dallas Hood; 16 Steve Snitch; 18 Olivier Elima; 25 Albert Talipeau.
Tries: Wrench (23, 64), Jeffries (28), Domic (47), Wainwright (72, 79);
Goals: Rooney 7/9; **Field goal:** Jeffries.
Rugby Leaguer & League Express Men of the Match: *Broncos:* Steve Trindall; *Wildcats:* David Wrench.
Penalty count: 12-10; **Half-time:** 6-14;
Referee: Ian Smith (Oldham); **Attendance:** 2,486.

Friday 9th April 2004

ST HELENS 21 WIGAN WARRIORS 21

SAINTS: 1 Paul Wellens; 5 Darren Albert; 6 Jason Hooper; 4 Willie Talau; 22 Dom Feaunati; 13 Paul Sculthorpe (C); 7 Sean Long; 8 Nick Fozzard; 9 Keiron Cunningham; 18 Mark Edmondson; 12 Lee Gilmour; 11 Chris Joynt; 21 Jon Wilkin. Subs: 2 Ade Gardner (not used); 14 Mick Higham; 20 Ricky Bibey; 16 Keith Mason.
Tries: Gilmour (12, 21), Wilkin (24), Talau (46);
Goals: Long 2/4; **Field goal:** Long.
Sin bin: Wilkin (59) - fighting.
On report: Brawl (59).
WARRIORS: 1 Kris Radlinski; 3 Martin Aspinwall; 19 Stephen Wild; 21 Kevin Brown; 2 Brett Dallas; 15 Sean O'Loughlin; 6 Danny Orr; 8 Terry O'Connor; 9 Terry Newton; 18 Quentin Pongia; 12 Danny Tickle; 11 Mick Cassidy; 13 Andy Farrell (C). Subs (all used): 17 Mark Smith; 10 Craig Smith; 20 Gareth Hock; 16 Danny Sculthorpe.
Tries: Brown (30), Orr (42), Newton (49);
Goals: Farrell 4/4; **Field goal:** Farrell.
Sin bin: Newton (59) - fighting.
On report: Brawl (59).
Rugby Leaguer & League Express Men of the Match: *Saints:* Sean Long; *Warriors:* Andy Farrell.
Penalty count: 7-6; **Half-time:** 14-8; **Referee:** Karl Kirkpatrick (Warrington); **Attendance:** 15,964.

WARRINGTON WOLVES 16 WIDNES VIKINGS 24

WOLVES: 1 Daryl Cardiss; 18 Paul Noone; 3 Brent Grose; 4 Ben Westwood; 12 Ian Sibbit; 19 Gary Hulse; 7 Nathan Wood (C); 16 Paul Wood; 9 Jon Clarke; 10 Mark Hilton; 15 Jerome Guisset; 23 Mike Wainwright; 13 Mike Forshaw. Subs (all used): 14 Mark Gleeson; 25 Richard Varkulis; 17 Warren Stevens; 22 Danny Lima.
Tries: Guisset (6, 38), Lima (48); **Goals:** Noone 2/3.
VIKINGS: 23 Steve Rowlands; 21 Nicky Royle (D); 4 Adam Hughes; 3 Aaron Moule; 5 Chris Giles; 6 Jules O'Neill; 20 Stephen Myler; 8 Robert Relf; 9 Shane Millard; 17 David Mills; 12 Andy Hay (C); 15 Troy Wozniak; 18 Simon Finnigan. Subs (all used): 1 Paul Atcheson; 11 Steve McCurrie; 14 Deon Bird; 10 Julian O'Neill.
Tries: Giles (15), Finnigan (22), Royle (43), Millard (56);
Goals: Jules O'Neill 4/4.
Rugby Leaguer & League Express Men of the Match: *Wolves:* Jerome Guisset; *Vikings:* Jules O'Neill.
Penalty count: 7-3; **Half-time:** 12-12; **Referee:** Ronnie Laughton (Barnsley); **Attendance:** 11,413.

HUDDERSFIELD GIANTS 24 SALFORD CITY REDS 16

GIANTS: 1 Paul Reilly; 2 Hefin O'Hare; 11 Chris Nero; 4 Julian Bailey; 34 Marcus St Hilaire; 13 Brandon Costin; 9 Paul March; 8 Mick Slicker; 15 Darren Turner; 25 Darren Fleary (C); 14 Stuart Jones; 17 Paul Smith; 6 Stanley Gene. Subs (all used): 3 Stuart Donlan; 7 Sean Penkywicz; 10 Jim Gannon; 18 Eorl Crabtree.
Tries: O'Hare (19), St Hilaire (25), Bailey (55), Nero (65); **Goals:** March 4/7.
Sin bin: Fleary (58) - late challenge on Clinch.
On report: Fleary (58) - late challenge on Clinch.
CITY REDS: 15 Karl Fitzpatrick; 4 Andy Kirk; 20 Scott Naylor; 3 Stuart Littler; 5 Anthony Stewart; 6 Cliff Beverley; 7 Gavin Clinch; 8 Andy Coley; 9 Malcolm Alker (C); 10 Sean Rutgerson; 11 Simon Baldwin; 18 Mark Shipway; 13 Chris Charles. Subs (all used): 19 Neil Baynes; 12 Andy Johnson; 14 Paul Highton; 17 Gareth Haggerty.
Tries: Stewart (39), Beverley (76); **Goals:** Charles 4/5.
Rugby Leaguer & League Express Men of the Match: *Giants:* Brandon Costin; *City Reds:* Gavin Clinch.
Penalty count: 10-9; **Half-time:** 12-8; **Referee:** Richard Silverwood (Dewsbury); **Attendance:** 4,062.

ROUND 6

Monday 12th April 2004

BRADFORD BULLS 54 ST HELENS 8

BULLS: 6 Michael Withers; 2 Tevita Vaikona; 16 Paul Johnson; 4 Shontayne Hape; 5 Lesley Vainikolo; 3 Leon Pryce; 7 Paul Deacon; 8 Joe Vagana; 1 Robbie Paul (C); 29 Stuart Fielden; 12 Jamie Peacock; 11 Lee Radford; 13 Logan Swann. Subs (all used): 17 Stuart Reardon; 27 Rob Parker; 19 Jamie Langley; 10 Paul Anderson.
Tries: Radford (6), Vaikona (17, 32), Vainikolo (25, 50), Langley (36), Hape (39, 61, 67), Withers (64, 72);
Goals: Withers 3/10, Deacon 1/1, Paul 1/1.
SAINTS: 25 Ian Hardman; 2 Ade Gardner; 3 Martin Gleeson; 21 Jon Wilkin; 22 Dom Feaunati; 26 James Roby; 28 Phil Anderton (D); 20 Ricky Bibey; 31 Liam Bostock (D); 16 Keith Mason; 11 Chris Joynt (C); 17 Tim Jonkers; 23 Maurie Fa'asavalu. Subs (all used): 32 Ian Kenny (D); 24 James Graham; 29 Mike Roby (D); 30 Peter Cook (D).
Tries: Gleeson (2), Feaunati (78); **Goals:** Hardman 0/2.
Dismissal: Wilkin (11) - high tackle on Deacon.
Rugby Leaguer & League Express Men of the Match: *Bulls:* Shontayne Hape; *Saints:* Ian Hardman.
Penalty count: 9-8; **Half-time:** 30-4; **Referee:** Richard Silverwood (Dewsbury); **Attendance:** 15,623.

WIDNES VIKINGS 32 HULL FC 18

VIKINGS: 23 Steve Rowlands; 21 Nicky Royle; 3 Aaron Moule; 4 Adam Hughes; 5 Chris Giles; 6 Jules O'Neill; 20 Stephen Myler; 8 Robert Relf; 9 Shane Millard; 17 David Mills; 12 Andy Hay (C); 15 Troy Wozniak; 18 Simon Finnigan. Subs (all used): 10 Julian O'Neill; 14 Deon Bird; 11 Steve McCurrie; 1 Paul Atcheson.
Tries: Hughes (23), Giles (37), Royle (60), McCurrie (66), Jules O'Neill (73); **Goals:** Jules O'Neill 5/8;
Field goals: Jules O'Neill 2.
HULL: 32 Shaun Briscoe; 5 Gareth Raynor; 14 Kirk Yeaman; 3 Richie Barnett (C); 2 Colin Best; 16 Paul Cooke; 6 Richard Horne; 18 Ewan Dowes; 9 Richard Swain; 10 Paul King; 15 Shayne McMenemy; 23 Paul McNicholas; 25 Peter Lupton. Subs (all used): 17 Chris Chester; 27 Liam Higgins; 30 Richard Whiting; 20 Garreth Carvell.
Tries: Briscoe (3), McMenemy (15), Cooke (41);
Goals: Cooke 3/4.
Rugby Leaguer & League Express Men of the Match: *Vikings:* Jules O'Neill; *Hull:* Richard Swain.
Penalty count: 5-3; **Half-time:** 14-12;
Referee: Steve Ganson (St Helens); **Attendance:** 6,059.

WIGAN WARRIORS 26 WARRINGTON WOLVES 24

WARRIORS: 1 Kris Radlinski; 3 Martin Aspinwall; 19 Stephen Wild; 21 Kevin Brown; 2 Brett Dallas; 15 Sean O'Loughlin; 6 Danny Orr; 8 Terry O'Connor; 17 Mark Smith; 10 Craig Smith; 11 Mick Cassidy; 20 Gareth Hock; 13 Andy Farrell (C). Subs (all used): 18 Quentin Pongia; 12 Danny Tickle; 16 Danny Sculthorpe; 7 Adrian Lam.
Tries: Aspinwall (14), Dallas (42, 61), Tickle (76);
Goals: Farrell 5/7.
WOLVES: 1 Daryl Cardiss; 20 Dean Gaskell; 18 Paul Noone; 4 Ben Westwood; 25 Richard Varkulis; 7 Nathan Wood (C); 9 Jon Clarke; 22 Danny Lima; 19 Gary Hulse; 10 Mark Hilton; 15 Jerome Guisset; 11 Darren Burns; 23 Mike Wainwright. Subs (all used): 21 Matt Sturm; 17 Warren Stevens; 13 Mike Forshaw; 14 Mark Gleeson.
Tries: Hulse (29), Gaskell (33), Varkulis (68), Clarke (71); **Goals:** Noone 4/4.
Rugby Leaguer & League Express Men of the Match: *Warriors:* Quentin Pongia; *Wolves:* Daryl Cardiss.
Penalty count: 9-6; **Half-time:** 4-12;
Referee: Ian Smith (Oldham); **Attendance:** 13,822.

WAKEFIELD TRINITY WILDCATS 17 HUDDERSFIELD GIANTS 24

WILDCATS: 14 Colum Halpenny; 24 Michael Wainwright; 1 Jason Demetriou; 4 Sid Domic; 5 Semi Tadulala; 6 Jamie Rooney; 7 Ben Jeffries; 8 Darrell Griffin; 9 David March; 10 Michael Korkidas; 11 David Solomona; 13 Jamie Field (C); 25 Albert Talipeau. Subs (all used): 12 Dallas Hood; 16 Steve Snitch; 18 Olivier Elima; 21 Mark Field.
Tries: Rooney (10), Halpenny (45); **Goals:** Rooney 4/5;
Field goal: Rooney.
GIANTS: 1 Paul Reilly; 2 Hefin O'Hare; 3 Stuart Donlan; 11 Chris Nero; 34 Marcus St Hilaire; 13 Brandon Costin; 9 Paul March; 10 Jim Gannon; 15 Darren Turner; 18 Eorl Crabtree; 12 Ben Roarty; 16 Iain Morrison; 17 Paul Smith. Subs (all used): 6 Stanley Gene; 7 Sean Penkywicz; 25 Darren Fleary (C); 14 Stuart Jones.
Tries: Roarty (6), O'Hare (37), Penkywicz (63), Turner (77); **Goals:** March 4/5.
On report: Roarty (2) - late tackle on Jeffries.
Rugby Leaguer & League Express Men of the Match: *Wildcats:* Ben Jeffries; *Giants:* Chris Nero.
Penalty count: 12-10; **Half-time:** 10-12;
Referee: Ashley Klein (London); **Attendance:** 4,702.

SALFORD CITY REDS 0 LEEDS RHINOS 44

CITY REDS: 2 Joel Caine; 4 Andy Kirk; 3 Stuart Littler; 12 Andy Johnson; 5 Anthony Stewart; 6 Cliff Beverley; 15 Karl Fitzpatrick; 10 Sean Rutgerson; 9 Malcolm Alker (C); 14 Paul Highton; 11 Simon Baldwin; 8 Andy Coley; 13 Chris Charles. Subs (all used): 24 Bryn Powell (D); 17 Gareth Haggerty; 18 Mark Shipway; 23 Vinny Myler (D).
RHINOS: 21 Richard Mathers; 18 Mark Calderwood; 5 Chev Walker; 2 Francis Cummins; 22 Marcus Bai; 6 Danny McGuire; 14 Andrew Dunemann; 8 Ryan Bailey; 9 Matt Diskin; 10 Barrie McDermott; 15 Chris Feather; 3 Chris McKenna; 13 Kevin Sinfield (C). Subs (all used): 7 Rob Burrow; 17 Wayne McDonald; 16 Willie Poching; 28 Liam Botham.
Tries: Walker (18, 73), McKenna (26), Bai (33, 44), Poching (46), Dunemann (65), Calderwood (66), McGuire (70); **Goals:** Sinfield 4/6, Burrow 0/1, Botham 0/2.
Rugby Leaguer & League Express Men of the Match: *City Reds:* Andy Kirk; *Rhinos:* Willie Poching.
Penalty count: 3-7; **Half-time:** 0-14; **Referee:** Karl Kirkpatrick (Warrington); **Attendance:** 5,462.

Tuesday 13th April 2004

CASTLEFORD TIGERS 34 LONDON BRONCOS 42

TIGERS: 1 Damian Gibson; 20 Tom Saxton; 19 Francis Maloney; 4 Paul Newlove; 5 Darren Rogers; 6 Sean Rudder; 16 Jon Hepworth; 8 Craig Greenhill; 13 Ryan Hudson (C); 10 Andy Lynch; 23 Michael Smith; 12 Sean Ryan; 11 Lee Harland. Subs (all used): 28 Dean Ripley; 9 Wayne Godwin; 17 Paul Jackson; 18 Jamie Thackray.
Tries: Hudson (4), Rogers (7), Saxton (30), Rudder (35), Ryan (73), Newlove (76), Saxton (78);
Goals: Maloney 3/5, Godwin 0/2.
BRONCOS: 1 Paul Sykes; 2 Jon Wells; 17 Tom Haughey; 3 Nigel Roy; 23 Lee Greenwood; 25 Scott Murrell; 7 Dennis Moran; 12 Steele Retchless; 9 Neil Budworth; 15 Mitchell Stringer; 14 Andrew Brocklehurst; 16 Joe Mbu; 13 Jim Dymock (C). Subs (all used): 10 Steve Trindall; 19 David Highton; 24 Andy McNally; 26 Jonny Williams.
Tries: Greenwood (10, 20), Mbu (15), Wells (38), Moran (41, 68), Murrell (48), Roy (70); **Goals:** Sykes 5/8.
Rugby Leaguer & League Express Men of the Match: *Tigers:* Andy Lynch; *Broncos:* Dennis Moran.
Penalty count: 2-3; **Half-time:** 18-20; **Referee:** Ronnie Laughton (Barnsley); **Attendance:** 4,710.

ROUND 7

Friday 16th April 2004

LEEDS RHINOS 38 HUDDERSFIELD GIANTS 6

RHINOS: 21 Richard Mathers; 2 Francis Cummins; 5 Chev Walker; 4 Keith Senior; 22 Marcus Bai; 6 Danny McGuire; 14 Andrew Dunemann; 10 Barrie McDermott; 9 Matt Diskin; 15 Chris Feather; 11 David Furner; 3 Chris McKenna; 13 Kevin Sinfield (C). Subs (all used): 17 Wayne McDonald; 16 Willie Poching; 7 Rob Burrow; 24 Nick Scruton.
Tries: Mathers (5), Walker (13, 33, 59), Furner (67, 78), McGuire (73); **Goals:** Sinfield 5/6, Burrow 0/1.
GIANTS: 5 Ben Cooper; 2 Hefin O'Hare; 3 Stuart Donlan; 4 Julian Bailey; 34 Marcus St Hilaire; 13 Brandon Costin; 7 Sean Penkywicz; 8 Mick Slicker (C); 22 Phil Joseph; 10 Jim Gannon; 16 Iain Morrison; 19 Matt Whitaker; 17 Paul Smith. Subs (all used): 14 Stuart Jones; 18 Eorl Crabtree; 11 Chris Nero; 20 Jon Grayshon.
Try: St Hilaire (22); **Goals:** Costin 1/2.
Rugby Leaguer & League Express Men of the Match: *Rhinos:* Richard Mathers; *Giants:* Brandon Costin.
Penalty count: 7-5; **Half-time:** 14-6;
Referee: Russell Smith (Castleford); **Attendance:** 11,701.

ST HELENS 40 SALFORD CITY REDS 4

SAINTS: 1 Paul Wellens; 25 Ian Hardman; 5 Darren Albert; 4 Willie Talau; 2 Ade Gardner; 6 Jason Hooper; 27 Carl Forber (D); 8 Nick Fozzard; 9 Keiron Cunningham; 16 Keith Mason; 18 Mark Edmondson; 12 Lee Gilmour; 13 Paul Sculthorpe (C). Subs (all used): 23 Maurie Fa'asavalu; 20 Ricky Bibey; 14 Mick Higham; 24 James Graham.
Tries: Albert (3, 40), Sculthorpe (11, 24, 36), Higham (44), Fa'asavalu (68); **Goals:** Forber 6/7.
CITY REDS: 6 Cliff Beverley; 4 Andy Kirk; 3 Stuart Littler; 5 Anthony Stewart; 2 Joel Caine; 16 Martin Moana; 7 Gavin Clinch; 8 Andy Coley; 9 Malcolm Alker (C); 10 Sean Rutgerson; 11 Simon Baldwin; 18 Mark Shipway; 13 Chris Charles. Subs (all used): 12 Andy Johnson; 17 Gareth Haggerty; 14 Paul Highton; 23 Vinny Myler.
Try: Littler (32); **Goals:** Charles 0/1.
Rugby Leaguer & League Express Men of the Match: *Saints:* Paul Sculthorpe; *City Reds:* Malcolm Alker.
Penalty count: 9-9; **Half-time:** 28-4;
Referee: Ian Smith (Oldham); **Attendance:** 7,649.

Saturday 17th April 2004

CASTLEFORD TIGERS 10
WAKEFIELD TRINITY WILDCATS 42

TIGERS: 20 Tom Saxton; 28 Dean Ripley; 14 Ryan Clayton; 4 Paul Newlove; 5 Darren Rogers; 6 Sean Rudder; 19 Francis Maloney; 17 Paul Jackson; 13 Ryan Hudson (C); 10 Andy Lynch; 23 Michael Smith; 12 Sean Ryan; 18 Jamie Thackray. Subs (all used): 15 Nathan Sykes; 16 Jon Hepworth; 25 Craig Huby; 29 Dominic Brambani (D).
Tries: Ryan (25), Ripley (29); **Goals:** Maloney 1/2.
WILDCATS: 14 Colum Halpenny; 24 Michael Wainwright; 1 Jason Demetriou; 4 Sid Domic; 5 Semi Tadulala; 6 Jamie Rooney; 7 Ben Jeffries; 8 Darrell Griffin; 9 David March; 10 Michael Korkidas; 11 David Solomona; 15 David Wrench; 3 Gareth Ellis (C). Subs (all used): 12 Dallas Hood; 2 Justin Ryder; 18 Olivier Elima; 25 Albert Talipeau.
Tries: Ellis (10, 62), Jeffries (39, 78), Tadulala (53, 66), Demetriou (56), Korkidas (70);
Goals: Rooney 1/2, March 4/7.
Rugby Leaguer & League Express Men of the Match: *Tigers:* Jamie Thackray; *Wildcats:* Gareth Ellis.
Penalty count: 7-10; **Half-time:** 10-10; **Referee:** Richard Silverwood (Dewsbury); **Attendance:** 5,427.

Sunday 18th April 2004

LONDON BRONCOS 34 WIDNES VIKINGS 18

BRONCOS: 1 Paul Sykes; 2 Jon Wells; 3 Nigel Roy; 17 Tom Haughey; 23 Lee Greenwood; 25 Scott Murrell; 7 Dennis Moran; 15 Mitchell Stringer; 9 Neil Budworth; 12 Steele Retchless (C); 16 Joe Mbu; 14 Andrew Brocklehurst; 18 Andrew Hart. Subs (all used): 19 David Highton; 24 Andy McNally; 26 Jonny Williams; 10 Steve Trindall.
Tries: Roy (7), Mbu (10), Haughey (27), Moran (34), Retchless (75), Greenwood (79); **Goals:** Sykes 5/6.
VIKINGS: 23 Steve Rowlands; 21 Nicky Royle; 3 Aaron Moule; 4 Adam Hughes; 5 Chris Giles; 6 Jules O'Neill; 20 Stephen Myler; 8 Robert Relf; 9 Shane Millard; 17 David Mills; 15 Troy Wozniak; 12 Andy Hay (C); 18 Simon Finnigan. Subs (all used): 1 Paul Atcheson; 10 Julian O'Neill; 11 Steve McCurrie; 14 Deon Bird.
Tries: Millard (17), Hughes (40, 68), Royle (55);
Goals: Jules O'Neill 1/4.
Rugby Leaguer & League Express Men of the Match: *Broncos:* Dennis Moran; *Vikings:* Shane Millard.
Penalty count: 4-5; **Half-time:** 22-10; **Referee:** Karl Kirkpatrick (Warrington); **Attendance:** 2,923.

Tuesday 27th April 2004 (re-scheduled from Sunday 18th April due to Challenge Cup)

WARRINGTON WOLVES 22 BRADFORD BULLS 22

WOLVES: 19 Gary Hulse; 25 Richard Varkulis; 3 Brent Grose; 4 Ben Westwood; 20 Dean Gaskell; 6 Lee Briers (C); 7 Nathan Wood; 22 Danny Lima; 9 Jon Clarke; 10 Mark Hilton; 18 Paul Noone; 23 Mike Wainwright; 13 Mike Forshaw. Subs (all used): 14 Mark Gleeson; 15 Jerome Guisset; 17 Warren Stevens; 11 Darren Burns.
Tries: Briers (19), Varkulis (22), Grose (27, 45), Gaskell (71); **Goals:** Briers 1/5.
BULLS: 6 Michael Withers; 17 Stuart Reardon; 16 Paul Johnson; 4 Shontayne Hape; 5 Lesley Vainikolo; 3 Leon Pryce; 7 Paul Deacon; 8 Joe Vagana; 24 Aaron Smith; 29 Stuart Fielden; 11 Lee Radford; 12 Jamie Peacock (C); 13 Logan Swann. Subs (all used): 26 Chris Bridge; 19 Jamie Langley; 27 Rob Parker; 30 Richard Moore.
Tries: Aaron Smith (3), Withers (52, 68), Vainikolo (77); **Goals:** Deacon 3/4.
Rugby Leaguer & League Express Men of the Match: *Wolves:* Danny Lima; *Bulls:* Lesley Vainikolo.
Penalty count: 3-5; **Half-time:** 14-6; **Referee:** Richard Silverwood (Dewsbury); **Attendance:** 8,111.

Tuesday 29th June 2004 (re-scheduled from Sunday 18th April due to Challenge Cup)

HULL FC 20 WIGAN WARRIORS 20

HULL: 32 Shaun Briscoe; 2 Colin Best; 4 Michael Eagar; 14 Kirk Yeaman; 5 Gareth Raynor; 16 Paul Cooke (C); 6 Richard Horne; 18 Ewan Dowes; 9 Richard Swain; 10 Paul King; 15 Shayne McMenemy; 23 Paul McNicholas; 25 Peter Lupton. Subs (all used): 26 Richie Barnett Jnr; 27 Liam Higgins; 30 Richard Whiting; 34 Nick Scruton.
Tries: McNicholas (44), Eagar (53), Best (58); **Goals:** Cooke 4/5.
Sin bin: Raynor (27) - holding down.
WARRIORS: 33 Gary Connolly; 2 Brett Dallas; 3 Martin Aspinwall; 19 Stephen Wild; 4 David Hodgson; 6 Danny Orr; 7 Adrian Lam; 10 Craig Smith; 9 Terry Newton; 12 Danny Tickle; 13 Andy Farrell (C); 20 Gareth Hock; 15 Sean O'Loughlin. Subs: 17 Mark Smith; 16 Danny Sculthorpe; 11 Mick Cassidy; 25 Liam Colbon (not used).
Tries: Wild (6), Farrell (17), Orr (36); **Goals:** Farrell 4/6.
Rugby Leaguer & League Express Men of the Match: *Hull:* Paul King; *Warriors:* Stephen Wild.
Penalty count: 10-7; **Half-time:** 4-18; **Referee:** Karl Kirkpatrick (Warrington); **Attendance:** 11,042.

ROUND 8

Friday 23rd April 2004

BRADFORD BULLS 18 HULL FC 26

BULLS: 6 Michael Withers; 22 Karl Pryce; 16 Paul Johnson; 4 Shontayne Hape; 17 Stuart Reardon; 3 Leon Pryce; 7 Paul Deacon; 8 Joe Vagana; 24 Aaron Smith; 29 Stuart Fielden; 27 Rob Parker; 12 Jamie Peacock (C); 13 Logan Swann. Subs (all used): 26 Chris Bridge; 11 Lee Radford; 19 Jamie Langley; 10 Paul Anderson.
Tries: Hape (8), Deacon (42); **Goals:** Deacon 5/5.
HULL: 32 Shaun Briscoe; 5 Gareth Raynor; 2 Colin Best; 14 Kirk Yeaman; 26 Richie Barnett Jnr; 16 Paul Cooke (C); 6 Richard Horne; 18 Ewan Dowes; 9 Richard Swain; 20 Garreth Carvell; 15 Shayne McMenemy; 23 Paul McNicholas; 17 Chris Chester. Subs (all used): 10 Paul King; 25 Peter Lupton; 30 Richard Whiting; 31 Danny Hill.
Tries: Briscoe (38, 52, 65, 78); **Goals:** Cooke 5/6.
Rugby Leaguer & League Express Men of the Match: *Bulls:* Michael Withers; *Hull:* Richard Swain.
Penalty count: 7-8; **Half-time:** 8-8;
Referee: Ian Smith (Oldham); **Attendance:** 12,684.

WAKEFIELD TRINITY WILDCATS 12 LEEDS RHINOS 36

WILDCATS: 14 Colum Halpenny; 24 Michael Wainwright; 1 Jason Demetriou; 2 Justin Ryder; 5 Semi Tadulala; 4 Sid Domic; 7 Ben Jeffries; 8 Darrell Griffin; 9 David March; 10 Michael Korkidas; 11 David Solomona; 18 Olivier Elima; 3 Gareth Ellis (C). Subs (all used): 16 Steve Snitch; 13 Jamie Field; 25 Albert Talipeau; 17 Paul Handforth.
Tries: Domic (6), Solomona (56); **Goals:** March 2/2.
RHINOS: 21 Richard Mathers; 2 Francis Cummins; 5 Chev Walker; 4 Keith Senior (C); 22 Marcus Bai; 6 Danny McGuire; 14 Andrew Dunemann; 8 Ryan Bailey; 9 Matt Diskin; 10 Barrie McDermott; 15 Chris Feather; 3 Chris McKenna; 11 David Furner. Subs (all used): 17 Wayne McDonald; 16 Willie Poching; 7 Rob Burrow; 19 Danny Ward.
Tries: Senior (9, 74), McGuire (25, 28), Cummins (51), Furner (69, 79); **Goals:** Furner 4/8.
Rugby Leaguer & League Express Men of the Match: *Wildcats:* Sid Domic; *Rhinos:* Rob Burrow.
Penalty count: 2-3; **Half-time:** 6-14;
Referee: Steve Ganson (St Helens); **Attendance:** 7,680.

Saturday 24th April 2004

SALFORD CITY REDS 18 WARRINGTON WOLVES 37

CITY REDS: 2 Joel Caine; 4 Andy Kirk; 3 Stuart Littler; 20 Scott Naylor; 5 Anthony Stewart; 6 Cliff Beverley; 7 Gavin Clinch; 8 Andy Coley; 13 Chris Charles; 10 Sean Rutgerson (C); 11 Simon Baldwin; 18 Mark Shipway; 12 Andy Johnson. Subs (all used): 14 Paul Highton; 15 Karl Fitzpatrick; 17 Gareth Haggerty; 23 Vinny Myler.
Tries: Johnson (31), Beverley (54), Fitzpatrick (55); **Goals:** Charles 3/3.
WOLVES: 1 Daryl Cardiss; 25 Richard Varkulis; 11 Darren Burns; 4 Ben Westwood; 20 Dean Gaskell; 6 Lee Briers (C); 7 Nathan Wood; 22 Danny Lima; 9 Jon Clarke; 16 Paul Wood; 18 Paul Noone; 23 Mike Wainwright; 13 Mike Forshaw. Subs (all used): 14 Mark Gleeson; 15 Jerome Guisset; 17 Warren Stevens; 19 Gary Hulse.
Tries: Burns (16), N Wood (27), Briers (40), P Wood (55), Gleeson (73), Varkulis (78);
Goals: Briers 5/5, Noone 1/1; **Field goal:** Briers.
Rugby Leaguer & League Express Men of the Match: *City Reds:* Karl Fitzpatrick; *Wolves:* Lee Briers.
Penalty count: 2-3; **Half-time:** 6-18;
Referee: Russell Smith (Castleford); **Attendance:** 3,624.

Sunday 25th April 2004

WIDNES VIKINGS 29 CASTLEFORD TIGERS 18

VIKINGS: 23 Steve Rowlands; 21 Nicky Royle; 3 Aaron Moule; 4 Adam Hughes; 5 Chris Giles; 6 Jules O'Neill; 20 Stephen Myler; 8 Robert Relf; 9 Shane Millard; 17 David Mills; 12 Andy Hay (C); 15 Troy Wozniak; 13 Daniel Frame. Subs (all used): 16 Andy Hobson; 14 Deon Bird; 11 Steve McCurrie; 1 Paul Atcheson.
Tries: Royle (40), Myler (41), McCurrie (48), Jules O'Neill (53); **Goals:** Jules O'Neill 6/6;
Field goal: Jules O'Neill.
TIGERS: 20 Tom Saxton; 28 Dean Ripley; 5 Darren Rogers; 4 Paul Newlove; 3 Paul Mellor; 19 Francis Maloney; 16 Jon Hepworth; 8 Craig Greenhill; 13 Ryan Hudson (C); 10 Andy Lynch; 23 Michael Smith; 18 Jamie Thackray; 12 Sean Ryan. Subs (all used): 14 Ryan Clayton; 17 Paul Jackson; 15 Nathan Sykes; 11 Lee Harland.
Tries: Rogers (36), Saxton (56), Thackray (66); **Goals:** Maloney 3/3.
Rugby Leaguer & League Express Men of the Match: *Vikings:* Troy Wozniak; *Tigers:* Michael Smith.
Penalty count: 10-6; **Half-time:** 8-6;
Referee: Ashley Klein (London); **Attendance:** 5,274.

WIGAN WARRIORS 64 LONDON BRONCOS 8

WARRIORS: 1 Kris Radlinski; 29 Desi Williams (D); 15 Sean O'Loughlin; 21 Kevin Brown; 2 Brett Dallas; 6 Danny Orr; 7 Adrian Lam; 18 Quentin Pongia; 9 Terry Newton; 10 Craig Smith; 12 Danny Tickle; 20 Gareth Hock; 13 Andy Farrell (C). Subs (all used): 8 Terry O'Connor; 16 Danny Sculthorpe; 17 Mark Smith; 19 Stephen Wild.
Tries: Dallas (4), Orr (11), Radlinski (14, 54), Brown (16), O'Loughlin (22), Farrell (32), Newton (36, 48, 79), C Smith (71); **Goals:** Farrell 10/11.
BRONCOS: 1 Paul Sykes; 23 Lee Greenwood; 3 Nigel Roy; 17 Tom Haughey; 2 Jon Wells; 25 Scott Murrell; 7 Dennis Moran; 15 Mitchell Stringer; 9 Neil Budworth; 12 Steele Retchless (C); 16 Joe Mbu; 14 Andrew Brocklehurst; 18 Andrew Hart. Subs (all used): 10 Steve Trindall; 19 David Highton; 26 Jonny Williams; 24 Andy McNally.
Tries: Wells (19), Roy (60); **Goals:** Murrell 0/1, Moran 0/1.
Rugby Leaguer & League Express Men of the Match: *Warriors:* Danny Orr; *Broncos:* David Highton.
Penalty count: 1-1; **Half-time:** 40-4; **Referee:** Ronnie Laughton (Barnsley); **Attendance:** 9,132.

Wednesday 7th July 2004 (re-scheduled from Sunday 25th April due to Challenge Cup)

HUDDERSFIELD GIANTS 8 ST HELENS 50

GIANTS: 1 Paul Reilly; 21 Paul White; 11 Chris Nero; 24 James Evans; 3 Stuart Donlan; 6 Stanley Gene; 7 Sean Penkywicz; 10 Jim Gannon; 2 Hefin O'Hare; 18 Eorl Crabtree; 14 Stuart Jones (C); 17 Paul Smith; 12 Ben Roarty. Subs (all used): 16 Iain Morrison; 20 Jon Grayshon; 22 Phil Joseph; 34 Marcus St Hilaire.
Try: Gannon (6); **Goals:** White 2/3.
SAINTS: 1 Paul Wellens; 2 Ade Gardner; 12 Lee Gilmour; 4 Willie Talau; 5 Darren Albert; 13 Paul Sculthorpe (C); 26 James Roby; 8 Nick Fozzard; 21 Jon Wilkin; 18 Mark Edmondson; 10 John Stankevitch; 15 Mike Bennett; 6 Jason Hooper. Subs (all used): 20 Ricky Bibey; 23 Maurie Fa'asavalu; 22 Dom Feaunati; 16 Keith Mason.
Tries: Stankevitch (16), Albert (35), Wellens (42), Gilmour (48), Sculthorpe (60), Wilkin (69), Gardner (75), Feaunati (80); **Goals:** Sculthorpe 9/9.
Rugby Leaguer & League Express Men of the Match: *Giants:* Eorl Crabtree; *Saints:* Paul Sculthorpe.
Penalty count: 9-11; **Half-time:** 8-14;
Referee: Ian Smith (Oldham); **Attendance:** 3,506.

ROUND 9

Friday 30th April 2004

ST HELENS 56 LEEDS RHINOS 10

SAINTS: 1 Paul Wellens; 2 Ade Gardner; 3 Martin Gleeson; 4 Willie Talau; 5 Darren Albert; 6 Jason Hooper; 7 Sean Long; 8 Nick Fozzard; 9 Keiron Cunningham; 16 Keith Mason; 11 Chris Joynt; 12 Lee Gilmour; 13 Paul Sculthorpe (C). Subs (all used): 18 Mark Edmondson; 20 Ricky Bibey; 23 Maurie Fa'asavalu; 25 Ian Hardman.
Tries: Gardner (6), Gilmour (8), Hooper (20, 29), Sculthorpe (23), Albert (53), Talau (57), Hardman (68), Edmondson (79); **Goals:** Long 8/9, Hooper 2/2.
Sin bin: Albert (66) - holding down.
RHINOS: 21 Richard Mathers; 2 Francis Cummins; 5 Chev Walker; 4 Keith Senior; 22 Marcus Bai; 6 Danny McGuire; 14 Andrew Dunemann; 15 Chris Feather; 7 Rob Burrow; 10 Barrie McDermott; 11 David Furner; 3 Chris McKenna; 13 Kevin Sinfield (C). Subs (all used): 8 Ryan Bailey; 12 Matt Adamson; 16 Willie Poching; 17 Wayne McDonald.
Tries: Burrow (61), Feather (75); **Goals:** Sinfield 1/2.
Rugby Leaguer & League Express Men of the Match: *Saints:* Jason Hooper; *Rhinos:* Ryan Bailey.
Penalty count: 8-6; **Half-time:** 28-0; **Referee:** Russell Smith (Castleford); **Attendance:** 11,059.

Saturday 1st May 2004

CASTLEFORD TIGERS 28 WIGAN WARRIORS 42

TIGERS: 20 Tom Saxton; 30 Michael Shenton (D); 5 Darren Rogers; 14 Ryan Clayton; 3 Paul Mellor; 19 Francis Maloney; 29 Dominic Brambani; 8 Craig Greenhill; 9 Wayne Godwin; 10 Andy Lynch; 23 Michael Smith; 11 Lee Harland; 13 Ryan Hudson (C). Subs (all used): 15 Nathan Sykes; 16 Jon Hepworth; 18 Jamie Thackray; 22 Byron Smith (D).
Tries: Mellor (8, 49, 66), Saxton (41), Thackray (54); **Goals:** Godwin 3/3, Maloney 1/4.
WARRIORS: 1 Kris Radlinski; 29 Desi Williams; 15 Sean O'Loughlin; 21 Kevin Brown; 2 Brett Dallas; 6 Danny Orr; 7 Adrian Lam; 18 Quentin Pongia; 9 Terry Newton; 10 Craig Smith; 11 Mick Cassidy; 12 Danny Tickle; 13 Andy Farrell (C). Subs (all used): 8 Terry O'Connor; 16 Danny Sculthorpe; 20 Gareth Hock; 19 Stephen Wild.
Tries: Dallas (5, 45), Brown (29), Newton (32, 64), Lam (61), C Smith (75), Radlinski (78); **Goals:** Farrell 5/8.
Rugby Leaguer & League Express Men of the Match: *Tigers:* Paul Mellor; *Warriors:* Terry Newton.
Penalty count: 7-5; **Half-time:** 8-14;
Referee: Ian Smith (Oldham); **Attendance:** 6,222.

Sunday 2nd May 2004

WARRINGTON WOLVES 20 HUDDERSFIELD GIANTS 26

WOLVES: 19 Gary Hulse; 20 Dean Gaskell; 4 Ben Westwood; 3 Brent Grose; 25 Richard Varkulis; 6 Lee Briers (C); 7 Nathan Wood; 16 Paul Wood; 9 Jon Clarke; 22 Danny Lima; 11 Darren Burns; 23 Mike Wainwright; 18 Paul Noone. Subs (all used): 12 Ian Sibbit; 15 Jerome Guisset; 10 Mark Hilton; 17 Warren Stevens.
Tries: Clarke (17), Guisset (39), Gaskell (49); **Goals:** Briers 4/5.
GIANTS: 1 Paul Reilly; 2 Hefin O'Hare; 6 Stanley Gene; 4 Julian Bailey; 3 Stuart Donlan; 13 Brandon Costin; 7 Sean Penkywicz; 25 Darren Fleary (C); 9 Paul March; 10 Jim Gannon; 14 Stuart Jones; 12 Ben Roarty; 11 Chris Nero. Subs (all used): 5 Ben Cooper; 16 Iain Morrison; 17 Paul Smith; 18 Eorl Crabtree.
Tries: Bailey (24), Roarty (28), Crabtree (69), Nero (73); **Goals:** March 5/5.
Rugby Leaguer & League Express Men of the Match: *Wolves:* Brent Grose; *Giants:* Eorl Crabtree.
Penalty count: 11-9; **Half-time:** 14-14; **Referee:** Richard Silverwood (Dewsbury); **Attendance:** 8,792.

HULL FC 82 SALFORD CITY REDS 6

HULL: 32 Shaun Briscoe; 2 Colin Best; 14 Kirk Yeaman; 30 Richard Whiting; 5 Gareth Raynor; 16 Paul Cooke (C); 6 Richard Horne; 10 Paul King; 9 Richard Swain; 18 Ewan Dowes; 15 Shayne McMenemy; 23 Paul McNicholas; 17 Chris Chester. Subs (all used): 25 Peter Lupton; 20 Garreth Carvell; 26 Richie Barnett Jnr; 31 Danny Hill.
Tries: Whiting (3, 64), Raynor (14, 46), Carvell (30, 33), Briscoe (37, 39, 41), Swain (43), R Horne (49), Yeaman (52), Lupton (55), Barnett Jnr (67), King (78);
Goals: Cooke 11/15.
CITY REDS: 2 Joel Caine; 4 Andy Kirk; 3 Stuart Littler; 5 Anthony Stewart; 24 Bryn Powell; 6 Cliff Beverley; 15 Karl Fitzpatrick; 14 Paul Highton; 13 Chris Charles; 10 Sean Rutgerson (C); 8 Andy Coley; 18 Mark Shipway; 12 Andy Johnson. Subs (all used): 7 Gavin Clinch; 11 Simon Baldwin; 17 Gareth Haggerty; 23 Vinny Myler.
Try: Littler (27); **Goal:** Charles 1/1.
Rugby Leaguer & League Express Men of the Match: *Hull:* Shaun Briscoe; *City Reds:* Chris Charles.
Penalty count: 12-4; **Half-time:** 32-6;
Referee: Ashley Klein (London); **Attendance:** 9,869.

WAKEFIELD TRINITY WILDCATS 40 WIDNES VIKINGS 10

WILDCATS: 14 Colum Halpenny; 24 Michael Wainwright; 1 Jason Demetriou; 19 Rob Spicer; 2 Justin Ryder; 4 Sid Domic; 7 Ben Jeffries; 8 Darrell Griffin; 9 David March; 10 Michael Korkidas; 11 David Solomona; 18 Olivier Elima; 3 Gareth Ellis (C). Subs (all used): 13 Jamie Field; 25 Albert Talipeau; 20 Liam Finn (D); 22 Mark Applegarth (D).
Tries: Elima (12), Halpenny (23), J Field (51), Domic (53), March (62), Jeffries (67), Applegarth (74);
Goals: March 6/7.
VIKINGS: 23 Steve Rowlands; 21 Nicky Royle; 3 Aaron Moule; 4 Adam Hughes; 22 John Robinson; 6 Jules O'Neill; 20 Stephen Myler; 8 Robert Relf; 9 Shane Millard; 10 Julian O'Neill; 15 Troy Wozniak; 12 Andy Hay (C); 13 Daniel Frame. Subs (all used): 1 Paul Atcheson; 11 Steve McCurrie; 14 Deon Bird; 17 David Mills.
Tries: Jules O'Neill (45, 78); **Goals:** Jules O'Neill 1/2.
Rugby Leaguer & League Express Men of the Match: *Wildcats:* David March; *Vikings:* Jules O'Neill.
Penalty count: 3-2; **Half-time:** 12-0;
Referee: Steve Ganson (St Helens); **Attendance:** 4,136.

Monday 3rd May 2004

LONDON BRONCOS 12 BRADFORD BULLS 24

BRONCOS: 24 Andy McNally; 2 Jon Wells; 29 Steve Thomas (D); 17 Tom Haughey; 23 Lee Greenwood; 27 Dwayne Barker (D); 7 Dennis Moran; 12 Steele Retchless (C); 9 Neil Budworth; 10 Steve Trindall; 16 Joe Mbu; 28 Jason Netherton (D); 18 Andrew Hart. Subs (all used): 14 Andrew Brocklehurst; 19 David Highton; 22

Lee Sanderson; 15 Mitchell Stringer.
Tries: Moran (50), Barker (67); **Goals:** Sanderson 2/2.
BULLS: 6 Michael Withers; 17 Stuart Reardon; 16 Paul Johnson; 4 Shontayne Hape; 32 Andy Smith (D); 3 Leon Pryce; 7 Paul Deacon; 10 Paul Anderson; 1 Robbie Paul (C); 27 Rob Parker; 19 Jamie Langley; 12 Jamie Peacock; 13 Logan Swann. Subs (all used): 26 Chris Bridge; 11 Lee Radford; 8 Joe Vagana; 29 Stuart Fielden.
Tries: Deacon (11), Langley (19), L Pryce (27), Reardon (62, 73); **Goals:** Deacon 2/5.
Sin bin: Fielden (66) - fighting.
Rugby Leaguer & League Express Men of the Match: *Broncos:* Dennis Moran; *Bulls:* Paul Deacon.
Penalty count: 7-4; **Half-time:** 0-16; **Referee:** Karl Kirkpatrick (Warrington); **Attendance:** 3,987.

ROUND 10

Friday 7th May 2004

HUDDERSFIELD GIANTS 0 HULL FC 20

GIANTS: 1 Paul Reilly; 2 Hefin O'Hare; 6 Stanley Gene; 4 Julian Bailey; 3 Stuart Donlan; 13 Brandon Costin; 7 Sean Penkywicz; 25 Darren Fleary (C); 9 Paul March; 10 Jim Gannon; 14 Stuart Jones; 12 Ben Roarty; 11 Chris Nero. Subs (all used): 5 Ben Cooper; 16 Iain Morrison; 8 Mick Slicker; 18 Eorl Crabtree.
Sin bin: Fleary (67) - dissent; March (78) - interference.
On report: Bailey (24) - high tackle.
HULL: 32 Shaun Briscoe; 2 Colin Best; 14 Kirk Yeaman; 3 Richie Barnett (C); 5 Gareth Raynor; 16 Paul Cooke; 6 Richard Horne; 20 Garreth Carvell; 9 Richard Swain; 18 Ewan Dowes; 15 Shayne McMenemy; 23 Paul McNicholas; 17 Chris Chester. Subs (all used): 25 Peter Lupton; 30 Richard Whiting; 24 Graeme Horne; 27 Liam Higgins.
Tries: McNicholas (8), Whiting (27), G Horne (78);
Goals: Cooke 4/7.
Rugby Leaguer & League Express Men of the Match: *Giants:* Paul Reilly; *Hull:* Paul McNicholas.
Penalty count: 7-14; **Half-time:** 0-14;
Referee: Russell Smith (Castleford); **Attendance:** 4,064.

LEEDS RHINOS 23 WARRINGTON WOLVES 10

RHINOS: 21 Richard Mathers; 18 Mark Calderwood; 3 Chris McKenna; 4 Keith Senior; 22 Marcus Bai; 6 Danny McGuire; 14 Andrew Dunemann; 8 Ryan Bailey; 9 Matt Diskin; 19 Danny Ward; 11 David Furner; 12 Matt Adamson; 13 Kevin Sinfield (C). Subs (all used): 10 Barrie McDermott; 16 Willie Poching; 7 Rob Burrow; 2 Francis Cummins.
Tries: Bai (28, 45), Calderwood (59), McGuire (79);
Goals: Sinfield 2/3, Furner 1/1; **Field goal:** Sinfield.
WOLVES: 1 Daryl Cardiss; 20 Dean Gaskell; 18 Paul Noone; 3 Brent Grose; 12 Ian Sibbit; 6 Lee Briers (C); 7 Nathan Wood; 16 Paul Wood; 9 Jon Clarke; 10 Mark Hilton; 23 Mike Wainwright; 11 Darren Burns; 13 Mike Forshaw. Subs (all used): 17 Warren Stevens; 14 Mark Gleeson; 15 Jerome Guisset; 19 Gary Hulse.
Try: Briers (37); **Goals:** Briers 3/3.
Rugby Leaguer & League Express Men of the Match: *Rhinos:* Marcus Bai; *Wolves:* Mike Forshaw.
Penalty count: 4-7; **Half-time:** 6-8;
Referee: Ian Smith (Oldham); **Attendance:** 16,065.

ST HELENS 26 WAKEFIELD TRINITY WILDCATS 20

SAINTS: 1 Paul Wellens; 5 Darren Albert; 3 Martin Gleeson; 4 Willie Talau; 22 Dom Feaunati; 6 Jason Hooper; 7 Sean Long (C); 8 Nick Fozzard; 9 Keiron Cunningham; 16 Keith Mason; 18 Mark Edmondson; 24 James Graham; 12 Lee Gilmour. Subs (all used): 23 Maurie Fa'asavalu; 20 Ricky Bibey; 25 Ian Hardman; 27 Carl Forber.
Tries: Feaunati (1), Albert (35), Cunningham (38), Talau (59), Hardman (64); **Goals:** Long 3/5.
WILDCATS: 14 Colum Halpenny; 24 Michael Wainwright; 1 Jason Demetriou; 2 Justin Ryder; 5 Semi Tadulala; 4 Sid Domic; 7 Ben Jeffries; 8 Darrell Griffin; 9 David March; 10 Michael Korkidas; 11 David Solomona; 22 Mark Applegarth; 3 Gareth Ellis (C). Subs (all used): 13 Jamie Field; 18 Olivier Elima; 19 Rob Spicer; 25 Albert Talipeau.
Tries: Ellis (17), Ryder (44), Korkidas (47);
Goals: March 3/3, Griffin 1/2.
On report: Solomona (28) - lifting in tackle.
Rugby Leaguer & League Express Men of the Match: *Saints:* Nick Fozzard; *Wildcats:* David March.
Penalty count: 13-14; **Half-time:** 18-10;
Referee: Ashley Klein (London); **Attendance:** 9,191.

WIGAN WARRIORS 26 WIDNES VIKINGS 8

WARRIORS: 1 Kris Radlinski; 4 David Hodgson; 19 Stephen Wild; 15 Sean O'Loughlin; 2 Brett Dallas; 6 Danny Orr; 7 Adrian Lam; 8 Terry O'Connor; 17 Mark Smith; 16 Danny Sculthorpe; 12 Danny Tickle; 20 Gareth Hock; 13 Andy Farrell (C). Subs (all used): 25 Liam Colbon (D); 10 Craig Smith; 18 Quentin Pongia; 11 Mick Cassidy.
Tries: Wild (10), Tickle (16), Orr (34), Hodgson (45), Hock (73); **Goals:** Farrell 3/5.
Sin bin: Pongia (76) - striking.
On report: Pongia (51) - high tackle on Bird.
VIKINGS: 14 Deon Bird; 21 Nicky Royle; 4 Adam Hughes; 3 Aaron Moule; 5 Chris Giles; 6 Jules O'Neill; 20 Stephen Myler; 8 Robert Relf; 25 Phil Wood (D); 10 Julian O'Neill; 15 Troy Wozniak; 12 Andy Hay (C); 13 Daniel Frame. Subs (all used): 16 Andy Hobson; 18 Simon Finnigan; 11 Steve McCurrie; 26 Adam Bibey (D).
Tries: Bird (40), Royle (53); **Goals:** Jules O'Neill 0/2.
Sin bin: Bibey (30) - holding down;
Relf (59) - holding down.
Rugby Leaguer & League Express Men of the Match: *Warriors:* Danny Sculthorpe; *Vikings:* Deon Bird.
Penalty count: 11-11; **Half-time:** 16-4; **Referee:** Richard Silverwood (Dewsbury); **Attendance:** 10,145.

Saturday 8th May 2004

SALFORD CITY REDS 30 LONDON BRONCOS 12

CITY REDS: 2 Joel Caine; 5 Anthony Stewart; 3 Stuart Littler; 33 Kevin McGuinness (D); 4 Andy Kirk; 6 Cliff Beverley; 7 Gavin Clinch; 19 Neil Baynes; 9 Malcolm Alker (C); 14 Paul Highton; 12 Andy Johnson; 8 Andy Coley; 13 Chris Charles. Subs (all used): 15 Karl Fitzpatrick; 16 Martin Moana; 11 Simon Baldwin; 17 Gareth Haggerty.
Tries: Littler (26), Caine (32), Beverley (36), Stewart (40), Charles (57); **Goals:** Charles 5/6.
Sin bin: Moana (69) - striking; Highton (72) - fighting.
On report: Littler (38) - high tackle on Greenwood.
BRONCOS: 1 Paul Sykes; 23 Lee Greenwood; 2 Jon Wells; 17 Tom Haughey; 29 Steve Thomas; 27 Dwayne Barker; 7 Dennis Moran; 12 Steele Retchless (C); 9 Neil Budworth; 15 Mitchell Stringer; 16 Joe Mbu; 28 Jason Netherton; 18 Andrew Hart. Subs (all used): 10 Steve Trindall; 14 Andrew Brocklehurst; 19 David Highton; 22 Lee Sanderson.
Tries: Greenwood (43, 80); **Goals:** Sanderson 2/2.
Sin bin: Netherton (72) - fighting.
Rugby Leaguer & League Express Men of the Match: *City Reds:* Chris Charles; *Broncos:* Lee Greenwood.
Penalty count: 7-2; **Half-time:** 24-0;
Referee: Steve Ganson (St Helens); **Attendance:** 2,529.

Sunday 9th May 2004

BRADFORD BULLS 44 CASTLEFORD TIGERS 18

BULLS: 6 Michael Withers; 17 Stuart Reardon; 3 Leon Pryce; 16 Paul Johnson; 5 Lesley Vainikolo; 1 Robbie Paul (C); 7 Paul Deacon; 10 Paul Anderson; 24 Aaron Smith; 27 Rob Parker; 19 Jamie Langley; 12 Jamie Peacock; 13 Logan Swann. Subs (all used): 26 Chris Bridge; 11 Lee Radford; 8 Joe Vagana; 29 Stuart Fielden.
Tries: Reardon (1, 16, 34, 50), Langley (11, 14), Vainikolo (55, 64); **Goals:** Deacon 6/8.
TIGERS: 26 Rob Worrincy (D); 5 Darren Rogers; 14 Ryan Clayton; 3 Paul Mellor; 16 Jon Hepworth; 19 Francis Maloney; 29 Dominic Brambani; 8 Craig Greenhill; 9 Wayne Godwin; 10 Andy Lynch; 18 Jamie Thackray; 11 Lee Harland; 13 Ryan Hudson (C). Subs (all used): 17 Paul Jackson; 22 Byron Smith; 12 Sean Ryan; 24 Andy Kain (D).
Tries: Rogers (8), Godwin (18), Mellor (69);
Goals: Godwin 3/4.
Rugby Leaguer & League Express Men of the Match: *Bulls:* Leon Pryce; *Tigers:* Jon Hepworth.
Penalty count: 5-7; **Half-time:** 26-12; **Referee:** Ronnie Laughton (Barnsley); **Attendance:** 12,877.

ROUND 11

Friday 21st May 2004

HULL FC 12 LEEDS RHINOS 23

HULL: 32 Shaun Briscoe; 2 Colin Best; 3 Richie Barnett (C); 14 Kirk Yeaman; 5 Gareth Raynor; 16 Paul Cooke; 6 Richard Horne; 10 Paul King; 9 Richard Swain; 18 Ewan Dowes; 15 Shayne McMenemy; 23 Paul McNicholas; 17 Chris Chester. Subs (all used): 30 Richard Whiting; 24 Graeme Horne; 25 Peter Lupton; 27 Liam Higgins.
Tries: R Horne (43), Cooke (59); **Goals:** Cooke 2/2.
RHINOS: 21 Richard Mathers; 18 Mark Calderwood; 3 Chris McKenna; 4 Keith Senior; 22 Marcus Bai; 6 Danny McGuire; 14 Andrew Dunemann; 8 Ryan Bailey; 9 Matt Diskin; 17 Wayne McDonald; 11 David Furner; 12 Matt Adamson; 13 Kevin Sinfield (C). Subs (all used): 7 Rob Burrow; 2 Francis Cummins; 10 Barrie McDermott; 15 Chris Feather.
Tries: Mathers (50), Burrow (52, 75), McGuire (54);
Goals: Sinfield 3/4; **Field goal:** Sinfield.
Rugby Leaguer & League Express Men of the Match: *Hull:* Richard Horne; *Rhinos:* Richard Mathers.
Penalty count: 2-0; **Half-time:** 0-0;
Referee: Steve Ganson (St Helens); **Attendance:** 16,528.

Saturday 22nd May 2004

WARRINGTON WOLVES 20 ST HELENS 50

WOLVES: 5 Graham Appo; 2 John Wilshere; 3 Brent Grose; 4 Ben Westwood; 1 Daryl Cardiss; 6 Lee Briers (C); 7 Nathan Wood; 16 Paul Wood; 9 Jon Clarke; 10 Mark Hilton; 18 Paul Noone; 23 Mike Wainwright; 13 Mike Forshaw. Subs (all used): 12 Ian Sibbit; 14 Mark Gleeson; 8 Chris Leikvoll; 17 Warren Stevens.
Tries: Westwood (8), Wainwright (24), Grose (56), Clarke (76); **Goals:** Briers 2/3, Noone 0/1.
SAINTS: 1 Paul Wellens; 2 Ade Gardner; 3 Martin Gleeson; 4 Willie Talau; 5 Darren Albert; 6 Jason Hooper; 7 Sean Long; 8 Nick Fozzard; 9 Keiron Cunningham; 16 Keith Mason; 11 Chris Joynt; 12 Lee Gilmour; 13 Paul Sculthorpe (C). Subs (all used): 18 Mark Edmondson; 20 Ricky Bibey; 21 Jon Wilkin; 25 Ian Hardman.
Tries: Cunningham (3), Wilkin (14), Albert (22, 35, 67), Long (28), Hooper (47), Gleeson (69), Gilmour (74);
Goals: Long 7/10.
On report: Mason (54) - high tackle on Stevens.
Rugby Leaguer & League Express Men of the Match: *Wolves:* Nathan Wood; *Saints:* Martin Gleeson.
Penalty count: 6-5; **Half-time:** 12-28;
Referee: Ian Smith (Oldham); **Attendance:** 11,328.

Sunday 23rd May 2004

LONDON BRONCOS 6 HUDDERSFIELD GIANTS 30

BRONCOS: 2 Jon Wells; 5 John Kirkpatrick (D); 4 Mark O'Halloran; 21 Rob Jackson; 23 Lee Greenwood; 27 Dwayne Barker; 7 Dennis Moran; 12 Steele Retchless (C); 19 David Highton; 14 Andrew Brocklehurst; 16 Joe Mbu; 28 Jason Netherton; 9 Neil Budworth. Subs (all used): 10 Steve Trindall; 17 Tom Haughey; 22 Lee Sanderson; 29 Steve Thomas.
Try: O'Halloran (38); **Goals:** Moran 1/2.
GIANTS: 1 Paul Reilly; 2 Hefin O'Hare; 3 Stuart Donlan; 4 Julian Bailey; 34 Marcus St Hilaire; 13 Brandon Costin (C); 9 Paul March; 8 Mick Slicker; 7 Sean Penkywicz; 10 Jim Gannon; 14 Stuart Jones; 12 Ben Roarty; 11 Chris Nero. Subs (all used): 16 Iain Morrison; 18 Eorl Crabtree; 22 Phil Joseph; 25 Darren Fleary.
Tries: Penkywicz (22), Jones (29), O'Hare (45), Donlan (56), St Hilaire (65), Reilly (73); **Goals:** March 3/7.
On report: Morrison (50) - high tackle on Wells.
Rugby Leaguer & League Express Men of the Match: *Broncos:* Mark O'Halloran; *Giants:* Paul March.
Penalty count: 12-4; **Half-time:** 6-12; **Referee:** Ronnie Laughton (Barnsley); **Attendance:** 2,627.

WIDNES VIKINGS 20 BRADFORD BULLS 30

VIKINGS: 14 Deon Bird; 21 Nicky Royle; 3 Aaron Moule; 4 Adam Hughes; 5 Chris Giles; 18 Simon Finnigan; 6 Jules O'Neill; 8 Robert Relf; 25 Phil Wood; 10 Julian O'Neill; 12 Andy Hay (C); 15 Troy Wozniak; 13 Daniel Frame. Subs (all used): 16 Andy Hobson; 17 David Mills; 11 Steve McCurrie; 20 Stephen Myler.
Tries: Finnigan (22), Bird (56), Wozniak (64);
Goals: Jules O'Neill 4/4.
Sin bin: Wozniak (48) - holding down.
BULLS: 6 Michael Withers; 17 Stuart Reardon; 16 Paul Johnson; 4 Shontayne Hape; 5 Lesley Vainikolo; 3 Leon Pryce; 7 Paul Deacon; 10 Paul Anderson; 24 Aaron Smith; 29 Stuart Fielden; 19 Jamie Langley; 12 Jamie Peacock (C); 13 Logan Swann. Subs (all used): 8 Joe Vagana; 1 Robbie Paul; 11 Lee Radford; 27 Rob Parker.
Tries: L Pryce (11, 44), Johnson (17), Hape (50), Aaron Smith (61); **Goals:** Deacon 5/6.
Rugby Leaguer & League Express Men of the Match: *Vikings:* Deon Bird; *Bulls:* Leon Pryce.
Penalty count: 6-7; **Half-time:** 8-12;
Referee: Ashley Klein (London); **Attendance:** 6,615.

CASTLEFORD TIGERS 32 SALFORD CITY REDS 36

TIGERS: 1 Damian Gibson; 5 Darren Rogers; 3 Paul Mellor; 4 Paul Newlove; 19 Francis Maloney; 6 Sean Rudder; 31 Luke Robinson (D); 8 Craig Greenhill; 9 Wayne Godwin; 10 Andy Lynch; 23 Michael Smith; 11 Lee Harland; 13 Ryan Hudson (C). Subs (all used): 17 Paul Jackson; 16 Jon Hepworth; 12 Sean Ryan; 24 Andy Kain.
Tries: Godwin (18), M Smith (30), Harland (49), Kain (59), Hudson (79); **Goals:** Godwin 6/7.
Sin bin: Mellor (39) - holding down.
CITY REDS: 2 Joel Caine; 27 Nathan McAvoy (D2); 3 Stuart Littler; 33 Kevin McGuinness; 5 Anthony Stewart; 6 Cliff Beverley; 7 Gavin Clinch; 19 Neil Baynes; 9 Malcolm Alker (C); 14 Paul Highton; 10 Sean Rutgerson; 8 Andy Coley; 13 Chris Charles. Subs (all used): 15 Karl Fitzpatrick; 12 Andy Johnson; 18 Mark Shipway; 17 Gareth Haggerty.
Tries: Baynes (40), Caine (46), Highton (60), Haggerty (66), Stewart (70), Johnson (76); **Goals:** Caine 6/7.
Rugby Leaguer & League Express Men of the Match: *Tigers:* Wayne Godwin; *City Reds:* Joel Caine.
Penalty count: 9-8; **Half-time:** 14-8;**Referee:** Karl Kirkpatrick (Warrington); **Attendance:** 6,961.

**WAKEFIELD TRINITY WILDCATS 14
WIGAN WARRIORS 20**

WILDCATS: 14 Colum Halpenny; 24 Michael Wainwright; 1 Jason Demetriou; 2 Justin Ryder; 5 Semi Tadulala; 4 Sid Domic; 7 Ben Jeffries; 8 Darrell Griffin; 9 David March; 10 Michael Korkidas; 13 Jamie Field; 22 Mark Applegarth; 3 Gareth Ellis (C). Subs (all used): 16 Steve Snitch; 17 Paul Handforth; 18 Olivier Elima; 19 Rob Spicer.
Tries: Ryder (62), Domic (72);
Goals: March 3/3, Handforth 0/2.
On report: Korkidas (20) - swinging arm in tackle.
WARRIORS: 1 Kris Radlinski; 2 Brett Dallas; 21 Kevin Brown; 33 Gary Connolly (D2); 4 David Hodgson; 6 Danny Orr; 7 Adrian Lam; 8 Terry O'Connor; 17 Mark Smith; 10 Craig Smith; 20 Gareth Hock; 13 Andy Farrell (C); 15 Sean O'Loughlin. Subs (all used): 11 Mick Cassidy; 12 Danny Tickle; 19 Stephen Wild; 25 Liam Colbon.
Tries: O'Loughlin (7), Brown (32), Radlinski (50);
Goals: Farrell 4/5.
Sin bin: Lam (36) - persistent offside.
On report: M Smith (25) - dangerous tackle.
Rugby Leaguer & League Express Men of the Match: *Wildcats:* Gareth Ellis; *Warriors:* Andy Farrell.
Penalty count: 9-8; **Half-time:** 6-12;
Referee: Russell Smith (Castleford); **Attendance:** 5,118.

ROUND 12

Friday 28th May 2004

LEEDS RHINOS 34 SALFORD CITY REDS 6

RHINOS: 21 Richard Mathers; 18 Mark Calderwood; 3 Chris McKenna; 4 Keith Senior; 2 Francis Cummins; 14 Andrew Dunemann; 7 Rob Burrow; 8 Ryan Bailey; 9 Matt Diskin; 17 Wayne McDonald; 12 Matt Adamson; 15 Chris Feather; 13 Kevin Sinfield (C). Subs (all used): 16

Willie Poching; 10 Barrie McDermott; 29 Ali Lauitiiti (D); 6 Danny McGuire.
Tries: Sinfield (9), Diskin (19), Calderwood (25), Senior (27), Cummins (36), McGuire (66); **Goals:** Sinfield 5/6.
CITY REDS: 1 Jason Flowers; 27 Nathan McAvoy; 5 Anthony Stewart; 33 Kevin McGuinness; 4 Andy Kirk; 16 Martin Moana; 2 Joel Caine; 19 Neil Baynes; 9 Malcolm Alker (C); 14 Paul Highton; 10 Sean Rutgerson; 20 Scott Naylor; 13 Chris Charles. Subs (all used): 8 Andy Coley; 12 Andy Johnson; 11 Simon Baldwin; 28 Tim Hartley (D).
Try: Baynes (52); **Goals:** Charles 1/1.
Rugby Leaguer & League Express Men of the Match: *Rhinos:* Kevin Sinfield; *City Reds:* Kevin McGuinness.
Penalty count: 5-5; **Half-time:** 28-0; **Referee:** Ronnie Laughton (Barnsley); **Attendance:** 14,239.

LONDON BRONCOS 10 CASTLEFORD TIGERS 12

BRONCOS: 2 Jon Wells; 23 Lee Greenwood; 21 Rob Jackson; 4 Mark O'Halloran; 5 John Kirkpatrick; 1 Paul Sykes; 7 Dennis Moran; 12 Steele Retchless; 9 Neil Budworth; 10 Steve Trindall; 16 Joe Mbu; 17 Tom Haughey; 13 Jim Dymock (C). Subs (all used): 15 Mitchell Stringer; 14 Andrew Brocklehurst; 30 Liam Botham (D); 19 David Highton.
Tries: Greenwood (15), Brocklehurst (35);
Goals: Moran 0/2, Botham 1/1.
TIGERS: 16 Jon Hepworth; 2 Waine Pryce; 5 Darren Rogers; 20 Tom Saxton; 3 Paul Mellor; 24 Andy Kain; 31 Luke Robinson; 8 Craig Greenhill; 9 Wayne Godwin; 10 Andy Lynch; 11 Lee Harland; 12 Sean Ryan; 13 Ryan Hudson (C). Subs (all used): 6 Sean Rudder; 15 Nathan Sykes; 23 Michael Smith; 17 Paul Jackson.
Tries: Robinson (12), Mellor (26);
Goals: Godwin 2/2, Robinson 0/2.
Sin bin: Robinson (70) - professional foul.
Rugby Leaguer & League Express Men of the Match: *Broncos:* Jon Wells; *Tigers:* Luke Robinson.
Penalty count: 3-8; **Half-time:** 8-10; **Referee:** Richard Silverwood (Dewsbury); **Attendance:** 2,562.

WARRINGTON WOLVES 34 WIGAN WARRIORS 18

WOLVES: 1 Daryl Cardiss; 5 Graham Appo; 3 Brent Grose; 4 Ben Westwood; 20 Dean Gaskell; 6 Lee Briers (C); 7 Nathan Wood; 10 Mark Hilton; 9 Jon Clarke; 16 Paul Wood; 18 Paul Noone; 23 Mike Wainwright; 13 Mike Forshaw. Subs (all used): 8 Chris Leikvoll; 12 Ian Sibbit; 14 Mark Gleeson; 17 Warren Stevens.
Tries: Forshaw (6), N Wood (22, 45, 49), Wainwright (26), Briers (71); **Goals:** Briers 5/6.
WARRIORS: 1 Kris Radlinski; 2 Brett Dallas; 33 Gary Connolly; 3 Martin Aspinwall; 4 David Hodgson; 6 Danny Orr; 7 Adrian Lam; 8 Terry O'Connor; 9 Terry Newton; 10 Craig Smith; 20 Gareth Hock; 13 Andy Farrell (C); 15 Sean O'Loughlin. Subs (all used): 11 Mick Cassidy; 12 Danny Tickle; 16 Danny Sculthorpe; 17 Mark Smith.
Tries: C Smith (49), Aspinwall (58), M Smith (72);
Goals: Farrell 3/3.
Rugby Leaguer & League Express Men of the Match: *Wolves:* Nathan Wood; *Warriors:* Andy Farrell.
Penalty count: 2-3; **Half-time:** 16-0;
Referee: Steve Ganson (St Helens); **Attendance:** 10,062.

Saturday 29th May 2004

ST HELENS 35 BRADFORD BULLS 30

SAINTS: 1 Paul Wellens; 2 Ade Gardner; 3 Martin Gleeson; 4 Willie Talau; 5 Darren Albert; 6 Jason Hooper; 7 Sean Long; 8 Nick Fozzard; 21 Jon Wilkin; 20 Ricky Bibey; 11 Chris Joynt; 12 Lee Gilmour; 13 Paul Sculthorpe (C). Subs: 18 Mark Edmondson; 22 Dom Feaunati; 24 James Graham; 26 James Roby (not used).
Tries: Hooper (2, 5, 58), Long (15), Gilmour (24);
Goals: Long 7/7; **Field goal:** Sculthorpe.
BULLS: 17 Stuart Reardon; 15 Karl Pratt; 16 Paul Johnson; 4 Shontayne Hape; 5 Lesley Vainikolo; 3 Leon Pryce; 7 Paul Deacon; 10 Paul Anderson; 1 Robbie Paul (C); 29 Stuart Fielden; 12 Jamie Peacock; 19 Jamie Langley; 13 Logan Swann. Subs (all used): 8 Joe Vagana; 11 Lee Radford; 32 Andy Smith; 27 Rob Parker.
Tries: Anderson (11), Parker (30), Pratt (54, 65, 67);
Goals: Deacon 5/5.
Rugby Leaguer & League Express Men of the Match: *Saints:* Jason Hooper; *Bulls:* Paul Deacon.
Penalty count: 7-7; **Half-time:** 26-12; **Referee:** Russell Smith (Castleford); **Attendance:** 10,933.

Sunday 30th May 2004

HUDDERSFIELD GIANTS 6 WAKEFIELD TRINITY WILDCATS 38

GIANTS: 1 Paul Reilly; 2 Hefin O'Hare; 3 Stuart Donlan; 4 Julian Bailey; 34 Marcus St Hilaire; 13 Brandon Costin; 9 Paul March; 8 Mick Slicker; 7 Sean Penkywicz; 10 Jim Gannon; 14 Stuart Jones; 12 Ben Roarty; 11 Chris Nero. Subs (all used): 22 Phil Joseph; 16 Iain Morrison; 18 Eorl Crabtree; 25 Darren Fleary (C).
Try: Penkywicz (48); **Goals:** March 1/2.
WILDCATS: 14 Colum Halpenny; 2 Justin Ryder; 1 Jason Demetriou; 4 Sid Domic; 5 Semi Tadulala; 3 Gareth Ellis (C); 7 Ben Jeffries; 8 Darrell Griffin; 9 David March; 10 Michael Korkidas; 11 David Solomona; 13 Jamie Field; 22 Mark Applegarth. Subs (all used): 16 Steve Snitch; 18 Olivier Elima; 24 Michael Wainwright; 19 Rob Spicer.
Tries: J Field (17, 70), Jeffries (25), Demetriou (51, 60), Korkidas (57), Ryder (75); **Goals:** March 5/8.
Rugby Leaguer & League Express Men of the Match: *Giants:* Darren Fleary; *Wildcats:* Gareth Ellis.
Penalty count: 7-5; **Half-time:** 0-12;
Referee: Ian Smith (Oldham); **Attendance:** 4,419.

Monday 31st May 2004

HULL FC 70 WIDNES VIKINGS 4

HULL: 32 Shaun Briscoe; 2 Colin Best; 3 Richie Barnett (C); 4 Michael Eagar; 26 Richie Barnett Jnr; 16 Paul Cooke; 6 Richard Horne; 18 Ewan Dowes; 9 Richard Swain; 10 Paul King; 15 Shayne McMenemy; 17 Chris Chester; 13 Jason Smith. Subs (all used): 14 Kirk Yeaman; 34 Nick Scruton (D); 25 Peter Lupton; 27 Liam Higgins.
Tries: Barnett Jnr (9, 35), Chester (22, 56), Smith (26), McMenemy (32), Briscoe (43, 54), Lupton (50), R Horne (65), Best (72), Yeaman (78); **Goals:** Cooke 11/13.
VIKINGS: 14 Deon Bird; 21 Nicky Royle; 3 Aaron Moule; 4 Adam Hughes; 5 Chris Giles; 6 Jules O'Neill; 20 Stephen Myler; 8 Robert Relf; 18 Simon Finnigan; 10 Julian O'Neill; 12 Andy Hay (C); 15 Troy Wozniak; 13 Daniel Frame. Subs (all used): 16 Andy Hobson; 17 David Mills; 11 Steve McCurrie; 27 Craig Weston (D2).
Try: Finnigan (69). **Goals:** Jules O'Neill 0/1.
Rugby Leaguer & League Express Men of the Match: *Hull:* Richard Horne; *Vikings:* Jules O'Neill.
Penalty count: 9-3; **Half-time:** 30-0; **Referee:** Karl Kirkpatrick (Warrington); **Attendance:** 9,946.

ROUND 13

Friday 4th June 2004

WIGAN WARRIORS 30 ST HELENS 14

WARRIORS: 1 Kris Radlinski; 4 David Hodgson; 33 Gary Connolly; 3 Martin Aspinwall; 2 Brett Dallas; 6 Danny Orr; 7 Adrian Lam; 8 Terry O'Connor; 9 Terry Newton; 10 Craig Smith; 20 Gareth Hock; 13 Andy Farrell (C); 15 Sean O'Loughlin. Subs (all used): 19 Stephen Wild; 12 Danny Tickle; 16 Danny Sculthorpe; 17 Mark Smith.
Tries: Lam (21), Aspinwall (23), Radlinski (34, 58);
Goals: Farrell 5/8, Tickle 2/2.
SAINTS: 1 Paul Wellens; 2 Ade Gardner; 3 Martin Gleeson; 4 Willie Talau; 5 Darren Albert; 6 Jason Hooper; 7 Sean Long; 8 Nick Fozzard; 21 Jon Wilkin; 18 Mark Edmondson; 12 Lee Gilmour; 11 Chris Joynt; 13 Paul Sculthorpe (C). Subs (all used): 23 Maurie Fa'asavalu; 25 Ian Hardman; 20 Ricky Bibey; 10 John Stankevitch.
Tries: Gleeson (66), Sculthorpe (74); **Goals:** Long 3/3.
Rugby Leaguer & League Express Men of the Match: *Warriors:* Adrian Lam; *Saints:* Nick Fozzard.
Penalty count: 15-9; **Half-time:** 20-2;
Referee: Ian Smith (Oldham); **Attendance:** 17,194.

Saturday 5th June 2004

BRADFORD BULLS 12 LEEDS RHINOS 26

BULLS: 6 Michael Withers; 17 Stuart Reardon; 16 Paul Johnson; 4 Shontayne Hape; 5 Lesley Vainikolo; 3 Leon Pryce; 7 Paul Deacon; 8 Joe Vagana; 15 Karl Pratt; 29 Stuart Fielden; 12 Jamie Peacock; 13 Logan Swann; 11 Lee Radford. Subs (all used): 1 Robbie Paul (C); 19 Jamie Langley; 10 Paul Anderson; 27 Rob Parker.
Tries: Vainikolo (46), Reardon (65); **Goals:** Deacon 2/3.
RHINOS: 21 Richard Mathers; 18 Mark Calderwood; 3 Chris McKenna; 4 Keith Senior; 22 Marcus Bai; 6 Danny McGuire; 14 Andrew Dunemann; 8 Ryan Bailey; 9 Matt Diskin; 17 Wayne McDonald; 11 David Furner; 15 Chris Feather; 13 Kevin Sinfield (C). Subs (all used): 16 Willie Poching; 10 Barrie McDermott; 29 Ali Lauitiiti; 7 Rob Burrow.
Tries: Senior (19), Poching (22), Lauitiiti (39), Dunemann (53); **Goals:** Sinfield 5/7.
Rugby Leaguer & League Express Men of the Match: *Bulls:* Lesley Vainikolo; *Rhinos:* Andrew Dunemann.
Penalty count: 6-6; **Half-time:** 2-18; **Referee:** Karl Kirkpatrick (Warrington); **Attendance:** 23,375.

Sunday 6th June 2004

SALFORD CITY REDS 18 HUDDERSFIELD GIANTS 25

CITY REDS: 2 Joel Caine; 4 Andy Kirk; 3 Stuart Littler; 33 Kevin McGuinness; 5 Anthony Stewart; 6 Cliff Beverley; 7 Gavin Clinch; 19 Neil Baynes; 9 Malcolm Alker (C); 14 Paul Highton; 8 Andy Coley; 10 Sean Rutgerson; 13 Chris Charles. Subs (all used): 15 Karl Fitzpatrick; 12 Andy Johnson; 18 Mark Shipway; 17 Gareth Haggerty.
Tries: Haggerty (25), McGuinness (51), Johnson (58);
Goals: Charles 3/4.
Sin bin: Alker (48) - fighting.
GIANTS: 1 Paul Reilly; 2 Hefin O'Hare; 24 James Evans (D); 4 Julian Bailey; 34 Marcus St Hilaire; 9 Paul March; 7 Sean Penkywicz; 25 Darren Fleary (C); 22 Phil Joseph; 12 Ben Roarty; 14 Stuart Jones; 17 Paul Smith; 11 Chris Nero. Subs (all used): 6 Stanley Gene; 10 Jim Gannon; 8 Mick Slicker; 3 Stuart Donlan.
Tries: Smith (2), O'Hare (7), Gene (32), Penkywicz (36);
Goals: March 4/5; **Field goal:** March.
Sin bin: Roarty (48) - fighting.
Rugby Leaguer & League Express Men of the Match: *City Reds:* Kevin McGuinness; *Giants:* Stanley Gene.
Penalty count: 11-10; **Half-time:** 8-20; **Referee:** Richard Silverwood (Dewsbury); **Attendance:** 3,271.

WIDNES VIKINGS 31 WARRINGTON WOLVES 10

VIKINGS: 14 Deon Bird; 21 Nicky Royle; 3 Aaron Moule; 4 Adam Hughes; 5 Chris Giles; 6 Jules O'Neill; 20 Stephen Myler; 8 Robert Relf; 9 Shane Millard; 10 Julian O'Neill; 12 Andy Hay (C); 15 Troy Wozniak; 18 Simon Finnigan. Subs (all used): 17 David Mills; 23 Steve Rowlands; 11 Steve McCurrie; 13 Daniel Frame.
Tries: Hughes (14, 80), Royle (45), Millard (58), Hay (74); **Goals:** Jules O'Neill 4/6, Myler 1/1;
Field goal: Jules O'Neill.
WOLVES: 1 Daryl Cardiss; 5 Graham Appo; 3 Brent Grose; 4 Ben Westwood; 20 Dean Gaskell; 6 Lee Briers (C); 7 Nathan Wood; 16 Paul Wood; 9 Jon Clarke; 10 Mark Hilton; 18 Paul Noone; 23 Mike Wainwright; 13 Mike Forshaw. Subs (all used): 14 Mark Gleeson; 22 Danny Lima; 8 Chris Leikvoll; 12 Ian Sibbit.
Try: Forshaw (35); **Goals:** Briers 3/3.
Rugby Leaguer & League Express Men of the Match: *Vikings:* Shane Millard; *Wolves:* Daryl Cardiss.
Penalty count: 10-9; **Half-time:** 8-10;
Referee: Robert Connolly (Wigan); **Attendance:** 8,315.

CASTLEFORD TIGERS 18 HULL FC 52

TIGERS: 16 Jon Hepworth; 5 Darren Rogers; 3 Paul Mellor; 20 Tom Saxton; 2 Waine Pryce; 32 Motu Tony (D); 31 Luke Robinson; 8 Craig Greenhill; 9 Wayne Godwin; 10 Andy Lynch; 12 Sean Ryan; 11 Lee Harland; 13 Ryan Hudson (C). Subs (all used): 14 Ryan Clayton; 6 Sean Rudder; 15 Nathan Sykes; 22 Byron Smith.
Tries: Clayton (53), Rudder (75), Mellor (79);
Goals: Hepworth 2/2, Godwin 1/1.
HULL: 32 Shaun Briscoe; 2 Colin Best; 14 Kirk Yeaman; 4 Michael Eagar; 5 Gareth Raynor; 16 Paul Cooke; 6 Richard Horne; 10 Paul King; 9 Richard Swain; 18 Ewan Dowes; 15 Shayne McMenemy; 17 Chris Chester; 13 Jason Smith (C). Subs (all used): 30 Richard Whiting; 23 Paul McNicholas; 25 Peter Lupton; 34 Nick Scruton.
Tries: R Horne (1), Smith (14), King (17), Best (26), Raynor (29, 68, 73), Yeaman (44, 47), Whiting (57);
Goals: Cooke 5/9, Whiting 1/1.
Rugby Leaguer & League Express Men of the Match: *Tigers:* Jon Hepworth; *Hull:* Gareth Raynor.
Penalty count: 3-6; **Half-time:** 0-24;
Referee: Ashley Klein (London); **Attendance:** 8,084.

WAKEFIELD TRINITY WILDCATS 48 LONDON BRONCOS 18

WILDCATS: 14 Colum Halpenny; 2 Justin Ryder; 1 Jason Demetriou; 4 Sid Domic; 5 Semi Tadulala; 3 Gareth Ellis (C); 7 Ben Jeffries; 8 Darrell Griffin; 9 David March; 10 Michael Korkidas; 11 David Solomona; 13 Jamie Field; 22 Mark Applegarth. Subs (all used): 16 Steve Snitch; 18 Olivier Elima; 24 Michael Wainwright; 19 Rob Spicer.
Tries: Solomona (3, 28, 61, 79), Elima (34), March (55), Domic (70), Jeffries (73); **Goals:** March 8/12.
BRONCOS: 2 Jon Wells; 5 John Kirkpatrick; 21 Rob Jackson; 4 Mark O'Halloran; 23 Lee Greenwood; 7 Dennis Moran; 22 Lee Sanderson; 31 Richard Moore (D2); 9 Neil Budworth; 12 Steele Retchless; 17 Tom Haughey; 14 Andrew Brocklehurst; 13 Jim Dymock (C). Subs (all used): 10 Steve Trindall; 15 Mitchell Stringer; 30 Liam Botham; 19 David Highton.
Tries: Sanderson (15), Budworth (41), Botham (47);
Goals: Sanderson 3/4.
Rugby Leaguer & League Express Men of the Match: *Wildcats:* David Solomona; *Broncos:* Jim Dymock.
Penalty count: 13-4; **Half-time:** 14-8; **Referee:** Ronnie Laughton (Barnsley); **Attendance:** 3,104.

ROUND 14

Friday 11th June 2004

LEEDS RHINOS 48 WIDNES VIKINGS 24

RHINOS: 21 Richard Mathers; 18 Mark Calderwood; 2 Francis Cummins; 4 Keith Senior (C); 22 Marcus Bai; 6 Danny McGuire; 7 Rob Burrow; 17 Wayne McDonald; 9 Matt Diskin; 10 Barrie McDermott; 29 Ali Lauitiiti; 16 Willie Poching; 11 David Furner. Subs (all used): 8 Ryan Bailey; 20 Jamie Jones-Buchanan; 19 Danny Ward; 15 Chris Feather.
Tries: Calderwood (4, 19), McGuire (31, 35, 59, 66, 72), Lauitiiti (39), Burrow (53); **Goals:** Furner 5/8, Burrow 1/1.
VIKINGS: 14 Deon Bird; 21 Nicky Royle; 3 Aaron Moule; 4 Adam Hughes; 5 Chris Giles; 18 Simon Finnigan; 20 Stephen Myler; 17 David Mills; 9 Shane Millard; 10 Julian O'Neill; 15 Troy Wozniak; 12 Andy Hay (C); 13 Daniel Frame. Subs (all used): 16 Andy Hobson; 11 Steve McCurrie; 27 Craig Weston; 23 Steve Rowlands.
Tries: Finnigan (1), Royle (27), Giles (51, 61);
Goals: Myler 4/5.
Rugby Leaguer & League Express Men of the Match: *Rhinos:* Danny McGuire; *Vikings:* Stephen Myler.
Penalty count: 11-11; **Half time:** 26-12;
Referee: Ian Smith (Oldham); **Attendance:** 13,419.

ST HELENS 52 CASTLEFORD TIGERS 8

SAINTS: 1 Paul Wellens; 5 Darren Albert; 3 Martin Gleeson; 4 Willie Talau; 2 Ade Gardner; 6 Jason Hooper; 7 Sean Long; 8 Nick Fozzard; 9 Keiron Cunningham; 16 Keith Mason; 21 Jon Wilkin; 10 John Stankevitch; 13 Paul Sculthorpe (C). Subs (all used): 18 Mark Edmondson; 23 Maurie Fa'asavalu; 11 Chris Joynt; 25 Ian Hardman.
Tries: Hooper (3), Albert (21, 24), Wellens (41, 56), Long (54), Joynt (62, 76), Sculthorpe (66);
Goals: Long 6/7, Sculthorpe 2/2.
TIGERS: 16 Jon Hepworth; 2 Waine Pryce; 20 Tom Saxton; 5 Darren Rogers; 3 Paul Mellor; 24 Andy Kain; 31 Luke Robinson; 8 Craig Greenhill; 9 Wayne Godwin; 10 Andy Lynch; 12 Sean Ryan; 14 Ryan Clayton; 13 Ryan Hudson (C). Subs (all used): 15 Nathan Sykes; 22 Byron Smith; 6 Sean Rudder; 32 Motu Tony.
Try: Hudson (19); **Goals:** Godwin 2/2.
Rugby Leaguer & League Express Men of the Match: *Saints:* Paul Wellens; *Tigers:* Ryan Hudson.
Penalty count: 7-8; **Half-time:** 18-8; **Referee:** Karl Kirkpatrick (Warrington); **Attendance:** 8,397.

Saturday 12th June 2004

WARRINGTON WOLVES 42 LONDON BRONCOS 12

WOLVES: 1 Daryl Cardiss; 5 Graham Appo; 3 Brent Grose; 4 Ben Westwood; 20 Dean Gaskell; 6 Lee Briers (C); 7 Nathan Wood; 22 Danny Lima; 9 Jon Clarke; 10 Mark Hilton; 15 Jerome Guisset; 23 Mike Wainwright; 18 Paul Noone. Subs (all used): 19 Gary Hulse; 14 Mark Gleeson; 17 Warren Stevens; 8 Chris Leikvoll.
Tries: Appo (5), N Wood (11), Noone (31, 79), Westwood (60, 66), Grose (68);
Goals: Briers 7/7, Noone 0/1.
BRONCOS: 2 Jon Wells; 5 John Kirkpatrick; 1 Paul Sykes; 4 Mark O'Halloran; 23 Lee Greenwood; 13 Jim Dymock (C); 7 Dennis Moran; 10 Steve Trindall; 9 Neil Budworth; 15 Mitchell Stringer; 12 Steele Retchless; 14 Andrew Brocklehurst; 30 Liam Botham. Subs (all used): 16 Joe Mbu; 19 David Highton; 22 Lee Sanderson; 31 Richard Moore.
Tries: Moran (47), O'Halloran (70); **Goals:** Sykes 2/2.
Sin bin: Kirkpatrick (76) - holding down.
Rugby Leaguer & League Express Men of the Match:
Wolves: Mark Gleeson; *Broncos:* Dennis Moran.
Penalty count: 7-5; **Half-time:** 20-0;
Referee: Russell Smith (Castleford); **Attendance:** 7,123.

Sunday 13th June 2004

SALFORD CITY REDS 28 BRADFORD BULLS 35

CITY REDS: 1 Jason Flowers; 2 Joel Caine; 3 Stuart Littler; 5 Anthony Stewart; 27 Nathan McAvoy; 6 Cliff Beverley; 7 Gavin Clinch; 19 Neil Baynes; 9 Malcolm Alker (C); 10 Sean Rutgerson; 11 Simon Baldwin; 8 Andy Coley; 13 Chris Charles. Subs (all used): 15 Karl Fitzpatrick; 16 Martin Moana; 12 Andy Johnson; 17 Gareth Haggerty.
Tries: Alker (8), Beverley (32), Caine (61), Coley (74);
Goals: Charles 6/6.
BULLS: 17 Stuart Reardon; 32 Andy Smith; 16 Paul Johnson; 4 Shontayne Hape; 5 Lesley Vainikolo; 6 Michael Withers; 1 Robbie Paul (C); 8 Joe Vagana; 24 Aaron Smith; 29 Stuart Fielden; 12 Jamie Peacock; 13 Logan Swann; 11 Lee Radford. Subs (all used): 26 Chris Bridge; 19 Jamie Langley; 27 Rob Parker; 10 Paul Anderson.
Tries: Hape (16), Johnson (20, 44), Vainikolo (46, 71), Bridge (56); **Goals:** Withers 1/2, Bridge 4/4;
Field goal: Withers.
Rugby Leaguer & League Express Men of the Match:
City Reds: Andy Coley; *Bulls:* Chris Bridge.
Penalty count: 4-8; **Half-time:** 16-10; **Referee:** Ronnie Laughton (Barnsley); **Attendance:** 5,006.

WIGAN WARRIORS 40 HUDDERSFIELD GIANTS 18

WARRIORS: 1 Kris Radlinski; 4 David Hodgson; 19 Stephen Wild; 33 Gary Connolly; 2 Brett Dallas; 6 Danny Orr; 7 Adrian Lam; 8 Terry O'Connor; 9 Terry Newton; 10 Craig Smith; 12 Danny Tickle; 13 Andy Farrell (C); 15 Sean O'Loughlin. Subs (all used): 11 Mick Cassidy; 20 Gareth Hock; 16 Danny Sculthorpe; 17 Mark Smith.
Tries: Farrell (7), Radlinski (17, 66), Dallas (24, 31), Sculthorpe (59), Orr (68); **Goals:** Farrell 6/7.
On report: O'Connor (12) - high tackle.
GIANTS: 3 Stuart Donlan; 2 Hefin O'Hare; 34 Marcus St Hilaire; 24 James Evans; 21 Paul White; 6 Stanley Gene; 9 Paul March; 25 Darren Fleary (C); 7 Sean Penkywicz; 10 Jim Gannon; 14 Stuart Jones; 12 Ben Roarty; 11 Chris Nero. Subs (all used): 8 Mick Slicker; 18 Eorl Crabtree; 20 Jon Grayshon; 22 Phil Joseph.
Tries: Slicker (37), Evans (48), Nero (52);
Goals: White 3/4.
On report: Roarty (28) - punching;
Gene (57) - stamping.
Rugby Leaguer & League Express Men of the Match:
Warriors: Adrian Lam; *Giants:* Paul White.
Penalty count: 6-5; **Half-time:** 22-8;
Referee: Steve Ganson (St Helens); **Attendance:** 9,162.

HULL FC 28 WAKEFIELD TRINITY WILDCATS 24

HULL: 32 Shaun Briscoe; 2 Colin Best; 30 Richard Whiting; 14 Kirk Yeaman; 5 Gareth Raynor; 6 Richard Horne; 16 Paul Cooke; 18 Ewan Dowes; 9 Richard Swain; 23 Paul McNicholas; 15 Shayne McMenemy; 17 Chris Chester; 13 Jason Smith (C). Subs: 26 Richie Barnett Jnr (not used); 10 Paul King; 25 Peter Lupton; 34 Nick Scruton.
Tries: Yeaman (11, 71), Raynor (20, 61), King (43), Best (48); **Goals:** Cooke 2/7.
WILDCATS: 14 Colum Halpenny; 2 Justin Ryder; 1 Jason Demetriou; 4 Sid Domic; 5 Semi Tadulala; 3 Gareth Ellis (C); 7 Ben Jeffries; 10 Michael Korkidas; 9 David March; 8 Darrell Griffin; 11 David Solomona; 13 Jamie Field; 22 Mark Applegarth. Subs (all used): 16 Steve Snitch; 19 Rob Spicer; 18 Olivier Elima; 24 Michael Wainwright.
Tries: Jeffries (52), Korkidas (57), Wainwright (68), Ryder (80); **Goals:** March 4/4.
Rugby Leaguer & League Express Men of the Match:
Hull: Kirk Yeaman; *Wildcats:* Gareth Ellis.
Penalty count: 9-9; **Half-time:** 8-0;
Referee: Robert Connolly (Wigan); **Attendance:** 9,928.

ROUND 15

Friday 18th June 2004

WIDNES VIKINGS 12 ST HELENS 40

VIKINGS: 14 Deon Bird; 23 Steve Rowlands; 3 Aaron Moule; 27 Craig Weston; 5 Chris Giles; 18 Simon Finnigan; 6 Jules O'Neill; 8 Robert Relf; 9 Shane Millard; 10 Julian O'Neill; 12 Andy Hay (C); 15 Troy Wozniak; 13 Daniel Frame. Subs (all used): 20 Stephen Myler; 16 Andy Hobson; 11 Steve McCurrie; 17 David Mills.
Tries: Rowlands (38), Moule (55); **Goals:** Jules O'Neill 2/2.
On report: Weston (49) - high tackle on Stankevitch.
SAINTS: 5 Darren Albert; 25 Ian Hardman; 12 Lee Gilmour; 4 Willie Talau; 2 Ade Gardner; 6 Jason Hooper; 1 Paul Wellens; 8 Nick Fozzard; 9 Keiron Cunningham; 16 Keith Mason; 11 Chris Joynt; 21 Jon Wilkin; 13 Paul Sculthorpe (C). Subs (all used): 18 Mark Edmondson; 22 Dom Feaunati; 10 John Stankevitch; 23 Maurie Fa'asavalu.
Tries: Gilmour (16), Albert (19), Cunningham (28), Hardman (39), Mason (52), Sculthorpe (69), Wilkin (75);
Goals: Sculthorpe 6/8.
Rugby Leaguer & League Express Men of the Match:
Vikings: Aaron Moule; *Saints:* Paul Sculthorpe.
Penalty count: 6-11; **Half-time:** 6-22;
Referee: Russell Smith (Castleford); **Attendance:** 7,482.

Saturday 19th June 2004

WIGAN WARRIORS 26 LEEDS RHINOS 22

WARRIORS: 1 Kris Radlinski; 4 David Hodgson; 3 Martin Aspinwall; 33 Gary Connolly; 2 Brett Dallas; 6 Danny Orr; 7 Adrian Lam; 8 Terry O'Connor; 9 Terry Newton; 10 Craig Smith; 12 Danny Tickle; 13 Andy Farrell (C); 15 Sean O'Loughlin. Subs: 16 Danny Sculthorpe; 17 Mark Smith; 19 Stephen Wild (not used); 20 Gareth Hock.
Tries: Radlinski (5), Newton (14), Hock (43), O'Loughlin (48); **Goals:** Farrell 4/4, Tickle 1/2.
On report: Aspinwall (73) - high tackle on McGuire.
RHINOS: 21 Richard Mathers; 2 Francis Cummins; 5 Chev Walker; 4 Keith Senior; 22 Marcus Bai; 6 Danny McGuire; 14 Andrew Dunemann; 8 Ryan Bailey; 9 Matt Diskin; 17 Wayne McDonald; 11 David Furner; 29 Ali Lauitiiti; 13 Kevin Sinfield (C). Subs (all used): 7 Rob Burrow; 16 Willie Poching; 19 Danny Ward; 20 Jamie Jones-Buchanan.
Tries: Bai (11), Lauitiiti (25), Jones-Buchanan (57);
Goals: Sinfield 5/6, Burrow 0/1.
Rugby Leaguer & League Express Men of the Match:
Warriors: Terry Newton; *Rhinos:* Matt Diskin.
Penalty count: 10-12; **Half-time:** 12-12; **Referee:** Richard Silverwood (Dewsbury); **Attendance:** 14,140.

Sunday 20th June 2004

LONDON BRONCOS 26 HULL FC 42

BRONCOS: 1 Paul Sykes; 23 Lee Greenwood; 21 Rob Jackson; 4 Mark O'Halloran; 5 John Kirkpatrick; 29 Steve Thomas; 7 Dennis Moran; 10 Steve Trindall; 9 Neil Budworth; 31 Richard Moore; 30 Liam Botham; 14 Andrew Brocklehurst; 12 Steele Retchless (C). Subs (all used): 15 Mitchell Stringer; 16 Joe Mbu; 17 Tom Haughey; 19 David Highton.
Tries: Botham (11), Jackson (30, 78), O'Halloran (45), Mbu (72); **Goals:** Sykes 3/5.
HULL: 32 Shaun Briscoe; 2 Colin Best; 14 Kirk Yeaman; 30 Richard Whiting; 5 Gareth Raynor; 16 Paul Cooke; 6 Richard Horne; 10 Paul King; 9 Richard Swain; 18 Ewan Dowes; 23 Paul McNicholas; 15 Shane McMenemy; 13 Jason Smith (C). Subs (all used): 25 Peter Lupton; 19 Alex Wilkinson; 27 Liam Higgins; 34 Nick Scruton.
Tries: Briscoe (19), Whiting (21, 57), McNicholas (34), Best (42), R Horne (53), Raynor (64), Lupton (70);
Goals: Cooke 4/8, Whiting 1/1.
Rugby Leaguer & League Express Men of the Match:
Broncos: Steele Retchless; *Hull:* Richard Horne.
Penalty count: 6-5; **Half-time:** 12-16;
Referee: Ian Smith (Oldham);
Attendance: 3,589 *(at Welford Road, Leicester).*

CASTLEFORD TIGERS 10 WARRINGTON WOLVES 32

TIGERS: 16 Jon Hepworth; 3 Paul Mellor; 32 Motu Tony; 20 Tom Saxton; 2 Waine Pryce; 6 Sean Rudder; 31 Luke Robinson; 8 Craig Greenhill; 9 Wayne Godwin; 10 Andy Lynch; 12 Sean Ryan; 23 Michael Smith; 13 Ryan Hudson (C). Subs (all used): 17 Paul Jackson; 21 Richard Blakeway; 1 Damian Gibson; 5 Darren Rogers.
Tries: Robinson (6, 67); **Goals:** Godwin 1/2.
Sin bin: Godwin (40) - fighting.
WOLVES: 1 Daryl Cardiss; 5 Graham Appo; 3 Brent Grose; 4 Ben Westwood; 20 Dean Gaskell; 9 Jon Clarke; 7 Nathan Wood (C); 22 Danny Lima; 18 Paul Noone; 10 Mark Hilton; 15 Jerome Guisset; 12 Ian Sibbit; 23 Mike Wainwright. Subs (all used): 19 Gary Hulse; 14 Mark Gleeson; 17 Warren Stevens; 8 Chris Leikvoll.
Tries: Westwood (20, 24, 55), Gaskell (48), Grose (72), N Wood (78); **Goals:** Noone 3/5, Appo 1/1.
Sin bin: Hilton (40) - fighting.
Rugby Leaguer & League Express Men of the Match:
Tigers: Wayne Godwin; *Wolves:* Nathan Wood.
Penalty count: 8-4; **Half-time:** 4-10;
Referee: Ashley Klein (London); **Attendance:** 6,111.

WAKEFIELD TRINITY WILDCATS 21
SALFORD CITY REDS 20

WILDCATS: 14 Colum Halpenny; 2 Justin Ryder; 1 Jason Demetriou; 4 Sid Domic; 5 Semi Tadulala; 3 Gareth Ellis (C); 7 Ben Jeffries; 8 Darrell Griffin; 9 David March; 10 Michael Korkidas; 11 David Solomona; 13 Jamie Field; 22 Mark Applegarth. Subs (all used): 16 Steve Snitch; 18 Olivier Elima; 19 Rob Spicer; 24 Michael Wainwright.
Tries: Ryder (4), Domic (45, 48), Ellis (56);
Goals: March 2/5; **Field goal:** Jeffries.
CITY REDS: 2 Joel Caine; 27 Nathan McAvoy; 3 Stuart Littler; 33 Kevin McGuinness; 5 Anthony Stewart; 6 Cliff Beverley; 7 Gavin Clinch; 19 Neil Baynes; 9 Malcolm Alker (C); 10 Sean Rutgerson; 11 Simon Baldwin; 8 Andy Coley; 13 Chris Charles. Subs (all used): 1 Jason Flowers; 14 Paul Highton; 12 Andy Johnson; 18 Mark Shipway.
Tries: Littler (16), Beverley (24), Coley (72);
Goals: Charles 4/5.
Rugby Leaguer & League Express Men of the Match:
Wildcats: David Solomona; *City Reds:* Stuart Littler.
Penalty count: 11-7; **Half-time:** 6-12;
Referee: Steve Ganson (St Helens); **Attendance:** 3,426.

BRADFORD BULLS 40 HUDDERSFIELD GIANTS 12

BULLS: 6 Michael Withers; 17 Stuart Reardon; 16 Paul Johnson; 4 Shontayne Hape; 32 Andy Smith; 3 Leon Pryce; 7 Paul Deacon; 8 Joe Vagana; 1 Robbie Paul (C); 29 Stuart Fielden; 13 Logan Swann; 12 Jamie Peacock; 11 Lee Radford. Subs (all used): 26 Chris Bridge; 19 Jamie Langley; 27 Rob Parker; 10 Paul Anderson.
Tries: Hape (19, 77), Swann (25), Fielden (50), Reardon (76); **Goals:** Deacon 10/10.
Sin bin: Fielden (59) - fighting.
GIANTS: 3 Stuart Donlan; 2 Hefin O'Hare; 34 Marcus St Hilaire; 24 James Evans; 21 Paul White; 6 Stanley Gene; 7 Sean Penkywicz; 25 Darren Fleary (C); 22 Phil Joseph; 10 Jim Gannon; 14 Stuart Jones; 12 Ben Roarty; 11 Chris Nero. Subs (all used): 27 Bolouagi Fagborun (D); 18 Eorl Crabtree; 26 Jason Southwell (D); 1 Paul Reilly.
Tries: Evans (54), White (63); **Goals:** White 2/2.
Sin bin: Gannon (59) - fighting; Donlan (75) - professional foul; Roarty (80) - off the ball tackle.
Rugby Leaguer & League Express Men of the Match:
Bulls: Stuart Fielden; *Giants:* Stanley Gene.
Penalty count: 13-9; **Half-time:** 18-2; **Referee:** Karl Kirkpatrick (Warrington); **Attendance:** 11,069.

ROUND 16

Friday 25th June 2004

LEEDS RHINOS 28 HULL FC 24

RHINOS: 21 Richard Mathers; 2 Francis Cummins; 5 Chev Walker; 4 Keith Senior; 22 Marcus Bai; 14 Andrew Dunemann; 7 Rob Burrow; 17 Wayne McDonald; 9 Matt Diskin; 8 Ryan Bailey; 29 Ali Lauitiiti; 15 Chris Feather; 13 Kevin Sinfield (C). Subs (all used): 20 Jamie Jones-Buchanan; 10 Barrie McDermott; 3 Chris McKenna; 19 Danny Ward.
Tries: Lauitiiti (17, 66), Senior (31), Walker (43), Jones-Buchanan (68); **Goals:** Sinfield 1/3, Burrow 3/3.
Sin bin: Mathers (35) - professional foul.
HULL: 32 Shaun Briscoe; 2 Colin Best; 30 Richard Whiting; 4 Michael Eagar; 5 Gareth Raynor; 16 Paul Cooke (C); 6 Richard Horne; 10 Paul King; 9 Richard Swain; 18 Ewan Dowes; 23 Paul McNicholas; 15 Shayne McMenemy; 25 Peter Lupton. Subs (all used): 34 Nick Scruton; 29 Andy Bailey; 27 Liam Higgins; 19 Alex Wilkinson.
Tries: R Horne (35, pen), Scruton (39), Briscoe (59), Best (79); **Goals:** Whiting 0/1, Cooke 4/5.
Rugby Leaguer & League Express Men of the Match:
Rhinos: Chev Walker; *Hull:* Richard Swain.
Penalty count: 6-5; **Half-time:** 10-12;
Referee: Steve Ganson (St Helens); **Attendance:** 15,153.

WIGAN WARRIORS 28
WAKEFIELD TRINITY WILDCATS 22

WARRIORS: 1 Kris Radlinski (C); 4 David Hodgson; 19 Stephen Wild; 3 Martin Aspinwall; 2 Brett Dallas; 6 Danny Orr; 7 Adrian Lam; 8 Terry O'Connor; 9 Terry Newton; 10 Craig Smith; 12 Danny Tickle; 20 Gareth Hock; 15 Sean O'Loughlin. Subs (all used): 11 Mick Cassidy; 17 Mark Smith; 23 Harrison Hansen (D); 25 Liam Colbon.
Tries: Radlinski (3, 30), Orr (18), Dallas (22), Hodgson (63); **Goals:** Tickle 4/5.
WILDCATS: 14 Colum Halpenny; 24 Michael Wainwright; 1 Jason Demetriou; 4 Sid Domic; 5 Semi Tadulala; 3 Gareth Ellis (C); 7 Ben Jeffries; 13 Jamie Field; 9 David March; 10 Michael Korkidas; 11 David Solomona; 22 Mark Applegarth; 19 Rob Spicer. Subs (all used): 12 Dallas Hood; 16 Steve Snitch; 17 Paul Handforth; 26 Matthew Blake.
Tries: Domic (43), J Field (46), March (57), Solomona (73); **Goals:** March 3/5.
Sin bin: Halpenny (16) - holding down.
Rugby Leaguer & League Express Men of the Match:
Warriors: Kris Radlinski; *Wildcats:* Rob Spicer.
Penalty count: 5-11; **Half-time:** 22-2;
Referee: Russell Smith (Castleford); **Attendance:** 9,274.

Saturday 26th June 2004

ST HELENS 28 WARRINGTON WOLVES 8

SAINTS: 1 Paul Wellens; 22 Dom Feaunati; 5 Darren Albert; 4 Willie Talau; 2 Ade Gardner; 13 Paul Sculthorpe (C); 6 Jason Hooper; 16 Keith Mason; 9 Keiron Cunningham; 18 Mark Edmondson; 11 Chris Joynt; 21 Jon Wilkin; 12 Lee Gilmour. Subs (all used): 8 Nick Fozzard; 10 John Stankevitch; 23 Maurie Fa'asavalu; 25 Ian Hardman.
Tries: Albert (49), Hardman (59), Talau (61), Fa'asavalu (64), Hooper (69); **Goals:** Sculthorpe 4/6.
WOLVES: 1 Daryl Cardiss; 4 Ben Westwood; 3 Brent Grose; 12 Ian Sibbit; 20 Dean Gaskell; 5 Graham Appo; 7 Nathan Wood (C); 22 Danny Lima; 14 Mark Gleeson; 8 Chris Leikvoll; 18 Paul Noone; 23 Mike Wainwright; 13 Mike Forshaw. Subs (all used): 10 Mark Hilton; 11 Darren Burns; 15 Jerome Guisset; 16 Paul Wood.
Try: N Wood (38); **Goals:** Noone 1/1, Cardiss 1/2.
Rugby Leaguer & League Express Men of the Match:
Saints: Jon Wilkin; *Wolves:* Mark Gleeson.
Penalty count: 7-11; **Half-time:** 2-6; **Referee:** Richard Silverwood (Dewsbury); **Attendance:** 8,783.

Sunday 27th June 2004

SALFORD CITY REDS 30 CASTLEFORD TIGERS 14

CITY REDS: 1 Jason Flowers; 2 Joel Caine; 3 Stuart Littler; 33 Kevin McGuinness; 5 Anthony Stewart; 6 Cliff Beverley; 7 Gavin Clinch; 19 Neil Baynes; 9 Malcolm Alker (C); 14 Paul Highton; 8 Andy Coley; 10 Sean Rutgerson; 13 Chris Charles. Subs (all used): 17 Gareth Haggerty; 15 Karl Fitzpatrick; 12 Andy Johnson; 18 Mark Shipway.
Tries: Coley (23), Alker (33, 73), Charles (52), Shipway (67); **Goals:** Charles 5/5.
TIGERS: 16 Jon Hepworth; 2 Waine Pryce; 32 Motu Tony; 1 Damian Gibson; 3 Paul Mellor; 33 Brad Davis (D2); 31 Luke Robinson; 17 Paul Jackson; 9 Wayne Godwin; 10 Andy Lynch; 23 Michael Smith; 12 Sean Ryan; 13 Ryan Hudson (C). Subs (all used): 22 Byron Smith; 14 Ryan Clayton; 20 Tom Saxton; 28 Dean Ripley.
Tries: Mellor (5), Lynch (18); **Goals:** Godwin 3/3.
On report: Hepworth (60) - use of the elbow.
Rugby Leaguer & League Express Men of the Match: *City Reds:* Gareth Haggerty; *Tigers:* Paul Mellor.
Penalty count: 5-9; **Half-time:** 12-14; **Referee:** Karl Kirkpatrick (Warrington); **Attendance:** 3,313.

HUDDERSFIELD GIANTS 35 LONDON BRONCOS 22

GIANTS: 1 Paul Reilly; 3 Stuart Donlan; 13 Brandon Costin; 11 Chris Nero; 34 Marcus St Hilaire; 24 James Evans; 6 Stanley Gene; 18 Eorl Crabtree; 7 Sean Penkywicz; 10 Jim Gannon; 17 Paul Smith; 12 Ben Roarty; 14 Stuart Jones. Subs (all used): 2 Hefin O'Hare; 21 Paul White; 25 Darren Fleary (C) (not used); 19 Matt Whitaker.
Tries: Evans (16, 24), Nero (38), St Hilaire (50, 79), Gene (72); **Goals:** Costin 4/6, White 1/1;
Field goal: Costin.
BRONCOS: 1 Paul Sykes; 5 John Kirkpatrick; 21 Rob Jackson; 4 Mark O'Halloran; 23 Lee Greenwood; 29 Steve Thomas; 7 Dennis Moran; 10 Steve Trindall; 9 Neil Budworth; 31 Richard Moore; 30 Liam Botham; 14 Andrew Brocklehurst; 12 Steele Retchless (C). Subs (all used): 8 Francis Stephenson; 15 Mitchell Stringer; 16 Joe Mbu; 19 David Highton.
Tries: Kirkpatrick (8), Moran (10), Sykes (34);
Goals: Sykes 5/5, Botham 0/1.
Rugby Leaguer & League Express Men of the Match: *Giants:* Brandon Costin; *Broncos:* Paul Sykes.
Penalty count: 9-7; **Half-time:** 14-20; **Referee:** Ronnie Laughton (Barnsley); **Attendance:** 3,009.

BRADFORD BULLS 38 WIDNES VIKINGS 30

BULLS: 17 Stuart Reardon; 15 Karl Pratt; 16 Paul Johnson; 4 Shontayne Hape; 32 Andy Smith; 3 Leon Pryce; 7 Paul Deacon; 8 Joe Vagana; 1 Robbie Paul (C); 29 Stuart Fielden; 13 Logan Swann; 12 Jamie Peacock; 11 Lee Radford. Subs (all used): 26 Chris Bridge; 19 Jamie Langley; 27 Rob Parker; 10 Paul Anderson.
Tries: Johnson (4), Pratt (9, 13), Andy Smith (20), L Pryce (23), Paul (46, 48); **Goals:** Deacon 3/4, Bridge 2/2.
VIKINGS: 23 Steve Rowlands; 21 Nicky Royle; 3 Aaron Moule; 4 Adam Hughes; 5 Chris Giles; 6 Jules O'Neill; 20 Stephen Myler; 17 David Mills; 9 Shane Millard; 10 Julian O'Neill; 12 Andy Hay (C); 15 Troy Wozniak; 13 Daniel Frame. Subs (all used): 27 Craig Weston; 16 Andy Hobson; 18 Simon Finnigan; 28 Bruce Johnson (D).
Tries: Finnigan (32), Moule (61), Hay (64), Frame (67), Jules O'Neill (72); **Goals:** Jules O'Neill 5/5.
Rugby Leaguer & League Express Men of the Match: *Bulls:* Robbie Paul; *Vikings:* Jules O'Neill.
Penalty count: 5-5; **Half-time:** 26-6;
Referee: Robert Connolly (Wigan); **Attendance:** 11,137.

ROUND 17

Sunday 28th March 2004 (re-scheduled from Sunday 4th July due to Challenge Cup)

LONDON BRONCOS 35 SALFORD CITY REDS 30

BRONCOS: 1 Paul Sykes; 23 Lee Greenwood; 4 Mark O'Halloran; 24 Andy McNally; 17 Tom Haughey; 13 Jim Dymock (C); 7 Dennis Moran; 15 Mitchell Stringer; 9 Neil Budworth; 10 Steve Trindall; 12 Steele Retchless; 18 Andrew Hart; 14 Andrew Brocklehurst. Subs (all used): 19 David Highton (D); 25 Scott Murrell (D); 26 Jonny Williams (D); 16 Joe Mbu.
Tries: Dymock (3), Moran (11), Greenwood (20), Budworth (60), O'Halloran (62), Murrell (74);
Goals: Sykes 5/6; **Field goal:** Dymock.
CITY REDS: 2 Joel Caine; 4 Andy Kirk; 20 Scott Naylor; 3 Stuart Littler; 5 Anthony Stewart; 15 Karl Fitzpatrick; 7 Gavin Clinch; 8 Andy Coley; 9 Malcolm Alker (C); 10 Sean Rutgerson; 11 Simon Baldwin; 18 Mark Shipway; 16 Martin Moana. Subs (all used): 6 Cliff Beverley; 12 Andy Johnson; 14 Paul Highton; 17 Gareth Haggerty.
Tries: Baldwin (26), Stewart (31), Beverley (35, 69), Haggerty (41), Moana (78);
Goals: Fitzpatrick 2/5, Caine 1/1.
Rugby Leaguer & League Express Men of the Match: *Broncos:* Steele Retchless; *City Reds:* Cliff Beverley.
Penalty count: 6-6; **Half-time:** 16-14;
Referee: Ian Smith (Oldham); **Attendance:** 2,198.

Friday 2nd July 2004

WAKEFIELD TRINITY WILDCATS 41 ST HELENS 22

WILDCATS: 14 Colum Halpenny; 24 Michael Wainwright; 1 Jason Demetriou; 4 Sid Domic; 5 Semi Tadulala; 3 Gareth Ellis (C); 7 Ben Jeffries; 13 Jamie Field; 9 David March; 10 Michael Korkidas; 11 David Solomona; 22 Mark Applegarth; 19 Rob Spicer. Subs (all used): 16 Steve Snitch; 17 Paul Handforth; 25 Albert Talipeau; 26 Matthew Blake.
Tries: Domic (8), Jeffries (12, 37), Wainwright (15), Snitch (54), Tadulala (58);
Goals: March 7/7, Handforth 1/1; **Field goal:** Jeffries.
SAINTS: 5 Darren Albert; 2 Ade Gardner; 12 Lee Gilmour; 4 Willie Talau; 25 Ian Hardman; 6 Jason Hooper; 1 Paul Wellens; 8 Nick Fozzard; 21 Jon Wilkin; 16 Keith Mason; 11 Chris Joynt; 18 Mark Edmondson; 13 Paul Sculthorpe (C). Subs (all used): 22 Dom Feaunati; 23 Maurie Fa'asavalu; 24 James Graham; 26 James Roby.
Tries: Sculthorpe (3), Gardner (50), J Roby (62), Talau (79); **Goals:** Sculthorpe 3/4.
Rugby Leaguer & League Express Men of the Match: *Wildcats:* Ben Jeffries; *Saints:* Paul Wellens.
Penalty count: 9-7; **Half-time:** 24-6; **Referee:** Karl Kirkpatrick (Warrington); **Attendance:** 4,151.

Saturday 3rd July 2004

WIDNES VIKINGS 8 WIGAN WARRIORS 56

VIKINGS: 27 Craig Weston; 21 Nicky Royle; 3 Aaron Moule; 4 Adam Hughes; 5 Chris Giles; 6 Jules O'Neill; 7 Willie Peters (D); 17 David Mills; 9 Shane Millard; 10 Julian O'Neill; 12 Andy Hay (C); 11 Steve McCurrie; 13 Daniel Frame. Subs (all used): 14 Deon Bird; 16 Andy Hobson; 15 Troy Wozniak; 28 Bruce Johnson.
Tries: Millard (20), Jules O'Neill (53);
Goals: Jules O'Neill 0/2.
WARRIORS: 33 Gary Connolly; 2 Brett Dallas; 3 Martin Aspinwall; 19 Stephen Wild; 25 Liam Colbon; 6 Danny Orr; 7 Adrian Lam; 12 Danny Tickle; 9 Terry Newton; 10 Craig Smith; 13 Andy Farrell (C); 20 Gareth Hock; 15 Sean O'Loughlin. Subs: 17 Mark Smith; 11 Mick Cassidy; 4 David Hodgson (not used); 23 Harrison Hansen.
Tries: Lam (10), Newton (13, 26, 65, 72), Wild (16, 23), O'Loughlin (69), M Smith (76);
Goals: Farrell 5/5, Tickle 1/1, Orr 4/4.
Rugby Leaguer & League Express Men of the Match: *Vikings:* Aaron Moule; *Warriors:* Terry Newton.
Penalty count: 5-8; **Half-time:** 4-30;
Referee: Ian Smith (Oldham); **Attendance:** 6,012.

Sunday 4th July 2004

WARRINGTON WOLVES 22 LEEDS RHINOS 38

WOLVES: 1 Daryl Cardiss; 5 Graham Appo; 3 Brent Grose; 4 Ben Westwood; 12 Ian Sibbit; 6 Lee Briers (C); 7 Nathan Wood; 8 Chris Leikvoll; 9 Jon Clarke; 10 Mark Hilton; 18 Paul Noone; 23 Mike Wainwright; 13 Mike Forshaw. Subs (all used): 11 Darren Burns; 16 Paul Wood; 15 Jerome Guisset; 22 Danny Lima.
Tries: Grose (17), N Wood (24), Burns (63), Noone (73);
Goals: Briers 3/4.
Sin bin: Wainwright (31) - obstruction.
RHINOS: 21 Richard Mathers; 2 Francis Cummins; 5 Chev Walker; 4 Keith Senior; 22 Marcus Bai; 14 Andrew Dunemann; 7 Rob Burrow; 17 Wayne McDonald; 9 Matt Diskin; 19 Danny Ward; 29 Ali Lauitiiti; 20 Jamie Jones-Buchanan; 13 Kevin Sinfield (C). Subs (all used): 6 Danny McGuire; 3 Chris McKenna; 16 Willie Poching; 10 Barrie McDermott.
Tries: Bai (9), Walker (13), Diskin (36), Cummins (38), McGuire (52, 78), McKenna (57);
Goals: Sinfield 4/6, Burrow 1/1.
On report: Dunemann (48) – high tackle on N Wood.
Rugby Leaguer & League Express Men of the Match: *Wolves:* Mark Hilton; *Rhinos:* Barrie McDermott.
Penalty count: 8-6; **Half-time:** 10-22; **Referee:** Russell Smith (Castleford); **Attendance:** 10,404.

HULL FC 40 HUDDERSFIELD GIANTS 12

HULL: 32 Shaun Briscoe; 2 Colin Best; 4 Michael Eagar; 30 Richard Whiting; 5 Gareth Raynor; 16 Paul Cooke; 6 Richard Horne; 18 Ewan Dowes; 9 Richard Swain; 10 Paul King; 15 Shayne McMenemy; 14 Kirk Yeaman; 25 Peter Lupton. Subs (all used): 13 Jason Smith (C); 23 Paul McNicholas; 29 Andy Bailey; 34 Nick Scruton.
Tries: Raynor (8), Eagar (14), Lupton (26), Dowes (53), R Horne (64), Whiting (69), Briscoe (76); **Goals:** Cooke 6/9.
GIANTS: 1 Paul Reilly; 3 Stuart Donlan; 24 James Evans; 11 Chris Nero; 34 Marcus St Hilaire; 6 Stanley Gene; 7 Sean Penkywicz; 18 Eorl Crabtree; 21 Paul White; 10 Jim Gannon; 17 Paul Smith; 14 Stuart Jones; 12 Ben Roarty. Subs (all used): 2 Hefin O'Hare; 22 Phil Joseph; 25 Darren Fleary (C); 19 Matt Whitaker.
Tries: White (6), Gannon (57); **Goals:** White 2/3.
Rugby Leaguer & League Express Men of the Match: *Hull:* Gareth Raynor; *Giants:* Paul Reilly.
Penalty count: 9-6; **Half-time:** 18-4;
Referee: Ashley Klein (London); **Attendance:** 9,706.

CASTLEFORD TIGERS 12 BRADFORD BULLS 60

TIGERS: 16 Jon Hepworth; 1 Damian Gibson; 32 Motu Tony; 3 Paul Mellor; 5 Darren Rogers; 33 Brad Davis (C); 31 Luke Robinson; 17 Paul Jackson; 9 Wayne Godwin; 10 Andy Lynch; 12 Sean Ryan; 23 Michael Smith; 14 Ryan Clayton. Subs (all used): 8 Craig Greenhill; 15 Nathan Sykes; 22 Byron Smith; 34 Kevin King (D).
Tries: Godwin (22), Rogers (65); **Goals:** Godwin 2/2.
Sin bin: Gibson (71) - holding down.
BULLS: 17 Stuart Reardon; 15 Karl Pratt; 16 Paul Johnson; 4 Shontayne Hape; 5 Lesley Vainikolo; 3 Leon Pryce; 7 Paul Deacon; 8 Joe Vagana; 1 Robbie Paul (C); 29 Stuart Fielden; 13 Logan Swann; 12 Jamie Peacock; 11 Lee Radford. Subs (all used): 32 Andy Smith; 19 Jamie Langley; 27 Rob Parker; 10 Paul Anderson.
Tries: L Pryce (3), Vainikolo (13, 16, 63, 78), Hape (29, 36), Deacon (48), Peacock (57), Parker (72);
Goals: Deacon 10/11.
Rugby Leaguer & League Express Men of the Match: *Tigers:* Michael Smith; *Bulls:* Lesley Vainikolo.
Penalty count: 7-7; **Half-time:** 6-32; **Referee:** Ronnie Laughton (Barnsley); **Attendance:** 6,606.

ROUND 18

Friday 9th July 2004

LEEDS RHINOS 46 CASTLEFORD TIGERS 14

RHINOS: 2 Francis Cummins; 18 Mark Calderwood; 5 Chev Walker; 4 Keith Senior; 22 Marcus Bai; 6 Danny McGuire; 14 Andrew Dunemann; 15 Chris Feather; 9 Matt Diskin; 10 Barrie McDermott; 3 Chris McKenna; 12 Matt Adamson; 13 Kevin Sinfield (C). Subs (all used): 19 Danny Ward; 20 Jamie Jones-Buchanan; 7 Rob Burrow; 16 Willie Poching.
Tries: Bai (2), McGuire (9, 28), Diskin (26), Poching (41, 51, 72); Calderwood (47); **Goals:** Sinfield 7/8.
On report: Senior (65) - alleged kicking.
TIGERS: 1 Damian Gibson; 28 Dean Ripley; 32 Motu Tony; 5 Darren Rogers; 3 Paul Mellor; 33 Brad Davis; 31 Luke Robinson; 8 Craig Greenhill; 13 Ryan Hudson (C); 15 Nathan Sykes; 23 Michael Smith; 11 Lee Harland; 14 Ryan Clayton. Subs (all used): 9 Wayne Godwin; 10 Andy Lynch; 16 Jon Hepworth; 20 Tom Saxton.
Tries: Lynch (23), Greenhill (58), Tony (75);
Goals: Godwin 1/2, Davis 0/1.
Rugby Leaguer & League Express Men of the Match: *Rhinos:* Kevin Sinfield; *Tigers:* Luke Robinson.
Penalty count: 10-9; **Half-time:** 24-4;
Referee: Ashley Klein (London); **Attendance:** 13,922.

Saturday 10th July 2004

ST HELENS 30 LONDON BRONCOS 10

SAINTS: 1 Paul Wellens; 2 Ade Gardner; 5 Darren Albert; 4 Willie Talau; 22 Dom Feaunati; 6 Jason Hooper; 26 James Roby; 20 Ricky Bibey; 9 Keiron Cunningham; 16 Keith Mason; 12 Lee Gilmour; 10 John Stankevitch; 13 Paul Sculthorpe (C). Subs (all used): 15 Mike Bennett; 21 Jon Wilkin; 23 Maurie Fa'asavalu; 18 Mark Edmondson.
Tries: Stankevitch (11), J Roby (15), Feaunati (23), Wellens (69), Mason (71); **Goals:** Sculthorpe 5/6.
BRONCOS: 1 Paul Sykes; 23 Lee Greenwood; 3 Nigel Roy; 21 Rob Jackson; 2 Jon Wells; 4 Mark O'Halloran; 7 Dennis Moran; 10 Steve Trindall; 9 Neil Budworth; 15 Mitchell Stringer; 14 Andrew Brocklehurst; 30 Liam Botham; 12 Steele Retchless (C). Subs(all used): 19 David Highton; 31 Richard Moore; 5 John Kirkpatrick; 8 Francis Stephenson.
Tries: Jackson (17), Wells (50); **Goals:** Sykes 1/2.
Rugby Leaguer & League Express Men of the Match: *Saints:* Paul Wellens; *Broncos:* Dennis Moran.
Penalty count: 6-3; **Half-time:** 16-6;
Referee: Robert Connolly (Wigan); **Attendance:** 6,828.

Sunday 11th July 2004

SALFORD CITY REDS 16 WIGAN WARRIORS 32

CITY REDS: 2 Joel Caine; 4 Andy Kirk; 3 Stuart Littler; 33 Kevin McGuinness; 5 Anthony Stewart; 6 Cliff Beverley; 7 Gavin Clinch; 14 Paul Highton; 9 Malcolm Alker (C); 10 Sean Rutgerson; 18 Mark Shipway; 8 Andy Coley; 13 Chris Charles. Subs (all used): 15 Karl Fitzpatrick; 30 Tim Jonkers (D); 12 Andy Johnson; 17 Gareth Haggerty.
Tries: Kirk (22), Johnson (49), Stewart (65);
Goals: Charles 2/4.
WARRIORS: 1 Kris Radlinski (C); 2 Brett Dallas; 33 Gary Connolly; 3 Martin Aspinwall; 5 Brian Carney; 6 Danny Orr; 7 Adrian Lam; 10 Craig Smith; 17 Mark Smith; 11 Mick Cassidy; 19 Stephen Wild; 12 Danny Tickle; 15 Sean O'Loughlin. Subs (all used): 30 Bryn Hargreaves (D); 23 Harrison Hansen; 4 David Hodgson; 24 Bob Beswick.
Tries: Dallas (6, 26), Tickle (30), Aspinwall (38), Hansen (57), O'Loughlin (68); **Goals:** Tickle 4/6.
Rugby Leaguer & League Express Men of the Match: *City Reds:* Malcolm Alker; *Warriors:* Danny Orr.
Penalty count: 7-8; **Half-time:** 6-22;
Referee: Russell Smith (Castleford); **Attendance:** 6,037.

WARRINGTON WOLVES 18 HULL FC 38

WOLVES: 19 Gary Hulse; 12 Ian Sibbit; 3 Brent Grose; 4 Ben Westwood; 20 Dean Gaskell; 6 Lee Briers (C); 5 Graham Appo; 8 Chris Leikvoll; 9 Jon Clarke; 10 Mark Hilton; 18 Paul Noone; 23 Mike Wainwright; 13 Mike Forshaw. Subs (all used): 11 Darren Burns; 15 Jerome Guisset; 16 Paul Wood; 22 Danny Lima.
Tries: Leikvoll (9), Grose (74), Wainwright (77);
Goals: Briers 3/3.
HULL: 32 Shaun Briscoe; 2 Colin Best; 30 Richard Whiting; 14 Kirk Yeaman; 5 Gareth Raynor; 16 Paul Cooke; 6 Richard Horne; 18 Ewan Dowes; 9 Richard Swain; 10 Paul King; 23 Paul McNicholas; 15 Shayne McMenemy; 13 Jason Smith (C). Subs (all used): 26 Richie Barnett Jnr; 29 Andy Bailey; 24 Graeme Horne; 34 Nick Scruton.
Tries: Barnett Jnr (15), Raynor (19), Whiting (24), Scruton (47), Briscoe (66), Smith (80); **Goals:** Cooke 7/7.
Rugby Leaguer & League Express Men of the Match: *Wolves:* Gary Hulse; *Hull:* Richard Whiting.
Penalty count: 2-4; **Half-time:** 6-20; **Referee:** Ronnie Laughton (Barnsley); **Attendance:** 8,166.

HUDDERSFIELD GIANTS 26 WIDNES VIKINGS 20

GIANTS: 1 Paul Reilly; 2 Hefin O'Hare; 11 Chris Nero; 24 James Evans; 3 Stuart Donlan; 13 Brandon Costin; 6 Stanley Gene; 25 Darren Fleary (C); 22 Phil Joseph; 18

Eorl Crabtree; 14 Stuart Jones; 17 Paul Smith; 12 Ben Roarty. Subs (all used): 20 Jon Grayshon; 7 Sean Penkywicz; 10 Jim Gannon; 21 Paul White.
Tries: Jones (21, 53), Evans (30), Costin (38);
Goals: Costin 5/6.
Sin bin: Penkywicz (66) - punching.
VIKINGS: 6 Jules O'Neill; 1 Paul Atcheson; 4 Adam Hughes; 14 Deon Bird; 5 Chris Giles; 20 Stephen Myler; 7 Willie Peters; 10 Julian O'Neill; 9 Shane Millard (C); 16 Andy Hobson; 15 Troy Wozniak; 11 Steve McCurrie; 13 Daniel Frame. Subs (all used): 17 David Mills; 27 Craig Weston; 28 Bruce Johnson; 18 Simon Finnigan.
Tries: Peters (13), Hughes (75), Giles (78);
Goals: Jules O'Neill 4/5.
Rugby Leaguer & League Express Men of the Match: *Giants:* Stuart Jones; *Vikings:* Jules O'Neill.
Penalty count: 7-8; **Half-time:** 20-10; **Referee:** Karl Kirkpatrick (Warrington); **Attendance:** 3,566.

BRADFORD BULLS 36
WAKEFIELD TRINITY WILDCATS 26

BULLS: 17 Stuart Reardon; 15 Karl Pratt; 19 Jamie Langley; 4 Shontayne Hape; 5 Lesley Vainikolo; 3 Leon Pryce; 7 Paul Deacon; 8 Joe Vagana; 1 Robbie Paul (C); 29 Stuart Fielden; 13 Logan Swann; 12 Jamie Peacock; 11 Lee Radford. Subs: 18 Iestyn Harris (D); 32 Andy Smith (not used); 27 Rob Parker; 10 Paul Anderson.
Tries: Peacock (3), Reardon (12), Deacon (32), Vainikolo (45, 79), Parker (47); **Goals:** Deacon 6/8.
Dismissal: Pratt (25) - fighting
Sin bin: L Pryce (25) - fighting.
On report: Brawl (25).
WILDCATS: 14 Colum Halpenny; 24 Michael Wainwright; 1 Jason Demetriou; 4 Sid Domic; 5 Semi Tadulala; 3 Gareth Ellis (C); 7 Ben Jeffries; 13 Jamie Field; 9 David March; 10 Michael Korkidas; 11 David Solomona; 22 Mark Applegarth; 19 Rob Spicer. Subs (all used): 16 Steve Snitch; 17 Paul Handforth; 2 Justin Ryder; 18 Olivier Elima.
Tries: Elima (20), J Field (37), Solomona (52), Ellis (66), Spicer (71); **Goals:** March 2/4, Handforth 1/1.
Sin bin: Tadulala (25) - fighting.
On report: Brawl (25).
Rugby Leaguer & League Express Men of the Match: *Bulls:* Stuart Reardon; *Wildcats:* Ben Jeffries.
Penalty count: 8-8; **Half-time:** 20-12;
Referee: Ian Smith (Oldham); **Attendance:** 12,670.

ROUND 19

Friday 16th July 2004

WIGAN WARRIORS 32 BRADFORD BULLS 16

WARRIORS: 1 Kris Radlinski; 5 Brian Carney; 19 Stephen Wild; 3 Martin Aspinwall; 2 Brett Dallas; 6 Danny Orr; 7 Adrian Lam; 10 Craig Smith; 9 Terry Newton; 13 Andy Farrell (C); 12 Danny Tickle; 20 Gareth Hock; 15 Sean O'Loughlin. Subs (all used): 11 Mick Cassidy; 17 Mark Smith; 23 Harrison Hansen; 33 Gary Connolly.
Tries: Farrell (4), Dallas (8), Cassidy (61), Radlinski (72), C Smith (76); **Goals:** Farrell 6/6.
BULLS: 17 Stuart Reardon; 32 Andy Smith; 3 Leon Pryce; 4 Shontayne Hape; 5 Lesley Vainikolo; 18 Iestyn Harris; 7 Paul Deacon; 8 Joe Vagana; 1 Robbie Paul (C); 29 Stuart Fielden; 12 Jamie Peacock; 13 Logan Swann; 11 Lee Radford. Subs (all used): 24 Aaron Smith; 19 Jamie Langley; 27 Rob Parker; 10 Paul Anderson.
Tries: Peacock (15), Swann (30), Hape (47);
Goals: Deacon 2/3.
Rugby Leaguer & League Express Men of the Match: *Warriors:* Andy Farrell; *Bulls:* Stuart Fielden.
Penalty count: 5-6; **Half-time:** 14-12; **Referee:** Russell Smith (Castleford); **Attendance:** 15,102.

Saturday 17th July 2004

HULL FC 34 ST HELENS 6

HULL: 32 Shaun Briscoe; 2 Colin Best; 30 Richard Whiting; 14 Kirk Yeaman; 5 Gareth Raynor; 16 Paul Cooke; 6 Richard Horne; 18 Ewan Dowes; 9 Richard Swain; 10 Paul King; 15 Shayne McMenemy; 23 Paul McNicholas; 13 Jason Smith (C). Subs (all used): 24 Graeme Horne; 26 Richie Barnett Jnr; 29 Andy Bailey; 34 Nick Scruton.
Tries: R Horne (11), Briscoe (14), Yeaman (37, 66), Best (47), Raynor (59); **Goals:** Cooke 5/8.
SAINTS: 1 Paul Wellens; 2 Ade Gardner; 12 Lee Gilmour; 4 Willie Talau; 5 Darren Albert; 6 Jason Hooper; 26 James Roby; 8 Nick Fozzard; 9 Keiron Cunningham; 16 Keith Mason; 21 Jon Wilkin; 10 John Stankevitch; 13 Paul Sculthorpe (C). Subs (all used): 20 Ricky Bibey; 25 Ian Hardman; 23 Maurie Fa'asavalu; 18 Mark Edmondson.
Try: Gilmour (77); **Goals:** Hooper 1/1.
Rugby Leaguer & League Express Men of the Match: *Hull:* Paul King; *Saints:* Lee Gilmour.
Penalty count: 7-6; **Half-time:** 18-0; **Referee:** Karl Kirkpatrick (Warrington); **Attendance:** 12,949.

Sunday 18th July 2004

LONDON BRONCOS 36 LEEDS RHINOS 36

BRONCOS: 1 Paul Sykes; 23 Lee Greenwood; 21 Rob Jackson; 3 Nigel Roy; 5 John Kirkpatrick; 4 Mark O'Halloran; 7 Dennis Moran; 10 Steve Trindall; 9 Neil Budworth; 31 Richard Moore; 30 Liam Botham; 18 Andrew Hart; 12 Steele Retchless (C). Subs (all used): 8 Francis Stephenson; 15 Mitchell Stringer; 19 David Highton; 6 Rob Purdham.
Tries: Roy (5), Greenwood (28, 80), Kirkpatrick (33), O'Halloran (37), Moran (61), Botham (69);
Goals: Sykes 0/2, Botham 4/5.
RHINOS: 21 Richard Mathers; 2 Francis Cummins; 5 Chev Walker; 3 Chris McKenna; 22 Marcus Bai; 6 Danny McGuire; 14 Andrew Dunemann; 8 Ryan Bailey; 7 Rob Burrow; 10 Barrie McDermott; 29 Ali Lauitiiti; 12 Matt Adamson; 13 Kevin Sinfield (C). Subs (all used): 19 Danny Ward; 17 Wayne McDonald; 20 Jamie Jones-Buchanan; 30 Carl Ablett (D).
Tries: McGuire (8), Bai (15, 18), McDonald (29), Sinfield (44), McKenna (46); **Goals:** Sinfield 6/6.
Rugby Leaguer & League Express Men of the Match: *Broncos:* Dennis Moran; *Rhinos:* Marcus Bai.
Penalty count: 8-8; **Half-time:** 18-24;
Referee: Ian Smith (Oldham); **Attendance:** 5,058.

WIDNES VIKINGS 14 SALFORD CITY REDS 15

VIKINGS: 1 Paul Atcheson; 27 Craig Weston; 14 Deon Bird; 4 Adam Hughes; 5 Chris Giles; 6 Jules O'Neill; 7 Willie Peters; 16 Andy Hobson; 9 Shane Millard; 10 Julian O'Neill; 12 Andy Hay (C); 11 Steve McCurrie; 18 Simon Finnigan. Subs (all used): 17 David Mills; 20 Stephen Myler; 15 Troy Wozniak; 13 Daniel Frame.
Tries: Myler (42), Frame (78);
Goals: Jules O'Neill 2/3, Myler 1/1.
Sin bin: Millard (28) - fighting; Finnigan (28) - fighting.
CITY REDS: 1 Jason Flowers; 4 Andy Kirk; 5 Anthony Stewart; 33 Kevin McGuinness; 2 Joel Caine; 6 Cliff Beverley; 7 Gavin Clinch; 14 Paul Highton; 9 Malcolm Alker (C); 19 Neil Baynes; 8 Andy Coley; 18 Mark Shipway; 13 Chris Charles. Subs (all used): 10 Sean Rutgerson; 15 Karl Fitzpatrick; 30 Tim Jonkers; 17 Gareth Haggerty.
Tries: Caine (15), Kirk (72); **Goals:** Charles 3/3;
Field goal: Clinch.
Sin bin: Haggerty (28) - fighting.
Rugby Leaguer & League Express Men of the Match: *Vikings:* Shane Millard; *City Reds:* Andy Coley.
Penalty count: 5-6; **Half-time:** 4-6; **Referee:** Ronnie Laughton (Barnsley); **Attendance:** 5,573.

CASTLEFORD TIGERS 24 HUDDERSFIELD GIANTS 20

TIGERS: 1 Damian Gibson; 2 Waine Pryce; 32 Motu Tony; 5 Darren Rogers; 3 Paul Mellor; 33 Brad Davis; 31 Luke Robinson; 8 Craig Greenhill; 9 Wayne Godwin; 10 Andy Lynch; 11 Lee Harland; 23 Michael Smith; 13 Ryan Hudson (C). Subs (all used): 35 Mark Tookey (D); 15 Nathan Sykes; 14 Ryan Clayton; 16 Jon Hepworth.
Tries: Mellor (38), Robinson (42), Hudson (50), Rogers (70); **Goals:** Robinson 3/4, Godwin 1/1, Hepworth 0/1.
GIANTS: 1 Paul Reilly; 2 Hefin O'Hare; 11 Chris Nero; 24 James Evans; 3 Stuart Donlan; 13 Brandon Costin; 9 Paul March; 25 Darren Fleary (C); 7 Sean Penkywicz; 10 Jim Gannon; 14 Stuart Jones; 17 Paul Smith; 12 Ben Roarty. Subs (all used): 20 Jon Grayshon; 8 Mick Slicker; 18 Eorl Crabtree; 21 Paul White.
Tries: Evans (5), Penkywicz (28), O'Hare (66);
Goals: Costin 4/6.
Sin bin: Nero (16) - holding down.
On report: Roarty (17) - alleged butting; Reilly (78) - kicking.
Rugby Leaguer & League Express Men of the Match: *Tigers:* Luke Robinson; *Giants:* Brandon Costin.
Penalty count: 15-9; **Half-time:** 6-16;
Referee: Steve Ganson (St Helens); **Attendance:** 5,321.

WAKEFIELD TRINITY WILDCATS 32
WARRINGTON WOLVES 26

WILDCATS: 14 Colum Halpenny; 2 Justin Ryder; 1 Jason Demetriou; 4 Sid Domic; 24 Michael Wainwright; 3 Gareth Ellis (C); 7 Ben Jeffries; 13 Jamie Field; 9 David March; 10 Michael Korkidas; 11 David Solomona; 22 Mark Applegarth; 19 Rob Spicer. Subs (all used): 15 David Wrench; 16 Steve Snitch; 17 Paul Handforth; 23 Duncan MacGillivray (D).
Tries: Jeffries (1), Wainwright (10), Domic (27), Solomona (57), Ryder (78);
Goals: March 6/9, Handforth 0/1.
Sin bin: Ryder (64) - holding down.
WOLVES: 3 Brent Grose; 20 Dean Gaskell; 9 Jon Clarke; 11 Darren Burns; 4 Ben Westwood; 6 Lee Briers (C); 7 Nathan Wood; 8 Chris Leikvoll; 19 Gary Hulse; 10 Mark Hilton; 16 Paul Wood; 23 Mike Wainwright; 13 Mike Forshaw. Subs (all used): 14 Mark Gleeson; 22 Danny Lima; 15 Jerome Guisset; 17 Warren Stevens.
Tries: P Wood (16), Forshaw (33), Lima (48), Burns (65, 71); **Goals:** Briers 3/5.
Rugby Leaguer & League Express Men of the Match: *Wildcats:* Ben Jeffries; *Wolves:* Darren Burns.
Penalty count: 10-7; **Half time:** 20-12;
Referee: Ashley Klein (London); **Attendance:** 4,309.

ROUND 20

Friday 23rd July 2004

LEEDS RHINOS 70 ST HELENS 0

RHINOS: 21 Richard Mathers; 2 Francis Cummins; 5 Chev Walker; 4 Keith Senior; 22 Marcus Bai; 13 Kevin Sinfield (C); 6 Danny McGuire; 19 Danny Ward; 9 Matt Diskin; 8 Ryan Bailey; 3 Chris McKenna; 29 Ali Lauitiiti; 16 Willie Poching. Subs (all used): 10 Barrie McDermott; 12 Matt Adamson; 7 Rob Burrow; 17 Wayne McDonald.
Tries: Bai (2, 26, 61), McGuire (4, 7, 13), McDonald (36, 45), Diskin (47), Mathers (50), Lauitiiti (63), Senior (75);
Goals: Sinfield 11/13.
SAINTS: 1 Paul Wellens; 2 Ade Gardner; 5 Darren Albert; 12 Lee Gilmour; 22 Dom Feaunati; 4 Willie Talau; 6 Jason Hooper; 8 Nick Fozzard; 9 Keiron Cunningham (C); 16 Keith Mason; 18 Mark Edmondson; 23 Maurie Fa'asavalu; 21 Jon Wilkin. Subs: 15 Mike Bennett; 20 Ricky Bibey; 26 James Roby; 25 Ian Hardman (not used).
On report: Bibey (24) – high tackle on Adamson.
Rugby Leaguer & League Express Men of the Match: *Rhinos:* Matt Diskin; *Saints:* Jason Hooper.
Penalty count: 8-3; **Half-time:** 38-0; **Referee:** Karl Kirkpatrick (Warrington); **Attendance:** 16,635.

WIGAN WARRIORS 48 CASTLEFORD TIGERS 18

WARRIORS: 33 Gary Connolly; 5 Brian Carney; 19 Stephen Wild; 3 Martin Aspinwall; 2 Brett Dallas; 15 Sean O'Loughlin; 14 Luke Robinson; 13 Andy Farrell (C); 9 Terry Newton; 11 Mick Cassidy; 12 Danny Tickle; 20 Gareth Hock; 1 Kris Radlinski. Subs (all used): 4 David Hodgson; 17 Mark Smith; 24 Bob Beswick; 31 Paul Prescott (D).
Tries: Dallas (9, 56, 73, 80), Robinson (12), Aspinwall (18), Newton (42, 59); **Goals:** Farrell 7/7, Tickle 1/1.
TIGERS: 1 Damian Gibson; 36 Matt Gardner (D); 20 Tom Saxton; 5 Darren Rogers; 2 Waine Pryce; 33 Brad Davis; 32 Motu Tony; 15 Nathan Sykes; 16 Jon Hepworth; 10 Andy Lynch; 11 Lee Harland; 23 Michael Smith; 13 Ryan Hudson (C). Subs (all used): 35 Mark Tookey; 14 Ryan Clayton; 22 Byron Smith; 30 Michael Shenton.
Tries: Pryce (6), Lynch (24), Gardner (52), Rogers (65);
Goals: Davis 0/1, Hepworth 1/3.
Rugby Leaguer & League Express Men of the Match: *Warriors:* Terry Newton; *Tigers:* Brad Davis.
Penalty count: 9-4; **Half-time:** 18-10;
Referee: Ian Smith (Oldham); **Attendance:** 10,032.

Saturday 24th July 2004

HUDDERSFIELD GIANTS 18 WARRINGTON WOLVES 34

GIANTS: 1 Paul Reilly; 3 Stuart Donlan; 24 James Evans; 4 Julian Bailey; 34 Marcus St Hilaire; 13 Brandon Costin; 9 Paul March; 25 Darren Fleary (C); 22 Phil Joseph; 18 Eorl Crabtree; 11 Chris Nero; 14 Stuart Jones; 12 Ben Roarty. Subs (all used): 7 Sean Penkywicz; 8 Mick Slicker; 10 Jim Gannon; 17 Paul Smith.
Tries: Donlan (8), Bailey (34), Smith (60);
Goals: Costin 2/4, March 1/1.
WOLVES: 19 Gary Hulse; 20 Dean Gaskell; 11 Darren Burns; 3 Brent Grose; 4 Ben Westwood; 6 Lee Briers (C); 5 Graham Appo; 22 Danny Lima; 9 Jon Clarke; 8 Chris Leikvoll; 23 Mike Wainwright; 16 Paul Wood; 13 Mike Forshaw. Subs (all used): 14 Mark Gleeson; 15 Jerome Guisset; 17 Warren Stevens; 12 Ian Sibbit.
Tries: Gaskell (15), Briers (36, 46), P Wood (44), Gleeson (63), Lima (76); **Goals:** Briers 5/7.
Sin bin: Gaskell (32) - holding down.
Rugby Leaguer & League Express Men of the Match: *Giants:* Paul Reilly; *Wolves:* Lee Briers.
Penalty count: 10-7; **Half-time:** 12-12; **Referee:** Ronnie Laughton (Barnsley); **Attendance:** 4,038.

Sunday 25th July 2004

SALFORD CITY REDS 20 HULL FC 44

CITY REDS: 1 Jason Flowers; 2 Joel Caine; 5 Anthony Stewart; 3 Stuart Littler; 4 Andy Kirk; 33 Kevin McGuinness; 15 Karl Fitzpatrick; 19 Neil Baynes; 9 Malcolm Alker (C); 14 Paul Highton; 8 Andy Coley; 18 Mark Shipway; 13 Chris Charles. Subs (all used): 12 Andy Johnson; 11 Simon Baldwin; 17 Gareth Haggerty; 30 Tim Jonkers.
Tries: Charles (13), Coley (41), Baynes (77);
Goals: Charles 3/3, Caine 1/1.
HULL: 32 Shaun Briscoe; 2 Colin Best; 30 Richard Whiting; 14 Kirk Yeaman; 26 Richie Barnett Jnr; 16 Paul Cooke; 6 Richard Horne; 18 Ewan Dowes; 9 Richard Swain; 10 Paul King; 15 Shayne McMenemy; 23 Paul McNicholas; 13 Jason Smith (C). Subs (all used): 27 Liam Higgins; 29 Andy Bailey; 25 Peter Lupton; 24 Graeme Horne.
Tries: Yeaman (5, 24, 33), Briscoe (16, 80), Barnett Jnr (57, 60), Best (66), R Horne (72); **Goals:** Cooke 4/9.
Rugby Leaguer & League Express Men of the Match: *City Reds:* Kevin McGuinness; *Hull:* Kirk Yeaman.
Penalty count: 7-2; **Half-time:** 8-18;
Referee: Ashley Klein (London); **Attendance:** 3,515.

WIDNES VIKINGS 25
WAKEFIELD TRINITY WILDCATS 24

VIKINGS: 6 Jules O'Neill; 21 Nicky Royle; 14 Deon Bird; 4 Adam Hughes; 5 Chris Giles; 20 Stephen Myler; 7 Willie Peters; 16 Andy Hobson; 9 Shane Millard; 17 David Mills; 13 Daniel Frame; 12 Andy Hay (C); 18 Simon Finnigan. Subs (all used): 1 Paul Atcheson; 11 Steve McCurrie; 15 Troy Wozniak; 30 Gary Middlehurst (D).
Tries: Frame (26, 73), Peters (36), Finnigan (50);
Goals: Myler 4/5; **Field goal:** Peters.
WILDCATS: 14 Colum Halpenny; 2 Justin Ryder; 1 Jason Demetriou; 4 Sid Domic; 24 Michael Wainwright; 6 Jamie Rooney; 7 Ben Jeffries; 13 Jamie Field (C); 9 David March; 10 Michael Korkidas; 11 David Solomona; 22 Mark Applegarth; 19 Rob Spicer. Subs (all used): 15 David Wrench; 16 Steve Snitch; 17 Paul Handforth; 23 Duncan MacGillivray.
Tries: Ryder (18), Rooney (22), Jeffries (30), Domic (62); **Goals:** March 3/4, Rooney 1/1.
Rugby Leaguer & League Express Men of the Match: *Vikings:* Daniel Frame; *Wildcats:* Ben Jeffries.
Penalty count: 8-8; **Half-time:** 12-18;
Referee: Russell Smith (Castleford); **Attendance:** 5,104.

BRADFORD BULLS 44 LONDON BRONCOS 16

BULLS: 17 Stuart Reardon; 32 Andy Smith; 3 Leon Pryce; 4 Shontayne Hape; 5 Lesley Vainikolo; 18 Iestyn Harris; 7 Paul Deacon; 10 Paul Anderson; 1 Robbie Paul

(C); 29 Stuart Fielden; 13 Logan Swann; 12 Jamie Peacock; 11 Lee Radford. Subs (all used): 26 Chris Bridge; 19 Jamie Langley; 8 Joe Vagana; 27 Rob Parker.
Tries: Andy Smith (14), Vainikolo (25, 79), Paul (42), Swann (46), Langley (51), Reardon (63), Fielden (75);
Goals: Deacon 4/6, Harris 2/3.
BRONCOS: 1 Paul Sykes; 2 Jon Wells; 21 Rob Jackson; 3 Nigel Roy; 5 John Kirkpatrick; 6 Rob Purdham; 7 Dennis Moran; 10 Steve Trindall; 9 Neil Budworth; 12 Steele Retchless (C); 30 Liam Botham; 18 Andrew Hart; 4 Mark O'Halloran. Subs (all used): 15 Mitchell Stringer; 19 David Highton; 8 Francis Stephenson; 23 Lee Greenwood.
Tries: Hart (39), Jackson (57), Moran (60);
Goals: Sykes 1/2, Botham 1/1.
Sin bin: Hart (17) - holding down;
Retchless (78) - holding down.
Rugby Leaguer & League Express Men of the Match:
Bulls: Lesley Vainikolo; *Broncos:* Dennis Moran.
Penalty count: 11-5; **Half-time:** 12-4;
Referee: Steve Ganson (St Helens); **Attendance:** 10,283.

ROUND 21

Friday 30th July 2004

ST HELENS 50 HUDDERSFIELD GIANTS 10

SAINTS: 5 Darren Albert; 2 Ade Gardner; 12 Lee Gilmour; 4 Willie Talau; 25 Ian Hardman; 1 Paul Wellens; 26 James Roby; 8 Nick Fozzard; 9 Keiron Cunningham (C); 18 Mark Edmondson; 10 John Stankevitch; 15 Mike Bennett; 6 Jason Hooper. Subs (all used): 16 Keith Mason; 21 Jon Wilkin; 22 Dom Feaunati; 23 Maurie Fa'asavalu.
Tries: Albert (7), Stankevitch (12, 77), Cunningham (20), Mason (28), Talau (38, 64), Hooper (66), Gardner (73);
Goals: Hooper 7/9.
GIANTS: 1 Paul Reilly; 34 Marcus St Hilaire; 4 Julian Bailey; 24 James Evans; 3 Stuart Donlan; 13 Brandon Costin; 9 Paul March; 25 Darren Fleary (C); 22 Phil Joseph; 18 Eorl Crabtree; 17 Paul Smith; 14 Stuart Jones; 12 Ben Roarty. Subs (all used): 7 Sean Penkywicz; 10 Jim Gannon; 16 Iain Morrison; 20 Jon Grayshon.
Tries: Smith (42), St Hilaire (70); **Goals:** Costin 1/2.
Rugby Leaguer & League Express Men of the Match:
Saints: Jason Hooper; *Giants:* Paul March.
Penalty count: 7-10; **Half-time:** 28-0;
Referee: Ashley Klein (London); **Attendance:** 7,218.

Saturday 31st July 2004

CASTLEFORD TIGERS 42 WIDNES VIKINGS 8

TIGERS: 1 Damian Gibson; 20 Tom Saxton; 32 Motu Tony; 5 Darren Rogers; 3 Paul Mellor; 33 Brad Davis; 19 Francis Maloney; 35 Mark Tookey; 9 Wayne Godwin; 10 Andy Lynch; 11 Lee Harland; 23 Michael Smith; 13 Ryan Hudson (C). Subs (all used): 8 Craig Greenhill; 15 Nathan Sykes; 22 Byron Smith; 16 Jon Hepworth.
Tries: Davis (2), Mellor (21, 55), M Smith (26), Hudson (34), Maloney (39), Godwin (65), Rogers (78);
Goals: Godwin 5/8, Maloney 0/1.
VIKINGS: 1 Paul Atcheson; 2 Paul Devlin; 14 Deon Bird; 4 Adam Hughes; 5 Chris Giles; 20 Stephen Myler; 7 Willie Peters; 16 Andy Hobson; 9 Shane Millard; 17 David Mills; 13 Daniel Frame; 12 Andy Hay (C); 18 Simon Finnigan. Subs (all used): 11 Steve McCurrie; 31 Matt Whitaker (D); 15 Troy Wozniak; 30 Gary Middlehurst.
Try: Millard (45); **Goals:** Myler 2/2.
Sin bin: Atcheson (76) – delaying tactics.
Rugby Leaguer & League Express Men of the Match:
Tigers: Brad Davis; *Vikings:* Shane Millard.
Penalty count: 6-4; **Half-time:** 26-2; **Referee:** Karl Kirkpatrick (Warrington); **Attendance:** 5,517.

Sunday 1st August 2004

HULL FC 25 BRADFORD BULLS 14

HULL: 32 Shaun Briscoe; 2 Colin Best; 14 Kirk Yeaman; 30 Richard Whiting; 26 Richie Barnett Jnr; 16 Paul Cooke; 6 Richard Horne; 18 Ewan Dowes; 9 Richard Swain; 10 Paul King; 15 Shayne McMenemy; 23 Paul McNicholas; 13 Jason Smith (C). Subs (all used): 24 Graeme Horne; 25 Peter Lupton; 27 Liam Higgins; 34 Nick Scruton.
Tries: Barnett Jnr (5), Briscoe (48), G Horne (57), Dowes (68); **Goals:** Cooke 4/4; **Field goal:** Whiting.
BULLS: 17 Stuart Reardon; 22 Karl Pratt; 3 Leon Pryce; 4 Shontayne Hape; 5 Lesley Vainikolo; 18 Iestyn Harris; 7 Paul Deacon; 10 Paul Anderson; 1 Robbie Paul (C); 29 Stuart Fielden; 13 Logan Swann; 12 Jamie Peacock; 11 Lee Radford. Subs (all used): 26 Chris Bridge; 19 Jamie Langley; 8 Joe Vagana; 27 Rob Parker.
Tries: Hape (34), Paul (62); **Goals:** Deacon 3/3.
Rugby Leaguer & League Express Men of the Match:
Hull: Paul Cooke; *Bulls:* Stuart Fielden.
Penalty count: 7-9; **Half-time:** 6-8; **Referee:** Russell Smith (Castleford); **Attendance:** 14,124.

LEEDS RHINOS 46 WAKEFIELD TRINITY WILDCATS 28

RHINOS: 21 Richard Mathers; 2 Francis Cummins; 3 Chris McKenna; 4 Keith Senior; 22 Marcus Bai; 6 Danny McGuire; 14 Andrew Dunemann; 19 Danny Ward; 9 Matt Diskin; 8 Ryan Bailey; 16 Willie Poching; 29 Ali Lauitiiti; 13 Kevin Sinfield (C). Subs (all used): 17 Wayne McDonald; 12 Matt Adamson; 7 Rob Burrow; 10 Barrie McDermott.
Tries: Ward (13), Poching (28, 43), McGuire (31), Burrow (45, 73), Senior (57), McKenna (73);
Goals: Sinfield 6/7, Burrow 1/1.
WILDCATS: 21 Mark Field; 2 Justin Ryder; 1 Jason Demetriou; 4 Sid Domic; 24 Michael Wainwright; 6 Jamie Rooney; 7 Ben Jeffries; 26 Matthew Blake; 9 David March; 10 Michael Korkidas; 11 David Solomona; 13 Jamie Field (C); 19 Rob Spicer. Subs (all used): 23 Duncan MacGillivray; 18 Olivier Elima; 17 Paul Handforth; 22 Mark Applegarth.
Tries: Rooney (17), Wainwright (26), Solomona (49), Demetriou (56, 69), Jeffries (79);
Goals: March 1/2, Rooney 1/4.
Rugby Leaguer & League Express Men of the Match:
Rhinos: Richard Mathers; *Wildcats:* David Solomona.
Penalty count: 4-4; **Half-time:** 18-10;
Referee: Steve Ganson (St Helens); **Attendance:** 15,629.

LONDON BRONCOS 22 WIGAN WARRIORS 20

BRONCOS: 2 Jon Wells; 23 Lee Greenwood; 4 Mark O'Halloran; 3 Nigel Roy; 5 John Kirkpatrick; 1 Paul Sykes; 7 Dennis Moran; 31 Richard Moore; 9 Neil Budworth; 8 Francis Stephenson; 12 Steele Retchless (C); 18 Andrew Hart; 6 Rob Purdham. Subs (all used): 10 Steve Trindall; 15 Mitchell Stringer; 19 David Highton; 21 Rob Jackson.
Tries: O'Halloran (27), Trindall (40), Wells (61), Moran (75); **Goals:** Sykes 3/4.
WARRIORS: 1 Kris Radlinski; 2 Brett Dallas; 3 Martin Aspinwall; 33 Gary Connolly; 5 Brian Carney; 15 Sean O'Loughlin; 14 Luke Robinson; 30 Bryn Hargreaves; 9 Terry Newton; 13 Andy Farrell (C); 19 Stephen Wild; 12 Danny Tickle; 20 Gareth Hock. Subs (all used): 31 Paul Prescott; 17 Mark Smith; 4 David Hodgson; 21 Kevin Brown.
Tries: Robinson (24), Radlinski (29), Aspinwall (65);
Goals: Farrell 4/4.
Rugby Leaguer & League Express Men of the Match:
Broncos: Dennis Moran; *Warriors:* Andy Farrell.
Penalty count: 5-4; **Half-time:** 10-12; **Referee:** Ronnie Laughton (Barnsley); **Attendance:** 4,352.

WARRINGTON WOLVES 46 SALFORD CITY REDS 20

WOLVES: 19 Gary Hulse; 4 Ben Westwood; 3 Brent Grose; 11 Darren Burns; 20 Dean Gaskell; 6 Lee Briers (C); 5 Graham Appo; 22 Danny Lima; 9 Jon Clarke; 8 Chris Leikvoll; 16 Paul Wood; 23 Mike Wainwright; 13 Mike Forshaw. Subs (all used): 14 Mark Gleeson; 15 Jerome Guisset; 17 Warren Stevens; 12 Ian Sibbit.
Tries: Hulse (19, 60), Forshaw (26), Burns (28, 38), Westwood (33), Appo (65), Guisset (76);
Goals: Briers 7/8.
Sin bin: Lima (46) - interference.
CITY REDS: 2 Joel Caine; 27 Nathan McAvoy; 5 Anthony Stewart; 3 Stuart Littler; 4 Andy Kirk; 33 Kevin McGuinness; 15 Karl Fitzpatrick; 19 Neil Baynes; 9 Malcolm Alker (C); 14 Paul Highton; 18 Mark Shipway; 8 Andy Coley; 13 Chris Charles. Subs (all used): 12 Andy Johnson; 17 Gareth Haggerty; 30 Tim Jonkers; 10 Sean Rutgerson.
Tries: McGuinness (14), McAvoy (53), Johnson (57), Littler (71); **Goals:** Charles 2/4.
Rugby Leaguer & League Express Men of the Match:
Wolves: Lee Briers; *City Reds:* Kevin McGuinness.
Penalty count: 6-9; **Half-time:** 30-6;
Referee: Ian Smith (Oldham); **Attendance:** 8,641.

ROUND 22

Friday 6th August 2004

WIGAN WARRIORS 13 HULL FC 13

WARRIORS: 1 Kris Radlinski; 4 David Hodgson; 19 Stephen Wild; 3 Martin Aspinwall; 2 Brett Dallas; 15 Sean O'Loughlin; 14 Luke Robinson; 13 Andy Farrell (C); 9 Terry Newton; 10 Craig Smith; 11 Mick Cassidy; 12 Danny Tickle; 20 Gareth Hock. Subs: 17 Mark Smith; 24 Bob Beswick; 30 Bryn Hargreaves (not used); 33 Gary Connolly.
Tries: Wild (7), Tickle (30); **Goals:** Farrell 2/2;
Field goal: Farrell.
HULL: 32 Shaun Briscoe; 2 Colin Best; 30 Richard Whiting; 14 Kirk Yeaman; 26 Richie Barnett Jnr; 16 Paul Cooke; 6 Richard Horne; 10 Paul King; 9 Richard Swain; 18 Ewan Dowes; 23 Paul McNicholas; 15 Shayne McMenemy; 13 Jason Smith (C). Subs (all used): 25 Peter Lupton; 24 Graeme Horne; 34 Nick Scruton; 11 Richard Fletcher.
Tries: Briscoe (35), R Horne (63);
Goals: Whiting 1/1, Cooke 1/1; **Field goal:** R Horne.
Rugby Leaguer & League Express Men of the Match:
Warriors: Sean O'Loughlin; *Hull:* Jason Smith.
Penalty count: 5-3; **Half-time:** 12-6;
Referee: Steve Ganson (St Helens); **Attendance:** 12,074.

Sunday 8th August 2004

SALFORD CITY REDS 30 ST HELENS 20

CITY REDS: 15 Karl Fitzpatrick; 2 Joel Caine; 3 Stuart Littler; 12 Andy Johnson; 5 Anthony Stewart; 33 Kevin McGuinness; 7 Gavin Clinch; 19 Neil Baynes; 9 Malcolm Alker (C); 10 Sean Rutgerson; 8 Andy Coley; 18 Mark Shipway; 13 Chris Charles. Subs (all used): 30 Tim Jonkers; 17 Gareth Haggerty; 11 Simon Baldwin; 23 Andrew Brocklehurst (D).
Tries: Alker (8, 78), Caine (11), Littler (23), Baynes (47);
Goals: Charles 5/6.
SAINTS: 1 Paul Wellens; 2 Ade Gardner; 5 Darren Albert; 4 Willie Talau; 25 Ian Hardman; 6 Jason Hooper; 26 James Roby; 8 Nick Fozzard; 9 Keiron Cunningham (C); 18 Mark Edmondson; 15 Mike Bennett; 10 John Stankevitch; 11 Chris Joynt. Subs (all used): 21 Jon Wilkin; 16 Keith Mason; 14 Mick Higham; 22 Dom Feaunati.
Tries: Gardner (29, 41), Albert (65), Higham (67);
Goals: Wellens 2/4.
Rugby Leaguer & League Express Men of the Match:
City Reds: Malcolm Alker; *Saints:* Paul Wellens.
Penalty count: 6-9; **Half-time:** 18-4;
Referee: Russell Smith (Castleford); **Attendance:** 4,897.

WIDNES VIKINGS 24 LONDON BRONCOS 38

VIKINGS: 33 Tim Holmes (D); 2 Paul Devlin; 14 Deon Bird; 4 Adam Hughes; 32 Steve Hall (D); 27 Craig Weston; 20 Stephen Myler; 16 Andy Hobson; 9 Shane Millard; 17 David Mills; 13 Daniel Frame; 12 Andy Hay (C); 18 Simon Finnigan. Subs (all used): 11 Steve McCurrie; 31 Matt Whitaker; 34 Tommy Gallagher (D); 25 Phil Wood.
Tries: Devlin (27, 52), Hughes (56), Mills (63);
Goals: Myler 4/5.
BRONCOS: 2 Jon Wells; 5 John Kirkpatrick; 3 Nigel Roy; 4 Mark O'Halloran; 23 Lee Greenwood; 1 Paul Sykes; 7 Dennis Moran; 15 Mitchell Stringer; 19 David Highton; 10 Steve Trindall; 12 Steele Retchless; 6 Rob Purdham; 13 Jim Dymock (C). Subs (all used): 32 Russell Bawden (D3); 16 Joe Mbu; 33 Paul Sampson (D); 29 Steve Thomas.
Tries: Wells (5, 23), Dymock (14), Purdham (21), O'Halloran (47, 69), Kirkpatrick (75); **Goals:** Sykes 5/7.
Rugby Leaguer & League Express Men of the Match:
Vikings: Shane Millard; *Broncos:* Paul Sykes.
Penalty count: 4-6; **Half-time:** 8-22;
Referee: Ian Smith (Oldham); **Attendance:** 4,829.

WAKEFIELD TRINITY WILDCATS 39 CASTLEFORD TIGERS 18

WILDCATS: 21 Mark Field; 2 Justin Ryder; 1 Jason Demetriou; 4 Sid Domic; 5 Semi Tadulala; 6 Jamie Rooney; 7 Ben Jeffries; 23 Duncan MacGillivray; 9 David March; 10 Michael Korkidas; 11 David Solomona; 13 Jamie Field; 3 Gareth Ellis (C). Subs (all used): 8 Darrell Griffin; 18 Olivier Elima; 19 Rob Spicer; 24 Michael Wainwright.
Tries: Demetriou (33, 60), Jeffries (42, 51), Domic (45), Ellis (54); **Goals:** Rooney 7/9; **Field goal:** Rooney.
Sin bin: Ellis (40) - holding down.
TIGERS: 1 Damian Gibson; 20 Tom Saxton; 19 Francis Maloney; 5 Darren Rogers; 3 Paul Mellor; 33 Brad Davis; 16 Jon Hepworth; 35 Mark Tookey; 9 Wayne Godwin; 10 Andy Lynch; 11 Lee Harland; 23 Michael Smith; 13 Ryan Hudson (C). Subs (all used): 8 Craig Greenhill; 15 Nathan Sykes; 29 Dominic Brambani; 37 Steve Crouch (D).
Tries: Hepworth (21), Crouch (71), Davis (76);
Goals: Hepworth 2/2, Godwin 1/2.
Sin bin: Harland (28) - striking.
Rugby Leaguer & League Express Men of the Match:
Wildcats: Ben Jeffries; *Tigers:* Brad Davis.
Penalty count: 9-5; **Half-time:** 10-8; **Referee:** Richard Silverwood (Dewsbury); **Attendance:** 6,673.

HUDDERSFIELD GIANTS 10 LEEDS RHINOS 42

GIANTS: 3 Stuart Donlan; 2 Hefin O'Hare; 24 James Evans; 4 Julian Bailey; 34 Marcus St Hilaire; 13 Brandon Costin; 9 Paul March; 10 Jim Gannon; 7 Sean Penkywicz; 20 Jon Grayshon; 11 Chris Nero; 14 Stuart Jones; 12 Ben Roarty. Subs (all used): 8 Mick Slicker; 17 Paul Smith; 21 Paul White; 25 Darren Fleary (C).
Tries: Costin (52), Evans (55);
Goals: White 1/1, Costin 0/2.
RHINOS: 21 Richard Mathers; 2 Francis Cummins; 3 Chris McKenna; 4 Keith Senior; 22 Marcus Bai; 6 Danny McGuire; 14 Andrew Dunemann; 17 Wayne McDonald; 9 Matt Diskin; 19 Danny Ward; 11 David Furner; 29 Ali Lauitiiti; 13 Kevin Sinfield (C). Subs (all used): 7 Rob Burrow; 10 Barrie McDermott; 12 Matt Adamson; 16 Willie Poching.
Tries: McDonald (4), Bai (9), McKenna (25, 80), Burrow (39), McGuire (42), Poching (77);
Goals: Sinfield 5/5, Burrow 2/2.
Rugby Leaguer & League Express Men of the Match:
Giants: Brandon Costin; *Rhinos:* Danny Ward.
Penalty count: 7-11; **Half-time:** 0-24; **Referee:** Karl Kirkpatrick (Warrington); **Attendance:** 6,011.

BRADFORD BULLS 36 WARRINGTON WOLVES 22

BULLS: 17 Stuart Reardon; 15 Karl Pratt; 3 Leon Pryce; 4 Shontayne Hape; 5 Lesley Vainikolo; 18 Iestyn Harris; 7 Paul Deacon; 10 Paul Anderson; 1 Robbie Paul (C); 29 Stuart Fielden; 13 Logan Swann; 12 Jamie Peacock; 19 Jamie Langley. Subs (all used): 26 Chris Bridge; 11 Lee Radford; 30 Richard Moore; 27 Rob Parker.
Tries: Hape (19), Reardon (27), Vainikolo (47, 53, 71), Bridge (64); **Goals:** Deacon 6/8.
WOLVES: 5 Graham Appo; 27 Henry Fa'afili (D); 3 Brent Grose; 11 Darren Burns; 20 Dean Gaskell; 6 Lee Briers (C); 7 Nathan Wood; 10 Mark Hilton; 9 Jon Clarke; 8 Chris Leikvoll; 16 Paul Wood; 23 Mike Wainwright; 13 Mike Forshaw. Subs (all used): 14 Mark Gleeson; 15 Jerome Guisset; 22 Danny Lima; 12 Ian Sibbit.
Tries: N Wood (23, 34), Grose (39), Gleeson (59);
Goals: Briers 3/4.
Rugby Leaguer & League Express Men of the Match:
Bulls: Lesley Vainikolo; *Wolves:* Nathan Wood.
Penalty count: 8-4; **Half-time:** 16-16;
Referee: Ashley Klein (London); **Attendance:** 12,981.

ROUND 23

Friday 13th August 2004

BRADFORD BULLS 38 WIGAN WARRIORS 12

BULLS: 17 Stuart Reardon; 6 Michael Withers; 3 Leon Pryce; 4 Shontayne Hape; 5 Lesley Vainikolo; 18 Iestyn Harris; 7 Paul Deacon; 27 Rob Parker; 1 Robbie Paul (C); 29 Stuart Fielden; 13 Logan Swann; 12 Jamie Peacock; 11 Lee Radford. Subs (all used): 19 Jamie Langley; 15

Karl Pratt; 30 Richard Moore; 16 Paul Johnson.
Tries: L Pryce (6), Paul (9), Langley (30), Vainikolo (45), Harris (59, 69), Hape (72); **Goals:** Deacon 4/5, Harris 1/2.
WARRIORS: 33 Gary Connolly; 5 Brian Carney; 19 Stephen Wild; 3 Martin Aspinwall; 2 Brett Dallas; 15 Sean O'Loughlin; 7 Adrian Lam; 13 Andy Farrell (C); 9 Terry Newton; 10 Craig Smith; 11 Mick Cassidy; 12 Danny Tickle; 20 Gareth Hock. Subs (all used): 17 Mark Smith; 24 Bob Beswick; 4 David Hodgson; 14 Luke Robinson.
Tries: Aspinwall (12), Carney (17); **Goals:** Farrell 2/3.
Rugby Leaguer & League Express Men of the Match: *Bulls:* Karl Pratt; *Warriors:* Sean O'Loughlin.
Penalty count: 8-2; **Half-time:** 18-10; **Referee:** Russell Smith (Castleford); **Attendance:** 12,610.

ST HELENS 22 LONDON BRONCOS 28

SAINTS: 1 Paul Wellens; 2 Ade Gardner; 4 Willie Talau; 12 Lee Gilmour; 5 Darren Albert; 13 Paul Sculthorpe (C); 6 Jason Hooper; 8 Nick Fozzard; 14 Mick Higham; 16 Keith Mason; 11 Chris Joynt; 21 Jon Wilkin; 9 Keiron Cunningham. Subs (all used): 26 James Roby; 20 Ricky Bibey; 15 Mike Bennett; 10 John Stankevitch.
Tries: Hooper (5), Wellens (29), Albert (42), Talau (76); **Goals:** Hooper 3/5.
BRONCOS: 2 Jon Wells; 23 Lee Greenwood; 4 Mark O'Halloran; 3 Nigel Roy; 5 John Kirkpatrick; 1 Paul Sykes; 7 Dennis Moran; 10 Steve Trindall; 19 David Highton; 8 Francis Stephenson; 12 Steele Retchless; 6 Rob Purdham; 13 Jim Dymock (C). Subs (all used): 9 Neil Budworth; 15 Mitchell Stringer; 16 Joe Mbu; 32 Russell Bawden.
Tries: Moran (7, 16, 67), Sykes (38); **Goals:** Sykes 6/6.
Rugby Leaguer & League Express Men of the Match: *Saints:* Paul Wellens; *Broncos:* Dennis Moran.
Penalty count: 6-6; **Half-time:** 12-18;
Referee: Glen Black (New Zealand); **Attendance:** 6,637.

Saturday 14th August 2004

SALFORD CITY REDS 14 WIDNES VIKINGS 13

CITY REDS: 15 Karl Fitzpatrick; 2 Joel Caine; 3 Stuart Littler; 12 Andy Johnson; 4 Andy Kirk; 33 Kevin McGuinness; 7 Gavin Clinch; 19 Neil Baynes; 9 Malcolm Alker (C); 10 Sean Rutgerson; 8 Andy Coley; 18 Mark Shipway; 13 Chris Charles. Subs (all used): 14 Paul Highton; 23 Andrew Brocklehurst; 11 Simon Baldwin; 17 Gareth Haggerty.
Tries: Kirk (19), Caine (49), Johnson (73);
Goals: Charles 1/3.
VIKINGS: 33 Tim Holmes; 2 Paul Devlin; 22 John Robinson; 14 Deon Bird; 5 Chris Giles; 6 Jules O'Neill; 7 Willie Peters; 10 Julian O'Neill; 9 Shane Millard; 11 Steve McCurrie; 12 Andy Hay (C); 31 Matt Whitaker; 18 Simon Finnigan. Subs (all used): 20 Stephen Myler; 17 David Mills; 13 Daniel Frame; 34 Tommy Gallagher.
Tries: Robinson (11), Jules O'Neill (58);
Goals: Jules O'Neill 2/2; **Field goal:** Peters.
Rugby Leaguer & League Express Men of the Match: *City Reds:* Karl Fitzpatrick; *Vikings:* Jules O'Neill.
Penalty count: 4-2; **Half-time:** 4-6; **Referee:** Karl Kirkpatrick (Warrington); **Attendance:** 3,067.

Sunday 15th August 2004

HUDDERSFIELD GIANTS 12 CASTLEFORD TIGERS 29

GIANTS: 3 Stuart Donlan; 2 Hefin O'Hare; 24 James Evans; 4 Julian Bailey; 34 Marcus St Hilaire; 13 Brandon Costin; 9 Paul March; 10 Jim Gannon; 7 Sean Penkywicz; 12 Ben Roarty; 11 Chris Nero; 14 Stuart Jones; 6 Stanley Gene. Subs (all used): 20 Jon Grayshon; 17 Paul Smith; 21 Paul White; 25 Darren Fleary (C).
Tries: White (48), Evans (69); **Goals:** Costin 2/2.
TIGERS: 1 Damian Gibson; 2 Waine Pryce; 20 Tom Saxton; 5 Darren Rogers; 3 Paul Mellor; 33 Brad Davis; 19 Francis Maloney; 15 Nathan Sykes; 9 Wayne Godwin; 10 Andy Lynch; 11 Lee Harland; 37 Steve Crouch; 13 Ryan Hudson (C). Subs (all used): 8 Craig Greenhill; 16 Jon Hepworth; 35 Mark Tookey; 17 Paul Jackson.
Tries: Pryce (2, 10), Hudson (57), Tookey (60);
Goals: Godwin 6/9; **Field goal:** Maloney.
Rugby Leaguer & League Express Men of the Match: *Giants:* Stuart Donlan; *Tigers:* Ryan Hudson.
Penalty count: 11-14; **Half-time:** 0-14;
Referee: Ian Smith (Oldham); **Attendance:** 3,231.

WARRINGTON WOLVES 12 LEEDS RHINOS 44

WOLVES: 1 Daryl Cardiss; 27 Henry Fa'afili; 3 Brent Grose; 4 Ben Westwood; 20 Dean Gaskell; 6 Lee Briers (C); 7 Nathan Wood; 8 Chris Leikvoll; 9 Jon Clarke; 10 Mark Hilton; 11 Darren Burns; 16 Paul Wood; 23 Mike Wainwright. Subs (all used): 19 Gary Hulse; 12 Ian Sibbit; 17 Warren Stevens; 22 Danny Lima.
Tries: Fa'afili (13), Stevens (32); **Goals:** Briers 2/3.
Sin bin: Westwood (65) - holding down.
RHINOS: 21 Richard Mathers; 2 Francis Cummins; 5 Chev Walker; 4 Keith Senior; 22 Marcus Bai; 6 Danny McGuire; 7 Rob Burrow; 19 Danny Ward; 9 Matt Diskin; 17 Wayne McDonald; 29 Ali Lauitiiti; 3 Chris McKenna; 13 Kevin Sinfield (C). Subs (all used): 10 Barrie McDermott; 16 Willie Poching; 8 Ryan Bailey; 12 Matt Adamson.
Tries: Diskin (8), Walker (18), McDermott (38), Bai (40), McGuire (42), Mathers (63), Sinfield (73);
Goals: Sinfield 8/8.
Sin bin: Adamson (47) - holding down;
Diskin (57) - holding down.
Rugby Leaguer & League Express Men of the Match: *Wolves:* Brent Grose; *Rhinos:* Kevin Sinfield.
Penalty count: 14-9; **Half-time:** 12-24; **Referee:** Richard Silverwood (Dewsbury); **Attendance:** 9,360.

HULL FC 38 WAKEFIELD TRINITY WILDCATS 24

HULL: 32 Shaun Briscoe; 2 Colin Best; 14 Kirk Yeaman; 30 Richard Whiting; 26 Richie Barnett Jnr; 16 Paul Cooke; 6 Richard Horne; 18 Ewan Dowes; 9 Richard Swain; 10 Paul King; 15 Shayne McMenemy; 24 Graeme Horne; 13 Jason Smith (C). Subs (all used): 11 Richard Fletcher; 29 Andy Bailey; 33 Kirk Dixon (D); 34 Nick Scruton.
Tries: R Horne (3), Yeaman (30), Briscoe (33, 59), Scruton (42), Cooke (73), Bailey (78); **Goals:** Cooke 5/7.
WILDCATS: 21 Mark Field; 2 Justin Ryder; 1 Jason Demetriou; 4 Sid Domic; 5 Semi Tadulala; 6 Jamie Rooney; 7 Ben Jeffries; 23 Duncan MacGillivray; 9 David March; 10 Michael Korkidas; 11 David Solomona; 13 Jamie Field; 3 Gareth Ellis (C). Subs (all used): 8 Darrell Griffin; 18 Olivier Elima; 19 Rob Spicer; 27 Chris Feather (D2).
Tries: Jeffries (16), Domic (23, 63), Demetriou (54);
Goals: Rooney 1/1, March 3/4.
Rugby Leaguer & League Express Men of the Match: *Hull:* Shayne McMenemy; *Wildcats:* Ben Jeffries.
Penalty count: 10-8; **Half-time:** 16-14;
Referee: Ashley Klein (London); **Attendance:** 11,048.

ROUND 24

Friday 20th August 2004

WIGAN WARRIORS 27 ST HELENS 18

WARRIORS: 1 Kris Radlinski; 5 Brian Carney; 3 Martin Aspinwall; 19 Stephen Wild; 2 Brett Dallas; 15 Sean O'Loughlin; 7 Adrian Lam; 13 Andy Farrell (C); 9 Terry Newton; 10 Craig Smith; 11 Mick Cassidy; 12 Danny Tickle; 20 Gareth Hock. Subs (all used): 8 Terry O'Connor; 17 Mark Smith; 24 Bob Beswick; 33 Gary Connolly.
Tries: Dallas (11), Lam (15), O'Loughlin (23), Radlinski (61); **Goals:** Farrell 5/5; **Field goal:** Farrell.
On report: Newton (75) - late tackle on Wilkin.
SAINTS: 1 Paul Wellens; 5 Darren Albert; 12 Lee Gilmour; 4 Willie Talau; 2 Ade Gardner; 6 Jason Hooper; 33 Scott Moore (D); 8 Nick Fozzard; 9 Keiron Cunningham; 16 Keith Mason; 11 Chris Joynt; 21 Jon Wilkin; 13 Paul Sculthorpe (C). Subs (all used): 26 James Roby; 20 Ricky Bibey; 15 Mike Bennett; 10 John Stankevitch.
Tries: Hooper (30), J Roby (55, 58);
Goals: Sculthorpe 3/3, Hooper 0/1.
Sin bin: Wilkin (29) - interference.
Rugby Leaguer & League Express Men of the Match: *Warriors:* Andy Farrell; *Saints:* Paul Sculthorpe.
Penalty count: 13-4; **Half-time:** 21-6;
Referee: Ian Smith (Oldham); **Attendance:** 16,424.

Sunday 22nd August 2004

LONDON BRONCOS 34 WARRINGTON WOLVES 26

BRONCOS: 34 Zebastian Luisi (D); 23 Lee Greenwood; 4 Mark O'Halloran; 3 Nigel Roy; 5 John Kirkpatrick; 1 Paul Sykes; 7 Dennis Moran; 10 Steve Trindall; 19 David Highton; 8 Francis Stephenson; 12 Steele Retchless; 6 Rob Purdham; 13 Jim Dymock (C). Subs (all used): 35 Mal Kaufusi (D); 15 Mitchell Stringer; 16 Joe Mbu; 9 Neil Budworth.
Tries: Sykes (16), Roy (38), Purdham (44), Retchless (48), Greenwood (72, 80); **Goals:** Sykes 5/7.
Sin bin: Roy (8) - professional foul.
WOLVES: 5 Graham Appo; 20 Dean Gaskell; 4 Ben Westwood; 3 Brent Grose; 27 Henry Fa'afili; 7 Nathan Wood (C); 19 Gary Hulse; 8 Chris Leikvoll; 9 Jon Clarke; 10 Mark Hilton; 23 Mike Wainwright; 11 Darren Burns; 16 Paul Wood. Subs (all used): 14 Mark Gleeson; 12 Ian Sibbit; 22 Danny Lima; 15 Jerome Guisset.
Tries: Clarke (9), Fa'afili (12, 31), Westwood (28), Sibbit (75); **Goals:** Appo 3/5.
Rugby Leaguer & League Express Men of the Match: *Broncos:* Rob Purdham; *Wolves:* Henry Fa'afili.
Penalty count: 2-2; **Half-time:** 12-22;
Referee: Steve Ganson (St Helens); **Attendance:** 3,526.

WIDNES VIKINGS 24 HUDDERSFIELD GIANTS 18

VIKINGS: 33 Tim Holmes; 2 Paul Devlin; 14 Deon Bird; 4 Adam Hughes; 35 Justin Murphy (D); 6 Jules O'Neill; 7 Willie Peters; 10 Julian O'Neill; 9 Shane Millard; 11 Steve McCurrie; 31 Matt Whitaker; 12 Andy Hay (C); 18 Simon Finnigan. Subs (all used): 13 Daniel Frame; 17 David Mills; 34 Tommy Gallagher; 20 Stephen Myler.
Tries: Murphy (2), Whitaker (11, 57), Peters (41);
Goals: Jules O'Neill 4/7.
GIANTS: 3 Stuart Donlan; 27 Bolouagi Fagborun; 24 James Evans; 13 Brandon Costin; 34 Marcus St Hilaire; 6 Stanley Gene; 9 Paul March; 10 Jim Gannon; 7 Sean Penkywicz; 25 Darren Fleary (C); 16 Iain Morrison; 17 Paul Smith; 12 Ben Roarty. Subs (all used): 20 Jon Grayshon; 14 Stuart Jones; 21 Paul White; 2 Hefin O'Hare.
Tries: Costin (31, 73), Gannon (71);
Goals: Costin 2/3, March 1/1.
Rugby Leaguer & League Express Men of the Match: *Vikings:* Matt Whitaker; *Giants:* Brandon Costin.
Penalty count: 9-5; **Half-time:** 10-8;
Referee: Ashley Klein (London); **Attendance:** 4,881.

CASTLEFORD TIGERS 21 HULL FC 14

TIGERS: 1 Damian Gibson; 2 Waine Pryce; 5 Darren Rogers; 20 Tom Saxton; 3 Paul Mellor; 33 Brad Davis; 19 Francis Maloney; 8 Craig Greenhill; 9 Wayne Godwin; 10 Andy Lynch; 11 Lee Harland; 37 Steve Crouch; 13 Ryan Hudson (C). Subs (all used): 15 Nathan Sykes; 35 Mark Tookey; 16 Jon Hepworth; 17 Paul Jackson.
Tries: Rogers (4), Gibson (51);
Goals: Godwin 5/6, Hepworth 1/1; **Field goal:** Davis.
Sin bin: Davis (80) - flopping.
HULL: 32 Shaun Briscoe; 2 Colin Best; 30 Richard Whiting; 14 Kirk Yeaman; 26 Richie Barnett Jnr; 16 Paul Cooke; 6 Richard Horne; 18 Ewan Dowes; 9 Richard Swain; 10 Paul King; 29 Andy Bailey; 15 Shayne McMenemy; 13 Jason Smith (C). Subs (all used): 24 Graeme Horne; 27 Liam Higgins; 11 Richard Fletcher; 34 Nick Scruton.
Tries: Cooke (28), Yeaman (56), Barnett Jnr (80);
Goals: Cooke 1/3.
Dismissal: King (64) - high tackle on Greenhill.
Sin bin: R Horne (46) - professional foul.
Rugby Leaguer & League Express Men of the Match: *Tigers:* Ryan Hudson; *Hull:* Richard Swain.
Penalty count: 10-10; **Half-time:** 10-4; **Referee:** Richard Silverwood (Dewsbury); **Attendance:** 8,054.

WAKEFIELD TRINITY WILDCATS 46 SALFORD CITY REDS 18

WILDCATS: 21 Mark Field; 2 Justin Ryder; 1 Jason Demetriou; 4 Sid Domic; 5 Semi Tadulala; 3 Gareth Ellis (C); 7 Ben Jeffries; 27 Chris Feather; 9 David March; 10 Michael Korkidas; 11 David Solomona; 13 Jamie Field; 19 Rob Spicer. Subs (all used): 8 Darrell Griffin; 15 David Wrench; 23 Duncan MacGillivray; 24 Michael Wainwright.
Tries: Domic (9, 22), Tadulala (39, 50), Demetriou (59, 76), M Field (43), Ryder (53), Feather (71); **Goals:** March 4/7, Demetriou 1/3.
CITY REDS: 15 Karl Fitzpatrick; 2 Joel Caine; 3 Stuart Littler; 5 Anthony Stewart; 4 Andy Kirk; 33 Kevin McGuinness; 7 Gavin Clinch; 19 Neil Baynes; 9 Malcolm Alker (C); 10 Sean Rutgerson; 8 Andy Coley; 18 Mark Shipway; 13 Chris Charles. Subs (all used): 14 Paul Highton; 23 Andrew Brocklehurst; 11 Simon Baldwin; 12 Andy Johnson.
Tries: Coley (14, 80), Caine (35); **Goals:** Charles 3/3.
Rugby Leaguer & League Express Men of the Match: *Wildcats:* David Solomona; *City Reds:* Chris Charles.
Penalty count: 7-2; **Half-time:** 18-12;
Referee: Glen Black (New Zealand); **Attendance:** 3,641.

LEEDS RHINOS 40 BRADFORD BULLS 12

RHINOS: 21 Richard Mathers; 5 Chev Walker; 3 Chris McKenna; 4 Keith Senior; 22 Marcus Bai; 13 Kevin Sinfield (C); 6 Danny McGuire; 19 Danny Ward; 9 Matt Diskin; 17 Wayne McDonald; 12 Matt Adamson; 29 Ali Lauitiiti; 16 Willie Poching. Subs (all used): 7 Rob Burrow; 8 Ryan Bailey; 20 Jamie Jones-Buchanan; 10 Barrie McDermott.
Tries: McGuire (1, 34), McKenna (12, 37), Lauitiiti (15), Bai (46), Jones-Buchanan (63); **Goals:** Sinfield 6/8.
BULLS: 17 Stuart Reardon; 6 Michael Withers; 3 Leon Pryce; 4 Shontayne Hape; 5 Lesley Vainikolo; 18 Iestyn Harris; 7 Paul Deacon; 29 Stuart Fielden; 1 Robbie Paul (C); 27 Rob Parker; 12 Jamie Peacock; 13 Logan Swann; 11 Lee Radford. Subs (all used): 15 Karl Pratt; 16 Paul Johnson; 19 Jamie Langley; 30 Richard Moore.
Tries: Swann (56), Harris (74); **Goals:** Deacon 2/2.
Sin bin: L Pryce (59) - interference, (77) - fighting.
Rugby Leaguer & League Express Men of the Match: *Rhinos:* Chris McKenna; *Bulls:* Logan Swann.
Penalty count: 7-8; **Half-time:** 26-0; **Referee:** Karl Kirkpatrick (Warrington); **Attendance:** 21,225.

ROUND 25

Friday 27th August 2004

LEEDS RHINOS 64 CASTLEFORD TIGERS 12

RHINOS: 21 Richard Mathers; 22 Marcus Bai; 5 Chev Walker; 4 Keith Senior; 18 Mark Calderwood; 14 Andrew Dunemann; 7 Rob Burrow; 19 Danny Ward; 9 Matt Diskin; 17 Wayne McDonald; 12 Matt Adamson; 29 Ali Lauitiiti; 13 Kevin Sinfield (C). Subs (all used): 8 Ryan Bailey; 16 Willie Poching; 10 Barrie McDermott; 20 Jamie Jones-Buchanan.
Tries: Burrow (8, 10), Senior (20), Walker (31, 37, 64, 79), Bai (34), Poching (43, 76), Dunemann (55), McDonald (57); **Goals:** Sinfield 8/11, Adamson 0/1.
Sin bin: Dunemann (70) - fighting.
TIGERS: 1 Damian Gibson; 2 Waine Pryce; 20 Tom Saxton; 14 Ryan Clayton; 5 Darren Rogers; 33 Brad Davis; 16 Jon Hepworth; 8 Craig Greenhill; 13 Ryan Hudson (C); 17 Paul Jackson; 10 Andy Lynch; 37 Steve Crouch; 11 Lee Harland. Subs (all used): 35 Mark Tookey; 15 Nathan Sykes; 30 Michael Shenton; 22 Byron Smith.
Tries: Crouch (25), Davis (48); **Goals:** Hepworth 2/2.
Rugby Leaguer & League Express Men of the Match: *Rhinos:* Keith Senior; *Tigers:* Steve Crouch.
Penalty count: 10-7; **Half-time:** 34-6;
Referee: Ashley Klein (London); **Attendance:** 14,605.

ST HELENS 48 HUDDERSFIELD GIANTS 12

SAINTS: 1 Paul Wellens; 25 Ian Hardman; 34 Gray Viane (D); 4 Willie Talau; 2 Ade Gardner; 6 Jason Hooper; 33 Scott Moore; 16 Keith Mason; 14 Mick Higham; 10 John Stankevitch; 12 Lee Gilmour; 9 Keiron Cunningham; 13 Paul Sculthorpe (C). Subs (all used): 15 Mike Bennett; 18 Mark Edmondson; 20 Ricky Bibey; 26 James Roby.
Tries: Stankevitch (4), Talau (16, 72), Moore (19), Hooper (23), Hardman (35), Cunningham (49, 70), Viane (61), J Roby (79); **Goals:** Sculthorpe 4/10.
GIANTS: 3 Stuart Donlan; 27 Bolouagi Fagborun; 24 James Evans; 13 Brandon Costin; 34 Marcus St Hilaire; 6 Stanley Gene; 9 Paul March; 25 Darren Fleary (C); 7 Sean Penkywicz; 10 Jim Gannon; 4 Julian Bailey; 17 Paul Smith; 14 Stuart Jones. Subs (all used): 2 Hefin O'Hare; 21 Paul White; 22 Phil Joseph; 20 Jon Grayshon.
Tries: Costin (39), St Hilaire (57); **Goals:** Costin 2/3.
Rugby Leaguer & League Express Men of the Match: *Saints:* Paul Sculthorpe; *Giants:* Brandon Costin.

Penalty count: 8-8; Half-time: 24-8; Referee: Richard Silverwood (Dewsbury); Attendance: 6,095.

Saturday 28th August 2004

WIDNES VIKINGS 20 WIGAN WARRIORS 16

VIKINGS: 33 Tim Holmes; 2 Paul Devlin; 14 Deon Bird; 4 Adam Hughes; 35 Justin Murphy; 6 Jules O'Neill; 7 Willie Peters; 10 Julian O'Neill; 9 Shane Millard; 11 Steve McCurrie; 13 Daniel Frame; 12 Andy Hay (C); 18 Simon Finnigan. Subs (all used): 31 Matt Whitaker; 17 David Mills; 34 Tommy Gallagher; 20 Stephen Myler. Tries: McCurrie (14), Whitaker (56), Finnigan (64); Goals: Jules O'Neill 3/3, Myler 1/1.
WARRIORS: 1 Kris Radlinski; 3 Martin Aspinwall; 19 Stephen Wild; 33 Gary Connolly; 2 Brett Dallas; 15 Sean O'Loughlin; 7 Adrian Lam; 8 Terry O'Connor; 17 Mark Smith; 31 Paul Prescott; 13 Andy Farrell (C); 12 Danny Tickle; 20 Gareth Hock. Subs (all used): 11 Mick Cassidy; 14 Luke Robinson; 21 Kevin Brown; 23 Harrison Hansen. Tries: Connolly (59), Wild (72), Lam (74); Goals: Farrell 2/3.
Rugby Leaguer & League Express Men of the Match: Vikings: Shane Millard; Warriors: Stephen Wild.
Penalty count: 7-6; Half-time: 8-0;
Referee: Glen Black (New Zealand); Attendance: 6,456.

Sunday 29th August 2004

LONDON BRONCOS 16
WAKEFIELD TRINITY WILDCATS 24

BRONCOS: 34 Zebastian Luisi; 23 Lee Greenwood; 3 Nigel Roy; 4 Mark O'Halloran; 5 John Kirkpatrick; 1 Paul Sykes; 7 Dennis Moran; 8 Francis Stephenson; 9 Neil Budworth; 35 Mal Kaufusi; 12 Steele Retchless; 6 Rob Purdham; 13 Jim Dymock (C). Subs (all used): 15 Mitchell Stringer; 19 David Highton; 11 Paul Toshack; 10 Steve Trindall. Tries: Purdham (12), Greenwood (17), Roy (50); Goals: Sykes 2/4.
WILDCATS: 21 Mark Field; 2 Justin Ryder; 1 Jason Demetriou; 4 Sid Domic; 5 Semi Tadulala; 20 Liam Finn; 7 Ben Jeffries; 27 Chris Feather; 9 David March; 10 Michael Korkidas; 11 David Solomona; 13 Jamie Field; 3 Gareth Ellis (C). Subs (all used): 8 Darrell Griffin; 15 David Wrench; 23 Duncan MacGillivray; 24 Michael Wainwright. Tries: Domic (33), Solomona (40, 61), Jeffries (45), Demetriou (72); Goals: March 1/5, Finn 1/1.
Rugby Leaguer & League Express Men of the Match: Broncos: Rob Purdham; Wildcats: David Solomona.
Penalty count: 12-7; Half-time: 10-10; Referee: Karl Kirkpatrick (Warrington); Attendance: 3,035.

SALFORD CITY REDS 6 WARRINGTON WOLVES 32

CITY REDS: 15 Karl Fitzpatrick; 2 Joel Caine; 3 Stuart Littler; 6 Cliff Beverley; 5 Anthony Stewart; 33 Kevin McGuinness; 7 Gavin Clinch; 19 Neil Baynes; 9 Malcolm Alker (C); 14 Paul Highton; 18 Mark Shipway; 8 Andy Coley; 13 Chris Charles. Subs (all used): 23 Andrew Brocklehurst; 11 Simon Baldwin; 17 Gareth Haggerty; 12 Andy Johnson. Try: Littler (20); Goals: Charles 1/1.
WOLVES: 19 Gary Hulse; 27 Henry Fa'afili; 3 Brent Grose; 11 Darren Burns; 20 Dean Gaskell; 5 Graham Appo; 7 Nathan Wood (C); 22 Danny Lima; 9 Jon Clarke; 8 Chris Leikvoll; 16 Paul Wood; 23 Mike Wainwright; 12 Ian Sibbit. Subs (all used): 14 Mark Gleeson; 1 Daryl Cardiss; 15 Jerome Guisset; 10 Mark Hilton. Tries: Fa'afili (27), Grose (28), Hilton (56), Hulse (63), P Wood (68), Sibbit (73); Goals: Appo 4/7.
Rugby Leaguer & League Express Men of the Match: City Reds: Andy Coley; Wolves: Ian Sibbit.
Penalty count: 9-8; Half-time: 6-12;
Referee: Ian Smith (Oldham); Attendance: 4,019.

Monday 30th August 2004

HULL FC 12 BRADFORD BULLS 26

HULL: 32 Shaun Briscoe; 2 Colin Best; 14 Kirk Yeaman; 30 Richard Whiting; 26 Richie Barnett Jnr; 16 Paul Cooke; 6 Richard Horne; 10 Paul King; 9 Richard Swain; 18 Ewan Dowes; 15 Shayne McMenemy; 23 Paul McNicholas; 13 Jason Smith (C). Subs (all used): 3 Richie Barnett; 11 Richard Fletcher; 20 Garreth Carvell; 34 Nick Scruton. Tries: Best (2), Smith (18); Goals: Cooke 2/3.
BULLS: 6 Michael Withers; 17 Stuart Reardon; 3 Leon Pryce; 4 Shontayne Hape; 5 Lesley Vainikolo; 18 Iestyn Harris; 7 Paul Deacon; 29 Stuart Fielden; 1 Robbie Paul (C); 8 Joe Vagana; 12 Jamie Peacock; 13 Logan Swann; 11 Lee Radford. Subs (all used): 15 Karl Pratt; 30 Richard Moore; 19 Jamie Langley; 27 Rob Parker. Tries: Vainikolo (27, 39, 44), Langley (57), Harris (78); Goals: Deacon 3/6.
Sin bin: Fielden (76) - fighting.
On report: L Pryce (34) - kicking out; Fielden (50) - high tackle on Smith.
Rugby Leaguer & League Express Men of the Match: Hull: Richard Swain; Bulls: Lesley Vainikolo.
Penalty count: 5-7; Half-time: 12-8;
Referee: Steve Ganson (St Helens); Attendance: 13,593.

ROUND 26

Friday 3rd September 2004

WIGAN WARRIORS 12 LEEDS RHINOS 12

WARRIORS: 1 Kris Radlinski; 5 Brian Carney; 19 Stephen Wild; 3 Martin Aspinwall; 2 Brett Dallas; 21 Kevin Brown;

Salford's Neil Baynes tackled by Castleford duo Wayne Godwin and Steve Crouch as the City Reds secure Super League safety with a narrow win at The Jungle

7 Adrian Lam; 13 Andy Farrell (C); 17 Mark Smith; 10 Craig Smith; 20 Gareth Hock; 12 Danny Tickle; 15 Sean O'Loughlin. Subs (all used): 8 Terry O'Connor; 11 Mick Cassidy; 14 Luke Robinson; 33 Gary Connolly. Try: Carney (3); Goals: Farrell 4/4.
RHINOS: 21 Richard Mathers; 18 Mark Calderwood; 5 Chev Walker; 4 Keith Senior; 22 Marcus Bai; 6 Danny McGuire; 7 Rob Burrow; 17 Wayne McDonald; 9 Matt Diskin; 19 Danny Ward; 3 Chris McKenna; 29 Ali Lauitiiti; 13 Kevin Sinfield (C). Subs (all used): 8 Ryan Bailey; 12 Matt Adamson; 16 Willie Poching; 20 Jamie Jones-Buchanan. Tries: McGuire (52, 59); Goals: Sinfield 2/2.
Rugby Leaguer & League Express Men of the Match: Warriors: Stephen Wild; Rhinos: Danny McGuire.
Penalty count: 6-10; Half-time: 8-0; Referee: Karl Kirkpatrick (Warrington); Attendance: 14,288.

Saturday 4th September 2004

HUDDERSFIELD GIANTS 22 HULL FC 20

GIANTS: 1 Paul Reilly; 3 Stuart Donlan; 24 James Evans; 13 Brandon Costin; 34 Marcus St Hilaire; 6 Stanley Gene; 9 Paul March; 25 Darren Fleary (C); 7 Sean Penkywicz; 10 Jim Gannon; 17 Paul Smith; 4 Julian Bailey; 14 Chris Nero. Subs (all used): 2 Hefin O'Hare; 11 Chris Nero; 20 Jon Grayshon; 21 Paul White. Tries: St Hilaire (27), Costin (75), Evans (78); Goals: Costin 5/5.
Sin bin: Gannon (72) - fighting; March (72) - dissent.
HULL: 32 Shaun Briscoe; 2 Colin Best; 14 Kirk Yeaman; 30 Richard Whiting; 26 Richie Barnett Jnr; 16 Paul Cooke; 6 Richard Horne; 18 Ewan Dowes; 9 Richard Swain; 10 Paul King; 15 Shayne McMenemy; 23 Paul McNicholas; 13 Jason Smith (C). Subs (all used): 11 Richard Fletcher; 24 Graeme Horne; 20 Garreth Carvell; 34 Nick Scruton. Tries: Carvell (39), King (57), Whiting (61); Goals: Cooke 4/6.
Sin bin: R Horne (72) - fighting.
Rugby Leaguer & League Express Men of the Match: Giants: Brandon Costin; Hull: Richard Swain.
Penalty count: 10-10; Half-time: 8-8;
Referee: Ian Smith (Oldham); Attendance: 3,541.

Sunday 5th September 2004

WARRINGTON WOLVES 24 ST HELENS 26

WOLVES: 1 Daryl Cardiss; 27 Henry Fa'afili; 5 Graham Appo; 11 Darren Burns; 20 Dean Gaskell; 6 Lee Briers (C); 7 Nathan Wood; 8 Chris Leikvoll; 9 Jon Clarke; 22 Danny Lima; 12 Ian Sibbit; 23 Mike Wainwright; 16 Paul Wood. Subs (all used): 14 Mark Gleeson; 19 Gary Hulse; 15 Jerome Guisset; 10 Mark Hilton. Tries: Gaskell (13), N Wood (23), Wainwright (27, 35), Appo (65); Goals: Appo 2/5, Briers 0/2.
SAINTS: 1 Paul Wellens; 5 Darren Albert; 4 Willie Talau; 34 Gray Viane; 2 Ade Gardner; 6 Jason Hooper; 14 Mick Higham; 8 Nick Fozzard; 9 Keiron Cunningham; 16 Keith Mason; 12 Lee Gilmour; 10 John Stankevitch; 13 Paul Sculthorpe (C). Subs (all used): 20 Ricky Bibey; 26 James Roby; 15 Mike Bennett; 11 Chris Joynt. Tries: Sculthorpe (2), Wellens (18), Higham (40), Hooper (78), Sculthorpe 5/5.
Rugby Leaguer & League Express Men of the Match: Wolves: Mike Wainwright; Saints: Paul Sculthorpe.
Penalty count: 4-7; Half-time: 18-20;
Referee: Ashley Klein (London); Attendance: 11,930.

WAKEFIELD TRINITY WILDCATS 40 WIDNES VIKINGS 6

WILDCATS: 21 Mark Field; 14 Colum Halpenny; 1 Jason Demetriou; 4 Sid Domic; 5 Semi Tadulala; 3 Gareth Ellis (C); 7 Ben Jeffries; 27 Chris Feather; 9 David March; 10 Michael Korkidas; 11 David Solomona; 13 Jamie Field; 15 David Wrench. Subs (all used): 8 Darrell Griffin; 17 Paul Handforth; 23 Duncan MacGillivray; 16 Steve Snitch. Tries: Domic (18, 51), Ellis (25), Handforth (43, 63), Demetriou (61); Goals: March 2/2, Handforth 3/4, Demetriou 1/1.
VIKINGS: 33 Tim Holmes; 2 Paul Devlin; 14 Deon Bird; 4 Adam Hughes; 35 Justin Murphy; 6 Jules O'Neill; 7 Willie Peters; 10 Julian O'Neill; 9 Shane Millard; 11 Steve McCurrie; 12 Andy Hay (C); 13 Daniel Frame; 18 Simon Finnigan. Subs (all used): 20 Stephen Myler; 31 Matt Whitaker; 17 David Mills; 36 Sala Fa'alogo (D). Try: Finnigan (14); Goals: Jules O'Neill 1/1.
Rugby Leaguer & League Express Men of the Match: Wildcats: Paul Handforth; Vikings: Adam Hughes.
Penalty count: 6-6; Half-time: 12-6; Referee: Richard Silverwood (Dewsbury); Attendance: 5,198.

BRADFORD BULLS 60 LONDON BRONCOS 18

BULLS: 6 Michael Withers; 17 Stuart Reardon; 3 Leon Pryce; 4 Shontayne Hape; 5 Lesley Vainikolo; 18 Iestyn Harris; 7 Paul Deacon; 8 Joe Vagana; 1 Robbie Paul (C); 29 Stuart Fielden; 13 Logan Swann; 12 Jamie Peacock; 11 Lee Radford. Subs (all used): 15 Karl Pratt; 19 Jamie Langley; 30 Richard Moore; 27 Rob Parker.
Tries: Hape (9, 15, 75), Fielden (20), Swann (25, 59), Withers (29), Parker (36, 52), Vagana (70);
Goals: Deacon 10/10.
BRONCOS: 2 Jon Wells; 23 Lee Greenwood; 3 Nigel Roy; 4 Mark O'Halloran; 5 John Kirkpatrick; 1 Paul Sykes; 7 Dennis Moran; 10 Steve Trindall; 19 David Highton; 8 Francis Stephenson; 11 Mat Toshack; 6 Rob Purdham; 13 Jim Dymock (C). Subs (all used): 15 Mitchell Stringer; 21 Rob Jackson; 9 Neil Budworth; 35 Mal Kaufusi.
Tries: Moran (41), Greenwood (58, 66);
Goals: Sykes 3/4.
Rugby Leaguer & League Express Men of the Match:
Bulls: Shontayne Hape; *Broncos:* Jim Dymock.
Penalty count: 6-3; **Half-time:** 36-2; **Referee:** Russell Smith (Castleford); **Attendance:** 11,319.

CASTLEFORD TIGERS 22 SALFORD CITY REDS 24

TIGERS: 1 Damian Gibson; 2 Waine Pryce; 5 Darren Rogers; 20 Tom Saxton; 3 Paul Mellor; 33 Brad Davis; 19 Francis Maloney; 8 Craig Greenhill; 9 Wayne Godwin; 10 Andy Lynch; 11 Lee Harland; 37 Steve Crouch; 13 Ryan Hudson (C). Subs (all used): 15 Nathan Sykes; 35 Mark Tookey; 16 Jon Hepworth; 17 Paul Jackson.
Tries: Mellor (24, 32, 70), Maloney (52);
Goals: Godwin 2/3, Maloney 1/1.
CITY REDS: 15 Karl Fitzpatrick; 2 Joel Caine; 3 Stuart Littler; 6 Cliff Beverley; 5 Anthony Stewart; 33 Kevin McGuinness; 7 Gavin Clinch; 19 Neil Baynes; 9 Malcolm Alker (C); 14 Paul Highton; 8 Andy Coley; 10 Sean Rutgerson; 13 Chris Charles. Subs (all used): 17 Gareth Haggerty; 12 Andy Johnson; 18 Mark Shipway; 11 Simon Baldwin.
Tries: Alker (14), Fitzpatrick (46, 61), Coley (49);
Goals: Charles 4/4.
Sin bin: Littler (58) - obstruction.
Rugby Leaguer & League Express Men of the Match:
Tigers: Brad Davis; *City Reds:* Karl Fitzpatrick.
Penalty count: 4-2; **Half-time:** 12-6;
Referee: Steve Ganson (St Helens); **Attendance:** 5,809.

ROUND 27

Friday 10th September 2004

ST HELENS 19 LEEDS RHINOS 25

SAINTS: 1 Paul Wellens; 2 Ade Gardner; 34 Gray Viane; 4 Willie Talau; 5 Darren Albert; 13 Paul Sculthorpe (C); 14 Mick Higham; 8 Nick Fozzard; 9 Keiron Cunningham; 10 John Stankevitch; 12 Lee Gilmour; 11 Chris Joynt; 21 Jon Wilkin. Subs (all used): 15 Mike Bennett; 16 Keith Mason; 18 Mark Edmondson; 26 James Roby.
Tries: Wilkin (14), Edmondson (31), Wellens (40);
Goals: Sculthorpe 3/4; **Field goal:** Sculthorpe.
RHINOS: 21 Richard Mathers; 18 Mark Calderwood; 5 Chev Walker; 4 Keith Senior; 22 Marcus Bai; 6 Danny McGuire; 14 Andrew Dunemann; 8 Ryan Bailey; 9 Matt Diskin; 19 Danny Ward; 3 Chris McKenna; 12 Matt Adamson; 13 Kevin Sinfield (C). Subs (all used): 29 Ali Lauitiiti; 17 Wayne McDonald; 16 Barrie McDermott; 16 Willie Poching.
Tries: Walker (3), Mathers (60), Senior (64), Diskin (78);
Goals: Sinfield 4/4; **Field goal:** Sinfield.
Sin bin: Dunemann (27) - holding down.
Rugby Leaguer & League Express Men of the Match:
Saints: Jon Wilkin; *Rhinos:* Kevin Sinfield.
Penalty count: 7-6; **Half-time:** 18-6; **Referee:** Russell Smith (Castleford); **Attendance:** 11,265.

WAKEFIELD TRINITY WILDCATS 21 HUDDERSFIELD GIANTS 20

WILDCATS: 21 Mark Field; 14 Colum Halpenny; 1 Jason Demetriou; 4 Sid Domic; 5 Semi Tadulala; 3 Gareth Ellis (C); 7 Ben Jeffries; 27 Chris Feather; 9 David March; 10 Michael Korkidas; 11 David Solomona; 15 David Wrench; 19 Rob Spicer. Subs (all used): 8 Darrell Griffin; 17 Paul Handforth; 23 Duncan MacGillivray; 16 Steve Snitch.
Tries: Domic (35), Halpenny (38), Tadulala (70);
Goals: March 3/4, Handforth 1/3; **Field goal:** Jeffries.
Sin bin: Snitch (53) - holding down.
GIANTS: 1 Paul Reilly; 3 Stuart Donlan; 24 James Evans; 13 Brandon Costin; 34 Marcus St Hilaire; 6 Stanley Gene; 9 Paul March; 25 Darren Fleary (C); 7 Sean Penkywicz; 10 Jim Gannon; 17 Paul Smith; 4 Julian Bailey; 14 Stuart Jones. Subs (all used): 2 Hefin O'Hare; 11 Chris Nero; 20 Jon Grayshon; 21 Paul White.
Tries: Penkywicz (17), Gannon (28), White (44);
Goals: Costin 4/4.
Sin bin: Bailey (32) - holding down;
On report: Bailey (75) - spear tackle.
Rugby Leaguer & League Express Men of the Match:
Wildcats: Ben Jeffries; *Giants:* Brandon Costin.
Penalty count: 13-9; **Half-time:** 12-12;
Referee: Steve Ganson (St Helens); **Attendance:** 4,311.

Saturday 11th September 2004

WIDNES VIKINGS 6 CASTLEFORD TIGERS 7

VIKINGS: 33 Tim Holmes; 2 Paul Devlin; 14 Deon Bird; 4 Adam Hughes; 35 Justin Murphy; 6 Jules O'Neill; 20 Stephen Myler; 10 Julian O'Neill; 9 Shane Millard; 11 Steve McCurrie; 13 Daniel Frame; 12 Andy Hay (C); 18 Simon Finnigan. Subs (all used): 31 Matt Whitaker; 17 David Mills; 34 Tommy Gallagher; 36 Sala Fa'alogo.
Try: Myler (36); **Goals:** Jules O'Neill 1/1.
TIGERS: 1 Damian Gibson; 2 Waine Pryce; 5 Darren Rogers; 20 Tom Saxton; 3 Paul Mellor; 33 Brad Davis; 19 Francis Maloney; 8 Craig Greenhill; 9 Wayne Godwin; 10 Andy Lynch; 11 Lee Harland; 23 Michael Smith; 13 Ryan Hudson (C). Subs (all used): 15 Nathan Sykes; 35 Mark Tookey; 16 Jon Hepworth; 17 Paul Jackson.
Try: Hepworth (66); **Goals:** Godwin 1/1;
Field goal: Maloney.
Rugby Leaguer & League Express Men of the Match:
Vikings: Stephen Myler; *Tigers:* Wayne Godwin.
Penalty count: 5-7; **Half-time:** 6-0; **Referee:** Karl Kirkpatrick (Warrington); **Attendance:** 7,005.

Sunday 12th September 2004

LONDON BRONCOS 22 WIGAN WARRIORS 26

BRONCOS: 34 Zebastian Luisi; 23 Lee Greenwood; 3 Nigel Roy; 4 Mark O'Halloran; 2 Jon Wells; 1 Paul Sykes; 7 Dennis Moran; 10 Steve Trindall; 9 Neil Budworth; 8 Francis Stephenson; 6 Rob Purdham; 11 Mat Toshack; 13 Jim Dymock (C). Subs (all used): 35 Mal Kaufusi; 15 Mitchell Stringer; 21 Rob Jackson; 33 Paul Sampson.
Tries: Roy (19), Luisi (26), Greenwood (36), Trindall (56); **Goals:** Sykes 3/4.
WARRIORS: 1 Kris Radlinski; 3 Martin Aspinwall; 19 Stephen Wild; 21 Kevin Brown; 2 Brett Dallas; 6 Danny Orr; 7 Adrian Lam; 10 Craig Smith; 9 Terry Newton; 11 Mick Cassidy; 20 Gareth Hock; 13 Andy Farrell (C); 15 Sean O'Loughlin. Subs (all used): 14 Luke Robinson; 23 Harrison Hansen; 33 Gary Connolly; 12 Danny Tickle.
Tries: Dallas (2), C Smith (7), Wild (48), Farrell (64); **Goals:** Farrell 5/5.
Rugby Leaguer & League Express Men of the Match:
Broncos: Steve Trindall; *Warriors:* Andy Farrell.
Penalty count: 6-12; **Half-time:** 16-12; **Referee:** Richard Silverwood (Dewsbury); **Attendance:** 4,151.

SALFORD CITY REDS 8 HULL FC 12

CITY REDS: 6 Cliff Beverley; 2 Joel Caine; 3 Stuart Littler; 27 Nathan McAvoy; 4 Andy Kirk; 33 Kevin McGuinness; 15 Karl Fitzpatrick; 14 Paul Highton; 9 Malcolm Alker (C); 10 Sean Rutgerson; 8 Andy Coley; 23 Andrew Brocklehurst; 13 Chris Charles. Subs (all used): 11 Simon Baldwin; 12 Andy Johnson; 17 Gareth Haggerty; 28 Tim Hartley.
Try: Alker (12); **Goals:** Charles 2/2.
Dismissal: Coley (25) - punching.
HULL: 32 Shaun Briscoe; 2 Colin Best; 5 Gareth Raynor; 14 Kirk Yeaman; 26 Richie Barnett Jnr; 16 Paul Cooke (C); 6 Richard Horne; 34 Nick Scruton; 9 Richard Swain; 18 Ewan Dowes; 15 Shayne McMenemy; 23 Paul McNicholas; 30 Richard Whiting. Subs (all used): 10 Paul King; 11 Richard Fletcher; 20 Garreth Carvell; 24 Graeme Horne.
Tries: Raynor (30), Yeaman (57);
Goals: Cooke 2/3, Whiting 0/1.
Rugby Leaguer & League Express Men of the Match:
City Reds: Sean Rutgerson; *Hull:* Kirk Yeaman.
Penalty count: 7-6; **Half-tim:** 8-8;
Referee: Ashley Klein (London); **Attendance:** 3,307.

WARRINGTON WOLVES 27 BRADFORD BULLS 28

WOLVES: 5 Graham Appo; 27 Henry Fa'afili; 3 Brent Grose; 11 Darren Burns; 20 Dean Gaskell; 6 Lee Briers (C); 7 Nathan Wood; 22 Danny Lima; 9 Jon Clarke; 10 Mark Hilton; 12 Ian Sibbit; 16 Paul Wood; 13 Mike Forshaw. Subs (all used): 14 Mark Gleeson; 19 Gary Hulse; 15 Jerome Guisset; 8 Chris Leikvoll.
Tries: Sibbit (3), Appo (47), P Wood (54), Grose (60), Gaskell (74); **Goals:** Briers 3/5; **Field goal:** Briers.
BULLS: 6 Michael Withers; 17 Stuart Reardon; 3 Leon Pryce; 4 Shontayne Hape; 5 Lesley Vainikolo; 18 Iestyn Harris; 7 Paul Deacon; 8 Joe Vagana; 1 Robbie Paul (C); 29 Stuart Fielden; 12 Jamie Peacock; 13 Logan Swann; 19 Jamie Langley. Subs (all used): 15 Karl Pratt; 16 Paul Johnson; 27 Rob Parker; 30 Richard Moore.
Tries: Langley (14), Vainikolo (16), Hape (19), Harris

London duo Rob Jackson and Mark O'Halloran wrestle Mick Cassidy to the ground as the Broncos lose a close encounter to Wigan

241

Super League IX - Round by Round

Castleford's Andy Lynch reflects on relegation following the Tigers' loss to Wakefield

CASTLEFORD TIGERS 28
WAKEFIELD TRINITY WILDCATS 32

TIGERS: 1 Damian Gibson; 2 Waine Pryce; 3 Paul Mellor; 20 Tom Saxton; 5 Darren Rogers; 33 Brad Davis; 19 Francis Maloney; 8 Craig Greenhill; 9 Wayne Godwin; 10 Andy Lynch; 11 Lee Harland; 23 Michael Smith; 13 Ryan Hudson (C). Subs (all used): 15 Nathan Sykes; 35 Mark Tookey; 16 Jon Hepworth; 17 Paul Jackson. **Tries:** Gibson (8), Saxton (11), Mellor (20, 56), M Smith (23), Godwin (75); **Goals:** Maloney 2/3, Godwin 0/2. **WILDCATS:** 21 Mark Field; 14 Colum Halpenny; 1 Jason Demetriou; 4 Sid Domic; 5 Semi Tadulala; 3 Gareth Ellis (C); 7 Ben Jeffries; 27 Chris Feather; 9 David March; 10 Michael Korkidas; 11 David Solomona; 23 Duncan MacGillivray; 19 Rob Spicer. Subs (all used): 8 Darrell Griffin; 17 Paul Handforth; 18 Olivier Elima; 2 Justin Ryder. **Tries:** Tadulala (2), Halpenny (15, 59), Solomona (39, 43), Handforth (49); **Goals:** March 3/6, Handforth 1/2. **Rugby Leaguer & League Express Men of the Match:** *Tigers:* Wayne Godwin; *Wildcats:* David Solomona. **Penalty count:** 8-9; **Half-time:** 18-18; **Referee:** Ian Smith (Oldham); **Attendance:** 11,055.

HULL FC 20 WIDNES VIKINGS 18

HULL: 32 Shaun Briscoe; 2 Colin Best; 5 Gareth Raynor; 14 Kirk Yeaman; 26 Richie Barnett Jnr; 30 Richard Whiting; 25 Peter Lupton; 34 Nick Scruton; 9 Richard Swain (C); 18 Ewan Dowes; 29 Andy Bailey; 23 Paul McNicholas; 24 Graeme Horne. Subs (all used): 11 Richard Fletcher; 20 Garreth Carvell; 27 Liam Higgins; 35 Andy Last. **Tries:** Whiting (12, 25), Barnett Jnr (48), Lupton (55), Best (70); **Goals:** Whiting 0/3, Swain 0/1, Lupton 0/1. **VIKINGS:** 33 Tim Holmes; 2 Paul Devlin; 14 Deon Bird; 4 Adam Hughes; 35 Justin Murphy; 6 Jules O'Neill; 20 Stephen Myler; 17 David Mills; 9 Shane Millard; 11 Steve McCurrie; 13 Daniel Frame; 12 Andy Hay (C); 18 Simon Finnigan. Subs (all used): 31 Matt Whitaker; 16 Andy Hobson; 34 Tommy Gallagher; 36 Sala Fa'alogo. **Tries:** Frame (19), Whitaker (38), Fa'alogo (64); **Goals:** Jules O'Neill 3/5. **Rugby Leaguer & League Express Men of the Match:** *Hull:* Richard Swain; *Vikings:* Jules O'Neill. **Penalty count:** 4-7; **Half-time:** 8-12; **Referee:** Richard Silverwood (Dewsbury); **Attendance:** 9,544.

HUDDERSFIELD GIANTS 28 SALFORD CITY REDS 22

GIANTS: 1 Paul Reilly; 3 Stuart Donlan; 24 James Evans; 13 Brandon Costin; 34 Marcus St Hilaire; 5 Stanley Gene; 9 Paul March; 25 Darren Fleary (C); 7 Sean Penkywicz; 10 Jim Gannon; 4 Julian Bailey; 11 Chris Nero; 14 Stuart Jones. Subs (all used): 2 Hefin O'Hare; 16 Iain Morrison; 20 Jon Grayshon; 21 Paul White. **Tries:** Grayshon (27), Evans (61), St Hilaire (62), White (78); **Goals:** Costin 6/8. **Sin bin:** Nero (33) - holding down; (74) - interference. **CITY REDS:** 6 Cliff Beverley; 2 Joel Caine; 3 Stuart Littler; 27 Nathan McAvoy; 5 Anthony Stewart; 33 Kevin McGuinness; 15 Karl Kirkpatrick; 8 Andy Coley; 9 Malcolm Alker (C); 10 Sean Rutgerson; 18 Mark Shipway; 12 Andy Johnson; 13 Chris Charles. Subs (all used): 11 Simon Baldwin; 17 Gareth Haggerty; 21 John Clough; 28 Tim Hartley. **Tries:** Littler (2, 46), Rutgerson (37), Caine (56); **Goals:** Charles 3/5. **Sin bin:** Beverley (60) - holding down. **On report:** Charles & Shipway (67) - foul play. **Rugby Leaguer & League Express Men of the Match:** *Giants:* Jon Grayshon; *City Reds:* Kevin McGuinness. **Penalty count:** 11-9; **Half-time:** 8-10; **Referee:** Russell Smith (Castleford); **Attendance:** 3,083.

(34, 74); **Goals:** Deacon 3/6; **Field goals:** Deacon 2. **Rugby Leaguer & League Express Men of the Match:** *Wolves:* Jerome Guisset; *Bulls:* Lesley Vainikolo. **Penalty count:** 5-5; **Half-time:** 6-22; **Referee:** Ian Smith (Oldham); **Attendance:** 10,008.

ROUND 28

Friday 17th September 2004

BRADFORD BULLS 64 ST HELENS 24

BULLS: 6 Michael Withers; 17 Stuart Reardon; 3 Leon Pryce; 4 Shontayne Hape; 5 Lesley Vainikolo; 18 Iestyn Harris; 7 Paul Deacon; 8 Joe Vagana; 1 Robbie Paul (C); 29 Stuart Fielden; 12 Jamie Peacock; 13 Logan Swann; 11 Lee Radford. Subs (all used): 15 Karl Pratt; 16 Paul Johnson; 27 Rob Parker; 30 Richard Moore. **Tries:** Hape (4, 8), Reardon (27, 54, 72), Vainikolo (36, 51, 57), Peacock (39), Withers (69), Deacon (79); **Goals:** Deacon 10/11. **SAINTS:** 1 Paul Wellens; 2 Ade Gardner; 34 Gray Viane; 4 Willie Talau; 25 Ian Hardman; 26 James Roby; 7 Sean Long (C); 16 Keith Mason; 14 Mick Higham; 23 Maurie Fa'asavalu; 11 Chris Joynt; 10 John Stankevitch; 21 Jon Wilkin. Subs (all used): 15 Mike Bennett; 24 James Graham; 22 Dom Feaunati; 35 Andy Bracek (D). **Tries:** Stankevitch (11), Bennett (42), Feaunati (61), Gardner (74); **Goals:** Long 4/5, Hardman 0/1. **Rugby Leaguer & League Express Men of the Match:** *Bulls:* Lesley Vainikolo; *Saints:* Sean Long. **Penalty count:** 7-7; **Half-time:** 28-10; **Referee:** Ashley Klein (London); **Attendance:** 13,127.

LEEDS RHINOS 42 LONDON BRONCOS 14

RHINOS: 21 Richard Mathers; 18 Mark Calderwood; 5 Chev Walker; 4 Keith Senior; 2 Francis Cummins; 13 Kevin Sinfield (C); 14 Andrew Dunemann; 8 Ryan Bailey; 9 Matt Diskin; 12 Matt Adamson; 3 Chris McKenna; 20 Jamie Jones-Buchanan; 11 David Furner. Subs (all used): 10 Barrie McDermott; 29 Ali Lauititi; 7 Rob Burrow; 17 Wayne McDonald. **Tries:** Senior (9), Calderwood (20, 65), Walker (28), Lauititi (48, 50), Diskin (54, 62); **Goals:** Sinfield 5/8. **BRONCOS:** 34 Zebastian Luisi; 23 Lee Greenwood; 3 Nigel Roy; 4 Mark O'Halloran; 33 Paul Sampson; 1 Paul Sykes; 7 Dennis Moran; 10 Steve Trindall; 9 Neil Budworth; 8 Francis Stephenson; 6 Rob Purdham; 11 Mat Toshack; 13 Jim Dymock (C). Subs (all used): 15 Mitchell Stringer; 2 Jon Wells; 21 Rob Jackson; 36 Ade Adebisi (D). **Tries:** Purdham (34), Sampson (44), Moran (78); **Goals:** Sykes 0/2, Budworth 1/1. **Rugby Leaguer & League Express Men of the Match:** *Rhinos:* David Furner; *Broncos:* Dennis Moran. **Penalty count:** 4-2; **Half-time:** 16-4; **Referee:** Ronnie Laughton (Barnsley); **Attendance:** 17,329.

WIGAN WARRIORS 21 WARRINGTON WOLVES 16

WARRIORS: 1 Kris Radlinski; 3 Martin Aspinwall; 19 Stephen Wild; 21 Kevin Brown; 2 Brett Dallas; 6 Danny Orr; 7 Adrian Lam; 8 Terry O'Connor; 17 Mark Smith; 10 Craig Smith; 13 Andy Farrell (C); 12 Danny Tickle; 15 Sean O'Loughlin. Subs (all used): 4 David Hodgson; 11 Mick Cassidy; 14 Luke Robinson; 20 Gareth Hock. **Tries:** Farrell (33), Aspinwall (42), Tickle (68), Brown (77); **Goals:** Farrell 1/1, Tickle 1/4; **Field goal:** Lam. **WOLVES:** 1 Daryl Cardiss; 27 Henry Fa'afili; 3 Brent Grose; 4 Ben Westwood; 20 Dean Gaskell; 6 Lee Briers; 7 Nathan Wood; 22 Danny Lima; 9 Jon Clarke; 10 Mark Hilton; 12 Ian Sibbit; 16 Paul Wood; 13 Mike Forshaw (C). Subs (all used): 14 Mark Gleeson; 19 Gary Hulse; 15 Jerome Guisset; 8 Chris Leikvoll. **Tries:** Guisset (19), Grose (55), Cardiss (61); **Goals:** Briers 2/3. **Sin bin:** P Wood (44) - obstruction. **Rugby Leaguer & League Express Men of the Match:** *Warriors:* Adrian Lam; *Wolves:* Dean Gaskell. **Penalty count:** 4-4; **Half-time:** 6-6; **Referee:** Steve Ganson (St Helens); **Attendance:** 15,132.

Widnes' Adam Hughes tackled by Colin Best and Graeme Horne as the Vikings survive in Super League, despite losing to Hull

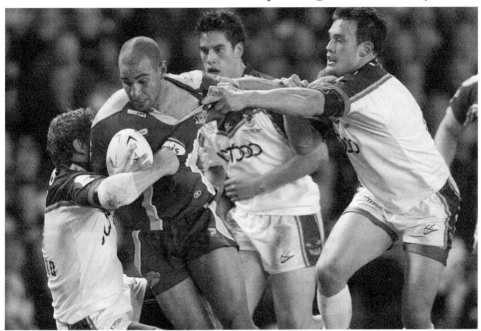

Bradford's Logan Swann gets to grips with Leeds' Chev Walker during the Super League Grand Final

PLAY-OFFS

Friday 24th September 2004

ELIMINATION PLAY-OFF

HULL FC 18 WAKEFIELD TRINITY WILDCATS 28

HULL: 32 Shaun Briscoe; 2 Colin Best; 30 Richard Whiting; 14 Kirk Yeaman; 5 Gareth Raynor; 16 Paul Cooke (C); 25 Peter Lupton; 18 Ewan Dowes; 9 Richard Swain; 20 Garreth Carvell; 11 Richard Fletcher; 23 Paul McNicholas; 15 Shayne McMenemy. Subs (all used): 24 Graeme Horne; 26 Richie Barnett Jnr; 29 Andy Bailey; 34 Nick Scruton.
Tries: Swain (12), McMenemy (17), Dowes (68);
Goals: Lupton 3/5.
WILDCATS: 21 Mark Field; 14 Colum Halpenny; 1 Jason Demetriou; 4 Sid Domic; 5 Semi Tadulala; 3 Gareth Ellis (C); 7 Ben Jeffries; 27 Chris Feather; 9 David March; 10 Michael Korkidas; 11 David Solomona; 23 Duncan MacGillivray; 19 Rob Spicer. Subs (all used): 8 Darrell Griffin; 17 Paul Handforth; 18 Olivier Elima; 16 Steve Snitch.
Tries: March (7), Halpenny (45), Feather (52), Tadulala (55), Demetriou (75); **Goals:** March 1/2, Handforth 3/4.
Sin bin: Jeffries (3) - interference;
Ellis (12) - holding down.
On report: Solomona (8) - foul tackle.
Rugby Leaguer & League Express Men of the Match:
Hull: Shayne McMenemy; *Wildcats:* Ben Jeffries.
Penalty count: 8-7; **Half-time:** 14-6; **Referee:** Karl Kirkpatrick (Warrington); **Attendance:** 10,550.

Saturday 25th September 2004

ELIMINATION PLAY-OFF

WIGAN WARRIORS 18 ST HELENS 12

WARRIORS: 1 Kris Radlinski; 3 Martin Aspinwall; 19 Stephen Wild; 21 Kevin Brown; 2 Brett Dallas; 6 Danny Orr; 7 Adrian Lam; 13 Andy Farrell (C); 9 Terry Newton; 10 Craig Smith; 20 Gareth Hock; 12 Danny Tickle; 15 Sean O'Loughlin. Subs (all used): 14 Luke Robinson; 33 Gary Connolly; 16 Danny Sculthorpe; 8 Terry O'Connor.
Tries: Robinson (32), Brown (37), Farrell (42);
Goals: Farrell 3/3.
SAINTS: 1 Paul Wellens; 25 Ian Hardman; 4 Willie Talau; 5 Darren Albert; 26 James Roby; 6 Jason Hooper; 7 Sean Long; 8 Nick Fozzard; 14 Mick Higham; 9 Keiron Cunningham; 12 Lee Gilmour; 11 Chris Joynt; 13 Paul Sculthorpe (C). Subs (all used): 2 Ade Gardner; 16 Keith Mason; 18 Mark Edmondson; 21 Jon Wilkin.
Try: Gardner (74); **Goals:** Long 4/4.
Rugby Leaguer & League Express Men of the Match:
Warriors: Sean O'Loughlin; *Saints:* Lee Gilmour.
Penalty count: 6-8; **Half-time:** 12-6; **Referee:** Russell Smith (Castleford); **Attendance:** 20,052.

Friday 1st October 2004

ELIMINATION SEMI-FINAL

WIGAN WARRIORS 18 WAKEFIELD TRINITY WILDCATS 14

WARRIORS: 1 Kris Radlinski; 3 Martin Aspinwall; 19 Stephen Wild; 21 Kevin Brown; 2 Brett Dallas; 6 Danny Orr; 7 Adrian Lam; 13 Andy Farrell (C); 9 Terry Newton; 10 Craig Smith; 20 Gareth Hock; 12 Danny Tickle; 15 Sean O'Loughlin. Subs (all used): 5 Brian Carney; 8 Terry O'Connor; 14 Luke Robinson; 16 Danny Sculthorpe.
Tries: Radlinski (21), Brown (24), Lam (70);
Goals: Farrell 3/6.
WILDCATS: 21 Mark Field; 14 Colum Halpenny; 1 Jason Demetriou; 4 Sid Domic; 5 Semi Tadulala; 3 Gareth Ellis (C); 7 Ben Jeffries; 27 Chris Feather; 9 David March; 10 Michael Korkidas; 11 David Solomona; 23 Duncan MacGillivray; 19 Rob Spicer. Subs (all used): 8 Darrell Griffin; 17 Paul Handforth; 13 Jamie Field; 16 Steve Snitch.
Tries: Halpenny (11), MacGillivray (13), Solomona (17);
Goals: March 1/3, Handforth 0/1.
Sin bin: Solomona (54) - professional foul.
Rugby Leaguer & League Express Men of the Match:
Warriors: Kris Radlinski; *Wildcats:* Ben Jeffries.
Penalty count: 7-5; **Half-time:** 10-14; **Referee:** Russell Smith (Castleford); **Attendance:** 16,179.

Saturday 2nd October 2004

QUALIFYING SEMI-FINAL

LEEDS RHINOS 12 BRADFORD BULLS 26

RHINOS: 21 Richard Mathers; 5 Chev Walker; 3 Chris McKenna; 4 Keith Senior; 22 Marcus Bai; 6 Danny McGuire; 14 Andrew Dunemann; 8 Ryan Bailey; 9 Matt Diskin; 19 Danny Ward; 11 David Furner; 12 Matt Adamson; 13 Kevin Sinfield (C). Subs (all used): 16 Willie Poching; 29 Ali Lauitiiti; 10 Barrie McDermott; 7 Rob Burrow.
Tries: McGuire (20), Poching (61); **Goals:** Sinfield 2/2.
BULLS: 6 Michael Withers; 17 Stuart Reardon; 3 Leon Pryce; 4 Shontayne Hape; 5 Lesley Vainikolo; 18 Iestyn Harris; 7 Paul Deacon; 8 Joe Vagana; 1 Robbie Paul (C); 29 Stuart Fielden; 12 Jamie Peacock; 13 Logan Swann; 11 Lee Radford. Subs (all used): 27 Rob Parker; 15 Karl Pratt; 16 Paul Johnson; 30 Richard Moore.
Tries: Hape (2, 14), Paul (52), Radford (54), Vainikolo (79); **Goals:** Deacon 3/5.
Rugby Leaguer & League Express Men of the Match:
Rhinos: Marcus Bai; *Bulls:* Iestyn Harris.
Penalty count: 4-3; **Half-time:** 6-8;
Referee: Steve Ganson (St Helens); **Attendance:** 21,225.

Friday 8th October 2004

FINAL ELIMINATOR

LEEDS RHINOS 40 WIGAN WARRIORS 12

RHINOS: 21 Richard Mathers; 18 Mark Calderwood; 5 Chev Walker; 4 Keith Senior; 22 Marcus Bai; 13 Kevin Sinfield (C); 6 Danny McGuire; 19 Danny Ward; 9 Matt Diskin; 8 Ryan Bailey; 3 Chris McKenna; 29 Ali Lauitiiti; 11 David Furner. Subs (all used): 16 Willie Poching; 10 Barrie McDermott; 20 Jamie Jones-Buchanan; 7 Rob Burrow.
Tries: Bai (10, 62, 69), Walker (23), McGuire (26), Mathers (33), Bailey (75);
Goals: Sinfield 5/6, Furner 1/1.
WARRIORS: 1 Kris Radlinski; 2 Brett Dallas; 21 Kevin Brown; 19 Stephen Wild; 3 Martin Aspinwall; 6 Danny Orr; 7 Adrian Lam; 10 Craig Smith; 9 Terry Newton; 13 Andy Farrell (C); 12 Danny Tickle; 20 Gareth Hock; 15 Sean O'Loughlin. Subs (all used): 8 Terry O'Connor; 14 Luke Robinson; 16 Danny Sculthorpe; 11 Mick Cassidy.
Tries: Farrell (37), Robinson (45); **Goals:** Farrell 2/2.
Rugby Leaguer & League Express Men of the Match:
Rhinos: Richard Mathers; *Warriors:* Adrian Lam.
Penalty count: 6-5; **Half-time:** 22-6; **Referee:** Karl Kirkpatrick (Warrington); **Attendance:** 20,119.

Saturday 16th October 2004

GRAND FINAL

BRADFORD BULLS 8 LEEDS RHINOS 16

BULLS: 6 Michael Withers; 17 Stuart Reardon; 16 Paul Johnson; 4 Shontayne Hape; 5 Lesley Vainikolo; 18 Iestyn Harris; 7 Paul Deacon; 8 Joe Vagana; 1 Robbie Paul (C); 29 Stuart Fielden; 12 Jamie Peacock; 13 Logan Swann; 11 Lee Radford. Subs: 10 Paul Anderson for Vagana (14); 15 Karl Pratt for Paul (23); 27 Rob Parker for Anderson (24); 19 Jamie Langley for Peacock (32); Paul for Withers (ht); Peacock for Radford (48); Radford for Swann (54); Vagana for Parker (56); Parker for Fielden (63); Fielden for Vagana (67); Swann for Langley (68).
Tries: Vainikolo (7), Hape (45); **Goals:** Deacon 0/2.
RHINOS: 21 Richard Mathers; 18 Mark Calderwood; 5 Chev Walker; 4 Keith Senior; 22 Marcus Bai; 13 Kevin Sinfield (C); 6 Danny McGuire; 19 Danny Ward; 9 Matt Diskin; 8 Ryan Bailey; 3 Chris McKenna; 29 Ali Lauitiiti; 11 David Furner. Subs: 16 Willie Poching for Furner (19); 10 Barrie McDermott for Ward (22); Ward for Bailey (29); 7 Rob Burrow for Lauitiiti (30); Bailey for McDermott (41); 20 Jamie Jones-Buchanan for McKenna (48); Lauitiiti for Ward (50); Furner for Sinfield (60); McKenna for Poching (63); Sinfield for Diskin (67); Poching for McKenna (72); Ward for Bailey (73).
Tries: Diskin (15), McGuire (75); **Goals:** Sinfield 4/4.
Rugby Leaguer & League Express Men of the Match:
Bulls: Lesley Vainikolo; *Rhinos:* Richard Mathers.
Penalty count: 5-5; **Half-time:** 4-10;
Referee: Steve Ganson (St Helens);
Attendance: 65,547 *(at Old Trafford, Manchester).*

SUPER LEAGUE IX
Opta Index Analysis

Richard Swain

SUPER LEAGUE IX TOP PERFORMERS *(BY CATEGORY)*

TACKLES
Richard Swain	Hull	933
Shane Millard	Widnes	881
Malcolm Alker	Salford	849
David March	Wakefield	811
Sean O'Loughlin	Wigan	792
Ryan Hudson	Castleford	780
Wayne Godwin	Castleford	730
Danny Tickle	Wigan	724
Steele Retchless	London	694
Matt Diskin	Leeds	685

TACKLES MADE *(% Success)*
Jon Clarke	Warrington	99%
Michael Smith	Castleford	98%
Paul Smith	Huddersfield	98%
Liam Higgins	Hull	98%
Chris Charles	Salford	97%
Richard Swain	Hull	97%
David Furner	Leeds	97%
Malcolm Alker	Salford	97%
Ryan Bailey	Leeds	97%
Wayne Godwin	Castleford	96%

CARRIES
Paul Wellens	St Helens	511
Andy Farrell	Wigan	468
Michael Korkidas	Wakefield	463
Ewan Dowes	Hull	439
Richard Mathers	Leeds	438
Steele Retchless	London	424
Shane Millard	Widnes	408
Andy Lynch	Castleford	408
Marcus Bai	Leeds	404
David Solomona	Wakefield	396

AVERAGE GAIN PER CARRY *(Metres)*
Brett Dallas	Wigan	10.33
Duncan MacGillivray	Wakefield	10.24
Mark Calderwood	Leeds	10.1
Lesley Vainikolo	Bradford	9.74
Chev Walker	Leeds	9.53
Julian Bailey	Huddersfield	9.52
Jason Hooper	St Helens	9.39
Marcus Bai	Leeds	9.27
Keith Senior	Leeds	9.12
Jamie Langley	Bradford	9.08

METRES
Michael Korkidas	Wakefield	4084
Marcus Bai	Leeds	3746
Brett Dallas	Wigan	3617
Lesley Vainikolo	Bradford	3593
Paul Wellens	St Helens	3556
Sid Domic	Wakefield	3384
Andy Farrell	Wigan	3312
Colin Best	Hull	3310
Andy Lynch	Castleford	3296
Ewan Dowes	Hull	3265

CLEAN BREAKS
Marcus Bai	Leeds	44
Danny McGuire	Leeds	43
Lesley Vainikolo	Bradford	40
Keith Senior	Leeds	33
Dennis Moran	London	32
Kirk Yeaman	Hull	29
Ben Jeffries	Wakefield	29
Jason Demetriou	Wakefield	28
Brett Dallas	Wigan	28
Sid Domic	Wakefield	27

OFFLOADS
David Solomona	Wakefield	81
Mike Forshaw	Warrington	66
Andy Lynch	Castleford	61
Michael Smith	Castleford	59
Wayne McDonald	Leeds	58
Keith Senior	Leeds	56
Andy Farrell	Wigan	55
Kevin Sinfield	Leeds	55
Colin Best	Hull	53
Barrie McDermott	Leeds	51

TACKLE BUSTS
Lesley Vainikolo	Bradford	132
Colin Best	Hull	84
Richard Mathers	Leeds	78
Brett Dallas	Wigan	77
Keith Senior	Leeds	75
Michael Smith	Castleford	74
Gareth Raynor	Hull	74
Stuart Fielden	Bradford	71
Dean Gaskell	Warrington	69
Sid Domic	Wakefield	69

MARKER TACKLES
Shane Millard	Widnes	114
David March	Wakefield	109
Sean O'Loughlin	Wigan	109
Richard Swain	Hull	103
Kevin Sinfield	Leeds	102
Mark Gleeson	Warrington	89
Gareth Ellis	Wakefield	89
Lee Radford	Bradford	88
Ryan Hudson	Castleford	85
Wayne Godwin	Castleford	80

TRY ASSISTS
Dennis Moran	London	33
Leon Pryce	Bradford	28
Lee Briers	Warrington	27
Ben Jeffries	Wakefield	24
Paul Deacon	Bradford	23
Kevin Sinfield	Leeds	22
Paul Cooke	Hull	21
Gavin Clinch	Salford	20
Keith Senior	Leeds	20
Paul Sculthorpe	St Helens	19

40/20s
Jules O'Neill	Widnes	3
Dennis Moran	London	3
Paul Deacon	Bradford	3
Stephen Myler	Widnes	2
Ben Jeffries	Wakefield	2
Adrian Lam	Wigan	2
Luke Robinson	Wigan	1
Jason Smith	Hull	1
Paul March	Huddersfield	1
Brandon Costin	Huddersfield	1

Leeds' Danny McGuire touches down against Wakefield to break Paul Newlove's record for tries in a Super League season, set in 1996. The Rhinos scored more tries than any other team in Super League IX.

SUPER LEAGUE IX AVERAGES PER MATCH

TACKLES		CARRIES		BREAKS		ERRORS	
Widnes Vikings	260	Leeds Rhinos	206	Leeds Rhinos	12	Leeds Rhinos	11
Salford City Reds	259	Hull FC	185	Bradford Bulls	10	Bradford Bulls	11
London Broncos	257	Wigan Warriors	183	St Helens	9	Wakefield T Wildcats	11
Castleford Tigers	256	Widnes Vikings	181	Wakefield T Wildcats	8	London Broncos	11
Wigan Warriors	256	Warrington Wolves	181	Hull FC	8	Huddersfield Giants	11
Warrington Wolves	255	Bradford Bulls	181	Warrington Wolves	8	St Helens	11
Hull FC	253	Wakefield T Wildcats	177	Wigan Warriors	7	Hull FC	10
Huddersfield Giants	251	St Helens	175	London Broncos	7	Salford City Reds	10
St Helens	249	Salford City Reds	173	Salford City Reds	6	Warrington Wolves	10
Leeds Rhinos	239	London Broncos	167	Castleford Tigers	6	Wigan Warriors	9
Bradford Bulls	230	Castleford Tigers	167	Widnes Vikings	5	Castleford Tigers	9
Wakefield T Wildcats	228	Huddersfield Giants	162	Huddersfield Giants	5	Widnes Vikings	9

MISSED TACKLES		METRES		OFFLOADS		KICKS	
Widnes Vikings	26	Leeds Rhinos	1592	Leeds Rhinos	21	Wigan Warriors	20
London Broncos	25	Bradford Bulls	1401	Bradford Bulls	14	Hull FC	20
Huddersfield Giants	24	Wakefield T Wildcats	1386	Wakefield T Wildcats	14	Salford City Reds	20
Wakefield T Wildcats	24	Hull FC	1383	Hull FC	14	Widnes Vikings	20
Castleford Tigers	20	Wigan Warriors	1358	Wigan Warriors	13	Castleford Tigers	19
Wigan Warriors	20	St Helens	1340	Salford City Reds	13	Warrington Wolves	19
Warrington Wolves	20	Warrington Wolves	1311	Warrington Wolves	12	London Broncos	18
St Helens	20	Widnes Vikings	1253	London Broncos	12	Huddersfield Giants	17
Bradford Bulls	20	Salford City Reds	1249	Castleford Tigers	12	Leeds Rhinos	17
Salford City Reds	19	Castleford Tigers	1211	Huddersfield Giants	12	Bradford Bulls	16
Hull FC	18	Huddersfield Giants	1153	Widnes Vikings	11	St Helens	15
Leeds Rhinos	16	London Broncos	1147	St Helens	10	Wakefield T Wildcats	15

SUPER LEAGUE IX TRIES SCORED/CONCEDED

TOTAL TRIES SCORED		TOTAL TRIES CONCEDED		TRIES SCORED (KICKS)		TRIES CONCEDED (KICKS)	
Leeds Rhinos	184	London Broncos	173	Leeds Rhinos	29	Salford City Reds	26
Bradford Bulls	160	Castleford Tigers	166	Bradford Bulls	28	London Broncos	25
Hull FC	151	Widnes Vikings	149	Castleford Tigers	22	Wigan Warriors	23
St Helens	144	Salford City Reds	148	Hull FC	21	Castleford Tigers	22
Wakefield T Wildcats	136	Huddersfield Giants	125	Warrington Wolves	21	Warrington Wolves	22
Warrington Wolves	123	Warrington Wolves	124	Wigan Warriors	20	Huddersfield Giants	21
Wigan Warriors	122	Wakefield T Wildcats	118	Wakefield T Wildcats	19	Widnes Vikings	19
London Broncos	101	St Helens	111	London Broncos	16	Hull FC	18
Castleford Tigers	89	Wigan Warriors	99	Huddersfield Giants	15	Leeds Rhinos	16
Salford City Reds	85	Bradford Bulls	97	St Helens	14	Bradford Bulls	15
Huddersfield Giants	85	Hull FC	78	Widnes Vikings	14	Wakefield T Wildcats	15
Widnes Vikings	77	Leeds Rhinos	76	Salford City Reds	13	St Helens	10

SUPER LEAGUE IX TRIES SCORED/CONCEDED

TRIES SCORED FROM OWN HALF

Leeds Rhinos	36
St Helens	35
Hull FC	30
Wakefield T Wildcats	27
Wigan Warriors	26
Bradford Bulls	25
London Broncos	20
Warrington Wolves	17
Huddersfield Giants	15
Salford City Reds	14
Castleford Tigers	14
Widnes Vikings	5

TRIES CONCEDED FROM OVER 50M

Widnes Vikings	43
Castleford Tigers	38
Salford City Reds	28
London Broncos	25
Warrington Wolves	25
St Helens	24
Wigan Warriors	16
Bradford Bulls	16
Leeds Rhinos	15
Huddersfield Giants	13
Hull FC	12
Wakefield T Wildcats	9

TRIES SCORED FROM UNDER 10M

Leeds Rhinos	66
St Helens	57
Bradford Bulls	57
Wakefield T Wildcats	54
Warrington Wolves	51
Hull FC	48
London Broncos	46
Widnes Vikings	44
Wigan Warriors	44
Castleford Tigers	41
Salford City Reds	39
Huddersfield Giants	26

TRIES CONCEDED FROM UNDER 10M

London Broncos	75
Castleford Tigers	68
Salford City Reds	63
Wakefield T Wildcats	58
Huddersfield Giants	53
Warrington Wolves	45
St Helens	41
Wigan Warriors	41
Widnes Vikings	39
Bradford Bulls	36
Leeds Rhinos	32
Hull FC	28

SUPER LEAGUE IX PENALTIES

TOTAL PENALTIES AWARDED

Huddersfield Giants	243
Wakefield T Wildcats	236
Castleford Tigers	218
St Helens	217
Hull FC	214
Bradford Bulls	208
Salford City Reds	204
Warrington Wolves	204
Wigan Warriors	198
Leeds Rhinos	193
London Broncos	184
Widnes Vikings	184

TOTAL PENALTIES CONCEDED

Huddersfield Giants	284
St Helens	239
Castleford Tigers	228
Wakefield T Wildcats	211
Wigan Warriors	210
Widnes Vikings	208
Warrington Wolves	202
Salford City Reds	189
London Broncos	186
Hull FC	183
Leeds Rhinos	182
Bradford Bulls	181

FOUL PLAY - AWARDED

Huddersfield Giants	55
Hull FC	55
Castleford Tigers	54
St Helens	54
Wakefield T Wildcats	50
Salford City Reds	50
Warrington Wolves	48
London Broncos	47
Wigan Warriors	46
Widnes Vikings	41
Bradford Bulls	34
Leeds Rhinos	33

FOUL PLAY - CONCEDED

Huddersfield Giants	75
St Helens	74
Warrington Wolves	54
Castleford Tigers	50
Wakefield T Wildcats	47
Wigan Warriors	47
Leeds Rhinos	40
Widnes Vikings	39
Salford City Reds	39
London Broncos	36
Hull FC	34
Bradford Bulls	32

OFFSIDE - AWARDED

Wakefield T Wildcats	38
St Helens	37
Castleford Tigers	35
Warrington Wolves	35
London Broncos	35
Wigan Warriors	35
Widnes Vikings	35
Bradford Bulls	32
Huddersfield Giants	28
Hull FC	28
Leeds Rhinos	26
Salford City Reds	25

OFFSIDE - CONCEDED

Castleford Tigers	44
Wakefield T Wildcats	41
Wigan Warriors	40
Widnes Vikings	38
Huddersfield Giants	35
London Broncos	34
Salford City Reds	33
Bradford Bulls	29
Warrington Wolves	27
Hull FC	27
Leeds Rhinos	24
St Helens	17

INTERFERENCE - AWARDED

Bradford Bulls	83
Leeds Rhinos	73
Wakefield T Wildcats	72
Huddersfield Giants	70
Salford City Reds	66
St Helens	61
Hull FC	59
Wigan Warriors	58
Castleford Tigers	50
Warrington Wolves	50
London Broncos	40
Widnes Vikings	36

INTERFERENCE - CONCEDED

Huddersfield Giants	93
Widnes Vikings	69
St Helens	68
Castleford Tigers	65
Warrington Wolves	61
Bradford Bulls	57
London Broncos	56
Hull FC	54
Wigan Warriors	51
Wakefield T Wildcats	49
Salford City Reds	49
Leeds Rhinos	46

OBSTRUCTION - AWARDED

St Helens	11
Huddersfield Giants	10
Castleford Tigers	10
Warrington Wolves	9
Leeds Rhinos	8
Wakefield T Wildcats	8
Hull FC	7
Widnes Vikings	7
Wigan Warriors	6
Salford City Reds	5
London Broncos	5
Bradford Bulls	2

OBSTRUCTION - CONCEDED

St Helens	13
Widnes Vikings	10
Leeds Rhinos	10
Warrington Wolves	9
Huddersfield Giants	8
Castleford Tigers	7
Hull FC	6
Salford City Reds	5
Bradford Bulls	5
Wigan Warriors	5
Wakefield T Wildcats	5
London Broncos	4

BALL STEALING - AWARDED

Widnes Vikings	22
Wakefield T Wildcats	21
St Helens	20
Hull FC	20
Huddersfield Giants	19
Bradford Bulls	19
London Broncos	16
Leeds Rhinos	15
Wigan Warriors	15
Castleford Tigers	11
Warrington Wolves	11
Salford City Reds	10

BALL STEALING - CONCEDED

Castleford Tigers	22
Salford City Reds	21
Wigan Warriors	20
St Helens	19
Warrington Wolves	18
Huddersfield Giants	18
Hull FC	16
Widnes Vikings	15
Wakefield T Wildcats	15
Bradford Bulls	14
London Broncos	11
Leeds Rhinos	10

OFFSIDE MARKERS - AWARDED

Castleford Tigers	28
Salford City Reds	22
Huddersfield Giants	18
Wakefield T Wildcats	17
Warrington Wolves	17
Wigan Warriors	16
Bradford Bulls	14
London Broncos	14
Leeds Rhinos	10
Hull FC	9
St Helens	6
Widnes Vikings	5

OFFSIDE MARKERS - CONCEDED

Wakefield T Wildcats	22
Leeds Rhinos	21
Wigan Warriors	20
St Helens	18
Huddersfield Giants	17
Hull FC	16
London Broncos	13
Bradford Bulls	12
Castleford Tigers	11
Salford City Reds	9
Widnes Vikings	9
Warrington Wolves	8

NOT PLAYING BALL CORRECTLY - AWARDED

Huddersfield Giants	12
London Broncos	9
Widnes Vikings	8
Warrington Wolves	7
Hull FC	7
Castleford Tigers	6
Wakefield T Wildcats	6
Bradford Bulls	6
Salford City Reds	5
Leeds Rhinos	5
St Helens	4
Wigan Warriors	3

NOT PLAYING BALL CORRECTLY - CONCEDED

Leeds Rhinos	17
Wakefield T Wildcats	10
Huddersfield Giants	10
Bradford Bulls	7
Widnes Vikings	7
St Helens	6
Hull FC	5
Warrington Wolves	5
Castleford Tigers	4
London Broncos	3
Wigan Warriors	2
Salford City Reds	2

DISSENT - AWARDED

Huddersfield Giants	9
Widnes Vikings	7
Hull FC	7
Castleford Tigers	7
Leeds Rhinos	7
St Helens	6
Warrington Wolves	5
Wakefield T Wildcats	5
Salford City Reds	5
London Broncos	4
Wigan Warriors	4
Bradford Bulls	3

DISSENT - CONCEDED

Huddersfield Giants	11
Bradford Bulls	8
Widnes Vikings	8
Wakefield T Wildcats	7
London Broncos	7
Salford City Reds	7
Warrington Wolves	5
St Helens	4
Castleford Tigers	4
Wigan Warriors	4
Hull FC	3
Leeds Rhinos	1

BRADFORD BULLS

Michael Withers

Lesley Vainikolo

TACKLES
Jamie Peacock...............614
Stuart Fielden 597
Lee Radford...................550
Logan Swann..................495
Rob Parker 492

CARRIES
Jamie Peacock...............395
Stuart Reardon 385
Stuart Fielden 383
Lesley Vainikolo..............369
Robbie Paul 271

METRES
Lesley Vainikolo............3593
Stuart Fielden 3181
Stuart Reardon 3060
Jamie Peacock...............3031
Joe Vagana 2175

CLEAN BREAKS
Lesley Vainikolo...............40
Shontayne Hape 26
Stuart Reardon 23
Leon Pryce 19
Paul Johnson...................19

OFFLOADS
Stuart Fielden 46
Leon Pryce 43
Jamie Peacock.................34
Lesley Vainikolo................31
Logan Swann...................27

TACKLE BUSTS
Lesley Vainikolo.............132
Stuart Fielden 71
Shontayne Hape 63
Jamie Peacock.................59
Stuart Reardon 58

MARKER TACKLES
Lee Radford.....................88
Rob Parker 79
Jamie Peacock.................77
Jamie Langley 70
Robbie Paul 70

AVERAGE OPTA INDEX
Lesley Vainikolo 954.5
Michael Withers 661.47
Stuart Fielden 658.89
Shontayne Hape 636.25
Stuart Reardon 614.89

CASTLEFORD TIGERS

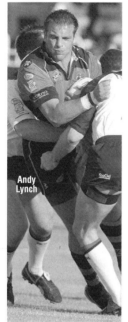

Andy Lynch

Michael Smith

TACKLES
Ryan Hudson..................780
Wayne Godwin................730
Andy Lynch 534
Lee Harland 413
Paul Jackson 394

CARRIES
Andy Lynch 408
Craig Greenhill................331
Ryan Hudson..................307
Damian Gibson 284
Michael Smith 274

METRES
Andy Lynch 3296
Craig Greenhill..............2329
Michael Smith 2217
Ryan Hudson..................2031
Jon Hepworth 1887

CLEAN BREAKS
Darren Rogers 19
Paul Mellor 16
Michael Smith 13
Ryan Hudson...................13
Tom Saxton 11

OFFLOADS
Andy Lynch 61
Michael Smith 59
Tom Saxton 36
Paul Mellor 26
Ryan Hudson...................23

TACKLE BUSTS
Michael Smith 74
Paul Mellor 44
Tom Saxton 41
Jamie Thackray 37
Jon Hepworth 35

MARKER TACKLES
Ryan Hudson...................85
Wayne Godwin.................80
Nathan Sykes...................55
Sean Ryan 45
Craig Greenhill.................40

AVERAGE OPTA INDEX
Michael Smith...........663.76
Andy Lynch................633.81
Wayne Godwin 604.46
Paul Mellor 591.26
Ryan Hudson..................552

HUDDERSFIELD GIANTS

Brandon Costin

Stanley Gene

TACKLES
Stuart Jones 660
Chris Nero 528
Ben Roarty...................510
Sean Penkywicz.............504
Jim Gannon 461

CARRIES
Paul Reilly 374
Stanley Gene 355
Jim Gannon 309
Ben Roarty....................305
Hefin O'Hare 277

METRES
Paul Reilly 2807
Jim Gannon 2289
Stanley Gene 2238
Hefin O'Hare 2119
Ben Roarty....................1984

CLEAN BREAKS
Brandon Costin 15
Julian Bailey 14
Paul March 12
James Evans 10
Marcus St Hilaire.............10

OFFLOADS
Ben Roarty......................33
James Evans 30
Jim Gannon 26
Eorl Crabtree 25
Darren Fleary..................22

TACKLE BUSTS
Paul Reilly 58
Brandon Costin 39
Stanley Gene 35
Marcus St Hilaire.............25
Stuart Donlan 23

MARKER TACKLES
Sean Penkywicz...............58
Stuart Jones 54
Paul Smith.......................48
Chris Nero 38
Eorl Crabtree 38

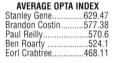
opta stats

AVERAGE OPTA INDEX
Stanley Gene.............629.47
Brandon Costin..........577.38
Paul Reilly...................570.6
Ben Roarty 524.1
Eorl Crabtree.............468.11

HULL F.C.

Richard Horne

Gareth Raynor

TACKLES
Richard Swain 933
Shayne McMenemy 589
Ewan Dowes 586
Paul Cooke 551
Richard Horne 523

CARRIES
Ewan Dowes 439
Shaun Briscoe 393
Paul King 383
Colin Best 379
Richard Horne 372

METRES
Colin Best 3310
Ewan Dowes 3265
Paul King 2998
Shaun Briscoe 2929
Kirk Yeaman 2624

CLEAN BREAKS
Kirk Yeaman 29
Colin Best 23
Richard Horne 22
Shaun Briscoe 21
Gareth Raynor 20

OFFLOADS
Colin Best 53
Shayne McMenemy 49
Gareth Raynor 36
Ewan Dowes 31
Richard Horne 31

TACKLE BUSTS
Colin Best 84
Gareth Raynor 74
Richard Horne 67
Kirk Yeaman 47
Shaun Briscoe 37

MARKER TACKLES
Richard Swain 103
Richard Whiting...............76
Paul Cooke 72
Shayne McMenemy 64
Richard Horne 63

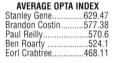
opta stats

AVERAGE OPTA INDEX
Gareth Raynor 757.13
Richard Horne 705.19
Colin Best 668.41
Shaun Briscoe 614.37
Richard Swain 604.44

LEEDS RHINOS

Marcus Bai

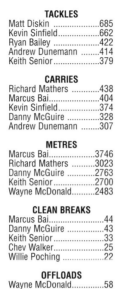

Danny McGuire

TACKLES
Matt Diskin 685
Kevin Sinfield.................662
Ryan Bailey 422
Andrew Dunemann 414
Keith Senior....................379

CARRIES
Richard Mathers 438
Marcus Bai.....................404
Kevin Sinfield.................374
Danny McGuire 328
Andrew Dunemann 307

METRES
Marcus Bai....................3746
Richard Mathers 3023
Danny McGuire 2763
Keith Senior.................2700
Wayne McDonald..........2483

CLEAN BREAKS
Marcus Bai.......................44
Danny McGuire 43
Keith Senior......................33
Chev Walker.....................25
Willie Poching 22

OFFLOADS
Wayne McDonald..............58
Keith Senior......................56
Kevin Sinfield...................55
Barrie McDermott 51
Ali Lauitiiti 45

TACKLE BUSTS
Richard Mathers 78
Keith Senior......................75
Marcus Bai.......................63
Danny McGuire 54
Willie Poching 52

MARKER TACKLES
Kevin Sinfield.................102
Willie Poching 64
Matt Diskin 63
Chris McKenna 55
Andrew Dunemann 52

AVERAGE OPTA INDEX
Danny McGuire...........876.12
Marcus Bai 820.04
Keith Senior 762.62
Kevin Sinfield 746.88
David Furner................727.4

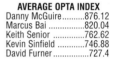

LONDON BRONCOS

Steele Retchless

Dennis Moran

TACKLES
Steele Retchless 694
Steve Trindall..................646
Neil Budworth 637
Joe Mbu 403
Mitchell Stringer 390

CARRIES
Steele Retchless 424
Steve Trindall..................344
Mitchell Stringer 305
Paul Sykes......................295
Dennis Moran 271

METRES
Steele Retchless 2653
Steve Trindall................2515
Dennis Moran 2255
Mitchell Stringer 2115
Paul Sykes....................2071

CLEAN BREAKS
Dennis Moran 32
Paul Sykes.......................16
Nigel Roy.........................14
Lee Greenwood 13
Mark O'Halloran...............11

OFFLOADS
Mitchell Stringer 39
Steve Trindall...................30
Andew Hart 27
Mark O'Halloran...............27
Jim Dymock 26

TACKLE BUSTS
Dennis Moran 51
Paul Sykes.......................46
Jim Dymock 32
Mitchell Stringer 30
Jon Wells.........................22

MARKER TACKLES
Steele Retchless 70
Steve Trindall...................57
Joe Mbu 55
Neil Budworth 50
Mark O'Halloran...............50

AVERAGE OPTA INDEX
Dennis Moran 692
Steele Retchless 584.52
Jim Dymock 569.47
Nigel Roy 536.26
Steve Trindall 498.43

SALFORD CITY REDS

Andy Coley

TACKLES
Malcolm Alker 849
Chris Charles 683
Andy Coley 582
Paul Highton 513
Sean Rutgerson.............490

CARRIES
Joel Caine 368
Andy Coley 368
Karl Fitzpatrick...............299
Chris Charles 297
Sean Rutgerson.............281

METRES
Andy Coley 2869
Joel Caine 2735
Karl Fitzpatrick..............2106
Sean Rutgerson...........2058
Paul Highton 1934

CLEAN BREAKS
Karl Fitzpatrick.................18
Stuart Littler 18
Cliff Beverley 17
Kevin McGuinness...........15
Andy Coley 14

OFFLOADS
Stuart Littler 43
Andy Coley 38
Neil Baynes 33
Chris Charles 30
Karl Fitzpatrick.................26

TACKLE BUSTS
Andy Coley 66
Kevin McGuinness...........52
Karl Fitzpatrick.................48
Joel Caine 40
Stuart Littler 36

MARKER TACKLES
Malcolm Alker 73
Sean Rutgerson..............57
Andy Coley 52
Kevin McGuinness...........51
Gavin Clinch 51

AVERAGE OPTA INDEX
Andy Coley 677.96
Cliff Beverley............636.59
Kevin McGuinness 576.88
Malcolm Alker...........557.96
Neil Baynes...............519.12

Cliff Beverley

ST HELENS

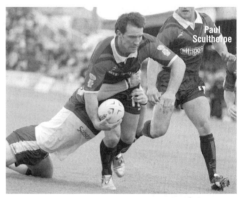

Paul Sculthorpe

TACKLES
Keiron Cunningham........606
Keith Mason 535
Nick Fozzard 518
Jason Hooper 508
Jon Wilkin 430

CARRIES
Paul Wellens 511
Paul Sculthorpe.............366
Ade Gardner 360
Nick Fozzard 334
Keith Mason 333

METRES
Paul Wellens 3556
Ade Gardner 2834
Paul Sculthorpe...........2747
Keith Mason 2720
Nick Fozzard 2520

CLEAN BREAKS
Paul Sculthorpe...............25
Jason Hooper 24
Paul Wellens 20
Willie Talau 16
Sean Long 16

OFFLOADS
Keiron Cunningham..........29
Paul Sculthorpe...............26
Nick Fozzard 23
Ricky Bibey 23
Willie Talau 15

TACKLE BUSTS
Paul Wellens 52
Keiron Cunningham.........50
Jason Hooper 41
Paul Sculthorpe...............37
Ade Gardner 36

MARKER TACKLES
Keiron Cunningham.........67
Chris Joynt 65
Keith Mason 51
Jason Hooper 50
Paul Wellens 48

AVERAGE OPTA INDEX
Paul Sculthorpe 833.1
Paul Wellens.............687.42
Keiron Cunningham ..652.36
Jason Hooper.............614.5
Nick Fozzard 508.17

Paul Wellens

WAKEFIELD T WILDCATS

Gareth Ellis

David Solomona

TACKLES
David March 811
Gareth Ellis 539
Jamie Field 435
David Solomona 431
Michael Korkidas 429

CARRIES
Michael Korkidas 463
David Solomona 396
Sid Domic 395
Gareth Ellis 331
Darrell Griffin 303

METRES
Michael Korkidas 4084
Sid Domic 3384
David Solomona 3014
Darrell Griffin...............2445
Jason Demetriou 2342

CLEAN BREAKS
Ben Jeffries 29
Jason Demetriou 28
Sid Domic 27
Gareth Ellis 19
Colum Halpenny 18

OFFLOADS
David Solomona 81
Gareth Ellis 43
Michael Korkidas 42
Jamie Field 34
Jason Demetriou 30

TACKLE BUSTS
Sid Domic 69
Jason Demetriou 58
Gareth Ellis 53
David Solomona 50
Ben Jeffries 48

MARKER TACKLES
David March 109
Gareth Ellis 89
Jason Demetriou 64
Mark Applegarth 62
Jamie Field 52

AVERAGE OPTA INDEX
David Solomona 667.74
Gareth Ellis 663.36
Michael Korkidas 643.3
Sid Domic.................614.64
Ben Jeffries..............605.36

Opta
opta stats

WARRINGTON WOLVES

Nathan Wood

Mike Forshaw

TACKLES
Mike Wainwright 587
Mike Forshaw 570
Jon Clarke 555
Mark Gleeson 523
Paul Wood 490

CARRIES
Paul Wood 354
Danny Lima 353
Mike Wainwright 333
Mike Forshaw 301
Nathan Wood..................297

METRES
Danny Lima 3081
Paul Wood 2568
Nathan Wood................2350
Mike Wainwright 2290
Mark Hilton 2048

CLEAN BREAKS
Brent Grose 24
Nathan Wood...................23
Lee Briers 21
Dean Gaskell 15
Darren Burns 11

OFFLOADS
Mike Forshaw 66
Nathan Wood...................43
Mike Wainwright 39
Danny Lima 28
Brent Grose 27

TACKLE BUSTS
Dean Gaskell 69
Nathan Wood...................54
Mike Forshaw 40
Danny Lima 40
Paul Wood 38

MARKER TACKLES
Mark Gleeson 89
Mike Wainwright 68
Brent Grose 62
Paul Wood 54
Mike Forshaw 48

AVERAGE OPTA INDEX
Mike Forshaw 674.9
Nathan Wood 586.75
Paul Wood 585.16
Brent Grose 565.36
Paul Noone 562.24

Opta
opta stats

WIDNES VIKINGS

Jules
O'Neill

Shane
Millard

TACKLES
Shane Millard 881
Simon Finnigan 606
Daniel Frame 586
Andy Hay 565
David Mills.....................503

CARRIES
Shane Millard 408
Daniel Frame 356
Deon Bird 338
Simon Finnigan 308
Julian O'Neill 287

METRES
Shane Millard 2726
Daniel Frame 2482
Deon Bird 2474
Julian O'Neill 2199
Andy Hay 2066

CLEAN BREAKS
Adam Hughes 14
Jules O'Neill....................14
Aaron Moule 13
Simon Finnigan 9
Nicky Royle 9

OFFLOADS
Julian O'Neill 41
Daniel Frame 35
Troy Wozniak 30
Adam Hughes 29
Simon Finnigan 20

TACKLE BUSTS
Jules O'Neill.....................44
Aaron Moule 40
Daniel Frame 34
Troy Wozniak 27
Chris Giles 27

MARKER TACKLES
Shane Millard 114
Daniel Frame 66
Simon Finnigan 64
Jules O'Neill....................56
David Mills......................43

AVERAGE OPTA INDEX
Shane Millard 767.5
Jules O'Neill 571.8
Daniel Frame...............560.4
Simon Finnigan...........535.8
Julian O'Neill 466.2

WIGAN WARRIORS

Kris
Radlinski

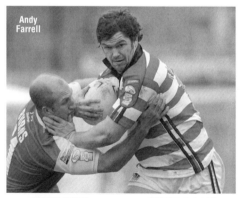

Andy
Farrell

TACKLES
Sean O'Loughlin 792
Danny Tickle 724
Craig Smith 520
Terry Newton 473
Danny Orr 455

CARRIES
Andy Farrell 468
Craig Smith 377
Brett Dallas 350
Danny Tickle 339
Kris Radlinski 339

METRES
Brett Dallas 3617
Andy Farrell 3312
Craig Smith 2873
Danny Tickle 2512
Gareth Hock.................2432

CLEAN BREAKS
Brett Dallas 28
Sean O'Loughlin 22
Stephen Wild 19
Andy Farrell 18
Danny Orr 16

OFFLOADS
Andy Farrell 55
Terry Newton 44
Gareth Hock....................39
Craig Smith 28
Kris Radlinski 28

TACKLE BUSTS
Brett Dallas 77
Andy Farrell 66
Danny Tickle 48
Gareth Hock....................46
Martin Aspinwall 41

MARKER TACKLES
Sean O'Loughlin 109
Craig Smith 79
Danny Tickle 72
Danny Orr 67
Terry Newton 64

AVERAGE OPTA INDEX
Andy Farrell 890.05
Kris Radlinski 626.2
Brett Dallas 623.96
Terry Newton 613.2
Sean O'Loughlin 584.89

NATIONAL LEAGUE 2004
Club by Club

BATLEY BULLDOGS

DATE	FIXTURE	RESULT	SCORERS	LGE	ATT
1/2/04	York (a) (NLC)	W22-24	t:Spurr,Flynn,Sibson,Berry g:Eaton(4)	2nd(NLC-Y)	2,039
8/2/04	Ince Rosebridge (a) (CCR3) ●	W8-42	t:Maun(3),Cass,Harrison,Richardson,Lingard,Molyneux g:Eaton(5)	N/A	750
15/2/04	Doncaster (h) (NLC)	W46-26	t:Flynn(2),Toohey,Richardson(2),Royston(2),Heptinstall g:Eaton(7)	1st(NLC-Y)	815
22/2/04	Featherstone (a) (NLC)	L20-19	t:Spink,Richardson,Flynn g:Eaton(3) fg:Eaton	2nd(NLC-Y)	1,309
28/2/04	Bradford-Dudley Hill (a) (CCR4) ●●	W14-76	t:Flynn(3),Spurr(2),Horsley,Royston(3),Cartledge,Maun,Sibson,Cass,Berry g:Eaton(10)	N/A	890
7/3/04	Dewsbury (h) (NLC)	W70-12	t:Toohey,Rourke,Spink,Berry(3),Richardson(2),Harrison,Spurr,Sibson(2) g:Eaton(11)	1st(NLC-Y)	868
14/3/04	Whitehaven (h) (CCR5)	L6-29	t:Harrison g:Eaton	N/A	1,186
21/3/04	York (h) (NLC)	W36-12	t:Rourke,Flynn(2),Maun,Spink,Royston g:Eaton(6)	1st(NLC-Y)	829
28/3/04	Doncaster (a) (NLC)	W30-44	t:Spink(2),Maun,Bramald,Lawford,Sibson,Richardson g:Eaton(8)	1st(NLC-Y)	707
4/4/04	Featherstone (h) (NLC)	W40-16	t:Leek,Spink,Harrison,Flynn,Spears,Maun g:Eaton(8)	1st(NLC-Y)	1,007
9/4/04	Dewsbury (a) (NLC)	W20-46	t:Richardson,Maun,Horsley(3),Flynn,Harrison,Evans g:Eaton(7)	1st(NLC-Y)	932
12/4/04	Rochdale (h)	W48-12	t:Sibson(3),Richardson,Maun,Rourke,Hill,Eaton g:Eaton(8)	2nd	639
18/4/04	Keighley (a)	W22-39	t:Horsley,Sibson(2),Flynn,Eaton,Spink,Horsley g:Eaton(5) fg:Heptinstall	1st	1,282
2/5/04	Doncaster (h)	W28-20	t:Hill,Spink,Sibson,Flynn,Royston g:Eaton(4)	2nd	801
9/5/04	Halifax (a)	L24-14	t:Spink,Toohey,Spurr g:Eaton	4th	2,155
23/5/04	Hull KR (h)	W34-28	t:Hill,Spink(2),Richardson,Sibson,Eaton g:Eaton(5)	3rd	1,211
30/5/04	Oldham (a) ●●●	W20-44	t:Royston(2),Harrison,Spurr,Powell(2),Rourke,Horsley g:Eaton(6)	2nd	1,541
6/6/04	Whitehaven (h) (NLCQF)	L16-22	t:Harrison,Royston,Bramald g:Eaton(2)	N/A	910
13/6/04	Whitehaven (a)	L28-17	t:Hill,Richardson,Powell g:Eaton(2) fg:Eaton	3rd	1,853
20/6/04	Featherstone (h)	L14-22	t:Sibson,Lythe g:Eaton(3)	4th	873
4/7/04	Leigh (a)	L27-22	t:Lingard,Toohey(2),Rourke g:Eaton(3)	4th	2,030
11/7/04	Keighley (h)	W30-14	t:Lawford(2),Royston,Sibson,Harrison g:Eaton(5)	4th	685
25/7/04	Doncaster (a)	L31-28	t:Lingard(2),Richardson,Powell,Harrison g:Eaton(4)	4th	830
1/8/04	Halifax (h)	L20-39	t:Toohey,Horsley,Sibson g:Eaton(4)	6th	941
8/8/04	Hull KR (a)	L29-18	t:Royston,Powell(2) g:Eaton(3)	7th	1,695
15/8/04	Oldham (h)	L18-34	t:Spink(3) g:Eaton(3)	7th	886
22/8/04	Whitehaven (h)	L22-48	t:Eaton,Powell,Toohey,Bates g:Eaton(3)	8th	605
29/8/04	Featherstone (a)	W18-28	t:Harrison,Maun,Powell,Royston,Horsley g:Eaton(4)	8th	1,298
5/9/04	Rochdale (a)	W24-32	t:Flynn,Spink,Maun,Sibson,Lythe g:Eaton(6)	7th	1,067
12/9/04	Leigh (h)	L22-29	t:Lythe(3),Maun g:Eaton(3)	7th	1,719

● Played at Robin Park Arena, Wigan
●● Played at Mount Pleasant
●●● Played at Bloomfield Road, Blackpool

		APP		TRIES		GOALS		FG		PTS	
	D.O.B.	ALL	NL1	ALL	NL1	ALL	NL1	ALL	NL1	ALL	NL1
David Bates	23/10/80	1(3)	1(3)	1	1	0	0	0	0	4	4
Steve Beard	21/6/79	2(2)	2(1)	0	0	0	0	0	0	0	0
Joe Berry	7/5/74	8(3)	(2)	5	0	0	0	0	0	20	0
Matt Bramald	6/2/73	11(1)	5	2	0	0	0	0	0	8	0
Will Cartledge	11/9/79	3(13)	2(7)	1	0	0	0	0	0	4	0
Mark Cass	17/11/71	6(6)	3(3)	2	0	0	0	0	0	8	0
Barry Eaton	30/9/73	30	18	4	4	144	72	2	1	306	161
Danny Evans	15/10/74	3(1)	0	1	0	0	0	0	0	4	0
Adrian Flynn	9/9/74	24	13	14	3	0	0	0	0	56	12
Nathan Graham	23/11/71	3(1)	3(1)	0	0	0	0	0	0	0	0
Paul Harrison	24/9/70	7(23)	5(13)	10	4	0	0	0	0	40	16
Andy Heptinstall	28/4/76	10(2)	6	1	0	0	0	1	1	5	1
Steve Hill	17/11/76	25(1)	17	4	4	0	0	0	0	16	16
Ryan Horsley	21/8/78	19(4)	11(3)	9	5	0	0	0	0	36	20
Dean Lawford	9/5/77	9	7	3	2	0	0	0	0	12	8
Adrian Leek	2/4/80	1(6)	1(3)	1	0	0	0	0	0	4	0
Craig Lingard	11/12/77	4(2)	4	3	0	0	0	0	0	16	12
Kris Lythe	29/3/83	6(1)	6(1)	5	5	0	0	0	0	20	20
Danny Maun	5/1/81	27	16	12	4	0	0	0	0	48	16
Chris Molyneux	5/5/80	9(13)	3(11)	1	0	0	0	0	0	4	0
Bryn Powell	5/9/79	14	13	8	8	0	0	0	0	32	32
Andy Rice	9/6/80	3(2)	0	0	0	0	0	0	0	0	0
Sean Richardson	20/8/73	14(15)	10(7)	12	4	0	0	0	0	48	16
David Rourke	12/3/81	19(3)	11(1)	5	3	0	0	0	0	20	12
Shad Royston	29/11/82	23(4)	14(2)	13	6	0	0	0	0	52	24
Gary Shillabeer	23/11/79	(2)	(2)	0	0	0	0	0	0	0	0
Mark Sibson	20/10/76	28	16	16	11	0	0	0	0	64	44
Tim Spears	27/7/84	8(9)	6(7)	1	0	0	0	0	0	4	0
Andy Spink	12/1/79	29	18	15	9	0	0	0	0	60	36
Chris Spurr	7/7/80	14	7	6	2	0	0	0	0	24	8
Danny Thomas	21/12/83	1(1)	1(1)	0	0	0	0	0	0	0	0
Mark Toohey	16/6/82	26(1)	15(1)	7	5	0	0	0	0	28	20
Craig Wright	8/9/71	3(1)	3(1)	0	0	0	0	0	0	0	0

Barry Eaton

LEAGUE RECORD
P18-W8-D0-L10
(7th, NL1)
F478, A469, Diff+9
16 points.

CHALLENGE CUP
Round Five

NATIONAL LEAGUE CUP
Quarter Finalists/1st, Yorkshire Division

ATTENDANCES
Best - v Leigh (NL1 - 1,719)
Worst - v Whitehaven (NL1 - 605)
Total (NL1 & NLC, inc QF, only) - 12,789
Average (NL1 & NLC, inc QF, only) - 914
(Up by 58 on 2003)

DONCASTER DRAGONS

DATE	FIXTURE	RESULT	SCORERS	LGE	ATT
8/2/04	West Hull (h) (CCR3)	W28-6	t:Muff,Woodcock,Lee(2),Billy g:Holroyd(4)	N/A	839
11/2/04	Sheffield (a) (NLC)	W6-38	t:Holroyd,Hough(2),Billy(2),Woodcock,Muff g:Holroyd(5)	1st(NLC-E)	945
15/2/04	Batley (a) (NLC)	L46-26	t:Lloyd,Lee(2),Lawton g:Holroyd(4),Woodcock	2nd(NLC-E)	815
22/2/04	Hull KR (a) (NLC)	L28-12	t:M Walker,Billy g:Holroyd(2)	2nd(NLC-E)	2,043
29/2/04	Hunslet (a) (CCR4)	W20-48	t:Lloyd,Woodcock(2),Handford,M Walker,Holroyd,Colton,Solomon g:Holroyd(8)	N/A	682
7/3/04	Sheffield (h) (NLC)	W34-4	t:Miles(2),Billy(2),Lloyd(2),Leaf g:Holroyd(3)	2nd(NLC-E)	734
14/3/04	Huddersfield (a) (CCR5)	L36-12	t:Handford,Woodcock g:Holroyd(2)	N/A	3,134
20/3/04	London Skolars (a) (NLC)	W6-24	t:Leaf(2),Solomon,Brentley g:Woodcock(4)	2nd(NLC-E)	375
28/3/04	Batley (h) (NLC)	L30-44	t:Muff,Holroyd,Miles(2),Solomon g:Holroyd(5)	2nd(NLC-E)	707
31/3/04	London Skolars (h) (NLC)	W58-20	t:Ostler,W Green(2),Lloyd,Hough,Brentley,P Green,Muff,Miles,Buckenham g:Holroyd(9)	2nd(NLC-E)	395
9/4/04	Hull KR (h) (NLC)	L8-38	t:W Green,Solomon	2nd(NLC-E)	914
12/4/04	Halifax (a)	W20-38	t:Muff,Cook,Colton,Solomon,Billy,Leaf g:Holroyd(7)	4th	2,290
18/4/04	Hull KR (h)	W27-14	t:Colton,Cook(2),Lawton g:Holroyd(5) fg:Hough	4th	1,302
25/4/04	Oldham (h) (NLCQFQ)	W32-28	t:Billy(2),Muff,Leaf,Colton(2) g:Holroyd(4)	N/A	835
2/5/04	Batley (a)	L28-20	t:Leaf,Horne,Solomon,Billy g:Holroyd(2)	5th	801
9/5/04	Whitehaven (h)	W31-24	t:Woodcock,Billy,Holroyd,Cook,M Walker g:Holroyd(3),Woodcock(2) fg:Hough	5th	853
23/5/04	Featherstone (a)	L44-18	t:Holroyd(2),Colton(2) g:Holroyd	5th	1,418
30/5/04	Leigh (h)	W19-14	t:Holroyd,Solomon g:Holroyd(5) fg:Holroyd	4th	1,140
6/6/04	Hull KR (h) (NLCQF)	L28-50	t:Lawton(2),Muff,Billy,Fisher g:Holroyd(3),Woodcock	N/A	1,181
13/6/04	Rochdale (h)	W38-18	t:Handford,Cook,Ostler,Holroyd(2),Colton g:Woodcock(7)	4th	645
20/6/04	Keighley (h)	W52-30	t:Woodcock(2),Horne(2),Hough,J Walker(2),P Green,Moana g:Woodcock(8)	3rd	827
4/7/04	Oldham (h)	W31-30	t:Hough,Leaf,J Walker,Horne g:Woodcock(2),Hough(4) fg:Holroyd(2),Cook	2nd	998
11/7/04	Hull KR (a)	L18-13	t:Colton g:Holroyd(4) fg:Hough	3rd	1,888
25/7/04	Batley (h)	W31-28	t:Holroyd(2),Billy,Colton,Horne(2) g:Holroyd(3) fg:Hough	3rd	830
1/8/04	Whitehaven (a)	L42-18	t:Billy,Moana(2) g:Holroyd(3)	3rd	1,814
8/8/04	Featherstone (h)	L18-33	t:O'Loughlin,Lloyd,Colton g:Holroyd	3rd	966
15/8/04	Leigh (a)	L46-32	t:P Green,Billy(3),Handford,J Walker g:Holroyd(4)	4th	1,793
21/8/04	Rochdale (a)	L52-18	t:Colton,Fisher,Billy g:Holroyd(2),Woodcock	6th	624
29/8/04	Keighley (a)	W20-39	t:Holroyd,Moana(3),W Green(2),Colton g:Woodcock(4),Holroyd fg:W Green	4th	760
5/9/04	Halifax (h)	L34-44	t:Cook,W Green,Colton,Fisher,Moana,Hough g:Woodcock(5)	6th	786
12/9/04	Oldham (a)	L29-26	t:Lawton(2),Hough,Colton g:Hough(5)	6th	1,448
19/9/04	Hull KR (a) (EPO)	L63-22	t:Moana(2),Muff,J Walker g:Hough(3)	N/A	2,319

		APP		TRIES		GOALS		FG		PTS	
	D.O.B.	ALL	NL1	ALL	NL1	ALL	NL1	ALL	NL1	ALL	NL1
Tony Atter	6/1/79	(3)	0	0	0	0	0	0	0	0	0
Marlon Billy	22/11/73	28(2)	16(2)	18	9	0	0	0	0	72	36
Liam Brentley	27/6/85	2(4)	(1)	2	0	0	0	0	0	8	0
Tom Buckenham	15/8/84	(4)	0	1	0	0	0	0	0	4	0
Dean Colton	18/2/83	24(4)	19	16	13	0	0	0	0	64	52
Craig Cook	26/5/83	29	18	6	6	0	0	1	1	25	25
Maea David	27/2/72	4(1)	4(1)	0	0	0	0	0	0	0	0
Allan Dunham	5/12/80	2(2)	2(2)	0	0	0	0	0	0	0	0
Jamie Fielden	9/5/78	4(1)	0	0	0	0	0	0	0	0	0
Andy Fisher	17/11/67	20(1)	14(1)	3	2	0	0	0	0	12	8
Peter Green	2/12/81	32	19	3	2	0	0	0	0	12	8
Wayne Green	1/1/83	8(3)	5(3)	6	3	0	0	1	1	25	13
Danny Grimshaw	25/2/86	2	1	0	0	0	0	0	0	0	0
Gareth Handford	22/4/80	25(1)	14	4	2	0	0	0	0	16	8
Chris Hemmings	24/12/83	2(9)		0	0	0	0	0	0	0	0
Graham Holroyd	25/10/75	30(1)	18(1)	12	9	90	41	3	3	231	121
Craig Horne	20/5/78	13(4)	12(4)	6	6	0	0	0	0	24	24
Chris Hough	30/8/81	22(7)	13(4)	7	4	12	12	4	4	56	44
Craig Lawton	17/2/81	25(1)	16(1)	6	3	0	0	0	0	24	12
Shaun Leaf	10/2/84	17(4)	6(4)	7	3	0	0	0	0	28	12
Jason Lee	16/1/71	6	0	4	0	0	0	0	0	16	0
Gareth Lloyd	12/8/75	17(4)	7(4)	6	1	0	0	0	0	24	4
Craig Miles	8/7/81	4	0	5	0	0	0	0	0	20	0
Martin Moana	13/8/73	12	12	9	9	0	0	0	0	36	36
Alex Muff	17/8/82	19(11)	14(4)	8	2	0	0	0	0	32	8
Dean O'Loughlin	25/9/82	(7)	(7)	1	1	0	0	0	0	4	4
Martin Ostler	21/6/80	20(1)	14	2	1	0	0	0	0	8	4
Carl Sayer	23/1/82	(2)	(1)	0	0	0	0	0	0	0	0
PJ Solomon	17/8/76	21	11	7	3	0	0	0	0	28	12
Carl Stannard	22/3/79	(7)	(5)	0	0	0	0	0	0	0	0
Martin Sykes	28/12/76	(1)	0	0	0	0	0	0	0	0	0
James Walker	15/4/77	2(23)	2(17)	5	5	0	0	0	0	20	20
Matt Walker	23/11/78	6(14)	1(8)	3	1	0	0	0	0	12	4
Johnny Woodcock	5/2/81	20(5)	9(5)	8	3	35	29	0	0	102	70

Graham Holroyd

LEAGUE RECORD
P18-W9-D0-L9
(6th, NL1/Elimination Play-Off)
F503, A534, Diff-31
18 points.

CHALLENGE CUP
Round Five

NATIONAL LEAGUE CUP
Quarter Finalists/2nd, East Division

ATTENDANCES
Best - v Hull KR (NL1 - 1,302)
Worst - v London Skolars (NLC - 395)
Total (NL1 & NLC,
inc QFQ & QF, only) - 13,113
Average (NL1 & NLC,
inc QFQ & QF, only) - 874
(Down by 76 on 2003)

FEATHERSTONE ROVERS

DATE	FIXTURE	RESULT	SCORERS	LGE	ATT
1/2/04	Dewsbury (a) (NLC)	W12-28	t:Hayes,Dooler,Newlove g:Briggs(8)	1st(NLC-Y)	1,489
8/2/04	Castleford Lock Lane (h) (CCR3)	W96-0	t:Ford(2),Presley(2),Stokes(3),Dooler(2),Hayes,Newlove(4),Blakeway,Briggs, Wray(2) g:Briggs(11),Blakeway	N/A	1,576
15/2/04	Hull KR (h) (NLC)	L16-22	t:Jarrett,Newlove(2) g:Briggs(2)	3rd(NLC-Y)	1,929
22/2/04	Batley (h) (NLC)	W20-19	t:Wray,Blakeway,Presley,Newlove g:Briggs(2)	3rd(NLC-Y)	1,309
29/2/04	London Skolars (a) (CCR4)	W6-52	t:Wray,Newlove,Ford,Henare,Coventry,Blakeway,Darley,Batty,Presley g:Briggs(8)	N/A	380
7/3/04	York (a) (NLC)	L18-16	t:Dickens(2),Wray g:Briggs(2)	3rd(NLC-Y)	1,942
14/3/04	York (h) (CCR5)	L26-29	t:Wray,Presley,Newlove(2),Darley g:Briggs(3)	N/A	2,234
21/3/04	Dewsbury (h) (NLC)	W48-4	t:Presley,Archibald,Newlove(2),Blakeway(2),Dickens,Chapman,Ford g:Briggs(6)	2nd(NLC-Y)	1,068
28/3/04	Hull KR (a) (NLC)	W16-18	t:Feehan,Presley g:Briggs(5)	2nd(NLC-Y)	1,755
4/4/04	Batley (a) (NLC)	L40-16	t:Stokes,Wray,Jarrett g:Briggs(2)	3rd(NLC-Y)	1,007
9/4/04	York (h) (NLC)	L26-36	t:Stokes(2),Wray,Dooler g:Briggs(5)	3rd(NLC-Y)	1,435
12/4/04	Oldham (a)	L50-24	t:Lowe,Chapman,Blakeway,Presley(2) g:Briggs(2)	8th	1,320
18/4/04	Leigh (a)	L50-12	t:Stokes,Newlove g:Briggs(2)	8th	1,790
25/4/04	York (a) (NLCQFQ)	L27-18	t:Blakeway,Dooler g:Briggs(5)	N/A	1,202
2/5/04	Rochdale (h)	W58-12	t:Zitter(2),Stokes(2),Hayes,Batty(2),Blakeway,Dooler,Wray g:Dickens(9)	7th	1,098
9/5/04	Keighley (a)	L42-18	t:Cardoza(2),Blakeway g:Dickens(3)	8th	1,251
23/5/04	Doncaster (h)	W44-18	t:Stokes,Newlove,Blakeway,Lowe,Wray,Ripley,Chapman,Zitter g:Dickens(6)	7th	1,418
30/5/04	Halifax (a)	W20-27	t:Newlove,Wray(2) g:Dickens(7) fg:Blakeway	6th	1,760
13/6/04	Hull KR (h)	L22-26	t:Zitter,Stokes,Newlove g:Dickens(4),Blakeway	7th	1,795
20/6/04	Batley (a)	W14-22	t:Batty,Stokes,Presley g:Dickens(5)	7th	873
4/7/04	Whitehaven (h)	W26-12	t:Wray,McNally,Stokes,Hayes g:McNally,Dickens(4)	5th	1,259
11/7/04	Leigh (h)	L20-75	t:Stokes(2),Newlove,Dooler g:Dickens(2)	7th	1,859
25/7/04	Rochdale (a)	D12-12	t:Hayes g:Blakeway(2),Dickens(2)	7th	804
1/8/04	Keighley (h)	W54-16	t:Wray(2),Greseque(2),Haughey,McNally(2),Zitter,Blakeway,Newlove g:Greseque(3),Dickens(4)	5th	1,089
8/8/04	Doncaster (a)	W18-33	t:Dooler(2),Newlove,Wray,Moss g:Dickens(6) fg:Blakeway	4th	966
15/8/04	Halifax (h)	W35-16	t:Zitter(2),McNally(2),Blakeway,Newlove g:Dickens(3),Greseque(2) fg:Blakeway	3rd	1,488
22/8/04	Hull KR (a)	L32-24	t:Blakeway,McNally,Greseque,Ripley g:Dickens(3),Greseque	4th	1,985
29/8/04	Batley (h)	L18-28	t:Hayes(2),McNally g:Dickens	5th	1,298
5/9/04	Oldham (h)	W35-26	t:Zitter,Stokes,Haughey,Lowe(2) g:Dickens(7) fg:Greseque	3rd	1,397
12/9/04	Whitehaven (a)	L24-16	t:Blakeway,Lowe g:Greseque(4)	5th	2,024
19/9/04	Oldham (a) (EPO)	W28-33	t:Haughey,Newlove,Lowe,Wray,McNally g:Dickens(2),Greseque(4) fg:Greseque	N/A	1,970
26/9/04	Hull KR (a) (ESF)	W18-19	t:Ford,Dooler g:Dickens(2),Greseque(3) fg:Greseque	N/A	3,075
3/10/04	Whitehaven (a) (FE)	L30-2	g:Dickens	N/A	2,374

		APP		TRIES		GOALS		FG		PTS	
	D.O.B.	ALL	NL1	ALL	NL1	ALL	NL1	ALL	NL1	ALL	NL1
Ben Archibald	21/10/82	5(3)	1	1	0	0	0	0	0	4	0
Nathan Batty	20/5/82	16	8	4	3	0	0	0	0	16	12
Richard Blakeway	22/7/83	28(1)	18(1)	14	8	4	3	3	3	67	41
Carl Briggs	27/9/74	13(2)	2(1)	1	0	58	4	0	0	120	8
Dale Cardoza	13/9/79	1(1)	1(1)	2	2	0	0	0	0	8	8
Jim Carlton	26/4/80	6(19)	3(11)	0	0	0	0	0	0	0	0
Richard Chapman	5/9/75	13(7)	8(3)	3	2	0	0	0	0	12	8
Steve Coulson	5/4/86	(1)	(1)	0	0	0	0	0	0	0	0
Jamie Coventry	9/2/77	6(1)	0	1	0	0	0	0	0	4	0
Paul Darley	26/1/74	31(1)	20	2	0	0	0	0	0	8	0
Stuart Dickens	23/3/80	28(3)	20(1)	3	0	78	73	0	0	168	146
Steve Dooler	31/12/77	27(5)	17(4)	10	5	0	0	0	0	40	20
Danny Evans	15/10/74	(4)	(4)	0	0	0	0	0	0	0	0
Ben Feehan	15/6/85	3	0	1	0	0	0	0	0	4	0
James Ford	29/9/82	8(12)	4(8)	5	1	0	0	0	0	20	4
Maxime Greseque	18/3/81	10(1)	10(1)	3	3	17	17	3	3	49	49
Tom Haughey	30/1/82	8	8	3	3	0	0	0	0	12	12
Adam Hayes	30/11/81	25(8)	14(7)	7	5	0	0	0	0	28	20
Bryan Henare	24/9/74	12(8)	3(6)	1	0	0	0	0	0	4	0
James Houston	28/12/82	(1)	0	0	0	0	0	0	0	0	0
Andy Jarrett	26/4/83	6(18)	5(9)	2	0	0	0	0	0	8	0
Neil Lowe	20/12/78	10(8)	9(8)	6	6	0	0	0	0	24	24
Andy McNally	9/1/82	14	14	8	8	1	1	0	0	34	34
Craig Milnthorpe	21/12/82	(1)	0	0	0	0	0	0	0	0	0
Craig Moss	4/8/84	8(2)	6	1	1	0	0	0	0	4	4
Richard Newlove	18/7/78	27(1)	18	22	9	0	0	0	0	88	36
Danny Patrickson	21/5/82	1(1)	0	0	0	0	0	0	0	0	0
Jon Presley	8/7/84	19(3)	8(2)	10	3	0	0	0	0	40	12
Dean Ripley	13/9/83	8(1)	8(1)	2	2	0	0	0	0	8	8
Jamie Stokes	13/8/79	21(6)	13(6)	16	10	0	0	0	0	64	40
Adam Sullivan	14/11/82	(1)	(1)	0	0	0	0	0	0	0	0
Brian Sutton	7/3/85	(1)	(1)	0	0	0	0	0	0	0	0
Ian Tonks	13/2/76	26(2)	19	0	0	0	0	0	0	0	0
Lee Williamson	21/9/80	1(2)	(2)	0	0	0	0	0	0	0	0
Matthew Wray	15/5/84	32	20	17	9	0	0	0	0	68	36
Freddie Zitter	28/10/79	15(4)	15(4)	8	8	0	0	0	0	32	32

Stuart Dickens

LEAGUE RECORD
P18-W9-D1-L8
(5th, NL1/Final Eliminator)
F500, A491, Diff+9
19 points.

CHALLENGE CUP
Round Five

NATIONAL LEAGUE CUP
3rd, Yorkshire Division
(Eliminated in Quarter Final Qualifiers)

ATTENDANCES
Best - v York (CC - 2,234)
Worst - v Dewsbury (NLC - 1,068)
Total (NL1 & NLC only) - 18,442
Average (NL1 & NLC only) - 1,419
(Down by 90 on 2003)

HALIFAX

DATE	FIXTURE	RESULT	SCORERS	LGE	ATT
1/2/04	Keighley (h) (NLC)	W18-12	t:Arnold,Bloem,Cantillon g:Bloem(3)	2nd(NLC-P)	3,360
8/2/04	Oulton (h) (CCR3)	W66-10	t:Smith(2),Chapman,Roper,Moxon.Marns(2),Hadcroft,Cantillon(2),Norman,Farrell g:Bloem(7),Roper(2)	N/A	1,675
15/2/04	Rochdale (a) (NLC)	W14-33	t:Smith,Arnold(2),Norman,Marns g:Bloem(4),Roper,W Corcoran fg:Weisner	2nd(NLC-P)	1,343
22/2/04	Hunslet (a) (NLC)	W14-38	t:Roper,Cantillon,Chapman,Moxon(2),Weisner,Law g:Bloem(5)	1st(NLC-P)	1,144
29/2/04	Limoux (a) (CCR4)	L19-18	t:Hadcroft,Cantillon,Bloem g:Bloem(2),W Corcoran	N/A	1,200
7/3/04	Rochdale (h) (NLC)	W21-6	t:Chapman,Davidson,Cantillon g:Bloem(4) fg:Bloem	1st(NLC-P)	2,096
21/3/04	Keighley (a) (NLC)	L26-8	t:Arnold,Hadcroft	1st(NLC-P)	1,926
28/3/04	Leigh (h) (NLC)	L16-27	t:Smith,Norman,Moxon g:Bloem(2)	2nd(NLC-P)	2,815
4/4/04	Hunslet (h) (NLC)	W20-4	t:Roper,Davidson,Chapman,Sheriffe g:Roper(2)	1st(NLC-P)	1,536
9/4/04	Leigh (a) (NLC)	L46-20	t:Norman,Sheriffe(2),Bates g:Roper(2)	1st(NLC-P)	2,563
12/4/04	Doncaster (h)	L20-38	t:Sheriffe,Hadcroft,Roper g:Bloem(2),Roper(2)	7th	2,290
18/4/04	Oldham (h)	L6-25	t:Moxon g:Bloem	7th	1,807
2/5/04	Hull KR (a)	L28-18	t:Simon Grix,Arnold,Sheriffe g:Bloem(3)	8th	2,393
9/5/04	Batley (h)	W24-14	t:G Corcoran,Simon Grix(2),Sheriffe,Davidson g:Bloem(2)	7th	2,155
23/5/04	Whitehaven (a)	L34-8	t:Sheriffe g:Bloem(2)	8th	1,648
30/5/04	Featherstone (h)	L20-27	t:Cantillon(2),Farrell,Haley g:Bloem(2)	8th	1,760
6/6/04	York (h) (NLCQF)	L14-37	t:Haley,Scott Grix g:Bloem(3)	N/A	1,840
13/6/04	Leigh (a)	L43-25	t:Feehan,Haley,Simon Grix g:W Corcoran(5),Roper fg:Weisner	8th	1,952
20/6/04	Rochdale (h)	W15-14	t:Davidson g:Roper(5) fg:Weisner	8th	1,301
4/7/04	Keighley (a)	W16-37	t:Bloem(2),Moxon,Birchall,Hadcroft,Simon Grix g:Bloem(6) fg:Weisner	8th	1,380
10/7/04	Oldham (a) ●	L24-14	t:Weisner,Haley,Greenwood g:Bloem	8th	850
25/7/04	Hull KR (h)	L14-20	t:G Corcoran,Scott Grix,Black g:Bloem	8th	1,556
1/8/04	Batley (a)	W20-39	t:Hadcroft,Farrell,Sheriffe,Scott Grix,Black(2),Bloem g:Bloem(4),Haley fg:Weisner	8th	941
8/8/04	Whitehaven (h)	L14-34	t:Sheriffe,Cantillon,Bunyan g:Bloem	9th	1,440
15/8/04	Featherstone (a)	L35-16	t:Simpson,Bloem,Scott Grix g:Bloem(2)	9th	1,488
22/8/04	Leigh (h)	W58-30	t:Haley(3),Bloem,Black(3),Sheriffe(2) g:Bloem(11)	9th	1,781
29/8/04	Rochdale (a)	L34-24	t:Feehan(2),Black,Bloem g:Bloem(4)	9th	1,230
5/9/04	Doncaster (a)	W34-44	t:Scott Grix(2),Haley,Feehan,Sheriffe,Black,Bloem,Moxon g:Bloem(5),Jones	9th	786
12/9/04	Keighley (h)	W30-22	t:Sheriffe(2),Black(2),Feehan g:Bloem(5)	9th	1,344
26/9/04	York (h) (NL1QS-QSF)	W37-20	t:Hadcroft(2),Simon Grix,Weisner,Scott Grix,Sheriffe,Feehan g:Bloem(4) fg:Black	N/A	2,213
10/10/04	York (NL1QS-F) ●●	W34-30	t:Hadcroft(2),Bunyan(2),Sheriffe,Scott Grix g:Bloem(5)	N/A	N/A

● Played at Victory Park, Chorley
●● Played at Halton Stadium, Widnes

	D.O.B.	APP		TRIES		GOALS		FG		PTS	
		ALL	NL1	ALL	NL1	ALL	NL1	ALL	NL1	ALL	NL1
Danny Arnold	15/4/77	13	5	5	1	0	0	0	0	20	4
Brad Attwood	24/11/84	2	0	0	0	0	0	0	0	0	0
David Bates	23/10/80	5(17)	2(10)	1	0	0	0	0	0	4	0
Chris Birchall	25/3/81	17(2)	16(2)	1	1	0	0	0	0	4	4
Ben Black	29/4/81	10	10	10	10	0	0	1	1	41	41
Jamie Bloem	26/5/71	26(1)	18(1)	9	7	91	61	1	0	219	150
Andy Boothroyd	7/1/85	1(1)	1(1)	0	0	0	0	0	0	0	0
James Bunyan	2/11/77	11	11	3	3	0	0	0	0	12	12
Phil Cantillon	2/6/76	22(4)	11(4)	9	3	0	0	0	0	36	12
Jaymes Chapman	17/12/83	8(4)	(3)	4	0	0	0	0	0	16	0
Ged Corcoran	28/3/83	20(3)	17(2)	2	2	0	0	0	0	8	8
Wayne Corcoran	10/7/85	5(7)	2(2)	0	0	7	5	0	0	14	10
Paul Davidson	1/8/69	8(7)	7(3)	4	2	0	0	0	0	16	8
Anthony Farrell	17/1/69	19(8)	11(7)	3	2	0	0	0	0	12	8
Danny Fearon	13/3/79	1(2)	0	0	0	0	0	0	0	0	0
Ben Feehan	15/6/85	9(4)	9(4)	6	6	0	0	0	0	24	24
Gareth Greenwood	14/1/83	9(2)	9(2)	1	1	0	0	0	0	4	4
Scott Grix	1/5/84	14(4)	12(1)	8	7	0	0	0	0	32	28
Simon Grix	28/9/85	18(5)	8(5)	6	6	0	0	0	0	24	24
Alan Hadcroft	31/3/77	23(1)	14(1)	10	7	0	0	0	0	40	28
James Haley	2/7/85	18	17	8	7	1	1	0	0	34	30
Danny Jones	6/3/86	2(1)	1(1)	0	0	1	1	0	0	2	2
Scott Law	19/2/85	(10)	(2)	1	0	0	0	0	0	4	0
Oliver Marns	10/10/78	9(1)	1	3	0	0	0	0	0	12	0
Gareth Matthews	27/10/82	(1)	0	0	0	0	0	0	0	0	0
Ryan McDonald	24/2/78	9(13)	7(10)	0	0	0	0	0	0	0	0
Chris Morley	22/9/73	9	0	0	0	0	0	0	0	0	0
Mark Moxon	22/8/80	22(7)	13(5)	7	3	0	0	0	0	28	12
Chris Norman	22/1/83	10(6)	3(3)	4	0	0	0	0	0	16	0
Jon Roper	5/5/76	17	8	4	1	15	8	0	0	46	20
Rikki Sheriffe	5/5/84	22	19	16	13	0	0	0	0	64	52
Jon Simpson	16/7/83	4(3)	4(2)	1	1	0	0	0	0	4	4
Richard Smith	18/6/73	9(5)	1(5)	4	0	0	0	0	0	16	0
Pat Weisner	17/3/82	25	17	3	2	0	0	5	4	17	12
Matt Whitaker	6/3/82	5	4	0	0	0	0	0	0	0	0

Anthony Farrell

LEAGUE RECORD
P18-W7-D0-L11
(9th, NL1)
(Winners, NL1 Qualifying Series)
F426, A492, Diff-66
14 points.

CHALLENGE CUP
Round Four

NATIONAL LEAGUE CUP
Quarter Finalists/1st, Pennine Division

ATTENDANCES
Best - v Keighley (NLC - 3,360)
Worst - v Rochdale (NL1 - 1,301)
Total (NL1, NL1QS &
NLC, inc QF, only) - 29,294
Average (NL1, NL1QS &
NLC, inc QF, only) - 1,953
(Down by 1,024 on 2003, SL)

HULL KINGSTON ROVERS

DATE	FIXTURE	RESULT	SCORERS	LGE	ATT
1/2/04	Sheffield (h) (NLC)	W24-2	t:Farrell,Holdstock,Mansson,McClarron,Mayberry g:Hasty,Poucher	1st(NLC-E)	2,391
8/2/04	Union Treiziste Catalane (h) (CCR3)	L22-23	t:Bovill,Seibold,McClarron,Hasty g:Stott(3)	N/A	2,066
15/2/04	Featherstone (a) (NLC)	W16-22	t:Hasty,Poucher,Parker g:Stott(5)	1st(NLC-E)	1,929
22/2/04	Doncaster (h) (NLC)	W28-12	t:McClarron,Stott(2) g:Stott(4)	1st(NLC-E)	2,043
7/3/04	London Skolars (h) (NLC)	W58-6	t:Mansson,Ellis,Calland(3),Seibold,Mayberry,Andrews,Holdstock,Thorburn,Parker g:Thorburn(7)	1st(NLC-E)	1,677
19/3/04	Sheffield (a) (NLC)	W18-22	t:Bovill,Thorburn,Hasty,McClarron g:Thorburn(3)	1st(NLC-E)	1,049
28/3/04	Featherstone (h) (NLC)	L16-18	t:Parker(2),Mansson g:Thorburn(2)	1st(NLC-E)	1,755
3/4/04	London Skolars (a) (NLC)	W8-50	t:Poucher,McClarron(2),Pickering,Parker,Mansson,Aston,Calland,Thorburn g:Thorburn(7)	1st(NLC-E)	656
9/4/04	Doncaster (a) (NLC)	W8-38	t:Aizue,Farrell,Parker,Stott,Hasty,Walker,Thorburn g:Stott(5)	1st(NLC-E)	914
12/4/04	Keighley (h)	W56-6	t:McClarron(4),Farrell,Thorburn,Stott,Hasty(2),Smith g:Stott(8)	1st	2,383
18/4/04	Doncaster (a)	L27-14	t:Farrell,Aizue g:Stott(3)	5th	1,302
2/5/04	Halifax (h)	W28-18	t:Poucher,Hasty,Holdstock,Mansson g:Stott(6)	4th	2,393
9/5/04	Oldham (h)	W29-22	t:McClarron,Mansson(2),Calland,Pinkney g:Stott(4) fg:Mansson	3rd	2,121
23/5/04	Batley (a)	L34-28	t:Mansson,Calland,Aston,Farrell,Pinkney g:Thorburn(4)	4th	1,211
30/5/04	Whitehaven (h)	L12-26	t:Gallagher,Fletcher g:Thorburn(2)	5th	1,954
6/6/04	Doncaster (a) (NLCQF)	W28-50	t:Bovill,Pinkney(2),Poucher(2),Stott,Ellis(2),Seibold g:Stott(2),Thorburn(5)	N/A	1,181
13/6/04	Featherstone (a)	W22-26	t:Holdstock,Mansson,Parker(3) g:Thorburn(3)	5th	1,795
20/6/04	Leigh (h)	L8-35	t:Andrews g:Thorburn(2)	6th	2,647
27/6/04	York (h) (NLCSF)	W32-0	t:Holdstock,Watene,Thorburn,Pinkney,Mansson g:Stott(6)	N/A	2,629
4/7/04	Rochdale (a)	L36-18	t:Gallagher,Poucher,Hasty,Holdstock g:Hasty	7th	1,094
11/7/04	Doncaster (h)	W18-13	t:Pinkney,Hasty,Pickering g:Stott(3)	6th	1,888
18/7/04	Leigh (NLCF) ●	L14-42	t:Poucher,Thorburn g:Stott(3)	N/A	4,383
25/7/04	Halifax (a)	W14-20	t:Mansson,Gallagher,Farrell,Pinkney g:Thorburn(2)	5th	1,556
1/8/04	Oldham (a)	L29-24	t:Stott(2),Ball,Bovill,Parker g:Stott(2)	7th	1,393
8/8/04	Batley (h)	W29-18	t:Netherton,Hasty,Bovill,Pinkney g:Stott(6) fg:Mansson	5th	1,695
15/8/04	Whitehaven (a)	L38-8	t:Parker,Pinkney	6th	1,857
22/8/04	Featherstone (h)	W32-24	t:McClarron(2),Parker,Walker,Aston,Hasty g:Poucher(4)	5th	1,985
29/8/04	Leigh (a)	L26-22	t:Poucher,Smith,Watene(2) g:Poucher(3)	6th	1,768
5/9/04	Keighley (a)	W22-52	t:Bovill,Hasty(3),Netherton,Parker,Aizue,McClarron,Mansson g:Poucher(8)	4th	1,152
12/9/04	Rochdale (h)	W42-18	t:Owen,Parker,Ball,Aizue(3) g:Poucher(9)	3rd	2,017
19/9/04	Doncaster (h) (EPO)	W63-22	t:McClarron(2),Netherton,Ellis(2),Pinkney(2),Mansson,Walker,Hasty,Watene g:Poucher(9) fg:Mansson	N/A	2,319
26/9/04	Featherstone (h) (ESF)	L18-19	t:Pinkney,Parker,McClarron(2) g:Hasty	N/A	3,075

● Played at Spotland, Rochdale

			APP		TRIES		GOALS		FG		PTS	
	D.O.B.	ALL	NL1	ALL	NL1	ALL	NL1	ALL	NL1	ALL	NL1	
Makali Aizue	30/12/77	22(7)	17(2)	6	5	0	0	0	0	24	20	
Dean Andrews	1/6/79	4(7)	2(4)	2	1	0	0	0	0	8	4	
Jon Aston	5/6/76	16(3)	7(1)	3	2	0	0	0	0	12	8	
Damian Ball	14/7/75	8	8	2	2	0	0	0	0	8	8	
Dwayne Barker	21/9/83	2	2	0	0	0	0	0	0	0	0	
Matthew Blake	17/3/83	1(1)	1(1)	0	0	0	0	0	0	0	0	
Jamie Bovill	21/3/83	26	16	6	3	0	0	0	0	24	12	
Matt Calland	20/8/71	12(2)	6(1)	6	2	0	0	0	0	24	8	
Andy Ellis	15/12/84	12	8	5	2	0	0	0	0	20	8	
Craig Farrell	8/10/81	14	6	6	4	0	0	0	0	24	16	
Paul Fletcher	17/3/70	(24)	(16)	1	1	0	0	0	0	4	4	
Tommy Gallagher	10/9/83	9(1)	6(1)	3	3	0	0	0	0	12	12	
Marvin Golden	21/12/76	5	2	0	0	0	0	0	0	0	0	
Phil Hasty	28/5/80	19(10)	13(5)	15	11	3	2	0	0	66	48	
Dale Holdstock	2/8/79	17	8	6	3	0	0	0	0	24	12	
Paul Mansson	13/3/72	32	20	13	8	0	0	3	3	55	35	
Casey Mayberry	19/12/81	4(2)	0	2	0	0	0	0	0	8	0	
Alasdair McClarron	19/6/73	23	15	20	12	0	0	0	0	80	48	
Jason Netherton	5/10/82	10	10	3	3	0	0	0	0	12	12	
Paul Owen	15/8/78	10	10	1	1	0	0	0	0	4	4	
Paul Parker	13/2/79	27	17	15	9	0	0	0	0	60	36	
Paul Pickering	16/12/82	18(1)	12	2	1	0	0	0	0	8	4	
Nick Pinkney	6/12/70	20(3)	16(3)	12	9	0	0	0	0	48	36	
Craig Poucher	12/9/80	25	15	8	3	34	33	0	0	100	78	
Anthony Seibold	3/10/74	28(2)	17(1)	3	0	0	0	0	0	12	0	
Andy Smith	4/1/76	18(7)	10(7)	2	2	0	0	0	0	8	8	
Lynton Stott	9/5/71	16	9	7	3	60	32	0	0	148	76	
Adam Sullivan	14/11/82	(5)	(3)	0	0	0	0	0	0	0	0	
Scott Thorburn	24/1/77	14(5)	7(2)	7	1	37	13	0	0	102	30	
Jimmy Walker	22/11/73	1(14)	(12)	3	2	0	0	0	0	12	8	
Frank Watene	15/2/77	2(28)	(19)	4	3	0	0	0	0	16	12	
Loz Wildbore	23/9/84	(2)	(2)	0	0	0	0	0	0	0	0	
Richard Wilson	5/2/75	1(4)	0	0	0	0	0	0	0	0	0	

Paul Mansson

LEAGUE RECORD
P18-W10-D0-L8
(3rd, NL1/Elimination Semi Finalists)
F466, A428, Diff+38
20 points.

CHALLENGE CUP
Round Three

NATIONAL LEAGUE CUP
Runners Up/1st, East Division

ATTENDANCES
Best - v Featherstone (ESF - 3,075)
Worst - v London Skolars (NLC - 1,677)
Total (NL1, inc play-offs,
& NLC, inc SF only) - 34,972
Average (NL1, inc play-offs,
& NLC, inc SF only) - 2,186
(Up by 624 on 2003)

KEIGHLEY COUGARS

DATE	FIXTURE	RESULT	SCORERS	LGE	ATT
1/2/04	Halifax (a) (NLC)	L18-12	t:Mervill(2) g:Mitchell(2)	3rd(NLC-P)	3,360
8/2/04	Bradford-Dudley Hill (a) (CCR3) ●	L16-14	t:Smith(2),Firth g:Mitchell	N/A	1,300
15/2/04	Workington (h) (NLC)	W42-6	t:Smith,Ekis,Parker,M Foster,Hoyle,Webster g:Mitchell(9)	3rd(NLC-P)	937
22/2/04	Rochdale (a) (NLC)	L18-14	t:Robinson,Patterson g:Mitchell(3)	3rd(NLC-P)	762
7/3/04	Hunslet (a) (NLC)	L42-24	t:D Foster,Mitchell(2),Wainwright g:Mitchell(4)	3rd(NLC-P)	640
21/3/04	Halifax (h) (NLC)	W26-8	t:Hoyle,Rushforth,Robinson,Ekis g:Mitchell(5)	3rd(NLC-P)	1,926
28/3/04	Workington (a) (NLC)	W12-33	t:M Foster,Hoyle,Rushforth,McDowell,Patterson g:Mitchell(4) fg:Mitchell	3rd(NLC-P)	567
4/4/04	Rochdale (h) (NLC)	D14-14	t:Robinson(2) g:Mitchell(3)	3rd(NLC-P)	1,171
9/4/04	Hunslet (h) (NLC)	W47-8	t:Parker,M Foster,Smith(2),Steel,McDowell,Rushforth,Mitchell(2) g:Mitchell(5) fg:McDowell	2nd(NLC-P)	1,297
12/4/04	Hull KR (a)	L56-6	t:Hoyle g:Mitchell	10th	2,383
18/4/04	Batley (h)	L22-39	t:M Foster(3) g:Mitchell(5)	9th	1,282
25/4/04	Barrow (a) (NLCQFQ)	L32-20	t:Firth,Smith,Beever g:Mitchell(4)	N/A	730
2/5/04	Whitehaven (a)	L38-6	t:Robinson g:Nipperess	9th	1,160
9/5/04	Featherstone (h)	W42-18	t:Wilson(2),M Foster(2),Clegg,Hoyle g:Nipperess(9)	9th	1,251
23/5/04	Leigh (a)	L30-12	t:Parker,Clegg g:Nipperess(2)	9th	1,683
30/5/04	Rochdale (h)	L32-46	t:Stephenson(2),M Foster(2),Hoyle,Nipperess g:Nipperess(2),Mitchell(2)	9th	1,041
13/6/04	Oldham (h)	L28-33	t:Fielden,Robinson(2),Mervill,Mitchell g:Nipperess(3),Mitchell	9th	1,153
20/6/04	Doncaster (a)	L52-30	t:Patterson,M Foster(2),Hoyle,D Foster g:Nipperess(4),Mitchell	9th	827
4/7/04	Halifax (h)	L16-37	t:M Foster,Firth,Robinson g:Mitchell(2)	10th	1,380
11/7/04	Batley (a)	L30-14	t:Hoyle,Beever,Robinson g:Mitchell	10th	685
25/7/04	Whitehaven (h)	L16-29	t:McDowell,Hoyle g:Mitchell(4)	10th	948
1/8/04	Featherstone (a)	L54-16	t:M Foster,Robinson,Nipperess g:Nipperess,Mitchell	10th	1,089
8/8/04	Leigh (h)	L10-48	t:Tomlinson,Wainwright g:Nipperess	10th	1,091
15/8/04	Rochdale (a)	L46-32	t:M Foster(3),Nipperess,Smith(2) g:Mitchell(4)	10th	822
22/8/04	Oldham (a)	L31-20	t:M Foster(3),Robinson,Mitchell	10th	1,202
29/8/04	Doncaster (h)	L20-39	t:Stephenson,M Foster g:Mitchell(5),Nipperess	10th	760
5/9/04	Hull KR (h)	L22-52	t:Stephenson,Bramald,Feather,Nipperess g:Nipperess(2),Bramald	10th	1,152
12/9/04	Halifax (a)	L30-22	t:Hoyle,D Foster,Patterson,Firth g:Nipperess(3)	10th	1,344

● Played at Cougar Park

		APP		TRIES		GOALS		FG		PTS	
	D.O.B.	ALL	NL1	ALL	NL1	ALL	NL1	ALL	NL1	ALL	NL1
Chris Beever	18/2/81	13(3)	8(3)	2	1	0	0	0	0	8	4
Matt Bramald	6/2/73	8	8	1	1	1	1	0	0	6	6
Jason Clegg	24/3/71	12(15)	12(6)	2	2	0	0	0	0	8	8
Danny Ekis	17/1/84	3(13)	1(6)	2	0	0	0	0	0	8	0
Andy Feather	3/11/84	(2)	(2)	1	1	0	0	0	0	4	4
Jamie Fielden	9/5/78	1(7)	1(7)	1	1	0	0	0	0	4	4
Matt Firth	19/2/81	28	18	4	2	0	0	0	0	16	8
David Foster	8/4/81	28	18	3	2	0	0	0	0	12	8
Matt Foster	10/6/76	22	13	21	18	0	0	0	0	84	72
Simeon Hoyle	18/9/79	23(2)	14(2)	11	7	0	0	0	0	44	28
Craig McDowell	5/11/81	25(1)	17(1)	3	1	0	0	1	0	13	4
Richard Mervill	24/6/81	11(9)	6(8)	3	1	0	0	0	0	12	4
Adam Mitchell	7/8/81	18(8)	9(7)	6	2	67	27	1	0	159	62
Danny Murgatroyd	23/10/80	2(2)	2(2)	0	0	0	0	0	0	0	0
Craig Nipperess	27/10/76	14(12)	13(4)	4	4	29	29	0	0	74	74
Chris Parker	9/9/78	18(2)	8(2)	3	1	0	0	0	0	12	4
Lee Patterson	5/7/81	21(2)	11(2)	4	2	0	0	0	0	16	8
Andy Robinson	15/11/78	28	18	11	7	0	0	0	0	44	28
Chris Roe	13/7/84	(7)	(4)	0	0	0	0	0	0	0	0
Jordan Ross	25/10/84	3	3	0	0	0	0	0	0	0	0
James Rushforth	9/2/77	6	2	3	0	0	0	0	0	12	0
Karl Smith	28/5/77	21(1)	13	8	2	0	0	0	0	32	8
Matthew Steel	5/10/84	7(1)	2	1	0	0	0	0	0	4	0
Phil Stephenson	17/6/72	28	18	4	4	0	0	0	0	16	16
Max Tomlinson	12/4/70	8(4)	7(2)	1	1	0	0	0	0	4	4
Chris Wainwright	18/10/79	13(7)	9(5)	2	1	0	0	0	0	8	4
Adam Webster	2/4/85	(4)	(2)	1	0	0	0	0	0	4	0
Eddie Wilson	18/3/85	3(6)	3(5)	2	2	0	0	0	0	8	8

Phil Stephenson

LEAGUE RECORD
P18-W1-D0-L17
(10th, NL1)
F366, A708, Diff-342
2 points.

CHALLENGE CUP
Round Three

NATIONAL LEAGUE CUP
2nd, Pennine Division
(Eliminated in Quarter Final Qualifiers)

ATTENDANCES
Best - v Halifax (NLC - 1,926)
Worst - v Doncaster (NL1 - 760)
Total (NL1 & NLC only) - 15,389
Average (NL1 & NLC only) - 1,184
(Up by 79 on 2003, NL2)

LEIGH CENTURIONS

DATE	FIXTURE	RESULT	SCORERS	LGE	ATT
1/2/04	Swinton (a) (NLC)	W6-22	t:Turley(2),Potter,Isherwood g:Turley(3)	2nd(NLC-W)	1,351
8/2/04	Elland (a) (CCR3) ●	W4-64	t:Percival(2),Turley,Cardoza,Martyn,McCully(2),Potter,Rowley(2),Isherwood(2) g:Turley(8)	N/A	1,365
15/2/04	Oldham (h) (NLC)	W51-32	t:McCully,Bradbury,Knott(2),Turley,Rowley,Martyn,Duffy g:Turley(9) fg:Turley	1st(NLC-W)	2,316
22/2/04	Chorley (h) (NLC)	W60-10	t:Rowley,Alstead,Isherwood(3),Callan(2),Larder,Wilkes,Maden,Knott g:Turley(8)	1st(NLC-W)	1,452
29/2/04	Hull (h) (CCR4)	L14-21	t:Martyn,Knott g:Turley(3)	N/A	3,324
7/3/04	Oldham (a) (NLC)	W10-54	t:Halliwell(3),Martyn,Alstead,Potter(3),Munro(2),Percival g:Knott(2),Martyn(3)	1st(NLC-W)	1,805
21/3/04	Swinton (h) (NLC)	W66-6	t:Rowley,Potter,Percival(2),Duffy(3),Knott(3),Munro(2) g:Turley(9)	1st(NLC-W)	1,475
28/3/04	Halifax (a) (NLC)	W16-27	t:Rowley,Larder,Turley,Potter,Percival g:Turley(3) fg:Turley	1st(NLC-W)	2,815
4/4/04	Chorley (a) (NLC)	W10-78	t:Martyn(2),Knott(2),Turley(5),Halliwell(2),Isherwood(2),Percival g:Turley(11)	1st(NLC-W)	770
9/4/04	Halifax (h) (NLC)	W46-20	t:Rowley(2),Halliwell,Alstead,Potter,Turley,McCully,Duffy g:Turley(7)	1st(NLC-W)	2,563
12/4/04	Whitehaven (a)	L31-24	t:Percival(2),Alstead,Wilkes g:Turley(4)	6th	2,104
18/4/04	Featherstone (h)	W50-12	t:Martyn,Knox(2),Isherwood,Percival,Bowker(2),Maden(2) g:Turley(7)	6th	1,790
2/5/04	Oldham (a)	W20-60	t:Duffy(2),Marshall,Turley,Martyn,Percival(2),Swann,Bowker,Maden g:Turley(10)	3rd	2,104
9/5/04	Rochdale (a)	W24-74	t:Percival(3),Potter,Knox,Knott(2),Rowley,Cruckshank,McConnell,Turley(2),Martyn g:Turley(11)	1st	1,303
23/5/04	Keighley (h)	W30-12	t:Rourke,Halliwell,Knott(2),Martyn,Rowley g:Turley(3)	1st	1,683
30/5/04	Doncaster (a)	L19-14	t:Potter,Smyth,Maden g:Smyth	3rd	1,140
6/6/04	Barrow (a) (NLCQF)	W20-24	t:Knox(2),Martyn,Munro g:Turley(4)	N/A	1,245
13/6/04	Halifax (h)	W43-25	t:Maden,Turley,Smyth,Swann,Martyn,Duffy,Knott g:Turley(7) fg:Martyn	2nd	1,952
20/6/04	Hull KR (a)	W8-35	t:Turley,Smyth,Potter,Swann(2) g:Turley(7) fg:Duffy	1st	2,647
27/6/04	Whitehaven (a) (NLCSF)	W30-34	t:Larder,Turley(2),Halliwell,Munro,Martyn g:Turley(5)	N/A	2,449
4/7/04	Batley (h)	W27-22	t:Wilkes(2),Turley,Isherwood g:Turley(5) fg:Turley	1st	2,030
11/7/04	Featherstone (a)	W20-75	t:Halliwell(3),Cruckshank,Smyth(2),Potter,Govin,Duffy,Martyn,Wilkes,Knox,Cooper g:Turley(7),Smyth(4) fg:Martyn	1st	1,859
18/7/04	Hull KR (NLCF) ●●	W14-42	t:Halliwell(2),Knox(2),Cooper,Turley,Martyn g:Turley(6) fg:Martyn,Turley	N/A	4,383
25/7/04	Oldham (h)	W36-12	t:Percival(3),Martyn,Cooper,Munro g:Turley(6)	1st	1,841
1/8/04	Rochdale (h)	L18-44	t:Larder,Turley,Martyn g:Turley,Smyth(2)	1st	1,662
8/8/04	Keighley (a)	W10-48	t:Halliwell,Smyth,Turley(3),Munro(2),Martyn g:Turley(8)	1st	1,091
15/8/04	Doncaster (h)	W46-32	t:Knott(2),Munro,Martyn(2),Potter,McConnell g:Smyth(9)	1st	1,793
22/8/04	Halifax (a)	L58-30	t:McConnell,Swann(2),Rourke,Duffy g:Smyth(3)	2nd	1,781
29/8/04	Hull KR (h)	W26-22	t:Percival,Wilkes g:Turley(7)	2nd	1,768
5/9/04	Whitehaven (h)	W21-14	t:Alstead(2),McConnell g:Turley(4) fg:Turley	1st	3,442
12/9/04	Batley (a)	W22-29	t:Wilkes(2),Cruckshank,Turley g:Turley(6) fg:Turley	1st	1,719
26/9/04	Whitehaven (h) (QSF)	W30-16	t:Smyth,Halliwell,Alstead(2),Larder(2) g:Turley(2) fg:Turley(2)	N/A	4,563
10/10/04	Whitehaven (GF) ●●●	W32-16 (aet)	t:Cooper(2),Martyn,Turley g:Turley(6) fg:Turley(2),Rowley,Martyn	N/A	11,005

● Played at The Coliseum
●● Played at Spotland, Rochdale
●●● Played at Halton Stadium, Widnes

		APP		TRIES		GOALS		FG		PTS	
	D.O.B.	ALL	NL1	ALL	NL1	ALL	NL1	ALL	NL1	ALL	NL1
David Alstead	18/2/82	10(4)	6(3)	8	5	0	0	0	0	32	20
Radney Bowker	5/2/79	4(3)	4(1)	3	3	0	0	0	0	12	12
David Bradbury	16/3/72	4(3)	1(1)	1	0	0	0	0	0	4	0
Mike Callan	8/8/83	1(5)	1(1)	2	0	0	0	0	0	8	0
Dale Cardoza	13/9/79	2	0	1	0	0	0	0	0	4	0
Mick Coates	8/3/80	(3)	0	0	0	0	0	0	0	0	0
Ben Cooper	8/10/79	12	9	5	4	0	0	0	0	20	16
Heath Cruckshank	28/6/76	13(17)	6(13)	3	3	0	0	0	0	12	12
John Duffy	2/7/80	28	17	10	5	0	0	1	1	41	21
Mick Govin	5/11/84	3(1)	3(1)	1	1	0	0	0	0	4	4
Danny Halliwell	23/3/81	21(3)	13(1)	15	6	0	0	0	0	60	24
Luke Isakka	1/11/80	(2)	(2)	0	0	0	0	0	0	0	0
Andrew Isherwood	23/11/79	7(16)	3(10)	10	2	0	0	0	0	40	8
Phil Jones	30/9/77	3	3	0	0	0	0	0	0	0	0
Ian Knott	2/10/76	28	15	16	7	2	0	0	0	68	28
Simon Knox	14/10/72	19(9)	11(5)	8	4	0	0	0	0	32	16
David Larder	5/6/76	28	17	6	3	0	0	0	0	24	12
Steve Maden	13/9/82	17(1)	8	6	5	0	0	0	0	24	20
Richard Marshall	9/10/75	8(15)	6(12)	1	1	0	0	0	0	4	4
Tommy Martyn	4/6/71	27	14	21	12	3	0	4	3	94	51
Dave McConnell	25/3/81	12(15)	9(7)	4	4	0	0	0	0	16	16
Mark McCully	24/10/79	5	1	4	0	0	0	0	0	16	0
Damian Munro	6/10/76	13(1)	6(1)	10	4	0	0	0	0	40	16
Paul Norman	25/3/74	3(7)	2(2)	0	0	0	0	0	0	0	0
Chris Percival	25/12/79	19(1)	12	20	13	0	0	0	0	80	52
Dan Potter	8/11/78	26(1)	14(1)	13	5	0	0	0	0	52	20
Gary Rourke	9/5/83	3	3	3	3	0	0	0	0	12	12
Paul Rowley	12/3/75	22(3)	12(1)	10	2	0	0	1	1	41	9
Rob Smyth	22/2/77	16(1)	14(1)	7	7	19	19	0	0	66	66
Matt Sturm	13/12/72	15	12	0	0	0	0	0	0	0	0
Willie Swann	25/2/74	1(17)	1(15)	6	6	0	0	0	0	24	24
Neil Turley	15/3/80	29	17	26	12	177	101	10	7	468	257
Craig Weston	20/12/73	4	4	0	0	0	0	0	0	0	0
Oliver Wilkes	2/5/80	26(4)	16(2)	8	7	0	0	0	0	32	28

Tommy Martyn

LEAGUE RECORD
P18-W14-D0-L4
(1st, NL1/Grand Final Winners, Champions)
F686, A407, Diff+279
28 points.

CHALLENGE CUP
Round Four

NATIONAL LEAGUE CUP
Winners/1st, West Division

ATTENDANCES
Best - v Whitehaven (QSF - 4,563)
Worst - v Chorley (NLC - 1,452)
Total (NL1, inc play-offs, & NLC only) - 30,330
Average (NL1, inc play-offs, & NLC only) - 2,166
(Down by 279 on 2003)

OLDHAM

DATE	FIXTURE	RESULT	SCORERS	LGE	ATT
1/2/04	Chorley (h) (NLC)	W64-14	t:N Johnson,Morgan,Goddard,Barber,Cowell,L Marsh,Elswood,I Marsh(2), Watson,Dodd g:Svabic(5),Barber(5)	1st(NLC-W)	1,096
6/2/04	Castleford Panthers (h) (CCR3)	W16-8	t:N Johnson,I Marsh,Cowell g:Barber(2)	N/A	1,003
15/2/04	Leigh (a) (NLC)	L51-32	t:I Marsh,Morgan(2),Doran,Watson g:Svabic(6)	2nd(NLC-W)	2,316
22/2/04	Swinton (a) (NLC)	W18-30	t:Goddard,L Marsh,Dodd,N Johnson,Bunyan g:Svabic(4),Barber	2nd(NLC-W)	731
3/3/04	Sharlston (h) (CCR4)	W24-4	t:I Marsh(2),L Marsh,N Johnson g:Svabic(4)	N/A	1,301
7/3/04	Leigh (h) (NLC)	L10-54	t:Dodd,Goddard g:L Marsh	2nd(NLC-W)	1,805
14/3/04	Warrington (h) (CCR5)	L10-44	t:Cowell,N Johnson g:L Marsh	N/A	2,859
21/3/04	Chorley (a) (NLC)	W10-40	t:Brennan,N Johnson(3),Southern,Dodd,Roden,Cowell g:Barber(4)	2nd(NLC-W)	370
28/3/04	Rochdale (h) (NLC)	W56-12	t:Roden(3),Dodd(2),Doran,Morgan,N Johnson(3) g:Barber(5),Svabic(3)	2nd(NLC-W)	1,214
4/4/04	Swinton (a) (NLC)	W42-15	t:Roden(2),Barber,N Johnson,Rich,Cowell(2),Elswood g:Rich(5)	2nd(NLC-W)	983
9/4/04	Rochdale (a) (NLC)	W12-48	t:L Marsh(2),Barber,Morgan,Dodd,Rich,N Johnson(2),Roden,Goddard g:Rich(3),Svabic	2nd(NLC-W)	1,305
12/4/04	Featherstone (h)	W50-24	t:Bunyan(4),Dodd(2),Goddard,Roden,Cowell g:L Marsh(7)	3rd	1,320
18/4/04	Halifax (a)	W6-25	t:Roden(2),Brennan g:Rich(6) fg:Watson	2nd	1,807
25/4/04	Doncaster (a) (NLCQFQ)	L32-28	t:Farrell,L Marsh(2),Watson g:Rich(6)	N/A	835
2/5/04	Leigh (h)	L20-60	t:N Johnson(2),Farrimond,Farrell g:Rich(2)	6th	2,104
9/5/04	Hull KR (a)	L29-22	t:Morgan(2),Farrell g:Rich(5)	6th	2,121
23/5/04	Rochdale (h)	W26-24	t:Roden,Goddard(3),Svabic g:Rich(3)	6th	1,243
30/5/04	Batley (h) ●	L20-44	t:L Marsh(2),Morgan g:Rich(3) fg:Brennan(2)	7th	1,541
13/6/04	Keighley (a)	W28-33	t:Brennan,N Johnson(2),Bunyan,Svabic,Watson g:Rich(2),Svabic(2) fg:Watson	6th	1,153
20/6/04	Whitehaven (h) ●●	W31-22	t:L Marsh,I Marsh,Bunyan,Dodd g:Rich(2),L Marsh(5) fg:Watson	5th	752
4/7/04	Doncaster (a)	L31-30	t:Dodd,I Marsh(2),Brennan,L Marsh g:Rich(5)	6th	998
10/7/04	Halifax (h) ●●	W24-14	t:I Marsh,N Johnson,L Marsh,Barber g:Rich(3) fg:Watson(2)	5th	850
25/7/04	Leigh (a)	L36-12	t:Roden g:Rich(4)	6th	1,841
1/8/04	Hull KR (h)	W29-24	t:L Marsh(2),N Johnson,Roden,Goddard,Watson g:L Marsh,Roper fg:L Marsh	4th	1,393
8/8/04	Rochdale (a)	L30-24	t:N Johnson,Dodd,Brennan,Roden g:Roper(4)	6th	1,403
15/8/04	Batley (a)	W18-34	t:Barber(2),Watson,N Johnson,Farrell,Goddard g:Roper(5)	5th	886
22/8/04	Keighley (h)	W31-20	t:N Johnson,Morgan,Goddard(2),Roden g:Watson(5) fg:Watson	3rd	1,202
29/8/04	Whitehaven (a)	L32-16	t:McLoughlin,Doran,Dodd g:L Marsh(2)	3rd	2,009
5/9/04	Featherstone (a)	L35-26	t:Goddard,Roden,L Marsh,Dodd(2) g:L Marsh(3)	5th	1,397
12/9/04	Doncaster (h)	W29-26	t:N Johnson,Barber,Morgan,I Marsh g:Roper(6) fg:Watson	4th	1,448
19/9/04	Featherstone (h) (EPO)	L28-33	t:I Marsh,Farrell,N Johnson,Barber,McLoughlin g:Roper(4)	N/A	1,970

● Played at Bloomfield Road, Blackpool
●● Played at Victory Park, Chorley

	D.O.B.	APP		TRIES		GOALS		FG		PTS	
		ALL	NL1	ALL	NL1	ALL	NL1	ALL	NL1	ALL	NL1
Gareth Barber	15/12/80	8(20)	3(14)	8	5	17	0	0	0	66	20
Keith Brennan	31/10/73	23(3)	15(1)	5	4	0	0	2	2	22	18
Chris Brett	24/10/79	(1)	(1)	0	0	0	0	0	0	0	0
James Bunyan	2/11/77	11(3)	6	7	6	0	0	0	0	28	24
Adam Clayton	14/3/85	(1)	(1)	0	0	0	0	0	0	0	0
Will Cowell	31/12/79	17	5	7	1	0	0	0	0	28	4
Gavin Dodd	28/2/81	27	16	15	8	0	0	0	0	60	32
Lee Doran	23/3/81	31	19	3	1	0	0	0	0	12	4
Martin Elswood	18/10/83	2(18)	1(10)	2	0	0	0	0	0	8	0
Phil Farrell	14/2/80	19	18	5	4	0	0	0	0	20	16
Craig Farrimond	20/11/82	(6)	(4)	1	1	0	0	0	0	4	4
David Gibbons	18/1/76	2	2	0	0	0	0	0	0	0	0
Jon Goddard	21/6/82	30	18	13	9	0	0	0	0	52	36
John Hough	14/4/76	8(4)	5(4)	0	0	0	0	0	0	0	0
Gavin Johnson	18/12/80	(6)	(5)	0	0	0	0	0	0	0	0
Nick Johnson	16/4/83	31	19	25	11	0	0	0	0	100	44
James Lomax	20/10/81	(1)	0	0	0	0	0	0	0	0	0
Iain Marsh	6/10/80	14(2)	8(2)	12	6	0	0	0	0	48	24
Lee Marsh	5/3/83	23(3)	12(2)	15	8	20	18	1	1	101	69
Martin McLoughlin	2/8/80	12(10)	11(8)	2	2	0	0	0	0	8	8
Steve Molloy	11/3/69	9(6)	7(6)	0	0	0	0	0	0	0	0
Dane Morgan	30/1/79	22	19	10	5	0	0	0	0	40	20
Danny Nanyn	8/10/84	(1)	(1)	0	0	0	0	0	0	0	0
Pat Rich	25/6/78	10	10	2	0	49	35	0	0	106	70
Mark Roberts	9/11/82	(4)	(4)	0	0	0	0	0	0	0	0
Neil Roden	9/4/80	11(4)	10(3)	16	9	0	0	0	0	64	36
Jon Roper	5/5/76	9	9	0	0	20	20	0	0	40	40
Adam Sharples	19/4/85	(7)	(6)	0	0	0	0	0	0	0	0
Paul Southern	18/3/76	14(1)	12	1	0	0	0	0	0	4	0
Simon Svabic	18/1/80	6(5)	5(4)	2	2	25	2	0	0	58	12
Ian Watson	27/10/76	20	17	6	3	5	5	7	7	41	29

Gavin Dodd

LEAGUE RECORD
P18-W10-D0-L8
(4th, NL1/Elimination Play-Off)
F482, A503, Diff-21
20 points.

CHALLENGE CUP
Round Five

NATIONAL LEAGUE CUP
2nd, West Division
(Eliminated in Quarter Final Qualifiers)

ATTENDANCES
Best - v Warrington (CC - 2,859)
Worst - v Whitehaven (NL1 - 752)
Total (NL1, inc play-offs,
& NLC only) - 18,921
Average (NL1, inc play-offs,
& NLC only) - 1,352
(Down by 220 on 2003)

ROCHDALE HORNETS

DATE	FIXTURE	RESULT	SCORERS	LGE	ATT
1/2/04	Hunslet (a) (NLC)	L24-8	t:Williams g:Birdseye(2)	4th(NLC-P)	519
8/2/04	Dinamo Moscow (h) (CCR3)	W60-24	t:Billings,Gorski(3),Anderson(2),Campbell(3),Birdseye,Butterworth g:Birdseye(8)	N/A	707
15/2/04	Halifax (h) (NLC)	L14-33	t:Varkulis(2) g:Birdseye(3)	4th(NLC-P)	1,343
22/2/04	Keighley (h) (NLC)	W18-14	t:Gorski,Varkulis,Costello g:Birdseye(3)	4th(NLC-P)	762
2/3/04	Warrington (h) (CCR4) ●	L0-80	No Scorers	N/A	6,761
7/3/04	Halifax (a) (NLC)	L21-6	g:Birdseye(3)	4th(NLC-P)	2,096
21/3/04	Hunslet (h) (NLC)	W37-6	t:Campbell(2),Billings,Platt(2),Anderson,Costello g:Butterworth(4) fg:Butterworth	4th(NLC-P)	674
28/3/04	Oldham (a) (NLC)	L56-12	t:Butterworth,Campbell g:Butterworth(2)	4th(NLC-P)	1,214
4/4/04	Keighley (a) (NLC)	D14-14	t:Platt,Braddish g:Birdseye(3)	4th(NLC-P)	1,171
9/4/04	Oldham (h) (NLC)	L12-48	t:Birdseye,Campbell g:Birdseye(2)	4th(NLC-P)	1,305
12/4/04	Batley (a)	L48-12	t:Price(2) g:Birdseye(2)	9th	639
18/4/04	Whitehaven (h)	L12-46	t:Platt,Birdseye g:Birdseye(2)	10th	702
2/5/04	Featherstone (a)	L58-12	t:Cunliffe,Butterworth g:Birdseye(2)	10th	1,098
9/5/04	Leigh (h)	L24-74	t:Butterworth,Cunliffe,Naulumata,Gorski g:Birdseye(4)	10th	1,303
23/5/04	Oldham (a)	L26-24	t:Platt,Gorski,Price,Robinson g:Birdseye(4)	10th	1,243
30/5/04	Keighley (a)	W32-46	t:Robinson,Campbell(2),Birdseye(3),Gorski,Cunliffe g:Birdseye(7)	10th	1,041
13/6/04	Doncaster (a)	L38-18	t:Saywell(2),Cunliffe g:Birdseye(3)	10th	645
20/6/04	Halifax (a)	L15-14	t:Saywell,McCully g:Birdseye(3)	10th	1,301
4/7/04	Hull KR (h)	W36-18	t:Goulding,Robinson,Gorski,Alstead,Butterworth g:Braddish(8)	9th	1,094
11/7/04	Whitehaven (a)	L30-14	t:Gorski,McCully,Campbell g:Braddish	9th	1,654
25/7/04	Featherstone (h)	D12-12	t:Robinson g:Goulding(4)	9th	804
1/8/04	Leigh (a)	W18-44	t:Picton,Braddish,Newton,Williams,Ratcliffe(2),Price,McGovern g:Braddish(6)	9th	1,662
8/8/04	Oldham (h)	W30-24	t:Robinson,Alstead,Butterworth,Campbell,Platt g:Braddish(5)	8th	1,403
15/8/04	Keighley (h)	W46-32	t:Platt(3),Shaw,Price(2),Robinson,Newton g:Braddish(3),McCully(4)	8th	822
21/8/04	Doncaster (h)	W52-18	t:Alstead(2),Birdseye,Goulding,Platt,Varkulis(2),Robinson,Braddish g:Birdseye(7),McCully	7th	624
29/8/04	Halifax (h)	W34-24	t:Ball,Saywell,Campbell,Robinson,Gorski,Birdseye g:Birdseye(5)	7th	1,230
5/9/04	Batley (h)	L24-32	t:McCully,Gorski,Butterworth(2) g:Birdseye(4)	8th	1,067
12/9/04	Hull KR (a)	L42-18	t:Hodgkinson,Robinson,Goulding g:Braddish(3)	8th	2,017

● Played at Halliwell Jones Stadium, Warrington

		APP		TRIES		GOALS		FG		PTS	
	D.O.B.	ALL	NL1	ALL	NL1	ALL	NL1	ALL	NL1	ALL	NL1
David Alstead	18/2/82	6	6	4	4	0	0	0	0	16	16
Paul Anderson	2/4/77	12	3	3	0	0	0	0	0	12	0
Rob Ball	22/3/76	18(3)	10(3)	1	1	0	0	0	0	4	4
Janan Billings	27/1/82	11(12)	3(12)	2	0	0	0	0	0	8	0
Lee Birdseye	5/8/79	18(5)	11(3)	8	6	67	43	0	0	166	110
Ryan Blake	11/7/81	1	1	0	0	0	0	0	0	0	0
John Braddish	25/1/81	23(2)	14(2)	3	2	26	26	0	0	64	60
Danny Butler	16/6/80	1	0	0	0	0	0	0	0	0	0
Sam Butterworth	12/2/78	11(13)	6(8)	6	6	0	0	1	0	45	24
Chris Campbell	2/12/80	20	10	12	5	0	0	0	0	48	20
Mark Costello	10/11/83	2(13)	(5)	2	0	0	0	0	0	8	0
Dave Cunliffe	15/1/80	18	17	4	4	0	0	0	0	16	16
Andy Gorski	31/3/81	27	18	11	7	0	0	0	0	44	28
Bobbie Goulding	4/2/72	5(4)	5(4)	3	3	4	4	0	0	20	20
Andy Grundy	19/1/77	2(7)	0	0	0	0	0	0	0	0	0
Lee Hansen	23/7/68	10(12)	4(9)	0	0	0	0	0	0	0	0
Tommy Hodgkinson	15/4/70	11(11)	11(6)	1	1	0	0	0	0	4	4
Tony Kirwan	1/7/78	(4)	(1)	0	0	0	0	0	0	0	0
Andy Leathem	30/3/77	12(4)	4(3)	0	0	0	0	0	0	0	0
Mark McCully	24/10/79	13	13	3	3	5	5	0	0	22	22
Liam McGovern	6/10/84	8(1)	7(1)	1	1	0	0	0	0	4	4
Komai Naulumata		1	1	1	1	0	0	0	0	4	4
Dave Newton	22/12/81	7(11)	6(10)	2	2	0	0	0	0	8	8
Kevin Picton	19/10/83	2	2	1	1	0	0	0	0	4	4
Michael Platt	23/3/84	22	13	10	7	0	0	0	0	40	28
Gareth Price	28/6/80	16	12	6	6	0	0	0	0	24	24
Kris Ratcliffe	28/5/81	6(6)	3(2)	2	2	0	0	0	0	8	8
Darren Robinson	28/5/79	13(2)	13(2)	9	9	0	0	0	0	36	36
Andy Saywell	1/1/79	8(1)	8(1)	4	4	0	0	0	0	16	16
Darren Shaw	5/10/71	25	17	1	1	0	0	0	0	4	4
Lepani Soro		2	2	0	0	0	0	0	0	0	0
Matt Sturm	13/12/72	3(1)	0	0	0	0	0	0	0	0	0
Alex Taylor	22/9/79	1	0	0	0	0	0	0	0	0	0
Richard Varkulis	21/5/82	9	6	5	2	0	0	0	0	20	8
Ashley Watmore	30/9/84	1	0	0	0	0	0	0	0	0	0
Liam Williams	21/10/83	18	8	2	1	0	0	0	0	8	4
Danny Yates	6/1/84	1	0	0	0	0	0	0	0	0	0

Andy Gorski

LEAGUE RECORD
P18-W7-D1-L10
(8th, NL1)
F472, A587, Diff-115
15 points.

CHALLENGE CUP
Round Four

NATIONAL LEAGUE CUP
4th, Pennine Division

ATTENDANCES
Best - v Oldham (NL1 - 1,403)
Worst - v Doncaster (NL1 - 624)
Total (NL1 & NLC only) - 13,133
Average (NL1 & NLC only) - 1,010
(Down by 52 on 2003)

WHITEHAVEN

DATE	FIXTURE	RESULT	SCORERS	LGE	ATT
1/2/04	Barrow (a) (NLC)	W18-32	t:Nanyn(4),Seeds(2),Fatialofa g:Nanyn(2)	2nd(NLC-N)	1,269
8/2/04	Thatto Heath (a) (CCR3) ●	W12-26	t:Kiddie(2),Seeds,Walsh,Lebbon g:Nanyn(3)	N/A	1,114
15/2/04	Swinton (h) (NLC)	W38-10	t:Nanyn,Hill,O'Neil,McDermott,Marshall(2),Walsh,Broadbent g:Nanyn(2),Wood	1st(NLC-N)	1,073
22/2/04	Gateshead (a) (NLC)	W14-54	t:Nanyn(2),Kiddie,Morton(2),Walsh(3),Hill,Miller g:Nanyn(7)	1st(NLC-N)	294
2/3/04	East Hull (a) (CCR4) ●●	W4-14	t:McDermott,Nanyn g:Nanyn(3)	N/A	1,400
7/3/04	Workington (h) (NLC)	W54-12	t:Joe,Miller,Kiddie(2),Broadbent(3),Wilson(2),Nanyn g:Nanyn(7)	1st(NLC-N)	2,156
14/3/04	Batley (a) (CCR5)	W6-29	t:Hill(2),O'Neil,Wilson,Nanyn g:Nanyn(4) fg:Joe	N/A	1,186
21/3/04	Barrow (h) (NLC)	W14-10	t:Lebbon,Seeds g:Nanyn(3)	1st(NLC-N)	1,249
28/3/04	Warrington (h) (CCQF)	L10-42	t:Kiddie,Nanyn g:Nanyn	N/A	5,328
30/3/04	Swinton (a) (NLC)	W6-34	t:Walsh(2),Sice(2),McDermott,Miller g:Wood(5)	1st(NLC-N)	346
4/4/04	Gateshead (h) (NLC)	W74-16	t:Obst(2),Marshall,Kiddie(3),Lester,Wilson,McKinney,Jackson,Walsh, Broadbent,Nanyn g:Nanyn(11)	1st(NLC-N)	1,017
9/4/04	Workington (a) (NLC)	W10-26	t:Walsh(2),Sice,Kirkbride,Purdham g:Nanyn(3)	1st(NLC-N)	1,419
12/4/04	Leigh (h)	W31-24	t:O'Neil(2),McDermott,Hill,Sice g:Nanyn(5) fg:Sice	5th	2,104
18/4/04	Rochdale (a)	W12-46	t:Seeds,Nanyn(2),Obst(2),O'Neil,Walsh,Sice,Kiddie g:Nanyn(5)	3rd	702
2/5/04	Keighley (h)	W38-6	t:Walsh(2),Obst,Lester,Morton,Sice g:Nanyn(7)	1st	1,160
9/5/04	Doncaster (a)	L31-24	t:McDermott,Obst,Nanyn,Marshall,O'Neil g:Nanyn(2)	2nd	853
23/5/04	Halifax (h)	W34-8	t:Seeds,Marshall,Obst,Walsh(2),Lester,Nanyn g:Nanyn(3)	2nd	1,648
30/5/04	Hull KR (a)	W12-26	t:Fatialofa,Obst(2) g:Nanyn(5) fg:Obst(3),Joe	1st	1,954
6/6/04	Batley (a) (NLCQF)	W16-22	t:Walsh,O'Neil,Seeds(2) g:Nanyn(3)	N/A	910
13/6/04	Batley (h)	W28-17	t:Hill,Nanyn(2),Broadbent,Walsh g:Nanyn(4)	1st	1,853
20/6/04	Oldham (a) ●●●	L31-22	t:Walsh,Fatialofa,Nanyn,Wood g:Nanyn(3)	2nd	752
27/6/04	Leigh (h) (NLCSF)	L30-34	t:Marshall(2),Wilson,Obst g:Nanyn(7)	N/A	2,449
4/7/04	Featherstone (a)	L26-12	t:Fatialofa,Kiddie g:O'Neil(2)	3rd	1,259
11/7/04	Rochdale (h)	W30-14	t:Calvert(2),Morton,Obst,O'Neil,Walsh g:O'Neil(3)	2nd	1,654
25/7/04	Keighley (a)	W16-29	t:Sice,Obst,Nanyn,Joe g:Nanyn(6) fg:Obst	2nd	948
1/8/04	Doncaster (h)	W42-18	t:Nanyn(3),Miller,Obst,Seeds,Calvert g:Nanyn(7)	2nd	1,814
8/8/04	Halifax (a)	W14-34	t:Calvert(2),Hill(2),Obst,Nanyn g:Nanyn(5)	2nd	1,440
15/8/04	Hull KR (h)	W38-8	t:Hill,Walsh(2),Obst,Calvert,Tandy,Miller g:Nanyn(5)	2nd	1,857
22/8/04	Batley (a)	W22-48	t:Nanyn(4),Walsh(2),Miller,Calvert g:Nanyn(8)	1st	605
29/8/04	Oldham (h)	W32-16	t:Tandy(2),Obst,Lester,Joe,Calvert g:Nanyn(4)	1st	2,009
5/9/04	Leigh (a)	L21-14	t:Fatialofa,Obst g:Nanyn(3)	2nd	3,442
12/9/04	Featherstone (h)	W24-16	t:Walsh,Calvert(2),Nanyn,Seeds g:Nanyn(2)	2nd	2,024
26/9/04	Leigh (a) (QSF)	L30-16	t:Tandy,Calvert g:Nanyn(4)	N/A	4,563
3/10/04	Featherstone (h) (FE)	W30-2	t:Davidson,Walsh(2),Obst,Wilson,Nanyn g:Nanyn(3)	N/A	2,374
10/10/04	Leigh (GF) ●●●●	L32-16		N/A	11,005
		(aet)	t:Wilson(2),Calvert g:Nanyn(2)		

● Played at Knowsley Road, St Helens
●● Played at New Craven Park, Hull
●●● Played at Victory Park, Chorley
●●●● Played at Halton Stadium, Widnes

		APP		TRIES		GOALS		FG		PTS	
	D.O.B.	ALL	NL1	ALL	NL1	ALL	NL1	ALL	NL1	ALL	NL1
Gary Broadbent	31/10/76	26(2)	16	6	1	0	0	0	0	24	4
Craig Calvert	10/2/84	12	12	12	12	0	0	0	0	48	48
Ryan Campbell	23/9/81	4(2)	1	0	0	0	0	0	0	0	0
Craig Chambers	25/4/73	4(6)	2(2)	0	0	0	0	0	0	0	0
Tony Cunningham	4/7/74	(7)	(4)	0	0	0	0	0	0	0	0
Paul Davidson	1/8/69	4(4)	4(4)	1	1	0	0	0	0	4	4
David Fatialofa	11/6/74	29	21	5	4	0	0	0	0	20	16
Howard Hill	16/1/75	31	21	9	5	0	0	0	0	36	20
Marc Jackson	21/8/79	7(17)	1(14)	1	0	0	0	0	0	4	0
Leroy Joe	31/12/74	23(2)	17(1)	3	2	0	0	2	1	14	9
Lee Kiddie	2/1/75	15(1)	5(1)	11	2	0	0	0	0	44	8
Steve Kirkbride	10/1/81	2	1	1	0	0	0	0	0	4	0
John Lebbon	30/12/84	3	0	2	0	0	0	0	0	8	0
Aaron Lester	16/5/73	28(2)	20	4	3	0	0	0	0	16	12
Jamie Marshall	17/7/78	15	5	7	2	0	0	0	0	28	8
Brett McDermott	10/9/78	14(4)	6(1)	5	2	0	0	0	0	20	8
Chris McKinney	12/11/76	9(16)	4(12)	1	0	0	0	0	0	4	0
Spencer Miller	27/2/80	14(14)	9(9)	6	3	0	0	0	0	24	12
Graeme Morton	15/1/73	9(5)	3(3)	4	2	0	0	0	0	16	8
Mick Nanyn	3/6/82	32	19	30	18	139	83	0	0	398	238
Paul O'Neil	23/11/79	22(1)	13	8	5	5	5	0	0	42	30
Sam Obst	26/11/80	24(1)	20	18	15	0	0	4	4	76	64
Garry Purdham	20/10/78	5(7)	(6)	1	0	0	0	0	0	4	0
David Seeds	23/6/74	24	16	10	4	0	0	0	0	40	16
Carl Sice	13/4/80	8(26)	1(20)	7	4	0	0	1	1	29	17
Gary Smith	29/3/82	2(4)	0	0	0	0	0	0	0	0	0
Ryan Tandy	20/9/81	7(2)	7(2)	4	4	0	0	0	0	16	16
Dean Vaughan	9/2/78	16(7)	9(5)	0	0	0	0	0	0	0	0
Mark Wallace	21/2/78	4(1)	1	0	0	0	0	0	0	0	0
Craig Walsh	19/9/78	30(1)	19	26	15	0	0	0	0	104	60
Wesley Wilson	30/5/77	27(2)	19	8	3	0	0	0	0	32	12
Steven Wood	28/1/77	5(4)	1	1	1	6	0	0	0	16	4

Sam Obst

LEAGUE RECORD
P18-W14-D0-L4
(2nd, NL1/Grand Final Runners Up)
F552, A312, Diff+240
28 points.

CHALLENGE CUP
Quarter Finalists

NATIONAL LEAGUE CUP
Semi Finalists/1st, North Division

ATTENDANCES
Best - v Warrington (CC - 5,328)
Worst - v Gateshead (NLC - 1,017)
Total (NL1, inc play-offs,
& NLC, inc SF, only) - 26,441
Average (NL1, inc play-offs,
& NLC, inc SF, only) - 1,763
(Up by 370 on 2003)

BARROW RAIDERS

DATE	FIXTURE	RESULT	SCORERS	LGE	ATT
1/2/04	Whitehaven (h) (NLC)	L18-32	t:McClure,Atkinson,Pate,P Jones g:Holt	3rd(NLC-N)	1,269
8/2/04	Pia (h) (CCR3)	L20-22	t:Lupton,Wilcock,Beech g:Holt(4)	N/A	921
15/2/04	Chorley (a) (NLC)	W6-40	t:Atkinson,Pate(3),Archer,Smith,Whitehead g:Holt(6)	2nd(NLC-N)	303
22/2/04	Workington (a) (NLC)	D24-24	t:Whitehead,Beech,Atkinson,Holt g:Holt(4)	2nd(NLC-N)	775
7/3/04	Gateshead (h) (NLC)	W68-18	t:Holt(2),Whitehead(2),Smith,Archer(2),Reid(2),Pate,Beech,Clark g:Holt(10)	2nd(NLC-N)	767
21/3/04	Whitehaven (a) (NLC)	L14-10	t:Atkinson,McClure g:Holt	2nd(NLC-N)	1,249
27/3/04	Chorley (h) (NLC)	W31-22	t:Leigh,Pate(2),McClure,Reid g:Holt(5) fg:Holt	2nd(NLC-N)	567
4/4/04	Workington (h) (NLC)	W48-0	t:Holt,Leigh,Reid(3),King,Beech(2),Bower g:Holt(6)	2nd(NLC-N)	713
9/4/04	Gateshead (a) (NLC)	W12-50	t:Evans(2),P Jones(2),Pate,Whitehead,Archer,King,Beech g:Holt(3),Pate(4)	2nd(NLC-N)	259
12/4/04	Dewsbury (h)	W40-12	t:P Jones,McClure(2),Archer,Wilcock,Reid,Bower g:Holt(6)	3rd	949
18/4/04	Workington (a)	W14-32	t:Whitehead,Beech(2),McClure,Reid g:Holt(6)	2nd	503
25/4/04	Keighley (h) (NLCQFQ)	W32-20	t:King(3),Leigh,McClure,Reid g:Holt(4)	N/A	730
2/5/04	Hunslet (h)	W21-12	t:King,Archer,Beech g:Holt(4) fg:Holt	2nd	868
9/5/04	York (h)	L16-30	t:Whitehead,Clark,Pate g:Holt(2)	3rd	1,048
23/5/04	Swinton (a)	W10-46	t:Bower(5),Dancer,Wakelin,P Jones g:Holt(7)	2nd	504
30/5/04	London Skolars (h)	W32-16	t:Bower,Pate,Atkinson,King,Irabor,P Jones g:Holt(4)	1st	646
6/6/04	Leigh (h) (NLCQF)	L20-24	t:Pate(2),King,Wakelin g:Holt(2)	N/A	1,245
13/6/04	Chorley (a)	W38-34	t:Archer,P Jones(2),Irabor,Leigh,Reid g:Holt(7)	3rd	775
20/6/04	Sheffield (a)	W16-24	t:Irabor,Reid g:Holt(5),Pate(3)	2nd	977
4/7/04	Gateshead (a) ●	W24-40	t:Atkinson,Reid,Whitehead,P Jones(2),Wakelin,Pate,Holt g:Holt(4)	1st	301
11/7/04	Workington (h)	W18-10	t:Lupton,P Jones,Pate g:Holt(3)	1st	1,201
25/7/04	Hunslet (a)	W22-32	t:Reid,Bower,King(2),Pate,Irabor g:Holt(4)	1st	545
1/8/04	York (a)	L30-16	t:P Jones,Archer g:Holt(3),Pate	1st	1,307
8/8/04	Swinton (h)	L12-22	t:Clark,Wilcock g:Holt(2)	2nd	865
15/8/04	London Skolars (a)	W14-30	t:King(2),Beech,Irabor g:Holt(6),Beech	1st	382
22/8/04	Chorley (a)	D24-24	t:Irabor,Gardner(2),P Jones g:Holt(4)	1st	369
29/8/04	Sheffield (h)	W29-10	t:Holt,McConnell,Leigh,Atkinson g:Holt(5) fg:Holt(3)	1st	1,222
5/9/04	Gateshead (h)	W45-34	t:McConnell,P Jones,Beech,Atkinson,Holt,Whitehead,Archer g:Holt(8) fg:Holt	1st	1,015
12/9/04	Dewsbury (a)	W12-26	t:Gardner,Atkinson,Pate g:Holt(6) fg:Holt(2)	1st	1,583

● Played at Preston Avenue, North Shields

		APP		TRIES		GOALS		FG		PTS	
	D.O.B.	ALL	NL2	ALL	NL2	ALL	NL2	ALL	NL2	ALL	NL2
Chris Archer	18/9/83	17(12)	11(7)	9	5	0	0	0	0	36	20
Phil Atkinson	25/9/74	13(4)	6(3)	9	5	0	0	0	0	36	20
Nick Beech	22/1/85	17(2)	9(2)	11	5	1	1	0	0	46	22
Craig Bower	1/5/80	20	13	9	8	0	0	0	0	36	32
Ryan Campbell	23/9/81	3(1)	3(1)	0	0	0	0	0	0	0	0
Darren Carter	8/1/72	(1)	(1)	0	0	0	0	0	0	0	0
Dave Clark	6/4/71	26(2)	18	3	2	0	0	0	0	12	8
Tony Cunningham	4/7/74	(4)	(4)	0	0	0	0	0	0	0	0
Stuart Dancer	9/10/74	28	18	1	1	0	0	0	0	4	4
Lee Dutton	3/11/80	(4)	0	0	0	0	0	0	0	0	0
Paul Evans	21/4/79	1(2)	0	2	0	0	0	0	0	8	0
James Finch	9/7/83	3	3	0	0	0	0	0	0	0	0
Liam Finch	19/3/85	3(4)	3(4)	0	0	0	0	0	0	0	0
Matt Gardner	24/8/84	4	4	3	3	0	0	0	0	12	12
Darren Holt	21/9/76	29	18	7	3	132	86	8	7	300	191
Shane Irabor	14/1/82	12	11	6	6	0	0	0	0	24	24
Matt Jefferson	10/3/84	2(2)	2(2)	0	0	0	0	0	0	0	0
Paul Jones	1/2/79	25(1)	18	14	11	0	0	0	0	56	44
Wayne Jones	20/10/74	(3)	(1)	0	0	0	0	0	0	0	0
James King	12/12/80	22	16	12	6	0	0	0	0	48	24
Matthew Leigh	24/2/78	9(18)	1(16)	5	2	0	0	0	0	20	8
Paul Lupton	12/2/81	8(16)	4(9)	2	1	0	0	0	0	8	4
Geoff Luxon	2/6/71	(12)	(4)	0	0	0	0	0	0	0	0
Andy McClure	30/9/77	7(7)	1(3)	7	3	0	0	0	0	28	12
Matt McConnell	30/4/83	3	3	2	2	0	0	0	0	8	8
James Nixon	10/8/85	1(1)	1(1)	0	0	0	0	0	0	0	0
Adam Pate	19/8/83	22	13	16	6	8	4	0	0	80	32
Barry Pugh	17/10/84	26(1)	16(1)	0	0	0	0	0	0	0	0
Damien Reid	14/3/84	16(2)	10(1)	13	6	0	0	0	0	52	24
Gary Ruddy	9/12/73	1	0	0	0	0	0	0	0	0	0
Jamie Smith	2/10/76	5	0	2	0	0	0	0	0	8	0
Tama Wakelin	2/8/77	4(8)	1(7)	3	2	0	0	0	0	12	8
Lee Washington	27/9/83	1(1)	0	0	0	0	0	0	0	0	0
Mike Whitehead	25/8/78	26(2)	16(2)	9	4	0	0	0	0	36	16
Paul Wilcock	9/12/78	23(4)	15(2)	3	2	0	0	0	0	12	8
Jon Williamson	30/10/86	(1)	0	0	0	0	0	0	0	0	0

Paul Jones

LEAGUE RECORD
P18-W14-D1-L3
(1st, NL2/Champions)
F521, A346, Diff+175
29 points.

CHALLENGE CUP
Round Three

NATIONAL LEAGUE CUP
Quarter Finalists/2nd, North Division

ATTENDANCES
Best - v Whitehaven (NLC - 1,269)
Worst - v Chorley (NLC - 567)
Total (NL2 & NLC,
inc QFQ & QF, only) - 13,880
Average (NL2 & NLC,
inc QFQ & QF, only) - 925
(Up by 118 on 2003)

CHORLEY LYNX

DATE	FIXTURE	RESULT	SCORERS	LGE	ATT
1/2/04	Oldham (a) (NLC)	L64-14	t:Smyth,Kilgannon,Patterson g:Capewell	4th(NLC-W)	1,096
6/2/04	Locomotiv Moscow (h) (CCR3)	W54-6	t:Gambles(2),Newall(3),Capewell,Patterson,O'Regan(2),Redford g:Capewell(7)	N/A	521
15/2/04	Barrow (h) (NLC)	L6-40	t:Newall g:Capewell	4th(NLC-W)	303
22/2/04	Leigh (a) (NLC)	L60-10	t:Newall,Kilgannon g:Capewell	4th(NLC-W)	1,452
27/2/04	Wakefield (h) (CCR4)	L6-88	t:Newall g:Capewell	N/A	696
7/3/04	Swinton (a) (NLC)	L27-24	t:Kilgannon,Newall,Murray,Redford g:Smyth(4)	4th(NLC-W)	430
21/3/04	Oldham (h) (NLC)	L10-40	t:Stenhouse,O'Regan g:Gambles	4th(NLC-W)	370
27/3/04	Barrow (a) (NLC)	L31-22	t:Patterson(3),G Smith g:Alexander(3)	4th(NLC-W)	567
4/4/04	Leigh (h) (NLC)	L10-78	t:O'Regan,Stenhouse g:Alexander	4th(NLC-W)	770
9/4/04	Swinton (h) (NLC)	W20-12	t:Meade,Ormesher,Stenhouse,Barton g:Roden(2)	4th(NLC-W)	307
12/4/04	York (a)	L32-18	t:Patterson,Ramsdale,Ormesher,Gambles g:Ramsdale	7th	1,401
18/4/04	Sheffield (h)	L18-32	t:Ormesher,Ramsdale,Kilgannon g:Ramsdale(3)	7th	257
2/5/04	Gateshead (h)	W42-20	t:Patterson,Gambles(3),Kilgannon,Capewell,Redford,Stenhouse g:Smyth(4),Capewell	6th	164
9/5/04	Dewsbury (a)	L29-14	t:Redford,Stenhouse,Gambles g:Capewell	7th	459
23/5/04	Workington (h)	W40-26	t:O'Regan(2),Redford,Patterson(2),Ormesher g:Capewell(8)	6th	248
30/5/04	Hunslet (h)	W30-26	t:O'Regan,Ramsdale,Stenhouse,Patterson(2),Barton g:Capewell(3)	6th	303
13/6/04	Barrow (a)	L38-34	t:O'Regan,Redford(2),Capewell,Patterson,G Smith g:Capewell(5)	6th	775
20/6/04	Swinton (a)	L26-20	t:Capewell,Meade,Redford g:Capewell(4)	6th	418
4/7/04	London Skolars (h)	W32-18	t:Redford(2),Newall,Grundy,Stenhouse g:Capewell(5),Johnstone	6th	211
11/7/04	Sheffield (a)	W24-31	t:Parry(2),Stenhouse,Barton g:Capewell(7) fg:Capewell	6th	852
25/7/04	Gateshead (a)	W16-30	t:Stenhouse(2),Patterson,Gambles(2) g:Capewell(5)	6th	301
1/8/04	Dewsbury (a)	D20-20	t:Barton,Stenhouse,Arnold,Gambles g:Capewell(2)	6th	255
8/8/04	Workington (a)	L48-24	t:Capewell,Ormesher,Patterson,Ramsdale g:Capewell(4)	7th	1,051
15/8/04	Hunslet (a)	L52-16	t:Ormesher(2),G Smith g:Capewell,Johnstone	7th	377
22/8/04	Barrow (h)	D24-24	t:Ormesher,Capewell,Patterson,Chamberlain g:Capewell(4)	7th	369
27/8/04	Swinton (h)	L30-43	t:Capewell,Arnold(2),Barton,Bithel g:Capewell(4),Ramsdale	7th	369
5/9/04	London Skolars (a)	L28-16	t:Barton,Capewell,Ramsdale g:Johnstone,Capewell	7th	386
12/9/04	York (h)	W21-20	t:Roden,Arnold,Kilgannon(2) g:Capewell(2) fg:Capewell	7th	616

		APP		TRIES		GOALS		FG		PTS	
	D.O.B.	ALL	NL2	ALL	NL2	ALL	NL2	ALL	NL2	ALL	NL2
Neil Alexander	18/2/77	3(6)	(2)	0	0	4	0	0	0	8	0
Danny Arnold	15/4/77	6(1)	6(1)	4	4	0	0	0	0	16	16
Danny Barton	7/9/83	23(1)	18	6	5	0	0	0	0	24	20
Grant Bithel	10/5/80	1(3)	1(3)	1	1	0	0	0	0	4	4
Adam Briggs	9/8/81	(1)	0	0	0	0	0	0	0	0	0
Brian Capewell	21/10/77	18(3)	13(3)	8	7	68	57	2	2	170	144
John Chamberlain	1/5/82	8(3)	8(3)	1	1	0	0	0	0	4	4
Damian Duncan	13/11/77	(1)	0	0	0	0	0	0	0	0	0
Martin Gambles	8/3/80	28	18	10	8	1	0	0	0	42	32
Michael Griffin	24/10/83	(1)	(1)	0	0	0	0	0	0	0	0
Andy Grundy	19/1/77	3(10)	3(10)	1	1	0	0	0	0	4	4
John Hill	7/10/81	27	18	0	0	0	0	0	0	0	0
Jake Johnstone	6/12/77	10	10	0	0	3	3	0	0	6	6
Gareth Jones	14/10/82	5(1)	0	0	0	0	0	0	0	0	0
Eddie Kilgannon	4/12/71	20	10	7	4	0	0	0	0	28	16
Daryl Lacey	1/7/81	3	0	0	0	0	0	0	0	0	0
James Lomax	20/10/81	1(11)	1(10)	0	0	0	0	0	0	0	0
Ade Meade	6/4/76	10(1)	7	2	1	0	0	0	0	8	4
Anthony Murray	25/5/77	7(7)	4(2)	1	0	0	0	0	0	4	0
Chris Newall	30/11/76	10(7)	2(6)	8	1	0	0	0	0	32	4
Gary O'Regan	5/6/84	13(2)	5(1)	8	4	0	0	0	0	32	16
Steve Ormesher	5/4/78	10(3)	8(1)	8	7	0	0	0	0	32	28
Ian Parry	2/4/81	25(2)	17	2	2	0	0	0	0	8	8
Lee Patterson	20/7/82	26	18	15	10	0	0	0	0	60	40
Chris Ramsdale	25/4/82	19(5)	16(2)	5	5	5	5	0	0	30	30
Mick Redford	24/6/81	26(1)	18	10	8	0	0	0	0	40	32
Martin Roden	26/12/79	10(8)	2(6)	1	1	2	0	0	0	8	4
Lee Rowley	3/2/83	(24)	(16)	0	0	0	0	0	0	0	0
Gary Smith	11/1/81	24(2)	15(2)	3	2	0	0	0	0	12	8
Simon Smith	23/7/74	2(3)	0	0	0	0	0	0	0	0	0
Rob Smyth	22/2/77	7	2	1	0	8	4	0	0	20	8
Jamie Stenhouse	9/10/80	19	14	11	8	0	0	0	0	44	32

Martin Gambles

LEAGUE RECORD
P18-W7-D2-L9
(7th, NL2)
F460, A522, Diff-62
16 points.

CHALLENGE CUP
Round Four

NATIONAL LEAGUE CUP
4th, West Division

ATTENDANCES
Best - v Leigh (NLC - 770)
Worst - v Gateshead (NL2 - 164)
Total (NL2 & NLC only) - 4,542
Average (NL2 & NLC only) - 349
(Down by 85 on 2003)

DEWSBURY RAMS

DATE	FIXTURE	RESULT	SCORERS	LGE	ATT
1/2/04	Featherstone (h) (NLC)	L12-28	t:Crouthers,Robinson g:A Thaler(2)	4th(NLC-Y)	1,489
6/2/04	Sharlston (a) (CCR3) ●	L30-28	t:Waddle,Miles,McHugh,Kershaw,A Thaler g:A Thaler(4)	N/A	2,027
15/2/04	Sheffield (a) (NLC)	W18-42	t:Robinson(2),Thewliss,McHugh,Redfearn,A Thaler,Senior g:A Thaler(6) fg:Robinson(2)	4th(NLC-Y)	867
22/2/04	York (h) (NLC)	L16-58	t:Senior,McHugh,Crouthers g:A Thaler(2)	4th(NLC-Y)	848
7/3/04	Batley (a) (NLC)	L70-12	t:Redfearn,Hawksley g:A Thaler(2)	4th(NLC-Y)	868
21/3/04	Featherstone (a) (NLC)	L48-4	t:Redfearn	4th(NLC-Y)	1,068
28/3/04	Sheffield (h) (NLC)	L22-28	t:Webber,Robinson,Crouthers,Williamson g:A Thaler(3)	4th(NLC-Y)	499
4/4/04	York (a) (NLC)	L44-7	t:Robinson g:A Thaler fg:Robinson	4th(NLC-Y)	1,204
9/4/04	Batley (h) (NLC)	L20-46	t:Spink(2),Booth,Hawksley g:Hill(2)	4th(NLC-Y)	932
12/4/04	Barrow (a)	L40-12	t:Thomas,McHugh g:A Thaler(2)	9th	949
18/4/04	Swinton (h)	L8-35	t:Hawksley g:A Thaler(2)	10th	509
1/5/04	London Skolars (a)	W24-36	t:R Thaler(2),Hawksley,Thewliss,Redfearn,A Thaler(2) g:A Thaler(4)	8th	426
9/5/04	Chorley (h)	W29-14	t:Hawksley,A Thaler,Preece,Spink,Benn g:Benn(4) fg:A Thaler	6th	459
21/5/04	Sheffield (a)	L24-12	t:Dyson,A Thaler g:Benn(2)	7th	1,352
30/5/04	Gateshead (h)	W26-8	t:Crouthers,Mycoe(2),Williamson,A Thaler g:Benn(3)	7th	590
13/6/04	York (h)	L2-48	g:A Thaler	7th	1,275
20/6/04	Workington (a)	L44-22	t:Hawksley(2),A Thaler,Preece g:A Thaler(3)	8th	667
4/7/04	Hunslet (h)	L12-23	t:Dyson,A Thaler g:A Thaler(2)	8th	831
11/7/04	Swinton (a)	L34-15	t:Fairbank,Naidole,Firth g:A Thaler fg:Dyson	9th	444
25/7/04	London Skolars (h)	L8-41	t:Waddle,Fairbank	9th	487
1/8/04	Chorley (a)	D20-20	t:A Thaler,Kirke,Stubley g:A Thaler(4)	9th	255
8/8/04	Sheffield (h)	L10-51	t:A Thaler,Fairbank g:A Thaler	9th	502
15/8/04	Gateshead (a)	L22-4	t:Firth	9th	293
22/8/04	York (a)	L64-6	t:Crouthers g:A Thaler	9th	1,761
29/8/04	Workington (h)	L30-41	t:Hicks,Waddle,McHugh,Redfearn,A Thaler g:A Thaler(5)	9th	520
5/9/04	Hunslet (a)	L36-20	t:A Thaler(3),Hawksley g:A Thaler(2)	9th	532
12/9/04	Barrow (h)	L12-26	t:McHugh,Redfearn g:A Thaler(2)	9th	1,583

● Played at Lionheart Stadium, Featherstone

		APP		TRIES		GOALS		FG		PTS	
	D.O.B.	ALL	NL2	ALL	NL2	ALL	NL2	ALL	NL2	ALL	NL2
Steve Beard	21/6/79	1	0	0	0	0	0	0	0	0	0
Jamie Benn	4/5/77	3(1)	3(1)	1	1	9	9	0	0	22	22
Marcus Bernard	7/10/70	1	0	0	0	0	0	0	0	0	0
Ian Booth	8/7/79	(5)	0	1	0	0	0	0	0	4	0
James Brown	27/9/79	1	0	0	0	0	0	0	0	0	0
Richard Chapman	5/9/75	4	4	0	0	0	0	0	0	0	0
Kevin Crouthers	3/1/76	19	13	5	2	0	0	0	0	20	8
Shane Davis	19/9/75	3(2)	3(2)	0	0	0	0	0	0	0	0
Scott Dyson	7/3/79	13	13	2	2	0	0	1	1	9	9
Chris Elliott	7/12/84	1	1	0	0	0	0	0	0	0	0
Oliver Fairbank	19/3/81	9	9	3	3	0	0	0	0	12	12
Jason Firth	16/6/77	8	8	2	2	0	0	0	0	8	8
Andy Fisher	17/11/67	1	0	0	0	0	0	0	0	0	0
Michael Forbes	12/1/82	1	0	0	0	0	0	0	0	0	0
Ashley Fortis	12/5/83	(1)	(1)	0	0	0	0	0	0	0	0
Michael Gibbons	12/5/81	2(15)	(13)	0	0	0	0	0	0	0	0
Chris Hall	12/12/82	1	0	0	0	0	0	0	0	0	0
Ryan Hardy	12/2/74	(2)	0	0	0	0	0	0	0	0	0
Mark Hawksley	23/2/73	17(5)	15(1)	8	6	0	0	0	0	32	24
Paul Hicks	22/6/77	26(1)	18	1	1	0	0	0	0	4	4
Mick Hill	3/9/84	1(2)	(2)	0	0	2	0	0	0	4	0
Lee Kelly	18/3/75	(8)	(8)	0	0	0	0	0	0	0	0
Billy Kershaw	22/11/78	8(3)	4(2)	1	0	0	0	0	0	4	0
Ian Kirke	26/12/80	23	16	1	1	0	0	0	0	4	4
Graham Law	24/7/79	3	2	0	0	0	0	0	0	0	0
Mark Lawton	4/8/81	(1)	0	0	0	0	0	0	0	0	0
Ashley Lyndsey	31/7/83	(1)	(1)	0	0	0	0	0	0	0	0
Wayne McHugh	1/2/80	15	10	6	3	0	0	0	0	24	12
Craig Miles	8/7/81	1	0	1	0	0	0	0	0	4	0
David Mycoe	1/5/72	14(4)	12(2)	2	2	0	0	0	0	8	8
Joe Naidole	23/12/67	3(9)	2(9)	1	1	0	0	0	0	4	4
Ian Preece	13/6/85	18(2)	12(2)	2	2	0	0	0	0	8	8
Chris Redfearn	4/12/80	23(4)	18	6	3	0	0	0	0	24	12
Darren Robinson	28/5/79	9(1)	2	5	0	0	0	3	0	23	0
John Rourke	17/7/85	1	1	0	0	0	0	0	0	0	0
Kurt Rudder	29/1/80	1(2)	(2)	0	0	0	0	0	0	0	0
Mick Senior	2/12/81	4	0	2	0	0	0	0	0	8	0
Paul Smith	31/5/84	2(3)	0	0	0	0	0	0	0	0	0
Tim Spears	27/7/84	6	0	0	0	0	0	0	0	0	0
Kevin Spink	1/4/81	6(4)	4(4)	3	1	0	0	0	0	12	4
Mark Stubley	27/6/82	6	6	1	1	0	0	0	0	4	4
Jamie Tennant	15/11/80	2(12)	1(8)	0	0	0	0	0	0	0	0
Adam Thaler	3/9/83	25(2)	17(1)	15	13	50	30	1	1	161	113
Richard Thaler	30/1/81	10	7	2	2	0	0	0	0	8	8
Anthony Thewliss	22/6/85	11(7)	5(5)	2	1	0	0	0	0	8	4
Danny Thomas	21/12/83	4(1)	2	1	1	0	0	0	0	4	4
Jon Waddle	6/1/84	13(2)	6(1)	3	2	0	0	0	0	12	8
Rob Ward	12/10/76	2	0	0	0	0	0	0	0	0	0
Andrew Webber	25/9/81	7	2	1	0	0	0	0	0	4	0
Leon Williamson	22/8/74	19	16	2	1	0	0	0	0	8	4
Chris Woolford	4/1/84	3(8)	2(7)	0	0	0	0	0	0	0	0

Adam Thaler

LEAGUE RECORD
P18-W3-D1-L14
(9th, NL2)
F284, A595, Diff-311
7 points.

CHALLENGE CUP
Round Three

NATIONAL LEAGUE CUP
4th, Yorkshire Division

ATTENDANCES
Best - v Barrow (NL2 - 1,583)
Worst - v Chorley (NL2 - 459)
Total (NL2 & NLC only) - 10,524
Average (NL2 & NLC only) - 809
(Down by 141 on 2003, NL1)

GATESHEAD THUNDER

DATE	FIXTURE	RESULT	SCORERS	LGE	ATT
1/2/04	Workington (a) (NLC)	L52-0	No Scorers	4th(NLC-N)	709
8/2/04	Limoux (h) (CCR3)	L22-26	t:Neighbour,Firth,Peers,Line g:P Thorman(3)	N/A	254
15/2/04	York (h) (NLC)	L24-56	t:Stephenson,Peers,N Thorman,P Thorman g:P Thorman(4)	4th(NLC-N)	366
22/2/04	Whitehaven (h) (NLC)	L14-54	t:Peers,Stannard,Firth g:P Thorman	4th(NLC-N)	294
7/3/04	Barrow (a) (NLC)	L68-18	t:Bradley(2),Rutherford g:P Thorman(3)	4th(NLC-N)	767
21/3/04	Workington (h) (NLC)	D24-24	t:Neighbour,Fisher,Kent,Rutherford g:P Thorman(4)	4th(NLC-N)	288
31/3/04	York (a) (NLC) ●	L54-26	t:Bradley,Neighbour,N Thorman,Peers,P Thorman g:P Thorman(3)	4th(NLC-N)	1,520
4/4/04	Whitehaven (a) (NLC)	L74-16	t:Peers,Fleming,Neighbour g:P Thorman(2)	4th(NLC-N)	1,017
9/4/04	Barrow (h) (NLC)	L12-50	t:Hodgson,Bunting,Bradley	4th(NLC-N)	259
12/4/04	Swinton (a)	L42-10	t:Neighbour,Peers g:P Thorman	10th	410
18/4/04	London Skolars (h)	L21-22	t:Peers,N Thorman,Bunting g:P Thorman(4) fg:P Thorman	8th	203
2/5/04	Chorley (a)	L42-20	t:P Thorman,Neighbour,N Thorman,Peers g:P Thorman(2)	9th	164
9/5/04	Sheffield (h)	L6-42	t:N Thorman g:P Thorman	10th	297
23/5/04	York (a)	L48-12	t:Peers,Hodgson,Neighbour	10th	2,519
30/5/04	Dewsbury (a)	L26-8	t:Bradley,Bunting	10th	590
13/6/04	Workington (h)	L12-44	t:Firth,N Thorman g:P Thorman(2)	10th	291
18/6/04	Hunslet (a)	L52-22	t:Massey,Peers,Morton,Stephenson,Bradley g:Garside	10th	349
27/6/04	London Skolars (a)	L52-20	t:Line,Neighbour,Peers,Staveley g:Massey(2)	10th	356
4/7/04	Barrow (h) ●●	L24-40	t:Firth(2),Massey(2),N Thorman g:P Thorman(2)	10th	301
25/7/04	Chorley (a)	L16-30	t:Peers,Neighbour,Bradley g:P Thorman(2)	10th	301
1/8/04	Sheffield (a)	L54-10	t:Dodsworth,P Thorman g:P Thorman	10th	744
8/8/04	York (h)	L18-30	t:Bradley,Massey,Rutherford g:P Thorman(3)	10th	429
15/8/04	Dewsbury (h)	W22-4	t:Stephenson,Neighbour,Peers,Morton g:P Thorman(3)	10th	293
22/8/04	Workington (a)	L80-8	t:Peers g:P Thorman(2)	10th	958
29/8/04	Hunslet (h)	L12-34	t:Bradley(2) g:P Thorman,Garside	10th	277
5/9/04	Barrow (a)	L45-34	t:Firth,Garside,N Thorman,P Thorman,Bradley,Morton g:P Thorman(5)	10th	1,015
12/9/04	Swinton (h)	L23-28	t:N Thorman(2),Bradley,Peers g:P Thorman(3) fg:P Thorman	10th	342

● Played at Bootham Crescent (York City FC)
●● Played at Preston Avenue, North Shields

		APP		TRIES		GOALS		FG		PTS	
	D.O.B.	ALL	NL2	ALL	NL2	ALL	NL2	ALL	NL2	ALL	NL2
Shawn Ackerley	22/2/84	1(3)	0	0	0	0	0	0	0	0	0
Joe Bagshaw		2		0	0	0	0	0	0	0	0
Ian Ball	15/3/84	1(14)	(8)	0	0	0	0	0	0	0	0
Steven Bradley	27/7/81	27	18	12	8	0	0	0	0	48	32
Clint Brown	27/9/75	10	10	0	0	0	0	0	0	0	0
Jaymes Bulman	6/7/77	3(1)	0	0	0	0	0	0	0	0	0
Michael Bunting	10/2/85	8	7	3	2	0	0	0	0	12	8
Ryan Clark	8/9/85	(4)	(4)	0	0	0	0	0	0	0	0
Tom Clough	16/5/83	1	0	0	0	0	0	0	0	0	0
Anthony Cowburn	19/6/71	(1)	(1)	0	0	0	0	0	0	0	0
Greg Dawson	22/3/80	1(1)	1(1)	0	0	0	0	0	0	0	0
Bernie de Beer		1(1)	1(1)	0	0	0	0	0	0	0	0
Matthew Dehaty	22/3/83	1	0	0	0	0	0	0	0	0	0
Paul Dodsworth	24/1/80	(7)	(7)	1	1	0	0	0	0	4	4
Tony Doherty	3/8/83	12(6)	7(4)	0	0	0	0	0	0	0	0
Adam Endersby	7/1/82	1(8)	1(8)	0	0	0	0	0	0	0	0
Craig Firth	4/11/82	16(3)	10(2)	6	4	0	0	0	0	24	16
Craig Fisher	16/9/77	14	6	1	0	0	0	0	0	4	0
Andy Fleming	16/8/67	1(5)	(2)	1	0	0	0	0	0	4	0
Liam Garside	9/10/82	13	13	1	1	2	2	0	0	8	8
Dave Griffiths	23/4/83	2(1)	1(1)	0	0	0	0	0	0	0	0
Dave Guthrie	24/3/70	1(3)	(2)	0	0	0	0	0	0	0	0
Scott Harrison	22/1/83	9(3)	5(3)	0	0	0	0	0	0	0	0
Ben Hodgson	4/8/76	(4)	(3)	2	1	0	0	0	0	8	4
Mick Jones	18/8/87	1(1)	1(1)	0	0	0	0	0	0	0	0
Peti Keni	24/6/76	1(1)	1	0	0	0	0	0	0	0	0
Mick Kent	25/9/66	5(2)	2(2)	1	0	0	0	0	0	4	0
Rob Line	13/10/82	26(1)	17(1)	2	1	0	0	0	0	8	4
Jon MacDonald	22/1/77	3(4)	3(4)	0	0	0	0	0	0	0	0
Will Massey	26/9/77	8(3)	8(3)	4	4	2	2	0	0	20	20
Seamus McCallion	3/4/64	3(2)	1	0	0	0	0	0	0	0	0
Richard Meads	17/7/67	1	0	0	0	0	0	0	0	0	0
Steve Morton	10/5/69	11	11	3	3	0	0	0	0	12	12
Kevin Neighbour	10/7/83	27	18	10	6	0	0	0	0	40	24
Robin Peers	18/1/82	25(2)	18	15	10	0	0	0	0	60	40
Phil Pitt	2/11/78	2(5)	(3)	0	0	0	0	0	0	0	0
Charlie Roe	15/1/75	(4)	(3)	0	0	0	0	0	0	0	0
Steve Rutherford	24/8/81	24	16	3	1	0	0	0	0	12	4
Carl Stannard	22/3/79	6(1)	0	1	0	0	0	0	0	4	0
Nick Staveley	24/6/82	6(4)	6(4)	1	1	0	0	0	0	4	4
Graham Stephenson	10/5/84	25	17	3	2	0	0	0	0	12	8
Neil Thorman	4/6/84	25(2)	18	10	8	0	0	0	0	40	32
Paul Thorman	28/9/82	26	17	5	3	52	32	2	2	126	78
Andy Walker	19/5/83	1(3)	0	0	0	0	0	0	0	0	0
Mark Walker	14/12/73	(5)	(2)	0	0	0	0	0	0	0	0

Paul Thorman

LEAGUE RECORD
P18-W1-D0-L17
(10th, NL2)
F298, A715, Diff-417
2 points.

CHALLENGE CUP
Round Three

NATIONAL LEAGUE CUP
4th, North Division

ATTENDANCES
Best - v York (NL2 - 429)
Worst - v London Skolars (NL2 - 203)
Total (NL2 & NLC only) - 3,941
Average (NL2 & NLC only) - 303
(Up by 24 on 2003)

HUNSLET HAWKS

DATE	FIXTURE	RESULT	SCORERS	LGE	ATT
1/2/04	Rochdale (h) (NLC)	W24-8	t:Sykes,Wood,Seal,Wray g:Wood(4)	1st(NLC-P)	519
7/2/04	Featherstone Lions (h) (CCR3)	W32-0	t:Lockwood,W Freeman(2),Sykes,Bastow,Booth g:Wood(2),Booth(2)	N/A	433
15/2/04	London Skolars (a) (NLC)	W0-48	t:Gleadhill,Hawley,Bastow(2),Sykes,Jessey(2),Ibbetson g:Booth(8)	1st(NLC-P)	375
22/2/04	Halifax (h) (NLC)	L14-38	t:Rayner(2),McGibbon g:Wood	2nd(NLC-P)	1,144
29/2/04	Doncaster (h) (CCR4)	L20-48	t:Wray,Coyle,W Freeman,Ibbetson g:Booth,Tawhai	N/A	682
7/3/04	Keighley (h) (NLC)	W42-24	t:Tawhai,Coyle,Longo,Shillabeer,McGibbon,Wray(2),C Hall g:Wood,Booth(4)	2nd(NLC-P)	640
21/3/04	Rochdale (a) (NLC)	L37-6	t:W Freeman g:Wood	2nd(NLC-P)	674
28/3/04	London Skolars (h) (NLC)	W36-18	t:Tawhai,Ibbetson,G Freeman,Ross,C Hall(2) g:Wood(6)	1st(NLC-P)	337
4/4/04	Halifax (a) (NLC)	L20-4	g:Wood(2)	2nd(NLC-P)	1,536
9/4/04	Keighley (a) (NLC)	L47-8	t:Doherty g:Wood,Liddell	3rd(NLC-P)	1,297
12/4/04	Workington (h)	W42-14	t:G Freeman,Shillabeer,Seal(3),Tawhai,C Hall,Liddell g:Liddell(5)	2nd	344
18/4/04	York (a)	W8-21	t:Seal,Coyle,Wray,Deakin g:Liddell(2) fg:Tawhai	3rd	1,262
2/5/04	Barrow (a)	L21-12	t:Coyle,C Hall g:Liddell(2)	3rd	868
9/5/04	Swinton (h)	W42-20	t:Bastow,W Freeman,Rayner(3),Mears,Tawhai g:Wood(7)	2nd	525
23/5/04	London Skolars (h)	W32-8	t:W Freeman,Liddell,Ross,C Hall,Evans,Rayner(2) g:Wood(2)	1st	366
30/5/04	Chorley (a)	L30-26	t:Coyle,Mears,Lockwood(2),Seal g:Tawhai(3)	4th	303
13/6/04	Sheffield (h)	L14-40	t:S Hall,W Freeman,Wray g:Liddell	4th	620
18/6/04	Gateshead (h)	W52-22	t:Coyle,W Freeman,Murrell,Mears(2),S Hall,Rayner,C Hall,Seal g:Wood(6),Booth(2)	4th	349
4/7/04	Dewsbury (a)	W12-23	t:Ross(2),Seal,Ibbetson g:Ross(3) fg:Tawhai	4th	831
11/7/04	York (h)	W19-8	t:Deakin,Lockwood g:Ross(5) fg:Booth	3rd	770
25/7/04	Barrow (h)	L22-32	t:Wray,Pryce,Rayner,Stevens g:Ross(3)	4th	545
1/8/04	Swinton (a)	L33-16	t:Duda,Gleadhill,Lockwood g:Ross,Gleadhill	4th	508
8/8/04	London Skolars (a)	L24-16	t:C Hall,Lockwood,Tawhai g:Ross(2)	5th	362
15/8/04	Chorley (h)	W52-16	t:Rayner,Tawhai,Pryce,W Freeman,Duda(2),Ross,Fearon(2) g:Ross(8)	4th	377
22/8/04	Sheffield (a)	L50-10	t:Murrell,Rayner g:Tawhai	6th	870
29/8/04	Gateshead (a)	W12-34	t:Gleadhill(2),Hawley,W Freeman,Murrell,Duda,C Hall g:Ross(3)	6th	277
5/9/04	Dewsbury (h)	W36-20	t:Hawley,Coyle,Rayner,Tawhai,Fearon,Lockwood g:Ross(6)	5th	532
12/9/04	Workington (a)	L24-6	t:Duda g:Ross	6th	978
19/9/04	Sheffield (a) (NL1QS-EPO)	W16-39	t:Cook,Seal,W Freeman,C Hall(2),Tawhai,Rayner g:Gleadhill(5) fg:Tawhai	N/A	531
26/9/04	Workington (a) (NL1QS-ESF)	L27-13	t:Bastow,Rayner g:Gleadhill(2) fg:Tawhai	N/A	1,274

		APP		TRIES		GOALS		FG		PTS	
	D.O.B.	ALL	NL2	ALL	NL2	ALL	NL2	ALL	NL2	ALL	NL2
Andy Bastow	25/5/78	19(1)	11(1)	5	2	0	0	0	0	20	8
Craig Booth	28/10/70	11	3	1	0	17	2	1	1	39	5
Andy Burland	5/11/77	1(3)	1(3)	0	0	0	0	0	0	0	0
Gareth Carey	17/10/86	2(1)	2(1)	0	0	0	0	0	0	0	0
Ben Cockayne	20/7/83	(2)	(2)	0	0	0	0	0	0	0	0
Danny Cook	14/10/81	6(2)	5(2)	1	1	0	0	0	0	4	4
Mick Coyle	5/3/71	23(5)	15(4)	7	5	0	0	0	0	28	20
Leigh Deakin	27/12/72	13(1)	9	2	2	0	0	0	0	8	8
Steve Doherty	8/3/78	3	2	1	0	0	0	0	0	4	0
Craig Duda	1/11/80	8	8	5	5	0	0	0	0	20	20
Danny Evans	15/10/74	(2)	(2)	1	1	0	0	0	0	4	4
Danny Fearon	13/3/79	11(6)	11(6)	3	3	0	0	0	0	12	12
Glen Freeman	9/4/72	2(23)	2(14)	2	1	0	0	0	0	8	4
Wayne Freeman	30/4/74	29	19	11	7	0	0	0	0	44	28
Paul Gleadhill	2/2/76	11	9	4	3	8	8	0	0	32	28
Chris Grice	26/5/87	(1)	(1)	0	0	0	0	0	0	0	0
Chris Hall	23/5/79	22	16	11	8	0	0	0	0	44	32
Steve Hall	13/4/79	2	2	2	2	0	0	0	0	8	8
Joe Hawley	11/2/85	16(2)	13	3	2	0	0	0	0	12	8
Danny Herbert	27/2/86	1(1)	1(1)	0	0	0	0	0	0	0	0
Shaun Ibbetson	13/4/85	13(6)	10(4)	4	1	0	0	0	0	16	4
Liam Jarvis	20/2/83	(2)	0	0	0	0	0	0	0	0	0
Dave Jessey	12/5/81	2(5)	1	2	0	0	0	0	0	8	0
Jon Liddell	25/8/82	16(2)	9(1)	2	2	11	10	0	0	30	28
Jonlee Lockwood	18/3/78	15(10)	10(10)	7	6	0	0	0	0	28	24
Davide Longo	9/12/75	4	0	1	0	0	0	0	0	4	0
Wes McGibbon	13/1/79	14(2)	4(2)	2	0	0	0	0	0	8	0
Neil Mears	9/1/79	3(11)	3(9)	4	4	0	0	0	0	16	16
Gareth Murrell	29/7/83	4(1)	4(1)	3	3	0	0	0	0	12	12
Steve Pryce	12/5/69	12(16)	8(10)	2	2	0	0	0	0	8	8
George Rayner	19/9/80	20	17	14	12	0	0	0	0	56	48
Chris Ross	23/8/78	19(4)	11(4)	5	4	32	32	0	0	84	80
Dean Sampson	27/6/67	5(1)	5(1)	0	0	0	0	0	0	0	0
Paul Seal	21/4/78	21	17	9	8	0	0	0	0	36	32
Gary Shillabeer	23/11/79	2(7)	(1)	2	1	0	0	0	0	8	4
Craig Stevens	3/12/78	2	2	1	1	0	0	0	0	4	4
Martin Sykes	28/12/76	5	0	3	0	0	0	0	0	12	0
Latham Tawhai	23/8/71	24	17	8	6	5	4	4	4	46	36
Ryan Taylor	5/2/84	2	0	0	0	0	0	0	0	0	0
Danny Wood	8/10/77	11(1)	4	1	0	33	15	0	0	70	30
Jamaine Wray	15/3/84	16(2)	9(1)	7	3	0	0	0	0	28	12

Latham Tawhai

LEAGUE RECORD
P18-W10-D0-L8
(6th, NL2)
(Elimination Semi Finalists,
NL1 Qualifying Series)
F475, A394, Diff+81
20 points.

CHALLENGE CUP
Round Four

NATIONAL LEAGUE CUP
3rd, Pennine Division

ATTENDANCES
Best - v Halifax (NLC - 1,144)
Worst - v London Skolars (NLC - 337)
Total (NL2 & NLC only) - 7,068
Average (NL2 & NLC only) - 544
(Up by 3 on 2003)

LONDON SKOLARS

DATE	FIXTURE	RESULT	SCORERS	LGE	ATT
7/2/04	Rochdale Mayfield (h) (CCR3)	W22-16	t:Honor,Aderiye(2) g:G Osborn(5)	N/A	275
15/2/04	Hunslet (h) (NLC)	L0-48	No Scorers	3rd(NLC-E)	375
22/2/04	Sheffield (a) (NLC)	L34-6	t:Rua g:Coleman	4th(NLC-E)	662
29/2/04	Featherstone (h) (CCR4)	L6-52	t:Katipa g:G Osborn	N/A	380
7/3/04	Hull KR (a) (NLC)	L58-6	t:Cantoni g:J Osborn	4th(NLC-E)	1,677
14/3/04	Sheffield (h) (NLC)	W16-14	t:Foster,Butterfield,Honor g:G Osborn(2)	4th(NLC-E)	142
20/3/04	Doncaster (h) (NLC)	L6-24	t:Rua g:G Osborn	4th(NLC-E)	375
28/3/04	Hunslet (a) (NLC)	L36-18	t:Kadima,Coleman,Lam(2) g:J Osborn	4th(NLC-E)	337
31/3/04	Doncaster (a) (NLC)	L58-20	t:Foster,Green,Coleman(2) g:G Osborn(2)	4th(NLC-E)	395
3/4/04	Hull KR (h) (NLC)	L8-50	t:J Osborn g:G Osborn(2)	4th(NLC-E)	656
9/4/04	Sheffield (h)	L18-24	t:Green,Jonker,Cantoni g:G Osborn(2),J Osborn	6th	401
18/4/04	Gateshead (a)	W21-22	t:J Osborn,Mushiso,McFarland,Honor g:Joyce(3)	6th	203
1/5/04	Dewsbury (h)	L24-36	t:G Osborn,J Osborn,Cantoni,Joyce,Aggrey g:G Osborn(2)	7th	426
9/5/04	Workington (a)	L48-18	t:J Osborn,Cantoni,Mushiso g:Pittman(2),G Osborn	8th	446
23/5/04	Hunslet (a)	L32-8	t:Jonker g:J Osborn(2)	9th	366
30/5/04	Barrow (a)	L32-16	t:Cantoni(2),Coleman g:J Osborn(2)	9th	646
13/6/04	Swinton (h)	W28-26	t:Pittman,Cantoni(2),Green,Jonker g:J Osborn,Pittman(3)	9th	465
20/6/04	York (a)	L50-6	t:Hannan g:Pittman	9th	1,367
27/6/04	Gateshead (h)	W52-20	t:Cantoni(5),Coleman,R Singleton,S Singleton,J Osborn,Pittman g:Pittman(4),J Osborn(2)	9th	356
4/7/04	Chorley (a)	L32-18	t:Cantoni,J Osborn,Jonker g:Pittman,J Osborn(2)	9th	211
25/7/04	Dewsbury (a)	W8-41	t:Kadima(4),Coleman,Parillon,Gardiner,Cantoni g:Pittman,J Osborn(2),G Osborn fg:Hannan	8th	487
1/8/04	Workington (h)	L20-30	t:J Osborn,Pittman,S Singleton g:J Osborn(4)	8th	314
8/8/04	Hunslet (h)	W24-16	t:Cantoni(2),Coleman,Parillon g:J Osborn(4)	8th	362
15/8/04	Barrow (h)	L14-30	t:Honor,Green,Kadima g:J Osborn	8th	382
22/8/04	Swinton (a)	L42-12	t:Green,Cantoni,Coleman	8th	424
29/8/04	York (h)	L6-58	t:McFadyen g:Pittman	8th	650
5/9/04	Chorley (h)	W28-16	t:R Singleton,Cantoni,Green,Gardiner,J Osborn g:J Osborn(4)	8th	386
12/9/04	Sheffield (a)	L62-6	t:Cantoni g:J Osborn	8th	825

		APP		TRIES		GOALS		FG		PTS	
	D.O.B.	ALL	NL2	ALL	NL2	ALL	NL2	ALL	NL2	ALL	NL2
Ade Aderiye	26/2/85	3(7)	(5)	2	0	0	0	0	0	8	0
Austin Aggrey	12/5/79	15	15	1	1	0	0	0	0	4	4
Ed Bayles	24/2/80	(1)	0	0	0	0	0	0	0	0	0
Keir Bell	14/6/85	2(5)	0	0	0	0	0	0	0	0	0
Tim Butterfield	29/1/81	7	1	1	0	0	0	0	0	4	0
Mark Cantoni	29/5/79	22	18	20	19	0	0	0	0	80	76
Mike Castle	21/5/85	1(4)	0	0	0	0	0	0	0	0	0
Jermaine Coleman	17/6/82	28	18	8	5	1	0	0	0	34	20
Neil Foster	13/8/80	12(1)	3(1)	2	0	0	0	0	0	8	0
Zane Gardiner	10/10/79	13(1)	12(1)	2	2	0	0	0	0	8	8
Andy Gould	4/8/83	6(3)	1(2)	0	0	0	0	0	0	0	0
Stephen Green	13/6/78	19(3)	14(2)	6	5	0	0	0	0	24	20
Peter Hannan	11/7/78	28	18	1	1	0	0	1	1	5	5
Bryan Hendry	23/7/84	(6)	(6)	0	0	0	0	0	0	0	0
Gareth Honor	1/10/81	13(11)	6(11)	4	2	0	0	0	0	16	8
Tom Howden	11/7/78	3	0	0	0	0	0	0	0	0	0
Rubert Jonker	7/1/79	21(1)	17(1)	4	4	0	0	0	0	16	16
Ben Joyce	13/2/80	8(9)	2(6)	1	1	3	3	0	0	10	10
Desi Kadima	21/3/80	7(1)	5(1)	6	5	0	0	0	0	24	20
Koben Katipa	5/8/76	10(3)	2(2)	1	0	0	0	0	0	4	0
Donny Lam	4/8/77	9	1	2	0	0	0	0	0	8	0
Huy Le	2/2/80	(3)	0	0	0	0	0	0	0	0	0
Deon McFadyen	5/8/78	14(4)	14(2)	1	1	0	0	0	0	4	4
Brad McFarland	9/12/81	(6)	(4)	1	1	0	0	0	0	4	4
Mal McGivern	7/2/78	(1)	0	0	0	0	0	0	0	0	0
Ronnie Mushiso	12/8/81	6	5	2	2	0	0	0	0	8	8
Mike Okwusogu	28/4/73	2(1)	1(1)	0	0	0	0	0	0	0	0
Glenn Osborn	17/8/83	16(6)	9(5)	1	1	19	6	0	0	42	16
Joel Osborn	22/12/81	23	17	8	7	28	26	0	0	88	80
Wayne Parillon	27/11/80	4(17)	1(14)	2	2	0	0	0	0	8	8
Kurt Pittman	11/10/77	14(1)	14(1)	3	3	13	13	0	0	38	38
Dan Reeds	22/12/80	2(7)	(1)	0	0	0	0	0	0	0	0
John Rua	23/8/75	12	4	2	0	0	0	0	0	8	0
Richard Singleton	12/5/78	6(1)	6(1)	2	2	0	0	0	0	8	8
Stuart Singleton	17/3/76	13	13	2	2	0	0	0	0	8	8
Alex Smits	5/8/74	25(2)	17(1)	0	0	0	0	0	0	0	0
Roger Teau	24/10/77	(3)	0	0	0	0	0	0	0	0	0
Bobby Wallis	7/1/83	(3)	(3)	0	0	0	0	0	0	0	0

Stephen Green

LEAGUE RECORD
P18-W6-D0-L12
(8th, NL2)
F361, A583, Diff-222
12 points.

CHALLENGE CUP
Round Four

NATIONAL LEAGUE CUP
4th, East Division

ATTENDANCES
Best - v Hull KR (NLC - 656)
Worst - v Sheffield (NLC - 142)
Total (NL2 & NLC only) - 5,290
Average (NL2 & NLC only) - 407
(Down by 23 on 2003)

SHEFFIELD EAGLES

DATE	FIXTURE	RESULT	SCORERS	LGE	ATT
1/2/04	Hull KR (a) (NLC)	L24-2	g:G Brown	4th(NLC-E)	2,391
6/2/04	Leigh Miners Rangers (a) (CCR3) ●	W12-14	t:Morton,G Brown g:G Brown(3)	N/A	591
11/2/04	Doncaster (h) (NLC)	L6-38	t:Raleigh g:G Brown	4th(NLC-E)	945
15/2/04	Dewsbury (h) (NLC)	L18-42	t:Breakingbury,Tillyer,Turnbull g:G Brown(3)	4th(NLC-E)	867
22/2/04	London Skolars (h) (NLC)	W34-6	t:De Chenu(3),Turnbull(2),Mills(2),Breakingbury g:Aston	3rd(NLC-E)	662
29/2/04	York (h) (CCR4)	L24-32	t:Turnbull,Poynter,Mills,Hurst g:Goddard(4)	N/A	764
7/3/04	Doncaster (a) (NLC)	L34-4	t:Hurst	3rd(NLC-E)	734
14/3/04	London Skolars (a) (NLC)	L16-14	t:G Brown,Reilly g:Goddard(3)	3rd(NLC-E)	142
19/3/04	Hull KR (h) (NLC)	L18-22	t:J James,G Brown g:Goddard(5)	3rd(NLC-E)	1,049
28/3/04	Dewsbury (a) (NLC)	W22-28	t:Breakingbury(2),J James,Tillyer,Howieson g:Goddard(4)	3rd(NLC-E)	499
9/4/04	London Skolars (a)	W18-24	t:Breakingbury,Poynter(2),Turnbull g:Goddard(4)	5th	401
18/4/04	Chorley (a)	W18-32	t:Tillyer,G Brown,K Collins(2),Hurst(2),Turnbull g:Goddard(2)	4th	257
2/5/04	York (a)	L34-16	t:K Collins,Breakingbury,Raleigh g:Goddard,G Brown	5th	1,389
9/5/04	Gateshead (a)	W6-42	t:Poynter(2),Hurst,A Dickinson(2),Turnbull(2),Howieson g:Goddard(5)	4th	297
21/5/04	Dewsbury (h)	W24-12	t:Hurst(2),Breakingbury,R Dickinson g:Goddard(4)	4th	1,352
30/5/04	Workington (a)	W32-36	t:Poynter,Sodje(2),Doherty,Raleigh g:A James(8)	3rd	652
6/6/04	Workington (h)	W21-8	t:Goddard,Poynter,S Collins g:Goddard(4) fg:Goddard	1st	979
13/6/04	Hunslet (a)	W14-40	t:G Brown,Turnbull,Doherty,Poynter,Raleigh(2) g:Goddard(7),A James	1st	620
20/6/04	Barrow (a)	L16-24	t:Turnbull,Hurst g:Goddard(2),G Brown(2)	3rd	977
4/7/04	Swinton (h)	L16-32	t:Turnbull,J James,Hurst g:G Brown(2)	3rd	957
11/7/04	Chorley (h)	L24-31	t:De Chenu,Hurst,J James,Turnbull g:G Brown(4)	4th	852
23/7/04	York (h)	W27-14	t:A Dickinson,Rice,G Brown,Poynter g:G Brown(4),A James fg:G Brown	2nd	1,018
1/8/04	Gateshead (h)	W54-10	t:A Dickinson,J James(2),C Brown(2),De Chenu(3),S Dickinson,Hurst g:G Brown(7)	2nd	744
8/8/04	Dewsbury (a)	W10-51	t:J James,A James,G Brown,Poynter(3),De Chenu,Raleigh g:G Brown(9) fg:G Brown	1st	502
22/8/04	Hunslet (h)	W50-10	t:A Dickinson,Poynter,Turnbull(2),A James(2),J James(3),Hurst g:G Brown(4),A James	3rd	870
29/8/04	Barrow (a)	L29-10	t:A Dickinson,J James g:G Brown	3rd	1,222
5/9/04	Swinton (a)	L32-24	t:R Dickinson,Poynter,Pearson,Sodje g:G Brown(4)	3rd	595
12/9/04	London Skolars (h)	W62-6	t:J James(2),Doherty(2),Poynter(2),De Chenu,Breakingbury(2),Tillyer, K Collins,Turnbull g:G Brown,Pearson(6)	3rd	825
19/9/04	Hunslet (h) (NL1QS-EPO)	L16-39	t:S Collins,J James,A James g:Pearson(2)	N/A	531

● Played at The Coliseum, Leigh

	D.O.B.	APP		TRIES		GOALS		FG		PTS	
		ALL	NL2	ALL	NL2	ALL	NL2	ALL	NL2	ALL	NL2
Guy Adams	1/9/76	1(5)	1(3)	0	0	0	0	0	0	0	0
Mark Aston	27/9/67	2(3)	0	0	0	1	0	0	0	2	0
Jon Breakingbury	5/10/82	15(2)	9	9	5	0	0	0	0	36	20
Craig Brown	2/12/80	24(3)	14(3)	2	2	0	0	0	0	8	8
Gavin Brown	18/9/77	23	16	7	4	47	39	2	2	124	96
Jon Bruce	30/10/71	25(3)	16(3)	0	0	0	0	0	0	0	0
Adam Carroll	14/2/84	3(1)	0	0	0	0	0	0	0	0	0
Kieron Collins	20/10/82	5(3)	5(1)	4	4	0	0	0	0	16	16
Scott Collins	9/5/79	16	16	2	2	0	0	0	0	8	8
Carl De Chenu	18/6/82	18	10	9	6	0	0	0	0	36	24
Alex Dickinson	27/11/84	13(1)	13(1)	6	6	0	0	0	0	24	24
Ryan Dickinson	9/6/86	2(2)	2(2)	2	2	0	0	0	0	8	8
Sean Dickinson	17/8/83	6(11)	5(10)	1	1	0	0	0	0	4	4
Steve Doherty	8/3/78	9(4)	9(4)	4	4	0	0	0	0	16	16
Wayne Flynn	19/11/76	(1)		0	0	0	0	0	0	0	0
Richard Goddard	28/4/74	13(1)	8	1	1	45	29	1	1	95	63
Jack Howieson	28/7/81	25	15	2	1	0	0	0	0	8	4
Greg Hurst	22/6/80	16(9)	11(5)	12	10	0	0	0	0	48	40
Aled James	17/2/82	10(1)	10(1)	4	4	11	11	0	0	38	38
Jordan James	24/5/80	27(1)	18	14	12	0	0	0	0	56	48
Danny Mills	10/8/82	14(2)	6	3	0	0	0	0	0	12	0
Simon Morton	4/10/82	(7)	(4)	1	0	0	0	0	0	4	0
Rob North	19/11/77	1(8)	(1)	0	0	0	0	0	0	0	0
Jimmy Pearson	25/7/78	1(5)	1(5)	1	1	8	8	0	0	20	20
Andy Poynter	24/10/78	25	15	16	15	0	0	0	0	64	60
Andy Raleigh	17/3/81	28	19	6	5	0	0	0	0	24	20
Peter Reilly	24/7/81	7	0	1	0	0	0	0	0	4	0
Andy Rice	9/6/80	2(14)	2(14)	1	1	0	0	0	0	4	4
Bright Sodje	21/4/67	9(1)	9	3	3	0	0	0	0	12	12
Gareth Stanley	20/5/81	11(2)	3	0	0	0	0	0	0	0	0
Richard Stone	19/10/84	(2)	(2)	0	0	0	0	0	0	0	0
Simon Tillyer	9/5/80	3(19)	1(13)	4	2	0	0	0	0	16	8
Nick Turnbull	22/11/82	23(4)	13(4)	15	11	0	0	0	0	60	44

Andy Raleigh

LEAGUE RECORD
P18-W12-D0-L6
(3rd, NL2) (Elimination Play-Off,
NL1 Qualifying Series)
F569, A340, Diff+229
24 points.

CHALLENGE CUP
Round Four

NATIONAL LEAGUE CUP
3rd, East Division

ATTENDANCES
Best - v Dewsbury (NL2 - 1,352)
Worst - v Hunslet (EPO - 531)
Total (NL2, inc play-offs,
& NLC only) - 12,628
Average (NL2, inc play-offs,
& NLC only) - 902
(Down by 41 on 2003)

SWINTON LIONS

DATE	FIXTURE	RESULT	SCORERS	LGE	ATT
1/2/04	Leigh (h) (NLC)	L6-22	t:Maye g:Ashton	3rd(NLC-W)	1,351
8/2/04	East Hull (h) (CCR3)	L14-26	t:Irwin,Ashton,Maye g:Ashton	N/A	532
15/2/04	Whitehaven (a) (NLC)	L38-10	t:English,Ayres g:Ashton	3rd(NLC-W)	1,073
22/2/04	Oldham (h) (NLC)	L18-30	t:Cushion(2),English,Llewellyn g:Ayres	3rd(NLC-W)	731
7/3/04	Chorley (h) (NLC)	W27-24	t:Roach,Irwin,Cannon,Bolton,Maye g:Maye,Ashton(2) fg:Ayres	3rd(NLC-W)	430
21/3/04	Leigh (a) (NLC)	L66-6	t:Heaton g:Wingfield	3rd(NLC-W)	1,475
30/3/04	Whitehaven (h) (NLC)	L6-34	t:Irwin g:Maye	3rd(NLC-W)	346
4/4/04	Oldham (a) (NLC)	L42-15	t:Ayres,Cannon g:Maye,Ashton(2) fg:Ashton	3rd(NLC-W)	983
9/4/04	Chorley (a) (NLC)	L20-12	t:Roach,Ayres g:Ayres(2)	3rd(NLC-W)	307
12/4/04	Gateshead (h)	W42-10	t:Maye(2),Bolton(2),Sinfield,Cannon,English,Patel g:Ayres(4),Ashton	1st	410
18/4/04	Dewsbury (a)	W8-35	t:Cannon(2),Maye(2),Wingfield,Thorpe g:Ayres(5) fg:Ayres	1st	509
2/5/04	Workington (h)	W64-26	t:Ayres,Bolton,English(3),Smith,Maye(2),Roach,Cannon,Barraclough g:Ayres(9),Smith	1st	454
9/5/04	Hunslet (a)	L42-20	t:Sinfield,Thorpe,English,Irwin g:Ayres(2)	1st	525
23/5/04	Barrow (h)	L10-46	t:Cannon,Stazicker g:Ayres	5th	504
30/5/04	York (a)	L44-24	t:Cushion,Irwin,English,Cannon g:Ayres(4)	5th	1,411
13/6/04	London Skolars (a)	L28-26	t:Cannon(2),Maye,Llewellyn,Irwin g:Ayres(3)	5th	465
20/6/04	Chorley (h)	W26-20	t:Hodson,Sinfield,English,Maye g:Ashton(5)	5th	418
4/7/04	Sheffield (a)	W16-32	t:Maye,Smith,Russell,Irwin,Cannon g:Ashton(6)	5th	957
11/7/04	Dewsbury (h)	W34-15	t:Rogers,Ashton,Roach(2),Irwin,Thorpe g:Ashton(5)	5th	444
25/7/04	Workington (a)	L40-22	t:Russell,Maye,Thorpe,Smith g:Ayres(3)	5th	1,046
1/8/04	Hunslet (h)	W33-16	t:Roach,Cannon,Hodson,English(2),Tyrell g:Ashton(2),Ayres(2) fg:Coates	5th	508
8/8/04	Barrow (a)	W12-22	t:English,Patel,Maye,Llewellyn g:Ashton(3)	4th	865
15/8/04	York (h)	L12-48	t:English g:Ashton(4)	5th	742
22/8/04	London Skolars (h)	W42-12	t:Russell,Maye,Coates,English,Gardner,Hodson,Thorpe,Roach g:Ayres,Smith(4)	4th	424
27/8/04	Chorley (a)	W30-43	t:Cushion,Maye(2),English,Hodson,Thorpe,Russell,Whittaker g:Smith(2),Russell(3) fg:Patel	4th	369
5/9/04	Sheffield (h)	W32-24	t:Thorpe,Patel,Smith,Maye(2),Cushion g:Russell(4)	4th	595
12/9/04	Gateshead (a)	W23-28	t:Smith,Maye(2),English,Llewellyn,Sinfield g:Russell(2)	4th	342
19/9/04	Workington (h) (NL1QS-EPO)	L38-44	t:English,Ayres,Llewellyn,Hodson(2),Thorpe,Coates g:Ashton(4),Russell	N/A	768

	APP		TRIES		GOALS		FG		PTS	
	D.O.B.	ALL	NL2	ALL	NL2	ALL	NL2	ALL	NL2	ALL	NL2
Paul Ashton	17/6/79	13(4)	8(3)	2	1	37	30	1	0	83	64
Warren Ayres	11/12/78	21(6)	12(6)	5	2	37	34	2	1	96	77
Rob Barraclough	27/9/78	2(3)	(2)	1	1	0	0	0	0	4	4
Grant Bithel	10/5/80	(2)	0	0	0	0	0	0	0	0	0
Mark Bolton	12/8/77	11(1)	5	4	3	0	0	0	0	16	12
Chris Brett	24/10/79	(3)	(1)	0	0	0	0	0	0	0	0
Peter Cannon	22/3/74	18(1)	13	12	10	0	0	0	0	48	40
Mick Coates	8/3/80	17(1)	16	2	2	0	0	1	1	9	9
Phil Cushion	15/6/78	19(1)	14(1)	5	3	0	0	0	0	20	12
Wayne English	8/3/80	27	19	17	15	0	0	0	0	68	60
Lee Gardner	24/8/82	3(5)	3(5)	1	1	0	0	0	0	4	4
Neil Hayden	25/11/82	4(2)	4	0	0	0	0	0	0	0	0
Danny Heaton	19/4/81	6(2)	0	1	0	0	0	0	0	4	0
Ian Hodson	23/10/81	23(2)	16(1)	6	6	0	0	0	0	24	24
Chris Irwin	11/3/82	17(2)	10(2)	8	5	0	0	0	0	32	20
Jake Johnstone	6/12/77	2(2)	0	0	0	0	0	0	0	0	0
Craig Kay	22/11/80	(1)	0	0	0	0	0	0	0	0	0
Alan Kilshaw	23/11/82	(1)	(1)	0	0	0	0	0	0	0	0
Tau Liku	21/2/71	7(8)	1(5)	0	0	0	0	0	0	0	0
Dave Llewellyn	3/12/82	15(2)	10(1)	5	4	0	0	0	0	20	16
Mike Loughlin	23/9/81	7(2)	6(1)	0	0	0	0	0	0	0	0
Chris Maye	28/2/84	25	18	21	18	3	0	0	0	90	72
Safraz Patel	20/10/76	5(13)	2(11)	3	3	0	0	1	1	13	13
Mark Pembroke	25/2/81	1(5)	(4)	0	0	0	0	0	0	0	0
Jason Roach	2/5/71	16(3)	8(3)	7	5	0	0	0	0	28	20
Wes Rogers	3/11/77	12(3)	7(3)	1	1	0	0	0	0	4	4
Robert Russell	12/3/79	8(5)	8(5)	4	4	10	10	0	0	36	36
Ian Sinfield	7/4/77	23	19	4	4	0	0	0	0	16	16
Kris Smith	20/8/78	21(1)	15	5	5	7	7	0	0	34	34
Darren Speakman	24/3/74	(1)	(1)	0	0	0	0	0	0	0	0
Ryan Stazicker	28/7/79	4(2)	4(2)	1	1	0	0	0	0	4	4
Hugh Thorpe	19/12/78	18(2)	16	8	8	0	0	0	0	32	32
Danny Tyrell	30/3/78	4	4	1	1	0	0	0	0	4	4
Andrew Wallace	1/12/81	(1)	(1)	0	0	0	0	0	0	0	0
Steve Warburton	9/1/82	3	3	0	0	0	0	0	0	0	0
Rob Whittaker	13/5/79	6(13)	2(11)	1	1	0	0	0	0	4	4
Craig Wingfield	6/9/80	6(10)	4(5)	1	1	1	0	0	0	6	4

Chris Maye

LEAGUE RECORD
P18-W12-D0-L6
(4th, NL2)
(Elimination Play-Off,
NL1 Qualifying Series)
F547, A460, Diff+87
24 points.

CHALLENGE CUP
Round Three

NATIONAL LEAGUE CUP
3rd, West Division

ATTENDANCES
Best - v Leigh (NLC - 1,351)
Worst - v Whitehaven (NLC - 346)
Total (NL2, NL1QS & NLC only) - 8,125
Average (NL2, NL1QS
& NLC only) - 580
(Up by 38 on 2003)

WORKINGTON TOWN

DATE	FIXTURE	RESULT	SCORERS	LGE	ATT
1/2/04	Gateshead (h) (NLC)	W52-0	t:B Smith(2),Skillen,Limmer(2),Johnson,C Stalker,King(2),Coulson g:Hetherington(6)	1st(NLC-N)	709
8/2/04	Crosfields (a) (CCR3) ●	W14-46	t:Coulson,B Smith(2),Hetherington,Limmer(4),Heaney g:Hetherington(5)	N/A	768
15/2/04	Keighley (a) (NLC)	L42-6	t:Robinson g:Hetherington	3rd(NLC-N)	937
22/2/04	Barrow (h) (NLC)	D24-24	t:Limmer,Skillen,B Smith(2),Lewthwaite g:Skillen(2)	3rd(NLC-N)	775
29/2/04	Leeds (h) (CCR4)	L18-68	t:M Stalker,B Smith,Lewthwaite g:Skillen(3)	N/A	4,829
7/3/04	Whitehaven (a) (NLC)	L54-12	t:Coulson,Frazer g:Skillen(2)	3rd(NLC-N)	2,156
21/3/04	Gateshead (a) (NLC)	D24-24	t:Beaumont,Pettit,Burgess,Frazer g:Skillen(4)	3rd(NLC-N)	288
28/3/04	Keighley (h) (NLC)	L12-33	t:Wright,Lewthwaite g:Heaney(2)	3rd(NLC-N)	567
4/4/04	Barrow (a) (NLC)	L48-0	No Scorers	3rd(NLC-N)	713
9/4/04	Whitehaven (h) (NLC)	L10-26	t:Heaney,Lewthwaite g:Heaney	3rd(NLC-N)	1,419
12/4/04	Hunslet (a)	L42-14	t:Frazer,Burgess g:Heaney(3)	8th	344
18/4/04	Barrow (h)	L14-32	t:B Smith,Limmer g:Heaney(3)	9th	503
2/5/04	Swinton (a)	L64-26	t:Manihera,Chilton,Fearon,Limmer,Frazer g:Heaney(3)	10th	454
9/5/04	London Skolars (h)	W48-18	t:Wilson(2),Beaumont,Limmer(2),Chilton,Lewthwaite,Tunstall(2) g:Heaney(6)	9th	446
23/5/04	Chorley (a)	L40-26	t:Manihera,Burgess,Limmer,Beaumont(2) g:Manihera(3)	8th	248
30/5/04	Sheffield (h)	L32-36	t:Frazer,McGlasson,Chilton,Beaumont,Tuimaualuga g:Manihera(6)	8th	652
6/6/04	Sheffield (a)	L21-8	t:Manihera g:Manihera(2)	8th	979
13/6/04	Gateshead (a)	W12-44	t:Chilton,Limmer(2),Manihera(2),Frazer,Tunstall(2) g:Manihera(6)	8th	291
20/6/04	Dewsbury (h)	W44-22	t:Limmer(2),Lewthwaite,Manihera,Wilson(2),Sione,Tuimaualuga,Boylan g:Manihera(4)	7th	667
4/7/04	York (h)	W44-20	t:Limmer,Pettit,Frazer(2),B Smith(2),Tunstall g:Manihera(8)	7th	1,020
11/7/04	Barrow (a)	L18-10	t:Sione(2) g:Manihera	7th	1,201
25/7/04	Swinton (h)	W40-22	t:Sione(3),Frazer(2),Wilson,Lewthwaite g:Manihera(6)	7th	1,046
1/8/04	London Skolars (a)	W20-30	t:Sione,C Stalker,Limmer,Wright,Frazer g:Manihera(5)	7th	314
8/8/04	Chorley (h)	W48-24	t:Frazer,Beaumont,Limmer,Manihera,Pettit,B Smith,Wilson,Wright g:Manihera(8)	6th	1,051
22/8/04	Gateshead (h)	W80-8	t:Manihera(3),Frazer,B Smith(3),Sione(3),Lewthwaite,Wilson,Tunstall,Limmer g:Manihera(12)	5th	958
29/8/04	Dewsbury (a)	W30-41	t:Tuimaualuga,B Smith,Johnson,Manihera,Chilton,Wilson,Burgess g:Manihera(6) fg:Manihera	5th	520
4/9/04	York (a)	L44-24	t:Burgess,Limmer,Johnson,Manihera,Dawes g:Manihera(2)	6th	1,346
12/9/04	Hunslet (h)	W24-6	t:B Smith,Dean,George,Dawes g:B Smith(4)	5th	978
19/9/04	Swinton (a) (NL1QS-EPO)	W38-44	t:Lewthwaite(2),George,Limmer(2),B Smith,Manihera g:Manihera(8)	N/A	768
26/9/04	Hunslet (h) (NL1QS-ESF)	W27-13	t:Wilson,Sione,Chilton,Limmer g:Manihera(5) fg:Manihera	N/A	1,274
3/10/04	York (a) (NL1QS-FE)	L70-10	t:Chilton,Manihera g:Manihera	N/A	2,017

● Played at Wilderspool, Warrington

		APP		TRIES		GOALS		FG		PTS	
	D.O.B.	ALL	NL2	ALL	NL2	ALL	NL2	ALL	NL2	ALL	NL2
Thomas Armstrong	29/10/81	1		0	0	0	0	0	0	0	0
Craig Barker	1/9/75	(8)	(5)	0	0	0	0	0	0	0	0
Jamie Beaumont	22/1/75	25(2)	15(2)	6	5	0	0	0	0	24	20
William Blackburn	26/8/72	(3)	(3)	0	0	0	0	0	0	0	0
Shaun Boylan	16/10/80	6	6	1	1	0	0	0	0	4	4
Dean Bragg	14/1/82	(14)	(14)	0	0	0	0	0	0	0	0
Dean Burgess	11/10/84	22(4)	18(3)	5	4	0	0	0	0	20	16
Malcolm Caton	24/11/82	(3)	(1)	0	0	0	0	0	0	0	0
Scott Chilton	26/10/80	19	13	7	7	0	0	0	0	28	28
Adam Coulson	14/2/83	9(1)	1(1)	3	0	0	0	0	0	12	0
Stephen Dawes	14/1/85	5(2)	5(2)	2	2	0	0	0	0	8	8
Gareth Dean	31/3/81	10	10	1	1	0	0	0	0	4	4
Andrew Fearon	21/9/74	13(1)	5(1)	1	1	0	0	0	0	4	4
Neil Frazer	7/3/76	22	15	13	11	0	0	0	0	52	44
Richard George	6/8/84	6	6	2	2	0	0	0	0	8	8
Jonathan Heaney	30/10/79	13	4	2	0	18	15	0	0	44	30
Bryan Hendry	23/7/84	(6)	0	0	0	0	0	0	0	0	0
Kevin Hetherington	7/6/76	4(1)	0	1	0	12	0	0	0	28	0
Karl Hocking	9/6/76	(2)	(2)	0	0	0	0	0	0	0	0
Matthew Johnson	18/3/82	11(3)	7(1)	3	2	0	0	0	0	12	8
Darren King	9/3/82	2	0	2	0	0	0	0	0	8	0
Graeme Lewthwaite	5/7/72	18(4)	13(1)	10	6	0	0	0	0	40	24
Jonny Limmer	8/5/79	31	21	24	17	0	0	0	0	96	68
Tane Manihera	6/8/74	18	18	14	14	83	83	2	2	224	224
Andy McGlasson	12/1/84	11(9)	10(3)	1	1	0	0	0	0	4	4
Allan McGuiness	30/6/82	(6)	(6)	0	0	0	0	0	0	0	0
David Pettit	23/10/79	11(11)	5(9)	3	2	0	0	0	0	12	8
James Robinson	4/3/79	5(18)	2(12)	1	0	0	0	0	0	4	0
Lusi Sione	26/12/74	11	11	11	11	0	0	0	0	44	44
Gareth Skillen	10/10/82	7	0	2	0	11	0	0	0	30	0
Brett Smith	17/10/77	20(4)	14(3)	17	10	4	4	0	0	76	48
Gary Smith	29/3/82	1	1	0	0	0	0	0	0	0	0
Craig Stalker	8/6/75	10	7	2	1	0	0	0	0	8	4
Martin Stalker	8/6/75	6(8)	2(3)	1	0	0	0	0	0	4	0
John Tuimaualuga	29/10/77	17	17	3	3	0	0	0	0	12	12
Matthew Tunstall	7/9/77	29	19	6	6	0	0	0	0	24	24
Martyn Wilson	22/10/82	25	19	9	9	0	0	0	0	36	36
Matthew Woodcock	26/10/77	7	7	0	0	0	0	0	0	0	0
Ricky Wright	15/3/77	8(12)	1(12)	3	2	0	0	0	0	12	8
John Young	21/9/78	(1)	0	0	0	0	0	0	0	0	0

Jonny Limmer

LEAGUE RECORD
P18-W10-D0-L8
(5th, NL2)
(Final Eliminator, NL1 Qualifying Series)
F597, A479, Diff+118
20 points.

CHALLENGE CUP
Round Four

NATIONAL LEAGUE CUP
3rd, North Division

ATTENDANCES
Best - v Leeds (CC - 4,829)
Worst - v London Skolars (NL2 - 446)
Total (NL2, NL1QS & NLC only) - 12,065
Average (NL2, NL1QS & NLC only) - 862
(Up by 336 on 2003)

YORK CITY KNIGHTS

DATE	FIXTURE	RESULT	SCORERS	LGE	ATT
1/2/04	Batley (h) (NLC)	L22-24	t:Seal,Callaghan,Langley g:Brough(5)	3rd(NLC-Y)	2,039
8/2/04	Villeneuve (h) (CCR3)	W28-8	t:Rhodes,Forsyth,Elston,Friend g:Brough(6)	N/A	1,203
15/2/04	Gateshead (a) (NLC)	W24-56	t:Ball,Godfrey(2),Langley,Elston(3),Callaghan,Briggs,C Smith g:Brough(8)	2nd(NLC-Y)	366
22/2/04	Dewsbury (a) (NLC)	W16-58	t:Ball,Elston,Godfrey,Callaghan,Jackson(2),Friend,Sozi,Graham,Brough g:Brough(9)	1st(NLC-Y)	848
29/2/04	Sheffield (a) (CCR4)	W24-32	t:C Smith,Rhodes,Briggs,Ball,Forsyth,Langley g:Brough(4)	N/A	764
7/3/04	Featherstone (h) (NLC)	W18-16	t:Rhodes,Sozi,Godfrey g:Brough(3)	2nd(NLC-Y)	1,942
14/3/04	Featherstone (a) (CCR5)	W26-29	t:Seal,Godfrey(2),Graham g:Brough(6) fg:Brough	N/A	2,234
21/3/04	Batley (a) (NLC)	L36-12	t:Friend,Wood g:Brough(2)	3rd(NLC-Y)	829
28/3/04	Huddersfield (a) (CCQF)	L50-12	t:Elston,Seal g:Brough(2)	N/A	4,286
31/3/04	Gateshead (h) (NLC) ●	W54-26	t:Godfrey(3),Benjafield,Rhodes(2),Ball,Seal,Langley g:Brough(7),Ball(2)	2nd(NLC-Y)	1,520
4/4/04	Dewsbury (h) (NLC)	W44-7	t:Godfrey(3),Benjafield,Friend,Graham,Rhodes,Langley g:Brough(6)	2nd(NLC-Y)	1,204
9/4/04	Featherstone (a) (NLC)	W26-36	t:Stewart(2),Godfrey,Brough,Callaghan,Elston g:Brough(6)	2nd(NLC-Y)	1,435
12/4/04	Chorley (h)	W32-18	t:Ball,Callaghan,Walker,Brough,Elston g:Brough(6)	4th	1,401
18/4/04	Hunslet (h)	L8-21	t:Callaghan,Langley	5th	1,262
25/4/04	Featherstone (h) (NLCQFQ)	W27-18	t:Graham,Langley,Elston,Ball g:Brough(5) fg:Rhodes	N/A	1,202
2/5/04	Sheffield (h)	W34-16	t:Walker,Stewart(2),Callaghan,Elston,Wood,Graham g:Brough(2) fg:Brough(2)	4th	1,389
9/5/04	Barrow (a)	W16-30	t:Friend,Callaghan,Cain,Langley,Walker,Stewart g:Brough(3)	5th	1,048
23/5/04	Gateshead (h)	W48-12	t:Godfrey,Rhodes,Buchanan,Friend,Langley(2),Brough(2),Cain g:Brough(5),Ball	3rd	2,519
30/5/04	Swinton (h)	W44-24	t:Rhodes,Brough,Langley,Jackson,Graham,Callaghan,Ball g:Brough(8)	2nd	1,411
6/6/04	Halifax (a) (NLCQF)	W14-37	t:Wood,Ball,Friend,Langley(2) g:Brough(8) fg:Brough	N/A	1,840
13/6/04	Dewsbury (a)	W2-48	t:Buchanan(3),Cain(2),Brough(2),Friend g:Brough(7),Graham	2nd	1,275
20/6/04	London Skolars (h)	W50-6	t:Sozi(2),Buchanan(2),Cain(2),Graham,Rhodes,Wood g:Brough(7)	1st	1,367
27/6/04	Hull KR (a) (NLCSF)	L32-0	No Scorers	N/A	2,629
4/7/04	Workington (a)	L44-20	t:Rhodes,Sozi,Ball(2) g:Brough(2)	2nd	1,020
11/7/04	Hunslet (a)	L19-8	t:Walker g:Brough(2)	2nd	770
23/7/04	Sheffield (a)	L27-14	t:Brough,Sozi,Cain g:Brough	3rd	1,018
1/8/04	Barrow (h)	W30-16	t:D Andrews,Farrell,Brough,Ramsden,Elston g:Brough(5)	3rd	1,307
8/8/04	Gateshead (a)	W18-30	t:Elston,Buchanan(3),J Smith,Farrell,Sullivan g:Brough	3rd	429
15/8/04	Swinton (a)	W12-48	t:Langley,Brough,Buchanan,Farrell,Jackson(2),Cain,J Smith g:Brough(8)	2nd	742
22/8/04	Dewsbury (h)	W64-6	t:Elston(2),Farrell,Spurr(2),Brough(3),Friend,Rhodes(2),C Smith g:Brough(8)	2nd	1,761
29/8/04	London Skolars (a)	W6-58	t:J Smith,Langley(3),Walker(2),Rhodes,Spurr,Jackson,Sozi g:Brough(9)	2nd	650
4/9/04	Workington (h)	W44-24	t:Brough,Farrell,Rhodes,Langley(2),Elston(2),C Smith g:Brough(6)	2nd	1,346
12/9/04	Chorley (a)	L21-20	t:Buchanan,Langley,Elston,Talipeau g:Brough(2)	2nd	616
26/9/04	Halifax (a) (NL1QS-QSF)	L37-20	t:Jackson,J Smith(2),Friend g:Brough(2)	N/A	2,213
3/10/04	Workington (h) (NL1QS-FE)	W70-10	t:Spurr,Cain(5),Buchanan(2),Rhodes,Farrell(2),Sullivan g:Brough(8),Jackson,Buchanan(2)	N/A	2,017
10/10/04	Halifax (NL1QS-F) ●●	L34-30	t:Elston,Buchanan(2),Cain,Langley g:Brough(5)	N/A	N/A

● Played at Bootham Crescent (York City FC)
●● Played at Halton Stadium, Widnes

		APP		TRIES		GOALS		FG		PTS	
	D.O.B.	ALL	NL2	ALL	NL2	ALL	NL2	ALL	NL2	ALL	NL2
Dean Andrews	1/6/79	2	2	1	1	0	0	0	0	4	4
Tom Andrews	30/6/82	4	0	0	0	0	0	0	0	0	0
Damian Ball	14/7/75	21(1)	11	10	4	3	1	0	0	46	18
Ryan Benjafield	3/8/82	5	0	2	0	0	0	0	0	8	0
Dan Briggs	15/7/79	3(5)	(1)	2	0	0	0	0	0	8	0
Danny Brough	15/1/83	36	21	15	13	174	97	4	2	412	248
Austin Buchanan	22/5/84	16	14	15	15	2	2	0	0	64	64
Andy Burland	5/11/77	1(2)	1	0	0	0	0	0	0	0	0
Mark Cain	3/5/76	11(22)	6(15)	14	14	0	0	0	0	56	56
Darren Callaghan	6/8/76	27(2)	15	9	5	0	0	0	0	36	20
Dale Cardoza	13/9/79	2(1)	2(1)	0	0	0	0	0	0	0	0
Jimmy Elston	8/12/79	9(22)	6(11)	18	10	0	0	0	0	72	40
Craig Farrell	8/10/81	10	10	7	7	0	0	0	0	28	28
Craig Forsyth	24/10/70	5(25)	2(15)	2	0	0	0	0	0	8	0
Simon Friend	6/5/77	32(1)	19	10	5	0	0	0	0	40	20
Alex Godfrey	2/12/78	14	2	14	1	0	0	0	0	56	4
Nathan Graham	23/11/71	25(1)	11	7	3	1	1	0	0	30	14
Richard Hayes	21/2/70	4	0	0	0	0	0	0	0	0	0
Lee Jackson	12/3/69	30(2)	17(2)	7	5	1	1	0	0	30	22
Rob Kama	5/8/76	5(3)	1(2)	0	0	0	0	0	0	0	0
Chris Langley	11/10/80	33(1)	21	21	13	0	0	0	0	84	52
Mick Ramsden	13/11/71	11(4)	8(1)	1	1	0	0	0	0	4	4
Damien Reid	14/3/84	1	0	0	0	0	0	0	0	0	0
Scott Rhodes	21/6/80	35	21	15	9	0	0	1	0	61	36
Danny Seal	15/3/76	3(3)	0	4	0	0	0	0	0	16	0
Chris Smith	31/10/75	12(1)	10	4	2	0	0	0	0	16	8
John Smith	14/8/80	8(19)	5(13)	5	5	0	0	0	0	20	20
Yusuf Sozi	20/12/81	27(7)	15(5)	7	5	0	0	0	0	28	20
Chris Spurr	7/7/80	8(1)	8(1)	4	4	0	0	0	0	16	16
Carl Stannard	22/3/79	(3)	(3)	0	0	0	0	0	0	0	0
Mark Stewart	11/2/81	7(4)	2(2)	5	3	0	0	0	0	20	12
Adam Sullivan	14/11/82	5(5)	5(5)	2	2	0	0	0	0	8	8
Albert Talipeau	5/8/81	1(4)	1(4)	1	1	0	0	0	0	4	4
John Wainhouse	12/1/84	1(3)	1(3)	0	0	0	0	0	0	0	0
Scott Walker	12/9/83	18(1)	11	6	6	0	0	0	0	24	24
Richard Wilson	5/2/75	21(1)	19(1)	0	0	0	0	0	0	0	0
Aaron Wood	5/2/79	15	6	4	2	0	0	0	0	16	8

Chris Langley

LEAGUE RECORD
P18-W13-D0-L5
(2nd, NL2)
(Runners Up, NL1 Qualifying Series)
F630, A308, Diff+322
26 points.

CHALLENGE CUP
Quarter Finalists

NATIONAL LEAGUE CUP
Semi Finalists/2nd, Yorkshire Division

ATTENDANCES
Best - v Gateshead (NL2 - 2,519)
Worst - v Featherstone (NLCQFQ - 1,202)
Total (NL2, NL1QS
& NLC, inc QFQ, only) - 23,687
Average (NL2, NL1QS
& NLC, inc QFQ, only) - 1,579
(Up by 214 on 2003)

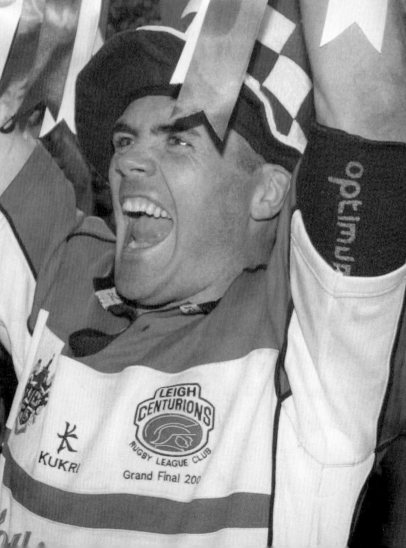

NATIONAL LEAGUE ONE 2004
Round by Round

WEEK 1

Monday 12th April 2004

BATLEY BULLDOGS 48 ROCHDALE HORNETS 12

BULLDOGS: 1 Mark Sibson; 2 Chris Spurr; 3 Shad Royston; 4 Danny Maun; 5 Adrian Flynn; 6 Mark Toohey; 7 Barry Eaton; 8 Steve Hill; 9 Andy Heptinstall; 10 David Rourke; 11 Sean Richardson; 12 Andy Spink; 13 Tim Spears. Subs (all used): 14 Adrian Leek; 15 Paul Harrison; 16 Joe Berry; 17 Will Cartledge.
Tries: Sibson (12, 62, 68), Richardson (15), Maun (35), Rourke (47), Hill (74), Eaton (78); **Goals:** Eaton 8/10.
HORNETS: 1 Michael Platt; 2 Liam Williams; 3 Paul Anderson; 4 Andy Gorski; 5 Dave Cunliffe; 6 Lee Birdseye; 7 Liam McGovern; 8 Andy Leathem; 9 Janan Billings; 10 Lee Hansen; 11 Rob Ball; 12 Gareth Price; 13 Darren Shaw. Subs (all used): 14 Kris Ratcliffe; 15 Dave Newton; 16 Tommy Hodgkinson; 17 Mark Costello.
Tries: Price (27, 76); **Goals:** Birdseye 2/3.
Rugby Leaguer & League Express Men of the Match:
Bulldogs: David Rourke; *Hornets:* Liam McGovern.
Penalty count: 8-3; **Half-time:** 16-6;
Referee: Peter Taberner (Wigan); **Attendance:** 639.

HALIFAX 20 DONCASTER DRAGONS 38

HALIFAX: 1 Simon Grix; 2 Rikki Sheriffe; 3 Chris Norman; 4 Alan Hadcroft; 5 Oliver Marns; 6 Pat Weisner; 7 Mark Moxon; 8 Anthony Farrell; 9 Phil Cantillon; 10 David Bates; 11 Jamie Bloem; 12 Ged Corcoran; 13 Jon Roper. Subs (all used): 14 Richard Smith; 15 Jaymes Chapman; 16 Scott Law; 17 Paul Davidson.
Tries: Sheriffe (48), Hadcroft (65), Roper (77);
Goals: Bloem 2/2, Roper 2/2.
Sin bin: Roper (23) - ball stealing; Farrell (51) - fighting.
DRAGONS: 1 Wayne Green; 2 Dean Colton; 3 Alex Muff; 4 PJ Solomon; 5 Marlon Billy; 6 Graham Holroyd; 7 Chris Hough; 8 Gareth Handford; 9 Craig Cook; 10 Andy Fisher; 11 Peter Green; 12 Craig Lawton; 13 Shaun Leaf. Subs (all used): 14 Carl Stannard; 15 James Walker; 16 Matt Walker; 17 Liam Brentley.
Tries: Muff (18), Cook (34), Colton (43), Solomon (56), Billy (73), Leaf (61); **Goals:** Holroyd 7/9.
Sin bin: M Walker (51) - fighting.
Rugby Leaguer & League Express Men of the Match:
Halifax: Rikki Sheriffe; *Dragons:* Graham Holroyd.
Penalty count: 7-7; **Half-time:** 2-14;
Referee: Russell Smith (Castleford); **Attendance:** 2,290.

HULL KINGSTON ROVERS 56 KEIGHLEY COUGARS 6

ROVERS: 1 Lynton Stott; 2 Craig Farrell; 3 Nick Pinkney; 4 Matt Calland; 5 Alasdair McClarron; 6 Paul Mansson; 7 Scott Thorburn; 8 Jamie Bovill; 9 Paul Pickering; 10 Jon Aston; 11 Dale Holdstock; 12 Andy Smith; 13 Anthony Seibold. Subs (all used): 14 Phil Hasty; 15 Jimmy Walker; 16 Makali Aizue; 17 Adam Sullivan.
Tries: McClarron (4, 10, 14, 73), Farrell (22), Thorburn (25), Stott (44), Hasty (49, 57), Smith (60);
Goals: Stott 8/10.
COUGARS: 1 James Rushforth; 2 Karl Smith; 3 David Foster; 4 Chris Wainwright; 5 Andy Robinson; 6 Adam Mitchell; 7 Matt Firth; 8 Phil Stephenson; 9 Simeon Hoyle; 10 Chris Parker; 11 Matthew Steel; 12 Lee Patterson; 13 Craig McDowell. Subs (all used): 14 Craig Nipperess; 15 Chris Wainwright; 16 Jason Clegg; 17 Danny Ekis.
Try: Hoyle (67); **Goals:** Mitchell 1/1.
Rugby Leaguer & League Express Men of the Match:
Rovers: Alasdair McClarron; *Cougars:* Adam Mitchell.
Penalty count: 6-6; **Half-time:** 30-0;
Referee: Robert Connolly (Wigan)- replaced (35) by Peter Brooke (Hull); **Attendance:** 2,383.

OLDHAM 50 FEATHERSTONE ROVERS 24

OLDHAM: 1 Gavin Dodd; 2 Will Cowell; 3 James Bunyan; 4 Jon Goddard; 5 Nick Johnson; 6 Neil Roden; 7 Ian Watson; 8 Steve Molloy; 9 Keith Brennan; 10 Paul Southern; 11 Lee Doran; 12 Dane Morgan; 13 Lee Marsh. Subs (all used): 14 Gareth Barber; 15 Simon Svabic; 16 Martin McLoughlin; 17 Martin Elswood.
Tries: Bunyan (4, 17, 25, 33), Dodd (9, 20), Goddard (41), Roden (48), Cowell (66); **Goals:** L Marsh 7/11.
ROVERS: 1 Ben Archibald; 2 Jamie Stokes; 3 Steve Dooler; 4 Richard Newlove; 5 Matthew Wray; 6 Jon Presley; 7 Carl Briggs; 8 Ian Tonks; 9 Richard Chapman; 10 Stuart Dickens; 11 Paul Darley; 12 Bryan Henare; 13 Adam Hayes. Subs (all used): 14 James Ford; 15 Richard Blakeway; 16 Neil Lowe; 17 Andy Jarrett.
Tries: Lowe (23), Chapman (31), Blakeway (40), Presley (51, 58); **Goals:** Briggs 2/5.
Sin bin: Chapman (44) - professional foul.
On report: Newlove (74) - high tackle.
Rugby Leaguer & League Express Men of the Match:
Oldham: James Bunyan; *Rovers:* Jon Presley.
Penalty count: 8-9; **Half-time:** 32-16;
Referee: Mike Dawber (Wigan); **Attendance:** 1,320.

WHITEHAVEN 31 LEIGH CENTURIONS 24

WHITEHAVEN: 1 Gary Broadbent; 2 Wesley Wilson; 3 Mick Nanyn; 4 David Seeds; 5 Paul O'Neil; 6 Lee Kiddie; 7 Sam Obst; 8 David Fatialofa; 9 Aaron Lester; 10 Dean Vaughan; 11 Brett McDermott; 12 Howard Hill; 13 Craig Walsh. Subs (all used): 14 Chris McKinney; 15 Carl Sice; 16 Craig Chambers; 17 Spencer Miller.
Tries: O'Neil (13, 67), McDermott (17), Hill (39), Sice (54); **Goals:** Nanyn 5/6; **Field goal:** Sice.
CENTURIONS: 1 Neil Turley; 2 Steve Maden; 3 Dan Potter; 4 Chris Percival; 5 Mark McCully; 6 Radney Bowker; 7 John Duffy; 8 Simon Knox; 9 Paul Rowley; 10 Heath Cruckshank; 11 David Larder; 12 Oliver Wilkes; 13 Ian Knott. Subs (all used): 14 Dave McConnell; 15 David Alstead; 16 Andrew Isherwood; 17 David Bradbury.
Tries: Percival (6, 59), Alstead (63), Wilkes (70);
Goals: Turley 4/5.
Sin bin: Rowley (63) - dissent.
Rugby Leaguer & League Express Men of the Match:
Whitehaven: Gary Broadbent; *Centurions:* Ian Knott.
Penalty count: 6-6; **Half-time:** 20-8; **Referee:** Colin Morris (Huddersfield); **Attendance:** 2,104.

WEEK 2

Sunday 18th April 2004

DONCASTER DRAGONS 27
HULL KINGSTON ROVERS 14

DRAGONS: 1 Wayne Green; 2 Dean Colton; 3 Alex Muff; 4 PJ Solomon; 5 Marlon Billy; 6 Graham Holroyd; 7 Chris Hough; 8 Gareth Handford; 9 Craig Cook; 10 Andy Fisher; 11 Martin Ostler; 12 Peter Green; 13 Craig Lawton. Subs (all used): 14 Carl Stannard; 15 James Walker; 16 Matt Walker; 17 Shaun Leaf.
Tries: Colton (24), Cook (43, 50), Lawton (52);
Goals: Holroyd 5/7; **Field goal:** Hough.
Sin bin: Fisher (18) - dissent.
ROVERS: 1 Lynton Stott; 2 Craig Farrell; 3 Nick Pinkney; 4 Matt Calland; 5 Alasdair McClarron; 6 Paul Mansson; 7 Scott Thorburn; 8 Jamie Bovill; 9 Paul Pickering; 10 Jon Aston; 11 Dale Holdstock; 12 Andy Smith; 13 Anthony Seibold. Subs (all used): 14 Phil Hasty; 15 Adam Sullivan; 16 Makali Aizue; 17 Frank Watene.
Tries: Farrell (11), Aizue (41); **Goals:** Stott 3/3.
Rugby Leaguer & League Express Men of the Match:
Dragons: Graham Holroyd; *Rovers:* Frank Watene.
Penalty count: 6-4; **Half-time:** 11-8; **Referee:** Colin Morris (Huddersfield); **Attendance:** 1,302.

HALIFAX 6 OLDHAM 25

HALIFAX: 1 Simon Grix; 2 Rikki Sheriffe; 3 Chris Norman; 4 Alan Hadcroft; 5 Richard Smith; 6 Pat Weisner; 7 Mark Moxon; 8 Anthony Farrell; 9 Phil Cantillon; 10 David Bates; 11 Jamie Bloem; 12 Chris Morley; 13 Jon Roper. Subs (all used): 14 Ged Corcoran; 15 Scott Law; 16 Jaymes Chapman; 17 Paul Davidson.
Try: Moxon (22); **Goals:** Bloem 1/1.
OLDHAM: 1 Jon Goddard; 2 Will Cowell; 3 James Bunyan; 4 Pat Rich; 5 Nick Johnson; 6 Neil Roden; 7 Ian Watson; 8 Steve Molloy; 9 Keith Brennan; 10 Paul Southern; 11 Lee Doran; 12 Dane Morgan; 13 Phil Farrell. Subs (all used): 14 Gareth Barber; 15 Martin McLoughlin; 16 Gavin Johnson; 17 Martin Elswood.
Tries: Roden (11, 70), Brennan (74); **Goals:** Rich 6/6;
Field goal: Watson.
Rugby Leaguer & League Express Men of the Match:
Halifax: Richard Smith; *Oldham:* Ian Watson.
Penalty count: 10-10; **Half-time:** 6-12; **Referee:** Steve Nicholson (Whitehaven); **Attendance:** 1,807.

KEIGHLEY COUGARS 22 BATLEY BULLDOGS 39

COUGARS: 1 Matt Foster; 2 Karl Smith; 3 David Foster; 4 Chris Wainwright; 5 Andy Robinson; 6 Adam Mitchell; 7 Matt Firth; 8 Phil Stephenson; 9 Simeon Hoyle; 10 Danny Ekis; 11 Matthew Steel; 12 Chris Parker; 13 Craig McDowell. Subs: 14 Craig Nipperess; 15 Max Tomlinson (not used); 16 Jason Clegg; 17 Chris Roe.
Tries: M Foster (19, 45, 70); **Goals:** Mitchell 5/5.
BULLDOGS: 1 Mark Sibson; 2 Chris Spurr; 3 Shad Royston; 4 Danny Maun; 5 Adrian Flynn; 6 Mark Toohey; 7 Barry Eaton; 8 Steve Hill; 9 Andy Heptinstall; 10 David Rourke; 11 Sean Richardson; 12 Andy Spink; 13 Ryan Horsley. Subs (all used): 14 Adrian Leek; 15 Paul Harrison; 16 Joe Berry; 17 Will Cartledge.
Tries: Horsley (5), Sibson (9, 52), Flynn (22), Eaton (56), Spink (64), Horsley (78); **Goals:** Eaton 5/7;
Field goal: Heptinstall.
Rugby Leaguer & League Express Men of the Match:
Cougars: Matt Foster; *Bulldogs:* Barry Eaton.
Penalty count: 6-5; **Half-time:** 10-19;
Referee: Mike Dawber (Wigan); **Attendance:** 1,282.

LEIGH CENTURIONS 50 FEATHERSTONE ROVERS 12

CENTURIONS: 1 Neil Turley; 2 Steve Maden; 3 Danny Halliwell; 4 Chris Percival; 5 Damian Munro; 6 John Duffy; 7 Tommy Martyn; 8 Paul Norman; 9 Dave McConnell; 10 David Bradbury; 11 Andrew Isherwood; 12 Oliver Wilkes; 13 Radney Bowker. Subs (all used): 14 Dan Potter; 15 Simon Knox; 16 David Alstead; 17 Heath Cruckshank.
Tries: Martyn (17), Knox (21, 39), Isherwood (24), Percival (41), Bowker (52, 60), Maden (59, 63);
Goals: Turley 7/9.
ROVERS: 1 Nathan Batty; 2 Jamie Stokes; 3 Steve Dooler; 4 Richard Newlove; 5 Matthew Wray; 6 Jon Presley; 7 Carl Briggs; 8 Ian Tonks; 9 Paul Darley; 10 Stuart Dickens; 11 Neil Lowe; 12 Richard Blakeway; 13 Adam Hayes. Subs (all used): 14 James Ford; 15 Bryan Henare; 16 Andy Jarrett; 17 Richard Chapman.
Tries: Stokes (30), Newlove (47); **Goals:** Briggs 2/3.
Rugby Leaguer & League Express Men of the Match:
Centurions: Dave McConnell; *Rovers:* Stuart Dickens.
Penalty count: 12-17; **Half-time:** 22-6; **Referee:** Ronnie Laughton (Barnsley); **Attendance:** 1,790.

ROCHDALE HORNETS 12 WHITEHAVEN 46

HORNETS: 1 Michael Platt; 2 Liam Williams; 3 Paul Anderson; 4 Dave Cunliffe; 5 Lepani Soro; 6 Lee Birdseye; 7 Liam McGovern; 8 Andy Leathem; 9 Janan Billings; 10 Tommy Hodgkinson; 11 Andy Gorski; 12 Gareth Price; 13 Darren Shaw. Subs (all used): 14 John Braddish; 15 Rob Ball; 16 Tony Kirwan; 17 Lee Hansen.
Tries: Platt (37), Birdseye (58); **Goals:** Birdseye 2/2.
Sin bin: Anderson (14) - professional foul.
WHITEHAVEN: 1 Wesley Wilson; 2 Mark Wallace; 3 David Seeds; 4 Mick Nanyn; 5 Paul O'Neil; 6 Lee Kiddie; 7 Sam Obst; 8 Dean Vaughan; 9 Aaron Lester; 10 David Fatialofa; 11 Craig Chambers; 12 Howard Hill; 13 Craig Walsh. Subs (all used): 14 Carl Sice; 15 Spencer Miller; 16 Garry Purdham; 17 Chris McKinney.
Tries: Seeds (5), Nanyn (17, 28), Obst (21, 47), O'Neil (25), Walsh (55), Sice (70), Kiddie (74); **Goals:** Nanyn 5/9.
Sin bin: Walsh (68) - holding down.
Rugby Leaguer & League Express Men of the Match:
Hornets: Darren Shaw; *Whitehaven:* Sam Obst.
Penalty count: 8-6; **Half-time:** 6-26;
Referee: Ashley Klein (London); **Attendance:** 702.

WEEK 3

Sunday 2nd May 2004

BATLEY BULLDOGS 28 DONCASTER DRAGONS 20

BULLDOGS: 1 Mark Sibson; 2 Matt Bramald; 3 Shad Royston; 4 Danny Maun; 5 Adrian Flynn; 6 Adrian Leek; 7 Barry Eaton; 8 Steve Hill; 9 Andy Heptinstall; 10 David Rourke; 11 Sean Richardson; 12 Andy Spink; 13 Ryan Horsley. Subs (all used): 14 Will Cartledge; 15 Paul Harrison; 16 Chris Molyneux; 17 Tim Spears.
Tries: Hill (11), Spink (18), Sibson (26), Flynn (39), Royston (64); **Goals:** Eaton 4/5.
DRAGONS: 1 Shaun Leaf; 2 Dean Colton; 3 Alex Muff; 4 PJ Solomon; 5 Marlon Billy; 6 Graham Holroyd; 7 Chris Hough; 8 Martin Ostler; 9 Craig Cook; 10 Andy Fisher; 11 Peter Green; 12 Gareth Lloyd; 13 Craig Lawton. Subs (all used): 14 Matt Walker; 15 James Walker; 16 Johnny Woodcock; 17 Craig Horne.
Tries: Leaf (6), Horne (44), Solomon (55), Billy (60);
Goals: Holroyd 2/4.
Rugby Leaguer & League Express Men of the Match:
Bulldogs: Shad Royston; *Dragons:* Peter Green.
Penalty count: 12-7; **Half-time:** 22-6;
Referee: Peter Taberner (Wigan); **Attendance:** 801.

FEATHERSTONE ROVERS 58 ROCHDALE HORNETS 12

ROVERS: 1 Nathan Batty; 2 Jamie Stokes; 3 Steve Dooler; 4 Freddie Zitter; 5 Matthew Wray; 6 Richard Blakeway; 7 Jon Presley; 8 Ian Tonks; 9 Paul Darley; 10 Stuart Dickens; 11 Bryan Henare; 12 Neil Lowe; 13 Adam Hayes. Subs (all used): 14 Carl Briggs; 15 Richard Chapman; 16 Andy Jarrett; 17 James Ford.
Tries: Zitter (8, 31), Stokes (14, 78), Hayes (21), Batty (27, 53), Blakeway (42), Dooler (64), Wray (74);
Goals: Dickens 9/12.
HORNETS: 1 Michael Platt; 2 Liam Williams; 3 Paul Anderson; 4 Dave Cunliffe; 5 Lepani Soro; 6 Lee Birdseye; 7 Liam McGovern; 8 Andy Leathem; 9 Darren Robinson; 10 Lee Hansen; 11 Andy Gorski; 12 Dave Newton; 13 Darren Shaw. Subs (all used): 14 Sam Butterworth; 15 John Braddish; 16 Janan Billings; 17 Tommy Hodgkinson.
Tries: Cunliffe (17), Butterworth (79); **Goals:** Birdseye 2/2.
Rugby Leaguer & League Express Men of the Match:
Rovers: Stuart Dickens; *Hornets:* Lee Birdseye.
Penalty count: 12-10; **Half-time:** 32-6; **Referee:** Gareth Hewer (Whitehaven); **Attendance:** 1,098.

HULL KINGSTON ROVERS 28 HALIFAX 18

ROVERS: 1 Craig Poucher; 2 Lynton Stott; 3 Paul Parker; 4 Matt Calland; 5 Alasdair McClarron; 6 Paul Mansson; 7 Phil Hasty; 8 Jamie Bovill; 9 Andy Ellis; 10 Jon Aston; 11 Dale Holdstock; 12 Andy Smith; 13 Anthony Seibold. Subs (all used): 14 Nick Pinkney; 15 Adam Sullivan; 16 Frank Watene; 17 Paul Fletcher.
Tries: Poucher (2), Hasty (9), Holdstock (28), Mansson (42); **Goals:** Stott 6/10.
Sin bin: Seibold (25) - interference.
HALIFAX: 1 Danny Arnold; 2 Chris Norman; 3 Jamie Bloem; 4 Simon Grix; 5 Rikki Sheriffe; 6 Jon Roper; 7 Pat Weisner; 8 Anthony Farrell; 9 Phil Cantillon; 10 Chris Birchall; 11 Paul Davidson; 12 Ged Corcoran; 13 Wayne Corcoran. Subs (all used): 14 Mark Moxon; 15 Jaymes Chapman; 16 Ryan McDonald; 17 David Bates.
Tries: Simon Grix (20), Arnold (54), Sheriffe (57);
Goals: Bloem 3/6.
Rugby Leaguer & League Express Men of the Match:
Rovers: Phil Hasty; *Halifax:* Pat Weisner.
Penalty count: 8-8; **Half-time:** 20-8; **Referee:** Ronnie Laughton (Barnsley); **Attendance:** 2,393.

OLDHAM 20 LEIGH CENTURIONS 60

OLDHAM: 1 Gavin Dodd; 2 Will Cowell; 3 Lee Marsh; 4 Pat Rich; 5 Nick Johnson; 6 Simon Svabic; 7 Ian Watson; 8 Steve Molloy; 9 Keith Brennan; 10 Martin McLoughlin; 11 Lee Doran; 12 Dane Morgan; 13 Phil Farrell. Subs (all used): 14 Gareth Barber; 15 Craig Farrimond; 16 Martin Elswood; 17 Adam Sharples.
Tries: N Johnson (9, 45), Farrimond (59), Farrell (69);
Goals: Rich 2/7.
Dismissals: Morgan (26) - punching;
Watson (65) - head-butt.
CENTURIONS: 1 Neil Turley; 2 Steve Maden; 3 Dan Potter; 4 Chris Percival; 5 Danny Halliwell; 6 John Duffy; 7 Tommy Martyn; 8 Richard Marshall; 9 Paul Rowley; 10 Oliver Wilkes; 11 David Larder; 12 Radney Bowker; 13 Ian Knott. Subs (all used): 14 Willie Swann; 15 Dave McConnell; 16 Simon Knox; 17 Heath Cruckshank.
Tries: Duffy (3, 50), Marshall (24), Turley (37), Martyn (39), Percival (54, 56), Swann (75), Bowker (78), Maden (80); **Goals:** Turley 10/10.

Rugby Leaguer & League Express Men of the Match: *Oldham:* Phil Farrell; *Centurions:* Ian Knott.
Penalty count: 12-5; **Half-time:** 8-24; **Referee:** Colin Morris (Huddersfield); **Attendance:** 2,104.

WHITEHAVEN 38 KEIGHLEY COUGARS 6

WHITEHAVEN: 1 Wesley Wilson; 2 Jamie Marshall; 3 Mick Nanyn; 4 Howard Hill; 5 Paul O'Neil; 6 Lee Kiddie; 7 Sam Obst; 8 Dean Vaughan; 9 Aaron Lester; 10 David Fatialofa; 11 Brett McDermott; 12 Craig Chambers; 13 Craig Walsh. Subs (all used): 14 Carl Sice; 15 Graeme Morton; 16 Spencer Miller; 17 Chris McKinney.
Tries: Walsh (7, 78), Obst (15), Lester (63), Morton (70), Sice (76); **Goals:** Nanyn 7/8.
Sin bin: Chambers (66) - fighting.
COUGARS: 1 Chris Beever; 2 Karl Smith; 3 Chris Wainwright; 4 Matt Foster; 5 Andy Robinson; 6 Craig Nipperess; 7 Matt Firth; 8 Phil Stephenson; 9 Simeon Hoyle; 10 Jason Clegg; 11 David Foster; 12 Chris Parker; 13 Craig McDowell. Subs (all used): 14 Adam Mitchell; 15 Adam Webster; 16 Eddie Wilson; 17 Chris Roe.
Try: Robinson (19); **Goals:** Nipperess 1/1.
Sin bin: Wainwright (45) - dissent; Roe (66) - fighting.
Rugby Leaguer & League Express Men of the Match: *Whitehaven:* Craig Walsh; *Cougars:* Craig McDowell.
Penalty count: 11-8; **Half-time:** 14-6;
Referee: Ben Thaler (Wakefield); **Attendance:** 1,160.

WEEK 4

Sunday 9th May 2004

DONCASTER DRAGONS 31 WHITEHAVEN 24

DRAGONS: 1 Johnny Woodcock; 2 Dean Colton; 3 Alex Muff; 4 PJ Solomon; 5 Marlon Billy; 6 Graham Holroyd; 7 Chris Hough; 8 Martin Ostler; 9 Craig Cook; 10 Andy Fisher; 11 Peter Green; 12 Gareth Lloyd; 13 Craig Lawton. Subs (all used): 14 Carl Stannard; 15 James Walker; 16 Matt Walker; 17 Craig Horne.
Tries: Woodcock (5), Billy (9), Holroyd (26), Cook (64), M Walker (69); **Goals:** Holroyd 3/5, Woodcock 2/2.
Field goal: Hough.
Sin bin: Holroyd (60) – kicking the ball away.
WHITEHAVEN: 1 Wesley Wilson; 2 Jamie Marshall; 3 Brett McDermott; 4 Mick Nanyn; 5 Paul O'Neil; 6 Lee Kiddie; 7 Sam Obst; 8 Dean Vaughan; 9 Aaron Lester; 10 David Fatialofa; 11 Howard Hill; 12 Spencer Miller; 13 Craig Walsh. Subs (all used): 14 Carl Sice; 15 Leroy Joe; 16 Craig Chambers; 17 Graeme Morton.
Tries: McDermott (13), Obst (16), Nanyn (38), Marshall (52), O'Neil (55); **Goals:** Nanyn 2/6.
Dismissal: McDermott (25) – use of the elbow.
Rugby Leaguer & League Express Men of the Match: *Dragons:* Andy Fisher; *Whitehaven:* Aaron Lester.
Penalty count: 7-7; **Half-time:** 17-16; **Referee:** Karl Kirkpatrick (Warrington); **Attendance:** 853.

HALIFAX 24 BATLEY BULLDOGS 14

HALIFAX: 1 Danny Arnold; 2 Rikki Sheriffe; 3 Ben Feehan; 4 Simon Grix; 5 James Haley; 6 Jon Roper; 7 Pat Weisner; 8 Anthony Farrell; 9 Phil Cantillon; 10 Chris Birchall; 11 Paul Davidson; 12 Ged Corcoran; 13 Jamie Bloem. Subs (all used): 14 Mark Moxon; 15 Wayne Corcoran; 16 Ryan McDonald; 17 David Bates.
Tries: G Corcoran (20), Simon Grix (31, 55), Sheriffe (60), Davidson (70); **Goals:** Bloem 2/6.
BULLDOGS: 1 Mark Sibson; 2 Matt Bramald; 3 Chris Spurr; 4 Tim Spears; 5 Adrian Flynn; 6 Mark Toohey; 7 Barry Eaton; 8 Chris Molyneux; 9 Andy Heptinstall; 10 Steve Hill; 11 Sean Richardson; 12 Andy Spink; 13 Ryan Horsley. Subs (all used): 14 Mark Cass; 15 Paul Harrison; 16 Adrian Leek; 17 Will Cartledge.
Tries: Spink (28), Toohey (68), Spurr (78);
Goals: Eaton 1/3.
Rugby Leaguer & League Express Men of the Match: *Halifax:* Paul Davidson; *Bulldogs:* Andy Spink.
Penalty count: 6-3; **Half-time:** 12-4; **Referee:** Colin Morris (Huddersfield); **Attendance:** 2,155.

HULL KINGSTON ROVERS 29 OLDHAM 22

ROVERS: 1 Craig Poucher; 2 Lynton Stott; 3 Paul Parker; 4 Matt Calland; 5 Alasdair McClarron; 6 Paul Mansson; 7 Phil Hasty; 8 Jamie Bovill; 9 Paul Pickering; 10 Makali Aizue; 11 Dale Holdstock; 12 Jon Aston; 13 Anthony Seibold. Subs (all used): 14 Nick Pinkney; 15 Dean Andrews; 16 Frank Watene; 17 Paul Fletcher.
Tries: McClarron (10), Mansson (24, 41), Calland (45), Pinkney (75); **Goals:** Stott 4/9; **Field goal:** Mansson.
On report: Mansson (16) - use of the elbow.
OLDHAM: 1 Jon Goddard; 2 Gavin Dodd; 3 James Bunyan; 4 Pat Rich; 5 Nick Johnson; 6 Gareth Barber; 7 Ian Watson; 8 Steve Molloy; 9 Keith Brennan; 10 Martin McLoughlin; 11 Lee Doran; 12 Dane Morgan; 13 Phil Farrell. Subs (all used): 14 Simon Svabic; 15 Craig Farrimond; 16 Martin Elswood; 17 Adam Sharples.
Tries: Morgan (4, 20), Farrell (61); **Goals:** Rich 5/5.
Rugby Leaguer & League Express Men of the Match: *Rovers:* Paul Mansson; *Oldham:* Ian Watson.
Penalty count: 10-8; **Half-time:** 10-14;
Referee: Ben Thaler (Wakefield); **Attendance:** 2,121.

KEIGHLEY COUGARS 42 FEATHERSTONE ROVERS 18

COUGARS: 1 Chris Beever; 2 Karl Smith; 3 Chris Wainwright; 4 Matt Foster; 5 Andy Robinson; 6 Craig Nipperess; 7 Matt Firth; 8 Phil Stephenson; 9 Simeon Hoyle; 10 Jason Clegg; 11 David Foster; 12 Chris Parker; 13 Craig McDowell. Subs (all used): 14 Adam Webster; 15 Adam Mitchell; 16 Eddie Wilson; 17 Chris Roe.
Tries: Wilson (18, 37), M Foster (67, 76), Clegg (73), Hoyle (79); **Goals:** Nipperess 9/11.
ROVERS: 1 Nathan Batty; 2 Jamie Stokes; 3 Steve Dooler; 4 Freddie Zitter; 5 Matthew Wray; 6 Richard Blakeway; 7 Jon Presley; 8 Ian Tonks; 9 Paul Darley; 10 Stuart Dickens; 11 Bryan Henare; 12 Neil Lowe; 13 Adam Hayes. Subs (all used): 14 Dale Cardoza; 15 Richard Chapman; 16 Andy Jarrett; 17 Brian Sutton.
Tries: Cardoza (23, 45), Blakeway (64);
Goals: Dickens 3/3.
Sin bin: Cardoza (31) - interference.
Rugby Leaguer & League Express Men of the Match: *Cougars:* Jason Clegg; *Rovers:* Stuart Dickens.
Penalty count: 15-3; **Half-time:** 18-6;
Referee: Peter Taberner (Wigan); **Attendance:** 1,251.

ROCHDALE HORNETS 24 LEIGH CENTURIONS 74

HORNETS: 1 Michael Platt; 2 Liam Williams; 3 Andy Gorski; 4 Dave Cunliffe; 5 Komai Naulumata; 6 Lee Birdseye; 7 John Braddish; 8 Andy Leathem; 9 Janan Billings; 10 Tommy Hodgkinson; 11 Kris Ratcliffe; 12 Dave Newton; 13 Darren Shaw. Subs (all used): 14 Sam Butterworth; 15 Rob Ball; 16 Darren Robinson; 17 Mark Costello.
Tries: Butterworth (47), Cunliffe (57), Naulumata (62), Gorski (80); **Goals:** Birdseye 4/4.
CENTURIONS: 1 Neil Turley; 2 Steve Maden; 3 Dan Potter; 4 Chris Percival; 5 Gary Rourke; 6 John Duffy; 7 Tommy Martyn; 8 Simon Knox; 9 Paul Rowley; 10 Richard Marshall; 11 David Larder; 12 Oliver Wilkes; 13 Ian Knott. Subs (all used): 14 Dave McConnell; 15 Heath Cruckshank; 16 Willie Swann; 17 Andrew Isherwood.
Tries: Percival (3, 22, 34), Potter (13), Knox (15), Knott (20, 28), Rowley (38), Cruckshank (51), McConnell (65), Turley (70, 78), Martyn (73); **Goals:** Turley 11/13.
Rugby Leaguer & League Express Men of the Match: *Hornets:* Michael Platt; *Centurions:* Tommy Martyn.
Penalty count: 6-5; **Half-time:** 0-46;
Referee: Mike Dawber (Wigan); **Attendance:** 1,303.

WEEK 5

Sunday 23rd May 2004

BATLEY BULLDOGS 34 HULL KINGSTON ROVERS 28

BULLDOGS: 1 Mark Sibson; 2 Steve Beard; 3 Chris Spurr; 4 Danny Maun; 5 Matt Bramald; 6 Mark Toohey; 7 Barry Eaton; 8 Steve Hill; 9 Andy Heptinstall; 10 David Rourke; 11 Tim Spears; 12 Andy Spink; 13 Ryan Horsley. Subs (all used): 14 Danny Thomas; 15 Paul Harrison; 16 Chris Molyneux; 17 Sean Richardson.
Tries: Hill (16), Spink (30, 42), Richardson (35), Sibson (50), Eaton (60); **Goals:** Eaton 5/6.
ROVERS: 1 Craig Poucher; 2 Craig Farrell; 3 Paul Parker; 4 Matt Calland; 5 Alasdair McClarron; 6 Paul Mansson; 7 Scott Thorburn; 8 Jamie Bovill; 9 Paul Pickering; 10 Makali Aizue; 11 Jon Aston; 12 Andy Smith; 13 Anthony Seibold. Subs (all used): 14 Nick Pinkney; 15 Jimmy Walker; 16 Frank Watene; 17 Paul Fletcher.
Tries: Mansson (14), Calland (55), Aston (67), Farrell (72), Pinkney (78); **Goals:** Thorburn 4/6.
Rugby Leaguer & League Express Men of the Match: *Bulldogs:* Barry Eaton; *Rovers:* Paul Mansson.
Penalty count: 7-7; **Half-time:** 18-8; **Referee:** Steve Nicholson (Whitehaven); **Attendance:** 1,211.

FEATHERSTONE ROVERS 44 DONCASTER DRAGONS 18

ROVERS: 1 Nathan Batty; 2 Matthew Wray; 3 Dale Cardoza; 4 Richard Newlove; 5 Freddie Zitter; 6 Richard Blakeway; 7 Jon Presley; 8 Ian Tonks; 9 Richard Chapman; 10 Stuart Dickens; 11 Steve Dooler; 12 Andy Jarrett; 13 Paul Darley. Subs (all used): 14 Jamie Stokes; 15 Dean Ripley; 16 Neil Lowe; 17 Adam Hayes.
Tries: Stokes (9), Newlove (31), Blakeway (38), Lowe (45), Wray (49), Ripley (55), Chapman (73), Zitter (77);
Goals: Dickens 6/12.
Sin bin: Tonks (55) - pushing.
DRAGONS: 1 Johnny Woodcock; 2 Dean Colton; 3 Alex Muff; 4 PJ Solomon; 5 Marlon Billy; 6 Graham Holroyd; 7 Chris Hough; 8 James Walker; 9 Craig Cook; 10 Andy Fisher; 11 Martin Ostler; 12 Peter Green; 13 Craig Lawton. Subs (all used): 14 Matt Walker; 15 Carl Stannard; 16 Craig Horne; 17 Shaun Leaf.
Tries: Holroyd (23, 52), Colton (28, 61);
Goals: Holroyd 1/5.
Dismissals: Solomon (15) - high tackle;
M Walker (73) - punching.
Sin bin: Colton (44) - obstruction,
and (71) - professional foul.
On report: M Walker (39) - off the ball incident.
Rugby Leaguer & League Express Men of the Match: *Rovers:* Stuart Dickens; *Dragons:* Andy Fisher.
Penalty count: 10-10; **Half-time:** 16-10;
Referee: Ben Thaler (Wakefield); **Attendance:** 1,418.

LEIGH CENTURIONS 30 KEIGHLEY COUGARS 12

CENTURIONS: 1 Neil Turley; 2 David Alstead; 3 Dan Potter; 4 Danny Halliwell; 5 Gary Rourke; 6 John Duffy; 7 Tommy Martyn; 8 Richard Marshall; 9 Paul Rowley; 10 Paul Norman; 11 Dave McConnell; 12 Oliver Wilkes; 13 Ian Knott. Subs (all used): 14 Andrew Isherwood; 15 Rob Smyth; 16 Radney Bowker; 17 Heath Cruckshank.
Tries: Rourke (12), Halliwell (24), Knott (26, 53), Martyn (43), Rowley (59); **Goals:** Turley 3/6.
COUGARS: 1 Chris Beever; 2 Karl Smith; 3 Chris Wainwright; 4 Matt Foster; 5 Andy Robinson; 6 Craig Nipperess; 7 Matt Firth; 8 Phil Stephenson; 9 Simeon Hoyle; 10 Jason Clegg; 11 Chris Parker; 12 David Foster; 13 Craig McDowell. Subs (all used): 14 Adam Mitchell; 15 Eddie Wilson; 16 Danny Ekis; 17 Richard Mervill.
Tries: Parker (17), Clegg (80); **Goals:** Nipperess 2/2.
Sin bin: Smith (50) - interference.
Rugby Leaguer & League Express Men of the Match: *Centurions:* Ian Knott; *Cougars:* Craig McDowell.
Penalty count: 7-10; **Half-time:** 16-6; **Referee:** Gareth Hewer (Whitehaven); **Attendance:** 1,683.

OLDHAM 26 ROCHDALE HORNETS 24

OLDHAM: 1 Jon Goddard; 2 Gavin Dodd; 3 James Bunyan; 4 Pat Rich; 5 Nick Johnson; 6 Gareth Barber; 7 Neil Roden; 8 Steve Molloy; 9 Keith Brennan; 10 Martin McLoughlin; 11 Lee Doran; 12 Dane Morgan; 13 Phil Farrell. Subs (all used): 14 John Hough; 15 Simon Svabic; 16 Martin Elswood; 17 Danny Nanyn.
Tries: Roden (26), Goddard (61, 64, 67), Svabic (73);
Goals: Rich 3/7.
Sin bin: Molloy (49) - holding down.
HORNETS: 1 Michael Platt; 2 Liam Williams; 3 Mark McCully; 4 Dave Cunliffe; 5 Chris Campbell; 6 Lee Birdseye; 7 John Braddish; 8 Rob Ball; 9 Darren Robinson; 10 Gareth Price; 11 Andy Gorski; 12 Dave Newton; 13 Darren Shaw. Subs (all used): 14 Janan Billings; 15 Kris Ratcliffe; 16 Sam Butterworth; 17 Mark Costello.
Tries: Platt (30), Gorski (34), Price (37), Robinson (45);
Goals: Birdseye 4/7.
Sin bin: McCully (59) - holding down.
Rugby Leaguer & League Express Men of the Match: *Oldham:* Dane Morgan; *Hornets:* Gareth Price.
Penalty count: 15-9; **Half-time:** 6-18; **Referee:** Richard Silverwood (Dewsbury); **Attendance:** 1,243.

WHITEHAVEN 34 HALIFAX 8

WHITEHAVEN: 1 Wesley Wilson; 2 Jamie Marshall; 3 David Seeds; 4 Mick Nanyn; 5 Paul O'Neil; 6 Leroy Joe; 7 Sam Obst; 8 Dean Vaughan; 9 Aaron Lester; 10 David Fatialofa; 11 Howard Hill; 12 Graeme Morton; 13 Craig Walsh. Subs (all used): 14 Carl Sice; 15 Spencer Miller; 16 Marc Jackson; 17 Tony Cunningham.
Tries: Seeds (15), Marshall (36), Obst (58), Walsh (61, 80), Lester (68), Nanyn (71); **Goals:** Nanyn 3/7.
HALIFAX: 1 Danny Arnold; 2 Rikki Sheriffe; 3 Matt Whitaker; 4 Simon Grix; 5 James Haley; 6 Jon Roper; 7 Pat Weisner; 8 Ryan McDonald; 9 Phil Cantillon; 10 Chris Birchall; 11 Paul Davidson; 12 Ged Corcoran; 13 Jamie Bloem. Subs (all used): 14 Mark Moxon; 15 Ben Feehan; 16 David Bates; 17 Wayne Corcoran.
Try: Sheriffe (75); **Goals:** Bloem 2/3.
Rugby Leaguer & League Express Men of the Match: *Whitehaven:* Aaron Lester; *Halifax:* Paul Davidson.
Penalty count: 4-12; **Half-time:** 10-2; **Referee:** Colin Morris (Huddersfield); **Attendance:** 1,648.

WEEK 6

Sunday 30th May 2004

DONCASTER DRAGONS 19 LEIGH CENTURIONS 14

DRAGONS: 1 Johnny Woodcock; 2 Dean Colton; 3 Craig Horne; 4 PJ Solomon; 5 Marlon Billy; 6 Graham Holroyd; 7 Sean Leaf; 8 Matt Walker; 9 Craig Cook; 10 Andy Fisher; 11 Martin Ostler; 12 Peter Green; 13 Craig Lawton. Subs (all used): 14 Carl Stannard; 15 James Walker; 16 Chris Hough; 17 Alex Muff.
Tries: Holroyd (5), Solomon (18); **Goals:** Holroyd 5/6;
Field goal: Holroyd.
CENTURIONS: 1 Steve Maden; 2 Rob Smyth; 3 Dan Potter; 4 Danny Halliwell; 5 Damian Munro; 6 Radney Bowker; 7 Willie Swann; 8 Richard Marshall; 9 Paul Rowley; 10 Heath Cruckshank; 11 David Larder; 12 Oliver Wilkes; 13 Dave McConnell. Subs (all used): 14 David Alstead; 15 Andrew Isherwood; 16 Simon Knox; 17 Paul Norman.
Tries: Potter (35), Smyth (41), Maden (67);
Goals: Smyth 1/3.
Rugby Leaguer & League Express Men of the Match: *Dragons:* Graham Holroyd; *Centurions:* Oliver Wilkes.
Penalty count: 15-8; **Half-time:** 14-4;
Referee: Ashley Klein (London); **Attendance:** 1,140.

HALIFAX 20 FEATHERSTONE ROVERS 27

HALIFAX: 1 Danny Arnold; 2 Rikki Sheriffe; 3 Ben Feehan; 4 Jon Roper; 5 James Haley; 6 Pat Weisner; 7 Mark Moxon; 8 Ryan McDonald; 9 Phil Cantillon; 10 Chris Birchall; 11 Paul Davidson; 12 Matt Whitaker; 13 Jamie Bloem. Subs (all used): 14 Scott Grix; 15 Ged Corcoran; 16 David Bates; 17 Anthony Farrell.
Tries: Cantillon (8, 50), Farrell (47), Haley (71);
Goals: Bloem 2/4.
ROVERS: 1 Craig Moss; 2 Jamie Stokes; 3 Freddie Zitter; 4 Richard Newlove; 5 Matthew Wray; 6 Richard Blakeway; 7 Dean Ripley; 8 Ian Tonks; 9 Richard Chapman; 10 Stuart Dickens; 11 Steve Dooler; 12 Andy Jarrett; 13 Paul Darley. Subs (all used): 14 James Ford; 15 Lee Williamson; 16 Neil Lowe; 17 Adam Hayes.
Tries: Newlove (24), Wray (31, 63); **Goals:** Dickens 7/7;
Field goal: Blakeway.
Rugby Leaguer & League Express Men of the Match: *Halifax:* Phil Cantillon; *Rovers:* Stuart Dickens.
Penalty count: 8-13; **Half-time:** 6-18; **Referee:** Steve Nicholson (Whitehaven); **Attendance:** 1,760.

HULL KINGSTON ROVERS 12 WHITEHAVEN 26

ROVERS: 1 Craig Poucher; 2 Nick Pinkney; 3 Paul Parker; 4 Matt Calland; 5 Alasdair McClarron; 6 Paul Mansson; 7 Scott Thorburn; 8 Jamie Bovill; 9 Paul Pickering; 10 Makali Aizue; 11 Anthony Seibold; 12 Dean Andrews; 13 Andy Smith. Subs (all used): 14 Phil Hasty;

15 Tommy Gallagher; 16 Frank Watene; 17 Paul Fletcher.
Tries: Gallagher (23), Fletcher (65); **Goals:** Thorburn 2/2.
Dismissal: Bovill (9) - use of the elbow.
WHITEHAVEN: 1 Gary Broadbent; 2 Wesley Wilson; 3 David Seeds; 4 Mick Nanyn; 5 Paul O'Neil; 6 Leroy Joe; 7 Sam Obst; 8 Dean Vaughan; 9 Aaron Lester; 10 David Fatialofa; 11 Brett McDermott; 12 Graeme Morton; 13 Howard Hill. Subs (all used): 14 Spencer Miller; 15 Carl Sice; 16 Marc Jackson; 17 Tony Cunningham.
Tries: Fatialofa (27), Obst (34, 37); **Goals:** Nanyn 5/6;
Field goals: Obst 3, Joe.
Rugby Leaguer & League Express Men of the Match: *Rovers:* Paul Pickering; *Whitehaven:* Sam Obst.
Penalty count: 4-6; **Half-time:** 6-23;
Referee: Robert Connolly (Wigan); **Attendance:** 1,954.

KEIGHLEY COUGARS 32 ROCHDALE HORNETS 46

COUGARS: 1 James Rushforth; 2 Karl Smith; 3 Chris Wainwright; 4 Matt Foster; 5 Andy Robinson; 6 Craig Nipperess; 7 Matt Firth; 8 Phil Stephenson; 9 Simeon Hoyle; 10 Jason Clegg; 11 Chris Parker; 12 David Foster; 13 Craig McDowell. Subs (all used): 14 Adam Mitchell; 15 Eddie Wilson; 16 Chris Beever; 17 Richard Mervill.
Tries: Stephenson (18, 24), M Foster (28, 50), Hoyle (75), Nipperess (79); **Goals:** Nipperess 2/3, Mitchell 2/3.
Sin bin: Smith (14) - dissent.
HORNETS: 1 Sam Butterworth; 2 Liam Williams; 3 Mark McCully; 4 Dave Cunliffe; 5 Chris Campbell; 6 Lee Birdseye; 7 John Braddish; 8 Rob Ball; 9 Darren Robinson; 10 Gareth Price; 11 Andy Gorski; 12 Dave Newton; 13 Darren Shaw. Subs (all used): 14 Janan Billings; 15 Tommy Hodgkinson; 16 Andy Saywell; 17 Andy Leathem.
Tries: Robinson (5), Campbell (7, 46), Birdseye (11, 13, 71), Gorski (38), Cunliffe (42); **Goals:** Birdseye 7/10.
Sin bin: McCully (23) - off the ball tackle.
On report: Birdseye (31) - use of knees.
Rugby Leaguer & League Express Men of the Match: *Cougars:* Phil Stephenson; *Hornets:* Lee Birdseye.
Penalty count: 9-10; **Half-time:** 16-24;
Referee: Ben Thaler (Wakefield); **Attendance:** 1,041.

OLDHAM 20 BATLEY BULLDOGS 44

OLDHAM: 1 Jon Goddard; 2 Gavin Dodd; 3 Gareth Barber; 4 Pat Rich; 5 Nick Johnson; 6 Neil Roden; 7 Keith Brennan; 8 Dane Morgan; 9 John Hough; 10 Martin McLoughlin; 11 Lee Doran; 12 Phil Farrell; 13 Lee Marsh. Subs (all used): 14 Simon Svabic; 15 Martin Elswood; 16 Adam Clayton; 17 Chris Brett.
Tries: L Marsh (11, 24), Morgan (14); **Goals:** Rich 3/4;
Field goals: Brennan 2.
BULLDOGS: 1 Mark Sibson; 2 Bryn Powell; 3 Chris Spurr; 4 Danny Maun; 5 Adrian Flynn; 6 Mark Toohey; 7 Barry Eaton; 8 David Rourke; 9 Andy Heptinstall; 10 Steve Hill; 11 Tim Spears; 12 Andy Spink; 13 Ryan Horsley. Subs (all used): 14 Shad Royston; 15 Paul Harrison; 16 Chris Molyneux; 17 Sean Richardson.
Tries: Royston (34, 37), Harrison (40), Spurr (45), Powell (55, 69), Rourke (64), Horsley (80);
Goals: Eaton 6/9.
Rugby Leaguer & League Express Men of the Match: *Oldham:* Dane Morgan; *Bulldogs:* Barry Eaton.
Penalty count: 7-10; **Half-time:** 20-16;
Referee: Peter Taberner (Wigan);
Attendance: 1,541 *(at Bloomfield Road, Blackpool).*

WEEK 7

Sunday 13th June 2004

DONCASTER DRAGONS 38 ROCHDALE HORNETS 18

DRAGONS: 1 Johnny Woodcock; 2 Dean Colton; 3 Craig Horne; 4 PJ Solomon; 5 Marlon Billy; 6 Graham Holroyd; 7 Danny Grimshaw; 8 Gareth Handford; 9 Craig Cook; 10 Martin Ostler; 11 Craig Lawton; 12 Peter Green; 13 Shaun Leaf. Subs (all used): 14 Carl Sayer; 15 James Walker; 16 Chris Hough; 17 Alex Muff.
Tries: Handford (13), Cook (47), Ostler (60), Holroyd (62, 73), Colton (68); **Goals:** Woodcock 7/8.
HORNETS: 1 Sam Butterworth; 2 Liam Williams; 3 Mark McCully; 4 Dave Cunliffe; 5 Andy Saywell; 6 Lee Birdseye; 7 John Braddish; 8 Rob Ball; 9 Darren Robinson; 10 Gareth Price; 11 Andy Gorski; 12 Dave Newton; 13 Darren Shaw. Subs (all used): 14 Janan Billings; 15 Tommy Hodgkinson; 16 Liam McGovern; 17 Andy Leathem.
Tries: Saywell (23, 37), Cunliffe (30); **Goals:** Birdseye 3/5.
Dismissal: Newton (58) - high tackle on Handford.
Sin bin: McCully (54) - persistent holding down.
Rugby Leaguer & League Express Men of the Match: *Dragons:* Chris Hough; *Hornets:* Andy Saywell.
Penalty count: 14-7; **Half-time:** 10-18;
Referee: Ashley Klein (London); **Attendance:** 645.

FEATHERSTONE ROVERS 22
HULL KINGSTON ROVERS 26

ROVERS: 1 Nathan Batty; 2 Jamie Stokes; 3 Freddie Zitter; 4 Richard Newlove; 5 Matthew Wray; 6 Richard Blakeway; 7 Dean Ripley; 8 Ian Tonks; 9 Richard Chapman; 10 Stuart Dickens; 11 Steve Dooler; 12 Andy Jarrett; 13 Paul Darley. Subs (all used): 14 Jon Presley; 15 James Ford; 16 Lee Williamson; 17 Adam Hayes.
Tries: Zitter (14), Stokes (32), Newlove (45);
Goals: Dickens 4/6, Blakeway 1/1.
ROBINS: 1 Lynton Stott; 2 Nick Pinkney; 3 Dale Holdstock; 4 Paul Parker; 5 Craig Farrell; 6 Paul Mansson; 7 Scott Thorburn; 8 Jamie Bovill; 9 Andy Ellis; 10 Makali Aizue; 11 Anthony Seibold; 12 Tommy Gallagher; 13 Andy Smith. Subs (all used): 14 Phil Hasty; 15 Dean Andrews; 16 Frank Watene; 17 Paul Fletcher.
Tries: Holdstock (41), Mansson (52), Parker (55, 70, 73);
Goals: Thorburn 3/6.
On report: Fletcher (77) - incident in tackle.
Rugby Leaguer & League Express Men of the Match: *Rovers:* Stuart Dickens; *Robins:* Makali Aizue.
Penalty count: 11-9; **Half-time:** 14-2; **Referee:** Richard Silverwood (Dewsbury); **Attendance:** 1,795.

KEIGHLEY COUGARS 28 OLDHAM 33

COUGARS: 1 Chris Beever; 2 Karl Smith; 3 David Foster; 4 Matt Foster; 5 Andy Robinson; 6 Craig Nipperess; 7 Matt Firth; 8 Phil Stephenson; 9 Simeon Hoyle; 10 Richard Mervill; 11 Chris Parker; 12 Eddie Wilson; 13 Craig McDowell. Subs (all used): 14 Adam Mitchell; 15 Lee Patterson; 16 Jamie Fielden; 17 Jason Clegg.
Tries: Fielden (17), Robinson (37, 72), Mervill (47), Mitchell (80); **Goals:** Nipperess 3/5, Mitchell 1/1.
OLDHAM: 1 Jon Goddard; 2 Gavin Dodd; 3 James Bunyan; 4 Pat Rich; 5 Nick Johnson; 6 Simon Svabic; 7 Ian Watson; 8 Paul Southern; 9 Keith Brennan; 10 Dane Morgan; 11 Lee Doran; 12 Phil Farrell; 13 Lee Marsh. Subs (all used): 14 John Hough; 15 Martin McLoughlin; 16 Iain Marsh; 17 Martin Elswood.
Tries: Brennan (6), N Johnson (10, 26), Bunyan (45), Svabic (63), Watson (69);
Goals: Rich 2/5, Svabic 2/2; **Field goal:** Watson.
Rugby Leaguer & League Express Men of the Match: *Cougars:* Matt Foster; *Oldham:* Nick Johnson.
Penalty count: 9-4; **Half-time:** 14-15;
Referee: Steve Nicholson (Whitehaven) - replaced (54) by Matthew Kidd (Castleford); **Attendance:** 1,153.

LEIGH CENTURIONS 43 HALIFAX 25

CENTURIONS: 1 Neil Turley; 2 Steve Maden; 3 Dan Potter; 4 Ben Cooper; 5 Rob Smyth; 6 John Duffy; 7 Tommy Martyn; 8 Simon Knox; 9 Paul Rowley; 10 Matt Sturm; 11 David Larder; 12 Andrew Isherwood; 13 Ian Knott. Subs (all used): 14 Paul Norman; 15 Richard Marshall; 16 Danny Halliwell; 17 Willie Swann.
Tries: Maden (40), Turley (44), Smyth (51), Swann (53), Martyn (60), Duffy (68), Knott (78); **Goals:** Turley 7/9;
Field goal: Martyn.
HALIFAX: 1 Scott Grix; 2 Rikki Sheriffe; 3 Ben Feehan; 4 Alan Hadcroft; 5 James Haley; 6 Pat Weisner; 7 Mark Moxon; 8 Anthony Farrell; 9 Andy Boothroyd; 10 Ged Corcoran; 11 Matt Whitaker; 12 Jon Roper; 13 Wayne Corcoran. Subs (all used): 14 Phil Cantillon; 15 Simon Grix; 16 Ryan McDonald; 17 Chris Birchall.
Tries: Feehan (11), Haley (34), Simon Grix (74);
Goals: W Corcoran 5/6, Roper 1/1; **Field goal:** Weisner.
Rugby Leaguer & League Express Men of the Match: *Centurions:* Ian Knott; *Halifax:* Pat Weisner.
Penalty count: 8-8; **Half-time:** 6-19; **Referee:** Colin Morris (Huddersfield); **Attendance:** 1,952.

WHITEHAVEN 28 BATLEY BULLDOGS 17

WHITEHAVEN: 1 Gary Broadbent; 2 Jamie Marshall; 3 Mick Nanyn; 4 Wesley Wilson; 5 Paul O'Neil; 6 Leroy Joe; 7 Sam Obst; 8 Dean Vaughan; 9 Aaron Lester; 10 David Fatialofa; 11 Brett McDermott; 12 Howard Hill; 13 Craig Walsh. Subs (all used): 14 Carl Sice; 15 Marc Jackson; 16 Spencer Miller; 17 Chris McKinney.
Tries: Hill (10), Nanyn (48, 58), Broadbent (52), Walsh (79); **Goals:** Nanyn 4/6.
BULLDOGS: 1 Mark Sibson; 2 Matt Bramald; 3 Chris Spurr; 4 Shad Royston; 5 Bryn Powell; 6 Mark Toohey; 7 Barry Eaton; 8 Steve Hill; 9 Kris Lythe; 10 David Rourke; 11 Paul Harrison; 12 Andy Spink; 13 Sean Richardson. Subs (all used): 14 Ryan Horsley; 15 Will Cartledge; 16 Tim Spears; 17 Chris Molyneux.
Tries: Hill (3), Richardson (22), Powell (45);
Goals: Eaton 2/3; **Field goal:** Eaton.
Rugby Leaguer & League Express Men of the Match: *Whitehaven:* Gary Broadbent; *Bulldogs:* Barry Eaton.
Penalty count: 7-4; **Half-time:** 8-13;
Referee: Peter Taberner (Wigan); **Attendance:** 1,853.

WEEK 8

Sunday 20th June 2004

BATLEY BULLDOGS 14 FEATHERSTONE ROVERS 22

BULLDOGS: 1 Mark Sibson; 2 Matt Bramald; 3 Chris Spurr; 4 Danny Maun; 5 Bryn Powell; 6 Dean Lawford; 7 Barry Eaton; 8 Steve Hill; 9 Mark Toohey; 10 David Rourke; 11 Paul Harrison; 12 Andy Spink; 13 Shad Royston. Subs (all used): 14 Ryan Horsley; 15 Kris Lythe; 16 Tim Spears; 17 Sean Richardson.
Tries: Sibson (7), Lythe (70); **Goals:** Eaton 3/3.
ROVERS: 1 Nathan Batty; 2 Jamie Stokes; 3 Steve Dooler; 4 Richard Newlove; 5 Matthew Wray; 6 Andy McNally; 7 Jon Presley; 8 Ian Tonks; 9 Richard Chapman; 10 Stuart Dickens; 11 Adam Hayes; 12 Neil Lowe; 13 Paul Darley. Subs (all used): 14 James Ford; 15 Freddie Zitter; 16 Bryan Henare; 17 Jim Carlton.
Tries: Batty (12), Stokes (38), Presley (49);
Goals: Dickens 5/7.
Rugby Leaguer & League Express Men of the Match: *Bulldogs:* Bryn Powell; *Rovers:* Jamie Stokes.
Penalty count: 4-7; **Half-time:** 8-16;
Referee: Colin Morris (Huddersfield); **Attendance:** 873.

DONCASTER DRAGONS 52 KEIGHLEY COUGARS 30

DRAGONS: 1 Craig Horne; 2 Dean Colton; 3 Alex Muff; 4 PJ Solomon; 5 Johnny Woodcock; 6 Graham Holroyd; 7 Chris Hough; 8 Gareth Handford; 9 Craig Cook; 10 Martin Ostler; 11 Craig Lawton; 12 Peter Green; 13 Martin Moana. Subs (all used): 14 Matt Walker; 15 James Walker; 16 Marlon Billy; 17 Wayne Green.
Tries: Woodcock (8, 50), Horne (12, 60), Hough (24), J Walker (29, 48), P Green (36), Moana (66);
Goals: Woodcock 8/9.
COUGARS: 1 Chris Wainwright; 2 Chris Beever; 3 David Foster; 4 Matt Foster; 5 Andy Robinson; 6 Lee Patterson; 7 Matt Firth; 8 Phil Stephenson; 9 Craig Nipperess; 10 Richard Mervill; 11 Chris Parker; 12 Eddie Wilson; 13 Craig McDowell. Subs (all used): 14 Adam Mitchell; 15 Simeon Hoyle; 16 Jamie Fielden; 17 Jason Clegg.
Tries: Patterson (34), M Foster (43, 71), Hoyle (64), D Foster (68); **Goals:** Nipperess 4/4, Mitchell 1/1.
Dismissal: Stephenson (15) - high tackle.
Rugby Leaguer & League Express Men of the Match: *Dragons:* Graham Holroyd; *Cougars:* Matt Foster.
Penalty count: 8-6; **Half-time:** 28-6;
Referee: Robert Connolly (Wigan); **Attendance:** 827.

HALIFAX 15 ROCHDALE HORNETS 14

HALIFAX: 1 Scott Grix; 2 Rikki Sheriffe; 3 Ben Feehan; 4 Alan Hadcroft; 5 James Haley; 6 Pat Weisner; 7 Mark Moxon; 8 Anthony Farrell; 9 Phil Cantillon; 10 Ged Corcoran; 11 Paul Davidson; 12 Matt Whitaker; 13 Jon Roper. Subs (all used): 14 Jamie Bloem; 15 Ryan McDonald; 16 Chris Birchall; 17 Simon Grix.
Try: Davidson (12); **Goals:** Roper 5/5;
Field goal: Weisner.
Sin bin: McDonald (20) - fighting.
HORNETS: 1 Sam Butterworth; 2 Kevin Picton; 3 Mark McCully; 4 Dave Cunliffe; 5 Andy Saywell; 6 Lee Birdseye; 7 John Braddish; 8 Rob Ball; 9 Darren Shaw; 10 Tommy Hodgkinson; 11 Dave Newton; 12 Gareth Price; 13 Andy Gorski. Subs (all used): 14 Janan Billings; 15 Bobbie Goulding; 16 Mark Costello; 17 Andy Leathem.
Tries: Saywell (35), McCully (72); **Goals:** Birdseye 3/3.
Sin bin: Cunliffe (20) - fighting.
Rugby Leaguer & League Express Men of the Match: *Halifax:* Matt Whitaker; *Hornets:* Bobbie Goulding.
Penalty count: 12-10; **Half-time:** 8-8;
Referee: Ben Thaler (Wakefield); **Attendance:** 1,301.

HULL KINGSTON ROVERS 8 LEIGH CENTURIONS 35

ROVERS: 1 Lynton Stott; 2 Craig Farrell; 3 Paul Parker; 4 Craig Poucher; 5 Alasdair McClarron; 6 Paul Mansson; 7 Scott Thorburn; 8 Jamie Bovill; 9 Andy Ellis; 10 Makali Aizue; 11 Dale Holdstock; 12 Tommy Gallagher; 13 Andy Smith. Subs (all used): 14 Phil Hasty; 15 Dean Andrews; 16 Frank Watene; 17 Paul Fletcher.
Try: Andrews (71); **Goals:** Thorburn 2/2.
CENTURIONS: 1 Neil Turley; 2 Steve Maden; 3 Danny Halliwell; 4 Ben Cooper; 5 Rob Smyth; 6 John Duffy; 7 Tommy Martyn; 8 Simon Knox; 9 Paul Rowley; 10 Matt Sturm; 11 David Larder; 12 Dan Potter; 13 Ian Knott. Subs (all used): 14 Willie Swann; 15 Heath Cruckshank; 16 Richard Marshall; 17 Oliver Wilkes.
Tries: Turley (7), Smyth (20), Potter (23), Swann (56, 67); **Goals:** Turley 7/8; **Field goal:** Duffy.
Sin bin: Larder (53) - persistent offside.
Rugby Leaguer & League Express Men of the Match: *Rovers:* Tommy Gallagher; *Centurions:* Neil Turley.
Penalty count: 11-10; **Half-time:** 2-23; **Referee:** Ronnie Laughton (Barnsley); **Attendance:** 2,647.

OLDHAM 31 WHITEHAVEN 22

OLDHAM: 1 Jon Goddard; 2 Gavin Dodd; 3 James Bunyan; 4 Pat Rich; 5 Nick Johnson; 6 Simon Svabic; 7 Ian Watson; 8 Martin McLoughlin; 9 Keith Brennan; 10 Dane Morgan; 11 Lee Doran; 12 Phil Farrell; 13 Lee Marsh. Subs (all used): 14 John Hough; 15 Iain Marsh; 16 Martin Elswood; 17 Steve Molloy.
Tries: L Marsh (21), I Marsh (46), Bunyan (62), Dodd (69); **Goals:** Rich 2/2, L Marsh 5/6; **Field goal:** Watson.
WHITEHAVEN: 1 Gary Broadbent; 2 Steven Wood; 3 Wesley Wilson; 4 Mick Nanyn; 5 Paul O'Neil; 6 Leroy Joe; 7 Steve Kirkbride; 8 Dean Vaughan; 9 Aaron Lester; 10 David Fatialofa; 11 Graeme Morton; 12 Howard Hill; 13 Craig Walsh. Subs (all used): 14 Garry Purdham; 15 Carl Sice; 16 Marc Jackson; 17 Chris McKinney.
Tries: Walsh (8), Fatialofa (31), Nanyn (55), Wood (74);
Goals: Nanyn 3/5.
On report: Lester (52) - high tackle on Morgan.
Rugby Leaguer & League Express Men of the Match: *Oldham:* Ian Watson; *Whitehaven:* Craig Walsh.
Penalty count: 8-6; **Half-time:** 10-12;
Referee: Mike Dawber (Wigan);
Attendance: 752 *(at Victory Park, Chorley).*

WEEK 9

Sunday 4th July 2004

DONCASTER DRAGONS 31 OLDHAM 30

DRAGONS: 1 Johnny Woodcock; 2 Dean Colton; 3 Craig Horne; 4 Alex Muff; 5 Marlon Billy; 6 Graham Holroyd; 7 Chris Hough; 8 Gareth Handford; 9 Craig Cook; 10 Martin Ostler; 11 Craig Lawton; 12 Peter Green; 13 Martin Moana. Subs (all used): 14 Matt Walker; 15 James Walker; 16 Shaun Leaf; 17 Gareth Lloyd.
Tries: Hough (11), Leaf (20), J Walker (31), Horne (42);
Goals: Woodcock 2/2, Holroyd 0/1, Hough 4/5;
Field goals: Holroyd 2, Cook.
OLDHAM: 1 Jon Goddard; 2 Gavin Dodd; 3 Iain Marsh; 4 Pat Rich; 5 Nick Johnson; 6 Simon Svabic; 7 Ian Watson; 8 Paul Southern; 9 John Hough; 10 Dane Morgan; 11 Lee Doran; 12 Phil Farrell; 13 Lee Marsh. Subs (all used): 14 Keith Brennan; 15 Gareth Barber; 16 Martin McLoughlin; 17 Gavin Johnson.
Tries: Dodd (39), I Marsh (53, 70), Brennan (55), L Marsh (65); **Goals:** Rich 5/6.
Rugby Leaguer & League Express Men of the Match: *Dragons:* Craig Cook; *Oldham:* Iain Marsh.

Penalty count: 7-7; **Half-time:** 21-6; **Referee:** Peter Taberner (Wigan); **Attendance:** 998.

FEATHERSTONE ROVERS 26 WHITEHAVEN 12

ROVERS: 1 Nathan Batty; 2 Jamie Stokes; 3 Andy McNally; 4 Richard Newlove; 5 Matthew Wray; 6 Richard Blakeway; 7 Jon Presley; 8 Ian Tonks; 9 Richard Chapman; 10 Stuart Dickens; 11 Steve Dooler; 12 Adam Hayes; 13 Paul Darley. Subs (all used): 14 Freddie Zitter; 15 Bryan Henare; 16 Andy Jarrett; 17 Jim Carlton.
Tries: Wray (9), McNally (36), Stokes (39), Hayes (79); **Goals:** McNally 1/2, Dickens 4/5.
WHITEHAVEN: 1 Gary Broadbent; 2 Jamie Marshall; 3 Wesley Wilson; 4 David Seeds; 5 Paul O'Neil; 6 Lee Kiddie; 7 Sam Obst; 8 Dean Vaughan; 9 Leroy Joe; 10 David Fatialofa; 11 Brett McDermott; 12 Howard Hill; 13 Aaron Lester. Subs (all used): 14 Garry Purdham; 15 Carl Sice; 16 Tony Cunningham; 17 Chris McKinney.
Tries: Fatialofa (26), Kiddie (64); **Goals:** O'Neil 2/3.
Rugby Leaguer & League Express Men of the Match: *Rovers:* Nathan Batty; *Whitehaven:* David Fatialofa.
Penalty count: 7-4; **Half-time:** 18-6; **Referee:** Robert Connolly (Wigan); **Attendance:** 1,259.

KEIGHLEY COUGARS 16 HALIFAX 37

COUGARS: 1 Chris Wainwright; 2 Karl Smith; 3 David Foster; 4 Matt Foster; 5 Andy Robinson; 6 Adam Mitchell; 7 Matt Firth; 8 Phil Stephenson; 9 Simeon Hoyle; 16 Jamie Fielden; 11 Richard Mervill; 12 Danny Murgatroyd; 13 Lee Patterson. Subs: 10 Jason Clegg; 14 Craig Nipperess (not used); 15 Craig McDowell; 17 Chris Parker.
Tries: M Foster (24), Firth (34), Robinson (71); **Goals:** Mitchell 2/4.
HALIFAX: 1 Scott Grix; 2 Rikki Sheriffe; 3 James Bunyan; 4 Alan Hadcroft; 5 James Haley; 6 Pat Weisner; 7 Mark Moxon; 8 Anthony Farrell; 9 Phil Cantillon; 10 Chris Birchall; 11 Ged Corcoran; 12 Chris Morley; 13 Jamie Bloem. Subs (all used): 14 Gareth Greenwood; 15 Simon Grix; 16 Ryan McDonald; 17 David Bates.
Tries: Bloem (3, 79), Moxon (17), Birchall (46), Hadcroft (67), Simon Grix (77); **Goals:** Bloem 6/7; **Field goal:** Weisner.
Rugby Leaguer & League Express Men of the Match: *Cougars:* Simeon Hoyle; *Halifax:* Pat Weisner.
Penalty count: 8-1; **Half-time:** 10-13; **Referee:** Colin Morris (Huddersfield); **Attendance:** 1,380.

LEIGH CENTURIONS 27 BATLEY BULLDOGS 22

CENTURIONS: 1 Neil Turley; 2 Steve Maden; 3 Danny Halliwell; 4 Ben Cooper; 5 Damian Munro; 6 John Duffy; 7 Tommy Martyn; 8 Matt Sturm; 9 Dave McConnell; 10 Heath Cruckshank; 11 David Larder; 12 Dan Potter; 13 Oliver Wilkes. Subs (all used): 14 Willie Swann; 15 Simon Knox; 16 Richard Marshall; 17 Andrew Isherwood.
Tries: Wilkes (4, 57), Turley (10), Isherwood (55); **Goals:** Turley 5/7; **Field goal:** Turley.
BULLDOGS: 1 Mark Sibson; 2 Steve Beard; 3 Shad Royston; 4 Danny Maun; 5 Bryn Powell; 6 Dean Lawford; 7 Barry Eaton; 8 Steve Hill; 9 Will Cartledge; 10 David Rourke; 11 Mark Toohey; 12 Andy Spink; 13 Sean Richardson. Subs (all used): 14 Mark Cass; 15 Paul Harrison; 16 Craig Lingard; 17 Chris Molyneux.
Tries: Lingard (34), Toohey (48, 74), Rourke (69); **Goals:** Eaton 3/4.
Rugby Leaguer & League Express Men of the Match: *Centurions:* Oliver Wilkes; *Bulldogs:* Barry Eaton.
Penalty count: 11-9; **Half-time:** 13-6; **Referee:** Ben Thaler (Wakefield); **Attendance:** 2,030.

ROCHDALE HORNETS 36 HULL KINGSTON ROVERS 18

HORNETS: 1 Michael Platt; 2 Andy Saywell; 3 Mark McCully; 4 David Alstead; 5 Chris Campbell; 6 John Braddish; 7 Bobbie Goulding; 8 Rob Ball; 9 Darren Robinson; 10 Gareth Price; 11 Andy Gorski; 12 Darren Shaw; 13 Dave Cunliffe. Subs (all used): 14 Janan Billings; 15 Tommy Hodgkinson; 16 Sam Butterworth; 17 Lee Hansen.
Tries: Goulding (3), Robinson (8), Gorski (24), Alstead (32), Butterworth (56); **Goals:** Braddish 8/9.
On report: Goulding (48) - high tackle on Bovill.
ROVERS: 1 Craig Poucher; 2 Nick Pinkney; 3 Paul Parker; 4 Marvin Golden; 5 Alasdair McClarron; 6 Paul Mansson; 7 Phil Hasty; 8 Jamie Bovill; 9 Paul Pickering; 10 Makali Aizue; 11 Dale Holdstock; 12 Anthony Seibold; 13 Tommy Gallagher. Subs (all used): 14 Scott Thorburn; 15 Dean Andrews; 16 Frank Watene; 17 Jon Aston.
Tries: Gallagher (37), Poucher (45), Hasty (65), Holdstock (68); **Goals:** Thorburn 0/2, Hasty 1/2.
Sin bin: Aizue (42) - holding down.
Rugby Leaguer & League Express Men of the Match: *Hornets:* Bobbie Goulding; *Rovers:* Phil Hasty.
Penalty count: 7-10; **Half-time:** 24-4; **Referee:** Richard Silverwood (Dewsbury); **Attendance:** 1,094.

Saturday 10th July 2004

OLDHAM 24 HALIFAX 14

OLDHAM: 1 Jon Goddard; 2 Gavin Dodd; 3 Iain Marsh; 4 Pat Rich; 5 Nick Johnson; 6 Simon Svabic; 7 Ian Watson; 8 Paul Southern; 9 Keith Brennan; 10 Dane Morgan; 11 Lee Doran; 12 Phil Farrell; 13 Lee Marsh. Subs (all used): 14 John Hough; 15 Gareth Barber; 16 Gavin Johnson; 17 Martin McLoughlin.
Tries: I Marsh (10), N Johnson (48), L Marsh (67), Barber (69); **Goals:** Rich 3/4; **Field goals:** Watson 2.
HALIFAX: 1 Scott Grix; 2 Rikki Sheriffe; 3 Ben Feehan; 4 Alan Hadcroft; 5 James Haley; 6 Pat Weisner; 7 Mark Moxon; 8 Anthony Farrell; 9 Phil Cantillon; 10 Chris Birchall; 11 Paul Davidson; 12 Gareth Greenwood; 13 Jamie Bloem. Subs: 14 Chris Norman; 15 Danny Arnold (not used); 16 David Bates; 17 Ryan McDonald.
Tries: Weisner (5), Haley (34), Greenwood (44); **Goals:** Bloem 1/4.
Rugby Leaguer & League Express Men of the Match: *Oldham:* Jon Goddard; *Halifax:* Jamie Bloem.
Penalty count: 3-1; **Half-time:** 6-10; **Referee:** Colin Morris (Huddersfield); **Attendance:** 850 *(at Victory Park, Chorley).*

WEEK 10

Sunday 11th July 2004

BATLEY BULLDOGS 30 KEIGHLEY COUGARS 14

BULLDOGS: 1 Mark Sibson; 2 Bryn Powell; 3 Shad Royston; 4 Danny Maun; 5 Adrian Flynn; 6 Dean Lawford; 7 Barry Eaton; 8 Steve Hill; 9 Will Cartledge; 10 David Rourke; 11 Mark Toohey; 12 Andy Spink; 13 Sean Richardson. Subs (all used): 14 Mark Cass; 15 Paul Harrison; 16 Craig Lingard; 17 Chris Molyneux.
Tries: Lawford (2, 62), Royston (8), Sibson (12), Harrison (79); **Goals:** Eaton 5/5.
COUGARS: 1 Chris Wainwright; 2 Max Tomlinson; 3 David Foster; 4 Andy Robinson; 5 Chris Beever; 6 Adam Mitchell; 7 Matt Firth; 8 Phil Stephenson; 9 Simeon Hoyle; 10 Danny Murgatroyd; 11 Lee Patterson; 12 Richard Mervill; 13 Craig McDowell. Subs (all used): 14 Craig Nipperess; 15 Chris Parker; 16 Jamie Fielden; 17 Jason Clegg.
Tries: Hoyle (25), Beever (55), Robinson (74); **Goals:** Mitchell 1/3.
Rugby Leaguer & League Express Men of the Match: *Bulldogs:* Bryn Powell; *Cougars:* David Foster.
Penalty count: 6-6; **Half-time:** 18-6; **Referee:** Mike Dawber (Wigan); **Attendance:** 685.

FEATHERSTONE ROVERS 20 LEIGH CENTURIONS 75

ROVERS: 1 Nathan Batty; 2 Jamie Stokes; 3 Andy McNally; 4 Richard Newlove; 5 Matthew Wray; 6 Richard Blakeway; 7 Jon Presley; 8 Ian Tonks; 9 Richard Chapman; 10 Stuart Dickens; 11 Steve Dooler; 12 Adam Hayes; 13 Paul Darley. Subs (all used): 14 Freddie Zitter; 15 Bryan Henare; 16 Neil Lowe; 17 Jim Carlton.
Tries: Stokes (46, 78), Newlove (48), Dooler (72); **Goals:** Dickens 2/4.
CENTURIONS: 1 Neil Turley; 2 Damian Munro; 3 Danny Halliwell; 4 Ben Cooper; 5 Rob Smyth; 6 John Duffy; 7 Tommy Martyn; 8 Matt Sturm; 9 Mick Govin; 10 Heath Cruckshank; 11 David Larder; 12 Dan Potter; 13 Oliver Wilkes. Subs (all used): 14 Simon Knox; 15 Willie Swann; 16 Richard Marshall; 17 Andrew Isherwood.
Tries: Halliwell (2, 19, 26), Cruckshank (5), Smyth (7, 12), Potter (14), Govin (23), Duffy (44), Martyn (53), Wilkes (60), Knox (63), Cooper (79); **Goals:** Turley 7/8, Smyth 4/6; **Field goal:** Martyn.
Rugby Leaguer & League Express Men of the Match: *Rovers:* Stuart Dickens; *Centurions:* John Duffy.
Penalty count: 5-5; **Half-time:** 0-47; **Referee:** Peter Taberner (Wigan); **Attendance:** 1,859.

HULL KINGSTON ROVERS 18 DONCASTER DRAGONS 13

ROVERS: 1 Craig Poucher; 2 Nick Pinkney; 3 Paul Parker; 4 Marvin Golden; 5 Lynton Stott; 6 Paul Mansson; 7 Phil Hasty; 8 Makali Aizue; 9 Paul Pickering; 10 Jon Aston; 11 Dale Holdstock; 12 Andy Smith; 13 Tommy Gallagher. Subs (all used): 14 Scott Thorburn; 15 Matt Calland; 16 Frank Watene; 17 Paul Fletcher.
Tries: Pinkney (22), Hasty (66), Pickering (77); **Goals:** Stott 3/6.
Dismissal: Poucher (38) - fighting.
On report: Brawl (38).
DRAGONS: 1 Shaun Leaf; 2 Dean Colton; 3 Alex Muff; 4 PJ Solomon; 5 Marlon Billy; 6 Graham Holroyd; 7 Chris Hough; 8 Gareth Handford; 9 Craig Cook; 10 Martin Ostler; 11 Peter Green; 12 Gareth Lloyd; 13 Martin Moana. Subs (all used): 14 Matt Walker; 15 James Walker; 16 Wayne Green; 17 Andy Fisher.
Try: Colton (3); **Goals:** Holroyd 4/5; **Field goal:** Hough.
Dismissals: J Walker (38) - fighting; Fisher (52) - dangerous tackle on Aizue.
On report: J Walker (32) - dangerous tackle on Fletcher; Brawl (38).
Rugby Leaguer & League Express Men of the Match: *Rovers:* Makali Aizue; *Dragons:* Graham Holroyd.
Penalty count: 12-14; **Half-time:** 6-11; **Referee:** Ben Thaler (Wakefield); **Attendance:** 1,888.

WHITEHAVEN 30 ROCHDALE HORNETS 14

WHITEHAVEN: 1 Wesley Wilson; 2 Craig Calvert; 3 David Seeds; 4 Ryan Campbell; 5 Paul O'Neil; 6 Leroy Joe; 7 Sam Obst; 8 Chris McKinney; 9 Aaron Lester; 10 David Fatialofa; 11 Spencer Miller; 12 Howard Hill; 13 Craig Walsh. Subs (all used): 14 Garry Purdham; 15 Carl Sice; 16 Graeme Morton; 17 Tony Cunningham.
Tries: Calvert (27, 45), Morton (41), Obst (57), O'Neil (74), Walsh (77); **Goals:** O'Neil 3/6.
HORNETS: 1 Michael Platt; 2 Andy Saywell; 3 Mark McCully; 4 David Alstead; 5 Chris Campbell; 6 John Braddish; 7 Bobbie Goulding; 8 Rob Ball; 9 Darren Robinson; 10 Gareth Price; 11 Andy Gorski; 12 Darren Shaw; 13 Dave Cunliffe. Subs (all used): 14 Janan Billings; 15 Tommy Hodgkinson; 16 Dave Newton; 17 Lee Hansen.
Tries: Gorski (8), McCully (39), Campbell (51); **Goals:** Braddish 1/4.
Rugby Leaguer & League Express Men of the Match: *Whitehaven:* Sam Obst; *Hornets:* Gareth Price.
Penalty count: 13-3; **Half time:** 4-10; **Referee:** Julian King (St Helens); **Attendance:** 1,654.

WEEK 11

Sunday 25th July 2004

DONCASTER DRAGONS 31 BATLEY BULLDOGS 28

DRAGONS: 1 Craig Horne; 2 Dean Colton; 3 Alex Muff; 4 PJ Solomon; 5 Marlon Billy; 6 Graham Holroyd; 7 Chris Hough; 8 Gareth Handford; 9 Craig Cook; 10 Andy Fisher; 11 Martin Ostler; 12 Peter Green; 13 Martin Moana. Subs (all used): 14 Gareth Lloyd; 15 James Walker; 16 Johnny Woodcock; 17 Shaun Leaf.
Tries: Holroyd (4, 15), Billy (24), Colton (48), Horne (72, 80); **Goals:** Holroyd 3/6; **Field goal:** Hough.
BULLDOGS: 1 Craig Lingard; 2 Mark Sibson; 3 Shad Royston; 4 Danny Maun; 5 Bryn Powell; 6 Dean Lawford; 7 Barry Eaton; 8 Steve Hill; 9 Kris Lythe; 10 David Rourke; 11 Mark Toohey; 12 Andy Spink; 13 Ryan Horsley. Subs (all used): 14 Tim Spears; 15 Paul Harrison; 16 Chris Molyneux; 17 Sean Richardson.
Tries: Lingard (8, 19), Richardson (41), Powell (55), Harrison (69); **Goals:** Eaton 4/5.
Rugby Leaguer & League Express Men of the Match: *Dragons:* Gareth Handford; *Bulldogs:* Craig Lingard.
Penalty count: 2-4; **Half-time:** 17-18; **Referee:** Colin Morris (Huddersfield); **Attendance:** 830.

HALIFAX 14 HULL KINGSTON ROVERS 20

HALIFAX: 1 Scott Grix; 2 Danny Arnold; 3 James Bunyan; 4 Alan Hadcroft; 5 James Haley; 6 Pat Weisner; 7 Ben Black; 8 Anthony Farrell; 9 Mark Moxon; 10 Chris Birchall; 11 Ged Corcoran; 12 Gareth Greenwood; 13 Jamie Bloem. Subs (all used): 14 Phil Cantillon; 15 Paul Davidson; 16 Chris Norman; 17 Ryan McDonald.
Tries: G Corcoran (2), Scott Grix (64), Black (68); **Goals:** Bloem 1/3.
ROVERS: 1 Paul Owen; 2 Nick Pinkney; 3 Dwayne Barker; 4 Dean Andrews; 5 Craig Farrell; 6 Paul Mansson; 7 Scott Thorburn; 8 Jamie Bovill; 9 Paul Pickering; 10 Makali Aizue; 11 Jason Netherton; 12 Anthony Seibold; 13 Tommy Gallagher. Subs (all used): 14 Jimmy Walker; 15 Andy Smith; 16 Frank Watene; 17 Paul Fletcher.
Tries: Mansson (16), Gallagher (34), Farrell (57), Pinkney (77); **Goals:** Thorburn 2/4.
Rugby Leaguer & League Express Men of the Match: *Halifax:* Ben Black; *Rovers:* Tommy Gallagher.
Penalty count: 10-4; **Half-time:** 4-10; **Referee:** Mike Dawber (Wigan); **Attendance:** 1,556.

KEIGHLEY COUGARS 16 WHITEHAVEN 29

COUGARS: 1 Matt Bramald; 2 Max Tomlinson; 3 David Foster; 4 Matt Foster; 5 Andy Robinson; 6 Adam Mitchell; 7 Matt Firth; 8 Phil Stephenson; 9 Simeon Hoyle; 10 Jason Clegg; 11 Lee Patterson; 12 Craig McDowell; 13 Craig Nipperess. Subs (all used): 14 Chris Beever; 15 Danny Ekis; 16 Jamie Fielden; 17 Richard Mervill.
Tries: McDowell (55), Hoyle (65); **Goals:** Mitchell 4/4.
WHITEHAVEN: 1 Gary Broadbent; 2 Craig Calvert; 3 David Seeds; 4 Mick Nanyn; 5 Wesley Wilson; 6 Leroy Joe; 7 Sam Obst; 8 Chris McKinney; 9 Carl Sice; 10 David Fatialofa; 11 Spencer Miller; 12 Howard Hill; 13 Craig Walsh. Subs (all used): 14 Dean Vaughan; 15 Lee Kiddie; 16 Garry Purdham; 17 Marc Jackson.
Tries: Sice (25), Obst (32), Nanyn (51), Joe (77); **Goals:** Nanyn 6/7; **Field goal:** Obst.
Sin bin: Walsh (41) - professional foul.
Rugby Leaguer & League Express Men of the Match: *Cougars:* Phil Stephenson; *Whitehaven:* Sam Obst.
Penalty count: 7-7; **Half-time:** 4-12; **Referee:** Peter Taberner (Wigan); **Attendance:** 948.

LEIGH CENTURIONS 36 OLDHAM 12

CENTURIONS: 1 Neil Turley; 2 Chris Percival; 3 Danny Halliwell; 4 Ben Cooper; 5 Rob Smyth; 6 John Duffy; 7 Tommy Martyn; 8 Heath Cruckshank; 9 Paul Rowley; 10 Richard Marshall; 11 David Larder; 12 Dan Potter; 13 Ian Knott. Subs (all used): 14 Dave McConnell; 15 Willie Swann; 16 Damian Munro; 17 Andrew Isherwood.
Tries: Percival (5, 16, 68), Martyn (43), Cooper (73), Munro (77); **Goals:** Turley 6/10.
OLDHAM: 1 Jon Goddard; 2 Will Cowell; 3 Jon Roper; 4 Pat Rich; 5 Nick Johnson; 6 Lee Marsh; 7 Ian Watson; 8 Paul Southern; 9 John Hough; 10 Dane Morgan; 11 Lee Doran; 12 Iain Marsh; 13 Phil Farrell. Subs (all used): 14 Neil Roden; 15 Gareth Barber; 16 Gavin Johnson; 17 Martin McLoughlin.
Try: Roden (32); **Goals:** Rich 4/4.
Dismissal: I Marsh (2) - high tackle on Marshall.
Rugby Leaguer & League Express Men of the Match: *Centurions:* Tommy Martyn; *Oldham:* Ian Watson.
Penalty count: 13-10; **Half-time:** 12-10; **Referee:** Richard Silverwood (Dewsbury); **Attendance:** 1,841.

ROCHDALE HORNETS 12 FEATHERSTONE ROVERS 12

HORNETS: 1 Michael Platt; 2 Andy Saywell; 3 Mark McCully; 4 David Alstead; 5 Chris Campbell; 6 John Braddish; 7 Bobbie Goulding; 8 Tommy Hodgkinson; 9 Darren Robinson; 10 Gareth Price; 11 Andy Gorski; 12 Darren Shaw; 13 Dave Cunliffe. Subs (all used): 14 Janan Billings; 15 Dave Newton; 16 Lee Birdseye; 17 Lee Hansen.
Try: Robinson (11); **Goals:** Goulding 4/5.
Dismissal: Alstead (62) - high tackle on Dooler.
Sin bin: Platt (21) - professional foul.
ROVERS: 1 Craig Moss; 2 Jamie Stokes; 3 Freddie Zitter; 4 Richard Newlove; 5 James Ford; 6 Richard Blakeway; 7 Andy McNally; 8 Jim Carlton; 9 Richard Chapman; 10 Stuart Dickens; 11 Steve Dooler; 12 Neil Lowe; 13 Tom Haughey. Subs (all used): 14 Maxime Greseque; 15 Adam Sullivan; 16 Bryan Henare; 17 Adam Hayes.
Try: Hayes (70); **Goals:** Blakeway 2/2, Dickens 2/2.

Sin bin: Ford (24) - obstruction.
Rugby Leaguer & League Express Men of the Match: *Hornets:* Darren Robinson; *Rovers:* Jim Carlton.
Penalty count: 7-13; **Half-time:** 6-0;
Referee: Ben Thaler (Wakefield); **Attendance:** 804.

WEEK 12

Sunday 1st August 2004

BATLEY BULLDOGS 20 HALIFAX 39

BULLDOGS: 1 Mark Sibson; 2 Bryn Powell; 3 Shad Royston; 4 Danny Maun; 5 Adrian Flynn; 6 Dean Lawford; 7 Barry Eaton; 8 Steve Hill; 9 Kris Lythe; 10 Sean Richardson; 11 Mark Toohey; 12 Andy Spink; 13 Ryan Horsley. Subs (all used): 14 Tim Spears; 15 Paul Harrison; 16 Chris Molyneux; 17 Nathan Graham.
Tries: Toohey (17), Horsley (45), Sibson (67);
Goals: Eaton 4/4.
Sin bin: Horsley (28) - fighting; Flynn (65) - fighting.
HALIFAX: 1 Scott Grix; 2 Rikki Sheriffe; 3 James Bunyan; 4 Alan Hadcroft; 5 James Haley; 6 Pat Weisner; 7 Ben Black; 8 Jon Simpson; 9 Gareth Greenwood; 10 Chris Birchall; 11 Ged Corcoran; 12 Paul Davidson; 13 Jamie Bloem. Subs (all used): 14 Phil Cantillon; 15 Ben Feehan; 16 Anthony Farrell; 17 Ryan McDonald.
Tries: Hadcroft (8), Farrell (28), Sheriffe (35), Scott Grix (53), Black (62, 79), Bloem (73);
Goals: Bloem 4/5, Haley 1/2; **Field goal:** Weisner.
Sin bin: Bloem (28) - fighting;
Black (43) - holding down; Bunyan (65) - fighting.
Rugby Leaguer & League Express Men of the Match: *Bulldogs:* Bryn Powell; *Halifax:* Jon Simpson.
Penalty count: 11-7; **Half-time:** 8-14;
Referee: Ben Thaler (Wakefield); **Attendance:** 941.

FEATHERSTONE ROVERS 54 KEIGHLEY COUGARS 16

ROVERS: 1 Craig Moss; 2 Freddie Zitter; 3 Andy McNally; 4 Richard Newlove; 5 Matthew Wray; 6 Richard Blakeway; 7 Maxime Greseque; 8 Ian Tonks; 9 Paul Darley; 10 Stuart Dickens; 11 Steve Dooler; 12 Tom Haughey; 13 Adam Hayes. Subs (all used): 14 James Ford; 15 Andy Jarrett; 16 Neil Lowe; 17 Jim Carlton.
Tries: Wray (5, 59), Greseque (9, 11), Haughey (15), McNally (24, 39), Zitter (29), Blakeway (49), Newlove (74); **Goals:** Greseque 3/5, Dickens 4/6.
COUGARS: 1 Matt Bramald; 2 Max Tomlinson; 3 David Foster; 4 Matt Foster; 5 Andy Robinson; 6 Adam Mitchell; 7 Matt Firth; 8 Phil Stephenson; 9 Simeon Hoyle; 10 Jason Clegg; 11 Craig McDowell; 12 Jordan Ross; 13 Lee Patterson. Subs (all used): 14 Craig Nipperess; 15 Chris Beever; 16 Jamie Fielden; 17 Richard Mervill.
Tries: M Foster (2), Robinson (69), Nipperess (78);
Goals: Nipperess 1/1, Mitchell 1/2.
Rugby Leaguer & League Express Men of the Match: *Rovers:* Maxime Greseque; *Cougars:* Simeon Hoyle.
Penalty count: 12-10; **Half-time:** 38-4; **Referee:** Richard Silverwood (Dewsbury); **Attendance:** 1,089.

LEIGH CENTURIONS 18 ROCHDALE HORNETS 44

CENTURIONS: 1 Neil Turley; 2 Rob Smyth; 3 Danny Halliwell; 4 Ben Cooper; 5 Chris Percival; 6 John Duffy; 7 Tommy Martyn; 8 Richard Marshall; 9 Paul Rowley; 10 Mike Callan; 11 David Larder; 12 Dan Potter; 13 Ian Knott. Subs (all used): 14 Dave McConnell; 15 Willie Swann; 16 Heath Cruckshank; 17 Oliver Wilkes.
Tries: Larder (52), Turley (67), Martyn (79);
Goals: Turley 1/1, Smyth 2/2.
HORNETS: 1 Chris Campbell; 2 Liam Williams; 3 Michael Platt; 4 Sam Butterworth; 5 Kevin Picton; 6 John Braddish; 7 Liam McGovern; 8 Lee Hansen; 9 Darren Robinson; 10 Tommy Hodgkinson; 11 Andy Gorski; 12 Gareth Price; 13 Kris Ratcliffe. Subs (all used): 14 Janan Billings; 15 Dave Newton; 16 Lee Birdseye; 17 Mark Costello.
Tries: Picton (10), Braddish (18), Newton (32), Williams (40), Ratcliffe (43, 46), Price (63), McGovern (75);
Goals: Braddish 6/8.
Sin bin: Ratcliffe (74) – interference.
Rugby Leaguer & League Express Men of the Match: *Centurions:* Oliver Wilkes; *Hornets:* Liam McGovern.
Penalty count: 10-3; **Half-time:** 0-20; **Referee:** Colin Morris (Huddersfield); **Attendance:** 1,662.

OLDHAM 29 HULL KINGSTON ROVERS 24

OLDHAM: 1 Jon Goddard; 2 Will Cowell; 3 Iain Marsh; 4 Jon Roper; 5 Nick Johnson; 6 Lee Marsh; 7 Ian Watson; 8 Paul Southern; 9 Keith Brennan; 10 Martin McLoughlin; 11 Lee Doran; 12 Dane Morgan; 13 Phil Farrell. Subs (all used): 14 Neil Roden; 15 Gareth Barber; 16 Martin Elswood; 17 Adam Sharples.
Tries: L Marsh (5, 11), N Johnson (8), Roden (44), Goddard (47), Watson (72); **Goals:** L Marsh 1/4, Barber 0/1, Roper 1/1; **Field goal:** L Marsh.
ROVERS: 1 Paul Owen; 2 Nick Pinkney; 3 Paul Parker; 4 Dwayne Barker; 5 Lynton Stott; 6 Paul Mansson; 7 Phil Hasty; 8 Jamie Bovill; 9 Paul Pickering; 10 Makali Aizue; 11 Jason Netherton; 12 Tommy Gallagher; 13 Damian Ball. Subs (all used): 14 Jimmy Walker; 15 Anthony Seibold; 16 Frank Watene; 17 Paul Fletcher.
Tries: Stott (2, 19), Ball (26), Bovill (52), Parker (78);
Goals: Stott 2/5.
Rugby Leaguer & League Express Men of the Match: *Oldham:* Jon Goddard; *Rovers:* Frank Watene.
Penalty count: 6-3; **Half-time:** 12-12;
Referee: Robert Connolly (Wigan); **Attendance:** 1,393.

WHITEHAVEN 42 DONCASTER DRAGONS 18

WHITEHAVEN: 1 Gary Broadbent; 2 Wesley Wilson; 3 Mick Nanyn; 4 David Seeds; 5 Craig Calvert; 6 Leroy Joe; 7 Sam Obst; 8 Chris McKinney; 9 Carl Sice; 10 David Fatialofa; 11 Spencer Miller; 12 Howard Hill; 13 Craig Walsh. Subs (all used): 14 Dean Vaughan; 15 Garry Purdham; 16 Carl Sice; 17 Marc Jackson.
Tries: Nanyn (7, 15, 32), Miller (21), Obst (36), Seeds (67), Calvert (72); **Goals:** Nanyn 7/10.
DRAGONS: 1 Craig Horne; 2 Dean Colton; 3 Alex Muff; 4 PJ Solomon; 5 Marlon Billy; 6 Graham Holroyd; 7 Shaun Leaf; 8 James Walker; 9 Craig Cook; 10 Andy Fisher; 11 Martin Ostler; 12 Peter Green; 13 Martin Moana. Subs (all used): 14 Gareth Lloyd; 15 Dean O'Loughlin; 16 Johnny Woodcock; 17 Craig Lawton.
Tries: Billy (18), Moana (27, 78); **Goals:** Holroyd 3/3.
Dismissal: Fisher (59) - high tackle on Sice.
Rugby Leaguer & League Express Men of the Match: *Whitehaven:* Sam Obst; *Dragons:* James Walker.
Penalty count: 9-6; **Half-time:** 26-12;
Referee: Mike Dawber (Wigan); **Attendance:** 1,814.

WEEK 13

Sunday 8th August 2004

DONCASTER DRAGONS 18 FEATHERSTONE ROVERS 33

DRAGONS: 1 Johnny Woodcock; 2 Dean Colton; 3 Gareth Lloyd; 4 Craig Lawton; 5 Marlon Billy; 6 Graham Holroyd; 7 Chris Hough; 8 Gareth Handford; 9 Craig Cook; 10 Andy Fisher; 11 Martin Ostler; 12 Peter Green; 13 Martin Moana. Subs (all used): 14 Dean O'Loughlin; 15 James Walker; 16 Alex Muff; 17 Craig Horne.
Tries: O'Loughlin (33), Lloyd (47), Colton (64, 76);
Goals: Holroyd 1/4.
ROVERS: 1 Craig Moss; 2 Freddie Zitter; 3 Andy McNally; 4 Richard Newlove; 5 Matthew Wray; 6 Richard Blakeway; 7 Maxime Greseque; 8 Ian Tonks; 9 Paul Darley; 10 Stuart Dickens; 11 Steve Dooler; 12 Tom Haughey; 13 Adam Hayes. Subs (all used): 14 James Ford; 15 Andy Jarrett; 16 Neil Lowe; 17 Jim Carlton.
Tries: Dooler (4, 58), Newlove (6), Wray (20), Moss (28); **Goals:** Dickens 6/8; **Field goal:** Blakeway.
Rugby Leaguer & League Express Men of the Match: *Dragons:* Craig Cook; *Rovers:* Steve Dooler.
Penalty count: 4-7; **Half-time:** 6-24;
Referee: Robert Connolly (Wigan); **Attendance:** 966.

HALIFAX 14 WHITEHAVEN 34

HALIFAX: 1 Scott Grix; 2 Rikki Sheriffe; 3 James Bunyan; 4 Alan Hadcroft; 5 James Haley; 6 Pat Weisner; 7 Ben Black; 8 Jon Simpson; 9 Phil Cantillon; 10 Chris Birchall; 11 Ged Corcoran; 12 Gareth Greenwood; 13 Jamie Bloem. Subs (all used): 14 Mark Moxon; 15 Ben Feehan; 16 Anthony Farrell; 17 Ryan McDonald.
Tries: Sheriffe (11), Cantillon (26), Bunyan (47);
Goals: Bloem 1/4.
Sin bin: Cantillon (63) - holding down.
WHITEHAVEN: 1 Gary Broadbent; 2 Craig Calvert; 3 David Seeds; 4 Mick Nanyn; 5 Paul O'Neil; 6 Leroy Joe; 7 Sam Obst; 8 Chris McKinney; 9 Aaron Lester; 10 David Fatialofa; 11 Spencer Miller; 12 Howard Hill; 13 Craig Walsh. Subs (all used): 14 Dean Vaughan; 15 Ryan Tandy; 16 Carl Sice; 17 Marc Jackson.
Tries: Calvert (5, 80), Hill (14, 68), Obst (17), Nanyn (20); **Goals:** Nanyn 5/6.
Sin bin: Joe (61) - holding down.
Rugby Leaguer & League Express Men of the Match: *Halifax:* Alan Hadcroft; *Whitehaven:* Sam Obst.
Penalty count: 12-9; **Half-time:** 10-22; **Referee:** Ronnie Laughton (Barnsley); **Attendance:** 1,440.

HULL KINGSTON ROVERS 29 BATLEY BULLDOGS 18

ROVERS: 1 Paul Owen; 2 Nick Pinkney; 3 Craig Poucher; 4 Paul Parker; 5 Lynton Stott; 6 Paul Mansson; 7 Phil Hasty; 8 Jamie Bovill; 9 Paul Pickering; 10 Makali Aizue; 11 Jason Netherton; 12 Anthony Seibold; 13 Damian Ball. Subs (all used): 14 Jimmy Walker; 15 Andy Smith; 16 Frank Watene; 17 Paul Fletcher.
Tries: Netherton (12), Hasty (16), Bovill (22), Pinkney (79); **Goals:** Stott 6/6; **Field goal:** Mansson.
BULLDOGS: 1 Nathan Graham; 2 Bryn Powell; 3 Shad Royston; 4 Danny Maun; 5 Adrian Flynn; 6 Dean Lawford; 7 Barry Eaton; 8 Chris Molyneux; 9 Mark Cass; 10 Steve Hill; 11 Sean Richardson; 12 Andy Spink; 13 Mark Toohey. Subs (all used): 14 Tim Spears; 15 Paul Harrison; 16 Will Cartledge; 17 David Bates.
Tries: Royston (25), Powell (38, 77); **Goals:** Eaton 3/4.
Sin bin: Richardson (52) - dissent;
Harrison (78) - dissent.
Rugby Leaguer & League Express Men of the Match: *Rovers:* Paul Mansson; *Bulldogs:* Barry Eaton.
Penalty count: 9-8; **Half-time:** 20-12; **Referee:** Colin Morris (Huddersfield); **Attendance:** 1,695.

KEIGHLEY COUGARS 10 LEIGH CENTURIONS 48

COUGARS: 1 Matt Bramald; 2 Karl Smith; 3 David Foster; 4 Andy Robinson; 5 Max Tomlinson; 6 Craig Nipperess; 7 Matt Firth; 8 Phil Stephenson; 9 Simeon Hoyle; 10 Jason Clegg; 11 Jordan Ross; 12 Craig McDowell; 13 Lee Patterson. Subs (all used): 14 Adam Mitchell; 15 Chris Wainwright; 16 Jamie Fielden; 17 Richard Mervill.
Tries: Tomlinson (31), Wainwright (79);
Goals: Nipperess 1/2.
On report: Stephenson (20) - high tackle on Wilkes.
CENTURIONS: 1 Neil Turley; 2 Rob Smyth; 3 Danny Halliwell; 4 Ben Cooper; 5 Damian Munro; 6 Mick Govin; 7 Tommy Martyn; 8 Heath Cruckshank; 9 Dave McConnell; 10 Matt Sturm; 11 Chris Percival; 12 Oliver Wilkes; 13 Ian Knott. Subs (all used): 14 Willie Swann; 15 Richard Marshall; 16 Mike Callan; 17 Andrew Isherwood.
Tries: Halliwell (2), Smyth (15), Turley (18, 36, 64), Munro (39, 69), Martyn (72); **Goals:** Turley 8/9.
Rugby Leaguer & League Express Men of the Match: *Cougars:* Phil Stephenson; *Centurions:* Neil Turley.
Penalty count: 9-5; **Half-time:** 6-30;
Referee: Glen Black (New Zealand); **Attendance:** 1,091.

ROCHDALE HORNETS 30 OLDHAM 24

HORNETS: 1 Michael Platt; 2 David Alstead; 3 Mark McCully; 4 Richard Varkulis; 5 Chris Campbell; 6 John Braddish; 7 Liam McGovern; 8 Tommy Hodgkinson; 9 Darren Robinson; 10 Gareth Price; 11 Andy Gorski; 12 Darren Shaw; 13 Dave Cunliffe. Subs (all used): 14 Janan Billings; 15 Dave Newton; 16 Sam Butterworth; 17 Lee Hansen.
Tries: Robinson (15), Alstead (47), Butterworth (50), Campbell (59), Platt (62); **Goals:** Braddish 5/8.
Sin bin: Alstead (22) - dissent; Robinson (74) - fighting.
On report:
Incident (55) - leaving McLoughlin with cut face.
OLDHAM: 1 Jon Goddard; 2 Gavin Dodd; 3 Iain Marsh; 4 Jon Roper; 5 Nick Johnson; 6 Lee Marsh; 7 Ian Watson; 8 Steve Molloy; 9 Keith Brennan; 10 Martin McLoughlin; 11 Lee Doran; 12 Dane Morgan; 13 Phil Farrell. Subs (all used): 14 Neil Roden; 15 Gareth Barber; 16 Gavin Johnson; 17 Adam Sharples.
Tries: N Johnson (11), Dodd (23), Brennan (34), Roden (55); **Goals:** Roper 4/7.
Sin bin: I Marsh (53) - holding down;
Roden (74) - fighting.
Rugby Leaguer & League Express Men of the Match: *Hornets:* Tommy Hodgkinson; *Oldham:* Jon Goddard.
Penalty count: 14-14; **Half-time:** 8-18;
Referee: Peter Taberner (Wigan); **Attendance:** 1,403.

WEEK 14

Sunday 15th August 2004

BATLEY BULLDOGS 18 OLDHAM 34

BULLDOGS: 1 Nathan Graham; 2 Bryn Powell; 3 Shad Royston; 4 Danny Maun; 5 Adrian Flynn; 6 Dean Lawford; 7 Barry Eaton; 8 Chris Molyneux; 9 Mark Cass; 10 Steve Hill; 11 Sean Richardson; 12 Andy Spink; 13 Mark Toohey. Subs (all used): 14 Ryan Horsley; 15 Paul Harrison; 16 David Bates; 17 David Rourke.
Tries: Spink (20, 51, 77); **Goals:** Eaton 3/3.
OLDHAM: 1 Jon Goddard; 2 Gavin Dodd; 3 Iain Marsh; 4 Jon Roper; 5 Nick Johnson; 6 Neil Roden; 7 Ian Watson; 8 Paul Southern; 9 Keith Brennan; 10 Martin McLoughlin; 11 Lee Doran; 12 Dane Morgan; 13 Phil Farrell. Subs (all used): 14 Gareth Barber; 15 Adam Sharples; 16 Martin Elswood; 17 Steve Molloy.
Tries: Watson (18), N Johnson (24), Barber (34, 73), Farrell (67), Goddard (79); **Goals:** Roper 5/7.
Rugby Leaguer & League Express Men of the Match: *Bulldogs:* Andy Spink; *Oldham:* Ian Watson.
Penalty count: 7-7; **Half-time:** 6-16;
Referee: Mike Dawber (Wigan); **Attendance:** 886.

FEATHERSTONE ROVERS 35 HALIFAX 16

ROVERS: 1 Craig Moss; 2 Freddie Zitter; 3 Andy McNally; 4 Richard Newlove; 5 Matthew Wray; 6 Richard Blakeway; 7 Maxime Greseque; 8 Ian Tonks; 9 Paul Darley; 10 Stuart Dickens; 11 Steve Dooler; 12 Tom Haughey; 13 Adam Hayes. Subs (all used): 14 Jamie Stokes; 15 Danny Evans; 16 Neil Lowe; 17 Jim Carlton.
Tries: Zitter (16, 68), McNally (32, 51), Blakeway (39), Newlove (45); **Goals:** Dickens 3/6, Greseque 2/3;
Field goal: Blakeway.
Sin bin: Darley (58) - minor altercation.
HALIFAX: 1 Scott Grix; 2 Rikki Sheriffe; 3 James Bunyan; 4 Alan Hadcroft; 5 James Haley; 6 Pat Weisner; 7 Ben Black; 8 Jon Simpson; 9 Phil Cantillon; 10 Chris Birchall; 11 Ged Corcoran; 12 Gareth Greenwood; 13 Jamie Bloem. Subs (all used): 14 Chris Norman; 15 Ben Feehan; 16 Anthony Farrell; 17 Ryan McDonald.
Tries: Simpson (9), Bloem (57), Scott Grix (77);
Goals: Bloem 2/2, Weisner 0/1.
Sin bin: Bloem (58) - minor altercation.
Rugby Leaguer & League Express Men of the Match: *Rovers:* Steve Dooler; *Halifax:* Pat Weisner.
Penalty count: 10-5; **Half-time:** 21-6;
Referee: Peter Taberner (Wigan); **Attendance:** 1,488.

LEIGH CENTURIONS 46 DONCASTER DRAGONS 32

CENTURIONS: 1 Rob Smyth; 2 Dan Potter; 3 Danny Halliwell; 4 Chris Percival; 5 Damian Munro; 6 Mick Govin; 7 Tommy Martyn; 8 Simon Knox; 9 Dave McConnell; 10 Matt Sturm; 11 David Larder; 12 Oliver Wilkes; 13 Ian Knott. Subs (all used): 14 Willie Swann; 15 Heath Cruckshank; 16 Richard Marshall; 17 Andrew Isherwood.
Tries: Knott (6, 14), Munro (28), Martyn (32, 40), Potter (72), McConnell (78); **Goals:** Smyth 9/9.
DRAGONS: 1 Craig Horne; 2 Dean Colton; 3 Alex Muff; 4 Craig Lawton; 5 Marlon Billy; 6 Graham Holroyd; 7 Chris Hough; 8 Gareth Handford; 9 Craig Cook; 10 Maea David; 11 Martin Ostler; 12 Peter Green; 13 Martin Moana. Subs (all used): 14 Dean O'Loughlin; 15 James Walker; 16 Johnny Woodcock; 17 Allan Dunham.
Tries: P Green (25), Billy (37, 48, 59), Handford (50), J Walker (65); **Goals:** Holroyd 4/6.
Rugby Leaguer & League Express Men of the Match: *Centurions:* David Larder; *Dragons:* Graham Holroyd.
Penalty count: 10-10; **Half-time:** 34-10; **Referee:** Ronnie Laughton (Barnsley); **Attendance:** 1,793.

ROCHDALE HORNETS 46 KEIGHLEY COUGARS 32

HORNETS: 1 Michael Platt; 2 David Alstead; 3 Mark McCully; 4 Richard Varkulis; 5 Chris Campbell; 6 John Braddish; 7 Bobbie Goulding; 8 Tommy Hodgkinson; 9 Darren Robinson; 10 Gareth Price; 11 Andy Gorski; 12 Darren Shaw; 13 Dave Cunliffe. Subs (all used): 14 Janan Billings; 15 Dave Newton; 16 Sam Butterworth; 17 Lee Hansen.
Tries: Platt (3, 31, 42), Shaw (25), Price (50, 67), Robinson (72), Newton (78);
Goals: Braddish 3/4, Butterworth 0/1, McCully 4/4.
COUGARS: 1 Matt Bramald; 2 Karl Smith; 3 David Foster; 4 Matt Foster; 5 Andy Robinson; 6 Adam Mitchell; 7 Matt Firth; 8 Phil Stephenson; 9 Craig Nipperess; 10 Jason Clegg; 11 Jordan Ross; 12 Craig McDowell; 13 Lee Patterson. Subs (all used): 14 Max Tomlinson; 15 Chris Wainwright; 16 Jamie Fielden; 17 Richard Mervill.
Tries: M Foster (6, 21, 38), Nipperess (9), Smith (47, 75); **Goals:** Mitchell 4/6.
Rugby Leaguer & League Express Men of the Match: *Hornets:* Michael Platt; *Cougars:* Matt Foster.
Penalty count: 6-4; **Half-time:** 18-22;
Referee: Colin Morris (Huddersfield); **Attendance:** 822.

WHITEHAVEN 38 HULL KINGSTON ROVERS 8

WHITEHAVEN: 1 Gary Broadbent; 2 Craig Calvert; 3 Mick Nanyn; 4 David Seeds; 5 Paul O'Neil; 6 Leroy Joe; 7 Sam Obst; 8 Ryan Tandy; 9 Aaron Lester; 10 David Fatialofa; 11 Spencer Miller; 12 Howard Hill; 13 Craig Walsh. Subs (all used): 14 Carl Sice; 15 Marc Jackson; 16 Chris McKinney; 17 Paul Davidson.
Tries: Hill (5), Walsh (10, 76), Obst (28), Calvert (58), Tandy (63), Miller (67); **Goals:** Nanyn 5/8.
ROVERS: 1 Paul Owen; 2 Nick Pinkney; 3 Craig Poucher; 4 Paul Parker; 5 Alasdair McClarron; 6 Paul Mansson; 7 Phil Hasty; 8 Matthew Blake; 9 Paul Pickering; 10 Makali Aizue; 11 Jason Netherton; 12 Anthony Seibold; 13 Damian Ball. Subs (all used): 14 Jimmy Walker; 15 Andy Smith; 16 Frank Watene; 17 Paul Fletcher.
Tries: Parker (35), Pinkney (72); **Goals:** Poucher 0/2.
Rugby Leaguer & League Express Men of the Match: *Whitehaven:* Howard Hill; *Rovers:* Paul Mansson.
Penalty count: 7-3; **Half-time:** 16-4;
Referee: Robert Connolly (Wigan); **Attendance:** 1,857.

Saturday 21st August 2004

ROCHDALE HORNETS 52 DONCASTER DRAGONS 18

HORNETS: 1 Michael Platt; 2 David Alstead; 3 Mark McCully; 4 Richard Varkulis; 5 Chris Campbell; 6 Lee Birdseye; 7 John Braddish; 8 Tommy Hodgkinson; 9 Darren Robinson; 10 Rob Ball; 11 Andy Gorski; 12 Darren Shaw; 13 Dave Cunliffe. Subs (all used): 14 Sam Butterworth; 15 Dave Newton; 16 Bobbie Goulding; 17 Lee Hansen.
Tries: Alstead (22, 30), Birdseye (39), Goulding (42), Platt (44), Varkulis (48, 61), Robinson (58), Braddish (76); **Goals:** Birdseye 7/10, McCully 1/1.
DRAGONS: 1 Craig Horne; 2 Dean Colton; 3 Alex Muff; 4 Craig Lawton; 5 Marlon Billy; 6 Martin Moana; 7 Graham Holroyd; 8 Gareth Handford; 9 Craig Cook; 10 Andy Fisher; 11 Martin Ostler; 12 Peter Green; 13 Maea David. Subs (all used): 14 Allan Dunham; 15 James Walker; 16 Gareth Lloyd; 17 Johnny Woodcock.
Tries: Colton (16), Fisher (68), Billy (80);
Goals: Holroyd 2/2, Woodcock 1/2.
Rugby Leaguer & League Express Men of the Match: *Hornets:* Michael Platt; *Dragons:* Craig Cook.
Penalty count: 7-9; **Half-time:** 22-8;
Referee: Russell Smith (Castleford); **Attendance:** 624.

WEEK 15

Sunday 22nd August 2004

BATLEY BULLDOGS 22 WHITEHAVEN 48

BULLDOGS: 1 Mark Sibson; 2 Bryn Powell; 3 Nathan Graham; 4 Danny Maun; 5 Adrian Flynn; 6 Danny Thomas; 7 Barry Eaton; 8 Steve Hill; 9 Mark Cass; 10 David Bates; 11 Mark Toohey; 12 Andy Spink; 13 Ryan Horsley. Subs (all used): 14 Shad Royston; 15 Paul Harrison; 16 Craig Wright; 17 Sean Richardson.
Tries: Eaton (48), Powell (68), Toohey (74), Bates (79);
Goals: Eaton 3/4.
WHITEHAVEN: 1 Gary Broadbent; 2 Craig Calvert; 3 Wesley Wilson; 4 Mick Nanyn; 5 Paul O'Neil; 6 Leroy Joe; 7 Sam Obst; 8 Ryan Tandy; 9 Aaron Lester; 10 David Fatialofa; 11 Spencer Miller; 12 Howard Hill; 13 Craig Walsh. Subs (all used): 14 Paul Davidson; 15 Carl Sice; 16 Dean Vaughan; 17 Marc Jackson.
Tries: Nanyn (2, 10, 13, 60), Walsh (6, 66), Miller (15), Calvert (28); **Goals:** Nanyn 8/10.
Rugby Leaguer & League Express Men of the Match: *Bulldogs:* Craig Wright; *Whitehaven:* Sam Obst.
Penalty count: 11-8; **Half-time:** 0-36;
Referee: Ronnie Laughton (Barnsley); **Attendance:** 605.

HALIFAX 58 LEIGH CENTURIONS 30

HALIFAX: 1 Ben Feehan; 2 Rikki Sheriffe; 3 James Bunyan; 4 Alan Hadcroft; 5 James Haley; 6 Pat Weisner; 7 Ben Black; 8 Ryan McDonald; 9 Gareth Greenwood; 10 Chris Birchall; 11 Anthony Farrell; 12 Ged Corcoran; 13 Jamie Bloem. Subs (all used): 14 Phil Cantillon; 15 Mark Moxon; 16 Richard Smith; 17 Jon Simpson.
Tries: Haley (4, 22, 39), Bloem (25), Black (33, 53, 63), Sheriffe (46, 56); **Goals:** Bloem 11/11.
CENTURIONS: 1 Rob Smyth; 2 Dan Potter; 3 Phil Jones; 4 Chris Percival; 5 Gary Rourke; 6 John Duffy; 7 Tommy Martyn; 8 Simon Knox; 9 Dave McConnell; 10 Matt Sturm; 11 David Larder; 12 Oliver Wilkes; 13 Ian Knott. Subs (all used): 14 Paul Rowley; 15 Willie Swann; 16 Richard Marshall; 17 Heath Cruckshank.
Tries: McConnell (30), Swann (59, 79), Rourke (70, 74), Duffy (77); **Goals:** Smyth 3/5, Jones 0/1.
Sin bin: Duffy (49) - professional foul.
Rugby Leaguer & League Express Men of the Match: *Halifax:* Jamie Bloem; *Centurions:* Gary Rourke.
Penalty count: 7-9; **Half-time:** 32-6; **Referee:** Gareth Hewer (Whitehaven); **Attendance:** 1,781.

HULL KINGSTON ROVERS 32 FEATHERSTONE ROVERS 24

ROBINS: 1 Paul Owen; 2 Nick Pinkney; 3 Paul Parker; 4 Craig Poucher; 5 Alasdair McClarron; 6 Paul Mansson; 7 Phil Hasty; 8 Jon Aston; 9 Andy Ellis; 10 Makali Aizue; 11 Jason Netherton; 12 Anthony Seibold; 13 Damian Ball. Subs (all used): 14 Jimmy Walker; 15 Andy Smith; 16 Frank Watene; 17 Paul Fletcher.
Tries: McClarron (5, 39), Parker (37), Walker (42), Aston (49), Hasty (58); **Goals:** Poucher 4/6.
ROVERS: 1 Craig Moss; 2 Freddie Zitter; 3 Andy McNally; 4 Dean Ripley; 5 Matthew Wray; 6 Richard Blakeway; 7 Maxime Greseque; 8 Ian Tonks; 9 Paul Darley; 10 Stuart Dickens; 11 Steve Dooler; 12 Andy Jarrett; 13 Adam Hayes. Subs (all used): 14 Jamie Stokes; 15 Bryan Henare; 16 Danny Evans; 17 Jim Carlton.
Tries: Blakeway (22), McNally (45), Greseque (67), Ripley (79); **Goals:** Dickens 3/4, Greseque 1/1.
Rugby Leaguer & League Express Men of the Match: *Robins:* Phil Hasty; *Rovers:* Richard Blakeway.
Penalty count: 4-2; **Half-time:** 16-8; **Referee:** Colin Morris (Huddersfield); **Attendance:** 1,985.

OLDHAM 31 KEIGHLEY COUGARS 20

OLDHAM: 1 Jon Goddard; 2 Gavin Dodd; 3 David Gibbons; 4 Jon Roper; 5 Nick Johnson; 6 Neil Roden; 7 Ian Watson; 8 Paul Southern; 9 John Hough; 10 Martin McLoughlin; 11 Lee Doran; 12 Dane Morgan; 13 Phil Farrell. Subs (all used): 14 Gareth Barber; 15 Craig Farrimond; 16 Lee Marsh; 17 Steve Molloy.
Tries: N Johnson (1), Morgan (18), Goddard (36, 44), Roden (73); **Goals:** Roper 0/1, Watson 5/5;
Field goal: Watson.
Sin bin: Doran (48) - fighting.
COUGARS: 1 Matt Bramald; 2 Max Tomlinson; 3 Karl Smith; 4 Matt Foster; 5 Andy Robinson; 6 Adam Mitchell; 7 Matt Firth; 8 Phil Stephenson; 9 Craig Nipperess; 10 Jason Clegg; 11 David Foster; 12 Craig McDowell; 13 Lee Patterson. Subs (all used): 14 Chris Wainwright; 15 Danny Murgatroyd; 16 Danny Ekis; 17 Richard Mervill.
Tries: M Foster (10, 23, 71), Robinson (13), Mitchell (32); **Goals:** Mitchell 0/5.
Sin bin: Mervill (48) - fighting.
Rugby Leaguer & League Express Men of the Match: *Oldham:* Ian Watson; *Cougars:* Matt Firth.
Penalty count: 6-6; **Half-time:** 16-16;
Referee: Robert Connolly (Wigan); **Attendance:** 1,202.

WEEK 16

Sunday 29th August 2004

FEATHERSTONE ROVERS 18 BATLEY BULLDOGS 28

ROVERS: 1 Andy McNally; 2 Jamie Stokes; 3 Dean Ripley; 4 Richard Newlove; 5 Matthew Wray; 6 Richard Blakeway; 7 Maxime Greseque; 8 Ian Tonks; 9 Paul Darley; 10 Stuart Dickens; 11 Steve Dooler; 12 Andy Jarrett; 13 Adam Hayes. Subs (all used): 14 Freddie Zitter; 15 Danny Evans; 16 Steve Coulson; 17 Jim Carlton.
Tries: Hayes (8, 55), McNally (21); **Goals:** Dickens 3/5.
BULLDOGS: 1 Mark Sibson; 2 Bryn Powell; 3 Shad Royston; 4 Danny Maun; 5 Adrian Flynn; 6 Mark Toohey; 7 Barry Eaton; 8 Craig Wright; 9 Kris Lythe; 10 David Rourke; 11 Paul Harrison; 12 Andy Spink; 13 Ryan Horsley. Subs (all used): 14 Tim Spears; 15 Will Cartledge; 16 David Bates; 17 Chris Molyneux.
Tries: Harrison (14), Maun (23), Powell (35), Royston (63), Horsley (74); **Goals:** Eaton 4/6.
Rugby Leaguer & League Express Men of the Match: *Rovers:* Adam Hayes; *Bulldogs:* David Rourke.
Penalty count: 10-4; **Half-time:** 12-18;
Referee: Ben Thaler (Wakefield); **Attendance:** 1,298.

KEIGHLEY COUGARS 20 DONCASTER DRAGONS 39

COUGARS: 1 Matt Bramald; 2 Max Tomlinson; 3 Karl Smith; 4 Matt Foster; 5 Andy Robinson; 6 Adam Mitchell; 7 Matt Firth; 8 Phil Stephenson; 9 Craig Nipperess; 10 Jason Clegg; 11 David Foster; 12 Craig McDowell; 13 Lee Patterson. Subs (all used): 14 Chris Wainwright; 15 Simeon Hoyle; 16 Danny Ekis; 17 Richard Mervill.
Tries: Stephenson (13), M Foster (74);
Goals: Mitchell 5/5, Nipperess 1/1.
DRAGONS: 1 Wayne Green; 2 Johnny Woodcock; 3 Gareth Lloyd; 4 Craig Horne; 5 Dean Colton; 6 Graham Holroyd; 7 Craig Cook; 8 Gareth Handford; 9 Peter Green; 10 Maea David; 11 Andy Fisher; 12 Craig Lawton; 13 Martin Moana. Subs (all used): 14 Dean O'Loughlin; 15 James Walker; 16 Chris Hough; 17 Marlon Billy.
Tries: Holroyd (6), Moana (23, 65, 80), W Green (30, 48), Colton (71); **Goals:** Woodcock 4/6, Holroyd 1/1;
Field goal: W Green.
Sin bin: W Green (32) - holding down.
On report: Moana (44) - high tackle on Wainwright.
Rugby Leaguer & League Express Men of the Match: *Cougars:* Phil Stephenson; *Dragons:* Martin Moana.
Penalty count: 9-7; **Half-time:** 8-16;
Referee: Mike Dawber (Wigan); **Attendance:** 760.

LEIGH CENTURIONS 26 HULL KINGSTON ROVERS 22

CENTURIONS: 1 Neil Turley; 2 Rob Smyth; 3 Craig Weston; 4 Chris Percival; 5 David Alstead; 6 Phil Jones; 7 John Duffy; 8 Simon Knox; 9 Paul Rowley; 10 Matt Sturm; 11 David Larder; 12 Andrew Isherwood; 13 Oliver Wilkes. Subs (all used): 14 Willie Swann; 15 Richard Marshall; 16 Luke Isakka; 17 Heath Cruckshank.
Tries: Percival (15, 55), Wilkes (45); **Goals:** Turley 7/8.
ROVERS: 1 Paul Owen; 2 Nick Pinkney; 3 Craig Poucher; 4 Paul Parker; 5 Alasdair McClarron; 6 Paul Mansson; 7 Phil Hasty; 8 Jason Netherton; 9 Andy Ellis; 10 Makali Aizue; 11 Andy Smith; 12 Anthony Seibold; 13 Damian Ball. Subs (all used): 14 Jimmy Walker; 15 Loz Wildbore; 16 Frank Watene; 17 Paul Fletcher.
Tries: Poucher (4), Smith (24), Watene (67, 78);
Goals: Poucher 3/4.
Sin bin: Walker (52) – holding down.
Rugby Leaguer & League Express Men of the Match: *Centurions:* David Larder; *Rovers:* Paul Mansson.
Penalty count: 15-14; **Half-time:** 14-10; **Referee:** Ronnie Laughton (Barnsley); **Attendance:** 1,768.

ROCHDALE HORNETS 34 HALIFAX 24

HORNETS: 1 Michael Platt; 2 Andy Saywell; 3 Mark McCully; 4 Richard Varkulis; 5 Chris Campbell; 6 Lee Birdseye; 7 John Braddish; 8 Tommy Hodgkinson; 9 Darren Robinson; 10 Rob Ball; 11 Andy Gorski; 12 Darren Shaw; 13 Dave Cunliffe. Subs (all used): 14 Sam Butterworth; 15 Dave Newton; 16 Bobbie Goulding; 17 Lee Hansen.
Tries: Ball (6), Saywell (12), Campbell (25), Robinson (44), Gorski (55), Birdseye (59); **Goals:** Birdseye 5/6.
HALIFAX: 1 Ben Feehan; 2 Rikki Sheriffe; 3 James Bunyan; 4 Alan Hadcroft; 5 James Haley; 6 Ben Black; 7 Mark Moxon; 8 Ryan McDonald; 9 Gareth Greenwood; 10 Chris Birchall; 11 Anthony Farrell; 12 Ged Corcoran; 13 Jamie Bloem. Subs (all used): 14 Andy Boothroyd; 15 Simon Grix; 16 Richard Smith; 17 Jon Simpson.
Tries: Feehan (18, 69), Black (30), Bloem (79);
Goals: Bloem 4/5.
Rugby Leaguer & League Express Men of the Match: *Hornets:* Andy Gorski; *Halifax:* Ben Feehan.
Penalty count: 8-9; **Half-time:** 16-12;
Referee: Robert Connolly (Wigan); **Attendance:** 1,230.

WHITEHAVEN 32 OLDHAM 16

WHITEHAVEN: 1 Gary Broadbent; 2 Craig Calvert; 3 Mick Nanyn; 4 David Seeds; 5 Wesley Wilson; 6 Leroy Joe; 7 Sam Obst; 8 Ryan Tandy; 9 Aaron Lester; 10 David Fatialofa; 11 Spencer Miller; 12 Howard Hill; 13 Craig Walsh. Subs (all used): 14 Brett McDermott; 15 Carl Sice; 16 Paul Davidson; 17 Marc Jackson.
Tries: Tandy (8, 13), Obst (15), Lester (28), Joe (66), Calvert (79); **Goals:** Nanyn 4/6.
OLDHAM: 1 Jon Goddard; 2 Gavin Dodd; 3 Lee Doran; 4 Jon Roper; 5 Nick Johnson; 6 Neil Roden; 7 Ian Watson; 8 Paul Southern; 9 Keith Brennan; 10 Dane Moran; 11 Martin Elswood; 12 Phil Farrell; 13 Lee Marsh. Subs (all used): 14 Gareth Barber; 15 Mark Roberts; 16 Martin McLoughlin; 17 Steve Molloy.
Tries: McLoughlin (22), Doran (64), Dodd (75);
Goals: L Marsh 2/2, Watson 0/1.
Rugby Leaguer & League Express Men of the Match: *Whitehaven:* Ryan Tandy; *Oldham:* Lee Marsh.
Penalty count: 5-5; **Half-time:** 22-4; **Referee:** Colin Morris (Huddersfield); **Attendance:** 2,009.

WEEK 17

Sunday 5th September 2004

DONCASTER DRAGONS 34 HALIFAX 44

DRAGONS: 1 Wayne Green; 2 Johnny Woodcock; 3 Gareth Lloyd; 4 Craig Horne; 5 Dean Colton; 6 Graham Holroyd; 7 Craig Cook; 8 Gareth Handford; 9 Peter Green; 10 Maea David; 11 Andy Fisher; 12 Craig Lawton; 13 Martin Moana. Subs (all used): 14 Dean O'Loughlin; 15 James Walker; 16 Chris Hough; 17 Alex Muff.
Tries: Cook (27), W Green (42), Colton (63), Fisher (67), Moana (74), Hough (77); **Goals:** Woodcock 5/6.
Sin bin: Handford (48) - fighting; Hough (50) - fighting.
HALIFAX: 1 Scott Grix; 2 Rikki Sheriffe; 3 James Bunyan; 4 Ben Feehan; 5 James Haley; 6 Simon Grix; 7 Ben Black; 8 Ryan McDonald; 9 Mark Moxon; 10 Chris Birchall; 11 Gareth Greenwood; 12 Ged Corcoran; 13 Jamie Bloem. Subs (all used): 14 Danny Jones; 15 Richard Smith; 16 David Bates; 17 Anthony Farrell.
Tries: Scott Grix (12, 33), Haley (16), Feehan (30), Sheriffe (35), Black (54), Bloem (58), Moxon (69);
Goals: Bloem 5/6, Jones 1/2.
Sin bin: Bunyan (48) - fighting; Feehan (50) - fighting.
Rugby Leaguer & League Express Men of the Match: *Dragons:* Andy Fisher; *Halifax:* Ben Black.
Penalty count: 4-4; **Half-time:** 6-28;
Referee: Colin Morris (Huddersfield); **Attendance:** 786.

FEATHERSTONE ROVERS 35 OLDHAM 26

ROVERS: 1 Andy McNally; 2 Jamie Stokes; 3 Freddie Zitter; 4 Richard Newlove; 5 Matthew Wray; 6 Dean Ripley; 7 Maxime Greseque; 8 Jim Carlton; 9 Paul Darley; 10 Stuart Dickens; 11 Tom Haughey; 12 Adam Hayes; 13 Richard Blakeway. Subs: 14 Jon Presley (not used); 15 Steve Dooler; 16 Neil Lowe; 17 Andy Jarrett.
Tries: Zitter (13), Stokes (25), Haughey (35), Lowe (62, 76); **Goals:** Dickens 7/10; **Field goal:** Greseque.

Leigh duo Oliver Wilkes and John Duffy halt Batley's Adrian Flynn as the Centurions secure the League Leadership

OLDHAM: 1 Jon Goddard; 2 Gavin Dodd; 3 David Gibbons; 4 Jon Roper; 5 Nick Johnson; 6 Neil Roden; 7 Ian Watson; 8 Paul Southern; 9 John Hough; 10 Dane Morgan; 11 Lee Doran; 12 Phil Farrell; 13 Lee Marsh. Subs (all used): 14 Gareth Barber; 15 Mark Roberts; 16 Martin McLoughlin; 17 Steve Molloy.
Tries: Goddard (12), Roden (21), L Marsh (29), Dodd (51, 71); **Goals:** L Marsh 3/5.
Rugby Leaguer & League Express Men of the Match: *Rovers:* Stuart Dickens; *Oldham:* Gavin Dodd.
Penalty count: 10-3; **Half-time:** 20-16;
Referee: Mike Dawber (Wigan); **Attendance:** 1,397.

KEIGHLEY COUGARS 22 HULL KINGSTON ROVERS 52

COUGARS: 1 Matt Bramald; 2 Chris Beever; 3 David Foster; 4 Andy Robinson; 5 Karl Smith; 6 Gavin Nipperess; 7 Matt Firth; 8 Phil Stephenson; 9 Simeon Hoyle; 10 Jason Clegg; 11 Richard Mervill; 12 Craig McDowell; 13 Lee Patterson. Subs (all used): 14 Andy Feather; 15 Eddie Wilson; 16 Danny Murgatroyd; 17 Danny Ekis.
Tries: Stephenson (21), Bramald (47), Feather (55), Nipperess (77); **Goals:** Nipperess 2/2, Bramald 1/2.
ROVERS: 1 Paul Owen; 2 Nick Pinkney; 3 Paul Parker; 4 Craig Poucher; 5 Alasdair McClarron; 6 Paul Mansson; 7 Phil Hasty; 8 Jamie Bovill; 9 Andy Ellis; 10 Makali Aizue; 11 Jason Netherton; 12 Andy Smith; 13 Anthony Seibold. Subs (all used): 14 Jimmy Walker; 15 Matthew Blake; 16 Frank Watene; 17 Paul Fletcher.
Tries: Bovill (6), Hasty (10, 27 ,40), Netherton (16), Parker (58), Aizue (63), McClarron (67), Mansson (73);
Goals: Poucher 8/10.
Rugby Leaguer & League Express Men of the Match: *Cougars:* Simeon Hoyle; *Rovers:* Paul Mansson.
Penalty count: 9-7; **Half-time:** 6-32; **Referee:** Gareth Hewer (Whitehaven). **Attendance:** 1,152.

LEIGH CENTURIONS 21 WHITEHAVEN 14

CENTURIONS: 1 Neil Turley; 2 Rob Smyth; 3 Craig Weston; 4 Chris Percival; 5 David Alstead; 6 Phil Jones; 7 John Duffy; 8 Simon Knox; 9 Dave McConnell; 10 Matt Sturm; 11 David Larder; 12 Oliver Wilkes; 13 Ian Knott. Subs (all used): 14 Willie Swann; 15 Richard Marshall; 16 Andrew Isherwood; 17 Heath Cruckshank.
Tries: Alstead (5, 29), McConnell (32);
Goals: Turley 4/5; **Field goal:** Turley.
WHITEHAVEN: 1 Gary Broadbent; 2 Craig Calvert; 3 David Seeds; 4 Mick Nanyn; 5 Wesley Wilson; 6 Leroy Joe; 7 Sam Obst; 8 Ryan Tandy; 9 Aaron Lester; 10 David Fatialofa; 11 Spencer Miller; 12 Howard Hill; 13 Craig Walsh. Subs (all used): 14 Paul Davidson; 15 Carl Sice; 16 Chris McKinney; 17 Marc Jackson.
Tries: Fatialofa (8), Obst (68); **Goals:** Nanyn 3/3.
Rugby Leaguer & League Express Men of the Match: *Centurions:* Dave McConnell; *Whitehaven:* Sam Obst.
Penalty count: 6-6; **Half-time:** 18-8;
Referee: Robert Connolly (Wigan). **Attendance:** 3,442.

ROCHDALE HORNETS 24 BATLEY BULLDOGS 32

HORNETS: 1 Sam Butterworth; 2 Andy Saywell; 3 Mark McCully; 4 Richard Varkulis; 5 Ryan Blake; 6 Lee Birdseye; 7 Liam McGovern; 8 Tommy Hodgkinson; 9 Darren Robinson; 10 Rob Ball; 11 Andy Gorski; 12 Darren Shaw; 13 Dave Cunliffe. Subs (all used): 14 Janan Billings; 15 Dave Newton; 16 Bobbie Goulding; 17 Lee Hansen.
Tries: McCully (17), Gorski (36), Butterworth (42, 79);

Goals: Birdseye 4/6.
Sin bin: Goulding (71) - dissent.
On report: Cunliffe (67) - use of knees.
BULLDOGS: 1 Mark Sibson; 2 Bryn Powell; 3 Shad Royston; 4 Andy Spink; 5 Adrian Flynn; 6 Danny Maun; 7 Barry Eaton; 8 Steve Hill; 9 Kris Lythe; 10 Craig Wright; 11 Paul Harrison; 12 Tim Spears; 13 Ryan Horsley. Subs (all used): 14 Steve Beard; 15 Sean Richardson; 16 Gary Shillabeer; 17 Chris Molyneux.
Tries: Flynn (1), Spink (4), Maun (59), Sibson (64), Lythe (77); **Goals:** Eaton 6/9.
Rugby Leaguer & League Express Men of the Match: *Hornets:* Dave Newton; *Bulldogs:* Danny Maun.
Penalty count: 7-16; **Half-time:** 12-12; **Referee:** Ronnie Laughton (Barnsley). **Attendance:** 1,067.

WEEK 18

Sunday 12th September 2004

BATLEY BULLDOGS 22 LEIGH CENTURIONS 29

BULLDOGS: 1 Mark Sibson; 2 Bryn Powell; 3 Shad Royston; 4 Andy Spink; 5 Adrian Flynn; 6 Danny Maun; 7 Barry Eaton; 8 Steve Hill; 9 Kris Lythe; 10 Craig Wright; 11 Paul Harrison; 12 Tim Spears; 13 Ryan Horsley. Subs (all used): 14 Mark Toohey; 15 Sean Richardson; 16 Gary Shillabeer; 17 Chris Molyneux.
Tries: Lythe (38, 64, 70), Maun (72); **Goals:** Eaton 3/4.
CENTURIONS: 1 Neil Turley; 2 Rob Smyth; 3 Dan Potter; 4 Chris Percival; 5 David Alstead; 6 Craig Weston; 7 John Duffy; 8 Simon Knox; 9 Dave McConnell; 10 Matt Sturm; 11 David Larder; 12 Oliver Wilkes; 13 Ian Knott. Subs (all used): 14 Willie Swann; 15 Luke Isakka; 16 Richard Marshall; 17 Heath Cruckshank.
Tries: Wilkes (15, 75), Cruckshank (23), Turley (33);
Goals: Turley 6/7; **Field goal:** Turley.
Rugby Leaguer & League Express Men of the Match: *Bulldogs:* Kris Lythe; *Centurions:* Oliver Wilkes.
Penalty count: 10-6; **Half-time:** 6-21;
Referee: Mike Dawber (Wigan). **Attendance:** 1,719.

HALIFAX 30 KEIGHLEY COUGARS 22

HALIFAX: 1 Scott Grix; 2 Rikki Sheriffe; 3 James Bunyan; 4 Ben Feehan; 5 James Haley; 6 Danny Jones; 7 Ben Black; 8 Ryan McDonald; 9 Mark Moxon; 10 Chris Birchall; 11 Gareth Greenwood; 12 Ged Corcoran; 13 Jamie Bloem. Subs (all used): 14 Simon Grix; 15 Richard Smith; 16 David Bates; 17 Alan Hadcroft.
Tries: Sheriffe (19, 37), Black (23, 53), Feehan (76);
Goals: Bloem 5/6.
COUGARS: 1 Matt Bramald; 2 Max Tomlinson; 3 David Foster; 4 Andy Robinson; 5 Chris Beever; 6 Craig Nipperess; 7 Matt Firth; 8 Phil Stephenson; 9 Simeon Hoyle; 10 Jason Clegg; 11 Richard Mervill; 12 Eddie Wilson; 13 Craig McDowell. Subs (all used): 14 Andy Feather; 15 Chris Wainwright; 16 Lee Patterson; 17 Chris Roe.
Tries: Hoyle (7), D Foster (28), Patterson (44), Firth (79); **Goals:** Nipperess 3/4.
Rugby Leaguer & League Express Men of the Match: *Halifax:* Ben Black; *Cougars:* Matt Firth.
Penalty count: 7-5; **Half-time:** 18-10;
Referee: Julian King (St Helens). **Attendance:** 1,344.

HULL KINGSTON ROVERS 42 ROCHDALE HORNETS 18

ROVERS: 1 Paul Owen; 2 Nick Pinkney; 3 Craig Poucher;

4 Paul Parker; 5 Alasdair McClarron; 6 Paul Mansson; 7 Phil Hasty; 8 Jamie Bovill; 9 Paul Pickering; 10 Makali Aizue; 11 Jason Netherton; 12 Anthony Seibold; 13 Damian Ball. Subs (all used): 14 Jimmy Walker; 15 Loz Wildbore; 16 Frank Watene; 17 Andy Smith.
Tries: Owen (8), Parker (22), Ball (39), Aizue (55, 64, 73); **Goals:** Poucher 9/10.
Sin bin: Hasty (12, 35) - fighting; Parker (70) - fighting.
HORNETS: 1 Mark McCully; 2 Andy Saywell; 3 Dave Cunliffe; 4 Richard Varkulis; 5 Sam Butterworth; 6 John Braddish; 7 Liam McGovern; 8 Lee Hansen; 9 Bobbie Goulding; 10 Tommy Hodgkinson; 11 Andy Gorski; 12 Kris Ratcliffe; 13 Darren Shaw. Subs (all used): 14 Lee Birdseye; 15 Dave Newton; 16 Darren Robinson; 17 Rob Ball.
Tries: Hodgkinson (16), Robinson (65), Goulding (78);
Goals: Braddish 3/3.
Sin bin: Goulding (12) - fighting;
McGovern (35) - fighting, Cunliffe (70) - fighting.
On report: Shaw (1) - late tackle.
Rugby Leaguer & League Express Men of the Match: *Rovers:* Damian Ball; *Hornets:* John Braddish.
Penalty count: 15-8; **Half-time:** 22-6;
Referee: Robert Connolly (Wigan). **Attendance:** 2,017.

OLDHAM 29 DONCASTER DRAGONS 26

OLDHAM: 1 Jon Goddard; 2 Gavin Dodd; 3 Iain Marsh; 4 Jon Roper; 5 Nick Johnson; 6 Neil Roden; 7 Ian Watson; 8 Steve Molloy; 9 Keith Brennan; 10 Martin McLoughlin; 11 Lee Doran; 12 Dane Morgan; 13 Phil Farrell. Subs (all used): 14 Gareth Barber; 15 Mark Roberts; 16 Lee Marsh; 17 Adam Sharples.
Tries: N Johnson (7), Barber (38), Morgan (53), I Marsh (72); **Goals:** Roper 6/9; **Field goal:** Watson.
DRAGONS: 1 Craig Horne; 2 Dean Colton; 3 Alex Muff; 4 Wayne Green; 5 Marlon Billy; 6 Martin Moana; 7 Chris Hough; 8 Gareth Handford; 9 Craig Cook; 10 Andy Fisher; 11 Allan Dunham; 12 Peter Green; 13 Craig Lawton. Subs: 14 Tom Buckenham (not used); 15 James Walker; 16 Graham Holroyd; 17 Dean O'Loughlin.
Tries: Lawton (31, 44), Hough (49), Colton (80);
Goals: Hough 5/7.
Rugby Leaguer & League Express Men of the Match: *Oldham:* Jon Goddard; *Dragons:* Chris Hough.
Penalty count: 14-8; **Half-time:** 14-8; **Referee:** Ronnie Laughton (Barnsley). **Attendance:** 1,448.

WHITEHAVEN 24 FEATHERSTONE ROVERS 16

WHITEHAVEN: 1 Gary Broadbent; 2 Craig Calvert; 3 David Seeds; 4 Mick Nanyn; 5 Wesley Wilson; 6 Leroy Joe; 7 Sam Obst; 8 Ryan Tandy; 9 Aaron Lester; 10 David Fatialofa; 11 Paul Davidson; 12 Howard Hill; 13 Craig Walsh. Subs (all used): 14 Chris McKinney; 15 Carl Sice; 16 Dean Vaughan; 17 Marc Jackson.
Tries: Walsh (24), Calvert (33, 43), Nanyn (71), Seeds (75); **Goals:** Nanyn 2/6.
Sin bin: Lester (39) - dissent.
ROVERS: 1 Andy McNally; 2 Jamie Stokes; 3 Freddie Zitter; 4 Richard Newlove; 5 Matthew Wray; 6 Richard Blakeway; 7 Maxime Gresegue; 8 Ian Tonks; 9 Paul Darley; 10 Jim Carlton; 11 Steve Dooler; 12 Neil Lowe; 13 Adam Hayes. Subs (all used): 14 Jon Presley; 15 Andy Jarrett; 16 Danny Evans; 17 Stuart Dickens.
Tries: Blakeway (13), Lowe (66); **Goals:** Gresegue 4/4.
Rugby Leaguer & League Express Men of the Match: *Whitehaven:* Howard Hill; *Rovers:* Maxime Gresegue.
Penalty count: 2-6; **Half-time:** 8-12; **Referee:** Colin Morris (Huddersfield); **Attendance:** 2,024.

Makali Aizue fends off Martin Moana as Hull KR eliminate Doncaster

James Ford drives forward as Featherstone defeat Hull KR in a thriller

PLAY-OFFS

Sunday 19th September 2004

ELIMINATION PLAY-OFFS

HULL KINGSTON ROVERS 63
DONCASTER DRAGONS 22

ROVERS: 1 Paul Owen; 2 Nick Pinkney; 3 Craig Poucher; 4 Paul Parker; 5 Alasdair McClarron; 6 Paul Mansson; 7 Phil Hasty; 8 Jamie Bovill; 9 Andy Ellis; 10 Makali Aizue; 11 Jason Netherton; 12 Anthony Seibold; 13 Damian Ball. Subs (all used): 14 Jimmy Walker; 15 Andy Smith; 16 Frank Watene; 17 Paul Fletcher.
Tries: McClarron (7, 71), Netherton (14), Ellis (18, 68), Pinkney (28, 39), Mansson (50), Walker (62), Hasty (74), Watene (77); **Goals:** Poucher 9/11;
Field goal: Mansson.
Sin bin: Owen (25) – holding down.
DRAGONS: 1 Craig Horne; 2 Dean Colton; 3 Alex Muff; 4 Gareth Lloyd; 5 Marlon Billy; 6 Graham Holroyd; 7 Chris Hough; 8 Gareth Handford; 9 Peter Green; 10 Andy Fisher; 11 Allan Dunham; 12 Craig Lawton; 13 Martin Moana. Subs (all used): 14 Wayne Green; 15 James Walker; 16 Maea David; 17 Dean O'Loughlin.
Tries: Moana (25, 34), Muff (57), J Walker (79);
Goals: Holroyd 0/1, Hough 3/3.
Rugby Leaguer & League Express Men of the Match: *Rovers:* Paul Mansson; *Dragons:* Chris Hough.
Penalty count: 13-11; **Half-time:** 30-10; **Referee:** Karl Kirkpatrick (Warrington); **Attendance:** 2,319.

OLDHAM 28 FEATHERSTONE ROVERS 33

OLDHAM: 1 Jon Goddard; 2 Gavin Dodd; 3 Iain Marsh; 4 Jon Roper; 5 Nick Johnson; 6 Neil Roden; 7 Ian Watson; 8 Paul Southern; 9 Keith Brennan; 10 Martin McLoughlin; 11 Lee Doran; 12 Dane Morgan; 13 Phil Farrell. Subs (all used): 14 Gareth Barber; 15 Mark Roberts; 16 Craig Farrimond; 17 Steve Molloy.
Tries: I Marsh (31), Farrell (39), N Johnson (45), Barber (57), McLoughlin (70); **Goals:** Roper 4/8.
ROVERS: 1 Andy McNally; 2 James Ford; 3 Freddie Zitter; 4 Richard Newlove; 5 Matthew Wray; 6 Dean Ripley; 7 Maxime Greseque; 8 Ian Tonks; 9 Paul Darley; 10 Stuart Dickens; 11 Tom Haughey; 12 Neil Lowe; 13 Richard Blakeway. Subs (all used): 14 Jamie Stokes; 15 Jim Carlton; 16 Steve Dooler; 17 Adam Hayes.
Tries: Haughey (10), Newlove (17), Lowe (26), Wray (68), McNally (74); **Goals:** Dickens 2/4, Greseque 4/4.
Field goal: Greseque.
Rugby Leaguer & League Express Men of the Match: *Oldham:* Mark Roberts; *Rovers:* Ian Tonks.
Penalty count: 8-6; **Half-time:** 12-14;
Referee: Robert Connolly (Wigan); **Attendance:** 1,970.

Sunday 26th September 2004

QUALIFYING SEMI-FINAL

LEIGH CENTURIONS 30 WHITEHAVEN 16

CENTURIONS: 1 Neil Turley; 2 Rob Smyth; 3 Danny Halliwell; 4 Ben Cooper; 5 David Alstead; 6 Craig Weston; 7 John Duffy; 8 Simon Knox; 9 Dave McConnell; 10 Matt Sturm; 11 David Larder; 12 Oliver Wilkes; 13 Ian Knott. Subs (all used): 14 Dave McConnell; 15 Richard Marshall; 16 Willie Swann; 17 Heath Cruckshank.
Tries: Smyth (6), Halliwell (11), Alstead (37, 76), Larder (49, 80); **Goals:** Turley 2/7; **Field goals:** Turley 2.
Sin bin: Larder (61) - holding down.
WHITEHAVEN: 1 Gary Broadbent; 2 Craig Calvert; 3 David Seeds; 4 Mick Nanyn; 5 Wesley Wilson; 6 Leroy Joe; 7 Sam Obst; 8 Ryan Tandy; 9 Aaron Lester; 10 David Fatialofa; 11 Paul Davidson; 12 Howard Hill; 13 Craig Walsh. Subs (all used): 14 Spencer Miller; 15 Carl Sice; 16 Chris McKinney; 17 Marc Jackson.
Tries: Tandy (23), Calvert (33); **Goals:** Nanyn 4/5.
Rugby Leaguer & League Express Men of the Match: *Centurions:* John Duffy; *Whitehaven:* Ryan Tandy.
Penalty count: 11-10; **Half-time:** 14-14;
Referee: Steve Ganson (St Helens); **Attendance:** 4,563.

ELIMINATION SEMI-FINAL

HULL KINGSTON ROVERS 18
FEATHERSTONE ROVERS 19

ROBINS: 1 Paul Owen; 2 Nick Pinkney; 3 Craig Poucher; 4 Paul Parker; 5 Alasdair McClarron; 6 Paul Mansson; 7 Phil Hasty; 8 Jamie Bovill; 9 Andy Ellis; 10 Makali Aizue; 11 Jason Netherton; 12 Anthony Seibold; 13 Damian Ball. Subs (all used): 14 Jimmy Walker; 15 Andy Smith; 16 Frank Watene; 17 Paul Fletcher.
Tries: Pinkney (3), Parker (14), McClarron (39, 74); **Goals:** Poucher 0/3, Hasty 1/1.
Sin bin: Walker (35) – fighting;
Bovill (65) – late tackle on Greseque.
ROVERS: 1 Andy McNally; 2 James Ford; 3 Freddie Zitter; 4 Richard Newlove; 5 Matthew Wray; 6 Dean Ripley; 7 Maxime Greseque; 8 Ian Tonks; 9 Paul Darley; 10 Stuart Dickens; 11 Tom Haughey; 12 Neil Lowe; 13 Richard Blakeway. Subs (all used): 14 Jamie Stokes; 15 Jim Carlton; 16 Steve Dooler; 17 Adam Hayes.
Tries: Ford (35), Dooler (66); **Goals:** Dickens 2/3, Greseque 3/3; **Field goal:** Greseque.
Sin bin: Darley (35) – fighting.
Rugby Leaguer & League Express Men of the Match: *Robins:* Phil Hasty; *Rovers:* Maxime Greseque.
Penalty count: 9-8; **Half-time:** 12-8;
Referee: Ian Smith (Oldham); **Attendance:** 3,075.

Leigh's David Larder halted by Whitehaven's Leroy Joe during the National League One Grand Final

Sunday 3rd October 2004

FINAL ELIMINATOR

WHITEHAVEN 30 FEATHERSTONE ROVERS 2

WHITEHAVEN: 1 Gary Broadbent; 2 Craig Calvert; 3 David Seeds; 4 Mick Nanyn; 5 Wesley Wilson; 6 Leroy Joe; 7 Sam Obst; 8 Ryan Tandy; 9 Aaron Lester; 10 David Fatialofa; 11 Paul Davidson; 12 Howard Hill; 13 Craig Walsh. Subs (all used): 14 Spencer Miller; 15 Carl Sice; 16 Chris McKinney; 17 Marc Jackson.
Tries: Davidson (21), Walsh (27, 63), Obst (37), Wilson (43), Nanyn (76); **Goals:** Nanyn 3/6.
ROVERS: 1 Andy McNally; 2 James Ford; 3 Freddie Zitter; 4 Richard Newlove; 5 Matthew Wray; 6 Dean Ripley; 7 Maxime Greseque; 8 Ian Tonks; 9 Paul Darley; 10 Stuart Dickens; 11 Tom Haughney; 12 Neil Lowe; 13 Richard Blakeway. Subs (all used): 14 Jamie Stokes; 15 Jim Carlton; 16 Steve Dooler; 17 Adam Hayes.
Goals: Dickens 1/1.
Rugby Leaguer & League Express Men of the Match: *Whitehaven:* Howard Hill; *Rovers:* Stuart Dickens.
Penalty count: 11-10; **Half-time:** 16-2; **Referee:** Karl Kirkpatrick (Warrington); **Attendance:** 2,374.

Sunday 10th October 2004

GRAND FINAL

LEIGH CENTURIONS 32 WHITEHAVEN 16
(After extra time)

CENTURIONS: 1 Neil Turley; 2 Rob Smyth; 3 Danny Halliwell; 4 Ben Cooper; 5 David Alstead; 6 John Duffy; 7 Tommy Martyn; 8 Simon Knox; 9 Paul Rowley; 10 Matt Sturm; 11 David Larder; 12 Oliver Wilkes; 13 Ian Knott. Subs (all used): 14 Dave McConnell; 15 Heath Cruckshank; 16 Richard Marshall; 17 Willie Swann.
Tries: Cooper (27, 83), Martyn (61), Turley (87); **Goals:** Turley 6/8; **Field goals:** Turley 2, Rowley, Martyn.
WHITEHAVEN: 1 Gary Broadbent; 2 Craig Calvert; 3 David Seeds; 4 Mick Nanyn; 5 Wesley Wilson; 6 Leroy Joe; 7 Sam Obst; 8 Marc Jackson; 9 Aaron Lester; 10 David Fatialofa; 11 Paul Davidson; 12 Howard Hill; 13 Craig Walsh. Subs (all used): 14 Spencer Miller; 15 Carl Sice; 16 Chris McKinney; 17 Ryan Tandy.
Tries: Wilson (2, 71), Calvert (45); **Goals:** Nanyn 2/6.
Rugby Leaguer & League Express Men of the Match: *Centurions:* Neil Turley; *Whitehaven:* Aaron Lester.
Penalty count: 5-9; **Half-time:** 7-6;
Referee: Ronnie Laughton (Barnsley);
Attendance: 11,005 *(at Halton Stadium, Widnes).*

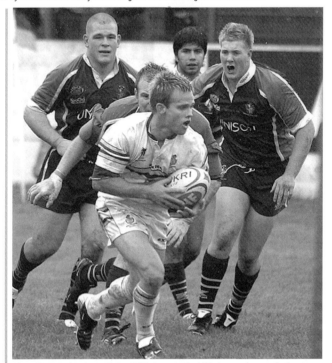

Sam Obst on the charge during Whitehaven's Final Eliminator win over Featherstone

NATIONAL LEAGUE TWO 2004
Round by Round

WEEK 1

Friday 9th April 2004

LONDON SKOLARS 18 SHEFFIELD EAGLES 24

SKOLARS: 1 Joel Osborn; 2 Ronnie Mushiso; 3 Donny Lam; 4 Stephen Green; 5 Neil Foster; 6 Jermaine Coleman; 7 Peter Hannan; 8 Koben Katipa; 9 Gareth Honor; 10 Alex Smits; 11 Glenn Osborn; 12 Mark Cantoni; 13 John Rua. Subs (all used): 14 Rubert Jonker; 15 Desi Kadima; 16 Ben Joyce; 17 Dan Reeds.
Tries: Green (6), Jonker (21), Cantoni (31);
Goals: G Osborn 2/3, J Osborn 1/1.
EAGLES: 1 Andy Poynter; 2 Carl De Chenu; 3 Nick Turnbull; 4 Jon Breakingbury; 5 Danny Mills; 6 Richard Goddard; 7 Gavin Brown; 8 Jack Howieson; 9 Gareth Stanley; 10 Jon Bruce; 11 Andy Raleigh; 12 Craig Brown; 13 Jordan James. Subs (all used): 14 Greg Hurst; 15 Andy Rice; 16 Sean Dickinson; 17 Simon Tillyer.
Tries: Breakingbury (15), Poynter (27, 44), Turnbull (75); **Goals:** Goddard 4/5.
Rugby Leaguer & League Express Men of the Match: *Skolars:* Alex Smits; *Eagles:* Gavin Brown.
Penalty count: 4-6; **Half-time:** 18-12;
Referee: Phil Bentham (Warrington); **Attendance:** 401.

Monday 12th April 2004

BARROW RAIDERS 40 DEWSBURY RAMS 12

RAIDERS: 1 Craig Bower; 2 Nick Beech; 3 Damien Reid; 4 Paul Jones; 5 Adam Pate; 6 Chris Archer; 7 Darren Holt; 8 Stuart Dancer; 9 Dave Clark; 10 Paul Wilcock; 11 Matthew Leigh; 12 James King; 13 Barry Pugh. Subs (all used): 14 Mike Whitehead; 15 Andy McClure; 16 Geoff Luxon; 17 Paul Lupton.
Tries: P Jones (17), McClure (32, 52), Archer (58), Wilcock (63), Reid (42), Bower (46); **Goals:** Holt 6/8.
RAMS: 1 Wayne McHugh; 2 Andrew Webber; 3 Chris Redfearn; 4 Ian Kirke; 5 Leon Williamson; 6 Danny Thomas; 7 Adam Thaler; 8 Paul Hicks; 9 Darren Robinson; 10 Joe Naidole; 11 Kevin Crouthers; 12 Billy Kershaw; 13 Graham Law. Subs (all used): 14 David Mycoe; 15 Kevin Spink; 16 Jamie Tennant; 17 Michael Gibbons.
Tries: Thomas (27), McHugh (78); **Goals:** A Thaler 2/2.
Rugby Leaguer & League Express Men of the Match: *Raiders:* Darren Holt; *Rams:* Adam Thaler.
Penalty count: 7-8; **Half-time:** 12-6; **Referee:** Steve Nicholson (Whitehaven); **Attendance:** 949.

SWINTON LIONS 42 GATESHEAD THUNDER 10

LIONS: 1 Wayne English; 2 Jason Roach; 3 Mark Bolton; 4 Chris Maye; 5 Chris Irwin; 6 Mick Coates; 7 Warren Ayres; 8 Mike Loughlin; 9 Peter Cannon; 10 Craig Wingfield; 11 Phil Cushion; 12 Kris Smith; 13 Ian Sinfield. Subs (all used): 14 Paul Ashton; 15 Safraz Patel; 16 Rob Whittaker; 17 Tau Liku.
Tries: Maye (4, 74), Bolton (25, 60), Sinfield (29), Cannon (39), English (55), Patel (65);
Goals: Ayres 4/6; Ashton 1/1; Wingfield 0/1.
Dismissal: Sinfield (44) - punching.
Sin bin: Ashton (71) - dissent.
THUNDER: 1 Graham Stephenson; 2 Michael Bunting; 3 Kevin Neighbour; 4 Dave Griffiths; 5 Robin Peers; 6 Paul Thorman; 7 Neil Thorman; 8 Rob Line; 9 Seamus McCallion; 10 Scott Harrison; 11 Steven Bradley; 12 Steve Rutherford; 13 Craig Fisher. Subs (all used): 14 Andy Fleming; 15 Phil Pitt; 16 Ian Ball; 17 Ben Hodgson.
Tries: Neighbour (17), Peers (31); **Goals:** P Thorman 1/2.
Rugby Leaguer & League Express Men of the Match: *Lions:* Peter Cannon; *Thunder:* Paul Thorman.
Penalty count: 9-11; **Half-time:** 20-10;
Referee: Gareth Hewer (Whitehaven); **Attendance:** 410.

YORK CITY KNIGHTS 32 CHORLEY LYNX 18

CITY KNIGHTS: 1 Nathan Graham; 2 Scott Walker; 3 Chris Langley; 4 Mark Cain; 5 Alex Godfrey; 6 Scott Rhodes; 7 Danny Brough; 8 Craig Forsyth; 9 Lee Jackson; 10 Yusuf Sozi; 11 Darren Callaghan; 12 Simon Friend; 13 Damian Ball. Subs (all used): 14 Jimmy Elston; 15 Mark Stewart; 16 Mick Ramsden; 17 John Smith.
Tries: Ball (16), Callaghan (27), Walker (53), Brough (56), Elston (73); **Goals:** Brough 6/7.
Sin bin: Rhodes (20) - high tackle.
LYNX: 1 Lee Patterson; 2 Ade Mead; 3 Eddie Kilgannon; 4 Jamie Stenhouse; 5 Steve Ormesher; 6 Chris Ramsdale; 7 Martin Gambles; 8 Ian Parry; 9 Martin Roden; 10 John Hill; 11 Mick Redford; 12 Gary Smith; 13 Danny Barton. Subs (all used): 14 Lee Rowley; 15 James Lomax; 16 Anthony Murray; 17 Neil Alexander.
Tries: Patterson (5), Ramsdale (23), Ormesher (43), Gambles (50);
Goals: Gambles 0/2, Ormesher 0/1, Ramsdale 1/1.
Sin bin: Stenhouse (35) - dissent.
Rugby Leaguer & League Express Men of the Match: *City Knights:* Darren Callaghan; *Lynx:* Martin Gambles.
Penalty count: 9-7; **Half-time:** 16-8;
Referee: Ben Thaler (Wakefield); **Attendance:** 1,401.

HUNSLET HAWKS 42 WORKINGTON TOWN 14

HAWKS: 1 Chris Hall; 2 Dave Jessey; 3 Paul Seal; 4 Wes McGibbon; 5 Leigh Deakin; 6 Steve Doherty; 7 Latham Tawhai; 8 Steve Pryce; 9 Jamaine Wray; 10 Mick Coyle; 11 Wayne Freeman; 12 Neil Mears; 13 Jon Liddell. Subs (all used): 14 Glen Freeman; 15 Gary Shillabeer; 16 Danny Fearon; 17 Jonlee Lockwood.
Tries: G Freeman (26), Shillabeer (35), Seal (43, 54, 68), Tawhai (50), C Hall (65), Liddell (73); **Goals:** Liddell 5/10.
TOWN: 1 Andrew Fearon; 2 Martyn Wilson; 3 Neil Frazer; 4 Craig Stalker; 5 Graeme Lewthwaite; 6 Jonathan Heaney; 7 Brett Smith; 8 Dean Burgess; 9 Jonny Limmer; 10 Matthew Tunstall; 11 Andy McGlasson; 12 Jamie Beaumont; 13 Martin Stalker. Subs (all used): 14 Matthew Johnson; 15 William Blackburn; 16 Craig Barker; 17 James Robinson.
Tries: Frazer (11), Burgess (20); **Goals:** Heaney 3/4.
Rugby Leaguer & League Express Men of the Match: *Hawks:* Latham Tawhai; *Town:* Jonny Limmer.
Penalty count: 13-6; **Half-time:** 10-14;
Referee: Phil Bentham (Warrington); **Attendance:** 344.

WEEK 2

Sunday 18th April 2004

CHORLEY LYNX 18 SHEFFIELD EAGLES 32

LYNX: 1 Lee Patterson; 2 Gary O'Regan; 3 Eddie Kilgannon; 4 Jamie Stenhouse; 5 Steve Ormesher; 6 Chris Ramsdale; 7 Martin Gambles; 8 Ian Parry; 9 Anthony Murray; 10 John Hill; 11 Mick Redford; 12 Gary Smith; 13 Danny Barton. Subs (all used): 14 Lee Rowley; 15 James Lomax; 16 Michael Griffin; 17 Neil Alexander.
Tries: Ormesher (42), Ramsdale (44), Kilgannon (47);
Goals: Ramsdale 3/3.
EAGLES: 1 Andy Poynter; 2 Kieron Collins; 3 Nick Turnbull; 4 Jon Breakingbury; 5 Greg Hurst; 6 Richard Goddard; 7 Gavin Brown; 8 Jack Howieson; 9 Gareth Stanley; 10 Jon Bruce; 11 Andy Raleigh; 12 Craig Brown; 13 Jordan James. Subs (all used): 14 Sean Dickinson; 15 Guy Adams; 16 Andy Rice; 17 Simon Tillyer.
Tries: Tillyer (31), G Brown (49), K Collins (57, 60), Hurst (63, 73), Turnbull (78); **Goals:** Goddard 2/7.
Rugby Leaguer & League Express Men of the Match: *Lynx:* Lee Patterson; *Eagles:* Gavin Brown.
Penalty count: 6-6; **Half-time:** 0-4;
Referee: Gareth Hewer (Whitehaven); **Attendance:** 257.

DEWSBURY RAMS 8 SWINTON LIONS 35

RAMS: 1 Wayne McHugh; 2 Richard Thaler; 3 Chris Redfearn; 4 Ian Kirke; 5 Leon Williamson; 6 Danny Thomas; 7 David Mycoe; 8 Paul Hicks; 9 Darren Robinson; 10 Joe Naidole; 11 Kevin Crouthers; 12 Billy Kershaw; 13 Graham Law. Subs (all used): 14 Adam Thaler; 15 Jamie Tennant; 16 Mark Hawksley; 17 Michael Gibbons.
Try: Hawksley (80); **Goals:** A Thaler 2/2.
On report: Gibbons (31) - illegal tackle.
LIONS: 1 Wayne English; 2 Hugh Thorpe; 3 Mark Bolton; 4 Chris Maye; 5 Chris Irwin; 6 Mick Coates; 7 Warren Ayres; 8 Mike Loughlin; 9 Peter Cannon; 10 Craig Wingfield; 11 Phil Cushion; 12 Ian Sinfield; 13 Ian Hodson. Subs (all used): 14 Safraz Patel; 15 Rob Whittaker; 16 Mark Pembroke; 17 Tau Liku.
Tries: Cannon (37, 64), Maye (61, 77), Wingfield (66), Thorpe (77); **Goals:** Ayres 5/7; **Field goal:** Ayres.
Rugby Leaguer & League Express Men of the Match: *Rams:* Wayne McHugh; *Lions:* Warren Ayres.
Penalty count: 8-9; **Half-time:** 2-8;
Referee: Phil Bentham (Warrington); **Attendance:** 509.

GATESHEAD THUNDER 21 LONDON SKOLARS 22

THUNDER: 1 Graham Stephenson; 2 Michael Bunting; 3 Mick Kent; 4 Kevin Neighbour; 5 Robin Peers; 6 Paul Thorman; 7 Craig Fisher; 8 Rob Line; 9 Neil Thorman; 10 Scott Harrison; 11 Liam Garside; 12 Steve Rutherford; 13 Steven Bradley. Subs (all used): 14 Mark Walker; 15 Ian Ball; 16 Andy Fleming; 17 Paul Dodsworth.
Tries: Peers (17), N Thorman (31), Bunting (45);
Goals: P Thorman 4/6; **Field goal:** P Thorman.
Sin bin: Kent (13) - persistent interference.
SKOLARS: 1 Joel Osborn; 2 Tim Butterfield; 3 Ben Joyce; 4 Ronnie Mushiso; 5 Neil Foster; 6 Jermaine Coleman; 7 Peter Hannan; 8 Rubert Jonker; 9 Gareth Honor; 10 Alex Smits; 11 Glenn Osborn; 12 Mark Cantoni; 13 John Rua. Subs (all used): 14 Koben Katipa; 15 Dean McFadyen; 16 Andy Gould; 17 Brad McFarland.
Tries: J Osborn (62), Mushiso (67), McFarland (70), Honor (78); **Goals:** J Osborn 0/1, Joyce 3/3.
Rugby Leaguer & League Express Men of the Match: *Thunder:* Robin Peers; *Skolars:* Joel Osborn.
Penalty count: 9-9; **Half-time:** 12-0; **Referee:** Matthew Thomasson (Warrington); **Attendance:** 203.

WORKINGTON TOWN 14 BARROW RAIDERS 32

TOWN: 1 Andrew Fearon; 2 Matthew Johnson; 3 Neil Frazer; 4 Craig Stalker; 5 Graeme Lewthwaite; 6 Brett Smith; 7 Jonathan Heaney; 8 Dean Burgess; 9 Jonny Limmer; 10 Andy McGlasson; 11 Martin Stalker; 12 Jamie Beaumont; 13 Martyn Wilson. Subs (all used): 14 Adam Coulson; 15 William Blackburn; 16 Craig Barker; 17 James Robinson.
Tries: B Smith (18), Limmer (77); **Goals:** Heaney 3/3.
Sin bin: Heaney (66) - fighting.
On report: Brawl (66).
RAIDERS: 1 Craig Bower; 2 Nick Beech; 3 Damien Reid; 4 Andy McClure; 5 Paul Jones; 6 Chris Archer; 7 Darren Holt; 8 Stuart Dancer; 9 Dave Clark; 10 Paul Wilcock; 11 Mike Whitehead; 12 James King; 13 Barry Pugh. Subs (all used): 14 Matthew Leigh; 15 Paul Lupton; 16 Geoff Luxon; 17 Wayne Jones.
Tries: Whitehead (31), Beech (34, 72), McClure (39), Reid (43); **Goals:** Holt 6/7.
Sin bin: Dancer (66) - fighting; King (67) - punching.
On report: Brawl (66).
Rugby Leaguer & League Express Men of the Match: *Town:* Jonny Limmer; *Raiders:* Darren Holt.
Penalty count: 8-6; **Half-time:** 8-22;
Referee: Peter Taberner (Wigan); **Attendance:** 503.

YORK CITY KNIGHTS 8 HUNSLET HAWKS 21

CITY KNIGHTS: 1 Nathan Graham; 2 Chris Smith; 3 Chris Langley; 4 Mark Cain; 5 Rob Kama; 6 Scott Rhodes; 7 Danny Brough; 8 Andy Burland; 9 Lee Jackson; 10 Yusuf Sozi; 11 Darren Callaghan; 12 Simon Friend; 13 Damian Ball. Subs (all used): 14 Jimmy Elston; 15 John Smith; 16 Richard Wilson; 17 Craig Forsyth.
Tries: Callaghan (15), Langley (51); **Goals:** Brough 0/2.
HAWKS: 1 Jon Liddell; 2 Chris Hall; 3 Paul Seal; 4 Wes McGibbon; 5 Leigh Deakin; 6 Steve Doherty; 7 Latham Tawhai; 8 Jonlee Lockwood; 9 Jamaine Wray; 10 Mick Coyle; 11 Wayne Freeman; 12 Shaun Ibbetson; 13 Andy Bastow. Subs (all used): 14 Steve Pryce; 15 Glen Freeman; 16 Danny Fearon; 17 Neil Mears.
Tries: Seal (1), Coyle (8), Wray (29), Deakin (41);
Goals: Liddell 2/4; **Field goal:** Tawhai.
On report: Fearon (78) - use of knees in the tackle.
Rugby Leaguer & League Express Men of the Match: *City Knights:* Lee Jackson; *Hawks:* Latham Tawhai.
Penalty count: 12-7; **Half-time:** 4-16;
Referee: Ben Thaler (Wakefield); **Attendance:** 1,262.

WEEK 3

Saturday 1st May 2004

LONDON SKOLARS 24 DEWSBURY RAMS 36

SKOLARS: 1 Joel Osborn; 2 Ronnie Mushiso; 3 Andy Gould; 4 Stephen Green; 5 Austin Aggrey; 6 Jermaine Coleman; 7 Peter Hannan; 8 Rubert Jonker; 9 Gareth Honor; 10 Koben Katipa; 11 Glenn Osborn; 12 Mark Cantoni; 13 John Rua. Subs (all used): 14 Ben Joyce; 15 Deon McFadyen; 16 Alex Smits; 17 Zane Gardiner.
Tries: G Osborn (2), J Osborn (12), Cantoni (41), Joyce (44), Aggrey (72); **Goals:** G Osborn 2/5.
RAMS: 1 Ian Preece; 2 Andrew Webber; 3 Ian Kirke; 4 Richard Thaler; 5 Leon Williamson; 6 Adam Thaler; 7 David Mycoe; 8 Paul Hicks; 9 Chris Woolford; 10 Mark Hawksley; 11 Kevin Crouthers; 12 Shane Davis; 13 Chris Redfearn. Subs (all used): 14 Kevin Spink; 15 Michael Gibbons; 16 Anthony Thewliss; 17 Joe Naidole.
Tries: R Thaler (6, 17), Hawksley (9), Thewliss (27), Redfearn (69), A Thaler (73, 80); **Goals:** A Thaler 4/7.
Rugby Leaguer & League Express Men of the Match: *Skolars:* Austin Aggrey; *Rams:* Adam Thaler.
Penalty count: 7-4; **Half-time:** 10-22;
Referee: Phil Bentham (Warrington); **Attendance:** 426.

WEEK 4

Sunday 2nd May 2004

BARROW RAIDERS 21 HUNSLET HAWKS 12

RAIDERS: 1 Craig Bower; 2 Nick Beech; 3 Damien Reid; 4 Paul Jones; 5 Adam Pate; 6 Chris Archer; 7 Darren Holt; 8 Stuart Dancer; 9 Dave Clark; 10 Paul Wilcock; 11 Mike Whitehead; 12 James King; 13 Barry Pugh. Subs (all used): 14 Andy McClure; 15 Matthew Leigh; 16 Paul Lupton; 17 Geoff Luxon.
Tries: King (34), Archer (40), Beech (53);
Goals: Holt 4/5; **Field goal:** Holt.
HAWKS: 1 Jon Liddell; 2 Chris Hall; 3 Paul Seal; 4 Wes McGibbon; 5 Leigh Deakin; 6 Andy Bastow; 7 Latham Tawhai; 8 Jonlee Lockwood; 9 Joe Hawley; 10 Neil Mears; 11 Wayne Freeman; 12 Shaun Ibbetson; 13 Mick Coyle. Subs (all used): 14 Steve Pryce; 15 Glen Freeman; 16 Danny Evans; 17 Chris Ross.
Tries: Coyle (17), C Hall (76); **Goals:** Liddell 2/3.
Dismissal: Evans (60) - high tackle on Holt.
Rugby Leaguer & League Express Men of the Match: *Raiders:* Darren Holt; *Hawks:* Andy Bastow.
Penalty count: 11-11; **Half-time:** 14-8;
Referee: Jamie Leahy (Dewsbury); **Attendance:** 868.

CHORLEY LYNX 42 GATESHEAD THUNDER 20

LYNX: 1 Lee Patterson; 2 Ade Mead; 3 Eddie Kilgannon; 4 Jamie Stenhouse; 5 Rob Smyth; 6 Chris Ramsdale; 7 Martin Gambles; 8 Ian Parry; 9 Anthony Murray; 10 John Hill; 11 Mick Redford; 12 Gary Smith; 13 Danny Barton. Subs (all used): 14 Lee Rowley; 15 Andy Grundy; 16 Brian Capewell; 17 James Lomax.
Tries: Patterson (5), Gambles (9, 52, 76), Kilgannon (18), Capewell (47, pen), Redford (57), Stenhouse (64);
Goals: Smyth 4/7, Capewell 1/1.
On report: Grundy (31) - knees in the tackle.
THUNDER: 1 Graham Stephenson; 2 Michael Bunting; 3 Craig Firth; 4 Kevin Neighbour; 5 Robin Peers; 6 Paul Thorman; 7 Craig Fisher; 8 Rob Line; 9 Neil Thorman; 10 Scott Harrison; 11 Liam Garside; 12 Steven Bradley; 13 Steve Rutherford. Subs (all used): 14 Mark Walker; 15 Tony Doherty; 16 Charlie Roe; 17 Adam Endersby.
Tries: P Thorman (12), Neighbour (22), N Thorman (36), Peers (80); **Goals:** P Thorman 2/4.
Sin bin: Bradley (43) - persistent interference.
Rugby Leaguer & League Express Men of the Match: *Lynx:* Jamie Stenhouse; *Thunder:* Paul Thorman.
Penalty count: 11-10; **Half-time:** 14-16;
Referee: Craig Halloran (Dewsbury); **Attendance:** 164.

SWINTON LIONS 64 WORKINGTON TOWN 26

LIONS: 1 Wayne English; 2 Hugh Thorpe; 3 Mark Bolton; 4 Chris Maye; 5 Chris Irwin; 6 Ian Hodson; 7 Warren Ayres; 8 Mike Loughlin; 9 Peter Cannon; 10 Craig Wingfield; 11 Phil Cushion; 12 Kris Smith; 13 Ian Sinfield. Subs (all used): 14 Jason Roach; 15 Rob Barraclough; 16 Ryan Stazicker; 17 Tau Liku.

Tries: Ayres (13), Bolton (15), English (20, 54, 79), Smith (28), Maye (39, 43), Roach (48), Cannon (52), Barraclough (58); **Goals:** Ayres 9/10, Smith 1/1.
Sin bin: Hodson (31) - fighting.
TOWN: 1 Scott Chilton; 2 Craig Stalker; 3 Neil Frazer; 4 Adam Coulson; 5 Andrew Fearon; 6 Tane Manihera; 7 Jonathan Heaney; 8 Adam Burgess; 9 Jonny Limmer; 10 Matthew Tunstall; 11 Andy McGlasson; 12 Jamie Beaumont; 13 David Pettit. Subs (all used): 14 Martin Stalker; 15 William Blackburn; 16 Craig Barker; 17 James Robinson.
Tries: Manihera (4), Chilton (6), Fearon (63), Limmer (64), Frazer (71); **Goals:** Heaney 3/5.
Sin bin: Beaumont (31) - fighting.
Rugby Leaguer & League Express Men of the Match: *Lions:* Warren Ayres; *Town:* Jonny Limmer.
Penalty count: 8-5; **Half-time:** 30-12; **Referee:** Matthew Thomasson (Warrington); **Attendance:** 454.

YORK CITY KNIGHTS 34 SHEFFIELD EAGLES 16

CITY KNIGHTS: 1 Nathan Graham; 2 Scott Walker; 3 Chris Langley; 4 Aaron Wood; 5 Mark Stewart; 6 Scott Rhodes; 7 Danny Brough; 8 Richard Wilson; 9 Lee Jackson; 10 Yusuf Sozi; 11 Darren Callaghan; 12 Simon Friend; 13 Damian Ball. Subs (all used): 14 Jimmy Elston; 15 Mark Cain; 16 John Smith; 17 Craig Forsyth.
Tries: Walker (10), Stewart (30, 50), Callaghan (40), Elston (57), Wood (66), Graham (80);
Goals: Brough 2/6, Walker 0/1; **Field goals:** Brough 2.
EAGLES: 1 Andy Poynter; 2 Kieron Collins; 3 Nick Turnbull; 4 Jon Breakingbury; 5 Greg Hurst; 6 Richard Goddard; 7 Gavin Brown; 8 Jack Howieson; 9 Gareth Stanley; 10 Jon Bruce; 11 Andy Raleigh; 12 Craig Brown; 13 Jordan James. Subs (all used): 14 Sean Dickinson; 15 Guy Adams; 16 Andy Rice; 17 Simon Tillyer.
Tries: K Collins (26), Breakingbury (44), Raleigh (73);
Goals: Goddard 1/2, G Brown 1/1.
Rugby Leaguer & League Express Men of the Match: *City Knights:* Darren Callaghan; *Eagles:* Jon Bruce.
Penalty count: 7-6; **Half-time:** 14-4;
Referee: Mike Dawber (Wigan); **Attendance:** 1,389.

WEEK 5

Sunday 9th May 2004

BARROW RAIDERS 16 YORK CITY KNIGHTS 30

RAIDERS: 1 Craig Bower; 2 Nick Beech; 3 Damien Reid; 4 Paul Jones; 5 Adam Pate; 6 Chris Archer; 7 Darren Holt; 8 Stuart Dancer; 9 Dave Clark; 10 Paul Wilcock; 11 Mike Whitehead; 12 James King; 13 Barry Pugh. Subs (all used): 14 Andy McClure; 15 Tama Wakelin; 16 Paul Lupton; 17 Geoff Luxon.
Tries: Whitehead (7), Clark (11), Pate (18);
Goals: Holt 2/3.
Sin bin: Holt (74) - punching.
CITY KNIGHTS: 1 Nathan Graham; 2 Scott Walker; 3 Chris Langley; 4 Darren Callaghan; 5 Mark Stewart; 6 Scott Rhodes; 7 Danny Brough; 8 Richard Wilson; 9 Lee Jackson; 10 Yusuf Sozi; 11 Mick Ramsden; 12 Simon Friend; 13 Damian Ball. Subs (all used): 14 Jimmy Elston; 15 Mark Cain; 16 John Smith; 17 Craig Forsyth.
Tries: Friend (25), Callaghan (29), Cain (32), Langley (40), Walker (46), Stewart (66); **Goals:** Brough 3/6.
Rugby Leaguer & League Express Men of the Match: *Raiders:* Paul Wilcock; *City Knights:* Danny Brough.
Penalty count: 12-7; **Half-time:** 16-16;
Referee: Phil Bentham (Warrington); **Attendance:** 1,048.

DEWSBURY RAMS 29 CHORLEY LYNX 14

RAMS: 1 Jamie Benn; 2 Richard Thaler; 3 Chris Redfearn; 4 Ian Kirke; 5 Leon Williamson; 6 Adam Thaler; 7 David Mycoe; 8 Paul Hicks; 9 Scott Dyson; 10 Mark Hawksley; 11 Kevin Spink; 12 Shane Davis; 13 Kevin Crouthers. Subs (all used): 14 Ian Preece; 15 Anthony Thewliss; 16 Michael Gibbons; 17 Joe Naidole.
Tries: Hawksley (12), A Thaler (15), Preece (61), Spink (68), Benn (76); **Goals:** Benn 4/6; **Field goal:** A Thaler.
Sin bin: Benn (28) - obstruction.
LYNX: 1 Lee Patterson; 2 Ade Mead; 3 Eddie Kilgannon; 4 Jamie Stenhouse; 5 Rob Smyth; 6 Chris Ramsdale; 7 Martin Gambles; 8 Ian Parry; 9 Anthony Murray; 10 John Hill; 11 Mick Redford; 12 Gary Smith; 13 Danny Barton. Subs (all used): 14 Lee Rowley; 15 Andy Grundy; 16 Brian Capewell; 17 Gary O'Regan.
Tries: Redford (29), Stenhouse (57), Gambles (79);
Goals: Capewell 1/2, Smyth 0/1.
Sin bin: Mead (45) - holding down.
On report: Ramsdale (37) - striking.
Rugby Leaguer & League Express Men of the Match: *Rams:* Kevin Crouthers; *Lynx:* John Hill.
Penalty count: 8-12; **Half-time:** 14-4; **Referee:** Matthew Thomasson (Warrington); **Attendance:** 459.

GATESHEAD THUNDER 6 SHEFFIELD EAGLES 42

THUNDER: 1 Graham Stephenson; 2 Michael Bunting; 3 Mick Kent; 4 Kevin Neighbour; 5 Robin Peers; 6 Paul Thorman; 7 Greg Dawson; 8 Rob Line; 9 Neil Thorman; 10 Peti Keni; 11 Liam Garside; 12 Steven Bradley; 13 Steve Rutherford. Subs (all used): 14 Charlie Roe; 15 Tony Doherty; 16 Adam Endersby; 17 Scott Harrison.
Try: N Thorman (56); **Goals:** P Thorman 1/1.
EAGLES: 1 Andy Poynter; 2 Greg Hurst; 3 Nick Turnbull; 4 Alex Dickinson; 5 Bright Sodje; 6 Steve Doherty; 7 Gavin Brown; 8 Jack Howieson; 9 Scott Collins; 10 Guy Adams; 11 Andy Raleigh; 12 Richard Goddard; 13 Simon Tillyer. Subs (all used): 14 Sean Dickinson; 15 Andy Rice; 16 Richard Stone; 17 Jon Bruce.
Tries: Poynter (2, 9), Hurst (24), A Dickinson (27, 30), Turnbull (42, 68), Howieson (78); **Goals:** Goddard 5/8.
Rugby Leaguer & League Express Men of the Match: *Thunder:* Graham Stephenson; *Eagles:* Jon Goddard.
Penalty count: 12-4; **Half-time:** 0-26;
Referee: Gareth Hewer (Whitehaven); **Attendance:** 297.

WORKINGTON TOWN 48 LONDON SKOLARS 18

TOWN: 1 Scott Chilton; 2 Matthew Johnson; 3 Neil Frazer; 4 Martyn Wilson; 5 Graeme Lewthwaite; 6 Tane Manihera; 7 Jonathan Heaney; 8 David Pettit; 9 Jonny Limmer; 10 Matthew Tunstall; 11 Andy McGlasson; 12 Gary Smith; 13 Jamie Beaumont. Subs (all used): 14 Andrew Fearon; 15 Martin Stalker; 16 Craig Barker; 17 Dean Burgess.
Tries: Wilson (10, 65), Beaumont (21), Limmer (24, 68), Chilton (26), Lewthwaite (33), Tunstall (45, 51);
Goals: Heaney 6/10.
SKOLARS: 1 Joel Osborn; 2 Neil Foster; 3 Kurt Pittman; 4 Stephen Green; 5 Ronnie Mushiso; 6 Jermaine Coleman; 7 Peter Hannan; 8 Rubert Jonker; 9 John Rua; 10 Alex Smits; 11 Glenn Osborn; 12 Deon McFadyen; 13 Mark Cantoni. Subs (all used): 14 Gareth Honor; 15 Wayne Parillon; 16 Andy Gould; 17 Koben Katipa.
Tries: J Osborn (60), Cantoni (71), Mushiso (79);
Goals: Pittman 2/2, G Osborn 1/2.
Sin bin: Honor (44) – dissent; Smits (78) – dissent.
Rugby Leaguer & League Express Men of the Match: *Town:* Tane Manihera; *Skolars:* Mark Cantoni.
Penalty count: 10-11; **Half-time:** 28–2;
Referee: Jamie Leahy (Dewsbury); **Attendance:** 446.

HUNSLET HAWKS 42 SWINTON LIONS 20

HAWKS: 1 Jon Liddell; 2 George Rayner; 3 Paul Seal; 4 Wes McGibbon; 5 Leigh Deakin; 6 Danny Wood; 7 Latham Tawhai; 8 Jonlee Lockwood; 9 Joe Hawley; 10 Steve Pryce; 11 Wayne Freeman; 12 Shaun Ibbetson; 13 Andy Bastow. Subs (all used): 14 Mick Coyle; 15 Neil Mears; 16 Andy Burland; 17 Chris Ross.
Tries: Bastow (11), W Freeman (20), Rayner (47, 66, 71), Mears (54), Tawhai (74); **Goals:** Wood 7/8.
LIONS: 1 Wayne English; 2 Hugh Thorpe; 3 Mark Bolton; 4 Phil Cushion; 5 Jason Roach; 6 Ian Hodson; 7 Warren Ayres; 8 Mike Loughlin; 9 Peter Cannon; 10 Rob Whittaker; 11 Ryan Stazicker; 12 Kris Smith; 13 Ian Sinfield. Subs (all used): 14 Chris Irwin; 15 Rob Barraclough; 16 Alan Kilshaw; 17 Craig Wingfield.
Tries: Sinfield (26), Thorpe (58), English (61), Irwin (79); **Goals:** Ayres 2/4.
Rugby Leaguer & League Express Men of the Match: *Hawks:* Latham Tawhai; *Lions:* Wayne English.
Penalty count: 5-4; **Half-time:** 12-4; **Referee:** Steve Nicholson (Whitehaven); **Attendance:** 525.

WEEK 6

Friday 21st May 2004

SHEFFIELD EAGLES 24 DEWSBURY RAMS 12

EAGLES: 1 Andy Poynter; 2 Greg Hurst; 3 Jon Breakingbury; 4 Alex Dickinson; 5 Bright Sodje; 6 Richard Goddard; 7 Ryan Dickinson; 8 Jack Howieson; 9 Scott Collins; 10 Jon Bruce; 11 Andy Raleigh; 12 Craig Brown; 13 Jordan James. Subs (all used): 14 Sean Dickinson; 15 Andy Rice; 16 Simon Tillyer; 17 Guy Adams.
Tries: Hurst (5, 42), Breakingbury (26), R Dickinson (65); **Goals:** Goddard 4/6.
Sin bin: Goddard (18) - fighting.
RAMS: 1 Jamie Benn; 2 Richard Thaler; 3 Chris Redfearn; 4 Ian Kirke; 5 Leon Williamson; 6 Adam Thaler; 7 David Mycoe; 8 Paul Hicks; 9 Scott Dyson; 10 Mark Hawksley; 11 Kevin Spink; 12 Shane Davis; 13 Kevin Crouthers. Subs (all used): 14 Ian Preece; 15 Billy Kershaw; 16 Michael Gibbons; 17 Joe Naidole.
Tries: Dyson (76), A Thaler (79); **Goals:** Benn 2/2.
Sin bin: Dyson (18) - fighting.
Rugby Leaguer & League Express Men of the Match: *Eagles:* Andy Poynter; *Rams:* Kevin Crouthers.
Penalty count: 7-4; **Half-time:** 12-0;
Referee: Mike Dawber (Wigan); **Attendance:** 1,352.

WEEK 7

Sunday 23rd May 2004

CHORLEY LYNX 40 WORKINGTON TOWN 26

LYNX: 1 Lee Patterson; 2 Ade Mead; 3 Eddie Kilgannon; 4 Jamie Stenhouse; 5 Gary O'Regan; 6 Brian Capewell; 7 Martin Gambles; 8 Ian Parry; 9 Anthony Murray; 10 John Hill; 11 Mick Redford; 12 Gary Smith; 13 Danny Barton. Subs (all used): 14 Lee Rowley; 15 James Lomax; 16 Steve Ormesher; 17 Chris Ramsdale.
Tries: O'Regan (2, 5), Redford (24), Patterson (43, 60), Ormesher (72); **Goals:** Capewell 8/8.
Sin bin: Stenhouse (20) - retaliation, and (38) - tripping.
TOWN: 1 Scott Chilton; 2 Craig Stalker; 3 Brett Smith; 4 Martyn Wilson; 5 Graeme Lewthwaite; 6 Shaun Boylan; 7 Tane Manihera; 8 Andy McGlasson; 9 Jonny Limmer; 10 Matthew Tunstall; 11 Ricky Wright; 12 John Tuimaualuga; 13 Jamie Beaumont. Subs (all used): 14 James Robinson; 15 David Pettit; 16 Dean Bragg; 17 Dean Burgess.
Tries: Manihera (13), Burgess (27), Limmer (31), Beaumont (34, 40); **Goals:** Manihera 3/6.
Sin bin: Beaumont (20) - fighting.
Rugby Leaguer & League Express Men of the Match: *Lynx:* Ian Parry; *Town:* Tane Manihera.
Penalty count: 12-7; **Half-time:** 22-24;
Referee: Phil Bentham (Warrington); **Attendance:** 248

SWINTON LIONS 10 BARROW RAIDERS 46

LIONS: 1 Wayne English; 2 Hugh Thorpe; 3 Mark Bolton; 4 Chris Maye; 5 Jason Roach; 6 Safraz Patel; 7 Warren Ayres; 8 Mike Loughlin; 9 Peter Cannon; 10 Phil Cushion; 11 Ryan Stazicker; 12 Kris Smith; 13 Ian Sinfield. Subs (all used): 14 Chris Irwin; 15 Ian Hodson; 16 Craig Wingfield; 17 Tau Liku.
Tries: Cannon (24), Stazicker (66); **Goals:** Ayres 1/2.
On report: Maye (70) - incident In tackle.
RAIDERS: 1 Craig Bower; 2 Shane Irabor; 3 Damien Reid; 4 Paul Jones; 5 Adam Pate; 6 Chris Archer; 7 Darren Holt; 8 Stuart Dancer; 9 Dave Clark; 10 Paul Lupton; 11 Mike Whitehead; 12 James King; 13 Barry Pugh. Subs (all used): 14 Tama Wakelin; 15 Matthew Leigh; 16 Phil Atkinson; 17 Nick Beech.
Tries: Bower (10, 16, 34, 51, 77), Dancer (39), Wakelin (42), P Jones (60); **Goals:** Holt 7/11.
Rugby Leaguer & League Express Men of the Match: *Lions:* Peter Cannon; *Raiders:* Darren Holt.
Penalty count: 5-5; **Half-time:** 6-28;
Referee: Robert Connolly (Wigan); **Attendance:** 504.

YORK CITY KNIGHTS 48 GATESHEAD THUNDER 12

CITY KNIGHTS: 1 Nathan Graham; 2 Austin Buchanan; 3 Chris Langley; 4 Darren Callaghan; 5 Alex Godfrey; 6 Scott Rhodes; 7 Danny Brough; 8 Richard Wilson; 9 Lee Jackson; 10 Yusuf Sozi; 11 John Smith; 12 Simon Friend; 13 Damian Ball. Subs (all used): 14 Jimmy Elston; 15 Mark Cain; 16 Mark Stewart; 17 Craig Forsyth.
Tries: Godfrey (7), Rhodes (10), Buchanan (18), Friend (20), Langley (35, 78), Brough (38, 45), Cain (61);
Goals: Brough 5/8, Ball 1/1.
Sin bin: Brough (69) - dissent.
THUNDER: 1 Graham Stephenson; 2 Michael Bunting; 3 Kevin Neighbour; 4 Craig Firth; 5 Robin Peers; 6 Paul Thorman; 7 Craig Fisher; 8 Rob Line; 9 Neil Thorman; 10 Steven Bradley; 11 Liam Garside; 12 Tony Doherty; 13 Steve Rutherford. Subs (all used): 14 Dave Griffiths; 15 Greg Dawson; 16 Adam Endersby; 17 Ben Hodgson.
Tries: Peers (49), Hodgson (55), Neighbour (71);
Goals: P Thorman 0/3.
Rugby Leaguer & League Express Men of the Match: *City Knights:* Damian Ball; *Thunder:* Paul Thorman.
Penalty count: 3-7; **Half-time:** 32-0;
Referee: Peter Taberner (Wigan); **Attendance:** 2,519.

HUNSLET HAWKS 32 LONDON SKOLARS 8

HAWKS: 1 Jon Liddell; 2 Chris Hall; 3 Paul Seal; 4 Chris Ross; 5 George Rayner; 6 Danny Wood; 7 Latham Tawhai; 8 Jonlee Lockwood; 9 Jamaine Wray; 10 Steve Pryce; 11 Wayne Freeman; 12 Shaun Ibbetson; 13 Andy Bastow. Subs (all used): 14 Glen Freeman; 15 Mick Coyle; 16 Neil Mears; 17 Danny Evans.
Tries: W Freeman (6), Liddell (31), Ross (43), C Hall (50), Evans (63), Rayner (65, 80); **Goals:** Wood 2/8.
SKOLARS: 1 Joel Osborn; 2 Ronnie Mushiso; 3 Stuart Singleton; 4 Stephen Green; 5 Austin Aggrey; 6 Jermaine Coleman; 7 Peter Hannan; 8 Rubert Jonker; 9 Gareth Honor; 10 Alex Smits; 11 Deon McFadyen; 12 Glenn Osborn; 13 Mark Cantoni. Subs (all used): 14 Neil Foster; 15 Bryan Hendry; 16 Kurt Pittman; 17 Wayne Parillon.
Try: Jonker (22); **Goals:** J Osborn 2/2.
Dismissal: Jonker (68) - spear tackle on Wray.
Rugby Leaguer & League Express Men of the Match: *Hawks:* Chris Ross; *Skolars:* Peter Hannan.
Penalty count: 10-8; **Half-time:** 8-8;
Referee: Jamie Leahy (Dewsbury); **Attendance:** 366.

WEEK 8

Sunday 30th May 2004

BARROW RAIDERS 32 LONDON SKOLARS 16

RAIDERS: 1 Craig Bower; 2 Shane Irabor; 3 Phil Atkinson; 4 Paul Jones; 5 Adam Pate; 6 Chris Archer; 7 Darren Holt; 8 Stuart Dancer; 9 Dave Clark; 10 Paul Lupton; 11 Mike Whitehead; 12 James King; 13 Barry Pugh. Subs (all used): 14 Tama Wakelin; 15 Paul Wilcock; 16 Nick Beech; 17 Matthew Leigh.
Tries: Bower (2), Pate (45), Atkinson (48), King (60), Irabor (73), P Jones (80); **Goals:** Holt 4/7.
SKOLARS: 1 Joel Osborn; 2 Austin Aggrey; 3 Stuart Singleton; 4 Stephen Green; 5 Mike Okwusogu; 6 Jermaine Coleman; 7 Peter Hannan; 8 Rubert Jonker; 9 Kurt Pittman; 10 Alex Smits; 11 Deon McFadyen; 12 Richard Singleton; 13 Mark Cantoni. Subs (all used): 14 Gareth Honor; 15 Wayne Parillon; 16 Bryan Hendry; 17 Brad McFarland.
Tries: Cantoni (20, 67), Coleman (37); **Goals:** J Osborn 2/3.
Rugby Leaguer & League Express Men of the Match: *Raiders:* Adam Pate; *Skolars:* Joel Osborn.
Penalty count: 6-5; **Half-time:** 8-10;
Referee: Mike Dawber (Wigan); **Attendance:** 646.

CHORLEY LYNX 30 HUNSLET HAWKS 26

LYNX: 1 Lee Patterson; 2 Ade Mead; 3 Eddie Kilgannon; 4 Jamie Stenhouse; 5 Gary O'Regan; 6 Brian Capewell; 7 Martin Gambles; 8 Ian Parry; 9 Chris Ramsdale; 10 John Hill; 11 Mick Redford; 12 Gary Smith; 13 Danny Barton. Subs (all used): 14 Lee Rowley; 15 Andy Grundy; 16 James Lomax; 17 Chris Newall.
Tries: O'Regan (4), Ramsdale (21), Stenhouse (24), Patterson (28, 73), Barton (79); **Goals:** Capewell 3/6.
HAWKS: 1 Jon Liddell; 2 Chris Hall; 3 Paul Seal; 4 Chris Ross; 5 George Rayner; 6 Danny Wood; 7 Latham Tawhai; 8 Andy Burland; 9 Jamaine Wray; 10 Steve Pryce; 11 Wayne Freeman; 12 Shaun Ibbetson; 13 Danny Fearon. Subs (all used): 14 Neil Mears; 15 Jonlee

Lockwood; 16 Glen Freeman; 17 Mick Coyle.
Tries: Coyle (53), Mears (60), Lockwood (63, 76), Seal (80); **Goals:** Tawhai 3/5.
Rugby Leaguer & League Express Men of the Match: *Lynx:* Danny Barton; *Hawks:* Jamaine Wray.
Penalty count: 7-3; **Half-time:** 22-0;
Referee: Colin Morris (Huddersfield); **Attendance:** 303.

DEWSBURY RAMS 26 GATESHEAD THUNDER 8

RAMS: 1 Jamie Benn; 2 Ian Preece; 3 Chris Redfearn; 4 Ian Kirke; 5 Leon Williamson; 6 Adam Thaler; 7 David Mycoe; 8 Paul Hicks; 9 Scott Dyson; 10 Mark Hawksley; 11 Billy Kershaw; 12 Kevin Spink; 13 Kevin Crouthers. Subs (all used): 14 Shane Davis; 15 Michael Gibbons; 16 Anthony Thewliss; 17 Joe Naidole.
Tries: Crouthers (15), Mycoe (21, 39), Williamson (36), A Thaler (52); **Goals:** Benn 3/5.
THUNDER: 1 Graham Stephenson; 2 Michael Bunting; 3 Kevin Neighbour; 4 Will Massey; 5 Robin Peers; 6 Paul Thorman; 7 Craig Fisher; 8 Rob Line; 9 Neil Thorman; 10 Steven Bradley; 11 Liam Garside; 12 Tony Doherty; 13 Steve Rutherford. Subs (all used): 14 Anthony Cowburn; 15 Scott Harrison; 16 Paul Dodsworth; 17 Ben Hodgson.
Tries: Bradley (6), Bunting (62); **Goals:** P Thorman 0/2.
Rugby Leaguer & League Express Men of the Match: *Rams:* Kevin Crouthers; *Thunder:* Steven Bradley.
Penalty count: 10-10; **Half-time:** 20-4;
Referee: Phil Bentham (Warrington); **Attendance:** 590.

WORKINGTON TOWN 32 SHEFFIELD EAGLES 36

TOWN: 1 Andrew Fearon; 2 Scott Chilton; 3 Neil Frazer; 4 Martyn Wilson; 5 Graeme Lewthwaite; 6 Brett Smith; 7 Tane Manihera; 8 Dean Burgess; 9 Jonny Limmer; 10 Matthew Tunstall; 11 Andy McGlasson; 12 John Tuimaualuga; 13 Jamie Beaumont. Subs (all used): 14 David Pettit; 15 Ricky Wright; 16 Dean Bragg; 17 Allan McGuiness.
Tries: Frazer (4), McGlasson (36), Chilton (62), Beaumont (67), Tuimaualuga (72); **Goals:** Manihera 6/6.
EAGLES: 1 Andy Poynter; 2 Greg Hurst; 3 Jon Breakingbury; 4 Alex Dickinson; 5 Bright Sodje; 6 Aled James; 7 Steve Doherty; 8 Jack Howieson; 9 Scott Collins; 10 Jon Bruce; 11 Andy Raleigh; 12 Craig Brown; 13 Jordan James. Subs (all used): 14 Jimmy Pearson; 15 Sean Dickinson; 16 Simon Tillyer; 17 Nick Turnbull.
Tries: Poynter (20), Sodje (22, 25), Doherty (47), Raleigh (51); **Goals:** A James 8/8.
Rugby Leaguer & League Express Men of the Match: *Town:* Jonny Limmer; *Eagles:* Aled James.
Penalty count: 8-8; **Half-time:** 14-22;
Referee: Jamie Leahy (Dewsbury); **Attendance:** 652.

YORK CITY KNIGHTS 44 SWINTON LIONS 24

CITY KNIGHTS: 1 Nathan Graham; 2 Austin Buchanan; 3 Chris Langley; 4 Aaron Wood; 5 Scott Walker; 6 Scott Rhodes; 7 Danny Brough; 8 Richard Wilson; 9 Lee Jackson; 10 Yusuf Sozi; 11 Darren Callaghan; 12 Simon Friend; 13 Damian Ball. Subs (all used): 14 Jimmy Elston; 15 Mark Cain; 16 John Smith; 17 Craig Forsyth.
Tries: Rhodes (12), Brough (14), Langley (18), Jackson (25), Graham (55), Callaghan (68), Ball (80);
Goals: Brough 8/10.
LIONS: 1 Wayne English; 2 Hugh Thorpe; 3 Dave Llewellyn; 4 Chris Maye; 5 Chris Irwin; 6 Mick Coates; 7 Warren Ayres; 8 Mike Loughlin; 9 Peter Cannon; 10 Tau Liku; 11 Phil Cushion; 12 Ian Sinfield; 13 Kris Smith. Subs (all used): 14 Paul Ashton; 15 Rob Russell; 16 Ryan Stazicker; 17 Craig Wingfield.
Tries: Cushion (5), Irwin (27), English (39), Cannon (75); **Goals:** Ayres 4/4.
Rugby Leaguer & League Express Men of the Match: *City Knights:* Lee Jackson; *Lions:* Kris Smith.
Penalty count: 8-5; **Half-time:** 24-18; **Referee:** Gareth Hewer (Whitehaven); **Attendance:** 1,411.

WEEK 9

Sunday 6th June 2004

SHEFFIELD EAGLES 21 WORKINGTON TOWN 8

EAGLES: 1 Andy Poynter; 2 Greg Hurst; 3 Nick Turnbull; 4 Alex Dickinson; 5 Kieron Collins; 6 Gavin Brown; 7 Steve Doherty; 8 Jack Howieson; 9 Scott Collins; 10 Jon Bruce; 11 Andy Raleigh; 12 Richard Goddard; 13 Jordan James. Subs (all used): 14 Jimmy Pearson; 15 Andy Rice; 16 Richard Stone; 17 Craig Brown.
Tries: Goddard (12), Poynter (56), S Collins (68);
Goals: Goddard 4/5; **Field goal:** Goddard.
TOWN: 1 Andrew Fearon; 2 Matthew Johnson; 3 Neil Frazer; 4 Jamie Beaumont; 5 Martyn Wilson; 6 Brett Smith; 7 Tane Manihera; 8 Matthew Tunstall; 9 David Pettit; 10 Dean Burgess; 11 Andy McGlasson; 12 John Tuimaualuga; 13 Jonny Limmer. Subs (all used): 14 Martin Stalker; 15 James Robinson; 16 Dean Bragg; 17 Allan McGuiness.
Try: Manihera (26); **Goals:** Manihera 2/2.
Rugby Leaguer & League Express Men of the Match: *Eagles:* Richard Goddard; *Town:* Tane Manihera.
Penalty count: 14-4; **Half-time:** 8-8;
Referee: Julian King (St Helens); **Attendance:** 979.

WEEK 10

Sunday 13th June 2004

BARROW RAIDERS 38 CHORLEY LYNX 34

RAIDERS: 1 Craig Bower; 2 Shane Irabor; 3 Damien Reid; 4 Paul Jones; 5 Adam Pate; 6 Chris Archer; 7 Darren Holt; 8 Stuart Dancer; 9 Dave Clark; 10 Paul Lupton; 11 Mike Whitehead; 12 James King; 13 Barry Pugh. Subs (used): 14 Tama Wakelin; 15 Matthew Leigh; 16 Phil Atkinson; 17 Paul Wilcock.
Tries: Archer (4), P Jones (22, 44), Irabor (34), Leigh (66), Reid (78); **Goals:** Holt 7/7.
LYNX: 1 Lee Patterson; 2 Jake Johnstone; 3 Eddie Kilgannon; 4 Jamie Stenhouse; 5 Gary O'Regan; 6 Brian Capewell; 7 Martin Gambles; 8 Ian Parry; 9 Chris Ramsdale; 10 John Hill; 11 Mick Redford; 12 Gary Smith; 13 Danny Barton. Subs: 14 Ade Mead (not used); 15 Lee Rowley; 16 Andy Grundy; 17 James Lomax (not used).
Tries: O'Regan (2), Redford (6, 55), Capewell (27), Patterson (38), G Smith (70); **Goals:** Capewell 5/6.
Rugby Leaguer & League Express Men of the Match: *Raiders:* Paul Jones; *Lynx:* Brian Capewell.
Penalty count: 7-4; **Half-time:** 18-22;
Referee: Julian King (St Helens); **Attendance:** 775.

DEWSBURY RAMS 2 YORK CITY KNIGHTS 48

RAMS: 1 Richard Thaler; 2 Ian Preece; 3 Chris Redfearn; 4 Ian Kirke; 5 Leon Williamson; 6 Adam Thaler; 7 David Mycoe; 8 Paul Hicks; 9 Scott Dyson; 10 Mark Hawksley; 11 Kevin Spink; 12 Billy Kershaw; 13 Jason Firth. Subs (all used): 14 Jon Waddle; 15 Shane Davis; 16 Michael Gibbons; 17 Joe Naidole.
Goal: A Thaler 1/1.
Sin bin: Naidole (45) - holding down.
CITY KNIGHTS: 1 Nathan Graham; 2 Austin Buchanan; 3 Chris Langley; 4 Aaron Wood; 5 Scott Walker; 6 Scott Rhodes; 7 Danny Brough; 8 Richard Wilson; 9 Lee Jackson; 10 Yusuf Sozi; 11 Darren Callaghan; 12 Simon Friend; 13 Damian Ball. Subs (all used): 14 John Wainhouse; 15 Mark Cain; 16 John Smith; 17 Craig Forsyth.
Tries: Buchanan (28, 75, 78), Cain (49, 51), Brough (54, 71), Friend (59); **Goals:** Brough 7/8, Graham 1/1.
Sin bin: Friend (39) - interference.
Rugby Leaguer & League Express Men of the Match: *Rams:* Mark Hawksley; *City Knights:* Danny Brough.
Penalty count: 9-15; **Half-time:** 2-6; **Referee:** Gareth Hewer (Whitehaven); **Attendance:** 1,275.

GATESHEAD THUNDER 12 WORKINGTON TOWN 44

THUNDER: 1 Graham Stephenson; 2 Steve Morton; 3 Kevin Neighbour; 4 Will Massey; 5 Robin Peers; 6 Paul Thorman; 7 Craig Fisher; 8 Rob Line; 9 Neil Thorman; 10 Scott Harrison; 11 Liam Garside; 12 Steven Bradley; 13 Steve Rutherford. Subs (all used): 14 Mick Kent; 15 Adam Endersby; 16 Craig Firth; 17 Charlie Roe.
Tries: Firth (39), N Thorman (55); **Goals:** P Thorman 2/3.
TOWN: 1 Scott Chilton; 2 Matthew Johnson; 3 Neil Frazer; 4 Martyn Wilson; 5 Matthew Woodcock; 6 Shaun Boylan; 7 Tane Manihera; 8 Dean Burgess; 9 Jonny Limmer; 10 Matthew Tunstall; 11 Andy McGlasson; 12 John Tuimaualuga; 13 Jamie Beaumont. Subs (all used): 14 Brett Smith; 15 Ricky Wright; 16 Dean Bragg; 17 Allan McGuiness.
Tries: Chilton (12), Limmer (21, 79), Manihera (28, 45), Frazer (50), Tunstall (60, 77); **Goals:** Manihera 6/8.
Sin bin: Tunstall (7) - persistent infringements.
Rugby Leaguer & League Express Men of the Match: *Thunder:* Neil Thorman; *Town:* Matthew Tunstall.
Penalty count: 10-10; **Half-time:** 8-18;
Referee: Ben Thaler (Wakefield); **Attendance:** 291.

LONDON SKOLARS 28 SWINTON LIONS 26

SKOLARS: 1 Joel Osborn; 2 Austin Aggrey; 3 Stuart Singleton; 4 Stephen Green; 5 Zane Gardiner; 6 Jermaine Coleman; 7 Peter Hannan; 8 Rubert Jonker; 9 Kurt Pittman; 10 Alex Smits; 11 Deon McFadyen; 12 Richard Singleton; 13 Mark Cantoni. Subs (all used): 14 Bryan Hendry; 15 Wayne Parillon; 16 Brad McFarland; 17 Gareth Honor.
Tries: Pittman (4), Cantoni (29, 69), Green (63), Jonker (73); **Goals:** J Osborn 1/1, Pittman 3/4.
Sin bin: Smits (20) - fighting.
LIONS: 1 Wayne English; 2 Hugh Thorpe; 3 Dave Llewellyn; 4 Chris Maye; 5 Chris Irwin; 6 Mick Coates; 7 Warren Ayres; 8 Craig Wingfield; 9 Peter Cannon; 10 Rob Whittaker; 11 Ryan Stazicker; 12 Ian Sinfield; 13 Ian Hodson. Subs (all used): 14 Paul Ashton; 15 Mark Pembroke; 16 Mike Loughlin; 17 Tau Liku.
Tries: Cannon (10, 40), Maye (36), Llewellyn (41), Irwin (60); **Goals:** Ayres 3/7.
Sin bin: Irwin (20) - fighting.
Rugby Leaguer & League Express Men of the Match: *Skolars:* Rubert Jonker; *Lions:* Peter Cannon.
Penalty count: 8-9; **Half-time:** 12-16;
Referee: Phil Bentham (Warrington); **Attendance:** 465.

HUNSLET HAWKS 14 SHEFFIELD EAGLES 40

HAWKS: 1 George Rayner; 2 Gareth Carey; 3 Paul Seal; 4 Jonlee Lockwood; 5 Steve Hall; 6 Jon Liddell; 7 Latham Tawhai; 8 Steve Pryce; 9 Jamaine Wray; 10 Mick Coyle; 11 Wayne Freeman; 12 Shaun Ibbetson; 13 Andy Bastow. Subs (all used): 14 Andy Burland; 15 Danny Fearon; 16 Glen Freeman; 17 Neil Mears.
Tries: S Hall (55), W Freeman (59), Wray (65);
Goals: Liddell 1/4.
EAGLES: 1 Andy Poynter; 2 Greg Hurst; 3 Nick Turnbull; 4 Alex Dickinson; 5 Bright Sodje; 6 Gavin Brown; 7 Steve Doherty; 8 Jack Howieson; 9 Scott Collins; 10 Jon Bruce; 11 Richard Goddard; 12 Andy Raleigh; 13 Jordan James. Subs (all used): 14 Aled James; 15 Andy Rice; 16 Simon Tillyer; 17 Sean Dickinson.
Tries: G Brown (10), Turnbull (15), Doherty (32), Poynter (38), Raleigh (42, 47);
Goals: Goddard 7/7, A James 1/1.
Dismissal: Howieson (78) - punching.
Rugby Leaguer & League Express Men of the Match: *Hawks:* Wayne Freeman; *Eagles:* Gavin Brown.
Penalty count: 12-11; **Half-time:** 2-24;
Referee: Jamie Leahy (Dewsbury); **Attendance:** 620.

Friday 18th June 2004

HUNSLET HAWKS 52 GATESHEAD THUNDER 22

HAWKS: 1 George Rayner; 2 Chris Hall; 3 Gareth Murrell; 4 Steve Hall; 5 Leigh Deakin; 6 Danny Wood; 7 Jon Liddell; 8 Craig Booth; 9 Joe Hawley; 10 Mick Coyle; 11 Wayne Freeman; 12 Paul Seal; 13 Danny Fearon. Subs (all used): 14 Andy Burland; 15 Neil Mears; 16 Glen Freeman; 17 Jonlee Lockwood.
Tries: Coyle (20), W Freeman (33), Murrell (44), Mears (50, 64), S Hall (57), Rayner (68), C Hall (78), Seal (79);
Goals: Wood 6/8, Booth 2/2.
THUNDER: 1 Graham Stephenson; 2 Steve Morton; 3 Will Massey; 4 Craig Firth; 5 Robin Peers; 6 Paul Thorman; 7 Neil Thorman; 8 Rob Line; 9 Steve Rutherford; 10 Steven Bradley; 11 Liam Garside; 12 Tony Doherty; 13 Kevin Neighbour. Subs (all used): 14 Adam Endersby; 15 Ian Ball; 16 Nick Staveley; 17 Scott Harrison.
Tries: Massey (7), Peers (50), Morton (53), Stephenson (62), Bradley (74); **Goals:** Garside 1/1, N Thorman 0/1, P Thorman 0/4.
Sin bin: Firth (39) - holding down.
Rugby Leaguer & League Express Men of the Match: *Hawks:* Joe Hawley; *Thunder:* Neil Thorman.
Penalty count: 10-9; **Half-time:** 14-4; **Referee:** Matthew Thomasson (Warrington); **Attendance:** 349.

WEEK 11

Sunday 20th June 2004

SWINTON LIONS 26 CHORLEY LYNX 20

LIONS: 1 Wayne English; 2 Jason Roach; 3 Dave Llewellyn; 4 Chris Maye; 5 Chris Irwin; 6 Mick Coates; 7 Paul Ashton; 8 Phil Cushion; 9 Peter Cannon; 10 Wes Rogers; 11 Ryan Stazicker; 12 Ian Sinfield; 13 Ian Hodson. Subs (all used): 14 Warren Ayres; 15 Robert Russell; 16 Rob Whittaker; 17 Craig Wingfield.
Tries: Hodson (3), Sinfield (16), English (46), Maye (62); **Goals:** Ashton 5/5.
Sin bin: Whittaker (63) - illegal tackle.
LYNX: 1 Lee Patterson; 2 Ade Meade; 3 James Lomax; 4 Jamie Stenhouse; 5 Gary O'Regan; 6 Brian Capewell; 7 Martin Gambles; 8 Ian Parry; 9 Chris Ramsdale; 10 John Hill; 11 Mick Redford; 12 Gary Smith; 13 Danny Barton. Subs (all used): 14 Lee Rowley; 15 Andy Grundy; 16 John Chamberlain; 17 Anthony Murray.
Tries: Capewell (24), Meade (64), Redford (80);
Goals: Capewell 4/5.
On report: Patterson (48) - high tackle on Irwin.
Rugby Leaguer & League Express Men of the Match: *Lions:* Ian Sinfield; *Lynx:* Lee Patterson.
Penalty count: 7-8; **Half-time:** 12-10;
Referee: Gareth Hewer (Whitehaven); **Attendance:** 418.

WORKINGTON TOWN 44 DEWSBURY RAMS 22

TOWN: 1 Lusi Sione; 2 Matthew Woodcock; 3 Neil Frazer; 4 Martyn Wilson; 5 Graeme Lewthwaite; 6 Shaun Boylan; 7 Tane Manihera; 8 Matthew Tunstall; 9 Jonny Limmer; 10 Dean Burgess; 11 Andy McGlasson; 12 John Tuimaualuga; 13 David Pettit. Subs (all used): 14 Brett Smith; 15 Ricky Wright; 16 Allan McGuiness; 17 James Robinson.
Tries: Limmer (8, 65), Lewthwaite (33), Manihera (39), Wilson (41, 57), Sione (49), Tuimaualuga (69), Boylan (78); **Goals:** Manihera 4/9.
RAMS: 1 Ian Preece; 2 Richard Thaler; 3 Chris Redfearn; 4 Ian Kirke; 5 Leon Williamson; 6 Adam Thaler; 7 David Mycoe; 8 Paul Hicks; 9 Scott Dyson; 10 Mark Hawksley; 11 Kevin Crouthers; 12 Anthony Thewliss; 13 Jason Firth. Subs (all used): 14 Jamie Benn; 15 Kevin Spink; 16 Billy Kershaw; 17 Joe Naidole.
Tries: Hawksley (13, 22), A Thaler (29), Preece (63);
Goals: A Thaler 3/3, Benn 0/1.
On report: Crouthers (52) - high tackle.
Rugby Leaguer & League Express Men of the Match: *Town:* Matthew Woodcock; *Rams:* Mark Hawksley.
Penalty count: 9-6; **Half-time:** 16-18;
Referee: Julian King (St Helens); **Attendance:** 667.

YORK CITY KNIGHTS 50 LONDON SKOLARS 6

CITY KNIGHTS: 1 Nathan Graham; 2 Austin Buchanan; 3 Chris Langley; 4 Aaron Wood; 5 Scott Walker; 6 Scott Rhodes; 7 Danny Brough; 8 Richard Wilson; 9 Lee Jackson; 10 Yusuf Sozi; 11 Darren Callaghan; 12 Simon Friend; 13 Damian Ball. Subs (all used): 14 John Wainhouse; 15 Mark Cain; 16 Dan Briggs; 17 Craig Forsyth.
Tries: Sozi (2, 47), Buchanan (16, 75), Cain (34, 52), Graham (39), Rhodes (61), Wood (64);
Goals: Brough 7/9.
Sin bin: Jackson (10) - punching.
SKOLARS: 1 Joel Osborn; 2 Austin Aggrey; 3 Stuart Singleton; 4 Stephen Green; 5 Zane Gardiner; 6 Jermaine Coleman; 7 Peter Hannan; 8 Rubert Jonker; 9 Kurt Pittman; 10 Alex Smits; 11 Deon McFadyen; 12 Richard Singleton; 13 Mark Cantoni. Subs (all used): 14 Glenn Osborn; 15 Wayne Parillon; 16 Brad McFarland; 17 Bryan Hendry.
Try: Hannan (10); **Goals:** Pittman 1/1.
Sin bin: Cantoni (44) - punching;
Smits (58) - lifting in the tackle.
Rugby Leaguer & League Express Men of the Match: *City Knights:* Mark Cain; *Skolars:* Kurt Pittman.

Penalty count: 17-5; **Half-time:** 22-6;
Referee: Jamie Leahy (Dewsbury); **Attendance:** 1,367.

SHEFFIELD EAGLES 16 BARROW RAIDERS 24

EAGLES: 1 Aled James; 2 Greg Hurst; 3 Nick Turnbull; 4 Alex Dickinson; 5 Bright Sodje; 6 Gavin Brown; 7 Steve Doherty; 8 Jack Howieson; 9 Scott Collins; 10 Jon Bruce; 11 Richard Goddard; 12 Andy Raleigh; 13 Jordan James. Subs (all used): 14 Sean Dickinson; 15 Andy Rice; 16 Simon Tillyer; 17 Craig Brown.
Tries: Turnbull (32), Hurst (78);
Goals: Goddard 2/2, G Brown 2/3, A James 0/1.
Sin bin: J James (60) - lying on.
RAIDERS: 1 Adam Pate; 2 Shane Irabor; 3 Damien Reid; 4 Paul Jones; 5 Nick Beech; 6 Chris Archer; 7 Darren Holt; 8 Stuart Dancer; 9 Dave Clark; 10 Paul Wilcock; 11 Mike Whitehead; 12 James King; 13 Phil Atkinson. Subs (all used): 14 Tama Wakelin; 15 Matthew Leigh; 16 Barry Pugh; 17 Paul Lupton.
Tries: Irabor (42), Reid (48); **Goals:** Holt 5/6, Pate 3/3.
Rugby Leaguer & League Express Men of the Match:
Eagles: Andy Raleigh; *Raiders:* Darren Holt.
Penalty count: 10-10; **Half-time:** 10-8;
Referee: Peter Taberner (Wigan); **Attendance:** 977.

WEEK 12

Sunday 27th June 2004

LONDON SKOLARS 52 GATESHEAD THUNDER 20

SKOLARS: 1 Joel Osborn; 2 Austin Aggrey; 3 Stuart Singleton; 4 Stephen Green; 5 Zane Gardiner; 6 Jermaine Coleman; 7 Peter Hannan; 8 Rubert Jonker; 9 Kurt Pittman; 10 Alex Smits; 11 Deon McFadyen; 12 Richard Singleton; 13 Mark Cantoni. Subs (all used): 14 Gareth Honor; 15 Wayne Parillon; 16 Bryan Hendry; 17 Glenn Osborn.
Tries: Cantoni (3, 20, 44, 51, 63), Coleman (16), R Singleton (30), S Singleton (40), J Osborn (75), Pittman (80); **Goals:** Pittman 4/7, J Osborn 2/4.
THUNDER: 1 Graham Stephenson; 2 Will Massey; 3 Kevin Neighbour; 4 Craig Firth; 5 Robin Peers; 6 Steven Bradley; 7 Steve Rutherford; 8 Rob Line; 9 Neil Thorman; 10 Scott Harrison; 11 Adam Endersby; 12 Clint Brown; 13 Tony Doherty. Subs (all used, three subs only): 14 Nick Staveley; 15 Ian Ball; 17 Paul Dodsworth.
Tries: Line (57), Neighbour (68), Peers (71), Staveley (79); **Goals:** Massey 2/4.
Rugby Leaguer & League Express Men of the Match:
Skolars: Mark Cantoni; *Thunder:* Neil Thorman.
Penalty count: 5-11; **Half-time:** 28-0;
Referee: Ben Thaler (Wakefield); **Attendance:** 356.

WEEK 13

Sunday 4th July 2004

CHORLEY LYNX 32 LONDON SKOLARS 18

LYNX: 1 Lee Patterson; 2 Jake Johnstone; 3 Mick Redford; 4 Jamie Stenhouse; 5 Ade Mead; 6 Brian Capewell; 7 Martin Gambles; 8 Ian Parry; 9 Chris Ramsdale; 10 John Hill; 11 John Chamberlain; 12 Gary Smith; 13 Danny Barton. Subs (all used): 14 Lee Rowley; 15 Andy Grundy; 16 James Lomax; 17 Chris Newall.
Tries: Redford (4, 52), Newall (32), Grundy (57), Stenhouse (68); **Goals:** Capewell 5/6, Johnstone 1/1.
Sin bin: Capewell (78) - infringement at play the ball.
SKOLARS: 1 Joel Osborn; 2 Austin Aggrey; 3 Stuart Singleton; 4 Zane Gardiner; 5 Desi Kadima; 6 Jermaine Coleman; 7 Peter Hannan; 8 Rubert Jonker; 9 Gareth Honor; 10 Alex Smits; 11 Mark Cantoni; 12 Deon McFadyen; 13 Kurt Pittman. Subs: 14 Ben Joyce; 15 Wayne Parillon; 16 Ade Aderiye (not used); 17 Mike Okwusogu.
Tries: Cantoni (18), J Osborn (46), Jonker (61);
Goals: Pittman 1/2, J Osborn 2/3.
Sin bin: Smits (74) - infringement at play the ball.
Rugby Leaguer & League Express Men of the Match:
Lynx: Andy Grundy; *Skolars:* Wayne Parillon.
Penalty count: 11-10; **Half-time:** 12-8;
Referee: Gareth Hewer (Whitehaven); **Attendance:** 211.

DEWSBURY RAMS 12 HUNSLET HAWKS 23

RAMS: 1 Ian Preece; 2 Richard Thaler; 3 Chris Redfearn; 4 Ian Kirke; 5 Leon Williamson; 6 Adam Thaler; 7 David Mycoe; 8 Paul Hicks; 9 Scott Dyson; 10 Mark Hawksley; 11 Kevin Crouthers; 12 Jon Waddle; 13 Jason Firth. Subs (all used): 14 Chris Woolford; 15 Kevin Spink; 16 Lee Kelly; 17 Joe Naidole.
Tries: Dyson (38), A Thaler (70); **Goals:** A Thaler 2/2.
HAWKS: 1 George Rayner; 2 Chris Hall; 3 Gareth Murrell; 4 Chris Ross; 5 Leigh Deakin; 6 Andy Bastow; 7 Latham Tawhai; 8 Jonlee Lockwood; 9 Joe Hawley; 10 Mick Coyle; 11 Wayne Freeman; 12 Paul Seal; 13 Danny Fearon. Subs (all used): 14 Steve Pryce; 15 Jamaine Wray; 16 Jon Liddell; 17 Shaun Ibbetson.
Tries: Ross (7, 64), Seal (27), Ibbetson (54);
Goals: Ross 3/5; **Field goal:** Tawhai.
Rugby Leaguer & League Express Men of the Match:
Rams: Scott Dyson; *Hawks:* George Rayner.
Penalty count: 8-6; **Half-time:** 6-13;
Referee: Mike Dawber (Wigan); **Attendance:** 831.

GATESHEAD THUNDER 24 BARROW RAIDERS 40

THUNDER: 1 Kevin Neighbour; 2 Steve Morton; 3 Michael Bunting; 4 Will Massey; 5 Robin Peers; 6 Paul Thorman; 7 Mick Jones; 8 Rob Line; 9 Neil Thorman; 10 Steven Bradley; 11 Clint Brown; 12 Tony Doherty; 13 Craig Firth. Subs (all used): 14 Jon MacDonald; 15 Bernie de Beer; 16 Ian Ball; 17 Nick Staveley.
Tries: Firth (16, 46), Massey (25, 28), N Thorman (75);
Goals: P Thorman 2/4, Massey 0/1.
RAIDERS: 1 Adam Pate; 2 Shane Irabor; 3 Damien Reid; 4 Paul Jones; 5 James Nixon; 6 Phil Atkinson; 7 Darren Holt; 8 Stuart Dancer; 9 Dave Clark; 10 Paul Wilcock; 11 Mike Whitehead; 12 James King; 13 Barry Pugh. Subs (all used): 14 Liam Finch; 15 Tama Wakelin; 16 Chris Archer; 17 Matthew Leigh.
Tries: Atkinson (3), Reid (8), Whitehead (12), P Jones (35, 53), Wakelin (50), Pate (63), Holt (71); **Goals:** Holt 4/9.
Sin bin: Reid (70) - throwing the ball away.
Rugby Leaguer & League Express Men of the Match:
Thunder: Kevin Neighbour; *Raiders:* Darren Holt.
Penalty count: 8-5; **Half-time:** 14-20;
Referee: Phil Bentham (Warrington);
Attendance: 301 *(at Preston Avenue, North Shields).*

SHEFFIELD EAGLES 16 SWINTON LIONS 32

EAGLES: 1 Greg Hurst; 2 Carl De Chenu; 3 Nick Turnbull; 4 Aled James; 5 Bright Sodje; 6 Gavin Brown; 7 Steve Doherty; 8 Andy Rice; 9 Scott Collins; 10 Jon Bruce; 11 Andy Raleigh; 12 Craig Brown; 13 Jordan James. Subs (all used): 14 Ryan Dickinson; 15 Sean Dickinson; 16 Kieron Collins; 17 Rob North.
Tries: Turnbull (47), J James (54), Hurst (79);
Goals: G Brown 2/3, A James 0/1.
LIONS: 1 Wayne English; 2 Hugh Thorpe; 3 Jason Roach; 4 Chris Maye; 5 Chris Irwin; 6 Mick Coates; 7 Paul Ashton; 8 Phil Cushion; 9 Peter Cannon; 10 Wes Rogers; 11 Kris Smith; 12 Ian Sinfield; 13 Ian Hodson. Subs (all used): 14 Warren Ayres; 15 Safraz Patel; 16 Robert Russell; 17 Mark Pembroke.
Tries: Maye (29), Smith (34), Russell (64), Irwin (70), Cannon (75); **Goals:** Ashton 6/7.
Rugby Leaguer & League Express Men of the Match:
Eagles: Andy Raleigh; *Lions:* Paul Ashton.
Penalty count: 4-7; **Half-time:** 2-14;
Referee: Julian King (St Helens); **Attendance:** 957.

WORKINGTON TOWN 44 YORK CITY KNIGHTS 20

TOWN: 1 Lusi Sione; 2 Matthew Woodcock; 3 Neil Frazer; 4 Martyn Wilson; 5 Scott Chilton; 6 Shaun Boylan; 7 Tane Manihera; 8 Matthew Tunstall; 9 Jonny Limmer; 10 Dean Burgess; 11 James Robinson; 12 John Tuimaualuga; 13 Brett Smith. Subs (all used): 14 Graeme Lewthwaite; 15 Andy McGlasson; 16 Dean Bragg; 17 David Pettit.
Tries: Limmer (7), Pettit (31), Frazer (35, 37), B Smith (43, 79), Tunstall (59); **Goals:** Manihera 8/9.
CITY KNIGHTS: 1 Nathan Graham; 2 Austin Buchanan; 3 Chris Langley; 4 Aaron Wood; 5 Scott Walker; 6 Scott Rhodes; 7 Danny Brough; 8 Richard Wilson; 9 Lee Jackson; 10 Yusuf Sozi; 11 John Smith; 12 Simon Friend; 13 Damian Ball. Subs (all used): 14 John Wainhouse; 15 Mark Cain; 16 Dale Cardoza; 17 Craig Forsyth.
Tries: Rhodes (23), Sozi (50), Ball (67, 78);
Goals: Brough 2/3, Ball 0/1.
Sin bin: Forsyth (30) – holding down.
Rugby Leaguer & League Express Men of the Match:
Town: Tane Manihera; *City Knights:* Damian Ball.
Penalty count: 11-10; **Half-time:** 26–4; **Referee:** Matthew Thomasson (Warrington); **Attendance:** 1,020.

WEEK 14

Sunday 11th July 2004

BARROW RAIDERS 18 WORKINGTON TOWN 10

RAIDERS: 1 Craig Bower; 2 Shane Irabor; 3 Damien Reid; 4 Paul Jones; 5 Adam Pate; 6 Phil Atkinson; 7 Darren Holt; 8 Stuart Dancer; 9 Dave Clark; 10 Paul Wilcock; 11 Mike Whitehead; 12 James King; 13 Barry Pugh. Subs (all used): 14 Paul Lupton; 15 Tama Wakelin; 16 Chris Archer; 17 Matthew Leigh.
Tries: Lupton (27), P Jones (37), Pate (73);
Goals: Holt 3/5.
Dismissal: Reid (64) - fighting.
TOWN: 1 Lusi Sione; 2 Matthew Woodcock; 3 Neil Frazer; 4 Martyn Wilson; 5 Craig Stalker; 6 Scott Chilton; 7 Tane Manihera; 8 Matthew Tunstall; 9 Jonny Limmer; 10 Dean Burgess; 11 Andy McGlasson; 12 John Tuimaualuga; 13 Brett Smith. Subs (all used): 14 David Pettit; 15 Ricky Wright; 16 Dean Bragg; 17 Allan McGuiness.
Tries: Sione (20, 50); **Goals:** Manihera 1/2.
Dismissal: Chilton (64) - fighting.
Rugby Leaguer & League Express Men of the Match:
Raiders: James King; *Town:* Lusi Sione.
Penalty count: 10-6; **Half-time:** 10-6;
Referee: Jamie Leahy (Dewsbury); **Attendance:** 1,201.

SWINTON LIONS 34 DEWSBURY RAMS 15

LIONS: 1 Wayne English; 2 Hugh Thorpe; 3 Jason Roach; 4 Chris Maye; 5 Chris Irwin; 6 Mick Coates; 7 Paul Ashton; 8 Ian Sinfield; 9 Peter Cannon; 10 Wes Rogers; 11 Kris Smith; 12 Robert Russell; 13 Ian Hodson. Subs (all used): 14 Warren Ayres; 15 Dave Llewellyn; 16 Mark Pembroke; 17 Lee Gardner.
Tries: Rogers (13), Ashton (29), Roach (52, 75), Irwin (57), Thorpe (66); **Goals:** Ashton 5/7.
Sin bin: Maye (24) - fighting.
RAMS: 1 Ian Preece; 2 Oliver Fairbank; 3 Chris Redfearn; 4 Ian Kirke; 5 Leon Williamson; 6 Adam Thaler; 7 David Mycoe; 8 Paul Hicks; 9 Scott Dyson; 10 Mark Hawksley; 11 Anthony Thewliss; 12 Chris Elliott; 13 Jason Firth. Subs (all used): 14 Chris Woolford; 15 Ashley Fortis; 16 Lee Kelly; 17 Joe Naidole.
Tries: Fairbank (3), Naidole (40), Firth (43);
Goals: A Thaler 1/4; **Field goal:** Dyson.
Sin bin: Redfearn (24) - fighting;
A Thaler (50) - holding down.
Rugby Leaguer & League Express Men of the Match:
Lions: Paul Ashton; *Rams:* Jason Firth.
Penalty count: 8-9; **Half-time:** 12-11; **Referee:** Matthew Thomasson (Warrington); **Attendance:** 444.

SHEFFIELD EAGLES 24 CHORLEY LYNX 31

EAGLES: 1 Greg Hurst; 2 Carl De Chenu; 3 Nick Turnbull; 4 Aled James; 5 Danny Mills; 6 Gavin Brown; 7 Steve Doherty; 8 Andy Rice; 9 Scott Collins; 10 Jon Bruce; 11 Andy Raleigh; 12 Craig Brown; 13 Jordan James. Subs (all used): 14 Sean Dickinson; 15 Alex Dickinson; 16 Simon Tillyer; 17 Simon Morton.
Tries: De Chenu (27), Hurst (39), J James (61), Turnbull (69); **Goals:** G Brown 4/4.
LYNX: 1 Lee Patterson; 2 Jake Johnstone; 3 Mick Redford; 4 Jamie Stenhouse; 5 Steve Ormesher; 6 Brian Capewell; 7 Martin Gambles; 8 Ian Parry; 9 Chris Ramsdale; 10 Andy Grundy; 11 John Chamberlain; 12 John Hill; 13 Danny Barton. Subs (all used): 14 Lee Rowley; 15 Gary Smith; 16 James Lomax; 17 Chris Newall.
Tries: Parry (42, 74), Stenhouse (55), Barton (65);
Goals: Capewell 7/7; **Field goal:** Capewell.
On report: Stenhouse (15) - alleged biting.
Rugby Leaguer & League Express Men of the Match:
Eagles: Andy Raleigh; *Lynx:* Martin Gambles.
Penalty count: 9-8; **Half-time:** 12-4;
Referee: Phil Bentham (Warrington); **Attendance:** 852.

HUNSLET HAWKS 19 YORK CITY KNIGHTS 8

HAWKS: 1 George Rayner; 2 Chris Hall; 3 Gareth Murrell; 4 Chris Ross; 5 Leigh Deakin; 6 Andy Bastow; 7 Latham Tawhai; 8 Craig Booth; 9 Jamaine Wray; 10 Mick Coyle; 11 Shaun Ibbetson; 12 Paul Seal; 13 Jon Liddell. Subs (all used): 14 Steve Pryce; 15 Neil Mears; 16 Jonlee Lockwood; 17 Danny Fearon.
Tries: Deakin (6), Lockwood (35); **Goals:** Ross 5/9;
Field goal: Booth.
Sin bin: Pryce (29) - holding down;
Coyle (63) - fighting.
CITY KNIGHTS: 1 Nathan Graham; 2 Chris Langley; 3 Dale Cardoza; 4 Aaron Wood; 5 Scott Walker; 6 Scott Rhodes; 7 Danny Brough; 8 Richard Wilson; 9 John Wainhouse; 10 Craig Forsyth; 11 Darren Callaghan; 12 Simon Friend; 13 Damian Ball. Subs (all used): 14 Lee Jackson; 15 Mark Cain; 16 Yusuf Sozi; 17 Carl Stannard.
Try: Walker (64); **Goals:** Brough 2/2.
Sin bin: Sozi (49) - holding down;
Forsyth (63) - fighting.
Rugby Leaguer & League Express Men of the Match:
Hawks: Latham Tawhai; *City Knights:* Lee Jackson.
Penalty count: 15-11; **Half-time:** 16-2;
Referee: Gareth Hewer (Whitehaven); **Attendance:** 770.

WEEK 15

Friday 23rd July 2004

SHEFFIELD EAGLES 27 YORK CITY KNIGHTS 14

EAGLES: 1 Andy Poynter; 2 Carl De Chenu; 3 Nick Turnbull; 4 Alex Dickinson; 5 Danny Mills; 6 Aled James; 7 Gavin Brown; 8 Jon Bruce; 9 Scott Collins; 10 Craig Brown; 11 Andy Raleigh; 12 Jordan James; 13 Sean Dickinson. Subs (all used): 14 Greg Hurst; 15 Steve Doherty; 16 Simon Tillyer; 17 Andy Rice.
Tries: A Dickinson (8), Rice (32), G Brown (38), Poynter (66); **Goals:** G Brown 4/6, A James 1/1;
Field goal: G Brown.
CITY KNIGHTS: 1 Nathan Graham; 2 Austin Buchanan; 3 Chris Langley; 4 Dale Cardoza; 5 Chris Smith; 6 Scott Rhodes; 7 Danny Brough; 8 Richard Wilson; 9 Lee Jackson; 10 Yusuf Sozi; 11 Mick Ramsden; 12 Simon Friend; 13 Damian Ball. Subs (all used): 14 Jimmy Elston; 15 Mark Cain; 16 Carl Stannard; 17 Craig Forsyth.
Tries: Brough (3), Sozi (48), Cain (50); **Goals:** Brough 1/4.
Sin bin: Wilson (29) - holding down.
Rugby Leaguer & League Express Men of the Match:
Eagles: Jordan James; *City Knights:* Craig Forsyth.
Penalty count: 7-8; **Half-time:** 16-4;
Referee: Julian King (St Helens); **Attendance:** 1,018.

WEEK 16

Sunday 25th July 2004

DEWSBURY RAMS 8 LONDON SKOLARS 41

RAMS: 1 Wayne McHugh; 2 Ian Preece; 3 Chris Redfearn; 4 Ian Kirke; 5 Oliver Fairbank; 6 Adam Thaler; 7 David Mycoe; 8 Paul Hicks; 9 Scott Dyson; 10 Mark Hawksley; 11 Kevin Crouthers; 12 Jon Waddle; 13 Jason Firth. Subs (all used): 14 Chris Woolford; 15 Anthony Thewliss; 16 Lee Kelly; 17 Joe Naidole.
Tries: Waddle (37), Fairbank (76); **Goals:** A Thaler 0/2.
Sin bin: Fairbank (60) - holding down.
SKOLARS: 1 Joel Osborn; 2 Austin Aggrey; 3 Stuart Singleton; 4 Zane Gardiner; 5 Desi Kadima; 6 Jermaine Coleman; 7 Peter Hannan; 8 Rubert Jonker; 9 Kurt Pittman; 10 Alex Smits; 11 Glenn Osborn; 12 Deon McFadyen; 13 Mark Cantoni. Subs (all used): 14 Gareth Honor; 15 Wayne Parillon; 16 Ben Joyce; 17 Stephen Green.
Tries: Kadima (2, 5, 40, 53), Coleman (10), Parillon (24), Gardiner (32), Cantoni (42); **Goals:** Pittman 1/3, J Osborn 2/3, Joyce 0/1, G Osborn 1/1;

Field goal: Hannan.
Rugby Leaguer & League Express Men of the Match: *Rams:* Kevin Crouthers; *Skolars:* Joel Osborn.
Penalty count: 7-10; **Half-time:** 4-28;
Referee: Paul Carr (Castleford); **Attendance:** 487.

GATESHEAD THUNDER 16 CHORLEY LYNX 30

THUNDER: 1 Graham Stephenson; 2 Steve Morton; 3 Will Massey; 4 Kevin Neighbour; 5 Robin Peers; 6 Paul Thorman; 7 Neil Thorman; 8 Clint Brown; 9 Bernie de Beer; 10 Steven Bradley; 11 Liam Garside; 12 Tony Doherty; 13 Steve Rutherford. Subs (all used): 14 Rob Line; 15 Jon MacDonald; 16 Nick Staveley; 17 Mick Kent.
Tries: Peers (39), Neighbour (70), Bradley (80);
Goals: P Thorman 2/3.
LYNX: 1 Lee Patterson; 2 Jake Johnstone; 3 Mick Redford; 4 Jamie Stenhouse; 5 Steve Ormesher; 6 Brian Capewell; 7 Martin Gambles; 8 John Hill; 9 Chris Ramsdale; 10 Andy Grundy; 11 John Chamberlain; 12 Gary Smith; 13 Danny Barton. Subs (all used): 14 Lee Rowley; 15 Martin Roden; 16 James Lomax; 17 Chris Newall.
Tries: Stenhouse (5, 16), Patterson (49), Gambles (73, 75); **Goals:** Capewell 5/6.
Rugby Leaguer & League Express Men of the Match: *Thunder:* Robin Peers; *Lynx:* Martin Gambles.
Penalty count: 9-9; **Half-time:** 6-12;
Referee: Jamie Leahy (Dewsbury); **Attendance:** 301.

WORKINGTON TOWN 40 SWINTON LIONS 22

TOWN: 1 Lusi Sione; 2 Matthew Woodcock; 3 Neil Frazer; 4 Martyn Wilson; 5 Graeme Lewthwaite; 6 Shaun Boylan; 7 Tane Manihera; 8 Matthew Tunstall; 9 Jonny Limmer; 10 Dean Burgess; 11 Gareth Dean; 12 John Tuimaualuga; 13 Jamie Beaumont. Subs (all used): 14 Brett Smith; 15 Ricky Wright; 16 Allan McGuiness; 17 Karl Hocking.
Tries: Sione (7, 17, 51), Frazer (9, 79), Wilson (13), Lewthwaite (54); **Goals:** Manihera 6/9.
LIONS: 1 Wayne English; 2 Hugh Thorpe; 3 Robert Russell; 4 Chris Maye; 5 Danny Tyrell; 6 Mick Coates; 7 Paul Ashton; 8 Phil Cushion; 9 Peter Cannon; 10 Lee Gardner; 11 Kris Smith; 12 Ian Sinfield; 13 Ian Hodson. Subs (all used): 14 Warren Ayres; 15 Safraz Patel; 16 Andrew Wallace; 17 Chris Brett.
Tries: Russell (27), Maye (33), Thorpe (43), Smith (62);
Goals: Ayres 3/5.
Rugby Leaguer & League Express Men of the Match: *Town:* Lusi Sione; *Lions:* Wayne English.
Penalty count: 6-7; **Half-time:** 20-10;
Referee: Phil Bentham (Warrington); **Attendance:** 1,046.

HUNSLET HAWKS 22 BARROW RAIDERS 32

HAWKS: 1 George Rayner; 2 Gareth Carey; 3 Paul Seal; 4 Chris Ross; 5 Leigh Deakin; 6 Craig Stevens; 7 Latham Tawhai; 8 Craig Booth; 9 Jamaine Wray; 10 Mick Coyle; 11 Wayne Freeman; 12 Shaun Ibbetson; 13 Danny Fearon. Subs (all used): 14 Steve Pryce; 15 Dean Sampson; 16 Neil Mears; 17 Jonlee Lockwood.
Tries: Wray (30), Pryce (53), Rayner (68), Stevens (79);
Goals: Ross 3/4.
Sin bin: Lockwood (33) - holding down.
RAIDERS: 1 Craig Bower; 2 Shane Irabor; 3 Tama Wakelin; 4 Paul Jones; 5 Adam Pate; 6 Chris Archer; 7 Darren Holt; 8 Stuart Dancer; 9 Dave Clark; 10 Paul Wilcock; 11 Mike Whitehead; 12 James King; 13 Barry Pugh. Subs (all used): 14 Damien Reid; 15 Paul Lupton; 16 Liam Finch; 17 Matthew Leigh.
Tries: Reid (7), Bower (15), King (18, 73), Pate (36), Irabor (47); **Goals:** Holt 4/9.
Rugby Leaguer & League Express Men of the Match: *Hawks:* George Rayner; *Raiders:* James King.
Penalty count: 12-12; **Half-time:** 6-22; **Referee:** Matthew Thomasson (Warrington); **Attendance:** 545.

WEEK 17

Sunday 1st August 2004

CHORLEY LYNX 20 DEWSBURY RAMS 20

LYNX: 1 Lee Patterson; 2 Jake Johnstone; 3 Mick Redford; 4 Jamie Stenhouse; 5 Steve Ormesher; 6 Brian Capewell; 7 Martin Gambles; 8 Ian Parry; 9 Chris Ramsdale; 10 John Hill; 11 John Chamberlain; 12 Chris Newall; 13 Danny Barton. Subs (all used): 14 Andy Grundy; 15 Gary Smith; 16 Danny Arnold; 17 Martin Roden.
Tries: Barton (42), Stenhouse (58), Arnold (63), Gambles (80); **Goals:** Capewell 2/4.
RAMS: 1 Wayne McHugh; 2 Ian Preece; 3 Chris Redfearn; 4 Kevin Crouthers; 5 Oliver Fairbank; 6 Adam Thaler; 7 David Mycoe; 8 Paul Hicks; 9 John Rourke; 10 Mark Hawksley; 11 Ian Kirke; 12 Mark Stubley; 13 Jason Firth. Subs (all used): 14 Ashley Lyndsey; 15 Jamie Tennant; 16 Michael Gibbons; 17 Lee Kelly.
Tries: A Thaler (29), Kirke (40), Stubley (67);
Goals: A Thaler 4/4.
Rugby Leaguer & League Express Men of the Match: *Lynx:* Danny Barton; *Rams:* Adam Thaler.
Penalty count: 9-11; **Half-time:** 0-14;
Referee: Gareth Hewer (Whitehaven); **Attendance:** 255.

LONDON SKOLARS 20 WORKINGTON TOWN 30

SKOLARS: 1 Joel Osborn; 2 Austin Aggrey; 3 Stuart Singleton; 4 Zane Gardiner; 5 Desi Kadima; 6 Jermaine Coleman; 7 Peter Hannan; 8 Rubert Jonker; 9 Kurt Pittman; 10 Alex Smits; 11 Glenn Osborn; 12 Deon McFadyen; 13 Mark Cantoni. Subs (all used): 14 Gareth Honor; 15 Wayne Parillon; 16 Ben Joyce; 17 Stephen Green.
Tries: J Osborn (19), Pittman (42), S Singleton (54);
Goals: J Osborn 4/4, Pittman 0/1.
TOWN: 1 Lusi Sione; 2 Scott Chilton; 3 Neil Frazer; 4 Martyn Wilson; 5 Craig Stalker; 6 Shaun Boylan; 7 Tane Manihera; 8 Matthew Tunstall; 9 Jonny Limmer; 10 Dean Burgess; 11 Gareth Dean; 12 John Tuimaualuga; 13 Jamie Beaumont. Subs (all used): 14 David Pettit; 15 Ricky Wright; 16 Andy McGlasson; 17 Karl Hocking.
Tries: Sione (10), C Stalker (13), Limmer (16), Wright (32), Frazer (73); **Goals:** Manihera 5/8.
Rugby Leaguer & League Express Men of the Match: *Skolars:* Kurt Pittman; *Town:* Jonny Limmer.
Penalty count: 11-13; **Half-time:** 4-22; **Referee:** Matthew Thomasson (Warrington); **Attendance:** 314.

SWINTON LIONS 33 HUNSLET HAWKS 16

LIONS: 1 Wayne English; 2 Jason Roach; 3 Dave Llewellyn; 4 Chris Maye; 5 Danny Tyrell; 6 Mick Coates; 7 Paul Ashton; 8 Phil Cushion; 9 Peter Cannon; 10 Wes Rogers; 11 Kris Smith; 12 Ian Sinfield; 13 Ian Hodson. Subs (all used): 14 Warren Ayres; 15 Safraz Patel; 16 Robert Russell; 17 Rob Whittaker.
Tries: Roach (8), Cannon (32), Hodson (50), English (63, 75), Tyrell (71); **Goals:** Ashton 2/5, Ayres 2/2;
Field goal: Coates.
HAWKS: 1 George Rayner; 2 Paul Gleadhill; 3 Paul Seal; 4 Craig Duda; 5 Leigh Deakin; 6 Chris Ross; 7 Craig Stevens; 8 Dean Sampson; 9 Jamaine Wray; 10 Mick Coyle; 11 Wayne Freeman; 12 Neil Mears; 13 Joe Hawley. Subs (all used): 14 Glen Freeman; 15 Jonlee Lockwood; 16 Danny Fearon; 17 Ben Cockayne.
Tries: Duda (12), Gleadhill (42), Lockwood (68);
Goals: Ross 1/3, Gleadhill 1/2.
Rugby Leaguer & League Express Men of the Match: *Lions:* Kris Smith; *Hawks:* Chris Ross.
Penalty count: 3-5; **Half-time:** 8-6;
Referee: Julian King (St Helens); **Attendance:** 508.

YORK CITY KNIGHTS 30 BARROW RAIDERS 16

CITY KNIGHTS: 1 Chris Smith; 2 Austin Buchanan; 3 Chris Langley; 4 Darren Callaghan; 5 Craig Farrell; 6 Scott Rhodes; 7 Danny Brough; 8 Richard Wilson; 9 Jimmy Elston; 10 Yusuf Sozi; 11 Mick Ramsden; 12 Dean Andrews; 13 Mark Cain. Subs (all used): 14 Rob Kama; 15 John Smith; 16 Adam Sullivan; 17 Carl Stannard.
Tries: D Andrews (16), Farrell (46), Brough (61), Ramsden (65), Elston (68); **Goals:** Brough 5/8.
RAIDERS: 1 Craig Bower; 2 Shane Irabor; 3 Damien Reid; 4 Paul Jones; 5 Adam Pate; 6 Chris Archer; 7 Darren Holt; 8 Stuart Dancer; 9 Dave Clark; 10 Paul Wilcock; 11 Mike Whitehead; 12 James King; 13 Barry Pugh. Subs (all used): 14 Liam Finch; 15 Paul Lupton; 16 Matthew Leigh; 17 Darren Carter.
Tries: P Jones (26), Archer (80); **Goals:** Holt 3/3, Pate 1/1.
Rugby Leaguer & League Express Men of the Match: *City Knights:* Jimmy Elston; *Raiders:* Darren Holt.
Penalty count: 15-11; **Half-time:** 10-8;
Referee: Peter Taberner (Wigan); **Attendance:** 1,307.

SHEFFIELD EAGLES 54 GATESHEAD THUNDER 10

EAGLES: 1 Greg Hurst; 2 Danny Mills; 3 Jon Breakingbury; 4 Alex Dickinson; 5 Carl De Chenu; 6 Aled James; 7 Gavin Brown; 8 Jon Bruce; 9 Scott Collins; 10 Craig Brown; 11 Andy Raleigh; 12 Jordan James; 13 Sean Dickinson. Subs (all used): 14 Steve Doherty; 15 Simon Tillyer; 16 Jimmy Pearson; 17 Andy Rice.
Tries: A Dickinson (6), J James (10, 13), C Brown (25, 72), De Chenu (32, 51, 77), S Dickinson (36), Hurst (55); **Goals:** G Brown 7/10.
THUNDER: 1 Graham Stephenson; 2 Steve Morton; 3 Will Massey; 4 Kevin Neighbour; 5 Robin Peers; 6 Paul Thorman; 7 Steve Rutherford; 8 Rob Line; 9 Neil Thorman; 10 Nick Staveley; 11 Clint Brown; 12 Liam Garside; 13 Steven Bradley. Subs (all used): 14 Craig Firth; 15 Jon MacDonald; 16 Mick Jones; 17 Paul Dodsworth.
Tries: Dodsworth (18), P Thorman (46);
Goals: P Thorman 1/2.
Rugby Leaguer & League Express Men of the Match: *Eagles:* Gavin Brown; *Thunder:* Paul Thorman.
Penalty count: 8-11; **Half-time:** 34-4;
Referee: Paul Carr (Castleford); **Attendance:** 744.

WEEK 18

Sunday 8th August 2004

BARROW RAIDERS 12 SWINTON LIONS 22

RAIDERS: 1 Adam Pate; 2 Shane Irabor; 3 James Finch; 4 Paul Jones; 5 Nick Beech; 6 Liam Finch; 7 Darren Holt; 8 Stuart Dancer; 9 Dave Clark; 10 Paul Wilcock; 11 Paul Lupton; 12 James King; 13 Mike Whitehead. Subs: 14 Matt Jefferson; 15 Matthew Leigh; 16 Chris Archer; 17 Jon Williamson (not used).
Tries: Clark (16), Wilcock (35); **Goals:** Holt 2/3.
LIONS: 1 Wayne English; 2 Hugh Thorpe; 3 Dave Llewellyn; 4 Chris Maye; 5 Danny Tyrell; 6 Mick Coates; 7 Paul Ashton; 8 Phil Cushion; 9 Peter Cannon; 10 Wes Rogers; 11 Kris Smith; 12 Ian Sinfield; 13 Ian Hodson. Subs: 14 Warren Ayres (not used); 15 Robert Russell; 16 Safraz Patel; 17 Rob Whittaker.
Tries: English (45), Patel (53), Maye (57), Llewellyn (79); **Goals:** Ashton 3/4.
Sin bin: Coates (30) - dissent.
Rugby Leaguer & League Express Men of the Match: *Raiders:* Stuart Dancer; *Lions:* Phil Cushion.
Penalty count: 9-7; **Half-time:** 10-0;
Referee: Gareth Hewer (Whitehaven); **Attendance:** 865.

DEWSBURY RAMS 10 SHEFFIELD EAGLES 51

RAMS: 1 Ian Preece; 2 Oliver Fairbank; 3 Wayne McHugh; 4 Kevin Crouthers; 5 Leon Williamson; 6 Chris Redfearn; 7 Adam Thaler; 8 Paul Hicks; 9 Richard Chapman; 10 Mark Hawksley; 11 Mark Stubley; 12 Jon Waddle; 13 Jason Firth. Subs (all used): 14 Chris Woolford; 15 Anthony Thewliss; 16 Jamie Tennant; 17 Lee Kelly.
Tries: A Thaler (37), Fairbank (41); **Goals:** A Thaler 1/2.
Dismissal: Chapman (50) - punching.
EAGLES: 1 Andy Poynter; 2 Danny Mills; 3 Jon Breakingbury; 4 Alex Dickinson; 5 Carl De Chenu; 6 Aled James; 7 Gavin Brown; 8 Jack Howieson; 9 Scott Collins; 10 Craig Brown; 11 Andy Raleigh; 12 Jordan James; 13 Sean Dickinson. Subs (all used): 14 Ryan Dickinson; 15 Andy Rice; 16 Nick Turnbull; 17 Jon Bruce.
Tries: J James (6), A James (16), G Brown (19), Poynter (22, 32, 60), De Chenu (63), Raleigh (74);
Goals: G Brown 9/12; **Field goal:** G Brown.
Rugby Leaguer & League Express Men of the Match: *Rams:* Mark Stubley; *Eagles:* Jack Howieson.
Penalty count: 5-6; **Half-time:** 6-26;
Referee: Julian King (St Helens); **Attendance:** 502.

GATESHEAD THUNDER 18 YORK CITY KNIGHTS 30

THUNDER: 1 Graham Stephenson; 2 Steve Morton; 3 Kevin Neighbour; 4 Craig Firth; 5 Robin Peers; 6 Paul Thorman; 7 Steve Rutherford; 8 Rob Line; 9 Neil Thorman; 10 Nick Staveley; 11 Jon MacDonald; 12 Clint Brown; 13 Steven Bradley. Subs (all used): 14 Dave Guthrie; 15 Will Massey; 16 Ian Ball; 17 Paul Dodsworth.
Tries: Bradley (19), Massey (36), Rutherford (54);
Goals: P Thorman 3/3.
CITY KNIGHTS: 1 Chris Smith; 2 Austin Buchanan; 3 Chris Langley; 4 Darren Callaghan; 5 Craig Farrell; 6 Scott Rhodes; 7 Danny Brough; 8 Richard Wilson; 9 Jimmy Elston; 10 Yusuf Sozi; 11 Mick Ramsden; 12 Dean Andrews; 13 Mark Cain. Subs (all used): 14 Adam Sullivan; 15 Rob Kama; 16 Chris Spurr; 17 John Smith.
Tries: Elston (10), Buchanan (16, 46, 72), J Smith (39), Farrell (64), Sullivan (78); **Goals:** Brough 1/7.
Rugby Leaguer & League Express Men of the Match: *Thunder:* Craig Firth; *City Knights:* Austin Buchanan.
Penalty count: 9-5; **Half-time:** 12-14;
Referee: Phil Bentham (Warrington); **Attendance:** 429.

LONDON SKOLARS 24 HUNSLET HAWKS 16

SKOLARS: 1 Joel Osborn; 2 Austin Aggrey; 3 Stuart Singleton; 4 Zane Gardiner; 5 Desi Kadima; 6 Jermaine Coleman; 7 Peter Hannan; 8 Rubert Jonker; 9 Kurt Pittman; 10 Alex Smits; 11 Stephen Green; 12 Deon McFadyen; 13 Mark Cantoni. Subs (all used): 14 Gareth Honor; 15 Glenn Osborn; 16 Bryan Hendry; 17 Wayne Parillon.
Tries: Cantoni (32, 41), Coleman (36), Parillon (78);
Goals: J Osborn 4/8.
Sin bin: McFadyen (40) - fighting.
HAWKS: 1 George Rayner; 2 Paul Gleadhill; 3 Paul Seal; 4 Jonlee Lockwood; 5 Chris Hall; 6 Chris Ross; 7 Latham Tawhai; 8 Steve Pryce; 9 Jamaine Wray; 10 Mick Coyle; 11 Wayne Freeman; 12 Glen Freeman; 13 Joe Hawley. Subs (all used): 14 Danny Fearon; 15 Neil Mears; 16 Andy Bastow; 17 Ben Cockayne.
Tries: C Hall (43), Lockwood (57), Tawhai (72);
Goals: Tawhai 0/1, Ross 2/4.
Dismissal: Mears (40) - fighting
Sin bin: Seal (40) - fighting.
Rugby Leaguer & League Express Men of the Match: *Skolars:* Stuart Singleton; *Hawks:* Chris Ross.
Penalty count: 10-9; **Half-time:** 16-2;
Referee: Jamie Leahy (Dewsbury); **Attendance:** 362.

WORKINGTON TOWN 48 CHORLEY LYNX 24

TOWN: 1 Lusi Sione; 2 Craig Stalker; 3 Neil Frazer; 4 Martyn Wilson; 5 Graeme Lewthwaite; 6 Brett Smith; 7 Tane Manihera; 8 Matthew Tunstall; 9 Jonny Limmer; 10 Dean Burgess; 11 Gareth Dean; 12 John Tuimaualuga; 13 Jamie Beaumont. Subs (all used): 14 David Pettit; 15 Ricky Wright; 16 Andy McGlasson; 17 Dean Bragg.
Tries: Frazer (4), Beaumont (14), Limmer (27), Manihera (34), Pettit (38), B Smith (55), Wilson (67), Wright (76);
Goals: Manihera 8/9.
LYNX: 1 Lee Patterson; 2 Danny Arnold; 3 Jake Johnstone; 4 Jamie Stenhouse; 5 Steve Ormesher; 6 Brian Capewell; 7 Martin Gambles; 8 Ian Parry; 9 Martin Roden; 10 Andy Grundy; 11 Mick Redford; 12 John Hill; 13 Danny Barton. Subs: 14 Lee Rowley (not used); 15 Chris Ramsdale; 16 Chris Newall; 17 John Chamberlain.
Tries: Capewell (42), Ormesher (50), Patterson (61), Ramsdale (79); **Goals:** Capewell 4/5.
Rugby Leaguer & League Express Men of the Match: *Town:* Tane Manihera; *Lynx:* Brian Capewell.
Penalty count: 8-5; **Half-time:** 30-2;
Referee: Mike Dawber (Wigan); **Attendance:** 1,051.

WEEK 19

Sunday 15th August 2004

GATESHEAD THUNDER 22 DEWSBURY RAMS 4

THUNDER: 1 Graham Stephenson; 2 Steve Morton; 3 Kevin Neighbour; 4 Craig Firth; 5 Robin Peers; 6 Paul Thorman; 7 Steve Rutherford; 8 Rob Line; 9 Neil Thorman; 10 Nick Staveley; 11 Liam Garside; 12 Clint Brown; 13 Steven Bradley. Subs (all used): 14 Adam Endersby; 15 Will Massey; 16 Ian Ball; 17 Dave Guthrie.
Tries: Stephenson (3), Neighbour (22), Peers (44), Morton (61); **Goals:** P Thorman 3/7.
RAMS: 1 Wayne McHugh; 2 Oliver Fairbank; 3 Chris Redfearn; 4 Kevin Crouthers; 5 Leon Williamson; 6 Scott Dyson; 7 Adam Thaler; 8 Paul Hicks; 9 Richard Chapman; 10 Mark Hawksley; 11 Ian Kirke; 12 Mark Stubley; 13 Jason Firth. Subs (all used): 14 Chris

National League Two 2004 - Round by Round

Woolford; 15 Jamie Tennant; 16 Michael Gibbons; 17 Lee Kelly.
Try: Firth (30); **Goals:** A Thaler 0/1.
Sin bin: Kelly (49) - obstruction.
Rugby Leaguer & League Express Men of the Match: *Thunder:* Paul Thorman; *Rams:* Leon Williamson.
Penalty count: 10-6; **Half-time:** 12-4;
Referee: Gareth Hewer (Whitehaven); **Attendance:** 293.

LONDON SKOLARS 14 BARROW RAIDERS 30

SKOLARS: 1 Joel Osborn; 2 Desi Kadima; 3 Stuart Singleton; 4 Zane Gardiner; 5 Austin Aggrey; 6 Jermaine Coleman; 7 Peter Hannan; 8 Rubert Jonker; 9 Kurt Pittman; 10 Alex Smits; 11 Stephen Green; 12 Deon McFadyen; 13 Mark Cantoni. Subs (all used): 14 Gareth Honor; 15 Ade Aderiye; 16 Wayne Parillon; 17 Glenn Osborn.
Tries: Honor (37), Green (40), Kadima (57);
Goals: J Osborn 1/3.
Dismissal: Parillon (31) - disrespectful behaviour.
RAIDERS: 1 Matt Jefferson; 2 Shane Irabor; 3 James Finch; 4 Paul Jones; 5 Nick Beech; 6 Liam Finch; 7 Darren Holt; 8 Stuart Dancer; 9 Dave Clark; 10 Paul Wilcock; 11 Mike Whitehead; 12 James King; 13 Barry Pugh. Subs (all used): 14 James Nixon; 15 Matthew Leigh; 16 Chris Archer; 17 Paul Lupton.
Tries: King (4, 67), Beech (50), Irabor (77);
Goals: Holt 6/7, Beech 1/2.
On report: Dancer (50) - punching.
Rugby Leaguer & League Express Men of the Match: *Skolars:* Jermaine Coleman; *Raiders:* James King.
Penalty count: 9-12; **Half-time:** 10-14;
Referee: Paul Carr (Castleford); **Attendance:** 382.

SWINTON LIONS 12 YORK CITY KNIGHTS 48

LIONS: 1 Wayne English; 2 Hugh Thorpe; 3 Dave Llewellyn; 4 Chris Maye; 5 Chris Irwin; 6 Mick Coates; 7 Paul Ashton; 8 Ian Sinfield; 9 Warren Ayres; 10 Wes Rogers; 11 Lee Gardner; 12 Robert Russell; 13 Ian Hodson. Subs (all used): 14 Jason Roach; 15 Safraz Patel; 16 Craig Wingfield; 17 Rob Whittaker.
Try: English (2); **Goals:** Ashton 4/4.
Sin bin: Russell (34) - obstruction, (52) - dissent; Ashton (74) - dissent.
CITY KNIGHTS: 1 Chris Smith; 2 Austin Buchanan; 3 Chris Langley; 4 Chris Spurr; 5 Craig Farrell; 6 Scott Rhodes; 7 Danny Brough; 8 Richard Wilson; 9 Jimmy Elston; 10 Adam Sullivan; 11 Mick Ramsden; 12 Darren Callaghan; 13 Simon Friend. Subs (all used): 14 Lee Jackson; 15 Mark Cain; 16 John Smith; 17 Craig Forsyth.
Tries: Langley (13), Brough (22), Buchanan (46), Farrell (52), Jackson (62, 67), Cain (74), J Smith (76);
Goals: Brough 8/9.
Sin bin: Elston (10) - obstruction.
Rugby Leaguer & League Express Men of the Match: *Lions:* Wayne English; *City Knights:* Richard Wilson.
Penalty count: 5-11; **Half-time:** 12-14;
Referee: Ben Thaler (Wakefield); **Attendance:** 742.

HUNSLET HAWKS 52 CHORLEY LYNX 16

HAWKS: 1 Chris Hall; 2 Paul Gleadhill; 3 Paul Seal; 4 Craig Duda; 5 George Rayner; 6 Chris Ross; 7 Latham Tawhai; 8 Steve Pryce; 9 Joe Hawley; 10 Mick Coyle; 11 Wayne Freeman; 12 Dean Sampson; 13 Danny Fearon. Subs (all used): 14 Jonlee Lockwood; 15 Glen Freeman; 16 Danny Herbert; 17 Danny Cook.
Tries: Rayner (2), Tawhai (8), Pryce (15), W Freeman (20), Duda (22, 44), Ross (29), Fearon (51, 56);
Goals: Ross 8/8, Duda 0/1.
LYNX: 1 Lee Patterson; 2 Danny Arnold; 3 Jake Johnstone; 4 Jamie Stenhouse; 5 Steve Ormesher; 6 Brian Capewell; 7 Martin Gambles; 8 Ian Parry; 9 Chris Ramsdale; 10 John Hill; 11 Mick Redford; 12 Gary Smith; 13 Danny Barton. Subs (all used): 14 Lee Rowley; 15 Andy Grundy; 16 John Chamberlain; 17 Martin Roden.
Tries: Ormesher (40, 67), G Smith (79);
Goals: Capewell 1/1, Ramsdale 0/1, Johnstone 1/1.
Rugby Leaguer & League Express Men of the Match: *Hawks:* Latham Tawhai; *Lynx:* Steve Ormesher.
Penalty count: 4-8; **Half-time:** 34-6;
Referee: Julian King (St Helens); **Attendance:** 377.

WEEK 20

Sunday 22nd August 2004

CHORLEY LYNX 24 BARROW RAIDERS 24

LYNX: 1 Lee Patterson; 2 Danny Arnold; 3 Jake Johnstone; 4 Mick Redford; 5 Steve Ormesher; 6 Brian Capewell; 7 Martin Gambles; 8 Ian Parry; 9 Chris Ramsdale; 10 John Hill; 11 John Chamberlain; 12 Gary Smith; 13 Danny Barton. Subs (all used): 14 Lee Rowley; 15 Andy Grundy; 16 Chris Newall; 17 Grant Bithel.
Tries: Ormesher (3), Capewell (22), Patterson (33), Chamberlain (78); **Goals:** Capewell 4/5.
Sin bin: Patterson (58) - interference.
RAIDERS: 1 Matt Jefferson; 2 Shane Irabor; 3 James Finch; 4 Paul Jones; 5 Matt Gardner; 6 Liam Finch; 7 Darren Holt; 8 Stuart Dancer; 9 Dave Clark; 10 Paul Wilcock; 11 Mike Whitehead; 12 James King; 13 Barry Pugh. Subs (all used): 14 Matthew Leigh; 15 Ryan Campbell; 16 Chris Archer; 17 Tony Cunningham.
Tries: Irabor (7), Gardner (47, 58), P Jones (63);
Goals: Holt 4/5.
Rugby Leaguer & League Express Men of the Match: *Lynx:* Brian Capewell; *Raiders:* Matt Gardner.
Penalty count: 4-10; **Half-time:** 16-8;
Referee: Mike Dawber (Wigan); **Attendance:** 369.

SWINTON LIONS 42 LONDON SKOLARS 12

LIONS: 1 Wayne English; 2 Hugh Thorpe; 3 Dave Llewellyn; 4 Chris Maye; 5 Chris Irwin; 6 Mick Coates; 7 Neil Hayden; 8 Ian Sinfield; 9 Warren Ayres; 10 Lee Gardner; 11 Kris Smith; 12 Robert Russell; 13 Ian Hodson. Subs (all used): 14 Jason Roach; 15 Safraz Patel; 16 Darren Speakman; 17 Rob Whittaker.
Tries: Russell (8), Maye (21), Coates (37), English (44), Gardner (64), Hodson (68), Thorpe (70), Roach (75);
Goals: Ayres 1/2, Smith 4/6.
Sin bin: Hodson (57) - dissent.
SKOLARS: 1 Joel Osborn; 2 Austin Aggrey; 3 Stuart Singleton; 4 Stephen Green; 5 Zane Gardiner; 6 Jermaine Coleman; 7 Peter Hannan; 8 Rubert Jonker; 9 Kurt Pittman; 10 Alex Smits; 11 Ben Joyce; 12 Deon McFadyen; 13 Mark Cantoni. Subs (all used): 14 Gareth Honor; 15 Ade Aderiye; 16 Wayne Parillon; 17 Glenn Osborn.
Tries: Green (30), Cantoni (33), Coleman (48);
Goals: G Osborn 0/3.
Sin bin: J Osborn (14) - obstruction; McFadyen (57) - dissent.
Rugby Leaguer & League Express Men of the Match: *Lions:* Ian Sinfield; *Skolars:* Peter Hannan.
Penalty count: 7-7; **Half-time:** 14-8; **Referee:** Steve Nicholson (Whitehaven); **Attendance:** 424.

WORKINGTON TOWN 80 GATESHEAD THUNDER 8

TOWN: 1 Lusi Sione; 2 Matthew Woodcock; 3 Neil Frazer; 4 Martyn Wilson; 5 Graeme Lewthwaite; 6 Richard George; 7 Tane Manihera; 8 Matthew Tunstall; 9 Jonny Limmer; 10 Dean Burgess; 11 Gareth Dean; 12 John Tuimaualuga; 13 Brett Smith. Subs (all used): 14 James Robinson; 15 Stephen Dawes; 16 Ricky Wright; 17 Dean Bragg.
Tries: Manihera (9, 39, 59), Frazer (11), B Smith (15, 42, 48), Sione (27, 45, 69), Lewthwaite (31), Wilson (36), Tunstall (64), Limmer (76); **Goals:** Manihera 12/14.
THUNDER: 1 Graham Stephenson; 2 Steve Morton; 3 Kevin Neighbour; 4 Craig Firth; 5 Robin Peers; 6 Paul Thorman; 7 Steve Rutherford; 8 Rob Line; 9 Neil Thorman; 10 Nick Staveley; 11 Clint Brown; 12 Tony Doherty; 13 Steven Bradley. Subs (all used): 14 Adam Endersby; 15 Will Massey; 16 Ian Ball; 17 Ryan Clark.
Try: Peers (3); **Goals:** P Thorman 2/2.
Rugby Leaguer & League Express Men of the Match: *Town:* Tane Manihera; *Thunder:* Neil Thorman.
Penalty count: 7-4; **Half-time:** 38–8;
Referee: Jamie Leahy (Dewsbury); **Attendance:** 958.

YORK CITY KNIGHTS 64 DEWSBURY RAMS 6

CITY KNIGHTS: 1 Chris Smith; 2 Austin Buchanan; 3 Chris Langley; 4 Chris Spurr; 5 Craig Farrell; 6 Scott Rhodes; 7 Danny Brough; 8 Richard Wilson; 9 Lee Jackson; 10 Adam Sullivan; 11 Darren Callaghan; 12 Simon Friend; 13 Jimmy Elston. Subs (all used): 14 Mark Cain; 15 Yusuf Sozi; 16 John Smith; 17 Craig Forsyth.
Tries: Elston (5, 59), Farrell (14), Spurr (22, 52), Brough (27, 46, 74), Friend (40), Rhodes (43, 77), C Smith (64);
Goals: Brough 8/12.
RAMS: 1 Ian Preece; 2 Oliver Fairbank; 3 Wayne McHugh; 4 Kevin Crouthers; 5 Leon Williamson; 6 Adam Thaler; 7 David Mycoe; 8 Paul Hicks; 9 Scott Dyson; 10 Anthony Thewliss; 11 Ian Kirke; 12 Mark Stubley; 13 Chris Redfearn. Subs (all used): 14 Mick Hill; 15 Jamie Tennant; 16 Michael Gibbons; 17 Lee Kelly.
Try: Crouthers (10); **Goals:** A Thaler 1/1.
Sin bin: Dyson (67) - dissent.
Rugby Leaguer & League Express Men of the Match: *City Knights:* Danny Brough; *Rams:* Kevin Crouthers.
Penalty count: 11-7; **Half-time:** 26-6;
Referee: Phil Bentham (Warrington); **Attendance:** 1,761.

SHEFFIELD EAGLES 50 HUNSLET HAWKS 10

EAGLES: 1 Andy Poynter; 2 Carl De Chenu; 3 Nick Turnbull; 4 Alex Dickinson; 5 Bright Sodje; 6 Aled James; 7 Gavin Brown; 8 Jack Howieson; 9 Scott Collins; 10 Craig Brown; 11 Andy Raleigh; 12 Jordan James; 13 Sean Dickinson. Subs (all used): 14 Steve Doherty; 15 Andy Rice; 16 Greg Hurst; 17 Jon Bruce.
Tries: A Dickinson (6), Poynter (14), Turnbull (19, 80), A James (23, 43), J James (48, 58, 77), Hurst (70);
Goals: G Brown 4/7, A James 1/3.
HAWKS: 1 Chris Hall; 2 Paul Gleadhill; 3 Gareth Murrell; 4 Craig Duda; 5 Danny Herbert; 6 George Rayner; 7 Latham Tawhai; 8 Steve Pryce; 9 Joe Hawley; 10 Mick Coyle; 11 Wayne Freeman; 12 Shaun Ibbetson; 13 Danny Fearon. Subs (all used): 14 Jonlee Lockwood; 15 Glen Freeman; 16 Danny Cook; 17 Chris Grice.
Tries: Murrell (9), Rayner (35); **Goals:** Tawhai 1/2.
Rugby Leaguer & League Express Men of the Match: *Eagles:* Jordan James; *Hawks:* George Rayner.
Penalty count: 8-7; **Half-time:** 20-10;
Referee: Ben Thaler (Wakefield); **Attendance:** 870.

Friday 27th August 2004

CHORLEY LYNX 30 SWINTON LIONS 43

LYNX: 1 Lee Patterson; 2 Eddie Kilgannon; 3 Chris Newall; 4 Mick Redford; 5 Danny Arnold; 6 Brian Capewell; 7 Martin Gambles; 8 Ian Parry; 9 Chris Ramsdale; 10 John Hill; 11 John Chamberlain; 12 Gary Smith; 13 Danny Barton. Subs (all used): 14 Lee Rowley; 15 Andy Grundy; 16 Martin Roden; 17 Grant Bithel.
Tries: Capewell (10), Arnold (13, 68), Barton (25), Bithel (79); **Goals:** Capewell 4/6, Ramsdale 1/1.
Sin bin: Kilgannon (56) - holding down; Capewell (64) - dissent.
LIONS: 1 Wayne English; 2 Hugh Thorpe; 3 Dave Llewellyn; 4 Chris Maye; 5 Jason Roach; 6 Mick Coates; 7 Neil Hayden; 8 Phil Cushion; 9 Safraz Patel; 10 Ian Sinfield; 11 Kris Smith; 12 Robert Russell; 13 Ian Hodson. Subs (all used): 14 Warren Ayres; 15 Wes Rogers; 16 Lee Gardner; 17 Rob Whittaker.
Tries: Cushion (3), Maye (6, 64), English (18), Hodson (34), Thorpe (39), Russell (59), Whittaker (62);
Goals: Smith 2/6, Russell 3/3; **Field goal:** Patel.
Sin bin: Ayres (57) - holding down.
Rugby Leaguer & League Express Men of the Match: *Lynx:* Gary Smith; *Lions:* Wayne English.
Penalty count: 9-11; **Half-time:** 18-25;
Referee: Gareth Hewer (Whitehaven); **Attendance:** 369.

WEEK 21

Sunday 29th August 2004

BARROW RAIDERS 29 SHEFFIELD EAGLES 10

RAIDERS: 1 Craig Bower; 2 Matt Gardner; 3 Ryan Campbell; 4 Paul Jones; 5 Nick Beech; 6 Chris Archer; 7 Darren Holt; 8 Stuart Dancer; 9 Dave Clark; 10 Paul Wilcock; 11 Mike Whitehead; 12 Matt McConnell; 13 Barry Pugh. Subs (all used): 14 Matt Jefferson; 15 Phil Atkinson; 16 Tony Cunningham; 17 Matthew Leigh.
Tries: Holt (2), McConnell (5), Leigh (45), Atkinson (73);
Goals: Holt 5/6; **Field goals:** Holt 3.
EAGLES: 1 Andy Poynter; 2 Carl De Chenu; 3 Nick Turnbull; 4 Alex Dickinson; 5 Bright Sodje; 6 Aled James; 7 Gavin Brown; 8 Jack Howieson; 9 Scott Collins; 10 Jon Bruce; 11 Andy Raleigh; 12 Jordan James; 13 Sean Dickinson. Subs (all used): 14 Greg Hurst; 15 Andy Rice; 16 Steve Doherty; 17 Craig Brown.
Tries: A Dickinson (57), J James (61);
Goals: G Brown 1/2.
Rugby Leaguer & League Express Men of the Match: *Raiders:* Darren Holt; *Eagles:* Jack Howieson.
Penalty count: 7-5; **Half-time:** 19-0; **Referee:** Steve Nicholson (Whitehaven); **Attendance:** 1,222.

DEWSBURY RAMS 30 WORKINGTON TOWN 41

RAMS: 1 Ian Preece; 2 Oliver Fairbank; 3 Wayne McHugh; 4 Jon Waddle; 5 Leon Williamson; 6 Scott Dyson; 7 Adam Thaler; 8 Paul Hicks; 9 Chris Woolford; 10 Mark Hawksley; 11 Anthony Thewliss; 12 Mark Stubley; 13 Chris Redfearn. Subs (all used): 14 Mick Hill; 15 Jamie Tennant; 16 Michael Gibbons; 17 Lee Kelly.
Tries: Hicks (10), Waddle (29), McHugh (46), Redfearn (65), A Thaler (70); **Goals:** A Thaler 5/5.
TOWN: 1 Lusi Sione; 2 Matthew Johnson; 3 Neil Frazer; 4 Martyn Wilson; 5 Scott Chilton; 6 Brett Smith; 7 Tane Manihera; 8 Matthew Tunstall; 9 Jonny Limmer; 10 Dean Burgess; 11 Gareth Dean; 12 John Tuimaualuga; 13 Jamie Beaumont. Subs (all used): 14 James Robinson; 15 Stephen Dawes; 16 David Pettit; 17 Dean Bragg.
Tries: Tuimaualuga (5), B Smith (17), Johnson (36), Manihera (50), Chilton (58), Wilson (62), Burgess (72);
Goals: Manihera 6/8; **Field goal:** Manihera.
Rugby Leaguer & League Express Men of the Match: *Rams:* Adam Thaler; *Town:* Tane Manihera.
Penalty count: 7-7; **Half-time:** 12-18;
Referee: Paul Carr (Castleford); **Attendance:** 520.

GATESHEAD THUNDER 12 HUNSLET HAWKS 34

THUNDER: 1 Graham Stephenson; 2 Steve Morton; 3 Will Massey; 4 Kevin Neighbour; 5 Robin Peers; 6 Paul Thorman; 7 Steve Rutherford; 8 Rob Line; 9 Neil Thorman; 10 Nick Staveley; 11 Liam Garside; 12 Clint Brown; 13 Steven Bradley. Subs (all used): 14 Tony Doherty; 15 Ryan Clark; 16 Adam Endersby; 17 Jon MacDonald.
Tries: Bradley (57, 74);
Goals: P Thorman 1/1, Garside 1/1.
HAWKS: 1 Chris Hall; 2 Paul Gleadhill; 3 Danny Cook; 4 Craig Duda; 5 George Rayner; 6 Chris Ross; 7 Latham Tawhai; 8 Glen Freeman; 9 Joe Hawley; 10 Mick Coyle; 11 Wayne Freeman; 12 Dean Sampson; 13 Danny Fearon. Subs (all used): 14 Jonlee Lockwood; 15 Shaun Ibbetson; 16 Steve Pryce; 17 Gareth Murrell.
Tries: Gleadhill (11, 42), Hawley (27), W Freeman (39), Murrell (47), Duda (62), C Hall (72);
Goals: Ross 3/7, Duda 0/1, Gleadhill 0/1.
Rugby Leaguer & League Express Men of the Match: *Thunder:* Kevin Neighbour; *Hawks:* Chris Hall.
Penalty count: 9-12; **Half-time:** 0-16;
Referee: Phil Bentham (Warrington); **Attendance:** 277.

LONDON SKOLARS 6 YORK CITY KNIGHTS 58

SKOLARS: 1 Jermaine Coleman; 2 Austin Aggrey; 3 Stuart Singleton; 4 Stephen Green; 5 Zane Gardiner; 6 Kurt Pittman; 7 Peter Hannan; 8 Wayne Parillon; 9 Gareth Honor; 10 Alex Smits; 11 Rubert Jonker; 12 Deon McFadyen; 13 Mark Cantoni. Subs (all used): 14 Richard Singleton; 15 Bobby Wallis; 16 Ade Aderiye; 17 Ben Joyce.
Try: McFadyen (45); **Goals:** Pittman 1/1.
Sin bin: Pittman (32) - holding down; Coleman (40), (75) - holding down.
CITY KNIGHTS: 1 Chris Smith; 2 Scott Walker; 3 Chris Langley; 4 Chris Spurr; 5 Craig Farrell; 6 Scott Rhodes; 7 Danny Brough; 8 Richard Wilson; 9 Lee Jackson; 10 Adam Sullivan; 11 Mick Ramsden; 12 John Smith; 13 Simon Friend. Subs (all used): 14 Jimmy Elston; 15 Mark Cain; 16 Yusuf Sozi; 17 Craig Forsyth.
Tries: J Smith (12), Langley (17, 33, 49), Walker (24, 59), Rhodes (40), Spurr (54), Jackson (57), Sozi (77);
Goals: Brough 9/10.
Rugby Leaguer & League Express Men of the Match: *Skolars:* Deon McFadyen; *City Knights:* Scott Rhodes.

Barrow celebrate promotion to National League One after a last-day regular season win at Dewsbury

Penalty count: 8-15; **Half-time:** 0-32;
Referee: Jamie Leahy (Dewsbury); **Attendance:** 650.

Saturday 4th September 2004

YORK CITY KNIGHTS 44 WORKINGTON TOWN 24

CITY KNIGHTS: 1 Chris Smith; 2 Scott Walker; 3 Chris Langley; 4 Chris Spurr; 5 Craig Farrell; 6 Scott Rhodes; 7 Danny Brough; 8 Richard Wilson; 9 Lee Jackson; 10 Adam Sullivan; 11 Mick Ramsden; 12 Simon Friend; 13 Mark Cain. Subs (all used): 14 Jimmy Elston; 15 Albert Talipeau; 16 John Smith; 17 Yusuf Sozi.
Tries: Brough (1), Farrell (7), Rhodes (15), Langley (27, 59), Elston (30, 63), C Smith (44); **Goals:** Brough 6/9.
TOWN: 1 Scott Chilton; 2 Matthew Johnson; 3 Jamie Beaumont; 4 Stephen Dawes; 5 Thomas Armstrong; 6 Richard George; 7 Tane Manihera; 8 John Tuimaualuga; 9 Jonny Limmer; 10 Dean Burgess; 11 James Robinson; 12 Gareth Dean; 13 David Pettit. Subs (all used): 14 Dean Bragg; 15 Ricky Wright; 16 Craig Barker; 17 Malcolm Caton.
Tries: Burgess (19), Limmer (34), Johnson (37), Manihera (68), Dawes (78);
Goals: Manihera 2/4, Bragg 0/1.
Rugby Leaguer & League Express Men of the Match:
City Knights: Scott Rhodes; *Town:* Tane Manihera.
Penalty count: 7-7; **Half-time:** 28-14;
Referee: Julian King (St Helens); **Attendance:** 1,346.

WEEK 22

Sunday 5th September 2004

BARROW RAIDERS 45 GATESHEAD THUNDER 34

RAIDERS: 1 Craig Bower; 2 Nick Beech; 3 Ryan Campbell; 4 Paul Jones; 5 Matt Gardner; 6 Phil Atkinson; 7 Darren Holt; 8 Stuart Dancer; 9 Dave Clark; 10 Paul Wilcock; 11 Mike Whitehead; 12 Matt McConnell; 13 Barry Pugh. Subs (all used): 14 Liam Finch; 15 Chris Archer; 16 Matthew Leigh; 17 Tony Cunningham.
Tries: McConnell (5), P Jones (15), Beech (20), Atkinson

(28), Holt (45), Whitehead (52), Archer (67);
Goals: Holt 8/8; **Field goal:** Holt.
THUNDER: 1 Graham Stephenson; 2 Steve Morton; 3 Jon MacDonald; 4 Craig Firth; 5 Robin Peers; 6 Steve Rutherford; 7 Kevin Neighbour; 8 Rob Line; 9 Neil Thorman; 10 Clint Brown; 11 Liam Garside; 12 Steven Bradley; 13 Paul Thorman. Subs: 14 Ryan Clark; 15 Phil Pitt; 16 Seamus McCallion (not used); 17 Paul Dodsworth.
Tries: Firth (35), Garside (50), N Thorman (57), P Thorman (61), Bradley (69), Morton (72);
Goals: P Thorman 5/6.
Rugby Leaguer & League Express Men of the Match:
Raiders: Dave Clark; *Thunder:* Paul Thorman.
Penalty count: 8-5; **Half-time:** 24-6;
Referee: Jamie Leahy (Dewsbury); **Attendance:** 1,015.

LONDON SKOLARS 28 CHORLEY LYNX 16

SKOLARS: 1 Joel Osborn; 2 Austin Aggrey; 3 Richard Singleton; 4 Stephen Green; 5 Zane Gardiner; 6 Jermaine Coleman; 7 Peter Hannan; 8 Glenn Osborn; 9 Kurt Pittman; 10 Alex Smits; 11 Rubert Jonker; 12 Deon McFadyen; 13 Mark Cantoni. Subs (all used): 14 Gareth Honor; 15 Wayne Parillon; 16 Ade Aderiye; 17 Bobby Wallis.
Tries: R Singleton (17), Cantoni (37), Green (45), Gardiner (48), J Osborn (58); **Goals:** J Osborn 4/5.
Sin bin: Cantoni (24) - fighting;
Hannan (78) - obstruction.
LYNX: 1 Lee Patterson; 2 Danny Arnold; 3 Jake Johnstone; 4 Mick Redford; 5 Eddie Kilgannon; 6 Grant Bithel; 7 Martin Gambles; 8 Ian Parry; 9 Chris Ramsdale; 10 John Hill; 11 John Chamberlain; 12 Gary Smith; 13 Danny Barton. Subs (all used): 14 Brian Capewell; 15 Lee Rowley; 16 James Lomax; 17 Martin Roden.
Tries: Barton (10), Capewell (32), Ramsdale (76);
Goals: Johnstone 1/1, Capewell 1/2.
Sin bin: Roden (14) - fighting.
Rugby Leaguer & League Express Men of the Match:
Skolars: Zane Gardiner; *Lynx:* Martin Gambles.
Penalty count: 1-7; **Half-time:** 10-12;
Referee: Ben Thaler (Wakefield); **Attendance:** 386.

SWINTON LIONS 32 SHEFFIELD EAGLES 24

LIONS: 1 Wayne English; 2 Hugh Thorpe; 3 Steve Warburton; 4 Chris Maye; 5 Danny Tyrell; 6 Mick Coates; 7 Neil Hayden; 8 Phil Cushion; 9 Warren Ayres; 10 Ian Sinfield; 11 Kris Smith; 12 Robert Russell; 13 Ian Hodson. Subs (all used): 14 Safraz Patel; 15 Wes Rogers; 16 Lee Gardner; 17 Rob Whittaker.
Tries: Thorpe (19), Patel (35), Smith (59), Maye (66, 73), Cushion (78); **Goals:** Russell 4/8.
EAGLES: 1 Andy Poynter; 2 Bright Sodje; 3 Jimmy Pearson; 4 Nick Turnbull; 5 Danny Mills; 6 Ryan Dickinson; 7 Gavin Brown; 8 Jack Howieson; 9 Scott Collins; 10 Jon Bruce; 11 Andy Raleigh; 12 Craig Brown; 13 Jordan James. Subs (all used): 14 Greg Hurst; 15 Andy Rice; 16 Simon Morton; 17 Simon Tillyer.
Tries: R Dickinson (1), Poynter (7), Pearson (15), Sodje (46); **Goals:** G Brown 4/5.
Rugby Leaguer & League Express Men of the Match:
Lions: Mick Coates; *Eagles:* Scott Collins.
Penalty count: 10-6; **Half-time:** 14-16;
Referee: Peter Taberner (Wigan); **Attendance:** 595.

HUNSLET HAWKS 36 DEWSBURY RAMS 20

HAWKS: 1 Chris Hall; 2 Paul Gleadhill; 3 Danny Cook; 4 Craig Duda; 5 George Rayner; 6 Chris Ross; 7 Latham Tawhai; 8 Danny Fearon; 9 Joe Hawley; 10 Mick Coyle; 11 Wayne Freeman; 12 Shaun Ibbetson; 13 Andy Bastow. Subs (all used): 14 Jonlee Lockwood; 15 Glen Freeman; 16 Steve Pryce; 17 Wes McGibbon.
Tries: Hawley (15), Coyle (17), Rayner (32), Tawhai (47), Fearon (58), Lockwood (69); **Goals:** Ross 6/7.
RAMS: 1 Ian Preece; 2 Oliver Fairbank; 3 Wayne McHugh; 4 Ian Kirke; 5 Leon Williamson; 6 Scott Dyson; 7 Adam Thaler; 8 Paul Hicks; 9 Richard Chapman; 10 Mark Hawksley; 11 Anthony Thewliss; 12 Jon Waddle; 13 Chris Redfearn. Subs (all used): 14 Chris Woolford; 15 Kurt Rudder; 16 Jamie Tennant; 17 Michael Gibbons.
Tries: A Thaler (3, 65, 71), Hawksley (6);
Goals: A Thaler 2/4.
Rugby Leaguer & League Express Men of the Match:
Hawks: Steve Pryce; *Rams:* Adam Thaler.
Penalty count: 7-8; **Half-time:** 18-12; **Referee:** Steve Nicholson (Whitehaven); **Attendance:** 532.

WEEK 23

Sunday 12th September 2004

CHORLEY LYNX 21 YORK CITY KNIGHTS 20

LYNX: 1 Lee Patterson; 2 Danny Arnold; 3 Mick Redford; 4 Jake Johnstone; 5 Eddie Kilgannon; 6 Brian Capewell; 7 Martin Gambles; 8 Ian Parry; 9 Chris Ramsdale; 10 John Hill; 11 John Chamberlain; 12 Gary Smith; 13 Danny Barton. Subs (all used): 14 Lee Rowley; 15 Jamie Lomax; 16 Grant Bithel; 17 Martin Roden.
Tries: Roden (39), Arnold (42), Kilgannon (72, 76);
Goals: Capewell 2/4; **Field goal:** Capewell.
CITY KNIGHTS: 1 Chris Smith; 2 Austin Buchanan; 3 Chris Langley; 4 Chris Spurr; 5 Craig Farrell; 6 Scott Rhodes; 7 Danny Brough; 8 Richard Wilson; 9 Lee Jackson; 10 Adam Sullivan; 11 Darren Callaghan; 12 Simon Friend; 13 Albert Talipeau. Subs (all used): 14 Jimmy Elston; 15 Mark Cain; 16 John Smith; 17 Yusuf Sozi.
Tries: Buchanan (17), Langley (27), Elston (36), Talipeau (46); **Goals:** Brough 2/5.
Sin bin: Brough (59) - dissent.
Rugby Leaguer & League Express Men of the Match: *Lynx:* Brian Capewell; *City Knights:* Albert Talipeau.
Penalty count: 9-9; **Half-time:** 6-16; **Referee:** Steve Nicholson (Whitehaven); **Attendance:** 616.

DEWSBURY RAMS 12 BARROW RAIDERS 26

RAMS: 1 Wayne McHugh; 2 Oliver Fairbank; 3 Jon Waddle; 4 Ian Kirke; 5 Leon Williamson; 6 Scott Dyson; 7 Adam Thaler; 8 Paul Hicks; 9 Richard Chapman; 10 Mark Hawksley; 11 Mark Stubley; 12 Jamie Tennant; 13 Chris Redfearn. Subs (all used): 14 Chris Woolford; 15 Kurt Rudder; 16 David Mycoe; 17 Michael Gibbons.
Tries: McHugh (24), Redfearn (43); **Goals:** A Thaler 2/2.
RAIDERS: 1 Craig Bower; 2 Matt Gardner; 3 Ryan Campbell; 4 Paul Jones; 5 Adam Pate; 6 Phil Atkinson; 7 Darren Holt; 8 Stuart Dancer; 9 Dave Clark; 10 Paul Wilcock; 11 Matt McConnell; 12 James King; 13 Barry Pugh. Subs (all used): 14 Mike Whitehead; 15 Tony Cunningham; 16 Chris Archer; 17 Matthew Leigh.
Tries: Gardner (46), Atkinson (56), Pate (66);
Goals: Holt 6/9; **Field goals:** Holt 2.
Rugby Leaguer & League Express Men of the Match: *Rams:* Wayne McHugh; *Raiders:* Stuart Dancer.
Penalty count: 4-6; **Half-time:** 6-4;
Referee: Peter Taberner (Wigan); **Attendance:** 1,583.

GATESHEAD THUNDER 23 SWINTON LIONS 28

THUNDER: 1 Graham Stephenson; 2 Steve Morton; 3 Jon MacDonald; 4 Craig Firth; 5 Robin Peers; 6 Steven Bradley; 7 Kevin Neighbour; 8 Rob Line; 9 Neil Thorman; 10 Nick Staveley; 11 Liam Garside; 12 Clint Brown; 13 Paul Thorman. Subs (all used): 14 Ryan Clark; 15 Phil Pitt; 16 Tony Doherty; 17 Paul Dodsworth.
Tries: N Thorman (14, 47), Bradley (61), Peers (66);
Goals: P Thorman 3/5; **Field goal:** P Thorman.
LIONS: 1 Wayne English; 2 Hugh Thorpe; 3 Dave Llewellyn; 4 Chris Maye; 5 Steve Warburton; 6 Mick Coates; 7 Neil Hayden; 8 Ian Sinfield; 9 Warren Ayres; 10 Wes Rogers; 11 Kris Smith; 12 Robert Russell; 13 Ian Hodson. Subs (all used): 14 Safraz Patel; 15 Phil Cushion; 16 Lee Gardner; 17 Rob Whittaker.
Tries: Smith (25), Maye (11, 20), English (32), Llewellyn (52), Sinfield (79); **Goals:** Russell 2/6.
Rugby Leaguer & League Express Men of the Match: *Thunder:* Neil Thorman; *Lions:* Chris Maye.
Penalty count: 7-4; **Half-time:** 6-18;
Referee: Phil Bentham (Warrington); **Attendance:** 342.

WORKINGTON TOWN 24 HUNSLET HAWKS 6

TOWN: 1 Scott Chilton; 2 Matthew Johnson; 3 Martyn Wilson; 4 Stephen Dawes; 5 Graeme Lewthwaite; 6 Richard George; 7 Brett Smith; 8 Matthew Tunstall; 9 Jonny Limmer; 10 Dean Burgess; 11 Gareth Dean; 12 John Tuimaualuga; 13 Jamie Beaumont. Subs (all used): 14 Dean Bragg; 15 Ricky Wright; 16 David Pettit; 17 James Robinson.
Tries: B Smith (7), Dean (27), George (43), Dawes (68);
Goals: B Smith 4/6.
HAWKS: 1 Chris Hall; 2 Paul Gleadhill; 3 Danny Cook; 4 Craig Duda; 5 George Rayner; 6 Andy Bastow; 7 Chris Ross; 8 Danny Fearon; 9 Joe Hawley; 10 Jonlee Lockwood; 11 Wayne Freeman; 12 Dean Sampson; 13 Paul Seal. Subs (all used): 14 Steve Pryce; 15 Glen Freeman; 16 Wes McGibbon; 17 Gareth Carey.
Try: Duda (12); **Goal:** Ross 1/2.
Sin bin: Fearon (73) – high tackle.
Rugby Leaguer & League Express Men of the Match: *Town:* Brett Smith; *Hawks:* Joe Hawley.
Penalty count: 12-9; **Half-time:** 14-6;
Referee: Ben Thaler (Wakefield); **Attendance:** 978.

SHEFFIELD EAGLES 62 LONDON SKOLARS 6

EAGLES: 1 Andy Poynter; 2 Kieron Collins; 3 Jon Breakingbury; 4 Alex Dickinson; 5 Carl De Chenu; 6 Steve Doherty; 7 Gavin Brown; 8 Jack Howieson; 9 Scott Collins; 10 Jon Bruce; 11 Andy Raleigh; 12 Craig Brown; 13 Jordan James. Subs (all used): 14 Jimmy Pearson; 15 Simon Morton; 16 Nick Turnbull; 17 Simon Tillyer.
Tries: J James (3, 49), Doherty (14, 22), Poynter (35, 37), De Chenu (55), Breakingbury (60, 69), Tillyer (72), K Collins (76), Turnbull (80);
Goals: G Brown 1/1, Pearson 6/11.
SKOLARS: 1 Joel Osborn; 2 Austin Aggrey; 3 Richard Singleton; 4 Stephen Green; 5 Zane Gardiner; 6 Jermaine Coleman; 7 Peter Hannan; 8 Glenn Osborn; 9 Kurt Pittman; 10 Alex Smits; 11 Rubert Jonker; 12

Martyn Wilson takes on Craig Duda as Workington eliminate Hunslet

Stuart Singleton; 13 Mark Cantoni. Subs (all used): 14 Gareth Honor; 15 Wayne Parrillon; 16 Ade Aderiye; 17 Bobby Wallis.
Try: Cantoni (65); **Goals:** J Osborn 1/1.
Sin bin: J Osborn (70) - holding down; Coleman (76) - holding down.
Rugby Leaguer & League Express Men of the Match: *Eagles:* Scott Collins; *Skolars:* Rubert Jonker.
Penalty count: 11-8; **Half-time:** 28-0;
Referee: Gareth Hewer (Whitehaven); **Attendance:** 825.

NATIONAL LEAGUE ONE QUALIFYING SERIES

Sunday 19th September 2004

ELIMINATION PLAY-OFFS

SWINTON LIONS 38 WORKINGTON TOWN 44

LIONS: 1 Wayne English; 2 Hugh Thorpe; 3 Dave Llewellyn; 4 Chris Maye; 5 Steve Warburton; 6 Mick Coates; 7 Paul Ashton; 8 Phil Cushion; 9 Warren Ayres; 10 Ian Sinfield; 11 Kris Smith; 12 Robert Russell; 13 Ian Hodson. Subs (all used): 14 Safraz Patel; 15 Wes Rogers; 16 Lee Gardner; 17 Rob Whittaker.
Tries: English (12), Ayres (28), Llewellyn (31), Hodson (45, 75), Thorpe (61), Coates (80);
Goals: Ashton 4/6, Russell 1/1.
TOWN: 1 Lusi Sione; 2 Matthew Woodcock; 3 Martyn Wilson; 4 Stephen Dawes; 5 Graeme Lewthwaite; 6 Richard George; 7 Tane Manihera; 8 Matthew Tunstall; 9 Jonny Limmer; 10 Dean Burgess; 11 Gareth Dean; 12 John Tuimaualuga; 13 Brett Smith. Subs (all used): 14 Dean Bragg; 15 Jamie Beaumont; 16 David Pettit; 17 James Robinson.
Tries: Lewthwaite (7, 38), George (18), Limmer (42, 51), B Smith (54), Manihera (79); **Goals:** Manihera 8/8.
Rugby Leaguer & League Express Men of the Match: *Lions:* Wayne English; *Town:* Jonny Limmer.
Penalty count: 7-6; **Half-time:** 16-18;
Referee: Ben Thaler (Wakefield); **Attendance:** 768.

SHEFFIELD EAGLES 16 HUNSLET HAWKS 39

EAGLES: 1 Andy Poynter; 2 Kieron Collins; 3 Jon Breakingbury; 4 Alex Dickinson; 5 Carl De Chenu; 6 Aled James; 7 Steve Doherty; 8 Jack Howieson; 9 Scott Collins; 10 Jon Bruce; 11 Andy Raleigh; 12 Craig Brown; 13 Jordan James. Subs (all used): 14 Jimmy Pearson; 15 Simon Morton; 16 Nick Turnbull; 17 Simon Tillyer.
Tries: S Collins (20), J James (48), A James (80);
Goals: A James 0/3, Pearson 2/2.
HAWKS: 1 Chris Hall; 2 Paul Gleadhill; 3 Danny Cook; 4 Craig Duda; 5 George Rayner; 6 Andy Bastow; 7 Latham Tawhai; 8 Danny Fearon; 9 Joe Hawley; 10 Dean Sampson; 11 Wayne Freeman; 12 Jonlee Lockwood; 13 Paul Seal. Subs (all used): 14 Mick Coyle; 15 Steve Pryce; 16 Glen Freeman; 17 Chris Ross.

Tries: Cook (16), Seal (25), W Freeman (29), C Hall (44, 52), Tawhai (60), Rayner (75);
Goals: Gleadhill 5/8; **Field goal:** Tawhai.
Rugby Leaguer & League Express Men of the Match: *Eagles:* Andy Raleigh; *Hawks:* Latham Tawhai.
Penalty count: 8-7; **Half-time:** 4-20;
Referee: Julian King (St Helens); **Attendance:** 531.

Sunday 26th September 2004

QUALIFYING SEMI-FINAL

HALIFAX 37 YORK CITY KNIGHTS 20

HALIFAX: 1 Scott Grix; 2 Rikki Sheriffe; 3 James Bunyan; 4 Alan Hadcroft; 5 James Haley; 6 Simon Grix; 7 Ben Black; 8 Ryan McDonald; 9 Mark Moxon; 10 Chris Birchall; 11 Jamie Bloem; 12 Ged Corcoran; 13 Pat Weisner. Subs (all used): 14 Gareth Greenwood; 15 Anthony Farrell; 16 David Bates; 17 Ben Feehan.
Tries: Hadcroft (12, 18), Simon Grix (21), Weisner (31), Scott Grix (48), Sheriffe (53), Feehan (78);
Goals: Bloem 4/8, Weisner 0/1; **Field goal:** Black.
CITY KNIGHTS: 1 Mark Cain; 2 Austin Buchanan; 3 Chris Langley; 4 Chris Spurr; 5 Craig Farrell; 6 Scott Rhodes; 7 Danny Brough; 8 Richard Wilson; 9 Lee Jackson; 10 Yusuf Sozi; 11 Mick Ramsden; 12 Darren Callaghan; 13 Simon Friend. Subs (all used): 14 Jimmy Elston; 15 Albert Talipeau; 16 John Smith; 17 Adam Sullivan.
Tries: Jackson (7), J Smith (38, 43), Friend (62);
Goals: Brough 2/4.
Rugby Leaguer & League Express Men of the Match: *Halifax:* Pat Weisner; *City Knights:* Jimmy Elston.
Penalty count: 5-9; **Half-time:** 23-12; **Referee:** Richard Silverwood (Dewsbury); **Attendance:** 2,213.

ELIMINATION SEMI-FINAL

WORKINGTON TOWN 27 HUNSLET HAWKS 13

TOWN: 1 Lusi Sione; 2 Scott Chilton; 3 Martyn Wilson; 4 Stephen Dawes; 5 Graeme Lewthwaite; 6 Richard George; 7 Tane Manihera; 8 Matthew Tunstall; 9 Jonny Limmer; 10 Dean Burgess; 11 Gareth Dean; 12 John Tuimaualuga; 13 Brett Smith. Subs (all used): 14 Dean Bragg; 15 Ricky Wright; 16 Jamie Beaumont; 17 James Robinson.
Tries: Wilson (22), Sione (33), Chilton (63), Limmer (68); **Goals:** Manihera 5/7; **Field goal:** Manihera.
HAWKS: 1 Chris Hall; 2 Paul Gleadhill; 3 Danny Cook; 4 Craig Duda; 5 George Rayner; 6 Andy Bastow; 7 Latham Tawhai; 8 Danny Fearon; 9 Joe Hawley; 10 Mick Coyle; 11 Wayne Freeman; 12 Jonlee Lockwood; 13 Paul Seal. Subs (all used): 14 Steve Pryce; 15 Glen Freeman; 16 Shaun Ibbetson; 17 Chris Ross.
Tries: Bastow (11), Rayner (59);
Goals: Gleadhill 2/3; **Field goal:** Tawhai.
Rugby Leaguer & League Express Men of the Match: *Town:* Tane Manihera; *Hawks:* Danny Fearon.
Penalty count: 12-10; **Half-time:** 14-7;
Referee: Ashley Klein (London); **Attendance:** 1,274.

Player-coach Anthony Farrell tackled by York's Scott Rhodes as Halifax survive in the National League One Qualifying Final

Sunday 3rd October 2004

FINAL ELIMINATOR

YORK CITY KNIGHTS 70 WORKINGTON TOWN 10

CITY KNIGHTS: 1 Chris Smith; 2 Austin Buchanan; 3 Chris Langley; 4 Chris Spurr; 5 Craig Farrell; 6 Scott Rhodes; 7 Danny Brough; 8 Richard Wilson; 9 Lee Jackson; 10 Yusuf Sozi; 11 John Smith; 12 Simon Friend; 13 Jimmy Elston. Subs (all used): 14 Mark Cain; 15 Albert Talipeau; 16 Adam Sullivan; 17 Craig Forsyth.
Tries: Spurr (1), Cain (12, 58, 61, 73, 76), Buchanan (31, 78), Rhodes (34), Farrell (36, 44), Sullivan (55); **Goals:** Brough 8/11, Jackson 1/1, Buchanan 2/2.
TOWN: 1 Lusi Sione; 2 Scott Chilton; 3 Martyn Wilson; 4 Stephen Dawes; 5 Graeme Lewthwaite; 6 Richard George; 7 Tane Manihera; 8 Matthew Tunstall; 9 Jonny Limmer; 10 John Tuimaualuga; 11 Gareth Dean; 12 Jamie Beaumont; 13 Brett Smith. Subs (all used): 14 Dean Bragg; 15 Ricky Wright; 16 Dean Burgess; 17 James Robinson.
Tries: Chilton (28), Manihera (69); **Goals:** Manihera 1/2.
Sin bin: B Smith (51) - punching.
Rugby Leaguer & League Express Men of the Match: *City Knights:* Lee Jackson; *Town:* Tane Manihera.
Penalty count: 8-6; **Half-time:** 26-6; **Referee:** Ronnie Laughton (Barnsley); **Attendance:** 2,017.

Sunday 10th October 2004

FINAL

HALIFAX 34 YORK CITY KNIGHTS 30

HALIFAX: 1 Scott Grix; 5 James Haley; 3 James Bunyan; 4 Alan Hadcroft; 2 Rikki Sheriffe; 6 Simon Grix; 7 Ben Black; 8 Jon Simpson; 9 Mark Moxon; 10 Chris Birchall; 11 Jamie Bloem; 12 Ged Corcoran; 13 Pat Weisner. Subs (all used): 14 Ben Feehan; 15 Anthony Farrell; 16 David Bates; 17 Gareth Greenwood.
Tries: Hadcroft (2, 71), Bunyan (9, 74), Sheriffe (22), Scott Grix (76); **Goals:** Bloem 5/7.
CITY KNIGHTS: 1 Scott Walker; 2 Austin Buchanan; 3 Chris Langley; 4 Chris Spurr; 5 Craig Farrell; 6 Scott Rhodes; 7 Danny Brough; 8 Richard Wilson; 9 Lee Jackson; 10 Yusuf Sozi; 11 John Smith; 12 Simon Friend; 13 Jimmy Elston. Subs (all used): 14 Mark Cain; 15 Albert Talipeau; 16 Adam Sullivan; 17 Craig Forsyth.
Tries: Elston (16), Buchanan (30, 37), Cain (61), Langley (64); **Goals:** Brough 5/7.
Rugby Leaguer & League Express Men of the Match: *Halifax:* Jamie Bloem; *City Knights:* Danny Brough.
Penalty count: 6-5; **Half-time:** 16-16; **Referee:** Robert Connolly (Wigan). *(at Halton Stadium, Widnes).*

Lee Jackson held by Jonny Limmer as York thrash Workington in the Final Eliminator

NATIONAL LEAGUE CUP 2004
Round by Round

National League Cup 2004 - Round by Round

WEEK 1

Sunday 1st February 2004

NORTH

BARROW RAIDERS 18 WHITEHAVEN 32

RAIDERS: 1 Craig Bower; 2 Adam Pate; 3 Jamie Smith; 4 Andy McClure; 5 Gary Ruddy; 6 Phil Atkinson; 7 Darren Holt; 8 Stuart Dancer; 9 Chris Archer; 10 James King; 11 Matthew Leigh; 12 Mike Whitehead; 13 Barry Pugh. Subs (all used): 14 Paul Jones; 15 Lee Dutton; 16 Dave Clark; 17 Paul Lupton.
Tries: McClure (3), Atkinson (62), Pate (66), P Jones (73); **Goal:** Holt.
WHITEHAVEN: 1 Gary Broadbent; 2 Jamie Marshall; 3 David Seeds; 4 Mick Nanyn; 5 Paul O'Neil; 6 Craig Walsh; 7 Lee Kiddie; 8 Chris McKinney; 9 Carl Sice; 10 David Fatialofa; 11 Spencer Miller; 12 Graeme Morton; 13 Howard Hill. Subs: 14 Steven Wood (not used); 15 Wesley Wilson; 16 Ryan Campbell; 17 Aaron Lester.
Tries: Nanyn (12, 22, 40, 51), Seeds (25, 47), Fatialofa (71); **Goals:** Nanyn 2.
Rugby Leaguer & League Express Men of the Match: *Raiders:* Matthew Leigh; *Whitehaven:* Mick Nanyn.
Penalty count: 7-7, **Half-time:** 6-18;
Referee: Mike Dawber (Wigan); **Attendance:** 1,269.

WORKINGTON TOWN 52 GATESHEAD THUNDER 0

TOWN: 1 Craig Stalker; 2 Matthew Johnson; 3 Jonathan Heaney; 4 Adam Coulson; 5 Scott Chilton; 6 Kevin Hetherington; 7 Gareth Skillen; 8 Jamie Beaumont; 9 Darren King; 10 Matthew Tunstall; 11 Jonny Limmer; 12 Ricky Wright; 13 Brett Smith. Subs (all used): 14 Graeme Lewthwaite; 15 David Pettit; 16 Andy McGlasson; 17 James Robinson.
Tries: B Smith (2, 14), Skillen (4), Limmer (11, 32), Johnson (19), C Stalker (50), King (59, 64), Coulson (68); **Goals:** Hetherington 6.
THUNDER: 1 Graham Stephenson; 2 Jaymes Bulman; 3 Kevin Neighbour; 4 Craig Firth; 5 Phil Pitt; 6 Paul Thorman; 7 Neil Thorman; 8 Rob Line; 9 Craig Fisher; 10 Steven Bradley; 11 Tony Doherty; 12 Andy Walker; 13 Steve Rutherford. Subs (all used): 14 Carl Stannard; 15 Shawn Ackerley; 16 Robin Peers; 17 Seamus McCallion.
Sin bin: Peers (36) – persistent interference.
Rugby Leaguer & League Express Men of the Match: *Town:* Darren King; *Thunder:* Steve Rutherford.
Penalty count: 8-7; **Half-time:** 28–0; **Referee:** Richard Silverwood (Dewsbury); **Attendance:** 709.

EAST

HULL KINGSTON ROVERS 24 SHEFFIELD EAGLES 2

ROVERS: 1 Craig Poucher; 2 Craig Farrell; 3 Paul Parker; 4 Matt Calland; 5 Alasdair McClarron; 6 Paul Mansson; 7 Phil Hasty; 8 Jamie Bovill; 9 Paul Pickering; 10 Jon Aston; 11 Dale Holdstock; 12 Andy Smith; 13 Anthony Seibold. Subs (all used): 14 Casey Mayberry; 15 Frank Watene; 16 Adam Sullivan; 17 Paul Fletcher.
Tries: Farrell (18), Holdstock (23), Mansson (37), McClarron (64), Mayberry (71); **Goals:** Hasty, Poucher.
EAGLES: 1 Andy Poynter; 2 Carl De Chenu; 3 Nick Turnbull; 4 Jon Breakingbury; 5 Danny Mills; 6 Peter Reilly; 7 Gavin Brown; 8 Jack Howieson; 9 Adam Carroll; 10 Jon Bruce; 11 Andy Raleigh; 12 Craig Brown; 13 Jordan James. Subs (all used): 14 Greg Hurst; 15 Gareth Stanley; 16 Simon Morton; 17 Rob North.
Goal: G Brown.
Sin bin: Bruce (17) - dissent.
Rugby Leaguer & League Express Men of the Match: *Rovers:* Paul Mansson; *Eagles:* Jordan James.
Penalty count: 10-8; **Half-time:** 14-2;
Referee: Robert Connolly (Wigan); **Attendance:** 2,391.

WEST

OLDHAM 64 CHORLEY LYNX 14

OLDHAM: 1 Gavin Dodd; 2 Will Cowell; 3 Iain Marsh; 4 Jon Goddard; 5 Nick Johnson; 6 Simon Svabic; 7 Ian Watson; 8 Steve Molloy; 9 John Hough; 10 Paul Southern; 11 Lee Doran; 12 Dane Morgan; 13 Lee Marsh. Subs (all used): 14 Keith Brennan; 15 Gareth Barber; 16 Martin Elswood; 17 Martin McLoughlin.
Tries: N Johnson (3), Morgan (9), Goddard (25), Barber (28), Cowell (39), L Marsh (43), Elswood (51), I Marsh (62, 65), Watson (78), Dodd (80);
Goals: Svabic 5, Barber 5.
LYNX: 1 Rob Smyth; 2 Lee Patterson; 3 Brian Capewell; 4 Eddie Kilgannon; 5 Gary O'Regan; 6 Neil Alexander; 7 Martin Gambles; 8 John Hill; 9 Martin Roden; 10 Gareth Jones; 11 Gary Smith; 12 Danny Barton; 13 Chris Newall. Subs (all used): 14 Anthony Murray; 15 Simon Smith; 16 Ian Parry; 17 Adam Briggs.
Tries: Smyth (15), Kilgannon (34), Patterson (57);
Goal: Capewell.
Rugby Leaguer & League Express Men of the Match: *Oldham:* Ian Watson; *Lynx:* John Hill.
Penalty count: 11-7; **Half-time:** 28-10;
Referee: Ben Thaler (Wakefield); **Attendance:** 1,096.

SWINTON LIONS 6 LEIGH CENTURIONS 22

LIONS: 1 Wayne English; 2 Jason Roach; 3 Chris Maye; 4 Dave Llewellyn; 5 Chris Irwin; 6 Warren Ayres; 7 Paul Ashton; 8 Tau Liku; 9 Safraz Patel; 10 Wes Rogers; 11 Kris Smith; 12 Ian Sinfield; 13 Ian Hodson. Subs (all used): 14 Hugh Thorpe; 15 Craig Wingfield; 16 Mike Loughlin; 17 Danny Heaton.
Try: Maye (37); **Goal:** Ashton.
CENTURIONS: 1 Neil Turley; 2 Steve Maden; 3 Dan Potter; 4 Chris Percival; 5 Damian Munro; 6 John Duffy; 7 Tommy Martyn; 8 Heath Cruckshank; 9 Dave McConnell; 10 David Bradbury; 11 David Larder; 12 Oliver Wilkes; 13 Ian Knott. Subs (all used): 14 Mick Coates; 15 Andrew Isherwood; 16 Simon Knox; 17 Richard Marshall.
Tries: Turley (46, 57), Potter (61), Isherwood (71);
Goals: Turley 3.
Rugby Leaguer & League Express Men of the Match: *Lions:* Wayne English; *Centurions:* Dave McConnell.
Penalty count: 13-10; **Half-time:** 6-0;
Referee: Peter Taberner (Wigan); **Attendance:** 1,351.

PENNINE

HALIFAX 18 KEIGHLEY COUGARS 12

HALIFAX: 1 Danny Arnold; 2 Chris Norman; 3 Jon Roper; 4 Alan Hadcroft; 5 Oliver Marns; 6 Pat Weisner; 7 Mark Moxon; 8 Anthony Farrell; 9 Phil Cantillon; 10 Ged Corcoran; 11 Jamie Bloem; 12 Chris Morley; 13 Wayne Corcoran. Subs: 14 Jaymes Chapman; 15 David Bates; 16 Danny Fearon; 17 Richard Smith (not used).
Tries: Arnold (15), Bloem (33), Cantillon (45);
Goals: Bloem 3.
Sin bin: Bloem (65) - persistent interference.
COUGARS: 1 Matt Foster; 2 Karl Smith; 3 David Foster; 4 Chris Wainwright; 5 Andy Robinson; 6 Adam Mitchell; 7 Matt Firth; 8 Phil Stephenson; 9 Simeon Hoyle; 10 Danny Ekis; 11 Richard Mervill; 12 Chris Parker; 13 Lee Patterson. Subs: 14 Craig Nipperess; 15 Adam Webster (not used); 16 Jason Clegg; 17 Chris Roe.
Tries: Mervill (51, 54); **Goals:** Mitchell 2.
Rugby Leaguer & League Express; Men of the Match: *Halifax:* Anthony Farrell; *Cougars:* Simeon Hoyle.
Penalty count: 11-12; **Half-time:** 12-4; **Referee:** Ronnie Laughton (Barnsley); **Attendance:** 3,360.

HUNSLET HAWKS 24 ROCHDALE HORNETS 8

HAWKS: 1 Jon Liddell; 2 Martin Sykes; 3 Paul Seal; 4 Wes McGibbon; 5 Leigh Deakin; 6 Danny Wood; 7 Chris Ross; 8 Craig Booth; 9 Jamaine Wray; 10 Mick Coyle; 11 Wayne Freeman; 12 Jonlee Lockwood; 13 Andy Bastow. Subs (all used): 14 Steve Pryce; 15 Glen Freeman; 16 Gary Shillabeer; 17 Dave Jessey.
Tries: Sykes (1), Wood (26), Seal (31), Wray (41);
Goals: Wood 4.
HORNETS: 1 Michael Platt; 2 Liam Williams; 3 Paul Anderson; 4 Ashley Watmore; 5 Chris Campbell; 6 John Braddish; 7 Lee Birdseye; 8 Andy Leathem; 9 Janan Billings; 10 Andy Grundy; 11 Rob Ball; 12 Andy Gorski; 13 Darren Shaw. Subs (all used): 14 Sam Butterworth; 15 Lee Hansen; 16 Kris Ratcliffe; 17 Mark Costello.
Try: Williams (73); **Goals:** Birdseye 2.
Rugby Leaguer & League Express Men of the Match: *Hawks:* Danny Wood; *Hornets:* Michael Platt.
Penalty count: 9-13; **Half-time:** 18-2;
Referee: Ian Smith (Oldham); **Attendance:** 519.

YORKSHIRE

DEWSBURY RAMS 12 FEATHERSTONE ROVERS 28

RAMS: 1 Richard Thaler; 2 Wayne McHugh; 3 Steve Beard; 4 Ian Kirke; 5 Jon Waddle; 6 Mick Senior; 7 Chris Redfearn; 8 Paul Hicks; 9 Adam Thaler; 10 Anthony Thewliss; 11 Billy Kershaw; 12 Tim Spears; 13 Kevin Crouthers. Subs (all used): 14 Darren Robinson; 15 Mark Hawksley; 16 Ian Booth; 17 Ryan Hardy.
Tries: Crouthers (78), Robinson (79); **Goals:** A Thaler 2.
ROVERS: 1 Nathan Batty; 2 Jamie Stokes; 3 Ben Archibald; 4 Richard Newlove; 5 Matthew Wray; 6 Jon Presley; 7 Carl Briggs; 8 Bryan Henare; 9 Paul Darley; 10 Lee Williamson; 11 Steve Dooler; 12 Richard Blakeway; 13 Adam Hayes. Subs (all used): 14 Jim Carlton; 15 Andy Jarrett; 16 James Houston; 17 James Ford.
Tries: Hayes (6), Dooler (33), Newlove (52);
Goals: Briggs 8.
Sin bin: Newlove (29) - dissent;
Wray (63) - throwing ball at opponent.
Rugby Leaguer & League Express Men of the Match: *Rams:* Mick Senior; *Rovers:* Carl Briggs.
Penalty count: 9-8; **Half-time:** 0-20; **Referee:** Colin Morris (Huddersfield); **Attendance:** 1,489.

YORK CITY KNIGHTS 22 BATLEY BULLDOGS 24

CITY KNIGHTS: 1 Nathan Graham; 2 Alex Godfrey; 3 Chris Langley; 4 Damien Reid; 5 Rob Kama; 6 Scott Rhodes; 7 Danny Brough; 8 Richard Hayes; 9 Lee Jackson; 10 Yusuf Sozi; 11 Darren Callaghan; 12 Damian Ball; 13 Danny Seal. Subs (all used): 14 Jimmy Elston; 15 Mark Cain; 16 Simon Friend; 17 Craig Forsyth.
Tries: Seal (3), Callaghan (28), Langley (64);
Goals: Brough 5.
Dismissal: Forsyth (32) - punching.
Sin bin: Kama (32) - fighting.
BULLDOGS: 1 Craig Lingard; 2 Mark Sibson; 3 Chris Spurr; 4 Danny Maun; 5 Adrian Flynn; 6 Barry Eaton; 7 Mark Cass; 8 Chris Molyneux; 9 Joe Berry; 10 Steve Hill; 11 Sean Richardson; 12 Andy Spink; 13 Ryan Horsley. Subs (all used): 14 Shad Royston; 15 Paul Harrison; 16 David Rourke; 17 Andy Rice.
Tries: Spurr (51), Flynn (60), Sibson (62), Berry (68);
Goals: Eaton 4.
Sin bin: Spurr (32) - fighting.
Rugby Leaguer & League Express Men of the Match: *City Knights:* Chris Langley; *Bulldogs:* Barry Eaton.
Penalty count: 10-6; **Half-time:** 14-0;
Referee: Ashley Klein (London); **Attendance:** 2,039.

WEEK 2

Wednesday 11th February 2004

EAST

SHEFFIELD EAGLES 6 DONCASTER DRAGONS 38

EAGLES: 1 Andy Poynter; 2 Danny Mills; 3 Nick Turnbull; 4 Greg Hurst; 5 Carl De Chenu; 6 Peter Reilly; 7 Gavin Brown; 8 Jack Howieson; 9 Gareth Stanley; 10 Jon Bruce; 11 Andy Raleigh; 12 Craig Brown; 13 Jordan James. Subs (all used): 14 Jon Breakingbury; 15 Rob North; 16 Simon Morton; 17 Simon Tillyer.
Try: Raleigh (74); **Goal:** G Brown.
Sin bin: James (47) - fighting; Mills (55) - retaliation.
DRAGONS: 1 Johnny Woodcock; 2 Jason Lee; 3 Gareth Lloyd; 4 PJ Solomon; 5 Marlon Billy; 6 Graham Holroyd; 7 Chris Hough; 8 Gareth Handford; 9 Craig Cook; 10 Jamie Fielden; 11 Peter Green; 12 Craig Lawton; 13 Shaun Leaf. Subs (all used): 14 Chris Hemmings; 15 Tony Atter; 16 Matt Walker; 17 Alex Muff.
Tries: Holroyd (15), Hough (21, 53), Billy (26, 39), Woodcock (43), Muff (70); **Goals:** Holroyd 5.
Sin bin: Walker (47) - fighting.
Rugby Leaguer & League Express Men of the Match: *Eagles:* Carl De Chenu; *Dragons:* Graham Holroyd.
Penalty count: 8-10; **Half-time:** 0-22;
Referee: Mike Dawber (Wigan); **Attendance:** 945.

WEEK 3

Sunday 15th February 2004

WEST

LEIGH CENTURIONS 51 OLDHAM 32

CENTURIONS: 1 Neil Turley; 2 Steve Maden; 3 Dan Potter; 4 Chris Percival; 5 Mark McCully; 6 John Duffy; 7 Tommy Martyn; 8 Richard Marshall; 9 Dave McConnell; 10 David Bradbury; 11 Oliver Wilkes; 12 David Larder; 13 Ian Knott. Subs (all used): 14 Paul Rowley; 15 Andrew Isherwood; 16 Simon Knox; 17 Heath Cruckshank.
Tries: McCully (5), Bradbury (18), Knott (34, 80), Turley (38), Rowley (54), Martyn (59), Duffy (78);
Goals: Turley 9; **Field goal:** Turley.
OLDHAM: 1 Gavin Dodd; 2 Will Cowell; 3 Iain Marsh; 4 Jon Goddard; 5 Nick Johnson; 6 Simon Svabic; 7 Ian Watson; 8 Steve Molloy; 9 John Hough; 10 Paul Southern; 11 Lee Doran; 12 Dane Morgan; 13 Lee Marsh. Subs (all used): 14 Gareth Barber; 15 Craig Farrimond; 16 Martin Elswood; 17 James Bunyan.
Tries: I Marsh (2), Morgan (48, 65), Doran (56), Watson (73); **Goals:** Svabic 6.
Rugby Leaguer & League Express Men of the Match: *Centurions:* Ian Knott; *Oldham:* Dane Morgan.
Penalty count: 9-14; **Half-time:** 27-8;
Referee: Ashley Klein (London); **Attendance:** 2,316.

PENNINE

ROCHDALE HORNETS 14 HALIFAX 33

HORNETS: 1 Michael Platt; 2 Liam Williams; 3 Paul Anderson; 4 Richard Varkulis; 5 Chris Campbell; 6 John Braddish; 7 Lee Birdseye; 8 Andy Leathem; 9 Janan Billings; 10 Lee Hansen; 11 Andy Gorski; 12 Rob Ball; 13 Darren Shaw. Subs (all used): 14 Sam Butterworth; 15 Andy Grundy; 16 Kris Ratcliffe; 17 Mark Costello.
Tries: Varkulis (56, 70); **Goals:** Birdseye 3.
HALIFAX: 1 Danny Arnold; 2 Richard Smith; 3 Jon Roper; 4 Alan Hadcroft; 5 Oliver Marns; 6 Simon Grix; 7 Mark Moxon; 8 Anthony Farrell; 9 Phil Cantillon; 10 Danny Fearon; 11 Jamie Bloem; 12 Chris Morley; 13 Pat Weisner. Subs (all used): 14 Wayne Corcoran; 15 Chris Norman; 16 David Bates; 17 Scott Law.
Tries: Smith (18), Arnold (32, 61), Norman (76), Marns (80); **Goals:** Bloem 4, Roper, W Corcoran;
Field goal: Weisner.
Rugby Leaguer & League Express Men of the Match: *Hornets:* Janan Billings; *Halifax:* Anthony Farrell.
Penalty count: 12-11; **Half-time:** 4-14;
Referee: Russell Smith (Castleford); **Attendance:** 1,343.

YORKSHIRE v EAST

BATLEY BULLDOGS 46 DONCASTER DRAGONS 26

BULLDOGS: 1 Craig Lingard; 2 Mark Sibson; 3 Shad Royston; 4 Danny Maun; 5 Adrian Flynn; 6 Mark Toohey; 7 Barry Eaton; 8 Chris Molyneux; 9 Joe Berry; 10 David Rourke; 11 Danny Evans; 12 Andy Spink; 13 Ryan Horsley. Subs (all used): 14 Andy Heptinstall; 15 Paul Harrison; 16 Will Cartledge; 17 Sean Richardson.
Tries: Flynn (3, 52), Toohey (13), Richardson (34, 42), Royston (40, 79), Heptinstall (48); **Goals:** Eaton 7.
DRAGONS: 1 Johnny Woodcock; 2 Jason Lee; 3 Gareth Lloyd; 4 PJ Solomon; 5 Marlon Billy; 6 Graham Holroyd; 7 Chris Hough; 8 Gareth Handford; 9 Craig Cook; 10 Jamie Fielden; 11 Peter Green; 12 Craig Lawton; 13 Shaun Leaf. Subs (all used): 14 James Walker; 15 Chris Hemmings; 16 Matt Walker; 17 Alex Muff.
Tries: Lloyd (18), Lee (20, 73), Lawton (62);
Goals: Holroyd 4, Woodcock.
Sin bin: Solomon (39) - punching;
Holroyd (55) - abusing official.
Rugby Leaguer & League Express Men of the Match: *Bulldogs:* Shad Royston; *Dragons:* Johnny Woodcock.
Penalty count: 9-8; **Half time:** 22-14; **Referee:** Richard Silverwood (Dewsbury); **Attendance:** 815.

WEST v NORTH

CHORLEY LYNX 6 BARROW RAIDERS 40

LYNX: 1 Lee Patterson; 2 Daryl Lacey; 3 Brian Capewell; 4 Eddie Kilgannon; 5 Gary O'Regan; 6 Neil Alexander; 7 Martin Gambles; 8 John Hill; 9 Martin Roden; 10 Ian Parry; 11 Gary Smith; 12 Mick Redford; 13 Chris Newall. Subs (all used): 14 Simon Smith; 15 Lee Rowley; 16 Gareth Jones; 17 Anthony Murray.
Try: Newall (30); **Goal:** Capewell.
RAIDERS: 1 Adam Pate; 2 Lee Washington; 3 Jamie Smith; 4 Andy McClure; 5 Nick Beech; 6 Phil Atkinson; 7 Darren Holt; 8 Stuart Dancer; 9 Dave Clark; 10 Paul Wilcock; 11 Matthew Leigh; 12 Mike Whitehead; 13 Barry Pugh. Subs (all used): 14 Chris Archer; 15 Geoff Luxon; 16 Paul Lupton; 17 Lee Dutton.
Tries: Atkinson (21), Pate (25, 39, 54), Archer (58), Smith (63), Whitehead (69); **Goals:** Holt 6.
Rugby Leaguer & League Express Men of the Match: *Lynx:* Chris Newall; *Raiders:* Adam Pate.
Penalty count: 9-8; **Half-time:** 6-16;
Referee: Robert Connolly (Wigan); **Attendance:** 303.

YORKSHIRE v EAST

FEATHERSTONE ROVERS 16
HULL KINGSTON ROVERS 22

ROVERS: 1 Nathan Batty; 2 Jamie Stokes; 3 Jamie Coventry; 4 Richard Newlove; 5 Matthew Wray; 6 Jon Presley; 7 Carl Briggs; 8 Ian Tonks; 9 Paul Darley; 10 Bryan Henare; 11 Steve Dooler; 12 Richard Blakeway; 13 Adam Hayes. Subs (all used): 14 Richard Chapman; 15 Stuart Dickens; 16 Andy Jarrett; 17 Jim Carlton.
Tries: Jarrett (29), Newlove (38, 53); **Goals:** Briggs: 2.
Sin bin: Darley (14) - fighting.
ROBINS: 1 Craig Poucher; 2 Lynton Stott; 3 Casey Mayberry; 4 Paul Parker; 5 Craig Farrell; 6 Paul Mansson; 7 Phil Hasty; 8 Jamie Bovill; 9 Paul Pickering; 10 Jon Aston; 11 Dale Holdstock; 12 Andy Smith; 13 Anthony Seibold. Subs (all used): 14 Scott Thorburn; 15 Makali Aizue; 16 Frank Watene; 17 Paul Fletcher.
Tries: Hasty (46), Poucher (61), Parker (74);
Goals: Stott 5.
Sin bin: Holdstock (14) - fighting.
Rugby Leaguer & League Express Men of the Match: *Rovers:* Richard Newlove; *Robins:* Dale Holdstock.
Penalty count: 12-10; **Half-time:** 12-4; **Referee:** Ronnie Laughton (Barnsley); **Attendance:** 1,929.

NORTH v YORKSHIRE

GATESHEAD THUNDER 24 YORK CITY KNIGHTS 56

THUNDER: 1 Graham Stephenson; 2 Jaymes Bulman; 3 Kevin Neighbour; 4 Craig Firth; 5 Robin Peers; 6 Paul Thorman; 7 Neil Thorman; 8 Rob Line; 9 Craig Fisher; 10 Richard Meads; 11 Carl Stannard; 12 Steven Bradley; 13 Steve Rutherford. Subs (all used): 14 Tony Doherty; 15 Andy Walker; 16 Ian Ball; 17 Seamus McCallion.
Tries: Stephenson (19), Peers (23), N Thorman (40), P Thorman (77); **Goals:** P Thorman 4.
Sin bin: McCallion (61) - persistent infringements.
CITY KNIGHTS: 1 Nathan Graham; 2 Scott Walker; 3 Chris Langley; 4 Aaron Wood; 5 Alex Godfrey; 6 Jimmy Elston; 7 Danny Brough; 8 Dan Briggs; 9 Lee Jackson; 10 Yusuf Sozi; 11 Darren Callaghan; 12 Simon Friend; 13 Damian Ball. Subs (all used): 14 Chris Smith; 15 Mark Cain; 16 Mick Ramsden; 17 John Smith.
Tries: Ball (4), Godfrey (8, 59), Langley (34), Elston (36, 44, 65), Callaghan (38), Briggs (47), C Smith (79);
Goals: Brough 8.
Rugby Leaguer & League Express Men of the Match: *Thunder:* Craig Fisher; *City Knights:* Jimmy Elston.
Penalty count: 7-9; **Half-time:** 18-28;
Referee: Craig Halloran (Dewsbury); **Attendance:** 366.

PENNINE v NORTH

KEIGHLEY COUGARS 42 WORKINGTON TOWN 6

COUGARS: 1 Chris Beever; 2 Karl Smith; 3 David Foster; 4 Matt Foster; 5 Andy Robinson; 6 Adam Mitchell; 7 Matt Firth; 8 Phil Stephenson; 9 Simeon Hoyle; 10 Richard Mervill; 11 Lee Patterson; 12 Chris Parker; 13 Craig McDowell. Subs (all used): 14 Craig Nipperess; 15 Adam Webster; 16 Jason Clegg; 17 Danny Ekis.
Tries: Smith (4), Ekis (35), Parker (49), M Foster (65), Hoyle (73), Webster (77); **Goals:** Mitchell 9.
TOWN: 1 Scott Chilton; 2 Matthew Johnson; 3 Neil Frazer; 4 Jonathan Heaney; 5 Andrew Fearon; 6 Kevin Hetherington; 7 Gareth Skillen; 8 Jamie Beaumont; 9 Jonny Limmer; 10 Matthew Tunstall; 11 Martin Stalker; 12 David Pettit; 13 Brett Smith. Subs (all used): 14 James Robinson; 15 Malcolm Caton; 16 Andy McGlasson; 17 Bryan Hendry.
Try: Robinson (42); **Goal:** Hetherington.
Sin bin: Beaumont (27) - persistent interference.
Rugby Leaguer & League Express Men of the Match: *Cougars:* Adam Mitchell; *Town:* Jonny Limmer.
Penalty count: 15-9; **Half-time:** 16-0;
Referee: Ben Thaler (Wakefield); **Attendance:** 937.

EAST v PENNINE

LONDON SKOLARS 0 HUNSLET HAWKS 48

SKOLARS: 1 Tom Howden; 2 Neil Foster; 3 Ade Aderiye; 4 Donny Lam; 5 Tim Butterfield; 6 Jermaine Coleman; 7 Peter Hannan; 8 Koben Katipa; 9 Gareth Honor; 10 Alex Smits; 11 Glenn Osborn; 12 Rubert Jonker; 13 John Rua. Subs (all used): 14 Wayne Parillon; 15 Roger Teau; 16 Huy Le; 17 Stephen Green.
HAWKS: 1 Chris Ross; 2 Paul Gleadhill; 3 Davide Longo; 4 Wes McGibbon; 5 Martin Sykes; 6 Andy Bastow; 7 Latham Tawhai; 8 Craig Booth; 9 Joe Hawley; 10 Mick Coyle; 11 Wayne Freeman; 12 Jonlee Lockwood; 13 Jon Liddell. Subs (all used): 14 Steve Pryce; 15 Shaun Ibbetson; 16 Jamaine Wray; 17 Dave Jessey.
Tries: Gleadhill (12), Hawley (17), Bastow (26, 55), Sykes (33), Jessey (40, 80), Ibbetson (58); **Goals:** Booth 8.
Rugby Leaguer & League Express Men of the Match: *Skolars:* Koben Katipa; *Hawks:* Craig Booth.
Penalty count: 9-7; **Half-time:** 0-32;
Referee: Peter Taberner (Wigan); **Attendance:** 375.

NORTH v WEST

WHITEHAVEN 38 SWINTON LIONS 10

WHITEHAVEN: 1 Wesley Wilson; 2 Jamie Marshall; 3 Brett McDermott; 4 Mick Nanyn; 5 Paul O'Neil; 6 Craig Walsh; 7 Lee Kiddie; 8 Marc Jackson; 9 Aaron Lester; 10 Dean Vaughan; 11 Craig Chambers; 12 Garry Purdham; 13 Howard Hill. Subs (all used): 14 Steven Wood; 15 Spencer Miller; 16 Gary Broadbent; 17 Gary Smith.
Tries: Nanyn (3), Hill (7), O'Neil (26), McDermott (32), Marshall (44, 75), Walsh (47), Broadbent (80);
Goals: Nanyn 2, Wood.
LIONS: 1 Wayne English; 2 Jake Johnstone; 3 Jason Roach; 4 Dave Llewellyn; 5 Chris Irwin; 6 Warren Ayres; 7 Paul Ashton; 8 Tau Liku; 9 Peter Cannon; 10 Mike Loughlin; 11 Craig Wingfield; 12 Danny Heaton; 13 Ian Hodson. Subs (all used): 14 Grant Bithel; 15 Mark Bolton; 16 Rob Barraclough; 17 Rob Whittaker.
Tries: English (12), Ayres (62); **Goal:** Ashton.
Rugby Leaguer & League Express Men of the Match: *Whitehaven:* Aaron Lester; *Lions:* Danny Heaton.
Penalty count: 10-5; **Half-time:** 20-6;
Referee: Ian Smith (Oldham); **Attendance:** 1,073.

EAST v YORKSHIRE

SHEFFIELD EAGLES 18 DEWSBURY RAMS 42

EAGLES: 1 Andy Poynter; 2 Greg Hurst; 3 Nick Turnbull; 4 Craig Brown; 5 Carl De Chenu; 6 Gavin Brown; 7 Gareth Stanley; 8 Jack Howieson; 9 Adam Carroll; 10 Jon Bruce; 11 Andy Raleigh; 12 Jordan James; 13 Simon Tillyer. Subs (all used): 14 Mark Aston; 15 Danny Mills; 16 Jon Breakingbury; 17 Rob North.
Tries: Breakingbury (30), Tillyer (55), Turnbull (79);
Goals: G Brown 3.
RAMS: 1 Ian Preece; 2 Andrew Webber; 3 Wayne McHugh; 4 Ian Kirke; 5 Jon Waddle; 6 Mick Senior; 7 Adam Thaler; 8 Paul Hicks; 9 Darren Robinson; 10 Rob Ward; 11 Anthony Thewliss; 12 Tim Spears; 13 Kevin Crouthers. Subs (all used): 14 Chris Redfearn; 15 Paul Smith; 16 Ian Booth; 17 Mark Hawksley.
Tries: Robinson (5, 34), Thewliss (15), McHugh (20), Redfearn (52), A Thaler (62), Senior (72);
Goals: A Thaler 6; **Field goals:** Robinson 2.
Rugby Leaguer & League Express Men of the Match: *Eagles:* Andy Raleigh; *Rams:* Darren Robinson.
Penalty count: 3-4; **Half-time:** 6-21;
Referee: Colin Morris (Huddersfield); **Attendance:** 867.

WEEK 4

Sunday 22nd February 2004

NORTH

GATESHEAD THUNDER 14 WHITEHAVEN 54

THUNDER: 1 Graham Stephenson; 2 Jaymes Bulman; 3 Kevin Neighbour; 4 Craig Firth; 5 Robin Peers; 6 Paul Thorman; 7 Neil Thorman; 8 Rob Line; 9 Seamus McCallion; 10 Carl Stannard; 11 Steven Bradley; 12 Tony Doherty; 13 Steve Rutherford. Subs (all used): 14 Shawn Ackerley; 15 Ian Ball; 16 Andy Walker; 17 Dave Guthrie.
Tries: Peers (28), Stannard (56), Firth (69);
Goal: P Thorman.
WHITEHAVEN: 1 Gary Broadbent; 2 Jamie Marshall; 3 David Seeds; 4 Mick Nanyn; 5 Mark Wallace; 6 Craig Walsh; 7 Lee Kiddie; 8 Marc Jackson; 9 Carl Sice; 10 Chris McKinney; 11 Spencer Miller; 12 Graeme Morton; 13 Howard Hill. Subs (all used): 14 Steven Wood; 15 Ryan Campbell; 16 Gary Smith; 17 Brett McDermott.
Tries: Nanyn (12, 43), Kiddie (23), Morton (35, 52), Walsh (39, 47, 76), Hill (64), Miller (66); **Goals:** Nanyn 7.
Rugby Leaguer & League Express Men of the Match: *Thunder:* Carl Stannard; *Whitehaven:* Lee Kiddie.
Penalty count: 10-9; **Half-time:** 6-22;
Referee: Jamie Leahy (Dewsbury); **Attendance:** 294.

WORKINGTON TOWN 24 BARROW RAIDERS 24

TOWN: 1 Scott Chilton; 2 Matthew Johnson; 3 Neil Frazer; 4 Adam Coulson; 5 Andrew Fearon; 6 Graeme Lewthwaite; 7 Gareth Skillen; 8 David Pettit; 9 Jonny Limmer; 10 Matthew Tunstall; 11 James Robinson; 12 Jamie Beaumont; 13 Brett Smith. Subs (all used): 14 Martin Stalker; 15 Malcolm Caton; 16 Andy McGlasson; 17 Bryan Hendry.
Tries: Limmer (7), Skillen (21), B Smith (58, 74), Lewthwaite (78); **Goals:** Skillen 2.
RAIDERS: 1 Adam Pate; 2 Jamie Smith; 3 Mike Whitehead; 4 Andy McClure; 5 Nick Beech; 6 Phil Atkinson; 7 Darren Holt; 8 Stuart Dancer; 9 Dave Clark; 10 Paul Wilcock; 11 Paul Lupton; 12 Matthew Leigh; 13 Barry Pugh. Subs (all used): 14 Paul Evans; 15 Chris Archer; 16 Geoff Luxon; 17 Lee Dutton.
Tries: Whitehead (30), Beech (32), Atkinson (37), Holt (44); **Goals:** Holt 4.
Rugby Leaguer & League Express Men of the Match: *Town:* Jonny Limmer; *Raiders:* Barry Pugh.
Penalty count: 10-7; **Half-time:** 8–18;
Referee: Colin Morris (Huddersfield); **Attendance:** 775.

EAST

HULL KINGSTON ROVERS 28
DONCASTER DRAGONS 12

ROVERS: 1 Craig Poucher; 2 Craig Farrell; 3 Paul Parker; 4 Lynton Stott; 5 Alasdair McClarron; 6 Paul Mansson; 7 Scott Thorburn; 8 Jamie Bovill; 9 Paul Pickering; 10 Frank Watene; 11 Jon Aston; 12 Andy Smith; 13 Anthony Seibold. Subs (all used): 14 Phil Hasty; 15 Richard Wilson; 16 Makali Aizue; 17 Paul Fletcher.
Tries: McClarron (7, 13, 71), Stott (44, 48);
Goals: Stott 4.
Sin bin: Aston (64) - professional foul.
DRAGONS: 1 Johnny Woodcock; 2 Jason Lee; 3 Alex Muff; 4 PJ Solomon; 5 Marlon Billy; 6 Graham Holroyd; 7 Chris Hough; 8 Gareth Handford; 9 Craig Cook; 10 Andy Fisher; 11 Peter Green; 12 Craig Lawton; 13 Shaun Leaf. Subs (all used): 14 Jamie Fielden; 15 Chris Hemmings; 16 Matt Walker; 17 Dean Colton.
Tries: M Walker (26), Billy (67); **Goals:** Holroyd 2.
Rugby Leaguer & League Express Men of the Match: *Rovers:* Paul Mansson; *Dragons:* Graham Holroyd.
Penalty count: 9-13; **Half-time:** 10-8;
Referee: Ashley Klein (London); **Attendance:** 2,043.

SHEFFIELD EAGLES 34 LONDON SKOLARS 6

EAGLES: 1 Andy Poynter; 2 Danny Mills; 3 Nick Turnbull; 4 Jon Breakingbury; 5 Carl De Chenu; 6 Peter Reilly; 7 Mark Aston; 8 Jack Howieson; 9 Gareth Stanley; 10 Jon Bruce; 11 Andy Raleigh; 12 Craig Brown; 13 Jordan James. Subs (all used): 14 Greg Hurst; 15 Adam Carroll; 16 Kieron Collins; 17 Rob North.
Tries: De Chenu (18, 47, 58), Turnbull (28, 34), Mills (41, 69), Breakingbury (51); **Goal:** Aston.
SKOLARS: 1 Tim Butterfield; 2 Neil Foster; 3 Andy Gould; 4 Donny Lam; 5 Ade Aderiye; 6 Jermaine Coleman; 7 Peter Hannan; 8 Koben Katipa; 9 Gareth Honor; 10 Alex Smits; 11 Wayne Parillon; 12 Mark Cantoni; 13 John Rua. Subs (all used): 14 Keir Bell; 15 Ben Joyce; 16 Dan Reeds; 17 Roger Teau.
Try: Rua (65); **Goal:** Coleman.
Rugby Leaguer & League Express Men of the Match: *Eagles:* Craig Brown; *Skolars:* Peter Hannan.
Penalty count: 4-11; **Half-time:** 14-2;
Referee: Phil Bentham (Warrington); **Attendance:** 662.

WEST

LEIGH CENTURIONS 60 CHORLEY LYNX 10

CENTURIONS: 1 Neil Turley; 2 David Alstead; 3 Danny Halliwell; 4 Chris Percival; 5 Mark McCully; 6 John Duffy; 7 Tommy Martyn; 8 Simon Knox; 9 Paul Rowley; 10 Oliver Wilkes; 11 David Larder; 12 Andrew Isherwood; 13 Ian Knott. Subs (all used): 14 Mick Coates; 15 Dave McConnell; 16 Steve Maden; 17 Mike Callan.
Tries: Rowley (6), Alstead (12), Isherwood (20, 34, 56), Callan (38, 60), Larder (48), Wilkes (67), Maden (69), Knott (79); **Goals:** Turley 8.
LYNX: 1 Lee Patterson; 2 Eddie Kilgannon; 3 Brian Capewell; 4 Mick Redford; 5 Gary O'Regan; 6 Anthony Murray; 7 Martin Gambles; 8 John Hill; 9 Martin Roden; 10 Simon Smith; 11 Gary Smith; 12 Gareth Jones; 13 Chris Newall. Subs (all used): 14 Lee Rowley; 15 Steve Ormesher; 16 Ian Parry; 17 Neil Alexander.
Tries: Newall (42), Kilgannon (52); **Goal:** Capewell.
Rugby Leaguer & League Express Men of the Match: *Centurions:* Neil Turley; *Lynx:* Ian Parry.
Penalty count: 7-7; **Half-time:** 30-0; **Referee:** Gareth Hewer (Whitehaven); **Attendance:** 1,452.

SWINTON LIONS 18 OLDHAM 30

LIONS: 1 Wayne English; 2 Jason Roach; 3 Mark Bolton; 4 Dave Llewellyn; 5 Chris Irwin; 6 Warren Ayres; 7 Paul Ashton; 8 Tau Liku; 9 Safraz Patel; 10 Wes Rogers; 11 Phil Cushion; 12 Danny Heaton; 13 Ian Sinfield. Subs (all used): 14 Jake Johnstone; 15 Ian Hodson; 16 Kris Smith; 17 Rob Whittaker.
Tries: Cushion (1, 71), English (77), Llewellyn (80);
Goal: Ayres.
Sin bin: Sinfield (44) - fighting;
Roach (53) - holding down.
OLDHAM: 1 Gavin Dodd; 2 Will Cowell; 3 James Bunyan; 4 Jon Goddard; 5 Nick Johnson; 6 Simon Svabic; 7 Ian Watson; 8 Steve Molloy; 9 Keith Brennan; 10 Dane Morgan; 11 Lee Doran; 12 Iain Marsh; 13 Lee Marsh. Subs (all used): 14 Gareth Barber; 15 Neil Roden; 16 Martin Elswood; 17 Martin McLoughlin.
Tries: Goddard (9), L Marsh (11), Dodd (36), N Johnson (47), Bunyan (69); **Goals:** Svabic 4, Barber.
Sin bin: I Marsh (44) - fighting.
Rugby Leaguer & League Express Men of the Match: *Lions:* Mark Bolton; *Oldham:* Lee Marsh.
Penalty count: 11-6; **Half-time:** 4-20;
Referee: Craig Halloran (Dewsbury); **Attendance:** 731.

PENNINE

ROCHDALE HORNETS 18 KEIGHLEY COUGARS 14

HORNETS: 1 Michael Platt; 2 Liam Williams; 3 Paul Anderson; 4 Richard Varkulis; 5 Chris Campbell; 6 John Braddish; 7 Lee Birdseye; 8 Andy Leathem; 9 Janan Billings; 10 Lee Hansen; 11 Andy Gorski; 12 Rob Ball; 13 Darren Shaw. Subs (all used): 14 Sam Butterworth; 15 Andy Grundy; 16 Tommy Hodgkinson; 17 Mark Costello.

Tries: Gorski (12), Varkulis (19), Costello (45);
Goals: Birdseye 3.
Sin bin: Anderson (66) - dissent.
COUGARS: 1 Chris Beever; 2 Karl Smith; 3 David Foster; 4 Matt Foster; 5 Andy Robinson; 6 Adam Mitchell; 7 Matt Firth; 8 Phil Stephenson; 9 Simeon Hoyle; 10 Richard Mervill; 11 Lee Patterson; 12 Chris Parker; 13 Craig McDowell. Subs (all used): 14 Craig Nipperess; 15 Chris Wainwright; 16 Jason Clegg; 17 Danny Ekis.
Tries: Robinson (41), Patterson (76); **Goals:** Mitchell 3.
Rugby Leaguer & League Express Men of the Match: *Hornets:* Lee Hansen; *Cougars:* Jason Clegg.
Penalty count: 10-12; **Half-time:** 12-2;
Referee: Peter Taberner (Wigan); **Attendance:** 762.

HUNSLET HAWKS 14 HALIFAX 38

HAWKS: 1 Chris Ross; 2 Leigh Deakin; 3 Davide Longo; 4 Wes McGibbon; 5 George Rayner; 6 Andy Bastow; 7 Latham Tawhai; 8 Craig Booth; 9 Joe Hawley; 10 Mick Coyle; 11 Wayne Freeman; 12 Jonlee Lockwood; 13 Jon Liddell. Subs (all used): 14 Steve Pryce; 15 Dave Jessey; 16 Glen Freeman; 17 Danny Wood.
Tries: Rayner (40, 44), McGibbon (47); **Goal:** Wood.
HALIFAX: 1 Danny Arnold; 2 Richard Smith; 3 Jon Roper; 4 Alan Hadcroft; 5 Oliver Marns; 6 Scott Grix; 7 Mark Moxon; 8 Anthony Farrell; 9 Phil Cantillon; 10 Jaymes Chapman; 11 Jamie Bloem; 12 Chris Morley; 13 Pat Weisner. Subs (all used): 14 Wayne Corcoran; 15 Chris Norman; 16 David Bates; 17 Scott Law.
Tries: Roper (8), Cantillon (16), Chapman (22), Moxon (34, 78), Weisner (69), Law (80); **Goals:** Bloem 5.
Rugby Leaguer & League Express Men of the Match: *Hawks:* Steve Pryce; *Halifax:* Pat Weisner.
Penalty count: 3-7; **Half-time:** 4-20;
Referee: Mike Dawber (Wigan); **Attendance:** 1,144.

YORKSHIRE

DEWSBURY RAMS 16 YORK CITY KNIGHTS 58

RAMS: 1 Ian Preece; 2 Andrew Webber; 3 Wayne McHugh; 4 Ian Kirke; 5 Jon Waddle; 6 Mick Senior; 7 Adam Thaler; 8 Paul Hicks; 9 Darren Robinson; 10 Rob Ward; 11 Anthony Thewliss; 12 Tim Spears; 13 Kevin Crouthers. Subs (all used): 14 Chris Redfearn; 15 Billy Kershaw; 16 Paul Smith; 17 Ian Booth.
Tries: Senior (20), McHugh (30), Crouthers (59);
Goals: A Thaler 2.
Sin bin: Senior (48) - fighting.
CITY KNIGHTS: 1 Nathan Graham; 2 Chris Smith; 3 Chris Langley; 4 Aaron Wood; 5 Alex Godfrey; 6 Scott Rhodes; 7 Danny Brough; 8 Ryan Benjafield; 9 Lee Jackson; 10 Yusuf Sozi; 11 Darren Callaghan; 12 Simon Friend; 13 Damian Ball. Subs (all used): 14 Jimmy Elston; 15 Mick Ramsden; 16 Dan Briggs; 17 Craig Forsyth.
Tries: Ball (6), Elston (24), Godfrey (40), Callaghan (43), Jackson (46, 69), Friend (51), Sozi (55), Graham (72), Brough (79); **Goals:** Brough 9.
Sin bin: Rhodes (48) - fighting.
Rugby Leaguer & League Express Men of the Match: *Rams:* Kevin Crouthers; *City Knights:* Danny Brough.
Penalty count: 9-10; **Half-time:** 10-18;
Referee: Andrew Leonard (Leeds); **Attendance:** 848.

FEATHERSTONE ROVERS 20 BATLEY BULLDOGS 19

ROVERS: 1 Nathan Batty; 2 Jamie Stokes; 3 Jamie Coventry; 4 Richard Newlove; 5 Matthew Wray; 6 Jon Presley; 7 Carl Briggs; 8 Ian Tonks; 9 Paul Darley; 10 Bryan Henare; 11 Steve Dooler; 12 Richard Blakeway; 13 Adam Hayes. Subs (all used): 14 Ben Archibald; 15 Stuart Dickens; 16 Andy Jarrett; 17 Jim Carlton.
Tries: Wray (10), Blakeway (15), Presley (31), Newlove (73); **Goals:** Briggs 2.
BULLDOGS: 1 Mark Sibson; 2 Matt Bramald; 3 Shad Royston; 4 Danny Maun; 5 Adrian Flynn; 6 Mark Toohey; 7 Barry Eaton; 8 Chris Molyneux; 9 Joe Berry; 10 David Rourke; 11 Danny Evans; 12 Andy Spink; 13 Sean Richardson. Subs (all used): 14 Andy Heptinstall; 15 Paul Harrison; 16 Andy Rice; 17 Will Cartledge.
Tries: Spink (18), Richardson (39), Flynn (52);
Goals: Eaton 3; **Field goal:** Eaton.
Sin bin: Heptinstall (58) - interference.
Rugby Leaguer & League Express Men of the Match: *Rovers:* Carl Briggs; *Bulldogs:* Sean Richardson.
Penalty count: 11-8; **Half-time:** 16-10;
Referee: Ben Thaler (Wakefield); **Attendance:** 1,309.

WEEK 5

Sunday 7th March 2004

NORTH

BARROW RAIDERS 68 GATESHEAD THUNDER 18

RAIDERS: 1 Adam Pate; 2 Tama Wakelin; 3 Jamie Smith; 4 Andy McClure; 5 Nick Beech; 6 Phil Atkinson; 7 Darren Holt; 8 Stuart Dancer; 9 Dave Clark; 10 Paul Lupton; 11 Matthew Leigh; 12 Mike Whitehead; 13 Barry Pugh. Subs (all used): 14 Damien Reid; 15 Chris Archer; 16 Geoff Luxon; 17 Paul Wilcock.
Tries: Holt (3, 13), Whitehead (10, 60), Smith (32), Archer (45, 72), Reid (51, 62), Pate (65), Beech (67), Clark (77); **Goals:** Holt 10.
THUNDER: 1 Kevin Neighbour; 2 Robin Peers; 3 Joe Bagshaw; 4 Matthew Dehaty; 5 Tom Clough; 6 Steve Rutherford; 7 Paul Thorman; 8 Rob Line; 9 Craig Fisher; 10 Dave Guthrie; 11 Carl Stannard; 12 Tony Doherty; 13 Steven Bradley. Subs (all used): 14 Ian Ball; 15 Neil Thorman; 16 Andy Fleming; 17 Craig Firth.
Tries: Bradley (6, 42), Rutherford (20);
Goals: P Thorman 3.
Rugby Leaguer & League Express Men of the Match: *Raiders:* Darren Holt; *Thunder:* Paul Thorman.
Penalty count: 5-7; **Half-time:** 28-12;
Referee: Phil Bentham (Warrington); **Attendance:** 767.

WHITEHAVEN 54 WORKINGTON TOWN 12

WHITEHAVEN: 1 Gary Broadbent; 2 Jamie Marshall; 3 Wesley Wilson; 4 Mick Nanyn; 5 Paul O'Neil; 6 Leroy Joe; 7 Lee Kiddie; 8 David Fatialofa; 9 Aaron Lester; 10 Marc Jackson; 11 Brett McDermott; 12 Spencer Miller; 13 Garry Purdham. Subs (all used): 14 Steven Wood; 15 Carl Sice; 16 Dean Vaughan; 17 Chris McKinney.
Tries: Joe (2), Miller (5), Kiddie (7, 16), Broadbent (26, 38, 74), Wilson (39, 56), Nanyn (65); **Goals:** Nanyn 7.
TOWN: 1 Andrew Fearon; 2 Jonathan Heaney; 3 Adam Coulson; 4 Neil Frazer; 5 Martyn Wilson; 6 Kevin Hetherington; 7 Gareth Skillen; 8 Jamie Beaumont; 9 Jonny Limmer; 10 Matthew Tunstall; 11 David Pettit; 12 Ricky Wright; 13 Brett Smith. Subs (all used): 14 James Robinson; 15 Martin Stalker; 16 Dean Burgess; 17 Bryan Hendry.
Tries: Coulson (22), Frazer (76); **Goals:** Skillen 2.
Rugby Leaguer & League Express Men of the Match: *Whitehaven:* Lee Kiddie; *Town:* Matthew Tunstall.
Penalty count: 13-4; **Half-time:** 38-6;
Referee: Peter Taberner (Wigan); **Attendance:** 2,156.

EAST

DONCASTER DRAGONS 34 SHEFFIELD EAGLES 4

DRAGONS: 1 Johnny Woodcock; 2 Craig Miles; 3 Gareth Lloyd; 4 PJ Solomon; 5 Marlon Billy; 6 Graham Holroyd; 7 Chris Hough; 8 Martin Ostler; 9 Craig Cook; 10 Matt Walker; 11 Craig Lawton; 12 Peter Green; 13 Shaun Leaf. Subs (all used): 14 Gareth Handford; 15 Chris Hemmings; 16 Alex Muff; 17 Liam Brentley.
Tries: Miles (8, 76), Billy (12, 70), Lloyd (19, 59), Leaf (50); **Goals:** Holroyd 3.
EAGLES: 1 Andy Poynter; 2 Danny Mills; 3 Nick Turnbull; 4 Jon Breakingbury; 5 Carl De Chenu; 6 Richard Goddard; 7 Peter Reilly; 8 Jack Howieson; 9 Gareth Stanley; 10 Rob North; 11 Andy Raleigh; 12 Craig Brown; 13 Jordan James. Subs (all used): 14 Greg Hurst; 15 Bright Sodje; 16 Mark Aston; 17 Simon Tillyer.
Try: Hurst (56).
Rugby Leaguer & League Express Men of the Match: *Dragons:* Johnny Woodcock; *Eagles:* Greg Hurst.
Penalty count: 10-8; **Half-time:** 16-0; **Referee:** Steve Nicholson (Whitehaven); **Attendance:** 734.

HULL KINGSTON ROVERS 58 LONDON SKOLARS 6

ROVERS: 1 Craig Poucher; 2 Alasdair McClarron; 3 Paul Parker; 4 Matt Calland; 5 Casey Mayberry; 6 Paul Mansson; 7 Scott Thorburn; 8 Jamie Bovill; 9 Andy Ellis; 10 Jon Aston; 11 Dean Andrews; 12 Dale Holdstock; 13 Anthony Seibold. Subs (all used): 14 Jimmy Walker; 15 Richard Wilson; 16 Makali Aizue; 17 Frank Watene.
Tries: Mansson (1), Ellis (10), Calland (13, 26, 34), Seibold (30), Mayberry (38), Andrews (48), Holdstock (50), Thorburn (68), Parker (71); **Goals:** Thorburn 7.
SKOLARS: 1 Joel Osborn; 2 Tom Howden; 3 Andy Gould; 4 Stephen Green; 5 Neil Foster; 6 Jermaine Coleman; 7 Peter Hannan; 8 Dan Reeds; 9 Mike Castle; 10 Alex Smits; 11 Ben Joyce; 12 Mark Cantoni; 13 Keir Bell. Subs (all used): 14 Ed Bayles; 15 Brad McFarland; 16 Ade Aderiye; 17 Mal McGivern.
Try: Cantoni (42); **Goal:** J Osborn.
Rugby Leaguer & League Express Men of the Match: *Rovers:* Scott Thorburn; *Skolars:* Mark Cantoni.
Penalty count: 12-6; **Half-time:** 36-0;
Referee: Jamie Leahy (Dewsbury); **Attendance:** 1,677.

WEST

OLDHAM 10 LEIGH CENTURIONS 54

OLDHAM: 1 Gavin Dodd; 2 Will Cowell; 3 James Bunyan; 4 Jon Goddard; 5 Nick Johnson; 6 Neil Roden; 7 Ian Watson; 8 Steve Molloy; 9 Keith Brennan; 10 Dane Morgan; 11 Lee Doran; 12 Iain Marsh; 13 Lee Marsh. Subs (all used): 14 Gareth Barber; 15 Simon Svabic; 16 Martin McLoughlin; 17 Paul Southern.
Tries: Dodd (63), Goddard (75); **Goal:** L Marsh.
CENTURIONS: 1 David Alstead; 2 Steve Maden; 3 Dan Potter; 4 Danny Halliwell; 5 Damian Munro; 6 John Duffy; 7 Tommy Martyn; 8 Simon Knox; 9 Paul Rowley; 10 Heath Cruckshank; 11 David Larder; 12 Oliver Wilkes; 13 Ian Knott. Subs (all used): 14 Dave McConnell; 15 Andrew Isherwood; 16 Paul Norman; 17 Chris Percival.
Tries: Halliwell (5, 39, 70), Martyn (9), Alstead (12), Potter (32, 55, 67), Munro (35, 45), Percival (60);
Goals: Knott 2, Martyn 3.
Rugby Leaguer & League Express Men of the Match: *Oldham:* Gavin Dodd; *Centurions:* Paul Rowley.
Penalty count: 13-6; **Half-time:** 0-30;
Referee: Mike Dawber (Wigan); **Attendance:** 1,805.

SWINTON LIONS 27 CHORLEY LYNX 24

LIONS: 1 Wayne English; 2 Jason Roach; 3 Mark Bolton; 4 Chris Maye; 5 Chris Irwin; 6 Ian Hodson; 7 Warren Ayres; 8 Tau Liku; 9 Peter Cannon; 10 Wes Rogers; 11 Phil Cushion; 12 Danny Heaton; 13 Kris Smith. Subs (all used): 14 Paul Ashton; 15 Dave Llewellyn; 16 Craig Wingfield; 17 Chris Brett.
Tries: Roach (2), Irwin (20), Cannon (32), Bolton (58), Maye (66); **Goals:** Maye, Ashton 2; **Field goal:** Ayres.
Sin bin: Bolton (45) - holding down;
Ayres (74) - holding down.
LYNX: 1 Chris Ramsdale; 2 Steve Ormesher; 3 Mick Redford; 4 Jamie Stenhouse; 5 Eddie Kilgannon; 6 Rob Smyth; 7 Martin Gambles; 8 John Hill; 9 Martin Roden; 10 Ian Parry; 11 Gary Smith; 12 Gareth Jones; 13 Chris Newall. Subs (all used): 14 Lee Rowley; 15 Danny Barton; 16 Gary O'Regan; 17 Anthony Murray.
Tries: Kilgannon (18), Newall (28), Murray (51), Redford (76); **Goals:** Smyth 4.
Rugby Leaguer & League Express Men of the Match: *Lions:* Danny Heaton; *Lynx:* Ian Parry.
Penalty count: 11-9; **Half-time:** 14-12;
Referee: Craig Halloran (Dewsbury); **Attendance:** 430.

PENNINE

HALIFAX 21 ROCHDALE HORNETS 6

HALIFAX: 1 Danny Arnold; 2 Richard Smith; 3 Chris Norman; 4 Alan Hadcroft; 5 Oliver Marns; 6 Simon Grix; 7 Mark Moxon; 8 Jaymes Chapman; 9 Phil Cantillon; 10 David Bates; 11 Jamie Bloem; 12 Chris Morley; 13 Jon Roper. Subs (all used): 14 Wayne Corcoran; 15 Scott Law; 16 Ryan McDonald; 17 Paul Davidson.
Tries: Chapman (10), Davidson (36), Cantillon (77);
Goals: Bloem 4. **Field goal:** Bloem.
Sin bin: Bloem (48) - fighting.
HORNETS: 1 Michael Platt; 2 Liam Williams; 3 Paul Anderson; 4 Richard Varkulis; 5 Chris Campbell; 6 Lee Birdseye; 7 Sam Butterworth; 8 Andy Leathem; 9 Janan Billings; 10 Lee Hansen; 11 Andy Gorski; 12 Rob Ball; 13 Darren Shaw. Subs (all used): 14 Tommy Hodgkinson; 15 Matt Sturm; 16 Andy Grundy; 17 Mark Costello.
Goals: Birdseye 3.
Sin bin: Butterworth (31) - interference; Billings (48) - fighting; Hodgkinson (80) - deliberate offside.
Rugby Leaguer & League Express Men of the Match: *Halifax:* Phil Cantillon; *Hornets:* Tommy Hodgkinson.
Penalty count: 12-13; **Half-time:** 10-4;
Referee: Gareth Hewer (Whitehaven); **Attendance:** 2,096.

HUNSLET HAWKS 42 KEIGHLEY COUGARS 24

HAWKS: 1 Chris Ross; 2 Martin Sykes; 3 Davide Longo; 4 Wes McGibbon; 5 Chris Hall; 6 Danny Wood; 7 Latham Tawhai; 8 Craig Booth; 9 Jamaine Wray; 10 Mick Coyle; 11 Wayne Freeman; 12 Shaun Ibbetson; 13 Andy Bastow. Subs (all used): 14 Steve Pryce; 15 Dave Jessey; 16 Glen Freeman; 17 Gary Shillabeer.
Tries: Tawhai (5), Coyle (11), Longo (33), Shillabeer (36), McGibbon (57), Wray (62, 69), C Hall (76);
Goals: Wood, Booth 4.
COUGARS: 1 Chris Wainwright; 2 Karl Smith; 3 David Foster; 4 Andy Robinson; 5 Chris Beever; 6 Adam Mitchell; 7 Matt Firth; 8 Phil Stephenson; 9 Simeon Hoyle; 10 Richard Mervill; 11 Lee Patterson; 12 Chris Parker; 13 Craig McDowell. Subs (all used): 14 Craig Nipperess; 15 Matthew Steel; 16 Jason Clegg; 17 Danny Ekis.
Tries: D Foster (2), Mitchell (49, 53), Wainwright (66);
Goals: Mitchell 4.
Rugby Leaguer & League Express Men of the Match: *Hawks:* Craig Booth/Mick Coyle; *Cougars:* Phil Stephenson.
Penalty count: 14-7; **Half-time:** 22-6;
Referee: Ben Thaler (Wakefield); **Attendance:** 640.

YORKSHIRE

BATLEY BULLDOGS 70 DEWSBURY RAMS 12

BULLDOGS: 1 Mark Sibson; 2 Chris Spurr; 3 Shad Royston; 4 Danny Maun; 5 Adrian Flynn; 6 Mark Toohey; 7 Barry Eaton; 8 Steve Hill; 9 Joe Berry; 10 David Rourke; 11 Andy Rice; 12 Andy Spink; 13 Ryan Horsley. Subs (all used): 14 Mark Cass; 15 Paul Harrison; 16 Will Cartledge; 17 Sean Richardson.
Tries: Toohey (12), Rourke (14), Spink (25), Berry (29, 54, 68), Richardson (43, 63), Harrison (47), Spurr (56), Sibson (73, 79); **Goals:** Eaton 11.
RAMS: 1 Ian Preece; 2 Andrew Webber; 3 Chris Redfearn; 4 Tim Spears; 5 Jon Waddle; 6 Kurt Rudder; 7 James Brown; 8 Paul Hicks; 9 Adam Thaler; 10 Paul Smith; 11 Anthony Thewliss; 12 Mark Hawksley; 13 Darren Robinson. Subs (all used): 14 Mark Lawton; 15 Ian Booth; 16 Jamie Tennant; 17 Chris Woolford.
Tries: Redfearn (7), Hawksley (16); **Goals:** A Thaler 2.
Rugby Leaguer & League Express Men of the Match: *Bulldogs:* Mark Toohey; *Rams:* Paul Hicks.
Penalty count: 7-2; **Half-time:** 22-12;
Referee: Colin Morris (Huddersfield); **Attendance:** 868.

YORK CITY KNIGHTS 18 FEATHERSTONE ROVERS 16

CITY KNIGHTS: 1 Nathan Graham; 2 Mark Stewart; 3 Chris Langley; 4 Aaron Wood; 5 Alex Godfrey; 6 Scott Rhodes; 7 Danny Brough; 8 Ryan Benjafield; 9 Lee Jackson; 10 Yusuf Sozi; 11 Mick Ramsden; 12 Tom Andrews; 13 Simon Friend. Subs (all used): 14 Jimmy Elston; 15 Mark Cain; 16 John Smith; 17 Craig Forsyth.
Tries: Rhodes (15), Sozi (20), Godfrey (69);
Goals: Brough 3.
Sin bin: Benjafield (49) - fighting.
ROVERS: 1 Nathan Batty; 2 James Ford; 3 Jamie Coventry; 4 Richard Newlove; 5 Matthew Wray; 6 Jon Presley; 7 Carl Briggs; 8 Ian Tonks; 9 Paul Darley; 10 Stuart Dickens; 11 Steve Dooler; 12 Richard Blakeway; 13 Adam Hayes. Subs: 14 Ben Archibald (not used); 15 Richard Chapman; 16 Danny Patrickson (not used); 17 Jim Carlton.
Tries: Dickens (9, 18), Wray (42); **Goals:** Briggs 2.
Sin bin: Briggs (5) - off the ball tackle;
Dickens (49) - fighting; Chapman (49) - fighting.
On report: Dooler (18) - high tackle;
Chapman (67) - high tackle.
Rugby Leaguer & League Express Men of the Match: *City Knights:* Jimmy Elston; *Rovers:* Carl Briggs.
Penalty count: 8-6; **Half-time:** 12-10;
Referee: Ashley Klein (London); **Attendance:** 1,942.

National League Cup 2004 - Round by Round

WEEK 6

Sunday 14th March 2004

EAST

LONDON SKOLARS 16 SHEFFIELD EAGLES 14

SKOLARS: 1 Joel Osborn; 2 Tim Butterfield; 3 Donny Lam; 4 Stephen Green; 5 Neil Foster; 6 Jermaine Coleman; 7 Peter Hannan; 8 Koben Katipa; 9 Gareth Honor; 10 Alex Smits; 11 Glenn Osborn; 12 Ben Joyce; 13 John Rua. Subs (all used): 14 Mike Castle; 15 Dan Reeds; 16 Andy Gould; 17 Keir Bell.
Tries: Foster (15), Butterfield (30), Honor (39);
Goals: G Osborn 2.
EAGLES: 1 Andy Poynter; 2 Danny Mills; 3 Nick Turnbull; 4 Richard Goddard; 5 Greg Hurst; 6 Gavin Brown; 7 Peter Reilly; 8 Jack Howieson; 9 Gareth Stanley; 10 Jon Bruce; 11 Andy Raleigh; 12 Craig Brown; 13 Sean Dickinson. Subs (all used): 14 Mark Aston; 15 Jordan James; 16 Kieron Collins; 17 Simon Tillyer.
Tries: G Brown (6), Reilly (54); **Goals:** Goddard 3.
Rugby Leaguer & League Express Men of the Match: *Skolars:* Donny Lam; *Eagles:* Jon Bruce.
Penalty count: 7-10; **Half-time:** 16-8; **Referee:** Steve Nicholson (Whitehaven); **Attendance:** 142.

Friday 19th March 2004

EAST

SHEFFIELD EAGLES 18 HULL KINGSTON ROVERS 22

EAGLES: 1 Andy Poynter; 2 Greg Hurst; 3 Nick Turnbull; 4 Richard Goddard; 5 Carl De Chenu; 6 Peter Reilly; 7 Gavin Brown; 8 Jack Howieson; 9 Gareth Stanley; 10 Jon Bruce; 11 Andy Raleigh; 12 Craig Brown; 13 Jordan James. Subs: 14 Danny Mills; 15 Guy Adams; 16 Jon Breakingbury (not used); 17 Simon Tillyer.
Tries: J James (24), G Brown (39); **Goals:** Goddard 5.
ROVERS: 1 Craig Poucher; 2 Craig Farrell; 3 Paul Parker; 4 Matt Calland; 5 Alasdair McClarron; 6 Paul Mansson; 7 Scott Thorburn; 8 Jamie Bovill; 9 Paul Pickering; 10 Frank Watene; 11 Dale Holdstock; 12 Dean Andrews; 13 Anthony Seibold. Subs (all used): 14 Phil Hasty; 15 Jon Aston; 16 Makali Aizue; 17 Paul Fletcher.
Tries: Bovill (19), Thorburn (35), Hasty (71), McClarron (79); **Goals:** Thorburn 3.
Rugby Leaguer & League Express Men of the Match: *Eagles:* Richard Goddard; *Rovers:* Scott Thorburn.
Penalty count: 10-9; **Half-time:** 16-12;
Referee: Steve Ganson (St Helens); **Attendance:** 1,049.

Saturday 20th March 2004

EAST

LONDON SKOLARS 6 DONCASTER DRAGONS 24

SKOLARS: 1 Joel Osborn; 2 Tim Butterfield; 3 Donny Lam; 4 Andy Gould; 5 Neil Foster; 6 Jermaine Coleman; 7 Peter Hannan; 8 Koben Katipa; 9 John Rua; 10 Alex Smits; 11 Glenn Osborn; 12 Rubert Jonker; 13 Ben Joyce. Subs (all used): 14 Huy Le; 15 Dan Reeds; 16 Mike Castle; 17 Wayne Parillon.
Try: Rua (69); **Goal:** G Osborn.
DRAGONS: 1 Johnny Woodcock; 2 Craig Miles; 3 Gareth Lloyd; 4 PJ Solomon; 5 Marlon Billy; 6 Sean Leaf; 7 Chris Hough; 8 Gareth Handford; 9 Craig Cook; 10 Chris Hemmings; 11 Peter Green; 12 Martin Ostler; 13 Matt Walker. Subs (all used): 14 Dean Colton; 15 James Walker; 16 Alex Muff; 17 Liam Brentley.
Tries: Leaf (27, 74), Solomon (35), Brentley (49);
Goals: Woodcock 4.
Rugby Leaguer & League Express Men of the Match: *Skolars:* Donny Lam; *Dragons:* Gareth Handford.
Penalty count: 12-14; **Half-time:** 0-12;
Referee: Phil Bentham (Warrington); **Attendance:** 375.

WEEK 7

Sunday 21st March 2004

NORTH

GATESHEAD THUNDER 24 WORKINGTON TOWN 24

THUNDER: 1 Graham Stephenson; 2 Mick Kent; 3 Kevin Neighbour; 4 Craig Firth; 5 Robin Peers; 6 Paul Thorman; 7 Craig Fisher; 8 Rob Line; 9 Neil Thorman; 10 Scott Harrison; 11 Carl Stannard; 12 Steven Bradley; 13 Steve Rutherford. Subs: 14 Phil Pitt; 15 Peti Keni; 16 Ian Ball; 17 Andy Fleming (not used).
Tries: Neighbour (12), Fisher (24), Kent (55), Rutherford (58); **Goals:** P Thorman 4.
TOWN: 1 Andrew Fearon; 2 Neil Frazer; 3 Martin Stalker; 4 Adam Coulson; 5 Martyn Wilson; 6 Jonathan Heaney; 7 Gareth Skillen; 8 Dean Burgess; 9 David Pettit; 10 Matthew Tunstall; 11 James Robinson; 12 Jamie Beaumont; 13 Jonny Limmer. Subs (all used): 14 Graeme Lewthwaite; 15 Craig Barker; 16 Andy McGlasson; 17 Matthew Johnson.
Tries: Beaumont (15), Pettit (29), Burgess (39), Frazer (74); **Goals:** Skillen 4.
Sin bin: Skillen (50) - punching.
Rugby Leaguer & League Express Men of the Match: *Thunder:* Mick Kent; *Town:* David Pettit.
Penalty count: 13-11; **Half-time:** 10-12;
Referee: Jamie Leahy (Dewsbury); **Attendance:** 288.

WHITEHAVEN 14 BARROW RAIDERS 10

WHITEHAVEN: 1 Wesley Wilson; 2 Mark Wallace; 3 Mick Nanyn; 4 David Seeds; 5 John Lebbon; 6 Craig Walsh; 7 Steven Wood; 8 Dean Vaughan; 9 Carl Sice; 10 Gary Smith; 11 Ryan Campbell; 12 Spencer Miller; 13 Garry Purdham. Subs (all used): 14 Paul O'Neil; 15 Craig Chambers; 16 Tony Cunningham; 17 Sam Obst.
Tries: Lebbon (26), Seeds (38); **Goals:** Nanyn 3.
RAIDERS: 1 Craig Bower; 2 Tama Wakelin; 3 Damien Reid; 4 Paul Jones; 5 Nick Beech; 6 Phil Atkinson; 7 Darren Holt; 8 Stuart Dancer; 9 Dave Clark; 10 Paul Wilcock; 11 Mike Whitehead; 12 Matthew Leigh; 13 Barry Pugh. Subs (all used): 14 Chris Archer; 15 Andy McClure; 16 Paul Lupton; 17 Geoff Luxon.
Tries: Atkinson (7), McClure (48); **Goal:** Holt.
Rugby Leaguer & League Express Men of the Match: *Whitehaven:* Garry Purdham; *Raiders:* Craig Bower.
Penalty count: 10-9; **Half-time:** 14-6;
Referee: Ben Thaler (Wakefield); **Attendance:** 1,249.

WEST

CHORLEY LYNX 10 OLDHAM 40

LYNX: 1 Lee Patterson; 2 Eddie Kilgannon; 3 Mick Redford; 4 Jamie Stenhouse; 5 Gary O'Regan; 6 Rob Smyth; 7 Martin Gambles; 8 Ian Parry; 9 Martin Roden; 10 John Hill; 11 Danny Barton; 12 Simon Smith; 13 Chris Newall. Subs (all used): 14 Lee Rowley; 15 Chris Ramsdale; 16 Ade Mead; 17 Anthony Murray.
Tries: Stenhouse (63), O'Regan (80); **Goal:** Gambles.
Sin bin: Ramsdale (75) - fighting.
OLDHAM: 1 Gavin Dodd; 2 Will Cowell; 3 Gareth Barber; 4 Jon Goddard; 5 Nick Johnson; 6 Neil Roden; 7 Ian Watson; 8 Steve Molloy; 9 Keith Brennan; 10 Paul Southern; 11 Lee Doran; 12 Dane Morgan; 13 Lee Marsh. Subs (all used): 14 Simon Svabic; 15 Martin McLoughlin; 16 Martin Elswood; 17 James Lomax.
Tries: Brennan (2), N Johnson (9, 39, 47), Southern (23), Dodd (33), Roden (42), Cowell (65); **Goals:** Barber 4.
Sin bin: Doran (75) - fighting.
Rugby Leaguer & League Express Men of the Match: *Lynx:* Jamie Stenhouse; *Oldham:* Nick Johnson.
Penalty count: 10-9; **Half-time:** 0-24; **Referee:** Steve Nicholson (Whitehaven); **Attendance:** 370.

LEIGH CENTURIONS 66 SWINTON LIONS 6

CENTURIONS: 1 David Alstead; 2 Neil Turley; 3 Danny Halliwell; 4 Chris Percival; 5 Damian Munro; 6 John Duffy; 7 Tommy Martyn; 8 Simon Knox; 9 Paul Rowley; 10 Heath Cruckshank; 11 David Larder; 12 Dan Potter; 13 Ian Knott. Subs (all used): 14 Mick Coates; 15 Paul Norman; 16 Dave McConnell; 17 Mike Callan.
Tries: Rowley (6), Potter (14), Percival (20, 51), Duffy (25, 43, 55), Knott (28, 36, 46), Munro (71, 75);
Goals: Turley 9.
LIONS: 1 Wayne English; 2 Dave Llewellyn; 3 Mark Bolton; 4 Chris Maye; 5 Chris Irwin; 6 Ian Hodson; 7 Warren Ayres; 8 Tau Liku; 9 Rob Barraclough; 10 Rob Whittaker; 11 Phil Cushion; 12 Danny Heaton; 13 Kris Smith. Subs (all used): 14 Neil Hayden; 15 Peter Cannon; 16 Chris Brett; 17 Craig Wingfield.
Try: Heaton (59); **Goal:** Wingfield.
Rugby Leaguer & League Express Men of the Match: *Centurions:* Paul Rowley; *Lions:* Danny Heaton.
Penalty count: 12-9; **Half-time:** 34-0; **Referee:** Gareth Hewer (Whitehaven); **Attendance:** 1,475.

PENNINE

KEIGHLEY COUGARS 26 HALIFAX 8

COUGARS: 1 James Rushforth; 2 Max Tomlinson; 3 David Foster; 4 Matt Foster; 5 Andy Robinson; 6 Adam Mitchell; 7 Matt Firth; 8 Phil Stephenson; 9 Simeon Hoyle; 10 Chris Parker; 11 Matthew Steel; 12 Lee Patterson; 13 Craig McDowell. Subs: 14 Craig Nipperess; 15 Chris Beever (not used); 16 Jason Clegg; 17 Danny Ekis.
Tries: Hoyle (2), Rushforth (18), Robinson (48), Ekis (57); **Goals:** Mitchell 5.
HALIFAX: 1 Scott Grix; 2 Richard Smith; 3 Chris Norman; 4 Alan Hadcroft; 5 Danny Arnold; 6 Simon Grix; 7 Mark Moxon; 8 Anthony Farrell; 9 Phil Cantillon; 10 Jaymes Chapman; 11 Wayne Corcoran; 12 Chris Morley; 13 Pat Weisner. Subs (all used): 14 Oliver Marns; 15 Danny Fearon; 16 Ryan McDonald; 17 Paul Davidson.
Tries: Arnold (5), Hadcroft (27).
Rugby Leaguer & League Express Men of the Match: *Cougars:* Danny Ekis; *Halifax:* Anthony Farrell.
Penalty count: 9-5; **Half-time:** 16-8;
Referee: Peter Taberner (Wigan); **Attendance:** 1,926.

ROCHDALE HORNETS 37 HUNSLET HAWKS 6

HORNETS: 1 Michael Platt; 2 Liam Williams; 3 Paul Anderson; 4 Andy Gorski; 5 Chris Campbell; 6 Sam Butterworth; 7 John Braddish; 8 Andy Leathem; 9 Janan Billings; 10 Mark Costello; 11 Matt Sturm; 12 Gareth Price; 13 Darren Shaw. Subs (all used): 14 Tommy Hodgkinson; 15 Andy Grundy; 16 Kris Ratcliffe; 17 Lee Hansen.
Tries: Campbell (21, 69), Billings (23), Platt (47, 67), Anderson (63), Costello (72);
Goals: Butterworth 4; **Field goal:** Butterworth.
HAWKS: 1 Chris Ross; 2 Martin Sykes; 3 Davide Longo; 4 Wes McGibbon; 5 Chris Hall; 6 Danny Wood; 7 Latham Tawhai; 8 Craig Booth; 9 Jamaine Wray; 10 Mick Coyle; 11 Wayne Freeman; 12 Gary Shillabeer; 13 Andy Bastow. Subs (all used): 14 Steve Pryce; 15 Jon Liddell; 16 Glen Freeman; 17 Leigh Deakin.
Try: W Freeman (15); **Goal:** Wood.
Rugby Leaguer & League Express Men of the Match: *Hornets:* Tommy Hodgkinson; *Hawks:* Jamaine Wray.
Penalty count: 6-10; **Half-time:** 11-6;
Referee: Colin Morris (Huddersfield); **Attendance:** 674.

YORKSHIRE

BATLEY BULLDOGS 36 YORK CITY KNIGHTS 12

BULLDOGS: 1 Mark Sibson; 2 Matt Bramald; 3 Shad Royston; 4 Danny Maun; 5 Adrian Flynn; 6 Dean Lawford; 7 Barry Eaton; 8 Steve Hill; 9 Andy Heptinstall; 10 David Rourke; 11 Paul Harrison; 12 Andy Spink; 13 Mark Toohey. Subs (all used): 14 Ryan Horsley; 15 Will Cartledge; 16 Chris Molyneux; 17 Sean Richardson.
Tries: Rourke (9), Flynn (29, 65), Maun (40), Spink (42), Royston (46); **Goals:** Eaton 6.
CITY KNIGHTS: 1 Nathan Graham; 2 Scott Walker; 3 Aaron Wood; 4 Darren Callaghan; 5 Alex Godfrey; 6 Scott Rhodes; 7 Danny Brough; 8 Ryan Benjafield; 9 Jimmy Elston; 10 Craig Forsyth; 11 Tom Andrews; 12 Danny Seal; 13 Simon Friend. Subs (all used): 14 Mark Stewart; 15 Dan Briggs; 16 Andy Burland; 17 Yusuf Sozi.
Tries: Friend (54), Wood (56); **Goals:** Brough 2.
Rugby Leaguer & League Express Men of the Match: *Bulldogs:* Dean Lawford; *City Knights:* Simon Friend.
Penalty count: 9-10; **Half-time:** 18-2;
Referee: Karl Kirkpatrick (Warrington); **Attendance:** 829.

FEATHERSTONE ROVERS 48 DEWSBURY RAMS 4

ROVERS: 1 Jamie Coventry; 2 Ben Archibald; 3 Steve Dooler; 4 Richard Newlove; 5 Matthew Wray; 6 Jon Presley; 7 Carl Briggs; 8 Ian Tonks; 9 Richard Chapman; 10 Stuart Dickens; 11 Paul Darley; 12 Bryan Henare; 13 Richard Blakeway. Subs (all used): 14 James Ford; 15 Danny Patrickson; 16 Adam Hayes; 17 Jim Carlton.
Tries: Presley (9), Archibald (21), Newlove (23, 40), Blakeway (31, 34), Dickens (57), Chapman (65), Ford (78); **Goals:** Briggs 6.
RAMS: 1 Ian Preece; 2 Jon Waddle; 3 Ian Kirke; 4 Richard Thaler; 5 Leon Williamson; 6 Danny Thomas; 7 Adam Thaler; 8 Paul Hicks; 9 Darren Robinson; 10 Michael Gibbons; 11 Tim Spears; 12 Billy Kershaw; 13 Chris Redfearn. Subs (all used): 14 David Mycoe; 15 Jamie Tennant; 16 Anthony Thewliss; 17 Mark Hawksley.
Try: Redfearn (51).
Rugby Leaguer & League Express Men of the Match: *Rovers:* Richard Chapman; *Rams:* Paul Hicks.
Penalty count: 11-6; **Half-time:** 34-0;
Referee: Mike Dawber (Wigan); **Attendance:** 1,068.

Saturday 27th March 2004

NORTH v WEST

BARROW RAIDERS 31 CHORLEY LYNX 22

RAIDERS: 1 Craig Bower; 2 Tama Wakelin; 3 Damien Reid; 4 Paul Jones; 5 Adam Pate; 6 Phil Atkinson; 7 Darren Holt; 8 Stuart Dancer; 9 Dave Clark; 10 Paul Wilcock; 11 Matthew Leigh; 12 James King; 13 Barry Pugh. Subs (all used): 14 Chris Archer; 15 Andy McClure; 16 Geoff Luxon; 17 Paul Lupton.
Tries: Leigh (34), Pate (39, 50), McClure (53), Reid (57);
Goals: Holt 5; **Field goal:** Holt.
LYNX: 1 Lee Patterson; 2 Ade Mead; 3 Eddie Kilgannon; 4 Jamie Stenhouse; 5 Gary O'Regan; 6 Rob Smyth; 7 Martin Gambles; 8 Ian Parry; 9 Chris Ramsdale; 10 John Hill; 11 Mick Redford; 12 Gary Smith; 13 Danny Barton. Subs (all used): 14 Lee Rowley; 15 Martin Roden; 16 Neil Alexander; 17 Anthony Murray.
Tries: Patterson (20, 65, 72), G Smith (38);
Goals: Alexander 3.
Rugby Leaguer & League Express Men of the Match: *Raiders:* Chris Archer; *Lynx:* Martin Gambles.
Penalty count: 6-4; **Half-time:** 12-12;
Referee: Gareth Hewer (Whitehaven); **Attendance:** 567.

WEEK 8

Sunday 28th March 2004

YORKSHIRE v EAST

DEWSBURY RAMS 22 SHEFFIELD EAGLES 28

RAMS: 1 Ian Preece; 2 Andrew Webber; 3 Ian Kirke; 4 Richard Thaler; 5 Leon Williamson; 6 Adam Thaler; 7 David Mycoe; 8 Paul Hicks; 9 Darren Robinson; 10 Mark Hawksley; 11 Kevin Crouthers; 12 Billy Kershaw; 13 Graham Law. Subs (all used): 14 Danny Thomas; 15 Chris Redfearn; 16 Jamie Tennant; 17 Michael Gibbons.
Tries: Webber (30), Robinson (41), Crouthers (44), Williamson (58); **Goals:** A Thaler 3.
EAGLES: 1 Andy Poynter; 2 Carl De Chenu; 3 Nick Turnbull; 4 Jon Breakingbury; 5 Danny Mills; 6 Richard Goddard; 7 Gavin Brown; 8 Jack Howieson; 9 Gareth Stanley; 10 Jon Bruce; 11 Andy Raleigh; 12 Craig Brown; 13 Jordan James. Subs (all used): 14 Sean Dickinson; 15 Guy Adams; 16 Rob North; 17 Simon Tillyer.
Tries: Breakingbury (6, 11), J James (20), Tillyer (25), Howieson (51); **Goals:** Goddard 4.
Rugby Leaguer & League Express Men of the Match: *Rams:* Paul Hicks; *Eagles:* Richard Goddard.
Penalty count: 8-9; **Half-time:** 4-22;
Referee: Colin Morris (Huddersfield); **Attendance:** 499.

EAST v YORKSHIRE

DONCASTER DRAGONS 30 BATLEY BULLDOGS 44

DRAGONS: 1 Wayne Green; 2 Craig Miles; 3 Alex Muff; 4 PJ Solomon; 5 Marlon Billy; 6 Graham Holroyd; 7 Dean Colton; 8 Gareth Handford; 9 Craig Cook; 10 Andy

Fisher; 11 Martin Ostler; 12 Peter Green; 13 Matt Walker. Subs (all used): 14 Chris Hemmings; 15 James Walker; 16 Martin Sykes; 17 Chris Hough.
Tries: Muff (2), Holroyd (9), Miles (20, 43), Solomon (33); **Goals:** Holroyd 5.
BULLDOGS: 1 Mark Sibson; 2 Matt Bramald; 3 Shad Royston; 4 Danny Maun; 5 Adrian Flynn; 6 Dean Lawford; 7 Barry Eaton; 8 Joe Berry; 9 Andy Heptinstall; 10 Steve Hill; 11 Danny Evans; 12 Andy Spink; 13 Mark Toohey. Subs (all used): 14 Adrian Leek; 15 Paul Harrison; 16 Tim Spears; 17 Sean Richardson.
Tries: Spink (4, 38), Maun (17), Bramald (27), Lawford (49), Sibson (52), Richardson (61); **Goals:** Eaton 8.
Rugby Leaguer & League Express Men of the Match: *Dragons:* Andy Fisher; *Bulldogs:* Barry Eaton.
Penalty count: 5-7; **Half-time:** 22-22; **Referee:** Steve Nicholson (Whitehaven); **Attendance:** 707.

PENNINE v WEST

HALIFAX 16 LEIGH CENTURIONS 27

HALIFAX: 1 Danny Arnold; 2 Richard Smith; 3 Chris Norman; 4 Alan Hadcroft; 5 Oliver Marns; 6 Simon Grix; 7 Pat Weisner; 8 Anthony Farrell; 9 Phil Cantillon; 10 Ryan McDonald; 11 Jaymes Chapman; 12 Wayne Corcoran; 13 Jamie Bloem. Subs (all used): 14 Mark Moxon; 15 Scott Law; 16 David Bates; 17 Paul Davidson.
Tries: Smith (58), Norman (63), Moxon (79);
Goals: Bloem 2.
CENTURIONS: 1 Neil Turley; 2 Steve Maden; 3 Dan Potter; 4 Chris Percival; 5 Damian Munro; 6 John Duffy; 7 Tommy Martyn; 8 Simon Knox; 9 Paul Rowley; 10 Heath Cruckshank; 11 David Larder; 12 Oliver Wilkes; 13 Ian Knott. Subs (all used): 14 Dave McConnell; 15 Andrew Isherwood; 16 Danny Halliwell; 17 Paul Norman.
Tries: Rowley (3), Larder (40), Turley (49), Potter (68), Percival (75); **Goals:** Turley 3; **Field goal:** Turley.
Rugby Leaguer & League Express Men of the Match: *Halifax:* Jaymes Chapman; *Centurions:* Paul Rowley.
Penalty count: 18-12; **Half-time:** 0-10;
Referee: Ben Thaler (Wakefield); **Attendance:** 2,815.

EAST v YORKSHIRE

HULL KINGSTON ROVERS 16 FEATHERSTONE ROVERS 18

ROBINS: 1 Casey Mayberry; 2 Craig Farrell; 3 Paul Parker; 4 Matt Calland; 5 Alasdair McClarron; 6 Paul Mansson; 7 Scott Thorburn; 8 Jamie Bovill; 9 Andy Ellis; 10 Makali Aizue; 11 Dale Holdstock; 12 Jon Aston; 13 Anthony Seibold. Subs (all used): 14 Phil Hasty; 15 Dean Andrews; 16 Richard Wilson; 17 Frank Watene.
Tries: Parker (9, 47), Mansson (74); **Goals:** Thorburn 2.
Dismissal: Watene (63) - high tackle on Carlton.
ROVERS: 1 Ben Archibald; 2 James Ford; 3 Steve Dooler; 4 Ben Feehan; 5 Matthew Wray; 6 Jon Presley; 7 Carl Briggs; 8 Jim Carlton; 9 Richard Chapman; 10 Stuart Dickens; 11 Paul Darley; 12 Richard Blakeway; 13 Adam Hayes. Subs (all used): 14 Craig Moss; 15 Bryan Henare; 16 Andy Jarrett; 17 Craig Milnthorpe.
Tries: Feehan (17), Presley (53); **Goals:** Briggs 5.
Sin bin: Jarrett (29) - interference;
Presley (74) - interference.
Rugby Leaguer & League Express Men of the Match: *Robins:* Dale Holdstock; *Rovers:* Carl Briggs.
Penalty count: 13-11; **Half-time:** 6-10; **Referee:** Richard Silverwood (Dewsbury); **Attendance:** 1,755.

WEST v PENNINE

OLDHAM 56 ROCHDALE HORNETS 12

OLDHAM: 1 Gavin Dodd; 2 Will Cowell; 3 Gareth Barber; 4 Jon Goddard; 5 Nick Johnson; 6 Neil Roden; 7 Ian Watson; 8 Steve Molloy; 9 Keith Brennan; 10 Paul Southern; 11 Lee Doran; 12 Dane Morgan; 13 Lee Marsh. Subs (all used): 14 Pat Rich; 15 Simon Svabic; 16 Martin McLoughlin; 17 Martin Elswood.
Tries: Roden (4, 54, 77), Dodd (7, 71), Doran (12), Morgan (30), N Johnson (34, 43, 50);
Goals: Barber 5, Svabic 3.
HORNETS: 1 Michael Platt; 2 Liam Williams; 3 Paul Anderson; 4 Andy Gorski; 5 Chris Campbell; 6 Sam Butterworth; 7 John Braddish; 8 Andy Leathem; 9 Janan Billings; 10 Lee Hansen; 11 Matt Sturm; 12 Gareth Price; 13 Darren Shaw. Subs (all used): 14 Lee Birdseye; 15 Andy Grundy; 16 Tommy Hodgkinson; 17 Mark Costello.
Tries: Butterworth (39), Campbell (65);
Goals: Butterworth 2.
Rugby Leaguer & League Express Men of the Match: *Oldham:* Nick Johnson; *Hornets:* Michael Platt.
Penalty count: 12-5; **Half-time:** 28-8;
Referee: Ashley Klein (London); **Attendance:** 1,214.

NORTH v PENNINE

WORKINGTON TOWN 12 KEIGHLEY COUGARS 33

TOWN: 1 Graeme Lewthwaite; 2 Matthew Johnson; 3 Neil Frazer; 4 Adam Coulson; 5 Martyn Wilson; 6 Jonathan Heaney; 7 Scott Chilton; 8 Dean Burgess; 9 David Pettit; 10 Matthew Tunstall; 11 Jonny Limmer; 12 Jamie Beaumont; 13 Ricky Wright. Subs (all used): 14 Martin Stalker; 15 Craig Barker; 16 James Robinson; 17 Bryan Hendry.
Tries: Wright (4), Lewthwaite (50); **Goals:** Heaney 2.
COUGARS: 1 James Rushforth; 2 Chris Beever; 3 David Foster; 4 Matt Foster; 5 Andy Robinson; 6 Adam Mitchell; 7 Matt Firth; 8 Phil Stephenson; 9 Simeon Hoyle; 10 Chris Parker; 11 Matthew Steel; 12 Lee Patterson; 13 Craig McDowell. Subs (all used): 14 Karl Smith; 15 Craig Nipperess; 16 Jason Clegg; 17 Danny Ekis.
Tries: M Foster (10), Hoyle (16, 21), Rushforth (45), McDowell (69), Patterson (73);
Goals: Mitchell 4; **Field goal:** Mitchell.
On report:
Unknown player (66) - late, high tackle on Wright.
Rugby Leaguer & League Express Men of the Match: *Town:* Adam Coulson; *Cougars:* Simeon Hoyle.
Penalty count: 13-7; **Half-time:** 6–20;
Referee: Mike Dawber (Wigan); **Attendance:** 567.

PENNINE v EAST

HUNSLET HAWKS 36 LONDON SKOLARS 18

HAWKS: 1 Chris Hall; 2 George Rayner; 3 Paul Seal; 4 Wes McGibbon; 5 Chris Ross; 6 Danny Wood; 7 Latham Tawhai; 8 Craig Booth; 9 Joe Hawley; 10 Steve Pryce; 11 Wayne Freeman; 12 Gary Shillabeer; 13 Andy Bastow. Subs (all used): 14 Glen Freeman; 15 Shaun Ibbetson; 16 Neil Mears; 17 Liam Jarvis.
Tries: Tawhai (25), Ibbetson (31), G Freeman (40), Ross (60), C Hall (63, 75); **Goals:** Wood 6.
Sin bin: Shillabeer (53) - late tackle.
On report: Unknown player (50) - high tackle.
SKOLARS: 1 Joel Osborn; 2 Mike Okwusogu; 3 Donny Lam; 4 Stephen Green; 5 Desi Kadima; 6 Jermaine Coleman; 7 Peter Hannan; 8 Rubert Jonker; 9 Gareth Honor; 10 Koben Katipa; 11 Mark Cantoni; 12 Ben Joyce; 13 John Rua. Subs (all used): 14 Keir Bell; 15 Alex Smits; 16 Glenn Osborn; 17 Deon McFadyen.
Tries: Kadima (3), Coleman (13), Lam (21, 72);
Goal: J Osborn.
On report: Jonker (68) - high tackle on Shillabeer.
Rugby Leaguer & League Express Men of the Match: *Hawks:* Latham Tawhai; *Skolars:* Jermaine Coleman.
Penalty count: 9-9; **Half-time:** 18-14;
Referee: Peter Taberner (Wigan); **Attendance:** 337.

Tuesday 30th March 2004

WEST v NORTH

SWINTON LIONS 6 WHITEHAVEN 34

LIONS: 1 Wayne English; 2 Jason Roach; 3 Mark Bolton; 4 Chris Maye; 5 Chris Irwin; 6 Ian Hodson; 7 Warren Ayres; 8 Rob Whittaker; 9 Rob Barraclough; 10 Wes Rogers; 11 Phil Cushion; 12 Danny Heaton; 13 Peter Cannon. Subs (all used): 14 Neil Hayden; 15 Safraz Patel; 16 Jake Johnstone; 17 Tau Liku.
Try: Irwin (51); **Goal:** Maye.
WHITEHAVEN: 1 Steven Wood; 2 Jamie Marshall; 3 Wesley Wilson; 4 Craig Walsh; 5 John Lebbon; 6 Leroy Joe; 7 Sam Obst; 8 Gary Smith; 9 Carl Sice; 10 Dean Vaughan; 11 Brett McDermott; 12 Ryan Campbell; 13 Garry Purdham. Subs (all used): 14 Gary Broadbent; 15 Spencer Miller; 16 Mark Wallace; 17 Tony Cunningham.
Tries: Walsh (16, 79), Sice (39, 77), McDermott (70), Miller (80); **Goals:** Wood 5.
On report: Wood (61) - high tackle.
Rugby Leaguer & League Express Men of the Match: *Lions:* Danny Heaton; *Whitehaven:* Carl Sice.
Penalty count: 8-7; **Half-time:** 0-12;
Referee: Mike Dawber (Wigan); **Attendance:** 346.

Wednesday 31st March 2004

EAST

DONCASTER DRAGONS 58 LONDON SKOLARS 20

DRAGONS: 1 Wayne Green; 2 Dean Colton; 3 Gareth Lloyd; 4 Alex Muff; 5 Craig Miles; 6 Graham Holroyd; 7 Shaun Leaf; 8 Gareth Handford; 9 Liam Brentley; 10 Chris Hemmings; 11 Martin Ostler; 12 Andy Fisher; 13 Peter Green. Subs (all used): 14 Tom Buckenham; 15 James Walker; 16 Matt Walker; 17 Chris Hough.
Tries: Ostler (2), W Green (6, 21), Lloyd (34), Hough (39), Brentley (55), P Green (58), Muff (66), Miles (74), Buckenham (77); **Goals:** Holroyd 9.
Sin bin: Ostler (46) - dissent.
SKOLARS: 1 Joel Osborn; 2 Zane Gardiner; 3 Donny Lam; 4 Stephen Green; 5 Neil Foster; 6 Jermaine Coleman; 7 Peter Hannan; 8 Rubert Jonker; 9 John Rua; 10 Alex Smits; 11 Glenn Osborn; 12 Wayne Parillon; 13 Ben Joyce. Subs (all used): 14 Brad McFarland; 15 Koben Katipa; 16 Dan Reeds; 17 Mike Castle.
Tries: Foster (13), Green (16), Coleman (24, 47);
Goals: G Osborn 2.
Rugby Leaguer & League Express Men of the Match: *Dragons:* Liam Brentley; *Skolars:* Jermaine Coleman.
Penalty count: 9-8; **Half-time:** 30-14;
Referee: Gareth Hewer (Whitehaven); **Attendance:** 395.

YORKSHIRE v NORTH

YORK CITY KNIGHTS 54 GATESHEAD THUNDER 26

CITY KNIGHTS: 1 Nathan Graham; 2 Rob Kama; 3 Chris Langley; 4 Mark Cain; 5 Alex Godfrey; 6 Scott Rhodes; 7 Danny Brough; 8 Ryan Benjafield; 9 Lee Jackson; 10 Yusuf Sozi; 11 Tom Andrews; 12 Damian Ball; 13 Simon Friend. Subs (all used): 14 Jimmy Elston; 15 Darren Callaghan; 16 Danny Seal; 17 Craig Forsyth.
Tries: Godfrey (2, 16, 47), Benjafield (14), Rhodes (26, 42), Ball (67), Seal (71), Langley (77);
Goals: Brough 7, Ball 2.
THUNDER: 1 Graham Stephenson; 2 Mick Kent; 3 Kevin Neighbour; 4 Craig Firth; 5 Robin Peers; 6 Paul Thorman; 7 Craig Fisher; 8 Rob Line; 9 Neil Thorman; 10 Scott Harrison; 11 Carl Stannard; 12 Steven Bradley; 13 Steve Rutherford. Subs (all used): 14 Andy Fleming; 15 Charlie Roe; 16 Tony Doherty; 17 Mark Walker.
Tries: Bradley (29), Neighbour (33), N Thorman (54), Peers (58), P Thorman (74); **Goals:** P Thorman 3.
Dismissal: Stephenson (16) - knees in the tackle.
Rugby Leaguer & League Express Men of the Match: *City Knights:* Lee Jackson; *Thunder:* Neil Thorman.
Penalty count: 10-7; **Half-time:** 24-12;
Referee: Ben Thaler (Wakefield);
Attendance: 1,520 *(at Bootham Crescent, York City FC).*

Saturday 3rd April 2004

EAST

LONDON SKOLARS 8 HULL KINGSTON ROVERS 50

SKOLARS: 1 Joel Osborn; 2 Desi Kadima; 3 Andy Gould; 4 Stephen Green; 5 Neil Foster; 6 Jermaine Coleman; 7 Peter Hannan; 8 Dan Reeds; 9 Gareth Honor; 10 Koben Katipa; 11 Glenn Osborn; 12 Mark Cantoni; 13 Ben Joyce. Subs (all used): 14 Keir Bell; 15 Mike Castle; 16 Deon McFadyen; 17 Ade Aderiye.
Try: J Osborn (26); **Goals:** G Osborn 2.
ROVERS: 1 Craig Poucher; 2 Casey Mayberry; 3 Paul Parker; 4 Matt Calland; 5 Alasdair McClarron; 6 Paul Mansson; 7 Scott Thorburn; 8 Jamie Bovill; 9 Paul Pickering; 10 Richard Wilson; 11 Dale Holdstock; 12 Andy Smith; 13 Anthony Seibold. Subs (all used): 14 Phil Hasty; 15 Jon Aston; 16 Makali Aizue; 17 Frank Watene.
Tries: Poucher (6), McClarron (16, 53), Pickering (29), Parker (33), Mansson (47), Aston (63), Calland (67), Thorburn (75); **Goals:** Thorburn 7.
Rugby Leaguer & League Express Men of the Match: *Skolars:* Mark Cantoni; *Rovers:* Paul Mansson.
Penalty count: 9-8; **Half-time:** 8-20;
Referee: Ben Thaler (Wakefield); **Attendance:** 656.

WEEK 9

Sunday 4th April 2004

NORTH

BARROW RAIDERS 48 WORKINGTON TOWN 0

RAIDERS: 1 Craig Bower; 2 Nick Beech; 3 Damien Reid; 4 Paul Jones; 5 Adam Pate; 6 Chris Archer; 7 Darren Holt; 8 Stuart Dancer; 9 Dave Clark; 10 Paul Wilcock; 11 Matthew Leigh; 12 James King; 13 Mike Whitehead. Subs (all used): 14 Paul Evans; 15 Paul Lupton; 16 Geoff Luxon; 17 Andy McClure.
Tries: Holt (3), Leigh (16), Reid (27, 66, 77), King (38), Beech (48, 71), Bower (55); **Goals:** Holt 6.
Sin bin: Leigh (48) - fighting.
TOWN: 1 Graeme Lewthwaite; 2 Martyn Wilson; 3 Neil Frazer; 4 Andrew Fearon; 5 Martin Stalker; 6 Jonathan Heaney; 7 Scott Chilton; 8 Dean Burgess; 9 Jonny Limmer; 10 Matthew Tunstall; 11 James Robinson; 12 Jamie Beaumont; 13 Ricky Wright. Subs (all used): 14 Matthew Johnson; 15 Craig Barker; 16 John Young; 17 Bryan Hendry.
Sin bin: Hendry (37) - interference;
Heaney (48) - fighting.
Rugby Leaguer & League Express Men of the Match: *Raiders:* Chris Archer; *Town:* Scott Chilton.
Penalty count: 5-7; **Half-time:** 22-0;
Referee: Jamie Leahy (Dewsbury); **Attendance:** 713.

WHITEHAVEN 74 GATESHEAD THUNDER 16

WHITEHAVEN: 1 Gary Broadbent; 2 Jamie Marshall; 3 David Seeds; 4 Mick Nanyn; 5 Wesley Wilson; 6 Lee Kiddie; 7 Sam Obst; 8 Dean Vaughan; 9 Aaron Lester; 10 David Fatialofa; 11 Brett McDermott; 12 Howard Hill; 13 Craig Walsh. Subs (all used): 14 Carl Sice; 15 Marc Jackson; 16 Garry Purdham; 17 Chris McKinney.
Tries: Obst (3, 37), Marshall (9), Kiddie (11, 19, 66), Lester (13), Wilson (15), McKinney (42), Jackson (51), Walsh (62), Broadbent (70), Nanyn (75); **Goals:** Nanyn 11.
THUNDER: 1 Graham Stephenson; 2 Mick Kent; 3 Steve Rutherford; 4 Kevin Neighbour; 5 Robin Peers; 6 Paul Thorman; 7 Craig Fisher; 8 Rob Line; 9 Neil Thorman; 10 Scott Harrison; 11 Tony Doherty; 12 Ian Ball; 13 Steven Bradley. Subs (all used): 14 Mark Walker; 15 Andy Fleming; 16 Shawn Ackerley; 17 Phil Pitt.
Tries: Peers (27), Fleming (29), Neighbour (55);
Goals: P Thorman 2.
Rugby Leaguer & League Express Men of the Match: *Whitehaven:* Marc Jackson; *Thunder:* Paul Thorman.
Penalty count: 6-5; **Half-time:** 38-10;
Referee: Phil Bentham (Warrington); **Attendance:** 1,017.

WEST

CHORLEY LYNX 10 LEIGH CENTURIONS 78

LYNX: 1 Lee Patterson; 2 Ade Mead; 3 Eddie Kilgannon; 4 Jamie Stenhouse; 5 Gary O'Regan; 6 Chris Ramsdale; 7 Martin Gambles; 8 Ian Parry; 9 Martin Roden; 10 John Hill; 11 Mick Redford; 12 Gary Smith; 13 Danny Barton. Subs (all used): 14 Lee Rowley; 15 Chris Newall; 16 Steve Ormesher; 17 Neil Alexander.
Tries: O'Regan (14), Stenhouse (47); **Goal:** Alexander.
CENTURIONS: 1 Neil Turley; 2 Steve Maden; 3 Dale Cardoza; 4 Chris Percival; 5 Danny Halliwell; 6 John Duffy; 7 Tommy Martyn; 8 Paul Norman; 9 Paul Rowley; 10 Oliver Wilkes; 11 Andrew Isherwood; 12 Dan Potter; 13 Ian Knott. Subs (all used): 14 Mike Callan; 15 Dave McConnell; 16 Radney Bowker; 17 David Bradbury.
Tries: Martyn (4, 70), Knott (9, 54), Turley (19, 37, 58, 76, 80), Halliwell (25, 62), Isherwood (28, 51), Percival (31); **Goals:** Turley 11.
Rugby Leaguer & League Express Men of the Match: *Lynx:* Jamie Stenhouse; *Centurions:* Neil Turley.
Penalty count: 9-4; **Half-time:** 4-38;
Referee: Peter Taberner (Wigan); **Attendance:** 770.

OLDHAM 42 SWINTON LIONS 15

OLDHAM: 1 Gavin Dodd; 2 Will Cowell; 3 Gareth Barber; 4 Jon Goddard; 5 Nick Johnson; 6 Neil Roden; 7 Ian Watson; 8 Steve Molloy; 9 Keith Brennan; 10 Paul Southern; 11 Lee Doran; 12 Martin Elswood; 13 Lee Marsh. Subs (all used): 14 Pat Rich; 15 Simon Svabic; 16 Adam Sharples; 17 Martin McLoughlin.
Tries: Roden (3, 66), Barber (16), N Johnson (41), Rich (55), Cowell (71, 77), Elswood (74); **Goals:** Rich 5.
Dismissal: L Marsh (51) - striking.
LIONS: 1 Jason Roach; 2 Jake Johnstone; 3 Mark Bolton; 4 Chris Maye; 5 Hugh Thorpe; 6 Warren Ayres; 7 Paul Ashton; 8 Rob Whittaker; 9 Peter Cannon; 10 Craig Wingfield; 11 Phil Cushion; 12 Kris Smith; 13 Ian Hodson. Subs (all used): 14 Mick Coates; 15 Craig Kay; 16 Mark Pembroke; 17 Tau Liku.
Tries: Ayres (22), Cannon (63); **Goals:** Maye, Ashton 2; **Field goal:** Ashton.
Rugby Leaguer & League Express Men of the Match: *Oldham:* Neil Roden; *Lions:* Peter Cannon.
Penalty count: 13-11; **Half-time:** 8-7;
Referee: Gareth Hewer (Whitehaven); **Attendance:** 983.

PENNINE

HALIFAX 20 HUNSLET HAWKS 4

HALIFAX: 1 Brad Attwood; 2 Rikki Sheriffe; 3 Richard Smith; 4 Chris Norman; 5 Oliver Marns; 6 Simon Grix; 7 Mark Moxon; 8 Anthony Farrell; 9 Phil Cantillon; 10 Ryan McDonald; 11 Jaymes Chapman; 12 Ged Corcoran; 13 Jon Roper. Subs (all used): 14 Scott Grix; 15 Scott Law; 16 David Bates; 17 Paul Davidson.
Tries: Roper (3), Davidson (42), Chapman (55), Sheriffe (57); **Goals:** Roper 2.
HAWKS: 1 Chris Hall; 2 Ryan Taylor; 3 Paul Seal; 4 Wes McGibbon; 5 Leigh Deakin; 6 Danny Wood; 7 Latham Tawhai; 8 Steve Pryce; 9 Jamaine Wray; 10 Mick Coyle; 11 Wayne Freeman; 12 Shaun Ibbetson; 13 Jon Liddell. Subs (all used): 14 Glen Freeman; 15 Gary Shillabeer; 16 Joe Hawley; 17 Neil Mears.
Goals: Wood 2.
Rugby Leaguer & League Express Men of the Match: *Halifax:* Jon Roper; *Hawks:* Jamaine Wray.
Penalty count: 8-11; **Half-time:** 4-4;
Referee: Ashley Klein (London); **Attendance:** 1,536.

KEIGHLEY COUGARS 14 ROCHDALE HORNETS 14

COUGARS: 1 James Rushforth; 2 Karl Smith; 3 David Foster; 4 Matt Foster; 5 Andy Robinson; 6 Adam Mitchell; 7 Matt Firth; 8 Phil Stephenson; 9 Simeon Hoyle; 10 Chris Parker; 11 Matthew Steel; 12 Lee Patterson; 13 Craig McDowell. Subs (all used): 14 Craig Nipperess; 15 Richard Mervill; 16 Jason Clegg; 17 Danny Ekis.
Tries: Robinson (12, 36); **Goals:** Mitchell 3.
HORNETS: 1 Michael Platt; 2 Liam Williams; 3 Paul Anderson; 4 Andy Gorski; 5 Chris Campbell; 6 Lee Birdseye; 7 John Braddish; 8 Rob Ball; 9 Janan Billings; 10 Mark Costello; 11 Matt Sturm; 12 Gareth Price; 13 Kris Ratcliffe. Subs (all used): 14 Sam Butterworth; 15 Lee Hansen; 16 Dave Newton; 17 Andy Leathem.
Tries: Platt (27), Braddish (47); **Goals:** Birdseye 3.
Rugby Leaguer & League Express Men of the Match: *Cougars:* Phil Stephenson; *Hornets:* Matt Sturm.
Penalty count: 11-7; **Half-time:** 8-8; **Referee:** Steve Nicholson (Whitehaven); **Attendance:** 1,171.

YORKSHIRE

BATLEY BULLDOGS 40 FEATHERSTONE ROVERS 16

BULLDOGS: 1 Mark Sibson; 2 Matt Bramald; 3 Shad Royston; 4 Danny Maun; 5 Adrian Flynn; 6 Mark Toohey; 7 Barry Eaton; 8 Steve Hill; 9 Andy Heptinstall; 10 David Rourke; 11 Sean Richardson; 12 Andy Spink; 13 Tim Spears. Subs (all used): 14 Adrian Leek; 15 Paul Harrison; 16 Joe Berry; 17 Will Cartledge.
Tries: Leek (32), Spink (36), Harrison (45), Flynn (53), Spears (58), Maun (70); **Goals:** Eaton 8.
ROVERS: 1 Ben Archibald; 2 Jamie Stokes; 3 Steve Dooler; 4 Ben Feehan; 5 Matthew Wray; 6 Jon Presley; 7 Carl Briggs; 8 Jim Carlton; 9 Richard Chapman; 10 Stuart Dickens; 11 Paul Darley; 12 Richard Blakeway; 13 Adam Hayes. Subs (all used): 14 Craig Moss; 15 Bryan Henare; 16 Andy Jarrett; 17 Richard Newlove.
Tries: Stokes (12), Wray (27), Jarrett (65);
Goals: Briggs 2.
Sin bin: Archibald (58) - interference.
Rugby Leaguer & League Express Men of the Match: *Bulldogs:* Paul Harrison; *Rovers:* Jon Presley.
Penalty count: 5-6; **Half-time:** 14-12;
Referee: Mike Dawber (Wigan); **Attendance:** 1,007.

YORK CITY KNIGHTS 44 DEWSBURY RAMS 7

CITY KNIGHTS: 1 Nathan Graham; 2 Scott Walker; 3 Chris Langley; 4 Aaron Wood; 5 Alex Godfrey; 6 Scott Rhodes; 7 Danny Brough; 8 Ryan Benjafield; 9 Lee Jackson; 10 Yusuf Sozi; 11 Tom Andrews; 12 Simon Friend; 13 Damian Ball. Subs (all used): 14 Jimmy Elston; 15 Danny Seal; 16 Darren Callaghan; 17 Craig Forsyth.
Tries: Godfrey (1, 39, 80), Benjafield (43), Friend (46), Graham (57), Rhodes (75), Langley (77);
Goals: Brough 6.
RAMS: 1 Ian Preece; 2 Marcus Bernard; 3 Chris Redfearn; 4 Ian Kirke; 5 Leon Williamson; 6 Danny Thomas; 7 Adam Thaler; 8 Paul Hicks; 9 Darren Robinson; 10 Joe Naidole; 11 Kevin Crouthers; 12 Anthony Thewliss; 13 Kevin Spink. Subs (all used): 14 David Mycoe; 15 Jamie Tennant; 16 Jon Waddle; 17 Michael Gibbons.
Try: Robinson (11); **Goal:** A Thaler; **Field goal:** Robinson.
Rugby Leaguer & League Express Men of the Match: *City Knights:* Simon Friend; *Rams:* Kevin Crouthers.
Penalty count: 9-11; **Half-time:** 10-7;
Referee: Robert Connolly (Wigan); **Attendance:** 1,204.

Friday 9th April 2004

NORTH

GATESHEAD THUNDER 12 BARROW RAIDERS 50

THUNDER: 1 Graham Stephenson; 2 Mike Bunting; 3 Phil Pitt; 4 Kevin Neighbour; 5 Dave Griffiths; 6 Paul Thorman; 7 Craig Fisher; 8 Rob Line; 9 Neil Thorman; 10 Scott Harrison; 11 Shawn Ackerley; 12 Andy Fleming; 13 Steven Bradley. Subs (all used): 14 Ben Hodgson; 15 Ian Ball; 16 Robin Peers; 17 Mark Walker.
Tries: Hodgson (35), Bunting (50), Bradley (59).
RAIDERS: 1 Craig Bower; 2 Nick Beech; 3 Damien Reid; 4 Paul Jones; 5 Adam Pate; 6 Chris Archer; 7 Darren Holt; 8 Paul Wilcock; 9 Paul Evans; 10 Paul Lupton; 11 Mike Whitehead; 12 James King; 13 Barry Pugh. Subs (all used): 14 Jon Williamson; 15 Andy McClure; 16 Lee Washington; 17 Wayne Jones.
Tries: Evans (3, 23), P Jones (10, 18), Pate (30), Whitehead (42), Archer (46), King (62), Beech (77);
Goals: Holt 3, Pate 4.
Rugby Leaguer & League Express Men of the Match: *Thunder:* Steven Bradley; *Raiders:* Mike Whitehead.
Penalty count: 9-2; **Half-time:** 4-28;
Referee: Craig Halloran (Dewsbury); **Attendance:** 259.

WORKINGTON TOWN 10 WHITEHAVEN 26

TOWN: 1 Andrew Fearon; 2 Martyn Wilson; 3 Neil Frazer; 4 Adam Coulson; 5 Graeme Lewthwaite; 6 Jonathan Heaney; 7 Scott Chilton; 8 Dean Burgess; 9 Jonny Limmer; 10 Matthew Tunstall; 11 Ricky Wright; 12 Jamie Beaumont; 13 Martin Stalker. Subs: 14 Matthew Johnson (not used); 15 Andy McGlasson; 16 Brett Smith; 17 James Robinson.
Tries: Heaney (8), Lewthwaite (76); **Goal:** Heaney.
WHITEHAVEN: 1 Steven Wood; 2 Jamie Marshall; 3 Craig Walsh; 4 Mick Nanyn; 5 Paul O'Neil; 6 Lee Kiddie; 7 Steve Kirkbride; 8 Chris McKinney; 9 Carl Sice; 10 Dean Vaughan; 11 Ryan Campbell; 12 Spencer Miller; 13 Garry Purdham. Subs (all used): 14 Aaron Lester; 15 Gary Smith; 16 Craig Chambers; 17 Tony Cunningham.
Tries: Walsh (16, 69), Sice (34), Kirkbride (62), Purdham (65); **Goals:** Nanyn 3.
Rugby Leaguer & League Express Men of the Match: *Town:* Jonny Limmer; *Whitehaven:* Carl Sice.
Penalty count: 12-10; **Half-time:** 4-10;
Referee: Ben Thaler (Wakefield); **Attendance:** 1,419.

EAST

DONCASTER DRAGONS 8 HULL KINGSTON ROVERS 38

DRAGONS: 1 Johnny Woodcock; 2 Wayne Green; 3 Gareth Lloyd; 4 PJ Solomon; 5 Marlon Billy; 6 Graham Holroyd; 7 Chris Hough; 8 Gareth Handford; 9 Liam Brentley; 10 Andy Fisher; 11 Martin Ostler; 12 Peter Green; 13 Craig Lawton. Subs (all used): 14 Carl Stannard; 15 Tom Buckenham; 16 Chris Hemmings; 17 Alex Muff.
Tries: W Green (7), Solomon (80).
Sin bin: Fisher (52) - fighting.
ROVERS: 1 Lynton Stott; 2 Craig Farrell; 3 Paul Parker; 4 Nick Pinkney; 5 Alasdair McClarron; 6 Paul Mansson; 7 Phil Hasty; 8 Makali Aizue; 9 Andy Ellis; 10 Jamie Bovill; 11 Jon Aston; 12 Andy Smith; 13 Anthony Seibold. Subs (all used): 14 Jimmy Walker; 15 Scott Thorburn; 16 Adam Sullivan; 17 Paul Pickering.
Tries: Aizue (1), Farrell (31), Parker (39), Stott (55), Hasty (60), Walker (69), Thorburn (75); **Goals:** Stott 5.
Sin bin: Bovill (52) - fighting.
Rugby Leaguer & League Express Men of the Match: *Dragons:* Wayne Green; *Rovers:* Jamie Bovill.
Penalty count: 11-11; **Half-time:** 4-14;
Referee: Mike Dawber (Wigan); **Attendance:** 914.

WEST

CHORLEY LYNX 20 SWINTON LIONS 12

LYNX: 1 Lee Patterson; 2 Ade Mead; 3 Eddie Kilgannon; 4 Jamie Stenhouse; 5 Steve Ormesher; 6 Chris Newall; 7 Martin Gambles; 8 Ian Parry; 9 Martin Roden; 10 John Hill; 11 Mick Redford; 12 Gary Smith; 13 Danny Barton. Subs: 14 Lee Rowley; 15 James Lomax; 16 Chris Ramsdale; 17 Gary O'Regan (not used).
Tries: Mead (11), Ormesher (24), Stenhouse (38), Barton (73); **Goals:** Roden 2.
LIONS: 1 Wayne English; 2 Jason Roach; 3 Mark Bolton; 4 Chris Maye; 5 Hugh Thorpe; 6 Mick Coates; 7 Warren Ayres; 8 Rob Whittaker; 9 Peter Cannon; 10 Mark Pembroke; 11 Danny Heaton; 12 Kris Smith; 13 Ian Sinfield. Subs: 14 Safraz Patel; 15 Jake Johnstone (not used); 16 Craig Wingfield; 17 Tau Liku.
Tries: Roach (5), Ayres (32); **Goals:** Ayres 2.
Rugby Leaguer & League Express Men of the Match: *Lynx:* Ian Parry; *Lions:* Warren Ayres.
Penalty count: 14-11; **Half-time:** 14-12;
Referee: Jamie Leahy (Dewsbury); **Attendance:** 307.

PENNINE

KEIGHLEY COUGARS 47 HUNSLET HAWKS 8

COUGARS: 1 James Rushforth; 2 Karl Smith; 3 David Foster; 4 Matt Foster; 5 Andy Robinson; 6 Adam Mitchell; 7 Matt Firth; 8 Phil Stephenson; 9 Simeon Hoyle; 10 Chris Parker; 11 Matthew Steel; 12 Lee Patterson; 13 Craig McDowell. Subs (all used): 14 Craig Nipperess; 15 Chris Wainwright; 16 Jason Clegg; 17 Danny Ekis.
Tries: Parker (14), M Foster (16), Smith (27, 75), Steel (37), McDowell (39), Rushforth (41), Mitchell (55, 80);
Goals: Mitchell 5; **Field goal:** McDowell.
Sin bin: Mitchell (23) - fighting.
On report: Incident (23) - leading to brawl.
HAWKS: 1 Chris Hall; 2 Ryan Taylor; 3 Danny Cook; 4 Wes McGibbon; 5 Leigh Deakin; 6 Danny Wood; 7 Steve Doherty; 8 Steve Pryce; 9 Jamaine Wray; 10 Mick Coyle; 11 Wayne Freeman; 12 Shaun Ibbetson; 13 Jon Liddell. Subs (all used): 14 Glen Freeman; 15 Gary Shillabeer; 16 Joe Hawley; 17 Liam Jarvis.
Try: Doherty (20); **Goals:** Wood, Liddell.
Sin bin: Wood (23) - fighting; Doherty (47) - punching.
On report: Incident (23) - leading to brawl.
Rugby Leaguer & League Express Men of the Match: *Cougars:* Matt Foster; *Hawks:* Mick Coyle.
Penalty count: 7-7; **Half-time:** 26-8;
Referee: Peter Taberner (Wigan); **Attendance:** 1,297.

YORKSHIRE

DEWSBURY RAMS 20 BATLEY BULLDOGS 46

RAMS: 1 Wayne McHugh; 2 Andrew Webber; 3 Chris Redfearn; 4 Jon Waddle; 5 Michael Forbes; 6 Mick Hill; 7 David Mycoe; 8 Paul Smith; 9 Chris Woolford; 10 Michael Gibbons; 11 Anthony Thewliss; 12 Jamie Tennant; 13 Kevin Spink. Subs (all used): 14 Adam Thaler; 15 Paul Hicks; 16 Mark Hawksley; 17 Ian Booth.
Tries: Spink (19, 40), Booth (35), Hawksley (60);
Goals: Hill 2.
BULLDOGS: 1 Mark Sibson; 2 Matt Bramald; 3 Chris Spurr; 4 Danny Maun; 5 Adrian Flynn; 6 Mark Toohey; 7 Barry Eaton; 8 Chris Molyneux; 9 Mark Cass; 10 Joe Berry; 11 Sean Richardson; 12 Andy Spink; 13 Ryan Horsley. Subs (all used): 14 Tim Spears; 15 Paul Harrison; 16 Danny Evans; 17 Steve Beard.
Tries: Richardson (1), Maun (5), Horsley (11, 19, 80), Flynn (46), Harrison (51), Evans (75); **Goals:** Eaton 7.
Rugby Leaguer & League Express Men of the Match: *Rams:* David Mycoe; *Bulldogs:* Barry Eaton.
Penalty count: 14-10; **Half-time:** 16-22;
Referee: Gareth Hewer (Whitehaven); **Attendance:** 932.

FEATHERSTONE ROVERS 26 YORK CITY KNIGHTS 36

ROVERS: 1 Craig Moss; 2 Jamie Stokes; 3 Ben Feehan; 4 Richard Newlove; 5 Matthew Wray; 6 Jon Presley; 7 Carl Briggs; 8 Andy Jarrett; 9 Richard Chapman; 10 Stuart Dickens; 11 Steve Dooler; 12 Bryan Henare; 13 Adam Hayes. Subs (all used): 14 James Ford; 15 Paul Darley; 16 Ian Tonks; 17 Jim Carlton.
Tries: Stokes (20, 78), Wray (27), Dooler (45);
Goals: Briggs 5.
Dismissals: Newlove (35) - high tackle;
Carlton (54) - swinging arm.
Sin bin: Newlove (7) - fighting; Henare (35) - dissent.
CITY KNIGHTS: 1 Scott Walker; 2 Rob Kama; 3 Darren Callaghan; 4 Mark Cain; 5 Alex Godfrey; 6 Scott Rhodes; 7 Danny Brough; 8 Dan Briggs; 9 Jimmy Elston; 10 Craig Forsyth; 11 Mick Ramsden; 12 John Smith; 13 Mark Stewart. Subs (all used): 14 Nathan Graham; 15 Chris Langley; 16 Andy Burland; 17 Damian Ball.
Tries: Stewart (3, 49), Godfrey (38), Brough (47), Callaghan (57), Elston (64); **Goals:** Brough 6.
Sin bin: Callaghan (7) - fighting; Rhodes (35) - dissent.
Rugby Leaguer & League Express Men of the Match: *Rovers:* Carl Briggs; *City Knights:* Jimmy Elston.
Penalty count: 13-10; **Half-time:** 16-14;
Referee: Colin Morris (Huddersfield); **Attendance:** 1,435.

WEST v PENNINE

LEIGH CENTURIONS 46 HALIFAX 20

CENTURIONS: 1 Neil Turley; 2 David Alstead; 3 Dan Potter; 4 Danny Halliwell; 5 Mark McCully; 6 John Duffy; 7 Tommy Martyn; 8 Simon Knox; 9 Paul Rowley; 10 Heath Cruckshank; 11 Andrew Isherwood; 12 Oliver Wilkes; 13 Ian Knott. Subs (all used): 14 Dave McConnell; 15 Radney Bowker; 16 Mike Callan; 17 David Bradbury.
Tries: Rowley (2, 43), Halliwell (15), Alstead (23), Potter (28), Turley (39), McCully (65), Duffy (77);
Goals: Turley 7.
HALIFAX: 1 Brad Attwood; 2 Rikki Sheriffe; 3 Chris Norman; 4 Alan Hadcroft; 5 Oliver Marns; 6 Simon Grix; 7 Mark Moxon; 8 Anthony Farrell; 9 Phil Cantillon; 10 David Bates; 11 Jaymes Chapman; 12 Ged Corcoran; 13 Jon Roper. Subs (all used): 14 Scott Grix; 15 Scott Law; 16 Jon Simpson; 17 Gareth Matthews.
Tries: Norman (32), Sheriffe (35, 74), Bates (53);
Goals: Roper 2.
Rugby Leaguer & League Express Men of the Match: *Centurions:* Paul Rowley; *Halifax:* Anthony Farrell.
Penalty count: 5-6; **Half-time:** 28-10;
Referee: Robert Connolly (Wigan); **Attendance:** 2,563.

PENNINE v WEST

ROCHDALE HORNETS 12 OLDHAM 48

HORNETS: 1 Liam Williams; 2 Sam Butterworth; 3 Dave Cunliffe; 4 Alex Taylor; 5 Chris Campbell; 6 John Braddish; 7 Liam McGovern; 8 Rob Ball; 9 Danny Butler; 10 Andy Grundy; 11 Dave Newton; 12 Gareth Price; 13 Kris Ratcliffe. Subs (all used): 14 Lee Birdseye; 15 Tony Kirwan; 16 Tommy Hodgkinson; 17 Mark Costello.
Tries: Birdseye (49), Campbell (52); **Goals:** Birdseye 2.
Dismissal: Price (35) - high tackle on Watson.
OLDHAM: 1 Gavin Dodd; 2 Will Cowell; 3 Pat Rich; 4

Jon Goddard; 5 Nick Johnson; 6 Gareth Barber; 7 Ian Watson; 8 Steve Molloy; 9 Neil Roden; 10 Martin McLoughlin; 11 Lee Doran; 12 Dane Morgan; 13 Lee Marsh. Subs (all used): 14 Simon Svabic; 15 James Bunyan; 16 Gavin Johnson; 17 Martin Elswood.
Tries: L Marsh (9, 80), Barber (13), Morgan (23), Dodd (44), Rich (57), N Johnson (63, 73), Roden (75), Goddard (77); **Goals:** Rich 3, Svabic.
Rugby Leaguer & League Express Men of the Match: *Hornets:* Liam McGovern; *Oldham:* Ian Watson.
Penalty count: 8-10; **Half-time:** 0-18; **Referee:** Steve Nicholson (Whitehaven); **Attendance:** 1,305.

FINAL TABLES

NORTH

	P	W	D	L	F	A	Diff	Pts
Whitehaven	8	8	0	0	326	96	230	16
Barrow	8	5	1	2	289	128	161	11
Workington	8	1	2	5	140	251	-111	4
Gateshead	8	0	1	7	134	432	-298	1

EAST

	P	W	D	L	F	A	Diff	Pts
Hull KR	8	7	0	1	258	88	170	14
Doncaster	8	4	0	4	230	192	38	8
Sheffield	8	2	0	6	124	204	-80	4
London Skolars	8	1	0	7	80	322	-242	2

WEST

	P	W	D	L	F	A	Diff	Pts
Leigh	8	8	0	0	404	110	294	16
Oldham	8	6	0	2	322	186	136	12
Swinton	8	1	0	7	100	276	-176	2
Chorley	8	1	0	7	116	352	-236	2

PENNINE

	P	W	D	L	F	A	Diff	Pts
Halifax	8	5	0	3	174	149	25	10
Keighley	8	4	1	3	212	126	86	9
Hunslet	8	4	0	4	182	192	-10	8
Rochdale	8	2	1	5	121	216	-95	5

YORKSHIRE

	P	W	D	L	F	A	Diff	Pts
Batley	8	7	0	1	325	158	167	14
York	8	6	0	2	300	175	125	12
Featherstone ●	8	4	0	4	188	167	21	8
Dewsbury	8	1	0	7	135	340	-205	2

Group winners progressed to Quarter Finals. Group runners-up and the best third placed team (●) progressed to Quarter Final Qualifiers.

QUARTER FINAL QUALIFIERS

Sunday 25th April 2004

BARROW RAIDERS 32 KEIGHLEY COUGARS 20

RAIDERS: 1 Craig Bower; 2 Nick Beech; 3 Damien Reid; 4 Andy McClure; 5 Paul Jones; 6 Chris Archer; 7 Darren Holt; 8 Paul Wilcock; 9 Dave Clark; 10 Stuart Dancer; 11 Mike Whitehead; 12 James King; 13 Barry Pugh. Subs (all used): 14 Geoff Luxon; 15 Wayne Jones; 16 Paul Lupton; 17 Matthew Leigh.
Tries: King (39, 43, 64), Leigh (48), McClure (53), Reid (77); **Goals:** Holt 4/6.
COUGARS: 1 Chris Beever; 2 Karl Smith; 3 Chris Wainwright; 4 Matt Foster; 5 Andy Robinson; 6 Adam Mitchell; 7 Matt Firth; 8 Phil Stephenson; 9 Lee Patterson; 10 Chris Parker; 11 Matthew Steel; 12 David Foster; 13 Craig McDowell. Subs (all used): 14 Max Tomlinson; 15 Adam Webster; 16 Eddie Wilson; 17 Chris Roe.
Tries: Firth (21), Smith (29), Beever (31);
Goals: Mitchell 4/4.
Rugby Leaguer & League Express Men of the Match: *Raiders:* James King; *Cougars:* Matt Firth.
Penalty count: 5-3; **Half-time:** 4-20;
Referee: Colin Morris (Huddersfield); **Attendance:** 730.

DONCASTER DRAGONS 32 OLDHAM 28

DRAGONS: 1 Johnny Woodcock; 2 Dean Colton; 3 Alex Muff; 4 PJ Solomon; 5 Marlon Billy; 6 Graham Holroyd; 7 Chris Hough; 8 Gareth Handford; 9 Craig Cook; 10 Andy Fisher; 11 Matt Walker; 12 Peter Green; 13 Shaun Leaf. Subs (all used): 14 Tom Buckenham; 15 James Walker; 16 Carl Stannard; 17 Liam Brentley.
Tries: Billy (2, 59), Muff (33), Leaf (47), Colton (50, 62);
Goals: Holroyd 4/9.
OLDHAM: 1 Jon Goddard; 2 Will Cowell; 3 James Bunyan; 4 Pat Rich; 5 Nick Johnson; 6 Neil Roden; 7 Ian Watson; 8 Steve Molloy; 9 Keith Brennan; 10 Paul Southern; 11 Lee Doran; 12 Dane Morgan; 13 Phil Farrell. Subs (all used): 14 Simon Svabic; 15 Martin McLoughlin; 16 Lee Marsh; 17 Martin Elswood.
Tries: Farrell (44), L Marsh (56, 78), Watson (65);
Goals: Rich 6/6.
Dismissal: McLoughlin (27) - swinging arm.
Rugby Leaguer & League Express Men of the Match: *Dragons:* Marlon Billy; *Oldham:* Lee Marsh.
Penalty count: 7-14; **Half-time:** 12-4; **Referee:** Steve Nicholson (Whitehaven); **Attendance:** 835.

Leigh's Tommy Martyn gets to grips with Hull KR's Paul Fletcher during the National League Cup Final

YORK CITY KNIGHTS 27 FEATHERSTONE ROVERS 18

CITY KNIGHTS: 1 Nathan Graham; 2 Scott Walker; 3 Chris Langley; 4 Aaron Wood; 5 Mark Stewart; 6 Scott Rhodes; 7 Danny Brough; 8 Richard Wilson; 9 Lee Jackson; 10 Yusuf Sozi; 11 Darren Callaghan; 12 Simon Friend; 13 Damian Ball. Subs (all used): 14 Jimmy Elston; 15 Mark Cain; 16 John Smith; 17 Craig Forsyth.
Tries: Graham (2), Langley (26), Elston (56), Ball (64);
Goals: Brough 5/6; **Field goal:** Rhodes.
ROVERS: 1 Craig Moss; 2 Jamie Stokes; 3 Steve Dooler; 4 Nathan Batty; 5 Matthew Wray; 6 Richard Blakeway; 7 Jon Presley; 8 Ian Tonks; 9 Paul Darley; 10 Stuart Dickens; 11 Bryan Henare; 12 Neil Lowe; 13 Adam Hayes. Subs (all used): 14 Ben Archibald; 15 Carl Briggs; 16 Andy Jarrett; 17 Richard Chapman.
Tries: Blakeway (6), Dooler (13); **Goals:** Dickens 5/5.
Rugby Leaguer & League Express Men of the Match: *City Knights:* Damian Ball; *Rovers:* Stuart Dickens.
Penalty count: 10-9; **Half-time:** 12-18; **Referee:** Richard Silverwood (Dewsbury); **Attendance:** 1,202.

QUARTER FINALS

Sunday 6th June 2004

BARROW RAIDERS 20 LEIGH CENTURIONS 24

RAIDERS: 1 Craig Bower; 2 Shane Irabor; 3 Damien Reid; 4 Paul Jones; 5 Adam Pate; 6 Chris Archer; 7 Darren Holt; 8 Stuart Dancer; 9 Dave Clark; 10 Paul Lupton; 11 Mike Whitehead; 12 James King; 13 Barry Pugh. Subs (all used): 14 Tama Wakelin; 15 Matthew Leigh; 16 Phil Atkinson; 17 Paul Wilcock.
Tries: Pate (15, 39), King (17), Wakelin (61);
Goals: Holt 2/7.
CENTURIONS: 1 Steve Maden; 2 Damian Munro; 3 Dan Potter; 4 Ben Cooper; 5 Rob Smyth; 6 Neil Turley; 7 Tommy Martyn; 8 Matt Sturm; 9 Paul Rowley; 10 Heath Cruckshank; 11 David Larder; 12 Andrew Isherwood; 13 Ian Knott. Subs (all used): 14 Simon Knox; 15 Paul Norman; 16 Danny Halliwell; 17 Oliver Wilkes.
Tries: Knox (6, 19), Martyn (31), Munro (57);
Goals: Turley 4/6.
Sin bin: Isherwood (26) - holding down;
Knott (50) - holding down.
Rugby Leaguer & League Express Men of the Match: *Raiders:* Adam Pate; *Centurions:* Neil Turley.
Penalty count: 17-14; **Half-time:** 16-18; **Referee:** Steve Nicholson (Whitehaven); **Attendance:** 1,245.

BATLEY BULLDOGS 16 WHITEHAVEN 22

BULLDOGS: 1 Mark Sibson; 2 Bryn Powell; 3 Chris Spurr; 4 Shad Royston; 5 Matt Bramald; 6 Mark Toohey; 7 Barry Eaton; 8 Steve Hill; 9 Andy Heptinstall; 10 David Rourke; 11 Tim Spears; 12 Andy Spink; 13 Ryan Horsley. Subs (all used): 14 Chris Molyneux; 15 Paul Harrison; 16 Sean Richardson; 17 Adrian Leek.
Tries: Harrison (34), Royston (50), Bramald (54);
Goals: Eaton 2/4.
WHITEHAVEN: 1 Gary Broadbent; 2 Jamie Marshall; 3 David Seeds; 4 Mick Nanyn; 5 Paul O'Neil; 6 Leroy Joe; 7 Sam Obst; 8 Dean Vaughan; 9 Aaron Lester; 10 David Fatialofa; 11 Brett McDermott; 12 Howard Hill; 13 Craig Walsh. Subs (all used): 14 Graeme Morton; 15 Carl Sice; 16 Marc Jackson; 17 Chris McKinney.
Tries: Walsh (4), O'Neil (8), Seeds (18, 38);
Goals: Nanyn 3/5.
Rugby Leaguer & League Express Men of the Match: *Bulldogs:* David Rourke; *Whitehaven:* Gary Broadbent.
Penalty count: 11-2; **Half-time:** 4-20;
Referee: Ben Thaler (Wakefield); **Attendance:** 910.

DONCASTER DRAGONS 28 HULL KINGSTON ROVERS 50

DRAGONS: 1 Johnny Woodcock; 2 Dean Colton; 3 Gareth Lloyd; 4 Craig Horne; 5 Marlon Billy; 6 Graham Holroyd; 7 Danny Grimshaw; 8 Martin Ostler; 9 Craig Cook; 10 Andy Fisher; 11 Craig Lawton; 12 Peter Green; 13 Shaun Leaf. Subs (all used): 14 Tom Buckenham; 15 James Walker; 16 Carl Sayer; 17 Alex Muff.
Tries: Lawton (5, 40), Muff (28), Billy (46), Fisher (69);
Goals: Holroyd 3/6, Woodcock 1/1.
Sin bin: Holroyd (59) – kicking the ball away.
ROVERS: 1 Lynton Stott; 2 Nick Pinkney; 3 Marvin Golden; 4 Craig Poucher; 5 Craig Farrell; 6 Paul Mansson; 7 Scott Thorburn; 8 Jamie Bovill; 9 Andy Ellis; 10 Makali Aizue; 11 Anthony Seibold; 12 Tommy Gallagher; 13 Andy Smith. Subs (all used): 14 Phil Hasty; 15 Dean Andrews; 16 Frank Watene; 17 Paul Fletcher.
Tries: Bovill (8), Pinkney (17, 55), Poucher (23, 75), Stott (59), Ellis (63, 72), Seibold (78);
Goals: Stott 2/4, Thorburn 5/5.
Rugby Leaguer & League Express Men of the Match: *Dragons:* Craig Lawton; *Rovers:* Anthony Seibold.
Penalty count: 5-5; **Half-time:** 18-14; **Referee:** Colin Morris (Huddersfield); **Attendance:** 1,181.

HALIFAX 14 YORK CITY KNIGHTS 37

HALIFAX: 1 Scott Grix; 2 Rikki Sheriffe; 3 Jon Roper; 4 Simon Grix; 5 James Haley; 6 Pat Weisner; 7 Danny Jones; 8 Anthony Farrell; 9 Phil Cantillon; 10 Chris Birchall; 11 Paul Davidson; 12 Matt Whitaker; 13 Jamie Bloem. Subs (all used): 14 Mark Moxon; 15 Ged Corcoran; 16 David Bates; 17 Ryan McDonald.
Tries: Haley (15), Scott Grix (65); **Goals:** Bloem 3/3.
Sin bin: Simon Grix (8) - interference.
CITY KNIGHTS: 1 Nathan Graham; 2 Austin Buchanan; 3 Chris Langley; 4 Aaron Wood; 5 Scott Walker; 6 Scott Rhodes; 7 Danny Brough; 8 Richard Wilson; 9 Lee Jackson; 10 John Smith; 11 Darren Callaghan; 12 Simon Friend; 13 Damian Ball. Subs (all used): 14 Jimmy Elston; 15 Mark Cain; 16 Dan Briggs; 17 Yusuf Sozi.
Tries: Wood (8), Ball (30), Friend (40), Langley (74, 77);
Goals: Brough 8/9; **Field goal:** Brough.
Rugby Leaguer & League Express Men of the Match: *Halifax:* Phil Cantillon; *City Knights:* Damian Ball.
Penalty count: 5-13; **Half-time:** 8-21;
Referee: Peter Taberner (Wigan); **Attendance:** 1,840.

SEMI FINALS

Sunday 27th June 2004

HULL KINGSTON ROVERS 32 YORK CITY KNIGHTS 0

ROVERS: 1 Craig Poucher; 2 Nick Pinkney; 3 Paul Parker; 4 Marvin Golden; 5 Lynton Stott; 6 Paul Mansson; 7 Phil Hasty; 8 Makali Aizue; 9 Paul Pickering; 10 Jon Aston; 11 Dale Holdstock; 12 Anthony Seibold; 13 Tommy Gallagher. Subs (all used): 14 Scott Thorburn; 15 Dean Andrews; 16 Frank Watene; 17 Paul Fletcher.
Tries: Holdstock (2), Watene (24), Thorburn (49), Pinkney (59), Mansson (65); **Goals:** Stott 6/7.
CITY KNIGHTS: 1 Nathan Graham; 2 Austin Buchanan; 3 Chris Langley; 4 Aaron Wood; 5 Scott Walker; 6 Scott Rhodes; 7 Danny Brough; 8 Craig Forsyth; 9 Lee Jackson; 10 Yusuf Sozi; 11 Darren Callaghan; 12 John Smith; 13 Simon Friend. Subs: 14 Mark Stewart; 15 Mark Cain; 16 Rob Kama; 17 Tom Andrews (not used).
Rugby Leaguer & League Express Men of the Match: *Rovers:* Phil Hasty; *City Knights:* Danny Brough.
Penalty count: 9-12; **Half-time:** 14-0; **Referee:** Colin Morris (Huddersfield); **Attendance:** 2,629.

WHITEHAVEN 30 LEIGH CENTURIONS 34

WHITEHAVEN: 1 Gary Broadbent; 2 Jamie Marshall; 3 Wesley Wilson; 4 Mick Nanyn; 5 Paul O'Neil; 6 Leroy Joe; 7 Sam Obst; 8 Dean Vaughan; 9 Aaron Lester; 10 David Fatialofa; 11 Brett McDermott; 12 Howard Hill; 13 Craig Walsh. Subs (all used): 14 Chris McKinney; 15 Carl Sice; 16 Graeme Morton; 17 Marc Jackson.
Tries: Marshall (32, 47), Wilson (35), Obst (57);
Goals: Nanyn 7/8.
CENTURIONS: 1 Neil Turley; 2 Steve Maden; 3 Danny Halliwell; 4 Ben Cooper; 5 Damian Munro; 6 John Duffy; 7 Tommy Martyn; 8 Simon Knox; 9 Paul Rowley; 10 Matt Sturm; 11 David Larder; 12 Dan Potter; 13 Ian Knott. Subs (all used): 14 Willie Swann; 15 Heath Cruckshank; 16 Richard Marshall; 17 Oliver Wilkes.
Tries: Larder (11), Turley (17, 26), Halliwell (40), Munro (50), Martyn (77); **Goals:** Turley 5/8.
Rugby Leaguer & League Express Men of the Match: *Whitehaven:* Sam Obst; *Centurions:* Neil Turley.
Penalty count: 15-12; **Half-time:** 14-24;
Referee: Ashley Klein (London); **Attendance:** 2,449.

FINAL

Sunday 18th July 2004

HULL KINGSTON ROVERS 14 LEIGH CENTURIONS 42

ROVERS: 1 Craig Poucher; 2 Nick Pinkney; 3 Paul Parker; 4 Marvin Golden; 5 Lynton Stott; 6 Paul Mansson; 7 Phil Hasty; 8 Makali Aizue; 9 Scott Thorburn; 10 Jon Aston; 11 Dale Holdstock; 12 Andy Smith; 13 Tommy Gallagher. Subs (all used): 14 Matt Calland; 15 Anthony Seibold; 16 Frank Watene; 17 Paul Fletcher.
Tries: Poucher (28), Thorburn (45); **Goals:** Stott 3/3.
CENTURIONS: 1 Neil Turley; 2 Dan Potter; 3 Danny Halliwell; 4 Ben Cooper; 5 Rob Smyth; 6 John Duffy; 7 Tommy Martyn; 8 Simon Knox; 9 Paul Rowley; 10 Matt Sturm; 11 David Larder; 12 Oliver Wilkes; 13 Ian Knott. Subs (all used): 14 Dave McConnell; 15 Willie Swann; 16 Richard Marshall; 17 Heath Cruckshank.
Tries: Halliwell (2, 19), Knox (10, 75), Cooper (37), Turley (51), Martyn (71); **Goals:** Turley 6/9;
Field goals: Martyn, Turley.
Rugby Leaguer & League Express Men of the Match: *Rovers:* Phil Hasty; *Centurions:* Tommy Martyn.
Penalty count: 4-5; **Half-time:** 8-26;
Referee: Colin Morris (Huddersfield);
Attendance: 4,383 *(at Spotland, Rochdale).*

CHALLENGE CUP 2004
Round by Round

ROUND 3

Friday 6th February 2004

CHORLEY LYNX 54 LOCOMOTIV MOSCOW 6

LYNX: 1 Lee Patterson; 2 Daryl Lacey; 3 Brian Capewell; 4 Eddie Kilgannon; 5 Gary O'Regan; 6 Rob Smyth; 7 Martin Gambles; 8 John Hill; 9 Anthony Murray; 10 Ian Parry; 11 Gary Smith; 12 Gareth Jones; 13 Chris Newall. Subs (all used): 14 Neil Alexander; 15 Mick Redford; 16 Simon Smith; 17 Martin Roden.
Tries: Gambles (18, 66), Newall (25, 63, 71), Capewell (40), Patterson (56), O'Regan (58, 75), Redford (76); **Goals:** Capewell 7.
LOCOMOTIV: 1 Oleg Logovnuv; 2 Vitolai Zagoski; 3 Vladimir Ovichinnikov; 4 Andrei Postnikov; 5 Valentin Baskakov; 6 Igor Gavrilin; 7 Denis Nikolskiy; 10 Taylor Polunise; 9 Roman Ovichinnikov; 20 Dana Wilson; 11 Robert Iliassov; 12 Alexander Bojoukov; 13 Eugueni Bojoukov. Subs (all used): 8 Andrei Koltykhov; 17 Irakli Chkhokvasze; 15 Rougian Izmailov; 14 Andrei Tcherevichnyi.
Try: R Ovichinnikov (10); **Goal:** Nikolskiy.
Rugby Leaguer & League Express Men of the Match: *Lynx:* Chris Newall; *Locomotiv:* Roman Ovichinnikov.
Penalty count: 7-7; **Half-time:** 18-6;
Referee: Steve Ganson (St Helens); **Attendance:** 521.

OLDHAM 16 CASTLEFORD PANTHERS 8

OLDHAM: 1 Gavin Dodd; 2 Will Cowell; 3 Iain Marsh; 4 Jon Goddard; 5 Nick Johnson; 6 Gareth Barber; 7 Ian Watson; 8 Paul Southern; 9 John Hough; 10 Martin McLoughlin; 11 Lee Doran; 12 Dane Morgan; 13 Lee Marsh. Subs (all used): 14 Keith Brennan; 15 James Bunyan; 16 Adam Sharples; 17 Craig Farrimond.
Tries: N Johnson (8), I Marsh (34), Cowell (58); **Goals:** Barber 2.
PANTHERS: 1 Chris Hepworth; 2 Simon Wassell; 3 Arron Gornall; 4 Neil Pycroft; 5 Keiron Hickman; 6 Jamie Benn; 7 Kevin Till; 8 Craig Potter; 9 Luke Varley; 10 Danny Pickering; 11 Paul Steel; 12 Andrew Smith; 13 Craig Pearson. Subs (all used): 14 Paul Walshaw; 15 Richard Leese; 16 Wayne Garwood; 17 Gary Wilders.
Try: Hickman (14); **Goals:** Benn 2.
Rugby Leaguer & League Express Men of the Match: *Oldham:* Gavin Dodd; *Panthers:* Kevin Till.
Penalty count: 9-9; **Half-time:** 10-8;
Referee: Steve Kilgallon (Leeds); **Attendance:** 1,003.

SHARLSTON ROVERS 30 DEWSBURY RAMS 28

ROVERS: 1 Shaun Taylor; 2 Lee Lingard; 3 Gareth Davis; 4 Keith Brook; 5 Dale Ferris; 6 Martyn Wood; 7 Danny Grimshaw; 8 Andy Booth; 9 Lee Bettinson; 10 Lee Kelly; 11 Chance Leake; 12 James Ward; 13 Stan Smith. Subs (all used): 14 Gordon Long; 15 Dale Potter; 16 Neil Shoesmith; 17 Carl Sayer.
Tries: Ferris (2), Smith (30), Grimshaw (32), Leake (37), Shoesmith (58); **Goals:** Lingard 5.
RAMS: 1 Chris Hall; 2 Craig Miles; 3 Wayne McHugh; 4 Ian Kirke; 5 Jon Waddle; 6 Mick Senior; 7 Adam Thaler; 8 Paul Hicks; 9 Darren Robinson; 10 Andy Fisher; 11 Kevin Crouthers; 12 Billy Kershaw; 13 Tim Spears. Subs (all used): 14 Chris Redfearn; 15 Anthony Thewliss; 16 Paul Smith; 17 Ryan Hardy.
Tries: Waddle (20), Miles (22), McHugh (51), Kershaw (63), A Thaler (78); **Goals:** A Thaler 4.
Rugby Leaguer & League Express Men of the Match: *Rovers:* Martyn Wood; *Rams:* Billy Kershaw.
Penalty count: 9-6; **Half-time:** 20-12;
Referee: Robert Connolly (Wigan);
Attendance: 2,027 *(at Lionheart Stadium, Featherstone).*

LEIGH MINERS RANGERS 12 SHEFFIELD EAGLES 14

MINERS RANGERS: 1 Darren Pilkington; 2 Neil Donlan; 3 Steve Warburton; 4 Chris Humphries; 5 Shaun Daley; 6 Alan Reddicliffe; 7 Shaun Phoenix; 8 Dave Powlesland; 9 Liam McCarthy; 10 Andy Forbar; 11 Dave Patterson; 12 Dave Radley; 13 Tommy Goulden. Subs (all used): 14 Craig Graham; 15 Mark Wallington; 16 Lee Lomax; 17 Steve Tooze.
Tries: Humphries (29), Reddicliffe (48); **Goals:** Radley 2.
EAGLES: 1 Andy Poynter; 2 Danny Mills; 3 Nick Turnbull; 4 Jon Breakingbury; 5 Greg Hurst; 6 Peter Reilly; 7 Gavin Brown; 8 Jack Howieson; 9 Gareth Stanley; 10 Jon Bruce; 11 Jordan James; 12 Craig Brown; 13 Simon Tillyer. Subs (all used): 14 Richard Goddard; 15 Simon Morton; 16 Wayne Flynn; 17 Rob North.
Tries: Morton (27), G Brown (70); **Goals:** G Brown 3.
Rugby Leaguer & League Express Men of the Match: *Miners Rangers:* Tommy Goulden; *Eagles:* Gavin Brown.
Penalty count: 7-7; **Half-time:** 6-6; **Referee:** Ben Thaler (Wakefield); **Attendance:** 591 *(at The Coliseum, Leigh).*

Saturday 7th February 2004

LONDON SKOLARS 22 ROCHDALE MAYFIELD 16

SKOLARS: 1 Tim Butterfield; 2 Neil Foster; 3 Ronnie Mushiso; 4 Donny Lam; 5 Ade Aderiye; 6 Jermaine Coleman; 7 Peter Hannan; 8 Koben Katipa; 9 Gareth Honor; 10 Alex Smits; 11 Glenn Osborn; 12 Keir Bell; 13 John Rua. Subs (all used): 14 Wayne Parillon; 15 Roger Teau; 16 Dan Reeds; 17 Ben Joyce.
Tries: Honor (3), Aderiye (8, 36); **Goals:** G Osborn 5.
MAYFIELD: 1 Steve Wood; 2 Austin Aggrey; 3 Chris Hilton; 4 Carl Platt; 5 Trevor Balzan; 6 Steve Gartland; 7 Ben Butterworth; 8 Andy Procter; 9 Neil Ramsden; 10 Tony Hilton; 11 Dave Chrimes; 12 Ben Simpson; 13 Chris Thair. Subs (all used): 14 Danny Mortin; 15 Leon Ashworth; 16 Shane Molloy; 17 Dave Harmer.
Tries: Simpson (14), Harmer (51), Procter (70); **Goals:** Gartland 2.
Rugby Leaguer & League Express Men of the Match: *Skolars:* Peter Hannan; *Mayfield:* Dave Chrimes.
Penalty count: 7-7; **Half-time:** 20-4;
Referee: Robert Hicks (Oldham); **Attendance:** 275.

HUNSLET HAWKS 32 FEATHERSTONE LIONS 0

HAWKS: 1 Jon Liddell; 2 Martin Sykes; 3 Paul Seal; 4 Wes McGibbon; 5 Paul Gleadhill; 6 Danny Wood; 7 Chris Ross; 8 Craig Booth; 9 Jamaine Wray; 10 Mick Coyle; 11 Wayne Freeman; 12 Jonlee Lockwood; 13 Andy Bastow. Subs (all used): 14 Steve Pryce; 15 Glen Freeman; 16 Gary Shillabeer; 17 Dave Jessey.
Tries: Lockwood (4), W Freeman (25, 61), Sykes (31), Bastow (39), Booth (58); **Goals:** Wood 2, Booth 2.
Sin bin: Booth (66) - fighting.
LIONS: 1 Craig Duda; 2 Peter Dawson; 3 Danny Tomkinson; 4 Anthony Slatter; 5 Scott Limb; 6 Jon Agar; 7 Chris Morgan; 8 Jason Wood; 9 Simon Child; 10 Mark Webster; 11 Andy Morgan; 12 Simon Thompson; 13 Kevin Spink. Subs (all used): 14 Shaun Walton; 15 Dave Raybould; 16 Wayne Simpson; 17 Stuart Early.
Sin bin: A Morgan (30) - interference at play the ball; Child (66) - fighting.
Rugby Leaguer & League Express Men of the Match: *Hawks:* Jamaine Wray; *Lions:* Jon Agar.
Penalty count: 16-2; **Half-time:** 20-0;
Referee: Andrew Leonard (Leeds); **Attendance:** 433.

Sunday 8th February 2004

INCE ROSEBRIDGE 8 BATLEY BULLDOGS 42

ROSEBRIDGE: 1 Lee Bamber; 2 Dean Kenny; 3 Lee Jones; 4 Ian Rostron; 5 Kevin Moran; 6 Stuart Cassidy; 7 Owen Lloyd; 8 Andy Eatock; 9 Lee Cassidy; 10 David Ashton; 11 Kevin Shepherd; 12 Chad Derbyshire; 13 Lee Jukes. Subs (all used): 14 Alan Wood; 15 Dean Farrimond; 16 Carl Roden; 17 Wesley Else.
Try: Jukes (23); **Goals:** Jukes 2.
BULLDOGS: 1 Craig Lingard; 2 Mark Sibson; 3 Chris Spurr; 4 Danny Maun; 5 Adrian Flynn; 6 Mark Toohey; 7 Barry Eaton; 8 Chris Molyneux; 9 Mark Cass; 10 David Rourke; 11 Paul Harrison; 12 Andy Rice; 13 Ryan Horsley. Subs (all used): 14 Shad Royston; 15 Matt Bramald; 16 Steve Hill; 17 Sean Richardson.
Tries: Maun (5, 40, 77), Cass (9), Harrison (17), Richardson (38), Lingard (58), Molyneux (67); **Goals:** Eaton 5.
Rugby Leaguer & League Express Men of the Match: *Rosebridge:* Lee Jukes; *Bulldogs:* Sean Richardson.
Penalty count: 5-8; **Half-time:** 8-26;
Referee: Matthew Thomasson (Warrington);
Attendance: 750 *(at Robin Park Arena, Wigan).*

BARROW RAIDERS 20 PIA DONKEYS 22

RAIDERS: 1 Jamie Smith; 2 Adam Pate; 3 Paul Jones; 4 Andy McClure; 5 Nick Beech; 6 Phil Atkinson; 7 Darren Holt; 8 Stuart Dancer; 9 Chris Archer; 10 Paul Wilcock; 11 Matthew Leigh; 12 Mike Whitehead; 13 Barry Pugh. Subs (all used): 14 Dave Clark; 15 Geoff Luxon; 16 Paul Lupton; 17 Lee Dutton.
Tries: Lupton (45), Wilcock (74), Beech (79); **Goals:** Holt 4.
DONKEYS: 1 Craig West; 2 Nicolas Athiel; 3 Florian Chaubet; 4 Lawrence Raleigh; 5 Sebastien Terrado; 6 Craig Field; 7 Maxime Greseque; 8 Franck Rovira; 9 Jim Serdaris; 10 Taboanitoga Cakacaka; 11 Emmanuel Bansept; 12 Mathieu Ambert; 13 Yannick Brousse. Subs (all used): 14 Karl Jaavuo; 15 David Romero; 16 Franck Traversa; 17 Michael Cousseau.
Tries: Athiel (27), Greseque (32), Field (70); **Goals:** Terrado 5.
Sin bin: Traversa (60) - holding down.
Rugby Leaguer & League Express Men of the Match: *Raiders:* Barry Pugh; *Donkeys:* Maxime Greseque.
Penalty count: 13-17; **Half-time:** 4-16;
Referee: Russell Smith (Castleford); **Attendance:** 921.

CROSFIELDS 14 WORKINGTON TOWN 46

CROSFIELDS: 1 Ian Hannon; 2 Ray Waring; 3 Matt Maloney; 4 Pete Royle; 5 Fraser Linaker; 6 Mike Redmond; 7 Dave Gibbons; 8 Terry Reid; 9 Richard Hough; 10 Andy Pucill; 11 Wade Rasmussen; 12 Chris Blackwell; 13 John Bannon. Subs (all used): 14 Eddie Bannon; 15 Dave Lucas; 16 Barry Lowe; 17 Dave Mather.
Tries: Pucill (19), Hough (57), Royle (65); **Goal:** Royle.
Dismissal: Hannon (49) - swinging arm.
Sin bin: Hannon (29) - ripping the ball out; Pucill (39) - interference.
TOWN: 1 Craig Stalker; 2 Martyn Wilson; 3 Jonathan Heaney; 4 Adam Coulson; 5 Andrew Fearon; 6 Kevin Hetherington; 7 Gareth Skillen; 8 Jamie Beaumont; 9 Darren King; 10 Matthew Tunstall; 11 Jonny Limmer; 12 Ricky Wright; 13 Brett Smith. Subs (all used): 14 Martin Stalker; 15 David Pettit; 16 Andy McGlasson; 17 Graeme Lewthwaite.
Tries: Coulson (8), B Smith (16, 52), Hetherington (32), Limmer (40, 42, 71, 80), Heaney (62); **Goals:** Hetherington 5.
Sin bin: Hetherington (57) - interference.
Rugby Leaguer & League Express Men of the Match: *Crosfields:* Andy Pucill; *Town:* Jonny Limmer.
Penalty count: 7-7; **Half-time:** 6-22;
Referee: Craig Halloran (Dewsbury);
Attendance: 768 *(at Wilderspool, Warrington).*

BRADFORD-DUDLEY HILL 16 KEIGHLEY COUGARS 14

DUDLEY HILL: 1 Craig Tyman; 2 Sheara Singh; 3 Lewis Evans; 4 Alex Dickinson; 5 Jamie Brentley; 6 Ryan Dickinson; 7 Chris Robinson; 8 Richard Bingley; 9 Liam Brentley; 10 Chris Walsh; 11 Victor Tordoff; 12 Anthony Huby; 13 Sean Dickinson. Subs (all used): 14 Marco Rossi; 15 Sam Broadley; 16 Jason Hoyland; 17 Jack Bradbury.
Tries: Huby (37), Rossi (76); **Goals:** Robinson 4.
COUGARS: 1 Matt Foster; 2 Karl Smith; 3 David Foster; 4 Chris Wainwright; 5 Andy Robinson; 6 Craig Nipperess; 7 Matt Firth; 8 Phil Stephenson; 9 Simeon Hoyle; 10 Danny Ekis; 11 Richard Mervill; 12 Chris Parker; 13 Lee Patterson. Subs (all used): 14 Adam Mitchell; 15 Max Tomlinson; 16 Jason Clegg; 17 Chris Roe.
Tries: Smith (63, 79), Firth (67); **Goal:** Mitchell.
Rugby Leaguer & League Express Men of the Match: *Dudley Hill:* Liam Brentley; *Cougars:* Matt Foster.
Penalty count: 7-7; **Half-time:** 8-0;
Referee: Mike Dawber (Wigan);
Attendance: 1,300 *(at Cougar Park, Keighley).*

DONCASTER DRAGONS 28 WEST HULL 6

DRAGONS: 1 Johnny Woodcock; 2 Jason Lee; 3 Craig Lawton; 4 Alex Muff; 5 Marlon Billy; 6 Graham Holroyd; 7 Dean Colton; 8 Gareth Handford; 9 Craig Cook; 10 Jamie Fielden; 11 Peter Green; 12 Gareth Lloyd; 13 Shaun Leaf. Subs (all used): 14 Chris Hemmings; 15 Matt Walker; 16 Tony Atter; 17 Chris Hough.
Tries: Muff (10), Woodcock (52), Lee (56, 61), Billy (70); **Goals:** Holroyd 4.
Sin bin: Fielden (3) - fighting; Handford (28) - fighting.
WEST HULL: 1 Loz Wildbore; 2 Lee Morton; 3 Brian Newby; 4 Mike Martinez; 5 Chris Lee; 6 Wayne Harris; 7 Terry Lynn; 8 Dave Wilkinson; 9 Danny Marquez-Laynez; 10 Gavin Last; 11 Scott Fletcher; 12 Paul Hatton; 13 Peter Stephenson. Subs (all used): 14 Johan Windley; 15 John Okul; 16 Rob Wilson; 17 Faz Balouchi.
Goals: Harris 3.
Sin bin: Lynn (3) - fighting; Morton (28) - fighting.
Rugby Leaguer & League Express Men of the Match: *Dragons:* Craig Cook; *West Hull:* Wayne Harris.
Penalty count: 11-6; **Half-time:** 4-6;
Referee: Peter Taberner (Wigan); **Attendance:** 839.

ELLAND 4 LEIGH CENTURIONS 64

ELLAND: 1 Jonathan Moore; 2 Oliver Fairbank; 3 Neil Foulds; 4 Dean Bishop; 5 Christopher Bradford; 6 Neil Walton; 7 Philip Taylor; 8 Marc Shickell; 9 Simon Bowker; 10 Andrew Shickell; 11 Jonathan Simpson; 12 Ian Simpson; 13 Lee Shackleton. Subs (all used): 14 James Fairbank; 15 Mark Bailey; 16 Stephen Wood; 17 Stephen Brocklehurst.
Try: Fairbank (27).
CENTURIONS: 1 Mark McCully; 2 Steve Maden; 3 Dan Potter; 4 Chris Percival; 5 Dale Cardoza; 6 Neil Turley; 7 Tommy Martyn; 8 Richard Marshall; 9 Dave McConnell; 10 David Bradbury; 11 David Larder; 12 Oliver Wilkes; 13 Ian Knott. Subs (all used): 14 Paul Rowley; 15 Andrew Isherwood; 16 Simon Knox; 17 Heath Cruckshank.
Tries: Percival (4, 75), Turley (12), Cardoza (31), Martyn (38), McCully (44, 70), Potter (48), Rowley (51, 59), Isherwood (57, 63); **Goals:** Turley 8.
Rugby Leaguer & League Express Men of the Match: *Elland:* Neil Foulds; *Centurions:* Neil Turley.
Penalty count: 12-6; **Half-time:** 4-22;
Referee: Gareth Hewer (Whitehaven);
Attendance: 1,365 *(at The Coliseum, Leigh).*

FEATHERSTONE ROVERS 96 CASTLEFORD LOCK LANE 0

ROVERS: 1 Nathan Batty; 2 Jamie Stokes; 3 James Ford; 4 Richard Newlove; 5 Matthew Wray; 6 Jon Presley; 7 Carl Briggs; 8 Bryan Henare; 9 Paul Darley; 10 Jim Carlton; 11 Steve Dooler; 12 Richard Blakeway; 13 Adam Hayes. Subs (all used): 14 Jamie Coventry; 15 Richard Chapman; 16 Andy Jarrett; 17 Ian Tonks.
Tries: Ford (1, 37), Presley (3, 62), Stokes (7, 57, 73), Dooler (10, 79), Blakeway (12), Hayes (16), Newlove (28, 39, 50, 67), Briggs (59), Wray (71, 76); **Goals:** Briggs 11, Blakeway.
LOCK LANE: 1 Martin Hunt; 2 John Astbury; 3 Matt Bateman; 4 Carl Saville; 5 Mick Beadle; 6 Mark Spears; 7 Dave Probert; 8 Dave Birdsall; 9 Dave Wolford; 10 Wayne Hardy; 11 Kalam Senior; 12 Tony Handford; 13 Steve Hall. Subs (all used): 14 Paul Couch; 15 Lee Loftus; 16 Darren Simms; 17 Jamie Price.
Rugby Leaguer & League Express Men of the Match: *Rovers:* Carl Briggs; *Lock Lane:* Martin Hunt.
Penalty count: 7-4; **Half-time:** 40-0; **Referee:** Richard Silverwood (Dewsbury); **Attendance:** 1,576.

GATESHEAD THUNDER 22 LIMOUX 26

THUNDER: 1 Graham Stephenson; 2 Kevin Neighbour; 3 Joe Bagshaw; 4 Craig Firth; 5 Robin Peers; 6 Paul Thorman; 7 Craig Fisher; 8 Rob Line; 9 Seamus McCallion; 10 Steven Bradley; 11 Carl Stannard; 12 Tony Doherty; 13 Steve Rutherford. Subs (all used): 14 Andy Walker; 15 Neil Thorman; 16 Ian Ball; 17 Jaymes Bulman.
Tries: Neighbour (4), Firth (52), Peers (62), Line (66); **Goals:** P Thorman 3.
LIMOUX: 1 Fabrice Estebanez; 2 Sylvain Teixido; 3 Freddie Zitter; 4 Boycie Nelson; 5 Sebastien Almarcha; 6 Nicolas Piccolo; 7 Mickael Murcia; 8 Walter Mackie; 9 Jerome Laffont; 10 Frederic Teixido; 11 Phillipe Laurent; 12 Tyrone Pau; 13 John Vaigafa. Subs (all used): 14 David Gagliazzo; 15 Christophe Grandjean; 16 Benoit Burgat; 17 Guillaume Mestre.
Tries: Piccolo (13, 17), Grandjean (34), Estebanez (40), Nelson (70); **Goals:** Mackie 3.
Rugby Leaguer & League Express Men of the Match: *Thunder:* Graham Stephenson; *Limoux:* John Vaigafa.

Penalty count: 10-4; **Half-time:** 6-22;
Referee: Colin Morris (Huddersfield); **Attendance:** 254.

HALIFAX 66 OULTON RAIDERS 10

HALIFAX: 1 Danny Arnold; 2 Richard Smith; 3 Jon Roper; 4 Alan Hadcroft; 5 Oliver Marns; 6 Simon Grix; 7 Mark Moxon; 8 Jaymes Chapman; 9 Phil Cantillon; 10 David Bates; 11 Jamie Bloem; 12 Chris Morley; 13 Pat Weisner. Subs (all used): 14 Chris Norman; 15 Wayne Corcoran; 16 Scott Law; 17 Anthony Farrell.
Tries: Smith (12, 43), Chapman (16), Roper (19), Moxon (31), Marns (32, 66), Hadcroft (46), Cantillon (50, 60), Norman (64), Farrell (78); **Goals:** Bloem 7, Roper 2.
RAIDERS: 1 Tommy Skerrett; 2 Steve McGreavy; 3 Dave White; 4 Neil Horton; 5 Geoff Hick; 6 Gavin Wood; 7 Alan White; 8 Rob Ward; 9 Matt White; 10 Neil Bradbrook; 11 Chris Brown; 12 Mark Taylor; 13 Carlos Sanchez. Subs (all used): 14 Sasch Brook; 15 Scott Collins; 16 Dave Wilkin; 17 Neil Shepherd.
Tries: Sanchez (40), Skerrett (69); **Goal:** Skerrett.
Rugby Leaguer & League Express Men of the Match:
Halifax: Phil Cantillon; *Raiders:* Tommy Skerrett.
Penalty count: 10-6; **Half-time:** 28-6;
Referee: Jamie Leahy (Dewsbury); **Attendance:** 1,675.

HULL KINGSTON ROVERS 22
UNION TREIZISTE CATALANE 23

ROVERS: 1 Lynton Stott; 2 Craig Farrell; 3 Craig Poucher; 4 Matt Calland; 5 Alasdair McClarron; 6 Paul Mansson; 7 Phil Hasty; 8 Jamie Bovill; 9 Jimmy Walker; 10 Jon Aston; 11 Dale Holdstock; 12 Andy Smith; 13 Anthony Seibold. Subs (all used): 14 Casey Mayberry; 15 Richard Wilson; 16 Frank Watene; 17 Paul Fletcher.
Tries: Bovill (21), Seibold (45), McClarron (57), Hasty (78); **Goals:** Stott 3.
UTC: 1 Craig Horne; 2 Patrice Gomez; 3 Said Tamghart; 4 Phil Howlett; 5 Bruno Verges; 6 Laurent Frayssinous; 7 Julien Rinaldi; 8 Adel Fellous; 9 David Berthezene; 10 Romain Gagliazzo; 11 Pascal Jampy; 12 Russell Bawden; 13 Djamel Fakir. Subs (all used): 14 Sebastien Argence; 15 Lionel Teixido; 16 Matthew Hill; 17 Sebastien Martin.
Tries: Gagliazzo (9), Rinaldi (27), Hill (61);
Goals: Frayssinous 5; **Field goal:** Rinaldi.
Rugby Leaguer & League Express Men of the Match:
Rovers: Dale Holdstock; *UTC:* Julien Rinaldi.
Penalty count: 6-12; **Half-time:** 4-14;
Referee: Ian Smith (Oldham); **Attendance:** 2,066.

ROCHDALE HORNETS 60 DINAMO MOSCOW 24

HORNETS: 1 Michael Platt; 2 Liam Williams; 3 Paul Anderson; 4 Sam Butterworth; 5 Chris Campbell; 6 John Braddish; 7 Lee Birdseye; 8 Andy Leathem; 9 Janan Billings; 10 Lee Hansen; 11 Andy Gorski; 12 Rob Ball; 13 Darren Shaw. Subs (all used): 14 Kris Ratcliffe; 15 Andy Grundy; 16 Tony Kirwan; 17 Mark Costello.
Tries: Billings (5), Gorski (8, 17, 22), Anderson (15, 72), Campbell (56, 60, 70), Birdseye (65), Butterworth (74);
Goals: Birdseye 8.
DINAMO: 1 Kurt Pittman; 2 Stanislav Zhiznyakov; 3 Vadim Fedchuk; 4 Rafael Yakubov; 5 Alexey Ruban; 6 Henry Turua; 7 Danila Mishukov; 8 Andrey Mamochka; 9 Mikhail Makarov; 10 Ian Vozdev; 11 Georgei Vinogradov; 12 Kirill Koulemine; 13 Siali Tufeao. Subs (all used): 14 Vladimir Lebedev; 15 Sergey Sidorov; 16 Andrey Darinsky; 17 Vitaly Katerinchuk.
Tries: Turua (31), Vinogradov (46, 80), Tufeao (51);
Goals: Pittman 4.
Sin bin: Sidorov (12) - holding down.
Rugby Leaguer & League Express Men of the Match:
Hornets: John Braddish; *Dinamo:* Siali Tufeao.
Penalty count: 7-7; **Half-time:** 28-6;
Referee: Ronnie Laughton (Barnsley); **Attendance:** 707.

SWINTON LIONS 14 EAST HULL 26

LIONS: 1 Wayne English; 2 Jason Roach; 3 Chris Maye; 4 Dave Llewellyn; 5 Chris Irwin; 6 Warren Ayres; 7 Paul Ashton; 8 Tau Liku; 9 Safraz Patel; 10 Wes Rogers; 11 Kris Smith; 12 Ian Sinfield; 13 Ian Hodson. Subs (all used): 14 Grant Bithel; 15 Hugh Thorpe; 16 Craig Wingfield; 17 Danny Heaton.
Tries: Irwin (6), Ashton (15), Maye (26); **Goal:** Ashton.
EAST HULL: 1 Phil Batty; 2 John McCracken; 3 Jordan Precious; 4 Gary Noble; 5 Graham Clark; 21 Mike Docherty; 7 Shaun Cooke; 8 Lee Brown; 9 Mark Moore; 10 Lee Roberts; 11 Paul Roberts; 12 Mark Woodcock; 13 Craig Bassett. Subs (all used): 14 James McCracken; 15 Ian Madley; 16 Dale Blakeley; 17 Lee Raspin.
Tries: Docherty (34), Madley (46), James McCracken (53), John McCracken (66); **Goals:** Docherty 5.
Rugby Leaguer & League Express Men of Match:
Lions: Wes Rogers; *East Hull:* Mike Docherty.
Penalty count: 7-10; **Half-time:** 14-6;
Referee: Phil Bentham (Warrington); **Attendance:** 532.

THATTO HEATH CRUSADERS 12 WHITEHAVEN 26

CRUSADERS: 1 Mike Wood; 2 Dave Hope; 3 Jamie Hill; 4 Mark Hayton; 5 Jason Delfarro; 6 Darren Harris; 7 Ian Haselden; 8 Martin Houghton; 9 Darren Mitchell; 10 Dave Smith; 11 Dave O'Donohue; 12 Dave Lloyd; 13 Tommy Hodgkinson. Subs (all used): 14 Steve Dutton; 15 John Highton; 16 Dave Gee; 17 Alan Dootson.
Tries: Mitchell (10), Wood (72); **Goals:** Wood 2.
Sin bin: Lloyd (40) - holding down.
WHITEHAVEN: 1 Gary Broadbent; 2 Mark Wallace; 3 David Seeds; 4 Mick Nanyn; 5 John Lebbon; 6 Craig Walsh; 7 Lee Kiddie; 8 Chris McKinney; 9 Carl Sice; 10 David Fatialofa; 11 Graeme Morton; 12 Howard Hill; 13 Aaron Lester. Subs (all used); 14 Steven Wood; 15 Wesley Wilson; 16 Dean Vaughan; 17 Brett McDermott.
Tries: Kiddie (5, 50), Seeds (27), Walsh (55), Lebbon (67); **Goals:** Nanyn 3.
Sin bin: Broadbent (10) - holding down.
Rugby Leaguer & League Express Men of the Match:
Crusaders: Tommy Hodgkinson; *Whitehaven:* Craig Walsh.
Penalty count: 7-7; **Half-time:** 6-14;
Referee: Paul Carr (Castleford);
Attendance: 1,114 *(at Knowsley Road, St Helens).*

YORK CITY KNIGHTS 28 VILLENEUVE LEOPARDS 8

CITY KNIGHTS: 1 Nathan Graham; 2 Rob Kama; 3 Chris Langley; 4 Mark Cain; 5 Alex Godfrey; 6 Scott Rhodes; 7 Danny Brough; 8 Richard Hayes; 9 Lee Jackson; 10 Yusuf Sozi; 11 Darren Callaghan; 12 Simon Friend; 13 Damian Ball. Subs (all used); 14 Jimmy Elston; 15 Mick Ramsden; 16 John Smith; 17 Craig Forsyth.
Tries: Rhodes (7), Forsyth (35), Elston (76), Friend (80);
Goals: Brough 6.
LEOPARDS: 1 Jason Webber; 2 Olivier Charles; 3 Andrew Bentley; 4 Jerome Hermet; 5 Regis Barre; 6 Michael Van Snick; 7 Brad Davis; 8 Philip Shead; 9 Vincent Wulf; 10 Unaloto Lamelagi; 11 Valu Bentley; 12 Pierre Sabatie; 13 Laurent Carrasco. Subs (all used): 14 Sabastien Gauffre; 15 Xavia Bemays; 16 Cyril Stacul; 17 Michael Jatz.
Try: Barre (9); **Goals:** Hermet 2.
Rugby Leaguer & League Express Men of the Match:
City Knights: Damian Ball; *Leopards:* Philip Shead.
Penalty count: 10-5; **Half-time:** 14-6;
Referee: Ashley Klein (London); **Attendance:** 1,203.

ROUND 4

Friday 27th February 2004

CHORLEY LYNX 6 WAKEFIELD TRINITY WILDCATS 88

LYNX: 1 Brian Capewell; 2 Eddie Kilgannon; 3 Daryl Lacey; 4 Mick Redford; 5 Gary O'Regan; 6 Neil Alexander; 7 Martin Gambles; 8 Gareth Jones; 9 Anthony Murray; 10 Ian Parry; 11 Gary Smith; 12 Martin Roden; 13 Chris Newall. Subs: 14 Lee Rowley; 15 Chris Ramsdale; 16 Damian Duncan; 17 Adam Briggs (not used).
Try: Newall (35); **Goals:** Capewell 1/1.
WILDCATS: 14 Colum Halpenny; 2 Justin Ryder; 3 Gareth Ellis (C); 4 Sid Domic; 5 Semi Tadulala; 6 Jamie Rooney; 7 Ben Jeffries; 18 Olivier Elima; 9 David March; 10 Michael Korkidas; 11 David Solomona; 12 Dallas Hood; 25 Albert Talipeau. Subs (all used): 1 Jason Demetriou; 8 Darrell Griffin; 15 David Wrench; 17 Paul Handforth.
Tries: Jeffries (5, 13, 24, 44, 80), Tadulala (11, 21), Korkidas (18), Ellis (29, 58), Domic (40), Rooney (42, 47, 62), March (67), Hood (75); **Goals:** Rooney 12/16.
Rugby Leaguer & League Express Men of the Match:
Lynx: Mick Redford; *Wildcats:* Jamie Rooney.
Penalty count: 10-5; **Half-time:** 6-46;
Referee: Ronnie Laughton (Barnsley); **Attendance:** 696.

Saturday 28th February 2004

BRADFORD-DUDLEY HILL 14 BATLEY BULLDOGS 76

DUDLEY HILL: 1 Craig Tyman; 2 Jack Bradbury; 3 Lewis Evans; 4 Alex Dickinson; 5 Jamie Brentley; 6 Ryan Dickinson; 7 Chris Robinson; 8 Richard Bingley; 9 Liam Brentley; 10 Gareth Shepherd; 11 Lee O'Connor; 12 Gareth Walker; 13 Sean Dickinson. Subs (all used): 14 Marco Rossi; 15 Sheara Singh; 16 Jason Hoyland; 17 John Exley.
Tries: Bingley (3), Robinson (26), Tyman (60);
Goals: Robinson 1/3.
BULLDOGS: 1 Mark Sibson; 2 Chris Spurr; 3 Shad Royston; 4 Danny Maun; 5 Adrian Flynn; 6 Mark Toohey; 7 Barry Eaton; 8 Steve Hill; 9 Joe Berry; 10 David Rourke; 11 Andy Rice; 12 Andy Spink; 13 Ryan Horsley. Subs (all used): 14 Mark Cass; 15 Paul Harrison; 16 Sean Richardson; 17 Will Cartledge.
Tries: Flynn (10, 23, 76), Spurr (13, 80), Horsley (32), Royston (36, 39, 64), Cartledge (44), Maun (53), Sibson (69), Cass (73), Berry (78); **Goals:** Eaton 10/14.
Sin bin: Spurr (57) - stealing ball after completion of tackle.
Rugby Leaguer & League Express Men of the Match:
Dudley Hill: Jason Hoyland; *Bulldogs:* Shad Royston.
Penalty count: 4-5; **Half-time:** 10-30;
Referee: Phil Bentham (Warrington);
Attendance: 890 *(at Mount Pleasant, Batley).*

CASTLEFORD TIGERS 32
UNION TREIZISTE CATALANE 20

TIGERS: 20 Tom Saxton; 1 Damian Gibson; 14 Ryan Clayton; 5 Darren Rogers; 2 Waine Pryce; 6 Sean Rudder; 7 Ryan Sheridan; 8 Craig Greenhill; 9 Wayne Godwin; 15 Nathan Sykes; 11 Lee Harland; 12 Sean Ryan; 13 Ryan Hudson (C). Subs (all used): 16 Jon Hepworth; 17 Paul Jackson; 23 Michael Smith; 18 Jamie Thackray.
Tries: Godwin (2), Gibson (8), Rudder (13), Thackray (34, 68), Pryce (54); **Goals:** Godwin 3/5, Hepworth 1/1.
On report: Ryan (35) – use of elbow in tackle.
UTC: 16 Craig Horne; 3 Matthew Hill; 4 Phil Howlett; 21 Steve Hall; 5 Bruno Verges; 6 Laurent Frayssinous; 7 Julien Rinaldi; 8 Russell Bawden; 9 David Berthezene; 20 Adel Fellous; 11 Pascal Jampy; 12 Djamel Fakir; 13 Aurelien Cologni. Subs (all used): 10 Sebastien Martin; 15 Lionel Teixido; 19 Gregory Mounis; 14 Thomas Bosc.
Tries: Cologni (24), Hall (26), Fakir (50), Howlett (74);
Goals: Frayssinous 2/5.
Rugby Leaguer & League Express Men of the Match:
Tigers: Craig Greenhill; *UTC:* Djamel Fakir.
Penalty count: 6-5; **Half-time:** 22-12;
Referee: Ashley Klein (London); **Attendance:** 3,435.

Sunday 29th February 2004

WIGAN WARRIORS 38 WIDNES VIKINGS 12

WARRIORS: 1 Kris Radlinski (C); 2 Brett Dallas; 3 Martin Aspinwall; 21 Kevin Brown; 5 Brian Carney; 6 Danny Orr; 14 Luke Robinson; 8 Terry O'Connor; 9 Terry Newton; 10 Craig Smith; 20 Gareth Hock; 12 Danny Tickle; 15 Sean O'Loughlin. Subs (all used): 16 Danny Sculthorpe; 17 Mark Smith; 18 Quentin Pongia; 22 David Allen.
Tries: Aspinwall (37), M Smith (52, 56), O'Loughlin (64), Newton (67), Brown (71), Orr (76);
Goals: Tickle 4/7, Robinson 1/1.
VIKINGS: 1 Paul Atcheson; 23 Steve Rowlands; 22 John Robinson; 14 Deon Bird; 5 Chris Giles; 6 Jules O'Neill; 7 Dean Lawford; 8 Robert Relf; 9 Shane Millard; 10 Julian O'Neill; 11 Steve McCurrie; 12 Andy Hay (C); 18 Simon Finnigan. Subs (all used): 4 Adam Hughes; 16 Andy Hobson; 17 David Mills; 19 Ryan McDonald.
Tries: Jules O'Neill (15), Bird (22); **Goals:** Jules O'Neill 2/2.
Rugby Leaguer & League Express Men of the Match:
Warriors: Sean O'Loughlin; *Vikings:* Jules O'Neill.
Penalty count: 11-8; **Half-time:** 4-12; **Referee:** Richard Silverwood (Dewsbury); **Attendance:** 6,737.

LIMOUX 19 HALIFAX 18

LIMOUX: 1 Sebastien Almarcha; 2 Freddie Zitter; 3 Tyrone Pau; 4 Boycie Nelson; 5 Michael Guiraud-Filh; 6 Nicolas Piccolo; 7 Mickael Murcia; 8 Walter Mackie; 9 Jerome Laffont; 10 Siose Muliumu; 11 Phillipe Laurent; 12 David Ferriol; 13 John Vaigafa. Subs (all used): 14 Christophe Grandjean; 15 David Gagliazzo; 16 Benoit Burgat; 17 Sebastien Planas.
Tries: Zitter (37), Pau (65), Nelson (68);
Goals: Mackie 3/5; **Field goal:** Murcia.
HALIFAX: 1 Danny Arnold; 2 Richard Smith; 3 Jon Roper; 4 Alan Hadcroft; 5 Chris Norman; 6 Simon Grix; 7 Mark Moxon; 8 Anthony Farrell; 9 Phil Cantillon; 10 Jaymes Chapman; 11 Jamie Bloem; 12 Chris Morley; 13 Pat Weisner. Subs (all used): 14 Wayne Corcoran; 15 Scott Grix; 16 David Bates; 17 Scott Law.
Tries: Hadcroft (42), Cantillon (56), Bloem (75);
Goals: Bloem 2/3, W Corcoran 1/1.
Rugby Leaguer & League Express Men of the Match:
Limoux: John Vaigafa; *Halifax:* Anthony Farrell.
Penalty count: 7-7; **Half-time:** 8-2;
Referee: Colin Morris (Huddersfield);
Attendance: 1,200 *(at Stade De L'Aiguille).*

BRADFORD BULLS 10 ST HELENS 30

BULLS: 6 Michael Withers; 2 Tevita Vaikona; 14 Toa Kohe-Love; 16 Paul Johnson; 5 Lesley Vainikolo; 3 Leon Pryce; 7 Paul Deacon; 10 Paul Anderson; 24 Aaron Smith; 29 Stuart Fielden; 11 Lee Radford; 12 Jamie Peacock (C); 19 Jamie Langley. Subs (all used): 8 Joe Vagana; 27 Rob Parker; 17 Stuart Reardon; 26 Chris Bridge.
Tries: Deacon (32), Radford (76); **Goals:** Deacon 1/3.
SAINTS: 1 Paul Wellens; 5 Darren Albert; 3 Martin Gleeson; 4 Willie Talau; 22 Dom Feaunati; 6 Jason Hooper; 7 Sean Long; 8 Nick Fozzard; 9 Keiron Cunningham; 18 Mark Edmondson; 15 Mike Bennett; 12 Lee Gilmour; 13 Paul Sculthorpe (C). Subs: 11 Chris Joynt; 25 Ian Hardman (not used); 14 Mick Higham; 16 Keith Mason.
Tries: Edmondson (10), Long (23), Gilmour (55), Gleeson (63), Sculthorpe (78);
Goals: Long 4/5, Sculthorpe 1/1.
Rugby Leaguer & League Express Men of the Match:
Bulls: Jamie Peacock; *Saints:* Paul Sculthorpe.
Penalty count: 6-3; **Half-time:** 6-14; **Referee:** Karl Kirkpatrick (Warrington); **Attendance:** 12,215.

HUDDERSFIELD GIANTS 50 PIA DONKEYS 16

GIANTS: 1 Paul Reilly; 2 Hefin O'Hare; 3 Stuart Donlan; 4 Julian Bailey; 34 Marcus St Hilaire; 6 Stanley Gene; 9 Paul March; 25 Darren Fleary (C); 15 Darren Turner; 8 Mick Slicker; 11 Chris Nero; 14 Stuart Jones; 13 Brandon Costin. Subs (all used): 5 Ben Cooper; 7 Sean Penkywicz; 12 Ben Roarty; 18 Eorl Crabtree.
Tries: St Hilaire (2, 45), March (6), Gene (24), Cooper (33), Jones (50), Reilly (56), Donlan (62), Roarty (72, 76); **Goals:** Costin 3/6, March 2/4.
Sin bin: Roarty (58) - obstruction.
DONKEYS: 1 Craig West; 2 Nicolas Athiel; 3 Lawrence Raleigh; 4 Florian Chaubet; 5 Sebastien Terrado; 6 Tom O'Reilly; 7 Maxime Greseque; 8 Karl Jaavuo; 9 Franck Traversa; 10 Taboanitoga Cakacaka; 11 Mathieu Ambert; 12 Emmanuel Bansept; 13 Jim Serdaris. Subs (all used): 14 Craig Field; 15 Michael Cousseau; 16 Franck Lagrange; 17 Franck Rovira.
Tries: Athiel (26), Terrado (35, 41); **Goals:** Terrado 2/3.
Sin bin: Jaavuo (52) - persistent interference.
Rugby Leaguer & League Express Men of the Match:
Giants: Marcus St Hilaire; *Donkeys:* Tom O'Reilly.
Penalty count: 13-7; **Half-time:** 20-12;
Referee: Robert Connolly (Wigan); **Attendance:** 1,392.

LEIGH CENTURIONS 14 HULL FC 21

CENTURIONS: 1 Neil Turley; 2 Steve Maden; 3 Dan Potter; 4 Danny Halliwell; 5 Damian Munro; 6 John Duffy; 7 Tommy Martyn; 8 Simon Knox; 9 Paul Rowley; 10 Heath Cruckshank; 11 David Larder; 12 Oliver Wilkes; 13 Ian Knott. Subs (all used): 14 David Alstead; 15 Dave McConnell; 16 Andrew Isherwood; 17 Paul Norman.
Tries: Martyn (2), Knott (64); **Goals:** Turley 3/5.
Sin bin: Rowley (42) - interference.
HULL: 32 Shaun Briscoe; 2 Colin Best; 3 Richie Barnett (C); 19 Alex Wilkinson; 5 Gareth Raynor; 16 Paul Cooke; 6 Richard Horne; 10 Paul King; 9 Richard Swain; 18 Ewan Dowes; 15 Shayne McMenemy; 23 Paul

Wakefield celebrate after defeating London at Griffin Park in Round 5

McNicholas; 17 Chris Chester. Subs (all used): 20 Garreth Carvell; 14 Kirk Yeaman; 25 Peter Lupton; 30 Richard Whiting (D).
Tries: Yeaman (24), Carvell (33), Best (45), Briscoe (59);
Goals: Cooke 2/4; **Field goal:** Lupton.
Dismissal: McNicholas (68) - high tackle.
Sin bin: Briscoe (63) - dissent.
Rugby Leaguer & League Express Men of the Match: *Centurions:* Simon Knox; *Hull:* Garreth Carvell.
Penalty count: 17-15; **Half-time:** 10-10;
Referee: Steve Ganson (St Helens); **Attendance:** 3,324.

LONDON BRONCOS 24 SALFORD CITY REDS 8

BRONCOS: 1 Paul Sykes; 2 Jon Wells; 21 Rob Jackson; 4 Mark O'Halloran; 3 Nigel Roy; 20 Radney Bowker; 7 Dennis Moran; 12 Steele Retchless; 9 Neil Budworth; 10 Steve Trindall; 18 Andrew Hart; 16 Joe Mbu; 13 Jim Dymock (C). Subs (all used): 14 Andrew Brocklehurst; 15 Mitchell Stringer; 8 Francis Stephenson; 17 Tom Haughey.
Tries: Mbu (2), Roy (29), Moran (55), Hart (63);
Goals: Sykes 4/5.
Sin bin: Hart (35) - holding down.
CITY REDS: 1 Jason Flowers; 4 Andy Kirk; 3 Stuart Littler; 20 Scott Naylor (D2); 5 Anthony Stewart; 6 Cliff Beverley; 7 Gavin Clinch; 8 Andy Coley; 9 Malcolm Alker (C); 17 Gareth Haggerty; 10 Sean Rutgerson; 18 Mark Shipway; 13 Chris Charles. Subs (all used): 12 Andy Johnson; 16 Martin Moana; 14 Paul Highton; 15 Karl Fitzpatrick.
Tries: Alker (73), Stewart (78); **Goals:** Charles 0/2.
Rugby Leaguer & League Express Men of the Match: *Broncos:* Jim Dymock; *City Reds:* Anthony Stewart.
Penalty count: 11-11; **Half-time:** 12-0;
Referee: Russell Smith (Castleford); **Attendance:** 2,454.

LONDON SKOLARS 6 FEATHERSTONE ROVERS 52

SKOLARS: 1 Tim Butterfield; 2 Tom Howden; 3 Andy Gould; 4 Donny Lam; 5 Dwayne Coleman; 7 Peter Hannan; 8 Koben Katipa; 9 Gareth Honor; 13 Alex Smits; 11 Wayne Parillon; 12 Glenn Osborn; 13 John Rua. Subs (all used): 14 Dan Reeds; 15 Keir Bell; 16 Huy Le; 17 Ben Joyce.
Try: Katipa (50); **Goals:** G Osborn 1/1.
Sin bin: Hannan (54) - holding down.
ROVERS: 1 Nathan Batty; 2 Jamie Stokes; 3 Jamie Coventry; 4 Richard Newlove; 5 Matthew Wray; 6 Danny Patrickson; 7 Carl Briggs; 8 Ian Tonks; 9 Paul Darley; 10 Stuart Dickens; 11 Bryan Henare; 12 Richard Blakeway; 13 Adam Hayes. Subs (all used): 14 Jon Presley; 15 James Ford; 16 Andy Jarrett; 17 Jim Carlton.
Tries: Wray (1), Newlove (14), Ford (20), Henare (28), Coventry (30), Blakeway (56), Darley (59), Batty (63), Presley (69); **Goals:** Briggs 8/9.
Rugby Leaguer & League Express Men of the Match: *Skolars:* Alex Smits; *Rovers:* Paul Darley.
Penalty count: 7-7; **Half-time:** 0-28;
Referee: Craig Halloran (Dewsbury); **Attendance:** 380.

WORKINGTON TOWN 18 LEEDS RHINOS 68

TOWN: 1 Craig Stalker; 2 Jonathan Heaney; 3 Andrew Fearon; 4 Adam Coulson; 5 Graeme Lewthwaite; 6 Brett Smith; 7 Gareth Skillen; 8 David Pettit; 9 Jonny Limmer; 10 Matthew Tunstall; 11 Jamie Beaumont; 12 Andy McGlasson; 13 Ricky Wright. Subs (all used): 14 Kevin Hetherington; 15 Martin Stalker; 16 James Robinson; 17 Bryan Hendry.
Tries: M Stalker (50), B Smith (57), Lewthwaite (79);
Goals: Skillen 3/3.
RHINOS: 21 Richard Mathers; 18 Mark Calderwood; 5 Chev Walker; 3 Chris McKenna; 2 Francis Cummins; 6 Danny McGuire; 7 Rob Burrow; 17 Wayne McDonald; 9 Matt Diskin; 10 Barrie McDermott; 11 David Furner; 16 Willie Poching; 13 Kevin Sinfield (C). Subs (all used): 14 Andrew Dunemann; 15 Chris Feather; 20 Jamie Jones-Buchanan; 19 Danny Ward.
Tries: McDermott (6), Calderwood (10, 38), Poching (12), Cummins (17, 22), McKenna (32), Burrow (36), Jones-Buchanan (41), Walker (63), Feather (66), Diskin (74); **Goals:** Sinfield 9/11, Burrow 1/1.
Rugby Leaguer & League Express Men of the Match:

Town: Brett Smith; *Rhinos:* Kevin Sinfield.
Penalty count: 7-7; **Half-time:** 0-46;
Referee: Ian Smith (Oldham); **Attendance:** 4,829.

SHEFFIELD EAGLES 24 YORK CITY KNIGHTS 32

EAGLES: 1 Andy Poynter; 2 Danny Mills; 3 Nick Turnbull; 4 Jon Breakingbury; 5 Carl De Chenu; 6 Richard Goddard; 7 Mark Aston; 8 Jack Howieson; 9 Adam Carroll; 10 Jon Bruce; 11 Andy Raleigh; 12 Craig Brown; 13 Jordan James. Subs (all used): 14 Greg Hurst; 15 Simon Tillyer; 16 Gareth Stanley; 17 Rob North.
Tries: Turnbull (3), Poynter (38), Mills (47), Hurst (79);
Goals: Goddard 4/5.
Sin bin: Aston (8) - retaliation; Raleigh (51) - holding down; Goddard (64) - persistent offside; Howieson (70) - holding down.
CITY KNIGHTS: 1 Nathan Graham; 2 Chris Smith; 3 Chris Langley; 4 Darren Callaghan; 5 Alex Godfrey; 6 Scott Rhodes; 7 Danny Brough; 8 Dan Briggs; 9 Lee Jackson; 10 Yusuf Sozi; 11 Mick Ramsden; 12 Simon Friend; 13 Damian Ball. Subs (all used): 14 Jimmy Elston; 15 Mark Cain; 16 John Smith; 17 Craig Forsyth.
Tries: C Smith (1), Rhodes (19), Briggs (22), Ball (35), Forsyth (59), Langley (71); **Goals:** Brough 4/7.
Sin bin: Callaghan (8) - punch in tackle; Rhodes (80) - holding down.
On report: Graham (47) - incident following Mills' try.
Rugby Leaguer & League Express Men of the Match: *Eagles:* Andy Poynter; *City Knights:* Danny Brough.
Penalty count: 12-9; **Half-time:** 12-22;
Referee: Gareth Hewer (Whitehaven); **Attendance:** 764.

HUNSLET HAWKS 20 DONCASTER DRAGONS 48

HAWKS: 1 Jon Liddell; 2 Chris Hall; 3 Dave Jessey; 4 Wes McGloasson; 5 George Rayner; 6 Andy Bastow; 7 Latham Tawhai; 8 Craig Booth; 9 Jamaine Wray; 10 Steve Pryce; 11 Wayne Freeman; 12 Jonlee Lockwood; 13 Chris Ross. Subs (all used): 14 Gary Shillabeer; 15 Mick Coyle; 16 Shaun Ibbetson; 17 Glen Freeman.
Tries: Wray (2), Coyle (30), W Freeman (72), Ibbetson (79); **Goals:** Booth 1/3, Tawhai 1/1.
DRAGONS: 1 Johnny Woodcock; 2 Jason Lee; 3 Gareth Lloyd; 4 PJ Solomon; 5 Marlon Billy; 6 Graham Holroyd; 7 Chris Hough; 8 Gareth Handford; 9 Craig Cook; 10 Jamie Fielden; 11 Craig Lawton; 12 Peter Green; 13 Shaun Leaf. Subs (all used): 14 Chris Hemmings; 15 Tony Atter; 16 Matt Walker; 17 Dean Colton.
Tries: Lloyd (17), Woodcock (20, 68), Handford (38), M Walker (43), Holroyd (54), Colton (76), Solomon (78);
Goals: Holroyd 8/8.
Rugby Leaguer & League Express Men of the Match: *Hawks:* Jamaine Wray; *Dragons:* Graham Holroyd.
Penalty count: 12-9; **Half-time:** 12-18;
Referee: Mike Dawber (Wigan); **Attendance:** 682.

Tuesday 2nd March 2004

EAST HULL 4 WHITEHAVEN 14

EAST HULL: 1 Phil Batty; 2 Lee James; 3 Jordan Precious; 4 John McCracken; 5 Jason Abdul; 6 Mike Docherty; 7 Shaun Cooke; 8 Lee Brown; 9 Mark Moore; 10 Lee Roberts; 11 Gary Noble; 12 Mark Woodcock; 13 Paul Roberts. Subs (all used): 14 Ian Madley; 15 Dale Blakeley; 16 James McCracken; 17 Paul Williamson.
Goals: Docherty 2/2.
Sin bin: P Roberts (64) - persistent interference.
WHITEHAVEN: 1 Gary Broadbent; 2 Jamie Marshall; 3 David Seeds; 4 Mick Nanyn; 5 Paul O'Neil; 6 Craig Walsh; 7 Lee Kiddie; 8 Marc Jackson; 9 Carl Sice; 10 Chris McKinney; 11 Craig Chambers; 12 Graeme Morton; 13 Howard Hill. Subs (all used): 14 Leroy Joe; 15 Gary Smith; 16 Spencer Miller; 17 Brett McDermott.
Tries: McDermott (46), Nanyn (57); **Goals:** Nanyn 3/3.
Sin bin: Morton (38) - interference.
Rugby Leaguer & League Express Men of the Match: *East Hull:* Lee Brown; *Whitehaven:* Brett McDermott.
Penalty count: 18-13; **Half-time:** 4-0;
Referee: Peter Taberner (Wigan);
Attendance: 1,400 *(at New Craven Park, Hull)*.

ROCHDALE HORNETS 0 WARRINGTON WOLVES 80

HORNETS: 1 Michael Platt; 2 Liam Williams; 3 Paul Anderson; 4 Danny Yates; 5 Chris Campbell; 6 John Braddish; 7 Lee Birdseye; 8 Andy Leathem; 9 Darren Shaw; 10 Lee Hansen; 11 Kris Ratcliffe; 12 Rob Ball; 13 Andy Gorski. Subs (all used): 14 Sam Butterworth; 15 Tony Kirwan; 16 Andy Grundy; 17 Mark Costello.
Dismissal: Ball (72) - high tackle on Hulse.
WOLVES: 1 Daryl Cardiss; 2 John Wilshere; 3 Brent Grose; 4 Ben Westwood; 20 Dean Gaskell; 5 Graham Appo; 7 Nathan Wood (C); 8 Chris Leikvoll; 14 Mark Gleeson; 22 Danny Lima; 16 Paul Wood; 23 Mike Wainwright; 18 Paul Noone. Subs (all used): 19 Gary Hulse; 12 Ian Sibbit; 15 Jerome Guisset; 17 Warren Stevens.
Tries: Appo (2, 31), P Wood (5, 20), Wilshere (8, 40), Guisset (25), Westwood (35, 49), Grose (38), Gaskell (42), Sibbit (57), Noone (68), Hulse (74), N Wood (77), Cardiss (80); **Goals:** Appo 3/8, Wilshere 5/7, Noone 0/1.
Rugby Leaguer & League Express Men of the Match: *Hornets:* Paul Anderson; *Wolves:* John Wilshere.
Penalty count: 10-8; **Half-time:** 0-46;
Referee: Ben Thaler (Wakefield); **Attendance:** 6,761 *(at Halliwell Jones Stadium, Warrington).*

Wednesday 3rd March 2004

OLDHAM 24 SHARLSTON ROVERS 4

OLDHAM: 1 Gavin Dodd; 2 Will Cowell; 3 James Bunyan; 4 Jon Goddard; 5 Nick Johnson; 6 Simon Svabic; 7 Ian Watson; 8 Steve Molloy; 9 Keith Brennan; 10 Dane Morgan; 11 Lee Doran; 12 Iain Marsh; 13 Lee Marsh. Subs (all used): 14 Gareth Barber; 15 Neil Roden; 16 Martin McLoughlin; 17 Paul Southern.
Tries: I Marsh (34, 55), L Marsh (43), N Johnson (76);
Goals: Svabic 4/7.
ROVERS: 1 Shaun Taylor; 2 Lee Lingard; 3 Gareth Davies; 4 Keith Brook; 5 Andy Martin; 6 Martyn Wood; 7 Danny Grimshaw; 8 Carl Sayer; 9 Lee Bettinson; 10 Andy Booth; 11 Chance Leake; 12 James Ward; 13 Stan Smith. Subs (all used): 14 Gordon Long; 15 Jamie Cox; 16 Dale Potter; 17 Lee Kelly.
Goals: Lingard 2/2.
Sin bin: Ward (30) - professional foul.
Rugby Leaguer & League Express Men of the Match: *Oldham:* Neil Roden; *Rovers:* Lee Bettinson.
Penalty count: 11-10; **Half-time:** 8-4;
Referee: Jamie Leahy (Dewsbury); **Attendance:** 1,301.

ROUND 5

Saturday 13th March 2004

ST HELENS 24 LEEDS RHINOS 14

SAINTS: 1 Paul Wellens; 5 Darren Albert; 12 Lee Gilmour; 4 Willie Talau; 22 Dom Feaunati; 6 Jason Hooper; 7 Sean Long; 8 Nick Fozzard; 9 Keiron Cunningham; 16 Keith Mason; 11 Chris Joynt; 13 Paul Sculthorpe (C); 14 Mick Higham. Subs: 21 Jon Wilkin; 18 Mark Edmondson; 23 Maurie Fa'asavalu (not used); 2 Ade Gardner.
Tries: Wellens (24, 44), Feaunati (38), Talau (70);
Goals: Long 4/6.
RHINOS: 1 Gary Connolly; 22 Marcus Bai; 5 Chev Walker; 4 Keith Senior; 18 Mark Calderwood; 6 Danny McGuire; 7 Rob Burrow; 17 Wayne McDonald; 9 Matt Diskin; 10 Barrie McDermott; 11 David Furner; 12 Matt Adamson; 13 Kevin Sinfield (C). Subs (all used): 19 Danny Ward; 16 Willie Poching; 8 Ryan Bailey; 14 Andrew Dunemann.
Tries: McGuire (13), Bailey (29); **Goals:** Sinfield 3/3.
Rugby Leaguer & League Express Men of the Match: *Saints:* Paul Wellens; *Rhinos:* Ryan Bailey.
Penalty count: 9-7; **Half-time:** 12-14;
Referee: Russell Smith (Castleford); **Attendance:** 13,699.

Challenge Cup 2004 - Round by Round

Sunday 14th March 2004

LIMOUX 20 WIGAN WARRIORS 80

LIMOUX: 1 Fabrice Estebanez; 2 Freddie Zitter; 3 Tyrone Pau; 4 Boycie Nelson; 5 Sebastien Almarcha; 6 Nicolas Piccolo; 7 Mickael Murcia; 8 Walter Mackie; 9 Jerome Laffont; 10 Siose Muliumu; 11 Phillipe Laurent; 12 David Ferriol; 13 John Vaigafa. Subs (all used): 14 Christophe Grandjean; 15 Benoit Burgat; 16 Guillaume Mestre; 17 Michael Guiraud-Filh.
Tries: Nelson (7), Almarcha (57), Grandjean (73), Mackie (80); **Goals:** Estebanez 2/4.
WARRIORS: 1 Kris Radlinski (C); 26 Chris Melling; 3 Martin Aspinwall; 21 Kevin Brown; 2 Brett Dallas; 6 Danny Orr; 14 Luke Robinson; 16 Danny Sculthorpe; 9 Terry Newton; 18 Quentin Pongia; 20 Gareth Hock; 19 Stephen Wild; 15 Sean O'Loughlin. Subs (all used): 17 Mark Smith; 10 Craig Smith; 12 Danny Tickle; 8 Terry O'Connor.
Tries: Melling (9), Newton (15), Aspinwall (18), O'Loughlin (21), Hock (27, 40), Orr (33), Radlinski (37), Brown (42), Robinson (45, 67, 70), M Smith (55), Dallas (60); **Goals:** Orr 2/2, Melling 10/12.
Rugby Leaguer & League Express Men of the Match: *Limoux:* Tyrone Pau; *Warriors:* Luke Robinson.
Penalty count: 5-12; **Half-time:** 4-42;
Referee: Karl Kirkpatrick (Warrington);
Attendance: 2,500 *(at Stade De L'Aiguille).*

BATLEY BULLDOGS 6 WHITEHAVEN 29

BULLDOGS: 1 Mark Sibson; 2 Chris Spurr; 3 Shad Royston; 4 Danny Maun; 5 Adrian Flynn; 6 Mark Toohey; 7 Barry Eaton; 8 Chris Molyneux; 9 Joe Berry; 10 Steve Hill; 11 Will Cartledge; 12 Andy Spink; 13 Ryan Horsley. Subs (all used): 14 Mark Cass; 15 Paul Harrison; 16 David Rourke; 17 Sean Richardson.
Try: Harrison (50); **Goals:** Eaton 1/1.
WHITEHAVEN: 1 Gary Broadbent; 2 Steven Wood; 3 Wesley Wilson; 4 Mick Nanyn; 5 Paul O'Neil; 6 Leroy Joe; 7 Lee Kiddie; 8 Marc Jackson; 9 Aaron Lester; 10 David Fatialofa; 11 Brett McDermott; 12 Graeme Morton; 13 Howard Hill. Subs: 14 Craig Walsh (not used); 15 Carl Sice; 16 Spencer Miller; 17 Craig Chambers.
Tries: Hill (4, 24), O'Neil (18), Wilson (35), Nanyn (48); **Goals:** Nanyn 4/7; **Field goal:** Joe.
Rugby Leaguer & League Express Men of the Match: *Bulldogs:* Mark Sibson; *Whitehaven:* David Fatialofa.
Penalty count: 7-4; **Half-time:** 0-22; **Referee:** Ronnie Laughton (Barnsley); **Attendance:** 1,186.

FEATHERSTONE ROVERS 26 YORK CITY KNIGHTS 29

ROVERS: 1 Nathan Batty; 2 James Ford; 3 Jamie Coventry; 4 Richard Newlove; 5 Matthew Wray; 6 Jon Presley; 7 Carl Briggs; 8 Ian Tonks; 9 Richard Chapman; 10 Stuart Dickens; 11 Paul Darley; 12 Bryan Henare; 13 Adam Hayes. Subs (all used): 14 Ben Archibald; 15 Steve Dooler; 16 Andy Jarrett; 17 Jim Carlton.
Tries: Wray (39), Presley (45), Newlove (54, 76), Darley (67); **Goals:** Briggs 3/5.
CITY KNIGHTS: 1 Nathan Graham; 2 Mark Stewart; 3 Mark Cain; 4 Aaron Wood; 5 Alex Godfrey; 6 Scott Rhodes; 7 Danny Brough; 8 Richard Hayes; 9 Lee Jackson; 10 Yusuf Sozi; 11 Darren Callaghan; 12 Danny Seal; 13 Simon Friend. Subs (all used): 14 Jimmy Elston; 15 Scott Walker; 16 Dan Briggs; 17 Craig Forsyth.
Tries: Seal (21), Godfrey (35, 79), Graham (73);
Goals: Brough 6/9; Field goal: Brough.
Dismissal: Wood (10) - high tackle.
Rugby Leaguer & League Express Men of the Match: *Rovers:* Paul Darley; *City Knights:* Danny Brough.
Penalty count: 10-9; **Half-time:** 4-17;
Referee: Robert Connolly (Wigan); **Attendance:** 2,234.

HUDDERSFIELD GIANTS 36 DONCASTER DRAGONS 12

GIANTS: 1 Paul Reilly; 2 Hefin O'Hare; 3 Stuart Donlan; 4 Julian Bailey; 34 Marcus St Hilaire; 6 Stanley Gene; 9 Paul March; 8 Mick Slicker; 22 Phil Joseph; 25 Darren Fleary (C); 14 Stuart Jones; 12 Ben Roarty; 11 Chris Nero. Subs (all used): 5 Ben Cooper; 7 Sean Penkywicz; 17 Paul Smith; 18 Eorl Crabtree.
Tries: O'Hare (9), Slicker (29), Donlan (31), Penkywicz (35), Jones (53), Smith (62), March (71);
Goals: March 4/7.
DRAGONS: 1 Johnny Woodcock; 2 Jason Lee; 3 Gareth Lloyd; 4 PJ Solomon; 5 Marlon Billy; 6 Graham Holroyd; 7 Chris Hough; 8 Gareth Handford; 9 Craig Cook; 10 Matt Walker; 11 Craig Lawton; 12 Peter Green; 13 Shaun Leaf. Subs (all used): 14 Chris Hemmings; 15 Martin Ostler; 16 Dean Colton; 17 Alex Muff.
Tries: Handford (17), Woodcock (49); **Goals:** Holroyd 2/3.
Rugby Leaguer & League Express Men of the Match: *Giants:* Ben Roarty; *Dragons:* Graham Holroyd.
Penalty count: 13-9; **Half-time:** 20-6;
Referee: Ashley Klein (London); **Attendance:** 3,134.

HULL FC 26 CASTLEFORD TIGERS 0

HULL: 32 Shaun Briscoe; 2 Colin Best; 3 Richie Barnett (C); 14 Kirk Yeaman; 26 Richie Barnett Jnr; 16 Paul Cooke; 6 Richard Horne; 10 Paul King; 9 Richard Swain; 18 Ewan Dowes; 15 Shayne McMenemy; 23 Paul McNicholas; 25 Peter Lupton. Subs (all used): 17 Chris Chester; 29 Andy Bailey (D); 30 Richard Whiting; 27 Liam Higgins.
Tries: Best (25, 33, 69), Whiting (73); **Goals:** Cooke 5/5.
TIGERS: 20 Tom Saxton; 5 Darren Rogers; 14 Ryan Clayton; 19 Francis Maloney; 1 Damian Gibson; 6 Sean Rudder; 7 Ryan Sheridan; 8 Craig Greenhill; 13 Ryan Hudson (C); 17 Paul Jackson; 23 Michael Smith; 12 Sean Ryan; 11 Lee Harland. Subs (all used): 16 Jon Hepworth; 10 Andy Lynch; 9 Wayne Godwin; 18 Jamie Thackray.
On report: Greenhill (53) - high tackle.
Rugby Leaguer & League Express Men of the Match: *Hull:* Colin Best; *Tigers:* Ryan Hudson.
Penalty count: 10-8; **Half-time:** 14-0; **Referee:** Richard Silverwood (Dewsbury); **Attendance:** 11,443.

LONDON BRONCOS 10
WAKEFIELD TRINITY WILDCATS 29

BRONCOS: 1 Paul Sykes; 2 Jon Wells; 3 Nigel Roy; 4 Mark O'Halloran; 24 Andy McNally (D); 20 Radney Bowker; 7 Dennis Moran; 12 Steele Retchless; 9 Neil Budworth; 10 Steve Trindall; 18 Andrew Hart; 16 Joe Mbu; 13 Jim Dymock (C). Subs (all used): 14 Andrew Brocklehurst; 15 Mitchell Stringer; 8 Francis Stephenson; 22 Lee Sanderson.
Tries: Wells (16), Sykes (70); **Goals:** Sykes 1/2.
Sin bin: O'Halloran (51) - late tackle.
On report: O'Halloran (51) - late tackle.
WILDCATS: 14 Colum Halpenny; 2 Justin Ryder; 1 Jason Demetriou; 4 Sid Domic; 5 Semi Tadulala; 6 Jamie Rooney; 7 Ben Jeffries; 8 Darrell Griffin; 9 David March; 18 Olivier Elima; 11 David Solomona; 15 David Wrench; 3 Gareth Ellis (C). Subs (all used): 12 Dallas Hood; 13 Jamie Field; 16 Steve Snitch; 25 Albert Talipeau.
Tries: Ryder (8), Rooney (44, 47), Domic (55, 80);
Goals: Rooney 4/7; **Field goal:** Rooney.
Rugby Leaguer & League Express Men of the Match: *Broncos:* Paul Sykes; *Wildcats:* Jamie Rooney.
Penalty count: 9-9; **Half-time:** 4-6;
Referee: Ian Smith (Oldham); **Attendance:** 2,654.

OLDHAM 10 WARRINGTON WOLVES 44

OLDHAM: 1 Gavin Dodd; 2 Will Cowell; 3 James Bunyan; 4 Jon Goddard; 5 Nick Johnson; 6 Neil Roden; 7 Ian Watson; 8 Steve Molloy; 9 Keith Brennan; 10 Paul Southern; 11 Lee Doran; 12 Dane Morgan; 13 Lee Marsh. Subs (all used): 14 Gareth Barber; 15 Simon Svabic; 16 Martin McLoughlin; 17 Martin Elswood.
Tries: Cowell (26), N Johnson (80);
Goals: L Marsh 1/2, Svabic 0/1.
WOLVES: 3 Brent Grose; 20 Dean Gaskell; 4 Ben Westwood; 12 Ian Sibbit; 2 John Wilshere; 7 Nathan Wood (C); 19 Gary Hulse; 10 Mark Hilton; 9 Jon Clarke; 22 Danny Lima; 23 Mike Wainwright; 11 Darren Burns; 18 Paul Noone. Subs (all used): 26 Jamie Durbin; 25 Richard Varkulis; 15 Jerome Guisset; 17 Warren Stevens.
Tries: Burns (6), Sibbit (20), Guisset (31), Hulse (35, 67), Grose (38), Varkulis (55), Westwood (57), Gaskell (62); **Goals:** Wilshere 1/3, Noone 3/6.
Rugby Leaguer & League Express Men of the Match: *Oldham:* Jon Goddard; *Wolves:* Paul Noone.
Penalty count: 6-6; **Half-time:** 6-26;
Referee: Steve Ganson (St Helens); **Attendance:** 2,859.

QUARTER FINALS

Friday 26th March 2004

WIGAN WARRIORS 20
WAKEFIELD TRINITY WILDCATS 4

WARRIORS: 1 Kris Radlinski; 3 Martin Aspinwall; 19 Stephen Wild; 21 Kevin Brown; 2 Brett Dallas; 6 Danny Orr; 14 Luke Robinson; 18 Quentin Pongia; 9 Terry Newton; 10 Craig Smith; 11 Mick Cassidy; 13 Andy Farrell (C); 15 Sean O'Loughlin. Subs (all used): 8 Terry O'Connor; 12 Danny Tickle; 17 Mark Smith; 20 Gareth Hock.
Tries: Radlinski (34), Brown (58), Aspinwall (68, 70);
Goals: Farrell 2/3, Tickle 0/1.
Sin bin: Farrell (52) - fighting.
On report: Cassidy (25) - late challenge on Ellis.
WILDCATS: 14 Colum Halpenny; 2 Justin Ryder; 1 Jason Demetriou; 4 Sid Domic; 5 Semi Tadulala; 6 Jamie Rooney; 7 Ben Jeffries; 8 Darrell Griffin; 9 David March; 18 Olivier Elima; 11 David Solomona; 15 David Wrench; 3 Gareth Ellis (C). Subs (all used): 12 Dallas Hood; 13 Jamie Field; 10 Michael Korkidas; 25 Albert Talipeau.
Goals: Rooney 2/2.
Sin bin: Field (52) - fighting.
Rugby Leaguer & League Express Men of the Match: *Warriors:* Terry Newton; *Wildcats:* Gareth Ellis.
Penalty count: 4-6; **Half-time:** 6-4;
Referee: Russell Smith (Castleford); **Attendance:** 9,728.

Sunday 28th March 2004

WHITEHAVEN 10 WARRINGTON WOLVES 42

WHITEHAVEN: 1 Gary Broadbent; 2 Wesley Wilson; 3 David Seeds; 4 Mick Nanyn; 5 Paul O'Neil; 6 Leroy Joe; 7 Lee Kiddie; 8 Marc Jackson; 9 Aaron Lester; 10 David Fatialofa; 11 Brett McDermott; 12 Graeme Morton; 13 Howard Hill. Subs (all used): 14 Craig Walsh; 15 Craig Chambers; 16 Spencer Miller; 17 Carl Sice.
Tries: Kiddie (29), Nanyn (67); **Goals:** Nanyn 1/3.
WOLVES: 3 Brent Grose; 1 Daryl Cardiss; 4 Ben Westwood; 18 Paul Noone; 2 John Wilshere; 6 Lee Briers (C); 7 Nathan Wood; 10 Mark Hilton; 9 Jon Clarke; 16 Paul Wood; 12 Ian Sibbit; 23 Mike Wainwright; 13 Mike Forshaw. Subs (all used): 14 Mark Gleeson; 15 Jerome Guisset; 17 Warren Stevens; 22 Danny Lima.
Tries: Wilshere (14), Westwood (25), N Wood (39, 49), Sibbit (47), Grose (59), P Wood (71), Stevens (79);
Goals: Briers 5/9.
Rugby Leaguer & League Express Men of the Match: *Whitehaven:* Brett McDermott; *Wolves:* Lee Briers.
Penalty count: 7-8; **Half time:** 6-14;
Referee: Steve Ganson (St Helens); **Attendance:** 5,328.

HUDDERSFIELD GIANTS 50 YORK CITY KNIGHTS 12

GIANTS: 5 Ben Cooper; 2 Hefin O'Hare; 11 Chris Nero; 4 Julian Bailey; 34 Marcus St Hilaire; 13 Brandon Costin; 9 Paul March; 8 Mick Slicker (C); 7 Sean Penkywicz; 10 Jim Gannon; 14 Stuart Jones; 12 Ben Roarty; 6 Stanley Gene. Subs (all used): 3 Stuart Donlan; 15 Darren Turner; 17 Paul Smith; 18 Eorl Crabtree.
Tries: Roarty (5, 59, 75), Costin (12, 66), Penkywicz (18), Cooper (22), O'Hare (25), St Hilaire (27), Bailey (34); **Goals:** March 5/10.
CITY KNIGHTS: 1 Nathan Graham; 2 Mark Stewart; 3 Chris Langley; 4 Mark Cain; 5 Alex Godfrey; 6 Scott Rhodes; 7 Danny Brough; 8 Richard Hayes; 9 Lee Jackson; 10 Yusuf Sozi; 11 Darren Callaghan; 12 Simon Friend; 13 Damian Ball. Subs (all used): 14 Jimmy Elston; 15 Danny Seal; 16 John Smith; 17 Craig Forsyth.
Tries: Elston (34), Seal (72); **Goals:** Brough 2/3.
Rugby Leaguer & League Express Men of the Match: *Giants:* Brandon Costin; *City Knights:* Danny Brough.
Penalty count: 11-10; **Half-time:** 38-6;
Referee: Ronnie Laughton (Barnsley); **Attendance:** 4,286.

Warrington duo Lee Briers and Daryl Cardiss close in on Whitehaven's David Seeds during the Quarter Final at the Recreation Ground

St Helens' Nick Fozzard takes on Wigan's Kris Radlinski during the Challenge Cup Final

ST HELENS 31 HULL FC 26

SAINTS: 1 Paul Wellens; 5 Darren Albert; 6 Jason Hooper; 4 Willie Talau; 22 Dom Feaunati; 13 Paul Sculthorpe (C); 7 Sean Long; 8 Nick Fozzard; 9 Keiron Cunningham; 16 Keith Mason; 12 Lee Gilmour; 18 Mark Edmondson; 11 Chris Joynt. Subs (all used): 2 Ade Gardner; 14 Mick Higham; 20 Ricky Bibey; 21 Jon Wilkin. **Tries:** Hooper (28, 36), Long (44), Cunningham (51), Sculthorpe (78); **Goals:** Long 5/7; **Field goal:** Sculthorpe.
HULL: 32 Shaun Briscoe; 2 Colin Best; 3 Richie Barnett (C); 14 Kirk Yeaman; 26 Richie Barnett Jnr; 16 Paul Cooke; 6 Richard Horne; 18 Ewan Dowes; 9 Richard Swain; 10 Paul King; 23 Paul McNicholas; 15 Shayne McMenemy; 25 Peter Lupton. Subs (all used): 17 Chris Chester; 27 Liam Higgins; 20 Garreth Carvell; 30 Richard Whiting. **Tries:** Briscoe (11, 42), R Horne (18), Barnett (40); **Goals:** Cooke 5/5.
Rugby Leaguer & League Express Men of the Match: *Saints:* Sean Long; *Hull:* Richard Horne.
Penalty count: 9-5; **Half-time:** 16-20; **Referee:** Karl Kirkpatrick (Warrington); **Attendance:** 11,184.

SEMI FINALS

Sunday 18th April 2004

WARRINGTON WOLVES 18 WIGAN WARRIORS 30

WOLVES: 1 Daryl Cardiss; 4 Ben Westwood; 11 Darren Burns; 12 Ian Sibbit; 20 Dean Gaskell; 6 Lee Briers (C); 7 Nathan Wood; 10 Mark Hilton; 9 Jon Clarke; 22 Danny Lima; 15 Jerome Guisset; 23 Mike Wainwright; 13 Mike Forshaw. Subs: 14 Mark Gleeson; 17 Warren Stevens; 18 Paul Noone; 19 Gary Hulse (not used). **Tries:** Westwood (46), Burns (67), Forshaw (80); **Goals:** Briers 3/4.

WARRIORS: 1 Kris Radlinski; 3 Martin Aspinwall; 19 Stephen Wild; 21 Kevin Brown; 2 Brett Dallas; 15 Sean O'Loughlin; 6 Danny Orr; 10 Craig Smith; 9 Terry Newton; 18 Quentin Pongia; 11 Mick Cassidy; 20 Gareth Hock; 13 Andy Farrell (C). Subs (all used): 7 Adrian Lam; 8 Terry O'Connor; 16 Danny Sculthorpe; 17 Mark Smith. **Tries:** Dallas (10, 63, 72), Radlinski (23), Wild (78); **Goals:** Farrell 5/6.
Rugby Leaguer & League Express Men of the Match: *Wolves:* Danny Lima; *Warriors:* Brett Dallas.
Penalty count: 4-5; **Half-time:** 2-12; **Referee:** Steve Ganson (St Helens); **Attendance:** 11,175 *(at Halton Stadium, Widnes).*

Sunday 25th April 2004

HUDDERSFIELD GIANTS 6 ST HELENS 46

GIANTS: 1 Paul Reilly; 2 Hefin O'Hare; 11 Chris Nero; 4 Julian Bailey; 34 Marcus St Hilaire; 13 Brandon Costin; 9 Paul March; 8 Mick Slicker; 15 Darren Turner; 25 Darren Fleary (C); 14 Stuart Jones; 12 Ben Roarty; 6 Stanley Gene. Subs (all used): 7 Sean Penkywicz; 10 Jim Gannon; 17 Paul Smith; 18 Eorl Crabtree. **Try:** March (31); **Goals:** March 1/1.
SAINTS: 1 Paul Wellens; 5 Darren Albert; 3 Martin Gleeson; 4 Willie Talau; 2 Ade Gardner; 6 Jason Hooper; 7 Sean Long; 8 Nick Fozzard; 9 Keiron Cunningham; 16 Keith Mason; 11 Chris Joynt; 12 Lee Gilmour; 13 Paul Sculthorpe (C). Subs: 14 Mick Higham (not used); 18 Mark Edmondson; 20 Ricky Bibey; 25 Ian Hardman. **Tries:** Cunningham (10), Hooper (14, 67), Gilmour (25), Talau (32), Gardner (40, 76), Long (51); **Goals:** Long 3/5, Sculthorpe 4/4.
Rugby Leaguer & League Express Men of the Match: *Giants:* Marcus St Hilaire; *Saints:* Sean Long.
Penalty count: 8-11; **Half-time:** 6-26; **Referee:** Karl Kirkpatrick (Warrington); **Attendance:** 13,134 *(at Halliwell Jones Stadium, Warrington).*

FINAL

Saturday 15th May 2004

ST HELENS 32 WIGAN WARRIORS 16

SAINTS: 1 Paul Wellens; 2 Ade Gardner; 3 Martin Gleeson; 4 Willie Talau; 5 Darren Albert; 6 Jason Hooper; 7 Sean Long; 8 Nick Fozzard; 9 Keiron Cunningham; 16 Keith Mason; 11 Chris Joynt; 12 Lee Gilmour; 13 Paul Sculthorpe (C). Subs: 18 Mark Edmondson for Mason (16); 22 Dom Feaunati for Gardner (24); Mason for Edmondson (36); Gardner for Feaunati (HT); Edmondson for Joynt (48); 21 Jon Wilkin for Mason (60); Feaunati for Gardner (66); Mason for Edmondson (70); 20 Ricky Bibey for Fozzard (70); Gardner for Feaunati (72); Joynt for Wilkin (75). **Tries:** Gilmour (3), Talau (23, 68), Wellens (39), Sculthorpe (50); **Goals:** Long 6/7.
On report: Feaunati (31) - high tackle on Brown.
WARRIORS: 1 Kris Radlinski; 4 David Hodgson; 15 Sean O'Loughlin; 21 Kevin Brown; 2 Brett Dallas; 6 Danny Orr; 7 Adrian Lam; 10 Craig Smith; 9 Terry Newton; 18 Quentin Pongia; 12 Danny Tickle; 20 Gareth Hock; 13 Andy Farrell (C). Subs: 8 Terry O'Connor for Smith (19); 16 Danny Sculthorpe for Pongia (20); 11 Mick Cassidy for Tickle (28); Smith for Sculthorpe (48); 19 Stephen Wild for Hock (52); Pongia for O'Connor (55); Tickle for Cassidy (61); Sculthorpe for Smith (66); Hock for Pongia (70). **Tries:** Newton (13), Dallas (33, 65); **Goals:** Farrell 2/3.
Rugby Leaguer & League Express Men of the Match: *Saints:* Sean Long; *Warriors:* Andy Farrell.
Penalty count: 2-4; **Half-time:** 20-10; **Referee:** Karl Kirkpatrick (Warrington); **Attendance:** 73,734 *(at Millennium Stadium, Cardiff).*

NATIONAL LEAGUE THREE

FINAL TABLE

	P	W	D	L	F	A	D	PTS
Coventry Bears	20	17	0	3	831	385	446	34
Bradford-Dudley H	20	16	0	4	942	317	625	32
Warr-Woolston	20	15	1	4	764	232	532	31
Sheff-Hillsborough	20	13	1	6	631	334	297	27
Bramley Buffaloes	20	13	1	6	592	368	224	27
Hemel Stags	20	13	0	7	721	424	297	26
St Albans C	20	12	0	8	724	406	318	24
Birmingham B	20	10	0	10	620	624	-4	20
Hudds-Underbank	20	9	1	10	671	519	152	19
South London S	20	8	2	10	496	510	-14	18
Manchester Knights	20	5	0	15	467	625	-158	10
Carlisle Centurions	20	3	0	17	290	948	-658	6
Gateshead Storm	20	2	0	18	290	1041	-751	4
Essex Eels	20	1	0	19	186	1492	-1306	2

PLAY-OFFS

Saturday 18th September 2004
Bradford-Dudley Hill 13 ....St Albans Centurions 30
Coventry Bears 32 ....Birmingham Bulldogs 26
Sheffield-Hillsborough Hawks 38 ....Bramley Buffaloes 6
Warrington-Woolston 36......Hemel Hempstead Stags 32

Saturday 25th September 2004
Sheffield-Hillsborough 26 ....Bradford-Dudley Hill 40
St Albans Centurions 18 ....Bramley Buffaloes 26

Saturday 2nd October 2004
Coventry Bears 32.........................Bramley Buffaloes 18
Warrington-Woolston 32 ....Bradford-Dudley Hill 18

GRAND FINAL

Sunday 10th October 2004
Coventry Bears 48 ....Warrington-Woolston Rovers 24
at Halton Stadium, Widnes

PLAYER OF THE YEAR
Adrian Veamatahau (Coventry Bears)
Nominees: Adam Cawley (Birmingham Bulldogs), Mark Roughneen (Warrington Woolston Rovers)

YOUNG PLAYER OF THE YEAR
Mike Jones (Birmingham Bulldogs)
Nominees: Liam Brentley (Bradford Dudley Hill), Bryn Evans (Sheffield Hillsborough Hawks)

COACH OF THE YEAR
Ken Roberts (Hemel Stags)
Nominees: Troy Perkins (Coventry Bears), Stuart Tighe (Bradford Dudley Hill)

RUGBY LEAGUE WORLD ALL STARS TEAM
1 Mark Roughneen (Warrington Woolston Rovers)
2 Mike Jones (Birmingham Bulldogs)
3 Adrian Veamatahau (Coventry Bears)
4 Tom Armstrong (Carlisle Centurions)
5 Phil Aiken (Hemel Stags)
6 Adam Cawley (Birmingham Bulldogs)
7 Bryn Evans (Sheffield Hillsborough Hawks)
8 Gareth Barron (Gateshead Storm)
9 Liam Brentley (Bradford Dudley Hill)
10 James Ellershaw (Hemel Stags)
11 Paul Rice (South London Storm)
12 Steve Warburton (Warrington Woolston Rovers)
13 Adam Cox (St Albans Centurions)

NATIONAL CONFERENCE

PREMIER DIVISION

	P	W	D	L	F	A	D	Pts
Siddal	26	20	0	6	539	394	145	40
Skirlaugh	26	19	1	6	527	312	215	39
West Hull	26	18	1	7	587	426	161	37
Thornhill Trojans	26	17	0	9	524	322	202	34
Leigh East	26	16	1	9	624	447	177	33
Leigh Miners R	26	15	1	10	639	477	162	31
Thatto Heath	26	14	0	12	557	539	18	28
Oldham St Annes	26	13	0	13	474	477	-3	26
West Bowling	26	12	1	13	420	441	-21	25
Oulton Raiders	26	11	2	13	567	443	124	24
Wigan St Patricks	26	10	1	15	529	506	23	21
Cas Lock Lane	26	9	0	17	407	617	-210	18
Ideal Isberg	26	3	0	23	358	759	-401	6
Featherstone Lions	26	1	0	25	242	829	-587	2

ELIMINATION PLAY-OFFS
Saturday 1st May 2004
Thornhill Trojans 20....................................Leigh East 23
West Hull 30 ....Leigh Miners Rangers 10

QUALIFYING SEMI-FINAL
Saturday 8th May 2004
Siddal 22...Skirlaugh 8
(after extra time - full time 8-8)

ELIMINATION SEMI FINAL
Saturday 8th May 2004
West Hull 38 ....Leigh East 12

GRAND FINAL
Saturday 22nd May 2004
Siddal 18 ....West Hull 16
at Mount Pleasant, Batley

DIVISION ONE

	P	W	D	L	F	A	D	Pts
Wath Brow Hornets	24	23	0	1	892	314	612	46
Wigan St Judes	24	20	0	4	659	312	347	40
Hull Dockers	24	16	1	7	687	415	238	33
Bradford-Dudley H	24	13	0	11	613	444	169	26
Milford Marlins	24	13	0	11	636	506	130	26
Shaw Cross Sharks	24	12	2	10	480	384	96	26
East Leeds	24	10	0	14	446	397	49	20
Walney Central	24	10	0	14	437	418	19	20
Askam	24	10	0	14	363	529	-166	20
Hunslet Warriors	24	9	1	14	388	557	-169	19
Eccles & Salford J	24	8	1	15	416	614	-198	17
Crosfields	24	8	0	16	489	682	-193	16
Saddleworth R	24	1	1	22	236	1183	-947	3

DIVISION TWO

	P	W	D	L	F	A	D	Pts
East Hull	24	20	2	2	846	337	509	42
Rochdale Mayfield	24	20	0	4	918	366	552	40
Castleford Panthers	24	20	0	4	643	298	345	40
Ince Rosebridge	24	15	1	8	726	412	314	31
Huddersfield S	24	14	2	8	437	445	-8	30
Normanton Knights	24	11	1	12	483	430	53	23
Eastmoor Dragons	24	11	1	12	488	458	30	23
Widnes St Maries	24	10	0	14	424	588	-164	20
Waterhead	24	9	1	14	495	648	-153	19
York Acorn	24	9	0	15	410	690	-280	18
Cottingham Tigers	24	7	0	17	281	644	-363	14
Heworth	24	4	0	20	361	739	-378	8
Millom	24	2	0	22	240	755	-515	4

NATIONAL CUP

QUARTER FINALS
Saturday 17th April 2004
Ideal Isberg 24...East Hull 16
Oldham St Annes 26 ....Bradford-Dudley Hill 8
Skirlaugh 38 ....Ellenborough Rangers 10
Wath Brow Hornets 31 ....Thornhill Trojans 10

SEMI-FINALS
Saturday 1st May 2004
Oldham St Annes 15.......................................Skirlaugh 6
Wath Brow Hornets 34 ....Ideal Isberg 27

FINAL
Saturday 29th May 2004
Oldham St Annes 19...................Wath Brow Hornets 25
at Bloomfield Road, Blackpool

TOTALRL.COM CONFERENCE

NORTH WEST

	P	W	D	L	F	A	D	PTS
Widnes Saints	10	9	0	1	524	152	372	18
Chester Wolves	10	9	0	1	475	186	289	18
Bolton le Moors	10	8	0	2	280	177	103	16
Liverpool B	10	6	0	4	289	204	85	12
Crewe Wolves	10	4	0	6	270	314	-44	8
Lancaster	10	3	0	7	208	294	-86	6
Blackpool Sea E	10	0	1	9	104	445	-341	1
North Wales C	10	0	1	9	160	538	-378	1

SOUTH

	P	W	D	L	F	A	D	PTS
West London S	8	7	0	1	424	116	308	14
Greenwich Admirals	8	7	0	1	274	180	94	14
Kingston Warriors	8	3	0	5	218	252	-34	6
Gosport & Fareham	8	3	0	5	182	248	-66	6
South London S	8	0	0	8	88	390	-302	0

SOUTH MIDLANDS

	P	W	D	L	F	A	D	PTS
Coventry Bears 'A'	10	8	0	2	447	226	221	16
Leicester Phoenix *	10	8	0	2	569	144	425	14
Birmingham B	10	6	0	4	276	248	28	12
St Albans C	10	4	0	6	340	303	37	8
Wolverhampton W	10	4	0	6	174	358	-184	8
Rugby Raiders	10	0	0	10	118	645	-527	0

** Points deducted*

NORTH MIDLANDS

	P	W	D	L	F	A	D	PTS
Rotherham Giants	10	9	0	1	510	94	416	18
Nottingham Outlaws	10	8	0	2	318	197	121	16
Derby City	10	7	0	3	210	160	50	14
Mansfield Storm	10	4	0	6	230	288	-58	8
Sheff-Hillsborough	10	2	0	8	142	394	-252	4
Worksop Sharks	10	0	0	10	138	415	-277	0

NORTH EAST

	P	W	D	L	F	A	D	PTS
Jarrow Vikings	10	9	0	1	382	128	254	18
Newcastle Knights	10	7	0	3	324	209	115	14
Sunderland City	10	7	0	3	270	213	57	14
Peterlee Pumas	10	4	0	6	287	166	121	8
Yorkshire Coast T	10	4	0	6	231	318	-87	8
Durham City	10	1	0	9	172	418	-246	2
Whitley Bay B	10	1	0	9	94	496	-402	2

EAST

	P	W	D	L	F	A	D	PTS
Ipswich Rhinos	10	10	0	0	531	116	415	20
North London	10	8	0	2	576	108	468	16
South Norfolk S	10	7	0	3	474	229	245	14
Luton Vipers	10	7	0	3	392	217	175	14
St Ives Roosters	10	4	0	6	200	424	-224	8
Hemel H Stags	10	2	0	8	212	440	-228	4
Cambridge Eagles	10	2	0	8	156	446	-290	4
Middlesex Lions	10	0	0	10	107	668	-561	0

SOUTH WEST

	P	W	D	L	F	A	D	PTS
Somerset Vikings	10	9	0	1	526	154	372	18
Gloucestershire W	10	8	0	2	434	200	234	16
Bristol Sonics	10	5	1	4	340	334	6	11
Oxford Cavaliers	10	4	1	5	254	416	-162	9
Telford Raiders	10	1	2	7	178	340	-162	4
Worcestershire S	10	1	0	9	202	490	-288	2

YORKSHIRE

	P	W	D	L	F	A	D	PTS
Leeds Akademiks	10	9	0	1	374	170	204	18
Wetherby Bulldogs	10	9	0	1	351	170	181	18
Hull Phoenix	10	5	1	4	368	217	151	11
Bridlington Bulls	10	5	1	4	335	276	59	11
South Wakefield S	10	5	0	5	235	306	-71	10
Thorne Moor M	10	3	1	6	213	297	-84	7
Bradford-Dudley H	10	1	1	8	206	435	-229	3
Hudds-Underbank	10	1	0	9	200	411	-211	2

CUMBRIA

	P	W	D	L	F	A	D	PTS
Barrow Shipbuilders	10	9	0	1	416	142	274	18
Penrith Pumas	10	5	2	3	391	222	169	12
West Cumbria	10	5	2	3	317	149	168	12
Copeland Athletic	10	5	2	3	240	223	17	12
Carlisle Centurions	10	0	0	10	72	512	-440	0

WALES

	P	W	D	L	F	A	D	PTS
Bridgend Blue Bulls	12	12	0	0	544	197	347	24
Aberavon Fighting I	12	9	0	3	464	291	173	18
Torfaen Tigers	12	7	0	5	459	289	170	14
Newport Titans	12	6	1	5	426	315	111	13
Cardiff Demons	12	3	0	9	358	442	-84	6
Swansea Valley M	12	2	1	9	235	647	-412	5
Valley Cougars	12	2	0	10	266	571	-305	4

HARRY JEPSON TROPHY PLAY-OFFS

Saturday 24th July 2004
Barrow Shipbuilders 0 ....Penrith Pumas 24
Bolton le Moors 8 ....Liverpool Buccaneers 36
Gloucestershire Warriors 68 ....Bristol Sonics 16
Greenwich Admirals 66....................Kingston Warriors 9
Hull Phoenix 56 ....Bridlington Bulls 14
Ipswich Rhinos 30 ....North London Skolars 22
Jarrow Vikings 22..........................Newcastle Knights 38
Leeds Akademiks 14 ....Wetherby Bulldogs 6
Leicester Phoenix 48 ....Birmingham Bulldogs 24
Nottingham Outlaws 28.............................Derby City 22
South Norfolk Saints 56 ....Luton Vipers 16
Sunderland City 12 ....Peterlee Pumas 36
West Cumbria 32............................Copeland Athletic 16
Widnes Saints 31 ....Chester Wolves 29

Saturday 31st July 2004
Aberavon Fighting Irish 27 ....Torfaen Tigers 22
Chester 16 ....Liverpool Buccaneers 14
Coventry Bears 12 ....Leicester Phoenix 30
Jarrow Vikings 18 ....Peterlee Pumas 36
North London Skolars 42 ....South Norfolk Saints 18
Rotherham Giants 24..................Nottingham Outlaws 36
Somerset Vikings 52 ....Gloucestershire Warriors 4
West London Sharks 52................Greenwich Admirals 6
Wetherby Bulldogs 28 ....Hull Phoenix 18

Saturday 7th August 2004
Aberavon Fighting Irish 21 ....Bridgend Blue Bulls 26
Ipswich Rhinos 18 ....North London Skolars 14
Leeds Akademiks 24 ....Wetherby Bulldogs 26
Newcastle Knights 34 ....Peterlee Pumas 12
Nottingham Outlaws 24 ....Leicester Phoenix 48
Widnes Saints 52 ....Chester Wolves 10

Saturday 14th August 2004
Bridgend Blue Bulls 18 ....West London Sharks 30
Ipswich Rhinos 54 ....Leicester Phoenix 12
Wetherby Bulldogs 54...................Newcastle Knights 14
Widnes Saints 52 ....Penrith Pumas 16

Sunday 22nd August 2004
Ipswich Rhinos 8 ....West London Sharks 40
Wetherby Bulldogs 4............................Widnes Saints 29

RLC SHIELD PLAY-OFFS

Saturday 24th July 2004
Blackpool Sea Eagles 36 ....North Wales Coasters 12
Bradford-Dudley Hill 38 ..Hudds-Underbank Rangers 16
Cambridge Eagles 42 ....Middlesex Lions 18
Crewe Wolves 24 ....Lancaster 18
Durham City 74.........................Whitley Bay Barbarians 4
Gosport & Fareham 2 ....South London Storm 26
Sheffield-Hillsborough 38 ....Worksop Sharks 44
South Wakefield Sharks 54 ..Thorne Moor Marauders 12
St Ives Roosters 32 ....Hemel Hempstead Stags 8
Telford Raiders 67.............................Worcester Saints 16
Wolverhampton Wizards 30 ....Rugby Raiders 6

Saturday 31st July 2004
Cardiff Demons 54..................Swansea Valley Miners 22
Hemel Stags 4 ....Cambridge Eagles 28
Lancaster 18..Blackpool 30
Mansfield Storm 32 ....Worksop Sharks 44
Newport Titans 30 ....Valley Cougars 6
Oxford Cavaliers 14 ....Telford Raiders 35
St Albans Centurions 38 ......Wolverhampton Wizards 28
Thorne Moor Marauders 46........Bradford-Dudley Hill 36

Saturday 7th August 2004
Crewe Wolves 35 ....Blackpool Sea Eagles 20
Newport Titans 35 ....Cardiff Demons 38
South Wakefield Sharks 6 ....Thorne Moor Marauders 34
St Albans Centurions 17 ....Worksop Sharks 15
St Ives Roosters 32.........................Cambridge Eagles 22
Telford Raiders 46 ....South London Storm 26

Saturday 14th August 2004
Cardiff Demons 46...............................Telford Raiders 6
St Albans Centurions 30 ....St Ives Roosters 22 (aet)
Thorne Moor Marauders 30 ....Durham City 29

Sunday 22nd August 2004
Cardiff Demons 66 ....St Albans Centurions 14
Thorne Moor Marauders 30.................Crewe Wolves 28

HARRY JEPSON TROPHY - GRAND FINAL

Sunday 5th September 2004
West London Sharks 28 ....Widnes Saints 36
at Woollams, St Albans

RLC SHIELD - GRAND FINAL

Sunday 5th September 2004
Cardiff Demons 29 ....Thorne Moor Marauders 20
at Woollams, St Albans

ACADEMY

SENIOR ACADEMY UNDER-21s CHAMPIONSHIP

	P	W	D	L	F	A	D	PTS
Leeds Rhinos	18	15	0	3	602	350	252	30
Wakefield T Wildcats	18	12	1	5	533	385	148	25
Hull FC	18	11	0	7	515	416	99	22
Bradford Bulls	18	10	0	8	550	446	104	20
Wigan Warriors	18	8	1	9	592	574	18	17
St Helens	18	8	0	10	505	548	-43	16
Halifax	18	8	0	10	474	554	-80	16
Widnes Vikings	18	8	0	10	442	535	-93	16
Castleford Tigers	18	7	0	11	368	431	-63	14
Warrington Wolves	18	2	0	16	358	700	-342	4

ELIMINATION PLAY-OFFS
Thursday 9th September 2004
Bradford Bulls 30 ....Wigan Warriors 22
Saturday 11th September 2004
Hull FC 27 ....St Helens 10

QUALIFYING SEMI-FINAL
Wednesday 15th September 2004
Leeds Rhinos 30 ....Wakefield Trinity Wildcats 16

ELIMINATION SEMI-FINAL
Saturday 18th September 2004
Hull FC 18 ....Bradford Bulls 28

FINAL ELIMINATOR
Thursday 23rd September 2004
Wakefield Trinity Wildcats 6 ....Bradford Bulls 64

GRAND FINAL
Wednesday 29th September 2004
Leeds Rhinos 18 ....Bradford Bulls 20

SENIOR ACADEMY UNDER-21 DIVISION ONE

	P	W	D	L	F	A	D	PTS
Leigh Centurions	14	13	1	0	621	206	415	27
Huddersfield Giants	14	10	1	3	600	322	278	21
Salford City Reds	14	10	0	4	429	303	126	20
Featherstone Rovers	14	7	0	7	414	358	56	14
Doncaster Dragons	14	5	0	9	339	500	-161	10
Oldham	14	3	1	10	261	479	-218	7
Dewsbury Rams	14	3	1	10	286	509	-223	7
Keighley Cougars	14	3	0	11	245	518	-273	6

PLAY-OFFS

Sunday 29th August 2004
Salford City Reds 24 ....Featherstone Rovers 26

Monday 30th August 2004
Leigh Centurions 48 ....Huddersfield Giants 12

Thursday 2nd September 2004
Huddersfield Giants 18 ....Featherstone Rovers 20

GRAND FINAL

Monday 13th September 2004
Leigh Centurions 36 ....Featherstone Rovers 10

Leeds' Dwayne Barker moves in on Bradford's Richard Johnson during the Senior Academy Grand Final

JUNIOR ACADEMY UNDER-18s CHAMPIONSHIP

	P	W	D	L	F	A	D	PTS
Castleford Tigers	14	10	1	3	412	290	122	21
St Helens	14	9	0	5	398	345	53	18
Wigan Warriors	14	8	1	5	423	288	135	17
Leeds Rhinos	14	8	1	5	458	344	114	17
Bradford Bulls	14	7	1	6	370	343	27	15
Hull FC	14	7	0	7	392	417	-25	14
Halifax	14	3	0	11	253	494	-241	6
Widnes Vikings	14	2	0	12	288	473	-185	4

ELIMINATION PLAY-OFFS
Friday 17th September 2004
Leeds Rhinos 33 ....Bradford Bulls 6
Saturday 18th September 2004
Wigan Warriors 42 ....Hull FC 18

QUALIFYING SEMI-FINAL
Saturday 25th September 2004
Castleford Tigers 44 ....St Helens 10

ELIMINATION SEMI-FINAL
Saturday 25th September 2004
Wigan Warriors 20 ....Leeds Rhinos 28

FINAL ELIMINATOR
Saturday 2nd October 2004
St Helens 36 ....Leeds Rhinos 12

GRAND FINAL
Saturday 9th October 2004
Castleford Tigers 26 ....St Helens 16

JUNIOR ACADEMY UNDER-18s DIVISION ONE

	P	W	D	L	F	A	D	PTS
Warrington Wolves	14	12	0	2	536	208	328	24
Huddersfield Giants	14	11	1	2	459	262	197	23
Salford City Reds	14	9	1	4	376	235	141	19
Wakefield T Wildcats	14	9	0	5	447	316	131	18
London Broncos	14	8	1	5	484	376	108	17
Hull KR	14	5	0	9	298	370	-72	10
Featherstone Rovers	14	3	1	10	247	508	-261	7
Keighley Cougars	14	2	0	12	279	520	-241	4
Leigh Centurions	14	2	0	12	233	572	-339	4

ELIMINATION PLAY-OFFS
Saturday 18th September 2004
Salford City Reds 34 ....Hull Kingston Rovers 4
Wakefield Trinity Wildcats 22...........London Broncos 44

ELIMINATION SEMI-FINAL
Thursday 23rd September 2004
Salford City Reds 28 ....London Broncos 0

QUALIFYING SEMI-FINAL
Saturday 25th September 2004
Warrington Wolves 40 ....Huddersfield Giants 16

FINAL ELIMINATOR
Saturday 2nd October 2004
Salford City Reds 12...................Huddersfield Giants 14

GRAND FINAL
Thursday 7th October 2004
Huddersfield Giants 12 ....Warrington Wolves 26

Castleford's Craig Huby grounded against St Helens during the Junior Academy Grand Final

SUPER LEAGUE 2005 FIXTURES

ROUND 1

FRIDAY 11 FEBRUARY 2005
Hull FC v Leeds Rhinos 8:00
St Helens v Widnes Vikings.................8:00
Wigan Warriors v Salford City Reds 8:00
SATURDAY 12 FEBRUARY 2005
Leigh Centurions v Huddersfield Giants ..6:05
SUNDAY 13 FEBRUARY 2005
Bradford Bulls v Wakefield T Wildcats..3:00
London Broncos v Warrington Wolves 3:00

ROUND 2

FRIDAY 18 FEBRUARY 2005
Leeds Rhinos v St Helens 8:00
Salford City Reds v London Broncos....8:00
SATURDAY 19 FEBRUARY 2005
Wakefield T Wildcats v Wigan Warriors ..6:05
SUNDAY 20 FEBRUARY 2005
Huddersfield Giants v Hull FC 3:00
Warrington Wolves v Leigh Centurions..3:00
Widnes Vikings v Bradford Bulls 3:00

ROUND 3

FRIDAY 25 FEBRUARY 2005
St Helens v Huddersfield Giants 8:00
Wigan Warriors v Bradford Bulls..........8:00
SATURDAY 26 FEBRUARY 2005
Leigh Centurions v Salford City Reds ..6:05
SUNDAY 27 FEBRUARY 2005
Hull FC v Warrington Wolves................3:15
Leeds Rhinos v Widnes Vikings 3:00
London Broncos v Wakefield T Wildcats..3:00

ROUND 4

FRIDAY 4 MARCH 2005
Warrington Wolves v St Helens 8:00
SATURDAY 5 MARCH 2005
Salford City Reds v Hull FC 6:05
SUNDAY 6 MARCH 2005
Bradford Bulls v London Broncos 3:00
Huddersfield Giants v Leeds Rhinos 3:00
Wakefield T Wildcats v Leigh Centurions..3:30
Widnes Vikings v Wigan Warriors 3:00

ROUND 5

FRIDAY 11 MARCH 2005
Huddersfield Giants v Widnes Vikings ..8:00
Leeds Rhinos v Warrington Wolves......8:00
Leigh Centurions v Bradford Bulls........8:00
St Helens v Salford City Reds 8:00
SATURDAY 12 MARCH 2005
London Broncos v Wigan Warriors 6:05
SUNDAY 13 MARCH 2005
Hull FC v Wakefield Trinity Wildcats 3:15

ROUND 6

FRIDAY 18 MARCH 2005
Bradford Bulls v Hull FC 8:00
Salford City Reds v Leeds Rhinos 8:00
Wigan Warriors v Leigh Centurions......8:00
SATURDAY 19 MARCH 2005
St Helens v Wakefield Trinity Wildcats..6:05
SUNDAY 20 MARCH 2005
London Broncos v Widnes Vikings 3:00
Warrington Wolves v Huddersfield Giants 3:00

ROUND 7

THURSDAY 24 MARCH 2005
Bradford Bulls v Leeds Rhinos..............TBA
FRIDAY 25 MARCH 2005
London Broncos v Hull FC....................3:00
Salford City Reds v Warrington Wolves ..3:00
Wakefield T Wildcats v Huddersfield Giants..7:30
Widnes Vikings v Leigh Centurions 3:00
Wigan Warriors v St Helens ....TBA

ROUND 8

MONDAY 28 MARCH 2005
Huddersfield Giants v Salford City Reds ..3:00
Hull FC v Wigan Warriors 3:15
Leeds Rhinos v Wakefield T Wildcats ..8:00
Leigh Centurions v London Broncos 3:00
St Helens v Bradford Bulls ....TBA
TUESDAY 29 MARCH 2005
Warrington Wolves v Widnes Vikings ..TBA

SUNDAY 3 APRIL 2005
POWERGEN CHALLENGE CUP
- FOURTH ROUND

ROUND 9

FRIDAY 8 APRIL 2005
Huddersfield Giants v Wigan Warriors..8:00
Salford City Reds v Wakefield T Wildcats..8:00
St Helens v Leigh Centurions 8:00
SATURDAY 09 APRIL 2005
Leeds Rhinos v London Broncos..........6:05
SUNDAY 10 APRIL 2005
Hull FC v Widnes Vikings.....................3:15
Warrington Wolves v Bradford Bulls 3:00

ROUND 10

FRIDAY 15 APRIL 2005
Wigan Warriors v Leeds Rhinos 8:00
SATURDAY 16 APRIL 2005
London Broncos v St Helens 6:05
SUNDAY 17 APRIL 2005
Bradford Bulls v Huddersfield Giants....3:00
Leigh Centurions v Hull FC 3:00
Wakefield T Wildcats v Warrington Wolves ..3:30
Widnes Vikings v Salford City Reds......3:00

ROUND 11

FRIDAY 22 APRIL 2005
Bradford Bulls v Wigan Warriors..........8:00
Salford City Reds v Leigh Centurions ..8:00
SATURDAY 23 APRIL 2005
Widnes Vikings v Leeds Rhinos 6:05
SUNDAY 24 APRIL 2005
Huddersfield Giants v St Helens 3:00
Wakefield T Wildcats v London Broncos..3:30
Warrington Wolves v Hull FC................3:00

ROUND 12

FRIDAY 29 APRIL 2005
Leeds Rhinos v Huddersfield Giants 8:00
St Helens v Warrington Wolves............8:00
Wigan Warriors v Widnes Vikings 8:00
SATURDAY 30 APRIL 2005
Leigh Centurions v Wakefield T Wildcats..6:05
SUNDAY 1 MAY 2005
Hull FC v Salford City Reds 3:15
MONDAY 2 MAY 2005
London Broncos v Bradford Bulls ....TBA

SUNDAY 8 MAY 2005
POWERGEN CHALLENGE CUP
- FIFTH ROUND

ROUND 13

FRIDAY 13 MAY 2005
Hull FC v St Helens 8:00
Leigh Centurions v Leeds Rhinos 8:00
Salford City Reds v Bradford Bulls 8:00
SATURDAY 14 MAY 2005
Wakefield T Wildcats v Widnes Vikings ..TBA
SUNDAY 15 MAY 2005
Huddersfield Giants v London Broncos..3:00
Warrington Wolves v Wigan Warriors ..3:00

ROUND 14

FRIDAY 20 MAY 2005
Leeds Rhinos v Leigh Centurions 8:00
Wigan Warriors v Huddersfield Giants..8:00
SATURDAY 21 MAY 2005
Widnes Vikings v St Helens..................6:05
SUNDAY 22 MAY 2005
Bradford Bulls v Warrington Wolves 3:00
London Broncos v Salford City Reds....3:00
Wakefield Trinity Wildcats v Hull FC 3:30

ROUND 15

FRIDAY 27 MAY 2005
St Helens v Leeds Rhinos 8:00
SATURDAY 28 MAY 2005
Hull FC v Bradford Bulls 6:05
SUNDAY 29 MAY 2005
London Broncos v Leigh Centurions 3:00
at TBA
Warrington Wolves v Wakefield T Wildcats ..3:00
Widnes Vikings v Huddersfield Giants ..3:00
MONDAY 30 MAY 2005
Salford City Reds v Wigan Warriors......TBA

ROUND 16

FRIDAY 3 JUNE 2005
Leeds Rhinos v Hull FC 8:00
Wigan Warriors v London Broncos 8:00
SATURDAY 04 JUNE 2005
Bradford Bulls v St Helens....................6:05
SUNDAY 05 JUNE 2005
Huddersfield Giants v Warrington Wolves ..3:00
Leigh Centurions v Widnes Vikings 3:00
Wakefield T Wildcats v Salford City Reds ..3:30

ROUND 17

FRIDAY 10 JUNE 2005
Salford City Reds v St Helens 8:00
Wakefield T Wildcats v Leeds Rhinos ..8:00
Wigan Warriors v Hull FC 8:00
SATURDAY 11 JUNE 2005
Huddersfield Giants v Bradford Bulls....6:05
SUNDAY 12 JUNE 2005
Leigh Centurions v Warrington Wolves ..3:00
Widnes Vikings v London Broncos 3:00

ROUND 18

FRIDAY 17 JUNE 2005
St Helens v London Broncos 8:00
SATURDAY 18 JUNE 2005
Leeds Rhinos v Wigan Warriors 6:05
SUNDAY 19 JUNE 2005
Bradford Bulls v Widnes Vikings 3:00
Huddersfield Giants v Wakefield T Wildcats ..3:00
Hull FC v Leigh Centurions 3:15
Warrington Wolves v Salford City Reds ..3:00

SUNDAY 26 JUNE 2005
POWERGEN CHALLENGE CUP
- QUARTER FINALS

ROUND 19

FRIDAY 1 JULY 2005
Leeds Rhinos v Bradford Bulls 8:00
Leigh Centurions v Wigan Warriors......8:00
SATURDAY 2 JULY 2005
Salford City Reds v Huddersfield Giants ..6:05
SUNDAY 3 JULY 2005
London Broncos v Hull FC....................3:00
at TBA
Wakefield Trinity Wildcats v St Helens..3:30
Widnes Vikings v Warrington Wolves ..3:00

ROUND 20

FRIDAY 8 JULY 2005
Salford City Reds v Widnes Vikings......8:00
St Helens v Hull FC 8:00
SATURDAY 09 JULY 2005
London Broncos v Leeds Rhinos..........6:00
at Perpignan
Wigan Warriors v Warrington Wolves ..6:05
SUNDAY 10 JULY 2005
Huddersfield Giants v Leigh Centurions ..3:00
Wakefield T Wildcats v Bradford Bulls..3:30

ROUND 21

FRIDAY 15 JULY 2005
St Helens v Wigan Warriors..................8:00
SATURDAY 16 JULY 2005
Hull FC v Huddersfield Giants 6:05
SUNDAY 17 JULY 2005
Bradford Bulls v Leigh Centurions........3:00
Leeds Rhinos v Salford City Reds 3:00
Warrington Wolves v London Broncos ..3:00
Widnes Vikings v Wakefield T Wildcats ..3:00

ROUND 22

FRIDAY 22 JULY 2005
Leigh Centurions v St Helens 8:00
Salford City Reds v Bradford Bulls 8:00
Wigan Warriors v Wakefield T Wildcats ..8:00
SATURDAY 23 JULY 2005
Warrington Wolves v Leeds Rhinos......6:05
SUNDAY 24 JULY 2005
London Broncos v Huddersfield Giants ..3:00
Widnes Vikings v Hull FC......................3:00

SUNDAY 31 JULY 2005
POWERGEN CHALLENGE CUP
- SEMI FINALS

ROUND 23

FRIDAY 5 AUGUST 2005
Leigh Centurions v Leeds Rhinos 8:00
Wigan Warriors v Salford City Reds 8:00
SUNDAY 7 AUGUST 2005
Bradford Bulls v Widnes Vikings 3:00
Hull FC v London Broncos....................3:15
Wakefield T Wildcats v Huddersfield Giants ..3:30
Warrington Wolves v St Helens 3:00

ROUND 24

FRIDAY 12 AUGUST 2005
Leeds Rhinos v London Broncos..........8:00
St Helens v Wakefield Trinity Wildcats..8:00
SUNDAY 14 AUGUST 2005
Bradford Bulls v Salford City Reds 3:00
Huddersfield Giants v Warrington Wolves ..3:00
Hull FC v Leigh Centurions 3:15
Widnes Vikings v Wigan Warriors 3:00

ROUND 25

FRIDAY 19 AUGUST 2005
Leeds Rhinos v Bradford Bulls 8:00
Salford City Reds v Wakefield T Wildcats ..8:00
St Helens v London Broncos 8:00
SUNDAY 21 AUGUST 2005
Huddersfield Giants v Leigh Centurions ..3:00
Hull FC v Wigan Warriors 3:15
Widnes Vikings v Warrington Wolves ..3:00

SATURDAY 27 AUGUST 2005
POWERGEN CHALLENGE CUP FINAL

ROUND 26

FRIDAY 2 SEPTEMBER 2005
Wigan Warriors v Leeds Rhinos 8:00
SUNDAY 4 SEPTEMBER 2005
Bradford Bulls v Hull FC 3:00
Leigh Centurions v St Helens 3:00
London Broncos v Huddersfield Giants ..3:00
Wakefield T Wildcats v Widnes Vikings ..3:30
Warrington Wolves v Salford City Reds ..3:00

ROUND 27

FRIDAY 9 SEPTEMBER 2005
Salford City Reds v London Broncos....8:00
Wigan Warriors v St Helens..................8:00
SUNDAY 11 SEPTEMBER 2005
Bradford Bulls v Huddersfield Giants....3:00
Wakefield Trinity Wildcats v Hull FC 3:30
Warrington Wolves v Leeds Rhinos......3:00
Widnes Vikings v Leigh Centurions 3:00

ROUND 28

FRIDAY 16 SEPTEMBER 2005
Leeds Rhinos v Wakefield T Wildcats ..8:00
Leigh Centurions v Salford City Reds ..8:00
St Helens v Bradford Bulls...................8:00
SUNDAY 18 SEPTEMBER 2005
Huddersfield Giants v Wigan Warriors..3:00
Hull FC v Warrington Wolves...............3:15
London Broncos v Widnes Vikings 3:00

PLAY-OFFS

FRIDAY 23 SEPTEMBER 2005
SUPER LEAGUE ELIMINATION PLAY OFFS

FRIDAY 30 SEPTEMBER 2005
SUPER LEAGUE PLAY OFF SEMI-FINALS

FRIDAY 07 OCTOBER 2005
SUPER LEAGUE PLAY OFF
- FINAL ELIMINATOR

SATURDAY 15 OCTOBER 2005
SUPER LEAGUE X GRAND FINAL

KEY DATES FOR THE 2005 AUSTRALIAN CALENDAR

MARCH 11-13
NRL PREMIERSHIP OPENING ROUND
Bulldogs v St George-Illawarra Dragons
Brisbane Broncos v North Qld Cowboys
Sydney Roosters v Souths Rabbitohs
Wests Tigers v Parramatta Eels
Melbourne Storm v Newcastle Knights
NZ Warriors v Manly Sea Eagles
Canberra Raiders bye

APRIL 22
ANZAC TEST
Australia v New Zealand (Suncorp Stadium)

MAY 6
CITY-COUNTRY
Country Origin v City Origin (Lismore)

MAY 25
STATE OF ORIGIN I
Queensland v NSW (Suncorp Stadium)

JUNE 15
STATE OF ORIGIN II
NSW v Queensland (Telstra Stadium)

JULY 6
STATE OF ORIGIN III
Queensland v NSW (Suncorp Stadium)

SEPTEMBER 9-11
NRL PREMIERSHIP
Finals series begins

OCTOBER 2
NRL PREMIERSHIP
Grand Final (Telstra Stadium)

311

NATIONAL LEAGUE 2005 FIXTURES

NATIONAL LEAGUE ONE

MONDAY 28 MARCH 2005
Barrow Raiders v Whitehaven 3:00
Doncaster Dragons v Castleford Tigers 7:30
Featherstone Rovers v Oldham 7:30
Halifax v Hull Kingston Rovers 7:30
Rochdale Hornets v Batley Bulldogs 7:30

SUNDAY 3 APRIL 2005
POWERGEN CHALLENGE CUP
- FOURTH ROUND

SUNDAY 10 APRIL 2005
Batley Bulldogs v Barrow Raiders 3:00
Castleford Tigers v Rochdale Hornets 3:30
Hull Kingston Rovers v Featherstone Rovers 3:00
Oldham v Doncaster Dragons 3:00
Whitehaven v Halifax 3:00

SUNDAY 17 APRIL 2005
Barrow Raiders v Rochdale Hornets 3:00
Doncaster Dragons v Hull Kingston Rovers..3:00
Featherstone Rovers v Whitehaven 3:00
Halifax v Batley Bulldogs 3:00
Oldham v Castleford Tigers 3:00

SUNDAY 24 APRIL 2005
Barrow Raiders v Castleford Tigers 3:00
Batley Bulldogs v Featherstone Rovers 3:00
Hull Kingston Rovers v Oldham 3:00
Rochdale Hornets v Halifax 3:00
Whitehaven v Doncaster Dragons 3:00

SUNDAY 1 MAY 2005
NATIONAL LEAGUE CUP - PLAY OFFS

SUNDAY 8 MAY 2005
POWERGEN CHALLENGE CUP - FIFTH ROUND

SUNDAY 15 MAY 2005
Castleford Tigers v Hull Kingston Rovers ..3:30
Doncaster Dragons v Batley Bulldogs 3:00
Featherstone Rovers v Rochdale Hornets ..3:00
Halifax v Barrow Raiders 3:00
Oldham v Whitehaven 3:00

SUNDAY 22 MAY 2005
Barrow Raiders v Featherstone Rovers 3:00
Batley Bulldogs v Oldham 3:00
Halifax v Castleford Tigers 3:00
Rochdale Hornets v Doncaster Dragons 3:00
Whitehaven v Hull Kingston Rovers 3:00

SUNDAY 29 MAY 2005
NATIONAL LEAGUE CUP - QUARTER FINALS

SUNDAY 05 JUNE 2005
Castleford Tigers v Whitehaven..................3:30
Doncaster Dragons v Barrow Raiders 3:00
Featherstone Rovers v Halifax 3:00
Hull Kingston Rovers v Batley Bulldogs 3:00
Oldham v Rochdale Hornets 3:00

SUNDAY 12 JUNE 2005
Barrow Raiders v Oldham 3:00
Batley Bulldogs v Whitehaven 3:00
Featherstone Rovers v Castleford Tigers 3:00
Halifax v Doncaster Dragons 3:00
Rochdale Hornets v Hull Kingston Rovers ..3:00

SUNDAY 19 JUNE 2005
NATIONAL LEAGUE CUP - SEMI FINALS

SUNDAY 26 JUNE 2005
Castleford Tigers v Batley Bulldogs 3:30
Doncaster Dragons v Featherstone Rovers ..3:00
Hull Kingston Rovers v Barrow Raiders 3:00
Oldham v Halifax 3:00
Whitehaven v Rochdale Hornets 3:00

POWERGEN CHALLENGE CUP
- QUARTER FINALS

SUNDAY 3 JULY 2005
Batley Bulldogs v Rochdale Hornets 3:00
Castleford Tigers v Doncaster Dragons 3:30
Hull Kingston Rovers v Halifax 3:00
Oldham v Featherstone Rovers 3:00
Whitehaven v Barrow Raiders 3:00

SUNDAY 10 JULY 2005
Barrow Raiders v Batley Bulldogs 3:00
Doncaster Dragons v Oldham 3:00
Featherstone Rovers v Hull Kingston Rovers..3:00
Halifax v Whitehaven 3:00
Rochdale Hornets v Castleford Tigers 3:00

SUNDAY 17 JULY 2005
NATIONAL LEAGUE CUP FINAL

SUNDAY 24 JULY 2005
Batley Bulldogs v Halifax 3:00
Castleford Tigers v Oldham 3:30
Hull Kingston Rovers v Doncaster Dragons ..3:00
Rochdale Hornets v Barrow Raiders 3:00
Whitehaven v Featherstone Rovers 3:00

SUNDAY 31 JULY 2005
Castleford Tigers v Barrow Raiders............3:30
Doncaster Dragons v Whitehaven 3:00
Featherstone Rovers v Batley Bulldogs 3:00
Halifax v Rochdale Hornets 3:00
Oldham v Hull Kingston Rovers 3:00

POWERGEN CHALLENGE CUP - SEMI FINALS

SUNDAY 7 AUGUST 2005
Barrow Raiders v Halifax 3:00
Batley Bulldogs v Doncaster Dragons 3:00
Hull Kingston Rovers v Castleford Tigers ...3:00
Rochdale Hornets v Featherstone Rovers ..3:00
Whitehaven v Oldham 3:00

SUNDAY 14 AUGUST 2005
Barrow Raiders v Doncaster Dragons 3:00
Batley Bulldogs v Hull Kingston Rovers 3:00
Halifax v Featherstone Rovers 3:00
Rochdale Hornets v Oldham 3:00
Whitehaven v Castleford Tigers.................3:00

SUNDAY 21 AUGUST 2005
Castleford Tigers v Halifax.........................3:30
Doncaster Dragons v Rochdale Hornets 3:00
Featherstone Rovers v Barrow Raiders 3:00
Hull Kingston Rovers v Whitehaven 3:00
Oldham v Batley Bulldogs 3:00

SATURDAY 27 AUGUST 2005
POWERGEN CHALLENGE CUP FINAL

SUNDAY 4 SEPTEMBER 2005
Castleford Tigers v Featherstone Rovers 3:30
Doncaster Dragons v Halifax 3:00
Hull Kingston Rovers v Rochdale Hornets 3:00
Oldham v Barrow Raiders 3:00
Whitehaven v Batley Bulldogs 3:00

SUNDAY 11 SEPTEMBER 2005
Barrow Raiders v Hull Kingston Rovers 3:00
Batley Bulldogs v Castleford Tigers 3:00
Featherstone Rovers v Doncaster Dragons ..3:00
Halifax v Oldham 3:00
Rochdale Hornets v Whitehaven 3:00

SUNDAY 18 SEPTEMBER 2005
LHF HEALTHPLAN
NATIONAL LEAGUE ONE - PLAY OFFS

SUNDAY 25 SEPTEMBER
LHF HEALTHPLAN
NATIONAL LEAGUE ONE - PLAY OFFS

SUNDAY 2 OCTOBER
LHF HEALTHPLAN
NATIONAL LEAGUE ONE - PLAY OFFS

SATURDAY 8 OCTOBER 2005
LHF HEALTHPLAN
NATIONAL LEAGUE ONE GRAND FINAL

NATIONAL LEAGUE TWO

MONDAY 28 MARCH 2005
Blackpool v Keighley Cougars 3:00
Dewsbury Rams v Hunslet Hawks.............3:00
London Skolars v Sheffield Eagles 3:00
Workington Town v Gateshead Thunder 3:00
York City Knights v Swinton Lions 3:00

SUNDAY 3 APRIL 2005
POWERGEN CHALLENGE CUP
- FOURTH ROUND

FRIDAY 8 APRIL 2005
Sheffield Eagles v Blackpool 8:00
SUNDAY 10 APRIL 2005
Gateshead Thunder v Dewsbury Rams 3:00
Hunslet Hawks v London Skolars 3:30
Keighley Cougars v York City Knights 3:00
Swinton Lions v Workington Town 3:00

SUNDAY 17 APRIL 2005
Blackpool v London Skolars 3:00
Dewsbury Rams v Swinton Lions 3:00
Gateshead Thunder v Hunslet Hawks 3:00
Workington Town v Keighley Cougars........3:00
York City Knights v Sheffield Eagles 3:00

FRIDAY 22 APRIL 2005
Sheffield Eagles v Keighley Cougars 8:00
SUNDAY 24 APRIL 2005
Blackpool v Gateshead Thunder 3:00
London Skolars v Swinton Lions...............3:00
Workington Town v Hunslet Hawks 3:00
York City Knights v Dewsbury Rams..........3:00

SUNDAY 1 MAY 2005
NATIONAL LEAGUE CUP - PLAY OFFS

SUNDAY 8 MAY 2005
POWERGEN CHALLENGE CUP - FIFTH ROUND

SUNDAY 15 MAY 2005
Dewsbury Rams v Workington Town 3:00
Gateshead Thunder v York City Knights 3:00
Hunslet Hawks v Sheffield Eagles 3:30
Keighley Cougars v London Skolars 3:00
Swinton Lions v Blackpool 3:00

FRIDAY 20 MAY 2005
Sheffield Eagles v Gateshead Thunder 8:00
SUNDAY 22 MAY 2005
Blackpool v Workington Town 3:00
Keighley Cougars v Swinton Lions 3:00
London Skolars v Dewsbury Rams 3:00
York City Knights v Hunslet Hawks 3:00

SUNDAY 29 MAY 2005
NATIONAL LEAGUE CUP - QUARTER FINALS

SUNDAY 5 JUNE 2005
Dewsbury Rams v Sheffield Eagles 3:00
Gateshead Thunder v Keighley Cougars 3:00
Hunslet Hawks v Swinton Lions 3:30
Workington Town v London Skolars 3:00
York City Knights v Blackpool 3:00

FRIDAY 10 JUNE 2005
Sheffield Eagles v Workington Town 8:00
SUNDAY 12 JUNE 2005
Blackpool v Hunslet Hawks 3:00
Keighley Cougars v Dewsbury Rams 3:00
London Skolars v York City Knights 3:00
Swinton Lions v Gateshead Thunder.........3:00

SUNDAY 19 JUNE 2005
NATIONAL LEAGUE CUP - SEMI FINALS

SUNDAY 26 JUNE 2005
Dewsbury Rams v Blackpool......................3:00
Gateshead Thunder v London Skolars.......3:00
Hunslet Hawks v Keighley Cougars 3:30
Swinton Lions v Sheffield Eagles 3:00
Workington Town v York City Knights 3:00

POWERGEN CHALLENGE CUP
- QUARTER FINALS

SUNDAY 3 JULY 2005
Blackpool v Sheffield Eagles 3:00
Dewsbury Rams v Gateshead Thunder 3:00
London Skolars v Hunslet Hawks 3:00
Workington Town v Swinton Lions 3:00
York City Knights v Keighley Cougars 3:00

FRIDAY 8 JULY 2005
Sheffield Eagles v London Skolars 8:00
SUNDAY 10 JULY 2005
Gateshead Thunder v Workington Town 3:00
Hunslet Hawks v Dewsbury Rams..............3:30
Keighley Cougars v Blackpool 3:00
Swinton Lions v York City Knights 3:00

SUNDAY 17 JULY 2005
NATIONAL LEAGUE CUP - FINAL

FRIDAY 22 JULY 2005
Sheffield Eagles v Hunslet Hawks 8:00
SUNDAY 24 JULY 2005
Blackpool v Swinton Lions 3:00
London Skolars v Keighley Cougars 3:00
Workington Town v Dewsbury Rams 3:00
York City Knights v Gateshead Thunder 3:00

SUNDAY 31 JULY 2005
Dewsbury Rams v York City Knights.........3:00
Gateshead Thunder v Blackpool 3:00
Hunslet Hawks v Workington Town............3:30
Keighley Cougars v Sheffield Eagles 3:00
Swinton Lions v London Skolars................3:00

POWERGEN CHALLENGE CUP - SEMI FINALS

FRIDAY 5 AUGUST 2005
Sheffield Eagles v Dewsbury Rams 8:00
SUNDAY 7 AUGUST 2005
Blackpool v York City Knights 3:00
Keighley Cougars v Gateshead Thunder 3:00
London Skolars v Workington Town 3:00
Swinton Lions v Hunslet Hawks 3:00

SUNDAY 14 AUGUST 2005
Dewsbury Rams v Keighley Cougars.........3:00
Gateshead Thunder v Swinton Lions.........3:00
Hunslet Hawks v Blackpool 3:30
Workington Town v Sheffield Eagles 3:00
York City Knights v London Skolars 3:00

SUNDAY 21 AUGUST 2005
Dewsbury Rams v London Skolars 3:00
Gateshead Thunder v Sheffield Eagles 3:00
Hunslet Hawks v York City Knights 3:30
Swinton Lions v Keighley Cougars 3:00
Workington Town v Blackpool....................3:00

SATURDAY 27 AUGUST 2005
POWERGEN CHALLENGE CUP - FINAL

FRIDAY 2 SEPTEMBER 2005
Sheffield Eagles v Swinton Lions 8:00
SUNDAY 4 SEPTEMBER 2005
Blackpool v Dewsbury Rams.....................3:00
Keighley Cougars v Hunslet Hawks 3:00
London Skolars v Gateshead Thunder.......3:00
York City Knights v Workington Town 3:00

FRIDAY 9 SEPTEMBER 2005
Sheffield Eagles v York City Knights 8:00
SUNDAY 11 SEPTEMBER 2005
Hunslet Hawks v Gateshead Thunder 3:30
Keighley Cougars v Workington Town........3:00
London Skolars v Blackpool 3:00
Swinton Lions v Dewsbury Rams 3:00

SUNDAY 18 SEPTEMBER 2005
LHF HEALTHPLAN
NATIONAL LEAGUE TWO - PLAY OFFS

SUNDAY 25 SEPTEMBER
LHF HEALTHPLAN
NATIONAL LEAGUE TWO - PLAY OFFS

SUNDAY 2 OCTOBER
LHF HEALTHPLAN
NATIONAL LEAGUE TWO - PLAY OFFS

SATURDAY 8 OCTOBER 2005
LHF HEALTHPLAN
NATIONAL LEAGUE TWO FINAL

NATIONAL LEAGUE CUP

FRIDAY 11 FEBRUARY 2005
Sheffield Eagles v Dewsbury Rams............8:00
SUNDAY 13 FEBRUARY 2005
Barrow Raiders v Gateshead Thunder 2:00
Batley Bulldogs v Doncaster Dragons 3:00
Castleford Tigers v York City Knights 3:30
Hunslet Hawks v Featherstone Rovers 3:30
Keighley Cougars v Hull Kingston Rovers..3:00
London Skolars v Halifax............................3:00
Oldham v Blackpool...................................3:00
Swinton Lions v Rochdale Hornets 3:00
Workington Town v Whitehaven 3:00

SUNDAY 20 FEBRUARY 2005
Blackpool v Swinton Lions 3:00
Dewsbury Rams v Batley Bulldogs 3:00
Doncaster Dragons v Sheffield Eagles......3:00
Featherstone Rovers v Castleford Tigers....3:00
Gateshead Thunder v Workington Town 3:00
Halifax v London Skolars 3:00
Hull Kingston Rovers v Keighley Cougars ..3:00
Rochdale Hornets v Oldham 3:00
Whitehaven v Barrow Raiders 3:00
York City Knights v Hunslet Hawks 3:00

SUNDAY 27 FEBRUARY 2005
Batley Bulldogs v Sheffield Eagles..............3:00
Castleford Tigers v Hunslet Hawks 3:30
Blackpool v Rochdale Hornets...................3:00
Dewsbury Rams v Doncaster Dragons 3:00
Featherstone Rovers v York City Knights ..3:00
Hull Kingston Rovers v Halifax...................3:00
Keighley Cougars v London Skolars 3:00
Swinton Lions v Oldham 3:00
Whitehaven v Gateshead Thunder 3:00
Workington Town v Barrow Raiders 3:00

FRIDAY 4 MARCH 2005
Sheffield Eagles v Batley Bulldogs.............8:00
SUNDAY 6 MARCH 2005
Barrow Raiders v Workington Town 2:00
Doncaster Dragons v Dewsbury Rams 3:00
Gateshead Thunder v Whitehaven 3:00
Halifax v Keighley Cougars 3:00
Hunslet Hawks v Castleford Tigers 3:30
London Skolars v Hull Kingston Rovers 3:00
Oldham v Swinton Lions 3:00
Rochdale Hornets v Blackpool...................3:00
York City Knights v Featherstone Rovers ..3:00

SUNDAY 13 MARCH 2005
POWERGEN CHALLENGE CUP
- THIRD ROUND

SUNDAY 20 MARCH 2005
Barrow Raiders v Whitehaven 2:00
Blackpool v Oldham...................................3:00
Dewsbury Rams v Sheffield Eagles............3:00
Doncaster Dragons v Batley Bulldogs 3:00
Featherstone Rovers v Hunslet Hawks 3:00
Halifax v Hull Kingston Rovers 3:00
London Skolars v Keighley Cougars 3:00
Rochdale Hornets v Swinton Lions 3:00
Workington Town v Gateshead Thunder 3:00
York City Knights v Castleford Tigers 3:00

FRIDAY 25 MARCH 2005
Batley Bulldogs v Dewsbury Rams 7:30
Castleford Tigers v Featherstone Rovers....7:30
Gateshead Thunder v Barrow Raiders 3:00
Hull Kingston Rovers v London Skolars 7:30
Hunslet Hawks v York City Knights 7:30
Keighley Cougars v Halifax 7:30
Oldham v Rochdale Hornets 3:00
Sheffield Eagles v Doncaster Dragons.......2:00
Swinton Lions v Blackpool 3:00
Whitehaven v Workington Town 3:00

● **Blackpool** - *proposed new name for Chorley
Lynx, not confirmed at time of going to press*

Grand Finals 1998-2003

1998...Jason Robinson and Robbie McCormack celebrate

1998

DIVISION ONE GRAND FINAL

Saturday 26th September 1998

FEATHERSTONE ROVERS 22 WAKEFIELD TRINITY 24

ROVERS: 1 Steve Collins; 2 Carl Hall; 3 Shaun Irwin; 4 Danny Baker; 5 Karl Pratt; 6 Jamie Coventry; 7 Ty Fallins; 8 Chico Jackson; 9 Richard Chapman; 10 Stuart Dickens; 11 Gary Price; 12 Neil Lowe; 13 Richard Slater. Subs: 14 Paddy Handley for Coventry (70); 15 Asa Amone for Lowe (50); 16 Micky Clarkson for Jackson (50); 17 Steve Dooler (not used).
Tries: Baker (15), Jackson (45), Collins (49), Hall (69);
Goals: Chapman 3.
TRINITY: 1 Martyn Holland; 2 Josh Bostock; 3 Adam Hughes; 4 Martin Law; 5 Kevin Gray; 6 Garen Casey; 7 Roger Kenworthy; 8 Francis Stephenson; 9 Roy Southernwood; 10 Gary Lord; 11 Ian Hughes; 12 Sonny Whakarau; 13 Matt Fuller. Subs: 14 Sean Richardson for I Hughes (32); 15 Andy Fisher for Lord (26); 16 David Mycoe (not used); 17 Wayne McDonald for Whakarau (70); Lord for Stephenson (40); Stephenson for Lord (70).
Tries: Southernwood (2), Bostock (7, 25), Casey (58), Stephenson (76); **Goals:** Casey 2.
League Express Men of the Match:
Rovers: Richard Chapman; *Trinity:* Garen Casey.
Penalty count: 8-3; **Half time:** 6-12; **Referee:** Nick Oddy (Halifax); **Attendance:** 8,224 *(at McAlpine Stadium, Huddersfield).*

1998...Garen Casey slots over the winning goal

SUPER LEAGUE GRAND FINAL

Saturday 24th October 1998

LEEDS RHINOS 4 WIGAN WARRIORS 10

RHINOS: 1 Iestyn Harris (C); 22 Leroy Rivett; 3 Richie Blackmore; 4 Brad Godden; 5 Francis Cummins; 13 Daryl Powell; 7 Ryan Sheridan; 8 Martin Masella; 21 Terry Newton; 25 Darren Fleary; 11 Adrian Morley; 17 Anthony Farrell; 12 Marc Glanville. Subs: 20 Jamie Mathiou for Masella (25); 24 Marcus St Hilaire for Powell (40); 14 Graham Holroyd for Newton (49); 27 Andy Hay for Fleary (54); Powell for Godden (58); Masella for Mathiou (71).
Try: Blackmore (20).
WARRIORS: 1 Kris Radlinski; 2 Jason Robinson; 3 Danny Moore; 4 Gary Connolly; 5 Mark Bell; 6 Henry Paul; 7 Tony Smith; 16 Terry O'Connor; 9 Robbie McCormack; 10 Tony Mestrov; 20 Lee Gilmour; 17 Stephen Holgate; 13 Andy Farrell (C). Subs: 8 Neil Cowie for O'Connor (18BB, rev 48); 14 Mick Cassidy for McCormack (19BB, rev 27); 25 Paul Johnson for Moore (37); 12 Simon Haughton for Gilmour (27BB, rev 33); Haughton for Holgate (33); Cowie for Mestrov (54); Cassidy for Haughton (64); Holgate for Cowie (68); Haughton for Gilmour (71BB, rev 75); Mestrov for O'Connor (75BB).
Try: Robinson (37); **Goals:** Farrell 3.
League Express Men of the Match:
Rhinos: Iestyn Harris; *Warriors:* Jason Robinson.
Penalty count: 7-13; **Half-time:** 4-6; **Referee:** Russell Smith (Castleford); **Attendance:** 43,553 *(at Old Trafford, Manchester).*

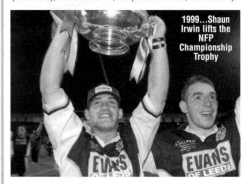

1999...Shaun Irwin lifts the NFP Championship Trophy

1999

NORTHERN FORD PREMIERSHIP GRAND FINAL

Saturday 25th September 1999

DEWSBURY RAMS 11 HUNSLET HAWKS 12

RAMS: 1 Nathan Graham; 2 Alex Godfrey; 3 Paul Evans; 4 Brendan O'Meara; 5 Adrian Flynn; 6 Richard Agar; 7 Barry Eaton; 8 Alan Boothroyd; 9 Paul Delaney; 10 Matthew Long; 11 Andy Spink; 12 Mark Haigh; 13 Damian Ball. Subs: 14 Brendan Williams for Eaton (5BB, rev 15); 15 Sean Richardson for Haigh (50); 16 Simon Hicks for Long (25); 17 Paul Medley for Spink (50); Williams for Evans (61); Long for Boothroyd (71); Spink for Long (78).
Tries: Flynn (27), Ball (54); **Goal:** Eaton; **Field goal:** Agar.
HAWKS: 1 Abraham Fatnowna; 2 Chris Ross; 3 Shaun Irwin; 4 Paul Cook; 5 Iain Higgins; 6 Marcus Vassilakopoulos; 7 Latham Tawhai; 8 Richard Hayes; 9 Richard Pachniuk; 10 Steve Pryce; 11 Rob Wilson; 12 Jamie Leighton; 13 Lee St Hilaire. Subs: 14 Mick Coyle for Wilson (57); 15 Phil Kennedy for Pryce (35); 16 Jamie Thackray for St Hilaire (25); 17 Richard Baker for Higgins (55); Higgins for Fatnowna (62); Pryce for Kennedy (65).
Tries: Cook (31), Higgins (46);
Goal: Ross; **Field goals:** Tawhai, Leighton.
League Express Men of the Match:
Rams: Barry Eaton; *Hawks:* Latham Tawhai.
Penalty count: 8-5; **Half-time:** 7-7; **Referee:** Steve Ganson (St Helens); **Attendance:** 5,783 *(at Headingley Stadium, Leeds).*

SUPER LEAGUE GRAND FINAL

Saturday 9th October 1999

BRADFORD BULLS 6 ST HELENS 8

BULLS: 28 Stuart Spruce; 2 Tevita Vaikona; 20 Scott Naylor; 5 Michael Withers; 17 Leon Pryce; 6 Henry Paul; 1 Robbie Paul (C); 10 Paul Anderson; 9 James Lowes; 29 Stuart Fielden; 15 David Boyle; 23 Bernard Dwyer; 13 Steve McNamara. Subs: 14 Paul Deacon for R Paul (53); 4 Nathan McAvoy (not used); 12 Mike Forshaw for McNamara (18); 22 Brian McDermott for Anderson (18); Anderson for Fielden (61); Fielden for Dwyer (65); R Paul for Deacon (72).
Try: H Paul (18); **Goal:** H Paul.
SAINTS: 1 Paul Atcheson; 14 Chris Smith; 3 Kevin Iro; 4 Paul Newlove; 5 Anthony Sullivan; 13 Paul Sculthorpe; 20 Tommy Martyn; 8 Apollo Perelini; 9 Keiron Cunningham; 10 Julian O'Neill; 2 Fereti Tuilagi; 21 Sonny Nickle; 11 Chris Joynt (C). Subs: 26 Paul Wellens for Martyn (52); 6 Sean Hoppe for Newlove (43); 16 Vila Matautia for O'Neill (20); 7 Sean Long for Perelini (24); Perelini for Matautia (46); O'Neill for Perelini (69).
Tries: Iro (65); **Goals:** Long 2.
League Express Men of the Match:
Bulls: Henry Paul; *Saints:* Kevin Iro.
Penalty count: 4-7; **Half-time:** 6-2; **Referee:** Stuart Cummings (Widnes); **Attendance:** 50,717 *(at Old Trafford, Manchester).*

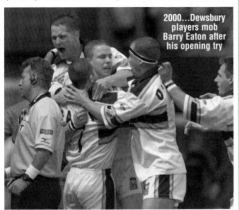

2000...Dewsbury players mob Barry Eaton after his opening try

2000

NORTHERN FORD PREMIERSHIP GRAND FINAL

Saturday 29th July 2000

DEWSBURY RAMS 13 LEIGH CENTURIONS 12

RAMS: 1 Nathan Graham; 2 Richard Baker; 4 Dan Potter; 3 Brendan O'Meara; 5 Adrian Flynn; 6 Richard Agar; 7 Barry Eaton; 8 Shayne Williams; 9 David Mycoe; 10 Mark Haigh; 11 Sean Richardson; 12 Daniel Frame; 13 Damian Ball. Subs: 14 Gavin Wood (not used); 15 Paul Delaney for Mycoe (53); 16 Ryan McDonald for Haigh (30); 17 Matthew Long for Williams (23); Haigh for McDonald (64).
Tries: Eaton (2), Long (23); **Goals:** Eaton 2; **Field goal:** Agar.
Sin bin: Williams (66) - use of the elbow.
On report: Richardson (20) - high tackle on Donlan.
CENTURIONS: 1 Stuart Donlan; 5 David Ingram; 3 Paul Anderson; 4 Andy Fairclough; 2 Alan Cross; 6 Liam Bretherton; 7 Kieron Purtill; 8 Tim Street; 9 Mick Higham; 10 Andy Leathem; 11 Simon Baldwin; 12 Heath Cruckshank; 13 Adam Bristow. Subs: 14 James Arkwright for Cross (68); 15 Paul Norman for Street (36); 16 Radney Bowker (not used); 17 David Whittle for Leathem (24); Street for Norman (62).
Tries: Higham (29, 69); **Goals:** Bretherton 2.
Sin bin: Whittle (66) - retaliation.
League Express Men of the Match:
Rams: Richard Agar; *Centurions:* Mick Higham.
Penalty count: 4-4; **Half-time:** 10-6; **Referee:** Robert Connolly (Wigan); **Attendance:** 8,487 *(at Gigg Lane, Bury).*

1999... St Helens celebrate Kevin Iro's winning try

SUPER LEAGUE GRAND FINAL

Saturday 14th October 2000

ST HELENS 29 WIGAN WARRIORS 16

SAINTS: 17 Paul Wellens; 24 Steve Hall; 3 Kevin Iro; 15 Sean Hoppe; 5 Anthony Sullivan; 20 Tommy Martyn; 7 Sean Long; 8 Apollo Perelini; 9 Keiron Cunningham; 10 Julian O'Neill; 11 Chris Joynt (C); 22 Tim Jonkers; 13 Paul Sculthorpe. Subs: 14 Fereti Tuilagi for O'Neill (20); 12 Sonny Nickle for Perelini (28); 26 John Stankevitch for Jonkers (50); 23 Scott Barrow (not used); Perelini for Nickle (52); Jonkers for Stankevitch (66); Stankevitch for Perelini (67BB); O'Neill for Hall (74).
Tries: Hoppe (7), Joynt (28, 50), Tuilagi (69), Jonkers (80); **Goals:** Long 4; **Field goal:** Sculthorpe.
WARRIORS: 5 Jason Robinson; 2 Brett Dallas; 1 Kris Radlinski; 3 Steve Renouf; 26 David Hodgson; 6 Tony Smith; 7 Willie Peters; 8 Terry O'Connor; 9 Terry Newton; 10 Neil Cowie; 11 Mick Cassidy; 12 Denis Betts; 13 Andy Farrell (C). Subs: 23 Brady Malam for Cowie (30); 17 Tony Mestrov for O'Connor (43); 19 Chris Chester for Cassidy (47BB, rev 69); 14 Lee Gilmour for Betts (51); O'Connor for Mestrov (61); Cowie for Malam (67); Chester for Newton (75).
Tries: Farrell (13), Hodgson (58), Smith (61); **Goals:** Farrell 2.
League Express Men of the Match:
Saints: Chris Joynt; *Warriors:* Andy Farrell.
Penalty count: 10-6; **Half-time:** 11-4; **Referee:** Russell Smith (Castleford); **Attendance:** 58,132 *(at Old Trafford, Manchester).*

2000... Tim Jonkers congratulated on scoring

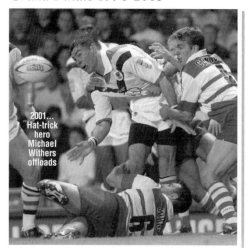

2001... Hat-trick hero Michael Withers offloads

2001

NORTHERN FORD PREMIERSHIP GRAND FINAL

Saturday 28th July 2001

OLDHAM 14 WIDNES VIKINGS 24

OLDHAM: 1 Mark Sibson; 2 Joey Hayes; 3 Anthony Gibbons; 4 Pat Rich; 5 Joe McNicholas; 6 David Gibbons; 7 Neil Roden; 8 Leo Casey; 9 Keith Brennan; 10 Paul Norton; 11 Phil Farrell; 12 Bryan Henare; 13 Kevin Mannion. Subs: 14 Mike Ford for Mannion (27); 15 Jason Clegg for Casey (18); 16 John Hough for Brennan (44); 17 Danny Guest for Norton (40BB, rev 54); Mannion for Henare (66); Guest for Clegg (73).
Tries: Brennan (9), Ford (74), Mannion (80); **Goal:** Rich.
VIKINGS: 1 Paul Atcheson; 2 Damian Munro; 3 Craig Weston; 4 Jason Demetriou; 5 Chris Percival; 6 Richard Agar; 7 Martin Crompton; 8 Simon Knox; 9 Phil Cantillon; 10 Stephen Holgate; 11 Steve Gee; 12 Sean Richardson; 13 Tommy Hodgkinson. Subs: 14 Andy Craig for Percival (65); 15 Chris McKinney for Gee (41); 16 Joe Faimalo for Knox (32); 17 Matthew Long for Holgate (23); Knox for Long (49BB, rev 61); Holgate for Long (74).
Tries: Gee (17), Demetriou (38, 60), Cantillon (50), Munro (69); **Goals:** Weston 2.
League Express Men of the Match:
Oldham: Jason Clegg; *Vikings:* Phil Cantillon.
Penalty count: 8-5; **Half-time:** 4-10; **Referee:** Steve Ganson (St Helens); **Attendance:** 8,974 *(at Spotland, Rochdale).*

2001...Tommy Hodgkinson held up by David Gibbons

SUPER LEAGUE GRAND FINAL

Saturday 13th October 2001

BRADFORD BULLS 37 WIGAN WARRIORS 6

BULLS: 5 Michael Withers; 2 Tevita Vaikona; 20 Scott Naylor; 23 Graham Mackay; 3 Leon Pryce; 6 Henry Paul; 1 Robbie Paul (C); 8 Joe Vagana; 9 James Lowes; 22 Brian McDermott; 11 Daniel Gartner; 19 Jamie Peacock; 12 Mike Forshaw. Subs: 29 Stuart Fielden for McDermott (21BB, rev 65); 10 Paul Anderson for Vagana (22); 15 Shane Rigon for Pryce (40); 7 Paul Deacon for R Paul (69); Vagana for Anderson (53); Fielden for Gartner (72); Anderson for Vagana (74).
Tries: Lowes (9), Withers (11, 27, 31), Fielden (65), Mackay (72); **Goals:** H Paul 5, Mackay; **Field goal:** H Paul.
WARRIORS: 1 Kris Radlinski; 2 Brett Dallas; 4 Gary Connolly; 3 Steve Renouf; 5 Brian Carney; 6 Matthew Johns; 7 Adrian Lam; 8 Terry O'Connor; 9 Terry Newton; 20 Harvey Howard; 11 Mick Cassidy; 14 David Furner; 13 Andy Farrell (C). Subs: 15 Paul Johnson for Carney (12BB); 10 Neil Cowie for Howard (17); 12 Denis Betts for O'Connor (32); 19 Chris Chester for Farrell (59); O'Connor for Cowie (55); Howard for Newton (64); Cowie for Cassidy (72).
Try: Lam (63); **Goal:** Furner.
League Express Men of the Match:
Bulls: Michael Withers; *Warriors:* Adrian Lam.
Penalty count: 6-7; **Half-time:** 26-0; **Referee:** Stuart Cummings (Widnes); **Attendance:** 60,164 *(at Old Trafford, Manchester).*

2002...Hefin O'Hare on the charge

2002

NORTHERN FORD PREMIERSHIP GRAND FINAL

Saturday 12th October 2002

HUDDERSFIELD GIANTS 38 LEIGH CENTURIONS 16

GIANTS: 1 Ben Cooper; 2 Hefin O'Hare; 3 Eorl Crabtree; 4 Graeme Hallas; 5 Marcus St Hilaire; 6 Stanley Gene; 7 Chris Thorman; 8 Michael Slicker; 9 Paul March; 10 Jeff Wittenberg; 11 David Atkins; 12 Robert Roberts; 13 Steve McNamara. Subs: 14 Heath Cruckshank for Roberts (24BB); 15 Chris Molyneux for Slicker (53); 16 Darren Turner for March (21); 17 Andy Rice for Cruckshank (57); Roberts for Wittenberg (34); Wittenberg for Roberts (74).
Tries: O'Hare (12, 78), St Hilaire (34, 53), Thorman (46), Gene (57); **Goals:** McNamara 7.
Sin bin: Roberts (47) - fighting.
CENTURIONS: 1 Neil Turley; 2 Leon Felton; 4 Jon Roper; 3 Dale Cardoza; 5 Oliver Marns; 6 Willie Swann; 7 Bobbie Goulding; 8 Vila Matautia; 9 Paul Rowley; 10 David Bradbury; 11 Simon Baldwin; 12 Andrew Isherwood; 13 Adam Bristow. Subs: 14 Gareth Price for Bradbury (24BB, rev 35); 15 John Duffy for Swann (32); 16 John Hamilton for Bristow (46BB, rev 57); 17 David Whittle for Matautia (22); Matautia for Bradbury (53BB); Swann for Goulding (58); Hamilton for Whittle (67); Bradbury for Turley (72); Goulding for Swann (75).
Tries: Cardoza (9), Marns (18), Hamilton (70); **Goals:** Turley 2.
Sin bin: Whittle (47) - fighting; Bristow (74) - interference.
On report: Isherwood (66) - high tackle on Roberts.
Rugby Leaguer & League Express Men of the Match:
Giants: Chris Thorman; *Centurions:* Adam Bristow.
Penalty count: 11-11; **Half-time:** 14-10; **Referee:** Karl Kirkpatrick (Warrington); **Attendance:** 9,051 *(at Halton Stadium, Widnes).*

SUPER LEAGUE GRAND FINAL

Saturday 19th October 2002

BRADFORD BULLS 18 ST HELENS 19

BULLS: 6 Michael Withers; 2 Tevita Vaikona; 20 Scott Naylor; 15 Brandon Costin; 5 Lesley Vainikolo; 1 Robbie Paul (C); 7 Paul Deacon; 8 Joe Vagana; 9 James Lowes; 29 Stuart Fielden; 11 Daniel Gartner; 12 Jamie Peacock; 13 Mike Forshaw. Subs: 14 Lee Gilmour for Gartner (21); 10 Paul Anderson for Vagana (25); 22 Brian McDermott for Fielden (34); 3 Leon Pryce for Vainikolo (53); Fielden for Anderson (55); Vainikolo for Paul (77).
Tries: Naylor (3), Paul (44), Withers (47); **Goals:** Deacon 3.
SAINTS: 1 Paul Wellens; 5 Darren Albert; 3 Martin Gleeson; 4 Paul Newlove; 19 Anthony Stewart; 13 Paul Sculthorpe; 7 Sean Long; 8 Darren Britt; 9 Keiron Cunningham; 10 Barry Ward; 23 Mike Bennett; 15 Tim Jonkers; 11 Chris Joynt (C). Subs: 2 Sean Hoppe for Wellens (3); 12 Peter Shiels for Ward (27); 14 John Stankevitch for Britt (31BB, rev 58); 17 Mick Higham for Joynt (54); Stankevitch for Shiels (58); Joynt for Britt (75); Shiels for Jonkers (77).
Tries: Bennett (24), Long (32), Gleeson (56);
Goals: Long 3; **Field goal:** Long.
Rugby Leaguer & League Express Men of the Match:
Bulls: Paul Deacon; *Saints:* Mike Bennett.
Penalty count: 5-4; **Half-time:** 12-8; **Referee:** Russell Smith (Castleford); **Attendance:** 61,138 *(at Old Trafford, Manchester).*

2002...
Sean Long
shows his
jubilation

2003

NATIONAL LEAGUE TWO GRAND FINAL

Sunday 5th October 2003

KEIGHLEY COUGARS 13 SHEFFIELD EAGLES 11

COUGARS: 1 Matt Foster; 2 Max Tomlinson; 3 David Foster; 4 James Rushforth; 5 Andy Robinson; 6 Paul Ashton; 7 Matt Firth; 8 Phil Stephenson; 9 Simeon Hoyle; 10 Danny Ekis; 11 Oliver Wilkes; 12 Ian Sinfield; 13 Lee Patterson. Subs (all used): 14 Chris Wainwright; 15 Richard Mervill; 16 Mick Durham; 17 Jason Ramshaw.

2003...
Matt Firth
collared

Tries: M Foster (7), Robinson (74); **Goals:** Ashton 2; **Field goal:** Firth.
EAGLES: 1 Andy Poynter; 2 Tony Weller; 3 Richard Goddard; 4 Tom O'Reilly; 5 Greg Hurst; 6 Gavin Brown; 7 Mark Aston; 8 Jack Howieson; 9 Gareth Stanley; 10 Dale Laughton; 11 Andy Raleigh; 12 Craig Brown; 13 Wayne Flynn. Subs (all used): 14 Peter Reilly; 15 Simon Tillyer; 16 Nick Turnbull; 17 Mitchell Stringer.
Try: O'Reilly (51); **Goals:** G Brown 3; **Field goal:** Reilly.
Rugby Leaguer & League Express Men of the Match:
Cougars: Simeon Hoyle; *Eagles:* Andy Raleigh.
Penalty count: 6-8; **Half-time:** 9-4; **Referee:** Peter Taberner (Wigan). *(At Halton Stadium, Widnes).*

NATIONAL LEAGUE ONE GRAND FINAL

Sunday 5th October 2003

LEIGH CENTURIONS 14 SALFORD CITY REDS 31

CENTURIONS: 1 Neil Turley; 2 Damian Munro; 3 Alan Hadcroft; 4 Danny Halliwell; 5 Leroy Rivett; 6 John Duffy; 7 Tommy Martyn; 8 Sonny Nickle; 9 Patrick Weisner; 10 Paul Norman; 11 Sean Richardson; 12 Willie Swann; 13 Adam Bristow. Subs (all used): 14 David Bradbury; 15 Lee Sanderson; 16 Bryan Henare; 17 Ricky Bibey.
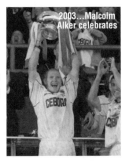
2003...Malcolm
Alker celebrates

Tries: Richardson (33), Halliwell (38), Swann (65);
Goal: Turley.
On report: Nickle (60) - late tackle on Clinch.
CITY REDS: 1 Jason Flowers; 2 Danny Arnold; 3 Stuart Littler; 4 Alan Hunte; 5 Andy Kirk; 6 Cliff Beverley; 7 Gavin Clinch; 8 Neil Baynes; 9 Malcolm Alker; 10 Andy Coley; 11 Simon Baldwin; 12 Paul Highton; 13 Chris Charles. Subs (all used): 14 Steve Blakeley; 15 David Highton; 16 Martin Moana; 17 Gareth Haggerty.
Tries: Hunte (3, 52), Beverley (23), Littler (73);
Goals: Charles 6, Blakeley; **Field goal:** Blakeley.
Rugby Leaguer & League Express Men of the Match:
Centurions: Willie Swann; *City Reds:* Gavin Clinch.
Penalty count: 10-10; **Half-time:** 10-16;
Referee: Richard Silverwood (Dewsbury);
Attendance: 9,186 *(at Halton Stadium, Widnes).*

2003...Shontayne
Hape mobbed by
teammates

SUPER LEAGUE GRAND FINAL

Saturday 18th October 2003

BRADFORD BULLS 25 WIGAN WARRIORS 12

BULLS: 17 Stuart Reardon; 2 Tevita Vaikona; 6 Michael Withers; 4 Shontayne Hape; 5 Lesley Vainikolo; 15 Karl Pratt; 7 Paul Deacon; 8 Joe Vagana; 9 James Lowes; 29 Stuart Fielden; 11 Daniel Gartner; 12 Jamie Peacock; 13 Mike Forshaw. Subs (all used): 10 Paul Anderson; 18 Lee Radford; 3 Leon Pryce; 1 Robbie Paul (C).
Tries: Reardon (51), Hape (59), Lowes (75);
Goals: Deacon 6/6; **Field goal:** Deacon.
WARRIORS: 1 Kris Radlinski; 5 Brian Carney; 18 Martin Aspinwall; 14 David Hodgson; 2 Brett Dallas; 15 Sean O'Loughlin; 20 Luke Robinson; 30 Quentin Pongia; 9 Terry Newton; 10 Craig Smith; 11 Mick Cassidy; 12 Danny Tickle; 13 Andy Farrell (C). Subs (all used): 4 Paul Johnson; 8 Terry O'Connor; 23 Gareth Hock; 17 Mark Smith.
Tries: Tickle (17), Radlinski (72); **Goals:** Farrell 2/3.
Rugby Leaguer & League Express Men of the Match:
Bulls: Stuart Reardon; *Warriors:* Kris Radlinski.
Penalty count: 7-6; **Half-time:** 4-6; **Referee:** Karl Kirkpatrick (Warrington); **Attendance:** 65,537 *(at Old Trafford, Manchester).*

SUPER LEAGUE

(Play-offs in brackets, inc. in totals)

TRIES
1 Lesley Vainikolo
   Bradford 38 (2)
   Danny McGuire
   Leeds 38 (3)
3 Marcus Bai
   Leeds 26 (3)
4 Shontayne Hape
   Bradford 24 (3)
5 Shaun Briscoe
   Hull 22 (0)
   Sid Domic
   Wakefield 22 (0)
7 Ben Jeffries
   Wakefield 19 (0)
8 Chev Walker
   Leeds 18 (1)
   Dennis Moran
   London ....18 (-)
   Brett Dallas
   Wigan 18 (0)

GOALS
1 Kevin Sinfield
   Leeds 140 (11)
2 Paul Deacon
   Bradford 123 (3)
3 Paul Cooke
   Hull 115 (0)
4 Andy Farrell
   Wigan 104 (8)
5 David March
   Wakefield 77 (2)
6 Lee Briers
   Warrington ....75 (-)
7 Chris Charles
   Salford ....68 (-)
8 Paul Sykes
   London ....63 (-)
9 Sean Long
   St Helens 59 (4)
   Jules O'Neill
   Widnes ....59 (-)

POINTS
1 Kevin Sinfield
   Leeds 299 (22)
2 Paul Deacon
   Bradford 276 (6)
3 Paul Cooke
   Hull 250 (0)
4 Andy Farrell
   Wigan 243 (24)
5 Lee Briers
   Warrington ......180 (-)
6 David March
   Wakefield 170 (8)
7 Jules O'Neill
   Widnes ....154 (-)
8 Danny McGuire
   Leeds 152 (12)
   Lesley Vainikolo
   Bradford 152 (8)
10 Chris Charles
   Salford ....148 (-)

Lesley Vainikolo

NATIONAL LEAGUE 1

(Play-offs in brackets, inc. in totals)

TRIES
1 Matt Foster
   Keighley ....18 (-)
   Mick Nanyn
   Whitehaven 18 (1)
3 Sam Obst
   Whitehaven 15 (1)
   Craig Walsh
   Whitehaven 15 (2)
5 Dean Colton
   Doncaster 13 (0)
   Rikki Sheriffe
   Halifax 13 (2)
   Chris Percival
   Leigh 13 (0)
8 Alasdair McClarron
   Hull KR 12 (4)
   Tommy Martyn
   Leigh 12 (1)
   Neil Turley
   Leigh 12 (1)
   Craig Calvert
   Whitehaven 12 (2)

GOALS
1 Neil Turley
   Leigh 101 (8)
2 Mick Nanyn
   Whitehaven 83 (9)
3 Stuart Dickens
   Featherstone 73 (5)
4 Barry Eaton
   Batley ....72 (-)
5 Jamie Bloem
   Halifax 61 (9)
6 Lee Birdseye
   Rochdale ....43 (-)
7 Graham Holroyd
   Doncaster 41 (0)
8 Pat Rich
   Oldham 35 (0)
9 Craig Poucher
   Hull KR 33 (9)
10 Lynton Stott
   Hull KR 32 (0)

POINTS
1 Neil Turley
   Leigh 257 (24)
2 Mick Nanyn
   Whitehaven 238 (22)
3 Barry Eaton
   Batley ....161 (-)
4 Jamie Bloem
   Halifax 150 (18)
5 Stuart Dickens
   Featherstone 146 (10)
6 Graham Holroyd
   Doncaster 121 (0)
7 Lee Birdseye
   Rochdale ....110 (-)
8 Craig Poucher
   Hull KR 78 (18)
9 Lynton Stott
   Hull KR 76 (0)
10 Craig Nipperess
   Keighley ....74 (-)

Matt Foster

NATIONAL LEAGUE 2

(Play-offs in brackets, inc. in totals)

TRIES
1 Mark Cantoni
   London Skolars ....19 (-)
2 Chris Maye
   Swinton 18 (0)
3 Jonny Limmer
   Workington 17 (3)
4 Andy Poynter
   Sheffield 15 (0)
   Wayne English
   Swinton 15 (1)
   Austin Buchanan
   York 15 (4)
7 Tane Manihera
   Workington 14 (2)
   Mark Cain
   York 14 (6)
9 Adam Thaler
   Dewsbury ....13 (-)
   Danny Brough
   York 13 (0)
   Chris Langley
   York 13 (1)

GOALS
1 Danny Brough
   York 97 (15)
2 Darren Holt
   Barrow ....86 (-)
3 Tane Manihera
   Workington 83 (14)
4 Brian Capewell
   Chorley ....57 (-)
5 Gavin Brown
   Sheffield 39 (0)
6 Warren Ayres
   Swinton 34 (0)
7 Chris Ross
   Hunslet 32 (0)
   Paul Thorman
   Gateshead ....32 (-)
9 Paul Ashton
   Swinton 30 (4)
   Adam Thaler
   Dewsbury ....30 (-)

POINTS
1 Danny Brough
   York 248 (30)
2 Tane Manihera
   Workington 224 (37)
3 Darren Holt
   Barrow ....191 (-)
4 Brian Capewell
   Chorley ....144 (-)
5 Adam Thaler
   Dewsbury ....113 (-)
6 Gavin Brown
   Sheffield 96 (0)
7 Joel Osborn
   London Skolars ...80 (-)
   Chris Ross
   Hunslet 80 (0)
9 Paul Thorman
   Gateshead ....78 (-)
10 Warren Ayres
   Swinton 77 (4)

Danny Brough

NAT LEAGUE CUP

TRIES
1 Neil Turley
  Leigh 13
2 Nick Johnson
  Oldham 11
  Alex Godfrey
  York 11
4 Adam Pate
  Barrow 10
  Craig Walsh
  Whitehaven 10
6 Danny Halliwell
  Leigh 9
  Mick Nanyn
  Whitehaven 9
8 Adrian Flynn
  Batley 8
  Marlon Billy
  Doncaster 8
  Ian Knott
  Leigh 8

GOALS
1 Neil Turley
  Leigh 65
2 Danny Brough
  York 59
3 Barry Eaton
  Batley 56
4 Mick Nanyn
  Whitehaven 45
5 Darren Holt
  Barrow 42
6 Adam Mitchell
  Keighley 39
7 Graham Holroyd
  Doncaster 35
8 Carl Briggs
  Featherstone 32
9 Lynton Stott
  Hull KR 25
10 Scott Thorburn
  Hull KR 24

POINTS
1 Neil Turley
  Leigh 185
2 Danny Brough
  York 127
3 Mick Nanyn
  Whitehaven 126
4 Barry Eaton
  Batley 113
5 Darren Holt
  Barrow 101
6 Adam Mitchell
  Keighley 95
7 Graham Holroyd
  Doncaster 78
8 Scott Thorburn
  Hull KR 72
9 Lynton Stott
  Hull KR 66
10 Carl Briggs
  Featherstone 64

CHALLENGE CUP

TRIES
1 Richard Newlove
  Featherstone 7
2 Brett Dallas
  Wigan 6
3 Ben Roarty
  Huddersfield 5
  Ben Jeffries
  Wakefield 5
  Jamie Rooney
  Wakefield 5
  Ben Westwood
  Warrington 5

GOALS
1 Sean Long
  St Helens 22
  Carl Briggs
  Featherstone 22
3 Danny Brough
  York 18
  Jamie Rooney
  Wakefield 18
5 Barry Eaton
  Batley 16
6 Graham Holroyd
  Doncaster 14
7 Paul Cooke
  Hull 12
  Paul March
  Huddersfield 12
  Kevin Sinfield
  Leeds 12
10 Mick Nanyn
  Whitehaven 11
  Neil Turley
  Leigh 11

POINTS
1 Jamie Rooney
  Wakefield 57
2 Sean Long
  St Helens 56
3 Carl Briggs
  Featherstone 48
4 Danny Brough
  York 37
5 Paul March
  Huddersfield 36
6 Mick Nanyn
  Whitehaven 34
7 Barry Eaton
  Batley 32
  Graham Holroyd
  Doncaster 32
9 Richard Newlove
  Featherstone 28
10 Neil Turley
  Leigh 26

ALL COMPETITIONS

TRIES
1 Danny McGuire
  Leeds 39
  Lesley Vainikolo
  Bradford 39
3 Mick Nanyn
  Whitehaven 30
4 Marcus Bai
  Leeds 26
  Neil Turley
  Leigh 26
  Craig Walsh
  Whitehaven 26
7 Shaun Briscoe
  Hull 25
  Sid Domic
  Wakefield 25
  Nick Johnson
  Oldham 25
10 Brett Dallas
  Wigan 24
  Shontayne Hape
  Bradford 24
  Ben Jeffries
  Wakefield 24
  Jonny Limmer
  Workington 24

GOALS
1 Neil Turley
  Leigh 177
2 Danny Brough
  York 174
3 Kevin Sinfield
  Leeds 152
4 Barry Eaton
  Batley 144
5 Mick Nanyn
  Whitehaven 139
6 Darren Holt
  Barrow 132
7 Paul Cooke
  Hull 127
8 Paul Deacon
  Bradford 124
9 Andy Farrell
  Wigan 113
10 Jamie Bloem
  Halifax 91

POINTS
1 Neil Turley
  Leigh 468
2 Danny Brough
  York 412
3 Mick Nanyn
  Whitehaven 398
4 Kevin Sinfield
  Leeds 323
5 Barry Eaton
  Batley 306
6 Darren Holt
  Barrow 300
7 Paul Deacon
  Bradford 282
8 Paul Cooke
  Hull 274
9 Andy Farrell
  Wigan 261
10 Graham Holroyd
  Doncaster 231

Neil Turley

Sean Long

Danny McGuire

FINAL TABLES

SUPER LEAGUE

	P	W	D	L	F	A	D	PTS
Leeds	28	24	2	2	1037	443	594	50
Bradford	28	20	1	7	918	565	353	41
Hull	28	19	2	7	843	478	365	40
Wigan	28	17	4	7	736	558	178	38
St Helens	28	17	1	10	821	662	159	35
Wakefield	28	15	0	13	788	662	126	30
Huddersfield	28	12	0	16	518	757	-239	24
Warrington	28	10	1	17	700	715	-15	21
Salford	28	8	0	20	507	828	-321	16
London	28	7	1	20	561	968	-407	15
Widnes	28	7	0	21	466	850	-384	14
Castleford	28	6	0	22	515	924	-409	12

NATIONAL LEAGUE ONE

	P	W	D	L	F	A	D	PTS
Leigh	18	14	0	4	686	407	279	28
Whitehaven	18	14	0	4	552	312	240	28
Hull KR	18	10	0	8	466	428	38	20
Oldham	18	10	0	8	482	503	-21	20
Featherstone	18	9	1	8	500	491	9	19
Doncaster	18	9	0	9	503	534	-31	18
Batley	18	8	0	10	478	469	9	16
Rochdale	18	7	1	10	472	587	-115	15
Halifax	18	7	0	11	426	492	-66	14
Keighley	18	1	0	17	366	708	-342	2

NATIONAL LEAGUE TWO

	P	W	D	L	F	A	D	PTS
Barrow	18	14	1	3	521	346	175	29
York	18	13	0	5	630	308	322	26
Sheffield	18	12	0	6	569	340	229	24
Swinton	18	12	0	6	547	460	87	24
Workington	18	10	0	8	597	479	118	20
Hunslet	18	10	0	8	475	394	81	20
Chorley	18	7	2	9	460	522	-62	16
London S	18	6	0	12	361	583	-222	12
Dewsbury	18	3	1	14	284	595	-311	7
Gateshead	18	1	0	17	298	715	-417	2

FIELD GOALS

1	Neil Turley	
	Leigh	10
2	Darren Holt	
	Barrow	8
3	Ian Watson	
	Oldham	7
4	Jamie Rooney	
	Wakefield	5
	Pat Weisner	
	Halifax	5
6	Danny Brough	
	York	4
	Chris Hough	
	Doncaster	4
	Ben Jeffries	
	Wakefield	4
	Tommy Martyn	
	Leigh	4
	Jules O'Neill	
	Widnes	4
	Sam Obst	
	Whitehaven	4
	Latham Tawhai	
	Hunslet	4

ATTENDANCES

SUPER LEAGUE

	2004 Avg	2003 Avg	Diff
Leeds	16,608	13,143	+3,465
Bradford	13,500	15,259	-1,759
Wigan	13,333	11,217	+2,116
Hull	11,397	11,598	-201
Warrington	9,889	7,031	+2,858
St Helens	9,507	9,643	-136
Castleford	7,035	7,199	-164
Widnes	6,167	6,511	-344
Wakefield	4,804	4,017	+787
Huddersfield	4,362	4,722	-360
Salford	3,994	2,322	+1,672
London	3,458	3,546	-88

'04 Avg 8,833 / **'03 Avg** 8,188 / **Diff** +645

BEST CROWDS

65,547	Bradford v Leeds (GF)	16/10/04
23,375	Bradford v Leeds (R13)	5/6/04
21,225	Leeds v Bradford (QSF)	2/10/04
21,225	Leeds v Bradford (R24)	22/8/04
21,225	Leeds v Bradford (R5)	8/4/04
20,119	Leeds v Wigan (FE)	8/10/04
20,052	Wigan v St Helens (EPO)	25/9/04
18,124	Leeds v Wigan (R3)	19/3/04
17,329	Leeds v London (R28)	17/9/04
17,267	Bradford v Wigan (R1)	20/2/04

WORST CROWDS

2,198	London v Salford (R17)	28/3/04
2,486	London v Wakefield (R5)	8/4/04
2,529	Salford v London (R10)	8/5/04
2,562	London v Castleford (R12)	28/5/04
2,627	London v Huddersfield (R11)	23/5/04
2,825	Salford v Wakefield (R3)	20/3/04
2,923	London v Widnes (R7)	18/4/04
3,009	Huddersfield v London (R16)	27/6/04
3,035	London v Wakefield (R25)	29/8/04
3,067	Salford v Widnes (R23)	14/8/04

NATIONAL LEAGUE ONE

	2004 Avg	2003 Avg	Diff
Hull KR	2,186	1,562	+624
Leigh	2,166	2,445	-279
Halifax	1,953	2,977	-1,024
Whitehaven	1,763	1,393	+370
Featherstone	1,419	1,509	-90
Oldham	1,352	1,572	-220
Keighley	1,184	1,105	+79
Rochdale	1,010	1,062	-52
Batley	914	856	+58
Doncaster	874	950	-76

'04 Avg 1,482 / **'03 Avg** 1,462 / **Diff** +20

BEST CROWDS

11,005	Leigh v Whitehaven (GF)	10/10/04
4,563	Leigh v Whitehaven (QSF)	26/9/04
3,442	Leigh v Whitehaven (W17)	5/9/04
3,075	Hull KR v Featherstone (ESF)	26/9/04
2,647	Leigh v Leigh (W8)	20/6/04
2,393	Hull KR v Halifax (W3)	2/5/04
2,383	Hull KR v Keighley (W1)	12/4/04
2,374	Whitehaven v Featherstone (FE)	3/10/04
2,319	Hull KR v Doncaster (EPO)	19/9/04
2,290	Halifax v Doncaster (W1)	12/4/04

WORST CROWDS

605	Batley v Whitehaven (W15)	22/8/04
624	Rochdale v Doncaster (W14)	21/8/04
639	Batley v Rochdale (W1)	12/4/04
645	Doncaster v Rochdale (W7)	13/6/04
685	Batley v Keighley (W10)	11/7/04
702	Rochdale v Whitehaven (W2)	18/4/04
752	Oldham v Whitehaven (W8)	20/6/04
760	Keighley v Doncaster (W16)	29/8/04
786	Doncaster v Halifax (W17)	5/9/04
801	Batley v Doncaster (W3)	2/5/04

NATIONAL LEAGUE TWO

	2004 Avg	2003 Avg	Diff
York	1,579	1,365	+214
Barrow	925	807	+118
Sheffield	902	943	-41
Workington	862	526	+336
Dewsbury	809	950	-141
Swinton	580	542	+38
Hunslet	544	541	+3
London S	407	430	-23
Chorley	349	434	-85
Gateshead	303	279	+24

'04 Avg 726 / **'03 Avg** 697 / **Diff** +29

BEST CROWDS

(Attendance figure unavailable for NL1QS-F)

2,519	York v Gateshead (W7)	23/5/04
2,213	Halifax v York (NL1QS-QSF)	26/9/04
2,017	York v Workington (NL1QS-FE)	3/10/04
1,761	York v Dewsbury (W2U)	22/8/04
1,583	Dewsbury v Barrow (W23)	12/9/04
1,411	York v Swinton (W8)	30/5/04
1,401	York v Chorley (W1)	12/4/04
1,389	York v Sheffield (W4)	2/5/04
1,367	York v London Skolars (W11)	20/6/04
1,352	Sheffield v Dewsbury (W6)	21/5/04

WORST CROWDS

164	Chorley v Gateshead (W4)	2/5/04
203	Gateshead v London Skolars (W2)	18/4/04
211	Chorley v London Skolars (W13)	4/7/04
248	Chorley v Workington (W7)	23/5/04
255	Chorley v Dewsbury (W17)	1/8/04
257	Chorley v Sheffield (W2)	18/4/04
277	Gateshead v Hunslet (W21)	29/8/04
291	Gateshead v Workington (W10)	13/6/04
293	Gateshead v Dewsbury (W19)	15/8/04
297	Gateshead v Sheffield (W5)	9/5/04

NATIONAL LEAGUE CUP

BEST CROWDS

4,383	Hull KR v Leigh (F)	18/7/04
3,360	Halifax v Keighley (W1)	1/2/04
2,815	Halifax v Leigh (W8)	28/3/04
2,629	Hull KR v York (SF)	27/6/04
2,563	Leigh v Halifax (W9)	9/4/04
2,449	Whitehaven v Leigh (SF)	27/6/04
2,391	Hull KR v Sheffield (W1)	1/2/04
2,316	Leigh v Oldham (W3)	15/2/04
2,156	Whitehaven v Workington (W5)	7/3/04
2,096	Halifax v Rochdale (W5)	7/3/04

WORST CROWDS

142	London Skolars v Sheffield (W6)	14/3/04
259	Gateshead v Barrow (W9)	9/4/04
288	Gateshead v Workington (W7)	21/3/04
294	Gateshead v Whitehaven (W4)	22/2/04
303	Chorley v Barrow (W3)	15/2/04
307	Chorley v Swinton (W9)	9/4/04
337	Hunslet v London Skolars (W8)	28/3/04
346	Swinton v Whitehaven (W8)	30/3/04
366	Gateshead v York (W3)	15/2/04
370	Chorley v Oldham (W7)	21/3/04

CHALLENGE CUP

BEST CROWDS

73,734	St Helens v Wigan (F)	15/5/04
13,699	St Helens v Leeds (R5)	13/3/04
13,134	Huddersfield v St Helens (SF)	25/4/04
12,215	Bradford v St Helens (R4)	29/2/04
11,443	Hull v Castleford (R5)	14/3/04
11,184	St Helens v Hull (QF)	28/3/04
11,175	Warrington v Wigan (R5)	14/3/04
9,728	Wigan v Wakefield (QF)	26/3/04
6,761	Rochdale v Warrington (R4)	2/3/04
	at Halliwell Jones Stadium	
6,737	Wigan v Widnes (R4)	29/2/04

WORST CROWDS

254	Gateshead v Limoux (R3)	8/2/04
275	London Skolars v Rochdale Mayfield (R3)	7/2/04
380	London Skolars v Featherstone (R4)	29/2/04
433	Hunslet v Featherstone Lions (R3)	7/2/04
521	Chorley v Locomotiv Moscow (R3)	6/2/04
532	Swinton v East Hull (R3)	8/2/04
591	Leigh Miners Rangers v Sheffield (R3)	6/2/04
682	Hunslet v Doncaster (R4)	29/2/04
696	Chorley v Wakefield (R4)	27/2/04
707	Rochdale v Dinamo Moscow (R3)	8/2/04